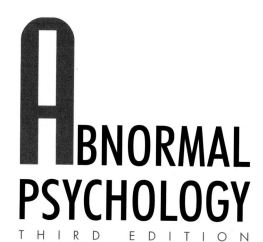

ABNORMAL PSYCHOLOGY

THIRD EDITION

ABNORMAL PSYCHOLOGY

THIRD EDITION

David L. Rosenhan Stanford University

Martin E. P. Seligman University of Pennsylvania

W · W · NORTON & COMPANY

New York · London

Library of Congress Cataloging-in-Publication Data
Rosenhan, David L.
    Abnormal psychology / David L. Rosenhan, Martin E. P. Seligman.—
    3rd ed.
        p.   cm.
    Includes bibliographical references and index.
    ISBN 0-393-96644-5
    1. Psychology, Pathological.   2. Psychotherapy—Case studies.
I. Seligman, Martin E. P.   II. Title.
RC454.R578   1995   94-27953
616.89—dc20   CIP

ISBN 0-393-96644-5

The text of this book is composed in Photina with the display set in Futura Medium
Composition by TSI Graphics
Manufacturing by Quebecor, Hawkins
Book design by Jack Meserole

Cover illustration: Will Barnet, *Nightfall*, 1979, oil on canvas, $40\frac{1}{2} \times 70\frac{1}{2}''$, private collection. Courtesy of the artist.

Acknowledgments and copyrights appear on pages A68–A72, which constitute a continuation of the copyright page.

W. W. Norton & Company, Inc., 500 Fifth Avenue, New York, N.Y. 10110
W. W. Norton & Company Ltd., 10 Coptic Street, London WC1A 1PU

1 2 3 4 5 6 7 8 9 0

For Irene Brown Seligman (b. 1905)
and Nuna Lurie Rosenhan (1900–1959)

CONTENTS IN BRIEF

PART 1 THE NATURE AND HISTORY OF ABNORMALITY

1 The Meanings of Abnormality   2
2 Abnormality across Time and Place   22

PART 2 MODELS AND TREATMENT OF ABNORMALITY

3 The Biomedical Model   46
4 Psychodynamic and Existential Approaches   70
5 The Learning Models: Behavioral and Cognitive Approaches   112

PART 3 INVESTIGATING AND DIAGNOSING ABNORMALITY

6 Investigating Abnormality   142
7 Psychological Assessment and Classification   172

PART 4 ANXIETY DISORDERS AND HEALTH PSYCHOLOGY

8 Phobia, Panic, and the Anxiety Disorders   208
9 Obsession, Hysteria, and Dissociation: Anxiety Inferred   264
10 Health Psychology   310

PART 5 DEPRESSION AND SCHIZOPHRENIA

11 Depression and Suicide   350
12 The Schizophrenias   418

PART 6 SOCIAL AND INTERPERSONAL DISORDERS

13 Sexual Dysfunction and Sexual Disorder   468
14 Psychoactive Substance Use Disorders   510
15 Personality Disorders   568

PART 7 ABNORMALITY ACROSS THE LIFESPAN

16 Childhood Disorders and Mental Retardation   598
17 Disorders of the Nervous System and Psychopathology   644

PART 8 ABNORMALITY, THE LAW, AND CHOOSING A A PSYCHOTHERAPY

18 The Law and Politics of Abnormality   694
19 A Consumer's Guide to Psychological Treatment   728

CONTENTS

PREFACE   xix

PART **1**

THE NATURE AND HISTORY OF ABNORMALITY

1 The Meanings of Abnormality   **2**

Abnormality   4
The Elements of Abnormality 6   Applying the Family
Resemblance Approach 11   DSM-IV and Psychological
Diagnosis 13   Hazards of the "Family Resemblance" Approach to
Abnormality 13

Normality   16
Positives and Negatives: The Meaning of Meaning 16

Beyond Normality: Living Optimally   17
Some Elements of Optimal Living 17

The Hazards of Self-Diagnosis   19

Summary   20

Questions for Critical Thinking   21

2 Abnormality across Time and Place   **22**

The Perceived Causes of Abnormal Behavior   24
Animistic Origins: Possession 25   Physical Causes 27
Psychogenic Origins 29

Treatment of the Mentally Distressed   33
Treating Demonic Possession 33   Treating Physical Causes 34
The Rise of Psychogenic Treatments 34

The Rise of the Psychiatric Hospital   35
Institutionalizing the Poor 36   Segregating the Insane 37
The Growth of Humane Treatment 39

Summary   42

Questions for Critical Thinking   43

PART **2**

**MODELS AND TREATMENTS
OF ABNORMALITY**

3 The Biomedical Model   46

Models of Abnormality   48

Principles of the Biomedical Model   49
Germs as Etiology: Syphilis and General Paresis 50   Genetics as
Etiology 53   Biochemistry as Etiology: Dopamine and
Schizophrenia 58   Neuroanatomy as Etiology: The Disordered
Brain 59

Treatment   61
Schizophrenia and the Antipsychotics 61   Depression and the
Antidepressants 62   Manic-Depression and Lithium 63
Anxiety and the Anti-anxiety Drugs 64

Evaluating the Biomedical Model   66
Strengths 66   Weaknesses 66

Reductionism: An Ongoing Debate   68

Summary   68

Questions for Critical Thinking   69

4 Psychodynamic and Existential Approaches   70

Freud and Psychoanalytic Theory   72
The Development of Personality 72   The Three Processes of
Personality 76   Unconscious Ideas and Impulses 78
Anxiety 79   Faults of Early Psychoanalytic Theory 80

The Neo-Freudians   81

Modern Psychodynamic Theory   82
The Self and Self Theory 82   Defenses and Consciousness 86
Growth and Existential Theories 97

Psychodynamic Treatment   102
Brief Psychotherapy 102   Client-Centered Therapy 106

Evaluating Psychodynamic Theory   107
Strengths of Psychodynamic Theories 107   Shortcomings of
Psychodynamic Theories 108

Summary   109

Questions for Critical Thinking   111

5 The Learning Models: Behavioral and Cognitive Approaches   112

History and Assumptions of the Learning Model   113
Empiricism and Associations 113   Behaviorism 114

Behavioral Psychology: Principles and Therapies   116
Pavlovian Conditioning 116   Operant Conditioning 121
Avoidance Learning 127

Cognitive Psychology: Principles and Applications   128
Assumptions of the Cognitive View 128   Cognitive
Therapy 129   Cognitive-Behavioral Therapy 135

Combining Cognitive-Behavioral Therapy and Psychodynamics   135

Evaluating the Behavioral and Cognitive Models   137

Summary   138

Questions for Critical Thinking   139

PART 3

INVESTIGATING AND DIAGNOSING ABNORMALITY

6 **Investigating Abnormality**   142

The Clinical Case History   144
A Clinical Case History 144   Evaluating the Clinical Case History 145

Scientific Experimentation   147
An Experiment 148   Experimental Confounds 150
Statistical Inference 153   Experiments with a Single Subject 155   Evaluation of the Experimental Method 158

Correlation   159
Correlation Coefficients 161   Correlation and Causality 162
Epidemiology 163   Evaluation of the Correlational Method 164

Experiments of Nature   165
Evaluation of Experiments of Nature 167

The Laboratory Model   167
Evaluation of the Laboratory Model 168

Combining Several Methods: A Woven Fabric   169

Summary   170

Questions for Critical Thinking   171

7 **Psychological Assessment and Classification**   172

Psychological Assessment   174
The Clinical Interview 174   Psychological Testing 175
Observations 183

Diagnosis   188
Reasons for Diagnosis 189   Historical Origins 189   Diagnosing with DSM-IV 191

Evaluating Psychological Diagnoses   193
Reliability 193   Validity 198   Conditions That Bias Diagnosis 200   Need for Categorization and Diagnosis 203

Summary   203

Questions for Critical Thinking   205

PART **4**

**ANXIETY DISORDERS AND
HEALTH PSYCHOLOGY**

8 **Phobia, Panic, and the Anxiety Disorders**   208

Fear and Anxiety   **209**
Fear 210   Anxiety 215

Phobia   **217**
Phobia Defined 217   Prevalence of Phobias 218   Kinds of
Phobias 219   The Psychoanalytic Account of Phobias 223
The Behavioral Account of Phobias 226   Therapies for
Phobias 229   Prepared Classical Conditioning and
Phobias 233

Post-Traumatic Stress Disorder   **237**
Precipitants of Post-Traumatic Stress Disorder 238   Course of
Post-Traumatic Stress Disorder 245   Vulnerability 247
Treatment 248

Disorders of Anxiety   **249**
Panic Disorder 250   Agoraphobia 255   Generalized Anxiety
Disorder 258

Coping with Everyday Anxiety   **261**

Summary   **261**

Questions for Critical Thinking   **263**

9 **Obsession, Hysteria, and Dissociation: Anxiety Inferred**   264

Obsessions and Compulsions   **266**
Obsessions and the Social Context 267   Anxiety, Depression, and
Obsessions 269   Vulnerability to Obsessive-Compulsive
Disorder 270   Theories of Obsessive-Compulsive Disorder 272
Treatment for Obsessive-Compulsive Disorder 277   Obsessive-
Compulsive Disorder: Anxiety Revisited 280

Somatoform Disorders   **281**
The Types of Somatoform Disorders 281   Diagnosing
Somatoform Disorder 284   Vulnerability to Somatoform
Disorders 286   Course of Somatoform Disorders 287
Comorbidity of Somatoform Disorders 288   The Etiology of
Somatoform Disorders 288   Treatment of Somatoform
Disorder 292

Dissociative Disorders   **294**
Dissociative Amnesia 295   Multiple Personality 297

The Neuroses   **306**

Summary   **307**

Questions for Critical Thinking   **309**

10 **Health Psychology**   310

Stigmata   **312**

An Overview of Psychosomatic Disorders   **313**

Peptic Ulcers   313
Symptoms of Peptic Ulcer 315   Physiological Development of an
Ulcer 315   Who Is Susceptible to Ulcers? 315   Psychological
Factors Influencing Peptic Ulcers 316   Treatment of Peptic
Ulcers 321

Cardiovascular Disorders   322
Defining the Type A Personality 322   Type A's at Risk for
CHD 323   Type A Dissected 324   Sudden Death 329

Psychoneuroimmunology (PNI)   332
Immunocompetence and Psychological States 332   The Mind-
Body Problem Re-examined 335

Theories of Psychosomatic Illness   337
The Biomedical Model of Psychosomatic Disorders 338   The
Psychodynamic Model 340   Behavioral and Cognitive
Models 341

Summary   345

Questions for Critical Thinking   347

PART **5**

**DEPRESSION AND
SCHIZOPHRENIA**

11 Depression and Suicide   350

Normal versus Clinical Depression   351

Unipolar Depression   353
Symptoms of Unipolar Depression 353   Classifying
Depression 360   Vulnerability to Depression 362   The Course
of Depression 369

Theories and Therapies of Unipolar Depression   370
The Biological Model of Depression 371   The Psychodynamic
Model of Depression 378   Cognitive Models of Depression 380
Integration of Theories of Unipolar Depression 398

Bipolar Depression (Manic-Depression)   400
Symptoms of Mania 400   Course and Characteristics of Manic-
Depression 403   Cause of Manic-Depression 404
Treatment 404   Seasonal Affective Disorder (SAD) 406

Suicide   407
Who Is at Risk for Suicide? 408   The Motivation for Suicide 413
Prevention of Suicide and Treatment of the Suicidal Person 414

Summary   415

Questions for Critical Thinking   417

12 The Schizophrenias   418

History and Background   420
Evolving Views of Schizophrenia 420   Schizophrenia Defined
Incidence and Prevalence of Schizophrenia 424

Types of Schizophrenia   425
Paranoid Schizophrenia 425   Disorganized Schizophrenia 426
Catatonic Schizophrenia 426   Residual Schizophrenia 427
Undifferentiated Schizophrenia 427

The Symptoms of Schizophrenia   427
Perceptual Difficulties 427   Thought Disorders 429   Affective
Disturbances 436   Meaning in Schizophrenia 437

The Dimensions of Schizophrenia   438
Acute and Chronic 438   Type I and Type II 439

The Causes of the Schizophrenias   440
The Genetics of Schizophrenia 440   The Biology of the
Schizophrenias 448   The Schizophrenogenic Family 453
Society and Schizophrenia 454

The Treatment of Schizophrenia   459
Drug Therapy 459   Psychological Treatment 462   Full
Treatment: Milieu and Therapeutic Communities 462

Summary   465

Questions for Critical Thinking   466

PART **6**

SOCIAL AND INTERPERSONAL DISORDERS

[3 **Sexual Dysfunction and Sexual Disorder   468**

**Five Layers of Erotic Life: Sexual Order and Sexual
Disorder   470**

Sexual Identity and Transsexualism: Layer I   472
Characteristics of Transsexuals 472   The Etiology of
Transsexualism 474   Therapy for Transsexualism: Sex-
Reassignment Operations 476

Sexual Orientation: Layer II   477
Origins of Male Homosexuality 477   Disordered Sexual
Orientation: Ego-Dystonic Homosexuality 480   Layer I (Sexual
Identity) Contrasted to Layer II (Sexual Orientation) 482

Sexual Interest: Layer III   483
Types of Paraphilias 483   The Causes of Paraphilias 492
Changing Sexual Interest 495   Layer III (Sexual Interest)
Compared to Layers I and (Sexual Identity) and II (Sexual
Orientation) 496

Sex Role: Layer IV   497

Sexual Performance: Layer V   498
The Physiology of the Human Sexual Response 499   Impairment
of Sexual Performance 500   The Causes of Sexual
Dysfunction 503   Treatment of Sexual Dysfunctions 506
Evaluation of Sexual Therapy 508

Summary   508

Questions for Critical Thinking   509

14 Psychoactive Substance Use Disorders 510

Ann E. Kelley

Diagnosing and Defining Drug Abuse   512
Historical Concepts of Drug Use and Dependence 512   DSM-IV Criteria 513   WHO Definition 514

Substance Dependence   515
Basic Effects of Drugs 515   Theoretical Models of Drug Dependence 518

Alcohol   524
Effects of Alcohol 524   Defining Alcoholism 528   Etiology of Alcoholism 528   Clinical Subgroups of Alcoholics 532   Treatment 532   Medical and Social Complications 535

Stimulants   536
Effects of Stimulants 537   Cocaine Dependence 539   Treatment 540   Medical and Social Complications 542

Opiates (Narcotics)   542
Effects of Opiates 543   Opiate Dependence 545   Treatment 547   Medical and Social Complications 549

Hallucinogens   549
Use of Hallucinogens 550   Medical and Social Complications 552   PCP and MDMA 552

Marijuana   554
Effects of Marijuana 554   Medical and Social Complications 556

Nicotine and Cigarette Smoking   557
Effects of Nicotine 557   Nicotine Dependence 558   Treatment 561   Medical and Social Complications of Smoking 561

Sedative-Hypnotics and Tranquilizers (Barbiturates, Benzodiazepines)   562
Effects of Sedatives 562   Sedative Dependence 563

Future Directions in Treatment and Prevention of Substance Abuse   564
Limiting Drug Availability 564   Drug Education and Prevention 565   Improved Treatment and Research 565

Summary   566

Questions for Critical Thinking   567

15 Personality Disorders 568

The Antisocial Personality Disorder   570
Disorders of Will 570   Characterizing the Antisocial Personality Disorder 572   The Sources of Sociopathy 574   The Antisocial Personality Disorder: An Overview 584

Other Personality Disorders   584
Paranoid Personality Disorder 584   Histrionic Personality Disorder 586   Narcissistic Personality Disorder 587   Avoidant Personality Disorder 588   Dependent Personality Disorder 588

Obsessive-Compulsive Personality Disorder 589 Schizoid Personality Disorder 590 Schizotypal Personality Disorder 590 Borderline Personality Disorder 591

The Personality Disorders: An Evaluation   593
Alternative Views of the Personality Disorders 594

Summary   595

Questions for Critical Thinking   596

16 Childhood Disorders and Mental Retardation   598
Susan Nolen-Hoeksema

Classifying Children's Disorders   600

Disruptive Behavior Disorders   602
Conduct Disorders 602   Attention-Deficit Hyperactivity Disorder (ADHD) 608

Emotional Disorders   611
Separation Anxiety Disorder 611   Phobias 612   Childhood Depression 615   Treatment of Emotional Disorders 616 Childhood Sexual Abuse 616

Habit Disorders and Eating Disorders   617
Enuresis 618   Stuttering 619   Eating Disorders: Anorexia and Bulimia 620

Developmental Disorders   624
Mental Retardation 624   Learning Disorders 632   Pervasive Developmental Disorders: Autism 633

Areas for Further Consideration   641

Summary   642

Questions for Critical Thinking   643

17 Disorders of the Nervous System and Psychopathology   644
Morris Moscovitch and Paul Rozin

Organization of the Nervous System in Relation to Organic Disorders   648
Structural and Functional Units: Neurons, Glia, Synapses, and Neurotransmitters 648   The Biochemical Organization of the Brain 649   The Spatial Organization of the Brain: Localization of Function 652

Damage to the Nervous System   659
Agents of Damage to the Nervous System 659   The Expression of Damage in the Nervous System 660   Susceptibility to Damage: Vulnerable Systems 660   Resistance to Damage: Redundancy in the Nervous System 661

Assessing Brain Damage   662
The Neurological Diagnosis 662   Neuroimaging 663

Some Selected Disorders of the Nervous System **665**
Disorders of Language: The Aphasias 665   Dyslexia 669
A Disorder of Memory: The Amnesic Syndrome 671
Dementia 677   Disorders Related to the Frontal Lobes 680

The Treatment of Disorders of the Nervous System **685**

The Expansion of the Neurological/Neurochemical Approaches **686**

The Virtues and Limitations of the Neurological Approach **688**

Summary **690**

Questions for Critical Thinking **692**

PART **8**

ABNORMALITY, THE LAW, AND CHOOSING A PSYCHOTHERAPY

18 **The Law and Politics of Abnormality** 695

Involuntary Commitment and Treatment **696**
Involuntary Commitment and Perceptions of Abnormality 696
Procedures to Commit 699   Treatment 704   The Patient's
Rights Movement 707   Abolish Involuntary
Hospitalization? 708

Criminal Commitment **710**
The Insanity Defense 710   Competence to Stand Trial 718

Identity, Memory, and the Nature of Evidence **719**
Multiple Personality 720   Recovered Memories 720

The Social and Political Abuse of Abnormal Psychology **722**
Abuse by State 723   Abuse by Society 725

Summary **726**

Questions for Critical Thinking **727**

19 **A Consumer's Guide to Psychological Treatment** 728

Who Treats? **730**

The Common Ingredients of Therapy **734**
Free Choice and Treatment 735   Hopes and Expectations 735
Characteristics of Therapist-Client Interactions 737
Therapeutic Effectiveness 742

The Variety of Treatment **744**
Specific Therapies 745   Global Therapies 749

The Choice of Treatment **752**
Specific Treatments 752   Global Treatments 763

Outreach and Prevention: The Hopes of Community Psychology **764**
Prevention 765   Containment 766   Rehabilitation 770

Summary **772**

Questions for Critical Thinking **773**

APPENDIX: NUMERICAL LISTING OF DSM-IV DIAGNOSES AND CODES   A1

GLOSSARY   A7

REFERENCES   A20

ACKNOWLEDGMENTS AND COPYRIGHTS   A68

NAME INDEX   A73

SUBJECT INDEX   A89

PREFACE

When one of us, David Rosenhan, was an undergraduate, he took a course in abnormal psychology. The textbook was the classic text in the area, Robert White's *Abnormal Psychology.* More than a decade later, now as a young instructor, he taught the course in abnormal psychology using the same edition of the same classic textbook. Over the years, nothing had really changed in abnormal psychology. So there was no need to produce a new edition.

That's hardly the case today. Rather, there is hardly a field that is so vital and changing as this one. The revealed truths and tired dogmas of only a decade ago are being replaced by vital new directions and insights. Genuine eclecticism and genuine hope abound more today than ever before. Each month, and sometimes more frequently, brings new and important discoveries. Indeed, we found ourselves writing new material for this edition right down to the wire.

The first edition of this book was conceived in, of all places, a psychiatric hospital. David Rosenhan was engaged in a study in which a diverse group of normal people went into mental hospitals pretending to have a single symptom: They heard voices that said "empty," "meaningless," and "thud." From the moment they were admitted, these pseudopatients abandoned that symptom and acted the way "normal" people do. But they were labeled as crazy and treated that way for reasons that will become clear as you read this book. Martin Seligman heard about the study and wrote Rosenhan a fan letter, expressing his admiration for the courage it involved. To his surprise, Seligman received a phone call several days later inviting him to enter a hospital with Rosenhan. So it came about that in October 1973 both of us assumed false names—you figure out why—and wound up on the locked men's ward of a state mental hospital.

One can hardly think of a better place for two psychologists to become fast friends than in such a fascinating trench. In the hours and days that followed, discussion ranged over an enormous variety of topics: how we and our fellow patients were being treated, and why we were treated that way; our personal and academic lives; the legal rights of mental patients; how to choose a therapist; the dehumanizing effects of labeling; the diagnosis (and frequent misdiagnosis) of schizophrenia and depression; the causes of suicide; and finally, teaching itself—how the experience of hospitalization, of psychopathology, of the richness of psychotherapy, the importance of diagnosis, and the panoramic range of psychological misery, could be communicated to students. We left the hospital good friends, and with the hope that we might some day attempt to do something to improve the teaching of abnormal psychology.

This book, now in its third edition, is the result of more than twenty years of collaboration, research, clinical experience, delving into a vast and burgeoning literature, writing, rewriting and rewriting yet again, and teaching abnormal psychology to thousands of undergraduates.

Though occasionally overwhelming, the work has been simply exhilarating, the revisions equally so. We have no regrets. During the lifetime of this book, the progress that has been made in understanding and treating psychological disorders has been extraordinary. Disorders that were wholly mysterious and untreatable in the past, like the schizophrenias, depression, the anxiety disorders, and the sexual dysfunctions, can now be treated, often with considerable success. They are not yet fully understood. But neither are they entirely shrouded. Indeed, we not only understand them better than ever before, but we are now enormously optimistic about the prospects of the immediate future. If the last twenty-five years were highly informative, the next twenty-five promise extraordinary discoveries.

The Excitement of the Past Quarter Century

Consider the new advances and emphases in abnormal psychology since the first edition of this book was published more than a decade ago:

- The latest diagnostic techniques in medicine—the PET and CAT scans as well as magnetic resonance imaging (MRIs)—have been used successfully in the study of schizophrenia and obsessive-compulsive disorder.
- Modern discoveries in genetics have led to better understanding of disorders like schizophrenia, depression, and substance abuse.
- The roles of cognitive and interpersonal therapy, as well as of psychopharmacology, in treating depression have been greatly elucidated.
- Remarkable advances have been achieved in psychoneuroimmunology, advances of such depth that they have altogether changed our understanding of the impact of psychological states on physical illness.
- A new psychological treatment has been implemented that cures panic disorder in almost 90 percent of the cases.
- Our knowledge of the action of neurotransmitters in anxiety, depression, and schizophrenia has been deepened.
- And most important, perhaps as the result of increasing concern with effective health care, there has been a sea change in people's insistence on *determining efficacious treatments* for all sorts of psychological disorders.

The third edition of *Abnormal Psychology* incorporates these new findings and attitudes, as well as new research on the outcome of specific psychotherapies for certain disorders, the epidemiology of psychological disorder, the lasting effects of post-traumatic stress and rape, the psychobiology of panic and obsessive-compulsive disorder. Further, this edition includes discussions of the new understandings about agoraphobia, generalized anxiety disorder, the neuroanatomy of the brains of schizophrenics, interpersonal therapy, further refinements on Type A behavior and hostility, recovered memories, multiple personality, preventing depressive symptoms in children, and the effects of Prozac, clomipramine, and Ritalin. And of course, all of these findings have been informed by the latest revision of the increasingly controversial *Diagnostic and Statistical Manual of Mental Disorders*, DSM-IV.

Psychological Theory and Efficacious Treatment

This revision continues the strong emphasis on theory that marked the book in its earlier editions. Rather than viewing psychopathology through a single theoretical lens, we discuss all of the theories and then say which one we feel best illuminates a particular disorder. But the applicability of theory to treatment and disorder changes over time. New theories, particularly those that emphasize the role of *self* and the nature of *systems,* are introduced for their utility in understanding the personality disorders, as well as forming the basis of couple and family therapies.

The Intrinsic Interest of Abnormal Psychology

Abnormal psychology is inherently interesting to anyone who is concerned with understanding people and what makes them tick. We have tried to augment that interest by using richly described case histories that convey the immediacy and drama of psychopathology. We hope, too, that we have sustained the reader's interest by writing clearly and directly, by treating research findings in a coherent manner, by avoiding shotgun citations, and by avoiding jargon. The book is written for the intelligent reader, likely but not invariably, an undergraduate who has a quarter or semester to give to this effort.

For that effort, we expect the reader will gain an intelligent grasp of, and sympathy for, the issues in abnormal psychology. We also hope that the reader will now be able to evaluate and appreciate the significance of new research that will emerge after the course is completed.

People and Science

One final point: The book emphasizes the science of abnormal psychology and, equally, the human suffering that abnormality spawns and its enormous social costs. We want to be clear about that joint emphasis. As we take up each disorder, the scientific theories that explain them and the therapies that best treat them, we have spared little effort to convey the human side of this ongoing endeavor. Scientific explorations into diagnosis and treatment promise wholesale amelioration of human misery. Nothing else does with any kind of reliability. But the "science" of abnormality has no meaning unless human suffering is kept centrally in mind.

New Pedagogy—Nailing the Facts Down and Thinking Critically

For the third edition, we have introduced a three-part pedagogy, which we hope will help students organize their reading assignments, focus on what is important in each chapter, and encourage broad and critical thinking about the issues in abnormal psychology. The first pedagogical element is the "Chapter Organizer," a combination chapter outline and learning objectives box, which opens each chapter. The second element comprises a series of "Focus Questions" in boxes in the margins throughout each chapter, which should help students to learn and remember the important points in each major section. The third pedagogical element consists of "Questions for Critical Thinking," which address fundamental and at times controversial issues in the field. Nothing can really substitute for coherent and organized writing, and we have worked hard to offer a "narrative" of abnormal psychology, but we hope that these added pedagogical elements will help students get even more out of the course.

The Plan of This Book

This book is designed to be used in one-semester or one-quarter courses in abnormal psychology. The definitions, history, and major schools of thought and treatment of abnormality are presented first. Then, each of the major disorders—their description, their causes, and their treatments—is laid out in light of the competing schools of thought.

The book opens with two chapters on abnormality across time and place (Part 1). In Chapter 1, we explore the meanings of abnormality and normality. We argue that there is no one element that cases of abnormality all have. Rather, several significant elements combine to yield the judgment of abnormality. Chapter 2 examines how the view of madness has changed across history. It emphasizes a notion that is now considered "common sense"—that the origins of madness may be either physical or psychological—a view that was not accepted until the twentieth century.

Part 2 describes the prominent schools of thought and their approaches to, and treatments of, abnormality. Chapter 3, which deals with the biomedical model, looks at abnormality as a disease of the body. It examines the role of germs, genes, biochemistry, and neuroanatomy in the production of abnormality. It also discusses the major psychotropic medications and their side effects. Chapter 4 takes up both the psychodynamic model of abnormality, the towering work of Sigmund Freud, and more modern views. Chapter 5 presents the learning models, incorporating the behavioral school of thought, which emphasizes the role of classical conditioning and of instrumental learning as potential causes and treatments of abnormality, and the cognitive school, which holds that psychological abnormality is produced by disordered conscious thinking, and that changing disordered thinking produces cure.

Having outlined the major schools of thought about abnormality, Part 3 turns to how abnormality is investigated and how it is diagnosed. Chapter 6 investigates the role of different methods of assessment for illuminating the cause and cure of abnormality. Case histories, laboratory experiments, correlational studies, experiments of nature, and experimental models are all examined and compared. All the methods contribute to our knowledge of abnormality, and we describe how they do so. This section ends with Chapter 7, which discusses the diagnosis and assessment of abnormality. The recently published DSM-IV is fully described and critically evaluated. (Part of it is reprinted in an appendix at the end of the book.) The varieties of psychological and neurological tests that assist in diagnosing abnormal conditions, are also examined.

Part 4 covers anxiety and psychosomatic disorders. The three chapters on anxiety and psychosomatic disorders are organized around the degree to which anxiety is apparent in the disorder itself. Chapter 8 discusses those anxiety disorders in which the sufferer actually feels fear and anxiety, and includes phobia, post-traumatic stress disorder, panic disorder, and generalized anxiety disorder. Chapter 9 turns to those disorders in which the existence of anxiety is inferred rather than apparent: obsessive-compulsive disorders, somatoform disorders, and dissociative disorders (including dissociative amnesia and multiple personality). Chapter 10 looks at health psychology and psychosomatic disorders, those disorders in which physical illness is influenced, and in the strongest case caused, by psychological factors. We examine in detail psychosomatic principles and illustrate these principles through discussing peptic ulcers and cardiovascular disorders (including Type A personality and sudden death). There is also a detailed discussion of psychoneuroimmunology.

Part 5 turns to the major depressive disorders and the schizophrenias. Chapter 11 deals with depression and suicide. It describes the symptoms of depression, the distinguishing features of manic-depressive disorder and unipolar depression, and it provides a description of the three major competing theories of and therapies for depression. We propose an integrative theory of depression, and then discuss the most tragic consequence of depression, suicide. Chapter 12 describes schizophrenia and its symptoms, illustrating the disorder with rich case history material. We conclude the section with an evaluation of competing psychological, genetic, biochemical, and societal theories of schizophrenia, and a discussion of the prospects of treatment and rehabilitation of people with this devastating disorder.

Part 6 examines some special social and interpersonal disorders. Chapter 13, on sexual disorders, begins with an examination of the five layers of human sexuality. We first examine sexual identity and transsexualism. We then turn to sexual orientation. Next we explore sexual interest (the paraphilias). We then go on to a discussion of sex roles. Finally, we examine sexual function and dysfunction. In Chapter 14, we examine psychoactive substance use disorders. We discuss diagnosing and defining drug abuse. We go into the basic effects of drugs and discuss theoretical models of drug dependence. We look at each of the major abused drugs, from alcohol, stimulants, opiates (narcotics), hallucinogens (including LSD, PCP, and MDMA), marijuana, and cigarette smoking, to sedative-hypnotics and tranquilizers, as well as their underlying psychological and biological causes and correlates. We also examine future directions in treatment and prevention of substance abuse. In Chapter 15, we discuss the personality disorders, that is, the disorders in which a person's entire character structure presents a problem for the individual or for society. We focus particularly on the antisocial personality disorder, but also include such other disorders as paranoid personality disorder, avoidant personality disorder, schizotypal personality disorder, and borderline personality disorder.

Part 7 considers abnormality throughout the lifespan. In Chapter 16, we examine disorders of childhood. In many respects, children and adults suffer similar problems: fears, phobias, eating disorders, and the like. But those problems in youngsters often create experiences and outcomes that adults might not predict or understand. In Chapter 17, we examine psychopathology and disorders of the nervous system, including disorders of language (the aphasias), dyslexia, a disorder of memory (the amnesic syndrome), dementia and especially Alzheimer's disease (which is a disorder that especially afflicts older people), and disorders related to the frontal lobes.

The final section of the book—Part 8—considers legal issues that are associated with psychological abnormality, and issues associated with effective treatment. In Chapter 18, we look at society's institutionalized reaction to abnormality, and our laws about voluntary and involuntary commitment. We then examine the insanity defense and ask: When, if ever, does insanity excuse wrongful actions? We also discuss a particularly difficult problem both for law and for psychology—the problem of repressed memories and their gradual or sudden reemergence. In the final chapter, Chapter 19, we ask: How can one use the information in this book to locate efficacious treatment? We review the panoply of available treatments for various disorders, and we offer suggestions about the most effective treatments for particular problems.

Acknowledgments

In the course of writing three editions of this book, we have accumulated intellectual and personal debts to colleagues, friends, students, and family. Many people have been more generous with time and critique than we had any right to anticipate. Chief among these is Paul Rozin (University of Pennsylvania), our friend and colleague and Norton's editorial adviser. He encouraged us when we flagged, and found merit when we seemed to be losing heart. He raised pointed questions in every draft of every chapter of the first edition, and continued to do so for the second and third editions.

Writing such a text is a challenging undertaking. There were three areas—psychoactive substance use disorders, child psychopathology, and disorders of the nervous system—where we felt that others, more expert in these areas, might best take up authorship. We particularly thank Ann E. Kelley (University of Wisconsin) for writing a completely new Chapter 14, Psychoactive Substance Use Disorders; Susan Nolen-Hoeksema (Stanford University) for thoroughly revising Chapter 16, Childhood Disorders and Mental Retardation; and Morris Moscovitch (University of Toronto) and Paul Rozin (University of Pennsylvania) for writing and revising Chapter 17, Disorders of the Nervous System.

From other colleagues we received comments on specific chapters in the book. For their time and thoughtful advice, which we occasionally risked neglecting, we thank the following:

Larry E. Beutler, *University of California, Santa Barbara*
Michael Bohn, *University of Wisconsin*
Irving Gottesman, *University of Virginia*
Will Grove, *University of Minnesota*
Janice Kiecolt-Glaser, *Ohio State University*
Gregory K. Lehne, *Private Practice, Maryland*
Sarnoff Mednick, *University of Southern California*
Patricia Minnes, *Queen's University, Canada*
John Monahan, *University of Virginia*

We thank teachers of courses in Abnormal Psychology on whom we came to rely for suggestions and changes for the third edition. They brought both their own expertise and especially their experience in the classroom.

Raymond M. Bergner, *Illinois State University*
Ron Boykin, *Salisbury State University*
Richard A. Gordon, *Bard College*
Charles Grunder, *University of Maine*
Laurie Heatherington, *Williams College*
Robert Hoff, *Mercyhurst College*
Mick Hunter, *University of Newcastle, Australia*
Gary G. Johnson, *Normandale Community College*
Mark Lenzenweger, *Cornell University*
Stanley Lynch, *Santa Fe Community College*
Joanne Marrow, *California State University, Sacramento*
E. George Nichols, *Mount Allison University, Canada*

Thomas Nielsen, *Aarhus University, Denmark*
J. Mitchell Noon, *University of Sussex, United Kingdom*
Demetrios Papageorgis, *University of British Columbia, Canada*
David Powley, *Mobile College*
Rena Repetti, *University of California, Los Angeles*
Georgina Rippon, *University of Warwick, United Kingdom*
Anita Rosenfield, *California State University, Los Angeles*
Jill A. Steinberg, *San Jose State University*
Laura Stephenson, *Washburn University*
Philip A. Street, *Saint Mary's University, Canada*
Steven Tiffany, *Purdue University*

The third edition of this book benefited enormously from the assistance of Chris Prokop, Shelly Zulman, Jennifer Ma, Midnight Toker, Dwight Owsley, Shulamit Magnus, and especially Justin Hayes. Administrative support came from Mary Tye, Elise McMahon, and Carol McSorley. Our debt to these people is great.

Finally, we thank those at Norton with whom we have worked for better than two decades across three editions of Abnormal Psychology. We are especially grateful to our editor, Don Fusting, who guided each edition. This was no mere acquiring editior. Don was passionately involved with the book, criticizing each chapter for its intellectual and educational message, offering conceptual and organizational suggestions. We learned to neglect Don's comments at the book's peril. Equally, we are grateful to our developmental editor, Sandra Lifland, whose efforts across the three editions simply defy description. Like Don, she took a collegial role in this revision, raising theoretical questions and pressing relentlessly for answers. She ferreted out every instance of awkward and inelegant prose—there are none left, we now believe—and made handsome remedial suggestions. Much of what is visually attractive about the book grew from her hard work, as well as the work of A. Deborah Malmud and Kate Brewster, the photo editors of the book. Timothy Holahan was a great help in taking care of innumerable editorial details. Roberta Flechner prepared the attractive page layouts, and Roy Tedoff, director of manufacturing, made sure that all our efforts were carried successfully through the book production process. All of their work was done with the incredible persistence and gentleness that evokes admiration, respect, and gratitude.

D.L.R.
M.E.P.S.
August 1994

THE NATURE AND HISTORY OF ABNORMALITY

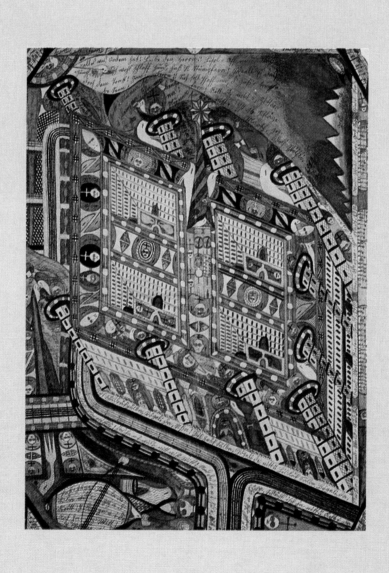

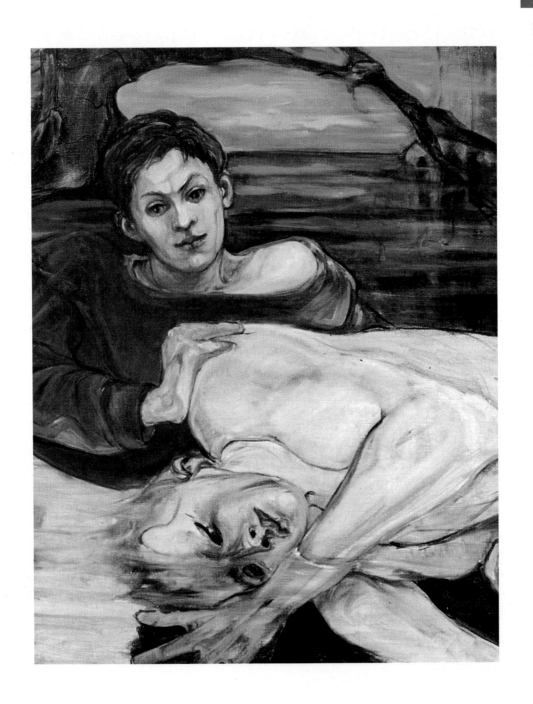

CHAPTER 1

The Meanings of Abnormality

CHAPTER ORGANIZER

ABNORMALITY
- Familiarize yourself with the seven elements of abnormality.
- Learn how the family resemblance approach can be applied when diagnosing behavior as abnormal, and what some of the pitfalls of the approach are.

NORMALITY
- In light of our definition of "abnormality," how do we define "normality"?

BEYOND NORMALITY
- Be able to describe the six areas of optimal living.

THE HAZARDS OF SELF-DIAGNOSIS
- Become aware of the hazards of self-diagnosis.

 hat does it mean to say that someone is "abnormal"? How do we *know* that person is abnormal? If we are right that the person is abnormal, how did he become that way? How can he be changed? By any means possible? Does he have any rights in this matter? These are the issues that concern this book. And they are not minor matters.

Junius Wilson* is now a free man. He was ninety-six years old when, in 1994, he was released from the locked ward of Cherry Hospital, a psychiatric institution located in Goldsboro, N.C. Black and deaf, he had been on the locked ward of that hospital for sixty-eight years, ever since 1925 when he was twenty-eight years old and was charged with assault with the intent to commit rape. He was never convicted of that (or any other) criminal offense. In fact, the charge was eventually dropped. Moreover, there is no evidence that he was ever insane. Nevertheless, he was declared insane and committed to what was then the state insane asylum for black people. Before he entered the hospital, the State had him castrated.

In 1970, hospital authorities realized that Mr. Wilson was perfectly sane and that he did not belong in the hospital. But by then, he had lived in Cherry Hospital for more than forty years. His family could not be found. And it was by no means

*Junius Wilson is his real name. We use it because his plight has been discussed in the news media. The identities of other people whose difficulties are described in this book have been carefully camouflaged.

clear that freeing him then would have improved his life. Living in a psychiatric hospital is not ideal preparation for living outside of it. So he remained on the locked ward, although he was given "privileges."

In 1991, John Wasson was appointed Wilson's legal guardian and social worker. Once he learned that Wilson was not insane, Wasson worked to get Wilson out of the locked ward of the hospital. Wasson threatened to sue the state for Wilson's release. It took three years, but in February 1994, North Carolina renovated a cottage on hospital grounds, and Wilson occupied it. A free man at last, Wilson could pass the rest of his life outside the locked psychiatric ward.

How could this have happened, you ask? How could a sane man, against whom no criminal charge had ever been sustained, have been locked up for sixty-eight years?

▲ Junius Wilson, declared insane and incarcerated for 68 years for a crime of which he was never convicted, after his release at the age of 96.

- Mr. Wilson was thought to be insane for at least forty-five years, until someone in 1970 recognized that he was not insane. How could his sanity have gone undetected for so long a period? We take up the question of what constitutes abnormality in this chapter, and the effects of hospitalization in Chapter 18.
- How much agreement is there about what constitutes normality and abnormality? Can we really spot abnormal people when we see them? This issue is taken up in this chapter.
- How much did Mr. Wilson's race have to do with his "treatment"? And how much did the fact that he was deaf make it difficult for professionals to understand that he was quite normal? These questions are addressed throughout the book, but especially in Chapter 7.
- Finally, is the State justified in using the instruments and insights of abnormal psychology to deal with legal issues and social policy? And if you feel that the State is justified in using psychological science that way, how can individuals be protected against potential abuse by the State? These matters are addressed in Chapter 18.

Before we begin to understand what happened to Junius Wilson, we need to understand what is normal and what is abnormal.

There are no clear-cut definitions of abnormality, and no infallible way to recognize abnormality. Many of us will have suspected as much from our own experience. Recall your descent from innocence when, after periods of special distress, you asked yourself "Am I normal?" or "Is she normal?" Those were difficult questions whose answers were not immediately forthcoming. And they were often questions that were quickly abandoned, lest they lead to uncharted areas in ourselves or others that were more difficult and distressing than the behaviors we were trying to understand in the first place.

ABNORMALITY

If abnormality cannot be defined simply and clearly, does that mean that there is no such thing as abnormal behavior? Far from it. Abnormality is recognized everywhere, in every culture, by nearly everyone. Sometimes the impression of abnormality comes through clearly and unambiguously. At other times, reasonable people will disagree as to whether a particular person, action, or thought is or is not abnormal. The following clinical vignettes make this clear.

- Don is viewed by nearly everyone as a quiet, mild-mannered executive. But one day, gripped by a sudden seizure in the temporal lobe of the brain, he picks up his sales manager, chair and all, and hurls her to death through the eleventh floor window of an office building.
- Vanessa, a teenage girl, eats nothing at all for several days, then gorges herself on eight hot-fudge sundaes within two hours, vomits explosively, and then eats nothing more for three days.
- Carla's religious principles forbid her from wearing makeup or drinking liquor. Her college friends do both. She is continually anxious when she is with them.

Of these cases, two things can be said immediately. First, they involve different behaviors, which arise from sources as diverse as brain pathology and religious beliefs. And second, while some people will be quite confident that all of these instances represent abnormality, not everyone will agree. Everyone will judge the first case abnormal. Nearly everyone will judge the second case abnormal. But there will be vigorous debate about the third.

The act of defining the word "abnormal" suggests that there is some single property that these three cases of abnormality, and all others, must share. This shared property is called a *necessary* condition for abnormality. But there is no common element among these three cases, for what is it that temporal lobe seizures, gorging oneself on hot-fudge sundaes, and conflict between religious conviction and social acceptance have in common? Moreover, a precise definition of "abnormal" requires that there be at least one distinguishing element that only cases of abnormality share and that no cases of "normality" share. This is called a *sufficient* condition of abnormality. But is there any one feature that separates all cases of abnormality from all those that we would call normal? Not any that we can find. In fact, as we will shortly see, there is no single element shared by all cases of abnormality, and no single element that distinguishes abnormality from normality.

In short, the word "abnormal" cannot be defined precisely. Indeed, few of the words we commonly use, and especially those that are used socially, are

▶ One of these images is by a commercial artist, one by a mental patient. Just as no single feature of the drawings sets them apart from each other, no single symptom or behavior is necessary or sufficient to define abnormality.

precisely defined, for the use of language often depends on flexible meanings. But the fact that abnormality cannot be defined "tightly" does not mean that abnormality doesn't exist or that it can't be recognized at all. It does exist, and it is recognized in much the same way that families are recognized. How do we know, for example, that Ed Smith is the *biological* offspring of Bill and Jane Smith? Well, he *looks* like them. He has Bill's blue eyes and sandy hair, and Jane's upturned nose and easy smile. Even though Ed is six inches taller than his father and has a rounder face than his mother, we sense a ***family resemblance*** among them because they have many significant elements in common. (But careful now: Ed might just be the *adopted* son of Bill and Jane Smith. Such are the hazards of family resemblances!)

Abnormality is recognized in the same way, by determining whether the behavior, thought, or person bears a family resemblance to the behaviors, thoughts, and people we would all recognize as abnormal. That determination is made by spelling out the properties of abnormality, the various *elements* that count toward defining a behavior as abnormal. The more such elements there are and the more clearly each one is present, the more likely it is that the behavior, thought, or person will be judged abnormal. Let's examine those elements.

The Elements of Abnormality

We will look at seven properties or elements that count toward deciding whether an action or a person is abnormal. Our analysis describes the way ordinary people and well-trained psychologists actually use the word. These elements or properties of abnormality are:

- Suffering
- Maladaptiveness
- Irrationality and incomprehensibility
- Unpredictability and loss of control
- Vividness and unconventionality
- Observer discomfort
- Violation of moral and ideal standards.

The more of these elements that are present, and the more clearly they can be seen, the more certain we are that the behavior or person is abnormal. At least one of these elements *must* be present for abnormality to exist. But no one particular element must always be present, and only rarely will all of the elements be present. Let us examine these elements in greater detail.

SUFFERING

Abnormality hurts. A depressed housewife feels miserable. For her, the prospect of going through another day seems unbearable.

We are likely to call people abnormal if they are suffering psychologically, and the more they suffer, the more certain we are. But suffering is not a *necessary* condition of abnormality: it does not have to be present for us to label a behavior as abnormal. Someone who phones the President in the middle of the night, certain that the Chief Executive wants to hear all about his health-care plan, can feel exuberant, cheerful, and full of hope. Nevertheless, such a person is viewed as abnormal, since the other elements of abnormality override the absence of suffering and convince us that his behavior is abnormal.

Suffering, moreover, is not a *sufficient* condition for abnormality because suffering is commonplace in the normal course of life. A child will grieve for a dead pet, for example, much as all of us mourn the loss of loved ones. If no other elements of abnormality are present, however, grief and suffering will not be judged as abnormal.

Suffering, then, is an element that counts toward the perception of abnormality. But it is neither necessary nor sufficient. The context in which the suffering occurs counts heavily toward whether it is seen as abnormal.

MALADAPTIVENESS

Whether a behavior is functional and adaptive—how well it enables the individual to achieve certain goals—is a fundamental element in deciding whether the behavior is normal or abnormal. In biology, the fundamental scientific yardstick of adaptiveness is applied to the three important questions: Does it promote survival of the species? Does it promote the well-being of the individual? And does it promote the well-being of society? Psychologists tend most strongly to ask the last two questions: How well does the behavior foster individual well-being? And how well does it foster the well-being of society? Behaviors that strongly interfere with individual or social well-being are maladaptive and would count as factors in assessing abnormality.

By individual well-being, we mean the ability to work and the ability to conduct satisfying relations with other people. Depression and anxiety interfere with love and work and, almost always, with an individual's sense of well-being. A fear of going out (agoraphobia) can be so strong that it keeps the sufferer locked inside an apartment, unable to fulfill any of the individual's goals. Such a fear grossly interferes with the enjoyment of life, the ability to work, and relations with others. The more there is such interference, the clearer the abnormality.

FOCUS QUESTIONS

1. What are the seven elements of abnormality?
2. Explain when each of the elements is used to determine abnormality.

It is abnormal to interfere strongly with the well-being of society. Murderers and arsonists are often called psychopaths, indicating society's judgment that their actions are abnormal. But are those actions truly abnormal? Are there enough elements of abnormality in these actions to make the family resemblance plausible? Or are these actions merely wrong or illegal? A "psychopathic" mobster may go about his work well, arranging theft and murder without the slightest pang of conscience. But he may also be an attentive husband, devoted father, and a lover of the good life. His behavior is maladaptive for the group, causing a negative social judgment of his behavior. But whether his behavior is ultimately held to be *abnormal* will depend on how many of the other elements of abnormality are present.

IRRATIONALITY AND INCOMPREHENSIBILITY

When a person's behavior seems to have no rational meaning, we are inclined to call that behavior and that person abnormal. People who, like Vanessa, alternately gorge themselves and vomit, who speak earnest gibberish, who somehow ensure that they will be disliked by precisely those from whom they most desire affection—these people exhibit incomprehensible and irrational behaviors that are elements of abnormality.

One kind of incomprehensibility that counts very strongly for the designation of abnormality is thought disorder, a major symptom of schizophrenia. Beliefs that are patently absurd and bizarre, perceptions that have no basis in objective reality, and mental processes that ramble from one idea to another unrelated one constitute thought disorders. A memorable example of such thought disorganization occurred during a formal experiment. The patient's task consisted of sorting colored blocks of various shapes and colors into a number of groups. The patient was cooperative and earnest. But he also exhibited an irresistible tendency to sort objects on the desk and on the experimenter's person, as well as parts of the room, things he pulled from his pockets, and even the experimenter himself, whom the patient recommended be remade of wood and cut into blocks. Here is what he said:

> I've got to pick it out of the whole room. I can't confine myself to this game . . . Three blues [test blocks] . . . now, how about that green blotter? Put it there too. Green peas you eat. You can't eat them unless you write on it (pointing to green blotter). Like that wristwatch (on the experimenter's wrist, a foot from the subject)—don't see three meals coming off that watch . . . To do this trick *you'd* have to be made of wood. You've got a white shirt on—and the white blocks. You have to have them cut out of *you!* You've got a white shirt on—this (white hexagonal block) will hold you and never let you go. I've got a blue shirt on, but it can't be a blue shirt and still go together. And the room's got to be the same . . . (Excerpted from Cameron, 1947, p. 59.)

UNPREDICTABILITY AND LOSS OF CONTROL

We expect people to be consistent from time to time, predictable from one occasion to the next, and very much in control of themselves. To be loved one day and hated the next is troubling. One hardly knows how to respond or what to expect. Our need to control our environment (Rotter, 1966; Seligman, 1975; Rothbaum, Weisz, and Snyder, 1982) and to retain our own freedom (Brehm and Brehm, 1981) require that other people be predictable. In a predictable world, there is consistency and control. In an unpredictable one, we feel vulnerable and threatened. Don, the mild-mannered executive who hurled his sales manager out the window, is frightening in much the same way that Dr. Jekyll's alter ego, Mr. Hyde, is: both are unpredictable and out of control.

The judgment that behavior is out of control will be made under two conditions. The first occurs when the ordinary guides and inhibitors of behavior suddenly break down. Don exemplifies this judgment. The second condition occurs when we do not know what causes an action. Imagine coming upon someone who is angry—raging and screaming in the streets. There may be good and socially acceptable reasons for such an anger. But if we do not know those reasons and are unable to elicit them at the time, we are likely to consider that the person is out of control and to designate those actions as abnormal.

Not all instances of loss of control, however, are abnormal. Flexible control, the ability to retain control or give it up as the self and situation require, is a hallmark of good psychological functioning (London and Rosenhan, 1968). The inability to relinquish control during sexual intercourse, for example, is likely to breed problems rather than reflect them.

VIVIDNESS AND UNCONVENTIONALITY

Generally, people recognize as acceptable and conventional those actions that they themselves are willing to do. Those who accede to a request to walk around campus wearing a sandwich board that reads "EAT AT JOE'S" are likely to estimate that a healthy majority of their peers would make the same choice. On the other hand, those who are unwilling to wear such a sign estimate that relatively *few* people would be willing. Thus, with the exception of behaviors that require great skill or daring, we tend to judge the abnormality of others' behavior by our own. Would *you* spend the winter in New York over a hot air vent on the Upper East Side? If you would, you would judge such behavior as conventional and normal. If you wouldn't, such behavior would stand out vividly as unconventional and abnormal (Ross, Greene, and House, 1977).

What is conventional and acceptable in any society is always changing. Those who are on the leading edge of that change are very visible compared to the rest of us (whose behavior is still conventional), and they run the risk of

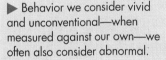
▶ Behavior we consider vivid and unconventional—when measured against our own—we often also consider abnormal.

being labeled as deviants, and therefore as abnormal. Forty-five years ago, for example, beards were rare. Those who wore them stood out in the crowd and were perceived as deviant and abnormal. Today, of course, those same beards would hardly be noticed.

The element of vividness is affected by whether an action is rare. Behaviors that are rare *and* undesirable are very likely to seem quite vivid, and hence to be considered abnormal. It hardly matters whether the behavior actually *is* rare, so long as it is *perceived* to be rare. Thus, there are many varieties of sexual and aggressive fantasies that are quite common but that are perceived to be rare and therefore abnormal. Nor is rareness itself a necessary condition for abnormality. Depression is a common disorder, as are anxiety states, and both are considered to be abnormal. But behavior that is both rare and socially undesirable is seen as abnormal. A rare behavior that is socially desirable, would be considered a "gift" and only abnormal in the statistical sense. Genius is rare. So is high moral character. But if they are abnormal, they are abnormalities to which most of us aspire.

OBSERVER DISCOMFORT

People who are very dependent on others, or ingratiating, or hostile, create discomfort in observers. Their behaviors often enable them to feel more comfortable, but the psychological conflicts they create are painful for others. In some ways, they are like people who are becoming gradually deaf and who turn up the volume on their radio to compensate. Suddenly, they can hear perfectly well again, but the noise that is created is intolerable to others.

We are most likely to experience vague observer discomfort when someone violates unwritten or **residual rules** of behavior (Scheff, 1966). Residual rules are rules that no one ever teaches but that we nonetheless know intuitively and use to guide our behavior. Violation of those rules creates the kind of discomfort that leads to the designation "abnormal."

For example, in some cultures, there is an unwritten rule which states that, except when angry or making love, one's face should be at least ten inches away from that of one's partner. Should that invisible boundary be overstepped, a residual rule will be violated, and the partner will feel uncomfortable. Similarly, there are unwritten rules about speech fluency (that one ought not to stutter) and about clothing one's genital area which, when violated, contribute to the impression that the person is abnormal.

VIOLATION OF MORAL AND IDEAL STANDARDS

There are times when behavior is assessed, not against our judgments of what is common and conventional, but against moral standards and idealized norms that are believed to characterize all right-thinking and right-acting people. This view starts with the notion that people *ought* to behave in a certain way, whether they really do or not, and it concludes with the view that it is normal to behave in the way one ought, and abnormal to fail to behave properly. Thus, it is normal to work, and abnormal not to do so (unless wealth, the unavailability of job openings, or illness exonerate one). It is normal to love, to be loyal, and to be supportive, and abnormal not to—regardless of the fact that evidence for these dispositions is not widely found in modern society. It is abnormal to be too aggressive or too restrained, too shy or too forward, too ambitious or not sufficiently ambitious. It is abnormal to believe in unidentified fly-

residual rules - unwritten rules of behavior that we know instinctively

"Anything wrong?"

(Drawing by Sempé; © 1981, The New Yorker Magazine, Inc.)

ing objects and abnormal *not* to believe in a good supernatural being. As far as ideal standards are concerned, abnormality becomes another word for all manner of behaviors that range from that which is down-right wicked to that which is best done without.

Applying the Family Resemblance Approach

Family members resemble each other across a fixed number of dimensions, such as height, hair and eye color, and shape of nose, mouth, and ears. Similarly, abnormality is assessed according to the match between an individual's characteristics and the seven elements of abnormality.

Examine the following case study with a view toward determining the "family resemblance" between the individual and the elements of abnormality.

> Ralph, the seventeen-year-old son of a physician and a pharmacist, moved with his family from a small farming town to a large suburban community during the middle of his junior year in high school. The move was sudden: both his parents were offered jobs that were simply too good to turn down. The abruptness of the move generated no complaint from Ralph, nor did he acknowledge any difficulty. Nevertheless, he seemed to withdraw. At the outset, his family hardly noticed, but once the family settled down, his distant behavior became apparent. He made no friends in his new school, and when the summer came, he seemed to withdraw even further. He spent a good deal of the summer in his room, emerging only to take extended walks around the house. He often seemed preoccupied, and occasionally seemed to be listening to sounds that only he could hear.
>
> Autumn approached and with it the time for Ralph to return to his senior year of high school. Ralph became even more withdrawn. He had difficulty sleeping, and he paced inside and outside the house. Shortly after he returned to school, his behavior deteriorated further. Sometimes, he seemed not to hear when called upon in class, while at other times his answers bore no relation to the questions. Both behaviors generated a good deal of mocking laughter in his classes, and his classmates actively avoided him. One day, he marched into class, stood up, and began to speak absolute gibberish. School authorities notified his parents, who came immediately to pick him up. When he saw them, he grimaced and began to roll a lock of hair between his fingers. He said nothing as he was brought to a psychiatric clinic. (Adapted from DSM-III Training Guide, 1981.)

Is Ralph abnormal according to the preceding criteria? Even this brief vignette, which fails to describe fully the richness of Ralph's problem, leaves us convinced that Ralph is suffering some kind of psychological abnormality. Let us return to the elements of abnormality, and examine the extent to which Ralph's actions reflect those elements.

- **Suffering.** We have no information about whether, or to what degree, Ralph is suffering. His withdrawal from his family *might* reflect subjective distress. But then again, it might not.
- **Maladaptiveness.** Ralph's behavior is highly dysfunctional. Not only does he needlessly draw negative attention to himself, but he obviously fails to respond to the demands of school. Such behavior neither serves his own needs nor those of society.

- ***Incomprehensibility and irrationality.*** There can be little doubt that Ralph's behavior is incomprehensible to observers, and that his verbalizations seem irrational to them.
- ***Unpredictability and loss of control.*** There is little evidence for loss of control in the vignette, but Ralph's parents would presumably find his behavior unpredictable. So too might his schoolmates.
- **Vividness.** Ralph's behavior is quite vivid. His silent withdrawal stands out noticeably and his speeches in class make him the center of undesirable attention.
- ***Observer discomfort.*** It is not clear from the vignette whether *all* observers are made uncomfortable by Ralph's behavior, but it is a fair guess that his schoolmates are avoiding him because they feel uncomfortable.
- ***Violation of moral and ideal standards.*** There is no evidence that Ralph's behavior violates widely held moral standards.

In the main, then, Ralph's behavior is dysfunctional and incomprehensible. These elements alone would have qualified his behavior as abnormal in most people's judgment. Additionally, there is some evidence that his behavior is unpredictable, vivid, and creates discomfort in observers. These elements lend additional strength to the judgment that his behavior is abnormal.

What is the locus of Ralph's abnormality? His behavior is abnormal. His thought is abnormal. And because these problems of behavior and thought last for such a long time and occur across so many different situations, we come to call Ralph himself abnormal. This is the convention; it invites us to generalize from the actions and thoughts of an individual to the individual himself. This linguistic convention is not without costs, however, for we can easily be misled into believing that a particular pattern of behavior or thought is much more disabling and pervasive than it really is. It is tragic enough that Ralph has the problems he is afflicted with. But it adds considerably to his tragedy to somehow infer that Ralph himself is flawed, rather than merely realizing that *sometimes* and in *some* situations Ralph's *behaviors and thoughts* are abnormal.

▶ The film *One Flew Over the Cuckoo's Nest,* based on the novel by Ken Kesey, is ambiguous about whether the main character is abnormal or not.

DSM-IV and Psychological Diagnosis

Abnormality is a global term. It serves only to indicate that something is judged to be wrong psychologically with a person's behavior or personality. But once the judgment is made that a person's behavior is abnormal, the question arises: How is it abnormal?

The specific ways in which people are judged to be abnormal are described in the revised *Diagnostic and Statistical Manual of Mental Disorders* (Fourth Edition), commonly called DSM-IV, which was published by the American Psychiatric Association in 1994. This catalog of psychological distress is large and all-embracing, and we will describe it at some length in Chapter 7. For the present, however, it is important to know that arriving at a specific disorder or diagnosis in DSM-IV itself amounts to using family resemblances. DSM-IV describes the elements that are said to characterize a particular disorder. Moreover, it describes the criteria for recognizing whether a particular element is present. The better the match between an individual's behavior and the elements offered for the disorder, the more confident we can be of the diagnosis (Cantor, Smith, French, and Mezzich, 1980).

Hazards of the "Family Resemblance" Approach to Abnormality

The virtue of a family resemblance approach to abnormality arises from the fact that, much as there is no *single* way in which all sons resemble all fathers, neither is there a *single* way in which all abnormal behaviors resemble each other. The notion that all abnormality must involve psychological suffering, or vividness, or observer discomfort is simply false, as we have seen. No single element exists that binds the behaviors of, say, a person who is deeply depressed, a person who is afraid to be alone, and a person who gorges herself and then vomits. Yet, we regard each of these people to be suffering an abnormality because their behaviors are members of the family of characteristics that we have come to regard as abnormal.

But there are some hazards to the family resemblance approach to abnormality. Let's look at three of these hazards: society's error, disagreement between observers, and disagreement between actor and observer.

SOCIETY MAY ERR IN WHOM IT CALLS ABNORMAL

Unlike the judgment of temperature, the judgment of abnormality is a social one. Look again at some of the elements: observer discomfort, vividness and unconventionality, and violation of moral and ideal standards. These all require the presence of other people, while the remaining elements of abnormality can also easily be interpreted socially. Social judgments, however, can easily be abused, and because the judgment of abnormality is so heavily social, it is even more susceptible to social abuse. That, in fact, is why Junius Wilson was locked up in a psychiatric hospital for sixty-eight years. A black man who was also deaf, he was an easy target for all kinds of social judgments that should have been absolutely irrelevant to judgments of psychological abnormality, but weren't.

The notion of abnormality can easily and erroneously be applied to all manner of behavior that society presently finds objectionable. As we indicated

3 problems: society error
disagreement b/w observers
dis b/w actor + observer

FOCUS QUESTIONS

1. What is the "family resemblance" approach to determining abnormality?
2. What are some of the pitfalls of psychological diagnosis?

---

earlier, those who wore beards forty-five years ago were seen as abnormal because they "stood out in the crowd." Their behavior matched one of the elements of abnormality, and they were, therefore, erroneously termed abnormal.

But it is not merely vivid behavior that can trigger allegations of abnormality. Behavior that creates discomfort in observers, for whatever reasons, risks triggering those allegations. The student who refuses to haze when his fraternity brothers are doing so, the person who, for deeply philosophic reasons, refuses to fight in any war, the person who works for social change, the political dissenter—these people march to their own drummers, and they create discomfort in the observers who disagree with them. Similarly, those who violate the ideal standards of others in the course of maintaining their *own* ideal standards risk being termed abnormal.

OBSERVERS WILL DISAGREE ABOUT PARTICULAR BEHAVIORS OR INDIVIDUALS

A family resemblance approach to abnormality is bound to generate some disagreements about whether or not a behavior qualifies as abnormal. Two observers might disagree that any given element was present. Moreover, they might disagree about whether enough elements were present, or whether they were present with sufficient intensity to constitute a clear case of abnormality.

In a study that will be more fully described in Chapter 7 (pp. 200–201), daily visitors came to large psychiatric hospitals to visit "pseudopatients," that is, people who were in the hospital to study it, not to be treated. These visitors quickly learned that they had to leave the hospital before the next staff shift came to work. Otherwise, they would be faced with the difficult task of proving that they, the visitors, were not patients. After all, they shared at least two visible elements with true patients: Like true patients, they had no keys! And like many of them, the visitors insisted that they did not belong there. That common family resemblance was occasionally strong enough to create some difficult moments for the visitors.

Such an approach generates disagreement for the further reason that the elements of abnormality are neither so precise nor so quantifiable that everyone will agree that a behavior or person fits the category. The more dramatic the behaviors and the longer they are sustained, the more agreement there will be among observers. The problem of observer disagreement is a serious one. As we shall see in Chapter 7, the problem is dealt with, to some extent, by stipulating as clearly as one can, the kinds of behaviors that are associated with each element of abnormality. When this is done, wider agreement occurs.

OBSERVERS AND ACTORS WILL OCCASIONALLY DISAGREE

There will occasionally be different opinions as to whether a behavior or person should be judged as abnormal, according to who is doing the judging: the individuals who are generating the behaviors in question—we call them actors—or those who observe the behaviors. Generally, actors will be less inclined to judge their own behaviors as abnormal for three reasons: First, they have much more information available to them about their own behaviors than do observers. What seems unpredictable or incomprehensible to an observer may seem quite predictable and comprehensible to an actor, and what generates discomfort in an observer may, as we indicated, generate none in the actor. Second, people who are psychologically distressed are not distressed all the time. Distress comes and goes. People, therefore, may be "crazy" at one time, but not crazy at another. Actors are uniquely positioned to recognize

FIGURE 1–1

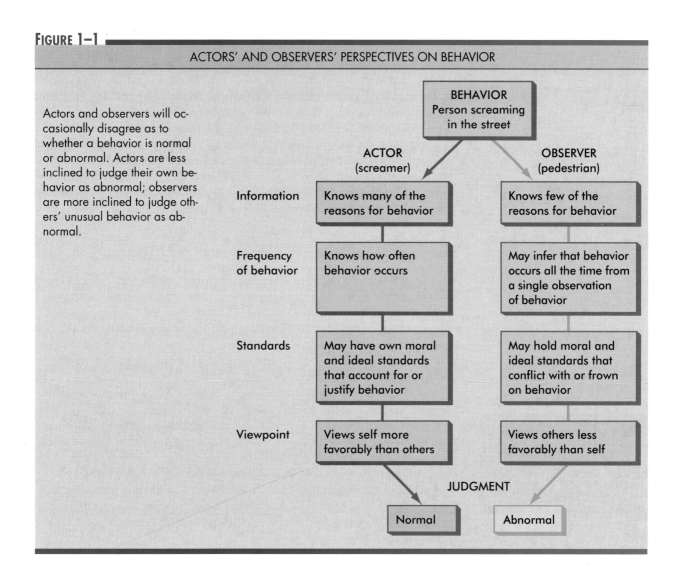

ACTORS' AND OBSERVERS' PERSPECTIVES ON BEHAVIOR

Actors and observers will occasionally disagree as to whether a behavior is normal or abnormal. Actors are less inclined to judge their own behavior as abnormal; observers are more inclined to judge others' unusual behavior as abnormal.

changes in themselves. Observers, however, often assume a continuity of psychological state that does not exist. Third, people generally are inclined to see themselves in a more favorable light than observers see them. As a result, actors will tend to see themselves and their behaviors more favorably, and hence more normally, than observers (see Figure 1–1). Such differences in the perspectives of actors and observers could alone account for the differing viewpoints of Junius Wilson and state and hospital authorities.

Thus, the family resemblance to abnormality is not perfect; it has its pitfalls, some of which are worse than others. We might wish that this were not the case and that abnormality were a more objective judgment. But our present wishes are beside the point, though eventually abnormality may be assessed with considerably greater objectivity. We are not endorsing the way abnormality is presently judged. Nor are we prescribing how the word "abnormal" should be used. Rather, we are merely describing how the word is actually used by laymen and professionals alike with the hope that such a description will help in both diagnosis and treatment.

We have dealt at length with the meaning of abnormality and the elements that are associated with it, but it will not take us as long to define normality. *Normality is simply the absence of abnormality.* It means nothing beyond that. If abnormality is a matter of judgment and social perspective, so is normality. If abnormality is much more a matter of degree than of kind, so too is normality. And if there are enormous gray areas associated with the judgment of abnormality, such that we often don't really know whether a behavior or person is abnormal, those same gray areas will apply to the question of normality.

Positives and Negatives: The Meaning of Meaning

Words can be stated in positive and negative forms. Usually, the positive form is well-defined, while the negative form is merely the opposite of the positive one. We know what "embarrassed" means, and it follows that "unembarrassed" means not embarrassed. The positive word is the primary member of the opposing pair and the "un" word gets its meaning only by negating the positive word. If we did not already know the meaning of the positive word, we would not understand its negation.

But this is not always the case. Sometimes the primary meaning resides in the *negative* case, and the positive word only makes sense as a negation of the negative word. The logic of "normal-abnormal" reflects the primacy of the negative case. Abnormal is the concept that makes primary sense. *Normal means nothing over and above "not abnormal."* To decide whether a person or an action is normal, we merely ask about the absence of the elements of abnormality. Are only a few of the elements of abnormality present, and those not intensely? Once we decide that actions or persons are *not* abnormal, we have simultaneously decided that they *are* normal. Normality has no meaning beyond the absence of abnormality.

We are occasionally uneasy about our own normality because of the logic of abnormality. Many things that we do have one or two elements of abnormality in them. While this is not enough for our actions to be termed abnormal, it is enough to make us uneasy about our own normality, particularly if we persist in the belief that normality is a state that has meaning beyond the absence of abnormality. Consider masturbation as a case in point. A fifteen-year-old boy who masturbates every day may wonder if he is normal. But if we examine that action against the elements of abnormality, we find very little to be concerned about. Is his masturbation *irrational?* Not at all. Is it *dysfunctional?* Not in any obvious way. Does he *suffer?* Quite the contrary (though worrying about it gives some pain). Does it produce *observer discomfort?* No, there are no observers. Is it *visible and unconventional?* No, over 90 percent of males acknowledge masturbation at one time or another, and adolescents who masturbate as often as three times a day are not uncommon. Is the behavior unacceptable because it *violates moral standards?* Marginally, with enormous variation from subculture to subculture. Overall, then, masturbation is somewhat unacceptable from some moral viewpoints, but it shares in no other element of abnormality. Why, then, would anyone be concerned about whether masturbation is normal? Because of that marginal unacceptability to some subcultures. The fact that it taps into one (and only one) element of abnormality is sufficient to make some people worry about its normality.

To be normal is not necessarily to live well, for there is more to living than being normal and avoiding abnormality. There are pleasures, maturities, insights, achievements, and wisdoms—the joys of life. They are mentioned here because without them, without the notion of **optimal living,** our conceptions of psychological life can become so oriented around abnormality that we fail to attend sufficiently to the positive aspects of living. These positive aspects constitute a good defense against abnormality itself (Rosenhan, 1969, 1970; Seligman, 1991), if only because it is difficult for suffering and irrationality to exist simultaneously with joy and wisdom.

Some Elements of Optimal Living

Like abnormality, optimal living is more a matter of degree than of kind. One doesn't live optimally all the time, any more than one is abnormal all the time. Rather, optimality is a goal that, on some days and under some conditions we feel more of, and at other times and conditions, less. No one lives optimally all the time.

There are six areas in which optimality can be recognized (Jahoda, 1958). They are:

- Positive attitudes toward self
- Growth and development
- Autonomy
- Accurate perception of reality
- Environmental competence
- Positive interpersonal relations.

▼ Positive aspects of living constitute a good defense against abnormality.

POSITIVE ATTITUDES TOWARD SELF

The phrase **self-acceptance** has many connotations, but generally it implies knowing ourselves, accepting rather than denying what we know, and feeling good about that knowledge. "Self-acceptance implies that a person has learned to live with himself, accepting both the limitations and possibilities he may find in himself" (Jahoda, 1958, p. 24). This does not mean we are thinking about ourselves all the time; rather, much of the time we take ourselves for granted. But when we do think about ourselves, we accept and like what we see.

GROWTH AND DEVELOPMENT

Living optimally involves a desire to utilize one's abilities instead of stagnating, to devote oneself to a mission or vocation, and to establish long-range goals (Maslow, 1954). At its best, this kind of growth involves a full investment in living, a capacity to get out of one's skin and to lose oneself in work, thought, sport, or other people (Allport, 1937).

AUTONOMY

Optimal living both requires and generates a degree of emotional freedom from the demands of the immediate social environment and greater responsiveness to one's own internal standards. Increasingly, *self*-regard—the approval of oneself by oneself—rather than the approval of others, becomes the mark of this kind of maturity. Often, it is the exercise of one's own standards that brings about such self-rewarded independence.

ACCURATE PERCEPTION OF REALITY

When we dislike someone, we prefer to believe that they are thoroughly unpleasant, rather than finding that in many ways they are really nice. If the latter perception is more accurate, however, it is also more constructive because it leads us to investigate the conditions that led to the difficulties in the first place. Is it possible that we misunderstood? Could her awful behavior have been accidental? In short, testing our perceptions against reality involves some risk that we may have been wrong, but also the greater gain that we can do something about it.

Closely related to that concern for accurately assessing reality is the ability to tolerate realities that are simply ambiguous without prematurely casting them into present molds. The ability to say "I don't know," to live with ignorance, to wait for information that is accurate—these abilities strongly influence our capacity to perceive reality accurately.

ENVIRONMENTAL COMPETENCE

Being competent in life's tasks—in work, love, and play—contributes enormously to the sense of living optimally. The reasons for this are obvious: competence brings with it not only external gratifications but also internal ones. Coping with the requirements of one's environment and meeting one's own standards of performance contribute to one's sense of efficacy (Bandura, 1977a).

POSITIVE INTERPERSONAL RELATIONS

The final area of optimal living involves positive interpersonal relations—the ability to enjoy the company of others, to empathize with them, to give and re-

▼ Positive relations with other people help us avoid emotional misery, alienation, and serious psychological disorders.

ceive support, to respect others regardless of their status, and the capacity to love and be loved—all of these are implied in the notion of positive interpersonal relations. Some theorists believe that the absence of such relations is a major source of emotional misery, resulting in alienation, loss of sense of community, and finally fear of one another (May, 1953).

THE HAZARDS OF SELF-DIAGNOSIS

There is almost no one who has not harbored secret doubts about his or her normality, "Do I cry too easily?" "Am I too afraid of speaking up in class?" "Do other people occasionally have fantasies about their parents dying in violent accidents?"

Related to our concern about our normality is a phenomenon called "interns' syndrome." In the course of early training, the fledgling medical student finds in himself symptoms of almost every disease he studies.

> I remember going to the British Museum one day to read up the treatment for some slight ailment of which I had a touch—hay fever, I fancy it was. I got down the book, and read all I came to read; and then, in an unthinking moment, I idly turned the leaves, and began to indolently study diseases, generally. I forgot which was the first distemper I plunged into—some fearful, devastating scourge, I know—and, before I had glanced half down the list of "premonitory symptoms," it was borne in upon me that I had fairly got it.
>
> I sat for a while frozen with horror, and then in the listlessness of despair, I again turned over the pages. I came to typhoid fever—read the symptoms—discovered that I had typhoid fever, must have had it for months without knowing it—wondered what else I had got; turned up St. Vitus's Dance—found, as I expected, that I had that too—began to get interested in my case, and determined to sift it to the bottom, and so started alphabetically—looked up ague, and learnt that I was sickening for it, and that the acute stage would commence in about another fortnight. Bright's disease, I was relieved to find, I had only in a modified form, and, so far as that was concerned, I might live for years. Cholera I had, with severe complications; and diptheria I seemed to have been born with. I plodded conscientiously through the twenty-six letters, and the only malady I could conclude I had not got was housemaid's knee.
>
> I felt rather hurt about this at first; it seemed somehow to be a sort of slight. Why hadn't I got housemaid's knee? Why this invidious reservation? After a while, however, less grasping feelings prevailed. I reflected that I had every other known malady in the pharmacology, and I grew less selfish, and determined to do without housemaid's knee. Gout, in its most malignant stage, it would appear, had seized me without my being aware of it; and zymosis I had evidently been suffering with from boyhood. There were no more diseases after zymosis, so I concluded there was nothing else the matter with me . . . I had walked into that reading-room a happy healthy man, I crawled out a decrepit wreck." (Jerome, 1880)

As you read this book, you too will encounter symptoms in yourself that will make you think you have each disorder in turn. Be forewarned: It is a very unpleasant experience and one about which neither authors nor readers can really do much. In part, it arises from the privacy that surrounds our lives. Many of our thoughts, and some of our actions, strike us as private, if not secret—things about which no one should know. If they did know, people, even (perhaps particularly) friends, might think less of us, or be offended, or both. One consequence of this privacy is the development of an exaggerated sense of the uniqueness of our forbidden thoughts and behaviors. Seeing them suddenly alluded to on these pages and associated with certain syndromes (commonly in contexts that are quite different from the contexts of our own behaviors—but we don't notice that) makes us believe that we have fallen prey to that problem too.

There are two things that can be done to combat the distress you may experience from reading this book and going to lectures. First, read carefully. You may, for example, be concerned when you read about depression: "Yes, I'm blue. I cry now more than I used to." But as you inquire deeply into the symptoms of depression, you will find that the absence of suicidal thoughts, your continued interest in sex or sports, your optimism about the future, all count against the diagnosis of depression.

Second, talk with your friends. Sometimes, merely mentioning that "when I read Chapter so-and-so, I get the feeling they're talking about me. Do you ever get that feeling?" will bring forth a chorus of "you bets," and relief for all of you.

SUMMARY

1. There are no hard and fast definitions of normality and abnormality, for there is no single element that all instances of abnormality share, nor any single property that distinguishes normality from abnormality.

2. *Abnormality* is recognized the way members of a family are recognized: because they share a *family resemblance* in that they have many significant elements in common.

3. With regard to abnormality, there are seven properties or elements that count toward deciding whether a person or an action is abnormal: suffering, maladaptiveness, irrationality and incomprehensibility, unpredictability and loss of control, vividness and unconventionality, observer discomfort, and violation of moral and ideal standards. The more of these elements that are present, and the more visible each element is, the more likely are we to judge the person or the action as abnormal.

4. Because the judgment of abnormality is a social judgment, there is sometimes disagreement about who is abnormal, and about which thoughts and actions qualify as being considered abnormal. Society occasionally errs about whom it calls abnormal, as sometimes do observers, even those who are qualified diagnosticians. But the absence of complete agreement should not be taken to mean that abnormality is always or frequently a matter of dispute.

5. *Normality* is simply the absence of abnormality, nothing more. To be normal is to possess so few of the elements of abnormality, and those at such a minimal degree, that no qualified observer would make the judgment of abnormality. But to be normal is not necessarily to live happily or well.

6. *Optimal living* requires some quite positive capacities, among them: positive attitudes toward oneself, capacity for growth and development, autonomy, an accurate perception of reality, social and vocational competence, and positive interpersonal relationships.

QUESTIONS FOR CRITICAL THINKING

1. Explain how authorities could have mistakenly believed that various of the elements of abnormality were present in Junius Wilson.

2. Why do you think that people may disagree as to whether a behavior or person should be judged as abnormal?

3. What do you think of the concept of defining normality as the absence of abnormality?

4. How can the elements of optimal living serve as a defense against abnormality?

Abnormality across Time and Place

Throughout human history, there have been many different notions about what behaviors can be defined as madness. This is only to be expected, for as the elements of abnormality change relative to historical context, so must the notions of what is normal and abnormal. Behaviors that have been revered in one time or place may have been defined as clear examples of madness in others. The ancient Hebrews and the ancient Greeks held in awe those who claimed to be prophets and had "the gift of tongues." Yet in the modern world, those who claim to see into the future generate suspicion, and those who speak in unknown words and rhythms are often classified as schizophrenics.

So too have there been different and contradictory theories about the causes of abnormal behavior. Shakespeare portrayed Ophelia as driven "mad" by Hamlet's cruel rejection, implying to his Elizabethan audiences that Ophelia's withdrawal and eventual suicide were products of the social influences in her immediate environment. Yet, during the same period in history, other "mad" women were accused of having willfully made pacts with Satan. Clearly, a society's definitions of madness and perceptions of its causes have played significant roles in how the abnormal have been viewed: they have influenced whether the mad were revered, feared, pitied, or simply accepted. In turn, these perceptions have determined the ways in which the mad have been treated: whether they were honored for their unique powers or incarcerated, treated, or abandoned for their madness.*

---

*Curiously, even the forms of abnormal behavior have been different in different ages and cultures. For example, hysteria, identified for more than two thousand years as a discrete syndrome, was especially prevalent at certain times. It was rife in the nineteenth century, if the historian is to judge by the notebooks of physicians and the guest registries of hostels like those in Lourdes. Yet, hysteria seems to have all but disappeared in the present century.

The history of abnormality, like the history of most other human phenomena, is not linear and logical but meandering and inconsistent. In this chapter, we will examine two significant issues in the history of madness: (1) theories of cause, and (2) methods of treatment and care. Remember that notions of abnormality change when values change, for notions of normality and abnormality are guided by the predominant values of a culture. We take it for granted, for example, that wearing a bikini to the pool is acceptable behavior today. But we know it would have been scandalous a hundred years ago. Why? Because our view of what is modest and immodest has undergone enormous change during the past century. So, too, has our view of abnormality.

THE PERCEIVED CAUSES OF ABNORMAL BEHAVIOR

There is very little about abnormality that tells what caused it, or that even provides clues about where to look for causes. Yet, because treatment and cure depend upon perceived cause—a complex relationship to which we will return many times in later chapters—people find it difficult to resist attributing causes to abnormality. Thus, there were times when abnormality was attributed to the wrath of the gods or to possession by demons. At other times and in other places, earthquakes and tides, germs and illness, interpersonal conflict and bad blood were separately and together used to explain the origins of abnormality. Notions about abnormality arise from the culture's world-view. If the culture has a theory of natural law that is animistic, abnormality will be viewed in animistic terms. If it is scientific and materialistic, as it is today, abnormality will be viewed in scientific terms. How our understanding of abnormality is articulated, therefore, depends distinctly on the beliefs that dominate in a culture and epoch. We will present three general explanations of abnormality, discussing in turn: animistic causes, physical causes, and psychogenic origins (see Table 2–1).

TABLE 2–1

EXPLANATIONS OF ABNORMALITY		
Historical Explanation	Causes	Treatment
animism/ Satanism	evil spirits or Satan possesses an individual	trephining exorcism ostracism
physical	wandering uterus	return uterus to its proper place
	animal magnetism	Mesmer's baquet
psychological	hysteria	hypnosis catharsis

trephines

▲ Paleolithic cave dwellers are believed to have made holes, or trephines, in skulls to free those who were "possessed" by evil spirits.

▼ This 20,000-year-old Paleolithic drawing, from a remote cave in the French Pyrenees, portrays a dancer disguised as an animal, and is thought to represent a sorcerer. (Cohn, 1975)

Animistic Origins: Possession

In premodern societies, the belief in ***animism***—that everyone and everything has a "soul"—was widespread, and mental disturbance was often ascribed to ***animistic*** causes. One of the most common explanations of madness was that evil spirits had taken possession of an individual and controlled that person's behavior. Much as a parasitic tapeworm lives in and weakens the body, so could a parasitic spirit inhabit and weaken the mind. Some skulls of Paleolithic cave dwellers have characteristic holes, called ***trephines,*** that appear to have been chipped out by stone instruments. It is thought that trephining was performed to provide an exit for demons or evil spirits trapped within the skull.

People could be possessed by many different kinds of spirits. The spirits of ancestors, animals, gods, and heroes, and of victims whose wrongs had not been redressed, were among those who could wreak madness. These spirits could enter a person through their own cunning, through the work of an evil-doer with magical powers, or through a lack of faith on the part of the possessed individual. Not surprisingly, because possession was a result of invisible forces, freeing the possessed individual from these spirits required special techniques. Across time and place, there has been the widespread belief in the power of some individuals to use magic both to induce evil and expel it; shamans, witch doctors, sorcerers, and witches were all believed to be able to influence animistic forces (Douglas, 1970). In medieval Europe, for example, individuals from all levels of society resorted to sorcerers and witches for spells, potents, and prophecies. Although they were often feared, witches were generally left alone unless they were thought to have murdered or to have destroyed property. But even then, they were prosecuted by secular, not religious, authorities (Currie, 1968).

Much of what is presently understood as originating from psychological distress was earlier attributed to animistic causes. Dancing ***manias,*** for example, often involved hundreds of people, who danced for days on end until they succumbed to exhaustion. These manias spread like an epidemic throughout much of Western Europe. ***Tarantism,*** a form of the dancing mania that occurred in Italy, was thought to have been brought on by the tarantula. Episodes of ***lycanthropy,*** in which groups of people believed they were wolves and acted accordingly, were common in rural areas. In these examples, ***animal possession*** was the dominant motif. In many other cases, individuals were thought to be possessed by evil spirits (Ellenberger, 1970).

By the middle of the fifteenth century, tolerance for bizarre behavior became strained. The perception of witches and the response to them changed radically, and for nearly three hundred years thereafter, Europe was caught up in a frenzied fear of witches—a fear that caused thousands to be led to their death. For modern students of abnormal psychology, these witch hunts provide a fascinating look at how animistic forces were used to explain madness and why it was such a convincing theory at the time.

Such changed attitudes toward witches arose out of the great social and intellectual upheavals prevailing during the late fifteenth century and the sixteenth century (McFarlane, 1970). With the rise of capitalism, individual values were replacing communal ones, towns were replacing rural communities, and the structure of the medieval family and village was being disturbed (Midelfort, 1972). Traditional authority was weakening. The Church itself was

MALLEVS
MALEFICARVM.
IN TRES DIVISVS
PARTES,

In quibus { Concurrentia ad maleficia,
{ Maleficiorum effectus,
{ Remedia aduersus maleficia,

Et modus procedendi, ac puniendi maleficos abundè continetur, præcipuè autem omnibus Inquisitoribus, & diuini uerbi concionatoribus utilis, ac necessarius.

Auctore R. P. F. IACOBO SPRENGER
Ordinis Prædicatorum, olim Inquisitore clarissimus.

Hac postrema editione per F. Raffaelem Maffeum Venetum. D. Iacobi a Iudeca instituti Seruorum, summo studio illustratus, & à multis erroribus uindicatus.

Hic adiecimus indicem rerum memorabilium, & quæstionum.

VENETIIS. Apud Io. Antonium Bertanum. 1576.

The frontispiece of one of the many editions of the *Malleus Maleficarum*, by Heinrich Kraemer and Johann Sprenger.

FOCUS QUESTIONS

1. What are the three perceived origins of abnormal behavior?
2. Describe each of the views of abnormality, and how they arose from the culture's world view.
3. Describe both the physical and the psychological explanations of the causes of hysteria.

rife with schism as the Protestant Reformation plunged much of Europe into religious civil wars that further upset social equilibrium (Trevor-Roper, 1970).

It was within this context of extensive social instability that a belief in witches flourished in Europe. Witches were those who made pacts with Satan and who took delight in harming others. A Biblical injunction, hardly used until that time, was recalled vividly and implemented:

Any man or woman among you who calls up ghosts or spirits shall be put to death.

The Church had earlier considered witchcraft mere "illusion" to be dealt with by secular authorities. Now it was heresy, treason against God, to be suppressed by the Church of Rome through its investigative agency, the Holy Inquisition. Two Dominican monks, Heinrich Kraemer and Johann Sprenger, wrote the *Malleus Maleficarum,* or *The Witches' Hammer,* a 1486 manual for hunting and disposing of witches. Printed on the recently invented printing press, the *Malleus Maleficarum* was widely distributed. Its official stamp and easy availability made it enormously popular, and more than thirty editions were published in the next hundred years (Summers, 1971). But it was not the only such treatise. Scores of "handbooks" on detecting the presence of witches flooded Europe.

Who were the witches? Overwhelmingly, they were women. "All witchcraft comes from carnal lust," the *Malleus Maleficarum* states, "which is in women insatiable." The association of evil with women's sexuality, and the fear of women's sexuality from which it arose, was probably widespread then, much as it is widespread today (see Gregor, 1985, for example). The most heinous crimes of which witches were accused were linked to reproduction: robbing men of their sexual potency, murdering born and unborn babies, and wanton lust. Men were protected from this heinous crime because Jesus was a man. The *Malleus Maleficarum,* then, was a religious document that reflected a strong fear of women's sexuality. Profoundly misogynist, it legitimized the persecution, torture, and death of women.

The occurrence of inexplicable events led one to suspect witchcraft. A sudden and dramatic illness in an otherwise healthy person might generate such suspicions. Or a roof that had collapsed on an unsuspecting bystander might lead one to ask why it had collapsed on *him.* That question, impermissible by modern scientific standards, was one that led to a quest for supernatural causes. Thus, the answer was sought in the following way: A collapsing roof is a rare event, and the fact that it had collapsed on this particular individual might well have made it rarer. Witchcraft too was rare, and if witches were present and active in this matter, they would have left other improbable traces. It was the presence of *other improbable facts* that lent credence to the view that witches had brought about this particular disaster.

There were a variety of ingenious tests for the presence of witches. One might hold molten lead over a sick person and then pour the lead into a bowl of water. If the lead condensed into an image, one might conclude that the sickness was due to witchcraft. Or one might lacerate a suspected witch. If there was no bleeding, one's suspicion would grow firmer. Or one might weight a suspect and throw her into a lake. If she floated inexplicably, she might well be a witch.

These were *strong* tests of witchcraft, and if they had been the only ones used, very few witches would have been discovered. But the belief in witchcraft was as strong as the fear of women's sexuality, and the presence of witchcraft was considered so widespread that two less reliable sorts of evidence were called upon. The first was the presence of *body marks* on the suspect. Any birthmark, scar, or mole on the woman's body indicated that she had entered into a pact with Satan. But because body marks are common in the first place, and more common among people who do manual labor, the test was likely to generate a substantial number of "false positives," that is, people who had body marks but were not witches.

The second indicator of witchcraft was *confession.* An individual's confession that she was a witch was held to be ideal. "Common justice demands that a witch should not be condemned to death unless she is convicted of her own confession." But because notions of "due process" were not highly developed then, confession could often be suggested or extracted. Again, false positives—people who were alleged to be witches on the basis of shaky evidence—were probably very common.

It was believed that there was no "cure" for witchcraft, except for the physical destruction of the witch. On the continent, the confessed witch was burned by the secular authorities. In England and the colonies, witches were hanged. Conservatively, between the middle of the fifteenth and seventeenth century, more than 100,000 people (mostly women) in Europe and in the American colonies died as a result of the witch trials (see Box 2–1) (Deutsch, 1949). Witch hunting was not the monopoly of the Church of Rome. With the Reformation, many Protestant sects also mounted zealous campaigns against the lustful consorts of Satan. Not surprisingly, charges of witchcraft were often hurled at members of rival religions (Thomas, 1971).

Physical Causes

While animistic beliefs served to explain psychological distress for centuries, an approach to abnormality that emphasizes **physical** causes can also be traced back to the ancient world. In fact, it is possible that the prehistoric peoples who practiced trephining were employing a primitive surgical technique to relieve the pain of severe headaches. One of the first psychological disorders that was thought to have arisen from physical causes was **hysteria.**

Papyri from early Egypt, as well as the writings of Greek physicians, record a remarkable disorder that was found mainly among women who were virgins or widows. Its symptoms included such complaints as epileptic-like fits, pains of all sorts in various parts of the body, aphonia (loss of voice), headaches, dizziness, paralysis, blindness, lameness, listlessness, and melancholia. The Greeks believed that all of these difficulties arose from a single source: a roaming uterus.

The Greeks believed that the uterus was an animated organ that had somehow dislodged itself from its normal place to rove around the body, perhaps in search of water and nourishment, but often enough, for no good reason. In the course of its wanderings, it would attach itself here or there and create havoc. If it attached itself to the liver, for instance, the person would lose her voice, grind her teeth, and her complexion would turn ashen. Lodged in the chest cavity, this roaming uterus would produce convulsions similar to epilepsy, and at the heart it would produce anxiety, oppression, and vomiting. The Greek word for uterus is *hystera,* and the Greeks believed so deeply that the uterus

Box 2–1

EVIDENCE AT THE SALEM WITCH TRIALS

The famous Salem Witch Trials, and the witchcraft mania that grew up in that town, evidently arose from the antics of children. A group of young girls used to play imaginary games at the village minister's house. Ghosts, devils, witches, and the whole invisible world were the subjects of their games, borrowed in the manner that children today borrow space explorations from the adult world that surrounds them. Their games of imagination, however, came to the attention of the village elders who solemnly concluded that these children were "bewitched." The children, perhaps stimulated by the attention they were receiving and the excitement they had caused, became more involved in their imaginings, feeding the concern of the elders.

Pressed by the elders to name those who had been casting evil spells over them, they named one person, then another, then still others, until it appeared that nearly half the people in the village had signed their souls over to the devil. Neighbors hurled wild accusations against each other. These accusations resulted in the arrest and trial of 250 persons in one year (1691–1692), of whom 50 were condemned, 19 executed, 2 died in prison, and 1 of torture.

It is important to remember that the elders of the community were "sane," sober, and intelligent people. Cotton Mather was a leading colonial figure, son of the president of Harvard University, and a founder of Yale. Deeply religious, he wanted to protect the community against dangers that, for him, were real. And precisely because he and the other elders were so deeply convinced of the dangers, they were remarkably credulous in weighing the evidence. An example of their gullibility is seen in the interrogation of Sarah Carrier, age eight, whose mother, Martha, was subsequently hanged as a witch.

"How long hast thou been a witch?"
"Ever since I was six years old."
"How old are you now?"
"Nearly eight years old."
"Who made you a witch?"
"My mother. She made me set my hand to the book."
"You said you saw a cat once. What did the cat say to you?"
"It said it would tear me to pieces if I would not set my hand to the book."
(Sarah is speaking here of the *Devil's Book*.)
"How did you know that it was your mother?"
"The cat told me so, that she was my mother."

SOURCE: Upham, 1867, cited in Deutsch, 1949, p. 35.

As a result of the witchcraft mania and fear of satanistic forces, 250 people were tried as witches in colonial Salem, Massachusetts.

was responsible for these difficulties that they named the entire disorder after it—hysteria (Veith, 1965).

This view of hysteria prevailed until the second century A.D., when it was challenged by Soranus and Galen, physicians who recognized that the uterus was not a living animal. Soranus wrote, ". . . the uterus does not issue forth like a wild animal from the lair, delighted by fragrant odors and fleeing bad odors; rather it is drawn together because of stricture caused by inflammation" (Veith, 1965, pp. 30–31). This new view of hysteria led to entirely different views about origins and treatment. Since the *hystera* was not a roaming animal but rather a malfunctioning sexual organ, might there be a similar organ in men which, when malfunctioning, could cause them to have similar symptoms? Galen believed there was. He had observed that both men and women suffer similar symptoms following periods of sexual abstinence. He, therefore, argued that hysteria has a sexual basis, a view that is widely accepted today.

Attributing psychological distress to physical causes took a peculiar twist hundreds of years later with the belief in ***animalism.*** This belief asserted that there were remarkable similarities between animals and mad people. Like animals, the mad could not control themselves and therefore needed to be severely controlled. Like animals, the insane were capable of violence, often suddenly and without provocation. Like animals, they could live without protest in miserable conditions, conditions under which normal people simply could not exist. One proponent of this view pointed to

> The ease with which certain of the insane of both sexes bear the most rigorous and prolonged cold. . . . On certain days when the thermometer indicated . . . as many as 16 degrees below freezing, a madman . . . could not endure his wool blanket, and remained sitting on the icy floor of his cell. In the morning, one no sooner opened his door than he ran in his shirt into the inner court, taking ice and snow by the fistful, applying it to his breast and letting it melt with a sort of delectation. (Foucault, 1965, pp. 74–75)

The relatively primitive notions of physical cause that are captured in the early Greek views of hysteria, or in animalism, gradually yielded to more sophisticated approaches. With the development of modern medicine, many physicians came to consider madness to be a form of illness amenable to the same kinds of treatment as physical illness. Purges, bleeding, and forced vomiting were choice medical remedies of the seventeenth and eighteenth centuries, and these were administered to the infirm and the insane alike. Gradually, these views and treatments were replaced by the kinds of approaches that characterize present-day medicine, in particular, surgery and pharmacology (see Chapter 3).

Psychogenic Origins

The quest for understanding psychological abnormality was pursued down still another path by the ancient Greeks and Romans, this time to its ***psychological*** origins. In addition to his observations about hysteria, Galen contributed important insights into the psychological causes of abnormality. In a particularly striking instance, Galen examined a woman who complained of sleeplessness, listlessness, and general malaise. He could find no direct evidence of physical illness and ultimately narrowed his inferences to two possibilities. Either she was suffering from melancholy, which was a physical disorder of one of the four body "humors," or fluids, "or else she was troubled about something she was unwilling to confess," a psychological explanation. He concluded:

> After I had diagnosed that there was no bodily trouble, and that the woman was suffering from some mental uneasiness, it happened that at the very time I was examining her, this was confirmed. Somebody came from the theatre and said he had seen Pylades dancing. Then both her expression and the colour of her face changed. Seeing this, I applied my hand to her wrist, and noticed that her pulse had suddenly become extremely irregular. This kind of pulse indicates that the mind is disturbed; thus it occurs also in people who are disputing over any subject. So on the next day I said to one of my followers that, when I paid my visit to the woman, he was to come a little later and announce to me, "Morphus is dancing today." When he said this, I found that the pulse was unaffected. Similarly also on the next day, when I had an announcement made about the third member of the troupe, the pulse remained unchanged as before. On the fourth evening I kept very careful watch when it was announced that Pylades was dancing, and noticed that the pulse was very much disturbed. Thus I found out that the woman was in love with Pylades, and by careful watch on the succeeding days my discovery was confirmed. (Galen, cited in Veith, 1965, p. 36)

Galen's assessment of possible cause is the hallmark of the scientific method that was eventually to advance our understanding and treatment of psychological disorders. Rather than leaping to a conclusion, Galen tested two alternative hypotheses and decided which was correct according to the evidence. In this case, the evidence favored the hypothesis that stressed psychological experience rather than physiology.

Galen's observations on the psychological origins of abnormality were forgotten for centuries. Thus, until the middle of the eighteenth century, hysteria was believed to be a female neurological disorder that had its origins in genital illness. The recognition that mental disorders were psychological in origin and could be treated by psychological means did not arise again until the middle of the eighteenth century. To understand how this view arose, we first need to look at one of the most colorful people in the history of abnormal psychology, Franz Anton Mesmer (1734–1815).

MESMERISM

Mesmer is not only one of the most colorful, but surely one of the most maligned characters in the history of abnormal psychology. Variously called a genius and a charlatan, he proposed that many diseases, from epilepsy to hysteria, develop from the obstruction of the flow of an invisible and impalpable entity that he first called "universal magnetic fluid" and later **animal magnetism.** Very much a man of the Enlightenment, Mesmer was influenced by contemporary discoveries in electricity and proposed the existence of a physical magnetic fluid which, when unequally distributed, causes disease in the body. He theorized that magnetic fluid was influenced by the lunar cycle, the tides, the planets, and the stars. Mesmer believed that health could be restored by using certain techniques which induced "crises" in the body. These crises would be provoked again and again, but each time would be experienced as less severe by the patient, until they disappeared and the body was back in equilibrium.

▲ The Greek physician Galen (circa 130–201 A.D.) was one of the first to believe that some apparently physical disorders were psychological in origin.

▶ Franz Anton Mesmer (1734–1815) and his patients around the baquet. The baquet was supposed to concentrate a patient's magnetic fluid and induce a crisis, which would eventually restore the body's equilibrium and the patient's health.

Mesmer went to Paris from Vienna in 1778. He opened a clinic where patients suffering from the various symptoms of hysteria were seen in groups. In a heavily curtained room, patients were arranged around a large wooden tub, or baquet, which was filled with water and magnetized iron filings. Iron rods protruded from the tub and were pointed by the patients to their ailing parts. The baquet was supposed to concentrate the magnetic fluid and induce the patient's crisis. Mesmer, dressed in a lavender cape, would pass among the patients to the accompaniment of gentle music, fixing his eye on them, and touching each with his iron wand. One patient would experience strange sensations, including trembling and convulsions. After the first succumbed, others were not long in having similar experiences, though there were always a few who were unaffected (Pattie, 1967).

Mesmer had departed from Vienna under a cloud: he had been accused of charlatanry. And, despite his therapeutic successes, it was not long before similar accusations were leveled against him in Paris. So heated and acrimonious were the charges and countercharges, that in 1783, Louis XVI appointed a Royal Commission to investigate animal magnetism. Its eminent members included the chemist Lavoisier, the astronomer Bailly, and Benjamin Franklin, who was then serving as U. S. ambassador to France. The Commission heard evidence, deliberated for five months, and concluded that there was no such thing as animal magnetism. Interestingly, the Commission did not question Mesmer's success in curing patients of their ills; rather, it addressed his theory that the ills themselves were the result of the imbalance of magnetic fluid in the body. The Commission found that there was no physical proof for the existence of this fluid. Thus, it concluded that Mesmer's cures were entirely due to "imagination." Crushingly defeated, Mesmer, a proud man, vanished into obscurity. But the *reality* of his "cures" remained. People in distress continued to seek this kind of help, and to benefit from it, so much so that animal magnetism came to be called **mesmerism.**

HYPNOTISM

The findings of the Royal Commission were deadly to the scientific theory of mesmerism, but the techniques themselves survived. Underground in France, but publicly in the United States and in Germany, mesmerism continued to be practiced and studied. (Indeed, one of the most famous patients to be treated by this method in America was Mary Baker Eddy, the founder of Christian Science.) While the quest for finding the elusive magnetic fluid led to a dead end and was finally abandoned, the cures that derived from mesmerism continued to excite interest. The process that had been called mesmerism underwent a name change and came to be known as **hypnotism.**

A major figure in the scientific study of hypnosis was Jean Martin Charcot (1825–1893), Medical Director of one of the largest sections at La Salpêtrière and Professor of Diseases of the Nervous System at the University of Paris. Charcot was widely regarded as a first-rate scientist, the most eminent neurologist of the nineteenth century, and an awesome and much-feared teacher. The latter characteristic, we shall see, was his scientific undoing.

While Charcot was at La Salpêtrière, one of the wards in his charge housed women patients who suffered from convulsions. Charcot sought to distinguish hysterical convulsions from those brought on by epilepsy. In order to distinguish hysteria from other neurological disorders, Charcot employed hypnosis. If, for example, a patient who suffered a paralyzed arm was able to move her arm under hypnosis, then the diagnosis of hysteria could be given; otherwise,

▶ Jean-Martin Charcot (1825–1893) demonstrating hypnosis to a class of medical students.

the appropriate diagnosis was a neurological disorder. Charcot extended his study to male patients as well, demonstrating that the symptoms of traumatic paralysis in the men were the same as those of hysterical paralysis (Ellenberger, 1970).

Hypnosis fascinated Charcot, and he quickly generated a neurological theory about it. His students, ever eager to please, tested his views and brought back confirmatory evidence. But Charcot himself never hypnotized his patients. Rather, his students "worked them up" and taught them how to perform, after which Charcot unwittingly used them as demonstration subjects. Other scientists, particularly Hyppolyte Bernheim in Nancy, were unable to replicate Charcot's findings, and quickly located the source of error. Once again, a theory of hypnosis fell into disrepute, though the fact that hypnosis could be used to cure was unquestioned.

Charcot trained a large number of neurologists and psychiatrists, among them Sigmund Freud, the father of psychoanalysis. Freud proposed psychogenic causes as the root of madness. His contribution to the psychological approach to abnormality is so great, however, that we will take it up separately in Chapter 4.

TREATMENT OF THE MENTALLY DISTRESSED

How a psychological disorder is treated depends heavily on how it is understood. When mental disturbance was deemed to be the result of animistic causes, supernatural means were often needed to rid the individual of the distress. Similarly, when its origins were believed to be physical or psychological, treatment tended to rely on those means.

Treating Demonic Possession

Possession by animistic forces—demons, spirits, and the like—was most commonly treated by *exorcism,* a ceremonial ritual during which the demons were expelled from the victim's bodies. Exhausting and often time-consuming, exorcism rituals generally involved a cooperative relationship between the shaman or priest, and the afflicted. Together they tried to make the alien spirits identify themselves and then to cajole, threaten, and overwhelm the intruders so that they would leave the poor unfortunates. The belief that mental distress is the result of possession by evil spirits has been a persistent one. While they are rare and commonly frowned upon, exorcism rituals are performed even today in the United States.

If exorcism failed, *ostracism*—casting out the person as well as his or her demons—might be used. It was with regard to ostracism that the myth of *narrenschiffen* arose (Foucault, 1965). These were thought to be ships full of "fools," quite possibly manned by madmen, which went from harbor to harbor, seeking but not finding safe port. While it is unlikely that such *narrenschiffen* ever existed—no such ship records have been found, and who after all, would entrust an expensive ship to a crew of madmen?—the myth conveys unequivocally the degree to which the mad were rejected (Maher and Maher, 1982).

▲ Exorcism was a particularly exhausting mode of psychological treatment, based on the persistent idea that demonic possession accounted for abnormality.

Treating Physical Causes

When hysteria was thought to result from a wandering uterus, there were a prodigious number of proposed cures. The Egyptians and Greeks based most of them on the pull-push principle: Draw the uterus back to its proper place with pleasant experiences and aromatic substances, and drive it away from its current attachment with fetid fumigations. Perfumes and gentle massage played a therapeutic role in pulling the uterus back to where it was supposed to be; garlic and burning dung were applied to the aching areas in order to drive the prodigal uterus away. Later, in the Middle Ages, human attempts to keep the uterus in its place appear to have been abandoned in favor of divine intercession, as in this tenth-century prayer: "I conjure thee, O womb . . . not to harm that maid of God, N., not to occupy her head, throat, neck, chest, . . . but to lie down quietly in the place which God chose for thee, so that this maid of God, N., be restored to health. . . . (From Zilboorg and Henry, 1941, pp. 131–32).

The Rise of Psychogenic Treatments

By the eighteenth century, the explanations that stressed animistic causes, while never completely abandoned, no longer commanded respect among serious thinkers, who emphasized rational rather than supernatural explanations. Thus, emphasis turned to two explanations, both of which, as we have seen, were first proposed in ancient times. One, following notions of physical cause, defined psychological distress as fundamentally *illness*, not different in kind from other physical illnesses. The other held that psychological disorder was fundamentally *psychological,* and *very* different in kind from physical illness. These theories continue to dominate our thinking today. Both views command considerable supportive evidence. We will examine the biological or medical view of psychological distress and its implications for treatment in the next chapter. Now, we focus on the treatments that grew out of psychogenic theories of madness.

Much of the excitement that was generated by the psychogenic viewpoint came about, as we have seen, through the study of hysteria. With its paralyses, anesthesias, and convulsions, its loss of voice, sight, or hearing, and occasional loss of consciousness, hysteria seemed patently a *physical* disorder. It was on the basis of his physical theory of animal magnetism that Mesmer developed the technique that came to be called hypnosis. Charcot, in his path-breaking work, was subsequently able to use hypnosis to distinguish between symptoms that had an organic cause and symptoms that were hysterical in nature. Subsequent theorists suggested that the therapeutic effects of hypnosis resulted from psychological suggestion (Bernheim, 1886, cited in Pattie, 1967). Thus, "psychotherapeutics" became an accepted treatment for the mentally disturbed.

By the end of the nineteenth century, hypnosis was widely used in Europe and in the United States for treating hysterical disorders. It formed the basis for the development of modern forms of psychotherapy, and it was a significant milestone in the psychogenic approach to mental disorders.

One of the people who used hypnosis in his treatment of patients was Josef Breuer (1842–1925), a distinguished Viennese internist whose practice included a large number of hysterical patients. Breuer's treatment often consisted of inducing these patients to talk about their problems and fantasies under hypnosis. Frequently patients would become emotional under hypnosis, reliving painful experiences, experiencing a deep **emotional catharsis,** and emerging from the hypnotic trance feeling much better. The patients, of course, were unaware of a relationship between what they discussed under hypnosis, how emotional they had become, and how they felt subsequently. But Breuer believed that because his patients had experienced a catharsis under hypnosis, their symptoms disappeared.

Just as Breuer was making these discoveries, Sigmund Freud, then a neurologist, returned to Vienna. Freud had just completed his studies with Charcot and began to work with Breuer. Together they utilized Breuer's "cathartic method," encouraging patients to report their experiences and fantasies under hypnosis. Freud, however, noticed that similar therapeutic effects could be obtained *without* hypnosis, so long as the patient reported everything that came to mind and experienced emotional catharsis. It was this discovery that led Freud to the theory and therapeutic technique called **psychoanalysis,** which is described in detail in Chapter 4.

FOCUS QUESTIONS

1. Relate exorcism, the Greek push-pull principle, and hypnosis to the three origins of abnormality.
2. Describe the rise of psychogenic treatments.
3. What was the cathartic method?

THE RISE OF THE PSYCHIATRIC HOSPITAL

There is no precise date to mark the beginning of modern treatments for madness. In fact, beliefs in animistic causes persisted into the twentieth century in some parts of the West. Nonetheless, most observers date the beginning of the modern psychological era with the establishment of the psychiatric hospital, an institution that itself has a rather special history.

Institutionalizing the Poor

The medical hospital and surely the psychiatric one are relatively modern inventions. Both evolved in the seventeenth century from institutions that were created to house and confine the poor, the homeless, the unemployed, and among them, the insane. Throughout the sixteenth and seventeenth centuries, poverty was widespread. War and economic depression had dislocated large numbers of people and reduced them to begging and petty crime. In 1532, in Paris, these problems were so severe that beggars were arrested and forced to work in pairs in the city's sewers. Two years later, a new decree forced "poor scholars and indigents" to leave the city. All to no avail, for at the beginning of the seventeenth century, Paris, which had a population of fewer than 100,000 people, had more than 30,000 beggars! In 1606, it was decreed that beggars should be publicly whipped, branded, shorn, and driven from the city. And a year later, in 1607, an ordinance established companies of archers who were located at the gates of the city—their sole task to forbid the return of these indigents.

It was in this social and economic climate that, in 1656, the Hôpital Général of Paris was founded for the poor "of both sexes, of all ages, and from all localities, of whatever breeding and birth, in whatever state they may be, able-bodied or invalid, sick or convalescent, curable or incurable" (Edict of 1656, cited in Foucault, 1965, p. 39). From a strictly humane point of view, the Hôpital Général, which included La Salpêtrière, La Pitie, and La Bicêtre—institutions that later became famous in their own right—was surely an improvement over the conditions that preceded it. For the first time in France, the government took responsibility for feeding and housing its "undesirables." But in return, those undesirables—the poor, the homeless, the mad—yielded up the privilege of roaming the streets. Personal liberty was traded for room and board. It was not a voluntary trade; shortly after the decree was proclaimed, the militia scoured the city, hunting and herding beggars into the various buildings of the Hôpital. Within four years, the Hôpital housed 1 percent of Paris's population.

Paris was not alone in its concern to confine undesirables. During the same period, all over France and throughout Europe, similar institutions were being established. To the modern mind, it seems inconceivable that the poor, the mad, the aged, the infirm, and even the petty criminal could somehow be lumped together and signed over to the same institution. Yet, a compelling commonality bound these people together. *They were not gainfully employed.* Unemployment was viewed, not as the result of economic depression, technological change, or bad luck, but as a personal, indeed a moral, failure. Simple indolence was its accepted name. The task of the Hôpital Général was a moral one: to prevent "mendicancy and idleness as the source of all disorders" (Edict of 1656, cited in Foucault, 1965, p. 47). Whatever restrictions were imposed, whatever behaviors required, and whatever punishments meted out, all were justified by the moral mission of the Hôpital Général.

The hospital was a place of confinement during periods of economic depression. But during economic growth, the hospital was easily and justifiably converted into a workhouse. It required that its residents work (but it paid them a mere fraction of what they would ordinarily make). With increasing industrialization in England, for example, many such workhouses were estab-

Paris

Europe

FOCUS QUESTIONS

1. Who were originally housed in seventeenth-century asylums?
2. Contrast the treatment of the insane at the Hôpital Général of Paris with their treatment at the community in Gheel, Belgium.
3. Why did Philippe Pinel unshackle the psychiatric patients at the Hôpital Général?
4. Describe "moral treatment" of the insane at Tuke's Retreat, the Friends Asylum, and Bloomingdale Asylum.

lished in industrial centers, providing cheap, forced labor to growing industries.

Segregating the Insane

While governments failed to distinguish the insane from the other unfortunates, within the hospital such distinctions were quickly made and were ultimately institutionalized. The insane were given much worse care than other residents of the hospital, and were subjected to brutal physical abuse. At the end of the eighteenth century, one visitor to La Bicêtre described the miserable condition in which he found one mad inmate:

> The unfortunate whose entire furniture consisted of this straw pallet, lying with his head, feet, and body pressed against the wall, could not enjoy sleep without being soaked by the water that trickled from that mass of stone. (Desportes, cited in Foucault, 1965, pp. 70–71)

The same reporter said of La Salpêtrière that what made the place more miserable, and often more fatal, was that in winter, "when the waters of the Seine rose, those cells situated at the level of the sewers became not only more unhealthy, but worse still, a refuge for a swarm of huge rats, which during the night attacked the unfortunates confined there and bit them wherever they could reach them; madwomen have been found with feet, hands, and face torn by bites which are often dangerous and from which several have died" (Desportes, cited in Foucault, 1965, pp. 70–71).

Paris was not unique. In the London hospital, St. Mary's of Bethlehem (which soon became known as Bedlam), patients were chained to the walls or

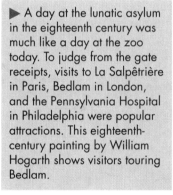

► A day at the lunatic asylum in the eighteenth century was much like a day at the zoo today. To judge from the gate receipts, visits to La Salpêtrière in Paris, Bedlam in London, and the Pennsylvania Hospital in Philadelphia were popular attractions. This eighteenth-century painting by William Hogarth shows visitors touring Bedlam.

kept on long leashes. Nearby, in Bethnal Green, patients were bound hand and foot, and confined in filthy quarters.

The United States established its first hospital, the Pennsylvania Hospital, in 1756. At the urging of Benjamin Franklin, the government set aside a section for "lunatics." They were consigned to the cellar and

> Their scalps were shaved and blistered; they were bled to the point of syncope; purged until the alimentary canal failed to yield anything but mucus, and in the intervals, they were chained by the waist or the ankle to the cell wall . . It was not considered unusual or improper for the keeper to carry a whip and use it freely. (Morton, 1897, cited in Deutsch, 1949, p. 600)

Clearly, to the modern mind, such treatment is cruel and inhumane. That judgment arises because, in the modern view, the insane are entitled to compassion and kindness. But it is not the case that our predecessors were less concerned with the treatment of the insane, or necessarily, morally obtuse. Rather, they had a different theory of insanity; they believed that madness resulted from animalism, that the insane had lost the one capacity that distinguished humans from beasts: *reason.* Because they had lost that capacity, their behavior was disordered, unruly, and wild. The first mandate of treatment, then, was to restore reason. *Fear* was believed to be the emotion that was best suited to restoring the disordered mind. The eminent physician William Cullen wrote that it was "necessary to employ a very constant impression of fear . . . awe and dread." Such emotions should be aroused by "all restraints that may occasionally be proper . . . even by stripes and blows" (Cullen, 1808, cited in Scull, 1981). Clearly, some unscrupulous madhouse operators took advantage of this view to abuse those in their care. But even the most eminent patients received similar treatment. King George III of England was a clear case in point. As Countess Harcourt later described his situation, "the unhappy patient . . . was no longer treated as a human being. His body was immediately encased in a machine which left it no liberty of motion. He was sometimes chained to a stake. He was frequently beaten and starved, and at best he was

▶ The cornerstone of a Dutch asylum shows the way such buildings themselves left little doubt about how people confined there were expected to behave.

kept in subjection by menacing and violent language." (Jones, 1955, cited in Bynum, 1981). In addition, he was bled, blistered, given emetics and various other drugs of the day. Again, such treatment arose from the belief that the insane did not have the physical sensitivities of human beings but rather were like animals in their lack of sensitivity to pain, temperature, and other external stimuli.

The Growth of Humane Treatment

By the end of the eighteenth century, the idea that the incarcerated insane should be treated as animals was under attack. No degree of intellectual or theological rationalization could conceal the torment that these punitive treatments imposed on patients. From a variety of respected sources, protest grew over the conditions of confinement, and especially over the shackles, the chains, the dungeons, and the whippings. Other models for treatment were sought. One was found at Gheel, a Belgian community that had been accepting the insane for quite some time. New ones were found through courageous experiments in Italy, France, England, and the United States.

GHEEL

As the site of a religious shrine in Belgium, the small town of Gheel had been a recuperative center for the insane since the Middle Ages. There, consistent with a religious ethos, "cure" was achieved through prayer and in the "laying on of the hands." Those who prayed were treated in a special, and for the time, unusual way. The deeply troubled were shown habitual kindness, courtesy, and gentleness. The insane lived in the community and, apart from being forbidden alcohol, suffered few restrictions. They took rooms in people's homes, where they were treated as guests. Gheel's reputation grew, and so did the number of people who went there. It provided a model of treatment that stressed sympathy, respect, and concern.

STRIKING PATIENTS' CHAINS

Gheel was not a hospital, but rather a refuge for those who were fortunate enough to make their way there. Although some of the insane were tolerated within their own communities, most of them were impoverished, abandoned, or simply unlucky. They filled the public institutions, which were cruel beyond the telling. But late in the eighteenth century, things began to change. The first hospital to remove the chains from psychiatric patients was St. Boniface in Florence, Italy. There, in 1774, by allowing patients freedom of movement, Vincenzo Chiarugi introduced a radical reform in patient care. It took hold. Later, in 1787, Joseph Dacquin initiated similar reforms in the Insane Department of the hospital at Chambéry, France. And in 1792, during the French Revolution, Philippe Pinel, the newly appointed director of La Bicêtre, unshackled the patients of the Hôpital Général of Paris from their chains, moved them from the cellar dungeons into sunny and airy rooms, and allowed them freedom of the hospital grounds. Pinel was not applying the dicta of liberty and equality to psychiatric patients. Indeed, he believed in the need for control and coercion in psychiatric care. But, he insisted that for coercion to be effective, it needed to be *psychological* rather than physical. The control exerted by shackles and chains would be ended just as soon as the patient was discharged.

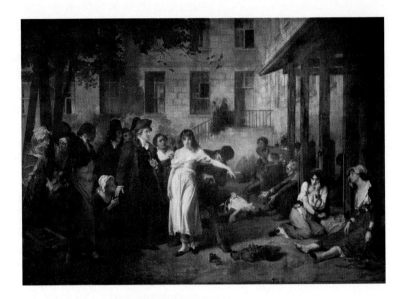

▶ The eighteenth-century French reformer Philippe Pinel ordering the removal of chains from mental patients.

What was required was internalized control that would endure after the patient left the hospital grounds.

His was not an easy decision. There was little public support for Pinel's views. Not only did the view that the insane were like animals linger on, but more important, the belief that they were "dangerous animals" also remained. Moreover, the political consequences of his decision were potentially disastrous. The function of La Bicêtre and its sister institutions was *confinement*. Most people believed that the hospitals existed in order to protect the civilized citizens of France from the dangerous and disturbing excesses of madmen. "Liberty, equality, and fraternity" were not meant to apply to the mentally deranged! An interchange between Pinel and Couthon, an aide to one of the Revolution's most radical leaders, reveals how foolhardy Pinel's reforms were thought to be. Couthon, after having been insulted and cursed by La Bicêtre's patients, had turned to Pinel and said:

> "Now citizen, are you mad yourself to seek to unchain such beasts?"

> Pinel replied calmly: "I am convinced that these madmen are so intractable only because they have been deprived of air and liberty."

> "Well, do as you like with them, but I fear you may become the victim of your own presumption."

> (Foucault, 1965, p. 242)

It is not difficult to appreciate Couthon's position in this debate. Abnormal behavior makes other people fearful and defensive. They worry much more about possible consequences than about causes. Couthon was concerned about what these people might do, and he failed to see, as Pinel had seen, that violent behavior might, at least partially, be a *result* of the cruel confinement.

RELIGIOUS REFORMS IN ENGLAND

Reforms in France were undertaken by secular authorities, but those in England developed from religious concerns. In 1791, Hannah Mills, a Quaker, was admitted to the Lunatick Asylum at York, one of the two major institutions for the insane in England (the other being Bedlam in London). Mills's friends came to visit her but were denied entry on the grounds that she was in no condition to see visitors. A few weeks later, Mills was dead. Her friends suspected that the treatment she had received at York caused or at least contributed to her death. Their suspicions were not entirely groundless, for the conditions in England's institutions for the insane were widely known to be horrible, even by the standards of those days.

Among Mills's friends was William Tuke who, moved by her death, urged the Yorkshire Society of Friends to establish a humanitarian institution for the insane. Despite stiff opposition, similar to the opposition Pinel faced in France, the Retreat at York was established in 1796. It was called a retreat in order to avoid the stigma of such words as "madhouse," "insane asylum," and "lunatickhouse." The name conveyed "the idea of what such an institution should be, namely, a place in which the unhappy might obtain a refuge; a quiet haven in which the shattered bark might find the means of reparation and safety." The kind of treatment that had originated at Gheel—long established, successful, but ignored—was finally being implemented elsewhere (Hunt, 1932, cited in Deutsch, 1949, p. 93).

From the outset, the Retreat's approach to care was dramatically different from practices elsewhere in England. Patients were guests, not "prisoners," as they were called at both Bedlam and the Lunatick Asylum at York. The cornerstones of care were kindness, consideration, courtesy, and dignity. To the extent that treatment principles were defined at the Retreat, two dominated: the need for esteem and the value of work, especially physical work. This emphasis on the therapeutic value of work was unique to the Retreat. The moral virtue of work is deeply embedded in Quaker philosophy. It was consistent with the widely held work ethic of the day and its concomitant distaste for unemployment and the unemployed. The need for esteem was an even more highly valued principle. Treatment took the form of encouraging the insane to acquire social skills, to utilize them, and to gain rewards for meeting the requirements of everyday social interaction. Thus, in the manner of the English during those times, the staff of the Retreat would regularly invite the guests to tea (Foucault, 1965, p. 249).

The effects of the Retreat upon some of its guests were dramatic. Samuel Tuke, the founder's grandson, tells of a guest who was brought to the Retreat in such a violent condition that even though he was chained and shackled, his escorts were afraid of him. Immediately upon entering the Retreat, however, his chains were removed. He was invited to dine with the staff and then was courteously shown to his room. So long as he was considerate of the needs of others, he was told, there would be no need for restraint. (Restraint was not entirely abolished. In emergencies, patients were bound in broad leather belts that left the arms free. In extreme circumstances, straitjackets were used.) The patient promised to restrain himself. When, however, he became agitated, he was reminded of the agreements he had made on his first day. After four months, he was able to leave the Retreat.

▲ A sketch of the English reformer William Tuke.

MORAL TREATMENT IN THE UNITED STATES

The ideas that led to the founding and success of Tuke's Retreat at York spread quickly to the United States. The essence of this form of treatment, called ***moral treatment,*** was enunciated by Dr. Romeyn Beck, of New York, in 1811.

He wrote:

> . . . The rules most proper to be observed are the following: Convince the lunatics that the power of the physician and keeper is absolute; have humane attendants, who shall act as servants to them; never threaten but execute; offer no indignities to them, as they have a high sense of honour; punish disobedience pre-emptorily, in the presence of other maniacs; if unruly, forbid them the company of others, use the strait waistcoats, confine them in a dark and quiet room, order spare diet. . . .; tolerate noisy ejaculations; . . . Let their fears and resentments be soothed without unnecessary opposition; thus acting, the patient will "minister to himself." (Beck, 1811, cited in Deutsch, 1949, pp. 91–92)

In 1817, the Friends Asylum at Frankford, Pennsylvania, was established. Shortly thereafter, in 1821, the Bloomingdale Asylum was founded through the efforts of Thomas Eddy, a Quaker businessman who had been much influenced by Samuel Tuke. The Bloomingdale Asylum, located on the site of the present campus of Columbia University in New York City, stressed the two features that were the hallmarks of humane care: kind treatment and the virtues of work. For the first time, moreover, records were kept of patients' progress in the hospital as well as of their condition before entering it. The efforts at the Bloomingdale Asylum served as the model for several later hospitals, including the Hartford Retreat and the McLean Hospital (Tourney, 1967; Rothman, 1971; Scull, 1981). Although not yet especially effective, treatment became increasingly humane. And that was a very important improvement over the past.

SUMMARY

1. The times and culture in which individuals live and the general way in which they perceive the world influence how abnormality is understood and treated.

2. When the world is perceived in animistic terms, abnormality is likely to be viewed as a *supernatural* phenomenon. Prehistoric people attributed abnormality to possession by spirits trapped in the head and chipped *trephines* in the skull to let the spirits out.

3. Some Greeks and Romans attributed abnormality to *physical* causes. For example, they believed that *hysteria* was caused by a wandering uterus that created discomfort wherever it settled. They treated it by trying to draw the uterus back to its proper place. Galen challenged this idea and said that hysteria was caused by a malfunctioning sexual organ. Furthermore, Galen also contributed important insights into *psychological* causes of abnormality.

4. In medieval Europe, some behaviors that might seem bizarre today were esteemed as being evidence of piety and holiness. Other behaviors, equally bizarre from a modern perspective, were held to be the result of *possession*. Individuals so possessed were subjected to rites of exorcism and were sometimes ostracized from their communities entirely.

5. During the Middle Ages and Renaissance, those suffering from psychological distress were often viewed as possessed, or accused of practicing

witchcraft and causing others to be possessed. Tens of thousands of people were accused of being witches and were hanged or burned during this period, as there was no known "cure" for witchcraft.

6. In the seventeenth century, hospitals grew out of institutions that were originally created to house and confine the poor, lame, dispossessed, and insane. The insane, however, were segregated from the other residents of the hospital and were subjected to brutal physical abuse. Treatment in the early insane asylum was predicated on the view that the insane lacked *reason* and displayed the characteristics of animals and could therefore be treated like animals.

7. In the middle of the eighteenth century, it gradually was recognized that mental disorders were *psychological* in origin and could be treated by psychological means. Mesmer tried to induce crises to restore the flow of *animal magnetism*. Charcot treated mental disorders by *hypnosis*, after distinguishing hysterical convulsions from symptoms with an organic cause. Both Breuer and Freud used hypnosis to induce *catharsis* in hysterical patients.

8. By the end of the eighteenth century, new and more humane treatments for the insane were found. The best hospitals began to stress the need for *moral treatment*, for patient dignity and work, and they began to keep records of patients' condition, both before they entered the hospital and while they were being treated.

QUESTIONS FOR CRITICAL THINKING

1. Why did extensive social instability in the late fifteenth and sixteenth centuries lead people to believe that mental illness could be caused by witches?

2. Why was Mesmer able to cure patients of their ills despite the fact that animal magnetism actually did not exist?

3. How did people justify the cruel and inhumane treatment of the insane in the early hospitals?

4. What aspects of moral treatment were likely to help less severely afflicted psychiatric patients?

PART **2** # MODELS AND TREATMENTS OF ABNORMALITY

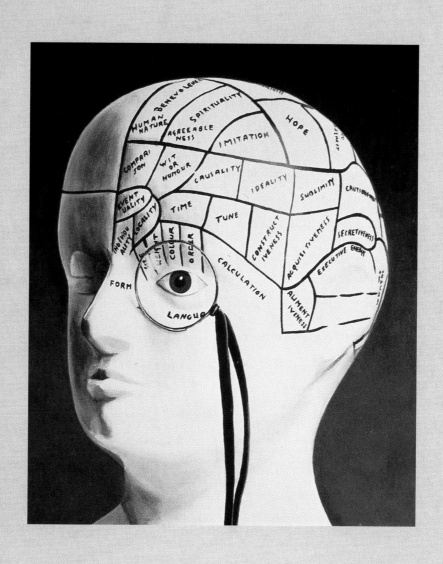

The Biomedical Model

CHAPTER ORGANIZER

MODELS OF ABNORMALITY
- Learn how each of the models of abnormality defines the causes of abnormality.

PRINCIPLES OF THE BIOMEDICAL MODEL
- Follow the story of general paresis to understand the syndrome-etiology-treatment approach of the biomedical model.
- Discover how biomedical researchers focus on germs, genetics, biochemistry, and neuroanatomy as possible causes of abnormal behavior.

TREATMENT
- Become familiar with the various kinds of drug treatment, and the side effects of each of these drugs.

EVALUATING THE BIOMEDICAL MODEL
- Know the strengths and weaknesses of the biomedical model.

REDUCTIONISM
- Learn what is meant by reductionism and its implications.

When anthropologists study how culture develops, they seek out existing "primitive" peoples, untouched by modern society and technology. To do this, anthropologists travel to remote corners of the world. For biomedical researchers, the challenges of studying the root causes of mental illness have been even greater. How can we best study the genetic origins of the major disorders and personality traits? How can we separate out the contributions of child rearing, of trauma, and of culture from the contribution of genes? A few years ago, a group of researchers at the University of Minnesota studied a pair of identical twins, both named Jim, who had been raised apart since birth, unaware of each other's existence. The Jims' psychological similarities were extraordinary, and their discovery opened the floodgates to the study of many more such twin pairs. Here was a way of separating the vicissitudes of growing up from the contributions of genes. The story of this study and how it illuminates the causes of human misery is told later in this chapter.

How one defines abnormality has been the subject of the previous two chapters. Chapter 1 presented the problem, and Chapter 2 discussed the different historical approaches to its definition. In this chapter, we begin our discussion of modern-day models of abnormality.

The biomedical model explains abnormality as a physical malfunction, such as a chemical or anatomical defect. Thus, it explains such symptoms as memory loss for recent events, language disorders, inability to deal with new situations, loss of personal skills and abilities, and neglect of bodily functions in an older person as physical malfunctions rather than psychological problems. It emphasizes the problems resulting from an abnormality in the synthesis of the neurotransmitter acetylcholine rather than considering poor adaptation to change or demoralization arising out of retirement and reduced income. Similarly it explains depression by concentrating on those symptoms of the depressive that are related to the depressive's biological processes rather than emphasizing distorted thinking or poor interpersonal relations. Thus, a biomedical scientist investigates the evidence that the chemistry of a depressive's brain changes when he is depressed. The biomedical scientist will experiment with these biochemical factors in order to see if they are the cause, or etiology, of the depression. Also, in an attempt to alleviate the disorder, the biomedical investigator will be more likely to develop chemical therapies or drugs that will counteract biochemical factors. This approach lies at the core of the lively field of "Biological Psychiatry."

MODELS OF ABNORMALITY

3 models of abnormality
① biomedical - body
② psychodynamic - personality
③ learning - behavior

What model we follow and how we define the causes of abnormality both help to determine how we will treat abnormality. Each approach to abnormality can be considered a **model** of abnormality. At present, there are three major models, which are sometimes complementary and often competing in their attempt to understand and cure abnormality. The **biomedical model,** discussed in this chapter, holds that abnormality is an illness of the body. The **psychodynamic model,** discussed in Chapter 4, holds that abnormality is driven by hidden conflicts within our personality. (Besides classical psychoanalysis, Chapter 4 discusses self theory and existential theory, which deals with questions of life's meaning, human potential, responsibility, and will.) The **learning model,** discussed in Chapter 5, includes the behavioral approach, which holds that we learn to be abnormal through conditioning and that we can unlearn these maladaptive ways of behaving, and the cognitive approach, which holds that abnormality springs from disordered conscious thought about oneself and the world.

▶ The biomedical model uses tools such as the PET scan to study how the chemistry of a depressive's brain differs from that of a normal's brain.

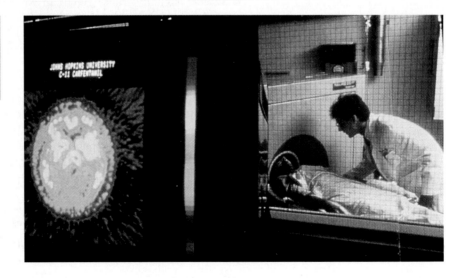

FOCUS QUESTIONS

1. What are the three principal models of abnormality?
2. Describe what each model considers to be the cause of abnormality.

Following a particular model of abnormality is a matter of choice, and the choice always involves risk. For example, an investigator might believe that early childhood experiences are the primary influence on adult psychopathology. He could spend years studying his manic-depressive patient's past history and never cure him, for it might turn out that manic-depression is caused by a biological problem and cured by a chemical. His strict adherence to a particular model would have blinded him to this other possibility—in this case, a biological explanation of manic-depression. In sum, there is a danger inherent in following any particular model of abnormality. By concentrating on one level of evidence, we might neglect some of the other, more crucial evidence. The kinds of abnormality vary so much that we do not believe that one particular model of abnormality will explain all mental disorders.

We now turn to our first model of abnormality, the biomedical model. We review the landmark findings that have convinced many investigators that mental illness might be, at bottom, physical illness.

PRINCIPLES OF THE BIOMEDICAL MODEL

biomedical model
syndrome
etiology (cause)
1) germs
2) genes
3) biochem
4) neuroanatomy
treatment

Those who advocate the biomedical model typically approach abnormality as medical researchers approach an illness: They will group diverse, but co-occurring, symptoms together into a coherent **syndrome.** Then they will search for the **etiology,** or cause, of the syndrome, examining four possible causes: (1) *germs,* (2) *genes,* (3) the *biochemistry* of the patient's brain, and (4) the patient's *neuroanatomy.* Once an etiology has been discovered, some biological **treatment** that attacks the cause, usually a drug, will be sought to alleviate the abnormality.

The idea that psychological disorders have physical etiologies is both ancient and venerable. We saw in the last chapter that the ancients believed that hysteria resulted from a wandering uterus. The Egyptians, Greeks, and Romans sought to cure this psychological abnormality by physical means: assaulting the body of the sufferer with a great variety of drugs, massages, fumigations, and so on. Behind all these treatments lay the belief that the cause of

▶ This 1530 painting by Jan Sanders van Hemessen shows physicians trying to remove the "Stone of Folly" from a bound patient possessed with madness. However gruesome this procedure, the theory and treatment of mental illness as a disorder of the body has survived; we now know that tumors in the brain sometimes bring about abnormality.

the psychological disorder was a physical disorder. It was not until the latter half of the nineteenth century, however, that anyone convincingly demonstrated that any form of psychological disorder was caused by organic illness. At that time, it was found that syphilis caused general paresis. This story illustrates how the isolation of a syndrome led to the discovery of an etiology, which in turn led to the discovery of a therapy. In addition, it illustrates how a mental disorder can be caused by a germ (one of the biomedical model's four possible causes of abnormality). This proved to be one of the great sagas in the history of biomedical science.

Germs as Etiology: Syphilis and General Paresis

The worst epidemic of madness in recorded history began a few years after Christopher Columbus discovered the New World and continued with mounting ferocity until the early 1900s. We have come to call this disorder **general paresis.** Beginning with a weakness in the arms and legs, it proceeds to symptoms of eccentricity and then downright delusions of grandeur, the false notion that one is more important than the objective facts warrant. It finally progresses to global paralysis, stupor, and death.

As early as 1672, Thomas Willis (1621–1675), an English anatomist, observed that some of these patients exhibited dullness of the mind and forgetfulness that seemed to develop into downright stupidity and foolishness. Later in life, these same people would fall into paralysis. This was not a precise observation. Rather, it served loosely to differentiate one group of madmen from others, based on signs of developing stupidity and paralysis. In 1805, a French physician, Jean Esquirol (1772–1840), added another significant observation: the mental deterioration and paralysis observed in this group of patients quickly culminated in death.

There the matter stood until 1826, when Esquirol's student, A. L. J. Bayle, undertook the first major step necessary for a disorder to be understood as biomedical: organization of symptoms into a syndrome, which allowed precise description and diagnosis of the illness. He formalized the diagnosis by giving a complete and exact description of the physical and psychological symptoms, and arguing strongly that these constituted a separate disease, a different madness, if you will, from all others then known. He argued that mental deterioration, paralysis, and subsequent death, among others, were a group of symptoms that clustered together and formed the distinct syndrome of general paresis.

Bayle's rigorous definition of the disorder led to considerable speculation about its etiology. Quite early, there had been some suspicion that it was caused by syphilis. But at the time, Wilhelm Griesinger (1817–1868), an eminent psychiatric authority of physiological bent, had dismissed that view on the seemingly sound basis that paresis occurred among people in whom no trace of syphilitic infection could be found. Reports of cases in which paretics were known to have had syphilis were clearly not sufficient, since these were contradicted by the paretics who adamantly denied they had ever had syphilis and who showed no evidence of syphilis.

Despite Griesinger's opinion and the support of his colleagues, evidence gradually emerged that syphilis was somehow implicated in general paresis. But that evidence was difficult to accumulate for three reasons. First, and per-

FOCUS QUESTIONS

1. How do biomedical researchers approach a mental disorder?
2. What four possible causes of abnormality are examined by adherents of the biomedical model?

haps most important, syphilis precedes paresis by as many as thirty years. The connection between the one and the other was difficult to see. Second, syphilis was then, as now, a disease about which there was considerable shame. People were often unable to admit to themselves, and surely not to others, that they had contracted the disease. Third, the diagnosis of syphilis was itself not an exact science. In the early part of the nineteenth century, techniques were still not available for ascertaining that someone had syphilis, because the overt symptoms that occur immediately after contracting it soon disappear. Not until there were improvements in microscopy was it ascertained that syphilitic organisms (spirochetes) remain in the body long after the overt symptoms vanish.

The evidence, then, accumulated slowly. By about 1860, it was possible to demonstrate that there was enormous destruction in the neural tissue of the brains of people who had died from general paresis. Later, in 1869, D. M. Argyll (1837–1909), a Scottish eye surgeon, demonstrated that the central nervous system was implicated in syphilis by showing that the eyes of syphilitics failed to show the standard pupillary reflex—the narrowing of the pupil to bright light. In 1884, Alfred Fournier (1832–1914), a French physician, provided highly suggestive **_epidemiological_** evidence (that is, evidence from many individuals) on the relation between syphilis and general paresis: some 65 percent of paretics had a demonstrable history of syphilis, compared to only 10 percent of nonparetics. That evidence, of course, was merely suggestive: it did not demonstrate cause since it did not show that 100 percent of paretics had prior histories of syphilis. But it added significantly to the mounting tide of data, turning belief away from Griesinger's view that strong spirits and cigars were the culprits, toward the syphilis-paresis link.

The overt symptoms of syphilis—the sores (chancres) on the genitals—may disappear in a few weeks, but the disease does not. It goes underground, attacking the central nervous system. Cures for syphilis were unknown then. Thus, not only was it true that if you had the disease you couldn't get rid of it, it was equally true and also known that _like measles, if you contracted syphilis once, you couldn't get it again._ More bluntly, if someone who has already become syphilitic (a paretic) comes in contact with another syphilitic germ, he will not develop sores on his genitals.

Consider the situation of those who believed that this psychological disorder (general paresis) was caused by the syphilitic germ. On the one hand, there was evidence that many paretics had syphilis. But some paretics claimed never to have contracted syphilis. The investigators had a hypothesis: perhaps those paretics who claimed not to have had syphilis actually had had the disease and did not know it or were too ashamed to admit it. If indeed these paretics were ignorant or not telling the truth, then the case for a biological cause of general paresis would be convincing. There was one means, but a risky one, of finding out by way of an experiment if these paretics had previously had syphilis. The investigators reasoned that if you inject these paretics with the syphilitic germ, one startling result would come about. The paretics would not contract the disease since you cannot get syphilis twice. Betting on this outcome, the German neurologist Richard von Krafft-Ebing (1840–1902) performed this critical experiment. In 1897, he innoculated nine paretics who had denied ever having had syphilis with material from syphilitic sores (see Box 3–1). None developed sores themselves, leading to the conclusion that they must have already been infected. The link between syphilis and general paresis was forged.

▼ The German neurologist Richard von Krafft-Ebing (1840–1902), an unsung hero of the biomedical model, performed the crucial experiment that forged the link between syphilis and general paresis.

Box 3–1

ETHICS AND EXPERIMENTATION

To test the hypothesis on the relationship between syphilis and general paresis, Richard von Krafft-Ebing used human guinea pigs. He injected with syphilitic germs paretics who claimed never to have had syphilis. He believed that these patients would not develop syphilitic sores because he was convinced that they actually already had had the disease and either did not know it or were lying. But had he been wrong, he would have knowingly injected these people with the incurable disease of syphilis.

It is worth pondering for a moment whether you would have done that experiment or permitted it to be done. Consider the facts. The year is 1897, nearly three-quarters of a century after Bayle defined the syndrome. General paresis is now a raging disorder, perhaps the most widespread of the psychoses, affecting the great (Henry VIII and Randolph Churchill, Winston's father, were probably both paretics) and the ordinary alike. There is no question that if a direct connection between paresis and syphilis can be demonstrated, there will be an enormous leap forward in the direction of understanding and therefore conquering the disease. But

in 1897, the relationship between syphilis and paresis is still speculative: a good hunch, but only a hunch. What if the hunch is wrong? Syphilis is still incurable. If the hunch is wrong, you will be taking people whose lives are already burdened by paresis and adding incurable syphilis to their misery. Can such an experiment be justified? Would you carry out such an experiment?

We suspect that such an experiment could not be done in our society today. The risks are deemed too large, regardless of the possibility that the gain may be overwhelming. But such a judgment is not an easy one to make. Many would argue that the benefits to each of us from huge advances in medicine are such that we are, each of us, obligated to contribute to those advances (Eisenberg, 1977). On the other hand, there may be other means to prove or disprove a hypothesis. Although Krafft-Ebing's experiment was a dramatic proof of the link between syphilis and general paresis, such a link might have been proven by other, less dangerous and more humane, experiments. But the less dangerous experiment is strictly hypothetical, and many lives would have been lost in the interim.

Evidence bearing Krafft-Ebing out soon cascaded in. In 1906, a German physician and bacteriologist, August von Wassermann (1866–1925), developed a blood test for detecting the presence of syphilis. More than 90 percent of paretics responded positively to the test. The causal connection between the syphilis germ and paresis, a mental disorder, was now understood.

Once the syndrome was isolated and its etiology understood, it was only a matter of time before investigators developed a treatment for general paresis. In 1909, a German bacteriologist, Paul Ehrlich (1854–1915), discovered "606," an arsenic compound that was given that name because it followed after 605 failures! Arsphenamine, the first effective cure of syphilis, acted by killing the syphilis germs in the bloodstream. By curing syphilis it prevented the occurrence of paresis. It was not until the 1940s that penicillin, a drug that arrests syphilis almost at any point in its development, replaced "606" as the preferred treatment.

So successful was Krafft-Ebing's work and that of others who followed him that the most common mental illness of the nineteenth century was eradicated within a generation. Today it is common to meet psychologists and psychiatrists who have never seen a case of general paresis. When we look for paretics in large American cities to instruct present-day medical students, we can no longer find them. Thus was general paresis, a psychological disorder characterized by stupidity and delusions of grandeur, understood and eradicated.

But Krafft-Ebing, this scientist of courage and genius, accomplished more than just discovering that a particular germ was the cause of paresis. With this discovery, he convinced the medical world of something much more global:

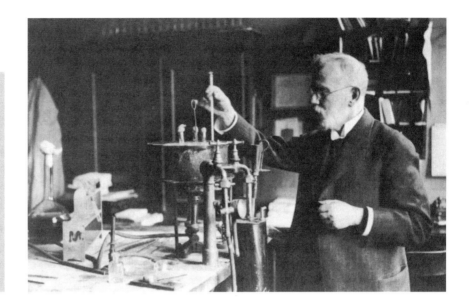

► The German bacteriologist Paul Ehrlich (1854–1915), shown in his laboratory, discovered an arsenic compound that was the first effective cure for syphilis, killing the syphilis germs in the bloodstream. The compound was named "606" because it was discovered after 605 failures. In the 1940s, penicillin, which arrests syphilis at any point in its development, replaced 606 as the preferred treatment.

that mental illness could be just an illness of the body. This became the first principle, the rallying cry, and the agenda for the field of biological psychiatry. A century of research searching for biological foundations of schizophrenia, depression, Alzheimer's, and many other disorders ensued.

Genetics as Etiology

Genetics is the second biomedical etiology that may lead researchers to consider a psychological disorder as being a physical illness. A generation ago, few mental health professionals believed that inherited vulnerabilities could be central to the development of mental illness. Fearing that discovery of a genetic predisposition might cast a stigma on patients and lead to a questioning of the need for psychotherapy, clinical researchers strongly leaned toward social and developmental explanations of the inescapable fact that some mental illness can run in families. Gradually, however, the genetic evidence became too compelling to ignore. Consider schizophrenia, for example.

GENES AND SCHIZOPHRENIA

Schizophrenia is a severe psychotic condition that strikes approximately 1 percent of the world's population. Usually beginning in adolescence or early adulthood, it results in highly disordered thinking, perception, and language. Schizophrenic individuals function poorly in complex and primitive societies alike. What causes schizophrenia? The biomedical model holds that it is an illness passed on genetically. Investigators have approached schizophrenia by studying twins.

There are two kinds of twins: identical and fraternal. Identical twins have all the same genes, whereas fraternal twins have an average of only half of their genes in common—exactly the same proportion of common genetic material as any two siblings share. Twins are an exquisite research tool for those who advocate the biomedical model because twins usually share very similar environments (same age, same social class, same food, similar social circles, etc.), while they differ systematically on how many genes they share.

FOCUS QUESTIONS

1. Explain how studies of twins help to determine that there is a genetic component to schizophrenia.
2. How do adoptive studies tease apart the contribution to personality of child rearing versus genes?

If there are genes that determine whether one will be schizophrenic or not, and if one twin becomes schizophrenic, what is the probability that the other twin will also be schizophrenic? (Assume, for the sake of the argument, that diagnosis of schizophrenia is infallible and environment has no influence.) Since identical twins share all of their genes, if one identical twin is schizophrenic, then the other *must* also be schizophrenic. This is not so with fraternal twins, since they share only half their genes. Depending on the nature of the alleged gene, the prediction would be 50 percent or 25 percent for fraternal twins (McGue, Gottesman, and Rao, 1985). Those who hold the biomedical view use this method of observing identical and fraternal twins. If they find that one twin is schizophrenic, they will then find out if the other twin is also schizophrenic. When both twins are schizophrenic, they are called ***concordant*** for schizophrenia; when only one is schizophrenic, they are called ***discordant.***

Many studies from Europe, Japan, and the U.S.A. have looked at hundreds of pairs of twins in this way. Overall, identical twins have a concordance rate for schizophrenia of about 50 percent, while fraternal twins have a concordance of about 10 percent. Keep in mind that the rate of schizophrenia in the population as a whole is about 1 percent. So when one of the identical twins is schizophrenic, the other is five times more likely to be schizophrenic than the fraternal twin of a schizophrenic, who is in turn ten times more likely than the average to be schizophrenic. This suggests a causal influence of genes, but not genetic determination, since concordance for identical twins is only 50 percent, not 100 percent. And since the concordance for identical twins is less than 100 percent, genes cannot be the whole etiological story. Environment also must have an influence on the cause of schizophrenia. This issue, the inheritance of schizophrenia, remains hotly debated. We will discuss it more fully in Chapter 12.

GENES AND PERSONALITY

It's not only mental illness that may have a genetic component, but almost all of personality as well. The idea that personality might have genetic components is so contrary to the political sensibilities of our time that its rediscovery has come as a shock. How did biological psychiatry come to believe in such an "unenlightened" idea? Consider a case in which several family members exhibit criminal behavior:

> Stewart is twelve years old. He likes to tag along with Joshua, his seventeen-year-old brother. Stewart follows Joshua everywhere. He especially likes to go to the store with Joshua where Joshua often shoplifts whatever catches his eye. Joshua always pockets a few candy bars for Stewart. All this came out when Stewart was picked up for shoplifting.
>
> Their father, Mark, was arrested several years ago for robbery, and Mark's father, their grandfather, was absent from home often because of his frequent arrests.

Environmentalists tell us that this cycle of crime is ingrained (Kolvin, Miller, Fleeting, and Kolvin, 1988). Stewart learned to shoplift by watching Joshua, who learned to steal by watching Mark. This explanation is quite possibly true: The children of criminals commit crimes more often than do children who were not exposed to criminal parents. But biomedical researchers remind us that this evidence is equally compatible with another theory. So unfashionable is this other theory that it is not even mentioned as a possibility by most of the social scientists who write about the generational transmission of crime.

Here is the alternative to learning criminal behavior: Some aspect of personality that contributes to crime—for example, lack of conscience, or present-mindedness, or aggression—may be inherited. According to this theory, people who commit crimes tend to lack conscience or tend to be present-minded or tend to be aggressive because they have a genetic makeup that contributes to these tendencies. Thus, if children have criminals as their biological parents, they will grow up to commit crimes—not because they learn anything at all from watching their parents, but because they inherit their parents' genetic tendencies.

Does the notion of "inheriting" aggression or present-mindedness or lack of conscience make any scientific sense? We are all used to the idea of genes controlling simple characteristics like eye color. But can something complex, like a personality trait, be inherited? To approach this it is useful to think about evolution: what does evolution work on and what gets selected for?

Consider for a moment the possibility that simple traits like eye color and the particular molecular string of DNA that leads to eye color, are selected only indirectly. These get selected because a person with this particular DNA string is more successful at reproducing and surviving than a person with different strings of DNA. What gets directly selected for are the global characteristics that cause their owners to out-reproduce and out-survive the competition. According to this analysis, it is complex, "molar" traits like beauty, intelligence, aggression, conscience that are the primary material of natural selection, not the "molecular" strings of DNA that are the building blocks of the molar traits.

Take the complex trait of sexual attractiveness, "beauty," for example. Evolution has certainly worked on beauty (Buss, 1989, 1991; Thornhill, 1989). Beauty is passed on from one generation to the next. Sexually attractive people have higher reproductive success than ugly people, and natural selection sees to it that their genetic makeup flourishes. Beauty is made up of simpler traits like eye color, and eye color in turn has even simpler building blocks like a particular chain of DNA. But beauty, like automobiles, comes in many models, and its definition changes within limits over time and culture. There are many ways to be sexually attractive: numerous combinations of eye color, teeth, and hair will all be attractive. More importantly, even more combinations will be ugly, and so will be eliminated from the gene pool. If there are myriad kinds of beauty, then there are myriad molecular ways to construct "beauty," all of which get selected for.

The upshot of this is that there is unlikely to be a molecular biology of beauty. There will not be "beauty genes," or there will be so many combinations of genes underlying beauty as to be scientifically unwieldy. But beauty will still be subject to natural selection and inherited. So too with conscience, aggression, and many of the complex traits that make up personality. It follows that the notion of "criminal genes" may not make much sense, but the notion of the heritability of criminal tendencies makes reasonable scientific sense.

If you can't find the actual genes underlying a personality trait, how can you possibly find out if a trait is inherited rather than learned? This formidable question has a surprisingly simple answer: Study adopted children or study twins.

The comparison of adopted children to their biological parents versus comparison to their adoptive parents is one way to tease apart the contribution of child rearing from genes. Hundreds of such "adoptive studies" have been done. Here is a typical one and it bears on the biomedical hypothesis that criminality might be heritable.

Denmark keeps complete records of adoptions and complete criminal records as well. The Danish Population Register is a gold mine for untangling child rearing from biology. The criminal records (or their absence) for the fathers, both biological and adoptive, of all the adopted children born in Copenhagen in 1953 and the criminal records (or their absence) of the sons have been scrutinized.

In the cases where neither the natural nor the adopted father was convicted of a crime, 10.5 percent of the sons turned out to be criminals. Where the adopted father was a criminal but the natural father was not, 11.5 percent of sons were criminals. So having an adoptive criminal father does *not* increase the son's risk of becoming a criminal.

If the natural father (whom the son hadn't seen since he was at most six months old) was a criminal but the adopted father was not, 22 percent of the sons were criminals. Crime rate is doubled by having "criminal genes." If *both* natural and adopted fathers were criminals, the sons' crime rate was 36.2 percent—triple the rate of the sons of noncriminal fathers.

▼ Twin researchers study the heritability of various traits and characteristics, as well as predispositions to mental disorders. In the Minnesota twin family studies, Dr. Thomas J. Bouchard, Jr., and his colleagues studied twins separated at birth and reared apart. When these twins were reunited, many were discovered to have similar personalities, mannerisms, likes, and dislikes, as did these two brothers. Both were fire chiefs and had the same mustache, sideburns, eyeglasses, drank the same beer, and used the same gestures.

Separated at birth, the Mallifert twins meet accidentally.

This means that there is a biological predisposition to commit crime (and get caught). If it is present and the son is reared by a criminal father, the son is at very high risk. This suggests a learning component as well. But merely having a criminal father rear the sons, without the biological predisposition, does not increase the son's risk (Hutchings and Mednick, 1977).

The best method of all for separating the learned from the genetic contribution to personality is to study twins who have been adopted away and reared apart from birth.

Over the last decade and a half, an iconoclastic group of University of Minnesota psychologists led by Tom Bouchard, David Lykken, and Auke Tellegen has studied the psychological profiles of such twins. They started with the "Jim" twins (both were named Jim), a pair whose reunion was covered in the press in the 1970s. The project snowballed. People who knew they had a long-lost twin came to the University of Minnesota for help in finding their other twin. Minnesota has now accumulated 110 pairs of identical twins reared apart and 27 pairs of fraternal twins reared apart. Many of the twins' very first reunions took place in the Minnesota laboratory. Stories of spooky similarity repeat over and over. For example, one pair of identicals both divorced a woman named Linda to marry a woman named Betty, and one identical twin named his son James Allen X while his co-twin named his son James Alan X. Could it just be coincidence? Unlikely. These "coincidences" do not seem to occur in the lives of the fraternal twins reared apart.

The degree of heritability and the range of personality traits that are heritable are impressive. All of the following are *strongly* related in identical twins reared apart, and they are much less related in fraternal twins reared apart (Bouchard, Lykken, McGue, Segal, and Tellegen, 1990; Plomin, Corley, De-

Fries, and Fulker, 1990; Waller, Kojetin, Bouchard, Lykken, and Tellegen, 1990; Bouchard and McGue, 1990):

IQ	authoritarianism
mental speed	extraversion
perceptual speed and accuracy	neuroticism
religiosity	amount of television viewing
traditionalism	well-being
alcohol and drug abuse	self-acceptance
crime and conduct problems	self-control
job satisfaction	dominance
actual choice of jobs	pessimism
cheerfulness	hostility
depressiveness	cynicism
danger seeking	

These findings have essentially been duplicated in another study carried out with 500 Swedish twins, identical and fraternal, reared apart and reared together, and now middle-aged (Pedersen, McClearn, Plomin, Nesselroade, Berg, and DeFaire, in press; Plomin, Scheier, Bergeman, Pedersen, Nesselroade, McClearn, submitted).

It is important to realize, however, that for every one of these heritable traits, the degree of heritability is much less than a perfect 1.00. (Degree of heritability for any trait is calculated by first subtracting the average correlation between fraternal twins, which results from common rearing and from commonality of half their genes, from the average correlation for identical twins, which results from both common rearing and from entirely common genes, and then doubling it.) Generally, heritability hovers a bit below .50. This means that genes do not determine at least half of any heritable personality traits, but it also means that genes do contribute much of what we are.

Biochemistry as Etiology: Dopamine and Schizophrenia

As we mentioned earlier, those believing in the biomedical model may also look for the cause of a disorder in a third category; irregularities in an individual's biochemistry. One hypothesis about schizophrenia is that it is caused by an unbalanced biochemistry. The "dopamine hypothesis," as it is called, states that schizophrenic behavior is caused by too much dopamine in the brain. Dopamine, like all neurotransmitters, is a chemical that is directly involved in transmitting nerve impulses from one nerve cell to the next. There is a considerable amount of evidence in favor of this hypothesis. But all of it is rather indirect, since it is still technically impossible to look into the brain of a living person and count how much of a given chemical is there. The most important evidence comes from the fact that drugs which usually relieve the symptoms of schizophrenia also lower the amount of usable dopamine in the brain. Such drugs do not completely cure schizophrenia, but they do reduce hallucinations and delusions, improve concentration, and make schizophrenic symptoms less bizarre. This action is called dopamine "blocking," and these drugs block dopamine by binding themselves to the nerve cells in the brain that receive dopamine, thus preventing naturally occurring dopamine from getting to

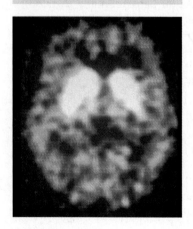

▼ The "dopamine hypothesis" states that schizophrenia may be caused by excess dopamine in the brain. Here is a PET (Positron Emission Tomography) scan of a human brain after it has been injected with a drug that enables researchers to visualize the distribution of dopamine receptors in the brain.

FOCUS QUESTIONS

1. Describe how irregularities in an individual's biochemistry can lead to schizophrenic behavior.
2. How might disorders in the anatomy of the brain lead to psychopathology?

these receptors. And the more dopamine that can be blocked by various drugs, the greater the ability of the drugs to relieve schizophrenic symptoms (Matthysse, 1973). Some investigators conclude that since these drugs decrease dopamine, an increase of dopamine causes schizophrenia (Krieckhaus, Donahoe, and Morgan, 1992).

Such evidence argues that the symptoms of schizophrenia are caused by too much dopamine in the brain. From the viewpoint of the biomedical school, evidence which shows that altering the biochemistry of the brain alters the symptoms of a disorder (for better or worse) suggests that the disorder is an illness. This supplements evidence that the disorder is caused by a germ and is relieved by killing that germ, or that a disorder can be transmitted genetically.

Neuroanatomy as Etiology: The Disordered Brain

Those who believe in the biomedical model also consider disorders in the anatomy of the brain as an explanation for psychopathology. Brain disorders may result from malfunctioning of specific areas of the brain (see Box 3–2). For example, the brain is organized in a hierarchy from bottom to top, with the higher levels generally controlling more abstract, cognitive, and voluntary functions. These higher areas are more fragile. So the sequence of symptoms of senility—problems in coping with new situations, confusion about when

Box 3–2

NUCLEAR MEDICINE AND OBSESSIVE-COMPULSIVE DISORDER

Modern techniques of nuclear medicine can now illuminate the anatomical and biochemical abnormalities present in the brains of patients with different forms of psychopathology. The brains of patients with schizophrenia, depression, or obsessive-compulsive disorder (OCD) have been examined in detail.

Obsessive-compulsive disorder is a disorder in which patients are plagued by recurring thoughts and rituals. New evidence suggests a defective circuit in the brains of obsessive-compulsive patients. Eighteen patients with OCD were given either drug therapy or behavior therapy. Prior to therapy, they had PET (Positron Emission Tomography) scans of their brains. In this procedure, patients are injected with a radioactively labeled glucose, which circulates through the bloodstream and becomes particularly concentrated in areas of high utilization. This means that areas of the brain that are particularly active will become more radioactive than less active areas of the brain. It follows that the brain areas involved in OCD may look "hot" when OCD patients in the throes of the disorder are given PET scans.

Of the eighteen patients, thirteen responded well to the two kinds of therapy, lowering their amount of obsessive thoughts and compulsive behavior markedly. They each then received a second PET scan, and this scan was compared to the pre-therapy scan to see what areas of the brain had "cooled down" after successful therapy. The head of the caudate nucleus had been hypothesized to be involved in OCD. Before therapy this structure (but only in the right hemisphere) was revealed by PET scans to be highly active. After either behavior or drug therapy, this structure became less active among patients whose obsessions and compulsions had waned. Further, the more the symptoms waned, the more the activity in this structure decreased (Baxter, Schwartz, Bergman, Szuba, et al., 1992).

This work suggests that a circuit in the brain including the right caudate nucleus is involved in "filtering" or "dampening" worry inputs from elsewhere in the brain. When the right caudate nucleus is defective, it does not inhibit worry adequately and allows worry to drive other parts of the brain, possibly leading to OCD. A decade ago, such speculation might have been dismissed as science fiction or as "neuromythologizing." Today, however, with advances in the resolution of brain scans, this type of theory can actually be tested, and the brain pathways involved in OCD may be isolated.

FIGURE 3–1

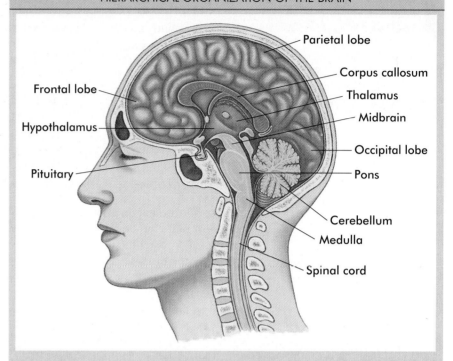

HIERARCHICAL ORGANIZATION OF THE BRAIN

Parietal lobe

Corpus callosum

Thalamus

Midbrain

Occipital lobe

Pons

Frontal lobe

Hypothalamus

Pituitary

Cerebellum

Medulla

Spinal cord

The brain is organized in a hierarchy, with the bottom levels (hindbrain and midbrain) controlling involuntary functions and the higher levels (forebrain) controlling voluntary functions. The medulla controls such functions as heartbeat, circulation, and respiration. The cerebellum controls bodily balance and muscular coordination. The midbrain controls some motor reactions and some auditory and visual functions. The hypothalamus is involved in the behavior related to drinking, eating, temperature control, and sexual activity. The thalamus receives input from the senses and passes it along to the cerebral cortex, which in turn is critical to thinking, memory, planning, and voluntary action. The higher levels will usually fail first, followed by malfunctioning of the lower systems. Such malfunctioning may account for physical and psychological disorders.

events occurred, intermittent memory loss, loss of personal skills, abilities, and social habits, and eventually failures in ability to perform basic bodily functions—can be explained by the biomedical model, which says that higher levels of brain function will malfunction first, followed by malfunctioning of the lower systems (see Figure 3–1).

Loss of other functions can also be explained by the biomedical model. Some functions of the brain are more vulnerable to damage than others; all parts of the brain are not equally resilient. A group of neurons may be more vulnerable because it has a relatively poor blood supply or because it has a higher requirement for oxygen or nutrients. Long-term memories, for example, are particularly vulnerable. They may be selectively damaged by general trauma, such as blows to the head, or by Vitamin B1 deficiency.

So the evidence that mental illness is at bottom physical illness comes from four sources: germs, genes, biochemical insufficiency, and anatomical malfunction. This has a straightforward implication for treatment: cure will follow only from getting rid of the physical illness.* Kill the syphilitic spirochetes with 606, for example, and stop the mental deterioration. Restore the right biochemical balance in schizophrenia and restore healthy cognition. Psychotherapy for a biological illness is at best cosmetic: this doctrine implies that a therapist might, at most, help a paretic adjust to his deteriorating mental and physical state or help a schizophrenic not to talk about his delusions. Treatment in the biomedical model takes place, with minor exceptions, in a single modality: drugs. But how well do these drugs work on the major mental disorders?

Schizophrenia and Antipsychotics

Horace shows up at his father's office one morning painted a dull brownish-red from head to toe, and daubed with slime. There is an enormous barbed fishhook sticking out of his cheek. He wears no clothes.

"I'm a worm!" he babbles as he crawls along the floor. The receptionist calls the police, and Horace is dragged off to the hospital.

In the hospital, Horace hallucinates floridly. He hears the sounds of fish in a feeding frenzy and believes he is the object of their frenzy. He has the unique delusion that he is a worm. ("You worm!" his girlfriend had shouted as she slammed the door and walked out of his life.) His mood gyrates from terror to giddiness to despair.

At Horace's case conference, there is a quarrel. The psychoanalysts advocate talking therapy. They believe that his delusion is a homosexual panic since all schizophrenia is "latent homosexuality." Drugging Horace will only be cosmetic and worse it may impede his gaining insight into the underlying conflict. But it is the summer of 1952 and one of the residents has just returned from a year in France. Before he left, he heard a paper at the French Congress of Psychiatrists and Neurologists. Professor Jean Delay, chief psychiatrist at the Hôpital Saint-Anne in Paris, announced a new drug treatment of psychosis. The resident argues doggedly, and Horace is injected with this drug, chlorpromazine. He relaxes right away. (The new drug is called a "major tranquilizer.") By the next weekend, the idea that he is a worm now seems as crazy to Horace as it does to those around him. Within three weeks, Horace is back at work as a delivery boy.

Until the mid-1950s, psychosis was an untreatable and ferocious mental illness. The back wards of mental hospitals were filled beyond their capacities with patients like Horace. The wards were called "snake pits." Many of the inmates were hallucinating and unreachable, or mutely catatonic, or wild with delusions and straitjacketed, or giggling out unrelated words, or broken with

*Some of the ideas in this section and elsewhere in this chapter are taken from M. Seligman, *What you can change and what you can't* (New York: Alfred Knopf, 1993), Chapter 3.

their faces turned toward the wall. Everything was tried to treat these schizophrenics: electroconvulsive shock therapy, artificial hibernation, lobotomy, insulin shock, cocktails of drugs. Nothing worked very noticeably. The psychotics might have remissions, but their future was widely believed to be life in the back ward.

Jean Delay and Pierre Deneker tried out a new antihistamine (chlorpromazine) that had been synthesized for hay fever by Rhône-Poulenc two years earlier. Their patients became calm, their delusions dissolved, and their contact with the real world resumed. Soon, at every major hospital, chlorpromazine was tried and, by and large, it worked. Many patients got better in a few weeks—some were astonishingly better. Even patients who had vegetated in the back wards for many years recovered and could be discharged. Beds in psychiatric wards became readily available for the first time in years.

Thus began the "third revolution" of psychiatry. The first began with Philippe Pinel's striking the chains of the insane; the second began with Freud's theories. The third revolution spread rapidly. Drugs are compatible with the biomedical model, and dispensing drugs rescued psychiatrists from the disdainful skepticism of their more traditional medical colleagues. Drugs are cheap. Drugs are quick. Drugs are very big business. All of these factors helped spread the third revolution.

Outcome studies of the new antipsychotics were done, and people on the drugs usually did better than those in control groups. The antipsychotic drugs "work" about 60 percent of the time, although, surprisingly, well-done outcome studies are scarce, and a large minority of patients do not benefit. The most optimistic recent estimate we know of percentage effectiveness of the antipsychotics is: complete eradication of delusions and hallucinations, 22.5 percent; partial improvement, 60 percent; no improvement, 17.5 percent (Chandler and Winokur, 1989).

Overcrowding of the back wards was ended, but it was soon replaced with a "revolving door." Many of the homeless people in large American cities were released, again and again, from mental hospitals by virtue of the antipsychotic drugs. Once out on the street, they deteriorated again—either because they stopped taking their drugs, or because the drug lost effect—and they wound up back in the hospital for the next round of drugs.

The antipsychotic drugs produce side effects, of which the most noticeable include: irregular heartbeat, low blood pressure, uncontrollable fidgeting, immobility of the face robbing the patient of the ability to smile, tremor, and a shuffling gait. But the worst is *tardive dyskinesia,* brought on because the drugs destroy something, still unknown, in the brain's control of movement. Victims suck and smack their lips uncontrollably like a frog catching an insect. Between one-quarter and one-third of patients who take antipsychotics develop tardive dyskinesia. The longer you take these drugs, the more likely it will develop, and once it starts, it is irreversible (ACNP-FDA Task Force, 1973; Wegner, Catalano, Gibralter, and Kane, 1985; Keck, Cohen, Baldessarini, and McElroy, 1989; Gualtieri, 1991).

Depression and the Antidepressants

As the drugs for psychotics showed promise, new drugs were tried on other disorders (Spiegel, 1989). The first antidepressant was discovered by accident. A

FOCUS QUESTIONS

1. Identify the four major categories of drug therapies and the disorders for which they are administered.
2. What are the side effects of the various drug treatments?
3. Why did the discovery of antipsychotic drugs produce a revolution in psychiatric treatment?

new drug was tried on tuberculosis, and the patients improved. The patients were pleased, very pleased. They danced in the corridors and shouted in ecstasy. The drug—an MAO inhibitor called iproniazid— was an euphoriant, and it also relieved depression. Within its first year, 1957, 400,000 patients were treated with it (Kline, 1970). Unfortunately, iproniazid is toxic, even occasionally lethal. It was soon outsold by milder antidepressants, called tricyclics. These also worked, and their side effects were less pronounced. A consensus figure is that about 65 percent of patients improve noticeably with tricyclics (Berger, 1977; Spiegel, 1989; White, Wykoff, Tynes, Schneider et al., 1990). The newest antidepressant, Prozac (generally, fluoxetine), works at just about the same rate as the old ones, but milder side effects were initially claimed (Hall, 1988). Like the antipsychotics, once you stop taking them, you are just as likely to relapse or have a fresh attack of depression as you were before you took them.

Antidepressants, like antipsychotics, have side effects: the MAO inhibitors, like iproniazid, can be fatal. The tricyclics are milder, but they can produce cardiac problems, mania, confusion and memory loss, and extreme fatigue. At least 25 percent of patients can't tolerate them. Serotonin reuptake inhibitors, such as Prozac, produce less drowsiness, dry mouth, and sweating than tricyclics, but they also produce more nausea, nervousness, and insomnia. There are a few case histories accumulating about Prozac causing suicidal preoccupation, but no well-controlled study has yet been done (Wernicke, 1985; Cooper, 1988; Teicher, Glod, and Cole, 1990; Beaumont, 1990; Preskorn and Jerkovich, 1990).

▲ Gerald Klerman (1928–1992) can be considered one of the driving forces of modern biological psychiatry. He was, until his untimely death, a professor of psychiatry and an active biomedical researcher specializing in the affective disorders. As head of the government agency in charge of mental health, he underwrote many therapy outcome studies to test which psychotherapies and drug therapies actually worked and he helped to launch the field of neuropsychology.

Manic-Depression and Lithium

As we have seen, the antidepressants are moderately helpful. In contrast, strong relief for mania comes from lithium carbonate. In 1947, John Cade, an Australian physician working under primitive conditions, found that the urine of his manic patients caused guinea pigs to tremble, twitch violently, and die. He injected them with lithium, an element known to be a poison. The guinea pigs now became calm and survived injections of the manics' urine. Cade tried lithium on the manic humans whose urine was so lethal. Within days their euphoric excitement gave way to calm (Cade, 1970).

By 1970, biological psychiatrists prescribed lithium routinely for manic-depression. Before the use of lithium, manic-depression was a crippling illness: 15 percent of manic-depressive patients killed themselves and most—many of whom were very talented—could not hold jobs. With lithium, this is no longer so. Roughly 80 percent of manic-depressives are helped, and most markedly.

Lithium is more effective for dampening manic episodes than it is for the depressive episodes in manic-depressive illness. It can also prevent manic episodes if taken regularly between episodes. Its main problem is that many manics refuse to take it because they like the feeling of being manic (Sack and De Fraites, 1977; Johnson, Olafsson, Andersen, Plenge, et al., 1989). From the outset, lithium was a known poison, so its potentially toxic and even lethal side effects—cardiac and gastrointestinal—were monitored carefully. Unlike the rest of the drugs, lithium therefore generated few unpleasant surprises (Jefferson, 1990).

Anxiety and Anti-Anxiety Drugs

In the mid-1950s, Miltown (meprobamate) was first used with anxious patients. Anxious patients relaxed profoundly in a few minutes, but they remained conscious and their troubles, which moments before had consumed them, now seemed far away. Sleep came more easily. Miltown was prescribed very widely. Librium (chlordiazepoxide) replaced Miltown and became the world's number one prescription drug. And Valium (diazepam), which is five times stronger, soon displaced Librium (Berger, 1970; Cohen, 1970).

Like the antidepressant and antipsychotic drugs, once you stop taking anxiolytics, anxiety usually returns in full force. When the anxiety stems from a real problem, you may find you have done nothing in the meantime to solve it. Anti-anxiety drugs do not have the *very* strong side effects that the antipsychotics and antidepressants have. They are probably not lethal, even in megadoses. But unlike the antipsychotic and antidepressant drugs, the anti-anxiety drugs become less potent the longer you take them, and they probably are addictive (Tinklenberg, 1977; Olivieri, Cantopher, and Edwards, 1986; Nagy, 1987; Roache, 1990). In addition, these drugs are probably without any effect on two of the major anxiety disorders: panic disorder and generalized anxiety disorder (Tyrer, Murphy, Kingdon, et al., 1988; Spiegel, 1989).

Overall, then, drug treatments are often effective for several specific disorders. But like most useful agents, they have drawbacks. They only work for exactly as long as they are taken, and each can produce unwanted side effects, some of them crippling (see Table 3–1). Perhaps most importantly, when you take a drug you come to depend on an external agent for your well-being, rather than on your own skills and abilities.

"AT THAT POINT THE MEETING BECAME CHAOTIC, AS EVERYONE'S MEDICATION SEEMED TO WEAR OFF AT THE SAME TIME."

TABLE 3–1

DRUG TREATMENTS			
Disorder	*Drug Treatment*	*Effectiveness*	*Side Effects*
Schizophrenia	antipsychotics	majority show partial improvement	irregular heartbeat, low blood pressure, uncontrolled fidgeting tardive dyskinesia, immobility of face
Depression	MAO inhibitors	majority show moderate improvement	toxicity
	tricyclics	majority show moderate improvement	cardiac problems, mania, confusion, memory loss, extreme fatigue
	serotonin reuptake inhibitors (e.g., Prozac)	majority show moderate improvement	nausea, nervousness, insomnia, possible preoccupation with suicide
Manic-Depression	lithium	large majority show substantial improvement	cardiac problems, gastrointestinal problems
Everyday Anxiety	anti-anxiety drugs (e.g., Miltown, Librium, Valium)	substantial majority show short-term improvement	less potent the longer you take them, may be addictive
Specific Phobias	anti-anxiety drugs	little relief	may be addictive
Social Phobia	MAO-inhibitors	majority show improvement	toxicity
Panic	anti-anxiety drugs (e.g., Xanax)	half show improvement	less potent the longer you take them, may be addictive
Agoraphobia	tricyclics	majority show moderate improvement	cardiac problems, mania, confusion, memory loss, extreme fatigue
	MAO-inhibitors	majority show moderate improvement	toxicity
Generalized Anxiety Disorder	anti-anxiety drugs	little to no improvement	may be addictive

As we discuss the various mental disorders in subsequent chapters, we will also take a closer look at particular biomedical treatments for these disorders. We will look at their underlying mechanisms (where they are known), we will examine their clinical use with patients, and we will discuss any side effects that are also produced by their use.

EVALUATING THE BIOMEDICAL MODEL

Here are the bulwarks of the biomedical model: First, a large body of research in the last ten years has shown that some mental disorders and many personality traits are heritable. Second, some mental disorders are caused by germs, some by biochemical disturbances, and some by neuroanatomical problems. Third, drugs can change our emotions and moods. These three together form a powerful view of psychopathology: mental illness as physical illness. Let us now take a look at both the strengths and weaknesses of this model.

Strengths

The biomedical model is grounded in mature sciences. Its basic components, such as the dopamine hypothesis, heritability, and the central nervous system, seem measurable and objective. It has a well-defined sequence of methods: syndrome, etiology, and treatment. One hundred years of biomedical research, highlighted by such stunning successes as the eradication of smallpox and of general paresis, make it clear that its hypotheses are testable and, when correct, applicable. The pursuit of the biological bases of abnormality is so extensive that all of Chapter 17 is devoted to it. There, we take up in detail the boundary between neurologically based disorders and psychologically based disorders.

FOCUS QUESTIONS

1. Describe the strengths and weaknesses of the biomedical model.
2. Describe the debate between the reductionists and the anti-reductionists regarding the cause of psychological phenomena.

Weaknesses

With all this, why don't we stop our search for models right here? Because the model also has several problems. The main bulwarks of the model are somewhat shakier than they first appear: First, that mental illness is physical illness has been demonstrated for only one mental illness—general paresis. The claim for schizophrenia, Alzheimer's disease, and manic-depression is plausible, but unproven—no biochemical cause has yet been isolated. The claim for depression, anxiety, sexual problems, and post-traumatic stress disorder is merely a research agenda, with little or no evidence to back it up.

Second, the claim that personality and mental disorder are inherited has strong evidence behind it. But personality is only *partly* genetic. Even by the most extreme estimates, only about half of personality is not inherited, and as it turns out, it is not just the environmental half of personality that can change. The heritable half is made up of both direct genetic effects and ***gene-environment covariances.*** Gene-environment covariance refers to the effective causal events in the environment that produce a trait, but that are correlated with genes, and so do not appear to be causes. So, for example, being very tall is heritable. Playing basketball professionally is also heritable. This is because tall people get into environments, eighth grade basketball teams, for example, in which they excel and which reward them. They go on to become top basketball players. The genes don't directly get you to the NBA; success at basketball does. Success at basketball is the effective, environmental cause—but it is correlated with the genes for tallness (see Figure 3–2).

FIGURE 3-2

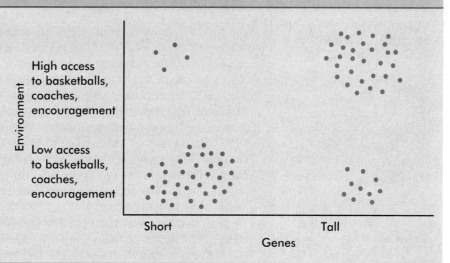

GENE-ENVIRONMENT COVARIANCE

The heritable part of personality and mental disorders are influenced by both genes and by their covariation with environment. The environment can bring out or prevent the expression of genetic potential. Thus, the tall person is more likely to have access to basketball courts and coaches than is the short person. And as the graph shows, a higher proportion of tall people get into environments in which they are encouraged and helped to do well at basketball.

Gene-environment covariance can be broken by intervention, allowing change to occur even in the heritable part of personality. Crime is, as we have seen, partly heritable, and the personality of children who become criminals tends to alienate their parents and teachers. Their parents and teachers often give up on them because they are so difficult to get along with. The children, lacking a relationship with an adult, often turn to the streets. This makes them street-smart and may cause them to turn to crime. This is gene-environment covariance. If the parents stay with it, however, and don't reject the child—breaking the covariance—they may prevent the child from becoming a criminal.

The third bulwark, the claims about drug treatment, should be viewed with skepticism. Medications warrant only modest enthusiasm. There are indeed drugs that alter mood and psychopathology for some, but not for all people. But the risk of relapse is unchanged once the patient stops taking the drug. Further, all drugs produce unwanted side effects, some of which are ruinous. Because of this, many patients cannot tolerate the biomedical treatments.

Finally, there is a great deal to be said for psychological intervention without any biomedical intervention. Psychological events sometimes cause psychopathology, and changing these events—without directly changing anything about the body—can indeed cure. Eliminating a phobic's fear of cats by behavioral procedures and changing a depressive's belief that he is useless by cognitive means can greatly help these patients. Some disorders may indeed be illnesses of the body, but others are ***problems in living*** (Szasz, 1961). General paresis is a disease, the consequence of syphilitic spirochetes. But marital discord, fear of public speaking, and depression following the death of one's child are not. These are psychological problems that can clearly be alleviated by psychological means.

[handwritten margin note: Atypical]

The thoroughgoing adherent of the biomedical model is a **reductionist.** A reductionist believes that *all psychological phenomena can be explained by and reduced to biological phenomena.* A reductionist points to *pellagra psychosis* as a clear example of a seemingly psychological disorder that can be wholly reduced to a biological disorder. In pellagra psychosis, formerly healthy individuals are stricken with confusion, inappropriate emotion (e.g., smiling and laughing at tragic events), hallucinations, and delirium (Ishii and Nishihara, 1985). On the surface, they appear to be schizophrenic. But there proves to be an underlying biological disorder: When people are deprived of niacin (a vitamin), either naturally or by taking an anti-tuberculosis drug (isoniazid), the skin lesions and intestinal problems of the vitamin deficiency disease, pellagra, follow along with psychosis.

[handwritten margin note: Psychological as well]

The **anti-reductionist** holds that *there are at least some psychological phenomena that cannot be reduced to biological phenomena.* The anti-reductionist points to the example of "deprivation dwarfism" (Foster and Wilson, 1985) to illustrate a biological phenomenon that is caused by a psychological rather than a physical state. In deprivation dwarfism a child living in a stressful environment, such as an abusive home, does not grow. The child may show no output of growth hormones and appears to have a malfunctioning pituitary gland. When the child is removed from the abusive home and placed in a foster home, however, pituitary hormones become normal and a growth spurt begins. This indicates that an underlying psychological state produces the biological changes in growth hormone.

The battle between reductionists and anti-reductionists is still very much alive. It has important implications for the biomedical model: Proponents of this model can take great comfort in such phenomena as paresis and syphilis, and pellagra psychosis. They must think seriously, however, about the challenge presented by instances in which psychological events precede the biological changes.

As a practical matter, it is important that disorders that seem largely biological can sometimes be modified psychologically, and that disorders that seem largely psychological can sometimes be modified biologically. Schizophrenia, as we will suggest in Chapter 12, fits the biomedical model well, but it can be exacerbated by emotionally laden criticism from relatives. On the other hand, the lack of confidence and sensitivity to rejection that depressives often display can be alleviated by antidepressant drugs. Thoroughgoing reductionists should be puzzled by the successful psychological treatment of some biological problems, and thoroughgoing anti-reductionists should likewise be puzzled by the successful drug treatment of some psychological problems. At this stage of knowledge, we believe that the most that can be concluded is that biological and psychological forces *interact* to produce mental illness.

SUMMARY

1. The *biomedical model* holds that psychological disorders are illnesses of the body.

2. The biomedical school of thought dictates an ideal procedure for isolating a psychological disorder as an illness: grouping the symptoms into a coherent *syndrome* that can be diagnosed reliably; searching for an *etiology*, or cause, of the syndrome; and finding a *treatment* and *prevention* that follow from knowing the cause.

3. Four sorts of evidence about etiology of a disorder point toward a psychological disorder being considered a physical illness: discovery of a *germ* causing the illness, *genetic transmission* of the disorder, a disordered *biochemistry* or *neuroanatomy of the brain* producing the disorder, or a combined *genetic* and *biochemical* etiology.

4. We discussed examples of each of these etiologies. The eradication of general paresis by the discovery that it was caused by the spirochete that caused syphilis exemplified the germ etiology. The evidence that schizophrenia is partly transmitted genetically and that personality traits are heritable exemplified the genetic etiology. The relationship between the blocking of dopamine and the alleviation of schizophrenia exemplified the biochemical etiology. The malfunctioning of higher and then lower levels of brain function illustrated the neuroanatomical etiology.

5. Biomedical therapy tries to correct disordered brain function by drugs and other agents. But these drugs only work while the patient continues to take them and may also have serious side effects.

6. The main strengths of the biomedical model are that it is grounded in well-established biological sciences, and that physical treatments are often able to bring relief.

7. The main weaknesses of the biomedical model are that the evidence about its central claims is incomplete, psychological treatments also are able to bring relief to individuals with psychological problems, some psychopathological problems are problems in living, and there are side effects to most biomedical treatments.

QUESTIONS FOR CRITICAL THINKING

1. What are the dangers of following only one particular model of abnormality?

2. How was the causal connection between syphilis and general paresis proven?

3. Why is there a causal influence of genes but not genetic determinism for schizophrenia?

4. What are the limitations of drug treatments?

CHAPTER 4

Psychodynamic and Existential Approaches

CHAPTER ORGANIZER

FREUD AND PSYCHOANALYTIC THEORY
- Become familiar with Freud's ideas on the development of personality (the oral, anal, phallic, latent, and genital stages), on the three processes of personality (id, ego, superego), and on the unconscious and underlying anxiety.

THE NEO-FREUDIANS
- Discover how Jung, Adler, and others departed from Freud's basic ideas.

MODERN PSYCHODYNAMIC THEORY
- Look carefully at the contemporary ideas of the "self," at our own everyday defense mechanisms and coping strategies, and at the basic notions of growth and existential theories.

PSYCHODYNAMIC TREATMENT
- Be able to distinguish the kinds of therapies derived from the personality theorists mentioned in this chapter.

EVALUATING PSYCHODYNAMIC THEORY
- Know the strengths and shortcomings of psychodynamic theory.

The psychodynamic theories of personality and abnormality are concerned with the psychological forces that—consciously or unconsciously—influence the mind. These inner forces, these desires and motives, often conflict. When these conflicts are well-resolved, they produce growth, vigor. But when they are poorly resolved, or remain unresolved, conflicts generate anxiety and unhappiness, against which people try to defend themselves. In this chapter, we examine some of the causes and consequences of conflict and the conditions that lead to its resolution, for better or for worse.

Psychodynamic approaches to personality and abnormality begin with the work of a single towering genius—a Viennese physician named Sigmund Freud. Freud's views were modified and elaborated by a group of clinicians who are commonly called **Neo-Freudians.** Finally, modern psychodynamic approaches culminate in the ideas of a large number of clinicians and scientists, whose observations and research have greatly revised Freud's original assertions about the nature of human development and the origins of psychological misery. We consider each in turn.

Born in 1856, Freud produced some twenty-four volumes of theoretical observations and case histories before he died in 1939. His own methods of studying and changing personality, as well as those of his students, are called **psychoanalysis.**

Throughout his life, Freud's consuming intellectual and clinical passion was with **psychic energy.** The natural scientists of his time were having a heyday with physical energy. Electricity had been harnessed during Freud's youth, and engines invented. In the spirit of the times, Freud turned his attention to the energies that fuel psychological life. People are endowed with a fixed amount of psychic energy, he assumed. Why is it, then, that sometimes people seem to be vigorous and full of life, while at others they seem listless? How is it that some people devote their energies to love and work, while others are largely concerned with their aches and pains? How is psychic energy used at the very beginning of life, and how do those uses become transformed as a person matures?

We begin our examination of psychoanalytic theories with the last question: How is psychic energy used very early in life, and how are its uses changed as a result of maturation? Conflict, anxiety, and defense play large roles here, and not only negative ones, for these matters play constructive as well as destructive roles in psychological development.

▲ Sigmund Freud
(1856–1939) in 1909.

The Development of Personality

From birth to maturity, people go through five overlapping stages of psychosexual development: the oral, anal, phallic, latency, and genital stages (see Table 4–1). Psychoanalysts call this kind of maturation **psychosexual** because it underscores the relationship between mind and pleasure. Sexuality, in Freudian usage, is not restricted to sexual intercourse, or even to the fantasies and behaviors that precede it. Rather, sexual energy is one important form of pleasurable psychic energy. Long before sexuality takes its adult form, sexual energy exists as **libido** (from the Latin, meaning desire or lust). Libido, then, is psychic energy that can become associated with a host of pleasurable activities. Early in life, during the oral stage, for example, those pleasures are associated with the gratification of biological needs. Later on, libido becomes attached to social and psychological needs.

TABLE 4–1

STAGES OF PSYCHOSOCIAL DEVELOPMENT			
Stage	Age (years)	Erogeneous Zones	Resolution of Conflict
Or	0-2	Mouth, tongue	Trust
Anal	2-4	Anal area	Autonomy
Phallic	3-6	Genitals	Identification with same-sex parent
Latency	6-12	(Asexual)	Mastery of social and cognitive skills
Genital	13-	(Heterosexual relations)	Love and competence at work

▲ During the oral stage, the mouth satisfies a baby's needs not only for food but for pleasure.

▼ Toilet training and accompanying issues of control dominate the anal stage.

ORAL STAGE

The first psychosexual stage, the **oral stage,** develops out of the central biological activity of very young infants: feeding. Their sucking response is instinctive, and it is through this behavior that a basic need is gratified. But quite independent of biological need, sucking provides pleasure of its own. The mouth and tongue are early pleasure centers: Freud called them **erogenous zones.** Sucking itself, then, engenders bliss.

Like all of the psychosexual stages, the oral stage is richly endowed with the capacity to disfigure development permanently. For many infants, it can be the stage of pleasurable dependency. Those who find this stage very gratifying and therefore become fixated here, develop **oral character traits,** which are enduring dispositions to react in the dependent ways of infants and young children. Like infants, they remain heavily dependent on others and overwhelmingly disposed to receive rather than give. On the other hand, those who experience intense conflict at the oral stage may well develop lifelong incapacities to trust others, perhaps especially to trust them to satisfy their needs.

ANAL STAGE

As infants begin to overcome their dependence, and as they become more autonomous and exploratory, they are confronted with social control. Social control takes many familiar forms, nearly all of them preceded by "don't." "Don't throw your food," "Don't go into the closet," "Don't play in the street"—these are the parental dicta to children in the "terrible two's." But a particular kind of parental control has been of interest to psychoanalysts because it centers on the body and provides yet another outlet for pleasurable energy as well as opportunity for conflict and defense. This is the control involved in toilet training.

From a parental perspective, toilet training is merely a way of controlling a child's mess. To the extent that parents speak of it at all, they speak of the gradual disappearance of diapers and the occasional occurrence of "accidents." From the child's viewpoint, toilet training may be an opportunity to savor the joys of increasing self-control, to please parents, and to be lavished with praise. Or it may be an opportunity to rebel, to pit a growing will against that of adults. But regardless of how the child views toilet training, one thing is certain from the psychoanalytic viewpoint: parental concern with toilet training makes the child attend to the anal area, to the sensations that arise there, and the body products that are eliminated. The anal region can now be stimulated through the voluntary retention and expulsion of feces as well as through manual stimulation. Thus, libido—pleasurable energy—is now associated with the anal area.

Opportunities for conflict and for fixation are rife in this stage. Early on, conflict may arise between children's natural inclination to eliminate when and where they will, and parental insistence that elimination occur in a particular place, and often at a particular time. If that conflict is not resolved, children may later manifest the remnants of that experience in character traits of messiness, disorderliness, and even rebelliousness. But even greater opportunities for conflict come later in the anal stage, when children have already learned to control their bowel movement. Then, a particularly strict toilet training will make children especially careful, or orderly, about their wastes. Moreover, because parents applaud their timely eliminations, they may come to consider their body wastes as especially valuable, and they may resist giving

FOCUS QUESTIONS

1. What are the five stages of psychosexual development?
2. Describe the interrelation among the three processes of personality.
3. List and describe three types of anxiety resulting from conflicts among the id, ego, and superego.
4. What did Freud mean by the perceptual unconscious, the preconscious, and the unconscious?

them up. Fixation can therefore generate enduring **anal character traits** of orderliness, stinginess, and stubbornness—a triad of traits that will persist into later life.

By the time children are approximately three years old, they will have traversed the anal stage more or less successfully. Now relatively autonomous and exploratory, they are ready to discover the pleasures of the third stage of psychosexual development. These pleasures lie in the genital area.

PHALLIC STAGE

The phallic stage is different from the stages that precede it in one important sense. In the oral stage, libido was associated with a biological process, feeding. In the anal stage, it was again associated with biological processes, defecation and urination, and also with social control. But phallic pleasures are self-initiated ones, arising from curiosity, first about one's own body, and gradually from curiosity about other people's bodies. At first, the idea that children stimulate themselves genitally horrified Freud's Victorian contemporaries. Gradually, the notion took hold, such that it is now commonly accepted that young children, from the ages of about three through six or seven, engage in pleasurable genital stimulation that is the rudimentary form of adult sexuality.

Adult sexual adjustment is often crucially determined at this stage by the outcome of what Freud called the **Oedipus complex.** That conflict takes its name from a Greek legend that is now more than 2,500 years old, in which Oedipus killed Laius, the king of Thebes, and married the queen, Jocasta, only later to find that the king was his father, and that he had therefore married his mother. Appalled by his unintentional crime, Oedipus gouged his eyes out. That legend symbolized for Freud the desire that all young children have: to do away with the parent of the same sex, and take possession of the parent of the opposite sex. That desire is often captured in the commonplace remarks of little boys—"when I grow up I'm going to marry you, mommy"—as well as in their fantasies.

What prevents young children from acting vigorously on their desire to take the opposite-sex parent for themselves and to do away with the same-sex one? Fear. The very curiosity that guided their interest in the opposite-sex parent teaches them quickly that the same-sex parent is bigger and stronger than they, and that that parent will resist their attempted conquest. Boys, especially, are vulnerable to this fear. During their childish explorations, sooner or later they come to know that women do not have a penis. Assuming that women once had a penis like themselves, they infer that their penis must have been cut off. The fear that they, too, will be castrated by their father if they persist in such longings is sufficient to dampen those desires considerably. **Castration anxiety,** then, terminates incestuous desire in boys.

For girls, the matter is more complicated and, in psychoanalytic theory, less well resolved. The young girl, too, sees the absence of a penis as a lack and may be angry with her mother for having created her incomplete and inferior. She continues to experience **penis envy,** which results in her further desire for her father, even in the desire to have a child by him and thereby to acquire a penis symbolically. Only the mother's greater strength, as well as her father's resistance to the idea, restrains the impulse to take him. These factors are less effective in terminating the Oedipal conflict in girls than is castration anxiety in boys.

▼ Freud believed children identify with and emulate their parents of the same sex. This boy is wearing his father's shirt.

▶ During the latency stage, children's sexual interest declines as they concentrate on mastering social and cognitive skills.

The outcome of this intense conflict is not merely withdrawal. It is ***identi-fication*** with the same-sex parent: becoming that person in a psychological sense, such that the adult's values, attitudes, standards, sexual orientation, and even mannerisms become the child's own. Identification is a defense that we will discuss later in the chapter. It resolves the Oedipal conflict because the child internalizes the very values that prohibit incest.

LATENCY STAGE

The Oedipal conflict is exhausting and frightening, and it is not surprising that by the age of six or seven, when it is over, sexual interest declines. Sexuality is repressed, that is, deflected from consciousness. This decline of sexual interest marks the beginning of the latency period. During latency, the child is relatively asexual. Attention is directed toward mastering social and cognitive skills.

GENITAL STAGE

The final stage of psychosexual development comes with the onset of puberty. Sexual impulse reawakens, but now in a more mature and socialized form. Earlier sexuality was fundamentally narcissistic, concerned nearly entirely with self-gratification. The developing adolescent is much more socialized than the child was, and adolescent sexual energies are channeled to reflect that growth. In the heterosexual sphere, others now are valued in their own right, and not merely as adjuncts for self-gratification. Love becomes possible and pleasurable, and altruism—the concern for another's welfare, independent of one's own—becomes possible too. Additionally, some sexual energy is channeled into work. Competence and efficacy in the workplace become rewarding in themselves, independent of the riches they bring.

Full-fledged genitality involves the capacities to love and to work, the two capacities that Freud felt were most significant for maturity. Psychoanalysts use the term ***sublimation*** to denote the transfer of libidinal energies from relatively narcissistic gratifications to those—like love and work—that gratify others and are highly socialized.

TABLE 4–2

THREE PROCESSES OF PERSONALITY			
Process	Principle	Reality Concerns?	Characteristics
Id	Pleasure principle	No	Aims to achieve immediate gratification of biological drives
Ego	Reality principle	Yes	Directs impulses toward targets that are appropriate and that can be achieved
Superego	(Idealism)	No	Directs actions toward morality, religion, ideals

The Three Processes of Personality

According to Freud, human personality is structured by three kinds of forces: the id, ego, and superego (see Table 4–2). These are neither objects nor places in the mind. Rather, they are dynamic and interactive ***processes,*** with their own origins and specific roles. The word ***id*** originates from the German "es," literally meaning "it," and connotes processes that seem to lie outside of an individual's control. ***Ego,*** in German, means "ich" or "I," and designates those capacities that enable a person to cope with reality, while ***superego*** (in German "Uberich" or "over I") describes those processes that are "above the self"—conscience, ideals, and morals.

THE ID

The id designates the mental representation of processes that are fundamentally biological in origin. In the newborn infant, nearly all psychic energy is devoted to such biological processes. And over the course of development, id processes continue to fuel personality, providing the energy for the diverse pursuits that are associated with psychological growth as well as biological survival.

Biological drives are raw and urgent. They create desires that clamor for immediate gratification, tensions that seek instantaneous relief. They are dominated by the ***pleasure principle,*** which demands immediate impulse gratification and tension reduction. The id is like a spoiled child. It wants what it wants when it wants it. When they seek external gratification, id drives know nothing of appropriateness, or even danger. Were people wholly dominated by id processes they would, like the spoiled child, eat any food when they were hungry, regardless of whether it was theirs, healthy, or even still alive.

THE EGO

Whereas the id seeks pleasure, the ego seeks reality. One function of the ego is to express and gratify the desires of the id in accordance with the requirements of reality. While the id operates on the pleasure principle, the ego utilizes the ***reality principle.*** It tests reality to determine whether the expression of an impulse is safe or dangerous. It delays the impulses of the id until the time is

▼ The id is dominated by the pleasure principle. It demands immediate gratification.

right, and may even divert those impulses toward appropriate targets. Freud describes the relations between ego and id this way:

> The ego's relation to the id might be compared with that of a rider to his horse. The horse supplies the locomotive energy, while the rider has the privilege of deciding on the goal and of guiding the powerful animal's movement. But only too often there arises between the ego and the id the not precisely ideal situation of the rider being obliged to guide the horse along the path by which it [the id] itself wants to go. (Freud, 1923, p. 77)

The ego's success in enabling impulses to be realistically and safely gratified depends on its ability to use thought processes, like reasoning, remembering, evaluating, and planning. The ego is the executive of the personality, carrying out the demands of the id in such a way as to minimize negative consequences.

THE SUPEREGO

Those processes of mind that comprise both conscience and idealistic striving are termed superego processes. Conscience is acquired through parents. It arises from the forceful resolution of the Oedipal conflict, and it results in the internalization of society's views of which thoughts, impulses, and behaviors are permissible and forbidden, as well as which goals and ideals should be pursued.

Superego processes are just as irrational as id processes; neither cares or knows much about reality. Conscience can also be overly harsh, suppressing not only permissible behaviors, but even the very thought of those behaviors. Whereas the person whose id processes are relatively uncontrolled seems impulse-ridden, the person who is overly dominated by his or her superego seems wooden and moralistic, unable to be comfortable with pleasure and overly sensitive to "Thou shalt not . . ."

▶ Through the superego, the child internalizes society's views of right and wrong, including religious ideas.

The processes that regulate normal personality and development are identical to those that regulate abnormal personality. What distinguishes normal from abnormal personality is the manner in which psychic energy is distributed between the three components of personality. In normal personality, psychic energy is strongly invested in ego processes, as well as those of the id and superego. In abnormal personality, psychic energy is distributed improperly, with the result that either the id or the superego is too strong, and ego processes are unable to control desire or conscience.

Id, ego, and superego regularly interact and often conflict. Sexual desires that arise in a classroom, for example, may be delayed by ego processes until a more permissible place is found. But even in such a place, they may be blocked by superego processes which proclaim that sex is sinful, or that the time might better be spent studying. As the executive, the ego is supposed to mediate these conflicts. But how does the ego do this? And what happens to desires that are blocked? The answers to these questions become clear when we examine additional ideas that have become central to psychodynamic thinking: unconscious ideas and impulses, and anxiety.

Unconscious Ideas and Impulses

Freud (1923) proposed that there are three levels of consciousness. The first is **_perceptual consciousness,_** consisting of the very small number of mental events to which the individual is presently attending. Being aware of reading a book and of the meaning of a passage would exemplify this kind of consciousness.

The second level of consciousness is the **_preconscious._** It consists of information and impulses that are not at the center of attention but that can be re-

▶ Freud seems best remembered by most people for his ideas on the expression of unconscious thoughts. (Drawing by Dana Fradon, © 1973, The New Yorker Magazine, Inc.)

3 levels of consciousness (memory)
① perceptual — present
② preconscious — not center of attention
③ unconscious — 1) forgotten
2) repressed

trieved more or less easily. Though not now part of one's central awareness, last night's dinner can be recalled with little difficulty.

The large mass of memory, experience, and impulse lies at the third level of consciousness: the **unconscious.** Two kinds of memories become unconscious: (1) those that are forgotten, and (2) those that, because of conflict are **repressed,** or actively barred from consciousness. Ordinary forgotten events, such as the cost of a loaf of bread last year, gradually decay and exert no subsequent influence on personality. But repressed events live on, and all the more vigorously, because they are not subject to rational control. They reveal their potent identities in normal fantasies and dreams, in slips of the tongue and "motivated" forgetting, under hypnosis and in a variety of abnormal psychological conditions. By far, unconscious forces are the dominant ones in personality.

> Ann was in love with two men, Michael and Jules. Both wanted to marry her, and she could not decide between them. Finally, after more than six months, she decided for Michael. The next night, she had the following dream:
>
> "I was climbing the fire-escape outside my dormitory. It was a dark and rainy night, and I was carrying a big box under my raincoat. I came to the fifth floor, opened the door silently, and tiptoed quickly to my room. Once inside, I double-locked the door, and put this box—it's a treasure chest—on my bed. I opened it and it was full of diamonds and rubies and emeralds."
>
> Now, there is no evidence at all that dreams *regularly* mean anything. Yet it is hard to escape the possibility that in Ann's dream, "diamonds and rubies and emeralds"=jewels=Jules. Her dream reveals her continuing attachment to her former lover, and quite possibly her desire to maintain the relationship secretly. The mind's extraordinary capacity to play on Jules's name and to transform it into visual symbols is revealed in this dream.

Certain personality processes operate more at the unconscious level than do others. Id impulses are entirely unconscious, as are many superego processes. In contrast, ego processes, because they must mediate between desire, conscience, and reality, are often preconscious or conscious.

Anxiety

Conflicts among the various personality processes regularly give rise to a kind of psychic pain that Freud termed **anxiety.** Anxiety can be conscious or unconscious, and its presence is always a signal that conflict is at hand. When the conflict causes the person to feel overwhelmed, helpless, and unable to cope, anxiety arises. The degree of experienced anxiety depends on the anticipated consequences to self.

Freud distinguished three kinds of anxiety, each of which arises from a different source of perceived danger. **Realistic anxiety** arises from the expectation that real-world events may be harmful to the self. Ordinarily, this is what is meant by fear. A person who slips while crossing the street may experience realistic anxiety as moving traffic approaches. **Neurotic anxiety** arises from the possibility that one will be overwhelmed by one's impulses, especially unconscious sexual and aggressive ones. The unconscious desire to vanquish some-one who controls an important destiny—say, a father, employer, or lover—may breed neurotic anxiety. Finally, **conscience** or **moral anxiety** arises when one anticipates that one's behavior will violate one's personal standards, or when that behavior has, in fact, violated those standards. The legend of Oedipus (described earlier) contains a classic instance of moral anxiety. Having learned that he has murdered his father and married his mother, Oedipus is overwhelmed with guilt, shame, and revulsion and, as a result, gouges out his eyes.

The experience of anxiety, even the anticipation of anxiety, is an uncomfortable experience that people try to relieve immediately. Humans are particularly well-endowed with strategies for alleviating anxiety. Beyond "overcoming fear" as we do when we learn to ride a bicycle, or "fleeing the field" when pursued by strong enemies, humans can, in their own minds, alter the very meaning and significance of troublesome drives and impulses. They perform these alterations by using coping strategies, or defenses. The more common of these include such defenses as repression and projection, as well as identification and rationalization, to name but a few. We discuss each in turn later in the chapter.

Faults of Early Psychoanalytic Theory

Early psychoanalytic theory suffered two major faults. First, it was simply non-verifiable. However interesting or compelling it might have been, there seemed no way at all to subject these notions to any kind of scientific test (Grunbaum, 1984). How does one test whether oral fixation really exists? How does one determine whether castration anxiety really leads to identification with the same-sex parent and thereby the resolution of the Oedipal conflict? Indeed, it seemed to some observers that it was the *belief* that present troubles are embedded in the deep past that led psychoanalytic thinkers to invent childhood *metaphors* that might make the present more cogent (Stern, 1985). Moreover, it became increasingly clear that modern evidence strongly disputed Freud's assertions about infancy and childhood (Flavell, 1977; Clarke-Stewart, 1973; Erdelyi, 1985). Freud, it should be remembered, had spent little time with infants and children (other than his own, presumably); as a result, his theories about childhood development could not have been much more than intelligent speculation. What would have greatly informed these speculations, and what might very well have altered them, was patient observation of, and experimentation with, infants and children.

Second, nearly all of psychoanalytic theory arose from carefully observing *individual clients* who had come for treatment. The virtue of this theory lay precisely in the fact that it arose from very detailed examination of individual personalities. But that was also its liability. Freud's clients, for example, were mainly Viennese women, in early and middle adulthood, who suffered a fairly restricted range of psychological symptoms. Yet his experience with such people led him to generalize to children as well as adults, to men as well as women, to normals as well as clients, and to the rest of the world as well as Vienna. His restricted experience, it has often been said (Eysenck, 1961; Mischel, 1968; Hall and Lindzey, 1970; Lamiell, 1987), hardly provided a basis for generalization, and many of his generalizations simply have proven to be wrong.

THE NEO-FREUDIANS

▲ Carl Jung (1875–1961).

▼ Alfred Adler (1870–1937).

Though they were rejected at first, Freud's ideas later came to attract a number of highly original thinkers who elaborated on his views and often disagreed with them. In some cases, the disagreements led to a break with Freud. Such was the case with Carl Jung (1875–1961) and Alfred Adler (1870–1937), both of whom came to be known as neo-Freudians.

What were the differences between Freud and the other thinkers? First, some theorists differed with Freud regarding the origins of motivation. Granting that motivation was mainly unconscious, these thinkers believed that Freud held much too narrow a view of *what* was unconscious. For example, Jung felt that there was also a **collective unconscious,** consisting of the memory traces of the experience of past generations and not just memories of early childhood as Freud thought. In Jung's view, we are born wiser than we think, already afraid of darkness and fire because our ancestors were, and already knowing of death because past generations have died. Jung called these universal ideas with which we are born **archetypes.** For Jung, these archetypes form the basis of personality, accounting for why people are not merely driven by their past experiences but also strive to grow and become something better. In essence, Jung saw the self as striving for wholeness.

Freud's emphasis on biological urges—the id impulses—as determinants of behavior is the basis of a second major dispute, particularly with Alfred Adler. In Freud's view, human activity serves fundamental sexual and aggressive needs arising from the id and mediated by the ego. But according to Alfred Adler, the self serves a more meaningful purpose. The self enables us to fulfill our lifestyle, to become more than the genes with which we are endowed and the environment that presses on us. The self creates something new, something unique, something that is not wholly determined by biological impulse or cultural press (Ansbacher and Ansbacher, 1956). As we will show, Adler's concerns foreshadowed the modern emphasis on self.

There is considerable difference in a third area, that of psycho*sexual* versus psycho*social* development. Fundamentally, that difference reduces to whether people are fundamentally biological or social animals. For example, Karen Horney (1885–1952) saw basic anxiety as a social rather than simply a biological experience. For her, that basic anxiety consisted of "the feeling a child has of being isolated and helpless in a potentially hostile world" (Horney, 1945, p. 41). That anxiety may lead children to develop one of three modes of coping. They may become hostile, seeking revenge against those who rejected them. Or they may become submissive, hoping thereby to regain the lost love. Or they may simply withdraw, giving up the quest entirely. These three strategies—moving against, moving toward, and moving away—are social responses to a fundamentally social anxiety.

Similarly, Harry Stack Sullivan (1892–1949) held that the very notion of personality is itself an illusion that cannot be separated from the social context in which it is seen and operates. According to Sullivan, psychological problems do not merely originate in faulty social development, they *consist* of faulty social relationships and need to be examined and treated as such. Sullivan's concerns are mirrored in the modern emphasis on the social context in which personality operates (Nisbett and Ross, 1980; Gergen, 1982).

erickson - psychosocial human personality develops through 8 stages

▶ *Left:* Karen Horney (1885–1952). *Right:* Harry Stack Sullivan (1892–1949).

FOCUS QUESTIONS

1. Distinguish between psychosexual and psychosocial development.
2. In what ways did each neo-Freudian explore beyond Freud's original psychoanalytic theory?

fromm - personality fundamentally social

Erik Erikson (1902–1994) has provided a broader theory of development, one that stresses the psycho*social* nature of people and the interrelations between individuals and society. Unlike Freud, who believed that the foundations of personality were essentially completed in childhood, Erikson saw human personality as developing and changing throughout life, from infancy on through adulthood and old age. Moreover, Erikson's eight stages of man, even where they overlap with Freud's stages during early childhood, emphasize the social aspects of development.

Erich Fromm (1900–1980) saw personality as fundamentally social. At birth and with development, humans find themselves increasingly isolated from others. That isolation—the fundamental human condition—is painful, and however much people cherish their freedom, they also seek to terminate their isolation. They can do this either through love and shared work—a constructive mode—or through conformity and submission to authority, a very destructive mode.

MODERN PSYCHODYNAMIC THEORY

As a group, the Neo-Freudians brought refinements to basic Freudian theory. Other theorists and practitioners have proposed further modifications to this theory. But these modern psychodynamic theorists still take as the basis for their work the approaches of Freud and the Neo-Freudians.

Today, there really is no single coherent theory of personality dynamics. Rather, the work that goes on in many clinics and laboratories sheds light on *aspects* of personality and human development, and it greatly revises Freud's notions and those of his immediate followers. The core of that revision has to do with the nature of the *self*—the processes and crises that shape it, the role of the defenses in shaping consciousness, and those aspects of the self that contribute to growth.

The Self and Self Theory

Let us grant, as Freud held, that personality is composed of the id, ego, and superego. But what gives personality its unity? What leads individuals to be-

► *Left:* Erik Erikson (1902–1994). *Right:* Erich Fromm (1900–1980).

lieve that they are the same person across time and place, that they are not fractured and fragmented psychologically? How is it that even though they are *doing* different things at different times with different people, they remain the very same person? For some, these questions have little meaning: they *are* the same person physically, and therefore psychologically. For others, however, especially those who have had a "shaky" self, or who see themselves as having undergone great change, such that they can say that "I am not the person that I was five years ago," these questions are significant and worth pursuing.

THE SELF

Modern psychodynamic theory is concerned with the **introcosm** (Jaynes, 1977), the vast subjective psychological space that is the storehouse of personal experience within each of us. Central to its theoretical formulations is the *self* in all its senses, and especially the ways in which it *emerges,* is *experienced,* and often becomes embattled and *defended* (Winnicott, 1971; Kohut, 1971, 1977; Mahler, 1979; Stern, 1985). There are three aspects of self that arise sequentially and are especially important in psychodynamic theory: the core self, the subjective self, and the verbal self (see Table 4–3).

TABLE 4–3

SELF THEORY			
Self	*Emerges*	*Features*	*Possible Problems*
Core Self	2-6 months	Agency/control Self-coherence Emotions Self-history	Sense of agency and control may break down
Subjective Self	7-9 months	Recognizing others Sharing attention Communicating intentions	Disturbances may result in being out of touch with self and others
Verbal Self	15-18 months	Using symbols and language to communicate particular thoughts	"False self" may develop

▲ Heinz Kohut (1913–1981).

self-objects

FOCUS QUESTIONS

1. Describe the core self, the subjective self, and the verbal self.
2. Explain each of the following defense mechanism or coping strategies:

   - repression
   - projection
   - reaction formation
   - displacement
   - identification
   - denial
   - isolation
   - intellectualization
   - rationalization
   - sublimation

3. Explain how notions of death and life, responsibility, and willing are central to growth and existential theories.

The Core Self The "first self" arises sometime between the second and sixth months of an infant's life, when he becomes aware that he and his caregiver are *physically separate.* The physical or **core self** that arises in this way is the "body self" and is pretty much taken for granted. Usually, people are unaware of their core selves. Nevertheless, it serves a very important function. The core self gives each person his sense of separateness, coherence, and identity. Moreover, it is the core self that enables individuals to confer coherence and identity on *others.*

The core self has four especially important features. First, it embraces a sense of *agency,* that we are the authors and controllers of our own actions (cf. Yalom, 1980) and correspondingly, we are *not* the controllers of other people's actions (nor they of ours). Daniel Stern (1985) describes a dramatic experiment that he and his colleagues conducted with a pair of "Siamese twins," Alice and Betty, young infants who were attached in such a way that they always faced each other. When Alice was sucking her own fingers and the experimenters tried to remove them from her mouth, they could sense resistance in Alice's arm, but no straining forward of her head. But when they tried to remove Betty's fingers from Alice's mouth, there was no resistance in Alice's arm, but her head strained forward. Clearly Alice knew whether she had her own or her sister's fingers in her mouth, and moreover, she understood best how she could control whether they remained in her mouth.

Second, the core self fosters and is promoted by a sense of *self-coherence,* that one is a physical unity. Third, the sense that the *emotions* one experiences are part of oneself contributes to the growth and maintenance of the core self. And finally, the core self promotes the sense of *self-history,* the perception of our continuity in time, despite the fact that we are not the same people we once were.

So long as these features of the core self remain strong, personality remains strong. But if there is a breakdown in say, the sense of agency and control, if one develops the sense that "things are happening to me outside of my control" or that "I can control other people's minds," there is also fertile ground for disruption.

The Subjective Self At about seven to nine months of age, a second sense of self emerges. It is the **subjective self,** and it encourages the development of **intersubjectivity**—the sense that we understand each others' intentions and feelings, as well as the sharing of experiences about things and events. At that age, children begin to draw their parents' attention to things, sharing that attention. They communicate intentions. And they share affective states. The result is meaningful exchanges between the infant and her caregivers, exchanges that are characterized by empathy and a sense of common understanding, exchanges that are distinctly human.

Disturbances in the subjective self may result in difficulties in feeling connected to other people and in empathizing with them or with oneself. The sense of being out of touch with self and others is what may arise when there are disturbances in the subjective self.

The Verbal Self At about fifteen to eighteen months of age, children begin to develop the third sense of self: the self as a storehouse of knowledge and experience. That **verbal self** develops by using symbols and language.

▲ *Left:* The subjective self is the self in relation to others. *Right:* The verbal self develops by using symbols and language.

The use of language, of course, opens a world of infinite variety and action for the infant. It permits rapid and direct communication, often about issues that are not behaviorally obvious. "Give me milk" is a precise request that might, without language, be misunderstood and very drawn out. Moreover, because the infant begins to use words such as "I" or "me" or "you," he can soon objectify the self, often seeing the self as others might.

But language has a special down side, for it can distort the same reality that it might otherwise extend and enrich. Imagine a child who is visibly bored or tired, and whose parent says, "My! Aren't we having a wonderful time!" Indeed, language has been implicated in the development of the "false self," the self that is a semantic construction of disavowed experiences and beliefs.

SELF-OBJECTS

The various selves are not sturdy and wholly independent structures. Much as they are formed by interactions between caregivers and infant, so they require support and sustenance from others throughout life. Those centrally important people who provide support for personality cohesiveness are called ***self-***

▶ Self-objects are people and things that support and sustain the self throughout life.

objects, people and things that each of us requires to keep our personalities functioning at their optimum level (Kohut, 1977). The notion of self-objects underscores the importance of the environment for optimal personality functioning. It shows that we are, none of us, islands into ourselves, free and independent of the contexts in which we are found. As we will see, self-object disturbances, in particular, are held to be important in the borderline personality disorders.

THE SIGNIFICANCE OF SELF

The notion of self is central to understanding the private world of experience. According to Carl Rogers (1902–1987), who was a leading theorist about the self, each person lives in a "continually changing world of experience of which he is the center." No one can understand a person's private world as well as that person does. But neither are we wholly barred from the private experience of others. **Empathy** is the gift and tool that enables us to understand others (Rogers, 1961; Kohut, 1978).

The self is the aspect of personality that embodies a person's perceptions and values. There are two kinds of values: those that are acquired from the experience of the subjective self, and those that are introjected or acquired from others, perhaps through the verbal self. Values that arise from experience are the ones that most commonly contribute to personal growth and self-knowledge. Values that are introjected, on the other hand, may be a source of confusion, for they often require that a person deny his or her own feelings in order to conform to the desires of another. Thus, when children are told that it is bad to be angry with a sibling, they may gradually come to avoid labeling their feelings toward siblings as anger in order to preserve parental affection. Their subjective self may be out of tune with their verbal self, and that may produce tension and conflict, particularly when they are with those siblings.

Defenses and Consciousness

Consciousness may be shaped by defenses against anxiety. An individual may turn to a variety of mechanisms to avoid and alter the psychological reality of consciousness. Modern psychodynamic theorists describe these mechanisms much as did Freud. But they depart from Freudian theory in that modern theorists organize these strategies in a hierarchy according to their level of maturity. First we will describe the various mechanisms, then we will discuss the hierarchical ordering of defenses as formulated by such theorists as George Vaillant, and finally we will describe how the defensive process can shape consciousness.

THE COPING STRATEGIES OF EVERYDAY LIFE

As we discussed earlier, Freud described anxiety as the psychic pain arising out of conflict. "The mind is its own place," the poet John Milton tells us. "It can make a heaven of hell or a hell of heaven." This is especially the case when the mind is experiencing conflict and anxiety. Then, the mind becomes enormously creative, finding all sorts of ways to reduce anxiety. The ways in which the mind accomplishes this are often automatic and unconscious, occurring outside the willful control of the individual. Sometimes it can be achieved in a direct and conscious effort to mitigate conflict and minimize psychic pain. We

[Handwritten marginal notes:]

defense mechanisms

- repression - unconsc forces
  unwanted thoughts / desires out
  of mind (affective memories)
  ~ mental inhibition
    images / memories blocked
  ~ attention withdrawal
    think of something else

- projection - attribute private
  understandings + matters
  "you" to "I"
  ~ assimilation projection
    something we are aware of
    feeling ourselves
  ~ disowning projection
    coping process
    attrib to others what feeling
    + experiences we deny
    having ourselves
  ~ psychological distress
    ① reduces distress by
       attrib anxiety-provoking
       impulse to someone else
    ② allows us to do something
       about anger

- reaction formation
  opposite reaction or feeling
  substitution
  seen in counterphobia
  pursue fear

- displacement
  replace true object w/ one less
  threatening + more innocent

- identification
  internalize the characteristics
  of others

- denial - does away w/ distressing
  external facts

- isolation - only affective components
  are repressed

- intellectualization - repress emotional
  component of experience +
  resisting it as intellectual analysis

- rationalization - edit facts + motives
  hypochondriasis - feeling ill

- sublimation - social undesirable goals to desireable ones

call the ways in which the mind alters painful psychological events **coping strategies** or **defense mechanisms.**

Repression   The most fundamental and widely used means for altering psychological realities is repression. In *Notes from Underground*, the Russian novelist Fyodor Dostoyevsky describes why repression is used and the role it plays. He writes:

> Every man has reminiscences which he would not tell to every one, but only to his friends. He has other matters in his mind which he would not reveal even to his friends, but only to himself, and that in secret. But there are other things which a man is afraid to tell even to himself, and every decent man has a number of such things stored away in his mind. The more decent he is, the greater the number of such things in his mind. (Dostoyevsky, 1864, pp. 57–59)

Repression is a defense by which the individual unconsciously forces unwanted thoughts or prohibited desires out of mind. Memories that evoke shame, guilt, humiliation, or self-deprecation—in short, affective memories (Davis and Schwartz, 1987)—are often repressed.

Not all painful memories are repressed nor, for that matter, are all repressed memories objectively painful. Whether repression occurs depends, at least partly, on the degree to which an experience or memory conflicts with self-image. People who think little of themselves and their abilities may well repress memories of the praise they received for a job well done. Such repression stabilizes their self-image and reduces anxiety that might arise from discrepant information.

Two processes facilitate repression: **mental inhibition** and **attention withdrawal.** Mental inhibition occurs when images or memories are blocked. Blocking can be either intentional and conscious (under which condition it is sometimes called suppression), or automatic and unconscious. Young children, for example, are frequently and uncomfortably concerned with dying. They may try to put those thoughts out of mind. But putting thoughts out of mind is difficult. Because thinking about death is painful, the entire blocking process may become unconscious and automatic, relieving the child of the difficult burden of repressing consciously.

Repression can also occur through withdrawing attention and redirecting it. If thinking about sex makes people feel guilty, for example, they can think about success and achievement instead, which makes them feel good. If repression is successful, each sexual impulse will be replaced by fantasies of fame and success.

Repression can be nearly complete, or it can be partial. When an idea or memory is partially repressed, some aspects may be consciously available, while others are not. For example, a person who had had a difficult relationship with a parent, may recall crying at that parent's funeral but may not recall what he or she cried about or anything else about the event. The available evidence also suggests that it is *partially* repressed conflicts and memories that play a significant role in abnormal behavior (Perkins and Reyher, 1971; Reyher and Smyth, 1971; Burns and Reyher, 1976; Silverman, 1976). In **multiple personality,** for example, an individual has two or more personalities that are alien to each other. When one personality is dominant, the others are repressed.

The capacity of the mind to be "its own place" is not limited merely to its ability to repress, to reject images and memories from consciousness, as important as that ability is. Rather, the mind is an editor, deleting whole chapters of experience and reorganizing others. Ordinarily, even in the absence of conflict, both perception and memory are reconstructive (Anderson and Bower, 1973). This is to say that minds take direct experience, edit, and make something "new" of it, by adding to, or subtracting from perception, by embellishing memory in ways that range from innocent decoration to filling memorial gaps with new "memories." It is no surprise, therefore, that these enlivening capacities of the mind should be used in the coping process, when anxiety is experienced or when conflict occurs between self-image and impulse or behavior. Here, sometimes consciously, but more often unconsciously, editing processes are invoked to enable the individual to cope by making perception and memory more pleasant.

The notion that memories and experiences can be partially or wholly repressed has been widely, though not universally accepted among psychologists (see, for example, Holmes, 1990). But recently that acceptance has been questioned as people report the "return" of repressed memories, and on the basis of those newly returned memories, accuse others of sexual molestation, satanic behaviors, and even murder (Loftus, 1993). We examine this matter at greater length in Chapter 18, where we explore the legal implications of "forgotten memories."

Projection   Fundamentally, projection consists of attributing private understandings and meanings to others, of substituting "you" for "I." It is the bedrock upon which language comprehension rests. Consider the sentence "I love Mary." Anyone reading that sentence will have little difficulty comprehending it because she will **project** her own notion of love onto the speaker's phrase and mind. Generally, when someone says that "she hurt my feelings" or "I'm worried about that exam," we feel we understand what she is saying, even though in another context, we would readily grant that our own "hurt" might feel different from hers, and our "worry" different, too. We call this **assimilative projection** because it is an attribution to another of something that we are quite aware of feeling ourselves. It is part of the general process of quickly assigning meanings to events. Such attributions can be correct or incorrect, and they can obviously lead to a host of wrong predictions and misunderstandings (Nisbett and Ross, 1980).

Another kind of projection, called **disowning projection,** is more common in the coping process. It consists in attributing to others those feelings and experiences that we personally *deny* having and that we usually repress. Think of the preacher who sees and decries sin everywhere but denies having a sinful impulse himself. That's disowning projection. Robert R. Sears (1936), in the first experimental validation of disowning projection, asked students in a dormitory to rate themselves and their fraternity brothers on four traits: stinginess, obstinacy, disorderliness, and bashfulness. The extent to which individuals actually possessed each trait was estimated from the average of the ratings assigned to them by their fraternity brothers. When that average departed significantly from the rating the person gave himself, it was assumed that the person lacked self-awareness and, as a result, it was predicted that he would project more of that trait onto his fraternity brothers. And indeed he did, as Figure 4–1 indicates. Similarly, people who deny or repress their own sexual impulses have been shown to project them on others and to rate others as more lustful than in fact they are (Halpern, 1977).

Psychodynamic thinkers point out that projection plays a double role in psychological distress. First, it reduces distress by allowing a person to attribute an anxiety-provoking impulse to another person, rather than the self. Thus, if anger makes us feel anxious, then the anxiety that anger creates can be reduced by attributing that anger to someone else. Second, projection allows us to do something about anger, for when someone is angry at us, are we

FIGURE 4–1

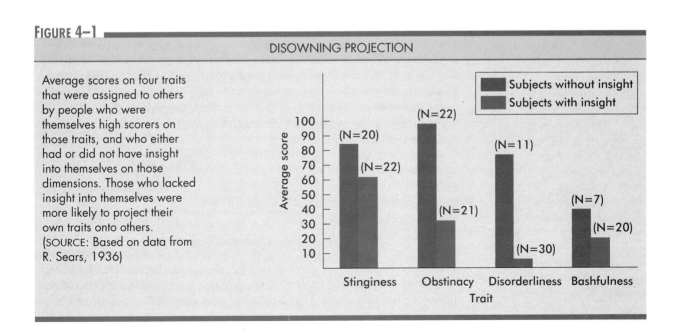

DISOWNING PROJECTION

Average scores on four traits that were assigned to others by people who were themselves high scorers on those traits, and who either had or did not have insight into themselves on those dimensions. Those who lacked insight into themselves were more likely to project their own traits onto others. (SOURCE: Based on data from R. Sears, 1936)

not permitted to take aggressive or retaliative action in our own defense? Thus, projection can provide the rationale for engaging in the behavior that would have been forbidden in the first place.

Reaction Formation   In the process of editing experience, we can delete a verb and substitute its opposite. Sometimes we say, "I hate her," when in fact we really mean "I love her." Such an editorial process is called *reaction formation,* because an opposite reaction is formed to the initial impulse.

Reaction formation, in fact, is a special case of a more generalized *feeling substitution,* which is easy to accomplish because feelings are often so ephemeral and difficult to label. For example, people in whom feelings of dependency are especially stressful may unwittingly experience and express anger each time they are in a situation that would ordinarily evoke dependency.

Reaction formation may be especially significant in mania. There, individuals behave as if they are full of joy and boundless energy, but one senses that their fundamental experience is one of sadness and depression, against which a reaction has been formed. Reaction formation is also seen in counterphobia, where individuals pursue precisely those activities that they deeply fear.

But if the mind can so easily revise experience and substitute a real feeling for its opposite, how can one tell the real feeling from its false opposite? When someone says "I love you!" how do we know he or she is not "really" feeling hatred? And conversely, if someone says "I can't stand you" should we not take that as a frank declaration of affection? Psychodynamic theorists offer two clues. First, because the conditions for experiencing and expressing the "real feeling" are not present in the reaction formation, the latter expressions of feeling tend to be thin, shallow, and seemingly wooden. Fabricated affections and genuine feelings are expressed in quite different ways. Second, the reaction formation is inflexible. Precisely because a stated fondness is formed, say, in reaction to hot anger, the anger must be avoided at all costs. Yet, anyone who has really liked someone knows that we are all occasionally annoyed or angry with people we truly care for. And we say so. Those who engage in reaction formation rarely are angry and rarely say so.

Displacement   When the strategy of *displacement* is used, the individual edits the target of his or her emotions by replacing the true object with one that is more innocent and less threatening. People who are angry and frustrated at work, but who cannot vent those feelings at work, are unconsciously using displacement strategies when they return home and vent their feelings on innocent spouses and children.

Identification   *Identification* describes the process by which we internalize the characteristics of others—their ideas, values, mannerisms, status, and power. Identification is the opposite of projection. It is a fairly common strategy for overcoming fear and inadequacy.

People identify with those who have power and status, and they try to do many of the things that those they identify with do. Thus, some people are willing to spend considerably more money for a house in a "proper" neighborhood than they would spend for the identical house at a less fashionable address, feeling that if their home is in a better neighborhood, they must perforce be "better" people. Similarly, people often rate themselves and each other by the college they attended, where they buy their clothes, or by the car they drive, even though we are, all of us, precisely what we are, no more and no less, regardless of the neighborhood we live in, the status of our college, where we buy our clothes, or the car we drive.

Identification relies heavily on people's sensitivity to context. Much as the perceived color of gray is changed according to whether it is seen against a black or white background, so are the perceived qualities of people altered by whether they are seen in an attractive or unattractive context.

There seems to be considerable clinical evidence for a special form of identification: identification with the aggressor. Bruno Bettelheim, a Jewish psychoanalyst who was interned at two notoriously cruel Nazi concentration camps during World War II, observed how people coped with concentration camp conditions. One of his most striking descriptions concerns how some of the old prisoners—those who had been in the camps more than three years—identified with their Nazi jailers. They used the language of the Gestapo, adopted its mannerisms and even its carriage. Occasionally, they wore scraps of discarded Nazi uniforms or altered their own clothing to resemble Nazi uniforms. At times, they appeared to use the same patterns of cruelty as the Gestapo used toward other prisoners. When it became necessary to kill another inmate, they would do so in a manner that was strikingly similar to that used by the Gestapo. Bettelheim sensed that the only way these prisoners could allay their own fears of the Gestapo was by identifying with the Gestapo and pretending to have its power (Bettelheim, 1943).

Identification is a particularly useful strategy for coping with fear. Anna Freud tells of a little girl who was afraid to cross the hall in the dark lest she meet a ghost. She handled this fear by making peculiar gestures as she crossed the hall. "There's no need to be afraid in the hall," she explained to her little brother, "you just have to pretend that you're the ghost who might meet you" (A. Freud, 1936, p. 119). Incidentally, this example points out what has been stressed previously: coping strategies need not be unconscious.

Identification plays an especially large role in psychodynamic views of depression (see Figure 4–2). People who are depressed, as we shall see in Chapter 11, often suffer enormously from self-deprecation, feelings of worthlessness,

FIGURE 4–2

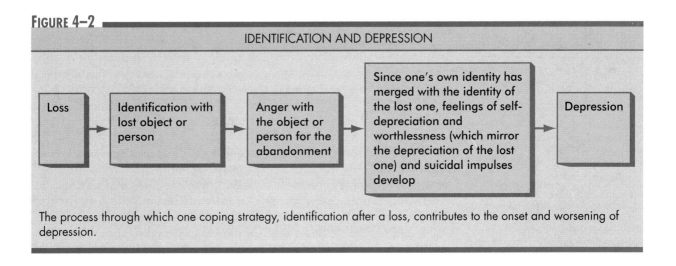

IDENTIFICATION AND DEPRESSION

Loss → Identification with lost object or person → Anger with the object or person for the abandonment → Since one's own identity has merged with the identity of the lost one, feelings of self-depreciation and worthlessness (which mirror the depreciation of the lost one) and suicidal impulses develop → Depression

The process through which one coping strategy, identification after a loss, contributes to the onset and worsening of depression.

and suicidal impulses. Such feelings arise from the combined action of mourning and identification. When people suffer a loss, either through death or rejection, they go through a period of mourning. That much is quite normal. Often, however, people identify with these lost objects, unwittingly merging these objects with themselves. Because they feel a good deal of unconscious anger toward these objects for having abandoned or rejected them, that anger now comes to be experienced toward the self, and they become depressed. An examination of their feelings of self-deprecation and worthlessness would reveal, in the psychoanalytic view, that these feelings are more properly directed toward those who have died or rejected them.

Denial If repression obliterates inner facts, ***denial*** does away with distressing external ones. Denial commonly occurs when our sense of security and of being loved is threatened. The fact that people generally find it difficult to perceive accurately negative feelings directed toward themselves suggests that the denial process is widespread (Taguiri, Bruner, and Blake, 1958). Denial is often used when people are threatened by death. The parents of a fatally ill child, much as the fatally ill themselves, often deny that anything is wrong, even though they have the diagnosis and prognosis in hand.

Isolation Whereas in repression and denial, both the affective and informational components of experience are deleted, in ***isolation*** only the affective ones (which, after all, are the sources of distress) are repressed, while information is retained. People who have suffered great brutality and humiliation, such as those in the German death camps during World War II, or those who have been raped, may utilize isolation. They may be able to recount their experience precisely and in copious detail but be unable to recall the accompanying intense feelings. The very experiences that would ordinarily bring tears to a teller's eyes or make a listener wince in empathic pain, may be related blandly, suggesting that the feelings that were originally associated with the experience have been isolated.

Isolation can also be a constructive strategy. The parent who responsibly reprimands a child cannot be too sensitive to the hurt feelings the reprimand engenders, else the reprimand will fail. Neither can a surgeon allow herself to be overly sensitive to the fact that the tissue she is cutting is human flesh. Isolation constructively permits these emotional concerns to be withheld from consciousness.

Intellectualization Related to denial and isolation, ***intellectualization*** consists of repressing the emotional component of experience, and restating the experience as an abstract intellectual analysis. Unable to deal with a particularly intense feeling, we sometimes seek to read all about it and to produce elaborate self-analyses that are all but devoid of feeling.

Rationalization In recalling experiences and accounting for them, people commonly edit not only the facts of the experience but the motives as well. The process of assigning to behavior socially desirable motives that an impartial analysis would not substantiate is called ***rationalization.*** Late to a party that they didn't want to attend in the first place, some people will offer socially desirable excuses: the car broke down, or their watch stopped. Those excuses are rationalizations.

The process of rationalization is beautifully illustrated in experiments involving posthypnotic suggestion (Hilgard, 1965). A person is hypnotized and told that upon awakening, he should attend carefully to the handkerchief in the hypnotist's pocket. When that handkerchief is removed, the subject is instructed to open the window. The subject is further given a posthypnotic amnesia, that is, he is instructed to forget that the hypnotist ever told him to open the window. He is then aroused from the hypnotic trance. He circulates among the people in the room, all the while keeping a careful eye on the hypnotist. The hypnotist removes his handkerchief. The subject hesitates: after all, one simply does not go around opening windows for no reason at all. "Isn't it a bit stuffy in here?" he finally asks—and then, having found a proper rationalization for his behavior, proceeds to raise the window.

Rationalization plays a dramatic role in the development of **hypochondriasis,** which is the conviction in the absence of medical evidence that one is ill or about to become ill. "I can't do the job, not because I fear failure or because I fear it won't be done as well as the next guy, but because I'm not feeling well." Because illness evokes concern from others, the seemingly ill are encouraged to abandon the job and given a good measure of comfort to boot. Thus, the tendency to rationalize is often supported by the positive reactions it evokes from others.

Sublimation   *Sublimation* is the process of rechanneling psychic energies from socially, undesirable goals to constructive and socially desirable ones. As we have seen, capacities for love, work, altruism, and even humor involve such rechanneling of raw sexual and aggressive impulses. According to Freud, love is an especially powerful form of sublimation because it allows people also to achieve sexual gratification in a socially acceptable context. Simultaneously, however, loving leaves one vulnerable to rejection or the death of a loved one. Thus, the gratifications of loving and working are often matched by the anxieties to which they give rise. Sublimation, in Freud's view, is therefore as fragile as it is constructive.

THE ORGANIZATION OF COPING STRATEGIES

Everyone uses coping strategies. But are some strategies better—more effective, more adaptive, more useful—than others? Psychodynamic theorists believe that some defenses are primitive and immature in the sense that they grossly distort reality; they believe that other defenses do less violence to reality and are therefore more mature. These strategies can be organized into a **maturational hierarchy** that has four levels (Vaillant, 1986). *Level I* is the least mature and involves strategies wherein the cloth of reality is either wholly invented or entirely discarded. Denial or outright distortion of external reality as well as delusional projection are included here. *Level II* strategies are somewhat more mature. They include projection as well as the strategies that result in hypochondriasis and passive-aggressive behavior. They also include **acting out,** the direct expression of unconscious impulses (without being aware of those impulses), as well as **dissociation,** the temporary but drastic modification of one's sense of self or character in order to avoid emotional distress. At *Level III,* one finds the mechanisms of intellectualization, isolation, repression, and displacement—strategies that are awfully common, although somewhat debilitating for all of us. The most mature strategies—*Level IV*—are the ones we all strive for. They include dealing with anxiety through sublima-

[handwritten margin notes:]
levels of maturation hierarchy
① cloth of reality invented or discarded ~ denial
② include projection + result in hypochondriasis + passive-aggression; acting out + dissociation
③ finds the mechanisms of intellectualization, isolation, repression, + displacement
④ dealing w/ anxiety through sublimation, altruism, humor, conscious suppression, and impulse delay

tion, and with it, the mechanisms of altruism, humor, conscious suppression, and impulse delay.

Several longitudinal studies have provided evidence that supports this notion of a maturational hierarchy of coping strategies. A group of men who graduated Harvard College between 1939 and 1944 were studied at graduation, and for thirty years subsequently. Initially selected because they were quite independent, there was, even in this highly qualified group, considerable variability in the maturity of their coping strategies. Thirty years after they were first studied, the following question was asked: Did differences in the way they coped as undergraduates result in differences in the quality of their lives some thirty years later? Indeed they did, and dramatically so, as can be seen in Table 4–4).

A similar study examined the psychological health of a vastly different group (Vaillant, Bond, and Vaillant, 1986). In this study, a group of inner-city

TABLE 4–4

USE OF MATURE VS. IMMATURE STRATEGIES		
	Mature Strategies (N = 25)	Immature Strategies (N=31)
Overall Adjustment		
1) Top third in adult adjustment	60%	0%
2) Bottom third in adult adjustment	4%	61%
3) "Happiness" (top third)	68%	16%
Career Adjustment		
1) Income over $20,000/year	88%	48%
2) Job meets ambition for self	92%	58%
3) Active public service outside job	56%	29%
Social Adjustment		
1) Rich friendship pattern	64%	6%
2) Marriage in least harmonious quartile or divorced	28%	61%
3) Barren friendship pattern	4%	52%
4) No competitive sports (ages 40–50)	24%	77%
Psychological Adjustment		
1) 10+ psychiatric visits	0%	45%
2) Ever diagnosed mentally ill	0%	55%
3) Emotional problems in childhood	20%	45%
4) Worst childhood environment (bottom fourth)	12%	39%
5) Fails to take full vacation	28%	61%
6) Able to be aggressive with other (top fourth)	36%	6%
Medical Adjustment		
1) Four or more adult hospitalizations	8%	26%
2) 5+ days sick leave/year	0%	23%
3) Recent health poor by objective exam	0%	36%
4) Subjective health consistently judged "excellent" since college	68%	48%

Note: All correlations are statistically significant except for the correlations for four or more adult hospitalizations under the Medical Adjustment category.
SOURCE: Adapted from Vaillant, 1977, p. 88.

FIGURE 4–3

ADAPTIVE STYLE AND PERSONAL ADEQUACY

The figure shows mature, intermediate, and immature coping strategies. The bars represent correlations of adaptive styles with global measures of personal adequacy. Those who utilized mature coping strategies functioned better in life (determined by a composite score that assessed happiness, career success, friendships, marriage, psychological and medical adjustment), as compared to those who utilized intermediate and immature strategies. Except for strategies of isolation, repression, and reaction formation, all the correlations are statistically significant. (SOURCE: Vaillant, Bond, and Vaillant, 1986)

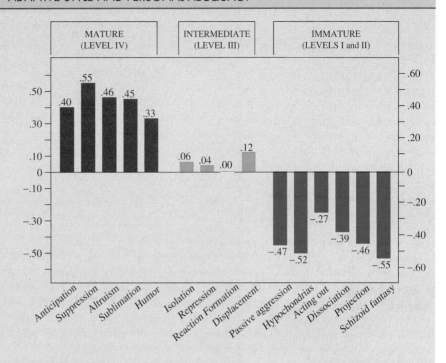

men who had first been interviewed between 1940 and 1945 were interviewed and rated again more than thirty years later, in 1977. The maturity of their defenses was established from the early interviews, when these men were in junior high school, while the adequacy of their present functioning was rated from the later interviews. The findings, once again, are remarkable, and are shown in Figure 4–3. Those men whose defenses can be characterized as mature functioned far better than those whose defenses were less mature.

Not only does the maturity of coping strategies affect overall psychological and social adjustment subsequently, but even *medical* adjustment is dramatically affected. People whose coping strategies were relatively immature tended in later years to be objectively in poorer health and to feel worse than those who coped more maturely.

THE SHAPING OF CONSCIOUS EXPERIENCE

Fueled by anxiety, the defenses shape conscious experience in dramatic ways. And the choice of defense, as well as its maturity, dictates the nature of subjective experience and the strength of coping. Consider the following case vignette (adapted from Vaillant, 1986):

> Married at the age of thirty, Mary Walt had one miscarriage and then tried for seven years to have children. When she was thirty-eight, a cervical biopsy examination revealed an early cancer. She immediately underwent surgery to remove her uterus.
>
> It was an awful blow. Both she and her husband had desperately wanted kids. Moreover, Mary had always felt inadequate in comparison to her younger sister,

who already had four children and had been the one in the family who had won praise for being good with kids. Below are a number of possible responses that Mary could have had to this crisis, each of which illustrates the use of a different defense.

Level IV:

Altruism. A month after surgery, Mary organized a group of other women who had breast and uterine surgery to visit and counsel patients who were now undergoing such surgery. From their own experience, these women gave information, counsel, and comfort, trying to answer questions and allay the fears that such surgery always engenders.

Sublimation. Mary took great pleasure from the get-well cards she received from her sister's children. She agreed to teach a Sunday School class for preschoolers. And she had a poem published in her local newspaper on the bittersweet joys of the maiden aunt.

Humor. The *Playboy* definition of a hysterectomy—"throwing out the baby carriage, but keeping the playpen"—made her laugh so hard that tears came to her eyes and her ribs ached.

Level III:

Repression. Mary found herself unable to remember the name of the operation. In addition, she forgot her first follow-up visit to the physician. And upon returning home, she burst into tears upon breaking an inexpensive vase. She had no idea why.

Intellectualization. She read a lot about uterine cancer, and asked the physician numerous questions. She concerned herself with the details of preventing postoperative infection.

Reaction Formation. She renewed an early interest in planned parenthood, and urged younger friends to limit their families. Moreover, she remembered that she had always been afraid of the pain of childbirth, and remarked to others that she was lucky to be spared that burden.

Level II:

Projection. Following a slight postoperative infection, she wrote long and angry letters blaming the hospital for unsanitary conditions. In addition, she blamed her doctor for not doing a Pap smear earlier, threatening to institute malpractice proceedings.

Hypochondriasis. Mary worried that the cancer might have spread to her lymph nodes, and could not be reassured by careful physical examination. She belabored her visitors with accounts of tiny lumps in her neck and groin.

Passive Aggression. While inserting her IV, the medical intern missed the vein. Mary smiled, told him not to worry, and said, "When you're *just* a medical student, it must be hard to get things right." Later, unable to sleep, Mary watched her IV run dry. At 4 A.M., the night nurse had to call the intern to restart the IV. Cheerfully, she told him that she had not rung for the nurse because she knew how busy everyone in the hospital was.

Level I:

Denial. Less than twenty-four hours after surgery, Mary ordered nurses to move her upstairs to the maternity ward. She then wandered about the hospital looking for *her* baby. She experienced no postoperative pain.

Delusional Projection. Mary complained that the hospital was being run by racists who were trying to sterilize her. She attempted to phone the FBI to report the hospital for genocide. She refused pain medication, claiming it was an experimental drug for thought control.

These defenses describe the variety of ways in which people cope with trauma. People characteristically use defenses from one or two adjacent levels. No one uses all of them.

Growth and Existential Theories

Recently, psychodynamically oriented theorists have sought to examine what is especially human in human experience, and particularly those aspects of human experience that contribute to growth or to abnormality. These existential theorists find three issues that are particularly important: fear of dying, personal responsibility, and will.

THE FUNDAMENTAL ANXIETY: DEATH AND LIFE

Existential psychologists assert that the central human fear and the one from which most psychopathology develops is the *fear of dying.* Anxiety about death is most prominent in, and best recalled from childhood. Perhaps because children are vulnerable, and because their worst imaginings are barely informed by reality, their fears are stark, vivid, and memorable. For them, the idea of death does not involve mere biological process. It is terrifyingly full of awful meanings. Death means being forgotten, being left out. Death means helplessness, aloneness, finiteness. In short, the idea of death is so awful that children and adults nearly universally employ coping strategies for dealing with it.

How does one deal with the fear of nonbeing? Broadly speaking, there are two kinds of strategies: by coming to believe oneself special, and by fusion. (Yalom, 1980).

Specialness One way through which some people protect themselves from death fears is by cultivating in themselves the notion that they are special. It is a peculiar notion in that it holds that the laws of nature apply to all mortals except oneself. The *notion of specialness* manifests itself in many ways. For example, the terminally ill simply cannot believe that it is they who are dying. They understand the laws of nature fully well, but they believe themselves somehow to be exempt from them. Similarly, people who smoke heavily, overeat, or fail to exercise sufficiently may also believe that somehow they are exempt from nature's laws.

The notion of specialness underlies many valued character traits. Physical courage may result from the belief that one is inviolable. So too may ambition and striving, and especially striving for power and control. But at the extreme, the unconscious belief in one's specialness may also lead to a spectrum of behavior disorders. The workaholic who compulsively strives to achieve success and power may also harbor the delusion that achieving that one kind of specialness may confer the other, immortal kind. Narcissistic people who devote enormous attention to themselves and are correspondingly insensitive to the requirements of others may believe that only that kind of self-nourishment will protect them from death and its associated anxieties.

Fusion Protection against the fear of death or nonbeing can also be achieved by fusing with others. *Fusion* is an especially useful strategy for those whose death fears take the form of loneliness. By attaching themselves to, and making themselves indistinguishable from others, they hope that their lot is cast

▲ One defense against the fear of death has been the idea that people can have immortal qualities or talents, as shown in this Chinese painting of a "thunderbolt bearer."

► People may attempt to protect themselves against nonbeing by fusing with others. These five people had plastic surgery to change their faces to those of rock stars Jim Croce, Linda Ronstadt, Kenny Rogers, Elvis Presley, and Buddy Holly, merging their identities with those of their favorite stars.

with them. They believe that much as these others continue to live, so will they. They also develop a fear of standing apart, as they believe that if they do stand apart, they will no longer be protected from death.

The fear of standing apart has socially valuable features. Why else would we marry and have children if not to create fusions? Why else would we form clubs, communities, and organizations? Such attachments protect against loneliness, against being separated from the flow of life. At the extreme, however, fusion is responsible for much unhappiness. Children who have grown up in brutal homes may be unwilling to leave them, not because they have nowhere else to go, but because they have established a fusion with their powerful parents and are afraid to destroy it. Similarly, spouses whose marriages have long ceased providing them satisfaction often find it difficult to separate lest in their old age, they find themselves alone. One example of an individual's need for fusion in order to ward off his fears of death is as follows:

> A well-trained, enormously presentable business executive had held seven positions in as many years, and he was now finding it difficult to gain employment. Each of his employers had been impressed both by his credentials and his industriousness. He was moved gradually into positions of greater responsibility. Oddly, however, just as he had begun to inspire faith in others, he would "foul up." His errors were as costly as they were inexcusable, and they led quickly to termination from the job. In the course of treatment with an existential therapist, it was found that success had a powerfully unconscious meaning for him. He feared success, for it meant isolation, standing apart from others. For him, success was analogous to death, in that it destroyed fusion. He unconsciously felt that it was better to be indistinguishable from the mass of people than to stand alone, even successfully.

Authenticity and Inauthenticity The desire for either specialness or fusion can lead to **inauthentic,** or false, modes of behavior. These ways of acting are false in that they are designed to achieve unattainable goals. Consider someone who tries to avoid the fear of nonbeing by fusing with others. He may say things to others that he hopes will please them, but that he does not really mean. For example, he may conform his opinions to theirs, bend his behaviors to suit them, do the things they do, even though his mind and body would rather believe and do something else. Gradually, he comes to lose sight of what *he* wants to do, while finding his conformity to others' opinions and behaviors only a pale pleasure. He has paid for a tenuous security against the fear of death by sacrificing his own authenticity.

The fear of death, then, promotes a host of irrational behaviors, according to existential thinkers. But that is not the only source of human irrationality. Whether one believes that one is fully responsible for one's life plays an equal role in determining human happiness or misery.

RESPONSIBILITY

The assumption of personal ***responsibility*** is central to existential thinking. It says that we are responsible for the way we perceive the world and for the way we react to those perceptions. To be responsible "is to be aware that one has created one's own self, destiny, life, predicament, feelings and, if such be the case, one's own suffering" (Yalom, 1980).

Existential psychologists generally pay careful attention to language; they are especially sensitive to the use of such words as "can't" and "it." People often say, "I just can't study" or "I can't get up in the morning," implying that the behavior is somehow removed from their control. What they really mean is, "I won't do it." They bury an act over which they have control beneath the appearance of disability. Young children who break something are inclined to say, "it broke," not "I broke it." Similarly, for adults to say that "something happened" or "it happened" is to imply that one is passively influenced by a capricious world. In short, they do not want to be held responsible. Generally, the use of the passive rather than the active voice, the avoidance of first person pronouns, as well as the attributions of the causes of current events to historical sources (i.e., my upbringing, my parents, the things I did as a child), are seen as signs of avoidance of responsibility.

Avoidance of responsibility is occasionally achieved by losing control. More accurately, it is achieved by *appearing* to lose control, by *seeming* to go out of one's mind, by *making it appear* that forbidden actions were taken because one was drunk or crazy. But behavior that is "out of control" is never really so. Otherwise, it could hardly be so purposive. For what is remarkable about "crazy" anger is the accuracy with which it is targeted: the blows fall, not on any random person, but precisely on the person toward whom the anger was experienced.

▶ Existentialists believe that we are responsible for the way we perceive the world and for the way we react to those perceptions. This includes taking responsibility for those close to us when they cannot help themselves.

Robert, age twenty-two, had just had an enormous fight with his father, and he was still furious. He went to his room and drank heavily. Inflamed, he took his bottle and went out for a drive—not in his own car, but in his father's sports car. At the end of the driveway, he turned too hard and accidentally dented the car's fender on a large oak tree.

Sara had been married for many years to a brutal and insensitive man who, without notice, one day asked for a divorce. She went "crazy." She followed him around town, repeatedly vandalized his apartment, and created wild scenes while he was dining with friends in a restaurant. Her crazy behavior defeated him. At first, he sought police protection, then he required emergency psychiatric hospitalization. Once he was hospitalized, she suddenly "regained her sanity." (Adapted from Yalom, 1980)

Because people can see themselves as responsible for their experiences and because they can plan for the future as well as live in the present, they are capable of *will,* which is a further theme in existential psychology.

WILLING

The capacity to will is as central a feature of existential views as are freedom and responsibility. Yet, despite its centrality, will is difficult to define unambiguously. Will is used psychologically in at least two senses. First, there is will as in willpower: the will of gritted teeth, clenched jaw, and tensed muscle. This is **exhortative will.** It can be useful at times, as when we force ourselves to work when we would rather play.

A second and more significant kind of will is associated with future goals. It is called **goal-directed will.** Much as memory is the organ of the past, goal-directed will has been called "the organ of the future" (Arendt, 1978). It is quite different from exhortative will, for it develops out of hope, expectation, and competence. Unlike exhortative will, it is not urged upon us but is rather a

▶ Goal-directed will arises from hope, expectation, and free choice, rather than grim determination.

freely chosen arousal in the service of a future that is willingly embraced. This kind of will cannot be created: it can only be unleashed or disinhibited.

> Susan was bright enough to do well in college but nevertheless was having a struggle. It was difficult for her to get up in the morning, difficult to crack the books, and difficult to put away the temptations that deflected her from achievement. She had no sense of what she wanted to study in college and, therefore, little motivation to work in her courses. After her midyear grades were posted, she went to the counseling center to "try to get myself down to work." During several counseling sessions, she realized that although she had plenty of intelligence, she lacked confidence in her ability to do well in college and, as a result, found it difficult to commit herself to any career. She had had a difficult start in the primary grades, and those bruises had remained with her. During one significant counseling session, she realized that grade school was far behind her and that, moreover, she had achieved a good deal since those experiences. Nearly simultaneously, a long-buried desire surfaced: to be a doctor.
>
> At the next session, she reported that "her life had come together during the past week." No longer did she find it difficult to get up in the morning or to resist going to the movies. It was easy to study now, and indeed, she bounded out of bed and headed for the books effortlessly. "Now that I know what I want to do, everything else has fallen into place. I no longer have to force myself."

Disorders of will are found among people who know what they should do, what they ought to do, and what they must do, but who have no notion of what they want to do. Lacking that knowledge of what they *want*, their goals seem apparently lusterless, and movement toward them is correspondingly difficult. People may fail to know what they want for three reasons. First, they may simply fear wanting. Wanting makes them vulnerable to failure and hurt, and that is especially difficult for those who wish to appear strong. Second, they may fail to know what they want because they fear rejection. They long ago learned that if their wishes departed from those of their friends or family, their wishes would infuriate and drive others away. Finally, they may fail to know what they wish because they want others, magically, to discover their silent wishes and fulfill them.

> Most graduate students complete a dissertation before receiving their doctoral degree, and the dissertation is often viewed by them as a significant hurdle in their graduate career. For some, however, that final hurdle is insurmountable. Such seemed to be the case for Cathy. She had done well until that point. Her course grades were excellent, and the research that she had completed while in graduate school had been quite interesting. But somehow she found it difficult to get down to the dissertation. In fact, she had begun three separate studies and had dropped each of them for no particular reason other than that she had lost interest. The fact of the matter was that she viewed the dissertation as a major undertaking, much bigger than anything she had undertaken before, and much beyond her abilities. Her fear of being criticized by her teachers or, worse, of failing her oral examination prevented her from finding a study that she really wanted to do.

For existential psychologists, then, goal-directed willing is more than just forcing oneself to do something (exhortative will). Rather, it is going through the pain and risk of finding what one really wants and then doing it.

Freud's own views and those of his disciples and descendants find expression in the modes of treatment that they have generated. Here, theory and practice come together. For it was from the clinic that Freud's most interesting ideas developed. We therefore turn to psychodynamic treatment in order to examine those views in practice. Much as psychoanalytic theory spawned a variety of psychodynamic theories, so did psychoanalysis, as a mode of treatment, give birth to numerous and varied treatment modes. Among these are a variety of brief psychoanalytically "inspired" treatments that alter classical treatment in a variety of important ways; existential therapies that focus on the meaning of thoughts and actions; psychodynamic family and couple therapies that focus on ameliorating the problems that arise among people who are significant to each other. We take up these forms of treatment in greater detail later in the book.

Brief Psychotherapy

FOCUS QUESTIONS

1. How does the case of Patty illustrate brief psychotherapy and the concepts of catharsis and transference?
2. Describe client-centered therapy.

Brief psychoanalytically inspired treatments have much in common with classical psychoanalysis. Both seek to alter thought and behavior. Both do so by examining early conflicts in the context of present relationships, and by making conscious that which is repressed. Both examine free associations, dreams, and resistances. In so doing, psychic energy is freed for more constructive purposes, and the individual is able to find more constructive resolutions for conflict. Anxiety is reduced because impulses now find "safe" methods of expression. And coping strategies, where they are required, are now more mature. These matters become much clearer when we examine an actual case of psychodynamic psychotherapy.

It had been more than two years since Patty had had a moment's peace. Her problems were in her head, quite literally. There, continually pounding headaches kept her in bed all day every day, unable to sleep, unable to rise, clawing at the sheets.

The headaches themselves were not unusual. What was unusual was the simultaneous presence of three of them, and their intensity. One was a drilling headache. "It's as if someone were drilling from the top of my head to the center of my brain." The second pulsed at the back of her head and felt as if someone were ripping the two lobes of her brain apart. And the third was a fairly common headache, one that felt as if there were a steel band around her head which was getting tighter and tighter.

Patty had sought help for these headaches for well over a year. She had had several medical and neurological work-ups. She had seen two allergists in the hope that they could find whether something she was ingesting was harmful to her. "In the hope . . ." is the appropriate phrase here, for, after searching for so long, anything that remotely promised an answer, however difficult, was more comforting than the perpetual pain.

She finally requested neurosurgery in the hope that the severing of nerve endings would alleviate the pain. Informed that nothing could be done surgically, she became exceedingly depressed. The situation by now seemed entirely hopeless to her. A burden to her husband, useless to her young children, there seemed little to do but end it all. It was then that she was referred for psychodynamic therapy.

The early part of her first meeting was spent describing the problem. With great pain, she described her headaches but quickly ran out of things to say. She didn't think that the problem was psychological, nor that anyone in their right mind would feel as she did under the circumstances. There being nothing more to say, she turned to the therapist and asked "What should I talk about now?"

Psychodynamically oriented psychotherapists seek to understand the present by relating it to the past. Having acquired as full an account of the patient's current status as possible, they inquire about the past. Therefore, in response to Patty's question, the therapist said, "Tell me about your childhood."

She began slowly and then, with growing animation, described her father. (Indeed, during the remainder of that very long interview, Patty alluded to her mother only in passing.) Her father had come originally from a stretch of land that borders Greece and Turkey. He was a man of violent passions and frustrations, a man who had once angrily left his family for four years, only to return as suddenly as he had gone. In her earliest memory of him, he threatened to take a train to a far off place, never to return.

He was, in her description, a drunk, a womanizer, an erratic supporter of the family, a man who often beat her mother. Despite this, Patty retained a hidden fount of fondness for him, one that was particularly evident (so it seemed to her therapist) in her description of the times he used to take her with him to the neighborhood saloon. He would put her up on the bar, and she would dance while everyone else clapped. It was a particularly warm memory in an otherwise distressing relationship.

"Did you ever go to bed with your father?" The question came suddenly, without warning.* Patty paled. "How did you know?" she asked. And then, not waiting for the answer, she burst into tears.

"Yes, it was him. And I still hate him. He's an old man now. And I still hate him. On Sunday morning, my mother would clean the house. All of us, except my mother, slept late on Sunday. When she cleaned my room, I went into her bed. I would get under the covers, close my eyes, and go back to sleep. My father was there. He would touch me . . . rub . . . the rat. How could he do that to his own daughter?"

In anger, in sadness, and in shame, she cried as she tore furiously into incidents that had occurred more than a quarter century ago, when she was eight years old.

Suddenly, she stopped crying, even talking. Then smiling in disbelief, she said "They're gone. The headaches are gone." She rose slowly and walked around the office, moving her head from side to side. For the first time in more than two years, she felt normal.

Before the session was over, those headaches would return again. But regardless, a connection had been made between her present suffering and her early memories of her father.

During subsequent sessions, Patty was able to retrieve from memory more experiences with her father. Her father, it appeared, had had another family, which he had left behind in Greece when he came to America and married her mother. Patty felt it was her responsibility to keep him in America by making him so happy that he would not want to return. The fear of abandonment ran deep in both Patty and her mother.

She could not recall what her father had done to her in bed, but she knew that it was bad and that even *he* must have thought so. Once, after an outing with a group

*Such questions are not usually asked so directly or so early in psychodynamic treatment. In this case, however, Patty's depression seemed so overwhelming that the therapist felt he had to quicken the therapeutic pace.

of friends, her father spotted her on a subway platform. He pulled her roughly aside from her schoolmates, slapped her hard across the face, and called her "Whore."

Those recaptured events—relived, remembered, re-experienced during therapy—brought relief over longer and longer periods. But certain experiences and even thoughts brought on headaches suddenly and fiercely, as when:

- she was shopping for a brassiere;
- Phil, her husband, was bouncing their young daughters on his lap, and the three of them were laughing;
- friends suggested that they go to a movie;
- she had gone with the family to a Greek wedding celebration, and all the young people were dancing; and
- she was washing the children's laundry.

All of these scenes vaguely connoted sexuality and therefore brought pain. Talking about them was difficult. There was a tension between exploring the psychodynamics of her situation and risking disturbing a trouble-free day. But she pushed on, pursuing her mental and emotional associations to early experiences and memories, not only about father and mother, but also about husband, children, friends, and later even about the therapist.

To a psychodynamic therapist, this search into Patty's past suggested that her headaches resulted from severe sexual conflicts that appeared to arise during the phallic stage. These conflicts paralyzed her, rendering her unable to even initiate caregiving activities on behalf of her husband, children, and increasingly, even herself.

The three headaches were themselves testimony to the power of the conflicts as well as the coping strategies. Those headaches—the drilling one, the one that felt as if the lobes of her brain were being torn apart, and the steel band that somehow refused to yield—symbolically suggested a conflict about rape. But since the conflict was going on in Patty's own mind, it suggested, too, a conflict about her *own* sexual desires. By some process which is not yet understood, these conflicting desires were repressed and displaced, not outward to other people, but upward to her head.

Patty clearly projected much of this conflict onto her husband and even her children. Their horseplay was seen, not as an innocent rumpus, but as a highly sexualized event. Shopping for underclothes, weddings, Greek dancing, and the weekly laundry were all similarly sexualized. Ego processes that normally differentiate these events and allow people to share social perceptions of them were clearly defective here. The defects, psychodynamic therapists hold, arose because of the intense and poorly contained pressure that was generated from Patty's own sexual conflicts.

It was **catharsis,** the uncovering and reliving of early traumatic conflicts, that mainly enabled Patty to remit her symptoms rapidly. But in psychodynamic theory, symptom remission is only part of the treatment, often the smallest part. Much more significant is the fact that enduring patterns of perceiving and reacting in adults are laid down in childhood and pervade all adult activities. They need to be altered because they are transferred from the people and impulses that originally stimulated the conflict to other significant people in one's life. Psychodynamic therapy seeks, therefore, not merely to relieve symptoms, but to alter personality—the very attitudes, perceptions, and behaviors that were misshaped by early experience.

How does psychodynamic treatment achieve personality changes? In practice, psychodynamic therapists must be nonreactive. They must listen calmly and intensely, but they must not be shocked by the client's revelations, nor should they commonly offer opinions or judgments. They should act as blank screens, onto which clients can project their own expectations, imaginings, and attributions. Over time, therapists themselves become central in the lives of their clients. This centrality is of such therapeutic importance that it is given a technical name in psychodynamic theory: ***transference.*** Transference describes the fact that during psychodynamic therapy, clients come to transfer emotions, conflicts, and expectations from the diverse sources from which they were acquired, onto their therapists. Therapists become mother, father, son, daughter, spouse, lover, and even employer or stranger, to their clients. In this emotional climate, clients are encouraged to speak frankly, to let their minds ramble, to free associate to emotionally charged ideas, even if the resulting ideas seem silly, embarrassing, or meaningless. Under these conditions, what was formerly repressed and distorted becomes available to consciousness and therefore more controllable by ego processes, as can be seen from further examination of Patty's case.

In less than three months, Patty's symptoms had abated. Her attention turned away from her headaches to other matters. Her mother, for example, was a "pain." She had always been melancholy and merely obedient, surely no fun to live with. Patty quickly related the impression that "she was no fun to live with" to her own relationship with her father. He had already abandoned a family in Greece. Had she been trying to keep him in the family? Might he not abandon them? More important, could her own sexual involvement with her father have been little more than an attempt to keep him at home? That possibility cast her memories in a much more positive light, relieving her of the guilt that the memories evoked. Shortly thereafter, she could observe her husband and children playing together, without suffering from headaches and guilt.

Gradually, attention turned from her parents, even from her husband and children, to the therapist himself. His lack of reacting now provoked discomfort; his occasional lateness caused her to feel anxiety; and when her therapist took a week-long vacation, she experienced dread. In turn, these feelings led to long, blocked silences during the therapy sessions. What thoughts lay behind these silences? It was difficult for her to say, and nearly impossible for her to free associate. But finally, she was able to allude to the embarrassing sexual fantasies that attended these events, fantasies now about the therapist himself. This was transference, for it shortly became clear that she interpreted his silences, lateness, and absences as abandonment, and she was unconsciously motivated to do what she had wanted to do in the past to retain the affections of significant others. She was, of course, initially unaware of the unconscious connection between abandonment and sexuality, and she was therefore deeply embarrassed by the thoughts that assailed her. Once she understood the reasons for those thoughts, however, she was able to see her relationship to the therapist in more objective terms, to recognize that an occasional lateness or absence is not the same as abandonment, and to find less self-demeaning and guilt-provoking ways to express her affections.

At about this time, and seemingly for no good reason, Patty began to explore an entirely new matter: what to do with her life. Upon graduating high school, she had considered going to college, but had given up that idea as "simply ridiculous." She had also been attracted to dance, but had not acted on that interest either. Now both ideas returned, as well as the desire to take a job again, and she began to explore those ideas with great enthusiasm. In Freud's view, energies that had once been bound up in repression and other defensive maneuvers, were now freed for other activities. Erik Erikson would point out that having resolved many of the guilts that were associated with sexuality, she was now free to take initiatives on her own behalf, to do something with her life.

Ultimately, over a period of a year, many of Patty's conflicts were resolved. She no longer felt that she had to be different from her mother, more sexual, more "fun to live with." Nor did she continue to feel that sexual behaviors were the only ones that would make her attractive and enable her to retain prized relationships. One result of these explorations was that her personal identity underwent considerable change. She had been an ineffectual, guilt-ridden person, dominated by forbidden impulses. She became an actively initiating and exploring person who trusted much more in others and took her own worth increasingly for granted.

Her stronger and more mature identity resulted from the greater understanding she had of herself and the greater control over impulses that this understanding brought. And it had one further result. The more Patty probed, the less clear it became that she had actually had a sexual relationship with her father. Eventually, that "memory" came to be seen as a false one, reflecting her own desire to retain his affections, rather than his actual behavior. In this, Patty repeated the experience of many of Freud's clients, for the mind, Freud observed, is a powerfully inventive place in which even "memories" can arise from desires, conflicts, and defenses.

Client-Centered Therapy

▲ Carl Rogers (1902–1987) developed client-centered therapy, which emphasizes unconditional positive regard and therapist empathy.

Client-centered therapy rests on two fundamental assumptions (Rogers, 1951, 1961, 1977). The first is that therapy proceeds best when the client experiences the therapist's **unconditional positive regard.** That regard arises from the therapist's belief that people are fundamentally good even when they are doing "bad" things. Indeed, they do "bad" things precisely because they have not experienced such unconditional respect. Thus, clients who are rude, boorish, liars, thieves, and brutes are both entitled to and needy of such unconditional regard. Without it, all people simply become defensive and when they are defensive, the process of change is retarded.

The second hallmark of client-centered therapy resides in the therapist's attempt to achieve **empathy** with the client, to see the world as he or she does. Client-centered therapists listen carefully to what the client says and then reflect or mirror their understanding back to the client. This enables clients to clarify and label their own experiences, and eventually to accept them.

CLIENT: Well, I made a very remarkable discovery. I know it's—*(laughs)* I found out that you actually *care* how this thing goes. *(Both laugh.)* It gave me the feeling, it's sort of well—"maybe I'll let you get in the act," sort of thing. It's—again you see, on an examination sheet, I would have had the correct answer. I mean—but it suddenly dawned on me that in the—client-counselor kind of thing, you *actually care* what happens to this thing. And it was a revelation, a—not that . . . That doesn't describe it. It was a—well, the closest I can come to it is a kind of relaxation, a—not letting down, but a *(pause)* more of a straightening out without tension, if that means anything. I don't know.

THERAPIST: Sounds as though it isn't as though this was a new idea, but it was a new *experience* of really *feeling* that I did care and if I get the rest of that, sort of willingness on your part to let me care.

CLIENT: Yes.

Because the client feels accepted and because he or she senses that the therapist is trying to understand, the client feels free to examine the host of feelings that lie just beneath surface behavior and that have been suppressed. That emphasis on feeling is one of the significant features of this therapy.

> CLIENT: You know over in this area of, of sexual disturbance, I have a feeling that I'm beginning to discover that it's pretty bad, pretty bad. I'm finding out that, that I'm bitter, really. Damn bitter. I—and I'm not turning it back in, into myself . . . I think what I probably feel is a certain element of "I've been cheated." *(Her voice is very tight and her throat chokes up.)* And I've covered up very nicely, to the point of consciously not caring. But I'm, I'm sort of amazed to find that in this practice of, what shall I call it, a kind of sublimation that right under it—again words—there's a, a kind of passive force that's, it's pas—it's very passive, but at the same time it's just kind of *murderous.*
>
> THERAPIST: So there's the feeling, "I've really been cheated. I've covered that up and seem not to care and yet underneath that there's a kind of a, a latent but very much present *bitterness* that is very, very strong."
>
> CLIENT: It's very strong. I—that I know. It's terribly powerful.
>
> THERAPIST: Almost a dominating kind of force.
>
> CLIENT: Of which I am rarely conscious. Almost never. . . . Well, the only way I can describe it, it's a kind of murderous thing, but without violence. . . . It's more like a feeling of wanting to get even. . . . And of course, I won't pay back, but I'd like to. I really would like to.

In the above excerpt, the feelings of bitterness and the desire for revenge begin to surface as a result of the therapist's patient understanding and reflection. Indeed, understanding and acceptance are the hallmarks of nearly all good treatments. And very often they give rise to the expression of feelings that seemed hitherto restrained and even impermissible.

EVALUATING PSYCHODYNAMIC THEORY

Strengths of Psychodynamic Theories

Psychodynamic theory is nothing less than a comprehensive description of human personality. This theory describes personality's development, the way personality functions, and every aspect of human thought, emotion, experience, and judgment—from dreams through slips of the tongue to normal and abnormal behavior.

Because of this, Freud is considered, along with Marx and Darwin, one of the great geniuses of the century. Perhaps the most important of his ideas is the view that the psychological processes that underlie normal and abnormal behaviors are fundamentally the same. Neither conflict, nor anxiety, nor defense, nor unconscious processes are the sole property of abnormal people. Rather, the *outcome* of conflict and the *nature* of defense will determine whether behavior will be normal or abnormal.

In addition, Freud developed a method for investigating psychodynamic processes and treating psychological distress. This was important for several reasons. First, his methods of investigation shed light on abnormal processes

FOCUS QUESTIONS

1. What are the strengths of psychodynamic theory?
2. What are the weaknesses of psychodynamic theory?

and thus demystified them. By accounting for why they behaved as they did, Freud "rehumanized" the distressed, making their suffering more comprehensible to the rest of humankind. Second, by providing a method of treatment, Freud encouraged an optimism regarding psychological distress that had been sorely lacking before him. Finally, while Freudian psychoanalysis must be distinguished sharply from modern psychodynamic therapies, the former was the progenitor of the modern efforts, and the modern therapies have been found to be quite effective (Smith, Glass, and Miller, 1980; Crits-Christoph, 1992; Gabbard, 1992).

Shortcomings of Psychodynamic Theories

Any theory that aspires to be as comprehensive as psychodynamic theory inevitably has faults, and Freud's theories and those of his successors have been no exception (see Table 4–5). We have already seen that not long after they were first enunciated, Freud's theories were attacked for several broad reasons (Gay, 1988). Over time, these deficiencies were remedied. But there are further criticisms of psychodynamic theory and therapy that have been more difficult to remedy: (1) the theory is simply too difficult to prove or disprove; (2) when studies have been conducted, psychodynamic theories have often failed to be supported; and (3) in emphasizing the role of the person, these theories neglect the situation. We will examine each of these criticisms in this section.

DIFFICULTIES OF PROOF

Psychodynamic theories are difficult to support or disprove. Some of the difficulty arises because they take complex views of personality and behavior. Many behaviors are held to be **overdetermined,** that is, determined by more than one force and with more than the required psychic energy. Altering a particular psychological force—for example, by recovering a crucial early memory—may have no visible effect on a particular trait or behavior because the latter are supported and sustained by many interrelated psychological forces.

Nevertheless, problems of proof are serious. Only rarely is it possible to confirm, for example, that a particular unconscious motive is really operating. Precisely because the motive is unconscious, it is invisible to the client and only **inferred** by the therapist. Even in Patty's case, where seeming confirmation was obtained because the headaches gradually disappeared, can we be sure

TABLE 4–5

EVALUATING PSYCHODYNAMIC THERAPY	
Strengths	*Weaknesses*
1. Provides a comprehensive description of human personality.	1. Difficult to disprove theories as behaviors are overdetermined and motives are inferred.
2. Psychological processes are the same in normal and abnormal behaviors.	2. Lack of scientific evidence.
3. Provides methodology for investigating and treating abnormal processes.	3. Underestimates role of situation and context, social class and gender.

that these changes were due to her increasing awareness of sexual motives and fears of abandonment? Might not the cure have arisen, with equal plausibility, from the fact that she had finally found someone whom she trusted and in whom she could confide?

LACK OF SCIENTIFIC EVIDENCE

Psychodynamic theories have been subjected to a variety of ingenious studies, many of which have failed to confirm the theories. Consider the Oedipus conflict, for example. The notion that boys desire to replace their fathers as their mothers' lovers has failed to find support in a variety of studies (Fisher and Greenberg, 1977). Similarly, the universality of castration anxiety remains to be demonstrated. Moreover, the idea that females, because they lack a penis, feel inferior to males has not been demonstrated either. Also, studies have not been able to prove Freud's notion that unresolved conflicts that occur during the oral stage of development are responsible for adult dependency. In short, many aspects of psychodynamic theories have yet to accrue sufficient scientific support to merit belief.

PERSON VERSUS SITUATION

Psychodynamic theories overwhelmingly emphasize the impact of traits and dispositions, those stable constellations of attitude and experience that are held to influence behavior. But what of situations? Because psychodynamic theories are derived mainly from information conveyed by clients during treatment, and because clients are encouraged to talk about their own reactions rather than the situation in which they find themselves, psychodynamic theory underestimates the role of situation and context. For example, it is much easier to infer that a person's continuing irritation with his employer results from unconscious and unresolved conflicts about authority when the employer's behavior has not been observed directly than when it has been. Similarly, it is easier to construe marital conflicts in terms of the traits of the spouse who has sought consultation precisely because one has no first-hand experience with that spouse's marital situation.

Freud's disciples, as well as modern psychodynamic theorists, have built on Freud's foundation. Many of his teachings have been found to be universally true. At the least, psychodynamic theory accords with everyday notions of personality. Most people believe, for example, that there is such a thing as the self, and they reflect that belief in their ordinary language when they say such things as "myself," "yourself," and "ourselves." They behave as if they and others are responsible, as if they are free to do what they will, as if their lives have meaning. Our laws reflect what each of us believes: that people act freely, for better or for worse, and that they are accountable for their actions. Rightly or wrongly, the modern psychodynamic perspective reflects a good deal of common sense.

SUMMARY

1. Psychodynamic theories are centrally concerned with conflict, anxiety, and defense. *Conflict* arises when desires cannot find immediate gratification because such gratification is not permitted by reality or conscience. Conflict generates *anxiety*, a form of psychic pain that arises when individ-

uals feel they cannot cope. Anxiety can be either conscious or unconscious and gives rise to *defense mechanisms,* which are the mind's flexible editing mechanisms that allow individuals to alter or entirely obliterate painful stimuli that arise from either desire or reality.

2. From birth to maturity, people move through five psychosexual stages, in which the use of *psychic energy* changes. The first is the *oral stage,* during which sensual pleasure is located around the mouth. Subsequently, they move through the *anal stage,* when pleasure is focused on the anus, and then the *phallic stage,* when pleasure is centered on the genitals. The *latency period* follows, during which time sexual instincts lie dormant. Individuals then emerge into the final stage of development, the *genital stage,* which marks the beginning of adult sexual functioning.

3. Adult sexual adjustment necessitates the child's resolution of the *Oedipal conflict.* Children desire to do away with the parent of the same sex and to take possession of the opposite-sex parent. *Castration anxiety* terminates the incestuous desire in boys. *Penis envy* is experienced by girls, who must also overcome their desire for the opposite-sex parent. *Identification* with the same-sex parent enables the child to resolve the Oedipus conflict.

4. Freud divided the personality into three kinds of processes: id, ego, and superego. The *id* is concerned with sexual and aggressive desires and is dominated by the *pleasure principle.* The *ego* is concerned with the individual's safety, allows desire to be expressed only when aversive consequences from other sources are minimal, and is dominated by the *reality principle.* The *superego* consists of the individual's conscience and ideals, and regardless of what reality permits, it either forbids individuals from expressing desires, or urges them toward the achievement of higher goals.

5. Freud proposed three levels of consciousness: perceptual consciousness, the preconscious, and the unconscious. The large mass of memory, experience, and impulse lies in the unconscious, which includes forgotten memories and repressed memories. Repressed memories live on because they are not subject to rational control; they are the dominant forces in personality.

6. There are three kinds of anxiety: realistic anxiety, neurotic anxiety, and moral anxiety. To relieve anxiety, individuals use such coping strategies as repression, projection, reaction formation, displacement, identification, denial, isolation, intellectualization, rationalization, and sublimation. Psychodynamic theorists believe that there is a maturational hierarchy of coping strategies and classify the strategies into four levels of maturity. Those that do less violence to reality are considered to be more mature strategies.

7. Jung asserted that the unconscious is not merely a concealed storehouse of sexual and aggressive desires, but that it contains a rich variety of attributes. Among these are the *collective unconscious,* which contains the memory traces of the experiences of past generations in the form of *archetypes,* or universal ideas.

8. Adler, Horney, Sullivan, Erikson, and Fromm stressed the impact of *social* relationships on psychological development, as well as the central role of ego processes in personality. According to these later theorists, ego

processes have energies of their own which generate goals that are neither sexual nor aggressive.

9. Modern psychodynamic theorists stress the importance of the *self* as the repository of values and the source of continuity across time and place. There are at least three significant aspects of self: the physical self, the subjective self, and the objective self. Self-objects are people and things that are especially important for maintaining the self.

10. Existentialists believe that the fundamental anxiety is *fear of death.* Psychologically, death means nonbeing. Because the fear of death is so threatening, people attempt to endow themselves with immortality by becoming *special* or by *fusion* with others, which may lead to *inauthentic,* or false, modes of behavior.

11. Existential theorists hold that we are the authors of our experience. We determine what we perceive and what we experience; we are *responsible* for how we behave. Freedom and responsibility, however, may create anxiety. Responsibility avoidance is occasionally achieved through denying ownership of behavior and thought. In extreme form, that denial appears as "craziness" or drunkenness, which are purposeful behaviors designed to make it seem that we are not responsible.

12. Existentialists often posit two kinds of will: *exhortative will* forces us to do what we know we should do, and *goal-directed will* is unleashed when we have freely chosen our goals and want to pursue and achieve them.

13. Psychodynamic therapies seek to make conscious that which is unconscious through encouraging the client to *free associate* and to examine dreams, resistances, and the *transference* that occurs between the client and therapist. Psychodynamic treatment aims to enable the client to reduce the amount of psychic energy that is invested in defensive maneuvers, and to achieve greater control over impulse expression.

14. *Client-centered* therapy stresses the role of *unconditional positive regard* and therapist empathy and warmth in enabling people to overcome their defensiveness and to begin to clarify and accept their own experiences.

15. Psychodynamic theories have demystified psychological processes and have offered the possibility of overcoming psychological distress. But critics cite difficulties of proof, their indifference to the scientific method and scientific proof, and their disregard of the situation.

QUESTIONS FOR CRITICAL THINKING

1. Describe how conflicts at the various stages of psychosexual development can lead to psychological problems later in life.

2. How does an overly strong id or superego lead to psychological problems?

3. What are the various ways that repressed thoughts can emerge in the conscious mind?

4. Which coping strategies are likely to lead to positive functioning, and which to maladjustment?

CHAPTER 5

The Learning Models:
Behavioral and Cognitive Approaches

CHAPTER ORGANIZER

HISTORY AND ASSUMPTIONS OF THE LEARNING MODEL
- Learn what the assumptions of behaviorism are.

BEHAVIORAL PSYCHOLOGY: PRINCIPLES AND THERAPIES
- Become familiar with the basic Pavlovian and operant phenomena and how specific therapies have been derived from them.

COGNITIVE THERAPY: PRINCIPLES AND APPLICATIONS
- Understand the importance of thoughts to the cognitive view and the therapies that have been derived from this view.

COMBINING COGNITIVE-BEHAVIORAL THERAPY AND PSYCHODYNAMICS
- Discover how some psychodynamically oriented psychologists have used cognitively oriented concepts to develop a new kind of psychodynamic therapy.

EVALUATING THE BEHAVIORAL AND COGNITIVE MODELS
- Examine the strengths and weaknesses of the behavioral and cognitive models.

s schizophrenia the result of conflicts over mother, or is it an inherited malady? Are phobias learned, or are they merely innate fears rekindled by environmental trauma? Is mental retardation acquired, or is it inherited from one's parents? Questions of this type bring to the forefront one of the major debates in psychology: the nature-nurture issue. Is our behavior determined by heredity or by our environment? The learning model takes a clear stand on these issues. It asserts that mental life and mental illness are a product of environmental learning and can be changed by changing the environment. This model includes both behavioral and cognitive theory. After discussing the common roots of these two arms of the learning model, we will discuss behavior therapy in the first half of this chapter, and then cognitive therapy.

HISTORY AND ASSUMPTIONS OF THE LEARNING MODEL

Empiricism and Associations

The seventeenth-century French philosopher, René Descartes (1596–1650), founded a movement called rationalism. Its adherents believed that many of the basic ideas that human beings hold—the ideas of self, of God, of space, of time, of causality—are inborn. This was called the *doctrine of innate ideas.* In contrast, the British empiricists believed that all knowledge comes from the senses, that all that we know and all that we are result from our experiences. John Locke (1632–1704), one of the founders of empiricism, claimed that at birth the mind of the child is a *tabula rasa,* a blank slate, on which experience "writes." A child's development is determined by what gets "written." If a certain child had had a wholly different set of experiences, he would be a wholly different person. But how does this child learn about the world? The empiricists answer "through associations." Associations between ideas are the mental glue holding the future to the present. David Hume (1711–1776), the most influential of the empiricists, claimed that the connections we make between ideas reduce to two simple principles: resemblance and contiguity. Through *resemblance,* the idea of a portrait of any individual looks like and therefore makes us think of the real individual. Through the principle of *contiguity,* or conjunction in time or place, imagining one part of a face will call up images of the rest of the face. For Hume, causality reduces to contiguity: we believe that A causes B, when each A is followed by a B. Since all knowledge consists only of ideas derived from the senses, and associations between ideas come only from our experience, it follows that we are creations of our environment, of our past. It was out of this empiricist tradition that behaviorism grew. And out of behaviorism that both behavior therapy and then cognitive therapy grew.

Behaviorism

A single movement—*behaviorism*—dominated academic psychology in the United States and Soviet Russia for almost fifty years, roughly from 1920 until the mid-1960s. Behaviorism is an ambitious effort to discover in the laboratory the general laws of human and animal learning and to apply these laws to the classroom, the workplace, the penitentiary, and to society as a whole. Thus, behaviorism is not only a model for the study of abnormal behavior, it is a world view. Its first assumption is *environmentalism,* which states that all organisms, including humans, are shaped by the environment. We learn about the future through the associations of the past. This is why our behavior is subject to rewards and punishments. If our employers paid us twice as much per hour for working one Saturday, we would be more likely to work on future Saturdays. If a child were denied T.V. for not eating her vegetables, her plate would be cleaned more often in the future.

The second assumption of behaviorism is *experimentalism,* which states that through an experiment, we can find out what aspect of the environment caused our behavior and how we can change it. If the crucial element is withheld, the present characteristic will disappear. If the crucial element is reinstated, the characteristic will reappear. For example, what causes us to work on Saturdays? Remove double-time pay, and work on Saturday will stop. Reinstate double-time pay, and work on Saturday will resume. This is the heart of the experimental method. From the experimental method, we can determine what causes people, in general, to forget, to be anxious, to fight, and we can then apply these general laws to individual cases. This is in contrast to the clinical method, which pervades the psychodynamic model. For the clinical model, the individual case must first be understood, and general laws then extrapolated. For the environmentalist it is the other way around.

behaviorism
① environmentalism
organisms shaped
by environ

② experimentalism
through experience
can find out what
part of environ
cause behavior + how
to change it

③ optimism
change

④ anti mentalism
mental events-feelings, +
thoughts not valid
objects of scientific
inquiry

▶ The child's development is affected by the environment. If that environment changes, the whole course of the child's life may be changed. When applied to social sciences, behaviorism claims that crime, prejudice, and stupidity can be overcome respectively by spreading wealth, learning, and environmental enrichment.

The third assumption of behaviorism is **optimism** concerning change. If an individual is a product of the environment and if those parts of the environment that have molded him can be known by experimentation, he will be changed when the environment is changed. When applied to social problems, behaviorism claims that crime is caused by poverty and other environmental circumstances and that it can be overcome by spreading wealth, that prejudice is caused by ignorance and can be overcome by learning, that stupidity is caused by deprivation and can be overcome by environmental enrichment, and so on.

These first three assumptions of behaviorism apply directly to abnormal psychology. First, abnormal as well as normal behavior is learned from past experiences. Psychopathology consists of acquired habits that are maladaptive. Second, we can find out by experiment what aspects of the environment cause abnormal behavior. Third, if we change these aspects of the environment the individual will unlearn his old, maladaptive habits and will learn new, adaptive habits.

There is also a fourth assumption of behaviorism: **anti-mentalism,** which is a view that mental events, feelings, and thoughts are not valid objects of scientific inquiry. While the environmentalism, experimentation, and optimism of behaviorism can all be traced directly to British empiricism, the disdain for mental events is behaviorism's very own. The empiricists were thoroughgoing mentalists; they believed that the building blocks of knowledge were mental ideas subject to introspection. (In fact, cognitive psychology, which we will discuss in the latter part of this chapter as the other pillar of the environmentalist model, is a science of mental events directly traceable to the empiricists.) The behaviorists, however, led in the 1920s by John B. Watson, reacted against the idea that an objective science could be built on an analysis of consciousness carried out by introspection. Consciousness, Watson argued, is not a material object, and the objects of science must be material. He believed that mental events do not cause behavior, and he further argued that introspection was not an objective method. Thoughts and feelings are essentially private and un-

verifiable. In contrast, behavior is material, and the study of behavior must be public and verifiable.

Behaviorism was founded on these four premises and it reigned supreme in academic psychology for fifty years. We now turn to the principles of behavioral psychology and to behavior therapy.

BEHAVIORAL PSYCHOLOGY: PRINCIPLES AND THERAPIES

How do we learn and what is it we learn? For the behavioral psychologist, two basic learning processes exist, and it is from these two that all behaviors, both normal and abnormal, derive. We can learn what goes with what through **Pavlovian** or **classical conditioning.** And we can learn what to do to obtain what we want and rid ourselves of what we do not want through **instrumental** or **operant conditioning.**

Pavlovian Conditioning

Just after the turn of the century, the Russian physiologist Ivan Pavlov (1849–1936) began work on a phenomenon that would change the nature of psychology. Pavlov was studying the digestive system of dogs, specifically the salivary reflex. He received the Nobel Prize in 1904 for his studies of digestive physiology. During his experiments, he would put food powder in the dog's mouth, and he would then measure the drops of saliva by way of a tube surgically inserted into the dog's mouth. But in the course of his work, Pavlov noticed that dogs began to salivate merely when he walked into the room. This salivation could not be a reflex since it did not occur the first few times Pavlov walked in; it only occurred once the dog had learned that Pavlov's appearance signaled food. That is, Pavlov's appearance became associated with a future event: food. He called this a psychic reflex, or a conditional reflex, since it was conditional upon past experience. It has come to be called, through mistrans-

lation, a ***conditioned response,*** or **CR.** A typical Pavlovian conditioning experiment goes as follows: we know that food (unconditioned stimulus, US) produces salivation (unconditioned response, UR)

$$\text{US (food)} \rightarrow \text{UR (salivation)}$$

We present a tone just prior to presenting the food. Because the tone itself does not produce salivation, it is a neutral stimulus. But after pairing the tone with the food several times we discover that salivation will occur upon presentation of the tone. The tone can now be called a conditioned stimulus (CS) because it produces salivation, the conditioned response (CR). In short:

$$\text{CS (tone)} \rightarrow \text{US (food)} \rightarrow \text{UR (salivation)}$$

After several pairings of CS and US:

$$\text{CS (tone)} \rightarrow \text{CR (salivation)}$$

This kind of experiment has been carried out using many species (Siamese fighting fish, rats, dogs, and humans), conditioned stimuli (tones, lights, tastes), and unconditioned responses (salivation, fear, nausea). It also can be used in therapeutic situations to eliminate unsatisfactory behaviors. For example, Pavlovian conditioning might be used to treat a foot fetishist, as in the following case:

> Steven has been in trouble with the police for fondling strange women's shoes in public places. He is a foot fetishist with strong erotic attachment to women's feet and footwear. He agrees to undergo Pavlovian therapy rather than go to jail.
>
> In the therapist's office, Steven fondles women's shoes. He then drinks ipecac, a drug that causes him to become nauseated in a few minutes. He vomits. A week later, the same procedure is repeated. The shoes are the CS, the US is ipecac, and the UR is nausea and vomiting. After several sessions the pairing of shoes and vomiting produces a major change in Steven's sexual preferences. He is no longer aroused by women's shoes, and he throws away his collection of five thousand pictures of shoes.

▶ Ivan Pavlov (1849–1936).

1. Describe how the conditioned stimulus leads to the conditioned response in Pavlovian conditioning.
2. Explain the following basic Pavlovian processes:
   • acquisition
   • extinction
   • stimulus generalization
   • discrimination
3. Describe how a phobia could result from Pavlovian conditioning.
4. Distinguish between flooding and systematic desensitization.

THE BASIC PAVLOVIAN PHENOMENA

There are two processes in Pavlovian conditioning that occur time and time again, regardless of what species, what kind of CS or US, or what kind of a response is tested. Pavlov discovered both: acquisition and extinction.

Acquisition is the learning of a response based on the contingency between a CS and US. Depending on the response to be learned, acquisition usually takes from three to fifteen pairings. *Extinction* is the loss of the CS's power to produce the formerly acquired resp+onse. This is brought about by presenting the CS, and no longer following it with the US. For example, it is possible to condition fear in humans. Fear can be measured by increased heart rate, perspiration, and muscle tension. When mild shocks (US) are given to humans, these measures become evident, that is, pain (UR) is produced. After several pairings of tone (CS) and shock (US), the tone (CS) alone begins to elicit fear (CR). That is what we call acquisition. But if we now repeatedly present the tone (CS) no longer followed with the shock (US), the individual no longer shows signs of fear. The tone (CS) no longer signals a shock (US). We call this process extinction.

In addition, there are two phenomena concerned with the stimulus properties of the CS. If the person has the CS of a high tone paired with shock, and then hears a lower-pitched tone, he may show a modified conditioned response to this new, but similar tone. This is called *stimulus generalization,* or the tendency of a response that has been conditioned to one stimulus to occur to similar stimuli. The more dissimilar the new stimulus from the original, the weaker will be the CR. Steven, for example, after becoming conditioned to pair women's shoes with vomiting, may show stimulus generalization to feet and become nauseated when imaging naked women's feet.

If a person has experienced the CS of a high tone paired with shock and a low tone repeatedly followed by no shock, he will give a CR to the high tone, but learn to give no CR to the low tone. This is *discrimination,* or showing a CR to a CS that has been paired with a US while showing no CR to similar stimuli that have been paired with the absence of the US. So, if Steven had ipecac after fondling shoes, but no ipecac after fondling boots, he would discriminate the two, becoming nauseated when imaging shoes but feeling fine when imaging boots.

PAVLOVIAN CONDITIONING, EMOTIONS, AND PSYCHOPATHOLOGY

There are situations in the world that arouse strong emotions in us. Some of these arouse the emotion *unconditionally,* or from our very first encounter with them: a loud clap of thunder startles us the very first time we hear it. Other objects acquire emotional significance: the face of a person we love produces a sense of well-being; seeing a stranger in a dark alleyway arouses dread. Pavlovian conditioning provides a powerful account of how objects take on emotional significance; it is this account that makes conditioning of great interest to the student of abnormality.

According to the behavioral account, the basic mechanism for all acquired emotional states is the pairing of a neutral object (CS) with an unconditioned emotional state (US). With enough pairings, the neutral object will lose its neutrality, become a CS, and all by itself produce the emotional state (CR). Consider the case of a child who is continually beaten with a tan hairbrush by his father. Before the beatings, the child had no feelings about the brush whatsoever. But, after several beatings (US), the brush becomes a CS and merely seeing the tan brush produces fear (CR).

If normal emotions are acquired in this way, the same should be true of acquired emotional disorders. Several of the psychopathological disorders explored in the following chapters involve the acquisition of an exaggerated or unusual emotional state in regard to inappropriate objects (see Figure 5–1). For example, phobias are said to be a result of Pavlovian conditioning. A ***phobia*** is a fear greatly out of proportion to how dangerous the phobic object actually is. For example, a cat phobic had a history of cats (CS) paired with painful events such as being scratched (US). As a result, cats became terrifying to the phobic individual, despite the fact that cats generally are not dangerous.

Here we can contrast the behavioral view of what causes emotional disorders with the biomedical model and the psychodynamic model. According to the behavioral view, the symptom of the disorder *is* the disorder. In the case above, the phobic individual's fear of cats is the disorder. There is no underlying pathological state that produces the symptoms. For the biomedical model, an underlying pathology such as a "virus," a disordered biochemistry, or a dysfunctional organ causes the symptoms. For the psychodynamic view, an intrapsychic conflict, usually sexual or aggressive in nature and stemming from childhood fixations, causes the symptoms.

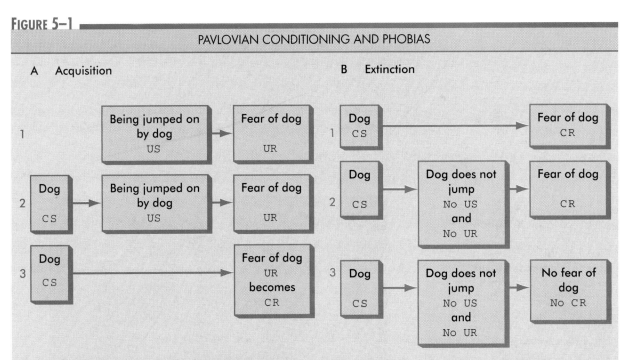

FIGURE 5–1

PAVLOVIAN CONDITIONING AND PHOBIAS

A   Acquisition

B   Extinction

A person who has a phobia has an exaggerated emotional reaction to an object. The person is terrified of the phobic object and unable to function in its presence. Pavlovian conditioning explains that the phobia is acquired when a neutral object (CS) is repeatedly paired with an unconditioned emotional state (US) until it loses its neutrality and evokes a conditioned fear response (CR) from the phobic person. Therapy consists of extinguishing the phobia by continuous pairing of the phobic object (CS) without the original trauma (US–UR) until the fear of the object (CR) is eliminated.

The therapeutic optimism of the behavioral view follows directly from its view of the cause of the disorder. If the disorders are the symptoms and do not reflect an underlying pathology, eliminating the symptoms will cure the disorder. Since the symptoms of emotional disorders are emotional responses acquired by Pavlovian conditioning, it follows that those techniques that have been found experimentally to extinguish conditioned emotional responses will cure emotional disorders. This contrasts with the biomedical and psychodynamic stance on therapy: for these models, getting rid of the symptoms is not enough; cure consists of removing the underlying disorder. For example, treating the symptoms of general paresis instead of attacking the syphilitic spirochete would not help much, for the underlying pathological process would remain intact. A strong test, then, of the behavioral view as opposed to the biomedical and psychodynamic views of emotional disorders would be whether the symptoms can be removed by extinction procedures, and whether other emotional problems will then occur, reflecting an uncured underlying pathology, after behavior therapy has removed one set of symptoms (see Chapter 8).

THE PAVLOVIAN THERAPIES

In the chapters on phobias and sexual dysfunction, we will look in detail at the therapies involving Pavlovian extinction of emotional disorders. But, some of the specific therapies should be briefly mentioned now.

Two Pavlovian therapies involving extinction have been applied to phobias and other anxiety disorders. In *flooding,* or *exposure,* the phobic patient is immersed in the phobic situation (either real or imagined) for several consecutive hours. For example, a claustrophobic (who is terrified of being in small enclosed places) would be placed in a closet (CS); the original trauma (US) would not occur, and the fear of being enclosed would diminish (Stampfl and Levis, 1967; Marks, 1969). Or a rape victim with post-traumatic stress disorder would be told to imagine the rape and to narrate the story repeatedly, in detail, and with emotion, to the therapist. The CS's here are sex, men, and the place, all of which produce terror after the rape, but the original trauma (US) no

▶ Pavlovian emotional conditioning begins with the pairing of an object or an event with an emotional state. The experience of being under water while being held and reassured by their parents increases the chances that these babies will enjoy swimming and decreases the chances that they will be afraid of water.

▲ In this mild form of flooding, or *exposure,* a child who has acquired a fear of dogs is gently prodded toward one. Upon learning that the dog no longer presents danger, the child's fear of dogs disappears.

Operant conditioning *punishment or* *reward*

longer occurs. This treatment diminishes anxiety symptoms (Foa, Rothbaum, Riggs, and Murdock, 1991).

In another kind of Pavlovian therapy, ***systematic desensitization*** (developed by Joseph Wolpe, then a South African psychiatrist), the phobic patient would imagine a set of gradually more frightening scenes involving the phobic object (CS), at the same time as he would be making a response incompatible with fear. Pavlovian extinction would occur with this exposure to the CS (thoughts about and eventually the actual phobic object) without the US (original trauma) and the UR (terror) (Wolpe, 1969).

Pavlovian conditioning, then, provides a theory of how we normally learn to feel a given emotion toward a given object. By applying its basic phenomena to emotional disorders, we can arrive at a theory of how emotional disorders come about, and we can deduce a set of therapies that should undo abnormal emotional responses.

Operant Conditioning

At about the same time that Pavlov discovered an objective way of studying how we learn "what goes with what," Edward L. Thorndike (1874–1949) began to study objectively how we learn "what to do to get what we want." Thorndike was studying animal intelligence. In one series of experiments he put hungry cats in puzzle boxes and observed how they learned to escape confinement and get food. He designed various boxes—some had levers to push, others had strings to pull, and some had shelves to jump on—and he left food—often fish—outside the box. The cat would have to make the correct response to escape from the puzzle box.

Thorndike's first major discovery was that learning what to do was gradual, not insightful. That is, the cat proceeded by trial and error. On the first few trials, the time to escape was very long; but with repeated success, the time gradually shortened to a few seconds. To explain his findings, Thorndike formulated the "law of effect." Still a major principle, this holds that when, in a given stimulus situation, a response is made and followed by positive consequences, the response will tend to be repeated; when followed by negative consequences, it will tend not to be repeated. Thorndike's work, like Pavlov's, was an objective way of studying the properties of learning.

This tradition was refined, popularized, and applied to a range of real-life settings by B. F. Skinner (1904–1990), who worked largely with rats pressing levers for food and with pigeons pecking lighted discs for grain. It was Skinner who formulated the basic concepts of operant conditioning.

THE CONCEPTS OF OPERANT CONDITIONING

Through his basic concepts, Skinner defined the elements of the law of effect rigorously. His three basic concepts consist of the reinforcer (both positive and negative), the operant, and the discriminative stimulus.

A ***positive reinforcer*** is an event whose onset increases the probability that a response preceding it will occur again. In effect, a positive reinforcer rewards behavior. A ***negative reinforcer*** is an event whose removal increases the probability of recurrence of a response that precedes it. ***Punishers,*** on the other hand, are events whose onset will decrease the probability of recurrence of a response that precedes it. The same stimulus whose onset acts as a punisher will usually act as a negative reinforcer when removed.

An ***operant*** is a response whose probability can either be increased by positive reinforcement or decreased by negative reinforcement. If a mother reinforces her twelve-month-old child with a hug every time he says "Daddy," the probability that he will say it again is increased. In this case, the operant is "saying Daddy." If the mother hugs the child for saying Daddy only when the child's father is in sight, and does not hug him for saying Daddy when the father is not around, she is teaching the child to respond to a discriminative stimulus. In this case, the father being in sight is the ***discriminative stimulus,*** a signal that means that reinforcement is available if the operant is made.

THE OPERANT PHENOMENA

Acquisition and Extinction The phenomena of ***acquisition*** and ***extinction*** in the operant conditioning of voluntary responses parallel the Pavlovian conditioning of involuntary responses. Consider a typical operant paradigm. A hungry rat is placed inside an operant chamber. The desired operant is the pressing of a lever. Each time the rat presses a lever, food is delivered down a chute. During this acquisition procedure, learning to lever press proceeds gradually, as shown in Figure 5–2. It takes about ten sessions for the rat to learn to press at a high and constant rate. Extinction is then begun (in session 22), and the reinforcer (food) is no longer delivered when the rat presses the lever. As a result, responding gradually diminishes back to zero.

▲ Edward L. Thorndike (1874–1949) studied animal intelligence and formulated the "law of effect."

▼ B. F. Skinner (1904–1990) formulated the basic concepts of operant conditioning.

FIGURE 5–2

ACQUISITION AND EXTINCTION

This typical curve depicts the growth in the frequency of lever pressing over the course of a number of experimental sessions, followed by its extinction when reinforcement is discontinued. (SOURCE: Adapted from Schwartz 1984)

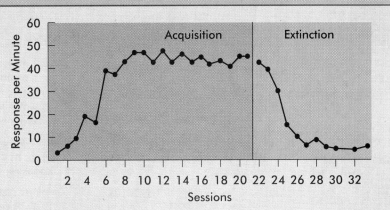

Partial Reinforcement and Schedules of Reinforcement An operant experimenter can arrange a rich variety of contingencies between the responses that his subjects make and the reinforcers they receive. In the simplest contingency, each and every time a subject makes a response a reinforcer is delivered. This is called *continuous reinforcement (CRF).* For example, every time the rat presses a lever, a food pellet arrives. In the real world, however, reinforcements do not usually come with such high consistency. More often, reinforcements only occur for some of the responses that are made, and many responses are in vain. To capture this, the experimenter arranges the contingencies such that reinforcement is delivered for only some of the responses that the subject makes. This is called a *partial* or *intermittent reinforcement* schedule. So, for example, the rat might receive one food pellet only when he has pressed the bar fifty times, rather than for each press.

Partial reinforcement schedules make initial learning slower, but these schedules have two other properties that are important for engineering human behavior. In the first place, a great deal of work can be produced for very little payoff. So, for one small food pellet, a rat or a person can be made to

▶ Winning at cards is a positive reinforcer for this little girl. She will probably play cards with the boys again in the future.

TABLE 5–1

OPERANT THERAPY			
Maladaptive Behavior	*Reinforcers That Maintain Behavior*	*Therapy*	*Response*
Not eating by anorexic	Staying thin	Selective positive reinforcement (e.g., anorexic not allowed to watch television until she has eaten)	Eating
Self-mutilation by autistic child	Self-stimulation	Selective punishment (e.g., pinches, spanking, cold water)	No self-mutilation
Hitting brother	Attention from parent	Selective punishment (e.g., television turned off)	No hitting brother
Patient disrupting nurses at nurses' station	Attention from nurses	Extinction (nurses ignore patient)	No disruptive visits

emit hundreds of responses. The second property has to do with extinction and is called the ***partial reinforcement extinction effect.*** After a subject has been partially reinforced for a response, and extinction (consisting of no reinforcement at all) has begun, a surprisingly large number of responses will occur before the subject gives up. A rat who had responded on a partial reinforcement schedule in which it pressed the lever fifty times in order to get one reinforcement will respond hundreds of times during extinction before it quits. In contrast, a rat who has had continuous reinforcement and whose behavior is then extinguished will stop pressing after only five to ten attempts.

Maladaptive human behavior in the real world is often highly resistant to extinction in the same way that partially reinforced operant behavior is in the laboratory. For example, a compulsive "checker" who fears that she left the gas in the stove on may check the stove hundreds of times a day. She is reinforced very little; that is, she almost never checks and finds that the gas is on. Most of her responding is in vain. The operant explanation of her behavior is partial reinforcement. Because once every several hundred times she was reinforced by finding the gas on, she will now check thousands of times in order to get one reinforcer (Rachman and Hodgson, 1980).

THE OPERANT THERAPIES

The operant therapist uses these principles in asking three essential questions: (1) What undesirable behavior or maladaptive operants does the patient engage in? (2) What reinforcers maintain these maladaptive responses? (3) What environmental changes, usually reinforcement or discriminative stimulus changes, can be made to change the maladaptive behavior into adaptive behavior? (Ullmann and Krasner, 1965). A variety of operant therapies have been employed for a variety of forms of psychopathology (see Table 5–1). We will look at a selection of them now and others will be discussed in more detail in the chapters that involve the specific disorders that these therapies treat.

▼ In baseball, as at school and home, a coach's consistent positive reinforcement teaches children what is expected of them.

▶ This autistic boy is fed each time he hits the drum with the stick. This use of selective positive reinforcement targets one of his symptoms—lack of social interaction—for change into adaptive behavior.

FOCUS QUESTIONS

1. Describe the basic concepts of operant conditioning:
   • positive reinforcer
   • negative reinforcer
   • punishers
   • operants
   • discriminative stimulus
   • schedules of reinforcement
2. Explain why maladaptive human behavior in the real world is often highly resistant to extinction.
3. Describe how the techniques of selective positive reinforcement and selective punishment can be used to treat maladaptive target behaviors.
4. What two relationships are learned in an avoidance situation?

Selective Positive Reinforcement   In the technique of selective positive reinforcement, the therapist selects a ***target behavior*** or adaptive behavior that is to be increased in probability. By the systematic delivery of positive reinforcement contingent on the occurrence of the target behavior, this behavior becomes more frequent.

Anorexia nervosa is a life-threatening disorder that, for the most part, afflicts women in their teens and early twenties. They literally starve themselves to death. By engaging in bizarre eating habits, such as eating only three Cheerios a day, an anorexic will lose 25 to 30 percent of her body weight within a couple of months. When they are hospitalized, the first problem with these patients (who may weigh as little as seventy-five pounds) is not curing them, but just saving their lives. Such patients usually do not cooperate with regimes that attempt to force them to eat. One highly effective way of saving the life of an anorexic woman is selectively to reinforce her for eating by using a reinforcer that is more highly desired than is eating. But, if you ask her what would be a reward that would induce her to eat, she will probably not tell you. In order to discover what is positively reinforcing, a therapist will look for a behavior that the patient engages in frequently and will only give her the opportunity to perform it if she first eats (Premack, 1959). If we observe and time what an anorexic does during the day, we might find, for example, that she watches television for an hour and a half, spends forty-five minutes talking with fellow patients, and spends an hour pacing the halls. An operant therapist would then set up a regime such that in order to be allowed to do any one of these three activities, the anorexic would first have to eat a fixed amount. For example, if she first ate a tablespoon of custard, she would then be allowed to watch television for ten minutes; if she ate all of her steak, she would then be allowed to pace the halls for twenty minutes (Stunkard, 1976).

During thirty years of research, selective positive reinforcement has been shown to be an effective technique across a very wide range of behavioral disorders. When a discrete and specifiable instrumental response is missing from the adaptive repertoire of an individual, application of selective positive reinforcement will generally produce and maintain that response.

Selective Punishment   In *selective punishment,* or selective negative reinforcement procedures, the therapist selects a target behavior that is maladaptive. By applying an aversive event when this target behavior occurs, the therapist causes its probability of occurrence to decrease.

Although we are not sure why, some autistic children engage in self-mutilation.* This maladaptive behavior is persistent, and most attempts at intervention on the part of a therapist will produce no or only temporary effects. In some of these cases, operant therapists have applied selective punishment. In one particular case, whenever the autistic child hit himself, a shock was delivered to him. The child soon learned that his behavior brought punishment, and he engaged less often in self-mutilation (Lovaas and Simmons, 1969; Dorsey, Iwata, Ong, and McSween, 1980). This procedure did not cure the child's autism, but it did stop his maladaptive behavior.

Punishment in the form of pinches, spanks, and cold water is now widely used to curtail the self-destructive behavior of autistic children. Punishment in this form strikes some people as cruel, and the Office for Children of the State of Massachusetts barred the use of such punishments in a school for autistic children in 1986. The children promptly regressed to their self-destructive behavior, and their parents went to court to overturn the ban, claiming that this was the only effective treatment their children had ever received. The court overturned the ban, charging that, out of sentimentalism, the Office for Children had played "Russian Roulette with the lives and safety of the students" by banning selective punishment (*New York Times,* June 5, 1986).

Extinction   Punishment involves imposing some noxious event on the patient, such as a loud noise, an electric shock, or a nausea-inducing drug. Even though such stimuli can be highly effective in removing unwanted behaviors, there are obvious undesirable aspects to such therapy. For example, patients may come to find the entire therapeutic setting aversive. Or many therapists, quite understandably, may feel uncomfortable with shocking, nauseating, and otherwise scaring fellow human beings, particularly those already burdened with psychological problems. Extinction is sometimes an alternative strategy: one can eliminate a behavior by merely omitting some highly desired event whenever the target behavior occurs.

The most common use of extinction in behavior therapy is when the therapist suspects that some maladaptive target behavior is being performed in order to get some positive reinforcement. The therapist then arranges the contingencies so that this behavior no longer produces the reinforcement. If the behavior decreases in frequency, extinction has been successful. For example, there was a case of a female psychotic patient who would make numerous disruptive visits to the nurses' office on the ward. An operant therapist believed that the attention the patient received from the nurses when she barged into their office was a positive reinforcer that maintained the disruptive behavior. So the therapist instructed the nurses to ignore the patient completely when the patient entered their office, thereby eliminating what was believed to be positive reinforcement. After seven weeks of treatment, the patient's visits dropped from an average of sixteen per day to two per day (Ayllon and Michel, 1959).

---

*Autism is characterized by severe social withdrawal (see Chapter 16).

Avoidance Learning

As we have seen, learning theorists regard human beings as capable of learning two sorts of relationships: the Pavlovian relationship—what goes with what—and the operant relationship—what to do in order to get what you want (see Table 5–2). There are many situations in which both sorts of learning go on at the same time. Prominent among such situations is learning to avoid aversive events. In an ***avoidance situation,*** two relationships have to be learned: (1) what predicts the aversive event, and (2) how to get away. The avoidance situation combines both a Pavlovian relationship and an operant relationship. To investigate avoidance, behavior theorists typically place a rat in a two-compartment chamber called a shuttlebox. After a while, a tone is turned on. Ten seconds after the tone has gone on, an electric shock is delivered through the floor of the apparatus. If the rat runs to the other side of the shuttlebox before the shock comes on, the tone terminates and the shock is prevented from occurring. Rats, dogs, and people usually learn to avoid shock altogether in these circumstances. In order to avoid the shock, the subject must learn two relationships (Mowrer, 1948; Rescorla and Solomon, 1967): (1) He must learn that the tone predicts shock, and he must become afraid of the tone. This is a Pavlovian relationship in which the CS is tone, the US is shock, and the CR is fear. (2) Having learned to fear the tone, he must learn what to do about it. He must learn that running to the other side of the shuttlebox terminates the fearful tone and prevents the shock from occurring. This is an operant relationship in which the discriminative stimulus is the tone, the operant is running to the other side of the shuttlebox, and the reinforcer is the termination of fear and the omission of shock.

An understanding of avoidance learning helps in the treatment of certain psychopathologies. The behavioral view of obsessive-compulsive disorders, for

TABLE 5–2

	Example of Problem	Origin	Therapy	Outcome
PAVLOVIAN VS. OPERANT THERAPIES				
Pavlovian Therapies	Fear (CR) of closed spaces (CS)	CS (closed space) associated with US (abuse)/UR (terror)	CS (closed space) presented without US (abuse)/UR (terror) through flooding or systematic desensitization	CS (closed space) no longer produces CR (debilitating fear)
Operant Therapies	No social skills	Insufficient rewards for acquiring operant response (social skills)	Desired operant response (social skills) is rewarded through selective positive reinforcement (e.g., gets ice cream after interacting with others)	Operant response (social skills) is learned; patient interacts better with others

example, involves the concept of avoidance learning. According to this view, the obsessive-compulsive checker believes that by engaging in the compulsive behavior of checking the stove several hundred times a day, she can prevent disaster from befalling her family. In this case, the occurrence and persistence of the compulsion may be explained by avoidance learning.

Behavior therapists often use both operant and Pavlovian relationships. Recall Steven, the foot fetishist who came to hate women's shoes after he received vomit-inducing ipecac. Whenever Steven made the operant response of reaching out to touch shoes, he felt queasy and withdrew his hand. By Pavlovian conditioning the sight and feel of shoes had become nauseating. By operant conditioning, Steven had learned that withdrawing his hand from the shoes would reduce his queasiness.

COGNITIVE PSYCHOLOGY: PRINCIPLES AND APPLICATIONS

The cognitive school is a modern outgrowth from, and reaction to, behaviorism. Implicit in the behavioral view is the assumption that the connection between the environment and behavior is direct. But over time, behaviorism has been challenged on this point, particularly by cognitive psychologists, who hold that behavior is influenced by more than just this direct relation between environment and response. Rather, cognitive psychologists contend that what a person thinks, believes, expects, attends to—in short, his or her mental life—influences how he or she behaves. Behaviorists, when pressed, frequently admit that mental life exists (Skinner, 1971). But they deny that such cognitions play a causal role in behavior. Rather, they dismiss cognitive processes, calling them *epiphenomena.* An epiphenomenon is a process that, while not causal, reflects the underlying process that is causal. A behaviorist who admits that mental processes exist likens them to the speedometer of an automobile. While a speedometer reflects how fast the automobile is going, it does not itself influence the speed.

Assumptions of the Cognitive View

The cognitive psychologist, as opposed to the behaviorist, believes that mental events are not mere epiphenomena, that cognitive processes influence behavior. Specifically, the cognitive psychologist contends that disordered cognitive processes cause some psychological disorders and that by changing these cognitions, the disorder can be alleviated and perhaps even cured.

The following case demonstrates the difference in emphasis between those holding the behavioral view and those holding the cognitive view:

> Two individuals have the same speaking skills, but one is very anxious when giving a public speech, and the other speaks with ease in public. On different occasions, each gives a public speech and, as is common during the course of almost any speech, a few members of the audience walk out of the room during each speech. When these two people record what they were thinking when a member of the audience walked out, a very different pattern emerges. The anxious individual thinks, "I must be boring. How much longer do I have to speak? This speech is

> going to be a failure." In contrast, the low-anxiety person says to herself, "The person walking out must have a class to make. Gee, that's too bad, he will miss the best part of my talk." The same environmental event—people walking out of the room during the speech—produces a very different set of thoughts: the high-anxiety individual has depressing and tension-inducing thoughts, whereas the low-anxiety individual does not. (Meichenbaum, 1977)

How do the behavioral and cognitive therapists look at this? On the one hand, the behaviorist will focus on the particular environmental event—people walking out during a speech—and how this affects behavior. (In this example the environmental event is the same, but the consequences are different.) The cognitive therapist, on the other hand, will focus on the difference in the *thoughts* of the two speakers, on how he or she *interprets* the event. For the cognitive therapist, a person's thoughts are of primary importance.

Cognitive Therapy

Underlying the cognitive model is the view that mental events—that is, expectations, beliefs, memories, and so on—can cause behavior. If these mental events are changed, behavior change will follow. Believing this, the cognitive therapist looks for the cause, or etiology, of psychological disorders in disordered mental events. For example, if someone is depressed, the cognitive therapist will look for the cause of the individual's depression in her beliefs or thoughts. Perhaps she believes that she has no control over the events of her life. Thinking that she has no control, the individual may well become passive, sad, and eventually clinically depressed. Successful therapy for such disorders will consist of changing these thoughts. In the case of the depressive, a cognitive therapist will draw out, analyze, and then help change the individual's thoughts, hoping to discover and then reverse the thoughts that caused the depressive's feeling of hopelessness.

To understand what a cognitive therapist does, let us return to the case study of the two speech givers. What if the high-anxiety speaker becomes increasingly depressed when he sees members of the audience walking out? He may label the speech, and himself, a failure. Perhaps he gets so depressed that he can no longer give a good speech, or worse, refuses to speak before an audience. Because of this problem, he may enter therapy. What will a cognitive therapist do?

Because a cognitive therapist is concerned primarily with what a person thinks and believes, he or she will inquire about the anxious speaker's thoughts. Upon finding out that the speaker thinks that he is boring his audience, the therapist will pursue two hypotheses. First, there is the hypothesis that the speaker in reality is boring. If, however, in the course of the therapy, the therapist learns that the person's speeches have in the past been received very well and that some have even been reprinted, the therapist will conclude that the first hypothesis is wrong.

After discarding the hypothesis that the speaker really is boring, the therapist will turn to the hypothesis that the speaker's thoughts are distorting reality. According to this hypothesis, the speaker is selecting negative evidence by focusing too narrowly on one event: he is thinking too much about those members of the audience who walked out. He believes that they think he is boring, that they dislike him, and so on. Here, the therapist gets the client to point out the contrary evidence. First, he has a fine speaking record. Second, only a very small number of people walked out; some probably had important appointments to catch and were glad to have heard at least part of the speech. Perhaps some of them were bored. But third, and most important, he minimized the fact that almost all of the audience remained, and he paid no attention to the fact that the audience applauded enthusiastically. The therapist's job is to draw out all of the distorted negative thoughts, to have the client confront the contrary evidence, and then to get the client to change these thoughts.

What kinds of mental events do cognitive therapists deal with? For the purposes of therapy, cognitive processes can be divided into short-term and long-term processes. The short-term processes are conscious. We are aware of them, or can become aware of them with practice. These include expectations, appraisals, and attributions. The long-term cognitive processes are not, generally speaking, available to consciousness. They are hypothetical constructs or dispositions that show themselves in the way they govern the short-term processes. One long-term process involves beliefs. We will discuss the short-term processes first.

OVERCOMING SELF-DEFEATING EXPECTATIONS

Expectations are cognitions that explicitly anticipate future events. The speech giver who, upon seeing a few people walk out, thought "this is going to be a failure" is reporting an expectation. He anticipates future consequences—in this case bad ones.

In his seminal work, Albert Bandura analyzed the notion of expectation and helped to usher in the cognitive school of therapy. In his early work, Bandura showed that people learned not only by direct reinforcement but also by observing others being reinforced. He concluded that the behavioral principles of reinforcement were insufficient and that such "vicarious learning" must involve the learning of expectations (Rotter, 1954; Bandura and Walters, 1959; Bandura, 1977a, 1978). For Bandura, a person in therapy has two kinds of expectancies: an ***outcome expectation*** is a person's estimate that a given behavior will lead to a desired outcome, and an ***efficacy expectation*** is the belief that he can successfully execute the behavior that produces the desired out-

[handwritten margin notes:]
expectations
① outcome
behavior → desired outcome

② efficacy
execute behavior → desired outcome

▼ Children's faces and gestures reflect their expectations of success or failure.

FOCUS QUESTIONS

1. Explain the importance of thoughts in the cognitive approach.
2. How does a cognitive therapist attempt to treat psychological disorders?
3. Describe cognitive therapeutic approaches to:
   - overcoming self-defeating expectations
   - modifying negative appraisals
   - changing attributions
   - overcoming irrational beliefs
4. What is multi-modal therapy?

come. Outcome and efficacy expectations are different because a person may be certain that a particular course of action will produce a given outcome, but he may doubt that he can perform this action. For example, he may realize that touching a snake will reduce his snake phobia, but he may still be unable to touch the snake. Bandura believes that the success of systematic desensitization and modeling therapies in curing phobias (Chapter 8) is attributable to changes in self-efficacy expectations. In both situations, the patient learns that he can make those responses—relaxation and approach—which will overcome the phobia. A "micro-analysis" of efficacy expectations and behavioral change in snake phobics has confirmed this speculation. Successful therapy created high efficacy expectations for approaching a boa constrictor. The higher the level of efficacy expectations at the end of treatment, the better was the approach behavior to the snake (Bandura, 1977a, 1982; Bandura and Adams, 1977; Staats, 1978; Biran and Wilson, 1981).

MODIFYING NEGATIVE APPRAISALS

We are constantly appraising and evaluating both what happens to us and what we do. These **appraisals** and evaluations are sometimes very obvious to us, but at other times we are unaware of them. For cognitive therapists, such automatic thoughts often precede and cause emotion (Beck, 1976). The speech giver becomes anxious and depressed once he thinks, "This is going to be a failure." He is not only expecting future consequences, he is also appraising his actions. He judges them to be failures, and this appraisal causes his negative emotions. This appraisal process is automatic. After a lifetime of practice, it occurs habitually and rapidly. The individual in therapy must be trained to slow down his thought process to become aware of such thoughts. Automatic thoughts are not vague and ill-formed, rather they are specific and discrete sentences. In addition, while they may seem implausible to the objective observer, they seem highly reasonable to the person who has them (see also Lazarus, 1976; Kanfer and Karoly, 1972; Mahoney and Thoresen, 1974; Rehm, 1978).

Test-anxious individuals are often found to make self-defeating appraisals. A student, for example, taking an examination may say to himself, "Look at that other student. She just left the room. She's much smarter than I am. My going so slowly means I will surely fail." In therapy, this person is taught to reappraise the situation: in short, to test his original appraisal of the event. "She left the room early because she didn't bother to check her answers. Chances are I probably won't fail. And even if I do people probably won't think I'm stupid. And even if they do that doesn't mean I *am* stupid." The goal of the therapist here is to get the individual to catch hold of his self-defeating thoughts as they come about, criticize them, control them, and thereby avoid the occurrence of anxiety (Goldfried, Decenteceo, and Wineburg, 1974; Goldfried, Linehan, and Smith, 1978; see also Langer, Janis, and Wolfer, 1975; Meichenbaum, 1977).

One instrument for discovering the frequency of automatic thoughts is the *Automatic Thoughts Questionnaire* (Hollon and Kendall, 1980). In answering its questions, clients record the frequency with which they make the following sorts of automatic appraisals of themselves, "I'm no good," "I'm so weak," "My life is a mess," "No one understands me," "It's just not worth it." The results show that when people are depressed, they have many more frequent negative automatic thoughts than when they are not depressed, and further, that these

thoughts are specific to depressives. Schizophrenics, substance abusers, and people with anxiety disorders do not record having frequent negative thoughts about themselves unless they are also depressed (Hollon, Kendall, and Lumry, 1986).

A major proponent of cognitive therapy, A. T. Beck (1976) argues that specific emotions are *always* preceded by discrete thoughts. Sadness is preceded by the thought "something of value has been lost." Anxiety is preceded by the thought "a threat of harm exists," and anger is preceded by the thought "my personal domain is being trespassed against." This is a sweeping and simple formulation of emotional life: the essence of sadness, anxiety, and anger consists of appraisals of loss, threat, and trespass, respectively. Thus, for cognitive therapists, modifying those thoughts will alter the emotion.

CHANGING ATTRIBUTIONS

Another kind of short-term mental event that cognitive therapists try to modify is attribution. An **attribution** is an individual's conception of *why* an event has befallen him. When a student fails an examination, he asks himself, "Why did I fail?" Depending on the causal analysis he makes, different consequences ensue. The student might make an **external** or **internal attribution** (Rotter, 1966). He might believe that the examination was unfair, an external cause. Alternatively, he might believe that he is stupid, an internal cause. A second dimension along which attributions for failure are made is **stable** or **unstable** (Weiner, 1974). A stable cause is one that persists in time; an unstable cause is one that is transient. For example, the student might believe that he failed because he did not get a good night's sleep, an unstable cause (which is also internal). Alternatively, the student might believe that he has no mathematical ability, a stable cause (which is also internal). Finally, an attribution for failure can be **global** or **specific** (Abramson, Seligman, and Teasdale, 1978; Seligman, 1991). An attribution to global factors means that failure must occur on many different tasks, and an attribution to specific factors means that failure must occur only on this task. For example, the student who fails might believe that he failed because he is stupid, a global cause (which is also stable and internal). Or he might believe that he failed because the form number of the test was 13, an unlucky number. This latter is a specific attribution (which is also external and stable). Table 5–3 presents these alternative attributions (Heider, 1958; Kelley, 1967; Weiner, 1972).

Cognitive therapists try to change an individual's attributions. For example, women with low self-esteem usually make internal attributions when they fail. They believe that they have failed because they are stupid, incompetent, and unlovable. To deal with this attribution, each week the therapist has them record five different bad events that have occurred during each week and then he has them write down *external* attributions for the events. For example, one woman might write, "my boyfriend criticized my behavior at a party last night, not because I am socially unskilled, but rather because he was in a bad mood." The goal is to get the woman to shift from internal to external what she believes to be the causes of bad events. After a few weeks, clients begin to see that there are alternative causes for their failures, and the low self-esteem and depression brought about by the internal attributions begin to lift (Beck et al., 1979).

CHANGING LONG-TERM BELIEFS

The short-term mental events that we have examined—expectations, appraisals, and attributions—are available to consciousness. Long-term cognitive processes are different. They are hypothetical constructs, inferred dispositions that govern the mental events now in consciousness. One of these long-term cognitive processes is ***beliefs.***

Albert Ellis, the founder of rational-emotive therapy, argues that psychological disorder stems largely from irrational beliefs. He gives an example of a

TABLE 5–3

ATTRIBUTIONS OF STUDENTS WHO DO POORLY ON THE GRADUATE RECORD EXAMINATION			
Internal		*External*	
Stable	*Unstable*	*Stable*	*Unstable*
Global Lack of intelligence	Exhaustion	ETS gives unfair tests.	Today is Friday the 13th.
(Laziness)	(Having a cold makes me stupid.)	(People are usually unlucky on the GRE.)	(ETS gave experimental tests this time that were too hard for everyone.)
Specific Lack of mathematical ability	Fed up with math problems	ETS gives unfair math tests.	The math test was form No. 13.
(Math always bores me.)	(Having a cold ruins my arithmetic.)	(People are usually unlucky on math tests.)	(Everyone's copy of the math test was blurred.)

NOTE: ETS = Educational Testing Service, the maker of graduate record examinations (GRE)
SOURCE: Abramson, Seligman, and Teasdale, 1978.

▲ Albert Ellis (1913–   ), founder of rational-emotive therapy, argues that psychological disorder stems largely from irrational beliefs.

client who, over the course of a lifetime, had had a set of destructive beliefs instilled in him by his parents and by society. Among these are the ideas that: (1) it is a dire necessity for an adult human being to be loved or approved by virtually every significant other person in his community; (2) one should be thoroughly competent, adequate, and achieving in all possible respects in order to be worthwhile; (3) it is awful and catastrophic when things are not the way one would very much like them to be; (4) human unhappiness is externally caused, and we have little or no ability to control our own sorrows; (5) our past history is an all-important determinant of our present behavior; if something once strongly affected our life, it should always have a similar effect; and (6) there is invariably a right, precise, and perfect solution to human problems, and it is catastrophic if this perfect solution is not found (Ellis, 1962).

These irrational and illogical beliefs shape the short-term distorted expectations, appraisals, and attributions that produce psychological disorder. The client is afflicted with a "tyranny of should's," and the job of the therapist is to break the hold of these "should's." Once the patient abandons the above beliefs, it is impossible for him to remain disturbed. The job of the therapist is to rid the individual of these beliefs. The therapy is an aggressive one. It makes a concerted attack on the client's beliefs in two ways: (1) the therapist is a frank counter-propagandist who contradicts superstitions and self-defeating propaganda embodied in the irrational beliefs of the patient, and (2) the therapist encourages, persuades, cajoles, and occasionally insists that the patient engage in behavior that will itself be forceful counter-propaganda against the irrational beliefs (Ellis, 1962).

This particular brand of cognitive therapy is called rational-emotive therapy, and it is among the most active and aggressive of psychotherapeutic procedures. The following case illustrates the force of therapeutic persuasion:

> During his therapy session, a twenty-three-year-old man said that he was very depressed and did not know why. A little questioning showed that this severely neurotic patient, whose main presenting problem was that he had been doing too much drinking during the last two years, had been putting off the inventory keeping he was required to do as part of his job as an apprentice glass-staining artist.
>
> PATIENT: I know that I should do the inventory before it piles up to enormous proportions, but I just keep putting it off. To be honest, I guess it's because I resent doing it so much.
> THERAPIST: But why do you resent it so much?
> PATIENT: It's boring. I just don't like it.
> THERAPIST: So it's boring. That's a good reason for disliking this work, but is it an equally good reason for resenting it?
> PATIENT: Aren't the two the same thing?
> THERAPIST: By no means. Dislike equals the sentence, "I don't enjoy doing this thing, and therefore I don't want to do it." And that's a perfectly sane sentence in most instances. But resentment is the sentence, "*Because* I dislike doing this thing, I shouldn't *have* to do it." And that's invariably a very crazy sentence.
> PATIENT: Why is it so crazy to resent something that you don't like to do?
> THERAPIST: There are several reasons. First of all, from a purely logical standpoint, it just makes no sense at all to say to yourself, "Because I dislike doing this thing, I shouldn't *have* to do it." The second part of this sentence just doesn't follow in any way from the first part. Your reasoning goes something like this: "Because *I* dislike doing this thing, *other people* and the *universe* should be so considerate of me

> that they should never make me do what I dislike." But, of course, this doesn't make any sense. Why *should* other people and the universe be that considerate of you? It might be nice if they were. But why the devil *should* they be? In order for your reasoning to be true, the entire universe, and all the people in it, would really have to revolve around and be uniquely considerate of you. (Ellis, 1962)

Here the therapist directly attacks the client's belief, arguing that it is irrational. This is an important distinction between cognitive therapists, on the one hand, and behavioral or psychodynamic therapists on the other. Behavioral and psychodynamic therapists point out that a client's actions and beliefs are maladaptive and self-defeating. Cognitive therapists emphasize that, in addition, the beliefs are irrational and illogical.

Cognitive-Behavioral Therapy

Cognitive therapists, then, believe that distorted thinking causes disordered behavior and that correcting the distorted thinking will alleviate and even cure the disordered behavior. Behavior therapists, in contrast, view disordered behavior as learned from past experience, and they attempt to alleviate the disorders by training the patients to use new, more adaptive behaviors. These two positions are not incompatible, and many therapists try both to correct distorted cognitions and to train patients to engage in new behaviors. When therapists combine both techniques, it is called cognitive-behavioral therapy (Ellis, 1962; Mahoney, 1974; Meichenbaum, 1977; Beck et al., 1979).

Arnold Lazarus is one of the therapists who integrates cognitive and behavioral techniques in therapy. Lazarus argues that disorder occurs in the same patient at seven different levels, and that there are levels of therapy appropriate to each level of disorder. The mnemonic device for these seven levels is BASIC ID, where B is behavior, A affect, S sensation, I imagery, C cognition, I interpersonal relations, D drugs. The job of the therapist using such **multimodal therapy** is to separate the disorder into its different levels and to choose appropriate techniques for each level. Lazarus is willing to use cognitive techniques, behavioral techniques, and even psychodynamic procedures. Table 5–4 shows the variety of treatments used in the course of the thirteen-month therapy for Mary Ann, a twenty-four-year-old woman diagnosed as a chronic undifferentiated schizophrenic with a very poor prognosis. She was overweight, apathetic, and withdrawn. She had been heavily medicated but with little effect. By the end of thirteen months of the techniques shown in Table 5–4, she was functioning well and engaged to be married.

COMBINING COGNITIVE-BEHAVIORAL THERAPY AND PSYCHODYNAMICS

There has been a movement among psychodynamically oriented therapists that augurs well for a fruitful combination of cognitively oriented concepts and psychodynamic therapy. Lester Luborsky (1984) argues that what a patient consciously thinks about in three spheres of life reveals the underlying, and often unconscious, core conflictual relationship theme (CCRT). The three spheres are: (1) current in-treatment relationship (the relationship with the

TABLE 5-4

BASIC ID TECHNIQUES

Modality	Problem	Proposed Treatment
Behavior	Inappropriate withdrawal responses Frequent crying Excessive eating	Assertiveness training Nonreinforcement Low-calorie regimen
Affect	Unable to express overt anger Frequent anxiety Absence of enthusiasm and spontaneous joy	Role playing Relaxation training and reassurance Positive imagery procedures
Sensation	Stomach spasms Out of touch with most sensual pleasures Tension in jaw and neck	Abdominal breathing and relaxing Sensate focus method Differential relaxation

Imagery	Distressing scenes of sister's funeral
	Recurring dreams about airplane
	    bombings
		Desensitization
		Vivid imagery invoking feelings of
		    being safe

Cognition	Irrational self-talk: "I am evil."
	    "I must suffer." "Sex is dirty."
	    "I am inferior."
	Overgeneralization
		Deliberate rational questioning
		    and corrective self-talk
		
		Critical analysis of irrational sentences

Interpersonal relationships	Childlike dependence Easily exploited and submissive Manipulative tendencies	Specific self-sufficiency assignments Assertiveness training Training in direct and confrontative behaviors
Drugs	Disordered biochemistry	Antipsychotic drugs

SOURCE: Adapted from Lazarus, 1976.

FOCUS QUESTIONS

1. What is the CCRT?
2. How can examining a patient's thoughts about three spheres of life reveal the CCRT and lead to positive therapeutic outcome?

therapist), (2) current out-of-treatment relationships, and (3) past relationships. Common cognitions about these spheres, their recurrent overlap, point to the patient's basic conflicted theme about interpersonal relations.

Ms. N. thinks, "I am trying to do well in my work," a thought about her current out-of treatment relationships. She tells this to the therapist, and she begins to cry. The therapist then remarks, "You get tearful and cry when I refer to your attractiveness," a result of her thoughts about the in-treatment relationship. Ms. N. then spontaneously thinks about her past, "Father could never stand my being attractive." The content of these three conscious spheres reflects the main unconscious CCRT. By disentangling the cognitions involved in the three spheres, the therapist can discover the client's *wish:* "I wish I could find a suitable man to provide me with the physical and emotional support I need." The therapist can also discover (and attempt to alter) the negative *consequence,* or automatic thoughts, that follow from the wish: "But I shouldn't because I am independent, and I can't because I will be rejected, and the man will not be able to provide that kind of support."

By attending to the conscious automatic thoughts that cognitive therapists emphasize, psychodynamically oriented therapists are beginning to bring these two disparate models closer together (Horowitz, Stinson, Curtis et al., 1993). The future will likely lead to more of such creative integrations across models.

There are several virtues of behavior therapy and cognitive therapy: they are effective in a number of discrete disorders; therapy is generally brief and inexpensive; they seem to be based on a science of behavioral and cognitive psychology; and their units of analysis—stimuli, responses, reinforcers, expectations, and attributions—can be measured. Behavioral and cognitive therapies, however, are not without problems. Perhaps the most serious allegation is that they are superficial.

Are humans more than just behavior and cognition? Are psychological disorders more than disordered behavior and disordered thinking? Must therapy, in order to be successful, do more than merely provide more adaptive behaviors and more rational ways of thinking? Because behavior therapists and cognitive therapists restrict themselves to an analysis of the discrete behaviors and cognitions of the human being, they miss the essence: that individuals are wholes, that individuals are free to choose. A phobic patient is more than a machine who happens to be afraid of cats. He is an individual whose symptoms are deeply rooted in his personality and psychodynamics. Alternatively, he is an individual who has made bad choices but who can still choose health. An autistic child who treats other human beings as if they were pieces of furniture may be taught by behaviorists to hug other people in order to receive food or to escape from shock. But in the end, all we have is an autistic child who hugs people. Merely changing how one behaves fails to change the underlying disorder.

Those who object to the behavioral and cognitive views feel that there are deeper disorders that produce symptoms. Because of this, seemingly superficial behavioral change may be short-lived, as in the case of what had been highly successful behavioral treatments of obesity. After one year and three years, obese individuals who had undergone behavior therapy had kept their weight down. But after five years, their weight returned (Stunkard and Penick, 1979). Although behavior therapy had led to change by removing the symptom of obesity, the underlying problem, probably biological in nature, remained and ultimately sabotaged the therapy.

How might behavioral and cognitive therapists respond to these charges of superficiality? A militant response might be to deny the concept of the "whole person." To radical behaviorists such a concept is romantic; it makes sense in literature and in poetry, but not for human beings in distress and in need of relief. We would make a less militant reply. Removing symptoms—either behavioral or cognitive—at least helps. Symptom substitution has rarely, if ever, followed successful behavioral or cognitive therapy. Some disorders are highly specific, peripheral to the heart of an individual's being, and amenable to behavioral and cognitive therapies. Phobias, obsessions, stuttering, and some sexual problems are such disorders. On the other hand, there may be deeper disorders left untouched by behavioral and cognitive therapy: schizophrenia and psychopathy, perhaps. For these disorders, change of personality, uncovering dynamics, and drugs are probably necessary.

We believe that human misery, including problems of psychological disorder, is sometimes, but not always, produced by an unfortunate set of environmental circumstances or by distorted cognition. To counteract such circum-

FOCUS QUESTIONS

1. What are the strengths of the behavioral and cognitive models?
2. What are the problems with the behavioral and cognitive models?

stances by applying behavioral and cognitive laws does not diminish or devalue human wholeness or freedom, but rather enlarges it. An individual who is so crippled by a phobia of leaving his apartment that he cannot work or see those he loves is not free. By applying behavioral and cognitive therapy to such an individual, one can remove this phobia. Such an individual will then be free to lead a rational life.

SUMMARY

1. The behavioral school of abnormality grew out of British empiricism, the view that knowledge is caused by experience and that *resemblance* and *contiguity* between ideas are the two simple principles that are the mental glue of experience.

2. The behavioral model sees the cause of abnormality as the *learning of maladaptive habits*. It aims to discover, by laboratory experiment, what aspect of the environment produced this learning, and it sees successful therapy as learning new and more adaptive ways of behaving.

3. Two kinds of basic learning processes exist: *Pavlovian* and *operant conditioning*. These have each generated a set of behavior therapies.

4. Pavlovian therapies begin with the assumption that emotional habits have been acquired by the contingency between a *conditioned stimulus* and an *unconditioned stimulus*. The formerly neutral conditioned stimulus now produces a *conditioned response*, which is the acquired emotion. Two Pavlovian therapies, *systematic desensitization* and *flooding*, extinguish some maladaptive emotional habits quite successfully.

5. Operant conditioning is based on three concepts: reinforcer, operant, and discriminative stimulus. Operant therapies are based on the assumption that people acquire voluntary habits by positive reinforcement and punishment. Operant therapies provide new and more adaptive repertoires of voluntary responses and extinguish maladaptive voluntary responses. Among such therapies are *selective positive reinforcement, selective punishment,* and *extinction*. These have been applied with some success to such disorders as *anorexia nervosa* and *autism*.

6. The understanding of *avoidance learning* combines operant and Pavlovian theory, and helps in the treatment of obsessive-compulsive disorders.

7. The cognitive school is an outgrowth and reaction to the behavioral school.

8. In contrast to the behaviorists, the cognitive school holds that mental events are not *epiphenomena*, rather they cause behavior. More particularly, disordered cognitions cause disordered behavior, and changing these disordered cognitions will alleviate and sometimes cure psychopathology.

9. Cognitive therapy is carried out by attempting to change different sorts of mental events, which can be divided into short-term mental events and long-term mental events. Cognitive therapy has been quite successful in the treatment of unipolar depression and panic disorder.

10. Short-term mental events consist of expectations, including *outcome and efficacy expectations, appraisals,* or mental evaluations of our experience, and *attributions,* the designation of causes concerning our experience.

11. Long-term mental events include *beliefs,* some of which are irrational and illogical. A prominent example is a set of beliefs called the "tyranny of should's," which has been viewed as a cause of depression.

12. Many therapists practice both cognitive and behavioral therapy and are called *cognitive-behavioral therapists. Multi-modal therapy* is an example of the use of cognitive and behavioral techniques along with techniques from the other models.

13. The cognitive and behavioral models have been seriously criticized. The most important criticisms argue that human beings are more than their behaviors and cognitions, and that it is superficial to treat only the symptoms rather than the whole person. The cognitive and behavioral schools reply by arguing that many times it is helpful to the client merely to remove the symptoms, and that the disorder *is* often just the symptoms.

QUESTIONS FOR CRITICAL THINKING

1. Examine the basic assumptions of behaviorism and explain why this movement dominated academic psychology for fifty years and why it lost its prominent position in the mid-1960s.

2. Give a Pavlovian explanation for how a child could develop a fear of the dark.

3. Give an explanation for compulsive gambling in terms of operant conditioning.

4. How do an individual's attributions affect whether he is able to bounce back quickly from a failed business or unhappy love affair?

PART **3** INVESTIGATING
AND DIAGNOSING
ABNORMALITY

CHAPTER 6

Investigating Abnormality

CHAPTER ORGANIZER

THE CLINICAL CASE HISTORY
- Learn how the clinical case history can be used in investigating psychological disorders.

SCIENTIFIC EXPERIMENTATION
- Become familiar with the experimental method and how it can be used to investigate psychological disorders.

CORRELATION
- Understand why correlational studies rather than experimental studies may sometimes be the method of choice for studying abnormality.

EXPERIMENTS OF NATURE
- Familiarize yourself with how investigators can use experiments of nature to observe the effects of traumatic stress.

THE LABORATORY MODEL
- Learn how the laboratory model can be used to test hypotheses about cause and treatment of abnormality.

COMBINING SEVERAL METHODS: A WOVEN FABRIC
- Understand how all the methods of investigation can converge to form a complete theory of specific disorders.

The chapters later in this book describe many individuals' abnormal behaviors. Some people are terrified at the thought of entering an elevator; some seem to act in a way that seems totally inappropriate, like laughing at a close friend's funeral. Others complain of physical ailments that have no biological basis. Why do they act this way? What can one do to treat these individuals?

These two questions arise from the human fascination with scientific phenomena. We take notice of various phenomena, and then we seek understanding of them. We ask "Why?" What is the cause, or *etiology,* of the phenomena? When we find the etiology, we seek a way of applying our newly found knowledge. Physicists and engineers developed nuclear power plants after they studied the whys of the atom. Psychologists and psychiatrists developed therapies after studying abnormal (and sometimes, normal) behavior. This chapter is devoted to examining the ways, or methods, in which we investigate abnormality. We will look closely at the two principal methods: clinical case histories and experimental studies.

We will begin with *clinical case histories,* which provide the major source of hypotheses and intuitions about the causes and cures of abnormality. While case histories provide rich hypotheses, however, they cannot isolate the causal elements. *Experimental studies,* which manipulate possible causes in order to isolate the crucial elements, are our next concern. Often, however, for ethical or practical reasons, experiments cannot be carried out on people who have problems of psychopathology. Three alternate methods are therefore available to the scientist: *correlational studies, experiments of nature,* and *laboratory models of psychopathology.* It is most satisfying when several or all of the methods converge to form a woven fabric of evidence.

Before we begin our examination of method, a warning is in order. Sound method is a means, not an end. The end is becoming justifiably convinced that *A* is the cause of *B;* where *A* is a past event and *B* a form of abnormality, or where *A* is a therapy and *B* the relief of abnormality. Understanding can be arrived at by any of the methods discussed here; no one of them is the only road to truth. It is easy to become a slave to method, and to forget that the study of method describes how scientists or clinicians have attained understanding in the past. The study of method does not prescribe how this must be done in the future. Great thinkers have often developed (sometimes by accident) new methods at the same time as they discovered new truths.

THE CLINICAL CASE HISTORY

If we keep in mind that the end point of any method is the discovery of evidence about cause, we will see that each of the methods we examine can lead toward this end. The first, the *clinical case history,* is the record of part of the life of an individual as seen during therapy. In developing his theories of personality, Sigmund Freud made extensive use of clinical case histories. For example, much of what we know about hysteria today came out of Freud's hypotheses based on his patient's case histories. After seeing a number of patients with hysterical symptoms, Freud hypothesized that repressed wishes were the cause of their hysteria. The clinician who is observing and recording the case history can not only make hypotheses, but sometimes he or she can test them and discover compelling evidence as to whether he or she is right or wrong. The following case of hysterical "anniversary blindness" is such an instance.

A Clinical Case History

> At age fifty, Jack went completely blind. For three months, he had been unable even to distinguish light from dark. His symptoms had begun, rather suddenly, at Christmas time. An exhaustive series of eye tests revealed nothing wrong physically. Medications and several types of psychotherapy had been tried, all to no avail.
>
> Jack was conscious of no incident that might have precipitated the blindness, and nothing in Jack's narration of his life provided a clue. At this point, his therapist formulated an hypothesis: hysterical blindness. This was indicated by the total absence of physical cause plus the absence of psychological insight (almost to the point of indifference) concerning precipitating events. If this were classical hysteria, then some event, so traumatic that it had been driven out of the patient's consciousness and repressed, should be responsible. If this were so, Jack might have access to the event under hypnosis, and reliving the trauma might bring about a cure. The therapist therefore decided to hypnotize Jack. Under hypnosis, he instructed Jack to go back to any period of his life that he could not remember when he was awake. Jack then relived an astonishing event.

Twenty-five years ago, Jack had been deeply in love. Both he and an acquaintance, Ronald, were courting Sarah in open competition. One day—it was Christmas—she confronted Jack with bad news: she was in love with Ronald and would no longer see Jack. In a state of wild jealousy, he went to Ronald and told him a tragic lie: Sarah, Jack said, was not in love with either of them, but with a third party. Ronald became extremely upset, jumped into his car, and drove off at high speed. In a frenzy of rage, he tried to race a train to a crossing, but his car was hit, and he was killed. Sarah found out soon afterward that Ronald had been killed, and she suspected that Jack was involved. Sarah made Jack come with her to the scene of the accident, and as they arrived, the wreckage was being cleared and Ronald's mangled body was being taken away by ambulance. Sarah accused Jack of being directly responsible for Ronald's death. The whole incident was described under hypnosis with extreme emotion, and Jack climaxed the narrative by sobbing out, "She made me go up and *see* what I had done; that I had killed him!"

This was the buried trauma that the therapist had guessed was there. At this point, he reassured Jack that although he had some responsibility, he had not foreseen or intended Ronald's death, that it was an accident.

At this point yet another revelation occurred: every Christmas, Sarah, who had married someone else, called Jack to remind him of what he had done. This last Christmas had been the twenty-fifth anniversary and shortly after the call, the blindness had begun. The therapist inferred that Jack could no longer bear to *see* what he had done, and the memory of both the calls and the initial trauma had been repressed.

With the trauma relived under hypnosis, the therapist told Jack that upon waking, if he wanted to see, his sight would gradually return in the next few days, which, in fact, it did. (Stinnett, 1978)

Here then is an exemplary case history. A skilled therapist is presented with a syndrome: blindness with no physical cause. He then hypothesizes that it is hysterical blindness. Drawing on his knowledge of past case histories, theory, and therapeutic technique, he tests his hypothesis by finding under hypnosis a precipitating trauma of tragic proportions. Once the trauma is relived, the blindness disappears. Under hypnosis, two missing pieces—the accident and the anniversary phone calls—fall into place, and the etiology of the blindness becomes clear.

In a lifetime, a therapist may come across only a handful of such dramatic encounters in which the causal chain is so clear. No experiment and no personality test could bolster our certainty about the origin of Jack's blindness. Much more common, however, are those cases in which painstaking work on the part of the therapist and patient results in only gradual understanding of the complex network of cause and in only gradual symptom relief. But in all cases, whether they be dramatic or more commonplace, the method is the same: with the aid of a therapist, the patient comes to grips with past events and their influences on his present problems. Based on a patient's history, a therapist will hypothesize about possible causes and then help the patient overcome his past.

Evaluating the Clinical Case History

As a method of inquiry, the study of the clinical case history has four advantages. First, it is not artificial. The investigation involves an actual person who has an actual problem. The reader can easily empathize with a well-reported

FOCUS QUESTIONS

1. What are the four advantages to studying the clinical case history?
2. Describe how each of the following is a limitation of clinical case histories:
• selectivity
• lack of repeatability
• lack of generality
• insufficient evidence of causality

case and understand the connection between past events and present problems, and between therapeutic actions and the patient's improvement. As we will see later, methods involving laboratory experiments and statistical surveys are more artificial in nature.

Second, the clinical case history can document a phenomenon so rare or bizarre that it probably could not be explored by other standard forms of investigation. The origin of Jack's blindness is such a phenomenon.

Third, the clinical case history is a major source of hypotheses about the etiology and cure of abnormality. At the present state of knowledge, no other method equals it in the generation of ideas and insights that can then be tested in the laboratory and the clinic. Finally, a convincing clinical case history can provide disconfirming evidence against a generally accepted hypothesis.

But there are also four major disadvantages to clinical case histories: selectivity of memory, lack of repeatability, lack of generality, and insufficient evidence for causality.

SELECTIVITY

The reported "evidence" may be distorted. Clinical reports are almost always *retrospective;* they deal with incidents in the past, often in the distant past. The patient may have an axe to grind; he may, for example, want to absolve himself of blame or, conversely, emphasize his guilt. To accomplish this, he may select the evidence that serves these purposes. While talking to his therapist, he may magnify trivial events and ignore important ones. Commonly, he has his own explanation about what happened, and he will remember and report the evidence that best fits this explanation.

Sometimes it is the therapist, not the patient, who has the axe to grind. A therapist might believe in a particular theory, which may influence what evidence she considers relevant and what evidence she ignores. If the therapist is an orthodox Freudian, she may seek and emphasize evidence about early life events, while ignoring evidence about present events. If the therapist is an orthodox behavior therapist, she may focus on ways to change the patient's present behavior, while neglecting childhood events. Although such selectivity does not invalidate the insights gained through the single case, we must keep in mind that this method is particularly susceptible to bias by patient and therapist.

LACK OF REPEATABILITY

Case histories, because they are part of the flow of real life, are not repeatable. If we could repeat an observation exactly, we could look carefully at the details, making certain that it happened the way it was reported to us. If an observation could be repeated, we would have a better chance of determining what caused it, for we could vary one and only one element and see if the observation changed. But this is not the case with clinical case histories; they each differ in one respect or another from one another.

LACK OF GENERALITY

Even a convincing case history, like Jack's, is specific to one person. Does *all* hysterical blindness begin with an unconscious wish not to see, and conversely, do *all* such wishes result in hysterical blindness? How many people have unconsciously not wanted to see something yet have not become hysterically blind? We simply do not know, and a single case history can, at best, tell

▲ The clinical case history of Bertha Pappenheim, known as Anna O. in *Studies on Hysteria,* helped Sigmund Freud to formulate his hypotheses on hysteria.

us only that one such case of hysterical blindness began in this way. By studying several case histories of hysterical blindness, we might find that each individual had an unconscious motivation not to see; this would indicate that such a desire is general to hysterical blindness. But we would still be ignorant about whether individuals who are not hysterically blind lack such a desire. And this is just what is needed to infer cause.

INSUFFICIENT EVIDENCE FOR CAUSALITY

Single clinical case histories only rarely convince us about etiology. In cases like Jack's, the cause was clear, but usually cause is more ambiguous. In most cases, there are several incidents, each of which might be the cause, or there is no obvious incident at all. This is the most serious problem with clinical case histories. In order to know that *A* causes *B*, we must at least know that when *A* occurs, *B* generally follows. If we collect many cases of *B*, we could determine if, in general, *B*'s are preceded by *A*'s. But here the causal question is the converse: When *A* occurs, does *B* regularly follow? Are unconscious wishes not to see followed, in general, by hysterical blindness? To determine this, we would have to look at many cases of people who are not hysterically blind and find that they lack the unconscious wish. The case history method, however, investigates only people with the disorder, not those without the disorder, and therefore it usually cannot isolate the cause.

Clinical case histories provide the richest source of hypotheses about the cause and cure of abnormality. Usually case histories generate several possible causes that cannot be unraveled even by adding further similar cases. The search for the cause among several possible causes is the theme of this chapter. This search provides the central rationale for us to move from examining the clinical case to discussing the experiment.

SCIENTIFIC EXPERIMENTATION

The grand ambition of all scientific experiments is to provide understanding by answering the question of cause. The basic experimental method is simple: (1) you make a guess (hypothesis) at the cause of an event; (2) you remove the suspected cause, and see if the event fails to occur; (3) you put the suspected cause back in and see if the event now reoccurs.

An experiment, then, consists of a procedure in which the hypothesized cause is manipulated and the occurrence of the effect is measured. The hypothesized cause, which the experimenter manipulates, is called the ***independent variable.*** The effect, which the experimenter measures, is called the ***dependent variable,*** because its occurrence depends on whether the cause precedes it. Both independent and dependent variables are operationally defined. An ***operational definition*** is the set of measurable and repeatable conditions under which a phenomenon is said to occur. So, for example, obesity can be operationally defined as being 15 percent or more above the "ideal" weights for a given height as given in a table of weights, or depression can be defined as having greater than a given score on a checklist of depressive symptoms. When manipulating an independent variable produces changes in a dependent variable, an ***experimental effect*** has been obtained.

FOCUS QUESTIONS

1. Describe the basic experimental method, referring to the following:
   • independent variable
   • dependent variable
   • operational definition
   • experimental group
   • control group
2. Explain how the following experimental confounds might lead to mistaken conclusions:
   • nonrandom assignment
   • experimenter bias
   • subject bias
   • demand characteristics
3. What are statistical inferences and when are effects statistically significant?
4. What are misses and false alarms?

Clinical case histories, you will recall, usually cannot answer the causal question definitively. While multiple similar cases can establish that hysterical blindness is generally preceded by unconscious wishes, they cannot establish whether such wishes are generally followed by the symptom in question. In principle, a well-done experiment can answer this question by imposing the wish (independent variable) on individuals and seeing if hysterical blindness (dependent variable) follows. There are a variety of ethical and practical reasons, however, why this experiment would never be done. We will now turn to an actual experiment designed to test the effectiveness of a novel therapy for depression.

An Experiment

Several clinical case histories about sleep deprivation recently came to the attention of researchers looking for cures of depression. It appeared that, in a few instances, depressed individuals who for one reason or another missed several whole nights of sleep surprisingly became less depressed. Putting this together with the fact that two antidepressant drugs, tricyclics and MAO inhibitors, incidentally reduce the amount of dreaming, investigators hypothesized that dream deprivation itself might relieve depression (Vogel, 1975).

When we dream, our eyes move rapidly back and forth beneath our closed lids; the muscles from the neck down lose their tone; and in males, the penis becomes erect. Since we can monitor when an individual is dreaming, we can deprive him of dreams by waking him up every time these signs appear. Such dream deprivation, carried out in a sleep laboratory for several nights running, was the independent variable that was manipulated in this experiment. Individuals who had been hospitalized for depression were the subjects, and the dependent variables were changes in ratings of the severity of depression on a variety of symptoms. The investigators obtained the expected experimental effect: when the depressed people were deprived of dreaming over a period of three weeks, they became markedly less depressed. But not all the depressed people improved. Only the subgroup who suffered from a specific kind of depression (called endogenous depression; see Chapter 11) showed signs of improvement.

Can we now conclude that dream deprivation causes relief from depression? Not yet. Perhaps it was not the dream deprivation that was effective, but some other aspect of what was done to the depressed patients. For example, the patients had electrodes strapped on them, got less total sleep than normal, and slept in a laboratory. Any one of these might have been effective, rather than the specific manipulation of preventing them from dreaming.

Factors other than the independent variable which might produce an experimental effect and which occur along with the independent variable are called **confounds.** In order to eliminate such confounds, experimenters use control procedures, the most typical of which is the **control group.** In principle, a control group is a group of subjects similar to those in the experimental group, who experience just the confounded factors that the experimental group had but who do not experience the hypothesized cause. In contrast, the **experimental group** experiences both the confounds and the hypothesized cause. In general, whenever there is reason to suspect that some factor confounded with the independent variable might produce the effect, groups that control for that confounding factor must be run (see Figure 6–1).

FIGURE 6–1

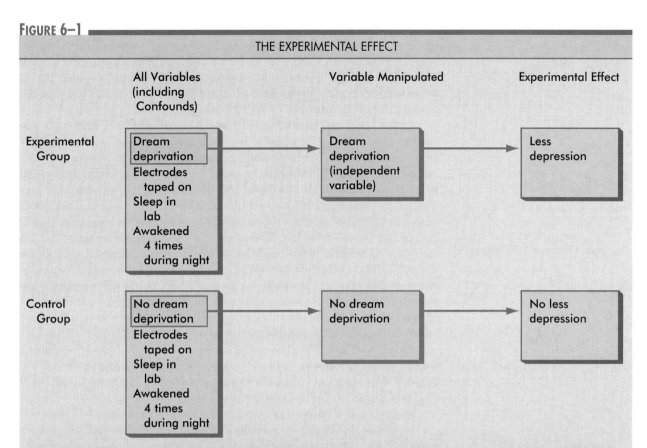

THE EXPERIMENTAL EFFECT

When manipulating an independent variable produces changes in a dependent variable, an experimental effect has been obtained. In the experiment above, the independent variable is dream deprivation, the dependent variable is depression, and the experimental effect is less depression as a result of the dream deprivation. To make sure that the experimental effect is not occurring because of the confounds (here, electrodes taped on, sleep in lab, awakened 4 times during the night), experimenters use control procedures. Control groups experience only the confounds; experimental groups experience both confounds and the hypothesized cause.

In this study, the investigators ran an appropriate control group, which controlled for a number of confounds. Other depressed patients were put through exactly the same procedure as above. They spent three weeks sleeping in the laboratory, electrodes were taped on them, and they were awakened the same number of times during each night as were those in the experimental group. But there was one crucial difference: the awakenings occurred, not when the patients were dreaming, but during non-dreaming phases of sleep. The patients in the control group did not become less depressed. This study is a good example of a ***therapy outcome study,*** in which the effects of a therapy are observed as it attempts to alleviate a disorder. Such experiments allow us to determine which therapies are effective. Here we can conclude that dream deprivation alleviates depression in endogenously depressed patients.

META-ANALYSIS

Any single therapy outcome study can be hard to evaluate and to generalize even to similar therapies. So, for example, if the therapy works on severely depressed young students, we cannot be sure it will work with middle-aged adults who are mildly depressed. If the therapy worked and the therapists were very experienced, is it likely to work even if the therapists are less experienced? These are important questions, since what therapy choices the public makes can depend upon the generalizability of such studies. To solve this dilemma the technique of *meta-analysis* of therapy outcome studies has arisen.

In meta-analysis, the analyst looks at a large number of therapy outcome studies, which may differ in many of their particulars, and attempts to integrate them statistically by concluding whether the therapy works and how large an effect it has. Consider the question of whether psychotherapy works at all. To answer this, Smith and Glass (1977) meta-analyzed 375 studies of psychotherapy involving 25,000 clients and 25,000 control subjects. These studies differed on many dimensions: age of clients, experience of therapists, type of disorder, duration of therapy, kind of therapy, and measure of outcome. But they were all similar in that each had a treated (experimental) group and a control condition. The analysts asked whether the experimental group benefited from therapy more than did the control group. In this meta-analysis, the average client under treatment did better than 75 percent of the untreated controls. So we can conclude that, in general, psychotherapy produces robust benefits relative to not being treated (Lipsey and Wilson, 1993).

The meta-analyst can then ask about specific forms of therapy or about specific kinds of problems. So, for example, clients undergoing systematic desensitization for phobias (Chapter 5) do better on average than 82 percent of untreated controls, and those undergoing psychodynamic therapy for interpersonal conflicts (Chapter 4) do better than 72 percent of untreated controls.

Meta-analysis has one large methodological problem: Each study gets exactly one "vote" no matter how well done it is. Thus, a study using a large sample that is well controlled has the same weight as a study using a smaller sample that is more poorly controlled (see Figure 6–2).

Experimental Confounds

A well-done experiment can allow us to determine whether *A* causes *B*. Experimenters, however, must be on their guard against a variety of subtle confounds that might actually produce the experimental effect. Common among these are nonrandom assignment, experimenter bias, subject bias, and demand characteristics.

NONRANDOM ASSIGNMENT

In an experiment that includes an experimental group and a control group, it is important that subjects be assigned to groups on a random basis. Such *random assignment* means that each subject should have had an equal chance of being assigned to each group. If subjects are not assigned by random selection, disastrously mistaken inferences, like the following example, can occur.

Who gets more stomach ulcers, individuals with a great deal of responsibility or individuals who have little responsibility? To decide this, four "executive" monkeys learned to lever press in order to avoid shock both for themselves and for their four yoked partners (Brady, 1958). In a *yoking* procedure, both experimental and control groups receive exactly the same physical events (shocks), but only the experimental group influences these events by its responses. In

▼ Executive monkeys learned to lever press to avoid shock for themselves and their yoked partners. Nonrandom assignment of subjects to the "executive group," however, may have confounded the results of this experiment and produced more ulcers in the executive group.

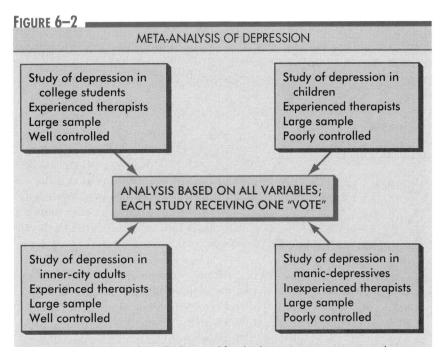

FIGURE 6–2

META-ANALYSIS OF DEPRESSION

Study of depression in
  college students
Experienced therapists
Large sample
Well controlled

Study of depression in
  children
Experienced therapists
Large sample
Poorly controlled

ANALYSIS BASED ON ALL VARIABLES;
EACH STUDY RECEIVING ONE "VOTE"

Study of depression in
  inner-city adults
Experienced therapists
Large sample
Well controlled

Study of depression in
  manic-depressives
Inexperienced therapists
Large sample
Poorly controlled

In a meta-analysis, each study that qualifies by having met some minimal standard (e.g., in this case the minimum standard is a large sample) carries the same weight, regardless of sophistication of diagnosis or how well controlled the experiment was. Thus, a meta-analysis of therapy for depression would have studies that differ as to age of clients, therapist experience, kinds of depression, duration of therapy, but all of these studies would be integrated statistically based on whether the experimental group in each study was deemed to have benefited from the therapy more than did those in the control group for each study.

the case of the executive monkeys, those in the experimental group could avoid the shocks by pressing a lever. The yoked control group, on the other hand, received exactly the same shock but had no responsibility for turning it off; they were helpless since no response they made enabled them to avoid shock. The study showed that the "executives" developed stomach ulcers and died, while their helpless partners remained healthy. Many readers drew the conclusion that executives run a higher risk of psychosomatic illness than more powerless individuals. Only years later did other scientists notice that the monkeys had not been randomly selected to the two groups. When the experiment began, all eight of the monkeys were shocked, and the first four to start pressing the lever were assigned to the "executive" group. We now realize that the more emotional the monkey was or the more the shock hurt him, the sooner he started banging at the lever. As it turned out, the four most emotionally reactive monkeys became the executives and the four most stolid became the yoked controls. Not surprisingly, the emotional "executives" died with ulcers, and the stolid but helpless monkeys stayed healthy. When the experiment was repeated thirteen years later, this time with randomly assigned subjects, the helpless animals developed more ulcers than the executives (Weiss, 1971).

EXPERIMENTER AND SUBJECT BIAS

Another source of mistaken inference from experiments comes from *experimenter bias.* If an experimenter wants or expects a particular result, he can subtly influence his subjects to produce that result, sometimes without being aware of it. If the experimenter merely nods his head agreeably at the crucial time he might be able to produce the experimental result spuriously (Greenspoon, 1955). An even bigger problem than experimenter bias is **subject bias.** Human subjects routinely form beliefs about what they are expected to do. When someone believes that a drug that is actually useless is going to help him, he may still sometimes get better after taking the drug. For example, following major surgery, pain is frequent and severe. Yet, about 35 percent of patients report marked relief after taking a useless drug, or **placebo** (Beecher, 1959). Morphine, even in large doses, relieves pain only 75 percent of the time. We can conclude from this that suggestion probably provides some of the pain-killing benefits of morphine (Melzack, 1973). To deal with subject bias, investigators use an experimental group that receives a real drug and a control group that is given a placebo. Both groups are given identical instructions. The mere belief on the part of all subjects that any pill should work has powerful effects. For it to be considered effective, the investigators must then find the real drug to be more potent than the placebo alone.

If neither the experimenter nor the subject knows whether the subject is in the experimental or the placebo control group, the results cannot be affected by either experimenter or subject bias. This elegant design in which both subject and experimenter are "blind" as to which subjects have received a drug or placebo is called a **double-blind experiment.** An experiment in which only the subject does not know whether he is receiving a drug or placebo is called a **single-blind experiment.** The design in which only the experimenter is blind and the subject is not is an **experimenter-blind design.** Notice that in an outcome study of a psychotherapy, as opposed to a drug, an experimenter-blind design is possible, but a single-blind or a double-blind design is nearly impossible and unnecessarily stringent. The person who assesses how well the patient is doing (the experimenter) may not know if the subject received psychotherapy or did not receive psychotherapy. It seems unlikely, however, that the patient will be ignorant of whether he himself had psychotherapy or did not. This does not seem to us to be a major impediment to studying the outcomes of psychotherapy.

DEMAND CHARACTERISTICS

Most subjects want to be good subjects and to confirm the experimenter's hypothesis. Frequently at the end of an experiment, subjects ask, "I hope I didn't ruin the experiment?" A few subjects want to be bad subjects and try to undermine the experiment. Both need, first, to figure out what the experimenter's hypothesis is and then to act accordingly. Campus scuttlebutt, the advertisement to get subjects, the personality of the experimenter, the explicit statement of the instructions, implicit suggestions in the instructions, and the setting of the laboratory all constitute a set of **demand characteristics** that may induce a subject to invent a hypothesis about how he should behave.

The demand characteristics can be powerful cues that lead to grossly mistaken inferences. In the 1950s, the topic of sensory deprivation was fashionable. In studies of this phenomenon, college students were paid $20 for a

"A Louie, Louie . . . wowoooo
. . . We gotta go now . . ."

▲ One pitfall of human research is subjects' tendency to form ideas of how they should behave.

twenty-four-hour day of lying on cots in darkened, sound-deadened rooms. They wore translucent goggles that made sight impossible, gloves and cuffs that made feeling impossible, and they listened to masking noise that blocked hearing (Bexton, Heron, and Scott, 1954). The investigators found that the subjects had hallucinations: first they saw simple patterns, later they saw complex, moving figures. They also felt highly stressed, nauseous, agitated, and fatigued. It was concluded that removing vision, touch, and hearing for normal human subjects produced stress-induced hallucinations.

But in reviewing these sensory deprivation experiments, Martin Orne and his associates noticed something fishy about their design. There seemed to be some powerful demand characteristics: subjects were first greeted by a doctor in a white coat; a sign "Sensory Deprivation Laboratory" was on the door; the subjects had to sign awesome release forms absolving the experimenter of responsibility should anything untoward happen; and they had a panic button that would release them from the experiment if "anything undesirable should happen." Could it be that these trappings communicated to the subject that he was expected to be stressed and perhaps to have hallucinations? This would mean that it was not the sensory deprivation but the demand characteristics that produced the experimental effect.

To test this, subjects were led into a room labeled "Memory Deprivation Laboratory," and they were greeted by a doctor in a white coat with a stethoscope. Awesome release forms were signed. Subjects were told that if the experiment proved to be too much for them, they could use the red panic button conspicuously installed in the wall of the experimental room. *No sensory deprivation whatsoever was imposed on the subjects.* Rather, they sat in a well-lighted room with two comfortable chairs, they were provided with ice water and sandwiches, and they were also given an optional task of adding numbers. In this situation, the subjects also reported stress-induced hallucinations, indicating that the demand characteristics and not the sensory deprivation may have caused the hallucinations (Orne, 1962).

▲ A subject participates in a sensory deprivation experiment. Will he have stress-induced hallucinations because of the isolation or because he believes he should be having hallucinations during such an experience?

Statistical Inference

Frequently there is room for doubt about whether an experimental manipulation really worked, even when experimental confounds have been ruled out. This is particularly true when there is an experimental and control group, each made up of several subjects. What happens when most, but not all subjects in the experimental group show an effect, and few, but not many subjects in the control group do not? How do we decide whether an effect is real, rather than due to chance?

Statistical inferences are the procedures we use to decide whether the **sample,** or particular observations we made, truly represents the **population,** or the entire set of potential observations we might have made.

Suppose we try out a new drug therapy on a sample of ten schizophrenics, and at the end of a year, six of them recover from schizophrenia. Did the drug cure the disorder? To begin with, we need to compare the drug therapy group to a control group of schizophrenics who were given placebos. Let's say we have an excellent control group: there is a control group consisting of 100 other wards in which each of the ten schizophrenic individuals is untreated, that is, merely given a placebo. On the average, for all of these wards, three out of ten schizophrenics have recovered by the end of the year. Is the difference between six out of ten recoveries with the drug and an average of three out of ten recoveries with the placebo real? Or, could as many as six out of ten of the patients have recovered, untreated, by chance alone? If this were so, the new drug would be of little value. It is vital to decide this, for unless we can, we will not know if it is worthwhile to use the drug for the population of schizophrenics as a whole.

To decide if the difference between six out of ten and three out of ten could have occurred by chance, we need to know the ***frequency distribution*** of recoveries from ward to ward. A frequency distribution is the number of occurrences in each given class observed; in this case, the number of wards showing no recoveries, one recovery, two recoveries, and so on. This frequency distribution shows how different numbers of recoveries among the wards are distributed. We know that the ***mean,*** or total number of recoveries divided by the total number of schizophrenics, is three out of ten, but for how many of the other wards did six (or more) out of ten schizophrenics recover? With a mean of three out of ten, six could be a very infrequent occurrence. For example, if exactly three out of ten recovered in each and every ward, then six out of ten would be very unlikely to occur by chance. With a different distribution, it could be a very frequent occurrence, for example, if for 50 of the wards, six out of ten recovered, but for the other 50 wards, zero out of ten recovered. In the first case, we could be very confident that the drug produced a real effect; in the second case, we would have very little confidence that the drug worked, and we would assume that six out of ten recoveries was just a chance fluctuation in the recovery rate.

Let us say we know the distribution of recovery for the 100 placebo wards (see Figure 6–3). In only 5 wards (noted by red) did six (or more) schizophrenics recover without treatment. This means that only 5 percent of the time (i.e., in 5 out of 100 placebo wards) will chance fluctuation produce recovery in as

FIGURE 6–3

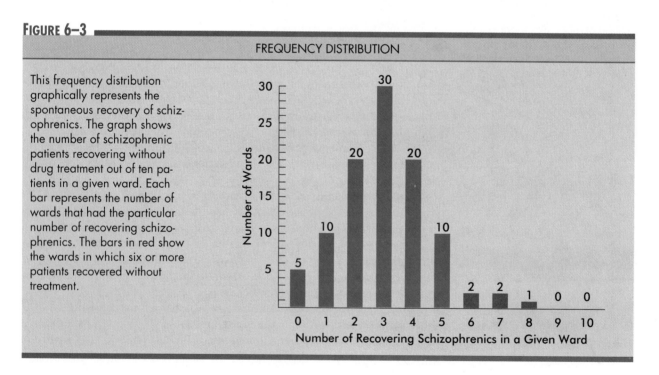

FREQUENCY DISTRIBUTION

This frequency distribution graphically represents the spontaneous recovery of schizophrenics. The graph shows the number of schizophrenic patients recovering without drug treatment out of ten patients in a given ward. Each bar represents the number of wards that had the particular number of recovering schizophrenics. The bars in red show the wards in which six or more patients recovered without treatment.

many as six out of ten cases. Scientists are generally quite conservative about making claims, and by convention, a real effect will be claimed only with at least 95 percent confidence that chance did not produce the result. When effects exceed this conventional confidence level, they are called ***statistically significant.***

Making inferences in this way, however, can result in two kinds of mistakes: ***misses*** (saying *x* is false when it is true) and ***false alarms*** (saying *x* is true when it is false). A miss can occur when, for example, confidence does not reach the 5 percent level: say we are only confident at the 10 percent level that the number of drug recoveries was not due to chance and so we reject the hypothesis that the drug causes recovery, and yet the drug really does cure schizophrenia. We have missed a real cure by our conservative procedure. On the other hand, a false alarm can occur when confidence does reach the 5 percent level: say we accept the hypothesis that the drug causes recovery, but this turns out to be one of the 5 percent of the wards in which six people would have recovered without treatment and the drug really does nothing. Here not being conservative enough caused us to adopt a therapy which was really ineffective.

These two kinds of mistakes have both occurred many times in science. In fact, they are inversely related; they stand in a trade-off relationship to each other. The choice of a confidence level is always a difficult and sometimes a life or death decision. If we require a very conservative level of confidence before we accept a new therapy, say 1 percent, then we will have very few false alarms. As a consequence, we will incorrectly believe a therapy works when it does not, only 1 percent of the time. But the cost of this is that we will miss many therapies that really are effective. On the other hand, if we set a much less conservative level—say 20 percent—we will not miss many real therapies, but we will believe that certain therapies work quite often when they are actually ineffective.

Experiments with a Single Subject

Most experiments involve an experimental group and a control group, each with several subjects. Several subjects, as opposed to one, increase our confidence in the causal inference made in an experiment because of two factors: (1) ***repeatability***—the experimental manipulation is repeated and has its effect on several individuals: and (2) ***generality***—several randomly chosen individuals, not just one, are affected, and this increases our confidence that any new individual, randomly chosen, would also be so affected.

But useful experiments can be carried out with just one subject, and a well-designed ***single-subject experiment*** can accomplish the goal of demonstrating repeatability. The demonstration of generality, however, always requires several subjects. An example of a single-subject experiment follows:

> Walter was a retarded ten-year-old, whose outbursts in his special education class were contagious, and therefore particularly disruptive. His teacher, in conjunction with several experimental and clinical psychologists, hypothesized that his outbursts, or "talk outs," were maintained by the teacher's attention to him when she reprimanded him, and that by ignoring the talk outs and giving attention to him for more constructive actions, the talk outs would extinguish. They de-

signed what is called an "A-B-A-B" experiment to test this. In such a design un-treated, or baseline, behavior is measured (A_1), then treatment is instituted (B_1), then there is a return to no treatment (A_2), then treatment is reinstituted (B_2). (You may notice, incidentally, that a clinical case history, like the case of Jack in which a therapeutic procedure is tried, is an A-B design: A_1, untreated, followed by B_1, treatment).

The experiment to change Walter's behavior was divided into four phases, during each of which the number of talk outs was counted. In the first five-day phase (A_1-untreated) the teacher handled the talk outs as she normally did, by repri-manding him. In the second five-day phase (B_1-treatment$_1$), the teacher ignored the talk outs and paid attention to Walter whenever he did anything constructive. The third phase (A_2-untreated$_2$) repeated the first phase: talk outs were again rep-rimanded. Finally, the fourth five-day phase (B_2-treatment$_2$) repeated the second phase: the talk outs were ignored, and the teacher only paid attention to him for constructive actions.

As you can see from Figure 6–4, the hypothesis proved correct. During A_1, there were about four outbursts in each session, but when contingent atten-tion was instituted (B_1), Walter rapidly learned to produce no outbursts. The most important and convincing part of the experiments, however, were the re-peated procedures, A_2 and B_2. These phases gave us evidence of repeatability. By reinstituting reprimands and showing that talk outs again increased, the experimenters showed that the decrease in talk outs during treatment was un-likely to have been caused by chance; rather the high rate of outbursts proba-bly was caused by the reprimands. Then, by reinstituting treatment and show-ing fewer outbursts once again, we can infer that treatment probably caused

FIGURE 6–4

REPEATABILITY IN A SINGLE-SUBJECT EXPERIMENT

This record of talking-out be-havior of a retarded student shows A_1 untreated—before experimental conditions; B_2 treatment—systematic ignoring of talking out and increased teacher attention to appropri-ate behavior; A_2 untreated—reinstatement of teacher atten-tion to talking-out behavior; and B_2 treatment—return to systematic ignoring of talking out and increased attention to appropriate behavior.
(SOURCE: Hall et al., 1971)

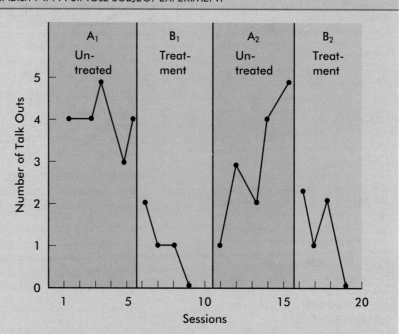

FIGURE 6–5

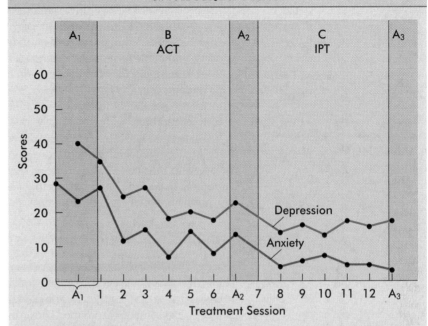

The figure shows weekly change in scores for anxiety on the Beck Anxiety Inventory and in scores for depression on the Beck Depression Inventory. A_1 is the baseline condition for two weeks during which time there was assessment for both anxiety and depression but no treatment; B is treatment with ACT (Anxiety Control Treatment); A_2 is an assessment week during which there was no treatment, and anxiety and depression both increased; C is treatment with IPT (Interpersonal Therapy, which is a treatment for depression); A_3 indicates another assessment week during which there was no treatment, and anxiety and depression both increased. Both treatments reduced anxiety and depression. (SOURCE: Adapted from Moras, Telfer, and Barlow, 1993)

his quieter behavior rather than chance. In addition, since the two conditions (each repeated) differed only in the direction of the teacher's attention—to bad behavior or to constructive behavior—cause is isolated in the same way that a control group isolates cause in a multi-subject experiment. The control condition occurs within the same subject and therefore does not require a separate control *group*.

It could be, however, that only Walter in particular, rather than misbehaving, retarded boys in general, would improve with attention to constructive behavior. Only repeating the procedure with several subjects would show generality. When there is only one subject available, however, as in a rare disorder or unique therapy, single-subject designs are the only way of determining causality.

The single-subject design can also be used to test the specificity of different therapies for different problems (see Figure 6–5). It is common for patients who have anxiety also to have depression. Anxiety control treatment (ACT) gives a patient training in breathing exercises to reduce the intensity of anxiety symptoms and provides cognitive restructuring to test the validity of anxiety-provoking thoughts and to marshal evidence against them. Interpersonal therapy (IPT; see Chapter 11) has been used to treat depression specifically. It consists of social skills training, dealing with grief, resolving interpersonal disputes, and mastering role transitions.

An A-B-A-C-A design can ask if anxiety control treatment works only on anxiety, and if interpersonal therapy works only on depression. In this design, *A* is for assessment for both anxiety and depression but no treatment, *B* is for ACT therapy, and *C* is for IPT therapy. The patient whose anxiety and depression scores are shown in Figure 6–5 had both strong anxiety and severe depressive symptoms.

As you can see, both anxiety and depression lessened when the patient was given anxiety control treatment in sessions 1–6. In addition, when the patient switched to interpersonal therapy in session 7, both depression and anxiety continued to decline. This suggests that each of these therapies is not specific to one problem; both may reduce anxiety as well as depression.

Evaluation of the Experimental Method

The experimental method has three strengths and three weaknesses. The first strength is that it is the foremost method for isolating causal elements. Second, it is general to the population sampled, when group—as opposed to single-subject—experiments are done. Third, it is repeatable. The first weakness is that an experiment is artificial; it does not capture the full reality of a disorder. Second, inferences made are probabilistic, not certain. Finally, performing certain experiments sometimes may be unethical or impractical. We now turn to a discussion of this last point: the practical and ethical difficulties of experimentation.

Often the road to experimental inquiry is completely blocked, and an alternate method must be used to attempt to investigate etiology. The reason an experiment cannot be done is often practical. It may be too expensive or time consuming. For example, will changing the child-rearing practices of schizophrenic parents lower the chances that their children will eventually become schizophrenic? An experiment may require more subjects than can be practically obtained. For example, "Will anti-anxiety drugs prevent hysterical blindness, which is a rare disorder?" The right technology may not yet exist. For example, "Will stimulating single brain cells related to satiation reduce obesity in humans?"

There are ethical, as well as practical, difficulties in experimentation (see Box 6–1). Protection of the welfare of human (and animal) subjects is presently a value on the rise in our society. But deciding to increase such protection is not made without cost (Miller, 1985). There is an unavoidable consequence: some research that might have benefited troubled people is left undone. There is, however, one set of values that investigators of abnormality generally do agree on: the less drastic experiment is preferable to the more drastic, less shock to more shock, less deceptive experiments to more deceptive ones, using animals to using humans. But even here there are costs, since we must presume that the results found with less drastic conditions are valid for more drastic conditions, or that the finding is general beyond the species investigated.

There are a variety of ethical and practical reasons why the road to experimentation is often blocked in the study of abnormal psychology. The most fre-

Box 6–1

Very often we do not experiment for ethical reasons. In 1920, an experiment was performed on a healthy nine-month-old infant, Little Albert (see Chapter 8). Investigators experimentally instilled in him a phobia of small animals by pairing a startling loud noise with his playing with a white rat (Watson and Rayner, 1920). There are two sides to this ethical issue. Look at the experiment from Little Albert's point of view. An innocent and healthy child, with no say in the matter, was caused to be terrified of small, furry creatures. Should he have had to endure this suffering? Further, Albert was taken from the hospital by his mother, who was a wet nurse there, before curative procedures could be tried out, and he was never heard from again. Was he victimized by a lifelong phobia of rats? The moral climate has changed, and this is an experiment that could not be undertaken today.

But now look at the Little Albert experiment from a real phobic's point of view. Forget, for a moment, Albert's suffering and the possibility that he became a phobic. As we shall see in the fear and phobia chapter, as a direct result of the Little Albert experiment, curative procedures were tried out in fearful children, experimental models of phobias were developed and refined in animals and then applied to human adults, and a cure for many phobias is now known. Thousands of phobic individuals today are free to lead normal lives because of a line of experimentation that began with Little Albert's suffering. There is a clear conflict of interest here, and it is very difficult to decide whose rights are more important: one innocent Albert made phobic through no choice of his own versus thousands of phobics who have been cured.

quent reason is that we value the right of the subjects in experiments to be treated humanely more than the right of humanity to possible experimental knowledge about cure and cause of abnormality. When the relevant experiment cannot be done, three other methods have been devised to provide information about etiology and cure: correlation, experiments of nature, and laboratory models.

CORRELATION

In an experiment, the experimenter manipulates the independent variable in order to discover cause. He or she imposes the independent variable on the subjects in the experimental group, but withholds it from subjects in the control group. If the experimental group but not the control group shows the effect, the experimenter infers causation. For ethical and practical reasons, such manipulation cannot be done in many settings of abnormality, so correlation is a widely used investigative technique. *Correlation* is pure observation, without manipulation. An observer performing a correlation measures two classes of events and records the relationship between them. There are three possible relationships: (1) As one increases, so does the other. This is called a *positive correlation.* Height, for example, correlates positively with weight, for the taller a person is, generally the more he weighs. This correlation is shown graphically in Figure 6–6A. (2) As one increases, the other decreases. This is called a *negative correlation.* Studying is, in general, negatively correlated with failure, for the more we study, the less likely we are to fail (Figure 6–6B). (3) As one changes, the other does not change in any systematic way. Two such events are said to be *uncorrelated.* Hair length is uncorrelated with failure on algebra exams, for how long our hair is, in general, makes no difference as to whether or not we fail (Figure 6–6C). The central point here is that

FIGURE 6–6

CORRELATIONS

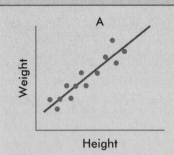
A

Weight

Height

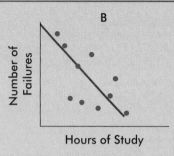
B

Number of Failures

Hours of Study

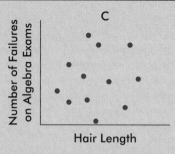
C

Number of Failures on Algebra Exams

Hair Length

Here are three scatterplots illustrating a positive correlation (A), a negative correlation (B), and a lack of correlation (C). The positive correlation indicates that taller individuals tend to weigh more. The negative correlation indicates that individuals who study less tend to fail more. The lack of correlation indicates no relationship between hair length and failure on algebra exams.

FOCUS QUESTIONS

1. Explain the relationships between variables in the following:
   • positive correlation
   • negative correlation
   • lack of correlation
2. Explain how the relationship between two classes of events is determined.
3. When is a correlation generally considered to be statistically significant?
4. What are the advantages and disadvantages of correlational studies of abnormality?

in correlational studies, we are observers of the variables; we do not manipulate weight, height, hair length, studying, or failure. Instead, we look at the relationships among variables.

Let us now see how correlation can be applied to important issues of abnormal psychology by working through an example of a negative correlation. One investigator proposed an elegantly simple theory of human depression: that depression is caused by having too few rewards in daily life (Lewinsohn, 1975). Experimentation on this is limited by ethical considerations; we cannot take nondepressed people and withhold rewards in their daily lives to see if depression results. But we can perform relevant correlations: Does depth of depression correlate with the number of pleasant activities that different individuals engage in? The experimenter predicted a negative correlation: as pleasant activities decrease, the degree of depression increases. Both variables can be operationally defined: degree of depression by a self-report test (Beck Depression Inventory), which totals up the number and severity of mood, thought, motivational, and physical symptoms that an individual reports; and a Pleasant Events Scale, which totals up the number of pleasant events, such as going on a date, listening to music, watching TV, dancing, that the individual has recently engaged in. The predicted negative correlation has been found: the higher the degree of depression, the fewer pleasant events that have been engaged in.

Consider the following hypothetical, but representative data, showing a negative correlation between depression and pleasant events in ten individuals (Table 6–1). The data show a strong negative correlation between depression and pleasant activities. Adam, who is far and away the most depressed, engaged in only one pleasant activity in the past week: watching TV. Sarah and Amy, who are not at all depressed, did many enjoyable things. In general, among the other seven individuals, the more the depression, the fewer pleasant activities they engaged in. The correlation is strong, but less than a perfect negative correlation, since, for example, Minerva was considerably more depressed than Davey (24 vs. 19) but engaged in more pleasant activities (4 vs. 2), although both were near the low end of activity.

TABLE 6–1

Name	Degree of Depression (the higher the score, the more depression)	Number of Pleasant Activities (in the past week)
NEGATIVE CORRELATION BETWEEN DEPRESSION AND NUMBER OF PLEASANT ACTIVITIES		
Adam	30	1
Minerva	24	4
Davey	19	2
Elmo	11	4
John	7	7
Alphonso	6	9
Lynn	3	6
Lauren	2	11
Sarah	0	13
Amy	0	10

This negative correlation can be seen graphically in Figure 6–7. Each person is represented by a point. A straight line is "fitted" to the points and the negative correlation is indicated by the descending line: the more depression, the fewer activities. If the correlation had turned out positive (the more depression, the more activities), the best fitting line would have been ascending.

Correlation Coefficients

The strength of the relationship between two classes of events can be expressed by a ***correlation coefficient,*** the symbol for which is *r* (representing the Pear-

FIGURE 6–7

The graph depicts the negative correlation between depression and number of pleasant events documented in Table 6–1. As pleasant events increase, severity of depression decreases.

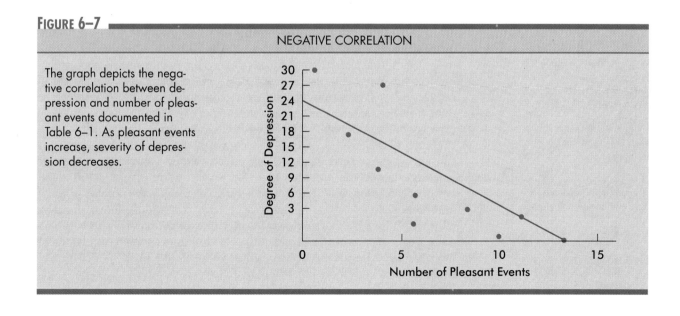

NEGATIVE CORRELATION

son Product Moment Correlation Coefficient, which is named after its inventor, Karl Pearson). The range for r is as follows: r can be as great as $+1.00$, for a perfect positive correlation; it can vary through 0.00, meaning no relationship at all; and it can go down to -1.00 for a perfect negative correlation. The r for our depression scores and pleasant activities turns out to be $-.87$, a strong negative correlation. The level of confidence that the relation did not occur by chance, or its **statistical significance,** can be determined for r by using logic similar to that used for deciding whether or not two groups really differ. In general, the farther the correlation coefficient is from $.00$, in either the positive or negative direction, and the more observations there are that contribute to the correlation, the higher is our confidence that the relationship did not occur by chance. Conventionally, the 95 percent level of confidence is chosen as statistically significant.

Correlation and Causality

Given the strong negative correlation in our example, can we conclude that a life with few rewards *causes* depression? The answer is no. And herein lies the main disadvantage of the correlational method as compared to the experimental method. There are really three causal possibilities and not just one: (1) engaging in only a few pleasant activities might cause depression; (2) depression itself might cause people to engage in fewer pleasant activities; for example, perhaps depression blunts the desire to be social; and (3) both depression and lower activity could be caused by some as yet unobserved third variable, such as some biochemical imbalance. In general, whether there is a correlation between X and Y, it can be either that X causes Y, that Y causes X, or that Z causes both X and Y.

Carrying out correlation studies, then, does not always lead us to discover cause. But there are ways of narrowing down the possible causes. One way is to perform an experiment. For example, an experiment has actually been done to test causation for the depression example above. In this experiment, depressed students were induced to increase the number of pleasant events they engaged in each day. Depressed students who increased their activities did not become any less depressed than the control group of depressed students, who did not change their activity level; rather they became more depressed (Hammen and Glass, 1975). So the fact that activity and depression correlate negatively does not seem to reflect a causal relationship. Having few rewards probably does not cause depression, rather depression either causes individuals to engage in fewer rewarding activities, or both are caused by an unobserved third variable. We infer this because the number of pleasant activities has been experimentally manipulated, yet depression has not been alleviated.

Doing the relevant experiment is one way of determining the direction of causality that has been suggested, but not proven, by a correlation. A second way has to do with the order in which the variables occur in time. For example, positive correlations have been found between illness and the number of major life events, such as divorce and job loss, in the year preceding illness; the more life events before, the more illnesses after (Holmes and Rahe, 1967). Here, temporal sequence narrows the possibilities of cause from three to two: a hassled life could produce illness, or some third variable, like unstable personality, could produce both more illness and more life events, but the hypothesis that the illness causes the increases in life events is ruled out.

Epidemiology

Since the advent of operational diagnostic criteria (as in DSM-III and DSM-IV), a concerted effort has taken place in the United States and Europe to determine just how much mental illness exists. These epidemiological studies represent some of the most productive uses of the correlational method. The initial purpose of these studies was practical: by determining how much of the different disorders existed, training and therapeutic resources could be allocated rationally. If there turned out to be a great deal of depression, for example, programs could be mounted to train more therapists to treat depressed patients, better antidepressant drugs could be developed, more money could be spent on research into the etiology of depression and to learn how to prevent depression.

In the best-done studies, such as the Epidemiologic Catchment Area (ECA) studies (Robins, Helzer, Weissman, et al., 1984) and the National Comorbidity Study (Kessler, McGonogle, Zhao, et al., 1994), trained diagnosticians went door-to-door to a representative sample of almost ten thousand individuals, and administered detailed structured diagnostic interviews. The disorders studied had clear operational definitions. The most important statistic they gathered was on the ***lifetime prevalence*** of each major disorder, the proportion of people in a sample who have ever experienced that particular disorder.

Table 6–2 presents the lifetime prevalence for the major disorders as discovered in three of the main sites of the Epidemiologic Catchment Area study. As you can see, the prevalence of mental disorder is alarmingly high—with almost one-third of the people in America suffering at least one major disorder in their lifetime.

TABLE 6–2

LIFETIME PREVALENCE RATES (PERCENT) OF DISORDERS			
Disorders	*New Haven (N = 3,058)*	*Baltimore (N = 3,481)*	*St. Louis (N = 3,004)*
Any disorder	28.8	38.0	31.0
Substance use disorders	15.0	17.0	18.1
Alcohol use/dependence	11.5	13.7	15.7
Drug abuse/dependence	5.8	5.6	5.5
Schizophrenia	1.9	1.6	1.0
Affective disorders	9.5	6.1	8.0
Manic episode	1.1	0.6	1.1
Major depressive episode	6.7	3.7	5.5
Dysthymia	3.2	2.1	3.8
Anxiety/somatoform disorders	10.4	25.1	11.1
Phobia	7.8	23.3	9.4
Panic	1.4	1.4	1.5
Obsessive-compulsive	2.6	3.0	1.9
Somatization	0.1	0.1	0.1
Anorexia	0.0	0.1	0.1
Antisocial personality	2.1	2.6	3.3
Cognitive impairment (severe)	1.3	1.3	1.0

SOURCE: Robins, Helzer, Weissman, et al., 1984.

TABLE 6–3

DEMOGRAPHIC CORRELATES (ODDS RATIOS) OF LIFETIME DISORDERS		
Any Affective *Disorder*	Any Anxiety Disorder	Any Substance-UseDisorder
Sex		
Male — 1.00	1.00	1.00
Female — 1.82	1.85	0.40
Age		
15-24 — 0.85	1.13	1.36
25-34 — 0.97	1.13	1.99
35-44 — 1.06	1.05	1.58
45-54 — 1.00	1.00	1.00
Race		
White — 1.00	1.00	1.00
Black — 0.63	0.77	0.35
Hispanic — 0.96	0.90	0.80
Income, $		
0-19,000 — 1.56	2.00	1.27
20,000-34,000 — 1.19	1.52	1.06
35,000-69,000 — 1.16	1.48	1.06
≥70,000 — 1.00	1.00	1.00
Education (years)		
0-11 — 0.98	1.86	0.99
12 — 1.00	1.76	1.25
13-15 — 1.05	1.44	1.20
≥16 — 1.00	1.00	1.00
Urbanicity		
Major metropolitan — 1.26	0.98	1.09
Other urban — 1.20	1.00	1.10
Rural — 1.00	1.00	1.00

SOURCE: Kessler, McGonogle, Zhao, et al., 1994.

The National Comorbidity Study sampled 8,098 Americans and examined the influence of sex, race, income, education, and "urbanicity" on the various disorders. The data on relative risk were presented in "odds ratios" (OR), where 1.00 equaled no increased risk, numbers greater than 1.00 equaled increased risk, and numbers lower than 1.00 equaled decreased risk (see Table 6–3).

Being female markedly increased risk for anxiety and depression (see Box 6–2), and markedly decreased risk for substance use. Being black lowered risk for anxiety and substance-use disorders. Being poor increased risk for all disorders, and living in a city increased risk for depression and substance abuse.

Evaluation of the Correlational Method

There are several advantages, and one major disadvantage, to correlational studies of abnormality. The use of correlations allows a quantitative and rigorous observation of relation between variables. Also, because the observations are on natural phenomenon, correlational studies do not have the artificiality of laboratory studies. Further, correlational studies are an option when performing an experiment is not a possibility, whether for practical or for ethical reasons. Lastly, correlations are repeatable. On the negative side, the major disadvantage in performing correlational studies is that the cause of a particular phenomenon usually cannot be isolated. One can move closer to discovering the cause, but other methods, such as experimental tests, are needed to determine causation more definitively.

EXPERIMENTS OF NATURE

Nature sometimes performs the experimental manipulation that scientists themselves could not do because of ethical or practical considerations. Sometimes a striking event occurs that changes the lives of individuals. An alert investigator can use such accidents to make inferences about what causes and cures abnormality. Because the accident is usually so striking, it is reasonable to suppose that *it*, and not some other extraneous event that happens to occur at the same time, is the cause. Such a strategy is an ***experiment of nature***, in short, a study in which the experimenter observes the effects of an unusual natural event.

An act of nature may permit us to study the effects of trauma on human behavior. We can go into villages to find survivors of earthquakes, volcano eruptions and so on, and we can observe their behavior. Ethical considerations (if not practical ones) prevent scientists from intentionally subjecting humans to traumatic stress. But because knowledge about the effects of trauma is so important to the study of abnormality, scientists will occasionally visit the scenes of natural disasters to observe the effects of such experiments of nature. One such study was of the survivors of a flood caused by the collapse of a dam in the Buffalo Creek area of Appalachia. For many months following the

Box 6–2

EPIDEMIOLOGY AND INFERRING CAUSE OF DEPRESSION

Epidemiology can be far more than just dry bean counting. The pattern of the information can be used to make inferences about the cause of disorders. This is a clever variant of the correlational method. McCarthy (1990) provides an example of how epidemiological data is used to answer deeper questions about cause—here, about a cause of depression in women.

In many parts of the world, epidemiological surveys have revealed that women are roughly twice as likely to be depressed as are men (Nolen-Hoeksema, 1990). The ECA study, among others, documented this. Women also have the great preponderance of the eating disorders, bulimia and anorexia. McCarthy wondered if the "thin ideal" fashionable in many Western nations might make women more depressed than men. After all, women diet more than men, and dieting usually leads to short-term success, followed by long-term failure—with the weight returning in 95 percent of dieters (Garner and Wooley, 1991). This kind of repeated failure along with the chronic female body dissatisfaction that the thin ideal engenders (the average American woman is markedly heavier than the thin ideal) might lead to more depression among women.

To test this, McCarthy compared the ratio of depression in women to men, the occurrence of the thin ideal, and the incidence of eating disorders across different cultures. Cultures that have the thin ideal (e.g., whites in America, New Zealand, England) also have a 2:1 ratio for female depression and a high incidence of eating disorders. Cultures without the thin ideal (there were not many with sufficient epidemiology) like India have a 1:1 female to male ratio in depression, and a low incidence of eating disorders. McCarthy inferred from these data that the thin ideal may be one cause both of more depression in women, as well as of eating disorders.

▶ Experiments of nature are often natural disasters, like the January 1994 earthquake in Los Angeles, whose aftermath is shown here, or the flood at Buffalo Creek in 1972.

trauma, the survivors showed symptoms of terror, disturbed sleep, guilt over surviving, and reliving of the events (Erikson, 1976). These symptoms characterize an anxiety disorder called "post-traumatic stress disorder" (see Chapter 8).

An experiment of nature is usually *retrospective,* with systematic observation beginning only after the precipitating event. But experiments of nature can also be *prospective,* with observation beginning before an expected outcome occurs. When prospective studies are *longitudinal* as well, looking at the same subjects on the same variables at different points over their lifetime, they are particularly powerful methods of investigation (Baltes, Reese, and Lipsitt, 1980). Consider the following prospective, longitudinal study of children vulnerable to schizophrenia by virtue of being born to a mother who was schizophrenic (Mednick, Parnas, and Schulsinger, 1987; Parnas, Cannon, Jacobsen, Schulsinger, Schulsinger, and Mednick, 1993). In this Copenhagen study, 207 children of schizophrenic mothers and 104 controls have been followed from 1962 until now. By 1972, 8.6 percent of the high-risk children had become schizophrenic, but only 1 percent of the children of normal mothers. Which of the vulnerable children became schizophrenic? Two factors emerge from this longitudinal study: (1) those high-risk children who had more traumatic births and birth complications tended to become schizophrenic, and (2) those high-risk children who had more unstable parenting tended to become schizophrenic.

The prospective, longitudinal method can also be used to predict who will become depressed. In one elegant study, the investigators combined this method with the twin studies method in order to look at genetic predisposition to depression at the same time as studying the contribution of recent life events, lifetime trauma, social relations, and personality (Kendler, Kessler, Neale, Heath, and Eaves, 1993). Six hundred and eighty female twin pairs were followed for a year to see if an episode of depression would occur during that time. Two-thirds of the pairs were identical twins and one-third were fra-

FOCUS QUESTIONS

1. Describe some symptoms of survivors of natural disasters.
2. How are prospective longitudinal studies used to study genetic and environmental factors that may trigger schizophrenia or depression?
3. What are the strengths and weaknesses of using experiments of nature to investigate abnormality?

ternal twins. Since identical twins have all the same genes, and fraternals only have an average of half their genes in common, the genetic contribution to depression could be assessed. Among identical twins, if one twin became depressed during the year, the probability was .27 that the co-twin did as well. But for fraternal twins, the probability for the co-twin to become depressed was only .09. This suggested a strong genetic contribution to depression.

How about other causes? Parental warmth, childhood loss, neuroticism, interpersonal difficulties, and depressive history were also measured. Each of these factors (along with genetics) was used separately and together to predict depression using correlational mathematics. Recent stressful events, prior depression, and neuroticism were strong predictors of depression. Interpersonal problems, lack of parental warmth, and lifetime trauma were intermediate predictors. Lack of social support and death or divorce of parents were only modest predictors. Studies like this are a fine beginning. They not only illuminate the multiple causes of depression, but point us toward the most efficacious interventions.

As more prospective, longitudinal studies are carried out, we will learn a great deal more about what environmental factors trigger psychopathology in individuals who are genetically vulnerable.

Evaluation of Experiments of Nature

Experiments of nature have three strengths as a method of inquiry: (1) like a case history, they document an actual happening and lack the artificiality of the laboratory experiment or the abstractness of a correlation; (2) no unethical manipulation is performed by the investigator since he merely observes an event produced by nature; and (3) the gross cause can be determined. In fact, the gross cause defines the investigation as an experiment of nature. However, the method also has three weaknesses: (1) we cannot isolate the elements in the gross cause that are active from those that are inactive; for example, we cannot know which aspects—the suddenness of the disaster or seeing others die or the uprooting of the community—of the Buffalo Creek Flood produced the stress disorder; (2) experiments of nature, as they are rare and conspicuous events, are not repeatable; and (3) like case histories, this method is also subject to retrospective bias by both victim and investigator. It is not irrelevant that the victims of the Buffalo Creek flood were suing the company that owned the dam for enormous sums.

THE LABORATORY MODEL

Correlations and experiments of nature are both used by investigators of abnormality when the road to experimentation is blocked. The final technique for getting around the impossibility of direct experimentation is the ***laboratory model.*** In the last decade, scientists have made considerable strides in understanding psychopathology by using such laboratory models.

A laboratory model is in essence the production, under controlled conditions, of phenomena analogous to naturally occurring mental disorders. That is, a particular symptom or constellation of symptoms is produced in miniature to test hypotheses about cause and cure. Confirmed hypotheses can then be further tested in situations outside the laboratory. Both human and animal subjects are utilized in laboratory models.

As an example, let us see how scientists have created an animal model of unipolar depression. About twenty-five years ago, investigators noticed that animals who received electric shock that was *uncontrollable*—that went on and off regardless of what the animal was doing—later became very passive. Later on in a different situation, they failed even to try to escape shock that was actually escapable. They just sat and took the shock (Seligman and Maier, 1967; Maier and Seligman, 1976). Evidence soon began to accumulate that such "learned helplessness" had many of the same symptoms as depression in humans.

Learned helplessness has been systematically evaluated to find if it is a valid model of depression (Weiss, Simson, Ambrose, Webster, and Hoffman, 1985). For a person to meet the DSM-IV criteria for diagnosis of depression, at least five of these nine symptoms must be present: (1) loss of interest in usual activities, (2) weight loss and poor appetite, (3) insomnia, (4) psychomotor alterations, (5) fatigue or loss of energy, (6) diminished ability to think or attend, (7) depressed mood, (8) feelings of worthlessness, and (9) suicidal thoughts.

Animals who have experienced uncontrollable events show each of the first six symptoms. They would receive a diagnosis of depression if they were human. The last three symptoms (depressed mood, feelings of worthlessness, and suicidal thoughts) cannot be displayed by animals. But the argument can be carried further. When humans are given uncontrollable noise, they display depressed mood and feelings of worthlessness in addition to the hallmark symptoms above (Hiroto and Seligman, 1975; Abramson, 1978). This means that eight of the nine symptoms of depression can be produced in the laboratory by uncontrollable events. The ninth, suicidal thoughts, cannot be produced, but probably because the intensity of the uncontrollable events in the laboratory is very mild.

This mapping of symptoms has inspired investigators to look for the biochemical basis of learned helplessness and to discover drug treatments that cure learned helplessness in animals. The brain chemistry of those suffering from learned helplessness has been explored and looks quite similar to what is known about the brain chemistry of those suffering from depression (Weiss et al., 1985). In addition, the drugs that break up helplessness in animals also alleviate depression in humans (Sherman and Petty, 1980).

All of this seems to argue that learned helplessness in animals is a convincing laboratory model of depression in humans. This model may help us to understand the brain chemistry of human depression, to understand how drugs can relieve depression, and to find new treatments for depression. The brain chemistry and experimental drug treatment of depression cannot be ethically carried out on humans, but such animal models enable us to understand and relieve human suffering with experimental rigor and to do so with fewer ethical dilemmas (Miller, 1985).

Evaluation of the Laboratory Model

Laboratory models have three strengths: (1) as experiments, they can isolate the cause of the disorder; (2) they are repeatable; (3) they minimize unethical manipulation. Like all other methods, they also have several weaknesses: (1) as laboratory creations, they are not the natural phenomenon, only a *model* of

FOCUS QUESTIONS

1. Explain how scientists tested in the laboratory the hypothesis concerning the learned helplessness model of depression.
2. What are the strengths and weaknesses of the laboratory model of investigating abnormality?

it. Thus, they are *analogous* to but not identical with the real disorder itself; (2) since observers often use animal subjects in laboratory models, they must infer that humans and the species being investigated are similarly susceptible to the disorder.

As similarity of symptoms, cause, physiology, cure, and prevention mount, we become more convinced that the model is the actual disorder. In later chapters, we will see examples of models that have given insight into the cause and cure of such disorders as depression, stomach ulcers, and phobias. Sophisticated laboratory modeling is a new development in the field of abnormality. The verdict is not entirely in on any one model, but the technique promises to add to our understanding of abnormality.

COMBINING SEVERAL METHODS: A WOVEN FABRIC

There is no single, most convincing way to understand abnormality. Each method has strengths and weaknesses (Table 6–4). But clinical case histories, experimental studies, correlational studies, experiments of nature, and laboratory models all can provide some insight. Each by itself can, on occasion, provide conclusive understanding. But most of the time, each taken in isolation resembles blind men groping at an elephant: one has hold of the tail, another

TABLE 6–4

STRENGTHS AND WEAKNESSES OF VARIOUS METHODS		
Method	*Strengths*	*Weaknesses*
Single Clinical Case	1. Is not artificial. 2. Documents rare events. 3. Generates causal hypotheses.	1. Is selective and susceptible to retrospective bias. 2. Is not repeatable. 3. Is not general. 4. Does not isolate causal elements.
Experiments	1. Isolate causal elements. 2. Are general to population sampled (not true of single subject-experiments). 3. Are repeatable.	1. Are artificial; don't capture full reality of the disorder. 2. Inferences are probabilistic or statistical, rather than certain. 3. It is unethical or impractical to manipulate many crucial variables.
Correlations	1. Quantify and observe relationships. 2. Are not artificial. 3. Are repeatable.	1. Do not isolate causal elements.
Experiments of Nature	1. Are not artificial. 2. There is no unethical manipulation. 3. Isolate gross cause.	1. Do not isolate active elements of the cause. 2. Are not repeatable. 3. Are susceptible to retrospective bias.
Laboratory Models	1. Isolate causal elements. 2. Are repeatable. 3. Minimize unethical manipulation.	1. Are analogous to but not identical with the real disorder. 2. Make cross-species inferences (with animal models).

FOCUS QUESTIONS

1. Why is the best understanding of a disorder formed when all the methods of investigating abnormality converge on a theory?
2. For which disorders have the various methods converged on a theory about the disorder?

the trunk, another a foot. Each captures only one aspect of being an elephant, but none captures the whole thing. Similarly, the clinical case, well done, best conveys the reality of a disorder, but it usually fails to isolate the cause. The experiment, well done, isolates the cause, but it remains artificial. The correlation, well done, picks out crucial relationships, but not necessarily causal ones. But when the methods together converge on a theory, a fabric of understanding is woven. In the particular disorders that we are close to understanding, case history evidence, experimental studies, correlations, experiments of nature, and laboratory models all play a role. A worthy scientific fabric of converging evidence has already been woven for phobias, for the genetics of schizophrenia, for depression, for certain kinds of brain damage, and for sexual identity. For some of the specific disorders that we will discuss in the ensuing chapters, the reader will realize that much still remains to be discovered before the disorder can be understood. For most others, the reader probably will feel that they are understood partially, but that pieces of the puzzle are still missing. But for several others, the reader should feel the pleasure and excitement of discovery and understanding, because these are examples of the woven fabric.

SUMMARY

1. The *clinical case history* is the record of part of the life of an individual as seen during therapy. Based on the patient's case history, the therapist will hypothesize about possible causes of a problem and then help the patient overcome his past.

2. A *scientific experiment* consists of a procedure in which the hypothesized cause (the *independent variable*) is manipulated and the occurrence of the effect (the *dependent variable*) is measured. Both independent and dependent variables are operationally defined. An *operational definition* is the set of measurable and repeatable conditions after which a phenomenon is said to occur. When manipulating an independent variable produces changes in a dependent variable, an *experimental effect* has been obtained.

3. *Confounds* are factors other than the independent variable that might produce an experimental effect. An *experimental group* experiences both the confounds and the hypothesized cause. The *control group* is similar to the experimental group, but the control group only experiences the confounds. Subtle confounds that might produce the experimental effect include nonrandom assignment, experimenter bias, subject bias, and demand characteristics.

4. *Statistical inferences* are the procedures used to determine whether the *sample* (the particular observations) truly represents the *population* (the entire set of potential observations). When effects exceed a conventional confidence level, they are called *statistically significant*.

5. If an hypothesis is rejected but it is really true, the mistake is called a *miss*. If an hypothesis is accepted but it is really false, the mistake is called a *false alarm*. Misses and false alarms stand in a trade-off relationship to each other; when there are many misses, there are few false alarms; when there are many false alarms, there are few misses.

6. *Correlation* is pure observation without manipulation. In a correlation, two classes of events are measured and the relationship between them is recorded. In a *positive correlation,* as one variable increases, the other does too. In a *negative correlation,* as one variable increases, the other decreases. Events are *uncorrelated* when, as one variable changes, the other does not change in any systematic way.

7. A relationship is *statistically significant* if it is unlikely to have occurred by chance. Generally, the farther the correlation is from .00 in either the positive or negative direction and the more observations that are made, the higher the level of confidence and the greater the likelihood that the relationship did not occur by chance.

8. *Epidemiological* data concerning the lifetime prevalence of disorders can be used to make inferences about the etiology of the disorder as well.

9. *Experiments of nature* are studies in which the experimenter observes the effects of an unusual natural event. *Prospective longitudinal* studies are a powerful means of assessing the effects of events on the development of psychopathology.

10. In a *laboratory model,* investigators produce, under controlled conditions, phenomena that are analogous to naturally occurring mental disorders. This is done to test hypotheses about biological and psychological causes and cures of symptoms.

11. No one method alone will provide complete understanding of psychopathology. But each method may lead us to an understanding of various aspects of abnormality. When all these methods converge in confirmation of a theory, we can say that a fabric of understanding has been woven.

QUESTIONS FOR CRITICAL THINKING

1. Why is the clinical case history method particularly susceptible to bias by patient and therapist?

2. Should insurance companies use meta-analysis to determine which psychological treatments are effective and should be covered under a health-care plan?

3. Do you think that confidence levels for a new drug to treat schizophrenia should be set at more or less conservative levels?

4. What are some possible causes for the positive correlation of living in a city with increased risk for depression and substance abuse?

CHAPTER 7

Psychological Assessment and Classification

CHAPTER ORGANIZER

PSYCHOLOGICAL ASSESSMENT
- Understand the importance of the reliability and validity of psychological tests.
- Familiarize yourself with the three kinds of psychological assessment techniques and how they are used to gather information about a client.

DIAGNOSIS
- Familiarize yourself with reasons to make a diagnosis.
- Understand how clinicians use DSM-IV to diagnose patients.

EVALUATING PSYCHOLOGICAL DIAGNOSES
- Be able to describe some factors that may influence the reliability and validity of diagnoses.
- Think about whether there is a need for diagnosis.

People differ psychologically. There are shy people and outgoing ones, industrious people and lazy ones, depressed people and happy ones. This observation is commonplace, but it leads to some very important ideas. Psychological classification permits us to group people according to their similarities, to ask how they came to be that way and how they can be changed. Without classification, there can be no science, no understanding of how things came to be and how they will evolve.

In this chapter, we take up the assessment and classification of abnormal psychological conditions. Because such classification often arises in a medical context and is modeled after medicine itself, it is often called psychological or psychiatric diagnosis. You know from the biological approach to abnormality (Chapter 3) that psychological diagnosis has already been a beneficial enterprise, for without it medical research could not have eliminated a disorder called general paresis. Those useful insights occurred nearly a century ago, however; here we will concern ourselves with modern psychological assessment and diagnosis. What kinds of assessment techniques promise reliable understanding of human misery and lead to useful diagnosis? What diagnostic categories seem most promising for understanding and treating psychological distress? Indeed, how do we assess whether an assessment procedure or diagnostic category is useful or promising?

Psychologists seek to understand individuals through a variety of procedures. They talk to people, administer psychological tests, and assess their behavior in real-life situations. The first theme of this chapter consists of the contribution of these assessment techniques to the process of classification. The second theme concerns diagnosis itself: the reliability and usefulness of current diagnostic schemes.

PSYCHOLOGICAL ASSESSMENT

assessment device must be reliable and valid

Assessment is undertaken to achieve a deep understanding of the client. That understanding may result in a diagnosis, but it commonly also results in much more. Commonly, assessment yields a sense of a person's individuality, the forces that generate his or her uniqueness. Often, it will give a sense of why a person is in difficulty, and occasionally a clue as to how the difficulty can be resolved.

In order for an assessment device to generate meaningful understandings about people, it must possess two characteristics. First, it must be **reliable,** that is, it must generate the same findings on repeated use; it must be stable. Imagine a physical universe in which yardsticks are made of rubber. Each time you would measure something, you would come up with different answers simply because of the nature of the rubber measuring instrument, which stretches. Such an instrument would be *un*reliable, which is to say you could not depend on it to come up with the same measurement each time it was used. Similarly, a psychological test that yields different findings on different occasions is also unreliable and has limited usefulness in understanding people. Second, an assessment device must be **valid.** It must be useful for the purposes for which it is intended. Even a good thermometer is useless for measuring a room. Similarly, a psychological test can be useful for one purpose and thoroughly invalid for others.

Psychological assessment techniques are divided into three processes: interviewing, testing, and observing. Each of these techniques can be used to gather information about a client's problems and disabilities.

FOCUS QUESTIONS

1. Describe how a structured interview differs from an unstructured interview.
2. What do the test items on the MMPI assess?
3. Describe what projective tests are used to assess and how they differ from objective psychological inventories like the MMPI.
4. Describe the techniques used to scan the brain and how they differ from each other.

The Clinical Interview

clinical interview ...met and talk w/ someone

The **clinical interview** is the favorite instrument of clinical psychologists and psychiatrists, reflecting the widespread view that we don't know someone well until we've met and talked with him. Good interviewers get information, not only from what people say, but from how they say it: their manner, tone of voice, body postures, and degree of eye contact (Exline and Winters, 1965; Ellsworth and Carlsmith, 1968; Ekman, Friesen, and Ellsworth, 1972). Of course, in order to get this information, there must be a good rapport between the client and interviewer. One should not expect people to be honest if they feel that their statements are going to incriminate them or lead to aversive decisions about their future. For an interview to be maximally informative, the client needs to perceive the interviewer as being nonthreatening, supportive, and encouraging of self-disclosure (Jourard, 1974).

The clinical interview may range from an unstructured conversation to a quite structured encounter. Fundamentally, an **unstructured interview** allows the interviewer to take advantage of the exigencies of the moment. The client may want to talk about a particular problem, and right now, rather than later. The unstructured interview permits that. Similarly, the interviewer may want to inquire into a particular issue. The unstructured interview, therefore, is very flexible, but it "pays a price" for that flexibility. Because they are unstructured, no two of these interviews are the same. They elicit different information and, therefore, the reliability and validity of the information that is elicited may be reduced (Fisher, Epstein, and Harris, 1967).

Although the unstructured interview may seem like a rambling event, it is not random. The kind of information interviewers attempt to elicit is heavily determined by their own orientation, by the theory that guides their own understanding of human behavior. For example, interviewers with a psychoanalytic orientation will often concentrate on early childhood experiences, sexual experiences, and dreams because such data enable them to form a psychoanalytic impression of personality. Behaviorists, on the other hand, tend to concentrate on current events, on behavior that is presently distressing and the events and experiences that surround it, again because these experiences are especially meaningful within their theoretical framework.

The fact that different interviewers pursue different issues and, therefore, often arrive at varying conclusions, has led increasingly to the use of **structured interviews** in which all of the interviewer's questions are prepared in an **interview schedule** and may, in fact, be read. The structured interview standardizes the questions that are asked by each interviewer. The amount of clinical judgment required in these interviews is substantially reduced, since the answers to the specific questions and probes lead automatically to the scoring of the symptoms, which can be processed by a computer. Such interview schedules remove much of the unreliability that is introduced by differences in the way clinicians elicit information in diagnostic interviews (Matarazzo, 1983) and make it possible for even lay interviewers to gather psychological information and make diagnoses.

Several structured interview schedules have been developed in recent years. Among the early attempts to structure clinical interviews was the Schedule of Affective Disorders and Schizophrenia (SADS), which was designed to elicit information about a person's symptoms and current level of functioning, as well as providing data that would lead to a diagnosis. SADS has been replaced, by and large, by the Structured Clinical Interview, known commonly as SCID. Unlike interview formats that are *linear*, requiring the interviewer to move without digression from question to question, SCID provides a *branching* format, enabling the interviewer to probe when required, and to move on to questions that relate to a different diagnosis (Shea, 1990).

Psychological Testing

Additional psychological information about the nature of an individual's problems and disabilities comes from psychological testing. Personality assessment is a subject that fascinates many people, so much so that there are thousands of personality tests, and hundreds of books written about them. Some tests are focal, designed to illuminate a single personality attribute, such as anxiety or depression, or to uncover a particular kind of brain damage. Others are omnibus, seeking to describe a larger portion of personality and abnormality. Many tests are unstructured or projective, requiring the client to draw a person or persons or a series of designs, to determine abnormality through careful

▲ Just as in everyday encounters with others, a patient speaks to a therapist in a clinical interview not only through words, but through her manner, posture, tone of voice, and degree of eye contact.

interviewing, while others aspire to the same goal through formal, structured examinations.

Most psychological testing procedures are relatively standardized. That important fact increases the likelihood that different examiners will obtain similar information from the client: that is, that the test will be reliable. If several examiners give the Wechsler Adult Intelligence Scale to the same client, for example, then the client's score should be approximately the same from one examination to the next.

Psychological tests fall into three categories: psychological inventories, "projective" tests, and intelligence tests.

PSYCHOLOGICAL INVENTORIES

Nearly everyone has taken an objective **psychological inventory** at one time or another for vocational guidance, or personal counseling, or in connection with a job. These tests are highly structured and contain a variety of statements that can be answered "true" or "false." The client is asked to indicate whether or not each statement applies to her. Inventories have enormous advantages: they are commonly highly reliable; they can often be given to several people simultaneously and are therefore relatively inexpensive to administer and score; and by providing statistical norms, they allow comparative judgments to be made.

By far, the most widely used and studied personality inventory in clinical assessment is the **Minnesota Multiphasic Personality Inventory** or the **MMPI** (Hathaway and McKinley, 1943). The MMPI consists of 550 test items that inquire into a wide array of behaviors, thoughts, and feelings. Although the MMPI can be administered separately to individual clients, it is most often administered to small groups of people. All respondents are usually given the same test items, but the meaning of those items may not be identical for each respondent. Thus, a college student who responds "yes" to the statement "I usually feel fine" obviously means something quite different from the hospitalized person who responded "yes" without reading the statement. As a consequence, the meanings of the MMPI items are by no means self-evident, and they have had to be ascertained by empirical research. Scales have been constructed by examining the responses of people with known characteristics, such as depressed versus nondepressed persons, manic versus non-manic, introverted versus extraverted. All in all, the MMPI provides scores for the ten categories shown in Table 7–1. These categories have been validated against diagnostic judgments that arose from psychiatric interviews and other tests (Wrobel and Lochar, 1982).

Any paper-and-pencil inventory is subject to a variety of distortions, and the MMPI is no exception. One can simply lie. One can be evasive. Or one can try to put oneself in the best possible social light. And one can do these things intentionally or unintentionally. However, the MMPI contains four "validity" scales that are designed to alert the diagnostician to such distortions. Thus, if a person were to respond "true" to the following items: "I never tell lies," and "I read the newspaper editorials every day," it might be reasonable to surmise that the test-taker is trying to present herself as favorably as she can—since it is a rare person who never tells lies and who reads the editorials daily. Notice that these judgments about social desirability and lying are *not* absolutely foolproof. Rather they are "best guesses." Most (but not all) people who respond positively to the above items will be, willingly or unwittingly, trying to improve

TABLE 7-1

PERSONALITY CHARACTERISTICS ASSOCIATED WITH ELEVATIONS ON THE BASIC MMPI SCALES

Scale	Characteristics
1 (Hs), Hypochondriasis	High scorers are described as cynical, defeatist, preoccupied with self, complaining, hostile, and presenting numerous physical problems.
2 (D), Depression	High scorers are described as moody, shy, despondent, pessimistic, and distressed. This scale is one of the most frequently elevated in clinical patients.
3 (Hy), Hysteria	High scorers tend to be repressed, dependent, naive, outgoing, and to have multiple physical complaints. They express psychological conflict through vague and unbased physical complaints.
4 (Pd), Psychopathic Deviate	High scorers often are rebellious, impulsive, hedonistic, and antisocial. They often have difficulty in marital or family relationships and trouble with the law or authority in general.
5 (MF), Masculinity-Femininity	High-scoring males are described as sensitive, aesthetic, passive, or feminine. High-scoring females are described as aggressive, rebellious, and unrealistic.
6 (Pa), Paranoia	Elevations on this scale are often associated with being suspicious, aloof, shrewd, guarded, worrisome, and overly sensitive. High scorers may project or externalize blame.
7 (Pt), Psychasthenia	High scorers are tense, anxious, ruminative, preoccupied, obsessional, phobic, rigid. They frequently are self-condemning and feel inferior and inadequate.
8 (Sc), Schizophrenia	High scorers are often withdrawn, shy, unusual, or strange and have peculiar thoughts or ideas. They may have poor reality contact and in severe cases bizarre sensory experiences—delusions and hallucinations.
9 (Ma), Mania	High scorers are called sociable, outgoing, impulsive, overly energetic, optimistic, and in some cases amoral, flighty, confused, disoriented.
0 (Si), Social Introversion-Extraversion	High scorers tend to be modest, shy, withdrawn, self-effacing, inhibited. Low scorers are outgoing, spontaneous, sociable, confident.

SOURCE: Butcher, 1969.

their image. For all we know, however, there may well be some people who read every editorial every day and who never tell lies (bless 'em!).

Assessment can be approached from a variety of angles. Some inventories examine thought. Others focus on behavior. Some concentrate on context and situation, others on traits. The content of the MMPI items has been compared to other personality inventories. The MMPI was found to have the highest percent of items dealing with the *cognitive* area of functioning, and the lowest percent dealing with *behavioral acts.* It was also lowest in terms of the proportion of items that referred to a situation, rather than a personal characteristic or trait (Werner and Pervin, 1986).

The results of the MMPI are recorded in the form of a profile (Figure 7–1A). The profile tells a clinician more than the individual scores would. By utilizing an MMPI atlas (e.g., Gilberstadt and Duker, 1965; Greene, 1991), the profile of a particular person can be compared with similar profiles obtained from individuals about whom a great deal is known (Figure 7–2B). The resulting personality assessment is more than the sum of the individual's MMPI scores. This larger assessment can then be examined against inferences from other sources

Figure 7—1

THE MINNESOTA MULTIPHASIC PERSONALITY INVENTORY

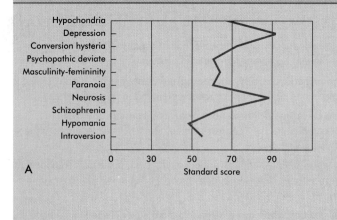

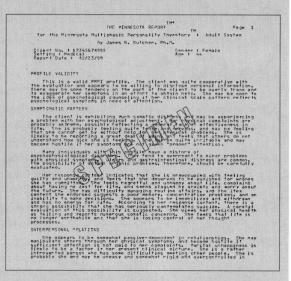

A

B

(A) An example of an MMPI profile. (B) An "automated" interpretation provided by a computer. The computer prints out statements that have been found to have some validity for other individuals with similar profiles. (SOURCES: Gleitman, 1981; NCS Interpretive Scoring Systems)

of information that the clinician has obtained, with the goal of noting consistencies and reconciling inconsistencies (Korchin, 1976).

The MMPI is more than fifty years old. Times change. Language changes. And tests may need to change to accommodate to new circumstances and new ways of describing individuals in those changed times. The MMPI-2 was designed to do precisely that. It modernized language, changing such phrases as "acid stomach" to "upset stomach." And it attempted to assess modern psychological concerns, such as vulnerability to drug abuse and eating disorders, as well as poor adaptation to work (Butcher, Dahlstrom, Graham, Tellegen, and Kraemer, 1989; Greene, 1991).

Opinion regarding the MMPI-2 is divided. Many clinicians obviously appreciate the modernization, as well as the fact that it was standardized on a larger and more representative sample than was the MMPI. But others find the new test significantly flawed, perhaps irremediably so. For example, although the standardization sample for MMPI-2 is larger and more representative than for the original MMPI, it is still biased in the direction of respondents who have more education and higher professional achievements than the population at large. More significantly, it seems that the two versions of the MMPI can be inconsistent with each other on some occasions. One can get a score on one version that indicates substantial depression, and a score on the other that is quite within normal range. Finally, it appears that the enormous amount of detail in the form of "profiles" that has been accumulated on the MMPI for more than half a century, will be inapplicable to the revised version—surely a major loss (Adler, 1989).

PROJECTIVE TESTS

For many psychologists, and especially those who are psychodynamically oriented, the focus of assessment is on unconscious conflicts, latent fears, sexual and aggressive impulses, and hidden anxieties. Structured inventories, because they inquire about *conscious* experience and feelings, obscure these deeper dynamics. But because ***projective tests*** utilize meaningless stimuli, such as inkblot forms, they minimize reality constraints, encourage imaginative processes, and maximize the opportunity for conflictual or unconscious concerns to emerge (Murray, 1951). Two of the most widely used projective tests are the Rorschach Test and the Thematic Apperception Test.

The Rorschach Test Invented by Hermann Rorschach (1884–1922), a Swiss psychiatrist, the ***Rorschach Test*** consists of ten bilaterally symmetrical "inkblots," some in color, some in black, gray, and white, and each on an individual card. The respondent is shown each card separately and asked to tell the examiner everything she sees on the card, that is, everything the inkblot could resemble. Figure 7–2 shows two inkblots that are similar to such cards.

Here are the responses made by one person to the card on the left (Exner, 1978, p. 170):

PATIENT: I think it could be a woman standing in the middle there . . . Should I try to find something else?
EXAMINER: Most people see more than one thing.
PATIENT: I suppose the entire thing could be a butterfly. . . . I don't see anything else.

Responses to these inkblots are scored in several ways. First, they are scored for the nature and quality of what has been seen. In this instance, the woman and the butterfly are well-formed percepts, indicative of someone whose view of the world is relatively clear. Second, whether the percept is commonly seen by others, or relatively rare (and if rare, whether creative or bizarre) is scored. Seeing a woman and a butterfly on this blot is a common occurrence. It suggests that this person is capable of seeing the world as others do. Additional scoring will examine whether the entire blot or only part of it was used, and whether color is used and integrated into the percept. These scores, as well as what is seen in the blot, are integrated to give an overall pic-

FIGURE 7–2

THE RORSCHACH TEST

Facsimiles of Rorschach Test cards. These projective instruments are composed of stimuli that seem like inkblots and that allow the respondent to project impressions of what those inkblots might be. (SOURCE: Based on Gleitman, 1981, p. 635)

ture of the vitality of the respondent's inner life, his conflicts, the degree to which he can control sexual and aggressive urges, and the like.

Perusal of the inkblot on the left in Figure 7–2 will give some sense of the thinking that goes into Rorschach interpretation. Imagine someone who has responded to the bits of ink that surround the central percept, but who failed to respond to the main part of the blot. You might hypothesize (and it is *only* a hypothesis) that this individual has difficulty confronting "central" realities and perhaps, as a result, turns her attention to trivia, as if *they* were central. Using the responses to a single blot, of course, would be merely one of any number of hypotheses you might entertain. There might, for example, be something about the central percept of this particular card that the respondent finds aversive. If so, the response would indicate little about generalized tendencies to avoid centralities. If, however, such responses were forthcoming on several cards—if on each of them the respondent "missed" the central percept and puttered about at the edges, an examiner might feel that the hunch was well-substantiated. This is the kind of thinking that is used to examine the use of color, of forms, of the popularity of the percept, and so on. A test record that reveals only commonly given percepts might be judged to be behaviorally conformist and cognitively banal, especially if all other indices were consistent with that view.

Interpreting the Rorschach requires enormous skill. It is a fascinating and complex process, whose full richness is not given by the above examples. But it is not without its hazards. Precisely because the interpretive logic is so compelling, there is a strong tendency to believe in it without validation, and to disregard contrary evidence. Indeed, the interpretation of Rorschach protocols turns out to be a place to examine the attributional errors that the intuitive mind makes (Ross, 1977: Nisbett and Ross, 1980). For example, clinicians might be asked to assess which of the following sets of responses given by a male respondent to the card on the right in Figure 7–2 indicates the presence of homosexual tendencies:

> *Protocol 1:* The whole thing looks ominous. There are violent monsters here. You can see them clawing at each other. I don't know what kind they are, but they sure are scary. . . . In fact, the entire blot looks like an angry centaur, rearing on its hind legs. You can see the human face and the animal body, and the arms there, the horse here.
>
> *Protocol 2:* Well, these in the center seem like sex organs. Male sex organs. . . . And over here, this looks like a dress and a bra. Kind of a padded bra, it looks like. . . . Here's someone's butt. Kind of a child's butt—you can even see the err . . . uh, rectum I think. . . . And this is—what do you call them—someone who is part man and part woman. The bottom part looks like it's a man, but when you look up, it's a woman.

Clinicians who examined many such protocols were emphatic in interpreting responses of the kind given in Protocol 2 as indicative of homosexuality, while responses like those in Protocol 1 were given much less weight (Chapman and Chapman, 1969). In fact, the responses shown in Protocol 2 are *entirely invalid* as indices of homosexual interest or behavior, having no research support whatsoever. Those in Protocol 1, however, though seemingly removed from homosexuality at the intuitive level, are moderately well-supported in validation studies as signs of homosexuality.

The conflict between intuition (or common sense) on the one hand and validated data on the other pervades assessment, as it pervades psychological judgment in general. Time and again, it will seem to clinicians that a certain sign makes sense as an indicator of a larger behavior, so much so that it hardly seems worth the effort to assess the validity of the sign empirically. And time and again, when that assessment *is* made, it will be found that the correlation between sign and indicator is *illusory* (Chapman and Chapman, 1969), based merely on a commonly held view and not on reality.

As might be expected with an instrument that is so complex and that is predicated on ambiguity, neither the reliability nor the validity of the Rorschach has been high. Reliability of scoring is low despite the variety of manuals that are available to assist the clinician (e.g., Exner, 1974, 1978; Aronow and Reznikoff, 1976). One attempt to objectify and standardize scoring has resulted in another set of inkblots (Holtzman, 1961; Hill, 1972), which has been used mainly in research rather than in clinical practice.

Tests that purport to reveal "underlying psychodynamics" are particularly difficult to validate because such dynamics are inferred. Technically, they are *hypothetical* constructs, assumed to be there for theoretical reasons since they cannot be examined directly nor verified directly. When, however, interpretations from the Rorschach have been susceptible to verification (as when the indices point to homosexuality or predict suicide), the evidence in the main has gone against the Rorschach (Zubin, Eron, and Schumer, 1965; Mischel, 1968, 1976; Peterson, 1978; see Weiner, 1969, for a more optimistic position).

Thematic Apperception Test   Another commonly used instrument is the ***Thematic Apperception Test,*** or the ***TAT.*** It consists of a series of pictures that are not as ambiguous as Rorschach cards, but not as clear as photographs either. Respondents are asked to look at each picture and to make up a story about it. They are told to tell how the story began, what is happening now, and how it will end. As with the Rorschach, it is assumed that because the pictures are ambiguous, the stories will reflect the respondent's proclivity to see situations in a particular way. A respondent who repeatedly uses the same theme to describe several different pictures may be revealing personal psychodynamics.

The TAT has been used extensively as a research instrument to explore a variety of motives, particularly the need for achievement (McClelland et al., 1953; Atkinson, 1958). Its use in that context has been fruitful and provocative. But its use as a clinical instrument for assessing individual personality is prey to the same problems that beset the Rorschach. Although reliability of scoring is adequate (Harrison, 1965), the interpretations of TAT protocols by different clinicians is quite diverse (Murstein, 1965).

INTELLIGENCE TESTS

Perhaps the most reliable and, for many purposes, the most valid of all psychological tests are those that measure intelligence. Originally designed by Alfred Binet to differentiate "slow" school children from those who were mentally retarded, the test underwent many revisions, culminating in the Stanford-Binet Intelligence Test for Children. Somewhat later, David Wechsler standardized individually administered intelligence tests for both adults and children. These tests include the Wechsler Adult Intelligence Scale (WAIS), the Wechsler Intelligence Scale for Children (WISC), and the Wechsler Preschool and Primary

▼ TAT pictures, such as this one, are designed to be sufficiently vague to allow respondents to project their own meaningful story onto it.

IQ tests:
WAIS
WISC

"WE REALIZE YOU DO BETTER ON YOUR IQ TESTS THAN YOU DO IN ANYTHING ELSE, BUT YOU JUST CANNOT MAJOR IN IQ."

Scale of Intelligence (WPPSI). The WAIS was revised and restandardized as the Wechsler Adult Intelligence Scale—Revised (WAIS-R) in 1981 to eliminate or modify items that were considered unfair to minority groups (Mishra and Brown, 1983), to update the test content, and to provide new norms. While there are high correlations between the WAIS and the WAIS-R, the overall scores on the latter tend to be substantially *lower* than those on the former (Urbina, Golden, and Ariel, 1982: Lippold and Claiborn, 1983; Mishra and Brown, 1983).

The Wechsler Scales provide a total IQ (Intelligence Quotient) which is composed of two subscores: Verbal IQ and Performance IQ. Verbal IQ comprises such matters as vocabulary, ability to comprehend verbal statements and problems, and general information. Performance IQ measures intelligence in ways that are less dependent upon verbal ability, such as the ability to copy designs and to associate symbols with numbers.

Intelligence tests play an important role in assessing mental retardation and brain damage. Moreover, they are the only psychological tests that are routinely administered to school children and that determine, in some measure, the kind of education that children will obtain. It is important, therefore, to understand what intelligence tests actually measure.

Intelligence itself is not directly knowable. It can only be inferred from behavior. Intelligence tests sample behaviors on certain standardized tasks, particularly those that predict success in school. Other behaviors, like the ability to make it "on the street" or the ability to appreciate classical music, are simply not measured. For that reason, intelligence has often been defined as what an intelligence test measures. That is not quite a satisfying definition, but it is accurate. If one's working definition of intelligence differs from the one that is implicit in a particular intelligence test, one should not be surprised that the test score fails to meet expectations. An intelligence test that measures verbal facility will not predict well ability on psychomotor tasks.

Observations

The assessment techniques reviewed so far—the interview, the standardized and projective tests, the intelligence test—have had one thing in common: all of them are verbal and all of them use words to portray psychological assets and liabilities. But words are often imprecise. Often they overstate the matter. Depressed people are wont to say that "My life is just miserable all the time," an expression that conveys the full sense of their feelings right now, but no sense at all of what the problem is, how often it occurs, and how to begin working on it. In marital conflict, for example, the following complaints are not uncommon.

> HE: She never has a meal on the table on time.
> SHE: He never takes me out.

Both clearly believe what they are saying and their beliefs amplify their anger with each other. The beliefs, however, are false. When they begin to take notice of actual behavior, rather than accusations, they find that most (but not all) of the meals are on the table on time, and they go out with some frequency (but not as often as she would like). Already the gap between them has narrowed, creating a smaller disagreement out of what seemed to be a major conflict.

More than a quarter century ago, Wendell Johnson (1946; cited in Goldfried and Davison, 1976) captured the significance of behavioral assessment for treatment:

> To say that Henry is mean implies that he has some sort of inherent trait, but it tells us nothing about what Henry has done. Consequently, it fails to suggest any specific means of improving Henry. If, on the other hand, it is said that Henry snatched Billy's cap and threw it in the bonfire, the situation is rendered somewhat more clear and actually more hopeful. You might never eliminate "meanness," but there are fairly definite steps to be taken in order to remove Henry's incentives or opportunities for throwing caps in bonfires . . . (What needs to be done) . . . is to get the person to tell him not what he *is* or what he *has*, but what he *does*, and the conditions under which he does it.

BEHAVIORAL ASSESSMENT

Behavioral assessment is commonly used in conjunction with treatment itself: to define the problem, to narrow it, to provide a record of what needs to be changed, and subsequently, of what progress has been made. The assessment does not stand apart from the treatment, nor is it an evaluation of the client for the therapist's use only. It is rather, part and parcel of the treatment, a procedure of interest to both client and therapist, and one in which they fully share.

Behavioral assessment consists in keeping as accurate a record as possible of the behaviors and thoughts one wishes to change: when they occur (incidence), how long they last (duration), and where possible, how intense they are. When the assessment includes not only the behaviors but also the stimuli that are presumed either to increase or decrease the incidence of those behaviors, the assessment is called a ***functional analysis.***

A person might report, for example, that she becomes nervous when she has to speak in public. If a fairly precise measure of how nervous she becomes were required, she could be asked to deliver a speech publicly (Paul, 1966).

One could then record, in good detail, not only how anxious she was—in blocks of thirty seconds throughout her speech—but what forms the anxiety took, utilizing the assessment form shown in Figure 7–3. Moreover, the overall degree of anxiety could be assessed by summing the scores on each of the twenty variables.

Behavioral assessment can also be done by clients themselves. People who desire to give up smoking are commonly asked to begin by recording when and under what conditions they smoke each cigarette. People who desire to lose weight are asked to record when, where, how much, and under what conditions they eat. Assessments by clients are not only useful for overt behaviors, but for private thoughts as well. Mahoney (1971), for example, asked a client to record each time she had a self-critical thought. Her record became the basis for evaluating whether subsequent interventions had any effect.

FIGURE 7–3

BEHAVIOR ASSESSMENT

This behavior rating form permits assessment of speech anxiety. Each time period is thirty seconds long. Evidence of any of the twenty anxiety-relevant behaviors during each time period is indicated by a (√) in the relevant boxes. (SOURCE: Paul, 1966)

Behavior observed	1	2	3	4	5	6	7	8	Σ
1. Paces									
2. Sways									
3. Shuffles feet									
4. Knees tremble									
5. Extraneous arm and hand movement (swings, scratches, toys, etc.)									
6. Arms rigid									
7. Hands restrained (in pockets, behind back, clasped)									
8. Hand tremors									
9. No eye contact									
10. Face muscles tense (drawn, tics, grimaces)									
11. Face "deadpan"									
12. Face pale									
13. Face flushed (blushes)									
14. Moistens lips									
15. Swallows									
16. Clears throat									
17. Breathes heavily									
18. Perspires (face, hands, armpits)									
19. Voice quivers									
20. Speech blocks or stammers									

(Column header group: Time period)

Sometimes behavioral assessment reveals causes for distress of which the respondent was unaware and that were not elicited in the interview. Metcalfe (1956; cited in Mischel, 1976) asked a patient who was hospitalized for asthma, but free to take leave from the hospital, to keep a careful record of the incidence, duration, and the events surrounding her asthma attacks. Attacks occurred on fifteen of the eighty-five days during which records were kept. Nine of the attacks occurred after contact with her mother. Moreover, on 80 percent of the days in which she had no asthma attacks, she also had had no contact with her mother. But while "contact with mother" seemed to be a source of the attacks, attempts to induce an attack by *discussing* her mother during an interview, or by presenting the patient with mother-relevant TAT cards, were unsuccessful. Because words, as symbols of experience, sometimes do not elicit the behaviors that the direct experiences themselves produce, interviews that rely heavily on words often fail to be fully diagnostic.

While behavioral assessment has clear advantages, it cannot be used with every psychological problem. Sometimes, tracking behavior in the required detail is simply too costly or time-consuming. Often, when the tracking is done by the client alone, the assessment fails for lack of motivation or precision. Finally, there are situations in which behavioral assessment may not work well: covert behaviors such as thoughts and feelings are not as amenable to reliable assessments as are overt behaviors.

PSYCHOPHYSIOLOGICAL ASSESSMENT

Some abnormal psychological states are reflected in physiological ones, while others grow directly out of physiological disorder. Careful diagnosis and treatment of abnormality therefore often requires psychophysiological assessment, which has become increasingly sophisticated during the past decade. The treatment of physical tension has been enhanced by using psychophysiological assessment.

Anxiety, fear, and tension often have physiological correlates. When people are anxious, they may feel it in their muscles or in the way they breathe or perspire. Psychophysiological assessment not only confirms whether there is a physiological component to the anxiety, but how intense that component is, and whether treatment affects it. Indeed, some treatments can actually be pegged to psychophysiological changes. Biofeedback proceeds by alerting the client to small psychophysiological changes, and to the psychological states that bring them about. Tension headaches often arise from contraction of frontalis muscles. Those contractions can be directly measured through the use of an **electromyagraph** (EMG) and communicated to the client. As the client is trained to relax, he can immediately see the effects of that relaxation on the EMG, and he can gradually eliminate muscle tension and headache by using the techniques he has learned (Budzynski, Stoyva, Adler, and Mullaney, 1973).

NEUROPSYCHOLOGICAL TESTING

Needless to say, the brain is exceedingly complex. Much of it remains to be mapped. But increasingly, we are able to see damage in certain parts of the brain that affect thought and behavior. Neuropsychological tests assess damage in the brain that appears to implicate thought and behavior. There are many widely used neuropsychological tests that attempt to fathom those kinds of difficulties, three of which will be discussed here.

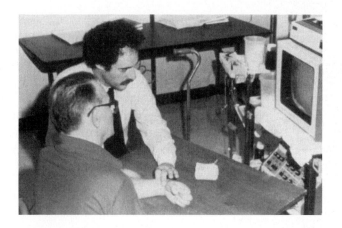

The Bender Visual-Motor Gestalt Test   This is one of the oldest and most widely used neuropsychological tests, perhaps because it is also the simplest to administer. Consisting of nine cards, each of which shows a design, the client is asked first to copy the design, and then to draw those designs from memory (Figure 7–4). Errors either in direct reproduction or in recall may well reflect neurological impairment. The emphasis here is on the possibility that test results *may* reflect disorder, for difficulties on the test may arise from multiple sources, not all of which are neurological. Thus, a tremor that shows itself in an inability to draw a straight line or to copy small circles may indeed arise from brain impairment. But it may also arise from simple "test nervousness." Good examiners will be sensitive to the difference.

The Halstead-Reitan Neuropsychological Battery   One wants to know not only whether a person is "neurologically impaired," but if so, what the nature of the impairment is, and where it is located. The Halstead-Reitan (Reitan and Davison, 1974) enables intelligent speculation about the location of the neurological deficit. The test assesses, among other capacities, an individual's ability:

- to categorize a variety of items as either similar or different;
- to place blocks quickly into slots on a board, while blindfolded;
- to detect whether the rhythm of pairs of sounds is similar or different;
- to tap rapidly on a small lever;
- to grasp vigorously a "dynamometer," which measures strength of grip;
- to identify correctly aurally transmitted "nonsense" words.

Serious deficiencies in the ability to categorize often point to gross brain damage, while deficiencies in the ability to grasp the dynamometer sometimes point to the area in the brain that contains the lesion. Equally important, the Halstead-Reitan provides very useful information about cognitive and motor repertoires, information that is often overlooked in standard psychological examinations (Hartlage, Asken, and Hornsby, 1987).

The Halstead-Reitan, however, is a very time-consuming test, requiring as many as six hours to administer. It consists of six simple subtests, as well as a variety of optional tests, the scores on which are interpreted in light of what is presently known about brain structures, thought, and behavior. The administration time, as well as the scoring effort, has spurred the use of a different approach—the Luria-Nebraska tests.

FIGURE 7-4

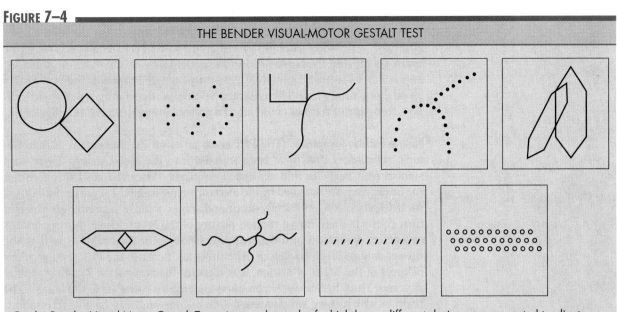

THE BENDER VISUAL-MOTOR GESTALT TEST

On the Bender Visual-Motor Gestalt Test, nine cards, each of which has a different design, are presented to clients. The clients must copy the designs and then draw them from memory.

Luria-Nebraska Neuropsychological Battery Based on the work of the eminent Russian psychologist, Alexander Luria (1902–1977), this 269-item battery provides information about a broad spectrum of psychological functions. Among the data that emerge from such an examination are information about tactile and kinesthetic skills, verbal and spatial skills, fine and complex motor coordination, writing, reading, speech and arithmetic skills, as well as intellectual and memorial processes. The patterns of scores across the entire test are thought to reveal impairments in various parts of the brain (Golden, Hammeke, and Puriosch, 1980). A children's version of the test permits diagnosis of brain disorders among children from ages eight to twelve (Golden, 1981). One virtue of the test lies in the fact that it takes less time to administer than the Halstead-Reitan. Psychologists believe that the Luria-Nebraska is able to detect effects of brain damage that are not yet discernible on neurological examination. Finally, the Luria-Nebraska permits control for level of education, such that a person who is less educated does not receive a lower score simply because of that fact (Brickman, McManus, Grapentine, and Alessi, 1984).

SCANNING THE BRAIN

As you saw in Chapter 3, perhaps the most exciting assessment possibilities arise from recent technological innovations in **brain imaging.** These advances in capturing the way the brain looks and functions are likely to have obvious and important implications for the study of abnormality. Among the most promising at present are three such techniques.

Computerized Axial Tomography Universally known as the **CAT scan,** it relies on X-ray technology, sending a moving beam of X-rays across the brain. The beam is captured on the other side of the skull by an X-ray detector that measures the amount of radioactivity that penetrates through the brain. Differences in radioactivity reflect differences in tissue density. Information so obtained is computerized, generating a detailed two-dimensional view of a cross-section of the brain. By moving the beam around the patient's head, the machine scans yet another cross-section, ultimately generating images that show the locations of blood clots, tumors, and/or enlarged ventricles. Depending upon their location, those abnormalities could affect a person's emotions and/or behavior.

Positron Emission Tomography The *PET scan* relies on the movement of radioisotopic substances that have been injected into the bloodstream. These substances emit particles that are called positrons. When the positrons arrive in the brain, they are detected by the electrons emitted by the scanner. Millions of such detections systematically occur and are recorded by a computer, which in turn converts them into a motion picture of the brain. These moving images can detect malignant and nonmalignant tumors in the brain, as well as the sites of damage from strokes or other injuries. Because the PET scan provides pictures of the brain *in motion*, it is a useful instrument for locating mental *processes*. Thus, because positron-carrying blood is conveyed to the areas of the brain in which there is heightened activity, one ought to be able to establish the locus in the brain for each of a variety of normal and disordered mental functions.

Nuclear Magnetic Resonance Imaging (MRI) The newest of the computer-based recorders of brain and brain activity, *MRI* does not require radioactive substances injected into the bloodstream, and nevertheless produces pictures of very high quality. It does so by creating a magnetic field that organizes the hydrogen atoms in particular organs. When the magnet is shut down, those atoms return to their normal place, thereby creating a signal that is read by the scanner. Such signals are translated by computer into pictures of the brain. Because of the quality of MRI pictures, and the non-invasiveness of the technique, MRI is gradually replacing CAT scans as the technology of choice for brain assessment. In addition to providing information on the sites of tumors, lesions, and strokes, in the future it is likely to provide insight into mental processes involved in behavior, thought, and emotion.

DIAGNOSIS

The first hallmark of a good assessment instrument—whether it is a structured or unstructured interview, an objective or projective test, or a behavioral rating system—is its **reliability.** Will two skilled users obtain the same findings? And provided nothing changes, will the test impressions obtained at one time be similar to those obtained at a later date? These are the first issues with which one is concerned. But they are not the only issues. Equally important are the purposes for which the test is being used. The purpose of assessment is to understand people, and one form of understanding is categorization, or **diagnosis.** We turn now to an examination of the reasons for, and nature of, diagnosis.

Reasons for Diagnosis

Properly executed, diagnosis is a long and complicated procedure. What does one gain from careful diagnosis? There are five important reasons to make a diagnosis: (1) diagnosis is a communication shorthand, (2) it tells something about treatment, (3) it may communicate etiology, (4) it aids scientific investigations and (5) it allows those who provide service to be paid for those services by third parties.

COMMUNICATION SHORTHAND

As we will shortly see, troubled people often have a host of symptoms. They may, for example, have trouble keeping their thoughts straight, often feel that people are out to get them, be unable to go to work, feel tense all the time, and have visual hallucinations. And they may be troubled by each of these symptoms simultaneously. A single diagnosis, in this case paranoid schizophrenia, incorporates all of these symptoms. Rather than going down an endless list of troubles, the diagnostician can merely indicate the ***syndrome*** (that is, the collection of symptoms that run together) in the single phrase: paranoid schizophrenia.

TREATMENT POSSIBILITIES

There is an ever-increasing fund of treatments available for psychological distress, and most are specific to certain disorders. Diagnosis enables the clinician to concentrate on the handful of treatments that might be useful in particular situations. Paranoid schizophrenia, for example, does not yield readily to verbal psychotherapies, nor is it effectively treated by Valium. But paranoid schizophrenics often respond well to a drug called chlorpromazine. A good diagnosis, then, suggests a small number of treatments that might alleviate the symptoms.

ETIOLOGY

People's problems arise from an infinity of sources, but certain problems are more reliably associated with particular causes or etiologies. For example, psychodynamic theorists believe that anxiety arises from poorly repressed conflicts and wishes. Knowing the diagnosis may tell something about the underlying cause.

AID TO SCIENTIFIC INVESTIGATIONS

Perhaps the main reason for psychological diagnosis is not clinical, but rather *scientific*. Abnormal psychology and psychiatry are developing sciences that have yet to discover all the causes and cures of human misery. By collecting together people with like symptoms, diagnosis allows psychological investigators to learn what those symptoms have in common by way of etiology and treatment. Indeed, for a developing science, this may be the single most important function of diagnosis.

ENABLING THIRD PARTY PAYMENTS

The care and treatment of those with psychological disorders is funded mainly by third-party payers—insurance companies, Medicare, and the like. Those in-

▲ People from all walks of life have tried to categorize abnormality. The French artist Théodore Géricault (1791–1824) painted a series of portraits of patients with "monomanies." This is *Monomanie du vol.*

▼ Emil Kraepelin (1856–1926) created the first comprehensive system of classification of psychological disorders.

stitutions that pay require patient diagnoses in order to be certain that the patient truly required care and occasionally to ascertain the quality of the care. Diagnosis, then, is essential for the economics of psychological treatment.

Historical Origins

The psychological diagnosis of personality has a long and interesting history. The Greeks, for example, recognized such diagnoses as senility (a disorder of aging), alcoholism, mania, melancholia (or depression), and paranoia. Many of these early diagnoses are still used today. Later, during the Middle Ages, it was widely believed that psychological disorders were caused by demons, and many different demonic "diagnoses" were described in such books as *The Witches' Hammer* (see Chapter 2).

The formal classification of human abnormalities, modeled upon biological classification of plants and animals, began with Philippe Pinel (1745–1826), the psychiatric reformer. He divided psychological disorders into melancholia, mania with and without delirium, dementia, and idiotism—a classification system that was to undergo many revisions and refinements during the next two centuries.

The first comprehensive system of classification of psychological disorders was created in 1896 by Emil Kraepelin (1856–1926). He believed that mental disorders have the same basis as physical ones and that the same diagnostic criteria and procedures should be applied to them. Above all, he insisted that diagnosis of mental disorders ought to be based on *symptoms* in much the sense that diagnosis of physical disorders proceeds from a careful assessment of physical symptoms. He might have stressed alternative bases for diagnosis such as drives, social deviance, level of adjustment, or social efficacy. But those bases were either merely inferred or social rather than physical. Inspired by the notion that there was a purely *physical* basis to psychological disorder, he proceeded to give psychological diagnosis the flavor of medical diagnosis, a flavor it still retains today.

Kraepelin's was not the only diagnostic system used for mental disorders. Early in the twentieth century, other clinicians, among them Eugen Bleuler, Adolf Meyer, and Ernst Kretschmer suggested other systems. Each of these systems enjoyed some popularity, with the result that different languages of diagnosis were invented and often used simultaneously. But because one basic function of diagnosis is communication, it is important to have a single and widely accepted language. This need for communication led to a search for one common system of diagnosis. One system evolved out of a classification of diseases, injuries, and causes of death. Developed by the World Health Organization, it included a listing of diagnoses of both physical and mental diseases and became known as the International Classification of Diseases and Related Health Problems.

Another system of classification designed specifically to diagnose psychological problems was developed in 1952 in the United States and was called the *Diagnostic and Statistical Manual of Mental Disorders* (DSM). Approved by the American Psychiatric Association, it was refined and ultimately replaced by DSM-II in 1968. The diagnostic categories in DSM-II were premised on psychoanalytic theory, and the diagnoses that arose from that system were heavily influenced by *inferred traits.* The diagnosis that were made using DSM-III were problematical; when asked to diagnose a troubled person, diagnosticians

DSM II
↓
DSM III
↓
DSM III - R
↓
DSM IV

had great difficulty agreeing with each other, and often they agreed no more than they would have by chance (Beck et al., 1962; Rosenhan, 1975; Spitzer, 1975). Those problems dictated the need for a new diagnostic system, culminating in the publication in 1980 of the *Diagnostic and Statistical Manual of Mental Disorders*, Third Edition (DSM-III).

DSM-III was a major diagnostic revision of DSM-II. The diagnostic categories in DSM-III were directly descriptive of *behaviors* rather than inferred traits. Moreover, it greatly expanded the number of diagnostic categories, from fewer than one hundred in DSM-II to well over two hundred in DSM-III.

Seven years after the publication of DSM-III, however, it was replaced by DSM-III-R (for revised). Published in 1987, it began as an attempt to fine-tune DSM-III but ended up as a major revision of its predecessor. Four of the five axes (which will be described shortly) were changed significantly. More than a third of the diagnostic categories were modified, some radically. And more than thirty new diagnostic categories were added.

Finally, DSM-III-R was replaced in 1994 by DSM-IV. DSM-IV bears a very close resemblance to DSM-III-R. It was created less to mark advances in diagnostic thinking—on that count it was hardly needed (Zimmerman, 1990; Kendell, 1991)—and much more to meet a treaty obligation that the United States has with the World Health Organization to maintain terminological consistency with the International Classification of Diseases and Related Health Problems, mentioned previously, which recently underwent its tenth revision (ICD-10). While it was touted as being based on empirical efforts (Widiger, Frances, Pincus, Davis, and First, 1991; Blashfield and Livesley, 1991), well-informed authorities consider that it relies mainly on expert opinion (Spitzer, 1991) and may continue to have the same problems with diagnosis as did its predecessors. In any event, DSM-IV is likely to remain the "diagnostic bible" for the coming decade.

FOCUS QUESTIONS

1. Give the five reasons why we diagnose.
2. What are the *Diagnostic and Statistical Manuals?*
3. How did DSM-II differ from DSM-III?
4. Describe the five axes on DSM-IV and why each individual is diagnosed on each of these axes.

Diagnosing with DSM-IV

In DSM-IV, a **mental disorder** is defined as a behavioral or psychological pattern that either has *caused* the individual distress or *disabled* the individual in one or more significant areas of functioning. One must be able to infer that there is a genuine **dysfunction,** and not merely a disturbance between the individual and society. The latter is social deviance, and social deviance is not a mental disorder. The full definition of mental disorder is given in Box 7–1.

Box 7–1

THE DEFINITION OF MENTAL DISORDER IN DSM-IV

In DSM-IV each of the mental disorders is conceptualized as a clinically significant behavioral or psychological syndrome or pattern that occurs in an individual and that is associated with present distress (a painful symptom) or disability (impairment in one or more important areas of functioning) or with significantly increased risk of suffering death, pain, disability, or an important loss of freedom. In addition, this syndrome or pattern must not be merely an expectable and culturally sanctioned response to a particular event, e.g., the death of a loved one. Whatever its original cause, it must currently be considered a manifestation of a behavioral, psychological, or biological dysfunction in the individual. Neither deviant behavior, e.g., political, religious, or sexual, nor conflicts that are primarily between the individual and society are mental disorders unless the deviance or conflict is a symptom of a dysfunction in the individual as described above. (DSM-IV)

Beyond defining mental disorder, DSM-IV, like its two predecessors, seeks to provide specific and operational diagnostic criteria for each mental disorder. To a substantial extent the shortcomings of previous diagnostic systems, especially DSM-II, arose from the fact that its definitions were vague and imprecise. For example, DSM-II described a depressive episode, but left it to the diagnostician to determine what precisely an "episode" consisted of. The definition left unresolved such practical questions as: Would a one-hour depressive experience qualify? Would depression that continued for a month be considered more than a single episode? The new diagnostic system takes some of the guesswork out of diagnosis by offering sharper definitions. With regard to a major depressive episode, for example, DSM-IV states that "At least five of the following symptoms have been present during the same two-week period . . . at least one of the symptoms is either (1) depressed mood or (2) loss of interest or pleasure . . . ," and it lists nine different symptoms. It was hoped that the use of functional definitions would contribute to the reliability of diagnosis.

Of course, in DSM-IV, as well as in its two major predecessors, DSM-III and DSM-III-R, diagnosis is not a single classifying statement, but rather it consists of multidimensional diagnostic guides. All told, there are five dimensions or axes that should be used, not only to classify a disorder, but to help plan treatment and predict outcome (see Appendix for Axes I and II categories and codes). This is an advance over former diagnostic systems that were used merely to classify individuals. DSM-IV provides useful information for functional diagnoses on the following axes:

- *Axis I—Clinical Syndromes.* The florid and fairly traditional clinical labels are included here, among them such familiar diagnostic terms as paranoid schizophrenia, major depression, and the various anxiety disorders. Also included on this axis are conditions that are *not* mental disorders but that may nevertheless require treatment. Among the latter are school, marital, and occupational problems that do not arise from psychological sources.
- *Axis II—Personality Disorders.* The personality disorders are not listed on Axis I but often accompany Axis I disorders. Axis II disorders generally begin in childhood or adolescence and persist in stable form into adulthood. Often, such disorders are overlooked by the diagnostician. Listing them as a separate axis ensures that they will be attended to. Axis I and II, then, comprise all of the psychological diagnoses.
- *Axis III—General Medical Conditions.* All medical problems that may be relevant to the psychological ones are listed here.
- *Axis IV—Psychosocial and Environmental Problems.* Included here are sources of difficulty during the past year, or anticipated difficulties such as retirement, which may be contributing to the individual's present difficulties.
- *Axis V—Global Assessment of Functioning.* The level of adaptive functioning has powerful prognostic significance, since individuals commonly return to their highest level of functioning when their psychological difficulties become less intense. The assessment on Axis V considers three areas: social relations with family and friends, occupational functioning, and use of leisure time, and is noted on a scale that runs from 1 (very low) to 100.

Information gathered along all five axes can yield greater understanding about a person's difficulty than can a simple descriptive diagnosis based on Axis I. Here is an example of the way a DSM-IV diagnosis would look using the multiple axes approach (DSM-IV):

Axis I:	296.23	Major Depression, Single Episode, severe without psychotic features
	305	Alcohol Abuse
Axis II:	301.6	Dependent Personality Disorder (Frequent use of denial)
Axis III:		None
Axis IV:	V62.2	Occupational Problem (Threat of job loss)
Axis V:	60	GAF (Global Assessment of Functioning)

The first two axes classify the disorders, with the other axes helping to get a fuller picture of the person, beyond the actual symptoms. A person's medical problems as well as any psychosocial and environmental stressors will certainly affect his condition. The level of the person's global functioning will be a factor in determining how well the individual can cope with his condition and the stressors in his life. DSM-IV, as did DSM-III and DSM-III-R, describes the essential and associated features of each diagnosis. It then provides the research findings about such factors as age of onset, predisposing conditions, and prevalence of each disorder. Finally, it describes the specific criteria for each category, using symptoms and their duration, that would warrant such a diagnosis. Using the various assessment measures discussed earlier in the chapter, clinicians then determine which categories of DSM-IV best describe the individual and his condition.

EVALUATING PSYCHOLOGICAL DIAGNOSES

As we mentioned earlier, assessment devices and diagnoses must be both reliable and valid to be of use to psychologists. When they are reliable, they generate the same findings on repeated use. When they are valid, they are of use for the purposes which they were intended.

Reliability

In order to arrive at a diagnosis, psychologists must use assessment devices that will give them a true picture of a patient and his or her problems. As mentioned earlier, they use clinical interviews, psychological tests, and observation. To arrive at a valid diagnosis, the tests must be reliable. Do two psychologists arrive at the same impression on the basis of psychological tests or interviews or observations? If they do, this is held to be evidence of ***interjudge reliability.*** To what extent will a test administered today yield the same results when given a week or month from now ***(test-retest reliability*** or ***test stability)?*** Reliability refers to the extent to which an instrument—be it a test or an observer—yields the same result in repeated trials or with different observers. When a group of psychologists examines a patient, and all arrive at the same conclusion, that conclusion is said to have ***high reliability.*** When,

FIGURE 7–5

LEVELS OF RELIABILITY

These diagrams depict various levels of reliability. Notice that even if reliability is relatively high, such as .67, there is considerable difference between the scores on Variable X and those on Variable Y that are supposed to measure the same thing.

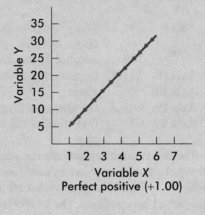

Variable X
Perfect positive (+1.00)

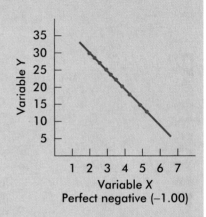

Variable X
Perfect negative (−1.00)

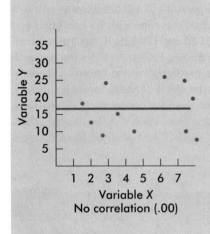

Variable X
No correlation (.00)

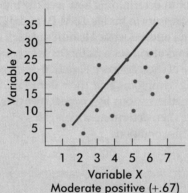

Variable X
Moderate positive (+.67)

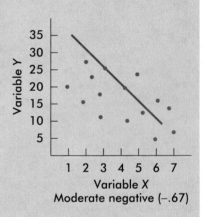

Variable X
Moderate negative (−.67)

however, they cannot agree, each proffered viewpoint is considered to have ***low reliability.*** Figure 7–5 describes reliability graphically. When two observers or tests are in complete agreement, their reliability is said to be +1.00. When they arrive at diametrically opposite conclusions, reliability is said to be −1.00. And when there seems to be no relationship between their conclusions, the reliability of those conclusions is 0.00.

As anyone who has tried to measure a floor knows, even using physical yardsticks, one rarely gets a reliability of 1.00. There are tiny measurement differences. Depending upon the purpose of the measurement, such differences may mean a great deal or nothing at all. A difference of an eighth of an inch means little to the height of an oak, but a lot to the diameter of a diamond. So it is with psychological measurement. How reliable an instrument needs to be depends upon many things, among them the purposes for which it is being used and the consequences of small and large errors (Cronbach et al., 1972). Generally, a high degree of reliability is required when individuals are being assessed, especially when the findings are to be used for individual care and treatment rather than, say, research. The human consequences of error in diagnosis and treatment are harsh: nothing less than individual well-being is at stake. Therefore, the reliability standards are stringent. A research diagnosis, however, is tentative until it is proven useful. Little harm is done with such diagnoses (Rosenhan, 1975). One cannot specify a degree of reliability that will be acceptable for all occasions of measurement and for all uses to which a measure will be put. But conservatively, a measure or observation whose reliability is below .80 should not be used for purposes of individual assessment or care, while one whose reliability descends below .60 is unreliable for research purposes.

FACTORS INFLUENCING RELIABILITY

Several factors influence both inter-judge reliability and test-retest reliability. Reliability coefficients calculated after separate interviews (test-retest reliability) are commonly lower than those from joint interviews (inter-judge reliability). These differences may arise from several sources: actual changes in the patient's condition between the interviews (occasion variance); different information obtained by each interviewer (information variance); and the absence of cues that are sometimes inadvertently provided by one observer to another in joint interview situations (Robins, 1985; Williams, Barefoot, and Shekele, 1985).

Reliability is also influenced by chance agreement between interviewers. The Kappa statistic (K) was developed to deal with this problem. The formula for K is:

$$K = \frac{P_o - P_c}{1 - P_c} ,$$

where P_o is the observed proportion for agreement, and P_c is the agreement expected by chance alone from the sample that is being studied. Kappa, therefore, indicates the proportion of agreement obtained over that which would have been expected to occur by chance in a particular sample. Kappa yields an index that ranges from +1.00 for perfect agreement to −1.00 for perfect disagreement. Technically, there are occasions when a low value of Kappa is satisfactory (Carey and Gottesman, 1978; Blashfield, 1984; Meehl, 1986). But generally, values of Kappa greater than 0.75 indicate chance-corrected agreement that is satisfactory, while values between roughly 0.40 and 0.74 indicate fair agreement. Values below 0.40 evidence poor agreement (Spitzer and Fleiss, 1974; Hasin and Grant, 1987).

THE RELIABILITY OF THE DIAGNOSTIC AND STATISTICAL MANUALS

It is still too soon to discuss the reliability of DSM-IV. While its reliability should have been determined before it was brought forth, it was not. Therefore, several years of using it will be necessary before reliability analyses can be done. As a result, we will discuss here the reliability of DSM-III, upon which DSM-IV is premised and for which there are available data.

Earlier *Diagnostic and Statistical Manuals* were badly flawed by problems of reliability. Experienced diagnosticians using DSM-II, for example, found they could not agree with each other. In some instances inter-judge reliability was so low as to make a diagnostic category functionally useless. Indeed, Spitzer and Fleiss (1974), in a review of all the reliability studies of DSM-II, found that only three broad categories were sufficiently reliable to be clinically useful:

1. Why is it important to have inter-judge reliability of diagnoses?

2. How did the compilers of DSM-III attempt to improve the reliability of diagnoses? Were they successful?

3. What are descriptive and predictive validity?

4. What conditions may bias diagnoses?

mental retardation, alcoholism, and organic brain syndrome. These are fairly broad categories, and when diagnosticians attempted to use finer categories—to distinguish the different kinds of alcoholism or brain damage, for example—diagnostic reliability fell further.

The compilers of DSM-III hoped to change all that. By making the categories more specific and precise, and by establishing criteria both for including and excluding behaviors in a particular diagnostic category, they hoped to increase reliability substantially.

Unfortunately, the reliability studies were quite disappointing, both for the manner in which they were conducted and in their actual outcome. Practicing clinicians were asked to examine patients and to arrive at independent diagnoses. They were asked not to confer before arriving at a diagnosis, and to submit their findings to a research committee even if they disagreed diagnostically. But because colleagues confer about diagnoses quite naturally, there needed to be a mechanism in place to prevent collaborative discussion. There was none. And because colleagues are likely to be more certain of efforts about which they agree than about those where they disagree, there needed to be some way to encourage submission of discrepant diagnostic findings. Again, there was none.

DSM-III encouraged clinicians to use multiple diagnoses, both within Axis I and Axis II, and between those axes. But multiple diagnoses, of course, *increase* the likelihood of agreement between clinicians. If clinician A makes six diagnoses and clinician B makes five, the likelihood that they will agree on *one of those diagnoses* is much higher than if each had only made a single diagnosis.

Thus, the reliability studies on DSM-III were "stacked" in favor of inflated reliabilities. Nevertheless, the actual reliabilities were quite disappointing, as seen in Table 7–2. The reliabilities given there are for clusters or classes of diagnosis, not for specific diagnoses. Thus, if two clinicians arrived at quite different diagnoses—if, for example, one found "agoraphobia with panic attacks" while the other found "obsessive-compulsive disorder"—diagnostic agreement would be considered "perfect" because the diagnoses were *in the same class*, even though there was no agreement on the specific diagnosis (Kirk and Kutchins, 1992). But no one is really interested in diagnostic classes. The central issue in diagnostic reliability is the reliability of the *specific* diagnoses.

It was disappointing to find that Axis I, *Clinical Syndromes*, describes nearly 200 specific disorders that are subsumed under seventeen major classes or clusters, but DSM-III provided reliabilities for only 16 of these specific disorders; the remaining diagnoses of Axis I are of unknown reliability. Other studies of reliability in diagnosis were equally disappointing, whether in the United States or elsewhere. Hanada and Takahashi (1983), for example, translated DSM-III into Japanese and asked experienced, university based psychiatrists who had had several seminars on DSM-III, to evaluate patients in seven psychiatric centers. Kappas on 10 of 17 diagnostic classes were below .70, while the Kappa for personality disorders was .43.

In the field trials, over half the adults and a quarter of the children received a diagnosis on Axis II, *Personality Disorders and Specific Developmental Disorders* (called *Personality Disorders* in DSM-IV). Nevertheless, no data on the reliability of the specific diagnoses have been published by the compilers of DSM-III. Moreover, as can be seen in Table 7–2, the reliability of the cluster diagnoses is disappointing. Subsequent studies (e.g., Mellsop and Varghese, 1983; Werry, Methven, Fitzpatrick, and Dixon, 1983) have confirmed the poor reliability of Axis II.

TABLE 7–2

AGREEMENT COEFFICIENTS (KAPPA) FOR CLUSTER AND SPECIFIC DIAGNOSES FOR ADULTS AND CHILDREN

	Study I		Study II	
	Adults	Children	Adults	Children
Axis I				
Disorders usually first evident in infancy, childhood, or adolescence	.65	.69	.73	.63
Mental retardation	.80	1.0	.83	
Attention-deficit hyperactivity disorder		.58		.50
Conduct disorder		.61		.61
Anxiety disorders of childhood and adolescence		.25		.44
Other disorders of infancy, childhood, or adolescence		.79		.73
Eating disorders	.59			
Organic mental disorders	.79		.76	
Disorders of the senium and presenium	.85		.91	
Substance induced	.63		.58	
Other	.66		.65	
Substance use disorders	.86		.80	.54
Schizophrenic disorders	.81		.81	
Psychotic disorders not elsewhere classified	.64		.69	
Affective disorders	.69	.53	.83	.30
Major affective disorders	.68	.36	.80	
Other specific affective disorders	.49		.69	
Atypical affective disorders	.29		.49	
Anxiety disorders	.63		.72	
Somatoform disorders	.54		.42	
Psychosexual disorders	.92		.75	
Disorders of impulse control not elsewhere classified	.28		.80	
Adjustment disorder	.67	.66	.68	.36
Axis II				
Specific developmental disorders		.77		.51
Personality disorders	.56	.56	.65	.61

*Cluster diagnoses in bold type. Subcluster and specific diagnoses in ordinary type. Numbers on the *left* in each category are Kappas for cluster diagnoses; numbers on the *right* are Kappas for subcluster and specific diagnoses. Only categories that include more than five diagnostic observations are included. Kappas of .75 and greater indicate satisfactory agreement (shown in green); between .60 and .74 indicate moderate agreement (shown in orange); between .40 and .59 indicate fair agreement (shown in blue); values below .40 indicate poor agreement (shown in red).
SOURCE: Data from DSM-III-R

Although the compilers of DSM-III report collecting data on all five axes, no reliability data are presented from Axis III, *Physical Disorders* (called *General Medical Conditions* in DSM-IV). The reliability of Axis IV, *Psychosocial Stressors* (called *Psychosocial and Environmental Problems* in DSM-IV), is modest at best (see Table 7–2). The reliability of Axis V, *Highest Level of Adaptive Functioning in the Past Year* (called *Global Assessment of Functioning* in DSM-IV), is quite good. That axis, however, has been greatly revised since these studies were done. Again, no reliability data for any of the DSM-IV categories are presently available.

Despite the fact that the built-in biases of DSM-III reliability created a favorable climate for *high* reliability, the general reliability of DSM-III was low. Why should that be? Why should experienced psychologists and psychiatrists have such difficulty in agreeing on the diagnosis they accord individuals? To a certain extent, this dilemma was anticipated in Chapter 1, where we examined "family resemblances," that is, how people determine whether two individuals are members of the same family or not. Despite the fact that there are important differences between the individuals, the fact that they nevertheless "look the same" goes a long way toward enabling a good guess about family membership—not always correct, but surely better than chance. But in the diagnostic context, the question is a closer one, requiring a more careful discrimination and analogous to asking, not whether two people are members of the same family, but whether they are *first cousins*. Nearly all diagnostic categories have much in common, as we saw in Chapter 1: pain, suffering, observer discomfort, irrationality, unpredictability, and the like—so much so that their commonalities often seem to outweigh their differences. The *specific* diagnoses, in practice, are often so close together that differentiating among them is substantially more difficult than the scientists who compiled DSM-III imagined. Often, the *context* in which the behavior occurs is of enormous importance in deciding the meaning of behavior (Rosenhan, 1973; 1975), and context is difficult to measure in the first place, and awfully hard to capture at the clinic, in the second.

In sum, the reliabilities of DSM-III are disappointing, and they provide little basis for optimism about the reliability of its next-of-kin, DSM-IV. They may well be a substantial improvement over the reliabilities of earlier diagnostic manuals, but they are still too low for credible clinical use.

Patently, there is a good deal that needs to be improved about psychological diagnosis. It is often unreliable; equally expert diagnosticians arrive at different diagnoses of the same individual. This is, of course, a problem in medicine too, but it is much more prevalent in psychological diagnosis since, as we mentioned earlier, there are few physical guideposts to support the psychological diagnostic effort. Moreover, psychological diagnosis is not always valid, for it often fails to suggest a clear-cut and useful treatment, and to communicate a known cause of the disorder. It is to the question of validity that we now turn.

Validity

The validity of an instrument is a measure of its ultimate usefulness, whether it does what it is supposed to do. People who obtain high scores on a good test of clerical ability, for example, should perform better in clerical tasks than those who obtain low scores. With regard to systems of diagnosis such as DSM-IV, we want to know whether the diagnostic categories satisfy the central functions of clinical diagnosis. Do they facilitate communication by describing patients, and particularly by differentiating patients in one category from those in another? This is called ***descriptive validity.*** Do diagnostic categories enable one to predict the course and especially the outcome of treatment? This is called ***outcome*** or ***predictive validity*** (Blashfield and Draguns, 1976). Of course, low reliability, as we have seen, undermines validity. To the extent that clinicians cannot agree about how the diagnostic categories should be applied, the usefulness of the diagnostic system is curtailed.

DESCRIPTIVE VALIDITY

To the extent that DSM-IV resembles its forebears, DSM-I and DSM-II, its descriptive validity is problematic. Most clinicians, when told that a patient is schizophrenic, for example, do not seem to get a rich sense of how that person will think, feel, and act. This failure has less to do with their imaginations and much more to do with the way clinical categories are used. A study by Zigler and Phillips (1961) exemplifies this problem. They investigated the relationship between the symptoms that patients presented to diagnosticians and the diagnoses that were made. In all, 793 patients were diagnosed in four broad categories: neurotic, manic-depressive, character disorder, and schizophrenic. Then the symptoms that these patients experienced were examined. A person whose symptom was "depressed" was likely to be diagnosed "manic-depressive." But he or she was also just as likely to be diagnosed "neurotic." Even of those diagnosed schizophrenic, better than one-quarter were likely to be depressed. Thus, the evidence from this study strongly suggests that diagnosis does not convey the kind of information about symptoms that might allow one to differentiate one patient from the other, or to have a reliable sense of what symptoms that patient has.

Perhaps that is the way it should be. After all, diagnosis does not proceed by simply listing symptoms and hoping they will *add* up to a particular diagnosis. Rather, a diagnosis emerges from a *pattern* of symptoms and from the current state of scientific understanding of abnormality. In the realm of physical disorder, "fever" yields a different diagnosis according to whether it is accompanied by a stuffed nose, swollen glands, or acute stomach pains. Similarly, symptoms such as "depressed" and "tense" mean different things when they are accompanied by other symptoms and form different patterns. Of course, this view of the diagnostic process only underscores the fact that summary diagnoses, such as schizophrenia and personality disorder, do not convey much information about a person.

PREDICTIVE VALIDITY

Predictive validity—demonstrating that the predictions that derive from a diagnosis are borne out by subsequent events—is especially crucial since it bears directly on the kind of treatment that is selected (Robins and Helzer, 1986). A diagnostic system with good outcome or predictive validity should also tell something about the future course of the disorder, and about what gave rise to the disorder. The validity of a system depends on the questions that are asked: Will the problem respond to particular kinds of treatment? Will the affected individual be violent or suicidal? What kinds of early childhood experiences are likely to bring about the disorder? These are the kinds of questions that can be answered if a diagnostic system has high predictive validity.

Predictive validity is high when a diagnosis can lead to an effective treatment for a disorder. For example, the predictive validity for "Bipolar Affective Disorder" is quite high when the disorder is treated with a drug called lithium. Here, the diagnosis performs a fine predictive function, in that a specific treatment is mandated. So, too, does "Premature Ejaculation," in that the disorder responds well to specific behavioral and social learning treatments. In these instances, the diagnosis indicates a treatment that has a high probability of succeeding. Unfortunately, in most diagnostic situations, merely having a diagnosis is of limited use. Often, the diagnosis does not dictate a particular course of treatment, nor can the outcome of particular treatments be predicted. More-over, the diagnosis does not say much about the causes of the disorder. When much more is learned about the nature of particular forms of abnormality, we may be able to say that a particular diagnostic scheme is valid. But right now, the predictive validity of many diagnostic categories of DSM-IV is still an open question.

Conditions That Bias Diagnoses

Psychological diagnoses are not at all like medical diagnoses. In the latter, there are physical data to support the final judgment. These include fever, X-ray results, and palpation. Often surgery and an array of laboratory reports back up the diagnosis. Psychological diagnosis is quite different. No evidence of psychological disorder can be found in feces, or blood, or on X-rays. You cannot palpate psychological disorder or see its physical presence. The evidence for psychological disorder is always transient, and highly subject to a variety of social and psychological considerations. Indeed, it is often those considerations that contribute to the unreliability of diagnoses. Three of the most important influences on diagnoses are context, expectation, and source credibility.

CONTEXT

The context in which a behavior is observed can dramatically affect the meaning that is ascribed to it (Asch, 1951; Gergen, 1982). In one study, a group of people who were free from major psychological symptoms *simulated* a particularly idiosyncratic symptom to the admitting doctors at general psychiatric hospitals. The "patients" alleged that they heard a voice—nothing particularly idiosyncratic about that—and that the voice said "dull," "empty," and "thud." Now *those* particular verbalizations were quite idiosyncratic, but nothing else about these people was unusual. Indeed, they had been carefully instructed to behave as they commonly behaved, and to give truthful answers to all questions, except those that dealt with their auditory hallucinations. Had they been outside of the hospital context, their simulation would have been detected, or at least suspected. Surely someone would have indicated that this single symptom with no accompanying symptoms was strange indeed. But that did not happen in the hospitals in which these patients sought admission. Rather, they were admitted mainly with the diagnosis of schizophrenia, and they were discharged with the diagnosis of schizophrenia in remission. The fact that most patients in hospitals who hallucinate are schizophrenics created a compelling context for these "pseudopatients" to be considered schizophrenics. Although their symptoms were not those of schizophrenia, the context of the symptoms mattered more in the diagnosis than did the symptoms themselves (Rosenhan, 1973).

Not only hospital settings, but the diagnoses themselves can constitute contexts that admit certain kinds of information and interpretations, bias other kinds, and disallow still others. For example, once the pseudopatients were admitted to the hospital, they of course began to observe their surroundings carefully and to take copious notes on their observations. Patients asked them what they were writing. Soon the patients concluded that the writers were not patients at all, but rather were journalists or college professors doing a study of the hospital. It was not an especially ingenious inference for the patients to make, since the pseudopatients did in fact behave quite differently than many of the real patients did. But the staff, on the other hand, made no such inference. They too noted that the pseudopatients often wrote. "Patient engages in writing behavior," the staff recorded about a particular patient. But they interpreted his writing within the context of the diagnosis itself, viewed the writing as yet another confirming bit of psychopathology, and closed off any explanation that lay outside of the diagnostic context.

Similar findings about the effects of contexts are demonstrated in a study in which clinicians were shown a videotape of a young man talking to an older, bearded man about his feelings and experiences in various jobs (Langer and Abelson, 1974). Some of the mental health professionals were told that the young man was a job applicant, while the others were told that he was a clinical patient. After seeing the videotape, all were asked for their observations about the young man. Those who saw the "job applicant" found him "attractive and conventional looking," "candid and innovative," an "upstanding middle-class citizen type." Those who saw the "patient" described him as a "tight, defensive person," "dependent, passive-aggressive," and "frightened of his own aggressive impulses."

In this study, the different labels—"job applicant" and "patient"—created not only a context for perceiving the person but also for explaining his behavior. The therapists were asked: "What do you think might explain Mr. Smith's outlook on life? Do you think he is realistic?" Those who saw the "patient" offered such observations as "Doesn't seem to be realistic because he seems to use denial (and rationalization and intellectualization) to center his problems in situations and other people," "seems afraid of his own drives, motives . . . outlook not based on realities of "objective world." But those who saw the "job applicant" explained the identical behavior in a quite different way. "His attitudes are consistent with a large subculture in the U.S. . . . the silent majority," "he seems fairly realistic, fairly reality oriented: recognizes injustices of large systems but doesn't seem to think that he can individually do anything to change them."

The descriptive comments that were made by the clinicians were subsequently quantified by raters who had no knowledge about either the experimental conditions (patient or job applicant) or the hypotheses that guided this study. These raters were simply asked to score the comments on a scale that ranged from 1 (very disturbed) to 10 (very well adjusted). The data are provided in Figure 7–6. Context clearly affected the evaluations of adjustment, as well as the perception of the causes of the behavior.

EXPECTATION

Whether a diagnostician is expecting to see a person in distress or a normal person may heavily influence diagnostic judgment. For example, one hospital administrator, having heard how easily the pseudopatients described earlier had been diagnosed as schizophrenic and had gained admission to a hospital, insisted that "it can't happen here." As a result, a simple study was devised (Rosenhan, 1973). The hospital was informed that sometime during the following three months, one or more pseudopatients would appear at the admissions office. During this period, each staff member—attendants, nurses, psychiatrists, and psychologists—was asked to rate each patient who sought admission or who was already on the ward, using a scale that indicated how likely it was that the patient was, in fact, a pseudopatient. More than 20 percent of the patients who were admitted for psychiatric treatment were judged,

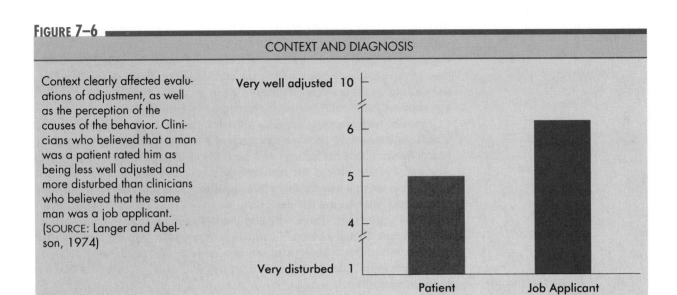

FIGURE 7–6

CONTEXT AND DIAGNOSIS

Context clearly affected evaluations of adjustment, as well as the perception of the causes of the behavior. Clinicians who believed that a man was a patient rated him as being less well adjusted and more disturbed than clinicians who believed that the same man was a job applicant. (SOURCE: Langer and Abelson, 1974)

with high confidence, to be pseudopatients by at least one staff member, and nearly 10 percent were thought to be pseudopatients by two staff members. Set in the direction of finding a pseudopatient, they found many. In fact, not a single pseudopatient ever presented himself for admission—at least not from this study!

SOURCE CREDIBILITY

Psychological diagnosis is particularly vulnerable to suggestions from "unimpeachable authorities." That vulnerability is demonstrated in a study in which groups of diagnosticians heard a taped interview of a man who seemed to be going through an especially happy and vigorous period in his life (Temerlin, 1970). His work was rewarding and going well, his relationships with others were cordial and gratifying, and he was happily married and enjoyed sexual relations. He was also entirely free of the symptoms that commonly generate a psychiatric diagnosis: depression, anxiety, psychosomatic symptoms, suspiciousness, hostility, and thought disturbance. After listening to the interview, one group of diagnosticians heard a respected authority say that the man seemed neurotic but was actually "quite psychotic." Other diagnosticians heard the same authority say that the person was quite healthy. Yet others heard someone on the tape say that it was an interview for a job. The results of this study are quite dramatic. Psychologically trained diagnosticians—psychiatrists, psychologists, and clinical psychology graduate students—were highly influenced by the assertions that this man might be quite disturbed. Indeed, they were somewhat more influenced by that assertion than were untrained diagnosticians, including law students and undergraduates. Correspondingly, when a composite group of diagnosticians (including both trained and untrained ones) was told that the individual was "healthy," their diagnoses mentioned no evidence of disturbance.

Need for Categorization and Diagnosis

Thus we see that there are problems with the reliability and validity of the current assessment devices and the present diagnostic devices and that psychological diagnosis is vulnerable to context, expectation, and source credibility effects. But can we do without diagnosis? Absolutely not. In the first place, seeing itself involves categorization. As we read these words, we may be aware that we are reading words (a categorization) rather than merely black ink (a categorization) on white paper (another categorization). And diagnosis is just another word for categorization, one that arises from a medical model. Second, and more important, there can be no science and no advance in understanding abnormality, without somehow segregating one kind of abnormality from another. That, you recall, is what initiated the understanding and, subsequently, the cure for general paresis (Chapter 3). Diagnosing general paresis as something quite different from other mental disorders ultimately made the treatment breakthrough possible. Without diagnosis, that advance would not have been possible. On the other hand, Jacqueline Persons (1986) criticizes diagnostic systems such as those in the *Diagnostic and Statistical Manuals* precisely because they do not lend themselves sufficiently to scientific advance. She urges a closer examination of the symptoms of distress themselves, rather than the more global diagnosis. Such an approach has a number of attractive features, not the least of which is that it is likely to augment the reliability of classification, allowing us to study important phenomena that are buried in traditional classification. Jerome Wakefield also criticizes the *Diagnostic and Statistical Manuals* (1992a, 1992b, 1993), arguing that, as currently constituted, the definition of mental disorder in the various *Diagnostic and Statistical Manuals* fails to embrace the notion of harmful dysfunction, and fails also to provide a diagnostic scheme that is likely to be valid.

We cannot live without diagnosis, but this does not mean that every diagnosis is accurate, or that every diagnostic term in DSM-IV truly reflects illness or mental disorder. The accuracy and utility of any diagnosis needs to be demonstrated. Indeed, as scientific understanding progresses, we come to understand which diagnoses are useful and which are not. Some diagnoses have proven usefulness and precision. They are already reliable and valid. Most, however, are promising at best. Eventually, they may shed light on the nature and treatment of particular kinds of psychological distress. Meanwhile, however, they are necessary if research is to proceed, with their utility mainly residing in their promise as ***research diagnoses*** (i.e., hunches that may prove useful in communicating about people and in treating them). The difference between a research and clinical diagnosis is very important; it rests on the reliability and validity of the diagnosis (Rosenhan, 1975). The remaining chapters of the book describe what is known about disorders for which we have fairly reliable research information.

▲ The power of psychological diagnosis can make it as dangerous as it is indispensable. This is a Romanian boy considered "irrecoverable" by hospital staff, a diagnosis that meant he would spend the rest of his life in these conditions.

SUMMARY

1. Personality assessment techniques may be divided into three processes: interviewing, testing, and observing. Assessment devices must be reliable and valid. *Reliability* refers to the stability of a measure, whether it yields

the same findings with repeated use. *Validity* refers to how useful the device is, whether it can be used for the purposes for which it is intended.

2. The clinical interview may be structured and have questions prepared in an *interview schedule*, or it may be unstructured and therefore more flexible.

3. Psychological tests fall into three categories: *psychological inventories* such as the MMPI and the MMPI-2; *projective tests*, including the Rorschach and the TAT; and *intelligence tests*, including the WAIS and the WISC. All of these are verbal tests and use words to portray psychological assets and liabilities.

4. *Behavioral assessment* is used in conjunction with treatment. It consists of a record of the patient's behavior and thoughts—their incidence, duration, and intensity. A *functional analysis* assesses the behavior and the stimuli affecting that behavior.

5. *Psychophysiological assessment* attempts to link physiological states to psychological ones. *Neuropsychological testing* attempts to link neurological states to psychological ones. Some of these test batteries, such as the Luria-Nebraska and the Halstead-Reitan, assess a variety of cognitive and motor skills that have known loci in the brain. Other technologies, such as *CAT* (computerized axial tomography) scans, *PET* (positron emission tomography) scans, and *MRI* (nuclear magnetic resonance imaging), search directly in the brain for abnormalities that may be relevant to behavior.

6. *Diagnosis* is the categorization of psychological disorders according to behavioral or psychological patterns. To be useful, or valid, the diagnosis should describe the patient's status, predict the course of the difficulty (with or without treatment), or aid in deepening our understanding of abnormality.

7. DSM-IV is a multidimensional diagnostic guide. It seeks to provide specific and operational diagnostic criteria for each mental disorder. Within DSM-IV, there are five dimensions, or axes, to classify a disorder and to help plan treatment and predict outcome.

8. When two psychologists arrive at the same assessment of a patient, there is said to be inter-judge *reliability*. The overall reliability of DSM-IV is unknown. The reliability of its progenitor, DSM-III, is only fair.

9. *Descriptive validity* refers to whether a diagnosis successfully differentiates patients in one category from those in another. *Outcome* or *predictive validity* refers to whether the diagnosis tells something about the future course of the disorder, what gave rise to the disorder, and whether the disorder will respond to treatment.

10. The accuracy and usefulness of a diagnosis may be compromised by the *context* in which it occurs and by the *expectations* and *credibility* of the diagnosticians and their informants.

11. Diagnosis and assessment are fundamental to treatment and necessary for scientific advancement. However, that does not mean that every assessment is useful or necessary. Some diagnoses may be useful for scientific purposes, but relatively useless for clinical ones.

1. Explain why psychological tests must be highly reliable when individuals are being assessed and diagnosed.

2. Why has there been increasing use of structured interviews?

3. Explain the problems of the *Diagnostic and Statistical Manuals* and speculate on whether you think DSM-IV will have fewer problems with reliability and validity.

4. How would you design an experiment to determine if a diagnosis is being made because of a real problem or because the context suggests a particular diagnosis?

4

ANXIETY DISORDERS AND HEALTH PSYCHOLOGY

SCOTTIE

CHAPTER 8

Phobia, Panic, and the Anxiety Disorders

CHAPTER ORGANIZER

FEAR AND PHOBIA
- Discover the difference between fear and anxiety.
- Learn the basic elements of fear.

PHOBIA
- Be able to describe the symptoms of a phobia and to distinguish the various kinds of phobias.
- Familiarize yourself with the major accounts of phobia and the therapies for the disorder.

POST-TRAUMATIC STRESS DISORDER (PTSD)
- Describe the events that that may be precipitants of PTSD and the symptoms that define the disorder.
- Find out who is more vulnerable to PTSD and how the disorder can be treated.

DISORDERS OF ANXIETY
- Be able to identify the symptoms of panic disorder and the biological and cognitive treatments for it.
- Describe the symptoms of agoraphobia and those of generalized anxiety disorder, and the range of treatments for both of these disorders.

COPING WITH EVERYDAY ANXIETY
- Discover some ways by which all of us can lessen our less serious anxieties.

We now begin our discussion of the psychological disorders themselves. In this chapter and in Chapter 9, we discuss the disorders that were once known as the "neuroses." In this chapter, we consider the disorders in which fear and anxiety are actually felt. In Chapter 9, we will deal with the obsessive-compulsive, somatoform, and dissociative disorders, in which anxiety typically is not felt, although its existence can be inferred from the individual's symptoms. In Chapter 10, we will examine the psychology of health and consider how psychological factors can affect physical conditions. Such problems were formerly called "psychosomatic"—disorders in which psychological factors, such as anxiety, contribute to the worsening or even the onset of a physical illness.

FEAR AND ANXIETY

There are five disorders in which fear and anxiety are actually felt by the individual, and these divide into two classes: the fear disorders and the anxiety disorders. Fear is distinguished from anxiety in that it is characterized by distress

FOCUS QUESTIONS

1. Distinguish among the cognitive, somatic, emotional, and behavioral elements of fear.
2. Describe the emergency reaction.
3. Explain how the fear response can vary in different people and across different situations.
4. What is the difference between fear and anxiety?

about a specific, dangerous object. Phobias and post-traumatic stress disorders constitute the fear disorders; in these disorders, a specified object causes the anxiety. In **phobic disorders,** the individual shows fear of an object (such as cats) which is out of all proportion to the reality of the danger that object presents. In **post-traumatic stress disorders,** the individual experiences anxiety, numbing, and repeated reliving of the trauma after experiencing an event that involves actual or threatened death or injury. For example, an undergraduate who was raped in her dormitory may subsequently relive the trauma repeatedly in memory and in her dreams, becoming numb to the world around her, avoiding men, and experiencing intense anxiety whenever she is alone with a man.

Panic disorder, agoraphobia, and generalized anxiety disorder are the anxiety disorders. In these disorders, no specific object threatens the individual, yet he or she still feels very anxious. In **panic disorder,** an individual is suddenly and repeatedly overwhelmed with brief attacks of intense anxiety and terror. In **agoraphobia,** the individual fears going out to public places because he fears that he will experience a panic attack and that no one will come to his aid. In **generalized anxiety disorder,** on the other hand, the individual experiences pervasive anxiety and worry that can be more or less continually present for months on end.

All five of these disorders share in common a grossly exaggerated version of normal and adaptive fear that each of us has felt on many occasions. We begin our discussion of these disorders by examining what fear and anxiety are.

Fear

All of us have experienced fear. The degree of danger we encounter has to do in large part with our job, where we live, and so on. Being a member of a team responsible for constructing an oil rig in the wintry North Sea exposes one to

▶ The degree of danger we encounter often has to do with our jobs. We can imagine that workers of this kind experience considerable fear.

TABLE 8–1

ELEMENTS OF FEAR			
Cognitive	Somatic	Emotional-Subjective	Behavioral

Thoughts of impending harm
Exaggerating the actual
   amount of danger
	Paleness of skin
	Goosebumps
	Tension of muscles
	Face of fear
	Heart rate increases
	Spleen contracts
	Respiration accelerates
	Respiration deepens
	Peripheral vessels dilate
	Liver releases
	   carbohydrates
	Bronchioles widen
	Pupils dilate
	Sweat glands secrete
	Coagulants and lymphocytes
	   increase in blood
	Adrenaline is secreted
	   from adrenal medulla
	Stomach acid is inhibited
	Loss of bladder and sphincter
	   control
	Salivation decreases
		Feelings of dread, terror, panic
		Queasiness and butterflies
		Tight stomach
		Creeping sensations
			Appetitive
			   responding
			   decreases
			Aversive
			   responding
			   increases
			Escape
			Avoidance
			Freezing
			Aggression

more danger than being an accountant. But an accountant living in New York City may experience more danger than one working in De Kalb, Illinois. When the oilman experiences fear, it is directly related to the danger of his situation; his reactions will be appropriate and normal. Similarly, the accountant's heart has every reason to beat rapidly upon hearing a noise at the window at three o'clock in the morning. Normal fear and anxiety, unlike the disorders we will discuss in this chapter, are in keeping with the reality of the danger.

ELEMENTS OF FEAR

When we experience danger, we undergo the various somatic and emotional changes that make up the fear response. There are four elements to the fear response: (1) cognitive elements—expectations of impending harm; (2) somatic elements—the body's emergency reaction to danger, as well as changes in our appearance; (3) emotional elements—feelings of dread and terror and panic; and (4) behavioral elements—fleeing and fighting (Lang, 1967; Rachman, 1978). These four elements of the fear response are summarized in Table 8–1.

Fear may take several forms, and different elements may be involved. No two individuals need display the same elements of fear when they are afraid. Nor is there any particular element that must be present. Fear is identified according to the following logic: (1) all of the elements need not be present; (2) some of the elements must be present, although there need not be the same combination every time; (3) no one element must be present; (4) the more intense any element and the more elements present, the more confident are we in labeling the state as "fear." What are each of these elements of fear?

Box 8-1

THE CHAIN OF COMMAND OF THE EMERGENCY REACTION

When faced with a potential attacker, a person may have certain thoughts or cognitions about what is going to happen. Terror or other emotions may overcome him. He may react or behave in several ways: by running or by attacking the assailant. He may begin breathing heavily, his muscles may tense up, and any number of other somatic changes may occur.

The somatic changes that begin in a few seconds after a person perceives danger constitute the emergency reaction, in which the body mobilizes to maximize its chances for survival. These internal changes are directly caused by our autonomic nervous system and our adrenal glands, which are in turn controlled by our central nervous system (CNS).

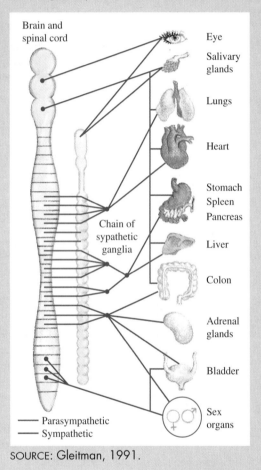

PARASYMPATHETIC SYSTEM

Constriction of pupil

Secretion of tear glands

Salivation

Inhibition of heart action

Constriction of respiratory passages

Stomach contraction: secretion of digestive fluids

Intestinal peristalsis

Contraction of bladder

Erection

SYMPATHETIC SYSTEM

Dilation of pupil

Inhibition of tear glands

Inhibition of salivation

Acceleration of heart action

Opens respiratory passages

Inhibits stomach contractions and digestive secretion

Inhibits intestinal peristalsis

Relaxes bladder

Inhibits erection

SOURCE: Gleitman, 1991.

The **cognitive elements** of fear are expectations of specific impending harm, usually in the immediate future. A large doberman growls menacingly at you. You think, "He's going to bite me," and you feel a surge of fear. On a dark and lonely street, you sense a sudden movement behind you. You think, "It's a mugger," and you freeze. You are unprepared at a recitation, and the teacher calls on you. You break into a cold sweat as you think, "I'm going to be humiliated." Notice that mental representations evoke the bodily reactions of fear (Lang, 1979; Foa and Kozak, 1986).

Somatic or bodily reactions also occur when we are afraid. There are two classes of bodily changes: external changes and internal changes. Like the octopus, who changes from green to red when afraid, human appearance

First, the danger registers, and this perception is transmitted from the sense organs and the higher centers of the brain (cortex) to the hypothalamus by wholly unknown processes. The hypothalamus is a brain structure about the size of a walnut, which lies under the cortex. (Roughly, if you follow the line of your nostrils up into your brain, you soon come to the hypothalamus.) The hypothalamus greatly influences eating, drinking, and sexual behavior, and is involved in regulating fundamental bodily processes, including metabolism and water balance. In times of emergency, it sends out messages of alarm.

The message from the hypothalamus activates the **sympathetic nervous system** (SNS) and, via this route, the **adrenal medulla**, the central part of the adrenal glands. These two systems then produce bodily changes by sending out adrenaline (epinephrine) and noradrenaline (norepinephrine) as their chemical messengers. The SNS releases norepinephrine from its neurons at the juncture with the neurons that excite the organ in question. The adrenal medulla amplifies the action of the SNS by releasing its chemical message into the blood, from where it diffuses into the organ tissues.

The chemicals released by the SNS and the adrenal medulla race throughout the body, producing the internal changes that constitute the emergency reaction. The heart beats faster and blood is pumped in greater volume. Peripheral blood vessels widen so that more oxygen will be pumped more rapidly around the body, and blood is redistributed from the skin and gut to the muscles and the brain. The spleen contracts, releasing stores of red blood cells to carry more oxygen. Breathing becomes deeper, and the air passages widen to take in more oxygen. The liver releases sugar for use by the muscles. Sweating increases to allow rapid cooling of the muscles and perhaps to increase tactile sensitivity. The content of the blood changes so that coagulation to seal possible wounds will occur more rapidly and lymphocyte cells that repair damage will increase in number.

The emergency reaction can be counteracted by the **parasympathetic nervous system** (PNS), which is responsible for producing a relaxation response. The PNS and the SNS generally oppose each other; together they make up the **autonomic nervous system** (ANS), which controls the organs that regulate the internal environment of the body, including the heart, stomach, adrenals, and intestines. Thus, when the PNS is excited, the heart slows down, whereas when the SNS is excited, the heart speeds up; while the PNS turns stomach acid secretions on, the SNS inhibits the secretion of acids. The SNS is an **adrenergic** system, using adrenaline and noradrenaline as the chemical messengers to produce an emergency reaction. The PNS is a **cholinergic** system, which uses the chemical transmitter acetylcholine to produce the relaxation reaction.

The completed mobilization of the body during the emergency reaction will increase the oxygen and energy resources that are available to the tissues, will increase circulation so that these resources can be moved through the body more quickly, will provide for waste product release, tactile sensitivity, surface protection, and quick repair of tissue damage. This will enable the individual to react to danger adaptively, so that he is able to run from an assailant or other fear-provoking situations. When the danger has passed, there will be a relaxation response, with a slowing down of the heart and breathing and a reduction in blood pressure.

changes, often dramatically, when we are afraid. A keen observer will notice the changes in bodily surface: our skin becomes pale, goosebumps may form, beads of sweat appear on our forehead, the palms of our hands become clammy, our lips tremble and shiver, and our muscles tense. But, most salient of all, fear can be seen in our face and those changes in the face can, by themselves, increase fear reactions elsewhere in the body (Lanzetta and Orr, 1980). In addition to the changes in appearance, there are internal changes within the body. In a matter of seconds after we perceive danger, our body's resources are mobilized in the **emergency reaction;** these internal changes are the physiological elements of fear (see Box 8–1).

Fear is also accompanied by the following strong **emotional elements:**

dread, terror, queasiness, the chills, creeping sensations, a lump in the pit of the stomach. These elements are familiar to us because we talk about them when describing our feelings of fear. We are also more conscious of the emotional elements, whereas we generally do not stop to reflect on our cognitions, nor are we particularly aware of the inner physiological workings set off by fear.

The **behavior** we engage in when afraid constitutes the fourth and final element of fear. There are two kinds of fear behavior: **classically conditioned** fear responses, which are involuntary reactions to being afraid, and **instrumental** responses, which are voluntary attempts to do something about the object we are afraid of.

In the world of elementary school children, bullies sometimes pick on a hapless child on his way home from school, perhaps in what was once a safe alley. After this occurs a few times, the child will become afraid when approaching the alley. He will display a number of involuntary fear reactions, like sweating and a faster heartbeat. This is an example of classical conditioning of fear. From Chapter 5, we know that classical fear conditioning takes place when a previously neutral signal is paired with a traumatic event. As a result of this pairing, the signal itself will cause fear reactions. In this case, the alley is the conditioned stimulus (CS), the encounter with the bullies is the unconditioned stimulus (US), and fear is the conditioned response (CR) (see Figure 8–1). Once conditioning has occurred, the signal alone causes the physiological emergency reaction to occur, profoundly changing other voluntary behavior. In our example, when the hapless child sees the alley, he will stop munching on potato chips and will cease reading his comic book.

Fleeing and fighting are the main instrumental behaviors in response to fear. There are two types of flight responses: escape and avoidance. In **escape**

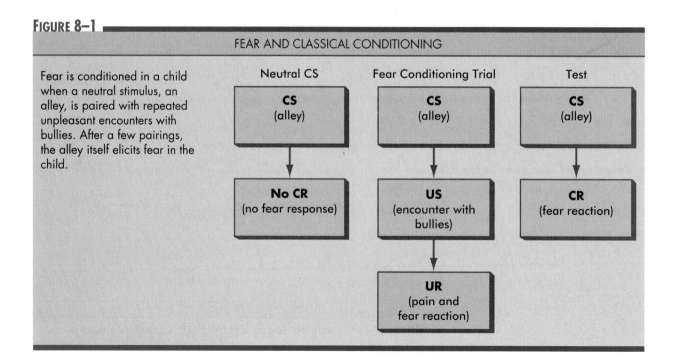

FIGURE 8–1

FEAR AND CLASSICAL CONDITIONING

Fear is conditioned in a child when a neutral stimulus, an alley, is paired with repeated unpleasant encounters with bullies. After a few pairings, the alley itself elicits fear in the child.

Neutral CS

CS (alley)

↓

No CR (no fear response)

Fear Conditioning Trial

CS (alley)

↓

US (encounter with bullies)

↓

UR (pain and fear reaction)

Test

CS (alley)

↓

CR (fear reaction)

▶ Fear is a quickly recognizable state, as shown by Vera Miles in Alfred Hitchcock's film *Psycho*.

responding, the harmful event actually occurs and the subject leaves the scene. For example, the child who is being beaten up by his schoolmates will run out of the alley if given the chance. Similarly, a rat will jump across a hurdle to escape from and terminate an electric shock. In contrast, in ***avoidance responding,*** the subject will leave *before* the harmful event occurs. A signal will herald the bad event; the alley is a signal that some bullies might await the child, just as a tone might signal shock to a rat. The child will run out of the alley and take another route home, even if no bullies are beating him up. Responding to the tone, a rat will avoid the shock before it comes on, thereby preventing the shock from occurring at all. The signal, because of its previous pairing with shock (in early trials, in which the subject failed to make the avoidance response, shock occurred), produces fear, and the subject responds during the signal to remove itself from fear.

DEGREE OF FEAR

The degree of fear varies in different people and in different situations. Some people actually like to step inside a cage with a chair and whip to teach lions tricks. Lion tamers probably experience some fear, whereas most of us would be terrified. Hence, we do not go into cages. Instead, we go to the circus or the zoo. This is considered normal behavior.

There is a range of dangerous situations, as well as a range of fear responses. We accept our fear response when it is in proportion to the degree of danger in the situation. But when the fear response is out of proportion to the amount of danger, we label it abnormal, in short, a phobia. While fear is normal and a phobia is abnormal, they are both on the same continuum; they differ in degree, not in kind (see Figure 8–2).

Anxiety

Anxiety has the same four components as fear but with one crucial difference: the cognitive component of fear is the expectation of a clear and specific danger, whereas the cognitive component of anxiety is the expectation of a more diffuse danger. In phobia, a typical thought is, "A dog might bite me." In generalized

FIGURE 8–2

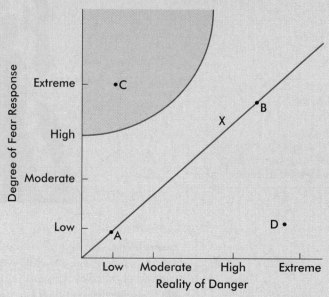

PHOBIA VERSUS NORMAL FEAR

This figure gives us a schematic way of distinguishing normal fear from a phobia. It plots the degree of the reality of the danger (as measured by societal consensus) against the degree of accompanying fear (as measured by the strength of the emergency reaction). The 45 degree line indicates normal fear. The area in red shows the phobic range. *A* plots an accountant at work, *B* plots an oil rig construction worker in the wintry North Sea. He probably feels more fear, but the level of fear is in proportion to what he should feel compared to an accountant. *C*, however, plots a phobic, whose reaction to the feared object is far out of proportion to the real danger. *D* plots decorated bomb disposers, who when placed in laboratory fear tasks, show a lack of reaction. Although these courageous individuals are in dangerous situations that would cause a high level of fear in most individuals, the bomb disposers display only a minimal emergency reaction (SOURCE: Based on Cox, Hallam, O'Connor, and Rachman, 1983).

anxiety disorder, in contrast, a typical thought is, "Something awful might happen to my child." The somatic component of anxiety is the same as that of fear: the elements of the emergency reaction. The emotional elements of anxiety are also the same as those of fear: dread, terror, apprehension, a lump in the pit of the stomach. Finally, the behavioral components of anxiety are also the same as those of fear: flight or fight is elicited. But the object that the afflicted individual should escape or avoid, or against which he should aggress, is less specific and sometimes shapeless. Thus, fear is based in reality, or an exaggeration of a real danger, whereas anxiety is based on a more formless danger.

We now turn to the specific disorders themselves. First, we will examine the two fear disorders: phobia and post-traumatic stress disorder. Then, we will discuss the anxiety disorders: panic disorder, agoraphobia, and generalized anxiety disorder. We begin with phobia.

We begin our discussion with phobia for several reasons: (1) phobia is an unusually well-defined phenomenon, and there is little trouble diagnosing it correctly; and (2) it is a disorder about which much is known concerning its cause and cure. Until four decades ago, phobias were a mysterious disorder from which there was no escape—unless you were one of the lucky individuals whose phobia disappeared just as inexplicably as it arrived. Today, most phobias can be successfully treated, and of all psychological disorders, phobias are among the best understood.

This section narrates the story of the conquest of phobia. We begin by defining phobia and then proceed to discuss what kinds of phobias exist. We discuss two rival theories of phobias: the psychoanalytic and the behavioral, and then we discuss the four therapies that seem to work on phobias. Finally, we present an integrated theory of phobia, which seems to account quite adequately for symptoms, cause, and treatment.

Phobia Defined

A **phobia** is a persistent fear reaction that is strongly out of proportion to the reality of the danger. For example, there are some people who, out of exaggerated fear, will not go to the circus or the zoo. In fact, a cat phobic cannot even be in the same room with a house cat because of her extreme fear of cats. Although we can repeatedly tell the cat phobic that house cats rarely attack humans, the fear will persist nonetheless.

A fear reaction may interfere with a phobic's entire life. Consider the following case in which fear is so great that the woman is even afraid to leave her home:

> Anna was housebound. Six months ago, the house next door had become vacant and the grass had begun to grow long. Soon, the garden had become a rendezvous for the local cats. Now Anna was terrified that if she left her house, a cat would spring on her and attack her. Her fear of cats was of thirty years' status, having begun at age four when she remembered watching in horror as her father drowned a kitten. In spite of saying that she believed it was unlikely that her father actually did such a thing, she was haunted by fear. At the sight of a cat, she would panic and sometimes be completely overwhelmed with terror. She could think of nothing else but her fear of cats. She interpreted any unexpected movement, shadow, or noise as a cat.

Anna is housebound because she is afraid that she might be attacked by a cat if she goes outside. Her fear is greatly out of proportion to the reality of the danger of actually being injured by a cat. The real danger is near zero, but her fear is extreme and irrational. Her problem is more than fear; it is a phobia. Very intense fear, however, does not constitute a phobia unless the actual danger is slight. For example, all of us would be housebound upon hearing about an approaching tornado. Here, the danger is great; the behavior is rational.

There is little trouble diagnosing a phobia when it is present, since its

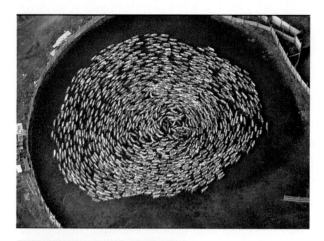

 Symptoms of fear are normal or abnormal according to context. In these frightened reindeer or these workers cleaning up after the 1993 World Trade Center explosion, we would expect to find the somatic, emotional, cognitive, and behavioral symptoms of fear.

symptoms are unambiguous: (1) persistent fear of a specific situation out of proportion to the reality of the danger, (2) great anxiety or even a panic attack produced by actual exposure to the situation, (3) avoidance of the phobic situation, (4) recognition that the fear is excessive or unreasonable, and (5) symptoms that are not due to another disorder, such as obsessive-compulsive disorder, post-traumatic stress disorder, or panic disorder. Finally, with the exception of agoraphobia, a phobic's psychological problems are quite isolated; typically, the only problem is the phobia itself, and phobics are able to function well in most other areas of their lives (Marks, 1969).

We must recognize that what we label a phobia is, by definition, partly a societal judgment. If the consensus of a society is that cats are extremely dangerous, it would not be considered a phobia to avoid them at all costs. Some superstitious societies attributed certain powers to animate and inanimate objects. Reacting to such objects with extreme fear would not constitute a phobia. For members of that society, such reactions made good rational sense.

There is no question that phobias cause one to suffer. They are maladaptive, since the individual's activities are greatly restricted; they are irrational, since the sense of danger is out of proportion to the reality of the danger. Phobics make others uncomfortable, and their behavior is considered socially unacceptable. Phobias are out of the individual's control, and phobics want to be rid of their fear. Thus, phobias are clearly abnormal.

Prevalence of Phobias

The most recent estimate of the prevalence of phobias puts the rate at 6.2 percent of the population with some phobic symptoms and about 1 percent of the population with severe phobias—phobias so strong that they keep the phobic housebound (Marks, 1986a; Regier, Narrow, and Rae, 1990). **Prevalence** is defined as the percentage of population having a disorder at any given time and is contrasted with **incidence,** which is the rate of new cases of a disorder in a given time period. So mild phobias are a widespread disorder, although crippling phobias are uncommon. In clinical practice, about 5 percent of all psychiatric patients have phobias. Moreover, there may be a genetic predisposition to phobias. In seven of eight pairs of identical twins, both of the twins had phobic features, but in only five of thirteen fraternal twins did both have phobic features (Carey and Gottesman, 1981; Marks, 1986a).

Kinds of Phobias

While there are reports of such unusual phobias as fear of flowers (anthophobia), the number 13 (triskaedekophobia), and snow (blanchophobia), these are very rare. The most common phobias in our society are social phobias and specific phobias.

THE SPECIFIC PHOBIAS

There are four classes of specific phobias: (1) fear of particular animals, usually cats, dogs, birds (most commonly pigeons), rats, snakes, and insects; (2) inanimate object phobias, including dirt, heights, closed spaces, darkness, and travel; (3) fear of illness, injury, or death; and (4) blood phobias (see Table 8–2). These make up about half of all phobias (Boyd, Rae, Thompson, and Burns, 1990).

Animal phobias, such as Anna's cat phobia, uniformly begin in early childhood, almost never beginning after puberty. While common in childhood, most animal phobias are outgrown by adulthood. Animal phobias are highly focused: Anna may be terrified of cats, but she is rather fond of dogs and birds. Untreated animal phobias can persist for decades with no period of remission. Only about 5 percent of all crippling phobias and perhaps 15 percent of milder phobias are of specific animals. The vast majority (95 percent) of animal pho-

TABLE 8–2

THE COMMON PHOBIAS			
Phobia		Sex Difference	Typical Age of Onset
Agoraphobias (fear of places of assembly, crowds, open spaces)		large majority are women	early adulthood
Social Phobias (fear of being observed doing something humiliating)		majority are women	adolescence
The Specific Phobias			
Animals		vast majority are women	childhood
Cats (ailurophobia)	Birds (avisophobia)		
Dogs (cynophobia)	Horses (equinophobia)		
Insects (insectophobia)	Snakes (ophidiophobia)		
Spiders (arachnophobia)	Rodents (rodentophobia)		
Inanimate Objects Phobias		none	any age
Dirt (mysophobia)	Darkness (nyctophobia)		
Storms (brontophobia)	Closed places (claustrophobia)		
Heights (acrophobia)			
Illness-Injury (nosophobia)		none	middle age
Death phobia (thanatophobia)			
Cancer (cancerophobia)			
Venereal disease (venerophobia)			
Blood Phobia		probably more women	late childhood

SOURCE: Marks, 1969.

bias are reported by women; they are rather healthy individuals and the phobia is apt to be their only psychological problem (Marks, 1969; Bourdon, Boyd, Rae, and Burns, 1988).

Animal phobics sometimes can describe a specific childhood incident that they believe set the phobia off. Anna seemed to recall that her father had drowned a kitten. Dog phobias may begin with a dog bite; a bird phobia may begin if a bird lands on a child's shoulder. Overall, about 60 percent of phobic patients can describe a clear precipitating trauma. But for the remaining 40 percent, no clear incident, only vague clues extracted from the mists of childhood memory can be isolated (Öst and Hugdahl, 1981). One child seemed to have developed a phobia by reading about a warrior dog in a fairy tale, and then hearing that a boy down the street had been bitten by a dog. Another child, already somewhat apprehensive about birds, was teased mercilessly with feathers by her playmates. In each case, there are a number of events, often several accumulating over time, that might contribute to the phobia. But uncovering the essential events, if such exist, can be enormously difficult. Usually animal phobias are outgrown, but for unknown reasons, a few remain robust and persist into adulthood.

Inanimate object phobias share many of the same characteristics as animal phobias. Heights, closed spaces, storms, dirt, darkness, running water, travel, flying in airplanes, and wind make up the majority of these phobias. As in animal phobias, the symptoms are focused on one object, and the individuals are otherwise psychologically normal. Onset is sometimes embedded in a traumatic incident. For example, a nineteen-year-old develops an airplane phobia after a plane he has just gotten off crashes at its next stop. An eight-year-old girl, who saw a boy hit by lightning and killed, develops a phobia of thunder and lightning. These phobias are somewhat more common than animal phobias, and they occur about equally in women and men. Unlike animal phobias, they can begin at any age.

Illness and injury phobias (nosophobias) are the final class of specific phobias. A person with such a phobia fears having one specific illness, although the kind of illness feared has changed throughout the centuries. In the nineteenth century, nosophobics feared they had tuberculosis or perhaps

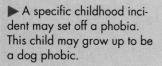

▶ A specific childhood incident may set off a phobia. This child may grow up to be a dog phobic.

FOCUS QUESTIONS

1. What is the difference between normal fear and phobia?
2. Describe the four classes of specific phobias.
3. What is a social phobia?
4. Distinguish between the psychoanalytic and behavioral accounts of phobia.

syphilis and other venereal diseases. More recently, cancer, heart disease, stroke, and AIDS have been the terrors.

A nosophobic is usually perfectly healthy, but he worries endlessly that he may have or will soon contract a particular disease. He searches his body for the slightest sign of the disease, and since fear itself produces symptoms like tightness in the chest and stomach pain, he interprets these symptoms as further evidence that the disease is upon him. And so it spirals to more stomach or chest pain and to more certainty that he has the dreaded disease.

There are no sex differences in overall reports of nosophobia, although cancer phobias tend to occur more in females and phobias of venereal disease almost always occur in males. Other psychological problems accompany the disorder frequently, and it usually arises in middle age. Nosophobics often know someone who has the feared disease.

Strangely enough, contracting the disease may cure the phobia. A man was admitted to a hospital, beside himself with syphilophobia. After discharge, he actually caught syphilis. The phobia disappeared at once, and the patient happily had his syphilis cured by medical treatment (Rogerson, 1951, cited in Marks, 1969).

Nosophobia is distinguished from **hypochondriasis.** Hypochondriacs have three defining characteristics: (1) They fear they have a serious disease that is undetected and they will not be reassured by negative medical evidence. (2) They are usually vigilant for a variety of illnesses in various parts of the body, unlike the phobic who is concerned with specific illness in one organ. (3) They are preoccupied with their body, its physiological functioning, and its appearance (Barsky, Wyshak, and Klerman, 1986; Noyes, Kathol, Fisher, and Phillips, 1993). In DSM-IV, hypochondriasis is not regarded as a phobia but as a somatoform disorder. It was originally believed to be a discrete disorder of a nonexistent organ, the *hypochondria,* located in the abdomen.

Blood phobias comprise the last category of specific phobias and are the newest phobic category, appearing for the first time in DSM-IV in 1994. Such phobics become highly anxious in situations involving the sight of blood, injections, and injuries. They often avoid medical procedures because of their phobia. They cannot bear to watch gory films. About 4 percent of the normal population show this phobia at least to a moderate extent (Agras, Sylvester, and Oliveau, 1969; Costello, 1982). It is probably somewhat more common in women than in men, and its onset is usually in late childhood (Öst, 1987; Kleinknecht and Lenz, 1989).

Blood phobics show a markedly different psychophysiological pattern of anxiety than do other kinds of phobics. When a cat phobic sees a cat, her blood pressure and heart rate soar. When a blood phobic sees a wound, in contrast, her blood pressure and heart rate markedly drop, and she might even faint. It is this atypical physiological reaction that puts blood phobia into a category by itself, and has led Lars-Goren Öst, a Swedish behavior therapist, to create a new treatment that seems to work almost all the time (Öst, Sterner, and Fellenius, 1989). We will examine this therapy and the theory behind it shortly.

SOCIAL PHOBIAS

All of us are, at times, anxious in social situations. Social phobias are exaggerations of such fears. In the 4th century B. C., Hippocrates, the Greek physician, described a classic social phobic who

. . . will not be seen abroad: loves darkness as life, and cannot endure the light, or to sit in lightsome places; his hat still in his eyes, he will neither see, nor be seen by his good will. He dare not come in company for fear he should be misused, disgraced, overshoot himself in gesture or speeches, or be sick, he thinks every man observes him. . . .(Burton, 1621, p. 272, quoted in Marks, 1969)

Social phobics fear being seen or observed. They fear that they will act in a way that will be humiliating or embarrassing and that being exposed to the situation may result in a panic attack. They are terrified of speaking or eating or drinking in front of other people. They may be unable to eat in a restaurant for fear of vomiting and being humiliated. A student may stop writing during an exam when watched by a teacher for fear of shaking violently. A factory worker may stop going to work lest he be unable to tie packages when observed. An actress may be terrified that she will begin to stutter or forget her lines when on stage. The fears are often unrealistic; individuals who fear they might shake, do not shake, nor do those who fear vomiting in public actually vomit in public.

DSM-IV divides social phobias into three classes: (1) *performance type*, in which the individual cannot perform in public certain acts—such as speaking, singing, writing, or urinating—that he can comfortably perform when he is alone; (2) *limited type*, in which the anxiety occurs only in specific social situations—such as going on a date or speaking to one's boss; and (3) *generalized type*, in which most social situations produce anxiety or panic.

Social phobias usually begin in adolescence, occasionally in childhood, and only rarely after age twenty-five (Schneier, Johnson, Hornig, et al., 1992). As we will see, both agoraphobics and social phobics are afraid of crowds, but for different reasons. The agoraphobic typically fears that she will not be able to get away from the crowd or that no one will help her if she has a panic attack. The social phobic, on the other hand, fears that some individuals in the crowd will look at him and observe him doing something embarrassing. Social phobias usually begin gradually. For example, while brooding about whether the groom is really good enough for her, a bride may begin to fear that she will tremble when she walks down the aisle with her father and that the guests will see how nervous she is. Thereafter, being observed by others in public may become more and more frightening for her. But sometimes a particularly dramatic incident will cause a social phobia. For example, a young man may actually vomit at a dance before making it to the toilet. This may so greatly embarrass him that he will no longer interact socially.

About 1 percent of adults have social phobias, and these phobias make up about 20 percent of all phobic cases. They are reported somewhat more often by women, and they are markedly more frequent among poor people. Unlike people with specific phobias, whose disorder is isolated, 70 percent of social phobics report other major disorders (Boyd, Rae, Thompson, and Burns, 1990; Schneier, Johnson, Hornig, et al., 1992).

We have now described the characteristics of the various kinds of phobias. How do phobias come about, and how can they be treated? There are two schools of thought that present comprehensive theories about phobias: the psychoanalytic and the behavioral (see Table 8–3). We now turn to these contrasting theories, and then we will discuss the therapies that work successfully on phobias.

▼ Social phobics often crave companionship, but avoid it out of fear of embarrassment. The phobia may begin gradually or after a dramatic event that really was embarrassing.

TABLE 8-3

	Cause	Mechanism of Maintenance	Treatment	Outcome
	FREUDIAN VS. BEHAVIORAL ACCOUNTS OF PHOBIAS			
Freudian account	Castration (or other) anxiety	Anxiety displaced onto feared object	Unconscious conflict discovered and re-solved in psycho-analysis	If symptoms, and not under-lying conflict removed, another symp-tom will arise
Behavioral account	Classically con-ditioned fear	Failure to reality test prevents extinction of fear	Extinction through pairing of CS with absence of fear, through modeling, flooding, or systematic desensitization	If symptoms re-moved, no new symptoms will arise

The Psychoanalytic Account of Phobias

The psychoanalytic account of phobias was put forward in 1909 by Sigmund Freud in the famous Little Hans case. To this day, psychodynamic accounts of phobia rely heavily on the logic of this case (Odier, 1956; Arieti, 1979). Freud's interpretation of a phobia consists of several steps: (1) the phobic (if he is male) is in love with and wants to seduce his mother; (2) he jealously hates his father, and wishes to kill him (these first two steps constitute the Oedipus complex); (3) the phobic fears that, in retaliation, his father will castrate him; (4) this conflict produces enormous anxiety in the phobic; because the wishes are un-acceptable to the conscious mind, the anxiety is displaced onto an innocent object (the phobic object), which symbolizes the conflict and is a more accept-able receptacle for fear; (5) the phobia is cured when the phobic gains insight into the nature of the underlying conflict.

THE LITTLE HANS CASE

Hans was a five-year-old boy who developed a fear of horses intense enough to keep him indoors. When he was four, he saw a horse fall down in the street and then thrash its legs violently in an apparent attempt to get up. Hans was very upset by this and thereafter was reluctant to leave the house, lest he be bitten by a horse who had fallen in the street. After extensive conversation with his father (who had been guided by Freud), Little Hans's phobia gradually weakened.

Freud weaved an enchanting story, and in the 150-page case history, mar-shaled evidence for each of the five premises of phobic origin. For example, Freud believed that Hans wanted to kill his father and replace him as his moth-er's lover. Hans had the following conversation with his father:

FATHER: Did you often get into bed with Mummy at Gmünden?
HANS: Yes.
FATHER: And you used to think to yourself you were Daddy?

HANS: Yes.
FATHER: And then you felt afraid of Daddy?
HANS: *You know everything; I didn't know anything.*
FATHER: When Fritzl fell down, you thought, "If only Daddy would fall down like that!" and when the lamb butted you, you thought, "If only it would butt Daddy!" Can you remember the funeral at Gmünden?
HANS: Yes. What about it?
FATHER: You thought then that, if only Daddy would die, you'd be Daddy.
HANS: Yes.

As the phobia waned, Freud told how Hans had the fantasy of a plumber giving him a new and bigger widdler, and that with this fantasy, Hans overcame his fear of castration and identified with his father (Freud, 1909a).

EVALUATION OF THE PSYCHOANALYTIC ACCOUNT

The psychoanalytic account of phobia is not compelling. There are three grounds for skepticism: (1) the account is based almost entirely on case history material, and the theoretical inferences from this material are loose; (2) psychoanalytic therapy for phobias works only infrequently, and then only with years of therapy; (3) there exists a viable alternative account—the behavioral analysis—which is based on both experimental evidence and case histories and which is associated with therapies that treat most phobias successfully.

First, we will consider the looseness of inference from the case history evidence. Did Hans really wish to kill and to replace his father? Hans never expressed fear or hatred for his father. He was told by Freud—who saw Hans only once—that he hated his father. Later, he was asked by his father about this, in a series of leading questions. First, Hans denied that it was so, and eventually he answered with a single "yes."

After 23 uneventful years at the zoo's snakehouse, curator Ernie Schwartz has a cumulative attack of the willies.

FATHER: Are you fond of Daddy?

HANS: Oh yes.

FATHER: Or perhaps not. . . . You're a little vexed with Daddy because Mummy's fond of him.

HANS: No.

FATHER: Then why do you always cry whenever Mummy gives me a kiss? It's because you're jealous.

HANS: Jealous, yes.

Hans's phobic improvement seems to be smooth and gradual through this period, not a sudden remission following his "insights." It has since been documented that children between the ages of two and six can suddenly develop strong fears of animals, which decline gradually on their own with no therapy (Holmes, 1935; MacFarland, Allen, and Honzik, 1954). Hans is well within the age in which fear spontaneously declines; this speculation is more consistent with the gradual elimination of his phobia than with the interpretation that his Oedipal conflict was suddenly resolved.

Would any evidence "count" as a disconfirmation of the theory? Hans's denial that he is vexed with his father does not count—in fact, it can be construed as confirmatory, by showing that Hans is defending himself against realizing his unacceptable hatred of his father. The theory is built in such a way that both denying and accepting an interpretation confirm that theory. This makes the theory difficult to test.

The success of a therapy can sometimes be relevant evidence for the theory from which the therapy is derived. What is the psychoanalytic therapy for phobia, and how does it fare? The psychoanalytic therapy for phobia follows from the theory that phobic fear is the displacement of anxiety generated by unacceptable intrapsychic conflict onto some innocent object. In post-Freudian accounts, any dynamic conflict symbolically displaced, not just the tenuous Oedipal conflict, can cause phobia. The therapist must then help the patient to bring the unconscious conflict to light, and to gain insight into the repressed traumatic incident that generated the phobia. In addition, some analysts recommend that the patient's attention should be focused away from the phobic object, but that as the patient comes to recognize the unconscious conflict, he should be encouraged to re-experience the phobic situation while learning that the fear is not intolerable. Psychoanalysts recognize that the prognosis for phobics under this regime is not good (Laughlin, 1967; Arieti, 1979).

> One must anticipate that many, many sessions will be required. A great deal of time and effort is generally required on the part of both doctor and patient alike. . . .
> Further, no guarantee as to the results can be given. . . . It may be a strenuous job, taking hundreds of therapeutic sessions over some years. (Laughlin, 1967, p. 601)

The Little Hans case history provides unsatisfactory evidence for the psychoanalytic view of phobias. The interpretations are large, uncompelling leaps. This alone would not necessarily be fatal to the theory if there existed experimental evidence to support the interpretation, or if psychoanalysis cured phobias. There is no such evidence, however, and psychoanalytic therapy is of doubtful value for overcoming phobias. Moreover, there exists an alternate account that is consistent with case history material and experimental evidence, and that is of considerable therapeutic value: the behavioral account.

▶ Classically conditioned fear of dogs would begin with the pairing of an unconditioned stimulus—dogs—with an unconditioned response—terror. A child who encountered dogs like these might develop a phobia (conditioned response) to all dogs (conditioned stimulus).

The Behavioral Account of Phobias

The behavioral analysis of phobias begins by assuming that normal fear and phobia are learned in the same way. According to this view, both fear and phobia arise when a neutral signal happens to be around at the same time as a bad event. If the bad event is mild, the neutral signal becomes mildly fear provoking. If, however, the bad event is particularly traumatic, the signal becomes terrifying, and the phobia develops. Phobic conditioning is simply an instance of classical fear being conditioned by a particularly traumatic unconditioned stimulus.

CLASSICAL CONDITIONING OF FEAR

Recall that classical conditioning consists of a procedure in which a conditioned stimulus (CS)—or signal—happens to occur at the same time as an unconditioned stimulus (US)—or traumatic event in the case of fear conditioning—which evokes a strong unconditioned reaction (UR). Thereafter, the previously neutral CS produces a conditioned response (CR) that resembles the UR. The CR is the phobic response and the CS is the phobic object. Hans's experience fits this description. Hans himself asserted that his phobia began suddenly when he saw a horse fall down in the street and violently thrash its legs. This gave him an awful fright. The sight of a horse, once not fearful, is a neutral CS. As he looks at the horse, it falls down and thrashes about (US) which evokes fear (UR). Thereafter, the CS of seeing a horse produces a CR of fear. Hans has been classically conditioned to fear horses; we need not postulate deeper fears or lusts. According to this analysis, Hans was not afraid of castration by his father; he was afraid of horses (Wolpe and Rachman, 1960). The precipitating trauma, when it occurs in phobic cases, can be well described by classical fear conditioning. Figure 8–3 details the classical fear conditioning analysis of several of our phobic case histories.

In addition to fitting many case histories, a substantial body of experimental evidence supports the hypothesis that pairing a neutral object with a frightening situation produces strong fear of the neutral object. In 1920, John B. Watson and Rosalie Rayner performed the first experiment on this topic. Little Albert B. was a normal, healthy eleven-month-old who, from birth, had been reared in the hospital in which his mother worked as a wet nurse. On the whole, he was big, stolid, and unemotional. One day, Albert was presented with a white rat, and he eagerly began to reach for it. Just as his hand touched the rat, the experimenters struck a metal bar suspended above Albert's head with a hammer. This produced such a loud and startling sound that Albert jerked violently, buried his head in the mattress, and whimpered. This pairing of the rat and the sound was repeated several times. When Albert was shown the rat later, he began to cry. He fell over on his side, and began to crawl away as rapidly as he could. A phobia had been conditioned.

This experiment was a primitive, but pioneering study. We will discuss below some of the flaws (Harris, 1979; Seligman, 1980). Nonetheless, since the Little Albert experiment, literally hundreds of studies of classically conditioned fear in animals and several in humans have been published. It is now well established that pairing a neutral CS with a traumatic US produces strong acquired fear to the CS. So classical conditioning of fear provides a potential experimental model of phobias because it fits many case histories and seems to be a sufficient condition for learning strong fear.

THE PERSISTENCE OF PHOBIAS

Can the behavioral analysis also offer an account of persistence, a defining feature of phobias? After fear is classically conditioned in the laboratory by pairing a tone a few times with shock, extinction will occur rapidly when the tone is presented without the shock. Within ten or twenty presentations of the tone

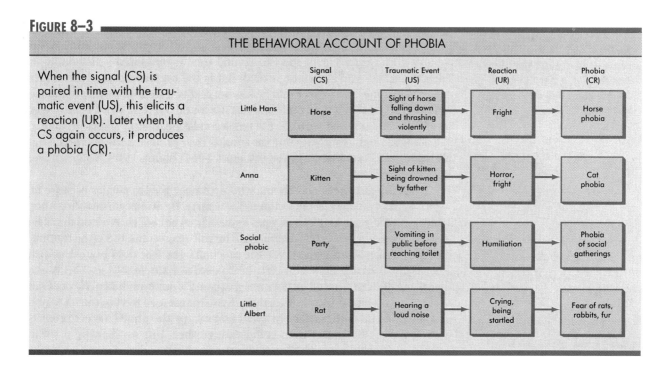

FIGURE 8–3

THE BEHAVIORAL ACCOUNT OF PHOBIA

When the signal (CS) is paired in time with the traumatic event (US), this elicits a reaction (UR). Later when the CS again occurs, it produces a phobia (CR).

	Signal (CS)	Traumatic Event (US)	Reaction (UR)	Phobia (CR)
Little Hans	Horse	Sight of horse falling down and thrashing violently	Fright	Horse phobia
Anna	Kitten	Sight of kitten being drowned by father	Horror, fright	Cat phobia
Social phobic	Party	Vomiting in public before reaching toilet	Humiliation	Phobia of social gatherings
Little Albert	Rat	Hearing a loud noise	Crying, being startled	Fear of rats, rabbits, fur

without shock, fear will always disappear. Even when shock is extremely painful, fear of the tone will extinguish in no more than forty trials (Annau and Kamin, 1961). Phobias, on the other hand, are very robust. They seem to resist extinction; some persist for a lifetime. How can a model based on an ephemeral phenomenon, classical fear conditioning, capture phobias that last and last?

An *extinction trial* in fear conditioning occurs when the fear-evoking signal is presented to the subject, but the traumatic event no longer follows. For example, a rat is put into the box in which it has received shocks. A fear-evoking tone that has been paired with shock comes on but no shock is presented. The rat can do nothing to escape the tone and is exposed to the fact that the tone no longer predicts shock. Because the rat cannot escape, it *reality tests* and finds out that the trauma no longer follows the signal. Under these conditions, fear extinguishes rapidly.

In contrast, phobics rarely test the reality of their fears. When the phobic object is around, they rarely sit there waiting to be passively exposed to an extinction trial. Rather, they run away as quickly as possible. For example, Anna would avoid cats as best she could, but if she did happen across a cat, she would flee as fast as she could. She would not reality test by staying in the presence of the cat and finding out what would happen.

Since phobias involve avoidance and escape from the phobic object, does fear of a signal that has been paired with trauma extinguish under the parallel laboratory conditions when the subject avoids the trauma by fleeing from the signal as soon as he is permitted to do so? Consider a rat in an avoidance procedure; a tone comes on, and at the end of ten seconds shock occurs. Remember that the tone equals the phobic object, and the shock equals the traumatic event that originally conditioned the phobia. If the rat jumps onto a platform before the ten seconds are up, the tone will go off, and shock will not occur. Soon the rat learns to jump up, and does so in less than two seconds on every trial. When extinction begins, the shock is disconnected (the phobic object no longer signals trauma). Now the rat undergoes one hundred trials in which he jumps up after two seconds of tone, the tone goes off promptly, but shock never occurs. If the rat's fear of the two-second tone is measured behaviorally or physiologically, fear has extinguished. But is the rat still afraid of the longer ten-second tone? Remember that he has not reality tested: he has *not* remained on the grid floor for ten seconds and has not found out that shock is no longer delivered. When tested with the full ten-second tone, the rat shows great fear. Escaping the signal and avoiding the trauma have protected the fear of the signal from extinction (Rescorla and Solomon, 1967; Baum, 1969; Seligman and Johnston, 1973).

Now consider the social phobic who no longer goes to parties because he was humiliated when he once vomited at a party. He avoids parties altogether, and if he must attend one, he escapes as quickly as he can. He is afraid that if he finds himself at a party (CS—the signal), he will again vomit (US—the trauma) and be publicly humiliated (UR—the reaction). His fear does not extinguish because he does not allow himself to be exposed to extinction trials—being at a party and finding out that he does not vomit and is not humiliated. He does not test the reality of the fact that parties (CS) no longer lead to vomiting (US) and humiliation (UR). The ability to avoid and escape the phobic object protects fear of the phobic object from being extinguished, just as allowing a rat to avoid reality testing protects fear from extinguishing.

▲ People with phobias severe enough to keep them housebound suffer from a problem that feeds on itself: they fail to test the reality of their fears. Whether afraid of cats, open spaces, or people, a phobic will not learn that they cannot hurt her if she never leaves her house.

The behavioral analysis can thus account for the persistence of phobias. Most importantly, it makes direct predictions about therapy: those procedures that extinguish fear conditioning in the laboratory should also cure phobias.

Therapies for Phobias

There are three classical therapies that have proven highly effective against phobias: systematic desensitization, flooding, and modeling. In addition, applied tension, a new therapy developed for blood phobia, has also been proven to be highly effective. All were developed within the framework of behavioral analysis. Historically, the first is systematic desensitization.

SYSTEMATIC DESENSITIZATION

In the 1950s, Joseph Wolpe, a South African psychiatrist, classically conditioned cats to fear a chamber in which they had been shocked. Using this animal model of phobias, Wolpe developed the therapy of **systematic desensitization.** First he cured his cats of their acquired fear, and then he successfully applied the therapy to human phobias.

Systematic desensitization is effective and brief, usually lasting at most a few months. It involves three phases: training in relaxation, hierarchy construction, and counterconditioning. First the therapist trains the phobic patient in deep muscle relaxation, a technique in which the subject sits or lies with eyes closed, with all his muscles completely relaxed. This state of relaxation will be used in the third phase to neutralize fear, since it is believed that individuals cannot be deeply relaxed and afraid at the same time (that is, fear and relaxation are incompatible responses). Second, with the aid of the therapist, the patient constructs a hierarchy of frightening situations, in which the most dreaded possible scene is on the highest rung and a scene evoking some, but minimal, fear is on the lowest rung. For example, a hierarchy constructed by a woman with a phobia of physical deformity (from Wolpe, 1969) might be as follows (from minimally feared situations to maximally feared situations):

1. Ambulances (minimally feared)
2. Hospitals
3. Wheelchairs
4. Nurses in uniform
5. Automobile accidents
6. The sight of somebody who is seriously ill
7. Someone in pain
8. The sight of physical deformity (maximally feared)

The third phase removes the fear of the phobic object by gradual counterconditioning; that is, causing a response that is incompatible with fear to occur at the same time as the feared CS. The patient goes into deep relaxation, and simultaneously imagines the first, least-arousing scene in the hierarchy. This serves two purposes. First, it pairs the CS, ambulances, with the absence of the original traumatic US. (You will recall that presenting the CS without the original US is an extinction procedure that will weaken the fear response to the CS.) Second, a new response, relaxation, which neutralizes the old response of fear, occurs in the presence of the CS. This is repeated until the patient can imagine scene 1 of the hierarchy without any fear at all. Then scene

FOCUS QUESTIONS

1. What are the three classical therapies for phobias?
2. How is blood phobia treated?
3. Evaluate the success of drug therapies for phobias.

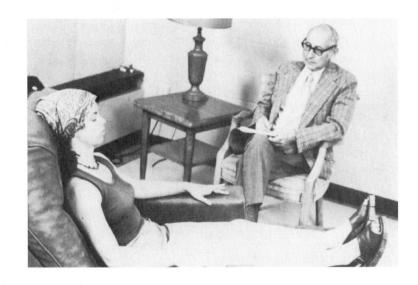

Psychiatrist Joseph Wolpe conducts systematic desensitization with a patient. The patient imagines a fear-evoking scene while engaging in deep muscle relaxation. She will signal by lifting her forefinger if the fear becomes unbearable.

2, which provokes a slightly greater fear than scene 1, is paired with relaxation. And so the patient progresses up the hierarchy by the graded extinction procedure until she reaches the most terrifying scene. Here the patient again relaxes and visualizes the final scene. When she can do this with no fear at all, the patient may be tested in real life by being confronted with an actual instance of something at the top of her hierarchy—in this case, with a real physical deformity. Therapy is considered successful when the patient can tolerate being in the actual presence of the most terrifying item on the hierarchy.

Eighty to 90 percent of specific phobias improve greatly with such treatment. These gains are usually maintained over follow-ups of a year or two. Follow-up studies universally report that new symptoms rarely, if ever, develop to replace the phobia. (For a sample of such studies, see Paul, 1967; Kazdin and Wilcoxon, 1976). This absence of "symptom substitution" is an apparent proof that Freud's theory of phobias, as anxiety displaced from deep intrapsychic conflict onto an innocent object, is mistaken. Characteristically, the psychoanalytic view of phobias claims that the phobia is merely a superficial symptom of a deeper, unresolved conflict, which is the genuine disorder. The psychoanalytic view maintains that removing the symptoms by desensitizing the phobic object cannot resolve the underlying conflict, and that therefore a new phobia or some other disorder will arise to bind the anxiety that can now no longer be displaced onto the newly desensitized object. This has not been shown to be the case.

FLOODING

▼ Through flooding, this woman is gradually losing her fear of water.

Recall that behaviorists believe that phobias persist because phobics will avoid the phobic object if at all possible, and if forced into its presence, they will escape rapidly. This failure to find out that the phobic object no longer predicts the original traumatic event will protect the phobia from extinction.

What happens when a phobic is forced or volunteers to be in the presence of a phobic object? What happens when rats, who are avoiding shock by escaping the tone in two seconds, are forced to sit repeatedly through the ten-second tone and find out that shock no longer occurs? Such a *flooding* of reality-testing procedure in rats reliably brings a reduced amount of fear and eliminates future avoidance (Baum, 1969; Tryon, 1976). The success of eliminating fear in animals by a flooding procedure encouraged behavior therapists to try, with caution, flooding in real phobic patients (Stampfl and Levis, 1967).

In a flooding procedure, the phobic patient agrees, usually with great apprehension, to imagine the phobic situation or to stay in its presence without attempting to escape for a long period. For example, a claustrophobic will be put in a closet for four hours, or an individual with a fear of flying (aviaphobia) will take a course including a real, aborted jet takeoff and a real flight (Serling, 1986).

In general, flooding has proven to be equal, and sometimes even superior, to systematic desensitization in its therapeutic effects. By forcing a patient to reality test and to stay in the phobic situation, and thereby find out that catastrophe does not ensue, extinction of the phobia can usually be accomplished. This directly confirms the hypothesis that phobias are so persistent because the object is avoided in real life and therefore not extinguished by the discovery that it is harmless.

MODELING

The third effective therapy for phobias is modeling. In a typical modeling procedure, the phobic watches someone who is not phobic perform the behavior that the phobic is unable to do himself. For example, a snake phobic will repeatedly watch a nonfearful model approach, pick up, and fondle a real snake (Bandura, Adams, and Beyer, 1977; Bandura, 1986). Seeing that the other person is not harmed, the phobic may become less fearful of the situation. However, if the phobic thinks that the model is endowed with special powers to deal with a snake, he may continue to fear the situation. In order to change this belief about the model, the therapist will attempt to find a model who resembles the phobic. Then, the therapist will gradually involve the phobic in the exercises. First, the phobic may be asked to describe aloud what he sees, then to approach the snake, and finally to touch it. The procedure will be repeated until the phobia diminishes.

Overall, modeling, when used in therapy, seems to work about as well as both desensitization and flooding in curing both mild and severe clinical phobias (Rachman, 1976). This therapy brings about cognitive change, as well as behavioral change. Once a patient has observed a model, the single best predictor of therapeutic progress is the extent to which he now expects that he will be

▼ In modeling therapy for snake phobia, a phobic learns to handle snakes by watching another person handle them, and eventually loses her fear.

able to perform the actions he formerly was unable to do (Bandura, Adams, and Beyer, 1977).

APPLIED TENSION

The latest effective therapy for phobias is **applied tension,** and it is the therapy of choice for blood phobias. It derives from the same logic that Wolpe used when he created systematic desensitization. Wolpe reasoned that relaxation would countercondition fear because it mobilized the opposite biological system: relaxation was incompatible with the muscular tension and sympathetic arousal components of fear. So the phobic could not be fearful at the same time that he was relaxing. Lars-Goren Öst noted that blood phobics, when confronted with the phobic stimulus of blood, have the opposite bodily reaction to that of other phobics when confronted with their phobic stimulus: blood phobics' blood pressure and heart rate drop, and they often faint. Öst reasoned that making blood phobics tense their muscles would raise their blood pressure and heart rate, so that they could not have the phobic reaction of fainting at the sight of blood.

In the applied tension technique, the patient tenses the muscles of his arms, legs, and chest until he feels warmth suffusing his face. Then he lets the tension go. He practices this repeatedly so that he can use it when he encounters blood. In an outcome study involving thirty blood phobics, Öst compared the applied tension technique to the relaxation technique and found that both helped considerably, but applied tension produced clinically meaningful improvement in 90 percent while relaxation produced meaningful improvement in only 60 percent (Öst, Sterner, and Fellenius, 1989).

A single underlying process—extinction—seems to be the operative element in all the effective therapies for phobias. In all four treatments, the patient is exposed, repeatedly and enduringly, to the phobic object in the absence of the original traumatic event. Each technique keeps the phobic in the presence of the phobic object by a different tactic so that extinction can take place: desensitization by having the patient relax and imagine the object, flooding by forcibly keeping the phobic in the phobic situation, modeling by encouraging the phobic to approach the phobic object as the model has done, and applied tension by preventing fainting in the presence of blood. The fact that each of these therapies works and employs classical fear extinction supports the view that the phobia was originally acquired by classical fear conditioning.

Classical fear extinction can also be described in alternative, cognitive language (see Chapter 5, p. 129). In order for permanent fear reduction to occur, two conditions must be met: First, information about the feared situation must be acquired forcefully enough to activate the entire fear memory, which consists of the fear response as well as the stimulus. Second, new information must be absorbed that is incompatible with the old fear memory, so that a new fear memory can be formed. Fear reduction occurs when this new information is integrated with the old memory (Lang, 1977; Foa and Kozak, 1986).

DRUGS

Drugs are not very useful with specific phobias. The anti-anxiety drugs produce calm and relaxation when the patient takes them in high doses during the phobic situation itself. The calm is accompanied by drowsiness and lethargy. So for a flying phobic who *must* suddenly take a plane, a minor tranquilizer will often help, but only temporarily. The calm is cosmetic, however. Once the drug wears off, the phobia is still there undiminished (Noyes, Chaudry, and Domingo, 1986).

The combination of anti-anxiety drugs and extinction therapy for specific phobias is also probably not useful. For extinction to work, Pavlovian conditioning suggests it is necessary to experience the fear and then have it wane in the presence of the phobic stimulus. Anti-anxiety drugs block the experience of fear, and so block extinction of fear. So the phobia remains intact.

Drugs do not seem very useful with social phobia, either. MAO inhibitors (a strong antidepressant) have been used with some success. About 60 percent of patients improve while on the drug. But the success is temporary, and the relapse rate is high once the drug is discontinued. Moreover, MAO inhibitors have dangerous side effects (see Chapter 3). Somewhat lower improvement (around 50 percent) occurs with the stronger anti-anxiety agents, like alprazolam (Xanax), and with beta-blockers. But again, the relapse rate is very high, and the drugs have marked side effects. A high relapse rate upon drug discontinuation suggests only a cosmetic effect on phobic anxiety (Versiani, Mundim, Nardi, et al. 1988; Levin, Scheier, and Liebowitz, 1989).

Prepared Classical Conditioning and Phobias

The behavioral model of phobias appears to be adequate—in fact, it is as good a model of a form of abnormality as any we know. It is consistent with case history material; it has generated four effective therapies based on classical fear extinction; and it is supported by a good deal of laboratory evidence. However, there are three main problems with this account: selectivity, irrationality, and lack of traumatic conditioning. We will now examine these three problems and will look at the theory that has been used to account for them: prepared classical conditioning.

SELECTIVITY OF PHOBIAS

Phobias occur almost entirely to a highly restricted set of objects, whereas ordinary classical conditioning of fear occurs to any object that happens to be around at the same time as trauma. Why are phobias of the dark so common but phobias of pillows are nonexistent, although both are paired with nighttime trauma? Why are phobias of knives so rare even though knives are often paired with injury? Why have we never heard of a phobia of electric outlets? Why are there rat, horse, dog, and spider phobias, but not lamb or kitten phobias?

Although Watson and Raynor had found it simple to condition Little Albert to fear rats, E. L. Thorndike (1874–1949), the American learning theorist, had difficulty trying to train his children to stay away from sharp objects and to stay out of the street, even though such trespasses were paired with spankings. In consequence, Thorndike decided to study this phenomenon experimentally. He brought young children to his laboratory and presented them with objects like curtains and wooden ducks which, unlike rats, do not contort and move themselves. These objects were paired with traumatic noise. No fear conditioning resulted, even after many pairings (Valentine, 1930; Bregman, 1934). Phobic conditioning, both in and out of the laboratory, is highly selective. Can the behavioral analysis accommodate this observation?

Yes, with some modification of its basic principles (Seligman, 1970; Eysenck, 1979; Mineka, 1985). Although ordinarily laboratory conditioning may be nonselective (as Pavlov claimed), there is a kind of classical conditioning that is highly selective, such as the conditioning of taste aversions. In an experiment by John Garcia, rats received sweet-tasting water at the same time as being subjected to light and noise, all signaling radiation sickness (see Figure 8–4). They learned to hate the sweet taste in only one trial, but the light and noise did not become at all aversive. Rats who received the same compound signals paired several times with shock, rather than stomach illness, learned to fear the light and noise, but they continued to love the sweet taste (Garcia and Koelling, 1966). Evolution seems to have selected rats who learn food aversions when taste is paired with stomach illness, but who learn to fear noise and light only when it is paired with shock.

The great majority of common phobias are of objects that were once actually dangerous to pre-technological man (De Silva, Rachman, and Seligman, 1977; Zafiropoulou and McPherson, 1986). Natural selection probably favored those of our ancestors who, once they had minimal exposure to trauma paired with such signals, were highly prepared to learn that strangers, crowds, heights, insects, large animals, and dirt were dangerous. Such primates would have had a clear reproductive and survival edge over others who learned only gradually about such real dangers. Thus, evolution seems to have selected a certain set of objects, all once dangerous to man, that are readily conditionable

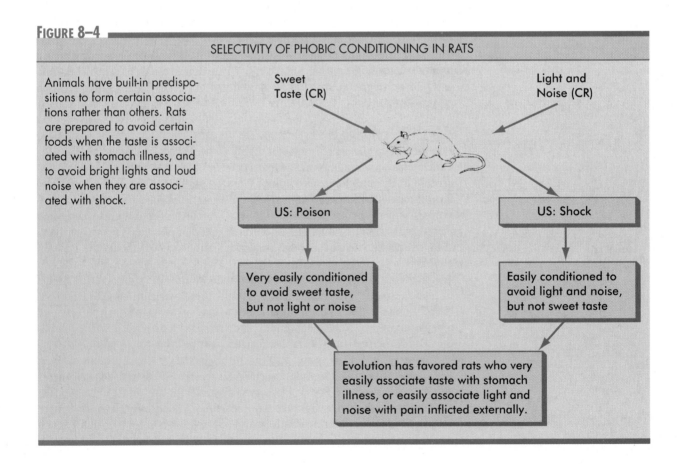

FIGURE 8–4

SELECTIVITY OF PHOBIC CONDITIONING IN RATS

Animals have built-in predispositions to form certain associations rather than others. Rats are prepared to avoid certain foods when the taste is associated with stomach illness, and to avoid bright lights and loud noise when they are associated with shock.

Sweet Taste (CR)

Light and Noise (CR)

US: Poison

US: Shock

Very easily conditioned to avoid sweet taste, but not light or noise

Easily conditioned to avoid light and noise, but not sweet taste

Evolution has favored rats who very easily associate taste with stomach illness, or easily associate light and noise with pain inflicted externally.

to trauma, and it seems to have left out other objects that are much more diffi-cult to condition to fear (such as lambs, electric outlets, knives), either because they were never dangerous or because their origin is too recent to have been subject to natural selection. One theory suggests that prepared phobic fear may reside in lower neural systems that are rekindled under adult stress (Ja-cobs and Nadel, 1985).

In an important series of experiments, Arne Öhman, Kenneth Hugdahl, and their collaborators at the University of Uppsala in Sweden created what appears to be a close laboratory model of phobias (Öhman, Fredrikson, Hug-dahl, and Rimmo, 1976). Fear was conditioned in student volunteers using a variety of prepared—once dangerous to Homo sapiens—or unprepared fear CSs: pictures of snakes or spiders (prepared) versus pictures of houses, faces, or flowers (unprepared). In a typical experiment, the "prepared" group was pre-sented with pictures of snakes that signaled the occurrence of a brief, painful electric shock ten seconds later. In the "unprepared" group, pictures of houses signaled shock. Fear conditioning, as measured by galvanic skin response (akin to sweating), occurred much more rapidly to prepared signals than to unprepared ones when each was paired with shock. In fact, conditioning took place in one pairing with snakes or spiders, but it took four or five pairings with shock for fear of unprepared signals to be conditioned.

This study demonstrates that humans seem more prepared to learn to be afraid of certain objects than of others. Consider guns, therefore, as a poten-tially phobic object. Guns are too recent to have been prepared for fear condi-tioning by evolution, but guns have had voluminous cultural preparation: sto-ries, TV shows, parental warnings. Does the fear conditioned to pictures of guns have the same properties as the fear of snakes and spiders, or the fear of houses and flowers? Guns turn out to resemble house and flowers, not spiders and snakes in their conditioning properties. This indicates that the prepared-ness to fear of spiders and snakes is biological, not cultural.

The behavioral reply to the selectivity of phobias is to assert that phobias are not instances of ordinary classical conditioning, but rather they are in-stances of **_prepared classical conditioning_** (McNally, 1987): certain evolu-tionarily dangerous objects are prepared to become phobic objects when paired with trauma, but others are not and require much more extensive and traumatic conditioning to become phobic objects. Phobias to snow, knives, lambs, and the like may be conditioned, but more trials and more intense trauma must occur. Thus, such unprepared phobias are very rare.

One researcher tells the story of a four-year-old girl who saw a snake while walking through a park in England. She found the snake interesting, but she was not greatly frightened by it. A short time later, she returned to the family car, and her hand was smashed in the car door. She developed a lifelong pho-bia, not of cars or doors but of snakes (Marks, 1977). So we see that phobias are selective, both in the laboratory and in real life.

IRRATIONALITY OF PHOBIAS

Laboratory fear conditioning seems very rational. When a signal predicts shock, the subject learns to expect shock and fear develops. When the signal predicts no shock (extinction or "inhibition"), the subject gradually learns to expect no shock, and fear accordingly is eliminated. When a signal is redun-dant and tells the subject no more than she already knows about when the shock will occur, no learning occurs (Rescorla and Wagner, 1972). Phobias, in

▲ What makes a bat more phobia-inducing than a ham-ster or an electrical outlet?

contrast, are not so rational. The elevator phobic, when far away from the elevator, may believe that the probability of the cable snapping is negligible. But, as she approaches and gets on, in her mind the probability grows to 1/100, then to 1/2, then to certainty, and panic sets in.

How can theories like the behavioral theory of fear conditioning, calling on the rationality of human beings, explain phobias? A phobic's life may be so impoverished by avoiding the phobic object that she cannot even leave her house. Why doesn't she merely give up the avoidance behavior and change her beliefs so that they match the realities of the danger?

Unprepared classical conditioning may be rational, but prepared classical conditioning is not. Taste aversions do not seem to be phenomena that accurately reflect the actual probability of danger. Once an aversion to Sauce Béarnaise is learned—based on vomiting after eating the sauce—merely knowing that a stomach virus rather than the Sauce Béarnaise caused the vomiting will not change the acquired distaste for Sauce Béarnaise. Instead, taste aversions are better seen as examples of blind, irrational conditioning (Garcia and Koelling, 1966; Rozin and Kalat, 1971; Seligman and Hager, 1972). If prepared conditioning is more like phobic fear than is unprepared fear conditioning, phobias should be irrational.

Kenneth Hugdahl and Arne Öhman (1977) have provided the relevant evidence for this conclusion. In the experiment mentioned earlier, Swedish students were conditioned to fear either snakes and spiders or houses and faces by pairing each CS with shock. At the end of the conditioning, the electrodes were removed, and the subjects were told that shock would not be delivered anymore. Fear extinguished immediately to houses and faces, but remained full-blown to snakes and spiders. Similarly, it is utterly futile to try to convince a cat phobic by arguing that cats aren't dangerous, while it is quite easy to convince the very same phobic that the building he works in has been effectively fireproofed. In general, the irrationality of phobic behavior may be due to the fact that it is prepared, rather than unprepared, learning (Eysenck, 1979).

▶ As far as we can tell, dinosaurs don't bother this child, even though he may have a phobia of the dark. Evidence like this suggests that we are conditioned by evolution to be more susceptible to some phobias than to others.

NONTRAUMATIC PHOBIAS

Classical fear conditioning requires an explicit pairing of the CS with a traumatic event. Sometimes phobias have such a history, but frequently they do not (Lazarus, 1971). For example, a phobia may develop gradually with minor impetus: the phobic's mother was always afraid of birds; when the patient was a child she saw a film in which people were attacked by flocks of birds, and she came to develop a phobia to birds. Can the behavioral analysis based on traumatic conditioning also account for nontraumatically induced phobias? It turns out that prepared fear conditioning, unlike unprepared, can occur with minimal relations between CS and US. In fact, this is the definition of prepared conditioning. Rhesus monkeys become phobic of snakes after merely observing their parents behave fearfully in the presence of a toy snake (Mineka, Davidson, Cook, and Keir, 1984). Even if six-hour delays occur between taste and illness, the taste aversion will still form (Garcia, Ervin, and Koelling, 1967).

Arne Öhman and his collaborators have also provided the direct evidence that prepared fear conditioning can occur without the experience of trauma paired with the signal. Verbal threat of shock alone produced robust fear conditioning following prepared signals, but fear conditioning did not follow unprepared signals (Hygge and Öhman, 1978). In addition, social modeling alone (without threat of shock) was more effective in producing robust fear conditioning to pictures of snakes and spiders than to flowers, mushrooms, and berries (Bandura, 1969; Hygge and Öhman, 1978).

SUSCEPTIBILITY TO PHOBIAS

One large mystery remains to be solved: Who becomes phobic and who does not? Some evidence indicates that phobias may be heritable (Carey, 1982). Although many people are exposed as children and young adults to potentially phobic signals paired with traumatic or subtraumatic events (they are bitten by large dogs; they are involved in auto accidents; they throw up in public), only a few develop phobias. Most show a transient disturbance that dissipates in time. The behavioral account does not now provide us with a way of telling in advance if a disturbance will become a phobia. A complete explanation of phobias will need to account for such individual differences as preparedness and proneness to spontaneous panic attacks (see McNally, 1987, for a critique of this theory).

POST-TRAUMATIC STRESS DISORDER

Trauma used to be a part of everyone's life—the incorrigible human condition. Until this century, most people experienced life as a vale of tears. But modern technology, medicine, and a growing sense of social justice have created a world in which the experience of trauma is not inevitable. Bad things still happen all too frequently: we get disappointing grades; our stocks go down; we don't get the job we had hoped for; people we love reject us; we age and die. But we are usually prepared for many losses, or at least we know ways to soften the blow. Once in a while, however, the ancient human condition intrudes, and something irredeemably awful, something beyond routine disappointment and setback occurs.

So devastating and long-lasting are the effects of certain types of trauma and extraordinary loss, they have been given a name and a diagnostic category of their own: ***post-traumatic stress disorder (PTSD).*** The following case shows an individual who is suffering from a delayed onset of post-traumatic stress disorder.

> Mr. A was raised as a Quaker until he was thirteen. In 1943 he was drafted into the Army and served as a machine gunner until the end of the war. A giant of a man, he could carry his fifty-five pound gun on his shoulder and run at full tilt. He was frequently in the center of combat and killed many enemy soldiers, often at close range. After the Battle of the Bulge, his sergeant and his assistant gunner were killed. For three days, he wandered the battlefield in a daze and crying, not noticing his own shrapnel wounds. There was one incident during the war of which he was ashamed. After machine-gunning a group of German attackers, he looked at the bodies and saw that many were teenage boys with imitation rifles. At the end of the war, only four of his original forty comrades remained alive, and Mr. A was awarded several of the nation's highest decorations for valor.
>
> Mr. A went on to become a very successful architect and remained in excellent health for the next twenty years. Aside from avoiding war movies, he seemed to show no immediate traces of his combat traumas. By 1975, thirty years after the war, because of diabetes and visual problems, he was forced to retire. At this point, he began to suffer nightmares about the war. In one recurring nightmare, his troop charged at and machine-gunned German teenagers, and he saw that they included his grandsons. When he revisited the battlefield as a guest of the German government in 1979, he broke down, distraught with anxiety about not being able to find the graves of his two comrades. He began to take many drugs to try to relieve his anxieties. (Van Dyke, Zilberg, and McKinnon, 1985)

Precipitants of Post-Traumatic Stress Disorder

The objects that set off a phobia are quite commonplace; for example, crowds, embarrassment, cats, and illness. But the precipitant of a post-traumatic stress disorder, in contrast, is unusual (see Table 8–4). There is debate about what kind of events should qualify as precipitants of the diagnosis of PTSD. At the most extreme, some claim that the events must be catastrophic, beyond the usual range of human suffering: living through an earthquake, watching one's children being tortured, being in a concentration camp, being kidnapped, experiencing hand-to-hand combat. This was the criterion in DSM-III, which followed the return of many psychologically crippled veterans of the Vietnam War. But it is important to note that some people endured the Holocaust with no trace of PTSD, and that others in contrast show full-blown PTSD when their spouse dies or even when sued in court. A wider, but more specific, criterion has therefore been given in DSM-IV: having witnessed or been confronted by threat of death, injury, or threat to the physical integrity of self or others. This would include rape, mugging, watching a bloody accident, committing an atrocity. Thus, the event merely need be an "exceptional" stressor, and what is crucial is the person's reaction: horror, helplessness, and a sense of ruination.

Three symptoms define the disorder: (1) the person *relives* the trauma recurrently, in dreams, in flashbacks, and in reverie; (2) the person becomes *numb* to the world, and avoids stimuli that remind him of the trauma; and (3) the person

TABLE 8–4

	Origin	Symptoms	Course	Therapy
		PHOBIAS AND PTSD COMPARED		
Single Phobia	Classical conditioning in which prepared (or occasionally unprepared) stimulus becomes a CS for fear reaction	Usually confined to phobic reaction to one object or situation; patient often functions well in other areas	Dissipates in most children, but unremitting if found in adults without therapy	Drugs ineffective; patient often responds well to brief behavioral/cognitive therapy
PTSD	Stressor outside normal range; confrontation with threat of death or injury responded to with horror or helplessness	Wide range of emotional, behavioral, and somatic symptoms; reliving of trauma, pervasive numbness and anxiety are common	Symptoms may persist and interfere with many areas of functioning for decades	Drugs largely ineffective; early intervention with both stress inoculation and exposure therapy may work well

experiences symptoms of *anxiety* and arousal that were not present before the trauma. The anxiety symptoms include trouble sleeping, over-alertness, trouble concentrating, exaggerated startle, and outbursts of anger. In addition, the individual may be wracked with guilt about surviving when others did not.

It was once thought that victims of disaster recovered briskly. An early psychiatric study of the aftermath of disaster was of the relatives of the victims of a catastrophic nightclub fire during the 1940s. Interviews with the survivors and the families of the dead led to the the belief that an "uncomplicated grief reaction" would be gone in four to six weeks (Lindemann, 1944). This has remained the lore ever since. When people took longer than a few weeks to recover after their lives had been devastated, it was considered "abnormal." Even today, in order to qualify for a certified diagnosis of PTSD, the symptoms have to last at least one month.

Dr. Camille Wortman, a psychologist at the State University of New York at Stony Brook, has changed the lore. She went through the microfilm records of every auto fatality in Michigan between 1976 and 1979. She randomly chose thirty-nine people who had lost a spouse and forty-one couples who had lost a child. She then interviewed them at length and compared them to matched controls.

Her interviews occurred four to seven years after the tragedy, and she found that the parents and spouses were still in decidedly poor shape. They were much more depressed than the controls. They were less optimistic about the future, and they did not feel good about their lives. They were more "worn out," "tense," and "unhappy." More of those who had lost a spouse or child had died than had the controls. While they did not differ on income before their child died, the bereaved parents now earned 25 percent less than did the controls. Twenty percent were now divorced (versus 2.5 percent of the controls). People were just as bad off seven years later as four years later, so there does not seem to be a noticeable natural healing process going on. Almost everyone asked "Why me?" Sixty percent could find no answer to this wrenching question (Lehman, Wortman, and Williams, 1987).

NATURALLY OCCURRING DISASTERS

The Los Angeles earthquake of 1994, the floods in the U. S. Midwest in 1993, and Hurricane Andrew in 1992 produced a large number of people with PTSD. Much of what we know about the suffering of these victims and the course of their problems begins with a study of a flood at Buffalo Creek in 1972. This flood produced devastation and death in a small West Virginia community, setting off many cases of post-traumatic stress disorder among its survivors (Erikson, 1976; Gleser, Green, and Winget, 1981). In the early morning of February 26, 1972, the dam on Buffalo Creek in the coal region of West Virginia collapsed, and within a few seconds, 132 million gallons of the sludge-filled black water roared upon the residents of the mountain hollows below. Wilbur, his wife Deborah, and their four children managed to survive. Here is how they describe what happened to them (Erikson, 1976, pp. 338–44):

> For some reason, I opened the inside door and looked up the road—and there it came. Just a big black cloud. It looked like 12 or 15 foot of water . . .
>
> Well, my neigbor's house was coming right up to where we live, coming down the creek . . . It was coming slow, but my wife was still asleep with the baby—she was about seven years old at the time—and the other kids were still asleep upstairs. I screamed for my wife in a bad tone of voice so I could get her attention real quick . . . I don't know how she got the girls downstairs so fast, but she run up there in her sliptail and she got the children out of bed and downstairs . . .
>
> We headed up the road . . . My wife and some of the children went up between the gons [railway gondonas]; me and my baby went under them because we didn't have much time . . . I looked around and our house was done gone. It didn't wash plumb away. It washed down about four or five house lots from where it was setting, tore all to pieces.

Two years after the disaster, Wilbur and Deborah describe their psychological scars, the defining symptoms of a post-traumatic stress disorder. First, Wilbur *relives* the trauma repeatedly in his dreams:

> What I went through on Buffalo Creek is the cause of my problem. The whole thing happens over to me even in my dreams, when I retire for the night. In my dreams, I

▼ While a specific object triggers the fear response in phobia, an unusually traumatic event—often a natural or man-made disaster—precipitates post-traumatic stress disorder. On the left, flood waters break a window during Hurricane Andrew in 1992; on the right, civilians and a U.N. soldier take cover during the war in Bosnia.

1. What are the three symptoms that define post-traumatic stress disorder?
2. What criterion for diagnosing PTSD is given in DSM-IV and who is likely to be most vulnerable to PTSD?
3. Describe how rape trauma syndrome resembles post-traumatic stress disorder.
4. How successful have drug treatments and psychotherapy been for relieving PTSD?

run from water all the time, all the time. The whole thing just happens over and over again in my dreams . . .

Second, Wilbur and Deborah have become *numb* psychologically. Affect is blunted and they are emotionally anesthetized to the sorrows and joys of the world around them. Wilbur says:

I didn't even go to the cemetery when my father died [about a year after the flood]. It didn't dawn on me that he was gone forever. And those people that dies around me now, it don't bother me like it did before the disaster . . . It just didn't bother me that my dad was dead and never would be back. I don't have the feeling I used to have about something like death. It just don't affect me like it used to.

And Deborah says:

I'm neglecting my children. I've just completely quit cooking. I don't do no housework. I just won't do nothing. Can't sleep. Can't eat. I just want to take me a lot of pills and just go to bed and go to sleep and not wake up. I enjoyed my home and my family, but outside of them, to me, everything else in life that I had any interest in is destroyed. I loved to cook. I loved to sew. I loved to keep house. I was all the time working and making improvements on my home. But now I've just got to the point where it don't mean a thing in the world to me. I haven't cooked a hot meal and put it on the table for my children in almost three weeks.

Third, Wilbur experiences symptoms of *anxiety*, including hyper-alertness and phobic reactions to events that remind him of the flood, such as rain and impending bad weather:

. . . I listen to the news, and if there is a storm warning out, why I don't go to bed that night. I sit up. I tell my wife, "Don't undress our little girls; just let them lay down like they are and go to bed and go to sleep and then if I see anything going to happen, I'll wake you in plenty of time to get you out of the house." I don't go to bed. I stay up.

My nerves is a problem. Every time it rains, every time it storms, I just can't take it. I walk the floor. I get so nervous I break out in a rash. I am taking shots for it now . . .

Wilbur also suffers from **_survival guilt:_**

At that time, why, I heard somebody holler at me, and I looked around and saw Mrs. Constable. . . . She had a little baby in her arms and she was hollering, "Hey, Wilbur, come and help me; if you can't help me, come get my baby." . . . But I didn't give it a thought to go back and help her. I blame myself a whole lot for that yet. She had her baby in her arms and looked as though she were going to throw it to me. Well, I never thought to go help that lady. I was thinking about my own family. They all six got drowned in that house. She was standing in water up to her waist, and they all got drowned.

These symptoms persisted. Fourteen years after the Buffalo Creek Flood, 193 survivors were examined. Sixty percent had PTSD initially, and 25 percent still had it fourteen years later. Thirty-five percent had major depression initially, and 19 percent had it fourteen years after the flood (Green, Lindy, Grace, and Leonard, 1992).

FIGURE 8–5

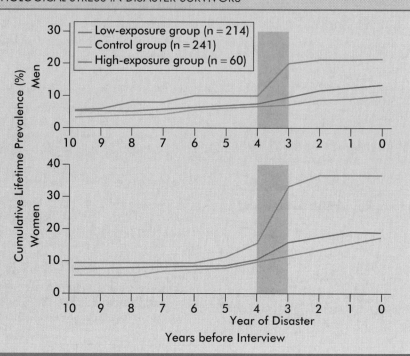

PSYCHOLOGICAL STRESS IN DISASTER SURVIVORS

The curves show lifetime prevalence of single-episode depression, generalized anxiety disorder, and post-traumatic stress disorder in men and women before and after the Mount St. Helens disaster. Those who were most affected by the disaster showed the highest rates of psychological disorders. (SOURCE: Shore, Tatum, and Vollmer, 1986, p. 592)

A similar naturally occurring disaster was the 1980 eruption of Mount St. Helens. Three years after the disaster, survivors were interviewed to see if they had symptoms of psychological stress. Those interviewed included 138 individuals who had high exposure (either death of a family member or substantial financial loss) to the disaster, 410 who had low exposure (merely lived in the affected area), and 477 control subjects. Eleven percent of the men in the high-exposure group had either post-traumatic stress disorder, depression, or anxiety disorders; 2.5 percent of the low-exposure group had these disorders; and 1 percent of the control group (see Figure 8–5). Women had double these rates in all groups (Shore, Tatum, and Vollmer, 1986). Similar findings occurred after the Three Mile Island Nuclear disaster (Davidson and Baum, 1986).

MANMADE CATASTROPHES

The catastrophe that brings out a post-traumatic stress reaction need not be a naturally occurring one like the Buffalo Creek Flood. Human beings have made a hell of the lives of other human beings since time immemorial: concentration camps, war, and torture ruin lives long after the victims have ceased to experience the original trauma. Unfortunately, the disorders following these catastrophes may be even more severe and long-lasting than those following natural disasters; it may be easier for us to deal with the "acts of God" than with the acts of men.

The survivors of the Nazi concentration camps illustrate how long-lasting and severe the post-traumatic stress reaction can be. In a study of 149 camp survivors, 142 (or 97 percent) were still troubled with anxiety twenty years after they were freed from the camps (Krystal, 1968). Anxiety symptoms were marked: 31 percent were troubled with fears that something terrible would happen to their mates or their children whenever they were out of sight. Many of them were phobic about certain people whose appearance or behavior reminded them of their jailors; for example, the sight of a uniformed policeman or the inquisitive behavior of a doctor might be enough to set off panic. Seven percent had such severe panic attacks that the individual became confused and disoriented, entering a dreamlike state in which he believed himself to be back in the concentration camp.

The survivors relived the trauma in dreams for twenty years: 71 percent of these patients had anxiety dreams and nightmares, with 41 percent having severe ones. These nightmares were usually of their persecution. Particularly terrifying were dreams in which only one detail was changed from the reality; for example, dreaming that their children who had not yet been born at the time of the camps had been imprisoned with them in the camps.

Eighty percent of the patients suffered survivor guilt, depression, and crying spells. Survival guilt was especially strong when the patient's children had been killed; those who were the most severely depressed had lost an only child or had lost all of their children, with no children being born since. Ninety-two percent expressed self-reproach for failing to save their relatives, and 14 percent wished they had been killed instead of their relatives (Krystal, 1968). One hundred twenty-four Holocaust survivors were examined more than forty years after the war, and the findings were grim. Almost half were suffering PTSD, with sleep disturbance the most pervasive symptom. Survivors of Auschwitz were three times as likely to still have PTSD as survivors who had not been in concentration camps (Kuch and Cox, 1992).

Human inhumanity to other humans did not abate after World War II, and among its more awful consequences has been lasting PTSD. Fifty-five survivors of the Lockerbie air disaster were examined, and the majority had PTSD, with victims over sixty-five, unlike younger victims, also having major depression (Livingston, Livingston, Brooks, and McKinlay, 1992; Brooks and McKinlay, 1992). Among evacuees of the SCUD missile attacks in Israel during the Gulf War, almost 80 percent met the criteria for PTSD. The more danger they encountered, the worse their symptoms (Solomon, Laor, Weiler, and Muller,

▶ These Jews in the Warsaw Ghetto were rounded up by German soldiers, then sent to concentration camps. Many survivors of the camps still suffer the psychological effects of one of the most deliberately evil acts of this century.

Survivors of war often suffer from PTSD even if they were not in the armed forces. This family was living in the ruins of a village in Kurdistan in 1991.

1993). Pol Pot's murderous regime left a wake of PTSD among Cambodian children. A group of forty-six refugees to North America who were children at the time have been followed and subsequently examined. PTSD was found to persist in many through their adolescence and into their adulthood, but depression markedly decreased from adolescence to adulthood (Sack, Clarke, Him, and Dickason, 1993).

RAPE TRAUMA SYNDROME

The event that brings about a post-traumatic stress disorder need not be experienced en masse, as in flood, war, and concentration camp; it can be solitary. Rape is, perhaps, the most common such trauma in modern American society. About 100,000 rapes are reported every year and possibly seven times as many go unreported. A woman's reaction to rape looks very much like the post-traumatic stress disorder, and so has been called the **rape trauma syndrome** (Burgess and Holmstrom, 1979).

When a woman is raped, her first reaction is called the phase of "disorganization." In one study, researchers found that immediately following rape, a roughly equal number of women exhibited one of two emotional styles: *expressive*—showing fear, anger, anxiety, crying, sobbing, and tenseness—or *controlled*—showing a calm exterior. The symptoms of post-traumatic stress disorder were usually present as well. As many as 95 percent of the victims may show the symptoms of post-traumatic stress disorder within two weeks (Rothbaum, Foa, Riggs, Murdock, and Walsh, 1992). The victim relives the rape time and again, in waking life and in dreams. Sleep disturbance sets in, and there is both trouble getting to sleep and sudden awakening. Rape victims startle easily. Women who were suddenly awakened by the rapist ("blitz" rape) find that they awake each night at about the same time, screaming from rape nightmares. Normal sexual activity is difficult to resume, and a complete avoidance of sex sometimes develops.

Most victims get over the phase of "disorganization" in time and enter the "reorganization" phase. In the long-term process of reorganization, most women take action to ensure safety. Many change their telephone numbers, and half of the women make special trips home to seek support from family

Rape trauma syndrome shares many symptoms with post-traumatic stress disorder, and as with PTSD, these symptoms are often profound and long-lasting.

members. Half of the victims move. One victim who couldn't afford to move first stayed with relatives and then rearranged her home. As the rape had occurred in her bedroom, she did what she could to change that room: "Wouldn't sleep in my own bed. Stayed with friends for a while. Changed my bedroom around, and got a new bedroom set." Many of the victims begin to read about rape and to write about their experience. Some become active in rape crisis centers and assist other victims, and of these, 70 percent recover in a few months (Burgess and Holmstrom, 1979; Meyer and Taylor, 1986).

Four to six years after the rape, about 75 percent of rape victims said they had recovered. More than half of these recovered in the first three months, and the rest within two years. Victims with the least fear and the fewest flashbacks in the week following the rape recovered more quickly. The very distressed or numbed victims had a poor outcome. The violence of the assault and how life-threatening it was also predicted worse long-term outcome. Distressingly, 25 percent of rape victims said they have not recovered, even after four to six years. Seventeen years later, 16 percent still had post-traumatic stress disorder (Girelli, Resick, Marhoefer-Dvorak, and Hutter, 1986; Kilpatrick, Saunders, Veronen, Best, and Von, 1987; Kilpatrick, Saunders, Amick-McMullan, et al., 1989; Rothbaum, Foa, Riggs, Murdock, and Walsh, 1992).

Course of Post-Traumatic Stress Disorder

Not much is known about the specific course of the post-traumatic stress disorder. Sometimes the symptoms disappear within a few months, resembling recovery from a depressive disorder (see Chapter 11). But overall, the prognosis is probably bleak, particularly for the victims of very severe trauma. As we saw, a high percentage of concentration camp victims are still troubled with anxiety and guilt twenty years later, and people who lose a child or spouse in a motor accident are still more depressed and anxious four to seven years later (Lehman, Wortman, and Williams, 1987). This also seems to be true of some veterans of combat. Sixty-two veterans of World War II who suffered chronic "combat fatigue," with symptoms of exaggerated jumpiness, recurrent night-

▶ Men who have been through combat, such as these American soldiers in Vietnam, may later suffer from chronic "combat fatigue."

FIGURE 8–6

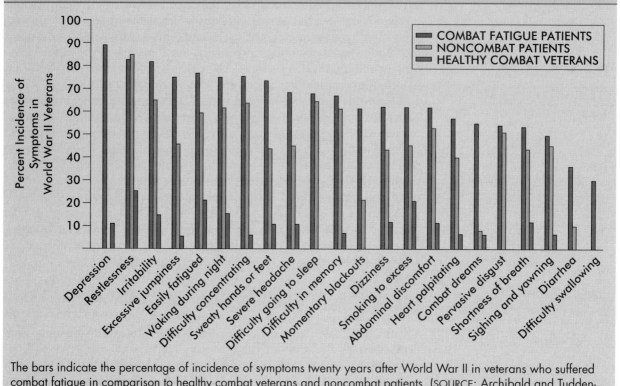

POST-TRAUMATIC STRESS DISORDER IN VETERANS

The bars indicate the percentage of incidence of symptoms twenty years after World War II in veterans who suffered combat fatigue in comparison to healthy combat veterans and noncombat patients. (SOURCE: Archibald and Tuddenham, 1965, p. 478)

mares, and irritability, were examined twenty years later. Irritability, depression, restlessness, difficulties in concentration and memory, blackouts, wakefulness, fatigability, and jumpiness persisted for twenty years. These symptoms were more prominent in the veterans suffering from combat fatigue than in noncombat patients or in healthy combat veterans. Combat fatigue victims still jumped when they heard noises of jets and firecrackers. Three-quarters of these men reported that their symptoms interfered with providing for their family. Half reported their sex lives were unsatisfactory, and that they were unduly irritable with their children. A third of the men were unemployed. Figure 8–6 presents the incidence of symptoms of World War II combat fatigue victims compared to control groups twenty years later (Archibald and Tuddenham, 1965).

Similar long-lasting symptoms are found among prisoners-of-war. Forty years after World War II, a random sample of Australian soldiers who were held in Japanese prison camps were compared to non-POW soldiers. The POWs were more depressed forty years later and had more stomach ulcers, but they did not have increased anxiety or alcohol problems (Tennant, Goulston, and Dent, 1986). Of 188 former World War II American POWs, about one-third had fully recovered, one-third still had mild post-traumatic stress symptoms, and one-third still had moderate to severe symptoms forty years later (Kluznik, Speed, Van Valkenberg, and Magraw, 1986).

Vietnam veterans have also experienced post-traumatic stress disorder, particularly those who saw buddies killed in action. Those who saw, and particularly those who participated in atrocities, have been shown to be at severe risk for post-traumatic stress disorder (Breslau and Davis, 1987). These extreme stressors seem to produce post-traumatic stress disorder specifically, since the risk for panic and depression has not been shown to be elevated. One group of Vietnam veterans interviewed six to fifteen years after participating in violent combat had lives fulls of problems. They had more arrests and convictions, more drinking, more drug addiction, and more stress than veterans who did not see combat. (Before Vietnam these two groups did not differ.) Men who took part in atrocities were in particularly bad shape (Yager, Laufer, and Gallops, 1984).

One caveat, which may sound hard-hearted, is in order, however. Post-traumatic stress disorder became an official disorder with the advent of DSM-III in 1980. It is now reimbursable under disability claims, and large lawsuits against the government and against private companies have been instituted. The lawyers for the victims of Buffalo Creek sued the Pittston Company, who owned the dam that burst, for enormous sums. We can no longer be sure that duration and severity of symptoms following disasters are disinterestedly reported, and future epidemiologists would do well to compare symptoms under reimbursable and nonreimbursable conditions to arrive at accurate severity and prevalence figures. Nonetheless, a similar picture also emerges from pre-DSM data and from victims who have little or nothing to gain; concentration camp survivors and rape victims have little more than sympathy to gain, and that hardly seems worth the cost of living the life of a PTSD victim. In a fourteen-year follow-up of 193 survivors of the Buffalo Creek flood, 117 were involved in the lawsuit against the coal company, and 76 were not. Rates of disorders, however, were the same in the two groups (Green, Grace, Lindy, et al., 1990). These data suggest that PTSD is both real and potentially very long-lasting.

Vulnerability

Who among us is particularly at risk? Psychologists comb over disasters looking for the people who survive them well (without signs of PTSD), and for those who crumble most readily. They then try to determine what factors predispose some people to PTSD. Here is what they have found:

- A prior life history free of mental problems predicted who did best after a catastrophic factory explosion in Norway.
- Among 469 firefighters caught in a disastrous Australian brushfire, those most at risk for getting chronic PTSD scored high on neuroticism and had a family history of mental disorders. These were better predictors than even how much physical trauma each one had experienced.
- After fighting in Lebanon, Israeli combat casualty veterans who were the children of Holocaust survivors (called "second-generation casualties") had higher rates of PTSD than control casualties.
- Among Israeli combat veterans of two wars, those who experienced PTSD after the second war had had more combat stress reactions during the first war.

These findings indicate that people who are psychologically most healthy before the trauma are at least risk for PTSD. This may be of some consolation—if you happen to be psychologically healthy. But if the bad event is awful enough, previously good psychological health will not protect you (Solomon, Kotler, and Mikulincer, 1988; Weisaeth, 1989; McFarlane, 1989; Malt and Weisaeth, 1989; Solomon, Opppenheimer, Elizur, and Waysman, 1990).

Another possible factor contributing to vulnerability to PTSD is genetic predisposition. The sheer scale of the American participation in the Vietnam War has allowed the first major study of the heritability of PTSD. Over 4,000 twin pairs who were Vietnam veterans were examined after the war for PTSD symptoms and for how intense their combat experience had been. PTSD symptoms occurred in roughly half the veterans who saw intense combat. Identical twins showed more similar level of PTSD symptoms than did fraternal twins, and identical twins also had more similar combat experience than did fraternal twins. But *both* genetics and the level of combat intensity contributed independently to PTSD. So PTSD has a heritable component *and* the more intense the combat experienced, the worse the PTSD (True, Rice, Eisen, et al., 1993).

Treatment

In spite of the fact that so many of our fellow human beings are victims of trauma, unfortunately little is known about how to alleviate post-traumatic stress reactions. Relatives, friends, and therapists are inclined to tell the victims of catastrophe to try to "forget it," but it should be apparent that such painful memories cannot be easily blotted out.

Therapists have tried both drug therapy and psychotherapy with victims of trauma. In the best controlled study, forty-six Vietnam veterans with post-traumatic stress disorder were given either antidepressants or a placebo. After the patients were given antidepressants, their nightmares and flashbacks decreased, but not down into the normal range. Numbing, a sense of distance from loved ones, and general anxiety were not relieved. More than a quarter, however, refused to take the drugs. It is not known what happened to the patients when the drugs were withdrawn. In another study, antidepressant drugs produced some relief, but at the end of treatment 64 percent of those in the antidepressant drug group and 72 percent of those in the placebo group still had post-traumatic stress disorder. Overall antidepressants and anti-anxiety drugs produce some symptom relief for some patients, but drug treatment alone is never sufficient to relieve the patient's suffering in post-traumatic stress disorder (Frank, Kosten, Giller, and Dan, 1988; Friedman, 1988; Davidson, Kudler, Smith, et al., 1990).

Several types of psychotherapy have been used to treat post-traumatic stress disorder. One takes its lead from Jamie Pennebaker's important work on silence. Pennebaker has found that Holocaust victims and rape victims who do not talk about the trauma later suffer worse physical health than do those who confide in somebody. Pennebaker got sixty Holocaust survivors to open up and to describe what happened to them. They finally related to others scenes that they had relived in their heads thousands of times over the last forty years.

> They were throwing babies from the second floor window of the orphanage. I can still see the pools of blood, the screams, and hear the thuds of their bodies. I just

stood there afraid to move. The Nazi soldiers faced us with their guns. (Pennebaker, 1990)

Ironically, the interviewers themselves had nightmares from hearing these long-buried stories, but the health of the disclosers improved. Similarly, Pennebaker had students write down their secret traumas: sexual abuse by a grandfather, death of a dog, a suicide attempt. The immediate consequence was increased depression. But in the long term, the number of physical illnesses of the students dropped—by 50 percent—and their immune systems became stronger (Pennebaker, 1990).

Prolonged exposure therapy, an extinction or habituation procedure like flooding in which individuals are repeatedly exposed to the feared stimulus, has also been used to treat post-traumatic stress disorder. In this kind of exposure treatment, victims relive the trauma in their imagination. They describe it aloud to the therapist, in the present tense. This is repeated session after session. In the best controlled study of exposure treatment, Edna Foa and her colleagues treated forty-five rape victims who had post-traumatic stress disorder (Foa, Rothbaum, Riggs, and Murdock, 1991). They compared the exposure treatment to stress inoculation training, which included deep muscle relaxation, thought-stopping for countering ruminations, and cognitive restructuring. Another group received supportive counseling. The fourth group was a control group consisting of those put on a waiting list for future treatment.

All groups, including those in the wait-list control group, improved. Immediately after the five weeks of treatment, stress inoculation training relieved post-traumatic stress disorder symptoms the most, but after another four months, prolonged exposure treatment produced the most lasting effects (Foa, Rothbaum, Riggs, and Murdock, 1991; see also Frank, Anderson, Stewart, Dacu, et al., 1988; Resick, Jordan, Girelli, Hutter, et al., 1988).

In an ongoing study conducted by Edna Foa, the combination of stress inoculation and prolonged exposure produced very good results. After five weeks of treatment (9 sessions), 80 percent of the victims were no longer showing post-traumatic stress disorder and symptoms were markedly reduced. No significant relapse was found. These new findings are the best outcome yet for treatment of rape victims. If they are replicated, rape victims, who are usually quite reluctant to go for treatment because they want to avoid thinking about the rape, should be encouraged to seek out this treatment promptly. So psychological treatment produces some relief, but as yet no cures, and future research in this domain is essential.

DISORDERS OF ANXIETY

In our discussion so far, we have focused on phobia and post-traumatic stress disorders, which we consider ***fear disorders.*** Both are problems in which anxiety is felt. Also, the individual afflicted by either of them experiences the four elements of fear: expectations of danger (the cognitive element); the emergency reaction (the somatic element); feelings of terror, apprehension, and dread (the emotional element); and avoidance and escape (the behavioral element). Phobia and post-traumatic stress disorder are similar in that they both stem from a specific object: the phobic object (cat, etc.) in the case of phobias, and the precipitating situation (flood, etc.) in the cases of post-traumatic stress disorder. In contrast, in the **anxiety disorders,** panic disorder, agoraphobia, and generalized anxiety disorder, anxiety is also felt. There is, however, no specific object that is feared. In these disorders, the anxiety felt by the individual is not focused on a clear and specific object. Panic disorder and its close relative, agoraphobia, involve acute experiences of anxiety, whereas generalized anxiety disorder is the chronic experience of anxiety.

Panic Disorder

How many of us have at some time been suddenly overwhelmed by intense apprehension? Physically, we feel jumpy and tense. Cognitively, we expect that something bad—we don't know what—is going to happen. Such an attack comes out of nowhere; no specific object or event sets it off, and the attack gradually subsides. But some people have more severe attacks, and they have them frequently. These people suffer from **panic disorder.** Panic disorder consists of recurrent panic attacks.

SYMPTOMS OF A PANIC ATTACK

A panic attack consists of the four elements of fear, with the emotional and physical elements most salient.

Emotionally, the individual is overwhelmed with intense apprehension, terror, or depersonalization.

> It was just like I was petrified with fear. If I were to meet a lion face to face, I couldn't be more scared. Everything got black, and I felt I would faint; but I didn't. I thought "I won't be able to hold on" . . . (Laughlin, 1967, p. 92)

Physically, a panic attack consists of an acute emergency reaction (including shortness of breath, dizziness, racing heart, trembling, chills, or chest pains).

▶ Cognitive and physical symptoms of anxiety make the world a frightening place for people who suffer from panic attacks. Their own symptoms can be as unpredictable and threatening as these creatures of Wifredo Lam's *The Jungle.*

FOCUS QUESTIONS

1. What is panic disorder?
2. Explain the emotional, physical, and cognitive symptoms of panic disorder.
3. What four questions do proponents of the biomedical model ask in approaching the etiology and treatment of panic disorder?
4. How does the cognitive model answer these questions?

My heart was beating so hard and fast it would jump out and hit my hand. I felt like I couldn't stand up—that my legs wouldn't support me. My hands got icy and my feet stung. There were horrible shooting pains in my forehead. My head felt tight, like someone had pulled the skin down too tight and I wanted to pull it away . . .

I couldn't breathe; I was short of breath. I literally got out of breath and panted like I had run up and down the stairs. I felt like I had run an eight-mile race. I couldn't do anything. I felt all in; weak, no strength. I can't even dial a telephone. . . . (Laughlin, 1967, p. 92)

Cognitively, the individual thinks he might have a heart attack and die, or go crazy, or lose control.

Even then I can't be still when I am like this. I am restless and I pace up and down. I feel like I am just not responsible. I don't know what I'll do. These things are terrible. I can go along real calmly for awhile. Then, without any warning, this happens. I just blow my top. (Laughlin, 1967, p. 92)

Such an attack begins abruptly, usually peaks within ten minutes, and subsides gradually. Panic attacks come in two forms: unexpected ("out of the blue") and situationally triggered. Unexpected panic attacks are the defining symptom of panic disorder. After a few attacks, the individual is likely to worry persistently about having another one and about the consequences (e. g., going crazy or dying). Situationally triggered panic attacks may be set off by social situations or specific objects (e. g., cats). An occasional panic attack is quite common, with as many as 20 percent of students and about 5 percent of senior citizens reporting one episode of panic in the preceding week (Barlow, 1988). When panic attacks are frequent, however—three in three weeks or four in a month—the condition is severe enough to warrant a diagnosis of panic disorder. Panic disorder has a prevalence rate of around 0.5 percent and may be more common in females than males. The first attack typically occurs when the individual is in the early twenties (Barlow, 1986, 1988; Joyce, Bushnell, Oakley-Browne, and Wells, 1989; Regier, Narrow, and Rae, 1990).

ETIOLOGY AND THERAPY: BIOMEDICAL VERSUS COGNITIVE

Biomedical Approach   There are four questions that each bear on whether a mental problem is primarily biomedical: (1) Can it be induced biologically?, (2) Is it heritable?, (3) Are specific brain functions involved?, and (4) Does a drug relieve it?

The answers to these four questions suggest that panic disorder may be a disease of the body. First, panic attacks can be induced chemically in the laboratory in patients who experience them frequently. Such patients are hooked up to an intravenous line that slowly infuses sodium lactate, a chemical that normally produces rapid, shallow breathing and heart palpitations, into their bloodstream. Within a few minutes about 60 to 90 percent of these patients have a panic attack. Normal controls rarely have panic attacks when infused with sodium lactate. Further, the induction is specific to people who are vulnerable to panic attacks, since sodium lactate rarely produces a panic attack in patients who have anxiety problems (Liebowitz, Gorman, Fyer, et al., 1985; Liebowitz, Fyer, Gorman, et al., 1985).

Second, panic disorder may have a genetic origin. If one of two identical twins has panic disorder, 31 percent of the co-twins are also found to have the disorder. But if one of two fraternal twins has panic disorder, none of the co-twins are so afflicted. Panic runs in families, and more than half of panic disorder patients have close relatives who have some anxiety disorder or suffer from alcoholism (Torgersen, 1983; Crowe, 1990).

Third, there is some evidence that panic disorder patients may have a neurochemical abnormality. The efficiency of the circuits in the brain that dampen and shut down the emergency reaction may be impaired (Nesse, Cameron, Curtis, McCann, and Huber-Smith, 1984; Charney and Heninger, 1986). In addition, PET scans have shown that patients who have panic attacks after being infused with sodium lactate have higher blood flow and oxygen use in relevant areas of their brains than patients who don't panic after lactate infusions (Reiman, Raichle, Robins, et al., 1986).

The fourth line of evidence for the biomedical view of panic comes from drug therapy. There are two kinds of drugs that relieve panic. Tricyclic antidepressant drugs and a potent anti-anxiety drug, Xanax (alprazolam), both work better than placebos. Panic attacks are dampened, and even sometimes eliminated. General anxiety and depression also decrease (Pecknold, Swinson, Kuch, and Lewis, 1988; Svebak, Cameron, and Levander, 1990; Tesar, 1990).

So by chemically inducing panic, by demonstrating some heritability, by finding biochemical abnormalities in the brain, and by relieving panic with drugs, a strong case existed for viewing panic disorder as a disease of the body—until very recently.

Cognitive Approach   The cognitive school has challenged the biomedical view by claiming that all four lines of biomedical evidence can be seen as stemming from a cognitive abnormality.

Cognitive therapists claim that panic disorder results from catastrophic misinterpretations of bodily sensations (Beck and Emery, 1985; Clark, 1988, 1989). The panic disorder patient misinterprets normal anxiety responses, such as heart racing, breathlessness, and dizziness, as indicating impending disaster. Palpitations are interpreted as meaning a heart attack is about to occur; dizziness as meaning insanity and loss of control. The cognitive view looks at each of the four pieces of evidence for the biomedical view in light of misinterpreting the meaning of bodily sensations. (1) Lactate induces panic because it makes your heart race. It then creates the first bodily sensations that you misinterpret as catastrophe. (2) Panic attacks are partially heritable because having a particularly noticeable bodily sensation, such as heart palpitations, is heritable, not because panic itself is directly heritable. (3) Brain areas that prevent the dampening of anxiety are active as a result of the panic attack, not as a cause of it. (4) Drugs relieve panic because they quiet the bodily sensations that get misinterpreted as catastrophe. When these drugs are no longer taken, panic attacks recur in full force.

So far, then, it is a tie. Both schools can adequately explain the four lines of evidence. But the cognitive school has carried out a series of additional experiments and created a new therapy. David Clark and Paul Salkovskis compared panic disorder patients with patients who had other anxiety disorders and with normal people. Everyone was asked to read the following sentences aloud, but the last word presented was blurred. For example:

> If I had palpitations I could be   *dying.*
> *excited.*

▼ David Clark (1954–   ) of Oxford University has designed and tested an effective form of cognitive therapy for panic disorder. Clark proposes that panic results from catastrophically misinterpreting bodily sensations of anxiety, such as a racing heart, as symptoms of a heart attack. He teaches people to correct these misinterpretations and to recognize that the symptoms signify anxiety, not physical catastrophe. This brief therapy eliminates panic disorder in more than 80 percent of patients.

If I were breathless I could be	*choking.*
	unfit.

When the sentences were about bodily sensations, the panic patients, but no one else, saw the catastrophic endings fastest. This indicates that panic patients possess the habit of thinking catastrophically.

Next Clark and Salkovskis asked if words alone would activate this habit of catastrophic thinking, thereby inducing panic. Everyone read a series of word pairs aloud. When panic patients got to "breathlessness-suffocation" and "palpitations-dying," 75 percent had a full-blown panic attack—right there in the laboratory. No normal people had panic attacks, no recovered panic patients had panic attacks, and only 17 percent of other anxious patients had panic attacks.

Clark and Salkovskis reasoned that if catastrophic misinterpretations of bodily sensations are the cause of panic disorder, then changing the misinterpretation should cure the disorder. The therapy they developed to do this is straightforward and brief. Patients are told that panic results when they mistake normal symptoms of mounting anxiety for symptoms of heart attack, going crazy, or dying. Anxiety itself, they are informed, produces shortness of breath, chest pain, and sweating. Once you misinterpret these normal bodily sensations as an imminent heart attack, this makes the symptoms even more pronounced because it changes your anxiety into terror. A vicious circle has set in, culminating in a full-blown panic attack.

Patients are taught to reinterpret the symptoms realistically—as mere anxiety symptoms. Then they are given practice in dealing with the anxiety symptoms. First, the symptoms of anxiety are brought on right in the office. Patients are told to breathe rapidly into a paper bag. This will cause a buildup of carbon dioxide and shortness of breath, mimicking the bodily sensations that provoke a panic attack. The therapist will then point out that the symptoms the patient is now experiencing—shortness of breath and heart racing— are harmless. They are simply the result of overbreathing, not a sign of a heart attack. The patient will then learn to interpret the sensations correctly. The following case illustrates how a cognitive therapist would proceed:

> One patient upon feeling somewhat faint would have a panic attack. He became afraid that he would actually faint and collapse. He interpreted his anxiety as a further symptom of fainting. This escalated to panic in a few seconds.
> THERAPIST: Why are you afraid of fainting? Have you never actually fainted?
> PATIENT: I always managed to avoid collapsing just in time by holding on to something.
> THERAPIST: That's one possibility. An alternative explanation is that the feeling of faintness that you get in a panic attack will never lead you to collapse, even if you don't control it. In order to decide which possibility is correct, we need to know what has to happen to your body for you to actually faint. Do you know?
> PATIENT: No.
> THERAPIST: Your blood pressure needs to drop. Do you know what happens to your blood pressure during a panic attack?
> PATIENT: Well, my pulse is racing. I guess my blood pressure must be up.
> THERAPIST: That's right. In anxiety, heart rate and blood pressure tend to go together. So you are actually *less* likely to faint when you are anxious than when you are not.

> PATIENT: But why do I feel so faint?
>
> THERAPIST: Your feeling of faintness is a sign that your body is reacting in a normal way to the perception of danger. When you perceive danger, more blood is sent to your muscles and less to your brain. This means that there is a small drop in oxygen to the brain and that is why you *feel* faint. However, this feeling is misleading because you will not actually faint since your blood pressure is up, not down.
>
> PATIENT: That's very clear. So next time I feel faint, I can check out whether I am going to faint by taking my pulse. If it's normal or quicker than normal, I know I won't faint. (Clark, 1989).

How well does this simple therapy work? Eighty to 90 percent of the patients treated with this therapy are panic free at the end of therapy (Klosko, Barlow, Tassarini, and Cerny, 1988; Michelson and Marchione, 1989; Clark, Gelder, Saldovskis, Hackman, Middleton, and Anastasiades, 1990; Beck, Sokol, Clark, Berchick, and Wright, 1991; Öst, 1991; Margraf and Schneider, 1991; Margraf, Barlow, Clark, and Telch, 1993).

This therapy can be characterized as a breakthrough: a simple, brief psychotherapy with no side effects showing 80 to 90 percent cure of a disorder that a decade ago was thought incurable. Such a high cure rate is actually unprecedented. There is not a single instance in the annals of psychotherapy or drug therapy where a therapy produced this high a cure rate with almost no recurrence. Lithium for manic-depression, at 80 percent effectiveness (with dangerous side effects and high recurrence when lithium is stopped), is the closest.

But still, the case isn't closed. Creating a cognitive therapy that works is not enough to show that the cause of panic is cognitive. The biological theory doesn't deny that some other therapy might work well on panic; it merely claims that at bottom panic is caused by some biochemical problem. The crucial experiment here would be one that tests between the biochemical theory and the cognitive theory.

The central pillar of the biochemical theory is that panic attacks are produced with infusions of sodium lactate. Carbon dioxide, yohimbine (a drug that stimulates the brain's fear system), and overbreathing, however, all induce panic as well. There is no known neurochemical pathway that all of these have in common. The cognitive theory claims that the common element is that all produce bodily sensations that get misinterpreted as catastrophe. The cognitive view holds that the single element that is *necessary* for a panic attack is the misinterpretation of the bodily sensations and predicts that you should therefore be able to block lactate-induced panic attacks merely by countering the misinterpretation. The biological theory, in contrast, predicts that sodium lactate is sufficient for panic attacks.

David Clark and his associates tested these predictions. They gave the usual sodium lactate infusion to ten panic patients, and nine of them panicked. They did the same thing with another ten patients, but added special instructions to allay the misinterpretation of the sensations. They simply told them: "Lactate is a natural bodily substance which produces sensations similar to exercise or alcohol. It is normal to experience intense sensations during infusion, but these do not indicate an adverse reaction." Only three out of the ten panicked.

In summary, both the biomedical and the cognitive schools have made major contributions to the understanding of panic disorder (see Table 8–5).

TABLE 8–5

THE BIOMEDICAL VS. THE COGNITIVE EXPLANATION OF PANIC DISORDER		
	Biomedical Explanation	*Cognitive Explanation*
Panic attacks can be induced by sodium lactate infusions	Lactate causes panic attacks in people with the disorder because lactate produces panic directly in biochemically vulnerable people	People with panic disorder panic to lactate because they misinterpret the drug-produced increases in heart rate and breathing; their cognitions produce acute anxiety, compounding those effects
Concordance for panic disorder is higher in identical twins than in fraternal twins	The biochemical vulnerability that produces panic is heritable because it is biochemical	Vulnerability to panic disorder is heritable either because the tendency to misinterpret certain physical symptoms is heritable or because higher heart rate is heritable
Patients with panic disorder enter the panic state and show less inhibition of the emergency reaction	Lack of inhibition of the emergency reaction is caused by a heritable brain abnormality and is not under patient's control	Lack of inhibition of the emergency reaction is a symptom of panic, caused ultimately by the patient's cognitions
Antidepressants and anti-anxiety drugs alleviate panic	Drugs block the biochemical process that produces panic	Drugs block the symptoms that are misinterpreted in ways that induce panic

Both have produced therapies that appear to relieve panic, as well as theories of how it is caused. But the cognitive approach seems to explain all of the biomedical evidence and to have created a therapy that the biomedical view cannot account for.

Agoraphobia

As the name ***agoraphobia,*** literally "fear of the marketplace," implies, this disorder was long thought to be a phobia. Two important facts gradually emerged, however, from careful study of many agoraphobics: (1) most cases begin with a panic attack, and (2) the individual is not afraid of the marketplace or of places of assembly in themselves, but of having an attack there, being helpless, and of no one coming to her aid. These facts strongly suggest that agoraphobia is not a true phobia, in the sense of fear of a specific situation, but rather it is a more global anxiety disorder. DSM-IV sensibly categorized agoraphobia as a subtype of panic disorder.

Agoraphobics are beset not only with a terror of being caught with panic in the marketplace, but they also fear open spaces, crowds, and streets, or being in any situation in which escape might be difficult or embarrassing, or in which help might not be available, in the event of suddenly getting sick. They typically believe that some disaster, usually a panic attack, will befall them when they are traveling away from the security of their homes, and that no one will help them. They then go to great lengths to avoid such places. Agora-

▶ Agoraphobia, commonly understood as the fear of open spaces, is more accurately the fear of illness or other disaster in a place where no one will come to one's aid.

phobia is crippling because many agoraphobics are unable to leave their homes. Agoraphobia is not uncommon, having a prevalence of about 3 percent (Thompson, Burns, Bartko, et al., 1988; Regier, Narrow, and Rae, 1990; Boyd, Rae, Thompson, and Burns, 1990). The large majority are women, and the first panic attack usually begins in late adolescence, followed shortly by avoidance of going out of the home as in the following case:

> A girl of nineteen suddenly came home from her work as a shop assistant and screamed that she was going to die. While standing at her counter, she had experienced the worst sensations in her life. Her heart began to pound like a jackhammer, she could not catch her breath, she was gripped by panic and dread, she felt the ground underneath her was about to give way, and she was convinced she was having a stroke or a heart attack. She spent the next two weeks in bed and, thereafter, she refused to walk beyond the front gate. She did not improve after four months as a psychiatric in-patient. After her discharge, she left her home only twice in the following seven years.

Here is an account of what an agoraphobic suffers:

> As a cold wind hit the hill, she stood holding her chin, looking back at the house in the distance. Her friends heard her mutter something—that she had snow in her boot, or needed the bathroom—some such lie. Then she began to run, looking down at the snow. She couldn't look at the house, it seemed too far away. She started to sweat and her legs went soft. She could not feel her feet, but they were running. Her heart was pounding, her face flushed. She began to pant. She felt as though she were coming apart, as if she had been running forever through the syrupy snow of a nightmare. Six Miltowns rattled against four Valiums in her pocket. The sweat on her body tripped triggers in her brain, the adrenaline signaled the nerves to further panic. "What if I die?" she thought. "Oh, my God, I'm going crazy." Then she was at the house, the "safe" place. But she had added more fears to an already long list. She was afraid of snow. She was afraid of hills. And, above all, she was afraid of ever again feeling the way she did running from that snowy hill in Vermont. (Baumgold, 1977)

Notice the woman's fear of open spaces, and the panic that occurs when she fears that she may not easily reach the safety of a contained space—the house. Agoraphobics dread a variety of objects connected with open space: smooth bodies of water, bleak landscapes, the street, train travel on clear days. These objects are much less terrifying when the space is more comfortably circumscribed, as by a snowstorm or trees, or when an enclosed space is easily within reach.

Agoraphobics are prone to panic attacks even when they are not in the agoraphobic situation. Moreover, they have more psychological problems—other than their disorder itself—than do true phobics. Agoraphobics are often globally anxious and generally depressed. Seventy percent of fifty-five patients with agoraphobia and panic also suffered depression as well (Breier, Charney, and Heninger, 1986). Substance abuse is also a frequent complication of agoraphobia. Obsessive-compulsive disorders occasionally accompany agoraphobia as well, and the relatives of agoraphobics are at greater risk for the entire range of anxiety disorders (Harris, Noyes, Crowe, and Chaudry, 1983). Untreated, agoraphobia will sometimes remit spontaneously, and then return mysteriously, or it may be unabating (Marks, 1969; Zitrin, Klein, Woerner, and Ross, 1983).

TREATMENT FOR AGORAPHOBIA

Two kinds of treatments have been quite effective for agoraphobia: behavior therapy—particularly flooding—and antidepressant drugs. In a flooding procedure, the agoraphobic agrees, usually with great apprehension, to enter a crowded public setting and to stay there without attempting to escape for a long period. This can be done first in imagination and then in reality. When it is done in imagination, an agoraphobic will listen to a long and vivid tape recording that describes a scenario in which she goes to a shopping center, falls down, is trampled by crowds, and hears them laugh as they observe her vomiting all over herself. Usually she is terrified for the first hour or two of flooding, and then gradually the terror will subside as she realizes that really nothing is going to happen to her. When she is actually taken to a shopping center subsequently, she will usually be greatly improved, and the anxiety may be gone. Treatment gains are maintained: four years after flooding, 75 percent of a group of seventy agoraphobics remained improved (Marks, Boulougouris, and Marset, 1971; Crowe, Marks, Agras, and Leitenberg, 1972; Emmelkamp and Kuipers, 1979).

Antidepressant and anti-anxiety drugs may also be helpful in alleviating agoraphobia, either alone or when given in concert with behavior therapy and supportive therapy. But there is an important distinction between who will benefit from medication and who will not. The distinction is between agoraphobics who do and who do not have spontaneous panic attacks. There is a small minority of agoraphobics who do not have panic attacks, and they may be considered true phobics rather than individuals with a subtype of panic disorder. They do not seem to benefit from medication (Marks, Gray, Cohen, Hill, Mawson, Ramm, and Stern, 1983; Zitrin, Klein, Woerner, and Ross, 1983; Charney and Heninger, 1985; Ballenger, 1986; Mavissakalian, Perel, Bowler, and Dealy, 1987; Pollard, Bronson, and Kenney, 1989).

The behavioral model suggests the following analysis of the acquisition of agoraphobia for those whose condition begins with a panic attack. The CS is the *agora* (a stimulus complex in which panic might occur and help not come),

FOCUS QUESTIONS

1. What is agoraphobia and why is it now considered a subtype of panic disorder rather than a phobia?
2. What kinds of treatments have been effective for agoraphobia?
3. Describe generalized anxiety disorder.
4. What kinds of treatment are most effective in providing lasting relief of generalized anxiety disorder?

the US is the first panic attack, the UR is the panic response, the CR is fear and avoidance of the agora. Based on this analysis, one way to cure agoraphobia would be to remove the possibility of panic attacks by drugs and then to show the agoraphobic that panic no longer occurs. In fact, it appears that the antidepressant imipramine reduces and removes panic. Groups that receive both imipramine and exposure therapy show improvement in that they experience less panic and tend to avoid the agora less. In contrast, groups that receive only exposure therapy show no less panic and only partial improvement in avoidance of the agora (Klein, Ross, and Cohen, 1987). This suggests that imipramine works by quelling the agoraphobic's spontaneous panic attacks. Once the panic attack is so controlled, the agoraphobic need no longer fear going into the street because the panic attack had been the traumatic event (the US) that he had feared and that he now knows will no longer occur.

There is still a rather heated controversy about the benefits of antidepressants alone and of flooding alone. One serious worry about medication is the high relapse rate, perhaps over 50 percent, when drugs are stopped (Noyes, Garvey, Cook, and Samuelson, 1989). Similarly, flooding therapy alone has some lasting benefit five years after termination, with about 50 percent of patients doing well, but few doing completely well (Lelliott, Marks, Monteiro, et al., 1987). So each alone may have some lasting benefit, but neither can be said to cure. The combination of exposure and antidepressants looks like the therapy of choice at present. Improvement rate may be as high as 90 percent with the combination. This makes theoretical sense: the combination of eliminating panic attacks by drugs and of eliminating the conditioned fear of the agora by flooding undercuts both the UR and the CR (Telch, Agras, Taylor, et al., 1985; Ballenger, 1986; Mavissakalian and Michelson, 1986; Mattick, Andrews, Hadzi-Pavlovic, and Christensen, 1990).

Generalized Anxiety Disorder

In contrast to a panic attack, which is sudden and acute, generalized anxiety is chronic, and may last for months on end, with the elements of anxiety more or less continually present. DSM-IV requires a period of six months during which most days are filled with worry and excessive anxiety for a diagnosis of **generalized anxiety disorder** (GAD). Emotionally, the individual feels jittery and tense, vigilant, and constantly on edge.

> I feel tense and fearful much of the time. I don't know what it is. I can't put my finger on it. . . . I just get all nervous inside. . . . I act like I'm scared to death of something. I guess maybe I am. (Laughlin, 1967, p. 107).

Cognitively the individual expects something awful but doesn't know what.

> I am frightened, but don't know what I fear. I keep expecting something bad to happen. . . . I have thought I could tie it to definite things, but this isn't true. It varies, and is unpredictable. I can't tell when it will come on. If I could just put my finger on what it is. . . . (Laughlin, 1967, p. 107)

Physically, the individual experiences a mild chronic emergency reaction: he sweats, his heart races, his stomach is usually upset, he feels cold, lightheaded, and his hands usually feel clammy.

Behaviorally, he is always ready to run away, flee, or hide.

For the past week or so I don't want to get away from the house. I fear I might go all to pieces, maybe become hysterical . . .
   Sometimes I get fearful and tense when I am talking to people and I just want to run away. (Laughlin, 1967, p. 107)

Considerably less is known about GAD than about any other anxiety disorder. Indeed, there is controversy about whether it is a disorder at all, because there are doubts that it can be reliably distinguished from panic and obsessive-compulsive disorder on the one hand and from normal worrying and fretting on the other (see Box 8–2). Here are a few of the better-documented findings: with a prevalence of 2.3 percent, GAD is somewhat more prevalent than panic disorder; it is more frequent in females; and it is mildly heritable. Family studies suggest that it is separable from panic disorder since relatives of GAD patients have more GAD than panic, and relatives of panic patients have more panic than GAD (Blazer, Hughes, and George, 1987; Noyes, Clarkson, Crowe, and Yates, 1987; Weissman, 1990; Rapee, 1991; Kendler, Neale, Kessler, and Heath, 1992).

Two kinds of treatment have been tested in controlled outcome studies of GAD: anti-anxiety drugs and cognitive-behavioral techniques. The drug evidence is consistent: anti-anxiety drugs produce clear reduction in anxiety symptoms for as long as the drug is taken. Because relapse is so likely once the drug is stopped and because the drugs have some potential for addiction, however, anti-anxiety agents are not an ideal treatment. It is regrettable that even well-controlled drug studies in this area have not seen fit to follow up patients after the drug has been discontinued (McLeod, Hoehn-Saric, Zimmerli, and de Souza, 1990; Schweizer, Rickels, Csanalosi, and London, 1990; Hunt and Singh, 1991; Enkelmann, 1991).

The range of cognitive and behavioral techniques have been tried on those with GAD, and there exist three well-done outcome studies. In one, fifty-seven GAD patients were randomly assigned to either cognitive-behavioral therapy (CBT), behavioral therapy alone, or wait-list control. Treatment lasted from four to twelve sessions and follow-up was continued for eighteen months. Cognitive-behavioral treatment fared best (Butler, Fennell, Robson, and Gelder,

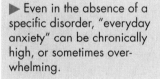
▶ Even in the absence of a specific disorder, "everyday anxiety" can be chronically high, or sometimes overwhelming.

Box 8–2

ANXIETY: STATE VERSUS TRAIT

As we have seen, some individuals have acute attacks of anxiety and do not have them again for some time (panic disorder); others seem to feel anxious all of the time (generalized anxiety disorder). Some have suggested that there is a **state** versus **trait** distinction that may explain this observation. That is, many of us at one time or another may feel panic whether or not we understand what it was in the situation that brought it on. In short, we fall into a state of anxiety. But others, those who feel anxious all the time, may have a predisposition to anxiety. They are always ready to feel anxiety; they are chronically anxious. We say that they have a trait of anxiety.

Various paper and pencil tests have been designed to determine whether one is in a state of anxiety, whether one has a trait for anxiety, or if neither measure applies. Among the most widely used are Janet Taylor Spence's Manifest Anxiety Scale (Taylor, 1951, 1953), Marvin Zuckerman's Affect Adjective Checklist (Zuckerman and Lubin, 1965), and Charles Spielberger's

State-Trait Anxiety Inventory (Spielberger, Gorsuch, and Lushene, 1970). These questionnaires ask about the four elements of anxiety.

An anxiety *state* questionnaire asks how the individual feels right now, whereas an anxiety *trait* questionnaire focuses on an individual's dispositions to display the elements of anxiety across time and across different situations. For example, the following questions might be asked: "Are you a steady person?" "Do unimportant thoughts run through your mind and bother you?" "Do you worry too much over something that really doesn't matter?" Affirmative answers to such questions point toward a trait of anxiety-proneness. Some sample items that seek to find state anxiety are shown on the facing page. This questionnaire was developed by Norman Endler and his colleagues at York University (Endler, Magnusson, Ekehammar, and Okada, 1975). The questions ask how the individual feels at the time that he or she is taking the test.

ANXIETY STATE QUESTIONNAIRE

Please circle a number from 1 to 5 for each of the items in response to the question: "HOW DO YOU FEEL AT THIS PARTICULAR MOMENT?"

Cognitive	1. Self-confident	Very Much 1	2	3	4	Not at All 5
	2. Able to focus my thoughts	Able to Focus 1	2	3	4	Unable to Focus 5
Emotional	3. Calm	Very Calm 1	2	3	4	Not at All 5
	4. Nervous	Not at All 1	2	3	4	Very Nervous 5
	5. Uneasy	Not at All 1	2	3	4	Very Uneasy 5
Somatic	6. Hands moist	Not at All 1	2	3	4	Very Moist 5
	7. Breathing is irregular	Not at All 1	2	3	4	Very Irregular 5
	8. Tense in my stomach	Not at All 1	2	3	4	Very Tense 5
Behavioral	9. Want to avoid this situation	Not at All 1	2	3	4	Very Much 5

SOURCE: Adapted from Endler, Magnusson, Ekehammar, and Okoda, 1975.

1991). The second compared cognitive-behavioral treatment to an anti-anxiety drug (diazepam) in 101 GAD patients. A six-month follow-up showed clear superiority for CBT, with the drug no more effective than a placebo (Power, Simpson, Swanson, and Wallace, 1990). The third found both CBT and relaxation superior to nondirective therapy, and emphasized imagery as an active ingredient (Borkovec and Costello, 1993).

Overall, anti-anxiety drugs appear to produce temporary relief from GAD until the drug is discontinued, while cognitive-behavioral techniques seem to produce more lasting gains.

COPING WITH EVERYDAY ANXIETY

FOCUS QUESTIONS

1. What is progressive relaxation and how does it relieve anxiety?
2. How does meditation relieve everyday anxiety?

Let's say you do not fit the diagnostic criteria for phobia or PTSD or panic or agoraphobia or GAD. Does this mean that all is well in your emotional life? Hardly. Your everyday anxiety may be unacceptably high and debilitating. Everyday anxiety level is not a category to which psychologists have devoted a lot of attention. The vast bulk of work on emotion is about "disorders."

There is enough research, however, for us to recommend two techniques that quite reliably lower everyday anxiety levels. Both techniques are cumulative, rather than quick fixes. They require devoting twenty to forty minutes a day of your time for them to work.

The first is **progressive relaxation** done once or twice a day (better) for at least ten minutes. In this technique, you tighten and then turn off each of the major muscle groups of your body, until your muscles are wholly flaccid. Relaxation engages a response system that competes with anxious arousal (Öst, 1987).

The second technique is regular **meditation.** "Transcendental Meditation" (TM) is one useful, widely available version of this. Twice a day for twenty minutes, in a quiet setting, you close your eyes and repeat a "mantra" (a syllable whose "sonic properties are known") to yourself. Meditation works by blocking thoughts that produce anxiety. It complements relaxation, which blocks the motor components of anxiety, but leaves the anxious thoughts untouched. Done regularly, most meditators enter a peaceful state of mind. Anxiety at other times of the day goes down, and hyperarousal to bad events is dampened. Done regularly, TM probably works better than relaxation alone (Eppley, Abrams, and Shear, 1989; Butler, Fennell, Robson, and Gelder, 1991; Kabat-Zinn, Massion, Kristeller, et al., 1992).

We urge you to weigh your everyday anxiety. If it is mild and not irrational or paralyzing, live with it. Listen to its dictates, and change your outer life accordingly. If it is intense or irrational or paralyzing, act now to reduce it. Intense everyday anxiety is sometimes quite changeable. Meditation and progressive relaxation practiced regularly may change it—and lastingly so.

SUMMARY

1. Phobias and post-traumatic stress disorder are both disorders in which fear is felt and in which specific objects or events set them off. Panic disorder, agoraphobia, and generalized anxiety disorder are anxiety disorders in

that the individual feels very anxious although the danger anticipated is less specific.

2. The state of fear consists of four elements: *cognitively*, the individual expects danger; *somatically*, the individual experiences the emergency reaction; *emotionally*, the individual feels apprehension, terror, or dread; and *behaviorally*, the individual tries to flee the feared situation. The elements of anxiety are identical to those of fear except for the cognitive element; the anxious individual does not expect a specific danger but simply that *something* bad will happen.

3. A *phobia* is a persistent fear of a specific object in which the fear is greatly out of proportion to the amount of danger actually present. There are social phobias and four specific phobias: phobias of particular animals and insects, phobias of inanimate objects, phobias of illness and injury (nosophobia), and blood phobia.

4. The psychoanalytic school holds that phobias occur when anxiety stemming from an intrapsychic conflict is displaced onto an innocent object.

5. The behavioral school holds that phobias are merely instances of the normal classical conditioning of fear to an innocent object that happened to be around when a traumatic event occurred. The behavioral model is consistent with case histories and laboratory evidence, and it has generated four effective therapies based on classical fear extinction: systematic desensitization, flooding, modeling, and applied tension for blood phobia. This latter appears to be a virtual cure for blood phobia.

6. The three problems with the behavioral model—selectivity of phobias, irrationality of phobias, and nontraumatic phobias—can be accounted for by the theory of *prepared classical conditioning*, which states that humans seem more prepared to learn to be afraid of certain objects than of others.

7. *Post-traumatic stress disorder* is a fear disorder that is set off by a specific event. In some cases, the specific event is a catastrophic happening such as natural disasters, combat, and imprisonment in a concentration camp. More commonplace adversities—death of a relative, divorce, and mugging—may also set off the symptoms of PTSD in some individuals. Following the event, symptoms of anxiety and avoidance, reliving the event in dreams and waking, and numbness toward the external world may develop. Also, the individual may experience survivor guilt. The symptoms may last a lifetime. Exposure therapy (extinction) shows some promise, particularly after rape, but medications do not.

8. *Panic attacks* come out of the blue, with no specific event or object setting them off. They last for only a few minutes and consist of the four elements of the anxiety reaction. *Panic disorder* consists of recurrent panic attacks. Panic disorders can be relieved by drugs and markedly relieved by learning to reinterpret frightening bodily sensations as resulting from stress and not impending doom. Both the biomedical and cognitive approaches have recently contributed to an understanding of panic, and the cognitive model may have created a cure.

9. *Agoraphobia* is a subtype of panic disorder and not a true phobia. It consists of anxiety about venturing into public places lest a panic attack occur

there, and it usually begins with a panic attack in a public place. The combination of antidepressant drugs and exposure therapy seems to be the treatment of choice.

10. *Generalized anxiety disorder* is similar to panic disorder in that there is no specific event that sets it off. In generalized anxiety disorder, however, the anxiety is milder and is chronic, with the elements of anxiety strongly present almost daily for months on end. Anti-anxiety drugs and cognitive-behavioral therapy both provide some relief.

11. Mild, *everyday anxiety* can be relieved by regular relaxation or meditation.

QUESTIONS FOR CRITICAL THINKING

1. Why do you think single phobias dissipate in most children but are unremitting in adults who are not in therapy?

2. How does prepared classical conditioning account for why humans seem more prepared to learn to be afraid of certain objects rather than others?

3. What is the reasoning behind the change from the criterion used by DSM-III to that used by DSM-IV to diagnose post-traumatic stress disorder?

4. Why is agoraphobia so debilitating and how can it interfere with a person's whole life if it goes untreated?

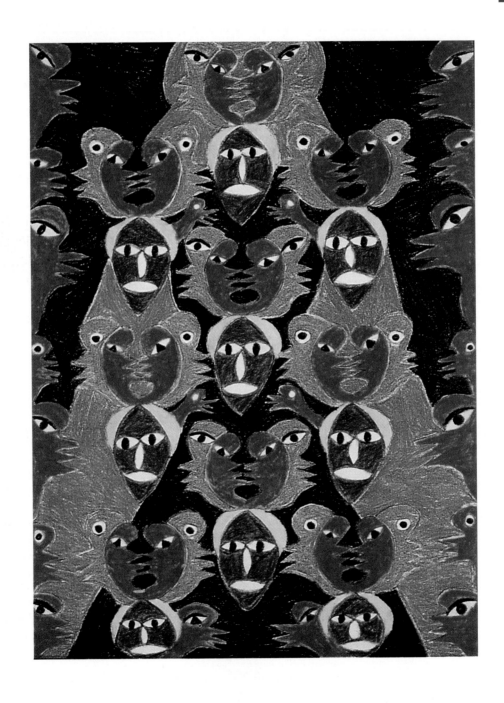

Obsession, Hysteria, and Dissociation: Anxiety Inferred

CHAPTER ORGANIZER

INTRODUCTION
- Distinguish between disorders in which anxiety is experienced by the sufferer and those in which anxiety is inferred.

OBSESSIONS AND COMPULSIONS
- Familiarize yourself with how obsessive-compulsives deal with anxiety.
- Be able to describe the various theoretical approaches to OCD as well as the efficacy of their concomitant therapies.

SOMATOFORM DISORDERS
- Be able to identify the five general symptoms of somatoform disorders.
- Familiarize yourself with the psychoanalytic, communicative, and percept blocking approaches to the somatoform disorders, and their respective treatments.

DISSOCIATIVE DISORDERS
- Be able to describe how dissociation can be experienced as amnesia, depersonalization, derealization, identity confusion, and identity alteration.
- Understand the multifaceted dimensions of multiple personality and its possible causes.

THE NEUROSES
- Understand how different models help to describe, explain, and formulate treatments for the various anxiety disorders.

We have divided anxiety disorders into two classes: those in which anxiety is actually experienced by the sufferer, and those in which anxiety is not experienced but is inferred to explain the various symptoms. In the last chapter, we discussed those disorders in which anxiety is manifest: phobia, post-traumatic stress disorder, panic disorder, and generalized anxiety disorder. In this chapter, we will discuss those disorders in which underlying anxiety has often been inferred as the cause of symptoms.

We will discuss three types of disorders. First is ***obsessive-compulsive disorder (OCD),*** in which the individual is plagued with uncontrollable, repulsive thoughts and engages in seemingly senseless rituals. An obsessive-compulsive may think that he left the gas stove on and get out of bed to check it twenty times during the night, or he may have continual thoughts of killing his children and keep all knives and sharp objects out of his own reach. The second disorder is the somatoform disorder called ***conversion.*** This disorder is characterized by a loss of physical functioning not due to any physical disorder but apparently resulting from psychological conflict. An individual may, for no biological reason, suddenly become blind, deaf, paralyzed, or suffer excruciating pain as a result of psychological stress. The third kind of disorder consists of **dissociative disorders,** in which the individual's very identity is fragmented. Among these are **amnesia,** in which an individual loses the memory of who he is, and **multiple personality,** in which more than one personality exists in the same individual, each with a relatively rich and stable life of its own.

In contrast to the disorders in the last chapter, anxiety is not usually felt by the victims of these three types of disorders. Although obsessive-compulsives often feel anxiety, they can ward off anxiety through quick and frequent rituals. Individuals with somatoform and dissociative disorders usually feel little anxiety. In fact, they may be surprisingly indifferent to their symptoms. But when psychoanalytic clinicians and researchers look at the conflicts that precede these disorders, they often infer that the symptoms are an attempt to control underlying anxiety that otherwise threatens to overwhelm the individual. For example, a man who believes he caused the paralysis of his friend may himself unconsciously assume the symptoms of paralysis; or a teenager who is plagued with unresolvable troubles at home and in school may forget who he is, wander to a new city, and assume a new identity. We begin our discussion of these disorders with obsessions and compulsions.

OBSESSIONS AND COMPULSIONS

All of us at least occasionally have distasteful and unacceptable thoughts. Many people at one time or another have had the following thoughts: "Might I do violence to someone I love?" "Am I absolutely sure that that I've locked all the doors and windows?" "Have I left the gas in the stove on?" Most of us pay little attention to these thoughts when they occur; if we do, we soon dismiss them. Such is not the case in individuals with obsessive-compulsive disorders. An example of such an individual follows:

> A thirty-eight-year-old mother of one child had been obsessed by fears of contamination during her entire adult life. Literally hundreds of times a day, thoughts of being infected by germs would occur to her. Once she began to think that either she or her child might become infected, she could not dismiss the thought. This constant concern about infection resulted in a series of washing and cleaning rituals that took up most of her day. Her child was confined to one room only, which the woman tried to keep entirely free of germs by scrubbing it—floor to ceiling—several times a day. Moreover, she opened and closed all doors with her feet, in order to avoid contaminating her own hands. (Rachman and Hodgson, 1980)

Obsessive-compulsive disorder consists of the two components from which we derive its name: obsessions and compulsions. **Obsessions** are repetitive thoughts, images, or impulses that invade consciousness, are often abhorrent, and are very difficult to dismiss or control. These thoughts are not mere excessive worries about real-life problems. The obsessive recognizes that the thoughts are products of his mind rather than imposed from outside. He is also aware that his obsessions are excessive and unreasonable, and he attempts to suppress or neutralize them with another thought or action. In the case above,

1. What is meant by anxiety felt and anxiety inferred?
2. Describe the two components of obsessive-compulsive disorder (OCD).
3. How does an obsessive-compulsive attempt to ward off anxiety?
4. What characterizes an obsessive-compulsive personality?

the mother is obsessed with repulsive thoughts and images of disease and infection that she cannot ward off.

Compulsions are the responses to obsessive thoughts. They consist of rigid rituals (such as handwashing or checking) or mental acts (such as counting or silently repeating words) that the person feels driven to perform in response to the obsession. The compulsions are aimed at preventing or reducing distress or averting some dreaded event; these actions, however, are not connected in a realistic way with what they are designed to prevent, and they are clearly excessive. The mother above, for example, reacts to her thoughts of germs by compulsively scrubbing her child's room.

Obsessions and compulsions cause marked distress, are time-consuming, and interfere with the person's normal routine, work, or social relations. Generally, individuals who are afflicted with obsessions also have compulsions (Rachman, 1978; Rachman and Hodgson, 1980). The terms "obsessive" and "compulsive" are often used interchangeably in the popular press, but they refer to two essential and distinct phenomena: obsessions are intrusive, recurrent, anxiety-producing thoughts, while compulsions are the stereotyped physical or mental acts performed in order to rid oneself of the anxiety produced by an obsession. The two are usually found together.

What distinguishes obsessions of clinical proportions from more harmless recurring thoughts? There are three hallmarks: (1) obsessions are *distressing* and *unwelcome* and intrude on consciousness; an obsessive complains, "The thought that I might strangle a child keeps returning and prevents me from concentrating on my work," whereas mere recurring thoughts do not interfere with work; (2) obsessions arise *from within,* not from an external situation; and (3) obsessions are very *difficult to control.* Someone with merely recurring thoughts can readily distract himself and think of something else; someone with an obsession, in contrast, complains, "I can't help myself—I keep saying the numbers over and over again."

Obsessions and the Social Context

The content of obsessions changes over time. In past centuries in the Western world, obsessions were often religious and sexual. John Bunyan, seventeenth-century author of *A Pilgrim's Progress,* was "fiercely assaulted" with the wicked suggestion to "sell Christ" running in his mind. "'Sell him, sell him, sell him, sell him,' as fast as a man could speak. Against which also in my mind I answered, 'No, no, not for thousands, thousands, thousands,' at least twenty times together." Other famous religious personalities believed they suffered from "pollution of the mind" with "naughty and blasphemous thoughts" of committing sexual sins "revolving in a restless circle." Today, obsessions about religion and sex have become somewhat rarer; obsessions about dirt and contamination, violence, and orderliness are more common (Hunter and MacAlpine, 1963; Akhtar, Wig, Varma, Pershard, and Verma, 1975; Rachman, 1978; Rachman and Hodgson, 1980). One patient embodied this historical trend in the course of her thirty-five-year-long disorder. For the first ten years, she was obsessed with contracting syphilis. She repeatedly scrubbed and disinfected herself, and took extraordinary care to avoid walking on used condoms in public places. The syphilis fear disappeared and gave way to obsessions about being infected with cancer, and she continued to wash and disinfect herself many times.

Obsessions about contamination are perhaps the most common kind of obsession today. Here is a description of a striking case:

Howard Hughes was one of America's richest and most colorful tycoons. During at least the last half of his life, Hughes was apparently afflicted with a severe obsessive-compulsive disorder about infection. He lived as a recluse, but unlike most obsessives, he was rich enough to be able to hire a retinue of servants to carry out his rituals for him, rather than doing them himself. Hughes's fear of germs and contamination dominated his life. He wrote numerous memos in which he explained in detail what he wanted done to prevent the "back transmission" of germs to him. For example, in a three-page memo, he explained how he wanted a can of fruit opened to prevent "fallout" of germs. He required that special equipment be used to open the can, writing, "The equipment used in connection with this operation will consist of the following items: 1 unopened newspaper, 1 sterile can opener; 1 large sterile plate; 1 sterile fork; 1 sterile spoon; 2 sterile brushes; 2 bars of soap; sterile paper towels." The ritual he devised for opening the can had nine steps: "preparing a table, procuring of fruit can, washing of can, drying the can, processing the hands, opening the can, removing the fruit from can, fallout rules while around can, and conclusion of operation." He worked out complicated procedures for each step of the operation; for example, to wash the can, he wrote:

> The man in charge then turns the valve in the bathtub on, using his bare hands to do so. He also adjusts the water temperatures so that it is not too hot nor too cold. He then takes one of the brushes, and, using one of the bars of soap, creates a good lather, and then scrubs the can from a point two inches below the top of the can. He should first soak and remove the label, and then brush the cylindrical part of the can over and over until all particles of dust, pieces of paper label, and, in general, all sources of contamination have been removed. Holding the can in the center at all times, he then processes the bottom of the can in the same manner, being very sure that all the bristles of the brush have thoroughly cleaned all the small indentations on the perimeter of the bottom of the can. He then rinses the soap from the cylindrical sides and bottom of the can. (Barlett and Steele, 1979, p. 233)

▲ Howard Hughes, pictured here, was afflicted in the last half of his life with a severe obsessive–compulsive disorder about germs.

Hughes's persistent fear of contamination led to a series of compulsive rituals that increasingly dominated his daily life. He eventually became a prisoner of his obsessions, confined to his "sterile" rooms, and seeing only his selected servants. He hired servants to wave newspapers to scare away imaginary flies, to wash everything in sight, and to open doors only with their feet (Fowler, 1986). Hughes's compulsive rituals bore a logical relationship to the obsession—if there really was rampant danger of infection from germs around food, the compulsion might have cut down the risk—but it was his obsession that germs were rampant that was illogical. The ritual to control contamination need not be so rational, as this next case illustrates.

A twenty-seven-year-old veterinarian described his severe compulsive ritual. His compulsion required him to flush the toilet a multiple of three times whenever he entered a bathroom. Sometimes he was "satisfied" with three times only; but on other occasions, nine, twenty-seven, or even more were needed. He was at a loss to control his compulsive ritual which had sometimes embarrassed him socially and was professionally handicapping. (Laughlin, 1967, p. 351)

Anxiety, Depression, and Obsessions

What motivates an obsessive-compulsive to perform such strange actions as flushing a toilet in multiples of three? How does he feel when he has obsessive thoughts and performs his compulsive rituals? The thoughts (the obsessive component) are very disturbing. Typically, the individual suffers considerable internal distress. A mild emergency reaction of the type described in the previous chapter is often present; he feels foreboding and dread. If the ritual is performed frequently and fast enough in response to the thoughts, he can reduce or even ward off the ensuing anxiety. This is why obsession-compulsion is put in the anxiety-inferred category. The obsessive finds ways of dealing with the anxiety—by acting out his compulsions. But if his compulsive ritual is prevented, he will first feel tension similar to what we would feel if someone prevented us from answering a ringing telephone. If the barrier persists, intense distress will sweep over the patient. Here, of course, the anxiety will be felt. The individual's distress then can only be alleviated by carrying out the compulsion, thereby neutralizing the anxiety evoked by the obsessive thoughts and images. The next case illustrates this.

> A middle-aged woman complained of an obsession concerning colors and heat, "The main problem is colors. I cannot look at any of the colors that are in the fire, red, orange or pink."
>
> She believed the colors blue, green, brown, white, and gray were neutral, and she used these colors to "neutralize" the fiery colors. "If I happen to see a fire color, I've got to immediately look at some other color to cancel it out. I've got to look at a tree or flowers out on the grounds, something brown or white, to neutralize it." She used to walk around with a small piece of green carpet in order to neutralize the effects of any orange colors she might happen upon and see or imagine.
>
> She described the traumatic feelings that images of colored stimuli (or hot stimuli) evoked:
>
>> It starts in my mind, and when I look at the color, I start to tremble and I go hot all over, just as though I'm on fire. I cannot stand up; I've got to sit down or else I'll fall. I feel sick, and all I can say is that it is a traumatic feeling, that's the only word I can think of to describe it. If it is the last color I look at before I get into bed, I just won't sleep all night. . . .
>>
>> I try to fight it, and get into bed and tell myself it is ridiculous. I know it can't hurt me physically, although it does harm me mentally. I lie there and this hot feeling comes over me, and I start to tremble. If that happens, I have to get up, put all my clothes on again and start once more, as though I am getting into bed. Sometimes I have to do this four or five times before finally getting to sleep. (Rachman and Hodgson, 1980)

Anxiety is in some way always there. And it is not the only negative effect associated with obsessions. Depression bears an intimate relationship as well. Obsessions and clinical depression appear frequently in the same person; as such, they are called **comorbid.** In fact, from 10 to 35 percent of depressed patients may have obsessions as well (Glittleson, 1966; Sakai, 1967; Beech and Vaughan, 1979). During their periods of depression, the incidence of obsessions triples over the rate before and after the depression (Videbech, 1975). Not only do depressed patients tend to develop obsessions, but obsessional patients are prone to develop depression as well (Wilner, Reich, Robins, Fishman, and Van Doren, 1976; Teasdale and Rezin, 1978).

Vulnerability to Obsessive-Compulsive Disorder

Obsessive-compulsive disorders are not uncommon. Between 2 and 3 percent of adults are diagnosed as obsessive-compulsive. Women are probably more vulnerable than men (Robins et al., 1984). The problem may be somewhat heritable, since identical twins show higher concordance than fraternal twins (Carey and Gottesman, 1981). Relatives of OCD patients often do not have obsessive-compulsive disorders themselves, but they do often suffer from other anxiety disorders as well as subclinical obsessions and compulsions (Black, Noyes, Goldstein, and Blum, 1992). The disorder usually comes on gradually, beginning in adolescence or early adulthood. Our patient with color obsession describes the typically vague and gradual onset of her disorder:

> It is hard to say exactly when the obsession started. It was gradual. My obsession about colors must have been coming on for a couple of years very, very gradually. I only noticed it fully during the past twelve years when it got worse and worse. I can't look at certain colors, can't bathe, can't do any cooking, have to repeat many activities over and over again. . . .
>
> I think it all began some years ago when I had a sort of nervous breakdown. At the onset, I went very hot; it seemed to happen overnight somehow. I was in bed, and woke up feeling very hot. It was connected with an obsession that I had about my ailing mother at the time. I feared for her safety, and when I got a horrible thought that she might have an accident or a serious illness, this horrible hot feeling came over me. (Rachman and Hodgson, 1980)

Is there a specific type of personality that is vulnerable to an obsessive-compulsive disorder? Based on case histories, psychodynamic theorists focus on the **obsessive-compulsive personality,** and this notion has crept into ordinary language. The person with an obsessive-compulsive personality is methodical and leads a very well-ordered life. He is always on time. He is meticulous in how he dresses and what he says. He pays exasperatingly close attention to detail, and he strongly dislikes dirt. He may have a distinct cognitive style, showing intellectual rigidity and focusing on details. He is deliberate in thought and action, and highly moralistic about himself and others. He is preoccupied with rules, lists, order, organization, or schedules to the point where he cannot see the forest through the trees. His perfectionism interferes with completing a task. He works so devotedly that he has no leisure and few friends. He is not a warm individual. In addition, he is reluctant to delegate tasks or to work with others (Sandler and Hazari, 1960; Shapiro, 1965; Pollack, 1979; DSM-III-R; DSM-IV Options Book).

What is the relationship between having an obsessive-compulsive *personality* and having an obsessive-compulsive *disorder?* One hypothesis is that when an individual with an obsessive-compulsive personality is under stress, he reacts by developing an obsessive-compulsive disorder (Shapiro, 1965). This is an important hypothesis, because if true, it would give us a way of predicting in advance who might be especially at risk for this disorder. Unfortunately, the evidence for this hypothesis is unconvincing. The crucial difference between having an obsessive-compulsive personality and having an obsessive-compulsive disorder has to do with how much the person *likes* having the symptoms. An obsessive-compulsive person views his meticulousness and love of detail with pride and self-esteem. For an individual with an obsessive-compulsive disorder, however, these characteristics are abhorrent, unwanted, and tormenting. They are "ego-alien."

When one actually looks at the personality of individuals with obsessive-compulsive disorders, little evidence emerges showing that they also have an obsessive-compulsive personality. A majority of OCD patients have no history of an obsessional personality, and few people with an obsessional personality develop OCD. To test this, S. J. Rachman and Ray Hodgson of the Maudsley Hospital in London developed a questionnaire that distinguishes between patients with anxiety disorders. Table 9–1 presents some of the questions from the Maudsley Obsessive-Compulsive Inventory. The questionnaire isolates three major components of obsessive-compulsive disorders: cleaning, checking, and doubting. Patients who had either an obsessive-compulsive disorder or some other anxiety disorder took both this inventory and an inventory that measured obsessive-compulsive personality by focusing on orderliness, perseverance, and rigidity. While there were extreme differences between patients with obsessive-compulsive disorders and those with other anxiety disorders on the Obsessive-Compulsive Inventory, there were no differences between these two groups on obsessive-compulsive personality measures. These results suggest that the obsessive-compulsive personality is not a precursor of obsessive-compulsive disorders, and that individuals who are meticulous and lead a well-ordered life are no more likely to develop an obsessive-compulsive disorder than any other individuals (Sandler and Hazari, 1960; Shapiro, 1965; Rosenberg, 1967; Rack, 1977; Pollack, 1979; Rachman and Hodgson, 1980).

TABLE 9–1

SAMPLE QUESTIONS FROM THE MAUDSLEY OBSESSIVE-COMPULSIVE INVENTORY

Components of Obsessive-Compulsive Disorder	Obsessive-Compulsive Disorder Answer
Cleaning	
1. I am not excessively concerned about cleanliness.	False
2. I avoid using public telephones because of possible contamination.	True
3. I can use well-kept toilets without any hesitation.	False
4. I take a rather long time to complete my washing in the morning.	True
Checking	
1. I frequently have to check things (gas or water taps, doors) more than once.	True
2. I do not check letters over and over again before mailing them.	False
3. I frequently get nasty thoughts and have difficulty getting rid of them.	True
Doubting-Conscience	
1. I have a very strict conscience.	True
2. I usually have serious doubts about the simple everyday things I do.	True
3. Neither of my parents was very strict during my childhood.	False

SOURCE: Rachman and Hodgson, 1980.

Theories of Obsessive-Compulsive Disorder

What causes an obsessive-compulsive disorder? There are three major theoretical views: psychodynamic, cognitive-behavioral, and biomedical (see Table 9–2). Their strengths complement each other well. The psychodynamic view wrestles with the question of the genesis of the obsession—who gets it and why it takes a particular form—but is less illuminating about why it persists for years once it has started. The cognitive-behavioral view illuminates its persistence, but leaves us in the dark as to who gets it and what its content will be. The biomedical view points to the brain structures underlying OCD.

THE PSYCHODYNAMICS OF THE OBSESSIVE-COMPULSIVE DISORDER

The questions "Who will get an obsessive-compulsive disorder?" and "What form will it take?" lie at the heart of the psychodynamic view of obsessive thoughts. According to this view, an obsessive thought is seen as a *defense* against an even more unwelcome and unconscious thought. This defensive process involves *displacement* and *substitution* (see Chapter 4). What happens is that an unconscious dangerous thought, such as "my mother might die of a fever" in the previously mentioned case of the woman with color and heat obsession, threatens to break into the individual's consciousness. This arouses

TABLE 9–2

	VIEWS OF OBSESSIVE-COMPULSIVE DISORDER			
Theoretical view	*Who develops OCD?*	*What happens?*	*How is it sustained?*	*How is it cured?*
Cognitive-behavioral view	People who cannot distract themselves easily from troubling thoughts, often combined with depression	Obsessive thoughts (present in normals also) become frequent and persistent, while depression simultaneously weakens ability to distract oneself	Patient discovers a ritual that temporarily relieves anxiety, which is then reinforced through repetition	Response blocking of compulsion extinguishes obsession
Psychodynamic view	People with specific unconscious conflicts (e.g., thoughts of injuring or murdering one's child or mother)	Obsessive thought begins as a defense against a more unacceptable thought	Obsession and accompanying compulsion are maintained because they successfully defend against anxiety	Unconscious conflict recognized and worked through
Biomedical view	People with overactive cortical-striatal-thalamic circuit	Perseveration may be poorly inhibited; anxiety may be inadequately dampened; filtering of irrelevant information may be inadequate	Obsessive thoughts and compulsive behaviors are directed toward objects and situations evolution has prepared us to see as threatening	Drugs (e.g., clomipramine) down-regulate overactive cortical-striatal-thalamic circuit

anxiety. To defend against this anxiety, the individual unconsciously displaces this anxiety from the original terrifying thought onto a less unwelcome substitute, like hot and fiery colors. The defense has a powerful internal logic, and the thoughts that are substituting for the underlying thought are not arbitrary. Fiery and hot colors symbolize the fever that her ailing mother might die of.

Freud's original case of obsessional neurosis, the "Rat Man," illustrates the logic of obsessional defenses (Freud, 1909b/1976):

> The Rat Man, whose name derives from his obsessional images of rats chewing their way into anuses, was plagued with a host of other obsessional thoughts, often of a violent nature. While a young man, the Rat Man lost some weeks of study because he was distressed about his girlfriend's absence. She had left him to nurse her seriously ill grandmother. While trying to study, an obsessional thought intruded—"If you were commanded to cut your throat with a razor, what then?" Freud interpreted this as caused by an unconscious rage that was even more threatening and more unacceptable: "I should like to go and kill that old woman for robbing me of my love!" The moral and high-minded Rat Man, with this horrendous thought knocking on the doors of consciousness, substitutes a more acceptable command "Kill yourself" and this is a fitting punishment for his savage and murderous passion. (Freud, 1909b/1976, pp. 187–98)

Psychodynamic theory explains *who* will develop an obsession in response to underlying conflict-arousing anxiety, and *what content* the obsession will take on to symbolize the underlying conflict. The following case of obsession about infanticide illustrates why the particular individual would be susceptible to the particular form of obsession she developed:

> A thirty-two-year-old mother of two had obsessional thoughts of injuring and murdering her children and more infrequently, her husband. These thoughts were almost as threatening and as guilt-provoking as the very act itself. Therapy uncovered even more threatening impulses from her childhood which had been displaced onto her children. She had been the eldest of three siblings and while very young had been given undue responsibility for their care. She felt deprived of affection from her parents and was greatly resentful of her younger sister and brother. She entertained murderous fantasies about them, which were accompanied by tremendous guilt and anxiety. As a result, these fantasies had been completely driven from consciousness. When she became an adult, her children symbolically stood for her siblings, whose destruction would make her the sole object of parental love and relieve her of her childhood burden. Her own mother's occasional visits triggered the obsessions. She was particularly susceptible because she had unresolved and anxiety-provoking resentment against her own parents and siblings. Her obsession had the content of death as it symbolized the death of her siblings, which would have solved her childhood problem. (Adapted from Laughlin, 1967, pp. 324–26)

Thus, the psychodynamic view of obsessions claims that powerful, abhorrent wishes and conflicts that have been repressed and threaten to break into consciousness put an individual at risk for obsessions, and that adopting the defense of displacement and substitution provides the immediate mechanism for relief. In addition, the particular content of the obsessions these individuals acquire will be a symbol for the underlying conflict.

Drawing by W. Miller, © 1992 The New Yorker Magazine, Inc.

COGNITIVE-BEHAVIORAL VIEW OF THE OBSESSIVE-COMPULSIVE DISORDER

S. J. Rachman and Ray Hodgson have formulated the most comprehensive cognitive-behavioral theory of obsessions (Rachman, 1978; Rachman and Hodgson, 1980). The theory begins with the assumption that we all experience obsessional thoughts occasionally. The thought "Step on a crack and you'll break your mother's back" followed by an avoidance of sidewalk cracks is a common obsessive-compulsive ritual in children. For others, memories of radio jingles often intrude, unbidden, into consciousness. But most of us outgrow the sidewalk ritual, and we easily are able to distract ourselves from or habituate to the radio jingles. We can also dismiss the more abhorrent thoughts that occasionally run through our heads. Individuals with obsessive-compulsive disorders, however, differ from the rest of us in that they are unable to habituate, dismiss, and distract themselves from abhorrent thoughts.

The more anxiety-provoking and depressing the content of the obsession, the more difficult it is for anyone—obsessive or non-obsessive—to dismiss the thought or distract himself from it. When normal individuals are shown a brief but stressful film, most of them have intrusive and repetitive thoughts. For example, a stressful film depicting a gruesome woodshop accident brought about anxiety and repetitive thoughts about the accident. The more emotionally upset an individual was made by the film, the more intrusive and repetitive the thoughts (Horowitz, 1975). Furthermore, anxious individuals find threatening words more intrusive than normal controls (Matthews and MacLeod, 1986). This supports two of the assumptions of the cognitive-behavioral view of obsession: (1) we all have unwanted and repetitive thoughts; and (2) the more stressed we are, the more frequent and intense are these thoughts.

Recall now the link between depression and obsession. To the extent that an individual is depressed beforehand, obsessive thoughts will be more disturbing and therefore more difficult to dismiss. In addition, as we will see in Chapter 11, depressed individuals display more helplessness (Seligman, 1975). This

▼ S.J. Rachman has formulated a comprehensive cognitive–behavioral theory of obsessions.

means that they are less able to initiate voluntary responses to relieve their own distress. The act of distracting oneself is a voluntary cognitive response, and like other such responses, it will be weakened by depression. A background of depression is therefore fertile soil for an obsessive-compulsive disorder.

Here, then, is the chain of events that distinguishes an obsessive-compulsive from a non-obsessive, according to the cognitive-behavioral view. For a non-obsessive, some initiating event, either internal or external, leads to a disturbing image or thought. A non-obsessive person may find this thought unacceptable but will not be made anxious by it. If he is not in a state of depression, he will easily dismiss the thought or distract himself from it. In contrast, the obsessive-compulsive will be made anxious by the thought, and the anxiety and depression will reduce his ability to dismiss it. The thought will persist, and the obsessive-compulsive's inability to turn the thought off will lead to further anxiety, helplessness, and depression, which will increase his susceptibility to the intrusive thought.

The cognitive-behavioral view also attempts to explain compulsive rituals. The rituals are reinforced by the temporary relief from anxiety that they bring. Since the obsessive-compulsive cannot remove the thoughts by the distraction and dismissal techniques that the rest of us readily use, he resorts to other tactics. He attempts to neutralize the bad thought, often by substituting a good thought. The fiery color obsessive-compulsive neutralized the color orange by looking at a swatch of green carpet. Alternatively, he attempts to neutralize the bad thoughts by an action that ensures safety. So, in an attempt to allay his fear of germs, the late millionaire Howard Hughes saw to it that his servants did not cough on the fruit he ate. Individuals who are obsessively afraid that their doors are not locked check them dozens of times a night. These compulsive rituals produce temporary relief, but they also produce a stronger tendency to check, wash, or seek reassurance, since they are followed by anxiety reduction and therefore strengthened. But the rituals can only be cosmetic; the relief they provide is only temporary. The obsessions are left intact, and they return with increased frequency and intensity. Each time a thought recurs, the ritual must be performed in order to produce any relief.

The strength of the cognitive-behavioral view is that it provides an account of why obsessions and compulsions, once started, might be maintained. The strength of the psychoanalytic view is that it tries to explain both the content of the obsessions and who is vulnerable. The next view we turn to, the biomedical view, can claim to be the most basic of the three: it looks for the brain structures underlying OCD.

THE BIOMEDICAL THEORY OF THE OBSESSIVE-COMPULSIVE DISORDER

Biomedical researchers claim that OCD is a brain disease. There are four lines of evidence for this view: (1) neurological signs, (2) brain scan abnormalities, (3) the primitive content of obsessions and compulsions, and (4) an effective drug (which we will discuss in more detail in the treatment section).

Neurological Signs OCD has been known to develop right after a brain trauma. On neurological examination, many OCD patients are said to show a number of abnormalities: poor fine motor coordination, more involuntary jerks, and poor visual-motor performance. The more pronounced such "soft signs" are, the more severe the obsessions (Hollander, Schiffman, Cohen, et al., 1990;

FOCUS QUESTIONS

1. Describe the three theories that explain the etiology of OCD.
2. What are the strengths of each of these explanations?
3. What are the neurological and brain abnormalities that have been found in many OCD patients?
4. Describe the therapies for OCD.

Tien, Pearlson, Machlin, et al., 1992). This is consistent with the presence of an underlying, but subtle, neurological disorder.

> Jacob, eight years old, was playing football in the backyard. He collapsed and went into a coma with a brain hemorrhage. When he came out of brain surgery, which went very well, he was now plagued by numbers. He had to touch everything in 7's. He swallowed in 7's and asked 7 times for everything. (Rapoport, 1990)

OCD is also comorbid with neurological disorders such as epilepsy. After the great sleeping sickness epidemic (a viral brain infection in Europe in 1916–1918) there was an apparent rise in the number of OCD patients (Rapaport, 1990). Tourette's syndrome is a compulsive-like disorder of motor tics and uncontrollable verbal outbursts, apparently of neurological origin. There is a high concordance between OCD and Tourette's syndrome in identical twins, and many patients who have Tourette's syndrome also have OCD (Robertson, Trimble, and Lees, 1988; Leonard, Lenane, Swedo, et al., 1992; George, Trimble, Ring, et al., 1993).

Brain Scan Abnormalities The second line of biomedical evidence comes from brain scan studies of patients with OCD. Several areas of the brain show high activity in OCD patients: the caudate nucleus, the orbito-frontal cortex, and the cingulate cortex. Together, they constitute a "cortical-striatal-thalamic" circuit (see Figure 9–1). These areas are related to filtering out of irrelevant information and perseveration of behavior. In fact, inability to turn off distracting thoughts and perseveration of behavior seem like central problems in obsessions and

FIGURE 9–1

THE CORTICAL-STRIATAL-THALAMIC CIRCUIT AND OCD

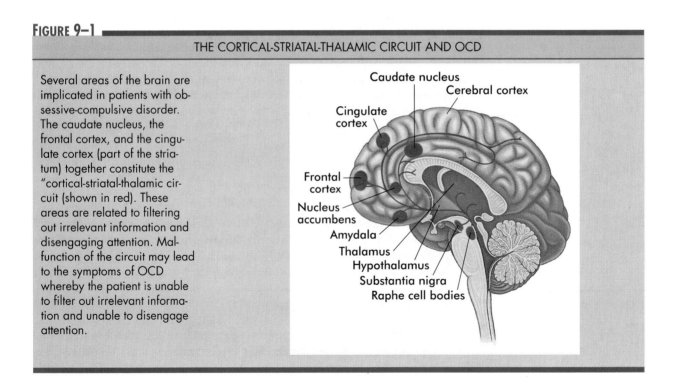

Several areas of the brain are implicated in patients with obsessive-compulsive disorder. The caudate nucleus, the frontal cortex, and the cingulate cortex (part of the striatum) together constitute the "cortical-striatal-thalamic circuit (shown in red). These areas are related to filtering out irrelevant information and disengaging attention. Malfunction of the circuit may lead to the symptoms of OCD whereby the patient is unable to filter out irrelevant information and unable to disengage attention.

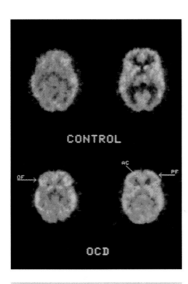

▲ PET scans of an OCD patient (top) and a normal control (bottom) reveal the differences in metabolic activity between OCD patients and normal controls. Red indicates the highest level of metabolic activity, and blue the lowest level.

compulsions. When these patients are treated successfully with drugs, these brain areas decrease their activity.

Unfortunately, different brain scan studies conflict on which brain areas increase and decrease in activity (Insel, 1992; Baxter, Schwartz, Bergman, Szuba, et al., 1992; Rubin, Villanueva-Meyer, Ananth, et al., 1992; Swedo, Pietrini, Leonard, et al., 1992). The remainder of the decade promises exciting research in this field, with the possibility of tracking down how the hyperactive cortical-striatal-thalamic circuit actually works and how drugs and behavior therapy affect this circuit. Consistent with this hypothesis is the finding that surgical interruption of this circuit produced substantial reduction in OCD symptoms in about one-third of thirty-three patients (Jenike, Baer, Ballantine, et al., 1991).

Primitive Content of Obsessions and Compulsions   The third line of evidence for a biological view concerns the specific content of OCD. The content of obsessions and compulsions is not arbitrary. Like the content of phobias, consisting mostly of objects that were once dangerous to the human species, the content of obsessions and of compulsive rituals is also narrow and selective. The vast majority of OCD patients are obsessed with germs or with violence, and they wash or they check in response. Why such a specific focus? Why not obsessions about particular shapes, like triangles, or about socializing only with people of the same height? Why no compulsions about push-ups, or about hand-clapping, or about crossword puzzles? Why germs and violence? Why washing and checking?

Across evolution, washing and checking have been very important. The grooming and physical security of oneself and one's children are central primate concerns. Perhaps the brain areas that kept our ancestors grooming and checking are the very areas gone awry in OCD. Perhaps the recurrent thoughts and the rituals in OCD are deep vestiges of primate habits run amok (Rapoport, 1990; Marks and Tobena, 1990).

Drug Therapy   Useful drug therapy is the final line of evidence for the biological theory. The drug clomipramine has been found to alleviate the symptoms of obsessions and compulsions in many OCD patients. We will discuss clomipramine in more detail as we examine the range of therapies available for OCD.

Treatment for Obsessive-Compulsive Disorder

Until recently, the prognosis for those with obsessive-compulsive disorders, either treated or untreated, was not particularly promising. Electroconvulsive shock, antidepressant drugs, supportive psychotherapy, and surgical removal of part of the brain (lobotomy) had all been tried frequently, but with poor short-term and worse long-turn results (Pollit, 1960; Grimshaw, 1964; Kringlen, 1965). At present, three kinds of treatments are being used for those with OCD—psychoanalytic therapy, behavior therapy, and drug therapy—with varying results.

PSYCHOANALYTIC THERAPY

In psychoanalytic therapy for obsessions, the central issue is to enable the patient to recognize the underlying conflict by undoing repression of this unconscious conflict. The mother with thoughts of infanticide must gain insight into her impulse to do away with her siblings during childhood and understand the connection of this conflict to her present problems. The psychodynamic treatment of the obsessive-compulsive patient involves a thorough analysis of the obsessive-compulsive's defenses and can be expected to take several years (Fenichel, 1945; Laughlin, 1967). Because there has been no controlled study of psychoanalytic treatment of obsessive-compulsive disorders, however, we can conclude little about its effectiveness.

BEHAVIOR THERAPIES

Behavior therapies for obsessive-compulsive disorders have been explored in several controlled studies (Marks and Rachman, 1978). The results have been promising, but are not usually cures. A combination of the three basic techniques of behavior therapy—response prevention, flooding, and modeling—are used in treating obsessive-compulsive disorders. These three procedures all encourage and persuade but do not force the patient to endure disturbing situations. For example, these techniques were used to treat a patient who had obsessive thoughts that he might be contaminated with germs and who as a result spent four hours a day washing himself. In therapy, he first watched the therapist contaminate himself with dirt (modeling). He then was urged to rub dirt and dust all over himself (flooding) and endure it without washing it off (response prevention). After a dozen sessions of covering himself with dirt and just sitting there without washing it off, the thoughts of contamination diminished and the washing rituals no longer occurred in his daily life.

In this case, flooding the patient and preventing him from washing off the dirt cured the compulsion. In addition to such case histories, there have been six controlled studies of response prevention, flooding, and modeling in obsessive-compulsive patients (Rachman, Hodgson, and Marks, 1971; Hodgson, Rachman, and Marks, 1972; Rachman, Marks, and Hodgson, 1973; Roper, Rachman, and Marks, 1975; Marks and Rachman, 1978; Salzman and Thaler, 1981). These studies indicated marked improvement in about two-thirds of the patients; follow-up for as long as six years indicates that improvement is maintained in all but about 10 percent of respondents (Emmelkamp, Hoekstra, and Visser, 1985; O'Sullivan, Noshirvani, Marks, et al., 1991; Foa and Kozak, 1993). The behavior therapies are specific in their effects: obsessive thoughts, compulsive rituals, and anxiety all decrease, but depression, sexual adjustment, and family harmony are not clearly helped. These results are not conclusive, however, since very few patients lose all their symptoms completely or are functioning well in all areas of life at follow-up. In addition, roughly 20 to 30 percent fail to improve at all (Meyer, 1966; Hackmann and McLean, 1975; Rabavilos, Boulougouris, and Stefanis, 1976; Beech and Vaughan, 1979; Rachman, Cobb, Grey, MacDonald, Mawson, Sartory, and Stern, 1979).

Why do flooding, response prevention, and modeling work, and what are their critical elements? Recall that in the laboratory, flooding and response prevention reliably extinguish avoidance responding. If a rat is prevented from making his habitual avoidance responses by a barrier interposed between him and safety (response prevention) while sitting and hearing a signal that used to predict shock (flooding), avoidance behavior extinguishes. On future trials, even when the animal is free to flee, he will sit still during the signal. Response prevention has forcibly exposed the rat to the fact that the signal is no longer

▼ The American behavior therapist Edna Foa, of the Medical College of Pennsylvania, has pioneered the use of exposure therapy for post–traumatic stress disorder following rape and contributed to the evaluation of behavior therapy for obsessive–compulsive disorder.

followed by shock and that he does not have to make the response in order to be safe (Seligman and Johnston, 1973).

Reconsider the man who washed himself for four hours a day. He had the obsession that some terrible illness would strike him if he did not wash. When he was persuaded to endure being dirty without washing, his obsessive thoughts of illness waned, and his compulsive rituals of washing vanished. What had he learned during flooding and response prevention? By covering himself with dirt and then not washing, his fear that dirt would lead to illness extinguished. The CS was the dirt, and the anticipated US was illness. He received stark exposure to being dirty without getting sick, and Pavlovian extinction occurred. In addition, he learned that illness did not happen even though he did not wash. This was an instrumental extinction procedure for the compulsive ritual of washing. So flooding and response prevention may work for two reasons: (1) by showing the patient that the dreaded event does not occur in the feared situation (Pavlovian extinction), and (2) by showing the patient that no dreaded event occurs even though the compulsive ritual is not performed (instrumental extinction of the compulsion).

DRUG THERAPY

There is a drug that works markedly better on OCD than do placebos. Clomipramine (trade name: Anafranil) has been used with thousands of OCD sufferers in more than a dozen controlled studies. Clomipramine is a potent antidepressant drug, a serotonin reuptake inhibitor. When OCD sufferers take clomipramine, obsessions wane and compulsions can be more easily resisted (Jenike, Baer, Summergrad, et al., 1989; Katz, DeVeaugh-Geiss, and Landau, 1990a, 1990b; Mavissakalian, Jones, Olson, and Perel, 1990; Trimble, 1990; Pato, Piggott, Hill, et al., 1991; Clomipramine Collaborative Study Group, 1991; Leonard, Swedo, Lenane, et al., 1991, 1993).

Clomipramine, however, is not a perfect drug. A large minority of patients (almost half) do not get better, or they will not take it because of its side effects, which include drowsiness, constipation, and loss of sexual interest. Those who benefit are rarely cured; their symptoms are dampened, but traces of the obsessive thoughts usually remain and the temptation to ritualize is still present. When those who do benefit stop taking the drug, many—perhaps most—of them relapse completely. But clomipramine is decidedly better than nothing (Pato, Zohar-Kadouch, Zohar, and Murphy, 1988; Piggott, Pato, Bernstein, et al., 1990; Greist, 1990; O'Sullivan, Noshirvani, Marks, et al., 1991).

COMPARISON OF TREATMENTS FOR OCD

Both the cognitive-behavioral and the biomedical models have generated treatments that improve the prognosis for OCD. Neither can be considered a cure. Flooding and response prevention reduce the obsessions and compulsions in more than half the cases of OCD, and these benefits seem to be long-lasting. Clomipramine reduces the obsessions and compulsions in more than half the cases as well. So both treatments are much more effective than placebos. Which is the treatment of choice?

The evidence is not yet definitive. More research is still needed that directly compares behavior therapy, clomipramine, and both, with a placebo, using large numbers of subjects with long-term follow-up. But the evidence that does exist points to an edge for behavior therapy. We can use two criteria: gain at the end of therapy and amount of relapse when therapy ends.

How much gain is produced by treatment with either drug or behavior therapy? In a summary of sixteen studies involving more than 300 OCD patients who were given behavior therapy, an average of 83 percent were judged "improved" by the end of therapy, and 76 percent were still improved over an average of two-and-one-half years of follow-up. This compares to an average of between 50 to 60 percent improvement for those treated with clomipramine (Foa and Kozak, 1993). So there is perhaps a small edge in treatment response for those treated with behavior therapy.

The evidence is clearer about what happens when clomipramine is no longer taken. Massive relapse occurs. For example, clomipramine produced at least moderate improvement in 55 percent of twenty-two OCD patients; in follow-up, however, of the six respondents who discontinued the drug, all relapsed (Thoren, Asberg, Chronholm, et al., 1980). Those treated with behavior therapy, in contrast, do not show much relapse once therapy is discontinued.

Overall when both amount of improvement and relapse are considered, behavior therapy appears to do better than clomipramine.

Obsessive-Compulsive Disorder: Anxiety Revisited

This chapter deals with those disorders in which anxiety is not directly felt by the afflicted individual. But we have assumed that anxiety underlies these disorders, specifically the obsessive-compulsive disorder. What is the evidence for this? There are four clues that anxiety underlies obsessive-compulsive disorder. First of all, the fact that flooding and response prevention seem to work suggest that obsessive-compulsive disorders are basically anxiety disorders. Since it is known from the laboratory that flooding and response prevention are techniques that produce extinction of conditioned fear and anxiety, we infer from the fact that they work that the obsessive suffered anxiety that is then extinguished in therapy.

The second clue relates to the integral relationship between the obsessive thought and the compulsive act. An obsessive-compulsive who continually thinks that he left the gas on will compulsively check the kitchen stove. In observing him we probably would not see him as particularly anxious. But what if we do not allow him to perform his checking ritual? In this case, the obsessive-compulsive may be overcome with anxiety, and think that his house will blow up as a result of the gas leak. This suggests that the function of the ritual is to ward off underlying anxiety. In short, when the compulsive symptoms are successful, they prevent anxiety from being experienced.

The third clue is that some obsessive-compulsives actually do experience some anxiety during the obsession but lose it when the compulsion is performed. The color obsessive-compulsive felt traumatized when she saw the color orange, and felt her anxiety turn off when she looked at the swatch of green carpet.

The fourth clue is the most intriguing of all. The content of the obsession can often be seen as a symbol of an underlying, unresolved conflict that when recognized provokes great anxiety. The mother with the infanticide obsession may have displaced her anxiety and guilt over wanting to murder her siblings onto a less unwelcome thought. During therapy, when she realized that she had done that even unconsciously, she felt very anxious.

Overall, then, there is reason to suspect that anxiety underlies obsessive-compulsive disorders. Sometimes the anxiety can actually be observed, as it is in phobias and panic attacks; but at most other times, the role of anxiety is inferred from clues about the patient's past, or by arranging special conditions such as response blocking to bring anxiety to the surface. In the next section, we will examine a set of disorders in which anxiety is almost never observed. In fact, it is the absence of anxiety that is often remarkable. These are the somatoform disorders, in which psychological factors cause the loss of some bodily function. We will look principally at hysterical conversions.

SOMATOFORM DISORDERS

As we learned in Chapter 2, Professor Jean Martin Charcot (1825–1893), a great French neurologist in Paris working at La Salpêtrière, saw a large number of female patients who had such symptoms as convulsive fits and muscular paralysis, although he could not find any clear organic basis for them. These symptoms characterized disorders that were called **hysterical conversions,** and Charcot believed that they were produced by psychological events. To show this, he hypnotized normal women and, by suggestion, produced in them symptoms identical to hysterical paralysis and hysterical convulsions. In addition, he hypnotized patients who had these symptoms and, by hypnotic suggestion, he was able to remove the symptoms. Charcot's demonstration that hysterical conversion, a somatoform disorder, could be induced and removed merely by influencing the mind formed the basis of the theories of anxiety disorders put forth by Pierre Janet (1859–1947), Josef Breuer (1842–1925), and most importantly, by Sigmund Freud himself (1856–1939).

The Types of Somatoform Disorders

What is a **somatoform disorder?** There are five factors to consider. First, there is lost or altered physical functioning. One may, for example, become deaf or paralyzed. Second, the symptom cannot be explained by a known physical or neurological condition. There is no evidence of neurological damage to produce the deafness or the paralysis. Third, there is positive evidence that psychological factors are related to the symptom. Fourth, the patient is often, but not always, indifferent to the physical loss. More specifically, he or she does not feel anxiety. Finally, the symptoms are not under voluntary control. Conversion, somatization disorder, and pain disorder are all categorized as somatoform disorders in DSM-IV.

CONVERSION

Before DSM-III and DSM-IV, **conversion** was called "hysterical conversion." It was renamed by DSM-III to remove the suggestion that it affects only women. "Hysteria," is derived from the Greek word *hystera,* which means womb, implying that the disorder is confined to women only. We now know this to be false: the large majority of patients are women, but a clear minority are men (Veith, 1965; Mezzich, Fabrega, Coffman, and Haley, 1989; Tomasson, Kent, and Coryell, 1991). The case below illustrates a conversion disorder, where psychological stress has been converted into physical symptoms:

▼ The French neurologist Jean-Martin Charcot (1825–1893) believed the symptoms of hysterical conversions were produced by psychological events.

Bear was a burly twenty-five-year-old construction worker who was paralyzed from the waist down—totally without movement or feeling—and had been so for three weeks. What's more, he was not particularly upset by his paralysis; that is, he was a bit concerned that he could not walk, but he was not emotional nor excessively anxious.

After three days of tests that failed to show anything, the neurologist examining Bear had decided that there was nothing wrong with him physically and had sent him to Psychiatry.

In Psychiatry, there was the same frustration as that experienced by the neurologist. Bear's recent life seemed uneventful to him, and he recalled no precipitating incident. He had used drugs occasionally, and he drank a bit, but he had no previous psychiatric history. Mystified, groping for any lead, one of the residents asked him if he knew anybody else who was paralyzed. At first, Bear couldn't think of anyone, but after a minute or so, he mumbled, without any show of emotion:

"Yeah, come to think of it, Tom, a good friend of mine, is paralyzed from the waist down. Broke his neck."

"How did that happen?"

"It was really sad, and, you know, I guess it was pretty much my fault. Tom's a virgin, like in every way possible. Doesn't even drink or smoke. Well, we were together at a party about a month ago, and I was riding him. I thought he should live a little, try some LSD. I guess he couldn't take it, so he gave in.

"Well, we downed a couple of tabs, and within a few minutes he was flying. Seeing all sorts of weird things. He ran out of the apartment, and I followed, a little afraid for him. God, it was awful! He was running away from something in his head. Next thing I knew, he jumped off the bridge. You know, the one over the tracks at 30th Street Station. He was still alive when the rescue squad got him down from the high tension lines. They say he'll never walk, or anything, again."

"Bear, tell me again when your problem started."

"Out of nowhere. About three weeks ago. I was at work, driving my forklift down at the station. As I crossed over the tracks under the high tension lines, suddenly I was all dead down there. I shouted for help, and my buddies took me off to. . . . Oh, my God! Don't you see what I've done!"

And within a few days, Bear walked home. (Stinnett, 1978)

Bear's paralysis has the five symptoms of somotoform disorder. First, he has lost physical functioning: he is paralyzed. Second, physical damage cannot explain the paralysis, since he is neurologically sound, and the paralysis is not under voluntary control. Third, Bear seems remarkably indifferent to his paralysis. Fourth, he feels no anxiety. And fifth, there is good evidence that psychological factors are certainly related to, and probably caused the symptoms: (1) he has a friend with paralysis caused partly by his actions; (2) the paralysis began at the same site that his friend's paralysis occurred; (3) Bear did not easily remember the incident when his friend was paralyzed, nor did he relate it to his own paralysis; and (4) Bear could not control his paralysis, but when he gained insight into this, his paralysis remitted.

SOMATIZATION DISORDER (BRIQUET'S SYNDROME)

In **somatization disorder,** also called **Briquet's syndrome,** the person has had many physical complaints that began before age thirty and that resulted in a complicated history of medical treatment. These complaints involve many different organs and cannot be fully explained from known physical causes. The symptoms include a history of pain from different areas such as the head, stomach, back, joints, arms and legs, rectum, chest, or pain on sexual intercourse, menstruation, and urination. In addition, the patient has gastrointestinal symptoms other than pain, such as nausea, diarrhea, vomiting, and food allergies. The patient also has a history of sexual symptoms, such as indifference to sex, irregular periods, excessive menstrual bleeding, or vomiting all through pregnancy. A history of conversion symptoms is also common. Unnecessary surgery, addiction to prescription medicines, depression, and attempted suicide are common complications of this syndrome. The fundamental difference between somatization and conversion is that the somatizer will suffer from many physical problems; the conversion patient generally has only one complaint.

There may be two distinct kinds of somatization disorders. The first is called "high frequency" and the second "diversiform." Individuals with high-frequency disorder have frequent stomach and back pains, along with psychiatric problems. These individuals have an extraordinarily large number of sick leaves, and they tend to abuse alcohol ten times as frequently as those in the normal population. Those with diversiform disorder have fewer back problems; instead, their complaints cover the rest of the body, although they also are prone to alcohol abuse. In a study of a Swedish population, the prevalence of these problems ran as high as 11 percent of all adult women (Cloninger, Sigvardsson, von Knorring, and Bohman, 1984).

PAIN DISORDER (PSYCHALGIA)

In addition to conversion and somatization, **pain disorder (psychalgia)** is also a somatoform disorder. In pain disorder, pain in one or more parts of the body, which causes marked distress or impairment, is the central symptom. Psychological factors account for its onset, or how severe it is, or its undue persistence, or for the worsening of the pain. Statistically, it may be the most frequent of the somatoform disorders (Watson and Buranen, 1979; Drossman, 1982). The following case illustrates an individual suffering from psychalgia:

> Harry, a forty-one-year-old man, suffered a sudden onset of severe abdominal pain. Emergency surgery was about to be performed, but there was no elevated white cell count, and other physical symptoms were normal. In addition, Harry seemed emotionally indifferent to the pain and the fact of impending surgery. He was obviously in pain, but not anxious about it.
>
> Upon consultation, it was decided to abandon urgent preparations for surgery, and to explore for a possible psychological basis. It emerged that Harry had had a childhood that predisposed him to psychalgia. His parents had been materially wealthy, but they had given him very little love and affection. The one break in this emotional barrenness in his childhood had been his appendectomy. The love he had received during this period was meaningful, real, and what he had "always longed for."
>
> The present abdominal pain was set off by an incident of domestic deceit. His wife had become infatuated with another man and had threatened to go off with him. At this very point, the abdominal pain had begun. (Adapted from Laughlin, 1967, pp. 667–68)

The hypothesis in Harry's case is that whenever he is under serious stress, he will suffer pain in his abdomen. This pain becomes a somatic excuse for not suffering the anxiety brought on by the stressful events.

Diagnosing Somatoform Disorder

A somatoform disorder is one of the most difficult disorders to diagnose correctly. In the case study discussed earlier, how can we tell if Bear was faking paralysis or if he had some obscure physical illness that was as yet undiagnosed?

In an attempt to make diagnosis clearer, let us distinguish somatoform disorders from four other disorders with which it can be confused, sometimes tragically. These disorders are malingering, psychosomatic disorders, factitious disorder, and undiagnosed physical illness. In principle, there are two differences between *malingering* (faking) and an authentic somatoform disorder—neither of which is easy to pin down in practice. First, the symptoms of a malingerer are under his voluntary control, whereas they are not under the voluntary control of an individual with a somatoform disorder. A malingerer can turn the paralysis on and off, although it may be difficult indeed to induce him to display this voluntary control for you. The individual suffering conversion cannot. For example, even if we had offered Bear an irresistibly large amount of money to get up out of his wheelchair and walk away, he would not have been able to do so. Second, the malingerer acquires an obvious environmental goal as a result of his symptom (e.g., getting out of the army by feigning paralysis), whereas an individual with a conversion disorder does not necessarily achieve anything obvious by his symptom (see Box 9–1).

Malingering itself should be distinguished from *secondary gain.* Secondary gain consists of deriving benefits from one's environment as a consequence of having abnormal symptoms. Individuals with somatoform disorders frequently get secondary gains. So, for example, a person with pain disorder

Box 9–1

CAMBODIAN WOMEN'S SIGHT LOSS: HYSTERICAL BLINDNESS?

Under the regime of Pol Pot, it is estimated that one million people (out of a total population of only seven million) were killed. Many were exiled from their homes in the city to the countryside, and there abused and even tortured. It became common for relatives to see the murder and torture of family members.

One woman watched as her three-month-old nephew was clubbed to death against a tree by Khmer Rouge soldiers. Soon after, she saw three other nephews and nieces beaten to death, and then her brother and his wife were murdered in front of her. She eventually emigrated to the United States and reacted to her Cambodian experiences by becoming blind. Two researchers have studied 150 cases of this sort just in the Long Beach, California, area. After finding no evidence of neurophysiological damage to the visual system, Gretchen Van Boehmel, an electrophysiologist, and Patrick Rozee, a psychologist, interviewed thirty of these women, aged fifty-one to seventy. They became convinced that the visual problems were conversion symptoms.

Unlike malingerers, these women had little to gain from blindness. Malingerers "play up" their symptoms by walking with exaggerated tripping motions and pretending they are not able to touch their nose with their fingers. But these women do not. Further, the longer the women spent under the Khmer Rouge and in Thai camps, the worse their visual problems were.

Using a skill building and group therapy intervention with ten of the women, Van Boehmel and Rozee reported improved vision in four of them.

These could possibly be cases of hysterical blindness on a massive scale in which the women no longer "wanted" to see. Alternatively, however, undiagnosed physical illness must be considered. Undetected neurological damage resulting from years of malnutrition and abuse might be the cause.

SOURCE: DeAngelis, 1990.

▼ These civilian survivors of the atrocities perpetuated by the Khmer Rouge are being forcibly marched 160 miles across the Thai border by Khmer Rouge guerillas. Countless others will die on the march, weakened by starvation and exhaustion.

may get more love and attention from his family when he is in pain. The use of secondary gain seems to be part of the universal human trait of making the best of a bad situation. A person with a somatoform disorder, who derives secondary gain, differs from a malingerer. The malingerer is faking the initial symptoms and then may, in addition, use them to benefit. The individual with the somatoform disorder, in contrast, is not faking the symptoms but may well derive benefit from having them. The pattern of symptoms sometimes distinguishes malingering from somatoform disorders. Hysterically blind patients do not crash into objects, but malingerers may (see pp. 291–92).

The second disorder that resembles somatoform disorders are **psychosomatic disorders,** which are subject of the next chapter. What distinguishes psychosomatic disorders from somatoform disorders is the existence of a physical basis that can explain the symptom. Although some individuals who have a peptic ulcer or high blood pressure may have these conditions exaggerated or even initiated by psychological factors, the ulcers and hypertension are actually being caused by specific known physical mechanisms. In contrast, **glove anesthesia,** a conversion symptom in which nothing can be felt in the hand and fingers, but in which sensation is intact from the wrist up, cannot be induced by any known pattern of damage to the nerves controlling the hand.

The third disorder from which somatoform disorder must be distinguished is **factitious disorder,** also called "Münchhausen syndrome." This disorder is characterized by multiple hospitalizations and operations in which the individual voluntarily produces the signs of illness, not through underlying anxiety, but by physiological tampering (Pope, Jonas, and Jones, 1982). He might, for example, take anticoagulant drugs, then seek treatment for his bleeding. There was one documented case of a thirty-four-year-old man who, over a decade, had made 200 visits to physicians under dozens of aliases at more than sixty-eight hospitals and who had cost Britain's health service $2,000,000. In contrast to malingering, a factitious disorder has no obvious goal other than gaining medical attention. It is crucially different from somatoform disorders because the symptoms are voluntarily produced by the person who has them and they are physically based.

Finally, a somatoform disorder may be misdiagnosed and actually result from an **undiagnosed physical illness.** The diagnosis of a somatoform disorder is for many people degrading, as the patient and his family are told that the disease is in his mind, not in his body. Current medical diagnosis is far from perfect, and occasionally an individual who has been labeled "hysteric" will eventually develop a full-blown physical disease, such as multiple sclerosis, which in fact had caused the earlier "hysterical" symptoms. This is one reason the diagnosis must be made with caution.

Table 9–3 summarizes the distinctions among conversion, malingering, psychosomatic disorders, factitious disorders, and undiagnosed physical illness.

Vulnerability to Somatoform Disorders

Conversion disorders are not common. Estimates vary widely, but probably not more than 5 percent of all nonpsychotic patients (or much less than 1 percent of the entire American population) have conversion disorders (Laughlin, 1967; Woodruff, Clayton, and Guze, 1971). Initially, conversion symptoms

FOCUS QUESTIONS

1. What five symptoms characterize somatoform disorders?
2. Describe conversion, somatization disorder (Briquet's syndrome), and pain disorder (psychalgia).
3. Distinguish somatoform disorders from malingering, psychosomatic disorders, and factitious disorder.
4. Describe the psychoanalytic, communicative, and percept blocking views of somatoform disorders.
5. Explain how suggestion, insight, advice, drug treatment, and family therapy are used to treat somatoform disorders.

TABLE 9–3

CRITERIA FOR DIFFERENTIAL DIAGNOSIS OF SYMPTOMS SUGGESTING PHYSICAL ILLNESS				
Classification	Can a known physical mechanism explain the symptom?	Are the symptoms linked to psychological causes?	Is the symptom under voluntary control?	Is there an obvious goal?
Conversion	Never	Always	Never	Sometimes
Malingering	Sometimes	Sometimes	Always	Always
Psychosomatic Disorders	Always	Always	Never	Sometimes
Factitious Disorder	Sometimes	Always	Always	Never (other than medical attention)
Undiagnosed Physical Illness	Sometimes	Sometimes	Never	Never

SOURCE: Based on Hyler and Spitzer, 1978.

usually are displayed from late adolescence to middle adulthood; they occur in children and old people, but rarely (Kotsopoulos and Snow, 1986; Lemkuhl, Blanz, Lemkuhl, and Braun-Scharm, 1989). Because conversion disorders were long regarded as hysteria, and hysteria (a wandering womb) was by definition a disorder of women, conversion disorders in men were overlooked. This is the basis of the myth that conversion afflicts only women. On the contrary, contemporary studies indicate that between 20 and 40 percent of conversion disorders occur in men (Chodoff, 1974; Tomasson, Kent, and Coryell, 1991).

Somatization disorder, in which the patient has a complicated medical history before the age of thirty-five, with a large number of symptoms ranging across many organ systems, and with no known medical explanations, is more common. As many as 2 to 10 percent of all adult women may display this disorder, and it is rarely diagnosed in men (Woodruff, Clayton, and Guze, 1971; Cloninger et al., 1984).

There is marginal evidence that somatoform disorders may run in families (Torgersen, 1986). Somatization disorder probably does run in families. The sisters, mothers, and daughters of women with this disorder are ten times more likely to develop it than women in the general population (Woodruff, Clayton, and Guze, 1971). Nothing is presently known about family patterns of pain disorder.

Course of Somatoform Disorders

What is the course of these disorders once they appear? Surprisingly, there has not been a single useful longitudinal study of conversion disorders, and our knowledge is based only on clinical impressions. Conversion disorders come on suddenly, and they remit suddenly and spontaneously. They probably do not last very long, and it has been estimated that 50 percent spontaneously disappear within two years of onset (Rachman and Wilson, 1979). It has been hypothesized that conversion disorders are early manifestations of slow-onset organic problems. In a follow-up of eighty-four conversion patients, however, only five went on to have a relevant organic disease (Spierings, Poels, Sijben, Gabreels, et al., 1990). Somatization disorder is much more insidious. Seventy percent of women who develop it probably will still have it fifteen years later, and as many as one-third of them will then be diagnosed as psychotic (Ziegler and Paul, 1954; Perley and Guze, 1962; Woodruff, Clayton and Guze, 1971; Coryell and Norten, 1981).

Comorbidity of Somatoform Disorders

As we will see, the cause of the somatoform disorders is a matter of debate and speculation. As research into these problems has become more empirical and rigorous, investigators have begun their search into cause by asking what other disorders co-occur with somatoform disorders. These facts may give us some hint about causes.

There is one disorder that very clearly co-occurs in the history of patients with either somatization, conversion, and pain disorder: depression. Anxiety also co-occurs, but to a lesser extent (Lecompte, 1989; Musetti, Perugi, Soriani, and Rossi, 1989; Brown, Golding, and Smith, 1990; Simon and Von Korff, 1991; Wessely, 1991). This suggests one of two etiological processes: that depression causes or somehow expresses itself in somatoform disorder, or that somatoform problems cause one to become depressed.

There is another, more modern disorder that is also comorbid with the somatoform disorders: ***chronic fatigue syndrome (CFS).*** This highly prevalent problem, usually thought to result from long-term consequences of the Epstein-Barr virus, is also seen frequently in somatization disorder. In one study, 15 out of 100 patients also had somatization disorder (Manu, Lane, and Matthews, 1989; see also Stewart, 1990; Wessely, 1991). Interestingly, cognitive-behavioral therapy as well as tricyclic antidepressants produce substantial relief in CFS when depression is comorbid with it (Butler, Chalder, Ron, and Wessely, 1991).

The Etiology of Somatoform Disorders

What causes the loss of the function of a bodily organ in the absence of any underlying physiological basis? This remains one of the great questions of psychopathology (see Table 9–4).

THE PSYCHOANALYTIC VIEW

The psychoanalytic view was put forth by Sigmund Freud in 1894 and remains a pillar of psychoanalytic thinking today. Freud believed that the physical symptom was a defense that absorbed and neutralized the anxiety generated by an unacceptable unconscious conflict (Freud, 1984/1976, p. 63). Today, the psychodynamic explanation of conversion still revolves around this notion, and postulates three distinct processes: First, the individual is made anxious by some unacceptable idea, and the conversion is a defense against this anxiety. Second, psychic energy is transmuted into a somatic loss. The anxiety is detached from the idea, rendering it neutral. Because anxiety is psychic energy it

TABLE 9–4

VIEWS OF SOMATOFORM DISORDERS			
Theory	*Who Is Vulnerable*	*Cause of Symptom*	*Therapy*
Psychoanalytic view	People with specific unresolved conflicts	Unconscious conflict causes anxiety; conversion into a physical symptom defends against anxiety while at the same time symbolizing the conflict	Recognize and work through unconscious conflict
Communicative view	People who have trouble expressing distress verbally	Physical symptom communicates distress to others in an acceptable and easily understood way	Recognize communicative function of symptom and find more acceptable means of expressing distress

must go some place, and in this case it is used to debilitate a physical organ. Third, the particular somatic loss symbolizes the underlying conflict. For Bear, the three processes seem to play a role: Bear is unconsciously anxious and guilty about causing Tom's paralysis, and he walls off these feelings from consciousness by transmuting the guilt and anxiety into his own paralysis. The particular symptom—paralysis—obviously symbolizes the real paralysis suffered by his friend.

This theory is just about the only idea that can explain one of the strangest symptoms of conversion: "la belle indifference." Unlike patients with actual physical loss due to injury, conversion patients are often strangely indifferent to their physical symptoms. For example, a patient with conversion paralysis may show much more concern over a minor skin irritation on his legs than the fact that he cannot move them (Laughlin, 1967, pp. 673–74). In the psychoanalytic view, a conversion symptom may absorb anxiety so well by transmuting it into a physical loss that the patient can actually be calm about being crippled, blind, deaf, or insensate.

While no complete behavioral view of somatoform disorders has been put forward, the psychoanalytic view gives a hint of what the behavioral view might look like. If conversion symptoms do, in fact, absorb anxiety, anxiety reduction reinforces the patient for having a symptom.

The concept of anxiety has exerted a mighty hold on theories about psychopathology for the last hundred years. For Freud and for the diagnostic systems prior to DSM-III, anxiety was the most important emotion we experienced. All the disorders discussed in Chapter 8 and in this chapter were said to be caused by the process of defending against anxiety. In phobias and panic attacks, in which anxiety was observed, the patient felt dread and displayed an emergency reaction; so its role could not be denied. But in other disorders, such as conversion, in which anxiety was not observed, its existence was inferred to explain the symptom.

Why did anxiety play such a central role in psychoanalytic theory? Part of the answer might have to do with the circumstances of Sigmund Freud's life. Freud grew up in Vienna in the declining days of the Hapsburg empire, in the last half of the nineteenth century, and much of his theorizing took place while his society was collapsing around him. The dissolution of the fixed order, with the attendant uncertainty about the future and about values, may have made anxiety a dominant emotion among the patients that Freud saw. The turn of the century in Vienna may truly have been the "age of anxiety."

THE COMMUNICATIVE VIEW

There are negative emotions other than anxiety: sadness, anger, guilt, awe, bewilderment, and shame are all elements of the human experience. Phobics and obsessive-compulsives experience these emotions as well as anxiety, particularly sadness and anger. Moreover, patients with conversions—if they are defending at all—might not be defending against anxiety but against depression, guilt, or anger. This possibility has spawned another theory of conversion, which emphasizes the *communicative,* rather than the defensive, function of the symptom. The communicative model claims that the patient uses the disorder to deal with a variety of distressing emotions—not only anxiety—and to negotiate difficult interpersonal transactions. He expresses his underlying distress to himself in terms of physical illness, thereby distracting himself from his distress. He then communicates the fact that he is distressed to others with his physical loss. He unconsciously chooses his symptoms according to his own conception of a physical illness—which will derive in part from the illnesses that important people in his life have had—and according to what in his time does and doesn't count as an illness. His particular symptoms will then simulate physical illness either expertly or crudely, depending on how much he knows (Ziegler and Imboden, 1962).

The communicative model views the case study of Bear in the following way: Bear is depressed, anxious, and guilty over his role in paralyzing his friend. In addition, he cannot *talk* about his distress because he is not verbal about his troubles. By paralyzing himself he is able to distract himself from these emotions, so he *shows* his distress to others by his paralysis. Bear's particular symptom derives directly from identification with his friend's paralysis. Bear is alexithymic. The term **alexithymia** (literally, no words for feelings) has been coined to categorize such people who cannot easily express their feelings (Sifneos, 1973). When asked about how they feel about highly charged events, such as the death of a spouse, they describe their physical symptoms or simply fail to understand the question. For example, they may say, "My headaches got worse . . . it was like a band around my head . . . that's all I felt" (Lesser, 1985). Alexithymic people are particularly susceptible to somatoform disorders and the psychosomatic problems discussed in the next chapter.

Experiencing a trauma but not talking about it may precede physical health problems. In a survey of 2,020 respondents, 367 reported having at one time experienced a sexual trauma. These people had higher rates of virtually all physical diseases inquired about than did those who had not experienced a trauma (Rubenstein, 1982; Pennebaker, 1985). In another study, 115 students were classified into a group that had not experienced a trauma, that had experienced a trauma but had confided in others, and a group that had experienced a trauma but had not told anybody. Those in the trauma/no confide group had more diseases, symptoms, and took more medication. Among nineteen people whose spouses had died by accident or suicide, the illness rate was substantially greater than in those who did not talk to their friends about the death (Pennebaker, 1985). In a study of Hmong refugees in the United States who were originally from Southeast Asia, considerable somatization was observed. Somatization was strongly associated with depression. Those who were most acculturated to America (had American friends, used the mass media, owned a car) were less likely to somatize (Westermeyer, Bouafuely, Neider, and Callies, 1989). This suggests that those refugees least able to communicate mental distress in their new world expressed it through bodily distress. While these studies are not definitive, the possibility that silence hurts is intriguing and important. The mechanism by which silence hurts may be rumination; the less people talk to others about tragedy or distress, the more they ruminate, and there may be some as yet unknown way in which rumination undermines physical health (Rachman and Hodgson, 1980). We will return to this idea in the next chapter.

The communicative model explains the odd fact that the kinds of physical losses produced by conversion have changed over the last hundred years, and that they vary with education. For Charcot in Paris in the 1880s, convulsions with frenzied, uncoordinated movements were the most common hysterical conversion. By the turn of the century in Vienna, Freud and his contemporaries saw in their upper-middle-class patients fewer convulsions and more paralysis, "glove" anesthesia, "stocking" anesthesia, blindness, and deafness. At the time of World War I, *clavus*—the painful sensation of a nail being driven into the head—and a severe low back pain producing forwardly bent back were common. Today in urban America, pain, dizziness, headache, loss of sensation, and weakness are the most common conversion reactions; whereas in backwoods America, conversion reactions of the type Freud saw still predominate (Laughlin, 1967; Chodoff, 1974; Woodruff, Goodwin, and Guze, 1974; Watson and Buranen, 1979).

The communicative model holds that conversion reactions "talk." They are a cry for help, particularly among individuals who are reluctant or unable to *talk* about their emotional distress. Such people may be forced to rely on physical symptoms to tell the people they love and their physicians that all is not well in their emotional lives. The physical losses that such individuals generate will correspond to what they know about illness. Once an age or a social class discovers that glove anesthesia is physically impossible, it is no longer a "plausible" symptom to communicate with. Pain, paralysis, and deafness are still plausible somatic symptoms in sophisticated, urban America, and so they are still seen as symptoms in conversion disorders.

THE PERCEPT BLOCKING VIEW

There is a third view of somatoform disorders compatible with either the psychoanalytic or communicative views. It focuses on how a perception can be blocked from conscious experience. This view is best illustrated by hysterical blindness, a conversion disorder in which blindness is the physical loss. Surprisingly, in spite of the claim that he is aware of no visual input at all, the behavior of a hysterically blind person is often controlled by visual input. Such individuals usually avoid walking in front of cars and tripping over furniture, even though they report no awareness of actually seeing anything. In the laboratory, they also give evidence that some visual material is getting through. When given discrimination tasks that can only be solved by visual cues, such as "pick the side—left or right—that has the square, as opposed to the circle, on it," they perform significantly *below* chance. They do worse than if they were guessing at random, and they systematically pick the side that has the circle. In order to be so wrong, the patient must be right—the square of which he is not aware must register at some level of his mind, and then be reacted to by choosing the circle (Theodor and Mandelcorn, 1978; see also Brady and Lind, 1961; Gross and Zimmerman, 1965; Bryant and McConkey, 1989).

What are we to make of this? If we assume that the hysterically blind individual is not lying when he says he is not aware of anything visual, then we are led to the following model: visual input can register in the sensory system and directly affect behavior (hence the avoidance of furniture and below-chance performance), while being blocked from conscious awareness (hence the report "I see nothing"). The conversion process consists in the blocking of the percept from awareness (Hilgard, 1977; Sackeim, Nordlie, and Gur, 1979). This is compatible with both the psychoanalytic and communicative models since it makes no claims about what motivations can cause blocking—a need to defend against anxiety or a desire to distract oneself from inner distress. This model is also physiologically possible. When some parts of the brain that control vision are destroyed, individuals report that they can see nothing at all in specific regions of their visual field. But in spite of consistent reports of blindness, such patients perform above chance on visual discrimination problems. When confronted with this fact, the patients, like the hysterically blind, insist they saw nothing at all and were merely guessing (Weiskrantz, Warrington, Sanders, and Marshall, 1974). So we conclude that the mechanism of hysterical blindness may be the blocking of a visual percept from awareness. The blocking could be motivated either by anxiety (as Freud held), by a need to communicate distress, or it might be reinforced by anxiety reduction (as a behaviorist would hold).

Treatment of Somatoform Disorder

There is an ancient Persian legend about a physician named Rhazes who was called into the palace for the purpose of diagnosing and treating a young prince. Apparently, the prince could not walk. After the usual examination of the day, Rhazes determined that there was nothing wrong with the prince's legs, at least not physically. With little more than a hunch, Rhazes set out to treat what may be the first recorded case of conversion. In doing so, he took a risk: Rhazes unexpectedly walked into the prince's bathroom brandishing a dagger and threatened to kill him. Upon seeing him, "the startled prince abruptly fled, leaving his clothes, his dignity, his symptom, and undoubtedly part of his self-esteem behind" (Laughlin, 1967, p. 678).

TREATMENT

Modern clinicians tend to approach their "princes" brandishing a less drastic treatment. They will sometimes confront a conversion patient and try to force him out of his symptom. For example, therapists may tell hysterically blind patients that they are performing significantly below or above chance on visual tasks in spite of seeing nothing, which may cause visual awareness gradually to return in the patient (Brady and Lind, 1961; but see also Gross and Zimmerman, 1965). But these recoveries are usually temporary, and they may produce conflict and loss of self-esteem in the patient. They also may make the patient feel that the therapist is unsympathetic, and so they may ultimately undermine therapy.

SUGGESTION

Simple suggestion, merely telling a patient in a convincing manner that the symptoms will go away, may fare somewhat better than confrontation does. Conversion patients are particularly suggestible, and certain therapists have found improvement by directly telling the patient, in an authoritative sounding way, that the symptom will go away. In an account of 100 cases of patients with conversion symptoms, one investigator found that following strong suggestion 75 percent of the patients were either symptom-free or much improved four to six years later (Carter, 1949). But since there was no comparison group that might have controlled for the spontaneous disappearance of conversion without suggestion, we cannot be sure that suggestion had any real effect (Bird, 1979).

INSIGHT

Insight, or coming to recognize the underlying conflict producing the physical loss, is psychoanalysts' therapy of choice for conversion disorders. According to these therapists, when the patient comes to see, and emotionally appreciate, that there is an underlying conflict that is producing a conversion disorder, the symptom should disappear. A number of dramatic case histories confirm this. For example, when Bear realized that his paralysis expressed his guilt over his friend's paralysis, the symptom remitted. Unfortunately, there does not exist a well-controlled study that tests whether psychoanalytic insight has any effect over and above suggestion, confrontation, spontaneous remission, or the mere formation of a helping alliance with a therapist.

OTHER THERAPIES

There are suggestions of promising effects from a variety of other approaches. Amitriptyline, an antidepressant with pain-killing effects, seems to have some beneficial effects on a minority of pain disorder patients, although its biochemical mechanism is unknown (Van Kempen, Zitman, Linssen, and Edelbroek, 1992). Sensible advice also helps pain disorder: telling the patient that the treatment goal is not to cure the pain, but to help him achieve a sense of control over pain and improve his functioning in life (Lipowski, 1990). Family therapy also may help. In a study of eighty-nine youngsters with conversion disorders, family therapy approaches produced recovery within two weeks for half the patients (Turgay, 1990). Because suggestion is such a strong factor in conversion, however, skepticism is in order. Placebo-controlled studies of therapy for somatoform disorders are *still* very much needed—more than one hundred years after the first cures were claimed by the very people who founded abnormal psychology as we know it.

Somatoform disorders still remain a great challenge for students of abnormality. These disorders are a real phenomenon—hysterically blind or paralyzed individuals are not feigning their symptoms. When Charcot showed that the symptoms could be produced by hypnotic suggestion and removed by hypnosis, he convinced most of the world that conversion disorders were psychological in origin. Thereupon Freud proposed that the symptoms defended against anxiety. More recent theorists have proposed that the symptoms are meant to communicate more global distress by individuals who find it impossible to talk about their problems. But we have not come much farther since Charcot. The theories of somatoform disorders have yet to be tested in a definitive way, and their cure remains a mystery.

DISSOCIATIVE DISORDERS

All of us have at time or another awakened in the middle of the night and being somewhat befuddled, wondered, "Where am I?" Sometimes the disorientation is more profound. "Who is the person sleeping next to me?" "Who am I, anyway?" When such an event happens—most commonly following fatigue, travel, or drinking—it usually wears off in a few seconds or minutes, and knowledge of our identity returns. But for others it is different. Such a loss of memory about identity sometimes occurs in people who have suffered a strong psychological trauma. It is then more profound, extends over a longer time, and is at the heart of the **dissociative disorders.** They are called "dissociative" because two or more mental processes co-exist or alternate without becoming connected or influencing each other (Gregory, 1987). Some area of memory is split off or dissociated from conscious awareness.

The dissociative disorders have much in common with our last topic, the somatoform disorders, particularly conversion. In conversion disorder, anxiety is not experienced by the victim; in fact, complete indifference is common. Rather, the symptom can be seen as a way to prevent underlying anxiety from surfacing. So it is with dissociative disorders. For example, when an individual suddenly loses his memory following an unbearable trauma, he is not necessarily overtly anxious. Rather, theorists infer that the loss of memory allows him to escape from intolerable anxiety brought on by the trauma (Spiegel and Cardena, 1991).

The experience of dissociation consists of either: (1) **amnesia,** in which a substantial block of time in one's life is forgotten—after the catastrophic collapse of the Hyatt Hotel skywalks in Nevada, 28 percent of the survivors had memory deficits (Wilkinson, 1983); (2) **depersonalization,** in which one feels detachment from oneself—as if one is just going through the motions or looking at oneself from the outside; 57 percent of survivors of a series of deadly tornadoes reported such detachment (Madakasira and O'Brien, 1987): (3) **derealization,** in which the world, not the self, seems unreal; 72 percent of survivors of life-threatening dangers reported feeling as if space and time had altered (Noyes and Kletti, 1977); (4) **identity confusion,** in which one is confused or uncertain about who one is; (5) **identity alteration,** in which one displays a surprising skill—e.g., speaking Flemish or tightrope walking—that one did not know one had (Steinberg, Rounsaville, and Cicchetti, 1990). Dissociative states are common, with 3 percent of the Dutch and Flemish population, mostly male, reporting serious dissociative experiences (Vanderlinden, Van Dyck, Vandereycken, and Vertommen, 1991).

We will discuss two dissociative disorders: **dissociative amnesia,** a loss of personal memory caused by severe trauma such as the death of a child or the dashing of a career; and **multiple personality,** in which two or more distinct personalities exist within the same individual and each leads a rather full life.

FOCUS QUESTIONS

1. What lies at the heart of dissociative disorders?
2. Describe how dissociation can be experienced as amnesia, depersonalization, derealization, identity confusion, and identity alteration.
3. What is a fugue state?
4. Distinguish between generalized amnesia and retrograde amnesia.

Dissociative Amnesia

> Timmy was fifteen years old and attending high school in upstate New York. He was teased mercilessly by his fellow students and was doing poorly in his schoolwork. In addition, he fought constantly with his parents. He was very upset about his problems, and it seemed to him that they had become absolutely unsolvable. One spring afternoon, he went home from school extremely distressed and threw his books down on the porch in disgust.
>
> At that moment, Timmy became a victim of amnesia. This was his last memory for a year, and we will never know exactly what happened next. The next thing we know with certainty is that a year later, a young soldier was admitted to an army hospital after a year of military service. He had severe stomach cramps and convulsions of no apparent physical origin. The following morning, he was better, calm and mentally clear. Astonishingly, he was at a total loss to explain where he was or how he got there. He asked how he came to be in the hospital, what town he was in, and who the people around him were. He was Timmy, all right, awake and in a military hospital with his last memory that of throwing his books down on the porch in disgust. Timmy's father was phoned, and he corroborated the story. At his father's request, Timmy was discharged from the service as underage. (Adapted from Laughlin, 1967, pp. 862–63)

Timmy was the victim of amnesia (the loss of memory of one's identity). As in many cases of amnesia, Timmy wandered and took up a new life by joining the army. Such unexpected travel away from home during amnesia is called a **fugue state,** from the Latin *fuga,* meaning flight. Timmy's loss of memory and fugue are understandable as a flight from intolerable anxiety caused by his problems at home and at school. Timmy adopted the most extreme defense against a painful situation: he became amnesic, not only for the situation, but for his very identity, and he took up a new identity. By becoming amnesic, he was able to escape from his anxiety. During his army life, he remembered nothing about his previous painful life and following recovery of his earlier memories, he was totally amnesic for his year in the army.

KINDS OF DISSOCIATIVE AMNESIA

What happened to Timmy was a **global** or **generalized amnesia:** all the details of his personal life had vanished when he joined the army. Amnesia can be less global than this. **Retrograde amnesia** is a more localized amnesia, in which all events immediately before some trauma are forgotten. For example, an uninjured survivor of an automobile accident may be unable to recall anything that happened during the twenty-four hours up to and including the accident that killed the rest of her family. **Post-traumatic amnesia** is the inability to recall events *after* the episode. Rarest is **anterograde amnesia,** in which there is difficulty remembering new material. This form of amnesia almost always has an organic cause, like a stroke (see pp. 673–74). Finally, there exists **selective** or **categorical amnesia,** in which only events related to a particular theme vanish (Hirst, 1982; Roediger, Weldon, and Challis, 1989).

DISSOCIATIVE VERSUS ORGANIC AMNESIA

Amnesia can also be caused by physical trauma, such as a blow to the head or a gunshot wound to the brain, alcoholism, Alzheimer's disease, and stroke (see

▶ In Alfred Hitchcock's film *Spellbound,* Gregory Peck plays an amnesic in the fugue state, who has lost his memory of his identity as a defense against unbearable guilt and anxiety.

Chapter 17). Such organically caused amnesia should be distinguished from dissociative amnesia. Aside from its physical basis, organic amnesia differs from dissociative amnesia in several ways. First, a dissociative amnesic is usually sorely troubled by marital, financial, or career stress before the amnesia, whereas an individual who suffers organic amnesia need not be (Coons, Bowman, Pellow, and Schneider, 1989). Second, dissociative amnesia resembles glove anesthesia—it does not result from any known neural damage.

A dissociative amnesic shows a fourfold pattern of memory loss that no organic amnesic has ever shown. First, a dissociative amnesic loses his past, both recent and remote—he cannot remember how many brothers and sisters he has; he cannot remember a well-learned fact from the distant past, nor can he remember what he had for breakfast right before the amnesia started. Organic amnesics, on the other hand, remember the distant past well—after a blow to the head, they can tell you perfectly well who taught them Sunday school when they were six years old, or the starting lineup of the 1964 Phillies—but they remember the recent past poorly. Second, an individual with dissociative amnesia loses his personal identity—name, address, occupation, and the like—but his store of general knowledge remains intact. He still remembers who the President is, what the date is, and what the capital of Saskatchewan is (Regina). Organic amnesics, in contrast, tend to lose both personal and general knowledge.

Third, psychogenic amnesics have no anterograde loss; they remember well events that happen after the moment amnesia starts. In contrast, organic amnesics have severe anterograde amnesia, and this is their primary symptom; they remember very little about episodes that happen after the organic damage (like the name of the doctor treating them for the blow to the head). Finally, dissociative amnesia often reverses abruptly. Dissociative amnesia often ends within a few hours or days, and within twenty-four hours of the return of his memory the individual may even recall the traumatic episode that set off the memory loss. In organic amnesia, memory only gradually returns for retrograde memories and hardly ever returns for anterograde memories following organic treatment, and memory of trauma is never revived (Suarez and Pittluck, 1976).

Only a few other facts about dissociative amnesia are known, and they tell us a bit more about vulnerability to this disorder. Dissociative amnesia and fugue states (assuming a new identity) are rare disorders in peacetime, but in times of war and natural disaster they are much more common. They apparently occur in men more than in women and in younger people more than in old people.

The cause of psychogenic amnesia is a mystery, more shrouded even than the causes of the somatoform disorders, which it resembles. We can speculate on how it might be caused, however. If we take the symptoms of conversion at face value, we assume that the mind sometimes can deal with emotionally distressing conflicts by producing physical losses. So, Bear, anxious and guilty about causing his friend's paralysis, converts his distress into his own paralysis. We do not know the mechanism of this conversion, but whatever it is, it might also be working in the amnesic. What happens when a vulnerable individual faces an even more traumatic conflict, such as occurs during war? What happens when one's phsycial existence is suddenly threatened, or when one's entire life plans are shattered? Enormous anxiety should be generated. Perhaps we have one ultimate psychological escape hatch—to forget who we are and thereby neutralize our anxiety about our possible death, our shattered future, or our insoluble problems. Both the psychoanalytic model and behavioral model are compatible with this explanation. For the psychoanalyst, the painful memory of who we are is repressed, and this defends successfully against anxiety. For the behaviorist, anxiety reduction reinforces the symptom of taking on a new identity. In short, amnesia may be the most global of defenses against anxiety produced by very traumatic and unacceptable circumstances.

We will now take up the final disorder in this chapter, multiple personality, in which amnesia plays a major role. Here it will be quite clear that the multiple personalities and their attendant amnesia for each other function to minimize unbearable anxiety.

Multiple Personality

Multiple personality disorder (MPD), which is called ***dissociative identity disorder*** by DSM-IV, is defined as the occurrence of two or more personalities in the same individual, each of which is sufficiently integrated to have a relatively stable life of its own and recurrently to take full control of the person's behavior (Taylor and Martin, 1944; DSM-IV). It is as astonishing a form of psychopathology as exists. Multiple personality was formerly thought of as a very rare disorder—only 200 cases had been reported—but now that clinicians are looking for it, much more of it seems to be around. One researcher, Eugene Bliss, saw 14 cases of it in the late 1970s, just in Utah (Bliss, 1980; Bliss and Jeppsen, 1985), and 100 other cases were reviewed by another group in the 1980s (Putnam, Guroff, Silberman, et al., 1986). At present, the rate of MPD may run as high as 5 percent of inpatient psychiatric admissions in some clinics (Ross, 1991; Ross, Anderson, Fleisher, and Norton, 1991).

The upsurge in the number of cases may be more than just a diagnostic fad. There seem to be three basic reasons for why so much more MPD is now seen. First, the diagnostic probe for amnesia is crucial ("Are there large swaths

▶ Multiple personalities may or may not know of each other's existence. When they do, they may conflict bitterly.

of the week that you can't remember?"). If the answer to the question turns out to be "yes" many times, there is a possibility that other personalities may exist. Thus, amnesia is now part of the diagnosis of MPD in DSM-IV, with "inability to recall important personal information that is too extensive to be explained by ordinary forgetfulness" a hallmark.

Second, MPD fits the psychoanalytic model to a T, and so psychodynamic therapists are highly prepared to diagnose it. As we shall see, MPD begins with childhood trauma that is repressed, and other personalities are generated as a defense against the trauma (Loewenstein and Ross, 1992). Treatment consists of cathartic reintegration of the personalities. It is not an exaggeration to say that MPD has breathed new life into the psychodynamic movement.

Third, diagnosis of MPD has surged with the new and highly visible awareness of child abuse. As we will see, the child abuse—often sexual abuse—is generally claimed to be the trigger for MPD. The immensely popular "Recovery Movement" sees such adult problems as depression, anxiety, eating disorders, and sexual dysfunction as resulting from child abuse (Bradshaw, 1990). Adherents of this movement believe that only by coming to grips with this early, and often unrecognized abuse, can an adult regain mental health. MPD is perhaps the best-documented example of the claims that child abuse has effects that last into adulthood. All these claims, however, are speculative and controversial.

MULTIPLE PERSONALITY DESCRIBED

Eugene Bliss, who is the pioneer of modern work on MPD, had his first introduction to multiple personality in 1978 when he received a call from a distressed supervisor of nurses at a Salt Lake City hospital. The supervisor suspected that one of her nurses had been secretly injecting herself with Demerol. The supervisor and Bliss called the nurse into the office and accused her of improper conduct. They asked the nurse to roll up her sleeves because they wanted to examine her arms for needle marks. The nurse complied, and the telltale marks were there. But in the process of complying, the nurse underwent a remarkable transformation. Her facial expression, her manner, and her voice all changed, claiming that she was not Lois, the demure nurse, but Lucy, the brazen drug addict. Almost everyone has heard of other famous multiple personalities, as in "The Three Faces of Eve" (Thigpen and Cleckley, 1954), Sybil (Schreiber, 1974), or Dr. Jekyll and Mr. Hyde. Among these cases is that of Julie-Jenny-Jerrie (Davis and Osherson, 1977):

Julie came to therapy through her son, Adam, age nine, who had been referred for counseling because of very poor school performance, poor relations with peers, and aggressive behavior at home. Eventually it was decided to see his thirty-six-year-old mother, Julie, in hope that she could help in the therapeutic process.

Julie was highly cooperative, sophisticated, and concerned about Adam. She seemed to have a good understanding of herself, and her general style of solving interpersonal problems was discussion and compromise. She felt that she had trouble setting limits for her son, and she worried that she sometimes behaved too rigidly toward him.

During a session in the sixth week of discussions with Julie, she suddenly announced that she wanted to introduce someone to the therapist. The therapist assumed there was someone out in the waiting room, but to his astonishment he witnessed the following: Julie closed her eyes for a few seconds, frowned, and then raised her eyelids slowly. Putting out her cigarette, she said, "I wish Julie would stop smoking. I hate the taste of tobacco." She introduced herself as Jerrie, and later in the hour and in the same way, she introduced Jenny, yet a third personality.

Jenny revealed that she was the original personality and said that she created Jerrie at age three and subsequently created Julie at age eight. Both times Jenny created the new personalities to cope with her disturbed family life. Jerrie emerged as the outer personality when Jenny was recovering from a severe case of measles, and Jerrie became a buffer who allowed Jenny to keep her distance from seven rejecting siblings and two frightening parents. Jenny said that observing Jerrie was like observing a character in a play.

Between the ages of three and eight, Jenny remembers that her physical welfare was neglected, that she was sexually molested by a neighbor, and was given away for permanent adoption at age eight, with her parents telling her she was "incorrigible." At this time, Jenny created Julie, a gentle personality who was better able to cope with rejection and not as vulnerable to cruelty as either Jerrie or Jenny. Remarkably, while Julie was allowed to know about Jenny, the original personality, Julie was kept unaware of the existence of Jerrie. Julie did not find out about Jerrie until age thirty-four, two years before therapy began.

At age eighteen, Julie-Jenny-Jerrie left home for good. Jerrie and Julie by this time were always the alternating outer personalities, and Jenny was always inside. In fact, Jenny had been "out" only twice since age seven. At age twenty-six, Jerrie married, and the couple adopted Adam, who was the husband's son by a woman with whom he was having an affair while he and Jerrie were married. Jerrie soon divorced him, but she kept Adam.

The three personalities were strikingly different. Jenny—the original—was a frightened person, very shy and vulnerable. She was the most insecure and child-like of the three and felt "exposed" whenever she was out. Jenny felt she had created two Frankensteins who were now out of her control. She liked Julie better, but she was put off by Julie's stubbornness and strong individuality. She felt Jerrie was tougher than Julie and better able to cope with the world, but she didn't like her as well. Jenny's main hope in therapy was that Julie and Jerrie would come to get along better with each other and therefore be better mothers to Adam.

Julie seemed to be the most integrated of the three personalities. Julie was heterosexual, and emotionally invested in being a good mother—this in spite of the fact that it was Jerrie who had adopted Adam.

Jerrie was the opposite of Julie. Jerrie was homosexual, dressed in masculine fashion, sophisticated, and sure of herself. She was accomplished and proficient in the business world, and she enjoyed it. Jerrie didn't smoke, whereas Julie was a heavy smoker, and Jerrie's blood pressure was a consistent twenty points higher than Julie's.

Jerrie had known about Julie since Julie was "born" at age eight, but she had been in touch with her only in the past two years. She wanted to have nothing to do with Julie because she was afraid Julie would have a mental breakdown. Julie and Jerrie did not get along. When one of them was out and having a good time, she would resist relinquishing her position. But when a crisis was at hand, the personality who was out would duck in, leaving the inner personality to face the problem. For example, Julie took LSD and then let Jerrie out so that Jerrie would be the victim of the hallucinations.

Ultimately Jerrie was able to tell Adam that there were two personalities who had been contributing to his misery, and Adam's immediate response was amusement and curiosity. He was able to accept the explanation that "Mother is two people who keep going in and out, but both of them love me." Adam appeared relieved rather than disturbed. Soon thereafter, Jerrie terminated therapy. Julie, in a suicidal depression, had gotten herself admitted to a state hospital against Jerrie's will, but Jerrie had gained control and talked her way out of the hospital. Julie wrote the therapist that she wanted to come to therapy, but Jerrie would not allow it and refused to come anymore. And this was the last that was seen of Julie-Jenny-Jerrie. (Adapted from Davis and Osherson, 1977)

This fascinating case exemplifies much of what is known about multiple personality. Amnesia of some kind or other almost always exists. It is common for one of the personalities to be aware of the experience of the other personalities (Jenny knew of both Julie and Jerrie, and Jerrie knew of Julie), and for one of the personalities to be amnesic about the others (Julie did not know of Jerrie). The presence of unexplained amnesia—hours or days each week that are missing—is a crucial clue to the undetected presence of multiple personality.

There is a personality who says, "I just have fun. I go out with the kids and drink beer." The patient, who had been instructed to listen, comments, "So that is the reason why I wake up drunk in the morning with terrible headaches." (Bliss, 1980)

In the history of multiple personalities, the several personalities within an individual—like Julie-Jenny-Jerrie—differ along many dimensions. Not only do they differ in their memories, but also in their wishes, attitudes, interests, learning ability, knowledge, morals, sexual orientation, age, rate of speech, personality test scores, and physiological indices such as heart rate, blood pressure, and EEG (Lester, 1977). In a systematic study of the autonomic patterns of nine MPD patients compared to five hypnotized controls at the National Institutes of Mental Health, the different personalities of the MPDs showed highly distinct patterns of breathing, sweating, heart rate, and habituation (Putnam, Zahn, and Post, 1990). Remarkably, women with MPD report that they menstruate much of the month because each personality has her own cycle (Jens and Evans, 1983). Most cases of multiple personality are women.

The personalities also differ in psychological health. Often, the dominant personality is the healthier personality. One patient, a proper Southern lady, was publicly accused of wanton sexuality, including intercourse with strangers. She made a clumsy attempt at a self-induced abortion, but she could

Dear Others,
    I would like all of you to sign your name and state your purpose in my ⊕ life. What exactly do you do for me.

Debbie - I give you happiness.
Elizabeth - you can't cry so I do it for you.
Margo - speak the words you can't.
Julie - Sex Sex Sex Sex Sex!!!!
Brenda - Knowledge, the ability to talk to people intellectually.
Kiara - I am gay (lesbian?)
Laurie - When a stranger talks to you I come around because I'm not afraid of people I don't know.
Christine - I express deep feelings.
Bobby - Fighting physically.
Deanne - the only thing I know how to do is run away.
Mellissa - I'm scared.
Valerie - Free Spirits.
Cynthia - I'm the comedian.
Bethanne - love all people and talk to as many as I can.
Monica - Partying is my game.
Sarah - I play games. You always worry that you're going to win but I don't.

▶ A patient with multiple personality disorder produced this handwriting sample, showing seventeen distinct personalities—each with distinct handwriting which emerged when that personality was dominant.

not remember it. Her submerged personality said, "I did it because I suspected a pregnancy. I took a sharp stick and shoved it inside, then I started to bleed badly" (Bliss, 1980). The dominant personality, however, is not always the healthiest, and a submerged personality may actually sympathize with an unhealthy dominant personality and try to help. In one case, the submerged personality wrote to the dominant personality giving her helpful information to try to make her healthier (Taylor and Martin, 1944).

MULTIPLE PERSONALITY AND SCHIZOPHRENIA

Multiple personality is commonly confused with schizophrenia by the layperson. This is because "schizophrenia" is mistakenly thought to refer to a "split personality." Schizophrenia actually refers to one mental process, such as emotion, being split off from another, such as judgment, rather than to the splitting of one entire personality from another. Schizophrenia, as we will see in Chapter 12, is characterized by incoherence of speech and thought, hallucinations, delusions, and blunted or inappropriate emotion, along with deterioration in work, social relationships, and self-care. The individual with multiple personalities, on the other hand, may show none of these symptoms. Multiple personality is diagnosed merely by the existence of two or more coherent and well-developed personalities in the same person. In a systematic comparison of twenty MPD patients versus schizophrenic, panic disorder, and eating disorder patients, MPD patients showed a distinct pattern: more physical and sexual abuse, more drug abuse, more sleepwalking, and more imaginary playmates as children. In addition, seven of the twenty MPD patients also had somatization disorder (Ross, Heber, Norton, and Anderson 1989a, 1989b). While some schizophrenics may have multiple personalities as well, and some individuals with multiple personality may be schizophrenic, the two disorders are distinct.

THE ETIOLOGY OF MULTIPLE PERSONALITY

Where does multiple personality come from? The fourteen cases of multiple personality that were seen by Bliss shared some important common features, and provide us with some clues as to how multiple personality begins and how it develops. Bliss's hypothesis about how multiple personality proceeds has three steps. First, an individual between ages four and six experiences a traumatic emotional problem. Indeed, multiple personality has much in common with post-traumatic stress disorder (Spiegel, 1984), and the rate of claims of child abuse experienced by those who develop multiple personalities may be as high as 97 percent (Putnam, Guroff, and Silberman, et al., 1986; Ross, Miller, Reagor, Bjornson, et al., 1990). She copes with the trauma by creating another personality to take the brunt of the problem. Second, the individual is particularly vulnerable because she is highly susceptible to self-hypnosis, a process by which one is able to put oneself at will into trance states that have the properties of formal hypnotic inductions. Third, the individual finds out that creating another personality by self-hypnosis relieves her of her emotional burden, so that in the future, when she confronts other emotional problems, she creates new personalities to take the brunt (see also Kluft, 1984).

There is some evidence for each of these three steps. First, all fourteen of the patients that Bliss saw did, in fact, create their first alternative personality between the ages of four and six, and each seemed to be created in order to cope with very difficult emotional circumstances. Roberta, for example, created the first of her eighteen personalities when her mother held her under water and tried to drown her. This personality had the purpose of controlling and feeling Roberta's anger and of handling Roberta's homicidal rage without Roberta having to do so. Another patient was molested at age four by an adult man; she created her first alternative personality in order to handle the molestation and thereafter used this personality to handle all sexual encounters.

Second, there is evidence that these patients are extraordinarily good at self-hypnosis. All fourteen of Bliss's patients were excellent hypnotic subjects. When Bliss hypnotized them, they went rapidly into a trance on the first induction. During the hypnosis, when he instructed them to have amnesia for what happened during hypnosis, they did this as well. In addition, when these patients reported the way in which they created the personalities, they described a process that sounds like hypnotic induction. One of the personalities of a patient said, "She creates personalities by blocking everything from her head, mentally relaxes, concentrates very hard and wishes." Another said, "She lies down, but can do it sitting up, concentrates very hard, clears her mind, blocks everything out and then wishes for the person, but she isn't aware of what she is doing." Once these patients were introduced to formal hypnosis in therapy,

FIGURE 9–2

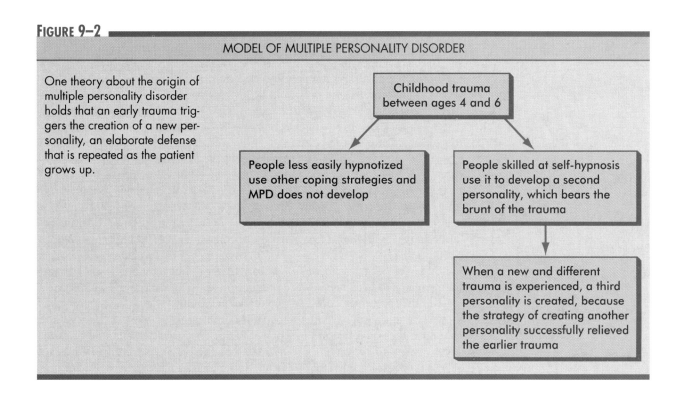

MODEL OF MULTIPLE PERSONALITY DISORDER

One theory about the origin of multiple personality disorder holds that an early trauma triggers the creation of a new personality, an elaborate defense that is repeated as the patient grows up.

Childhood trauma between ages 4 and 6

People less easily hypnotized use other coping strategies and MPD does not develop

People skilled at self-hypnosis use it to develop a second personality, which bears the brunt of the trauma

When a new and different trauma is experienced, a third personality is created, because the strategy of creating another personality successfully relieved the earlier trauma

most reported that this experience was identical to experiences they had had dating back to their childhood, and that an inordinate amount of their lives had been spent in this altered state of consciousness. One patient said, "I spent an awful lot of time in hypnosis when I was young. . . . I've always lived in a dream world. Now that I know what hypnosis is, I can say that I was in a trance often. There was a little place where I could sit, close my eyes and imagine, until I felt very relaxed, just like hypnosis—and it could be very deep."

Third, patients used new personalties to defend against distress later in life. Jenny, you will recall, created Julie, a gentle personality, to cope with her parents' putting her up for adoption at age eight. Most of the patients reported instances in which they created new personalities to cope with new stresses even when they were adults.

In short, multiple personality may come about in the following way: An individual, who is particularly good at self-hypnosis, confronts a serious trauma while a young child. She copes with this by producing a second personality to endure the trauma, rather than enduring it herself. She finds out that this tactic relieves her of emotional stress and, in the future, when she confronts new problems, she creates new personalities to bear them (see Figure 9–2).

PSYCHOTHERAPY FOR MULTIPLE PERSONALITY

As in the case of Julie-Jenny-Jerrie, the treatment of patients with multiple personalties is difficult and frustrating. Therapy for MPD has been conceptualized both in psychodynamic terms and as "tactical integration," a cognitive therapy approach (Fine, 1991). In the cognitive approach, the therapist collects the automatic thoughts of the patient, teaches skills of disputing and challenging irrational thoughts, and tries to find the basis for why these irrational thoughts were credible to the patient. Hypnosis is used in both the cognitive treatment and the more widely used psychodynamic treatment.

In the psychodynamic treatment, the first step is to make the patient aware of the problem. Although she may have lived in this strange state for many years, had amnesia, and been told by others about her bizarre behavior, she may not yet have confronted the fact of other personalities. Under hypnosis, the therapist calls up the alter-egos and allows them to speak freely. In addition, the patient herself is asked to listen and then is introduced to some of these personalities. She is told to remember the experience when she emerges from hypnosis. Enormous distress and turmoil often follow this discovery, but it is important for her to keep hold of the facts of many personalities. At this point, she may display one of the most troublesome problems for therapy—dodging back into a self-hypnotic state and so avoiding the unpleasant reality. The therapist may then try to enlist the aid of various personalities (Kluft, 1987).

After the patient is made fully aware of her many personalities, the therapist explains to her that they are products of self-hypnosis induced at an early age and without any conscious or malicious intent. The patient is told that now she is an adult, strong and capable, and that if she has the courage, she can flush these specters out and defeat them. The other personalities may object, or want to continue their own life, but she is the only real person here. There is only one body and one head, and the other personalities are her creations. She will have the privilege of deciding what aspects of the personalities she will retain. In one study of thirty-four patients treated by an experienced therapist, 94 percent apparently showed strong improvement, with a two-year follow-up (Kluft, 1987).

In a survey of 305 clinicians who treat MPD, Putnam and Loewenstein (1993) found the the average patient is in treatment for almost four years. Individual therapy (both psychodynamic and cognitive) and hypnosis were most widely used. Antidepressant and anti-anxiety drugs were also used by two-thirds of the clinicians with "moderate" relief reported. The remainder of the decade promises more systematic outcome studies of the effectiveness of psychotherapy and drugs for patients with MPD.

Overall, multiple personality, like somatoform disorders and amnesia, can be seen as an attempt to defend against severe emotional distress. A child of four to six who is unusually capable of self-hypnosis creates a new personality—an imaginary companion and ally—to help her deal with the anxiety generated by a possible traumatic experience. This innocent, childhood ploy inadvertently becomes an adult disaster as the patient repeatedly uses this technique to cope with the stresses she encounters as she grows up.

CAVEAT: IS THE STORY OF ABUSE REAL?

The story of MPD in recent times is a story of a hard-won struggle for scientific credibility. A central element concerns the veracity of the physical and sexual abuse in childhood that is said to trigger MPD (Ganaway, 1989). Most studies of MPD patients are based solely on the adult patient's uncorroborated, retrospective report that abuse occurred when she was a small child. More recently, however, investigators have begun to look prospectively at children who were known to have been abused, and tentative findings show the use of dissociation in these children (Putnam, 1989).

Society has become much more willing to listen to buried family secrets and to "believe the children." But there is also a growing trend toward facile acceptance of extensive, incredible, and contradictory accounts of abuse. This trend places the hard-won scientific credibility of the MPD field into jeopardy. David Spiegel (1990) points to the existence of the "grade 5" hypnotizable person. Only 5 percent of the population falls into this category. Grade 5's are extremely hypnotizable, very suggestible, show pathological compliance with their therapists, and give up critical judgment. They report vivid, rich, detailed "memories" from trance states—that are without factual foundation. Virtually all MPD patients are "grade 5's" (Ganaway, 1989).

The reports of MPD patients must be considered at high risk for contamination by such pseudo-memories. Ganaway's many MPD patients have told him in vivid detail of encounters with demons, angels, lobsters, chickens, tigers, God, and a unicorn. In one case, Sarah, a fifty-year-old MPD, was shocked when Carrie a five-year-old "alter" (jargon for one of the personalities) relived in vivid detail the brutal rape and murder of twelve girls from her Sunday school class. Carrie was spared by the cult leader because she was unlucky number 13. On further exploration, Sherry, another alter, revealed that she had created Carrie to absorb the terror she had felt when her grandmother read grisly murder stories to her (Ganaway, 1989).

At this point, we should remain skeptical of the validity of some of the MPD patients' tales of abuse, particularly the more outlandish ones. Some may be true, and some may be false. Their truth or falsity, however, does not matter nearly as much as the fact of their telling, the needs that such telling reveals about the patient, and the usefulness of such material for healing.

FAKING MULTIPLE PERSONALITY: THE HILLSIDE STRANGLER

As much as there is evidence for the existence and treatment of multiple personality, there can also be abuses of and faking of the symptoms of this disorder. Consider the case of the Hillside Strangler:

> Ten attractive young females were murdered, and some of their bodies were left conspicuously displayed on Los Angeles hillsides during the winter of 1977–1978. A year later, two similar murders took place in Bellingham, Washington, and Kenneth Bianchi was arrested. Bianchi claimed that he was totally ignorant of what had happened, and he insisted he was innocent. During the next six weeks, he reported a number of alibis, which could not be confirmed. Upon psychiatric examination, it was suggested that hypnosis be used to break through his "shell" of defenses.
>
> Under hypnosis, a new personality, Steve, appeared. Steve took credit for the murders and described them in detail. Steve displayed pleasure in "fixing" Ken and showed no remorse. Ken claimed to be ignorant of Steve's existence.

Was Bianchi really a multiple personality, and therefore perhaps not guilty of murder by reason of insanity (see Chapter 18)? Or had Bianchi made up Steve in an attempt to fake multiple personality?

Leading experts on the dissociative disorders and hypnosis were brought in, among them Martin Orne of the University of Pennsylvania. They argued that Bianchi was faking, on four grounds: (1) Steve's personality changed over time. Early on Steve was polite, passive, and unaggressive. Later he became

▼ Experts determined that Kenneth Bianchi, known as the Hillside Strangler and shown here during his trial, was faking multiple personality.

abusive and aggressive. Multiples, it was argued, show stable patterns, particularly when the personality has existed for nineteen years. (2) When it was suggested to Ken that "real" multiples have three or more personalities, not just two, a new one, nine-year-old "Billy" appeared. (3) When real multiple personality exists, it is noticed by many others and for a long time. Adam, Julie-Jenny-Jerrie's son, could have corroborated the existence of two distinct personalities in his mother. But there was no external corroboration of Steve's existence. (4) Most interestingly, it appeared that Bianchi was simulating hypnosis, rather than being in a deep trance. There are some striking differences between simulators and those in a trance, and Bianchi had the characteristics of a simulator. For example, Bianchi shook hands with a hallucination that he was induced to have, and he did not engage in trance logic during hypnotically induced anesthesia.

The experts argued that Bianchi was simulating multiple personality, but that he did warrant the diagnosis of antisocial personality disorder with sexual sadism, a diagnosis that does not excuse crime in the state of California. The court agreed (after Orne, Dinges, and Orne, 1984; Spanos, Weekes, and Bertrand, 1985).

THE NEUROSES

In this chapter and Chapter 8, we have examined disorders that appear, on the surface, to be quite varied: phobia, post-traumatic stress disorder, panic disorder, generalized anxiety disorder, obsessions, somatoform disorders, dissociative amnesia, and multiple personality. In the past, these disorders looked more like a coherent whole than they do today. Historically, they were all viewed as "neuroses" and all were thought to involve anxiety as the central process. In the case of phobia and post-traumatic stress disorder, fear is on the surface; in panic disorder and generalized anxiety disorder, anxiety (fear without a specific object) is also on the surface. The individual with one of these problems feels anxiety, apprehension, fear, terror, and dread in his daily life. In obsessive-compulsive disorders, on the other hand, anxiety is sometimes felt, but not if the compulsion is frequent and effective. In contrast, in the somatoform disorders and the dissociative disorders, anxiety is not usually observed. But in order to explain the bizarre symptoms of these disorders, theorists have inferred that, with his symptoms, the individual is defending against underlying anxiety. To the extent that the defense is successful, the symptoms will appear, and anxiety will not be felt.

The last twenty years have witnessed a sea change in the field of psychopathology: our categories have become more descriptive and less theoretical. DSM-IV disavows a common process—defending against anxiety—as the mechanism of these disorders. The dissociative disorders and somatoform disorders no longer fall under the larger class "Anxiety Disorders." Rather, DSM-IV includes as anxiety disorders only those disorders in which anxiety is observed: phobia, panic disorder, generalized anxiety disorder, post-traumatic stress disorder, and obsessive-compulsive disorder. Descriptively it makes good sense to segregate those disorders in which anxiety is observed from those in which anxiety is only inferred by a theory. But at a theoretical level, these disorders cry out for a common explanation.

For phobia and post-traumatic stress disorder, theories that come out of behavioral models seem appropriate. In both of these disorders we can postulate a trauma that imbued parts of the environment with terror, and the symptoms, the course, and the therapies roughly follow known behavioral laws. Obsessive-compulsive disorder is not as easy to handle in this way. How obsessions stay around once they have been acquired fits reasonably well within behavioral views, as do therapies that alleviate obsessions. But this is only part of the story. The questions of who is vulnerable to obsessions and what content obsessions will take are not answered by the behavioral school, nor is there even a useful theory from this tradition. These questions may be best viewed within a psychodynamic tradition, in which emotional distress lurks beneath the surface. Finally, we have somatoform disorders, dissociative amnesia, and multiple personality. Here theories of surface anxiety are useless, nor does there exist an adequate behavioral theory of these three disorders. Anxiety, or some other dysphoric emotion that lies beneath the surface and is being defended against, seems to make more sense of the symptoms of these disorders, but the details of their etiology and which therapy is best for them remain a mystery.

Overall, then, we find that when fear and anxiety are on the surface, behavioral models serve us well. As fear and anxiety tend to disappear from the surface, however, we find ourselves in need of models to attempt to explain what we do observe. It seems likely that for the present we still need, at least for disorders like conversion, amnesia, and multiple personality, theories such as the psychodynamic model, which postulates deep, unobserved emotional conflict and psychological defenses that are so rich as to still inspire awe in those who study these disorders closely.

SUMMARY

1. This chapter examined the disorders in which anxiety is inferred to exist as opposed to being observed. Three kinds of disorders were considered: obsessive-compulsive disorders, somatoform disorders, and dissociative disorders.

2. *Obsessive-compulsive disorders* (OCD) consist of *obsessions*, which are repetitive thoughts, images, or impulses that invade consciousness, are often abhorrent, and are very difficult to dismiss or control. In addition, most obsessions are associated with *compulsions*, which are repetitive, stereotyped, and unwanted thoughts or actions to counter the obsession. Compulsions can be resisted only with difficulty.

3. The content of obsessions has changed over history. In past centuries, they were mostly religious and sexual; now they are concerned mostly with dirt and contamination, violence, and orderliness.

4. An obsessive-compulsive individual displays anxiety when his or her rituals are blocked. In addition, depression is associated with this disorder. When such an individual is depressed, obsessions occur much more frequently, and such individuals are more prone to depression than the normal population. There is no personality type that seems predisposed to

obsessive-compulsive disorders. Individuals who are obsessive-compulsive in their daily life and concerned with order are not more vulnerable to obsessive-compulsive disorder. What distinguishes these individuals from individuals with the disorder is that individuals with the obsessive-compulsive personality are proud of their meticulousness and love of detail, whereas individuals who have the disorder are tormented by their symptoms.

5. Cognitive-behavioral theory explains why the disorder and its rituals are maintained. The theory claims that individuals with the disorder are unable to habituate, dismiss, or distract themselves from disturbing thoughts. Behavior therapies for obsessive-compulsive disorders include *flooding*, forcing the patient to endure the aversive situation, *response blocking*, preventing the individual from engaging in the ritual, and *modeling*, watching another person refrain from the ritual. These therapies bring about marked improvement in about two-thirds of the patients with obsessive-compulsive disorders.

6. Psychoanalytic theory explains who is vulnerable to the disorder and why it has the particular content it does. It claims that the obsessive thought is a *defense* against an even more unwelcome unconscious thought. The anxiety the unconscious thought arouses is displaced onto a less unwelcome substitute that symbolically stands for the underlying conflict.

7. The biomedical view holds that OCD is a disorder of the brain. Neurological signs, brain scan findings, the evolutionarily primitive content of obsessions and compulsions, and the success of clomipramine, an antidepressant drug, are all evidence for this view.

8. Clomipramine produces improvement in 50 to 60 percent of OCD patients, but relapse is almost universal when the drug is stopped.

9. The *somatoform disorders* have five symptoms: (1) lost or altered physical functioning, (2) the absence of a known physical cause, (3) positive evidence that psychological factors are associated with the symptom, (4) indifference to the physical loss, and (5) the absence of voluntary control over the symptom.

10. Three kinds of somatoform disorders are: (1) *conversion*, in which one physical function is lost or altered, (2) *somatization disorder*, in which there is a dramatic and complicated medical history for multiple and recurrent bodily complaints in many organs, although the symptoms are not physically caused, and (3) *pain disorder*, in which the onset, severity, or persistence of pain is not attributed to physical cause. Pain disorder is the most common somatoform disorder today. Somatoform disorders should be distinguished from malingering, secondary gain, psychosomatic disorders, and undiagnosed physical illness.

11. Psychoanalytic theory holds that somatoform disorders are a defense against anxiety, that psychic energy is transmuted into somatic loss, and that the particular somatic loss symbolizes the underlying conflict.

12. The experience of dissociation consists of either: (1) *amnesia*, in which a substantial block of one's life is forgotten, (2) *depersonalization*, in which one feels detachment from oneself, (3) *derealization*, in which the world, not

the self, seems unreal, (4) *identity confusion,* in which one is confused or uncertain about who one is, or (5) *identity alteration,* in which a surprising skill, like speaking a novel language, is displayed. In *dissociative disorders,* some area of memory is split off or dissociated from conscious awareness.

13. *Dissociative amnesia* is a loss of memory caused by unbearable trauma and can either be general or highly specific. *Retrograde amnesia* is a specific amnesia in which events immediately *before* some trauma are forgotten. *Anterograde amnesia* is an amnesia in which events *after* a trauma are not learned about.

14. *Multiple personality disorder* (MPD) is the existence of two or more personalities in the same individual, each personality being sufficiently integrated to have a relatively stable life of its own and to be able recurrently to take full control over the person's behavior. This disorder is more frequent than previously believed and seems to involve individuals who are highly susceptible to self-hypnosis, who claim to have experienced a serious trauma between ages four and six, and who use the creation of alternative personalities to bear this trauma, which they are unable to cope with in any other way.

15. Most studies of MPD are based solely on the adult patient's uncorroborated report that brutal abuse occurred when she was a small child. MPDs are extremely hypnotizable, very suggestible, and show strong compliance with their therapists. The reports of MPD patients should be considered at high risk for contamination by pseudo-memories. The truth or falsity of the reported abuse, however, does not matter as much as the usefulness of such material for healing.

QUESTIONS FOR CRITICAL THINKING

1. Explain why obsessions and depression often occur in the same person.

2. Why do you think women are more likely to develop somatoform disorders than are men?

3. Why is it possible that an undiagnosed physical disorder may be misdiagnosed as a somatoform disorder?

4. Do you think that someone with multiple personality disorder should be held accountable for the actions or crimes of each of his or her personalities?

Health Psychology

CHAPTER ORGANIZER

STIGMATA
- Discover one of the more dramatic examples of psychosomatic disorders.

OVERVIEW OF PSYCHOSOMATIC DISORDERS
- Be able to describe the two criteria for diagnosing psychosomatic disorders.

PEPTIC ULCERS
- Follow how the diathesis-stress model can explain the symptoms, development, and treatment of peptic ulcers.

CARDIOVASCULAR DISORDERS
- Learn how our physical health, especially regarding our heart, can be heavily influenced by emotional states.

PSYCHONEUROIMMUNOLOGY (PNI)
- Familiarize yourself with how emotional states, especially hopelessness, helplessness, and pessimism, can influence our immune system, the body's defense against disease.

THEORIES OF PSYCHOSOMATIC ILLNESS
- Understand how proponents of the biomedical, psychodynamic, and the behavioral-cognitive views offer insights into psychosomatic disorders.

Does what we think and what we feel change our physical well-being? We have learned from our discussion of emotion in the last two chapters that our thoughts and emotions can modify how our body reacts. One of our bodily reactions is, of course, disease, and we do not usually think of physical disease—stomach ulcers, coronary heart disease, cancer, tuberculosis, asthma—as reactions that can be influenced by thoughts and feelings. But there is a good deal of evidence that the course, and perhaps the very occurrence, of such illnesses can be influenced by the psychological states of their victims. Such a disorder is called a ***psychosomatic disorder*** and is defined as a disorder of the body (the soma) that is influenced by, or in the strongest case, caused by the mind (the psyche). The field that deals with these disorders stands at the border of psychology and medicine, and is called ***health psychology*** (Stone, Weiss, Matarazzo, Miller, Rodin, Belar, Follick, and Singer, 1987).

We will present an overview of psychosomatic disorders, followed by a close look at two examples of such problems: peptic ulcers and coronary heart disease. We will then look at ***psychoneuroimmunology (PNI),*** which investigates how mental state and behavior influence the immune system and disease. Finally, we will distill the principles used to analyze these examples by discussing various theoretical approaches to psychosomatics. We begin with a striking example of psychosomatic phenomenon on the skin: stigmata.

STIGMATA

FOCUS QUESTIONS

1. What are stigmata?
2. How do stigmata exemplify a psychosomatic disorder?

One of the most dramatic examples of psychosomatic disorder is the rare phenomenon of **stigmata.** Stigmata are marks on the skin—usually bleeding or bruises—often of high religious or personal significance, brought on by an emotional state. About 300 instances of stigmata, many of them called miracles, have been reported in the last 2,000 years. Most are found in religious histories, but only a handful of these are documented well enough to take seriously scientifically. This handful provides the quintessential demonstration of a psychosomatic phenomenon: a mental state causing the body to react in a way usually thought of as being purely physical. Consider the following case history:

> Since childhood, Steven had suffered from nightmares and sleepwalking. His sleepwalking became a particular problem when, in 1935, he was hospitalized because of an infection. To prevent him from sleepwalking about the ward in the middle of the night, he was restrained physically while he slept; his hands were tightly bound behind his back when he went to sleep. On one such occasion he awoke, and in a half-conscious state, found himself tied down. Although he could not untie his hands, he was still able to evade his bodyguard and escape into the surrounding countryside, from which he returned a few hours later.
>
> Some ten years later, at age thirty-five, Steven was again admitted to a hospital—this time in an attempt to cure his recurrent sleepwalking. One evening at about midnight the nurse saw him struggling violently on his bed, apparently having a nightmare. He was holding his hands behind his back and seemed to be trying to free them from some imaginary bond. After carrying on in this way for about an hour, he crept out of bed still holding his hands behind his back, and disappeared into the hospital grounds. He returned twenty minutes later in a state of normal consciousness. As the nurse put him into bed, she noted deep weals like rope marks on each arm, but until then Steven seemed unaware of their presence. The next day the marks were still visible and were observed by the hospital staff. Three nights later the marks had disappeared.
>
> His physician believed that the marks were stigmata caused by reliving the traumatic event of a decade earlier. To test this, he caused Steven to relive the experience of ten years before under a hypnotic drug. While reliving the experience, Steven writhed violently on the couch for about three-quarters of an hour. After a few minutes weals appeared on both forearms. Gradually these became deeply indented and finally blood appeared along their course. Next morning the marks were still clearly visible. (Moody, 1946)

▼ Steven's right forearm shows indented weals, resembling rope marks. They appeared when he relived, under a hypnotic drug, an earlier traumatic experience.

Here is a clear example of an essentially psychosomatic phenomenon. A process that we usually believe to be strictly physical—the appearance of rope marks and bleeding—is induced by the mental state of recalling a traumatic incident with high emotion. The patient was carefully observed during the development of the rope marks, and there is no ready explanation other than emotional state influencing a physical state.

It is already clear that psychosomatic illness may take a bizarre form. In the case of Steven, there is little doubt of the existence of a psychosomatic disorder. But what about those cases where there is less dramatic evidence? Many believe that some ulcers, heart attacks, and other physical problems are partly caused by an adverse psychological state. But how does a clinician know this, and when there is evidence, how does he or she classify it?

The diagnosis of psychosomatic disorder is made if (1) there is a disorder of known physical pathology present, *and* (2) psychologically meaningful events preceded and are judged to contribute to the onset or worsening of the disorder. When psychological factors influence physical illness, the individual commonly denies that he is ill, refuses to take medication, and may ignore the presence of risk factors that will likely worsen the physical condition (DSM-IV).

The first criterion distinguishes psychosomatic disorders from somatoform disorders. Conversion, dissociative amnesia, and the like have no known physical basis, whereas psychosomatic disorders do. By these two criteria, Steven's forearm weals are a clear case of psychosomatic disorder, since symptoms of known physical pathology are present—rope marks and bleeding—and a psychologically traumatic incident—being bound while asleep—preceded these symptoms.

These two defining criteria of psychosomatic disorder have been incorporated into a particular model: ***the diathesis-stress model.*** "Diathesis" refers to the constitutional weakness that underlies the physical pathology, and "stress" to the psychological reaction to meaningful events. According to this model, an individual develops a psychosomatic disorder when he both has some physical vulnerability (diathesis) and experiences psychological disturbance (stress). If an individual is extremely weak constitutionally, very little stress will be needed to trigger the illness; if, on the other hand, extreme stress occurs, even individuals who are constitutionally strong may fall ill. In effect, the model suggests that individuals who develop peptic ulcers are both constitutionally vulnerable to gastrointestinal problems and experience sufficient stress to trigger the pathology.

Psychological factors can affect many physical conditions in a large number of organ systems: the skin, the skeletal-musculature, the respiratory, the cardiovascular, the blood and lymphatic, the gastrointestinal, the genito-urinary, the endocrine systems, or the sense organs (Looney, Lipp, and Spitzer, 1978). There is no evidence, however, that the process causing psychosomatic effects is different for each different organ, although any given individual may be especially vulnerable to psychosomatic influence in only one organ system. Some of us react to stress with the stomach, others by sweating, some by muscle tension, and still others with a racing heart.

PEPTIC ULCERS

A ***peptic ulcer*** is a circumscribed erosion of the mucous membrane of the stomach or of the duodenum, the upper portion of the small intestine. Such ulcers are called "peptic" because it is commonly thought that they are at least partially caused by pepsin, which is contained in the acidic juices normally secreted by the stomach. There are two sorts of peptic ulcers that derive their names from their location: stomach (gastric) ulcers and duodenal ulcers.

Roughly two million people in the United States today have a peptic ulcer, and about five thousand people die of peptic ulcer each year in the United States (Center for Disease Control, 1982). We begin our discussion of psychosomatic disorders with the peptic ulcers because they are so widespread and because much is known, both about the physical pathology underlying ulcers and about psychological influence on their development and course. Carlos's gastrointestinal problems illustrate the ways in which environmental stress influences peptic ulcers.

Carlos has had an ulcer for the last seventeen years. Until recently he had it under control; for whenever he experienced gastric pain, drinking a quart of milk or eating eggs would relieve it. Three years ago he was promoted to manager of a major department store and moved from his home town to a distant city. Since he took on this increased responsibility, he has experienced severe ulcer pain.

He had been born and raised in a small New England town. His father was wealthy and the head of a chain of department stores. Although his father was in general domineering and intolerant (and also had an ulcer), he was kind and generous to Carlos. After graduation from college Carlos entered the department store business and even now, at age forty-one, he feels incapable of holding a job without his father's intervention, influence, and support.

As soon as Carlos took over the management of the store, he became tense and anxious and began to brood over trivial details. He was afraid the store would catch fire; he was afraid that there would be bookkeeping errors that he might not catch; he was afraid the store would not make a big profit. Convinced he was a complete failure, and plagued with severe pains from his duodenal ulcer, he entered psychotherapy. During these sessions, Carlos and his therapist learned how much the psychological factors in his life contributed to the worsening of the ulcer. The following three incidents particularly illustrate this.

First, on a day when the store was full of people a large ventilating fan broke. The store began to shake as the customers rushed to the street, and Carlos went into a panic. As soon as the excitement subsided and his panic diminished, severe ulcer pains started.

Second, Carlos's mother had for many years complained of a "heart condition." While his mother's physician had never isolated a physical cause, Carlos nevertheless worried about it. One day Carlos saw a hearse pass in front of the store. Immediately he thought that his mother had died and in panic ran several miles to her home finding her quite alive. As he started to run the stomach pains broke out, and these pains remained until he saw his mother was not ill.

Third, one night Carlos's store burned to the ground. He was highly anxious that he would be found negligent during the ensuing insurance investigation. As he awaited the results of the inquiry, his wife called and told him that his daughter had broken a leg. He ran home and found his wife in tears, and he immediately developed severe stomach pains.

Before he had become manager of the store he had occasionally had stomach pains while on the job, but he had found a technique for reliably and immediately alleviating them: he would go to an older person for comfort. Upon being reassured by an authority figure, his ulcer pain would disappear. In his new job, however, he was the authority figure, there was no one to turn to, and his ulcer pains persisted, unrelieved. (Adapted from Weisman, 1956)

FOCUS QUESTIONS

1. How can peptic ulcers exemplify the two criteria for a diagnosis of psychosomatic disorder?
2. Describe some psychological factors that influence peptic ulcers.
3. What have animal models shown us about conflict, unpredictability, uncontrollability, and peptic ulcers?
4. What can be done to treat peptic ulcers?

Symptoms of Peptic Ulcer

Carlos suffered the main symptom of peptic ulcer: abdominal pain. Such abdominal pain can vary from mild discomfort to severe and penetrating, extreme pain. Pain may be steady, aching, and gnawing, or it may be sharp and cramp-like. Pain is usually not present before breakfast; it generally starts from one to four hours after meals. Bland foods and antacids usually alleviate the pain, while peppery food, alcohol, and aspirin usually intensify it (Lachman, 1972; Weiner, 1977). Peptic ulcers that become very serious sometimes perforate or bleed. Without well-timed surgery, a perforated ulcer can lead to death from internal bleeding.

Physiological Development of an Ulcer

In order to understand how these symptoms come to be, we must first take a brief look at the actions of the digestive system. Digestion breaks down food in the stomach so that when the food passes through the intestines, the appropriate materials can be absorbed for use by the body. In order to digest food, the stomach secretes two highly corrosive juices: hydrochloric acid, which breaks food down, and pepsin, which decomposes protein. Why, you might wonder, does the stomach not digest itself? Fortunately, the stomach and the small intestine are lined with a mucous membrane that protects them from corrosion by the hydrochloric acid the stomach secretes. In addition, gastric juices are normally secreted only when there is food in the stomach to absorb most of the corrosive acid. But sometimes the system develops a problem. A break may occur in the mucous coating of the stomach or duodenum. Such a break may occur when some of the thin lining is worn away in the normal course of digestion. It may also occur when an overdose of aspirin, particularly in combination with alcohol, is ingested, or when naturally secreted bile attacks the membrane. If a break occurs in the absence of too much gastric juice, it will repair itself and no ulcer will form, since cell growth completely renews the stomach lining every three days (Davenport, 1972). If an excess of hydrochloric acid or pepsin is around, however, particularly when food is not in the stomach, the abrasion will worsen and an ulcer will form.

Who Is Susceptible to Ulcers?

The way an ulcer develops gives us clues about what diathesis, or constitutional weakness, makes ulcers more likely. Individuals who secrete excess hydrochloric acid or pepsin, individuals with an especially weak mucous defense against acid, and individuals whose stomach lining regenerates slowly may generally be more susceptible to ulcers. This condition may be genetically inherited.

The prevalence of peptic ulcer varies widely from country to country, and from decade to decade. Today, approximately 1 percent of the adult American population has an ulcer, and almost four hundred thousand Americans are hospitalized yearly for peptic ulcers. The frequency of peptic ulcers has, for unexplained reasons, declined by about 25 percent over the last decade in the

United States and Europe (McConnell, 1966; Lachman, 1972; Weiner, 1977; Elashoff and Grossman, 1980).

The susceptibility of women versus men seems to have undergone a major change over the past 100 years. Before 1900, peptic ulcers occurred more frequently in women than in men, but in the beginning of the twentieth century a shift occurred, with men becoming considerably more ulcer prone. By the late 1950s, men had 3.5 times as many duodenal ulcers as women (Watkins, 1960). In recent years, the male/female ratio has been changing (Elashoff and Grossman, 1980). By 1978, men had only 1.2 times as many peptic ulcers as women in America. Ulcers in men had become less frequent and ulcers in women had either stayed the same or slightly increased (Sturdevant, 1976).

Social class also influences the incidence of ulcers. For a time it was commonly believed that highly pressured, upwardly mobile and professionally successful individuals develop the most ulcers. But in fact many patients with peptic ulcer are poor and wholly unsuccessful, and those presently at highest risk for peptic ulcer are in the lower classes (Susser, 1967; Langman, 1974).

Age does not make much of a difference beyond the age of twenty. Children probably have ulcers less frequently than adults. Among children, girls have peptic ulcers about twice as frequently as boys (Christodoulou, Gergoulas, Paploukas, Marinopoulou, and Sideris, 1977; Medley, 1978).

Ulcers clearly run in families. The relatives of patients with duodenal and gastric ulcers are about three times as likely to have an ulcer as those in the general population (McConnell, 1966). Further, healthy individuals who have relatives with peptic ulcers secrete more gastric juice than individuals without relatives with ulcers (Fodor, Vestea, and Urcan, 1968). This increased susceptibility in families could either be genetic or environmental, since family members share many of the same stresses, as well as genes. But twin data suggest it is genetic. If one of a pair of identical twins has a peptic ulcer, the chances are 54 out of 100 that the co-twin will also have a peptic ulcer; whereas if one of a pair of fraternal twins has a peptic ulcer, there is only a 17 percent chance that the co-twin will also have a peptic ulcer (Eberhard, 1968).

There is a newly discovered risk factor, a bacterium called *Helicobacter pylori* that can survive in the acidic gastrointestinal tract. Killing the bacteria works well: When ulcer patients were treated with antibiotics, duodenal ulcers recurred in only 8 percent, but recurred in 86 percent of untreated controls (Graham, Lew, Klein, et al., 1992; Alper, 1993; Hentschel, Brandstetter, Dragosics, et al., 1993).

Here then is the foundation of the diathesis in the diathesis-stress model of peptic ulcers (see Figure 10–1). How much acid and pepsin the stomach secretes contributes to the formation of an ulcer. High acid and pepsin secretion runs in families and may be the constitutional weakness that makes individuals more susceptible to ulcers once the bacterium is present (Mirsky, 1958).

Psychological Factors Influencing Peptic Ulcers

To what extent does stress influence the development or worsening of peptic ulcers? When individuals who have a constitutional weakness of the intestinal system—such as hereditary oversecretion of acid—encounter certain kinds of stress, peptic ulcers may result. By "stress" researchers refer to the reaction of an individual to disturbing events in the environment. A stress reaction can either be a short-term emotional reaction induced by a specific situation, or it

"I'd say the sales chart is the ulcer, the phone is the hypertension, the paperwork is the migraine. . . ."

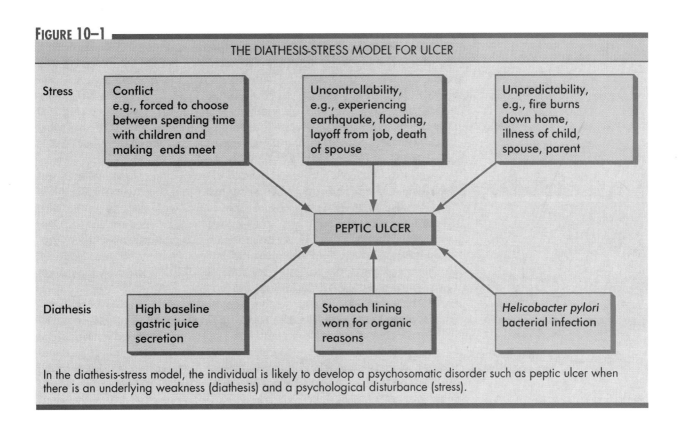

FIGURE 10–1

THE DIATHESIS-STRESS MODEL FOR ULCER

Stress

Conflict
e.g., forced to choose
between spending time
with children and
making ends meet

Uncontrollability,
e.g., experiencing
earthquake, flooding,
layoff from job, death
of spouse

Unpredictability,
e.g., fire burns
down home,
illness of child,
spouse, parent

PEPTIC ULCER

Diathesis

High baseline
gastric juice
secretion

Stomach lining
worn for organic
reasons

Helicobacter pylori
bacterial infection

In the diathesis-stress model, the individual is likely to develop a psychosomatic disorder such as peptic ulcer when there is an underlying weakness (diathesis) and a psychological disturbance (stress).

can be a long-term pattern of such emotional reactions, adding up to an ulcer-prone personality. We turn first to the evidence that emotional states influence peptic ulcer, and then we examine the possibility that individuals who have a certain personality pattern of reacting to stress are ulcer prone.

GASTRIC SECRETION, PEPTIC ULCER, AND EMOTIONAL STATES

Let us now take a look at the evidence that emotional states affect gastric secretion. Two researchers were afforded a rare opportunity to study directly the effects of anxiety and depression on digestion when they discovered a man who, because of a childhood experience, was forced to feed himself through a hole in his stomach.

> Tom was a fifty-seven-year-old workman who at age seven swallowed some very hot soup, which so burnt his esophagus that it had to be surgically sealed off. After many unsuccessful attempts at corrective surgery, Tom had to resort to feeding himself by chewing his food (to satisfy his taste) and then depositing the food directly into his stomach using a funnel and a rubber tube. He was secretive about this for many years, but when he was in his fifties, Tom allowed himself to be experimented upon. Investigators directly examined his gastric secretions under different emotional conditions. When Tom was anxious, angry, or resentful, gastric secretions increased. When he was sad, his gastric secretions decreased. (Wolff, 1965)

In another study, thirteen patients with ulcers and thirteen normal subjects were interviewed under emotion-provoking conditions. The patients with ulcers showed a greater secretion of hydrochloric acid in the stomach and more stomach motility than the patients without ulcers (Mittelmann, Wolff, and Scharf, 1942). Findings with normal individuals under hypnosis also confirmed that gastric secretions are influenced by emotion. Hypnotically induced thoughts of anger and anxiety produced high gastric secretion, while thoughts of depression, helplessness, and hopelessness produced low secretion (Kehoe and Ironside, 1963).

High rates of peptic ulcers were found in people in occupations that produce high anxiety. For example, air traffic controllers have twice the ulcer rate of matched control groups, and those controllers who work at towers with much traffic have twice the ulcer rate of those who work at towers with less traffic (Cobb and Rose, 1973). We must be cautious, however, about this correlation between occupation and ulcers. It could be that ulcer-prone individuals, for some reason, choose anxiety-provoking jobs. If this is the case, it need not be the anxiety of the job that causes the ulcer.

The evidence presented above does suggest that emotional states like anxiety and anger cause excess stomach acid; this in turn, contributes to the development of peptic ulcers. Also, certain anxiety-producing occupations may lead to more employees with stomach ulcers. Here again, greater anxiety produces excess acid in the stomach. This latter point fits in with Carlos's story narrated earlier. Like many individuals with ulcers, Carlos's ulcer worsened and caused more pain after emotional crises. When he was anxious, needed reassurance, and felt excessive demands for responsibility, his ulcer flared up. When he allowed himself to be dependent, his ulcer was inactive.

ANIMAL MODELS OF PEPTIC ULCER

Some investigators have shed light on the relation between emotional states and ulcers by studying animals. In doing so, they have put animals in conditions that change the emotional state of the animal. We will look at three such situations: conflict, unpredictability, and uncontrollability. All of these factors increase anxiety.

Conflict   Can "conflict" be aroused in a rat in order to find out whether or not conflict produces ulcers? One way to bring about conflict is to make a hungry rat run through shock in order to get food. This is called an "avoidance-approach" conflict. In one experiment, one group of rats was required to cross a shock grid in order to obtain food and water for forty-seven out of forty-eight hour cycles. During one hour, the grid was not electrified so that the animals could have sufficient water and food. Six of nine rats in this group developed ulcers, whereas none of the comparison group rats did. Control groups with shock alone, food and water deprivation alone, or nothing got fewer ulcers. So avoidance-approach conflict is more likely to produce stomach ulcers than is electric shock, hunger, or thirst without conflict (Sawrey, Conger, and Turrell, 1956; Sawrey and Weiss, 1956). Conflict, a psychological state that produces anxiety, can thus engender ulcers in rats.

Unpredictability   When noxious events are experienced by an individual, they can either be signaled, and therefore predictable, or unsignaled, and therefore

▲ Fighting oil fires in Kuwait is one example of an anxiety-producing job. We might expect these workers, like air traffic controllers, to have a high incidence of peptic ulcers.

▶ The gas masks these Saudi Arabians wear, even during prayer, are evidence of the unpredictable and uncontrollable sources of stress they endured during the 1991 Persian Gulf war. The constitutionally vulnerable among them would have been likely to develop ulcers.

unpredictable. For example, the rockets that fell on London in World War II were signaled by an air raid siren. But when a concentration camp guard arbitrarily singled out a prisoner for a beating, this was entirely unsignaled. There is considerable evidence, both in rats and humans, that when noxious events are signaled, individuals are terrified during the signal. But they also learn that when the signal is not on, the noxious event does not occur, so they are safe and can relax. Also, if something can be done, a signal allows a person to prepare for the bad event. In contrast, when the identical noxious event occurs without a signal, individuals are afraid all the time because they have no signal of safety that tells them they can relax (Seligman and Binik, 1977). Since oversecretion of gastric juices occurs during anxiety and more anxiety occurs with unpredictability, we might expect that more ulcers would occur as well. It has been found that they do.

In one study, investigators took two groups of rats and deprived them of food. Each group received occasional brief electric shocks. For one group, the shocks were predictable: each shock was preceded by a tone or a light. Another group of rats received exactly the same shocks and at the same times, but they had no signal to tell them when shock would occur and therefore no absence of signal to tell them when they were safe. More of the rats who received unpredictable shock formed ulcers, and the ulcers they formed were larger than those in the predictable shock group. Being in the presence of chronic anxiety—as produced by unpredictable shock—causes ulcers in rats (Seligman, 1968; Weiss, 1968).

Uncontrollability When noxious events occur, sometimes you can do something about them, but at other times you are helpless. So, for example, being a victim of lung cancer is at least partly controllable; you can take action to avoid lung cancer by not smoking cigarettes. Losing your job during a national depression, however, is quite uncontrollable. There is very little you can do to protect your job once economic panic has set in and most of your colleagues are being fired. More precisely, an event is *uncontrollable* when no response an individual can make will change the probability of the event. An event is *controllable* when at least one response the individual has in his repertoire can change the proba-

▶ People who work on the stock exchange may feel they can do little to protect their jobs if economic panic sets in. They may be more prone to ulcers than people in other jobs.

▼ Uncontrollable life events like the death of a close relative can be a factor in psychosomatic problems. This boy is attending his father's funeral in Bosnia.

bility of the event. Which produces more ulcers, controllable or uncontrollable dangers?

In 1958, a study now known as the "executive monkey" study was performed. (See Chapter 6, where we discussed this study in the context of the confound of nonrandom assignment.) Eight monkeys were given occasional electric shocks. Four of them could avoid the shocks by pressing a lever. The other four received exactly the same shocks as their four executive partners, but they were helpless; no response that they made would affect whether or not they were shocked. Only their executive partners' actions made any difference. The monkeys could not see or hear each other. The executives in each of the four pairs developed duodenal ulcers and died; their helpless partners remained healthy (Brady, 1958). The conclusion from this study was that having control over threat would cause ulcers. The moral was that executives, or others in a position of great responsibility, would be more prone to ulcers than their employees.

This study was widely publicized, and for years many believed it was valid. It is, however, an artifact. When experimenters in the 1960s had trouble replicating it, the details of the procedure were scrutinized. As it turned out, the eight monkeys had not been randomly assigned to the executive group. The four monkeys who probably had been the most emotionally reactive had become the executives and had developed the ulcers; but it probably had been their preexisting high emotionality (which was indicated by their readiness to lever press when shocked) and not the fact of having to execute a controlling response, which had produced the ulcers.

In another study, the methodological problems of the executive monkey study were avoided and the opposite results were obtained. Rats were divided into six groups. Two of the groups received escapable shock, shock they could turn off by rotating a wheel in front of them. Two of the groups were "yoked." They received exactly the same pattern of shock, but it was inescapable—no response they made affected the shock; it went on and off for them at the same time as for their "executive" partners in the "escapable" group. Two of the groups received no shock. Within each of these groups, shock was either signaled or unsignaled. In this experiment, then, both the controllability and pre-

TABLE 10-1

MEDIAN NUMBER OF ULCERS AND WHEEL TURNS

	Ulcers	Wheel Turns
Escape Groups		
Signaled	2.0	3,717
Unsignaled	3.5	13,992
Yoked, Inescapable Groups		
Signaled	3.5	1,404
Unsignaled	6.0	4,357
No Shock Groups		
Signaled	1.0	60
Unsignaled	1.0	51

SOURCE: Adapted from Weiss, 1971.

dictability of the shock were varied. The rats were assigned to these six groups randomly, thereby distributing any preexisting emotionality equally among the groups (Weiss, 1971).

As can be seen from Table 10–1, two basic findings emerged. First, unpredictability leads to ulcers—the rats developed more ulcers when they were subjected to unsignaled than to signaled shock, whether or not they could escape it. Second, uncontrollability leads to ulcers—rats who received inescapable shock developed more ulcers than rats who could escape shock, whether or not the shock was signaled.

What are we to conclude from this and other animal studies? First of all, it seems clear that the "executives" were actually less likely to develop ulcers. Second, this and other studies set up three conditions—conflict, unpredictability, and uncontrollability—that produce anxiety, and eventually a greater number of ulcers. Research on how humans react in parallel situations continues. Indeed, our environment may well be constructed in a way to produce ulcers in some individuals.

Treatment of Peptic Ulcers

In times past, peptic ulcers were treated primarily by giving patients antacid drugs in an attempt to lower stomach acidity. In addition, bland diets that restricted intake of foods that stimulate hydrochloric acid secretion were recommended to patients. Smoking, drinking alcohol, and drinking coffee or tea were also restricted. About half of the ulcers usually healed under such a regimen. In the late 1970s, a new drug—cimetidine—came into use. Cimetidine reduces stomach acid by about two-thirds, and it produces healing in 70 to 95 percent of patients with peptic ulcers in a few months. Relapse rate is high, however, with 50 percent recurrence in six months (Bardhan, 1980; Alper, 1993).

Psychological treatments of ulcers are less well charted. Rest, relaxation, anxiety management, and removal from the external sources of psychological stress are often prescribed for ulcer patients, and there is at least strong clinical evidence that these are effective. Psychoanalytic therapy has been reported to be effective with ulcer patients, but the appropriate controlled studies have yet to be done (Orgel, 1985).

To summarize, peptic ulcers are best viewed within a diathesis-stress model. A peptic ulcer is caused when gastric juice that is naturally secreted in the stomach eats a hole into the protective mucous membrane of the stomach or the duodenum. This erosion is the ulcer. Three kinds of constitutional weaknesses or "diatheses," can make an individual prone to ulcers: (1) an oversecretion of gastric juices, which may be genetically inherited; (2) a weak mucous membrane; and (3) a stomach lining that regenerates slowly. Psychological factors can also influence the formation of a peptic ulcer in individuals who have such a diathesis. There is evidence that emotional states, particularly anxiety, cause oversecretion of acid in the stomach. In addition, there is further experimental evidence that rats who experience anxiety when placed in conflict, in the presence of unpredictable stressors, or in the presence of uncontrollable stressors develop peptic ulcers. This suggests that chronic or frequent anxiety may cause oversecretion of stomach acid which, in turn, may produce ulcers in individuals whose gastrointestinal system is genetically vulnerable.

CARDIOVASCULAR DISORDERS

In the last century, Sir William Osler (1849–1919), a famous Canadian physician, prefigured what was to be learned in our century about personality and heart attacks:

> A man who has early risen and late taken rest, who has eaten the bread of carefulness, striving for success in commercial, professional, or political life, after twenty-five or thirty years of incessant toil, reaches the point where he can say, perhaps with just satisfaction, "Soul, thou has much goods laid up for many years; take thine ease," all unconscious that the fell sergeant has already issued the warrant. (Osler, 1897)

Coronary heart disease (CHD) kills more people than any other disease in the Western world. In the United States, over half the deaths of individuals over forty-five are caused by some form of heart or circulatory problem (Lachman, 1972; Weiner, 1977). The underlying condition in most instances of heart attack and sudden death is ***arteriosclerosis,*** a building up of fat on the inner walls of the coronary arteries. Such clogging blocks blood from reaching the heart muscle; heart attack and sudden death can result (Diamond, 1982).

Epidemiologists have thoroughly studied risk factors for CHD. There are seven major physical risk factors: (1) growing old, (2) being male, (3) smoking cigarettes, (4) having high blood pressure, (5) having high serum cholesterol, (6) physical inactivity, and (7) genetics. A psychological risk factor now joins the list: the Type A personality, which we will consider here.

Defining the Type A Personality

Type A personality was said to have been discovered by an upholsterer. When he came to reupholster the chairs in the office of a physician who spe-

FOCUS QUESTIONS

1. Distinguish between Type A and Type B personalities.
2. What components of Type A may lead to coronary heart disease?
3. What role might helplessness play in CHD, and why might a Type A's reaction to helplessness predispose him to CHD?
4. Why might Type A's have prolonged emergency reactions, and why might this make them at greater risk for CHD?

FIGURE 10-2

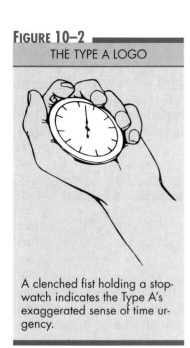

A clenched fist holding a stopwatch indicates the Type A's exaggerated sense of time urgency.

cialized in seeing patients who had had heart attacks, he noticed that the chairs were worn in the front of the seat, not the back. Coronary-prone individuals, Type A's, sit on the edge of their chair. They are defined by (1) an exaggerated sense of time urgency—deadlines are always with them (see Figure 10–2), (2) competitiveness and ambition, and (3) aggressiveness and hostility, particularly when things get in their way. They contrast to **Type B personalities,** who are relaxed, serene, and have no sense of time urgency. When Type A's miss a bus, they become upset. When Type B's miss a bus, they say to themselves, "Why worry? There will always be another bus coming along." The Type A sees the environment as threatening, and seems to be engaged in prolonged emergency reactions. Type A characteristics may begin when a person is as young as three or four years old (Steinberg, 1986).

Classifying individuals into Type A's and Type B's is done either by a standard stress interview or by a self-administered questionnaire (Jenkins, Rosenman, and Friedman, 1967; Glass, 1977). Typical questions are:

1. "Has your spouse or friend ever told you that you eat too fast?" Type A's say, "yes, often." Type B's say "yes, once or twice" or "no."
2. "How would your spouse (or best friend) rate your general level of activity?" Type A's say, "too active, need to slow down." Type B's say, "too slow, should be more active."
3. "Do you ever set deadlines or quotas for yourself at work or at home?" Type A's say, "yes, once a week or more often." Type B's say, "no" or "only occasionally."
4. "When you are in the midst of doing a job and someone (not your boss) interrupts you, how do you feel inside?" Type A's say, "I really feel irritated because most such interruptions are unnecessary." Type B's say, "I feel O.K. because I work better after an occasional break."

Type A's at Risk for CHD

Several excellent prospective studies exist of the Type A personality as a risk factor for CHD in the population at large:

- *The Western Collaborative Study.* Beginning in 1960, 3,200 working men who had no history of CHD were followed in a longitudinal study. Men who had been judged Type A by the structured interview had 2.2 times as much CHD as Type B's. When the physical risk factors were statistically controlled, Type A's still had double the risk for CHD (Rosenman, Brand, Jenkins, Friedman, Straus, and Wurm, 1975; Hecker, Chesney, Black, and Frautschi, 1988; Carmelli, Dame, Swan, and Rosenman, 1991).
- *The Framingham Heart Study.* More than 1,600 men and women, who were classified Type A or B by a questionnaire and who were free of any CHD, were followed for eight years. White-collar Type A men had almost three times the risk of CHD as white-collar Type B's (Haynes, Feinleib, and Kannel, 1980; Eaker, Haynes, and Feinleib, 1983).
- *The Belgian Heart Disease Prevention Trial.* Two thousand men, having demonstrated good health by passing a strenuous exercise test, were rated along the Type A–B continuum and followed for five years. The upper third had 1.9 times the risk for CHD as the lower third (Kittel, Kornitzer, deBacker, and Dramaix, 1982).

The conclusion that Type A is a risk factor for CHD has not gone unchallenged. When the population at large is studied, as above, the relationship holds; but when the population is selected to be at high risk already or at low risk already, Type A does not predict CHD. In the Honolulu Heart Program study, 2,200 Japanese-Americans, a low-risk group, were followed for eight years; this sample had only about half the incidence of heart attacks as a Caucasian sample. Type A did not predict increased risk here (Cohen and Reed, 1985). In the MRFIT (Multiple Risk Factor Intervention Trial), a very high-risk group was followed for seven years. These men were selected because they scored in the top 10 percent for risk, based on smoking, cholesterol, and blood pressure. Here, also, being Type A did not confer extra risk for CHD (Shekelle, Hulley, Neaton, et al., 1985).

Type A Dissected

From these studies, we could conclude that Type A confers extra risk for CHD in the general population. But Type A is a global and heterogeneous concept, that is, researchers have defined Type A using four factors: aggressiveness, time urgency, competitiveness, and ambitiousness. In addition to these defining components, there are many factors that correlate with these components: People who are time urgent and ambitious might have more encounters with defeat, failure, and helplessness. People who are competitive might spend more time in the emergency reaction. Could it be that one of the components, or a correlated factor, is the killer? We will examine two possibilities—hostility and helplessness—and then propose a third—more total emergency reaction—that seem to integrate the evidence.

HOSTILITY AND THE TYPE A

Hostility and anger may be the killing components of Type A. It has long been suspected that high blood pressure, also called **hypertension,** may be intimately related to hostility and to how we deal with our anger (Diamond, 1982). Psychodynamic theorists believe that dammed-up hostility underlies the hypertensive personality. Franz Alexander theorized that individuals with high blood pressure were struggling against their own aggressive impulses (Alexander, French, and Pollack, 1968). Later studies also suggested that hypertensives are particularly sensitive to hostility and respond with blood pressure elevation to threat in general and anger toward the threat in particular (Wolf, Cardon, Shepard, and Wolff, 1955; Kaplan, Gottschalk, Magliocco, Rohobit, and Ross, 1960). Other studies showed that opportunities to vent hostility lower blood pressure, and the failure to release hostility may keep blood pressure high (Hokanson, 1961; Hokanson and Burgess, 1962; Hokanson, Willers, and Koropsak, 1968; Dimsdale, Pierce, Schoenfeld, Brown, Zusman, and Graham, 1986).

Two very long-term studies directly relate hostility to CHD. Two hundred and fifty-five physicians were given the MMPI in medical school and were followed for twenty-five years (see Figure 10–3). One component of the MMPI is the Cook-Medley hostility score (Cook and Medley, 1954). High hostility scores strongly predicted CHD (Barefoot, Dahlstrom, and Williams, 1983; Williams, Barefoot, and Shekelle, 1985). This relationship was replicated in the Western Electric Study of 1,877 men followed for ten years. The high hostility men had five times the incidence of CHD (Shekelle, Gale, Ostfeld, and Paul, 1983).

▼ Hostility and anger may lead to hypertension, although the opportunity to vent hostility may lower blood pressure.

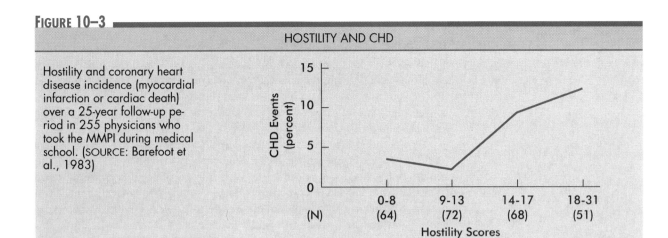

FIGURE 10–3

HOSTILITY AND CHD

Hostility and coronary heart disease incidence (myocardial infarction or cardiac death) over a 25-year follow-up period in 255 physicians who took the MMPI during medical school. (SOURCE: Barefoot et al., 1983)

Hostility is not distributed evenly over the American population, however. Poor, black males both have the most measured hostility and the highest rates of overall poor health and specifically CHD (Barefoot, Peterson, Dahlstrom, et al., 1991; Anderson, 1993; Treiber, Davis, Musante, et al., 1993). The direction of the causal arrow, however, remains to be determined. It could be that hostility directly causes poor health, particularly among poor minority men, or that poor health causes hostility, or that the frustrating grind of poverty causes both hostility and poor health (Smith, 1992). It could even be that some unmeasured third variable, like genetics, causes both a predisposition to hostility and poor health.

The studies of the Type A personality seem to indicate that where hostility and anger exist and are not released in Type A's, there is more likelihood of CHD and heart attacks. In two of the prospective studies of Type A and CHD, separate analyses were done for different components of Type A. In the Western Collaborative Study, those men who had heart attacks had been judged at the outset to have had significantly more "potential for anger," more explosive voices, more irritation when waiting, and frequent outwardly directed anger. In the Framingham Study, Type A white-collar men who did not outwardly express anger and Type A women who did not discuss their anger had more CHD (Matthews and Haynes, 1986).

In an exploration of the mechanism by which hostility might damage the heart, eighteen men angrily recounted incidents from their lives that had annoyed them. As they spoke, the pumping efficiency of their heart dropped by 5 percent on average, suggesting a drop in blood flow to the heart itself. Pumping efficiency was not changed by other stressors (Ironson, Taylor, Boltwood, et al., 1992; see also Krantz, Helmers, Bairey, et al., 1991). It has been speculated that hormonal changes during anger may provide a link from anger to CHD. To test this, the blood of 90 newlywed couples was monitored for hormonal changes during conflict. Hostile behavior was associated with significant changes in five different hormones (Williams, Lane, Kuhn, et al., 1982; Malarkey, Kiecolt-Glaser, Pearl, and Glaser, 1994). Whether it is expressing anger, damming up anger, or just underlying anger that produces CHD, and how the link from anger to hormonal changes to coronary changes actually works remain two of the most intriguing questions in health psychology today.

HELPLESSNESS AND THE TYPE A

Helplessness is not one of the defining components of the Type A personality, but it may correlate highly with it. People who are ambitious, competitive, and time urgent may get themselves into more situations that produce more frustration, failure, and helplessness, and they may react more strongly to helplessness than do Type B's (see Figure 10–4).

Type A individuals seem to be engaged in a lifelong struggle to control a world they see as threatening. David Glass suggests that it is this struggle for control that crucially distinguishes a Type A from a Type B personality. Glass postulates that a cycle of desperate efforts to control the environment, alternating with giving up when the environment proves uncontrollable, is repeated over and over again during the lifetime of the Type A individual. This struggle may result in high blood pressure and other physiological changes that in turn cause heart attacks.

Glass has demonstrated that Type A's and Type B's show a different reaction to helplessness and that it is this reaction that may predispose them to CHD (see Chapter 11). Both Type A and Type B subjects are presented with cognitive problems that are unsolvable, and failure is made highly salient. Type A's response to this uncontrollable and highly stressful situation is

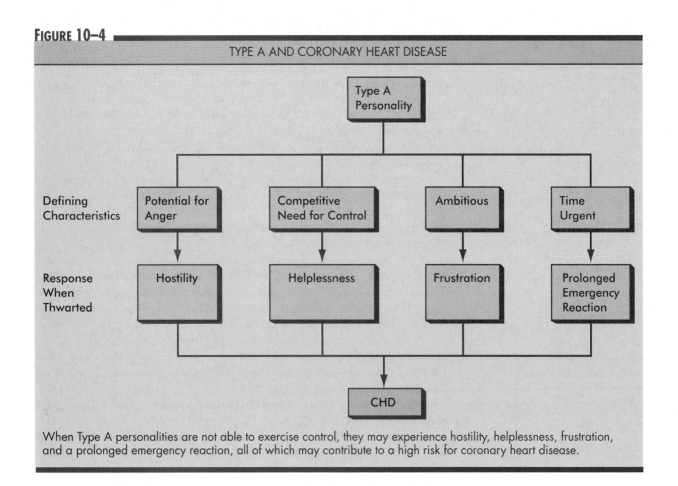

FIGURE 10–4

TYPE A AND CORONARY HEART DISEASE

When Type A personalities are not able to exercise control, they may experience hostility, helplessness, frustration, and a prolonged emergency reaction, all of which may contribute to a high risk for coronary heart disease.

twofold: (1) they respond to salient and stressful threats to their sense of control with desperate efforts to keep control, and (2) when they are forced into the recognition that they are helpless, their giving up is profound, and they fail to solve cognitive problems given later in the experiment. Type B individuals do not give up in such a profound way, and they end up solving more easily the solvable problems given later. This confirms Glass's suggestion that a life of attempting to control, then giving up, then trying all over again, may characterize Type A individuals and predispose them to CHD.

A second line of evidence comes from a study of "inhibited need for power" and hypertension. Seventy-eight Harvard juniors were tested in the late 1930s and early 1940s for high blood pressure and various personality characteristics. Ten years later, these individuals were given a projective test in which they told stories about five pictures from the TAT (see Chapter 7). The themes of the stories they told were used as indications of what their personalities were like. Twenty years later, in the early 1970s, these men were tested for high blood pressure. The findings were remarkable.

The expression of need for power and need for affiliation was judged from their TAT stories. A person was scored as having a high need for power if his story contained a reference to having an impact on others by aggression, persuasion, and prestige. A person was scored as having a high need for affiliation if his story included being friendly with other people. Finally, a person was judged for the amount of "inhibition of the need for power" by the number of times the word "not" appeared in his stories. Those of particular theoretical interest were the men who had a high need for power (which was greater than their need for affiliation), but who showed high inhibition in their stories. Twenty-three of the men fell into this group at approximately age thirty. By the time these men were in their fifties, 61 percent had shown definite signs of hypertensive pathology, whereas only 23 percent of the remaining forty-seven men showed hypertensive pathology. These findings become even more remarkable when we realize that they are unrelated to the blood pressure of these men when they were in their thirties. In other words, at age thirty the need for power combined with its inhibition predicted that individuals would be at risk for severe high blood pressure at age fifty, irrespective of what their blood pressure was when they were thirty years old (McClelland, 1979). We can view the inhibited need for power as a sign of the repeated helplessness in these individuals' lives.

THE EMERGENCY REACTION AND TYPE A

There is one simple way to view the evidence on Type A, CHD, and hypertension. Consider the heart as a glorified pump. As a pump breaks after some fixed number of uses, so the heart fails after it has exceeded its genetically allotted number of beats. The more beats you use up, the earlier your heart will fail. Being a Type A, continually viewing the world as a hostile and threatening place, will lead to the beats being used up earlier. We saw in Chapter 8 that when we are threatened we go into an emergency reaction that involves increased heart rate and increased blood pressure (Southard, Coates, Kolodner, Parker, Padgett, and Kennedy, 1986). Continuing threat leads to a ***continual emergency reaction.*** Perhaps the Type A views the world as a more threatening place than does the Type B. Such a view may lead the Type A to experience a sustained emergency reaction, which on average will use up his allotted beats more quickly.

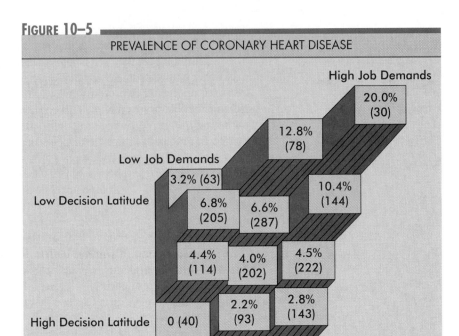

FIGURE 10–5

PREVALENCE OF CORONARY HEART DISEASE

High Job Demands

20.0% (30)

12.8% (78)

Low Job Demands

3.2% (63)

Low Decision Latitude

10.4% (144)

6.8% (205)

6.6% (287)

4.4% (114)

4.0% (202)

4.5% (222)

2.2% (93)

2.8% (143)

High Decision Latitude   0 (40)

The risk for coronary heart disease is increased where job characteristics include high demands and low decision latitude. The vertical bars indicate the percent of people developing CHD according to whether their job characteristics include high, medium, or low job demands and high, medium, or low decision latitude. There was a grand total of 1,621 men who at the beginning of the study in 1968 did not have CHD. The numbers in parentheses are the number of people in each subgroup, and the percentage is the percent of those people in the subgroup who developed symptoms of CHD over the six-year course of the study. (SOURCE: Adapted from Karasek, Baker, Marxer, Ahlbom, and Theorell, 1981)

Data on **overload** at work is compatible with this simple hypothesis (Jenkins, 1982). In the Western Collaborative Study, men who carried two jobs were at greater risk for CHD. In a particularly elegant analysis, job demand and decision latitude were related to CHD (Karasek, Baker, Marxer, Ahlbom, and Theorell, 1981). Among over 1,500 Swedish workers, a hectic and demanding job increased the risk for CHD, as did low amount of choice (see Figure 10–5). We might infer from this that workers whose jobs create the most frequent emergency reactions (high demand, low choice) use up their beats faster than those with other kinds of jobs, and such workers are at greater CHD risk.

Further evidence for the possibility that people who have prolonged emergency reactions are at greater risk for CHD comes from a prospective, longitudinal study of 126 alumni from the Harvard classes of 1952–1954. As students, these men were given an experimental stress test in which there was persistent criticism and harassment from the experimenter. Thirty-five years later, the amount of CHD was 2.5 times as great in those who experienced severe anxiety during the stress test than in those who did not (Russek, King, Russek, and Russek, 1990).

Finally, it is of considerable importance that physical activity and exercise lower the risk for CHD. In a review of forty-three studies, inactivity presented a consistent risk for CHD of about the same size as high blood pressure, smoking, or high cholesterol (Powell, Thompson, Caspersen, and Kendrick, 1987). The practical importance of this study is that in prevention programs, regular exercise should be promoted strongly. The theoretical importance concerns the emergency reaction: While vigorous exercise increases heart rate and blood pressure when you are engaged in it, its long-term consequences are to lower resting heart rate and blood pressure, thereby conserving the pump.

Sudden Death

In the phenomenon of **sudden death,** the individual perceives the environment as threatening, but gives up rather than mobilizing against the danger. Sudden death is believed to have a cardiovascular basis and, as mentioned previously, may result from arteriosclerosis. The following case describes how sudden death may result when an individual is convinced that she is about to die and so gives up:

> In 1967 a distraught woman, pleading for help, entered the Baltimore City Hospital a few days before her 23rd birthday. She and two other girls had been born of different mothers assisted by the same midwife in the Okefenokee Swamp on a Friday the 13th. The midwife cursed all three babies, saying one would die before her 16th birthday, another before her 21st birthday, and the third before her 23rd birthday. The first had died in a car crash during her 15th year; the second was accidentally shot to death in a nightclub fight on the evening of her 21st birthday. Now she, the third, waited in terror for her own death. The hospital somewhat skeptically admitted her for observation. The next morning two days before her 23rd birthday, she was found dead in her hospital bed—physical cause unknown. (Seligman, 1975, p. 5)

One sequence of events that could produce sudden death seems to be the following: (1) perceiving a strong threat to life followed by giving up and accepting one's fate, (2) a depressed, quiescent state; and (3) death.

THE EFFECTS OF HOPELESSNESS AND HELPLESSNESS

Curt Richter, an American psychologist, studied the phenomenon of sudden death in animals. Richter found that, on occasion, when he held a wild rat tightly it would die—right there, in his hand (Richter, 1957b). He hypothesized that when animals gave up in the face of threat and entered a state of hopelessness, they would die. To test this, he took wild rats and held them in his (chain-mailed) gloved hand until they stopped struggling. (For a wild rat, being held by a human is probably like being grabbed by a hawk.) Then Richter put them in a vat of water three feet deep with a jet of water playing down on them to stop them from floating. The rats would swim for three to five minutes, then dive to the bottom and drown. Death probably involved cardiac failure. In contrast, wild rats who had not been restrained in the experimenter's hand until they gave up would swim from sixty to eighty hours—vigorously trying to survive.

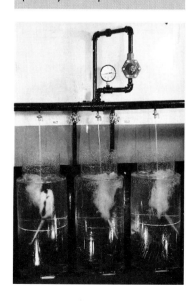

▼ This is the apparatus Curt Richter used in his experiments on sudden death. Richter found that some rats drowned within a few minutes of being placed in the apparatus, apparently of "hopelessness."

There were two findings that led Richter to believe that these were deaths from hopelessness. The first was that if he took the rat and held it in his hand until it stopped struggling, then released the rat "showing the rat there was hope," held the rat in his hand again, released it, then held it until it stopped struggling, and finally put it in the vat, the rat would swim for between sixty and eighty hours. Second, if he restrained the rat in his hand until it gave up, then put the rat in the water and waited three to five minutes until the rat started to go down, plucked it out, released it—again "showing it there was hope"—and then repeated the process several times, when the rat was finally placed in the water it would swim for sixty to eighty hours.

In another study, depression predicted high risk for death in the ten years following a stroke. One hundred and three patients were assessed for depression within two weeks of having a stroke. These patients were then followed for the next ten years. Patients who were most depressed after their strokes were 3.4 times more likely to die, and 90 percent of the depressed people who had few social contacts died. The rate of death for depressed patients exceeded that predicted by other risk factors like sex, age, and amount of brain damage (Morris, Robinson, Andrzejewski, et al., 1993).

Loss of one's spouse by death can be an experience that engenders profound hopelessness. Following the death of their wives, 4,500 British widowers fifty-five years or older were identified from British records. During the first six months of their bereavement, 213 of them died. This is 40 percent more than the expected mortality for men of this age. Susceptibility to death during bereavement seems to be concentrated in the first six months, since the death rate returns to normal thereafter. Most of these men died from cardiac problems (Parkes, Benjamin, and Fitzgerald, 1969; Helsing, Szklo, and Comstock, 1981).

The structure of some institutions may promote helplessness and hopelessness on a massive scale. Consider patient care in nursing homes. When we arrange care for the elderly, there is sometimes a tendency to try to do everything for them. On the one hand, this seems benevolent, but on the other hand, we end up taking all of their control away. By treating them as total patients, we undermine self-care (Bandura, 1982).

FIGURE 10–6

SCHEMA OF THE IMMUNE RESPONSE

Once the immune system recognizes an antigen such as a tumor, it takes action to inactivate and remove it. B-cells specific to the antigen multiply and produce antibodies that activate K-cells that work to destroy the antigen. T-cells multiply and either directly kill the antigen or activate macrophages and NK cells that work to destroy the antigen.

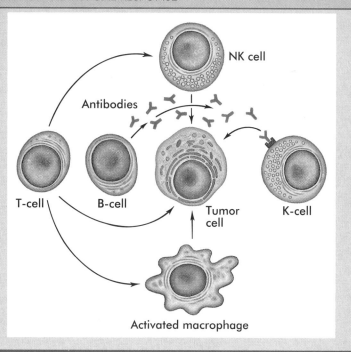

on the antigen the first time will multiply more rapidly the second time this antigen is spotted. This memory is responsible for **immunization. Immunocompetence,** the degree to which these events proceed efficiently to protect the organism, is measured in several ways: assessing the amount of immunoglobulin (antibodies formed after immunization) in the blood or saliva, assessing the amount of T-cell multiplication when antigens are challenged, assessing the ability of Natural Killer cells to kill tumors, and measuring how much the skin reddens and swells when injected with an antigen (the greater the reaction, the better the immune system is working) through the delayed hypersensitivity test.

LOWERED IMMUNOCOMPETENCE IN HUMANS

Evidence is accumulating that psychological states produce immune and disease changes in humans (see Box 10–1). There are several examples of how depression, helplessness, hopelessness, and stressful life events seem linked to immune change in people. In one study, infectious illness and number of doctor visits were counted for undergraduates who had either an optimistic or pessimistic explanatory style. In the year following the test for explanatory style, pessimists had about twice as many infectious illnesses and made about twice as many visits to doctors as optimists (Peterson and Seligman, 1987). In another study, twenty-six spouses whose mates had died were followed for six weeks after the death of their spouses; the bereaved group showed depressed T-cell multiplication to antigens (Bartrop, Luckhurst, Lazarus, Kiloh, and Penny, 1977). In a different study of senior citizens, blood was drawn after explanatory style had been

Box 10-1

PSYCHOTHERAPY FOR BREAST CANCER

One of the most insidious of all illnesses influenced by psychological factors is cancer. There is mounting evidence that hopelessness may play a role in susceptibility to cancer. Fifty-one women who entered a Rochester, New York, clinic for a cancer test were interviewed upon arriving. Each of these women had previously shown suspicious cells in her cervix which might indicate cancer, but which could not definitely be diagnosed as cancer without further testing. The investigators found that eighteen of these fifty-one women had experienced significant losses in the last six months to which they reacted with feelings of hopelessness and helplessness. The others had experienced no such life event. Of the eighteen who had experienced hopelessness, eleven were found to have cancer. Of the thirty-three, only eight had cancer. The difference between the two groups was statistically significant (Schmale and Iker, 1966). Similarly, lack of meaning in one's life, job instability, and no plans for the future predict who has lung cancer better than does the amount of smoking (Horne and Picard, 1979). Conversely, breast cancer patients who responded with a fighting spirit rather than stoic acceptance had a better chance of recurrence-free survival five years later (Greer, Morris, Pettingale, 1979).

David Spiegel and his colleagues at Stanford University have been pioneers in taking the knowledge that there are psychological influences on disease, specifically breast cancer, and working to develop psychological therapies to treat this physical disease (Spiegel, Bloom, Kraemer, and Gottheil, 1989). To this end, they followed a group of eighty-six women for ten years who had been referred to them for psychotherapy after the diagnosis of metastatic breast cancer. The women were randomly assigned either to therapy or to be controls without psychotherapy. Psychotherapy lasted for a year, while routine physical treatment for breast cancer continued. Therapy focused on expressing their feelings about their illness and talking about the effect of the illness on their lives. Self-hypnosis for pain control was also taught. At no time were patients led to expect that psychotherapy would affect the course of the illness.

Ten years later, Spiegel looked at survival rates of the women in the two groups. On average, women in the psychotherapy group lived twice as long as women in the control group. The figure below represents the survival curves for the two groups of women.

Spiegel's results have been confirmed in a study of patients with malignant melanoma. After surgery for melanoma, sixty-eight patients had either six weeks of structured group psychotherapy or no psychotherapy. Five years later, thirteen of the thirty-four control patients had a recurrence of melanoma, and ten of those having the recurrence died. In contrast, only seven of the thirty-four patients who had psychotherapy had a recurrence of melanoma, and only three of those having the recurrence died. Lower initial distress at intake and more active behavioral coping predicted lower recurrence and death (Fawzy, Fawzy, Hyun, et al., 1993).

The mechanism by which this psychotherapy prolonged survival is a matter of sheer speculation, but studies such as these give us hope that the next decade will see the development of psychological interventions that may treat, and may even prevent, such illnesses as breast cancer and heart attack.

SOURCE: Spiegel, Bloom, Kraemer, and Gottheil, 1989.

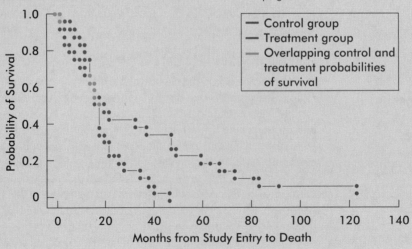

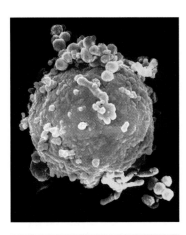

▲ B-cells are lymphocytes that are specific to a particular antigen and that can make antibodies only against that antigen. Pictured here is a B-lymphocyte (the large round body) and chlamydia bacteria (the clusters of small, round bodies). The photograph has a magnification of 14,000 times the actual size.

measured. Antigens were placed in the blood samples, and the efficiency of the immune reaction was measured. Pessimists had poorer T-cell function than optimists (Kamen-Siegel, Rodin, Seligman, and Dwyer, 1991).

In another study, Natural Killer cell activity was found to be lower in women who had recently experienced major life events like the death of their spouse; the more depressed the woman, the more both NK and T-cell functions were impaired (Irwin, Daniels, Bloom, Smith, and Weiner, 1987). In a fifth study, blood was drawn twice from seventy-five first-year medical students, one month before and then on the day of final exams. NK activity was lower just at finals time; the more loneliness and the more stressful life events reported, the lower the NK activity (Kiecolt-Glaser, Garner, Speicher, Penn, Holliday, and Glaser, 1984; Kiecolt-Glaser and Glaser, 1987).

As the population ages, more people are suffering from senile dementia (Alzheimer's disease), and many relatives have now become caregivers of Alzheimer's patients. Taking care of such a patient is a difficult and helplessness-inducing, full-time task. In a longitudinal study of the consequences of taking care of such relatives, sixty-nine spouses of Alzheimer's patients were followed for thirteen months. They were compared to a matched control group of non-caregivers. Caregivers had more days of infectious illness, primarily colds. They had more depression, and the functioning of their immune system, as measured by multiplication of cells to antigen challenge, was poorer than that of controls (Kiecolt-Glaser, Dura, Speicher, Trask, and Glaser, 1991).

Susceptibility to the common cold is now being investigated in the laboratory to determine the effects of psychological factors on the immune-disease link. In one study, 394 healthy volunteers were given controlled amounts of cold virus in a nasal spray, and the severity of the ensuing cold was measured. Subjects who had recently had more negative events in their lives, who had felt more negative affect, and who had had more perceived stress came down with worse colds (Cohen, Tyrrell, and Smith, 1993).

These studies indicate that depression, helplessness, hopelessness, and stressful life events can lower immunocompetence.

The Mind-Body Problem Re-Examined

At the beginning of this chapter we wondered how psychological states could influence physical illness. At this point, for at least one chain of events, we can speculate about a plausible route (see Figure 10–7). Consider how the experience of a loss might bring about cancer: (1) The individual whose husband has died perceives that she has lost something valuable. (2) She believes she is helpless to do anything about it, and if she has a pessimistic explanatory style she becomes severely depressed. (3) Depression and helplessness, as we will see in Chapter 11, are accompanied by depletion of certain neurotransmitters in the brain, as well as by an increase in endorphins, internal morphine-like substances that block pain. (4) The immune system has receptors for endorphins that may then lower immunocompetence. (5) If there are pathogens in the body, say the beginnings of a tumor in the uterus, NK cells and T-cells may be too inactivated to kill it. (6) A tumor that would ordinarily have been lysed in its early stages can now grow to life-threatening size.

We do not know if this schema is correct, but there is now evidence for each stage of this chain. If such a chain illuminates how tragedy can make us physically ill, there are important implications for prevention and therapy. Pro-

FIGURE 10–7

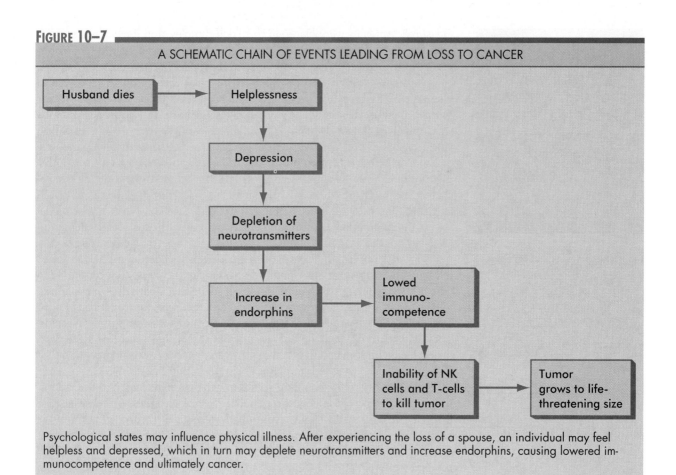

A SCHEMATIC CHAIN OF EVENTS LEADING FROM LOSS TO CANCER

Husband dies → Helplessness → Depression → Depletion of neurotransmitters → Increase in endorphins → Lowed immuno-competence → Inability of NK cells and T-cells to kill tumor → Tumor grows to life-threatening size

Psychological states may influence physical illness. After experiencing the loss of a spouse, an individual may feel helpless and depressed, which in turn may deplete neurotransmitters and increase endorphins, causing lowered immunocompetence and ultimately cancer.

cedures that intervene at each of the steps might prevent or even reverse such illnesses. So, for example, cognitive therapy might be used to prevent the perception of helplessness or the depressive response, thereby interrupting the chain. Or drug therapy that breaks the catecholamine-endorphin link or blocks the immune receptors to endorphin stimulation might also interrupt the chain. We believe the final decade of this century will see major advances in this area.

There is no mysterious connection between mind and body with such a chain of events. Depression and pessimism, just like neurotransmitter level, endorphin level, and the lysing of tumor cells are variables that can be operationally defined and measured. An error of measurement can be computed for both the "mental" and the "physical" variables, and the size of both these kinds of errors are usually quite comparable. These variables are then entered into a correlational chain that computes the effect of one variable on the next in the temporal sequence. When an earlier variable predicts the occurrence of a later variable, over and above the other variables, a causal link is confirmed. Links between mental events like depression and physical events like the lysing of tumor cells are correlational in nature, in exactly the same way that the links between neurotransmitter changes and endorphin changes are merely correlational in nature. The links between different kinds of physical events are identical to the links between mental and physical events. Neither are like the observation of one billiard ball hitting another, the old-fashioned causal model that gave rise to the mind-body problem in the first place, and so this kind of science dissolves the hoary mind-body problem.

THEORIES OF PSYCHOSOMATIC ILLNESS

We have now had a detailed look at two physical problems that are influenced by psychological factors: stomach ulcers and coronary heart disease. In addition to these two, many other diseases are often thought to have psychosomatic components: migraine headaches, arthritis, chronic pain, and asthma, among others (see Box 10–2).

Let us now look at the different principles that recur through explanations of the cause and the alleviation of these psychosomatic disorders. There are four theories, and they correspond to four of the schools of abnormality: biomedical, psychodynamic, behavioral, and cognitive. All are compatible with the diathesis-stress perspective.

Box 10–2

ASTHMA IN CHILDREN AND FAMILY SEPARATION

Asthma is a condition in which the air passages of the bronchia narrow, swell, and secrete excess fluid to a variety of stimuli. This results in wheezing, which in its worst form can be severe and can produce a convulsive struggle for breath. Asthma can be caused by infection, by allergy, or by psychological factors. It has been estimated that each of these plays the dominant role in about a third of the cases (Weiner, 1977). Put differently, asthma stems from psychological sources in only a minority of cases. In this minority, the personal relations between parents and the asthmatic child have long been suspected to be the major source of psychological disturbance.

Anecdotes indicated that when European children with asthma were sent off by their parents to spas "to take the waters" they cheerfully ignored their parents' long lists of instructions, showed few signs of asthma, and seemed to be psychologically improved as well. To test the possibility that separation from parents might alleviate asthma, Dennis Purcell and his colleagues chose twenty-five chronically asthmatic school children who lived with their families (Purcell, Brady, Chai, Muser, Molk, Gordon, and Means, 1969). They divided these children into two groups—those in whom emotional factors had usually preceded past attacks of asthma at home, and those in whom emotional factors seemed

irrelevant to the onset of past attacks. The first group was expected to benefit from separation, but not the second.

The parents and siblings were removed from the home and sent to a motel for two weeks, while the child continued to live in his home environment. A surrogate parent was provided, and the child continued normal attendance at school and normal play activities. After two weeks of not seeing their child, the parents returned to the home and life went on as usual.

As predicted, the effects were beneficial for the group suspected of emotionally induced asthma. Their medication during separation was reduced by half during daily physician checks, and on top of this the number of asthma attacks and amount of wheezing was reduced by half as well. When the parents returned, wheezing, number of attacks, and amount of necessary medication all increased. Beneficial effects of separation on asthma did not appear for the group in which emotional factors had been judged unimportant.

So, for some children, emotional factors are probably irrelevant to asthma. For others, however, family stresses may set off or worsen asthmatic attacks. In these cases, if the family members learn more effective and less stressful ways of dealing with each other, the child's asthma may get better.

1. How does the biomedical model explain psychosomatic disorders through genetics, specific organ vulnerability, evolution, and stress?
2. What is the psychodynamic explanation of psychosomatic disorder?
3. What roles do conditioning, cognitions, life events (controllable vs. uncontrollable), and lifestyle play in psychosomatic disorders?

The Biomedical Model of Psychosomatic Disorders

The biomedical model emphasizes the diathesis underlying psychosomatic illness. There are four components that fall under the biomedical view: genetic, specific organ vulnerability, evolutionary selection, and the general adaptation syndrome. These components do not all exclude one another, and most biomedical theorists emphasize more than one of them when explaining psychosomatic disorders.

GENETIC

Is the predisposition to psychosomatic disorders genetically inherited? We have seen evidence that this is so for ulcers. If one identical twin has ulcers, then his co-twin is more likely to have ulcers than is the case between fraternal twins. All the genes of two identical twins are the same, but only half the genes of fraternal twins are the same. The higher concordance of identical twins is most likely explained by genetics, since the environment fraternal twins share is probably almost as similar as that of identical twins. Thus, similar oversecretion of gastric juices or weakness of the mucous membrane of the stomach, each producing similar vulnerability to ulcers, is probably what is inherited.

SPECIFIC ORGAN VULNERABILITY

A variant of the genetic view holds that it is weakness in a specific organ that is inherited. That is, when an individual is stressed, the weakest link in his bodily chain snaps. The hypothesis that oversecretion of stomach acid is an inherited cause of ulcers is an instance of the specific organ vulnerability hypothesis. Organ specificity is confirmed by the fact that individuals tend to react to stress with one characteristic part of the body. Some of us usually react to stress with a queasy stomach, others with headache, others with sweating, and still others with a racing heart. Patients with ulcers react with gastric secretion, and patients with recurrent headaches tend to react with increased muscle tension (Malmo and Shagass, 1949; Lacey, 1950).

More recent evidence challenges the view that the same specific organ remains vulnerable to stress across an individual's lifespan. Ninety-five men were followed for thirty years. Men who reported one pattern of physical symptoms under stress at one time in their lives reported different patterns later. There did seem to be a natural progression of locus of symptoms over the lifespan, however. People who as adolescents reported experiencing stress with many physical symptoms—hay fever, diarrhea, asthma, palpitations—as adults experienced stress with mental symptoms—headache, insomnia, irritability (Vaillant, 1978).

EVOLUTION

Evolution may have actually favored the development of certain psychosomatic disorders. Consider the emergency reaction for which evolution has clearly selected. In a generally threatening environment, individuals who tended to perceive the world as hostile and responded crisply with elevation of blood pressure, muscle tension, and the like would be those most likely to survive and reproduce. Only under modern conditions, in which the level of physical threat has been reduced from the days of the cave and the jungle, is hypertension considered a disorder rather than a strength. Notice that hypertension

FIGURE 10–8

CHARACTERISTIC SYMPTOMS OF THE GENERAL ADAPTATION SYNDROME

Normal	Alarmed

A

B

C

Note the enlarged adrenals (A), the shrunken thymus (B) and the shrunken lymph nodes (C). (SOURCE: Selye, 1956)

does not kill young persons; it is deadly to individuals who are many years past the prime age of reproduction. This seems to suggest that tendencies to various psychosomatic disorders are inherited because at one time in history these "diseases" actually favored survival and reproduction.

STRESS AND THE GENERAL ADAPTATION SYNDROME

Hans Selye (1907–1983) integrated the emergency reaction of the sympathetic nervous system into the major theory of reaction to stress. He emphasized the stress side of the diathesis-stress model. Selye believed that the general adaptation syndrome is nonspecific, that one and the same stress reaction will occur to the whole gamut of disturbing events. He held that when a human being or an animal is stressed, a sequence of three stages called the **general adaptation syndrome** ensues. The first stage is the *alarm reaction.* After an initial phase of lowered resistance, the system goes into *counter shock*—the pituitary gland releases ACTH (adrenocorticotrophic hormone) into the bloodstream, which stimulates the adrenal cortex. This throws the organism into the emergency reaction. If the alarm reaction stage is successful, it restores bodily balance. The alarm reaction is followed by a second stage—the stage of *resistance,* in which defense and adaptation are sustained and optimal. If the stressor persists, the final stage, *exhaustion,* ensues, and adaptive responding ceases. Illness and, in some cases, death may follow (Selye, 1956).

The reaction of rats to long-term exposure to the stress of continuous cold temperatures illustrates the general adaptation syndrome. Rats were placed in a refrigerated room where the temperature was near freezing. During the first forty-eight hours, the rats showed the alarm reaction. They developed stomach ulcers, had swollen adrenals, and showed the changes of the thymus gland illustrated in Figure 10–8. The rats continued to live in this environment for many weeks. After five weeks, they had apparently entered the stage of resistance, for when these animals were placed in a still colder chamber they survived temperatures that animals who had not become adapted could not withstand. Finally, the stage of exhaustion was demonstrated. After several months

▶ Disasters like the nuclear accidents at Chernobyl and Three Mile Island have allowed researchers to develop more sophisticated theories of stress. This family living near Chernobyl was forced to move.

in the cold room, these rats could not survive a change to cold temperature that normal rats could survive.

From the point of view of this theory, symptoms such as high blood pressure and stomach ulcer may indicate that the individual is in an alarm reaction to stress. The theory postulates that psychosomatic symptoms are general stress reactions underlying the general adaptation syndrome (Selye, 1975; but see Mason, 1971, 1975).

Stress theorists traditionally rely on three basic concepts—stress, life events, and social support. Each of these concepts, however, has proven to be too global: stressors produce both good as well as the expected bad effects, life events produce illness as expected but also sometimes spurts of growth, and social support sometimes bolsters but sometimes undermines adaptive functioning (Veiel, 1993). Modern stress theorists now attempt to decompose these global notions into their constituent parts and their mechanisms. So, for example, Andrew Baum has proposed that one mechanism by which stress produces illness is by setting off intrusive thoughts—ruminations, automatic thoughts, and traumatic memories. Baum and his colleagues have followed the residents of Three Mile Island, who lived near the site of a threatened nuclear power plant explosion, since the radioactive accident in March 1979. They find that the more intrusive memories an individual has the greater the number of symptoms of somatic distress (Baum, Cohen, and Hall, 1993). Stress theory now shows promise of increasing sophistication.

The Psychodynamic Model

Diathesis and other biological considerations play a large role in the predisposition to psychosomatic disorders, but there is also evidence that personality and psychodynamics play a role as well. These factors contribute to the stress side of the diathesis-stress model.

Franz Alexander (1950) is the most influential psychoanalytic theorist of psychosomatic disorders. His view integrates genetic organ vulnerability, personality factors, and life stress. A person who is genetically vulnerable in a specific organ and has specific psychodynamic conflicts will develop disease of that organ when the stress of living arouses his psychodynamic conflicts and he is no longer able to defend against them. All three factors—a vulnerable organ system, an underlying dynamic conflict, and a precipitating life situation—interact to produce the disorder. The essence of the personality constellation for an individual who will develop peptic ulcer is conflict over dependent needs versus independent self-assertion. Alexander postulates other conflicts for asthma, arthritis, and skin disorders.

Some evidence supports this theory: from the psychological profile alone, researchers have been able to pick out which male patients have ulcer well beyond the level of chance. Further, gastric secretion occurs when the relevant emotions are aroused in individuals who have ulcers. Some evidence contradicts this theory as well, however. In Vaillant's thirty-year longitudinal study of ninety-five men, fifty developed one of the classic psychosomatic illnesses. But the locus of physical symptoms under stress did not predict which psychosomatic illness would develop. So the eleven men who eventually developed ulcers were not the same men who had earlier reported abdominal pain under stress (Vaillant, 1978).

Behavioral and Cognitive Models

Theories that stem from behavioral and cognitive views hold that learning or cognition produces psychosomatic disorders, and they emphasize the stress side of diathesis-stress. The stress can be produced by conditioning, by cognitions, or by life events.

CONDITIONING

The conditioning view of psychosomatic disorders maintains that the symptoms are a conditioned response acquired when a neutral stimulus was paired with an unconditioned stimulus that produced the disorder. For example, asthma has been conditioned in the laboratory:

> A thirty-seven-year-old shop assistant suffered from severe bronchial asthma that could be reliably set off by house dust. In the laboratory, she was sprayed with an aerosol having a neutral solvent; the aerosol was to be the conditioned stimulus. Following being sprayed with the aerosol, she inhaled house dust (unconditioned stimulus), and an asthma attack (unconditioned response) followed. Thereafter, upon inhaling from the aerosol, asthma attacks ensued. (Dekker, Pelse, and Groen, 1957)

Since individuals who suffer from asthma sometimes have attacks following exposure to highly specific events, such as experiencing a family argument or other emotional conflicts, this is an appealing model of psychosomatic illness (see again Box 10–2). It has, however, only been demonstrated under limited laboratory conditions and only some patients can be so conditioned.

COGNITIONS AND PSYCHOSOMATIC DISORDERS

Could it be that specific thoughts set off physical symptoms? William Grace and David Graham argue that an individual's perception of the world and what he thinks about threat predicts what psychosomatic disorder will develop. This argument antedates, but is wholly compatible with the cognitive model of abnormality. Grace and Graham interviewed 128 patients with a variety of diseases to find out what situations immediately preceded the onset of the symptoms and how the individual perceived what was happening to him. They found specific thoughts associated with specific illnesses. For example, individuals with high blood pressure were in a state of constant preparation to meet all threats, and when confronted with threat they thought, "Nobody is ever going to beat me. I'm ready for everything." Table 10–2 lists other illnesses that have specific thoughts associated with them (Grace and Graham, 1952). The modern cognitive school has yet to put forward a more articulate, research-supported view, but Baum may be moving stress theory toward an integration with cognitive theory (Baum, 1990).

LIFE EVENTS

Another behavioral theory of psychological influence on illness involves life stressors. It holds that stressful life events set off disease. If our reaction to stress makes us susceptible to physical disease, then frequent stressful life events should correlate with frequent disease. In the early pioneering research

TABLE 10–2

	COGNITIONS AND PSYCHOSOMATIC DISORDERS	
Illness	*Cognition*	*Examples of thoughts during illness-producing event*
1. Hives	Perception of mistreatment	"My fiance knocked me down and walked all over me, but what could I do?"
2. Eczema	Being prevented from doing something and helpless to deal with the frustration.	"I want to make my mother understand but I can't."
3. Asthma	Wishing the situation would go away or someone else would take over the responsibility for it.	"I just couldn't face it."
4. Diarrhea	Wishing to be done with the situation and have it over with.	"If the war was only over with."
5. Constipation	Grim determination to carry on when faced with an unsolvable problem.	"This marriage is never going to be any better but I won't quit."
6. Ulcer	Revenge seeking.	"He hurt me, so I wanted to hurt him."
7. Migraine headache	Engaged in an intense effort to carry out a definite plan.	"I had a million things to do before lunch."

SOURCE: Based on Grace and Graham, 1952.

on this question, Thomas Holmes and Richard Rahe devised a life events scale, the Social Readjustment Rating Scale, by having individuals rank the amount of stress different life events would cause them. Based on these rankings, Holmes and Rahe assigned a number to each stressful event (see Table 10–3). Death of a spouse was the most stressful life event; divorce and separation were near the top; taking a new job in the middle; holidays, vacations, minor violations of the law were considered the least stressful.

The more life events an individual experiences, the more likely he or she is to get sick from a variety of disorders. For example, individuals who had heart attacks had more total significant life events in the six months prior to their heart attack than in the year before. Similarly, individuals who became depressed had a larger number of life events, particularly losses, than those who did not (Holmes and Rahe, 1967; Paykel, Meyers, Dienelt, Klerman, Lindenthal, and Pfeffer, 1969; Theorell and Rahe, 1971).

Since the construction of the Social Readjustment Rating Scale, investigators have taken a closer look at the nature of the life events themselves. First of all, some of the life events listed by Holmes and Rahe could themselves reflect the fact of ongoing illness. An individual might be forced to retire (item 10) because he had high blood pressure, as opposed to getting high blood pressure as a consequence of retiring. Investigations of life events now distinguish between events that are confounded with illness and those that might contribute to it (Dohrenwend and Dohrenwend, 1974).

Second, some of the life events are positive *entrances*, such as item 25, outstanding personal achievement, while others are negative *exits*, like item 1, the

TABLE 10–3

	SOCIAL READJUSTMENT RATING SCALE	
Rank	Life event	Mean value
1	Death of spouse	100
2	Divorce	73
3	Marital separation	65
4	Jail term	63
5	Death of close family member	63
6	Personal injury or illness	53
7	Marriage	50
8	Fired at work	47
9	Marital reconciliation	45
10	Retirement	45
11	Change in health of family member	44
12	Pregnancy	40
13	Sex difficulties	39
14	Gain of new family member	39
15	Business readjustment	39
16	Change in financial state	38
17	Death of close friend	37
18	Change to different line of work	36
19	Change in number of arguments with spouse	35
20	Large mortgage	31
21	Foreclosure of mortgage or loan	30
22	Change in responsibilities at work	29
23	Son or daughter leaving home	29
24	Trouble with in-laws	29
25	Outstanding personal achievement	28
26	Wife begins or stops work	26
27	Begin or end school	26
28	Change in living conditions	25
29	Revision of personal habits	24
30	Trouble with boss	23
31	Change in work hours or conditions	20
32	Change in residence	20
33	Change in schools	20
34	Change in recreation	19
35	Change in church activities	19
36	Change in social activities	18
37	Small mortgage	17
38	Change in sleeping habits	16
39	Change in number of family get-togethers	15
40	Change in eating habits	15
41	Vacation	13
42	Christmas	12
43	Minor violations of the law	11

SOURCE: Adapted from Holmes and Rahe, 1967.

Stressful life events, even those not accompanied by the kind of grief shown by these women in India, may increase susceptibility to illness.

death of a spouse. Losses or exits seem to produce more problems than do entrances (Paykel, 1974a, 1974b).

Third, repetitive, daily hassles of life may be better predictors of illness than major life events. Losing your wallet, a price rise in the weekly food bill, and the breaking of a window may ultimately push health around more than deaths, divorces, and pregnancies (Kanner, Coyne, Schaefer, and Lazarus, 1981; Dohrenwend and Shrout, 1985). The gradual chipping away at an individual by stresses may wear him down to a point where susceptibility to illness jumps dramatically (Depue and Monroe, 1986).

Controllable Versus Uncontrollable Life Events   Another development in life events research concerns control over one's life. David Glass predicted that it is not life events themselves but ***uncontrollable life events*** that precede heart attacks, especially among Type A's. He differentiates between uncontrollable and controllable life events, categorizing death of a close family member, death of a best friend, and being laid off from work as uncontrollable losses, but divorce, separation, and changes in eating habits as controllable life events (Dohrenwend and Martin, 1978). Glass identified three groups of patients who had experienced the same total number of life events in the preceding year. Those who had had heart attacks (who tended to be Type A's) and those who had been hospitalized for noncoronary illnesses experienced more helplessness-inducing life events than did the healthy controls, indicating that a combination of being a Type A and experiencing uncontrollable life events—as opposed to a large number of life events per se—may be a formula for heart attack (Glass, 1977).

Life Events, Personality, and Lifestyle   Partly because of how easily the questionnaire in Table 10–3 can be given, investigators of life events have regarded such events as an independent and deep explanation of illness. In contrast, we regard the fact that many hassles or life events predict illness to be superficial, itself in need of deeper explanation. Perhaps it is personality and lifestyle that cause both the illness frequency and the number of life events.

Heroin addicts and alcoholics experience many life changes. In contrast, those who are aging experience fewer life events. What is causal here? It would be foolish to say that many life events cause the substance abuse or that the dearth of life changes causes aging. Here life events are caused by personality, by lifestyle, and by the normal changes of the life course; these factors may be the risk or protective factors for illness (Kasl, 1983). Personality can modify what the response to life events is. In one study, two groups of executives had comparable numbers of life events over the previous three years, but only one group tended to become ill. The *hardy* group, characterized by a strong sense of self, a strong sense of meaning, and vigor resisted illness (Garrity, Somes, and Marx, 1977; Kobasa, 1979). Social support can similarly buffer the effects of life events. Individuals who are isolated from friends and relatives are at higher risk for illness and death (Berkman, 1984, 1986).

VOLUNTARY BEHAVIOR

Most of the classic work on psychosomatic disorders from the psychodynamic and biomedical models focused on behaviors over which we have little or no voluntary control. Specific organ vulnerability, unconscious conflicts, and release of ACTH happen to us, we do not make them happen. The behavioral and cognitive models have shifted the focus onto behaviors that we can control voluntarily. A major part of health psychology emphasizes that we choose lifestyles and particular actions that can produce illness, and that by knowing this we can choose to lead healthier lives.

In our discussion of CHD, we emphasized that some of the risk factors are chosen: lack of exercise, eating cholesterol-laden foods, and smoking. We can choose not to engage in these behaviors. Others, like the time urgency component of the Type A personality, we can learn to change with counseling. In our discussion of psychoneuroimmunology (PNI), we saw that pessimists may be at risk for more chronic illness and early death. One source of this may be their belief that they are helpless, that they will not be able to lose weight through dieting, that if they see a doctor their lump will still not go away. The failure to seek out and follow medical advice is part of a lifestyle that can be voluntarily changed by knowledge and by counseling.

Why would some individuals voluntarily continue to smoke even though they know smoking is a risk factor for CHD? Is it because smoking is an addiction that cannot be changed or because it is a human frailty that is maintained by the contingencies of the environment? There is evidence that nicotine rapidly, but temporarily, improves performance and affect. Smokers may use cigarettes as a coping response to do better or feel better during the demands of daily living. Such choices may contribute to smoking above and beyond addiction, the avoidance of nicotine withdrawal (Pomerleau and Pomerleau, 1984). From the behavioral and cognitive point of view, a major part of the cause, the cure, and the prevention of psychosomatic disorders comes from the choices we make every day about how we will lead our lives.

SUMMARY

1. Psychological factors can influence the course, and even the beginning, of a physical illness. Health psychology studies *psychosomatic disorders,* which are defined as physical illnesses whose course or onset can be influenced by psychological factors.

2. Psychosomatic disorders can be viewed within a *diathesis-stress model.* In this view, psychosomatic disorder occurs when an individual is both constitutionally vulnerable to a particular physical problem and experiences life stress.

3. *Peptic ulcers* occur when the naturally secreted hydrochloric acid of the stomach erodes the protective mucous membrane of the stomach or duodenum. Emotional states, particularly anxiety, can cause an oversecretion of hydrochloric acid in the stomach.

4. Coronary heart disease (CHD) is the leading cause of death in the Western world. The Type A personality—characterized by aggressiveness, time urgency, and competitiveness—is a risk factor for CHD.

5. Hostility may be the active, insidious component of Type A. People high in hostility and anger have more CHD than those who are low in hostility and anger. More helplessness in the face of uncontrollable events might also be an insidious component of the Type A personality. Frequent engagement in the emergency reaction may be the process by which Type A's, hostile people, and overloaded people are at greater risk for CHD.

6. The immune system recognizes and destroys antigens and its activity can be influenced by psychological states. Psychoneuroimmunology is the field that studies this process.

7. Depression, stressful life events, and helplessness decrease immunocompetence and increase immune-related diseases.

8. Individuals with pessimistic explanatory style may suffer more illness and die earlier than optimists. One chain of events by which pessimism might produce immune-related illness may go from the occurrence of loss, to depression, followed by neurotransmitter depletion and endorphin increase, leading to immunosuppression, resulting in failure of the immune system to destroy threatening pathogens.

9. Biomedical, psychodynamic, behavioral, and cognitive models have all shed light on the causes and treatment of psychosomatic disorders. All are compatible with the diathesis-stress perspective.

10. The biomedical view emphasizes the "diathesis" of the diathesis-stress model, and it argues that genetic inheritance and vulnerability in a specific organ contribute to psychosomatic disorders.

11. The psychodynamic view emphasizes the personality types in whom underlying dynamic conflicts, a vulnerable organ system, and a precipitating life situation interact to produce psychosomatic disorders.

12. The behavioral and cognitive views emphasize the "stress" of the diathesis-stress model. They hold that the way individuals learn to cope with threat, think about threat, and the actual stressful and uncontrollable life events that they experience play the major role in the way psychological factors cause and aggravate physical illness. They emphasize that choice and voluntary behavior are central to the cause and prevention of psychosomatic disorders.

1. Describe some psychological factors that would explain why peptic ulcers occurred more frequently in women before 1900, more frequently in men by the late 1950s, and almost equally in men and women by 1978.

2. Describe the characteristics of Type A individuals that cause them to engage in a lifelong struggle to control a world they see as threatening. Why does this make them at risk for CHD?

3. Explain why hopelessness and helplessness contribute to susceptibility to death during bereavement, after a stroke, or after a heart attack.

4. Apply the diathesis-stress model to asthma in children.

PART 5

DEPRESSION
AND
SCHIZOPHRENIA

CHAPTER 11

Depression and Suicide

CHAPTER ORGANIZER

NORMAL VERSUS CLINICAL DEPRESSION
- Learn the differences between normal and clinical depression and the differences among unipolar depression, bipolar depression, and mania.

UNIPOLAR DEPRESSION
- Be able to enumerate the emotional, cognitive, motivational, and somatic symptoms of depression.
- Find out who is more vulnerable to depression and what the course of depression is like.

THEORIES AND THERAPIES OF UNIPOLAR DEPRESSION
- Be able to distinguish among the three main theories of depression: the biological, psychodynamic, and cognitive models.

- Familiarize yourself with the therapies for unipolar depression.

BIPOLAR DEPRESSION (MANIC-DEPRESSION)
- Familiarize yourself with the symptoms of bipolar depression.
- Learn about the course, probable cause, and treatment of bipolar depression and seasonal affective disorder (SAD).

SUICIDE
- Try to grasp the most grim outcome of affective disorders—suicide.
- Learn who is at risk for suicide, how it is motivated, and how it might be prevented.

Depression is the most widespread psychological disorder. And it has been strongly on the rise recently. If you were born after 1970, you are ten times more likely to become depressed than were your grandparents. If you are a teenager today, your risk for becoming depressed in the next year has never been higher. Depression is the common cold of mental illness. Almost everyone has felt depression, at least in its mild forms. Feeling blue, low, sad, downhearted, discouraged, and unhappy are all common depressive experiences. But familiarity does not produce understanding; for it is only in the last three decades that major advances have been made. Today the great majority of individuals suffering from severe depression can be helped. We also now know a great deal about its causes.

NORMAL VERSUS CLINICAL DEPRESSION

Loss and pain are inevitable parts of growing up and growing older. Sometimes people we care for reject us, we write bad papers, our stocks go down, we fail to get the job we want, people we love die. When these losses occur we go into mourning, and then emerge, our lives poorer, but with hope for the future. Almost everyone reacts to loss with some of the symptoms of depression. We become sad and discouraged, apathetic and passive, the future looks bleak, some of the zest goes out of living. Such a reaction is normal—and we have repeatedly found that at any given moment 25 to 30 percent of college undergraduates will have such symptoms, at least to some extent (Seligman, unpublished). In the following case, Nancy's depression is mild and within the normal range of reaction to loss.

> Within a two-day period, Nancy got a C on her Abnormal Psychology midterm and found out that the boy she had loved in her home town during high school had become engaged. The week that followed was awful; her future looked empty since she believed she would now not get into graduate school in clinical psychology and that she would never find anyone she could deeply love again. She blamed herself for these failures in the two most important arenas of her life. For the first few days she had trouble getting out of bed to go to class. She burst into tears over dinner one evening and had to leave the table. Missing dinner didn't much matter anyway since she wasn't hungry. After one week, the world started to look better. The instructor said that because the grades were so low on the midterm, everyone had the option of writing a paper to cancel out their midterm grade, and Nancy found herself looking forward to a blind date that her roommate had arranged for the weekend. Her usual bounce and enthusiasm for life began to return, and with it her appetite. She thought, "It will be an uphill battle, but I'm basically O.K. and I think I may find love and success."

How does such "normal" depression relate to the more serious depressive disorders? There are two kinds of depressive disorders, **_unipolar depression_** in which the individual suffers only depressive symptoms without ever experiencing mania, and **_bipolar depression_** (or **_manic-depression_**) in which both depression and mania occur. **_Mania_** is defined by excessive elation, expansiveness, irritability, talkativeness, inflated self-esteem, and flight of ideas. The existence of these two mood disorders, which go in apparently opposite directions, has given rise to the name **_affective disorders_** to embrace unipolar depression, bipolar depression, and mania. Normal depression differs in degree from unipolar depression; both have the same kinds of symptoms, but the unipolar depressive has more symptoms, more severely, more frequently, and for a longer time. The line between a "normal" depressive disturbance and a clinically significant depressive disorder is blurry.

Bipolar depressions, on the other hand, are clearly distinguishable from normal and unipolar depressions. They involve swings between episodes of mania and episodes of depression, and as we shall see, they probably have a genetic component. Bipolar depression develops at a younger age, and is often more crippling to the individual. Fortunately, a specific drug, lithium carbonate, seems to help considerably.

For many years, all depression was viewed as part of manic-depression. In the last decade, it has become clear that the large majority of depressions are unipolar and unrelated to manic-depression. Depression usually occurs in people who have never had mania, and mania may occur in people who have never been depressed. For this reason, we shall first discuss unipolar depression. We will then take up bipolar depression (manic-depression). We conclude by examining the most catastrophic outcome of both unipolar and bipolar depression: suicide.

FOCUS QUESTIONS

1. What is the difference between normal and clinical depression?
2. Offer broad definitions of the affective disorders: unipolar depression, bipolar depression, and mania.

▲ *Sorrow,* by Vincent van Gogh.

▶ Sixty-four percent of depressed patients lose their feelings for other people.

Symptoms of Unipolar Depression

Depression is widely regarded as a disorder of mood, but this is an oversimplification. There are actually four sets of symptoms in depression. In addition to mood or emotional symptoms, there are thought or cognitive symptoms, motivational symptoms, and physical or somatic symptoms. An individual does not have to have all these symptoms to be correctly diagnosed as "depressed," but the more symptoms he or she has and the more intense is each set, the more confident we can be that the individual is suffering from depression.

EMOTIONAL SYMPTOMS

When a depressed patient is asked how she feels, the most common adjectives she uses are: "sad, blue, miserable, helpless, hopeless, lonely, unhappy, downhearted, worthless, humiliated, ashamed, worried, useless, guilty."

Sadness is the most salient and widespread emotional symptom in depression. One person's life was so dominated by sadness that she cried during almost all her waking hours. She was unable to carry on a social conversation because of excessive crying. This occurred even in therapy to such an extent that almost no therapy was taking place (Beck et al., 1979). This melancholic mood varies with time of day. Most commonly, depressed people feel worse in the morning, and the mood seems to lighten a bit as the day goes on. Along with feelings of sadness, feelings of anxiety are very often present in depression (Fowles and Gersh, 1979).

Almost as pervasive as sadness in depression is loss of gratification, the numbing of the joy of living. Activities that used to bring satisfaction feel dull and flat. Loss of interest usually starts in only a few activities, such as work. But as depression increases in severity, it spreads through practically everything the individual does. The pleasure derived from hobbies, recreation, and family diminishes. Gregarious individuals who used to enjoy partygoing avoid

Box 11-1

DEPRESSION AND THE PERCEPTION OF REALITY

Depressed people clearly have more negative beliefs about themselves and their future than nondepressed people. But who is accurate? Sometimes the distortion from reality is in the mind of the depressive as in the example of the man who believed his wallpaper job was a failure because a couple of the panels weren't perfect. But is it possible that depressed individuals are sometimes more in touch with reality about their abilities than are nondepressed individuals? Perhaps it is nondepressed individuals who are making optimistic distortions. Lauren Alloy and Lyn Abramson (1979) conducted a study in which depressed and nondepressed college students performed a task where they pushed a button on some trials and refrained from button pushing on other trials. When the button was pushed, a green light sometimes went on. They were asked to judge how much control they had. For one group (75–0), the green light went on 75 percent of the time they pressed the button, and never went on when they didn't press the button. Their actual control was 75. For another group (75–50), the green light went on 75 percent of the time they pressed the button, but also went on 50 percent of the time when they didn't press the button, resulting in actual control of 25. In the most interesting group (75–75), the green light went on 75 percent of the time, whether or not they pressed the button. In this condition, actual control was zero since the green light went on regardless of whether they pressed the button.

The figure below shows the surprising results. Depressed people accurately judge how much control they have. When they exert control, they judge the contingency correctly. When they do not have control, they say that they do not. There *is* a net difference between depressed and nondepressed individuals, but the distortion resides in nondepressed individuals who believe they have control even when they do not. Alloy and Abramson speculated that depressed people are sadder, but wiser. What needs explaining on this account is not why people are sometimes depressed, but how nondepressed people successfully defend themselves from a grim reality (Alloy and Abramson, 1979).

This conclusion has been borne out in studies of perception of social ability. Depressed patients' assessment of their social skills is closer to the assessment of their skills by a panel of judges than is the assessment of nondepressed patients to the assessment of the judges. The nondepressed patients tend to believe that they are more socially skilled than the judges believe they are (Lewinsohn, Mischel, Chaplin, and Barton, 1980). Depressed people have low self-esteem, but this low self-evaluation may not always be a distortion; sometimes it may be merely a sober and accurate assessment of reality, which contrasts to that of others who may overinflate their views of themselves.

Does the illusion of control actually buffer nondepressed people against depression or is it just a correlate of not being depressed? Conversely, does being realistic *cause* a higher risk of becoming depressed or is being realistic just a consequence of being depressed?

To answer these questions, 145 students were tested for how large their illusions of control were using the contingency judgment task. Then they were given a laboratory-induced failure and their mood was measured. The students with little illusion of control became sadder after they failed than the students with large illu-

social gatherings. Finally, even biological functions, such as eating and sex, lose their appeal. Ninety-two percent of depressed patients no longer derive gratification from some major interests in their life, and 64 percent of depressed patients lose their feeling for other people (Beck, 1967).

COGNITIVE SYMPTOMS

A depressed person thinks of himself in a very negative light. These negative thoughts color his view of himself and of the future.

Negative View of the Self　A depressed individual often has low self-esteem. He believes he has failed and that he is the cause of his own failures. He believes he is inferior, inadequate, and incompetent. He believes that he lacks the qualities necessary to succeed in those areas of his life that are important to him, be

sions of control. These students were then followed through the natural course of their lives for the next month. The students with little illusion of control had more depression following bad events in their lives, and they became more discouraged during the month than the students with large illusions of control. This suggests that seeing the world as it is puts one at more risk for depression when bad events occur and that incorrectly seeing these events as controllable may protect a person from depression (Alloy and Clements, 1992).

Judgment of control in depressed and nondepressed students is assessed based on the probability of the green light going on when a response is made versus the probability of the green light going on when a response is not made. Depressed students accurately judge that they exert control over a green light when they in fact have control (75–0, 75–50), and they are also accurate in judging that they do not have control when the light goes on 75 percent of the time, whether or not they button press (75–75). Nondepressed students judge that they exert control even when they do not. (SOURCE: Alloy and Abramson, 1979)

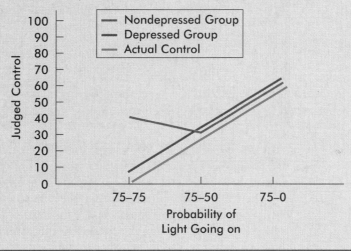

they intelligence, attractiveness, wealth, health, or talent (see Box 11–1). These views of failure and incompetence are often distortions.

One patient managed to wallpaper a kitchen although very depressed. Here is how he distorted this achievement into a failure:

THERAPIST: Why didn't you rate wallpapering the kitchen as a mastery experience?
PATIENT: Because the flowers didn't line up.
THERAPIST: You did in fact complete the job?
PATIENT: Yes.
THERAPIST: Your kitchen?
PATIENT: No. I helped a neighbor do his kitchen.

THERAPIST: Did he do most of the work?
PATIENT: No, I really did almost all of it. He hadn't wallpapered before.
THERAPIST: Did anything else go wrong? Did you spill the paste all over? Ruin a lot of wallpaper? Leave a big mess?
PATIENT: No, no, the only problem was that the flowers did not line up.
THERAPIST: So, since it was not perfect, you get no credit at all.
PATIENT: Well . . . yes.
THERAPIST: Just how far off was the alignment of the flowers?
PATIENT: (holds out fingers about 1/8 of an inch apart) About that much.
THERAPIST: On each strip of paper?
PATIENT: No . . . on two or three pieces.
THERAPIST: Out of how many?
PATIENT: About 20–30.
THERAPIST: Did anyone else notice it?
PATIENT: No. In fact, my neighbor thought it was great.
THERAPIST: Did your wife see it?
PATIENT: Yeah, she admired the job.
THERAPIST: Could you see the defect when you stood back and looked at the whole wall?
PATIENT: Well . . . not really.
THERAPIST: So you've selectively attended to a real but very small flaw in your effort to wallpaper. Is it logical that such a small defect should entirely cancel the credit you deserve?
PATIENT: Well, it wasn't as good as it should have been.
THERAPIST: If your neighbor had done the same quality job in your kitchen, what would you say?
PATIENT: . . . pretty good job!

(Beck et al., 1979)

Depressed people not only have low self-esteem, but they blame themselves and feel guilty for the troubles that afflict them. When failure occurs, depressed individuals tend to take the responsibility on themselves.

When failure has not yet occurred, they imagine that it will soon and that it will be caused by them. Those who are the most severely depressed may even believe that they are responsible for the violence and suffering of the world and that they should be greatly punished for their sins.

Belief in a Hopeless Future In addition to negative beliefs and guilt about the self, the depressed individual almost always views the future with great pessimism and hopelessness. A depressed individual believes that his actions, even if he could undertake them, are doomed. For example, when a middle-aged, depressed woman was told by her therapist that it would be a good idea for her to get a job, she replied, "I just couldn't possibly do it. How would I find the number of an employment agency? Even if I found the phone number, no one would want to hire me because I'm unqualified." Upon being reminded that she held a Ph.D. she replied, "Well, they might hire me, but they will surely fire me because I'm incompetent; and even if they kept me on it wouldn't be because of competence, but only because I'm so pathetic" (Seligman, unpublished). The depressed individual is equipped with a host of reasons for future failure, and no reasons at all for why success might occur.

Small obstacles in the path of a depressive seem insuperable barriers. One patient wanted to go swimming but was overwhelmed by the difficulties she saw in her way:

▲ Depressed patients show low self-esteem and pessimism about the future.

PATIENT: There is nowhere I could go swimming.
THERAPIST: How could you find a place?
PATIENT: There is a YWCA if I could get there . . . I'd get my hair wet and get a cold.
THERAPIST: How could you get there?
PATIENT: My husband would take me.
THERAPIST: How about your wet hair?
PATIENT: I couldn't take a hair dryer; someone would steal it.
THERAPIST: Could you do something about that?
PATIENT: They don't have lockers.
THERAPIST: How do you know?
PATIENT: I just don't think they do.

(Beck et al., 1979)

The depressive's belief that future action will be ineffective has been demonstrated experimentally. Hospitalized depressives worked on a task of skill and a task of chance. When they succeeded at the task of skill, their expectancies for future success did not go up, and when they failed, their expectancies that they would succeed did not go down. Unlike nondepressed individuals and unlike schizophrenics (either depressed or nondepressed), whose expectancies rise when they succeed and lower when they fail, depressed patients did not seem to believe that their responses could make any difference to future success (Abramson, Garber, Edwards, and Seligman, 1978). One theory of depression, hopelessness theory, regards this symptom as the proximal cause of depression (Abramson, Metalsky, and Alloy, 1989).

MOTIVATIONAL SYMPTOMS

People vary as to how motivated they are. Most of us, however, are able to get up in the morning, go to work, find ways of entertaining ourselves and others, and so on. But depressed individuals have great trouble getting started. An advertising executive loses his initiative in planning a major sales campaign; a college professor cannot bring herself to prepare her lectures; a student loses the desire to study.

One depressed man who was hospitalized after a suicide attempt merely sat motionless day after day in the lounge. His therapist decided to prepare a schedule of activities to get the patient engaged:

THERAPIST: I understand that you spend most of your day in the lounge. Is that true?
PATIENT: Yes, being quiet gives me the peace of mind I need.
THERAPIST: When you sit here, how's your mood?
PATIENT: I feel awful all the time. I just wish I could fall in a hole somewhere and die.
THERAPIST: Do you feel better after sitting for two or three hours?
PATIENT: No, the same.
THERAPIST: So you're sitting in the hope that you'll find peace of mind, but it doesn't sound like your depression improves.
PATIENT: I get so bored.
THERAPIST: Would you consider being more active? There are a number of reasons why I think increasing your activity level might help.
PATIENT: There's nothing to do around here.

> THERAPIST: Would you consider trying some activities if I could come up with a list?
>
> PATIENT: If you think it will help, but I think you're wasting your time. I don't have any interests.
>
> (Beck et al., 1979)

In extreme form, lack of response initiation is "paralysis of the will." Such a patient cannot bring himself to do even those things that are necessary to life. He has to be pushed and prodded out of bed, clothed, and fed. In severe depression, there may be **psychomotor retardation** in which movements slow down and the patient walks and talks excruciatingly slowly.

Lack of response initiation in depression has been seen clearly in the laboratory. Depressed college students fail to escape loud noise when performing tasks in which all that is required to turn off the noise is moving the hand two feet. This lack of response initiation occurs not only in instrumental motor behavior but also in cognitive tasks as well. Depressed students and depressed patients fail to solve anagrams that nondepressed individuals solve readily. The more depressed an individual is, the more severe are these deficits (Miller and Seligman, 1975, 1976; Price, Tryon, and Raps, 1978).

Difficulty in making a decision also seems to be a common symptom of depression (Hammen and Padesky, 1977). The following case illustrates how indecisiveness can overwhelm a depressed individual:

> Sylvia is a very bright college student whose life is being ruined by her depression. She finds it increasingly difficult to get on with routine studying because she can't take the initial steps. Now a major life decision has paralyzed her for the last three weeks. She has been accepted to two good graduate schools and has to make up her mind which to accept. One school offers a large scholarship, the other is more prestigious. She constantly ruminates over being selfish if she chooses the prestigious one without money, versus the cowardliness of giving in to her parents by choosing the other. Sylvia has managed to turn a can't-lose situation into a can't-win situation. (After Beck et al., 1979)

For a depressed individual, making a decision may be overwhelming and frightening. Every decision seems momentous, of make or break significance, and the fear of the wrong decision can be paralyzing.

SOMATIC SYMPTOMS

Perhaps the most insidious set of symptoms in depression are the physical changes. As depression worsens, every biological and psychological joy that makes life worth living is eroded.

Loss of appetite is common. A gourmet finds that food does not taste good to her anymore. Weight loss occurs in moderate and severe depression, although in mild depression weight gain sometimes occurs. Sleep disturbance occurs as well. Depressed individuals may experience trouble getting to sleep at night, or they may experience early morning awakening, with great difficulty getting back to sleep for the rest of the night. Sleep disturbance and weight loss both lead to weakness and fatigue. A depressed individual also may lose inter-

Box 11-2

MEASURING DEPRESSIVE SYMPTOMS

Lenore Radloff at the Center for Epidemiological Studies of the National Institute of Mental Health has developed a widely used inventory of depressive symptoms. Each of the questions describes one of the symptoms of depression, and each question provides a severity score of 0 through 3 for that symptom. The person circles the answer that best describes how he or she feels right now. The symptoms divide into mood, thought, motivational, and physical sets. The statements below show responses to eight of the twenty questions of the CES-D (Center for Epidemiological Studies–Depression).

This test is designed, not as a way of diagnosing depression, but as a way of knowing how many symptoms are present and how severe they are once depression is clinically diagnosed. A high score alone is not diagnostic of clinical depression or mental illness. Generally speaking, research has shown that the average score (for the total of the numbers from the eight questions) in a North American college population is about 3 or 4, and students who score below this can be considered nondepressed. Mildly depressed students typically have scores from about 5 to 9, and scores of 10 or higher suggest moderate to severe depression. If an individual scores 10 or more for a period of one or two weeks, it would probably be in his best interest to seek help. If he has serious or persistent thoughts of suicide, regardless of his score, it is imperative that he seek aid.

Center for Epidemiological Studies–Depression Inventory

Mood A (Sadness)
I felt sad.
0   Rarely or none of the time (less than 1 day)
1   Some or a little of the time (1–2 days)
2   Occasionally or a moderate amount of time (3–4 days)
3   Most or all of the time (5–7 days)

Mood B (Enjoyment of life)
I did not enjoy life.
0   Rarely or none of the time (less than 1 day)
1   Some or a little of the time (1–2 days)
2   Occasionally or a moderate amount of time (3–4 days)
3   Most or all of the time (5–7 days)

Thought C (Pessimism)
I felt hopeless about the future.
0   Rarely or none of the time (less than 1 day)
1   Some or a little of the time (1–2 days)
2   Occasionally or a moderate amount of time (3–4 days)
3   Most or all of the time (5–7 days)

Thought D (Failure)
I thought my life had been a failure.
0   Rarely or none of the time (less than 1 day)
1   Some or a little of the time (1–2 days)
2   Occasionally or a moderate amount of time (3–4 days)
3   Most or all of the time (5–7 days)

Motivation E (Work initiation)
I felt that everything I did was an effort.
0   Rarely or none of the time (less than 1 day)
1   Some or a little of the time (1–2 days)
2   Occasionally or a moderate amount of time (3–4 days)
3   Most or all of the time (5–7 days)

Motivation F (Sociability)
I talked less than usual.
0   Rarely or none of the time (less than 1 day)
1   Some or a little of the time (1–2 days)
2   Occasionally or a moderate amount of time (3–4 days)
3   Most or all of the time (5–7 days)

Physical G (Appetite)
I did not feel like eating; my appetite was poor.
0   Rarely or none of the time (less than 1 day)
1   Some or a little of the time (1–2 days)
2   Occasionally or a moderate amount of time (3–4 days)
3   Most or all of the time (5–7 days)

Physical H (Sleep loss)
My sleep was restless.
0   Rarely or none of the time (less than 1 day)
1   Some or a little of the time (1–2 days)
2   Occasionally or a moderate amount of time (3–4 days)
3   Most or all of the time (5–7 days)

SOURCE: Seligman, 1993.

est in sex. Erectile difficulties in men and lack of arousal in women are common side effects of depression.

A depressed individual is often self-absorbed and focused on the present. His body absorbs his attention, and increased worry about aches and pains can occur. In addition to more worrying about health, depressed individuals may, in fact, be more susceptible to physical illness, since depression as it be-

FOCUS QUESTIONS

1. List and describe the four main categories of symptoms of unipolar depression.
2. What roles do a negative view of self and belief in a hopeless future play in unipolar depression?
3. What is the distinction between endogenous and exogenous depression?

comes severe may erode basic biological drives. For example, when a flu swept through an Army base, those individuals who had been depressed took significantly longer to recover (Imboden, Cantor, and Cluff, 1961).

Classifying Depression

Depression of all kinds produces emotional, motivational, and somatic deficits. What kinds of depression exist? DSM-IV uses the most reliable and basic distinction in depression: the unipolar-bipolar distinction, which we defined above. In addition to the bipolar-unipolar distinction, however, DSM-IV also distinguishes between *episodic* and *chronic* depressions. In chronic depression, **dysthymic disorder,** the individual has been depressed for at least two solid years without having had a remission to normality of at least two months in duration. An **episodic depression,** which is much more common, is of less than two years' duration and has a clear onset, which distinguishes it from previous nondepressed functioning. Some unfortunate people have **double depression,** consisting of a depressive episode on top of an underlying dysthymic disorder. Those suffering from double depression have more severe symptoms and a low rate of remission (Keller and Shapiro, 1982; Wells, Burnam, Rogers, and Hays, 1992).

MELANCHOLIA: DO BAD EVENTS SET OFF DEPRESSION?

The endogenous vs. exogenous distinction in depression, which DSM-IV calls depression with melancholia vs. depression without melancholia, is an attempt to separate biologically based from psychologically based depressions (see Table 11–1). *Melancholia* is characterized chiefly by loss of pleasure in all activities and general lack of reaction to pleasurable events. The woman in the following case suffered from recurrent depression with melancholia:

> Mrs. Walters is fifty-four years old and has four grown children. Her latest depression began following a small quarrel at the airport with her daughter who was about to fly back to college. Mrs. Walters worried that she had destroyed her relationship with her daughter, and she imagined that her daughter was so distraught that she would neglect her studies and drop out of college.
>
> Mrs. Walters stopped going to parties and other social gatherings, lost interest in cleaning her house, found preparing meals and even just sitting with her husband a chore. She rejected comfort from him, and she could not concentrate—even on TV sitcoms. Over the past month she has lost fifteen pounds and just picks at her food. She wakes before dawn every morning and stares into the darkness, thinking about suicide. She is overcome with guilt and believes her children and husband would be better off if she ended her life.
>
> She has had three similar depressions in the last ten years. Each lasted three to six months and spontaneously remitted. (Adapted from Perry, Frances, and Clarkin, 1990, pp. 166–72)

The word *endogenous* (biological—with melancholia) means "coming from within the body," and *exogenous* (psychological—without melancholia) means "coming from outside the body." The implication of these terms is that an exogenous depression is precipitated by a life stressor, while an endogenous depression arises from a disordered biology. But in practice, endogenous depres-

TABLE 11-1

SYMPTOMS OF MELANCHOLIC DEPRESSION			
Emotional	*Cognitive*	*Motivational*	*Physical*
Loss of pleasure in any activities; lack of reactivity to good events	Pervasive pessimism, pervasive guilt, unchanged, even if the environment improves	Trouble getting up in the morning; psychomotor retardation	No appetite; weight loss; early morning awakening

sions have been found to have no fewer precipitating events than exogenous depressions (Paykel, Meyers, Dienelt, Klerman, Linderthal, and Pfefer, 1969; Leff, Roatch, and Bunney, 1970). Moreover, the distinction between endogenous and exogenous depressions has also been compromised by the findings from a major family study of depression (Andreasen, Scheftner, Reich, Hirschfeld, Endicott, and Keller, 1986). The researchers examined 3,000 first-degree relatives (immediate family) of 566 individuals with major depressive disorder to determine if the relatives also suffered from depressive disorder. Since endogenous depression is assumed to be genetic, a noticeably higher rate of depression was expected in relatives of endogenous depressives. But the rate of depression (of all subtypes) was found to be the same for relatives of the endogenous and the exogenous depressives.

Despite the lack of a difference in number of precipitating events and the findings of the family study, however, the endogenous-exogenous distinction has still been found to be a useful distinction. Two fairly reliable symptom clusters have been found for the two kinds of depression. Those who are diagnosed with endogenous depressions have been found to experience psychomotor retardation, more severe symptoms, a lack of reaction to environmental changes during the depression, loss of interest in life, and somatic symptoms. Those with exogenous depressions have experienced fewer of these characteristics. In addition, early morning awakening, guilt, and suicidal behavior may be more associated with endogenous than exogenous depressions (Mendels and Cochran, 1968).

To mark the distinction between endogenous and exogenous depressions, DSM-IV recommends specifying whether the depression has "melancholic features": loss of pleasure and numbing, which is worse in the morning; early morning awakening; psychomotor retardation; weight loss; and guilt. This distinction has treatment implications since melancholic depressions may respond better to antidepressant drugs and electroconvulsive shock, while nonmelancholic depressions may fare better with psychotherapy alone. The results of differential treatment studies have not been uniform, however, and the distinction must be viewed with caution (Fowles and Gersh, 1979; Nelson, Mazure, and Jatlow, 1990; Abrams and Vedak, 1991; Parker and Hazdi-Pavlovic, 1993).

Finally, there is also a good possibility that the distinction between mild and severe depression may be the basis of melancholia, with the melancholic depressions merely being more severe. This would mean that there is only one underlying type of unipolar depression but that there are important differences in intensity.

FOCUS QUESTIONS

1. Describe the evidence for generational differences in the risk for depression.
2. Explain why women are at greater risk for depression than men.
3. What is anaclitic depression?
4. What roles do early childhood loss or recent loss play in vulnerability to depression?

Vulnerability to Depression

How specific can we be about this "common cold of mental illness"? At the very moment about one out of twenty Americans is severely depressed, and chances are one in ten—or higher—of having a depressive episode of clinical proportions at least once in your lifetime (Myers et al., 1984; Robins et al., 1984; Angst, 1992).

Who, among our population, is vulnerable to depression? Everyone. No group—not blacks or whites, not women or men, not young or old, not rich or poor—is wholly spared. While depression is found among all segments of mankind, some groups, however, are more susceptible than others.

MODERNITY AND DEPRESSION: AN AGE OF MELANCHOLY?

There is growing evidence that we now live in an Age of Melancholy. Three lines of evidence point this way: (1) epidemiological studies of large groups of Americans, randomly sampled, show that people born earlier in this century have experienced less depression in their lifetime than people born later; (2) diagnostic studies of relatives of people who have clinically severe depression show that older relatives are less susceptible than younger relatives; (3) a study of a premodern culture, the Old Order Amish of Lancaster County, Pennsylvania, that lives surrounded by modern America, but has a rate of unipolar depression much lower than ours.

The Epidemiological Catchment Area (ECA) Study   The lifetime prevalence of a disorder is the percent of a population that has had the disorder at least once in their lifetime. Because this is a cumulative statistic, if the disorder has the same risk across historical time, older people will have a higher lifetime prevalence than younger people, simply because older people have had more years in which to get the disorder. The occurrence of a major depressive disorder was ascertained by asking 10,000 adults, sampled randomly across New Haven, Baltimore, and St. Louis, if enough symptoms of depression had occurred at any time of life, and Table 11–2 shows the lifetime prevalence of different age groups across the three sites.

These data are remarkable. They suggest that those born around 1910 had only a 1.3 percent chance of having a major depressive episode, even though they have had at least eighty-five years to get it. In contrast, those born after

TABLE 11–2

LIFETIME PREVALENCE OF MAJOR DEPRESSIVE EPISODES BY AGE			
	18–24 years *born c. 1960* *n = 1397*	*25–44 years* *c. 1945* *n = 3722*	*45–64 years* *c. 1925* *n = 2351*	*over 65* *c. 1910* *n = 1654*
New Haven	7.5	10.4	4.2	1.8
Baltimore	4.1	7.5	4.2	1.4
St. Louis	4.5	8.0	5.2	0.8

SOURCE: Adapted from Robins et al., 1984.

FIGURE 11–1

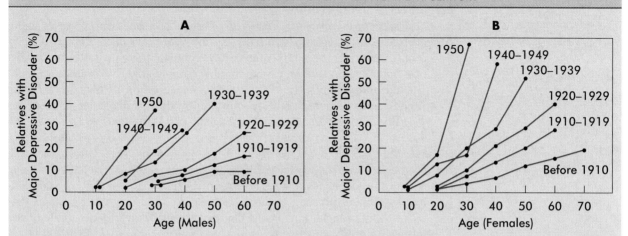

INCREASES IN DEPRESSION OVER THE TWENTIETH CENTURY

(A) Cumulative probability of diagnosable major depressive disorder in male relatives by birth cohort. (B) Cumulative probability of diagnosable major depressive disorder in female relatives by birth cohort. (SOURCE: Klerman, Lavori, Rice, et al., 1985)

1960 have already had a 5.3 percent chance, even though they have had only thirty years of opportunity. These are whopping differences, suggesting a roughly tenfold increase in risk for depression across two generations (Robins et al., 1984).

Birth Cohort Study of Relatives of Unipolar Depressives   Relatives of individuals with major depressive disorders are themselves at heightened risk for depression, probably for genetic reasons. Do the same trends for groups of people born within the same period hold with relatives at risk?

To ask this question, 2,289 relatives of 523 people with affective disorders were given the structured diagnostic interview probing for their lifetime prevalence of major depressive disorder. Figure 11–1 plots the percentage of relatives who have had at least one episode against their age. Men and women are plotted separately (Klerman, Lavori, Rice, et al., 1985).

Again the effects of historical time are enormous—about one order of magnitude. Consider, for example, women born in 1950 versus women born before 1910. By age thirty about 65 percent of the women born in 1950 had had one depressive episode, whereas fewer than 5 percent of women in the 1910 cohort had had such an episode by the time they were thirty. At almost all corresponding points, a more recent year of birth confers more and earlier risk for major depressive disorder. Overall, we can again estimate a risk increase of roughly tenfold across two generations.

The Old Order Amish   During just the period of these two studies, the rate of depression among the 12,500 Amish living in Lancaster County, Pennsylvania, was assessed using a parallel diagnostic interview. The Amish are an ultraconservative Protestant sect. No electricity is permitted in their homes, horses and buggies are used for transportation, alcoholism and crime are unknown, and pacifism is absolute. They are a closed population, descended entirely from thirty eighteenth-century progenitors.

For the five-year period from 1976–1980, forty-one active cases of major depressive disorder were found; this is a five-year prevalence of about 0.5 percent (there are 8,186 adult Amish). If we compare this rate to the parallel figures from the ECA studies, we can roughly estimate that the Amish have about one-fifth to one-tenth the risk for unipolar depression as their neighboring Americans from modern culture. Importantly, the rate of bipolar depression is the same as for modern Americans (Egeland and Hostetter, 1983).

SEX DIFFERENCES IN DEPRESSION

Women seem to have twice the risk for depression as men (Nolen-Hoeksema, 1988). Methodologically strong studies of depression (those that use standardized assessment procedures, large sample sizes, and diagnostic systems that separate out unipolar and bipolar depression) can be divided into treated cases (people undergoing therapy) and community samples (in which the researchers go door-to-door). In seven of the eight studies of treated cases in the United States, females were significantly more depressed than males, with a mean ratio of 2:1. In the ten studies of treated cases outside the United States, nine showed more females than males with depression, with a mean ratio of 2.3:1. Treated cases may not reveal underlying sex differences in depression, however, because women might be more likely to seek out treatment than men. To get around this problem, a large number of community studies have been conducted; most of these studies show a preponderance of depression in females over males, with a mean ratio slightly under 2:1.

Overall, the preponderance of depression among women is clearly established. Why this is so is much less clear. Several hypotheses have been advanced to account for this sex difference in depression. First, women may be more willing to express depressive symptoms than men are in our society. When they confront loss, women are more reinforced for passivity and crying,

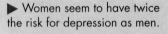

▶ Women seem to have twice the risk for depression as men.

while men are more reinforced for anger or indifference (Weissman and Paykel, 1974). Second, biological hypotheses suggest that chemical enzyme activity, genetic proneness, and a monthly bout of premenstrual depression influence vulnerability in women. Also there is the possibility that female carriers of a depressive gene become depressed, whereas male carriers of the same gene become alcoholic (Robinson, Davis, Nies, Ravaris, and Sylvester, 1971; Winokur, 1972). A third hypothesis grows out of the learned helplessness theory of depression (see pp. 384–89). If depression is related to helplessness, then to the extent that women learn to be more helpless than men, depression will appear more frequently in women than in men. A society that rewards women for brooding and becoming passive in the face of loss while rewarding men for active coping attempts may pay a heavy price in later female depression (Radloff, 1975). Fourth, women are *more state-oriented* than men, and so are inclined to worry about and explain bad life events (foremost among them, depression itself), whereas men are inclined to more *action* and less thought (Nolen-Hoeksema, 1988). State-orientation about depression will amplify depression (Zullow and Seligman, 1985), whereas action-orientation may dampen a depressive mood and bring about the resolution of the life problems.

The fifth explanation of the findings that women show more depression than men concerns premenstrual mood changes. In any survey, 25 percent of adult women will be within one week of menstruating, but zero percent of the men will be. If there is a valid phenomenon of *premenstrual depression*, its occurrence would inflate the amount of female depression. Does premenstrual depression exist?

This is a controversial topic, so much so that the DSM-IV committee consigned "premenstrual dysphoric disorder" to an appendix because it felt the disorder was in need of yet more study. Characterizing this disorder are: (1) in most cycles in the last year, emotional changes have occurred before menses, which remit with the onset of menses; (2) the presence of at least five symptoms, including emotional lability, anger, tension, depression, low interest, fatigability, feeling overwhelmed, difficulty concentrating, appetite changes, oversensitivity to rejection, sleep changes, or physical symptoms; and (3) the serious impairment of work or social functioning by these symptoms.

Overall at least 40 percent of adult women experience some of these symptoms premenstrually. Most of these women rate the symptoms as mild and are not impaired by them, but about 2 to 10 percent rate them as severe. This group may be significantly impaired by them (Logue and Moos, 1986; Nolen-Hoeksema, 1988; McMillan and Pihl, 1987). Depression is a prominent symptom in this cluster. One major study of 335 women found that 145 met criteria for premenstrual increases in depressive symptoms (Halbreich, Endicott, and Nee, 1983).

The sixth, and most intriguing hypothesis, has to do with body image and the pursuit of thinness through dieting common to women in developed nations. As we will see, one root cause of depression is failure and helplessness. Dieting sets up a cycle of failure and helplessness: pitting the goal of slimming to an almost unattainable "ideal" weight against untiring biological defenses. At first, dieters lose weight, and with it, the depression about being overweight. Ultimately, however, dieters become dismayed as the pounds come back, as they do in 95 percent of diets. Repeated failure and all the daily reminders of being overweight again bring depression in their wake (Wadden, Stunkard, and Smoller, 1986; Seligman, 1993). On the other hand, about 5 percent of dieters keep the weight from coming back, but they have to stay indefinitely on an unsatisfying low-calorie diet to do so. A side effect of prolonged malnutrition is depression. Either way, the pursuit of thinness makes people vulnerable to depression (Garner and Wooley, 1991).

The cultures—among them, white America, Sweden, Great Britain, Czechoslovakia—that have a thin ideal for women have a fascinating regularity. All thin-ideal cultures also have eating disorders—anorexia nervosa and bulimia. They all also have roughly twice as much depression in women as men. In these cultures, women diet twice as much as men, with an estimated 13 percent of adult men and 25 percent of adult women on a diet (Jeffrey, Adlis, and Forster, 1991). None of the cultures—among them, Egypt, Iran, India, Uganda—without the thin ideal have eating disorders, and the amount of depression in women and men is roughly the same in all of these cultures. These findings suggest that around the world the thin ideal and dieting not only cause eating disorders, they also cause women to be more depressed then men (McCarthy, 1990).

AGE AND DEPRESSION

No age group is exempt from depression. Comparison of the frequency of depression across age is controversial since depression may have different manifestations at different times of life, and a cohort effect clearly exists, with people born early in this century reporting much less depression than people born midway and later through the century.

Not only is severe depression more common now; it also attacks its victims when they are much younger. People born in the 1930s who have a depressed relative have their own first depression, if they have one at all, between the ages of thirty and thirty-five. People born in the 1956 cohort have their first depression between the ages of twenty and twenty-five—ten years sooner (Reich, Van Eerdewegh, Rice, and Mullaney, 1987). This trend toward younger and younger first incidence of depression continues. Peter Lewinsohn and his colleagues gave diagnostic interviews to 1,710 randomly selected western Oregon adolescents. By age fourteen, 7.2 percent of the youngest adolescents, born in 1972–1974, had had a severe depression; in contrast, 4.5 percent of the older adolescents, born in 1968–1971, had had a severe depression (Lewinsohn, Rohde, Seeley, and Fischer, 1993). In a study of over 3,000 twelve- to fourteen-year-olds in the southeastern United States, 9 percent had experienced major depressive disorder (Garrison, Addy, Jackson, McKeown, and Waller, 1992). This high a percentage of children suffering severe depression and at such a young age is dismaying. Since severe depression recurs in about half of those who have had it once, the extra years of depression resulting from earlier first occurrences add up to an ocean of tears.

The earliest psychological state that may be related to depression was described by the American psychiatrist René Spitz in 1946 and was called ***anaclitic depression.*** Spitz observed that when infants between the ages of six and eighteen months were separated from their mothers for prolonged periods of time, a state of unresponsive apathy, listlessness, weight loss, increased susceptibility to serious childhood illness, and even death occurred. The mothers' return, or the substitution of a different, permanent mother, reversed these effects (Spitz, 1946). Similar effects have been observed when infant rhesus monkeys are separated from their mothers. A regular sequence of the reaction to the separation—first protest, then despair, then reattachment—has

▲ Children show as high a rate of depressive symptoms as do adults.

been documented (Bowlby, 1960; Kaufman and Rosenblum, 1967; McKinney, Suomi, and Harlow, 1972).

Childhood depression is a controversial issue (Schulterbrand and Raven, 1977). It was formerly alleged that depression in childhood with the core symptoms of passivity, negative cognitions, resigned behavior, sadness, and inhibition in working and loving, was relatively rare. Instead, reaction to loss was thought to take other forms, such as hyperactivity, aggression, and delinquency (Cytryn and McKnew, 1972). More sensitive tests of depression in childhood have been developed, however, and have revealed as high a rate of depressive symptoms in children as among adults, along with accompanying intellectual deficits (Kovacs and Beck, 1977; Kaslow, Tanenbaum, Abramson, Peterson, and Seligman, 1983; Blumberg and Izard, 1985).

Another form of loss for a child is divorce and separation, as well as its precursor, parental turmoil. In a longitudinal study of 400 children who were followed as they went from third grade through sixth grade, 20 percent developed moderate to severe depressive symptoms (Nolen-Hoeksema, Girgus, and Seligman, 1986, 1992). Among the most salient precipitants of depression was parental turmoil—the report that parents had been fighting more lately. Parents' fighting probably undermines the child's sense of security and often leads to a string of bad life events, such as separation and economic problems, and so increases a child's risk for depression. Finally, when divorce occurs, and the child "loses" the parent through the divorce, the child may start to exhibit depressive symptoms, as in the following case:

> Peter, age nine, had not seen his father, who lived nearby, more than once every two to three months. We expected that he would be troubled, but we were entirely unprepared for the extent of this child's misery. The interviewer observed: "I asked Peter when he had last seen his dad. The child looked at me blankly and his thinking became confused, his speech halting. Just then, a police car went by with its siren screaming. The child's stared into space and seemed lost in reverie. As this continued for a few minutes, I gently suggested that the police car had reminded him of his father, a police officer. Peter began to cry and sobbed without stopping for 35 minutes. (Wallerstein and Kelly, 1980)

In adolescents, depression has all the symptoms that we saw for depression in adults. In addition to the core symptoms of depression, depressed adolescents, particularly boys, are commonly negativistic and even antisocial. Restlessness, grouchiness, aggression, and strong desire to leave home are also common symptoms; and sulkiness, uncooperativeness in family activities, school difficulties, alcohol and drug abuse can also be symptoms of adolescent depression.

Depression among adults does not increase in frequency and in severity with age as used to be believed (Myers et al., 1984; Robins et al., 1984). Although depression in old age is compounded by the helplessness induced by increasing physical and mental incapacities, as a visit to any old-age home will dramatically confirm, the frequency of depression among old people is at present much lower than among younger people.

RACE AND SOCIAL CLASS

For many years, depression was thought to be uncommon among North American blacks. Recent research, however, does not bear this out. The National Comorbidity Study of 8,098 Americans shows that the rate of affective disorder among blacks is about two-thirds that of whites and Hispanics, and that poorer people have somewhat more affective disorder (Kessler, McGonagle, Zhao, et al., 1994). Caution should be used, however, in interpreting any study of cross-racial, cross-age, cross-sex, or cross-cultural psychological disorders. Since diagnosis is, for the most part, made by middle-class white psychiatrists and psychologists, insensitivity to symptoms of depression within another culture or elicitation of greater hostility among the patients may easily contaminate the results (Tonks, Paykel, and Klerman, 1970).

No strong differences occur in depression among social classes. Unlike schizophrenia, which is less frequent in middle and upper classes, depression is democratic. Again, however, it is possible that depression may have different manifestations according to the patient's social class: lower-class patients may show more feelings of powerlessness and hopelessness, middle-class patients stronger feelings of loneliness and rejection, and upper-class patients greater pessimism and social withdrawal (Schwab, Bialow, Holzer, Brown, and Stevenson, 1967). At any rate, the similarities in the occurrence of depression between black people and white people and between rich people and poor people far outweigh the differences.

EFFECTS OF LIFE EVENTS

Are the lives of depressed people, before the onset of their depression, different from the lives of people who do not become depressed? Depressed individuals have experienced more early childhood losses than nondepressed individuals and more frequent stressful losses within a year or two before the onset of depression. Yet, many individuals suffer both early childhood loss and recent loss without becoming depressed, and a substantial number of depressed individuals do not suffer early childhood loss or recent loss. So we are far from saying that such life events *cause* depression, but some events do seem to increase the risk of depression.

Early Childhood Loss The death of a person's mother before the child is eleven years old may predispose an individual to depression in adulthood. In a study of depression in its natural setting, the English sociologists George W. Brown and Tirril Harris interviewed women door-to-door in the working class borough of Camberwell in London. They found that an alarmingly high percentage—15 to 20 percent—were moderately to severely depressed and that these women were not receiving treatment for their depression. The rate of depression was almost three times higher among women who, before age eleven, had lost their mother and who also had experienced a severe recent loss than among women who, before age eleven, had not lost their mother but who had experienced a similar recent loss. Death of the mother after the child reached age eleven had no effect on risk for depression according to this study (Brown and Harris, 1978). Death of the father while the child is young is also probably associated with later depression (Barnes and Prosin, 1985).

Recent Loss Most depressions are preceded by a recent stressful loss. Failure at work, marital separation, failure at school, loss of a job, rejection by a loved one, death of a child, illness of a family member, and physical illness are common precipitants of depression. Individuals who become depressed show more such losses preceding their depression than matched controls (Leff, Roach

and Bunney, 1970; Paykel, 1973; Brown and Harris, 1978; Littlefield and Rushton, 1986; Breslau and Davis, 1986).

But such losses do not always bring on depressions, by any means. Only about 10 percent of those persons who experience losses equivalent in severity to those of an average depressed person become depressed themselves. Why is it that the other 90 percent do *not* become depressed? Only half the women who, before age eleven, had lost their mother and who also had suffered a recent loss became depressed. What about the other half? Brown and Harris proposed that there are four invulnerability factors that can help prevent depression from occurring, even in the presence of the predisposing factors and recent loss. The vulnerable women had either (1) an intimate relationship with a spouse or a lover, or (2) a part-time or full-time job away from home, or (3) fewer than three children still at home, or (4) a serious religious commitment. So intimacy, employment, a life not overburdened by child care, and strong religious belief may protect against depression. Perhaps what these four invulnerability factors have in common is that they contribute self-esteem and a sense of mastery, while undercutting the formation of an outlook pervaded by hopelessness. All of these, in effect, help to ward off depression.

The Course of Depression

When a vulnerable individual becomes depressed, what is likely to happen if the individual fails to seek out treatment? If anything good about depression can be said, it is that it usually dissipates in time. After the initial attack, which comes on suddenly about three-quarters of the time, depression seems to last an average of about three months in outpatients. Among inpatients, who are usually more severely depressed, it lasts about six months on the average. At first, the depression gets progressively worse, eventually reaching the bottom, but then the depressed individual begins to recover gradually to the state that existed before the onset (Beck, 1967; Robins and Guze, 1972). What our grandmothers told us about our own personal tragedies—time heals all wounds—is certainly true for depression. The mind, or the body, seems incapable of sustaining a dark mood forever, and unknown homeostatic mechanisms take over and, in time, correct the disorder.

The time that a depressive episode lasts, however, is painfully long, and to an individual suffering from it, it seems like forever. For this reason, a therapist will always emphasize that the depressive episode will go away in time. Without minimizing the suffering the patient is feeling now, the therapist should tell the patient that complete recovery from the episode occurs in 70 to 95 percent of the cases. For some, this ray of hope may speed the time when the depression will lift.

Once a depressive episode has occurred, one of three patterns may develop. The first is *recovery without recurrence*. **Recurrence** is defined as the return of symptoms following at least six months without significant symptoms of depression. This should be differentiated from **relapse** into the same episode, which may occur when drug therapy or psychotherapy relieves symptoms for only a short while. If the patient goes for six months free of symptoms, however, it is generally believed that the episode has run its course. About half the patients who have had a depressive episode will not have another one, at least during the following ten years. Generally, the more stable a person is before the episode, the less likely depression will recur. On the other hand, half of depressed individuals will show the second pattern: *recovery with recurrence.*

The second depressive episode, if it occurs, will tend to be of about the same duration as the first attack. On the average, however, most individuals who have recurrent episodes of depression can expect an average symptom-free interval of more than three years before the next episode. But the interval between episodes in recurrent depression tends to become shorter over the years. The period of greatest risk for recurrence is in the first six months after recovery. And substance abuse increases the risk for recurrence (NIMH, 1984). For some individuals, a third pattern will develop: *chronic depression.* Roughly 10 percent of those individuals who have a major depressive episode will not recover and will remain chronically depressed (Perris, 1968; Kerr, Roth, Schapira, and Gurney, 1972; Schuyler, 1974; Angst and Wicki, 1991; Keller, Lavori, Mueller, and Endicott, 1992). Therapy for depression usually attempts to make the current episode shorter or to postpone the time at which another episode might strike. The therapies for depression derive from three different theories, and it is to these theories and therapies that we now turn.

THEORIES AND THERAPIES OF UNIPOLAR DEPRESSION

What causes depression, and how is depression most effectively treated? In the last thirty years, we have moved out of the dark ages in our understanding of depression. Substantial strides have been made in the understanding and treatment of the disorder. Between 80 and 90 percent of severe depressions can now be markedly alleviated with a brief course of therapy. Although several theories, with substantial research support, have emerged to explain the origins of depression, we still cannot say with certainty what the cause of depression is or how it can best be treated. We can, however, make highly educated guesses. There are three main theories and therapies for depression: the biological model, the psychodynamic model, and the cognitive model. These theo-

FOCUS QUESTIONS

1. What are the four clues that indicate that there is a biological basis of depression?
2. Describe the evidence for the genetic basis of depression.
3. Describe the neurochemical mechanisms that might explain depression.
4. How do certain drugs alter this neurochemical mechanism?
5. What is the possible neuroanatomical basis of depression?
6. What is electroconvulsive shock therapy (ECT)?

ries overlap, and there is also a good deal of overlap in the therapies each recommends, but each tends to focus on one aspect of depression. At the end of this section, we will attempt a synthesis of these models.

The Biological Model of Depression

According to the biological model, depression is a disorder of the body. While in principle, depression could be caused by a problem in any bodily organ, speculation has centered almost entirely on the brain, and in particular on depletion of a class of substances (biogenic amines) that help transmit nerve impulses across the gaps (synapses) between nerve cells (neurons). There are four clues that the body is intimately involved in depression (Schuyler, 1974). First of all, depression occurs with some frequency following periods of natural physiological change in women: after giving birth to a child, at menopause, and just before menstruation. Second, there is considerable similarity of symptoms across cultures, sexes, ages, and races, indicating an underlying biological process. Third, somatic therapies, in particular drugs like tricyclic antidepressants and MAO inhibitors, and electroconvulsive shock, are effective treatments of depression. Fourth, depression is occasionally induced in normal individuals as a side effect of medications; in particular, depression may be induced by reserpine, a high-blood-pressure-reducing drug (Schuyler, 1974). These clues have fueled the search for a biological basis of depression.

GENETICS AND UNIPOLAR DEPRESSION

First-degree relatives of unipolar depressives have between two and five times the risk for depression above the risk for those in the normal population (Weissman, Kidd, and Prusoff, 1982; Keller, Beardslee, Dorer, Lavori, Samuelson, and Klerman, 1986). If the depressive is alcoholic as well, the risk for both depression and alcoholism increases; but if the relative is not alcoholic, there is increased risk for only depression (Merikangas, Leckman, Prusoff, Pauls, and Weissman, 1985; Winokur and Coryell, 1992). Is this increased risk genetic?

While there is evidence that bipolar depression can be strongly inherited, unipolar depression is only weakly inherited. Only 28 percent of identical twins are discordant for bipolar depression, but at least 60 percent of identical twins are discordant for unipolar depression (Allen, 1976). The most recent twin study does not find evidence for concordance for unipolar depression (Torgersen, 1986a). Better evidence comes from studies of adoptive versus biological relatives of depressed patients. Biological relatives had an eightfold increased risk for unipolar depression relative to adoptive relatives (Wender, Kety, Rosenthal, Schulsinger, Ortmann, and Lunde, 1986). Overall it is clear that having a depressed family member confers risk for depression, but whether this risk is genetic awaits more evidence. Thus, the genetic evidence gives some support for a biomedical approach to unipolar depression. The drug and biochemical evidence, however, is stronger.

THE NEUROCHEMICAL BASIS OF DEPRESSION

The biological model holds that depression is a disorder of motivation caused by insufficiencies of the biogenic amines. The **biogenic amines** are neurochemicals that facilitate neural transmission. They divide into two groups with different chemical structures: the **catecholamines,** which include norepi-

FIGURE 11–2

THE NEUROCHEMICAL BASIS OF DEPRESSION

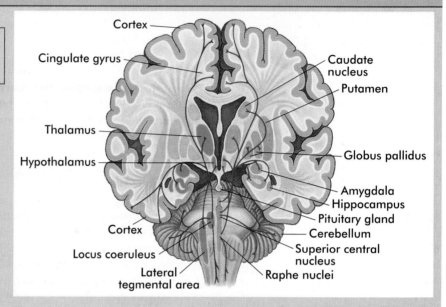

—— Norepinephrine
Pathways
—— Serotonin Pathways

The biogenic amines are neurochemicals that facilitate neural transmission. Depression may result from decreased availability of one of the catecholamines—norepinephrine—and one of the indoleamines—serotonin. Researchers have mapped norepinephrine and serotonin neurons in the brain. There is a high concentration of such neurons in the limbic system, which regulates emotional behavior, and hence may be implicated in depression. The figure shows a schematic representation of norepinephrine and serotonin pathways. Although these pathways are not limited to being located on the left and right sides of the brain, the figure attempts to simplify the depiction of these pathways by representing norepinephrine pathways on the left side of the drawing and representing serotonin pathways on the right side of the drawing. (SOURCE: Based on Snyder, 1986, p. 108)

nephrine, epinephrine, and dopamine; and the **indoleamines,** which include serotonin and histamine (see Figure 11–2).

The biogenic amines play significant roles in neural transmission in the medial forebrain bundle (MFB) and the periventricular system (PVS). The MFB and PVS are two major pathways that run through lower centers of the brain. Research with animals indicates that the neuroanatomical basis of reward and punishment may lie in the MFB and PVS respectively (Stein, 1968). Electrical stimulation of the MFB is highly reinforcing to rats, that is, they will work hard to receive that stimulation. Electrical stimulation of the periventricular system is very punishing. The MFB may function as a "go" system that facilitates active behavior, whereas the PVS may act as a "stop" system. When the biogenic amines are depleted, the functioning of these systems is reduced and depression, with its loss of motivation, may ensue. Speculation about the neurochemical basis of depression has centered primarily around decreased availability of one of the catecholamines, **norepinephrine (NE)** (Schildkraut, 1965), and one of the indoleamines, **serotonin** (Maas, 1975; McNeal and Cimbolic, 1986).

Norepinephrine and the Catecholamine Hypothesis Figure 11–3 depicts the hypothesized mode of action of norepinephrine in transmission of a nerve impulse from one neuron across the synapse to a second neuron. When a nerve impulse occurs in neuron 1, norepinephrine is discharged into the synapse (the gap between neuron 1 and neuron 2). This stimulates neuron 2 to fire when the NE makes contact with the receptors on the membrane of neuron 2. Norepinephrine is now sitting in the synapse and on the membrane of neuron 2. Neuron 2 will continue to fire until the NE is inactivated. There are two relevant ways that norepinephrine can now be inactivated. The first way is by **reuptake,** in which neuron 1 reabsorbs norepinephrine, thereby decreasing the amount of norepinephrine at the receptors. The second is by **breakdown.** This is facilitated by the enzyme monoamine oxidase (MAO) among others. This enzyme breaks down the norepinephrine chemically and renders it inactive. As we said above, norepinephrine is a catecholamine, which is one of two classes of biogenic amines. The biogenic amines affect our motivation. And when we decrease the amount of biogenic amines (in this case, norepinephrine), we will have less motivation. The catecholamine hypothesis claims that when reuptake and/or breakdown are doing their job too well, our norepinephrine level drops too low, and we become highly unmotivated, in short, depressed.

Two groups of drugs use these routes to treat depression: tricyclic antidepressants and MAO inhibitors. Each affects the availability of NE in the brain. It was a serendipitous finding that led to their use as antidepressants. Individuals with tuberculosis, who are frequently depressed, were tested with a new drug, iproniazid. It turned out that the drug didn't help cure their tuberculosis, but it did produce a much brighter mood in the patients, and they became less

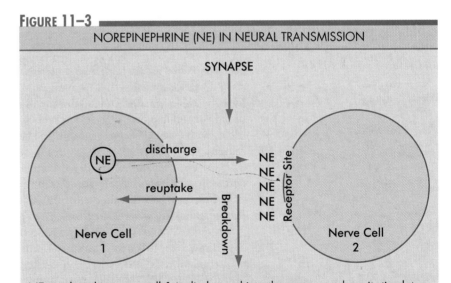

FIGURE 11–3

NOREPINEPHRINE (NE) IN NEURAL TRANSMISSION

NE produced in nerve cell 1 is discharged into the synapse, where it stimulates nerve cell 2 to fire. In order to stop the NE from stimulating nerve cell 2, NE can be inactivated either by being reabsorbed back into nerve cell 1 (reuptake) or by being broken down and excreted out of the synapse (breakdown). Antidepressant drugs keep NE available in the synapse by blocking its reuptake (tricyclics) or slowing its breakdown (MAO inhibitors). The same logic holds for the serotonin model, with drugs like fluoxetine (Prozac) blocking the reuptake of serotonin.

depressed. Why did this happen? The drug, iproniazid, is an MAO inhibitor. As we have seen, the enzyme MAO facilitates breakdown, thereby making less norepinephrine available for neural transmission. So this drug, iproniazid, inhibited the enzyme MAO in the patients with tuberculosis, and in part prevented breakdown of NE. The catecholamine hypothesis claims that, as a result, more norepinephrine was available, and with more NE available, the tuberculosis patients became less depressed. Since then, MAO inhibitors have been successfully used in treating depression, thereby lending support to the biological model, specifically the catecholamine hypothesis.

Also discovered by accident, the tricyclic antidepressants affect the availability of NE. These drugs block the process of reuptake. As we saw above, reuptake occurs when the neuron that released NE absorbs it back. If reuptake is blocked, then less NE is absorbed, and more will be available. As a result of more NE, the patient will become less depressed. This provides additional support for the catecholamine hypothesis.

Further evidence of this hypothesis has come from reserpine-induced depression. Reserpine is a powerful sedative given to high blood pressure patients. Physicians discovered that it produces an unwanted side effect, depression with suicidal tendencies, in about 15 percent of the people who take it. It turns out that reserpine, among other actions, depletes norepinephrine. With less NE, these high blood pressure patients became depressed.

Despite the favorable evidence supporting the catecholamine hypothesis based on the action of these drugs, advocates of the hypothesis are appropriately cautious. The reason is that reserpine, the tricyclics, and the MAO inhibitors all have a large number of effects other than their effect on norepinephrine. Because of this, it is very possible that their effects might be due to some other properties of the drugs and not necessarily to their effect on norepinephrine.

Fluoxetine (Prozac) and the Indoleamine Hypothesis   While the catecholamine hypothesis of depression claims that unavailability of NE is the cause, the indoleamine hypothesis claims that unavailability of serotonin is the cause. The drugs that keep NE available are "dirty" drugs: they are nonspecific in that they change the availability of NE *and* serotonin in the brain, as well as other neurotransmitters. As a result, scientists set out to find a drug that would only affect the availability of serotonin. In 1974, chemists reported that the chemical compound fluoxetine specifically inhibits only the reuptake of serotonin with negligible effects on NE and other transmitters (Wong, Horng, et al., 1974). Dubbed Prozac, this drug was released in 1987.

In severe depression, Prozac has about the same efficacy as the other antidepressants, the tricyclics and MAO inhibitors, producing relief in 60 to 70 percent of cases. It produces less drowsiness, dry mouth, sweating, and risk of overdose than the NE drugs, but it produces more nausea, nervousness, and insomnia (Wernicke, 1985; Cooper, 1988; Beaumont, 1990; Henry, 1992; Boulos, Kutcher, Gardner, and Young, 1992). There are case histories that implicate Prozac in unprecedented suicidal preoccupation, although it is disputed whether Prozac produces any more thoughts about suicide than does a placebo (Teicher, Glod, and Cole, 1990; Beasley, Dornseif, Bosomworth, et al., 1992).

This side effect profile allowed clinicians to prescribe Prozac freely, and it is currently in very wide use, particularly for less severe depression. There are intriguing suggestions that it works not as a global mood elevator, but through changing personality: lowering sensitivity to rejection and raising self-esteem (Kramer, 1993). Such "cosmetic psychopharmacology," if true, is important, but the hypothesis has yet to be subjected to controlled tests.

THE NEUROANATOMICAL BASIS OF DEPRESSION

There is also an anatomical theory of depression that claims that overactivity of the right frontal lobes in the brain produces depression. Subjects express more negativity about pictures of faces presented to the right hemisphere (left visual field) than about pictures presented to the left hemisphere (right visual field). This is particularly accentuated in depressed people (Davidson, Schaffer, and Saron, 1985). Brain damage to the left hemisphere due to stroke (oxygen starvation in part of the brain) more often results in depression than does damage to the right hemisphere (Sackheim, Greenberg, et al., 1982).

SOMATIC THERAPIES FOR DEPRESSION

Advocates of the biological model approach the treatment of unipolar depression, particularly when it is severe, in two ways. The first is to treat the patient with drugs; fluoxetine (Prozac), the tricyclics, and the MAO inhibitors may be used (see Figure 11–4). The second approach is to administer electroconvulsive shock (ECT). Relief is moderate, but relapse rate is high.

Drug Treatment   Fluoxetine (Prozac) is currently widely prescribed, particularly for less severe depressions. As we saw, it specifically inhibits only the reuptake of serotonin. It produces relief in 60 to 70 percent of those who have major depressions, with low risk of overdose. But it produces nausea, nervousness, and insomnia in some patients (Beaumont, 1990; Henry, 1992). It may also produce preoccupation with suicide (Teicher, Glod, and Cole, 1990; Beasley, Dornseif, Bosomworth, et al., 1992).

Tricyclic antidepressants, you will recall, block the reuptake of norepinephrine. As a result, NE is available and the patient becomes less depressed. On average, between 63 and 75 percent of depressed patients given tricyclics show significant clinical improvement (Beck, 1973). Further, maintaining a patient with recurrent depression on tricyclics between attacks reduces recurrence (Gelenberg and Klerman, 1978; NIMH, 1984).

The MAO inhibitors prevent the breakdown of norepinephrine by inhibiting the enzyme MAO. With more NE available, the patient becomes less depressed. But MAO inhibitors are now prescribed less often than fluoxetine or tricyclics, largely because the MAO inhibitors can have lethal side effects. When combined with cheese, alcohol, pickled herring, narcotics, or high-blood-pressure-reducing drugs, MAO inhibitors can be fatal. Most studies show MAO inhibitors to be superior to placebos in alleviating depression, however, and if fluoxetine or the tricyclics fail, the MAO inhibitors should be tried.

What all of the drug therapies for depression have in common is that while the relief produced is moderate to good, relapse and recurrence rates are high once the drug is stopped. Patients who respond well to drugs may have to take the drug indefinitely to prevent recurrence (Kupfer, Frank, Perel, et al., 1992). It has been suggested that drug treatments work better than psychotherapy for depression, particularly when depression is severe (Schulberg and Rush, 1994). Comparisons of psychotherapy and drugs, however, reveals an equal effect for severe depression (Munoz, Hollon, McGrath, et al., 1994).

FIGURE 11–4

DRUG TREATMENTS FOR DEPRESSION

Norepinephrine is discharged into the synapse when a nerve impulse from neuron 1 to neuron 2 fires. In a normal person, the norepinephrine is inactivated by either reuptake, whereby neuron 1 reabsorbs the norepinephrine, or breakdown of the norepinephrine by the enzyme MAO. In a depressed person, breakdown or reuptake or both of either norepinephrine (indicated by the blue part of the arrow) or serotonin (indicated by the red part of the arrow) removes the norepinephrine or serotonin, leaving the person depressed. MAO inhibitors work by preventing the breakdown of norepinephrine; tricyclic antidepressants work by preventing the reuptake of norepinephrine; fluoxetine works by preventing the reuptake of serotonin.

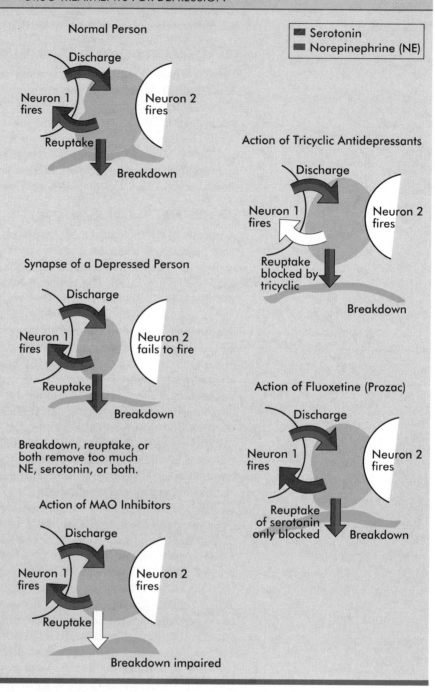

Electroconvulsive Shock (ECT) Electroconvulsive shock is, to the layman, the scariest of the antidepressant treatments. In the two decades following ECT's discovery as a psychotherapeutic treatment in 1938, enthusiasm was high, and it was promiscuously prescribed for a very broad range of disorders. The treatment, particularly in its less refined forms, can have very serious side effects, how-

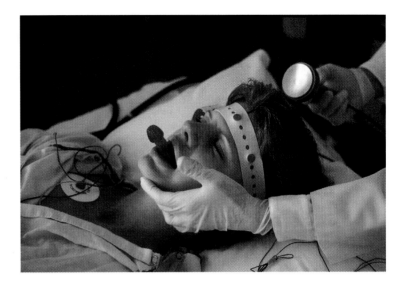

▶ A patient is prepared for electroconvulsive shock treatment. The object in her mouth is to prevent her from swallowing her tongue when the electric current passes through her body.

ever, and it has come to be regarded by the general public as "barbaric" and "punitive." But strong evidence exists that ECT, when given to severely depressed unipolar depressive patients, is a highly effective antidepressant therapy. Modern techniques have greatly reduced the common and severe side effects of yesteryear, and about 80 percent of patients with major depression respond to ECT (Fink, 1979; Malitz et al., 1984; Devanand, Sackeim, and Prudic, 1991).

Typically, ECT is administered by a medical team consisting of a psychiatrist, anesthesiologist, and a nurse. Metal electrodes are taped to either side of the patient's forehead, and the patient is anesthetized. The patient is given drugs to induce muscular relaxation in order to prevent the breaking of bones during the convulsion. A high current is then passed through the brain for approximately a half second. This is followed by convulsions that last for almost one minute. As the anesthetic wears off, the patient wakens and will not remember the period of treatment. Within twenty minutes, the patient is functioning reasonably well and has little, if any, physical discomfort. A course of ECT usually consists of a half dozen treatments, one every other day (Schuyler, 1974).

Electroconvulsive shock is often administered unilaterally, that is, to only half of the brain. Producing the convulsion on the side of the brain that does not contain the speech centers (in the nondominant hemisphere, see Chapter 17) greatly reduces the possibility of the side effect of impaired speech following ECT. Unilateral ECT is an effective antidepressant, but it is not as effective as bilateral ECT (Scovern and Killman, 1980; Abrams, Taylor, Faber, Ts'o, Williams, and Almy, 1983). The rate of response for bilateral ECT is about 50 percent greater than for unilateral ECT, but the intensity of the patient's disorientation and amnesia in the following week is also much greater. Recurrence of depression after ECT is substantial, with almost 60 percent of those treated with ECT becoming depressed again the next year (Sackeim, Prudic, Devanand, et al., 1993).

Exactly how ECT works is unknown, but it probably increases available norepinephrine and other biogenic amines. Isolating the effective ingredient in

ECT is quite difficult, however, as it is such a gross technique—shocking the entire brain—and has so many other effects, including memory loss and motivational changes (Squire, 1986).

The Psychodynamic Model of Depression

Psychodynamic theorists have stressed three causes of depression: anger turned against the self, excessive dependence on others for self-esteem, and helplessness at achieving one's goals.

ANGER TURNED UPON THE SELF

The first contributions of the psychodynamic model to the understanding of depression came from the early psychoanalysts. Karl Abraham (1911) and Sigmund Freud (1917) in his classic paper, "Mourning and Melancholia," both stressed the importance of anger turned inward upon the self in producing depression.

On the surface, depressed individuals often seem drained of anger, and this leads to the suspicion that their anger may be bound up inside them. For Freud, the main clue to their inner state came from the difference between normal bereavement (mourning) and depression (melancholia). The normal individual and the depressive have two strikingly different reactions to the loss of a person they love. For the mourner, the world now seems empty, but his self-esteem is not threatened. The mourner will survive the loss. In contrast, according to Freud, the depressive will begin to feel a powerful sense of worthlessness and self-blame. He will feel rotten and guilty; he will accuse himself of being a failure. This self-reproach is usually moral, grossly unjustified, and most remarkable, publicly and shamelessly declared. It provides the clue that anger turned against the self is actively motivated and generates the low self-esteem of depression.

▼ On the surface, depressed individuals may seem drained of anger, but they may bind up anger and turn it against themselves.

How could it come about that some individuals react to loss or rejection by turning their fury against themselves? For Freud, such a motivation for self-punishment follows from events in the depressive's childhood. During childhood, the future depressive forms an intense love that is undermined by disappointment with the other person. The depressive feels rage at having been disappointed. The libidinal energy underlying love is freed, but it does not become attached to any other person. Instead, the ego identifies with or "incorporates" the lost person, and the released libido attaches to this part of the ego. The rage originally felt for the person now is direct against the self.

Subsequent losses and rejection reactivate the primal loss and cause the depressive's rage to be turned again toward the original traitorous person, who has now been fused with the depressive's own ego. Such turning of anger in upon the self is the crucial step in producing the symptoms of low self-esteem, public accusation, the need for punishment, and in the most extreme cases, suicide. Depression ends either when the rage has spent itself or when the new loss is devalued—ends, that is, until a new loss starts the depressive sequence yet again.

The incorporation of a lost love object and anger turned inward upon the self producing depression is well illustrated by the following case:

Debby was a nineteen-year-old who was hospitalized because of strong suicidal impulses. During her hospitalization, she made a number of unsuccessful suicide attempts, and in addition, she engaged in a bizarre form of self-mutilation: clawing terribly at a particular spot on her left arm. These actions and impulses frightened her because she experienced them as originating outside of herself. On the other hand, however, she saw them as justified because she wanted to atone for her own worthlessness and promiscuity.

Debby's depression seemed to be closely related to her feelings about her mother, who had died a few years earlier under compromising circumstances; she had been murdered by a soldier with whom she had been spending the night. The body was so badly battered that it was identified only by a large distinctive birthmark on the left arm.

After her mother's death, Debby felt more warmth toward her mother than ever before. She became her mother's staunchest defender. When her mother was accused of ruining the family's reputation, Debby maintained that her mother had been badly misunderstood and ill treated by the family, and that this had caused her to carry on with other men. At the same time, however, Debby began to drop her former friends and to take up new friendships with people who had "bad reputations." She began to think of herself as a "bad person." As if to satisfy her new self-image, she began for the first time to behave promiscuously.

Debby's promiscuity seemed to result from identification with her mother, for this new part of herself provided the perfect target for the rage that her mother's death provoked. Debby's genuine feelings were mixed: both love and anger. We do not easily condemn the dead in our society, so instead Debby vented her anger by hating the part of herself that had become her mother. This was expressed most concretely through her self-mutilation. The specific part of her arm that she scratched so terribly was the exact location of her mother's birthmark. By mutilating herself, she was simultaneously able to *identify* with her mother by creating an ugly disfigurement on her left arm and to express her anger toward her mother.

Once Debby began to acknowledge her feelings of anger toward her mother consciously during therapy, her depression begin to lift. The crisis and resolution came violently, when Debby smashed every pane of glass in a door with her fist. During this experience she believed she was hitting not a door but an image of her mother. The conscious acknowledgment of this rage removed the need for indirect and symbolic expression, and Debby's feelings of worthlessness and self-hatred began to disappear. (Adapted from Fancher, 1973)

THE DEPRESSIVE PERSONALITY

Psychodynamic theorists since Freud have emphasized a personality style that may make individuals especially vulnerable to depression: the depressive depends excessively on others for his self-esteem. The depressive desperately needs to be showered with love and admiration. He goes through the world in a state of perpetual greediness for love, and when his need for love is not satisfied, his self-esteem plummets. When he is disappointed he has difficulty tolerating frustration, and even trivial losses upset his self-regard and result in immediate and frantic efforts to relieve discomfort. So depressives are seen as love addicts, who have become exquisitely skilled at producing demonstrations of love from others and who insist on a constant flow of love. Beyond receiving such love, however, the depressive cares little for the actual personality of the person he loves (Rado, 1928; Fenichel, 1945; Arieti and Bemporad, 1978).

FOCUS QUESTIONS

1. Describe the anger-turned-inward view of psychodynamic theorists.
2. Describe the depressive personality.
3. How might perceived helplessness lead to loss of self-esteem and depression?

HELPLESSNESS AT ACHIEVING ONE'S GOALS

The third major strand in psychodynamic theorizing about depression comes from the psychoanalyst Edward Bibring's (1953) claim that depression results when the ego feels helpless before its aspirations. Perceived helplessness at achieving the ego's high goals produces loss of self-esteem, the central feature in depression. The depression-prone individual has extremely high standards, and this increases his vulnerability to feeling helpless in the face of his goals. The combination of strongly held goals to be worthy, to be strong, and to be good, along with the ego's acute awareness of its helplessness and incapacity to live up to these goals, is for Bibring the mechanism of depression.

PSYCHODYNAMIC THERAPY FOR DEPRESSION

In general, psychodynamic theory emphasizes the long-term predisposition to depression, rather than the losses that happen to set it off in the short term. Psychodynamic therapies similarly are directed toward long-term change, rather than short-term alleviation of depression. Several therapeutic strategies follow from the three strands of psychodynamic theorizing about depression. First, psychodynamic therapists inclined toward the anger-turned-inward theory of depression will (as in Debby's case) attempt to make the patient conscious of his misdirected anger and the early conflicts that produced it. Learning to come to terms with the anger that loss and rejection produce and to direct it toward more appropriate objects should prevent and relieve depression. Second, psychodynamic therapists who deal with the depressive's strong dependence on others for self-esteem will attempt to get the patient to discover and then resolve the conflicts that make him perpetually greedy for love and esteem from others. Such a patient must learn that true self-esteem comes only from within. And third, therapists who work within Bibring's helplessness approach try to end the patient's depression by getting him to perceive his goals as being within reach, to modify his goals so that they can now be realized, or to give up these goals altogether.

Cognitive Models of Depression

The two cognitive models of depression view particular thoughts as the crucial cause of depressive symptoms. The first, developed by Aaron T. Beck, derives mainly from extensive therapeutic experience with depressed patients, and it views depression as caused by negative thoughts about the self, about ongoing experience, and about the future. The second, developed by Martin E. P. Seligman, derives mainly from experiments with dogs, rats, and mildly depressed people, and it views depression as caused by the expectation of future helplessness. A depressed person expects bad events to occur and believes that there is nothing he can do to prevent them from occurring.

BECK'S COGNITIVE THEORY OF DEPRESSION

Aaron T. Beck (along with Albert Ellis) founded a new type of therapy, called cognitive therapy, which we reviewed in Chapter 5. For Beck, two mechanisms, the **cognitive triad** and **errors in logic,** produce depression.

The Cognitive Triad   The cognitive triad consists of negative thoughts about the self, about ongoing experience, and about the future. The negative thoughts

▼ Aaron T. Beck has developed cognitive treatments for depression.

about the self consist of the depressive's belief that he is defective, worthless, and inadequate. The symptom of low self-esteem derives from his belief that he is defective. When he has unpleasant experiences, he attributes them to personal unworthiness. Since he believes he is defective, he believes that he will never attain happiness.

The depressive's negative thoughts about experience consist of his interpretation that what happens to him is bad. He misinterprets small obstacles as impassable barriers. Even when there are more plausible positive views of his experience, he is drawn to the most negative possible interpretation of what has happened to him. Finally, the depressive's negative view of the future is one of helplessness. When he thinks of the future, he believes the negative things that are happening to him now will continue unabated because of his personal defects. The following case illustrates how a depressive person may negatively interpret her experiences:

> Stella, a thirty-six-year-old depressed woman, had withdrawn from the tennis games she had previously enjoyed. Instead, her daily behavior pattern consisted of "sleeping and trying to do the housework I've neglected." Stella firmly believed that she was unable to engage in activities as "strenuous" as tennis and that she had become so poor at tennis that no one would ever want to play with her. Her husband arranged for a private tennis lesson in an attempt to help his wife overcome her depression. She reluctantly attended the lesson and appeared to be "a different person" in the eyes of her husband. She stroked the ball well and was agile in following instructions. Despite her good performance during the lesson, Stella concluded that her skills had "deteriorated" beyond the point at which lessons would do any good. She misinterpreted her husband's positive response to her lesson as an indication of how bad her game had become because in her view, "He thinks I'm so hopeless that the only time I can hit the ball is when I'm taking a lesson." She rejected the obvious reason for her husband's enthusiasm in favor of an explanation derived from her negative image of herself. She also stated that she didn't enjoy the tennis session because she wasn't "deserving" of any recreation time. (Adapted from Beck et al., 1979)

Stella's depression exemplifies the negative triad: (1) She believed that her tennis abilities had deteriorated (negative view of self), (2) she misinterpreted her husband's praise as indication of how poor her game was (negative view of experience), and (3) she believed that no one would ever want to play with her again (negative view of the future). Her motivational and cognitive symptoms stemmed from her negative cognitive triad. Her passivity (giving up tennis for sleeping and housework) resulted from her hopelessness about her abilities. Her cognitive symptoms were the direct expressions of her negative views of herself, her experience, and her future. Beck also claims that the other two classes of depressive symptoms—emotional and physical—result from the depressive's belief that he is doomed to failure.

Errors in Logic   Beck believes that systematic errors in logic are the second mechanism of depression. According to Beck, the depressive makes five different logical errors in thinking, and each of these darkens his experiences: arbitrary inference, selective abstraction, overgeneralization, magnification and minimization, and personalization.

__Arbitrary inference__ refers to drawing a conclusion when there is little or no evidence to support it. For example, an intern became discouraged when

FOCUS QUESTIONS

1. According to Aaron Beck, how do the mechanisms of the cognitive triad and errors in logic produce depression?
2. Explain the four specific cognitive therapy techniques: detection of automatic thoughts, reality testing automatic thoughts, reattribution training, and changing depressogenic assumptions.

she received an announcement which said that in the future all patients worked on by interns would be reexamined by residents. She thought, incorrectly, "The chief doesn't have any faith in my work." **Selective abstraction** consists of focusing on one insignificant detail while ignoring the more important features of a situation. In one case, an employer praised an employee at length about his secretarial work. Midway through the conversation, the boss suggested that he need not make extra carbon copies of her letters anymore. The employee's selective abstraction was, "The boss is dissatisfied with my work." In spite of all the good things said, only this was remembered.

Overgeneralization refers to drawing global conclusions about worth, ability, or performance on the basis of a single fact. Consider a man who fails to fix a leaky faucet in his house. Most husbands would call a plumber and then forget it. But the depressive will overgeneralize and may go so far as to believe that he is a poor husband. **Magnification and minimization** are gross errors of evaluation, in which small bad events are magnified and large good events are minimized. The inability to find the right color shirt is considered a disaster, but a large raise and praise for his good work are considered trivial. And lastly, **personalization** refers to incorrectly taking responsibility for bad events in the world. A neighbor slips and falls on her own icy walk, but the depressed next-door neighbor blames himself unremittingly for not having alerted her to her icy walk and for not insisting that she shovel it.

Cognitive Therapy   Beck's cognitive theory of depression considers that depression is caused by negative thoughts of self, ongoing experience, and future, and by errors in logic. Cognitive therapy for depression attempts to counter these cognitions (Beck, 1967; Beck, Rush, Shaw, and Emery, 1979). Its aim is to identify and correct the distorted thinking and dysfunctional assumptions underlying depression (Rehm, 1977; Beck et al., 1979). In addition, the patient is taught to conquer problems and master situations that he previously believed were insuperable. Cognitive therapy differs from most other forms of psychotherapy. In contrast to the psychoanalyst, the cognitive therapist actively guides the patient into reorganizing his thinking and his actions. The cognitive therapist talks a lot and is directive. She argues with the patient. She persuades; she cajoles; she leads. Beck claims that nondirective classical psychoanalytic techniques, such as free association, cause depressives to "dissolve in the morass of their negative thinking." Cognitive therapy also contrasts with psychoanalysis by being centered in the present. Childhood problems are rarely discussed; rather, the major focus is the patient's current thoughts and feelings. One of the central foci is not to be depressed about depression itself (Teasdale, 1985).

Cognitive therapy uses such behavioral therapy techniques as activity raising (rewarding the depressive for participating in more activities), graded task assignment (reinforcing the depressive for taking one small step at a time, and gradually increasing the difficulty of these steps), and social skills training against depressive symptoms. But in cognitive therapy, these techniques for changing behavioral symptoms are just tools for changing thoughts and assumptions that are seen as the underlying causes of depressed behavior. So, for example, the cognitive therapist believes that teaching a depressive to behave assertively works only insofar as it changes what the depressive believes about his own abilities and his future.

We discuss four specific cognitive therapy techniques: detecting automatic thoughts, reality testing automatic thoughts, reattribution training, and changing depressogenic assumptions.

Detection of Automatic Thoughts   Beck argues that there are discrete, negative sentences that depressed patients say to themselves quickly and habitually. These automatic thoughts maintain depression. Cognitive therapy helps patients to identify such automatic thoughts. Here is a case in which the patient had been unaware of her automatic thoughts:

> A mother of three found that her depression was at its worst from seven to nine in the morning when she prepared breakfast for her children. She was unable to explain this until she was taught to record her thoughts in writing as they occurred. As a result, she discovered she consistently compared herself with her mother, whom she remembered as irritable and argumentative in the morning. When her children misbehaved or made unreasonable requests, the patient often thought, "Don't get angry, or they'll resent you," with the result that she typically ignored them. With increasing frequency, however, she "exploded" at the children and then thought, "I'm worse than my mother ever was. I'm not fit to care for my children. They'd be better off if I were dead." (Beck et al., 1979)

Reality Testing Automatic Thoughts   Once the patient has learned to identify such thoughts, the cognitive therapist engages in a dialogue with the patient in which evidence for and against the thoughts is scrutinized. This is not an attempt to induce spurious optimism, rather to encourage the patient to use the reasonable standards of self-evaluation that nondepressed people use. The mother who thought she was unfit would be encouraged to remember that her children were flourishing in school, partly as a result of her tutoring them. Similarly a young student despondent over the belief that she would not get into a particular college was taught to criticize her automatic negative thoughts.

> THERAPIST: Why do you think you won't be able to get into the university of your choice?
> PATIENT: Because my grades were really not so hot.
> THERAPIST: Well, what was your grade average?
> PATIENT: Well, pretty good up until the last semester in high school.
> THERAPIST: What was your grade average in general?
> PATIENT: A's and B's.
> THERAPIST: Well, how many of each?
> PATIENT: Well, I guess almost all of my grades were A's, but I got terrible grades in my last semester.
> THERAPIST: What were your grades then?
> PATIENT: I got two A's and two B's.
> THERAPIST: So your grade average would seem to me to come to almost all A's. Why don't you think you'll be able to get into the university?
> PATIENT: Because of competition being so tough.
> THERAPIST: Have you found out what the average grades are for admission to the college?
> PATIENT: Well, somebody told me that a B+ average should suffice.
> THERAPIST: Isn't your average better than that?
> PATIENT: I guess so.
>
> (Beck et al., 1979)

By learning to scrutinize and criticize her automatic thoughts and marshaling evidence against them, the patient undermines her negative automatic thoughts, and they wane.

Reattribution Training   Depressed patients tend to blame themselves for bad events for which they are not, in fact, responsible. To counteract such irrational blame, the therapist and the patient review the events, applying the standards of nondepressed individuals in order to come up with an assignment of blame. This is not to absolve the patient of blame, but to let him see that there may be other factors besides his own incompetence that contribute to a bad event.

> A fifty-one-year-old bank manager in a state of deep depression believed he was ineffective in his job. His therapy session proceeded as follows:
>
> PATIENT: I can't tell you how much of a mess I've made of things. I made another major error in judgment which should cost me my job.
>
> THERAPIST: Tell me what the error in judgment was.
>
> PATIENT: I approved a loan which fell through completely. I made a very poor decision.
>
> THERAPIST: Can you recall the specifics about the decision?
>
> PATIENT: Yes, I remember it looked good on paper, good collateral, good credit rating, but I should have known that there was going to be a problem.
>
> THERAPIST: Did you have all the pertinent information at the time of your decision?
>
> PATIENT: Not at the time, but I sure found out six weeks later. I'm paid to make profitable decisions, not to give the bank's money away.
>
> THERAPIST: I understand your position. But I'd like to review the information which you had at the time your decision was required, not six weeks after the decision had been made.
>
> When the patient and the therapist reviewed this information, they concluded that the patient had made his judgment on sound banking principles. He recalled that he had even made an intensive check into the client's financial background, which he had forgotten. (Beck et al., 1979)

Such reattribution training enables patients to find sources of blame other than themselves, and it thereby raises their low self-esteem.

Changing Depressogenic Assumptions   The final technique of cognitive therapy is the explicit change of depressogenic assumptions (Ellis, 1962). Beck outlines six assumptions that depressed individuals base their life upon, thereby predisposing themselves to sadness, despair, and disappointment: (1) in order to be happy, I have to be successful in whatever I undertake; (2) to be happy, I must be accepted by all people at all times; (3) if I make a mistake, it means I am inept; (4) I can't live without love; (5) if somebody disagrees with me, it means he doesn't like me; and (6) my value as a person depends on what others think of me. When the patient and therapist identify one of these assumptions, it is vigorously attacked. The validity of the assumption is examined, counterarguments are marshaled, plausible alternative assumptions are presented, and the disastrous consequences of holding the assumption are exposed.

THE LEARNED HELPLESSNESS MODEL OF DEPRESSION

The second cognitive model of depression is the ***learned helplessness model.*** It is cognitive because it holds that the basic cause of depression is an expecta-

LACK OF CONTROL AND LEARNED HELPLESSNESS

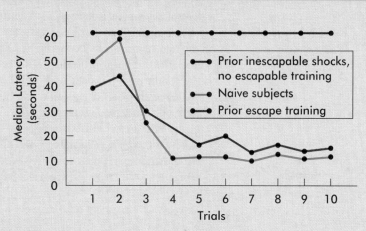

The figure shows the effects of matched escapable and inescapable shocks on later escape learning. It shows the escape latencies in the shuttlebox for three groups of dogs: (a) those given escape training in the shuttlebox as naive subjects, (b) those given prior escape training in a different situation, and (c) those given prior inescapable shocks, but matched in duration and temporal distribution to the shocks for the escape-training groups. (SOURCE: Maier, Seligman, and Solomon, 1969)

tion: the individual expects that bad events will occur to him and that there is nothing he can do to prevent their occurrence. We will discuss the phenomenon and theory of learned helplessness, and then we will discuss the relationship between learned helplessness and depression.

Experimental Discovery of Learned Helplessness   Learned helplessness was discovered quite by accident. In the course of experiments on the effects of prior Pavlovian conditioning on later instrumental learning, Steven Maier, Bruce Overmier, and Martin Seligman found that dogs first given Pavlovian conditioning with inescapable shock became profoundly passive later on when they were given escapable shock. In the latter condition, although they had the opportunity to flee the shock, they *did not* even attempt to escape. This behavior is in marked contrast to the behavior of two other groups of dogs who first received escapable shock or who received no shock. These dogs responded readily later, and learned to escape and avoid shock. This use of these three groups (the triadic design) tells us it is not shock *per se*, but the uncontrollability of the shock that produces the motivational deficits (see Figure 11–5).

There is another basic deficit of learned helplessness found in dogs, rats, and people. This is the failure to learn that responding can be successful, even once a response is made and it succeeds in controlling the outcome. Dogs and rats often sat for three or four trials, failing to escape shock when given a later opportunity to escape in a shuttle. On the fifth trial, the animal might successfully terminate shock. Such an animal, surprisingly, often did not catch on: during later trials it would revert to taking the shock, even though it had made a successful response (Overmier and Seligman, 1967; Maier and Seligman, 1976).

Learned Helplessness in Humans Following the exploration of learned helplessness in animals, it became important for investigators to find out whether or not learned helplessness occurred in normal human beings (see Figure 11–6). It does. In the basic procedure that produces learned helplessness in humans, the triadic design is used with nondepressed volunteers who receive loud noise delivered through earphones. For the first group, the noise is *inescapable;* it is preprogrammed to go on and off independently of what they do. The second group can *escape* noise by pressing a series of buttons in front of them. The third group receives *no noise.* Then all three groups are taken to a human shuttlebox, and noise goes on. If they move their hand from one side of the shuttlebox to the other, the noise goes off. The results parallel those in animals. Indi-

FIGURE 11–6

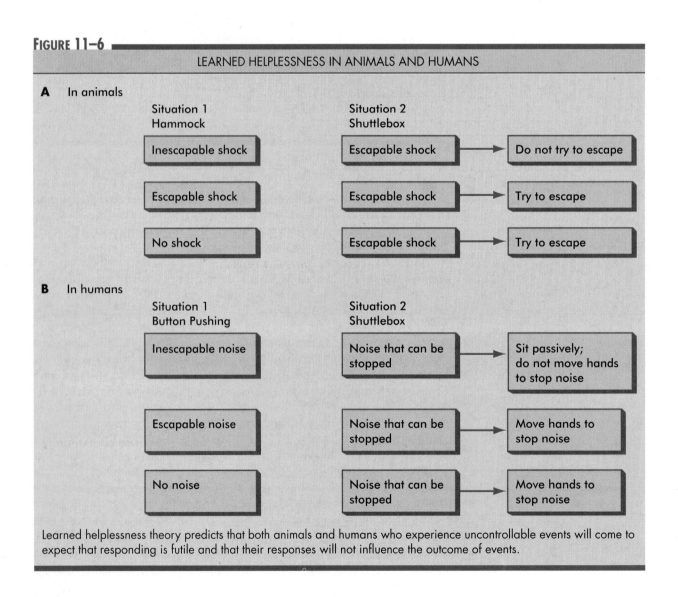

LEARNED HELPLESSNESS IN ANIMALS AND HUMANS

A In animals

Situation 1
Hammock

Situation 2
Shuttlebox

Inescapable shock	Escapable shock → Do not try to escape
Escapable shock	Escapable shock → Try to escape
No shock	Escapable shock → Try to escape

B In humans

Situation 1
Button Pushing

Situation 2
Shuttlebox

Inescapable noise	Noise that can be stopped → Sit passively; do not move hands to stop noise
Escapable noise	Noise that can be stopped → Move hands to stop noise
No noise	Noise that can be stopped → Move hands to stop noise

Learned helplessness theory predicts that both animals and humans who experience uncontrollable events will come to expect that responding is futile and that their responses will not influence the outcome of events.

1. What is the learned helplessness model of depression?
2. Describe the laboratory experiment on which the learned helplessness model is based.
3. What roles do attributions and explanatory style play in unipolar depression?
4. Describe the parallels between the symptoms, cause, and therapies for learned helplessness and those for depression.
5. What are three problems with the cognitive model of depression?

viduals who have received inescapable noise sit there passively and fail to escape, but those who have previously learned to escape noise escape it readily in the shuttlebox (Hiroto, 1974).

The deficits produced by learned helplessness in humans are quite general. Experience with inescapable noise produces deficits at later noise escape, deficits in cognitive tasks such as the solution of anagrams, deficits in seeing patterns in anagrams, and lowered expectancy change following success and failure in skilled tasks. The inducing events for helplessness in man need not be aversive. Not only do inescapable noise and shock produce the phenomenon, but also unsolvable cognitive problems produce it.

Learned helplessness theory argues that the basic cause of all the deficits observed in helpless animals and humans after uncontrollable events is the expectation of future noncontingency between responding and outcomes. This expectation that future responding will be futile causes the two helplessness deficits: (1) it produces deficits in responding by undermining the motivation to respond, and (2) it produces later difficulty in seeing that outcomes are contingent upon responding when they are. The three-group design is the basic evidence for this hypothesis. Recall that just the experience of shock, noise, or problems in themselves does not produce the motivational and cognitive deficits, only *uncontrollable* shock, noise, and problems produce these deficits. This strongly suggests that both animals and humans learn during uncontrollable events that their responding is futile and come to expect this in future situations.

Attributions in Human Helplessness   When a human being experiences inescapable noise or unsolvable problems and perceives that his responding is ineffective, he goes on to ask an important question: What causes my present helplessness? The causal attribution (explanation) that a person makes is a crucial determinant of when and where expectancies for future failure will recur. There are three attributional dimensions that govern when and where future helplessness deficits will be displayed (Abramson, Seligman, and Teasdale, 1978).

The first dimension is ***internal-external.*** Consider an individual who has received unsolvable problems in an experiment. When he discovers that responding is ineffective, he can either decide that he is stupid and the problem is solvable, or that the problems are rigged to be unsolvable and he is not stupid. The first explanation for this failure is internal (stupidity) and the second is external (unsolvable problem). Evidence suggests that when individuals fail at important tasks and make internal explanations for their failure, passivity appears and self-esteem drops markedly. When individuals make external explanations for failure, passivity ensues but self-esteem stays high (Abramson, 1978).

In addition to deciding whether or not the cause of failure is internal or external, an individual who has failed also considers the ***stable-unstable*** dimension: "Is the cause of my failure something permanent or transient?" An individual who has failed may decide that the cause of the failure is stable and that it will persist into the future. Examples of such stable factors are stupidity (which is internal as well as stable), or the difficulty of the task (which is stable but external). In contrast, an individual may decide that the cause of his failure is unstable. An individual who has failed an exam can believe that the cause was his bad night's sleep the night before, an unstable cause that is internal. Alternatively, he might decide that he failed because it was an unlucky day, an unstable cause that is external. The attributional theory of helplessness postulates that when the cause of failure is attributed to a stable factor, the helplessness deficits will persist in time. Conversely, if the individual believes that the cause of his failure is unstable, he will not necessarily fail again when he encounters the task months hence. According to the attributional model of learned helplessness, stable explanations lead to permanent deficits, and unstable explanations to transient deficits.

The third and final dimension is ***global-specific*** (see Figure 11–7). When an individual finds that he has failed, he must ask himself whether or not the cause of his failure is global—a factor that will produce failure in a wide variety of circumstances—or specific—a factor that will produce failure only in similar circumstances. For example, an individual who has failed to solve a laboratory problem may decide that he is unskilled at solving laboratory problems and probably unskilled at other tasks as well. In this instance, being unskilled is global and the expectation of failure will recur in a wide variety of other situations. It is also a stable and internal factor. Alternatively, he might decide that

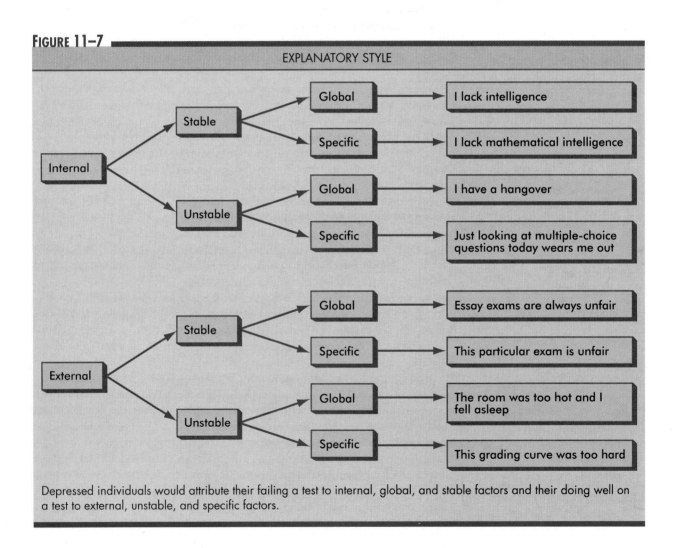

FIGURE 11–7

EXPLANATORY STYLE

Internal → Stable → Global	I lack intelligence
Internal → Stable → Specific	I lack mathematical intelligence
Internal → Unstable → Global	I have a hangover
Internal → Unstable → Specific	Just looking at multiple-choice questions today wears me out
External → Stable → Global	Essay exams are always unfair
External → Stable → Specific	This particular exam is unfair
External → Unstable → Global	The room was too hot and I fell asleep
External → Unstable → Specific	This grading curve was too hard

Depressed individuals would attribute their failing a test to internal, global, and stable factors and their doing well on a test to external, unstable, and specific factors.

▲ Explanatory style is a crucial factor in depression. Depressives tend to believe they are helpless for reasons that are internal, stable, and global.

these particular laboratory problems are too hard. The difficulty of laboratory problems is a specific factor, since it will only produce the expectation that future responding will be ineffective in other laboratory problems and not in real life. This factor, aside from being specific, is stable and external. The attributional model of helplessness holds that when individuals make global explanations for their failure, helplessness deficits will occur in a wide variety of situations. When individuals believe that specific factors cause their failures, the expectation of response ineffectiveness will be narrow, and only a narrow band of situations will produce helplessness.

EVIDENCE FOR EXPLANATORY STYLE AND DEPRESSION

The helplessness model suggests that an insidious explanatory or attributional style (attributing failure to internal, global, and stable factors; attributing success to external, unstable, and specific factors) predisposes an individual to depression. A variation is the ***hopelessness theory of depression*** (Abramson, Metalsky, and Alloy, 1989; Alloy, Lipman, and Abramson, 1992). This theory emphasizes the stable and global dimensions for negative events as determinants of hopelessness, and proposes a subtype of depression, ***hopelessness depression.*** Three types of recent evidence confirm these theories: longitudinal studies, experiments of nature, and therapy studies.

Longitudinal Studies   Longitudinal studies look at the same individual across time, taking the same set of measurements at each point in time. This allows us to find out if explanatory style at an earlier time influences susceptibility to depression later, *over and above how depressed the individual was at the earlier time.* A five-year longitudinal study of 350 third-graders and their parents predicted depression and poor school achievement from explanatory style. The researchers predicted which of these children would become depressed based on the pessimistic explanatory style, bad life events, and lack of popularity of these children as third-graders. Each of these factors made a separate contribution to predicting which third-graders experienced depression by the end of sixth grade (Nolen-Hoeksema, Girgus, and Seligman, 1986; 1992; Quiggle, Garber, Panak, and Dodge, 1992). Parallel questions have been asked of college students by Zullow and Seligman (1985). One hundred and fifty-four students took the ASQ (Attributional Style Questionnaire) and the BDI (Beck Depression Inventory) in three waves over three months. Again depressive explanatory style predicted later depression over and above earlier depression. More specifically, it was the severe end of depression that was particularly affected by their explanatory style. "Keepers and Gainers" were defined as individuals who either *became depressed* or stayed depressed (BDI stayed above sixteen). Of the thirteen Keepers and Gainers, ten came from the quartile that had the most depressive explanatory style.

The last longitudinal study is an unusual one because it involved only one patient. It made, however, a very accurate prediction of his behavior. The subject was a patient, Mr. Q, who demonstrated precipitous shifts in mood during psychotherapy sessions conducted over four years. Three types of sessions were analyzed: those in which Mr. Q became more depressed, those in which he became less depressed, and those in which no shift at all occurred. Explanations for bad events were extracted from these sessions before and after the mood swings, and were rated for internality, stability, and globality. Explanations for bad events were extracted from the 400 words (spoken by Mr. Q) be-

FIGURE 11–8

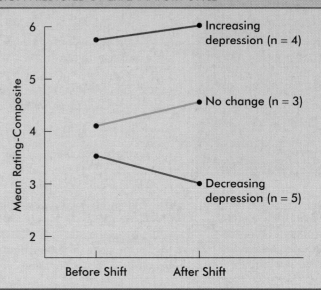

SHIFTS IN DEPRESSION PREDICTED BY EXPLANATORY STYLE

Means of internal, stable, and global ratings of explanation before and after mood shifts for the different types of sessions. (Numbers of sessions on which means are based are in parentheses.) (SOURCE: Peterson, Luborsky, and Seligman, 1983)

fore the swing and from the 400 words following the swing. For comparison purposes, causal explanations were also extracted from randomly chosen 800-word segments of three sessions in which no swing occurred. Means for the different types of sessions are shown in Figure 11–8. The differences predicted were present right before the swings in mood. Highly internal, stable, and global causal explanations preceded increased depression, whereas much more external, unstable, and specific statements preceded decreased depression. *There was no overlap between the ratings of causal explanations before swings to more versus less depression* (Peterson, Luborsky, and Seligman, 1983).

Experiments of Nature   The ideal way to test the helplessness reformulation is to measure the explanatory style of individuals and then to choose randomly from among them half of those who have experienced some naturally occurring bad event. The most severe depression is predicted to ensue for subjects with the preexisting depressive explanatory style who also then experienced the bad event.

In one study, the naturally occurring bad event was a poor grade on a midterm exam. The participants were undergraduates in an introductory psychology course. At Time 1, they took the ASQ and filled out a questionnaire about the midterm grades with which they would be happy and unhappy. Just prior to the midterm examination, at Time 2, students' level of depressed mood was assessed with a mood checklist. At Time 3, immediately following receipt of the midterm grade, students again completed the mood checklist. Explanatory style predicted the particular explanation for the midterm failure. The particular explanation in turn predicted depressive reaction. Students who made stable and global explanations for their poor grade became depressed (Metalsky, Halberstadt, and Abramson, 1987). Explanatory style, however, had no effect on depressive reaction over and above its effect on the particular explanation for the poor grade.

Therapy Studies Sixty-four unipolar depressed patients were randomly assigned to either tricyclic drug therapy, cognitive therapy, or both, and they were given twelve weeks of treatment (Hollon, DuRubeis, Evans, and Weimer, 1992). Each treatment produced strong relief from depression. Explanatory style was measured by the ASQ at the beginning, middle, and end of therapy. What was the relation between relief from depression and change for the better in explanatory style? In the tricyclic drug group, the correlation was negative and nonsignificant. In the group getting both cognitive therapy and tricyclics, the relation was strongly positive. In the cognitive therapy group, the relationship was very strong. Thus, as patients' explanatory style changed for the better during cognitive therapy, they became less depressed. But with drug therapy, improving explanatory style was unrelated to improvement. This suggests that cognitive therapy and drug therapy break up depression by different means. Perhaps drug therapy merely activates patients, but cognitive therapy changes the entire way they look at causes. Evidence suggests that those patients whose explanatory style did not change for the better tended to relapse over the next two years (Evans, Hollon, DuRubeis, and Piasecki, 1992). Drug therapy may result in a higher relapse rate because it does not improve explanatory style.

In summary, we have described three interlocking types of research investigating attributional style in the helplessness model of depression. A characteristic way of explaining bad events with internal, stable, and global causes co-occurs with depressive symptoms. The longitudinal studies showed that this explanatory style preceded the development of depressive symptoms. The experiment of nature indicated that this style resulted in depression once bad events were encountered. The study of therapy suggested that changing explanatory style for the better relieves depression.

PARALLELS BETWEEN DEPRESSION AND LEARNED HELPLESSNESS

We have now examined the basic learned helplessness phenomena in animals and humans and the theory behind it. Learned helplessness has been suggested as a model for depression. Table 11–3 outlines the similarity in symptoms, cause, cure, prevention, and predisposition between learned helplessness in the laboratory and unipolar depression as it occurs in real life (Seligman, 1975; Weiss, Simson, et al., 1985).

Symptoms The failure to escape noise and to solve problems after experience with uncontrollable events is the basic *passivity deficit* of learned helplessness. This passivity seems similar to the motivational deficits of depression (Miller and Seligman, 1975, 1976; Price, Tryon, and Raps, 1978).

Nondepressed individuals given inescapable noise or unsolvable problems show the *cognitive deficit* of learned helplessness: they have difficulty learning that responding is successful, even when it is. Depressed individuals show exactly the same deficit. Nondepressed human beings made helpless fail to see patterns in anagrams and fail to change expectancy for future success when they succeed and fail in skill tasks. Depressed students and patients show these same deficits in the laboratory (Miller and Seligman, 1975, 1976; Abramson, Garber, Edwards, and Seligman, 1978).

When individuals are made helpless by inescapable noise and attribute their failure to their own shortcomings as opposed to external causes, not only are the motivational and cognitive deficits of helplessness and depression ob-

TABLE 11–3

	Learned Helplessness	Depression
	SIMILARITY OF LEARNED HELPLESSNESS AND DEPRESSION	
Symptoms	Passivity Cognitive deficits Self-esteem deficits Sadness, hostility, anxiety Loss of appetite Loss of aggression Sleep loss Norepinephrine and serotonin depletion	Passivity Negative cognitive triad Low self-esteem Sadness, hostility, anxiety Loss of appetite Loss of aggression Sleep loss Norepinephrine and serotonin depletion
Cause	Learned belief that responding is independent of important outcomes (plus attributions to internal, global, and stable factors)	Generalized belief that responding will be ineffective
Therapy	Change belief in response futility to belief in response effectiveness ECT, MAO-I, tricyclics, fluoxetine REM deprivation Time	Cognitive and behavioral antidepressant therapy ECT, MAO-I, tricyclics, fluoxetine REM deprivation Time
Prevention	Immunization	Optimism training
Predisposition	Insidious explanatory style	Insidious explanatory style

served, but *self-esteem* drops as well. In contrast, when helpless subjects are led to make external attributions and blame the task difficulty for their failure, the motivational and cognitive deficits are observed but self-esteem deficits are not. This parallels the low self-esteem that occurs in depressives, particularly among individuals who blame themselves for their troubles (Abramson, 1978).

Parallel *mood changes* occur both in learned helplessness and depression. When nondepressed subjects are made helpless by inescapable noise or unsolvable problems, they become sadder, more hostile, and more anxious. These reports parallel the emotional changes in depression: more sadness, anxiety, and perhaps more hostility.

In the laboratory, rats who receive inescapable shock eat less food, lose more weight, aggress less against other rats, and lose out in competition for food with rats who had received either escapable shock or no shock. This *loss of appetite* and *loss of aggression* produced by helplessness in the laboratory parallel the somatic symptoms of depressives: they lose weight, eat less, lose sleep, their social desires and status drop, and they become less aggressive.

Finally, learned helplessness in the rat is accompanied by *norepinephrine depletion*. Jay Weiss has demonstrated that the brains of rats who have received inescapable shock have less available norepinephrine than the brains of animals who receive no shock or escapable shock (Weiss, Glazer, and Pohoresky, 1976).

In summary, there are several parallel symptoms in laboratory-created learned helplessness and depression as found in nature. In both conditions, the four basic symptoms of depression are displayed: motivational deficits, cognitive deficits, emotional deficits, and somatic deficits. These four deficits were created in the laboratory by a known factor—by imposing the expectation that future responses and important outcomes will be independent. Could it be that when we observe the same four symptoms in nature and call the condition depression, that the same cause—a belief in the futility of responding—is at work?

Cause   The learned helplessness hypothesis says that depressive deficits, which parallel the learned helplessness deficits, are produced when an individual expects that bad events may occur and that they will be independent of his responding. When this is attributed to internal factors, self-esteem will drop; to stable factors, the depression will be long-lived; and to global factors, the depression will be general. The experimental evidence confirms this. This insidious attributional style has been found in depressed students, children, and patients. Depressed patients, moreover, believe that the important goals in their life are less under their control than do other psychiatric patients (Eidelson, 1977; Seligman et al., 1979; Raps, Reinhard, and Seligman, 1980). Most important, individuals who have this explanatory style but are not depressed, become depressed when they later encounter bad events (Peterson and Seligman, 1984).

Therapy   Since the cause of learned helplessness and depression is hypothesized to be the expectation that responding will be ineffective in controlling future events, the basic therapeutic theme should be to change this belief to one in which the individual believes that responding will be effective and anticipated bad events will be avoided. The attributional theory of learned helplessness suggests some basic strategies for doing this. So, for example, learned helplessness theory suggests that therapies such as teaching social skills and assertiveness training should be antidepressive because they teach the individual that he can control affection and the esteem of other people by his own actions. Further tactics such as criticizing automatic thoughts (it's not that I'm an unfit mother, rather I'm grouchy at 7 A.M.) help alleviate depression because they change attributions for failure from internal, stable, and global (unfit mother) to external, unstable, and specific (7 A.M.). Notice how similar these strategies are to the techniques of cognitive and behavioral therapies that we have just reviewed.

In addition to cognitive and behavior therapy parallels, there are *somatic therapy* parallels as well. Five kinds of somatic therapy appear to break up learned helplessness in animals: electroconvulsive shock, MAO inhibitors, tricyclics, serotonin enhancers (e.g., fluoxetine), and dream deprivation (Dorworth, 1971; Porsolt et al., 1978; Brett, Burling, and Pavlik, 1981; Peterson, Maier, and Seligman, 1993). These are the five somatic therapies that also can break up unipolar depression. In summary, there is reason to believe that the somatic and cognitive therapies that reverse learned helplessness also reverse depression.

Prevention and Predisposition   Learned helplessness in animals is prevented by prior experience with mastery and immunization. If an animal first controls important events, such as shock and food, then later helplessness never occurs. In effect, it is prevented. Such immunization seems to be lifelong: rats who learn to escape shock as weanlings do not become helpless when as adults they are

Box 11–3

FLEXIBLE OPTIMISM

People who have the skill of making unstable, specific, and external explanations for the bad events that occur to them do better in several realms of life. Seligman (1991) calls them "optimists." They fight off depression better, achieve more in school, sports, and the workplace, and enjoy better physical health than do "pessimists," people who see bad events as stable, global, and internal.

Optimism is no panacea. For one thing, it may sometimes keep us from seeing reality with the necessary clarity (see Box 11–1). For another, it may help us to evade responsibility for failure by blaming it on others. But these limits are just that, limits. They do not nullify the benefits of optimism; rather they put it in perspective.

Until the development of cognitive therapy, if you were a pessimist, you had no choice but to live with the pessimism. You would endure frequent depressions; your work and your health would suffer. In exchange for this you might have a keener sense of reality and a stronger sense of responsibility.

You now have a choice. If you undergo cognitive therapy and learn to make unstable, specific, and external explanations for failures more readily, you can choose to use its techniques whenever you need them—without becoming a slave to them.

For example, let's say you are now able to curtail depression by disputing the catastrophic thoughts that used to plague you. Along comes a new setback. You fail your Psychology and your English midterms. You are not a brilliant student, and you didn't study enough for them. You might, if you choose, launch into all the disputations that would let you continue thinking that you are so smart you don't need to study: the exam was unfair, the grading was too hard, the professor is a poor teacher, the curve was too stringent. But you can also choose not to dispute. You can say to yourself that this is one of those moments that call for seeing yourself with merciless clarity, not one of those moments that call

for warding off your own depression. Your academic future is at stake. The cost of being wrong here outweighs the importance of fighting off demoralization. Rather it is the time to take stock and appreciate your need to study hard more clearly. You can choose *not* to dispute the pessimistic thoughts.

What you now have is more freedom—an additional choice. You can choose to use optimism when you judge less depression is the issue, or more achievement, or better health. But you can also choose not to use it, when you judge that clear sight or taking responsibility are called for. Learning optimism does not erode your sense of values or your judgment. Rather it frees you to use cognitive techniques as a tool to achieve the goals you set.

What criteria should guide you when deciding whether to use optimism or pessimism? The fundamental guideline for *not* deploying the skills of optimism and cognitive therapy is to ask what the *cost of failure* is in the particular situation. If the cost is high, optimism is the wrong strategy. In the cases of the pilot in the cockpit deciding whether to de-ice the plane one more time, the partygoer deciding whether to drive home after drinking, the student deciding to go skiing for the weekend rather than studying for the critical final exams, the costs of failure are, respectively, death, an auto accident, failing. Using techniques that minimize those costs are a disservice. On the other hand, if the cost of failure is low, use optimism. The sales agent deciding whether to make one more call only loses her time if she fails. The shy person deciding whether to attempt to open a conversation only risks rejection. The teenager contemplating learning a new sport only risks frustration. The disgruntled executive, passed over for promotion, only risks some refusals if he quietly puts out feelers for a new position. All should use optimism.

SOURCE: Adapted from Seligman, 1991.

given inescapable shock. Conversely, lifelong vulnerability to helplessness is produced by early experience with inescapable shock: rats who receive inescapable shock as weanlings become helpless adults (Hannum, Rosellini, and Seligman, 1976). This parallels the data on the prevention of and vulnerability to depression (see Box 11–3). Individuals whose mother dies before the child is eleven years old are more vulnerable to depression than those whose mother does not. There are, however, invulnerability factors that prevent depression from occurring in such individuals: a job, an intimate relationship with a spouse or lover, not having life burdened with child care, and religious belief

(Brown and Harris, 1978). These invulnerability factors may all increase the expectation of future control, and vitiate the expectations of future helplessness.

Explanatory Style as a Predisposition   The final parallel in the predisposition to helplessness and depression is that depressed individuals have an insidious explanatory style. As we said above, when they fail, they tend to attribute their failure to internal, global, and stable factors; but when they succeed, they attribute their success to external, unstable, and specific factors (Seligman, Abramson, Semmel, and von Baeyer, 1979; Sweeney, Anderson, and Bailey, 1986). This is a style that maximizes the expectation that responding will be ineffective in the future. The helplessness model suggests that it is this explanatory style that predisposes an individual to depression, and as we have seen, the evidence confirms this.

THE OUTCOME OF COGNITIVE THERAPY

The National Institutes of Mental Health (NIMH) sponsored a landmark collaborative study on the effectiveness of cognitive therapy, interpersonal therapy (IPT), and tricyclic antidepressants for overcoming unipolar depression (Elkin, Shea, Imber, Pilkonis, Sotsky, Glass, Watkins, Leber, and Collins, 1986; Elkin, Shea, Watkins, Imber, et at., 1989; Imber, Pilkonis, Sotsky, and Elkin, 1990; Shea, Elkin, Imber, and Sotsky, 1992). This study is the most extensive and thorough trial of any psychotherapy ever done.

Two hundred and fifty unipolar patients were randomly assigned to one of four groups, and the design was carried out at three different treatment centers. The patients were moderately to severely depressed, and 70 percent were female. Twenty-eight trained therapists were used. Cognitive therapy focused on detecting and changing negative thoughts and assumptions. IPT focused on interpersonal problems (see Box 11–4); these therapists taught depressives better techniques for resolving conflicts with others (Klerman, Weissman, Rounsaville, and Chevron, 1984). The drug group was given tricyclic antidepressant drugs, and a fourth group was given a placebo. Therapy was brief: sixteen weeks. Recovery from depression was carefully assessed by a battery of tests and interviews.

▶ Explanatory style is not only a depressive symptom, but may precede and predict other symptoms. Even if she is not now depressed, if this woman believes she is alone for reasons that will not change, she may be vulnerable to depression.

Box 11–4

INTERPERSONAL THERAPY

A very curious thing happened during the NIMH outcome study. Interpersonal therapy (IPT) was originally regarded as a control for nonspecific effects in the study. Researchers thought it would work about as well as a placebo. To the investigators' surprise, when the sealed envelope was opened, IPT worked at least as well as both cognitive therapy and tricyclic antidepressant drugs (Elkin, Shea, Watkins, Imber, et al., 1989).

IPT focuses on social relations. It originated in the psychoanalytic treatments of Harry Stack Sullivan and Frieda Fromm-Reichman. IPT is not psychoanalytic, however; it does not deal with childhood, the defenses, or the dynamics of getting on with others. IPT hones in on current interpersonal problems. Ongoing disputes, frustrations, anxieties, and disappointments are the main material of therapy.

IPT looks at four problem areas: grief, fights, role transitions, and social deficits. When dealing with grief, IPT looks for abnormal grief reactions. It brings out the delayed mourning process and helps the patient find new social relationships that can substitute. When dealing with fights, the IPT therapist helps determine where the disrupted relationship is going: Does it need renegotiation? Is it at an impasse? Is it irretrievably lost? Communication, negotiation, and assertiveness skills are taught. When dealing with role transitions, including retirement, divorce, and leaving home, the IPT therapist gets the patient to re-evaluate the lost role, to express emotions about the loss, to develop social skills suitable for the new role, and to establish new social supports. When dealing with social deficits, the IPT therapist looks for recurrent patterns in past relationships. Emotional expression is encouraged. Both recurrent social strengths and weaknesses are uncovered. When weaknesses are found, role playing and enhanced communication skills are used.

The main virtues of this approach are that it is brief, sensible, and inexpensive (a few months). It has no known bad side effects, and it has been shown to be quite effective against depression, bringing relief in around 70 percent of cases. A manual for it exists (Klerman, Weissman, Rounsaville, and Chevron, 1984). Its main problem is that it has not become very widely practiced, so little research has been done to find its active ingredients. This also means it is hard to find an IPT therapist outside of New York City.

More than 50 percent of the patients recovered in the two psychotherapy groups and in the drug group. Only 29 percent recovered in the placebo group. The drug treatment produced faster improvement, but by the end of the sixteen weeks patients in the two psychotherapies had caught up.

Relapse data from the collaborative study were unclear. While most treated subjects were improved, only 25 percent both recovered and remained well across all follow-ups (Shea, Elkin, Imber, and Sotsky, 1992). This suggests that the sixteen weeks of psychotherapy were insufficient for maintained antidepressant effects. There is evidence from other studies, however, which suggests that patients in cognitive therapy have learned a skill to cope with depression that the patients given drugs have not, and that this results in lower relapse of those treated with cognitive therapy. For example, in one study, forty-four depressed outpatients were randomly assigned for twelve weeks either to individual cognitive therapy or to therapy with tricyclic antidepressants (Rush, Beck, Kovacs, and Hollon, 1977; Kovacs, Rush, Beck, and Hollon, 1981). Their depressions were quite severe: on the average, the current episode of depression had lasted for twelve months, and patients had already been unsuccessfully treated by two previous therapists. During the course of therapy, the patients in the cognitive therapy group had a maximum of twenty sessions, and the patients in the drug group were given a tricyclic daily, plus twelve brief sessions with the therapist who had prescribed the drugs.

By the end of treatment, both groups had improved according to both self-report and therapist ratings of depression. Only one of the nineteen patients assigned to cognitive therapy had dropped out, whereas eight of the twenty-five assigned to drug therapy had dropped out. This is not surprising since there is usually notable attrition due to side effects and reluctance to take drugs in drug treatment. Of the cognitive therapy patients, 79 percent showed marked improvement or complete remission, but only 20 percent of the drug patients showed such a strong response. Follow-up at three months, six months, and twelve months after treatment indicated that both groups maintained their improvement. The group that had received cognitive therapy, however, continued to be less depressed than the group that had received drug therapy. In addition, the cognitive group had half the relapse rate of the drug group (see also Reynolds and Coats, 1986).

Overall then two systematic psychotherapies—cognitive therapy and interpersonal therapy—work as well as tricyclic antidepressant drugs against unipolar depression. And all three treatments work better than placebos. Tricyclics work faster, but the psychotherapies may produce more lasting relief.

PREVENTING DEPRESSION: HOPE FOR AT-RISK CHILDREN

Throughout this book, we have examined many controlled studies of therapies for sufferers of mental disorders. But for many years, psychologists have also called for studies that might explore the prevention of mental illness. Very few controlled studies of prevention have been performed, however. In one of the first, the Pennsylvania Prevention Project, researchers from the University of Pennsylvania used the principles of cognitive therapy with normal children to see if depressive symptoms could be prevented in advance (see Figure 11–9; Jaycox, Reivich, Gillham, and Seligman, 1994; Gillham, Reivich, Jaycox, and Seligman, 1994). Children were chosen because they were at risk for depression by one of two criteria: either they had mild symptoms of depression already, or their parents were fighting.

At-risk ten- to thirteen-year-olds learned the cognitive and problem-solving skills that already depressed patients are taught during cognitive therapy. The program was taught by advanced graduate students in clinical psychology in a

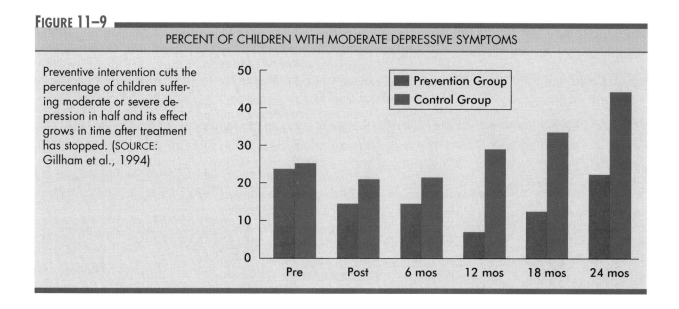

FIGURE 11–9

PERCENT OF CHILDREN WITH MODERATE DEPRESSIVE SYMPTOMS

Preventive intervention cuts the percentage of children suffering moderate or severe depression in half and its effect grows in time after treatment has stopped. (SOURCE: Gillham et al., 1994)

group format (ten to twelve children) according to a manual. There were twelve two-hour sessions held after school. Sixty-nine children participated in prevention groups and were compared to seventy-three children in control groups. The results showed that depressive symptoms were markedly reduced in the prevention groups as compared to in the control groups at post-test. A six-month follow-up showed prevention of depressive symptoms as well as significantly fewer behavioral problems in the treated children than in the controls.

The most unusual findings began to show up in the one-year follow-up. It is a universal finding in therapy outcome studies that even "successful" effects wane. Surprisingly, the Pennsylvania Project found that the prevention effects got larger over time. One-year, eighteen-month, and two-year follow-ups showed increasing gains and increasing separation between the treated groups and control groups on depressive symptoms. At the eighteen-month point, 33.3 percent of the control children had moderate or severe depressive symptoms, but only 12.2 percent of the treated children showed such symptoms. In addition, prevention was most effective in the children who were most at risk.

The researchers may have found a critical age to teach skills to guard against depression. The skills become incorporated into the child's repertoire; as the child goes into puberty, and depression becomes commonplace, he or she can use these skills repeatedly and increasingly to navigate the new shoals of adolescence.

PROBLEMS OF THE COGNITIVE MODEL OF DEPRESSION

FOCUS QUESTIONS

1. Explain how each theory of depression contributes to our understanding of depression.
2. Describe how cognitive, biological, and psychodynamic factors all play a role in accounting for predisposition, symptoms, precipitating incidents, and success in therapy.

The cognitive model of depression has three main problems. First, it is vague on what kind of depression is modeled (Depue and Monroe, 1978). It is probably not an especially good model of the subclasses of unipolar depression that are "biological" and "endogenous." Biological depressions may be better treated by somatic therapy than by cognitive-behavioral therapies, although this has yet to be tested.

Second, cognitive theory is weak in accounting for the somatic symptoms of depression; these seem better explained by the biological model. Similarly, although the cognitive model does not predict that somatic therapy would be effective, the effective somatic therapies do succeed in breaking up learned helplessness in animals, as well as depression in humans.

Third, experimental controversy still rages over many of the major points of the learned helplessness model of depression. Some critics doubt whether learned helplessness in animals is produced by an expectation, believing it to be either learned inactivity or norepinephrine depletion (Glazer and Weiss, 1976; Weiss, Glazer, and Pohoresky, 1976; Anisman, 1978). Others have argued that the learned helplessness deficits seen in human beings do not follow closely from the theory (Buchwald, Coyne, and Cole, 1978; Costello, 1978). There also has been difficulty in replicating some of the basic human phenomena (McNitt and Thornton, 1978; Willis and Blaney, 1978). Finally, it is still controversial whether helplessness and depressive explanatory style are consequences or causes of depression (Peterson and Seligman, 1984).

Integration of Theories of Unipolar Depression

No one theory of depression—not the biological, not the psychodynamic, and not the cognitive—explain all the phenomena of depression. But each of them seems to have a piece of the truth and most important of all, the theories are not, by and large, incompatible. Depression is, in fact, a disorder that occurs on at least three levels. There are clear cognitive deficits—hopelessness and worthlessness being the most prominent; there are clear biological deficits—the somatic symptoms and their biogenic amine correlates; and there may well be psychodynamic predispositions—the dependent and helpless personality style. Cognitive, biological, and psychodynamic factors all may play a role in accounting for the predisposition, the symptoms, the causal mediation, and in producing success in therapy (Akiskal and McKinney, 1973, 1975).

PREDISPOSITION

Predisposition to become depressed and invulnerability from depression may have determinants at all levels of analysis. Biological evidence suggests that individuals who are predisposed to alterations in functional levels of biogenic amines may be more vulnerable to depression. At the psychodynamic level, individuals who are heavily dependent on other people and who set such high standards that they frequently find themselves helpless before these standards may also be more vulnerable. At the cognitive level, individuals who have had early experience with loss and who have developed a pessimistic explanatory style in which loss is construed as internal, global, and stable may be more vulnerable to depression.

SYMPTOMS

The symptoms of depression can be described at the cognitive and biological levels of analysis. Cognitive symptoms, motivational symptoms, emotional symptoms, and somatic symptoms all make up depression. The duration and generality of these symptoms may be governed by the attributions an individual makes about loss, with those losses that stem from internal, stable, and global causes producing the most sweeping and long-lasting symptoms.

PRECIPITATING INCIDENTS

Cognitive theory explains precipitating incidents well: the experience of loss or threat of loss seems to set off most depressions, at least those in which precipitants can be identified. The biomedical model gives the depletion of biogenic amines as a possible explanation for why depression begins when no obvious loss has occurred. The evidence is not in about which of these causes is primary, but we suspect that neither is the sole cause and that either taken alone will produce many of the symptoms of depression.

THERAPY

All three theories have contributed insights into therapy for depression, although none of them has yet adequately accounted for the episodic rather than permanent nature of depression. An episode of depression, even severe depression, is no longer cause for despair. A combination of the biological treatments and the cognitive treatments of depression can probably alleviate severe depression roughly 90 percent of the time. In addition, to the extent that there is a depressive personality, dependent and inclined to helplessness, psychodynamic therapies may help to prevent the recurrence of depression.

Thus, biological, psychodynamic, and cognitive views can all be usefully brought to bear on depression. By taking the best from each, a woven fabric may be created in which the predisposition, the symptoms, and the precipitating incidents may be understandable. Ultimately any complete theory must tell us not only how depression starts and how to cure it, but also why it will, in and of itself, usually stop. In the meanwhile, however, what is most important of all is that depression can now be effectively treated.

BIPOLAR DEPRESSION (MANIC-DEPRESSION)

We have now explored the great majority of depressions: 80 to 95 percent of depressions are unipolar and occur without mania. This leaves between 5 and 20 percent of depressions that occur as part of *manic-depression.* These are called *bipolar depressions.*

We classify bipolar depressions in the following way: Given the presence of manic symptoms, an individual is judged to be manic-depressive if he has had one or more depressive episodes in the past. On the other hand, he is diagnosed as having experienced only a *manic episode* if he has never had a depressive episode. Mania itself can occur without depression, although this is very rare. Usually, a depressive episode will occur eventually, once a manic episode has happened. A chronic form of mania is called *chronic hypomanic disorder* or *hypomanic personality.* This diagnosis is made when an individual has experienced an unbroken two-year-long manic state. Finally, when depression is regularly set off by the approach of winter, it is characterized as *seasonal affective disorder (SAD).*

Since the symptoms of the depressive component of manic-depression are similar to what we described for unipolar depression, we need only describe mania here in order to have a clear picture of bipolar depression. Here is what it feels like to be in the manic state of a manic-depressive disorder:

> When I start going into a high, I no longer feel like an ordinary housewife. Instead, I feel organized and accomplished, and I begin to feel I am my most creative self. I can write poetry easily, I can compose melodies without effort. I can paint. My mind feels facile and absorbs everything. I have countless ideas about improving the conditions of mentally retarded children, how a hospital for these children should be run, what they should have around them to keep them happy and calm and unafraid. I see myself as being able to accomplish a great deal for the good of people. I have countless ideas about how the environmental problem could inspire a crusade for the health and betterment of everyone. I feel able to accomplish a great deal for the good of my family and others. I feel pleasure, a sense of euphoria or elation. I want it to last forever. I don't seem to need much sleep. I've lost weight and feel healthy, and I like myself. I've just bought six new dresses, in fact, and they look quite good on me. I feel sexy and men stare at me. Maybe I'll have an affair, or perhaps several. I feel capable of speaking and doing good in politics. I would like to help people with problems similar to mine so they won't feel hopeless. (Fieve, 1975, p. 17)

Symptoms of Mania

The onset of a manic episode usually occurs fairly suddenly, and the euphoric mood, racing thoughts, frenetic acts, and resulting insomnia stand in marked contrast to the person's usual functioning. Mania presents four sets of symptoms: emotional, cognitive, motivational, and somatic symptoms.

MOOD OR EMOTIONAL SYMPTOMS

The mood of an individual in a manic state is euphoric, expansive, and elevated. A highly successful manic artist describes his mood:

> I feel no sense of restriction or censorship whatsoever. I'm afraid of nothing and no one. During this elated state, when no inhibition is present, I feel I can race a car with my foot on the floorboard, fly a plane when I have never flown a plane before, and speak languages I hardly know. Above all, as an artist, I feel I can write poems and paint paintings that I could never dream of when just my normal self. I don't want others to restrict me during this period of complete and utter freedom. (Fieve, 1975)

Grandiose euphoria is not universal in mania, however. Often the dominant mood is irritability, and this is particularly so when a manic individual is thwarted in his ambitions. Manics, even when high, are peculiarly close to tears, and when frustrated may burst out crying. This is one reason to believe that mania is not wholly the opposite state of depression, but that a strong depressive element coexists with it.

THOUGHT OR COGNITIVE SYMPTOMS

The manic cognitions are appropriate to the mood. They are grandiose. The manic does not believe in limits to his ability, and worse, he does not recognize the painful consequences that will ensue when he carries out his plans. A manic who spends $100,000 buying three automobiles in a week does not recognize that he will have a great deal of trouble trying to pay for them over the coming years; a manic who calls the President in the middle of the night to tell him about her latest health care proposal does not recognize that this call may bring the police down on her; the manic who enters one sexual affair after another does not realize the permanent damage to her reputation that may ensue.

A manic may have thoughts or ideas racing through his mind faster than he can write them down or say them. This ***flight of ideas*** easily becomes derailed because the manic is highly distractible. In some extreme cases, the manic has delusional ideas about himself. He may believe that he is a special messenger of God; he may believe that he is an intimate friend of famous political and show business figures. The manic's thinking about other people is black and white: the individuals he knows are either all good or all bad; they are his best friends or his sworn enemies. The following is a case showing a manic's flight of ideas:

> "I went mad at the winter Olympics in Innsbruck. My brain got cloudy, as if a fog from the Alps has enveloped it. In that condition I came face to face with one gentleman—the Devil. He looked the part! He had hooves, fur, horns, and rotten teeth that looked hundreds of years old. With this figure in mind I climbed the hills above Innsbruck and torched a farm building. I was convinced that only a brilliant bonfire could burn off that fog. As I was leading the cows and horses from the barn, the Austrian police arrived. They handcuffed me and took me down into the valley . . . Back over the border I was delivered to the doctors in Prague . . .

> "Then the bad times began. The doctors, with their pills, got me into a state in which I realized I was mad. That is sadness, when you know that you are no Christ but a wretch whose brain, which makes a man a man, is sick . . .
>
> ". . . I know I suffered terribly. There are no words to describe it. And if there were such words, people would not believe them because they do not want to hear about madness. It frightens them.
>
> "When I felt better, I tried to remember what had been beautiful in my life. I did not think about love or how I had wandered all over the world . . . I remembered most the river I had loved most in my life. Before I could fish in it again I would take its water in the shell of my hands and kiss it as I would kiss a woman. . . Sometimes, when I sat at the barred window and fished in memory, the pain was almost unbearable. I had to block it out, the beauty, and I had to remind myself that dirt, foulness, and muddy waters also ran the world. When I succeeded in this, I did not long so much for my freedom . . .
>
> "I wanted to kill myself a hundred times when I felt I couldn't go on, but I never did. Maybe my desire to kiss the river and catch the silver fish again kept me going. Fishing taught me patience and my memories helped me go on." (Pavel, 1990)

Ota Pavel (1930–1973) was diagnosed manic-depressive in 1964. He never fully recovered. This passage is from the epilogue of Pavel's *How I Came To Know Fish.*

MOTIVATIONAL SYMPTOMS

Manic behavior is hyperactive. The manic engages in frenetic activity, be it in his occupation, in political or religious circles, in sexual relationships, or elsewhere. Describing the mania of a woman, one author wrote:

> Her friends noticed that she was going out every night, dating many new men, attending church meetings, language classes, and dances, and showing a rather frenetic emotional state. Her seductiveness at the office resulted in her going to bed with two of the available married men, who didn't realize she was ill. She burst into tears on several occasions without provocation and told risqué jokes that were quite out of character. She became more talkative and restless, stopped eating and didn't seem to need any sleep. She began to talk with religious feeling about being in contact with God and insisted that several things were now necessary to carry out God's wishes. This included giving herself sexually to all who needed her. When she was admitted to the hospital, she asked the resident psychiatrist on call to kiss her. Because he refused to do so, she became suddenly silent. Later, she talked incessantly, accusing the doctor of trying to seduce her and began to talk about how God knew every sexual thought that she or the doctor might have. (Fieve, 1975, pp. 22–23)

The activity of the manic has an intrusive, demanding, and domineering quality to it. Manics sometimes make us uncomfortable because of this. It is difficult to spend much time with an individual who delivers a rapid succession of thoughts and who behaves in a frenetic way almost in disregard of those around him. Other behaviors that commonly occur during mania are compulsive gambling, reckless driving, poor financial investments, and flamboyant dress and makeup.

With all this flurry of activity comes a greatly lessened need for sleep. Such hyposomnia virtually always occurs during mania. After a couple of days of this, exhaustion inevitably sets in and the mania slows down.

Course and Characteristics of Manic-Depression

Between .6 and 1.1 percent of the population of the United States will have manic-depression in their lifetime (Robins et al., 1984; Keller and Baker, 1991). Unlike unipolar depression, which affects more women than men, manic-depression affects both sexes equally. The onset of manic-depression is sudden, usually a matter of hours or days, and typically no precipitating event is obvious. The first episode is usually manic, not depressive, and it generally appears between the ages of twenty and thirty. This first attack occurs somewhat earlier than a first attack in unipolar depression. Ninety percent of manic-depressives will have had their first attack before they are fifty years old. Manic-depressive illness tends to recur, and each episode lasts from several days to several months. Over the first ten years of the disorder, the frequency and intensity of the episodes tend to worsen. Surprisingly, however, not many episodes occur twenty years after the initial onset. Both manic and depressive episodes occur in the disorder, but regular cycling (e.g., three months manic, followed by three months depressive, and so on) is rare. The depressive component of manic-depressive illness is similar in kind to that of unipolar depression, but it is often more severe (Angst, Baastrup, Grof, Hippius, Poldinger, and Weiss, 1973; Depue and Monroe, 1978; Loranger and Levine, 1978).

Manic-depressive illness is not a benign, remitting disorder. For some, extreme manic episodes may bring about much hardship. Their hyperactivity and bizarre behavior may be self-defeating. Employers may become annoyed at their behavior, and some manic-depressives may then find themselves without a job. For others, entire careers may be lost. In addition, manic-depressives' social relationships also tend to break down. The manic person is hard to deal with. A much higher percentage of married manic-depressives divorce than do married unipolar depressives. Alcohol abuse, either in attempted self-medication or due to poor judgment and impulsiveness, is very high in manic-depression. The more severe the mania, the more frequent the alcoholism. In all, between 20 and 50 percent of manic-depressives suffer chronic social and occupational impairment. In most extreme cases, hospitalization is required. And for a few, suicide is a constant threat. The rate of attempted and successful suicides is also higher in bipolar than in unipolar depressions. As many as 15 percent of manic-depressives may end their life by suicide (Brodie and Leff, 1971; Carlson, Kotin, Davenport, and Adland, 1974; Reich, Davies, and Himmelhoch, 1974; Dunner, Gershom, and Goodwin, 1976). Of 100 Hungarian depressed patients who committed suicide, almost half (47 percent) had been diagnosed with bipolar depression. Since bipolar depression is much less common than unipolar, this underscores the high suicide risk for bipolar patients (Rihmer, Barsi, Arato, and Demeter, 1990).

When the mania is more moderate and the depressions are not too debilitating, however, the manic-depressive's ambition, hyperactivity, talkativeness, and grandiosity may lead to great achievements. This behavior is conducive to

▼ There is evidence that Theodore Roosevelt was a manic-depressive, and that the mania contributed to his political success.

FOCUS QUESTIONS

1. Give general definitions of bipolar depression (manic-depression) and manic episodes.
2. What are the four broad symptoms of mania?
3. Describe the evidence for a genetic predisposition to manic-depression.
4. How is manic-depressive disorder treated?
5. What is seasonal affective disorder (SAD) and how is it treated?

success in our society. It is no surprise that many creative people, leaders of industry, entertainment, politics, and religion may have been able to use and control their less severe levels of manic-depression. Abraham Lincoln, Winston Churchill, and Theodore Roosevelt probably all were manic-depressives. One study reported that among forty-seven top British writers and artists, one-third suffer from severe mood swings; among fifteen writers at Iowa's prestigious Writers' Workshop, almost all reported manic and hypomanic states (Holden, 1987). Finally, another study indicates that first-degree relatives of manic-depressives have also been judged to be significantly higher in creativity than normals (Holden, 1986a). It is probably the mania, and not the depression, that contributes to bursts of creativity (Andreasen and Glick, 1988).

Cause of Manic-Depression

The cause of manic-depressive illness is unknown. On the surface, with its euphoria and hyperactivity, it looks like the opposite state of depression. But as we have seen, feelings of depression are close at hand during the mania. The bipolar individual, when manic, is close to tears; he voices more hopelessness and has more suicidal thoughts than normal individuals. This has led some theorists to believe that mania is a defense against an underlying depression, with a brittle euphoria warding off more fundamental sadness.

Other theorists believe that manic-depression results from self-correcting biological processes that have become ungoverned. When a normal individual becomes depressed, the depression is allegedly ended by switching in an opposite, euphoric state that cancels it out. Conversely, when a normal individual becomes euphoric, this state is kept from spiraling out of bounds by switching in a depressive state that neutralizes the euphoria. Investigations of the biochemistry of this switching process seem to indicate that a disturbance in the balance of mania and depression, with the reaction to either overshooting its mark, may be responsible for the manic-depressive disorder (see Figure 11–10). Investigations of the biochemistry of the switching process from mania to depression may illuminate the biological underpinnings of the disorder in the future, and it has been proposed that sleep reduction may be the trigger of the switching process (Bunney, Murphy, Goodwin, and Borge, 1972; Solomon and Corbit, 1974; Wehr, Sack, and Rosenthal, 1987; Strober, Lampert, Schmidt, and Morrell, 1993).

Individuals are genetically vulnerable to manic-depressive illness. Manic-depressive individuals are more often found in families in which successive generations have experienced depression or manic-depression. Relatives of manic-depressives have five times the normal 1 percent risk for developing the disorder (Rice, Reich, Andreasen, Endicott, Van Eerdewegh, Fishman, Hirschfeld, and Klerman, 1987). Identical twins have five times the concordance for manic-depressive disorder than do fraternal twins. Thus, the familial risk is probably genetic, at least in part for manic-depression, but less so for unipolar depression (Allen, 1976; McGuffin and Katz, 1989).

Treatment

By and large, manic-depressive illness can be successfully contained by lithium salts. Lithium was originally used as a table salt substitute. In 1949, John

FIGURE 11–10

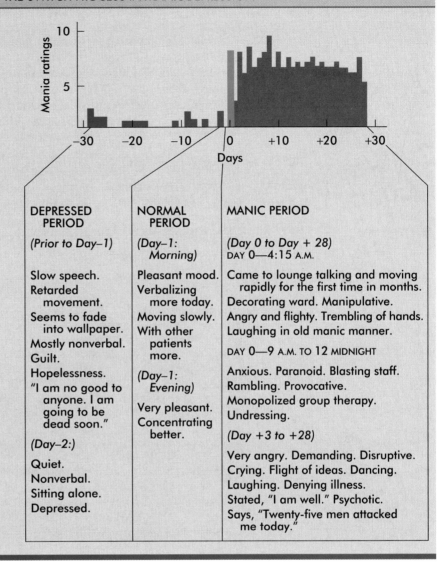

THE SWITCH PROCESS IN MANIC-DEPRESSION

This illustrates the striking changes in behavior as a bipolar patient switches from depression to mania. (SOURCE: Bunney and Murphy, 1974)

Mania ratings

Days

DEPRESSED PERIOD

(Prior to Day–1)

Slow speech.
Retarded movement.
Seems to fade into wallpaper.
Mostly nonverbal.
Guilt.
Hopelessness.
"I am no good to anyone. I am going to be dead soon."

(Day–2:)

Quiet.
Nonverbal.
Sitting alone.
Depressed.

NORMAL PERIOD

(Day–1: Morning)

Pleasant mood.
Verbalizing more today.
Moving slowly.
With other patients more.

(Day–1: Evening)

Very pleasant.
Concentrating better.

MANIC PERIOD

(Day 0 to Day + 28)
DAY 0—4:15 A.M.

Came to lounge talking and moving rapidly for the first time in months.
Decorating ward. Manipulative.
Angry and flighty. Trembling of hands.
Laughing in old manic manner.

DAY 0—9 A.M. TO 12 MIDNIGHT

Anxious. Paranoid. Blasting staff.
Rambling. Provocative.
Monopolized group therapy.
Undressing.

(Day +3 to +28)

Very angry. Demanding. Disruptive.
Crying. Flight of ideas. Dancing.
Laughing. Denying illness.
Stated, "I am well." Psychotic.
Says, "Twenty-five men attacked me today."

Cade, an Australian physician, having found that lithium made guinea pigs lethargic, tried it to dampen mania in humans and found that lithium ended severe manic attacks. Since that time, lithium carbonate has been shown to be an effective treatment both for mania and for the depressive aspects of manic-depression. Approximately 80 percent of manic-depressives will show a full or partial alleviation of symptoms during lithium administration. It is also clear, however, that the other 20 percent of bipolar depressives do not respond (Depue, 1979). Lithium has also been used as a preventative treatment for manic-depression, and repeated dosage with lithium in a vulnerable individual may prevent manic-depressive relapses (Depue, 1979). Patients with ***rapid cycling bipolar disorder,*** a subclass of manic-depression in which four or more episodes per year occur, often show inadequate response to lithium, however. For them, anticonvulsant drugs as well as levothyroxine added to lithium improve response (Post, Kramlinger, Altshuler, and Ketter, 1990; Bauer and Whybrow, 1990).

While lithium can be viewed as a miracle drug for manic-depression, its side effects, particularly its cardiovascular, digestive, and central nervous system effects, can be quite serious. Close medical supervision should always accompany the administration of lithium. Both the evidence on the effectiveness of lithium and the evidence on genetic vulnerability suggest that manic-depression is best understood within the framework of the biological model.

Seasonal Affective Disorder (SAD)

The most recent addition to the bipolar family has been dubbed ***seasonal affective disorder (SAD).*** For millennia, human activity in the temperate zones has been strongly influenced by the seasons, with highly active behavior occurring during spring and summer, and withdrawal from the frenzy of life tending to occur during fall and winter. This may be the evolutionary basis for SAD.

> When John moved to Washington, D.C., from Florida at age twenty-one, he experienced his first depression. He went there to attend medical school, and for each of the next four winters the depression recurred. He was hospitalized and became hopeless about his goal of becoming a physician because of his depression problem. He plodded on through his internship in Maryland with the depressions continuing yearly.
>
> He noticed that each year his depression remitted in the spring. The depressions started around the first of December, when the days were getting short, and they lifted by the first of April. In some years, the depressions came on gradually, but in other years a bad event, like a patient dying, precipitated the depression. His mood was worse in the morning; he had trouble sleeping; he craved carbohydrates and gained weight. He was apathetic, irritable, and felt pessimistic.
>
> After reading about SAD, he entered light therapy treatment at the National Institutes of Mental Health. He found that brilliant grow lights, on for two hours before dawn, markedly relieved his depression. Finally, he treated himself. He moved, and opened a practice in San Diego. He has not experienced a winter depression since. (Adapted from Spitzer, Gibbon, Skodol, Williams, and First, 1989, pp. 19–21)

SAD is characterized by depression beginning each year in October or November and fully remitting, sometimes switching toward mania, when the days start to lengthen (March and April). Patients complain of fatigue, oversleeping, and carbohydrate craving as well as the more typical symptoms of depression. Women outnumber men, and young children show the problem as well. In a nationwide Japanese survey, only 1 percent of the over 5,000 depressed outpatients were identified with SAD (Sakamoto, Kamo, Nakadaira, and Tamura, 1993). In contrast, among a random sample of 283 Alaskans, who have less sunlight, twenty-six (9.2 percent) had SAD (Booker and Hellekson, 1992). In one of the first major studies, twenty-nine SAD patients reported their clinical history of depression by month. The remarkable data shown in Figure 11–11 documents how depressive episodes are yoked to the sunlight and temperature of each month. Not only is depression governed by the amount of sunlight

FIGURE 11–11

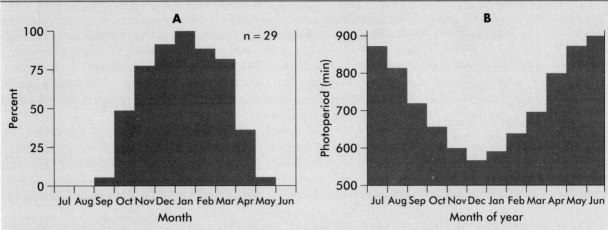

DEPRESSION AND LENGTH OF DAYLIGHT

(A) Percentage of patients depressed per month (based on history) compared with (B) mean minutes of daylight (39°) in Rockville, Maryland (Smithsonian Radiation Biology Laboratory). (SOURCE: Rosenthal et al., 1984)

where these patients live, but when they travel the depression changes. When they travel south in the winter, depression remits in a few days and when they travel north in the winter it tends to worsen (Rosenthal, Sack, Gillin, et al., 1984; Rosenthal, Carpenter, and James, et al., 1986).

These findings led to the use of artificial light as therapy. Bright "grow-lights" are strategically located in the homes of the patients and come on very early in the morning and after sunset to artificially lengthen daylight hours. Prompt relief of depressive symptoms, particularly with the morning lights, has been reported, and relapse has been reported when light is withdrawn (Hellekson, Kline, and Rosenthal, 1986; Lewy, Sack, Miller, and Hoban, 1987; Rosenthal, Moul, Hellekson, and Oren, 1993). Placebo-controlled studies of light therapy are now beginning. In one such study using thirty-two patients, no effect over and above the antidepressive effect found when using placebos occurred when using artificially supplied morning light (Eastman, Lehmeyer, Watell, and Good, 1992). SAD is a new category, and we await more research on its prevalence, its cause, and on therapy. Topics of active investigation include studies on how much light is needed, when during the day the light treatment will be most effective, and the mechanism by which light combats SAD (Wirz-Justice, Graw, Krauchi, et al., 1993).

SUICIDE

Suicide is the most disastrous consequence of depression, bipolar or unipolar. Depression is the precursor of a vast majority of suicides. Death only rarely results directly from other psychological disorders: the anorexic patient who re-

▲ Richard Bosman's *Witness*, 1983.

fuses food; the hallucinating schizophrenic, who believing he is Christ, attempts to walk on water; the heroin addict who administers an overdose. But it is depression that most frequently results in irreversible harm: death, by suicide.

Suicide is the second most frequent cause of death, after accidents, among high school and college students (U.S. Department of Health and Human Services, 1987). Further, it is on the rise in this age group. The death of a young person, because of all his unfulfilled promise, is a keenly felt tragedy. As a young man, Beethoven almost took his own life before composing his second symphony. What held him back was the thought that he had not yet produced the best that might be inside him.

Suicide is an act that most societies forbid. Many religions regard it as a sin; and it is, ironically, a crime in several states. No act leaves such a bitter and lasting legacy among friends and relatives. It leaves in its wake bewilderment, guilt, shame, and stigma that relatives may carry to their own graves.

Suicide is sometimes thought of as an act of high rationality. Seneca, the first century Roman stoic, said:

> Living is not good, but living well. The wise man, therefore, lives as well as he should, not as long as he can . . . He will always think of life in terms of quality, not quantity . . . Dying early or late is of no relevance, dying well or ill is . . . Even if it is true that while there is life, there is hope, life is not to be bought at any cost. (Seneca Epistle #70)

More often, however, even though the decision seems rational to the individual who takes his life, he is usually strongly ambivalent about the decision. One vote can tip the balance, as in a declaration of war (see Table 11–4). For example, when a physician canceled an appointment with a patient, this last straw in a series of disappointments tipped the balance toward suicidal death.

The ethical quandaries of suicide are immensely difficult. Does an individual have a right to take his own life, not interfered with by others, just as he has a right to dispose, unimpeded, of his own property? (Szasz, 1974).

Who Is at Risk for Suicide?

The list of famous suicides is very long: Marilyn Monroe, Samson, Ernest Hemingway, Cleopatra, Kurt Cobain, Virginia Woolf, Jack London, Modigliani, Adolph Hitler, Jim Jones and his People's Temple victims, to name a very few. At the very least, 25,000 people end their lives by suicide every year in the United States. There are also estimated to be at least ten times as many suicide attempts as successful suicides, and it has been estimated that in the United States today, five million people are alive who have attempted suicide.

The estimate of 25,000 suicidal deaths per year in the United States is highly conservative, and the real number is probably between 50,000 and 100,000. There are several reasons for the underreporting of suicide. Such stigma attaches to the act that the influential can often get coroners to label a relative's death as an accident rather than a suicide, and there is often family pressure on physicians not to report deaths as suicides. Many one-car accidents on clear roads are suicides, but they are usually labeled accidental death. Some life insurance policies do not cover death by suicide. Those individuals who flirt with death by high-risk hobbies or occupations, by adopting lethal

FOCUS QUESTIONS

1. Which group is most vulnerable to suicide?
2. Describe the sex and age differences regarding suicide.
3. Describe the surcease and manipulation motivations for suicide.
4. What steps can be taken to prevent suicide?

TABLE 11-4

FABLES AND FACTS ABOUT SUICIDE

Fable	Fact
Individuals who talk about killing themselves do not kill themselves.	Of every ten persons who have killed themselves, eight gave definite warnings of their intentions.
Suicidal individuals have made a clear decision to die.	Most are undecided about living or dying. They often gamble with death, leaving it to others to save them.
Once an individual is suicidal, he is forever suicidal.	Usually individuals who wish to kill themselves are suicidal only for a limited period. Suicidal wishes are often linked to depression, and depression usually dissipates in time.
The suicidal risk is over when improvement occurs following a suicidal crisis.	Most suicides occur while the individual is still depressed, but within about three months after the beginning of "improvement." It is at that time that the individual has better access to weapons and more energy to put his suicidal plans into effect than when he is in the hospital or at the nadir of his depression.
Suicide occurs more often among the rich.	Suicide is equally frequent at all levels of society.
The suicidal act is the act of a sick person.	While the suicidal person is almost always extremely unhappy, he is not necessarily "mentally ill." Suicide can be a rational act.

SOURCE: Adapted from Shneidman, 1976.

habits such as heavy smoking, drinking, and drugs, as well as the physically ill who terminate their own life by discontinuing medication are not counted as suicidal deaths. In subcultures in which suicide is seen as feminine and passive, but murder is seen as active and masculine, "victim-induced homicide"— for example, an adolescent provoking a policeman to kill him—is not counted as a suicide (Schuyler, 1974; Diggory, 1976; Linden and Breed, 1976).

Suicide may run in families, and to the extent that the depressive disorders are heritable, suicide itself may be heritable. All twenty-six suicides among the Amish of Lancaster County, Pennsylvania, over the last hundred years were analyzed. Twenty-four of these individuals had had major affective disorders; 16 percent of the families accounted for 73 percent of the suicides (Egeland and Sussex, 1985).

Suicide may even have a biochemistry. Among depressed patients, suicide attempts were most frequent in those having low serotonin levels, and when low-serotonin patients attempted suicide, they used more violent means (Asberg, Traskman, and Thoren, 1976). The brains of suicide victims have lower serotonin in their brainstem and cerebrospinal fluid, but not in their frontal cortex (Mann, Arango and Underwood, 1990; Bourgeois, 1991; Traskman-Bendz, Alling, Alsen, et al., 1993).

DEPRESSION AND SUICIDE

Depressed individuals are the single group most at risk for suicide. While suicide occasionally occurs in the absence of depression and the large majority of

▶ In 1993, followers of a religious sect headed by David Koresh were still with him, despite his warnings of mass suicide, when his compound in Waco, Texas, burned to the ground.

depressed people do not commit suicide, depression is a strong predisposing factor to suicide. An estimated 80 percent of suicidal patients are significantly depressed. Depressed patients ultimately commit suicide at a rate that is at least twenty-five times as high as control populations (Pokorny, 1964; Flood and Seager, 1968; Robins and Guze, 1972).

SEX DIFFERENCES AND SUICIDE

Women make roughly three times as many suicide attempts as men, but men actually succeed in killing themselves three times more often than women. These discrepancies seem to have diminished a bit over the last few years. The greater rate of suicide attempts in women is probably related to the fact that more depression occurs in women, whereas the greater completed suicide rate in men probably has to do with choice of methods: women tend to choose less lethal means, such as cutting their wrists and overdosing on sleeping pills; whereas men tend to shoot themselves and jump off buildings. The suicide rate for both men and women is higher among individuals who have been divorced and widowed; loneliness as well as a sense of failure in interpersonal affairs surely contributes to this statistic. Men who kill themselves tend to be motivated by failure at work, and women who kill themselves tend to be motivated by failure at love (Mendels, 1970; Linden and Breed, 1976; Shneidman, 1976). As one female patient who tried to find surcease in suicide after being rejected by her lover said, "There's no sense in living. There's nothing here for me. I need love and I don't have it anymore. I can't be happy without love—only miserable. It will just be the same misery, day in and day out. It's senseless to go on" (Beck, 1976).

CULTURAL DIFFERENCES AND SUICIDE

Race, religion, and nationality contribute somewhat to vulnerability to suicide. The suicide rate of young black and white men is approximately the same (Hendin, 1969; Linden and Breed, 1976; McIntosh, 1989), but black women and older black men probably kill themselves less often than whites (Swanson and Breed, 1976; McIntosh, 1989). There is some evidence that American Indians may have a higher suicide rate than the rest of the population (Frederick, 1978). Religion, at least in the United States, does not offer any protection against suicide in spite of varyingly strong strictures against it. The rate of suicide is roughly the same whether the individual is nonreligious, or Catholic, Protestant, or Jewish.

Suicide occurs in all cultures, even primitive ones, but it seems to be more common in industrialized countries. At the present time, the countries of central Europe (Hungary, Austria, and the former Czechoslovakia) and northern Europe (Finland and Denmark) seem to have the highest suicide rate. The suicide rate in the former Soviet Union almost doubled over the period from 1965 to 1984. Then during the period of democratization from 1984–1988, the suicide rate halved again. In regions of strong political antagonism (Baltic States) and of forced social changes (Russia) the rate was high, but in regions where families and religious faith were strong, the rate was low (Varnik and Wasserman, 1992). Ireland and Egypt have very low suicide rates, perhaps because suicide is considered a mortal sin in these cultures. The United States has, on the world scale, an average suicide rate. Sweden has a middling high rate of suicide. Some have blamed this on the lack of incentive provided by its social welfare system, but its suicide rate has remained the same since about 1910, before the introduction of social welfare (Shneidman, 1976; Department of International Economic and Social Affairs, 1985).

AGE AND SUICIDE

Among children, suicide is rare, with probably fewer than 200 suicides committed in a year in the United States by children who are under the age of fourteen. But among those preschoolers who are suicidal, they tend to be more impulsive and hyperactive, show less pain and crying when hurt, and have parents who abuse and neglect them (Rosenthal and Rosenthal, 1984).

Discussing her wish to die, Michelle, age nine, talks with Joaquim Puig-Antich, a leading expert on childhood depression:

JOAQUIM PUIG-ANTICH: Do you feel you should be punished?
MICHELLE: Yes.
JPA: Why?
M: I don't know.
JPA: Have you ever had the thought that you might want to hurt yourself?
M: Yes.
JPA: How would you hurt yourself?
M: By drinking a lot of alcohol, or jumping off the balcony.
JPA: Have you ever tried to jump?
M: I once stood on the edge of the terrace and put one leg over the railing, but my mother caught me.
JPA: Did you really want to jump?
M: Yes.
JPA: What would have happened if you had jumped?
M: I would have killed myself.
JPA: Did you want to get killed?
M: Uh-huh.
JPA: Why?
M: Because I don't like the life I live.
JPA: What kind of life do you live?
M: A sad and miserable life.

(Jerome, 1979)

Suicide among young people is on the rise. In the past thirty-five years, the suicide rate among college-age groups has tripled. Males between the ages of twenty and twenty-four are hardest hit, with a rate of about 28 per 100,000 compared to a rate of 12 per 100,000 in the general population. Two studies of the psychological "autopsies" of young suicides have strongly implicated substance abuse and untreated depression as precursors.

In one study, Mohammad Shafi examined the lives of 21 youths who killed themselves in the University of Kentucky area from 1980 to 1983. Seventy percent of them had been drug or alcohol abusers, and 76 percent had been diagnosed as depressed. They strongly exceeded matched controls in substance abuse and depression. In the other study, David Shaffer of Columbia University analyzed 160 youths who killed themselves in New York from 1984–1986. He found the same preponderance of substance abuse, but less depressive disorder. Males made up the bulk of these suicides, but choice of a more lethal weapon,

▶ The "will" of a suicidal 8-year-old girl, whose parents later arranged psychiatric care for her.

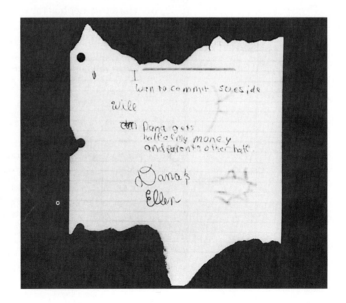

rather than the number of attempts, accounted for the male preponderance (Holden, 1986b).

Suicide rate rises dramatically through middle age and into old age. Increasing depression, loneliness, moving to a strange setting, loss of a meaningful role in family and society, and loss of people they love all surely contribute to the high rate of suicide among old people. In cultures and communities in which the aged are revered and remain important in the life of the family, suicide is infrequent.

Within two years of the death of her beloved husband with whom she had spent fifty joyous years, Mrs. K. committed suicide. "Alan," she told her son a few days before, "I wasn't made to sleep alone." Percy Bridgman, Nobel Prize winner in physics and famous American positivist, shot himself at age eighty. He had cancer and was in great pain. The day before he killed himself, he mailed the index for his collected works to Harvard University Press. He had repeatedly asked for euthanasia and had been refused. His suicide note was published in the *Bulletin of the Atomic Scientists* (1962): "It is indecent for Society to make a man do this thing himself. Probably this is the last day I will be able to do it myself. PWB" (Shneidman, 1976).

The Motivation for Suicide

In the first major modern study of suicide, the French sociologist Émile Durkheim (1858–1917) distinguished three motivations for suicide, all of them intimately related to the way an individual sees his place in society. He called these motives anomic, egoistic, and altruistic. **Anomic suicide** is precipitated by a shattering break in an individual's relationship to his society: the loss of a job, economic depression, even sudden wealth. **Egoistic suicide** occurs when the individual has too few ties to his fellow humans. Societal demands, principal among them the demand to live, do not reach the egoistic individual. Finally, **altruistic suicide** is required by the society. The individual takes his own life in order to benefit his community. Hara-kiri is an altruistic suicide. The Buddhist monks who burned themselves to death to protest the injustices of the Vietnam War are recent reminders of individuals who committed altruistic suicide.

Modern thinkers see two more fundamental motivations for suicide: **surcease** and **manipulation.** Those who wish surcease have simply given up. Their emotional distress is intolerable, and they see no alternative solution. In death, they see an end to their problems. Fifty-six percent of the suicide attempts observed in a systematic study were classified as individuals trying to achieve surcease. These suicide attempts involved more depression, more hopelessness, and they tended to be more lethal than the remaining suicide attempts (Beck, 1976).

The other motivation for suicide is the wish to manipulate other people by a suicide attempt. Some wish to manipulate the world that remains by dying: to have the final word in an argument, to have revenge on a rejecting lover, to ruin the life of another person. More commonly in manipulative suicide, the individual intends to remain alive, but by showing the seriousness of his dilemma, he is crying for help from those who are important to him. Trying to prevent a lover from leaving, getting into the hospital and having a temporary respite from problems, and being taken seriously are all manipulative motives for suicide with intent to live.

▲ Buddhist monks in Vietnam burned themselves to death to protest their government's policies in the late 1960s and early 1970s.

Thirteen percent of suicide attempts were found to be manipulative; these involved less depression, less hopelessness, and less lethal means than did the surcease attempts (Beck, 1976). Those suicides that are manipulative are clearly cries for help, but it should be apparent that all suicides are not cries for help (see Box 11–5). The individual who wishes to escape because life is not worth living is not crying out for help, but for an end to his troubles. The remaining 31 percent of suicide attempts combine surcease and manipulative motivation. Here the individual is not at all sure whether he wishes to live or die, whether he wishes surcease or a change in the world. In this undecided group, the more hopeless and the more depressed the individual is, the stronger are the surcease reasons for the suicide attempt (Beck, Rush, Shaw, and Emery, 1979).

Prevention of Suicide and Treatment of the Suicidal Person

In the initial therapeutic interview with a depressed individual, suicide is the overriding question in the back of the therapist's mind. If clear suicidal intent and hopelessness are pervading themes, crisis intervention, close observation, and hospitalization will probably ensue. If they are not, therapy will proceed at a somewhat more leisurely pace, directed toward careful understanding of the other depressive problems.

In the late 1960s, a network of more than 300 suicide prevention centers was established in the United States to deal with suicidal crises. In addition, hospitals and outpatient units set up hot-lines to deal with the crises of acutely suicidal individuals. It was believed that if someone was available for the suicidal individual to talk to, the suicide could be prevented.

In terms of prevention of suicide, once the suicidal person makes contact with a telephone hot-line volunteer, a psychologist, a psychiatrist, a family physician, a pastor, or emergency room doctor, evaluation of the suicidal risk takes first priority. Does the individual have a clear plan? Does he have access to a weapon? Does he have a past history of suicidal acts? Does he live alone? Once suicidal risk in a crisis is assessed, a treatment decision must be hastily made: home visit, hospitalization, medication, the police, or outpatient psychotherapy. In some cases, merely holding the person on the phone may be appropriate action. Long-term follow-up and after-care must then occur.

Success of the suicide prevention centers is uncertain, but some evidence points to modest success. The total number of prevention centers in each state was tabulated, and the number of suicides in that state over the next decade was compared to the rates that existed before the prevention centers were started. The more suicide centers that had been established, the larger the drop in suicide rate. The effect, however, was not large, and whether the centers caused the drop, or some other demographic variable did, was unclear (Diekstra, 1992; Hazell and Lewin, 1993; Lester, 1993).

In addition to suicide prevention, psychological intervention in the lives of the surviving relatives is also important (Hazell and Lewin, 1993). As we have seen, the survivors are themselves more vulnerable to later depression and suicide. They are faced with shame, guilt, bewilderment, and stigma. This is a group that has been neglected and that might benefit greatly from systematic care.

Box 11-5

About one-sixth of those individuals who die by their own hand leave suicide notes. A romantic view would lead us to expect that these final words, like those that are supposed to be uttered on the deathbed, would be masterful summaries of a life that preceded them and of the reasons for dying. Only occasionally are they:

"There should be little sadness, and no searching for who is at fault; for the act and result are not sad, and no one is at fault.

"My only sorrow is for my parents who will not easily be able to accept that this is so much better for me. Please, folks, it's all right, really it is.

"I wanted to be too many things, and greatness besides—it was a hopeless task. I never managed to really love another person—only to make the sounds of it. I never could believe what my society taught me to believe, yet I could never manage to quite find the truth.

"Two-fifteen p.m.—I'm about to will myself to stop my heartbeat and respiration. This is a very mystical experience. I have no fear. That surprises me. I thought I would be terrified. Soon I will know what death is like—how many people out there can say that?"

But much more often the notes are commonplace. Creative, unique, and expansive pieces of writing are rare in suicide notes. The individual is usually constricted, his field of consciousness has narrowed, and he is in despair. This is not a state conducive to creativity.

"Dearest darling I want you to know that you are the only one in my life I love you so much I could not do without you please forgive me I drove myself sick honey please believe me I love you you again and the baby honey don't be mean with me please I've lived 50 years since I met you, I love you—I love you. Dearest darling I love you, I love you. PLease don't discriminate me darling I know that I will die don't be mean with me please I love you more than you will ever know. Darling please and honey, Tom, I don't tell Tom why his daddy said goodbye honey. Can't stand it anymore. Darling I love you. Darling I love you."

A good number of suicide notes merely contain instructions and directions:

"Dear Mary. I am writing you, as our divorce is not final, and will not be til next month, so the way things stand now you are still my wife, which makes you entitled to the things which belong to me, and I want you to have them. Don't let anyone take them from you as they are yours. Please see a lawyer and get them as soon as you can. I am listing some of the things, they are: a blue davenport and chair, a Magic Chef Stove, a large mattress, an electrolux cleaner, a 9 x 12 rug, reddish flower design and pad. All the things listed above are almost new. Then there is my 30-30 rifle, books, typewriter, tools and a hand contract for a house in Chicago, a savings account in Boston, Massachusetts. Your husband."

And some are simple and starkly practical. A workman before hanging himself in an abandoned house chalked his suicide note on the wall outside.

"Sorry about this. There's a corpse in here. Inform police."

SOURCE: Adapted from Shneidman, 1976.

SUMMARY

1. The *affective disorders* consist of three types: unipolar depression, bipolar depression, and mania.

2. *Unipolar depression* consists of depressive symptoms only and involves no symptoms of mania. It is by far the most common of the depressive disorders, and has become much more frequent since World War II. *Dysthymic disorder* consists of chronic (more than two years) depressive symptoms.

3. *Bipolar depression* occurs in individuals who have both periods of depression and periods of mania as well.

4. *Mania* consists of four sets of symptoms: euphoric mood, grandiose thoughts, overactivity, and lack of sleep.

5. There are four basic symptoms of unipolar depression: emotional symptoms, largely sadness; motivational symptoms, largely passivity; cognitive symptoms, largely hopelessness and pessimism; and somatic symptoms, including loss of weight and loss of appetite. Untreated, these symptoms will usually dissipate within about three months.

6. Women are more at risk than men for unipolar depression.

7. Three theories—biological, psychodynamic, and cognitive—have all shed light on unipolar depression.

8. Biological models have generated four effective therapies; *tricyclic antidepressant drugs*, *MAO inhibitors*, *serotonin reuptake inhibitors*, and *electroconvulsive therapy* (ECT). The biomedical school holds that depression is due to depletions in certain central nervous system neurotransmitters, *serotonin* or *norepinephrine.*

9. Psychodynamic theories concentrate on the personality that predisposes one to depression. These theories hold that depression stems from *anger turned upon the self,* and that individuals who are predisposed to depression are overdependent on other people for their self-esteem and that they feel helpless to achieve their goals.

10. Cognitive models concentrate on particular ways of thinking and how these cause and sustain depression. There are two prominent cognitive models: the view of Aaron Beck, which holds that depression stems from a *negative cognitive triad,* and Seligman's *learned helplessness model* of depression. Cognitive therapy and interpersonal therapy relieve depression as effectively as tricyclic antidepressant drugs.

11. A pessimistic explanatory style predicts risk for depression. Changing this attribution style to optimistic may reverse depression.

12. Unipolar depression can now be effectively treated: nine out of ten people who suffer a severe unipolar depressive episode can be markedly helped either by drugs, ECT, cognitive therapy, or interpersonal therapy.

13. Depressive symptoms can be prevented among pre-teenagers. Learning social and cognitive antidepressant skills reduced symptoms of depression over two-year follow-up.

14. Bipolar depression, or *manic-depressive illness,* is the most crippling of the affective disorders. It results in ruined marriages, irreparable damage to reputation, and not uncommonly, suicide. Eighty percent of bipolar depressions can now be greatly helped by *lithium.* This disorder is best viewed within the biomedical model.

15. *Seasonal affective disorder* is characterized by depression that begins each year in October or November and ends in the early spring.

16. *Suicide* is the most disastrous consequence of bipolar and unipolar depression. Its frequency is rising among young people, and it is the second most frequent cause of death among college students. Women make more suicide attempts than men, but men actually succeed in killing themselves more often than women. There are two fundamental motivations for suicide: *surcease,* or desire to end it all, and *manipulation,* or desire to change the world or other individuals by a suicide attempt.

1. Since students with little illusions of control had more depression and became more discouraged than those with large illusions of control, do you think that therapy should try to help people see uncontrollable events as controllable? What do you think of "flexible optimism"?

2. Why do you think depressed individuals have difficulty initiating responses and making decisions?

3. Describe how Prozac works and its side effects. Do you think the benefits of Prozac outweigh its side effects?

4. How do you think creative people are able to use and control their manic-depression? What can happen when manic episodes get out of control?

5. Why does knowing or reading about someone who has committed suicide often trigger others to commit suicide?

CHAPTER 12

The Schizophrenias

CHAPTER ORGANIZER

HISTORY AND BACKGROUND
- Learn about schizophrenia's major symptoms and how they have been perceived in history.

TYPES OF SCHIZOPHRENIA
- Learn to distinguish among the five subtypes of schizophrenia.

THE SYMPTOMS OF SCHIZOPHRENIA
- Be able to describe perceptual difficulties and thought disorders typical of schizophrenia.
- You should have an idea of how schizophrenics violate our standards of "meaning."

THE DIMENSIONS OF SCHIZOPHRENIA
- Learn about the basis of the acute/chronic and Type I/Type II distinctions.

THE CAUSES OF THE SCHIZOPHRENIAS
- Be able to summarize evidence for the heritability and neurochemistry of schizophrenia.

THE TREATMENT OF SCHIZOPHRENIA
- Understand how neuroleptics like chlorpromazine changed the lives of schizophrenics.

There is no more puzzling and profound psychological disorder than schizophrenia. Many theories try to account for it, but a complete understanding of this complex disorder continues to elude us. Briefly, ***schizophrenia*** is a disorder of thinking and troubled mood. This thought disorder is manifested by difficulties in maintaining and focusing attention and in forming concepts. It can result in false perceptions and beliefs, in enormous difficulties in understanding reality, and in corresponding difficulties with language and emotional expression.

"Schizophrenia" is not a single disorder but rather a group of psychoses. As such, we often refer to these disorders as "the schizophrenias." We will try to understand the schizophrenic disorders by examining the symptoms that are part of them, and the psychological and biological determinants that promote them. Then we will examine the various treatments that are available for the schizophrenias. But before doing any of this, it is important to sketch out a general picture of the history, prevalence, and dimensions of the schizophrenias.

Evolving Views of Schizophrenia

▲ Society's view of the schizo-phrenic as dangerous, unpre-dictable, and out of control is reflected in this illustration by Charles Bell.

Until about 1880, little progress was made in differentiating one form of disor-der from another. There was a *sense* that there were different kinds of madness, but no shared view of what those differences might be. Indeed, it was not until 1809 that the set of symptoms that are presently called schizophrenia was clearly identified clinically (Gottesman, 1991). The first widely accepted classi-ficatory system for severe psychological disorders was advanced by the German psychiatrist, Emil Kraepelin (1856–1926). One of the disorders he de-scribed in 1896 was **dementia praecox**, literally, early or premature dete-rioration.

For Kraepelin, the diagnosis of *dementia praecox* was indicated when indi-viduals displayed certain unusual symptoms and showed a deteriorating course thereafter. Included among these were inappropriate emotional re-sponses such as laughter at a funeral or crying at a joke; stereotyped motor be-havior, such as bowing repeatedly before entering a room, or clapping five times before putting head to pillow; attentional difficulties such as inability to read because of shifting shadows; sensory experiences in the absence of appro-priate stimuli, such as seeing people when none are present, or smelling sul-phur in a jasmine garden; and beliefs sustained in spite of overwhelming con-trary evidence, such as insisting that one is an historical personage like Napoleon, or that one is held together by wire. Kraepelin's views powerfully in-fluenced succeeding generations of psychiatrists, and are important histori-cally for distinguishing and classifying the various forms of madness (Carpen-ter, 1992).

The term "schizophrenia" (*schizo* = split, *phreno* = mind) was coined by the Swiss psychiatrist Eugen Bleuler (1857–1939) in 1911. Bleuler believed that certain psychological *functions*, ordinarily coordinated in normal people, are somehow divided in schizophrenics (see Box 12–1). When non-schizophrenics perceive, say, a horrifying incident, they immediately have an emotional reac-tion that corresponds to their perception. But according to Bleuler, this does not happen to schizophrenics, for whom thought and emotion are split. Bleuler believed that the disorder was part of one's biological makeup and was likely to recur. He felt that schizophrenia could first occur at any time during a person's life, and while he recognized that schizophrenia was undoubtedly se-rious, and in many cases chronic, Bleuler asserted that recovery was possible.

Both Kraepelin and Bleuler were convinced that the causes of schizophre-nia were biological and that the ultimate cure would be biomedical. Kraepelin hypothesized that a chemical imbalance was produced by malfunctioning sex glands and somehow interfered with the nervous system. Bleuler was con-vinced that brain disease caused schizophrenia, and he continually resorted to hypothetical brain pathology to account for schizophrenic symptoms. The search for a biological basis for schizophrenia was begun by these two pioneer-ing scientists.

A completely different approach to understanding the origins and cure of schizophrenia was propounded by a contemporary of Kraepelin and Bleuler, Adolf Meyer (1866–1950). Meyer, a brain pathologist, later became recog-

▼ Eugen Bleuler (1857–1939).

nized as the dean of American psychiatry. He maintained that there were no fundamental biological differences between schizophrenics and normals and that there were not any fundamental differences in their respective psychological processes. Rather, he believed that the cognitive and behavioral disorganization that was associated with schizophrenia arose from inadequate early learning, and reflected "adjustive insufficiency" and habit deterioration and that individual maladjustment rather than biological malfunction lay at the root of the disorder. Meyer's approach mandated research in different areas than did Bleuler's or Kraepelin's. While Bleuler and Kraepelin strengthened the biological tradition of research in schizophrenia, Meyer gave impetus to a tradition that focused on learning and biosocial processes. Let us consider some of the modern views of this disorder.

Schizophrenia Defined

What schizophrenia is, as well as who is and who is not schizophrenic, has generated heated debate ever since Kraepelin described the symptoms of *dementia praecox* in his *Psychiatrie* in 1896. In part, the diagnosis of schizophre-

---

Box 12–1

SOME MYTHS ABOUT SCHIZOPHRENIA

Schizophrenics have been called lunatics, madmen, raving maniacs, unhinged, deranged, and demented. These words suggest that schizophrenics are dangerous, unpredictable, impossible to understand, and completely out of control. These notations, however, say more about non-schizophrenics' fear and ignorance than they do about the nature of schizophrenia itself.

Rather than being raving maniacs on the rampage, schizophrenics are often withdrawn and preoccupied with their own problems. Sometimes they yell and scream, and occasionally they strike someone. But it is by no means clear whether these behaviors arise from the actual disorder, or from the way schizophrenics are treated. Like others, schizophrenics often mirror their treatment. When the treatment is civilized, so are the patients. The mistaken notion that criminals are less dangerous than schizophrenics, and that one would be better off living near a prison than near a hospital, rests squarely on ignorance and fear.

Another common misconception about schizophrenia is that it involves a split personality of the Dr. Jekyll and Mr. Hyde sort, with its attendant unpredictability and potential for violence. This error arises from the origins of the word schizophrenia (*schizo* = split, *phreno* = mind). When Eugen Bleuler coined the term, he intended to suggest that certain psychological functions were divided in schizophrenics, not that there were two or more alternating personalities residing in the schizophrenic. Although Bleuler's view is no longer as widely accepted as it once was, the misconception that arose from his view continues to exist, fostered by Hollywood and television in such productions as *The Three Faces of Eve* (see Chapter 9 on dissociative disorders).

A third myth about schizophrenia is that once a person is found to be a schizophrenic, he or she will always be a schizophrenic. But in fact, the schizophrenic disorders are not necessarily durable, and surely not lifelong for all schizophrenics. Often, a single episode will occur and then disappear, never to recur. Sometimes, after a long period in which the individual has been symptom-free, another episode may occur. Much as one may suffer several colds during a lifetime and yet not always have a runny nose, so too can a person suffer several schizophrenic episodes during a lifetime, and be quite same in between. Many people who have suffered a schizophrenic disorder engage in athletics, read newspapers and novels, watch television, obtain college degrees, and relate to their friends and families in much the same way that others do. Long stretches of time can pass without evidence of their distress. We do not know why a schizophrenic episode occurs any more than we understand why we come down with a cold. As when the symptoms of a cold are absent and the individual is considered healthy, so when the symptoms of schizophrenia are absent the individual is considered sane. Finally, it goes without saying that schizophrenics are as human as the rest of us.

FOCUS QUESTIONS

1. What are the substantive criteria used by DSM-IV for a diagnosis of schizophrenia?
2. What are the temporal criteria used by DSM-IV to diagnose schizophrenia?
3. Who is most at risk for schizophrenia?

nia is controversial because each of its symptoms is quite similar to the symptoms that may arise from other mental or physical illnesses, traumatic stress, prescription medications, street drugs, and brain injury (Gottesman, 1991). The most recent definition was offered in 1994 in DSM-IV. In order to be diagnosed as a schizophrenic now, the symptoms must last for at least six months, and those symptoms must have induced a marked deterioration from the individual's previous level of functioning at work, in social relations, and in self-care. Those are the *temporal* criteria.

There are also two *substantive* criteria for the diagnosis: (1) There must be a gross impairment of reality testing, that is, the individual must evaluate the accuracy of his or her thoughts incorrectly and, as a consequence, must make obviously incorrect inferences about reality. Such an impairment in reality testing is called a ***psychosis.*** Psychoses reflect major disruptions of contact with reality. Minor impairments, such as a tendency to undervalue one's abilities or attractiveness, do not qualify. (2) The disturbance typically must affect several psychological processes, including thought, perception, emotion, communication, and psychomotor behavior. Disturbances of thought characteristically take the form of delusions and hallucinations.

Delusions are false beliefs that resist all argument and are sustained in the face of evidence that normally would be sufficient to destroy them. An individ-

▶ Entitled "Holy Sweat Miracle on the Insole," this drawing was done by a patient with a systematic delusion of poisoning and murder culminating in a miracle of the Holy Ghost. According to the patient, it was a "miracle in the insole of the victim ruthlessly sacrificed, disinherited, declared dead, by the secret violent poisoning and brain crushing of assassins possessed by Satan and mentally disturbed. . ."

ual who believes that he has drunk of the Fountain of Youth and is therefore immortal suffers a delusion. And the individual who believes that he not only has knowledge of these legendary waters but also that others are conspiring to pry his secret knowledge from him, is probably suffering from several delusions.

Hallucinations are false sensory perceptions that have a compelling sense of reality, even in the absence of external stimuli that ordinarily provoke such perceptions. In schizophrenia, hallucinations are commonly auditory, consisting either of a voice that maintains a running commentary on the individual's behavior, or two or more voices conversing with each other about the patient. But they can also be visual or implicate other sense organs, such as taste and smell. An individual who is convinced that she has seen, shook hands with, and had dinner with a minotaur has had an hallucination.

The examples of delusion and hallucination that were just given have their roots in colorful myths. But when experienced by real patients, these disturbances and others that we will examine later are considerably more painful, as the following case (first discussed in Chapter 8) illustrates:

> Carl was twenty-seven years old when he was first admitted to a psychiatric facility. Gangling and intensely shy, he was so incommunicative at the outset that his family had to supply initial information about him. They, it seemed, had been unhappy and uncomfortable with him for quite some time. His father dated the trouble from "sometime in high school." He reported, "Carl turned inward, spent a lot of time alone, had no friends and did no schoolwork." His mother was especially troubled about his untidiness. "He was really an embarrassment to us then, and things haven't improved since. You could never take him anywhere without an argument about washing up. And once he was there, he wouldn't say anything to anyone." His twin sisters, six years younger than Carl, said very little during the family interview, but rather passively agreed with their parents.
>
> One would hardly have guessed from their report that Carl graduated high school in the upper quarter of his class and had gone on to college where he studied engineering for three years. Though he had always been shy, he had had one close friend, John Winters, throughout high school and college. John had been killed in a car accident a year earlier. (Asked about Winters, his father said, "Oh, him. We don't consider him much of anything at all. He didn't go to church either. And he didn't do any schoolwork.")
>
> Carl and John were unusually close. They went through high school together, served in the army at the same time and when discharged, began college together and roomed in the same house. Both left college before graduating, much to the chagrin of Carl's parents, took jobs as machinists in the same firm, and moved into a nearby apartment.
>
> They lived together for three years until John was killed. Two months later the company for which they worked went out of business. John's death left Carl enormously distraught. When the company closed, he found himself without the energy and motivation to look for a job. He moved back home. Disagreements between Carl and his family became more frequent and intense. He became more reclusive, as well as sloppy and bizarre; they, more irritable and isolating. Finally they could bear his behavior no longer and took him to the hospital. He went without any resistance.
>
> After ten days in the hospital, Carl told the psychologist who was working with him: "I am un unreal person. I am made of stone, or else I am made of glass. I am wired precisely wrong, precisely. But you will not find my key. I have tried to lose the key to me. You can look at me closely if you wish, but you see more from far away."

▲ "I am an unreal person. I am made of stone. . ." *The Song of the Violet,* a painting by Magritte.

Shortly thereafter, the psychologist noted that Carl ". . . smiles when he is uncomfortable, and smiles more when in pain. He cries during television comedies. He seems angry when justice is done, frightened when someone compliments him, and roars with laughter on reading that a young child was burned in a tragic fire. He grimaces often. He eats very little but always carries food away."

After two weeks, the psychologist said to him: "You hide a lot. As you say, you are wired precisely wrong. But why won't you let me see the diagram?"

Carl answered: "Never, ever will you find the lever, the eternalever that will sever me forever with my real, seal, deal, heel. It is not on my shoe, not even on the sole. It walks away."

Incidence and Prevalence of Schizophrenia

Schizophrenia is one of the most prevalent of the severe psychological disorders. The various types are conservatively estimated to occur in less than 1 percent of the U.S. population (Dohrenwend and Dohrenwend, 1974; DSM-III, 1980), although some national estimates run as high as 3 or 4 percent (Heston, 1970). Moreover, among certain populations, such as college students, some estimates go as high as 18 percent (Koh and Peterson, 1974). These latter estimates are probably exaggerated, but even the conservative estimates mark the schizophrenias as a distressingly prevalent disorder.

The first episode of schizophrenia can occur anytime from puberty and adolescence up through the late forties. The episode, if untreated, may last for as little as a few weeks or may extend for several years. Although many treated schizophrenics return to a level of functioning called "social recovery," they may recover only to the bare level tolerated by society or, at worst, recover enough to leave the hospital while continuing in a chronic condition of disability as homeless people, or living in "SROs," or living in geriatric hostels, even though they are young (Gottesman, 1991). There are substantial sex differences in the time of first occurrence: men are at risk for schizophrenia when they are younger, mainly before age twenty-five, with peak incidence occurring at age twenty-four. Women are at risk after age twenty-five (Lewine, 1981; Zigler and Levine, 1981, Sartorius, Jablensky, Korten, Ernberg, Anker, Cooper, and Day, 1986; Saugstad, 1989). Moreover, these sex differences persist. Women are hospitalized less often than men, and for shorter periods (Goldstein, 1988). The long-term prognosis for women is better than it is for men (Nyman and Jonsson, 1983), perhaps because women seem to have better social skills (Mueser, Bellack, Morrison, and Wade, 1990).

Over the course of a lifetime, 1 in 100 people will develop symptoms of schizophrenia. And 1.85 million Americans over age sixteen have had an episode of schizophrenia (Gottesman, 1991). Compared to incidence among the wealthy, the incidence of the schizophrenias among the poor is three times greater, while its prevalence (the proportion of schizophrenics in the population at any one time) is eight times as high, mainly due to downward social drift (Dohrenwend et al., 1992). It especially affects the urban poor.

At the time of admission to a hospital or day treatment center, the typical schizophrenic is relatively young and relatively poor. Occasionally, schizophrenics come for treatment on their own, but more commonly their family or the police bring them to a treatment center after a disturbing incident triggers painful behavioral anomalies that are stressful for family and friends.

Although we speak of schizophrenia and schizophrenics as if this is a unitary disorder, the differences between the various types of schizophrenia overwhelm their similarities. The clinical heterogeneity of schizophrenia is so vast that some believe that the schizophrenias may even represent a number of potentially separable diagnostic entities (Fenton and McGlashan, 1991). We will focus on five subtypes of schizophrenia: paranoid, disorganized, catatonic, residual, and undifferentiated (see Table 12–1).

Paranoid Schizophrenia

The presence of systematized delusions or extensive auditory hallucinations marks this subtype. The ***paranoid schizophrenic*** suffers delusions of persecution or grandeur that are remarkably systematized and complex, often like the plots of dark mysteries. This complexity renders his experiences comprehensible to the schizophrenic—a matter of no small importance to which we will return—while simultaneously making it impenetrable to the outsider.

Paranoid schizophrenics (as well as others who suffer from delusional disorders) are often attracted to prominent places, such as the White House, 10 Downing Street, or the Vatican. Each year, the Secret Service arrests about 100 people after they approach the White House for money, relief from persecution, or to advise the government on how to run the country, and remands them to St. Elizabeth's Hospital for further evaluation (Gottesman, 1991).

Beyond experiencing delusions of persecution and/or grandeur, paranoid schizophrenics may also experience delusional jealousy, the deep belief that their sexual partner is unfaithful. But despite the intensity of their feelings, paranoid schizophrenics seldom display severely disorganized behavior, incoherence, or loose associations. Nor do they experience flat or inappropriate emotion. Rather, their demeanor tends to be extremely formal or quite intense.

TABLE 12–1

THOUGHT AND EMOTION IN THE SCHIZOPHRENIAS		
Type	*Thought*	*Emotion*
Paranoid	Delusions of persecution are complex and coherent	Either intensely emotional or very formal
Disorganized	Less coherent delusions, often centered on own body	Inappropriate and voluble
Catatonic	Delusions often centered on death and destruction	Very inappropriate, either very excited or "frozen" behavior
Residual	No delusions	May be flattened; may show impairment of hygiene or peculiar behavior

FOCUS QUESTIONS

1. What are five subtypes of schizophrenia?
2. What are the salient features of each type of schizophrenia?

Disorganized Schizophrenia

Formerly called hebephrenic schizophrenia, the most striking behavioral characteristic of ***disorganized schizophrenics*** is apparent silliness and incoherence. They burst into laughter, grimaces, or giggles without an appropriate stimulus. Their behavior is jovial, but quite bizarre and absurd, suggesting extreme sensitivity to internal cues and extreme insensitivity to external ones. Correspondingly, they are voluble, bursting into meaningless conversation for long periods of time.

Disorganized schizophrenics may experience delusions and hallucinations that tend to be more disorganized and diffused than those experienced by paranoid schizophrenics and that often center on their own bodies. For example, disorganized schizophrenics may complain that their intestines are congealed or that their brains have been removed. Sometimes, however, the delusions may be quite pleasant and contribute to the silliness of their behavior.

Disorganized schizophrenics often disregard bathing and grooming. They may not only become incontinent but also frequently eat their own body products, as well as other dirt. Again, a marked insensitivity is found here, similar to their insensitivity to social surroundings.

Catatonic Schizophrenia

The salient feature of ***catatonic schizophrenia*** is motor behavior that is either enormously excited or strikingly frozen, and that may occasionally alternate between the two states. The onset of the disorder is sudden. When behavior is excited, the individual may seem quite agitated, even wild, vigorously resisting all attempts at control, and dangerous to self and others. Affect is quite inappropriate, while agitation is enormously energetic and surprisingly prolonged, commonly yielding only to strong medication.

Stuporous or frozen behavior is also quite striking in this subtype of schizophrenia. Individuals may be entirely immobile, often adopting quite uncomfortable postures and maintaining them for long periods. If someone moves

▶ Catatonic schizophrenics may be entirely immobile, sometimes maintaining uncomfortable positions for hours.

them, they will freeze in a new position. A kind of statuesque "waxy flexibility" is characteristic. After emerging from such a stuporous episode, patients sometimes report that they had been experiencing hallucinations or delusions. These sometimes center on death and destruction, conveying the sense that any movement will provoke an enormous catastrophe.

Negativism—the apparently motiveless resistance to all instructions or attempts to be moved—is a common characteristic of catatonic schizophrenia, so much so that, in addition to the excited and stuporous behaviors, some theorists take negativism to define the category (Maher, 1966). Forbidden to sit, the catatonic will sit. Told to sit, the catatonic will insist on standing. Today this subtype is rare, possibly because the behavior is being controlled with antipsychotic drugs (Jablensky, Sartorius, Ernberg, Anker, Korten, Cooper, Day, and Bertelsen, 1992).

Residual Schizophrenia

This form of schizophrenia is characterized by the *absence* of prominent symptoms, such as delusions, hallucinations, incoherence, or grossly disorganized behavior. Rather, continuing evidence of the disorder is indicated by the presence of two or more symptoms which, though they are *relatively* minor, are nevertheless very distressing. These symptoms include: (a) marked social isolation or withdrawal; (b) marked impairment in role functioning; (c) very peculiar behavior; (d) serious impairment of personal hygiene and grooming; (e) blunt, flat, or inappropriate emotional expression; (f) odd, magical, or bizarre thinking; (g) unusual perceptual experiences; or (h) apathy or lack of initiative (DSM-IV, 1994).

Undifferentiated Schizophrenia

This designation is used to categorize individuals who do not otherwise fit neatly into other classifications. It is a diagnosis for disturbed individuals who present evidence of thought disorder, as well as behavioral and affective anomalies, but who are not classifiable under the other subtypes.

THE SYMPTOMS OF SCHIZOPHRENIA

In the case history presented earlier, Carl exhibited many of the characteristics associated with schizophrenia: lack of interest in life, withdrawal from social activity, seemingly bizarre behavior, incomprehensible communications, and increasing preoccupation with private matters. These symptoms, like many of the others that are common in schizophrenia, involve three areas of psychological functioning: perception, thought, and emotion.

Perceptual Difficulties

Perceptual anomalies often accompany schizophrenia. Patients sometimes report spatial distortions, such that a room may seem much smaller and more constricting than it really is, or objects may seem farther away. Controlled lab-

FOCUS QUESTIONS

1. What perceptual difficulties are often experienced by schizophrenics?
2. What deficit is most likely at the heart of the thought disorders in schizophrenics?
3. Why are emotional responses in schizophrenics likely to be blunted?
4. Why are schizophrenic communications often incomprehensible?

oratory studies indicate that compared to non-schizophrenics, schizophrenics are less able to discriminate faces and, more interesting, less able to decode the emotions that are being facially communicated (Feinberg, Rifkin, Schaffer, and Walker, 1986). Moreover, they are less able to estimate sizes accurately (Strauss, Foureman, and Parwatikar, 1974) and less able to judge the passage of time (Petzel and Johnson, 1972).

Generally, upon admission to a hospital, schizophrenics report a great number of perceptual difficulties, such as difficulties in understanding others' speech or identifying them, or overly acute auditory perception. These perceptual difficulties may provide a fertile soil for hallucinations, which are discussed below. Other people, as well as the self, may be described and apparently experienced as hollow, flat, or two-dimensional. Carl, for example, feels that he is made of steel or of glass.

HALLUCINATIONS

As we noted earlier, hallucinations are false sensory experiences that have a compelling sense of reality. In fact, PET scans show that the visual cortex is energized during visual hallucinations (Buchsbaum and Heier, 1987). Hallucinations are often gripping, and they are sometimes terrifying. Everyone knows what a visual hallucination is because everyone dreams. But for most people, dreams occur only during a certain portion of sleep, called "rapid eye movement," or REM sleep. They do not occur when we are awake, presumably because there is a neurotransmitter-mediated mechanism that inhibits them. Some researchers believe that this mechanism has failed in schizophrenics who hallucinate (Assad and Shapiro, 1986).

Auditory hallucinations are the most common hallucinations in schizophrenia (Heilbrun, 1993). One finds their origins in ordinary thought, where it is common enough to conduct a private dialogue by imagining oneself talking to others and others talking back. And it is quite common for people actually to talk to themselves, or to talk with deities whose presence can only be presumed. (The psychiatrist Thomas Szasz [1970] observes that it is quite nor-

▶ A schizophrenic may have visual and auditory hallucinations that have a compelling sense of reality.

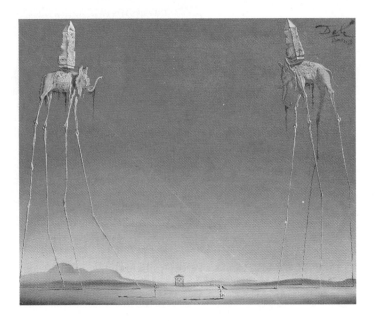

mal to talk with God, and that when we do so it is called prayer. Only when God responds is it called an hallucination!) Of course, the non-schizophrenic has considerably greater control over the internal dialogue than does the schizophrenic. The latter, when experiencing an auditory hallucination, does not believe that the voices originate within the self, or that she has the ability to begin or end the talk. The inability to distinguish between external and internal, real and imagined, controllable and imposed, is central to the schizophrenic experience.

Thought Disorders

Insofar as schizophrenics' speech reflects their thought, schizophrenics' thought can be disordered in a variety of ways. Sometimes the *process* of thinking is disordered, and sometimes it is the *content* of thought that is peculiar.

THE DISORDERED PROCESS OF THOUGHT

When the process of thinking is disturbed, the train of thought seems moved by the *sound* of words rather than by their meaning. ***Clang associations,*** that is, associations produced by the rhyme of words, such as ". . . my real, seal, deal, heel," abound. Schizophrenics like Carl may also come up with ***neologisms,*** new words like "eternalever" that have only private meaning. In addition, their use of vague, overly abstract or overly concrete, repetitive, or stereotyped words can impoverish the content of their speech, such that little information is communicated. These communication disturbances seem not to arise from lack of education or low intelligence but apparently from the disorder itself. Finally, some of the most interesting evidence about schizophrenic thought arises from studies of attention and distractibility.

Attentional Deficits   Everyone at one time or another has had trouble paying attention or concentrating, in spite of trying hard to do both. Tired or upset, we find our attention roaming, and we cannot direct it. What we have experienced briefly and in microcosm, acute schizophrenics experience profoundly. One patient explains his problem with attention in this way:

> I can't concentrate. It's diversion of attention that troubles me . . . The sounds are coming through to me, but I feel my mind cannot cope with everything. It's difficult to concentrate on any one sound. It's like trying to do two or three different things at one time. (McGhie and Chapman, 1961, p. 104)

Consider for a moment what normal attention involves. We are continuously bombarded by an enormous number of stimuli, much more than our limited channel capacity can absorb. So we need some mechanism for sorting out stimuli to determine which ones will be admitted and which ones barred. That mechanism has been referred to metaphorically as a ***cognitive*** or ***selective filter*** (Broadbent, 1958). Normally, that filter is flexible, sensitive, and sturdy. Sometimes it permits several different stimuli to enter simultaneously, and other times it bars some of those same stimuli. When you drive a car on a clear road, for example, you usually can conduct a conversation with a passenger, often while listening to background music. But when the roads are treacherous, and below you is a several hundred foot drop, attention narrows: it becomes impossible to conduct a conversation and what was formerly soothing

music is now quite an irritant. All of the mind's energy, as it were, is directed to one thing and one thing only: driving safely. Everything else is filtered out.

Among schizophrenics, something seems wrong with the attentional filter, so wrong, in fact, that attentional deficits have long been thought to be at the heart of the thought disorder that characterizes schizophrenia (Kraepelin, 1919; Bleuler, 1924; Chapman and Chapman, 1973; Garmezy, 1977b; Place and Gilmore, 1980). The sense that there is a breakdown of the filter, that the world's hodgepodge has simply invaded the mind, that one cannot control one's attention and therefore one's thoughts or speech, that it is difficult to focus the mind or sustain that focus once it is achieved—all of these experiences are said to be central to schizophrenia. A former patient puts it well:

> Each of us is capable of coping with a large number of stimuli, invading our being through any one of the senses. We could hear every sound within earshot and see every object, line and colour within the field of vision, and so on. It's obvious that we would be incapable of carrying on any of our daily activities if even one-hundredth of all these available stimuli invade us at once. So the mind must have a filter which functions without our conscious thought, sorting stimuli and allowing only those which are relevant to the situation in hand to disturb consciousness. And this filter must be working at maximum efficiency at all times, particularly when a high degree of concentration is required. What happened to me . . . was a breakdown in the filter, and a hodge-podge of unrelated stimuli were distracting me from things which should have had my undivided attention. (MacDonald, 1960, p. 218)

Some schizophrenics seem to suffer generalized attentional deficits; they seem not to be attending to anything at all. Others pay too much attention to some stimuli, and not enough to others. For example, someone who is experiencing hallucinations is likely to be hyperattentive to the hallucinations and correspondingly insensitive to external social stimuli.

Overinclusiveness   Schizophrenic thinking generally also tends to be overinclusive (Cameron, 1938, 1947; Chapman and Taylor, 1957; Payne, 1966; Yates, 1966; Marengo, Harrow and Edell, 1993). ***Overinclusiveness*** refers to the tendency to form concepts from both relevant and irrelevant information. This thought defect arises from an impaired capacity to resist distracting information, and it strongly suggests a defect in cognitive filtering.

Generally, then, schizophrenics may be processing much more information than normals, by virtue of overinclusiveness. Evidence from other research indicates that psychotic states generally tax and deplete information processing, slowing and straining a system that is already quite limited, and impairing performance for tasks that require full use of processing capabilities (Braff and Saccuzzo, 1985; Grove and Andreasen, 1985; Ohman, Nordby, and d'Elia, 1986; Patterson, Spohn, Bogia, and Hayes, 1986; Saccuzzo and Braff, 1986).

Cognitive Distractibility   The notion of a defective filter that gives rise to overinclusiveness in schizophrenic thinking merits further examination. Are there rules that determine what is relevant information and what irrelevant? Of course not. Very likely all of us differ with regard to the kind of information that we attend to and exclude, even on simple tasks. In what ways, then, may the thought and attentional processes of schizophrenics be different from those of normals?

The difference between schizophrenic and normal thinking is unlikely to be a qualitative one, since all of us have associations to a stimulus that may or may not prove to be relevant. The difference lies in the number of associative intrusions, the context in which they arise, and in how they are integrated conceptually. Imagine yourself writing a New Year's greeting to a friend. You wish her a happy and healthy year and then refer to the pleasures and sadnesses of the previous year. Compare your greeting to that written by one of Eugen Bleuler's patients:

▶ Hospitalized in a mental asylum and labeled a schizophrenic, August Klotz spent his time drawing such pictures as this. Here he depicts a person's hair as a combination of worms, fingers with nails, and heads of caterpillars, describing the drawing through free association: "Worm holes (bath faces), worm paths (pianomusicstickteeth), worm strings (spitbathlife of the arch-lyregallery-tin-timeler-reflections: ad mothersugarmoon in the sevensaltnose water . . ."

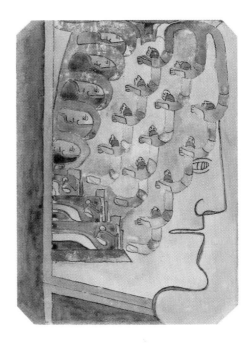

I wish you then a good, happy, joyful, healthy, blessed and fruitful year, and many good wine-years to come, as well as a healthy and good apple-year, and sauerkraut and cabbage and squash and seed year. (Bleuler, 1950, cited in Martin, 1977)

Here, there are many more associations than are found in normal greetings. These associations, moreover, arise in chains that appear to be generated by specific words that seem to distract the patient from his ultimate goal and impair the overall meaning of the greeting. The word fruitful seems to evoke associations to wine, apple, sauerkraut, cabbage, squash, and the like. Moreover, in this context, wine and sauerkraut are not normally the dominant associations of the word fruitful; abundance is. But the patient seems to have centered on "fruit" and to have generated associations that are appropriate for that word but not for "fruitfulness."

Many words have a variety of meanings, connotations, and associations. And all of us, schizophrenics and normals alike, are sensitive to those meanings and associations. But schizophrenics seem especially sensitive to the dominant associations of words, and are less influenced by the contexts in which they are used. In the following test item:

Pool means the same as
   1. puddle
   2. notebook
   3. swim
   4. none of the above.

The correct answer is "puddle." Many schizophrenics as well as some normals, however, will err and offer "swim" as the correct answer. The difference between normal and schizophrenic thought processes in items of this sort is a quantitative rather than a qualitative one (Chapman and Chapman, 1973; Rattan and Chapman, 1973).

THE DISORDERED CONTENT OF THOUGHT

Evidence for disordered thought is as commonly found in the content as the process of thinking. Sometimes the schizophrenic person develops the belief that certain events and people have special significance for him—that television newscasters are speaking to him, for example, or that strangers in the street are looking at him. These beliefs are called ***ideas of reference.*** When such beliefs become organized into a larger and coherent framework, they are called delusions.

Kinds of Delusions   Earlier we noted that a ***delusion*** is a private theory, deeply held, that often persists despite sound contradictory evidence, and that often does not fit with the individual's level of knowledge or cultural group. These beliefs are so deeply held that psychological lore tells of a delusional patient who was once wired to a lie detector and asked if she were the Virgin Mary. "No," she replied. But the detector indicated that she was lying! Delusions are common in a variety of psychoses. What differentiates schizophrenic delusions from those of, say, depressives, is their mood incongruence. Unlike depressives, whose delusions bear a strong relationship to their moods, schizophrenics have delusions that seem incongruent with their present feelings (Winokur, Scharfetter, and Angst, 1985; Farmer, McGuffin, and Gottesman, 1987; Junginger, Barker, and Coe, 1992).

There are five prominent kinds of schizophrenic delusions: delusions of grandeur, delusions of control, delusions of persecution, delusions of reference, and somatic delusions. **Delusions of grandeur** consist of convictions that one is especially important. The belief that one is Jesus Christ or fourth in line to the throne of Denmark would indicate a delusion of grandeur.

Delusions of control are characterized by beliefs that one's thoughts or behaviors are being controlled from without. The patient attributes the source of angry, sexual, or otherwise sinful thoughts to external agents. For example, someone who believes that beings from another universe are giving him instructions is suffering from a delusion of control.

Delusions of persecution consist of fears that individuals, groups, or the government have malevolent intentions and are "out to get me." The focus of the delusion may be quite specific: a neighbor, one's boss, the FBI, or a rather vague "they." When these delusions combine with hallucinations so that the subject "sees" and "hears" evidence of a plot, they can induce continual panic. Confirmation for these imaginings can often be found in misinterpretations of everyday experience, as shown in the following case:

> Arthur, who had been insecure and shy for as long as he could remember, took a job in a large office. Unsure of his clerical abilities, he worked long and hard at his job, rejecting invitations to have lunch or coffee with his colleagues. Gradually they stopped inviting him, going off merrily by themselves, and returning full of laughter and cheer.
>
> One day Arthur's supervisor found a substantial error in his work. Although it was his first error and the supervisor would easily have forgiven it, Arthur simply could not forget it. It seemed to underscore his own perception of his abilities, a perception that he was quite anxious to conceal. He came to believe that his supervisor knew of other mistakes he had made, and that his colleagues and supervisor were collaboratively examining his work daily. He "knew" that they were excluding him and talking about him, and that their lunchtime laughter was entirely at his expense. Moreover, he felt that their interest in his performance gradually overflowed into an interest in his personal life. When he encountered his co-workers after hours or on the weekend he felt certain that they were following him.
>
> Six weeks after his error had been discovered, he began to "sense" that people had been through his drawers, both at home and in the office. Moreover, certain papers that were necessary for his work were missing, leading him to believe that others were now actively plotting his vocational downfall. Their failure to invite him to lunch was taken as further evidence of the plot.
>
> He became very fearful and disorganized. Continually preoccupied with his troubles, he found it difficult to sleep, eat, or concentrate. His work deteriorated both in quality and in output. When his supervisor finally asked him what was wrong, he blurted out, "You know what's wrong. You and they have made it wrong ever since I came here." He then ran out of the office, never to return. Within the year, Arthur's behavior had so deteriorated that he was hospitalized with the diagnosis of paranoid schizophrenia.

Arthur's sense that others were actively seeking his errors and taking his papers constituted a delusion of persecution. But the continual misinterpretation of others' laughter, as well as their failure to invite him to lunch, constituted the fourth kind of delusion: a **delusion of reference**. Such delusions rest

on the incorrect assumption that the casual remarks or behaviors of others apply to oneself, and can extend to how others act in the street or subway, as well as to the behavior of actors on television. Depending on what they refer to, referential delusions can make a person miserably unhappy, as in the above instance, or quite joyful.

Finally, *somatic delusions* are characterized by the unverified belief that something is drastically wrong with one's body. A schizophrenic who suffers somatic delusions might believe, for example, that something is rotting inside her body.

Delusions: A Normal Cognitive Activity?   Delusions are among the most striking symptoms of schizophrenia. To the observer, the content of a delusion seems so bizarre that it automatically suggests the thought disorder that is characteristic of schizophrenia. How else does one explain the feeling that one is being intensely persecuted, or that one is infinitely superior to ordinary mortals, all in the absence of confirming evidence? Indeed, it is the flowering of a delusion in the absence of confirmation, and its resistance to ordinary persuasion, that leads us to believe that the thought processes that are implicated in delusional activity are different from our own (see Figure 12–1).

Before we consider the delusions from the schizophrenic's own vantage point, we might first look for analogies to delusional activity. These, of course, are only analogies, and likely rude analogies at that, but they give us some basis for understanding schizophrenic delusions.

Imagine that you have experienced a partial loss of hearing, and that you are unaware of that loss. You are with two other people who are talking, laughing, making funny faces, and looking at you. All three of you have to work together, but it seems that those two are doing a better job of it than you are. What are you likely to think? Remember that you can't *hear* what's going on very well, so you don't really *know* why they are laughing and looking at you. But that doesn't stop you from trying to make sense of the peculiar situation. One very real possibility is that you will infer that they are talking about *you* and laughing at *you*.

Such an experiment was in fact conducted among normal people who were highly hypnotizable and in whom partial deafness was induced. Subjects who were unaware that they were deaf were rated by judges (who had no knowledge of the subjects' hearing status) as being more agitated, irritated, hostile, and confused than either nondeaf subjects or subjects who were aware of the source of their deafness. Moreover, the experimental subjects rated themselves in very much the same way. Finally, formal measures of psychopathology, such as the Minnesota Multiphasic Personality Inventory (MMPI) and the Thematic Apperception Test (TAT), revealed much higher paranoia scores among subjects who were deaf and unaware of it (Zimbardo, Andersen, and Kabat, 1981).

While the sources of our feelings and perceptions are not always available to us, we do, in fact, develop theories to account for our experiences. These theories arise from the causal attributions we make about our experiences (Nisbett and Ross, 1980). In this sense, we behave like ordinary scientists: given a set of facts or experiences, we seek to explain them (Maher, 1974; Oltmanns and Maher, 1988).

A similar process may occur with schizophrenics. Like the normal person, the schizophrenic asks: What is happening? How is it happening? And why is it happening to me and not to others? Because their attention is overinclusive, schizophrenics will frequently "see" aspects of their environment that they are at a loss to explain, and be inundated by stimuli that they cannot control (Venables, 1964). Moreover, there is growing evidence that schizophrenics actually suffer impairments of a physical sort. The sensory quality of their perceptual experience may be more vivid, intense, or defective than in normals (Cooper, Garside, and Kay, 1976; Cooper and Porter, 1976). Much as it is common for older people whose hearing is fading to believe that people are whispering about them, so it may be that schizophrenics' delusions derive from actual perceptual deficits. Such deficits and the experiences to which they give rise are

FIGURE 12–1

NORMAL VS. DISTURBED THOUGHT PROCESSES		
In schizophrenia normal thought processes (described on the left side of the spectrum) become the disturbed processes of the right side. The difference for most processes is quantitative, not qualitative.	Cognitive filter is flexible, selective, sensitive, and sturdy, and functioning nearly all the time	Breakdown in filter, so that stimuli seem to invade the mind, causing attentional deficits and overinclusiveness
	Words and phrases provoke associations, but these are edited in ways appropriate to situation	Associations seem rampant and uncontrolled, and can interfere with accurate communication of meaning
	Experiences or situations are met with efforts to explain them, with an inherent bias toward one's own point of view	Owing partly to other disturbed processes, theories and explanations of events often lose touch with reality

genuine. But they lead schizophrenics to experience their world differently than the rest of us do.

Schizophrenics know that their own experiences are *real*. When others deny the reality of those experiences, schizophrenics have two alternative explanations: either the others are lying, or they are telling the truth. If schizophrenics decide that the others are lying, they feel victimized, and they suffer delusions of persecution. If schizophrenics decide that others are telling the truth, then they feel privileged because of their special ability to perceive "realities" that are unavailable to others, and they suffer delusions of grandiosity.

"But why me and not others?," the schizophrenic asks. It is in explaining his special fate that the personal history of the schizophrenic may become relevant. If, for example, he harbors a guilty secret in his past, he may conclude that this is why he is being so terribly punished now. If he has done something that he views as especially praiseworthy, he may now see himself as anointed from above. The variety of possible explanations is limited only by the variety of life histories that exist among schizophrenics, while the regularity with which certain explanations occur derives from the common life experiences that a culture provides.

Finally, it is schizophrenics' persistence in maintaining their delusions despite contrary evidence that requires explanation. Reality is not a solid, concrete thing. It can and has been used by normal people to arrive at conclusions that other normals find tenuous. All theories about how the world operates, including scientific ones, are overthrown only when a more satisfactory theory can be found to replace it. Because schizophrenics' theories often rest on invisible agencies, what seems ridiculous to the observer provides schizophrenics with a cohesive and satisfactory account of their situation. On those occasions when it is contradicted by particular kinds of data, the theory (i.e., the delusion) becomes more elaborate and comprehensive to account for the seeming contradiction, much as scientific theories do when they must account for anomalies. For example, if a schizophrenic believes that he is being poisoned and he encounters a nurse who seems particularly kind, he may expand his delusion to include people who seem kind, but who are really poisoners. This occurs not because the schizophrenic fails to test reality, but because he has no more satisfactory explanations.

▼ The schizophrenic may avoid social contacts, withdrawing behind a blank mask.

Affective Disturbances

Emotions, or affects, are jointly a function of perception, cognition, and physiological arousal. *Perceiving* a mad dog quickly generates some worrisome *cognitions* (or thoughts) that in turn generate an *emotion*, fear. Because schizophrenia arises from disorders of perception and cognition, it follows that there should be affective disturbances also.

For some schizophrenics, affect is characteristically flat or bland. Their voice may be monotonous and their face immobile. They seem entirely unresponsive emotionally. So much is this the case that flat or restricted affect is still considered a diagnostic hallmark of the schizophrenic disturbance (Carpenter, Strauss, and Bartko, 1974), although one with very low reliability. The apparent inability of some schizophrenics to display affect should not, however, be mistaken for absence of *any* affective experience. Schizophrenics are deeply emotional and deeply responsive to cognitions (Arieti, 1974). But the cognitions that affect them are not the ones that are evocative for most of us, and vice versa. In one respect, the schizophrenic experience is like our own when we visit unfamiliar places. For example, American guests at a Thai wedding, not knowing what all of the symbols mean, would hardly know how to act or what to feel. Shared symbolic meanings allow feelings to arise, be expressed, and be understood by others. Because schizophrenics have lost contact with the socially shared domain of symbols and meanings, their affective responses to those stimuli are likely to be blunted.

Sometimes, schizophrenic affect is best characterized as inappropriate. Carl's affect seemed to take that form:

> He smiles when he is uncomfortable, and smiles more when in pain. He cries during television comedies. He seems angry when justice is done. . . . and roars with laughter on reading that a young child was burned in a tragic fire.

Affective disturbance can take yet another form: intense ambivalence. A person or situation may arouse opposite feelings simultaneously. Such ambivalence may lead to behavioral paralysis, or to seemingly bizarre attempts to resolve the situation by expressing one affect overwhelmingly and suppressing the other entirely.

Finally, schizophrenics often experience recurrent depression, a depression so intense that it may result in suicide. In fact, suicide is the most frequent cause of mortality among schizophrenics, far surpassing any other cause (Gottesman, 1991). Because more than 10 percent of schizophrenics end their lives through suicide, battling depression is often as important in helping schizophrenics as dealing with the other symptoms of the schizophrenic disorder.

Meaning in Schizophrenia

Most people who read Carl's words are struck and upset by their incomprehensibility. "I am made of stone," he says, "or else I am made of glass. I am wired precisely wrong, precisely . . ." Neurotic communications evoke understanding. If you are told "I'm afraid to go outside" or "I can't stop daydreaming," you have little difficulty comprehending the communication, even empathizing with the speaker. But schizophrenic communications often seem to be gibberish; they seem to result in word salads and syllabic stews. Ideas are not transmitted. Unable to understand, people often turn away from schizophrenics, treating what schizophrenics say as part of the symptomatology of the disorder, and not as communication.

Do schizophrenics attempt to communicate? Is what they say gibberish? Was Carl saying anything that was meaningful? It appears that he was. But from the listener's viewpoint, it was difficult to find the communication in the thicket of strange verbalization.

> I am an unreal person. . . . I am wired precisely wrong, precisely. But you will not find my key. . . . You can look at me closely if you wish, but you see more from far away.

Carl is hiding. That is, he is trying "precisely" to mislead his observers. When angry, he pretends friendship; when sad, happiness. He wants to maintain privacy, and he may also feel in danger of being exposed. He is, therefore, all the more in need of concealment. When hiding by means of transparent opposites fails—as when he is asked an intrusive question—he hides more energetically. Or, he hides in more bizarre ways: by generating neologisms, by using clang associations to speak—in short, by talking a lot and saying little, by conveying his need to hide in his talk.

The divided self is a self that operates at two levels (Laing, 1965b). On one level, there is the silent self—clearly active but vulnerable and afraid to emerge. There is also a smoke-screen self, a mask, a disguise, designed to conceal and protect that silent self. There is no strong evidence for this two-self view, but many psychologists and psychiatrists who have worked with schizophrenics find merit in it. For example, later in his treatment, when his need to hide had abated, Carl had this to say of himself:

> When it's all over, it's hard to remember what you said and how you said it. I wouldn't want to talk that way now even if I could. I was putting people off almost consciously by talking that way. It would have been impossible for me to let on how I really felt. It's still hard. . . . But at the same time, while I was putting you off, I really wanted you to know. But I couldn't come out with it—that was too risky. Sometimes I would say things in a special way, hoping you'd take special notice. When I said I'm not angry. . . . I wagged my hand back and forth, making a "no" sign—telling but not saying that I'm angry. I don't know why I wanted someone to know. After all, I was hiding. But it was a prison I had made for myself. I didn't know how to get out myself. So I kept throwing out little keys, hoping someone would get at the lock.

THE DIMENSIONS OF SCHIZOPHRENIA

In DSM-IV, schizophrenics are categorized according to their symptoms. But they can also be categorized according to the onset of schizophrenia, the way the symptoms develop, and the ways in which they respond to treatment. The most common clinical dimension for categorizing schizophrenia is acute versus chronic, while a research mode of characterizing this set of disorders is Type I versus Type II.

Acute and Chronic

The distinction between acute and chronic conditions is based on how quickly the symptoms have developed and how long they have been present. **Acute schizophrenics** are characterized by rapid and sudden onset of very florid symptoms. Quite frequently, one can point to a specific precipitating incident that led to the difficulties: a **reactive** crisis that was precipitated by a severe social or emotional upset, often an upset from which the individual perceives no escape (Zigler and Phillips, 1961; Arieti, 1974). For some schizophrenics, that crisis may involve leaving home, leaving school for a job, their first sexual experience, the loss of a parent or sibling, or marriage. Prior to that upset, their history seems well within normal bounds.

FOCUS QUESTIONS

1. What criteria are used to distinguish between acute and chronic schizophrenia?
2. How does Type I schizophrenia differ from Type II schizophrenia?
3. What are the positive and negative symptoms of schizophrenia?

In contrast, **chronic schizophrenics** seem to manifest a rather gradual and prolonged history of withdrawal. No single crisis or identifiable stresses trigger the disorder. Rather, early history gives evidence of familial and peer rejection, inferior school and social adjustment, and intense shyness and social withdrawal, such that peer relations are impaired over a long period of time.

In clinical practice, the acute-chronic distinction rests on how many episodes a person has had and how long she has been hospitalized. First episodes that result in hospitalization for less than a year, or several episodes that lead to a series of very brief hospitalizations, qualify a person for an acute designation. Hospitalization that extends for more than two years invariably results in a chronic classification. When a person has been hospitalized from roughly eighteen to twenty-eight months, it is difficult to distinguish between acute and chronic conditions. That fact alone largely accounts for the low reliability of the classification.

Type I and Type II

The dimensions of the schizophrenias can be examined not only from the precipitants, but rather from the symptoms that are generated, the response to certain kinds of treatment, and the long-term outcome. **Type I** schizophrenia is characterized by a sudden onset of disorder in a person who seemed to be functioning well before the episode (Fenton and McGlashan, 1991), and by such symptoms as delusions, hallucinations, and prominent thought disorder. These are called "positive symptoms" because they reflect marked departures from ordinary cognition. Such positive symptoms are reversible. They are thought to arise from a disturbance in brain chemistry, specifically the neurotransmission of dopamine, an important matter that we will examine shortly. And they are thought to be responsive to a class of medications called **neuroleptics,** which alter brain chemistry.

The **Type II** syndrome is characterized by such symptoms as flat affect, poverty of speech, and loss of volition. There "negative symptoms" are more difficult to define because they reflect the absence or diminution of normal everyday functions, and "absence" is often more difficult to define and more elusive to measure. Negative symptoms are occasionally found in disorders other than schizophrenia. But they are a central and common aspect of schizophrenia and may even represent a distinct pathological process within schizophrenia (McGlashan and Fenton, 1992). Negative symptoms seem much more difficult to reverse than positive symptoms, and they are more closely associated with poor long-term outcome. The symptoms are unrelated to dopamine transmission, but may well be associated with structural changes in the brain, as well as intellectual impairment. Type II symptoms have a much poorer prognosis.

Type I and Type II syndromes are believed to reflect relatively independent processes that can coexist in the same individual but that follow different time courses. And perhaps because they can coexist simultaneously, they do not quite map on to the acute and chronic dimensions. Paranoid schizophrenia, however, reflects a chronic Type I syndrome, while disorganized schizophrenia includes a strong component of the Type II syndrome (Crow, 1985; Fenton and McGlashan, 1991).

The relationship between negative and positive symptoms within schizophrenia remains controversial. One view holds that negative and positive symptoms define relatively distinct subtypes of schizophrenia. This view posits an inverse correlation between positive and negative symptoms (Andreasen and Olsen, 1982). But another model argues that positive and negative symptoms reflect partially independent psychopathological processes that can coexist in the same individual (Crow, 1985; Fenton and McGlashan, 1991; Carpenter, 1992).

THE CAUSES OF THE SCHIZOPHRENIAS

While the schizophrenias have been studied for more than a century, progress in understanding them has been painfully slow. We know less about the origins and treatment of the schizophrenias than we do about some other disorders. In the following sections, we will outline the dominant approaches currently used in the search for the causes and treatment of the schizophrenias.

Knowledge about the origins of schizophrenia is concentrated in four major areas: genetics, neurochemistry, the role of the family, and the role of society. Research on the schizophrenias, like that on other psychological questions, is two-pronged, involving both biological and social questions. Some consider schizophrenia to be rooted in nature; others say that it is the product of social experience. Still others are convinced that nature-nurture interactions are involved, and that these interactions of genetic, biochemical, familial, and social factors predispose a person to schizophrenia (Zubin and Spring, 1977).

The Genetics of Schizophrenia

Various researchers have examined the notion of a genetic vulnerability to schizophrenia. Twin studies, family studies, and adoption studies have demonstrated a strong basis for the genetic component in schizophrenia (Gottesman, 1993).

CONCORDANCE FOR SCHIZOPHRENIA IN TWINS

MZ and DZ Twins We can best understand a possible genetic contribution to behavior by examining the similarities and differences between twins. As we discussed in Chapter 3, twins are of two kinds: identical and fraternal. Both kinds descend from the zygote, the fertilized egg from which all life begins. Identical twins are *monozygotic* (MZ), which means that both individuals developed from a single egg fertilized by a single sperm which divided and produced two individuals. Because all of the cells of these two individuals derived from a single egg, the genes and chromosomes—in short, the heredity—of these individuals is identical. They will, of course, have the identical physical makeup: genes, blood type, and eye color will be the same. There may be differences between them, but such differences will be entirely attributable to different life experiences: one may be thinner because of nutritional differences, or the other may limp because of an accident.

Fraternal, or *dizygotic* (DZ) twins develop from two different eggs and two different sperm. Except for the fact that they are born at the same time, DZ twins are like ordinary siblings. Their heredity makeup is quite different. They

FOCUS QUESTIONS

1. What is the genetic evidence for schizophrenia?
2. What is the dopamine hypothesis?
3. What brain abnormalities may lead to Type II schizophrenia?
4. What environmental factors may foster schizophrenia?

may be of different gender; they may have different eye color. They have different fingerprints. They can be accurately distinguished from MZ twins on the basis of these characteristics alone, and certainty can be increased by DNA "fingerprinting" as used in paternity testing or by the FBI.

The logic of a genetic study is really quite simple: if all other things are equal, the more similar people are in their genetic makeup, the more traits they will have in common if those traits are genetically influenced. MZ twins should resemble each other more than DZ twins or ordinary siblings. And DZ twins and siblings should have more in common than unrelated individuals. If both members of a twin set have a trait in common, we say that that twin set is **concordant** for that particular trait. If, however, one member has the trait and one does not, we call the twin set **discordant** for the trait. For quantitative differences, correlations are examined.

MZ twins are wholly identical in their genes and chromosomes. If the traits that subsequently develop are entirely determined by their genetic makeup, there should be 100 percent concordance. If one twin has the trait, the other should have it too. Anything less than 100 percent concordance (but more than the percentage found in DZ twins) will suggest that heredity *influences*, but does not actually determine, the presence of the trait. What is more, that influence depends on the assumption that all other possible influences, such as nutrition, physical health, and psychological environment, are themselves about the same. If one twin's physical and social environment diverges from the other's, that difference could explain any discrepancy between the pair.

Linking Genetics and Schizophrenia Although genetic studies of schizophrenia have been conducted for over fifty years, Irving Gottesman and James Shields (1972) conducted one of the very few studies that were planned in advance. From 1948 through 1964, every patient admitted for treatment to the psychiatric unit at the Maudsley and Bethlem Royal Hospital in London was routinely asked if he or she was a twin. Over these sixteen years, the investigators located 55 patients (out of more than 45,000 admitted) who were twins and whose twin could be located and would cooperate in the study. For analytic purposes, the twin who was first seen at the psychiatric clinic is called the **index case** or **proband.** The other twin, who will be examined for the presence or absence of schizophrenia, is called the **co-twin.**

Of these fifty-five sets of twins, it was determined that twenty-two were MZ twins and thirty-three were DZ twins. The twins ranged in age from nineteen to sixty-four, with a median age of thirty-seven initially. Concordance for schizophrenia, where it was already present in the co-twin at the time the proband was admitted to the hospital, could of course be determined immediately. Discordant pairs were followed for at least 13 and as long as 26 years to determine if schizophrenia subsequently developed in the co-twin (Gottesman, McGuffin, and Farmer, 1987).

Such a lengthy study examines more than simple diagnosis. In analyzing an enormous variety of psychological, medical, and social data for each twin pair, Gottesman and Shields observed two findings of special relevance to our own investigation into the genetic causes of schizophrenia. First, they found strict concordance when the proband's co-twin had been hospitalized and diagnosed schizophrenic: 50 percent of MZ twins and 9 percent of DZ twins were concordant for schizophrenia, a ratio of roughly 4:1. Despite the small sample, this is a very significant finding, one consistent with other genetic studies.

TABLE 12–2

CONCORDANCE RATES FOR SCHIZOPHRENIA IN TWIN STUDIES

Study	MZ		DZ	
	Pairs	Rate	Pairs	Rate
Finland 1963, 1971	17	35	20	13
Norway 1967	55	45	90	15
Denmark 1973	21	56	41	27
United Kingdom 1966, 1987	22	58	33	15
Norway 1991	31	48	28	4
United States 1969, 1983	164	31	268	6
Pooled concordance (excluding U.S.)				
Median	146	48	212	15
Weighted mean		48		16
Pooled concordance (all studies)				
Median	310	46	480	14
Weighted mean		39		10

SOURCE: Adapted from Gottesman, 1991.

Second, using length of hospitalization to indicate severity of schizophrenia, Gottesman and Shields found substantial concordance differences between MZ twins whose probands had been hospitalized for more than two years and those whose probands had been hospitalized for less than two years. Hospitalization for more than two years is critical to a diagnosis of chronic schizophrenia. It is therefore of enormous interest that concordance rates rose to 77 percent in this sample. For those who were hospitalized less than two years (very likely the acute, reactive schizophrenics), the concordance rate was only 27 percent (Gottesman and Shields, 1972). What this finding means practically is that severity of schizophrenia in a proband also increases the chances that the co-twin will become disabled (Torrey, 1992).

The evidence from the many studies summarized in Table 12–2 is strong: concordance rates for MZ twins are higher than they are for DZ twins; concordance rates for DZ twins are higher than the rate for unrelated persons in the general population (about 1 percent). Concordance, however, is never 100 percent because the genetic component of schizophrenia does not guarantee occurrence. Genetics only makes one vulnerable to schizophrenia; it does not guarantee that it will occur. Indeed, 89 percent of diagnosed schizophrenics have no known relative who is schizophrenic (Cromwell, 1993).

CONCORDANCE FOR SCHIZOPHRENIA IN FAMILIES

Family studies begin from the same premise as twin studies: individuals who have a similar heredity are more likely to possess a particular trait than those who are unrelated. Parents and siblings of a schizophrenic proband should be more likely to be or become schizophrenic than remote relatives, who in turn are more prone to schizophrenia than are those who are not related. The data from more than a dozen studies support this conclusion (Rosenthal, 1970a). As can be seen in Figure 12–2, the likelihood that ordinary siblings of a proband will also be schizophrenic is about 9 percent—much higher than the

1 percent one finds among the general population, but much lower than the 48 percent we find among identical twins. Similarly, the child of two schizophrenic parents has about a 46 percent chance of becoming schizophrenic. The evidence clearly supports genetic vulnerability—but only vulnerability. In no study do concordance and risk rise to 100 percent. Once again, it takes more than genetic vulnerability to produce schizophrenia.

BUT IS IT REALLY GENETIC?

We have assumed that if all other things are equal, the more similar people are in their genetic makeup, the more traits they will have in common if those traits are genetically influenced. But are all other things equal? Consider the finding that children of two schizophrenic parents stand a 46 percent chance of becoming schizophrenic themselves. Is that because they share a common gene pool, or is it because schizophrenic parents may be terrible parents, fully capable of inducing schizophrenia in their children, regardless of their common gene pool? Or consider again the twin studies. We know that MZ twins share a unique environment with each other. They tend to mature and to develop language more slowly than other children. They tend to be mistaken for

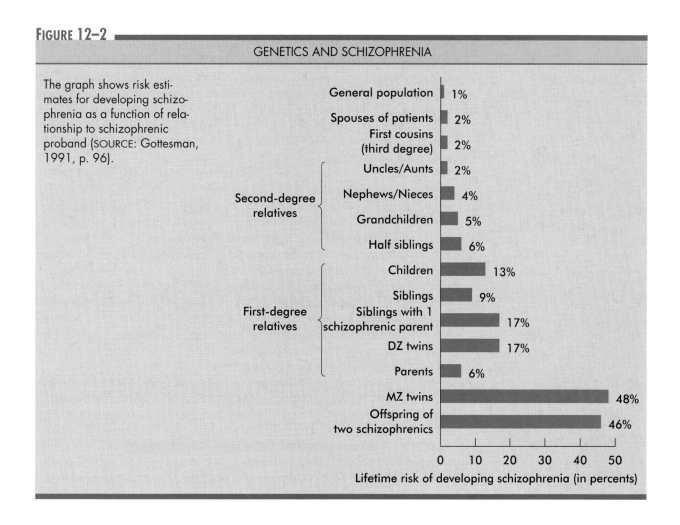

FIGURE 12–2

GENETICS AND SCHIZOPHRENIA

The graph shows risk estimates for developing schizophrenia as a function of relationship to schizophrenic proband (SOURCE: Gottesman, 1991, p. 96).

General population 1%
Spouses of patients 2%
First cousins (third degree) 2%

Second-degree relatives
Uncles/Aunts 2%
Nephews/Nieces 4%
Grandchildren 5%
Half siblings 6%

First-degree relatives
Children 13%
Siblings 9%
Siblings with 1 schizophrenic parent 17%
DZ twins 17%
Parents 6%

MZ twins 48%
Offspring of two schizophrenics 46%

0 10 20 30 40 50
Lifetime risk of developing schizophrenia (in percents)

one another and therefore to suffer identity problems of indeterminate magnitude. Could not these environmental problems, rather than genetics, be a major factor in their eventual schizophrenia?

Behavior geneticists have responded to these questions in three ways. First, they have tried to locate probands and co-siblings who have been reared apart. Studies of this kind are called **_adoption studies._** Second, they have conducted studies of people who are presumed to be at risk for schizophrenia because other members of their families are schizophrenic. These high-risk studies seek to map the development of behavior before schizophrenia occurs, in the hope of relating causative, correlative, and especially preventive factors. Finally, there are studies of non-schizophrenic twins which bear on this question.

Adoption Studies   Leonard Heston (1966) studied forty-seven children of schizophrenic mothers who had been placed in adoptive or foster homes less than one month after birth. He compared them to fifty control offspring. The environments for both groups were similar, and they were not environments produced by the schizophrenic mothers. All forty-seven offspring took intelligence tests and psychological tests. Each was interviewed by a psychiatrist. Then two other psychiatrists not previously involved in the experiment came in to evaluate the offspring's dossiers and, if necessary, to diagnose them. Neither psychiatrist knew the offspring's origins, or the nature of the mothers' illness. Even so, the two evaluating psychiatrists diagnosed five of the children of schizophrenic mothers as schizophrenic. None of those from the control group were so diagnosed. Moreover, thirty-seven of the forty-seven children of schizophrenic mothers were given some kind of psychiatric diagnosis, as compared with nine of the fifty offspring from the control group. Considering that the environments were matched for both groups and the very early age at which the children were placed, the much higher incidence of disordered behavior among the children of schizophrenic mothers points to a strong genetic component in the origins of schizophrenia.

Seymour Kety, David Rosenthal, Paul Wender, and Fini Schulsinger (1968) examined the records of all children born between 1924 and 1947 in Copenhagen, Denmark, who were adopted when quite young. From this large group, they selected those adoptees who were subsequently admitted to a psychiatric hospital and diagnosed as schizophrenic. Thirty-three such probands were compared with a control group drawn from the same population but lacking any psychiatric history. The family histories of biological (but not adoptive) relatives of the schizophrenic index cases revealed a higher incidence of disturbance (which included schizophrenia, uncertain schizophrenia, and inadequate personality) than did those of the controls (8.7 percent to 1.9 percent). A replication of the Copenhagen Adoption Study by Kety and his colleagues yielded roughly the same findings, and provided further evidence for a genetic vulnerability to schizophrenia (Tienari, 1991).

Because these two studies have measured the separate influences of genetics and of environment, and because both have documented the persistence of the genetic link, their combined impact is clear. When environmental and genetic factors are compared for their effect on rates of schizophrenia in relatives of probands, heredity has more influence than does environment. It is important, however, to state this case precisely, and not to overstate it. Genes contribute to vulnerability to schizophrenia, but they do not in themselves completely explain its presence.

Although most schizophrenia researchers agree that genetics remains a central etiologic factor in schizophrenia, debate continues regarding the magnitude of the genetic contribution. Torrey, for example, tends to minimize the contribution of genetics. He reviewed concordance rates for eight twin studies of schizophrenia which used representative samples of twins and determined whether they were MZ or DZ twins with reasonable certainty through using such techniques as DNA and red cell typing. (A representative sample is one that, for example, uses a population in which birth registers have recorded every twin.) The eight studies showed a pairwise concordance rate for schizophrenia that is 28 percent for MZ twins and 6 percent for DZ twins. The pairwise concordance rates support a lower genetic contribution to schizophrenia (Torrey, 1992). Others set those estimates much higher (Gottesman, 1991; McGue, 1992).

Children At Risk For Schizophrenia At-risk studies are important because they can identify those children who are most likely to develop schizophrenia, and the investigators can then observe the effects of specific influences on such children in order to reduce the incidence of schizophrenia. At-risk children are more vulnerable to schizophrenia than are other children. Their vulnerability may derive from several factors. Often, at-risk children are defined as those whose parents or siblings are schizophrenic. As we will see later, other factors also make children vulnerable; these are factors that relate to environment and to social class: poverty, broken homes, families where the ***double-bind*** reigns. (This latter hypothesis, formulated by Gregory Bateson, refers to two mutually exclusive messages from one person, which can neither be satisfied nor avoided.) All of these sources contribute to a child's vulnerability, or high risk for schizophrenia, and all can be studied in an at-risk program (Watt, Anthony, Wynne, and Rolf, 1984).

Perhaps the most extensive at-risk study of schizophrenia was a Danish study begun in 1962 by Sarnoff Mednick and Fini Schulsinger (Mednick, Cudeck, Griffith, Talovic, and Schulsinger, 1984; Parnas, Cannon, Jacobsen, Schulsinger, Schulsinger, and Mednick, 1993). These investigators isolated 207 subjects who were at significant risk for schizophrenia, and 104 low-risk people who were matched on such variables as age, gender, years of education, father's occupation, and place of residence. When the study began, the average age of the subjects was about fifteen years, and none of them was schizophrenic. Ten years later, 17 of the high-risk (and only 1 of the low-risk) people were diagnosed schizophrenic. The mothers of these schizophrenics were distinguished from the rest of the sample on a variety of characteristics. Most striking among these were the facts that the mothers' own psychotic episodes were precipitated by the childbirth, and that more generally, the mothers were unstable in their relations with men, and were not emotionally attached to the father when pregnancy occurred. Moreover, the fathers themselves were unstable at work and often addicted to drugs or alcohol (Talovic, Mednick, Schulsinger, and Falloon, 1981). The mothers of these disturbed offspring, moreover, were quite temperamental and tended to direct their emotions outward in highly aggressive forms (Mednick, 1973).

In another study of those at high risk for schizophrenia, investigators from the United States and Israel studied a group of preadolescent children who were born to a schizophrenic parent and who were raised either on a kibbutz or in a town. These index children were matched to kibbutz or town controls.

These children were first examined when they were eleven, and again at sixteen and at twenty-five. The first two examinations found the index group to be more impaired on such indices as severity of psychopathology (Nagler and Glueck, 1985), on psychophysiological measures (Kugelmass, Marcus, and Schmueli, 1985), and in the quality of their social and school adjustment (Sohlberg and Yaniv, 1985). No differences between kibbutz and town child-rearing were found, suggesting that the impairment was due wholly to the genetic predisposition. But the third examination at age twenty-five reversed all that and revealed that children of the kibbutz had the highest incidence of psychological disorder (Mirsky, Silberman, Latz, and Nagler, 1985; and see Kaffman, 1986, for a different interpretation). Why such a difference should occur, especially when the kibbutz has been viewed as a *benign* place in which to raise children, is not clear. Perhaps because the kibbutz is a relatively small community, it provides fewer opportunities for privacy and for familial peculiarities to be forgotten than exist in towns and cities (Mirsky and Duncan-Johnson, 1984).

Although the Danish and Israeli at-risk studies confirm the genetic hypothesis, their primary importance resides in understanding the influence of nongenetic factors—nutrition, psychophysiology, family, social and academic history, personal skills and liabilities—on the development of schizophrenia. Ultimately, it is hoped that at-risk studies will suggest biological and social interventions that can break the chain that leads to schizophrenia.

The Twin Factor   MZ twins grow up sharing a common environment that often treats them as if they were a single person. They are often dressed alike, confused for one another, compared to one another, and generally scrutinized more closely than are DZ twins or mere siblings. These experiences collectively create a distinct environment for MZ twins in addition to their identical genetic makeup. Could that environment account for the greater probability of schizophrenia in the co-twin when the proband is schizophrenic? Probably not. If the special environment and psychological factors common to MZ twins were the factors that produced schizophrenia, then the rate of schizophrenia among MZ twins would be higher than that of the general population. But that is not the case. MZ twins are not more likely to become schizophrenic than are non-twins. A co-twin is more likely to become schizophrenic if, and only if, the proband is schizophrenic, and not otherwise (Rosenthal, 1970b). Thus, the identical environment in which MZ twins develop has no bearing on whether the twins become schizophrenic.

LINKAGE ANALYSIS

Some genetic disorders, such as muscular dystrophy or cystic fibrosis, arise from defects at single genes. Schizophrenia, however, is not such a disorder. Rather, it is a complex disorder in which defects at *several* genes influence the risk for a variety of forms of schizophrenia. Schizophrenia is like cancer in the following way. A single process, analogous to uncontrolled cell division in cancer, may be at the core of a variety of forms of schizophrenia, whose multiplicity is brought about by additional and distinct genetic mechanisms.

When a disorder arises at more than a single major locus, a research technique in genetics known as ***linkage analysis*** is often employed. That technique seeks to evaluate the occurrence of a familial disorder alongside a known genetic marker. A decade ago, there were just a few known genetic markers, but with the advent of the Human Genome Project, markers that span the entire genome have been developed. Right now, findings from linkage analysis are conflicting and unclear, but in the fullness of time, these markers promise to enable us to locate the genetic regions that harbor the origins of the disorder (Kendler and Diehl, 1993).

ANOTHER SIDE OF SCHIZOPHRENIA: CREATIVITY

Any comprehensive treatment of the role of genetics in schizophrenia must take into account the possible relationship between schizophrenia and creativity. Being related to a schizophrenic may not be all bad. In fact, it may have some distinct advantages. Reporting on a follow-up study of children born to schizophrenic mothers and placed in adoptive or foster homes shortly after birth, Leonard Heston and Duane Denney note that the children who did not become schizophrenic were more "spontaneous," "had more colorful life histories," "held more creative jobs," and "followed the more imaginative hobbies. . . ." than normals (Heston and Denney, 1968, p. 371). Indeed, one study reports that non-paranoid schizophrenics score higher on a test of creativity than either paranoid schizophrenics or non-paranoid controls (Keefe and Magaro, 1980; Magaro, 1981).

A study of genetics and schizophrenia in Iceland by Karlsson (1972) further supports the connection between creativity and schizophrenia. Karlsson observes that the "genetic carriers" of schizophrenia often exhibit "unusual ability" and display "a superior capacity for associative thinking" (Karlsson, 1972, p. 61). Fascinated by this finding, Karlsson proposes that society may even depend upon "persons with a schizophrenic constitution" for its social and scientific progress. He remarks that a disproportionate number of the most creative people in philosophy, physics, music, literature, mathematics, and the fine arts often developed psychiatric disorders. *Superphrenic* is Karlsson's term for these people who are both related to schizophrenics and recognizably outstanding in politics, science, and the arts.

▶ Representations of irrationality. Left: Plate from *Urizen* by William Blake; right: *Agony-Raving Madness* by Richard Dadd, a nineteenth-century English artist who was hospitalized as a schizophrenic after he killed his father.

From this discussion of the genetic connection in schizophrenia, it is clear that a link exists. Although it does not embrace every important influence leading to schizophrenia, it does constitute one major influence. As David Rosenthal observed (1970b), "genetic factors do contribute appreciably and beyond a reasonable doubt" to the development of schizophrenia.

The Biology of the Schizophrenias

Over the past decade, enormous progress has been made in understanding the biology of the schizophrenias. Two lines of research have been particularly illuminating. The first has looked at irregularities in the neurochemistry of the schizophrenias, the second at differences in brain structure between schizophrenics and normals. Both lines of investigation have important consequences for understanding Type I and Type II schizophrenia.

THE NEUROCHEMISTRY OF THE SCHIZOPHRENIAS: THE DOPAMINE HYPOTHESIS

The idea that there may be biochemical antecedents to schizophrenia is not new. Researchers have frequently tried to find the biochemical differences between schizophrenics and normals, but with little luck. Reports of vast differences in the chemistry of blood or urine of normals as opposed to hospitalized schizophrenics have turned out merely to reflect differences in the diets of hospitalized and non-hospitalized people, or bad lab technique, or the absence of control groups, or experimenter bias.

More recently, the strategy has shifted. Instead of looking for biochemical substances that differentiate schizophrenics from normals, scientists are now searching for abnormalities in neurochemical functioning. Specifically, they are looking at special chemicals in the brain, called **neurotransmitters.** The way these chemicals function, and how increases or decreases in the available quantities of neurotransmitters affect behavior and perhaps influence the development of schizophrenia—these are presently the dominant research concerns. By focusing on these chemicals and by drawing connections between schizophrenia, the amphetamine psychosis, and Parkinson's disease, scientists have constructed what is now called the **dopamine hypothesis** (as we first mentioned in Chapter 3).

First, consider the similarities between the symptoms of schizophrenia and the effects of the amphetamines, or "speed." Large doses of amphetamines can create a psychosis, with symptoms indistinguishable from those of acute paranoid schizophrenia. Patients suffering amphetamine psychosis have, in fact, been wrongly diagnosed as schizophrenics (Snyder, 1947b). What is more, a very low dose of a drug related to the amphetamines, methylphenidate, will exacerbate a schizophrenic's symptoms almost immediately: paranoid schizophrenics, for example, become increasingly paranoid. Finally, the drugs most helpful in treating the symptoms of schizophrenia—the neuroleptics—are also the best antidotes for amphetamine psychosis and for the exacerbated schizophrenic symptoms induced by amphetamines (Snyder et al., 1974).

These neuroleptics produce varying effects on schizophrenia. One class of neuroleptic, the phenothiazines, blocks the brain's receptors for a neurotransmitter called dopamine. Neurotransmitters are chemicals that facilitate the transmission of electrical impulses between the brain's nerve endings. There are perhaps twenty different neurotransmitters, of which dopamine is particularly important. Since the phenothiazines both decrease the amount of available dopamine and also relieve the symptoms of schizophrenia, it seems to follow that schizophrenia results from excess dopamine. These findings have opened the door for the dopamine hypothesis, with the connection between Parkinson's disease and dopamine offering more support for the hypothesis (see Figure 12–3).

Characterized by growing stiffness in the arms and legs, Parkinson's disease is particularly noticeable because it renders facial expressions flat and dull, and causes tremors, especially in the hands. It happens that the main pathway in the brain for dopamine is the corpus striatum—an area that helps coordinate motor activity. This pathway deteriorates in Parkinson's disease, thus explaining the patient's inability to move and tendency to shake. When victims of Parkinson's disease are treated with L-DOPA, a drug that increases the amount of dopamine available in the brain, their symptoms are relieved. Curiously, when individuals suffering from schizophrenia are treated with heavy doses of phenothiazines for a prolonged period of time, they display symptoms very much like those associated with Parkinson's disease. They, too, develop motor difficulties: they have tremors in their extremities and problems in controlling their body movements in general. While there is no direct proof of a connection, is it possible that the neurotransmitter, dopamine, is involved in schizophrenia? In Parkinson's disease, L-DOPA is given to overcome the insufficiency of dopamine. In schizophrenia, the phenothiazines seem to calm

FIGURE 12–3

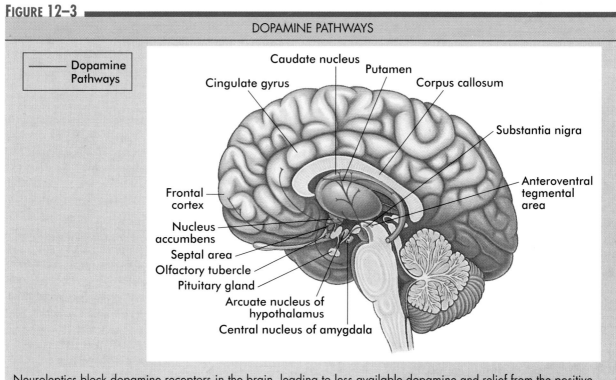

DOPAMINE PATHWAYS

Neuroleptics block dopamine receptors in the brain, leading to less available dopamine and relief from the positive symptoms of schizophrenia. By mapping the dopamine pathways, we arrive at a better understanding of how excess dopamine in the brain leads to the symptoms of schizophrenia. (SOURCE: Based on Snyder, 1986, p. 85)

disordered behavior by reducing the amount of dopamine available in the brain. Over time, however, they seem to cause an insufficiency of dopamine, and bring about symptoms of Parkinson's disease. That an excess of dopamine is one of the roots of schizophrenia has been shown in the PET (Positron Emission Tomography) scans, which show that there is increased dopamine receptor density in a schizophrenic's brain, and which suggest that an excess of cells that are sensitive to dopamine may be the crucial biochemical deficit in schizophrenia.

Let us summarize the evidence that supports the dopamine hypothesis thus far. First, the symptoms of acute paranoid schizophrenia and of amphetamine psychosis are nearly indistinguishable. Amphetamine psychosis seems to result from an overproduction of dopamine. Is it not reasonable to assume a similar mechanism for schizophrenia (Snyder, 1981)?

Further evidence comes from animal research, where it has been shown that the phenothiazines block dopamine receptors specifically, and not other neurotransmitters. In addition, the more potent the phenothiazine, the more powerfully it blocks dopamine receptors in animals.

The combined evidence suggests that dopamine overload, that is, excess dopamine at the synapse, produces many of the symptoms of acute schizophrenia (see Figure 12–4). Consider the attentional difficulties that are so characteristic of schizophrenia. When the substantia nigra, a bundle of nerves that goes from the brain stem to the corpus striatum, is destroyed on one side of the brain, rats stop attending to stimulation on the other side of their bodies (Understedt, 1971). (The left brain controls the right side of the body; the right brain, the left.) It is not that the rats lose their sensory perception. It seems rather that they fail to attend. Phenothiazines may have a similar effect: by blocking dopamine receptors, attention may be diminished.

FIGURE 12–4

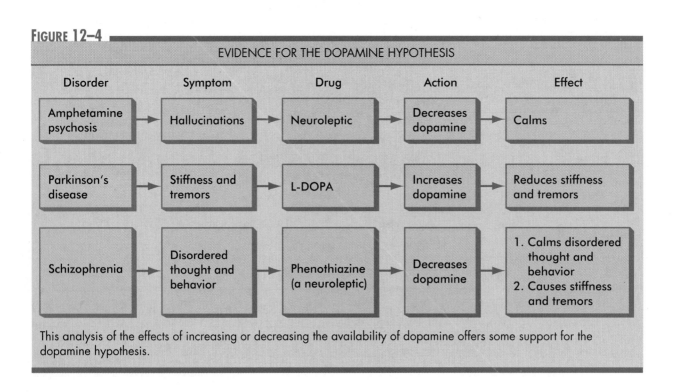

This analysis of the effects of increasing or decreasing the availability of dopamine offers some support for the dopamine hypothesis.

PET scans showing differing effects of a dose of haloperidol on a normal person and a patient with schizophrenia. The dopamine receptors were blocked in the normal person but not in the schizophrenic, indicating increased dopamine receptor density in schizophrenics.

There is now mounting evidence that confirms the dopamine hypothesis. Post-mortem examination of the brains of schizophrenics confirms what PET scans reveal: a marked increase in the number of dopamine receptor sites. While the precise cause of this increase is not yet known, it is clearly *not* the result of drug treatment. Patients who had been drug-free for at least a year before death also showed a greater number of dopamine receptors (Crow, 1980, 1982; Mackay, 1980).

Increased production of dopamine was once thought to be characteristic of all forms of schizophrenia. But recent thinking limits the dopamine hypothesis to Type I schizophrenia (see the discussion of Types I and II on pp. 439–40). Type I is associated with the dramatic positive symptoms of the disorder: delusions, hallucinations, and thought disorders. Those are the symptoms that are alleviated by the phenothiazines, which decrease the amount of dopamine in the brain. Type II schizophrenia is characterized by the "negative" or deficit symptoms of the disorder, such as flat affect, loss of motivation, and poverty of speech. Those symptoms seem unrelated to dopamine and are unaffected by the phenothiazines. Indeed, they seem presently to have no consistent neuroendocrinological basis (Lieberman and Koreen, 1993). Instead, they seem to arise from a wholly different source—peculiarly abnormal structures in the brain.

BRAIN STRUCTURE IN SCHIZOPHRENICS

Over the past two decades there has been growing evidence that schizophrenics who manifest Type II symptoms—particularly flat emotion, loss of motivation, and poverty of speech—may be suffering from one or several abnormalities in the structure of the brain. So far, three kinds of abnormalities seem to have been located. The first relates to the **frontal lobes,** which are known to be important in attention, motivation, and in planning and organizing behavior. Type II schizophrenics may have smaller frontal lobes (as well as smaller cerebrums and craniums) than do normals (Andreasen, Nasrallah, Dunn, Olson, Grove, Ehrhardt, Coffman, and Crossett, 1986). PET scans and other cerebral blood flow studies have confirmed considerably reduced function, as well as decreased metabolism, in the frontal regions of the brains of schizophrenics (Buchsbaum, 1990). Disturbances in gait, posture, and eye movements, which are important neurological signs in schizophrenia, often arise from frontal-lobe dysfunction (Weinberger, 1988; Robbins, 1990; Sweeney, Haas, and Li, 1992). Indeed, such a high proportion of schizophrenics show abnormalities in certain kinds of eye movements, that those have become genetic markers for schizophrenia (Clementz, Sweeney, Hirt, and Haas, 1990; Iacono, Moreau, Beiser, Fleming, and Lin, 1992). Finally, the reduction of memory capacity in schizophrenia has been found to be consistent with frontal-lobe abnormalities (Gold, Randolph, Carpenter, Goldberg, and Weinberger, 1992).

The second type of abnormality relates to the size and proportion of the **brain ventricles.** Ventricles are cavities in the brain, spaces that are filled with fluid. The ventricles of schizophrenics are substantially larger than those of normal people. Moreover, those on the left side of the schizophrenic brain appear to be substantially larger than those on the right side (Losonczy et al., 1986). Ventricular enlargement suggests a process of deterioration or atrophy in brain tissue whose precise effects can only be speculated upon (Brown, Colter, Corsellis, Crow, Frith, Jagoe, Johnstone, and Marsh, 1986; Bogerts, 1993). But whether such atrophy is the cause or the consequence of schizophrenia is still an open question (Suddath, Christison, Torrey, Casanova, and Weinberger, 1990).

Finally, there is mounting evidence of **neuronal degeneration,** especially in the cortex of schizophrenics (Benes, Davidson, and Bird, 1986), as well as evidence for decreased blood flow in that region (Weinberger, Berman, and Zec, 1986).

While the evidence for differences in brain structure mounts daily, just how those differences are related to schizophrenic symptoms—especially Type II symptoms—remains unclear. But the emerging picture seems to support the view that there are at least two forms of schizophrenia. Type I results from difficulties in **neurotransmission,** and particularly from an overabundance of dopamine receptors. That form of schizophrenia seems to be quite responsive to neuroleptic medications. Type II schizophrenia, on the other hand, results from abnormalities in **brain structure,** and is largely unaffected by neuroleptic treatment.

▶ MRIs of the brains of normal and schizophrenic twins have revealed that the ventricles (cavities filled with fluid) of schizophrenics (indicated in the right MRI) are larger than those of normals (indicated in the left MRI).

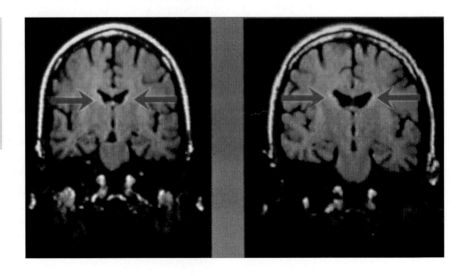

The Schizophrenogenic Family

The above evidence convinces us that heredity and biology play a role in the development of schizophrenia. But other factors—family and society—contribute in as yet unknown ways and proportions to one's vulnerability to schizophrenia. Heredity tells us about a biological component of schizophrenia. It can suggest, perhaps, that an individual will be prone to attentional difficulties, to overinclusive thinking, to delusions, and to hallucinations. But heredity does not assure that a propensity will become a certainty. Nor does heredity specify the content of disordered thought and the social reaction it will elicit. In all likelihood, the family plays some role in the development of schizophrenia, although establishing the nature of its contribution with precision is difficult. Families that seem to foster the emergence of schizophrenia in one or more family members are called **schizophrenogenic families.** Such families may themselves be disordered in the way they communicate and in the family structure itself.

Since schizophrenia is centrally marked by a thought disorder and since we are examining the families from which schizophrenics come, it follows that we should look at communication within the family as a correlate or cause of such thought disorder. Many researchers believe that the parents of schizophrenics distort their children's perceptions in two principal ways: by encouraging them to doubt their own feelings, perceptions, and experiences (a process that is called **mystification**), and by catching them in double-binds (Bateson, Jackson, Haley, and Weakland, 1956; Laing and Esterson, 1964). Whatever one calls it, this "effort to drive the other person crazy" (Searles, 1959) involves distorting the child's reality both verbally and nonverbally.

There are three characteristics of family communication that seem to bear striking relationships to the development of schizophrenia, particularly among those who are genetically predisposed to such symptoms. Those characteristics are expressed emotion, affective style, and communication deviance. **Expressed emotion** refers to attitudes of cynicism, hostility, or overinvolvement that an important relative expresses toward a schizophrenic person. **Affective style** describes the relative's emotional and verbal behavior when interacting with the schizophrenic person. **Communication deviance** describes the degree to which that relative's conversations and messages are unclear, arising when a parent is unable to establish and maintain a shared area of attention with a child. High expressed emotion is correlated with communication deviance (Miklowitz, Strachan, Goldstein, Doane, Snyder, Hogarty, and Falloon, 1986). And, in fact, all three characteristics are interrelated, and all three appear to run in families.

Investigations of familial influences have centered mainly on expressed emotion. When criticism and hostility are directed at an offspring, the offspring is more likely to develop the spectrum of symptoms associated with schizophrenia (Rodnick, Goldstein, Lewis, and Doane, 1984). Correspondingly, living in an environment where expressed emotion is low calms those who are already schizophrenic and contributes to their remission (Falloon, 1988). Moreover, the rate of relapse among those who are returning home after suffering a schizophrenic episode is more than twice as high among people who are returning to families that are high rather than low in expressed emotion (Goldstein, Strachan, and Wynne, 1994; Miklowitz, 1994).

Three processes occurring within the families of schizophrenics seem to influence thought disorders: injection of meaning, concealment of meaning, and denial of meaning. Although all three are clearly connected, each of these processes has particular manifestations (Wynne, Singer, Bartko, and Toohey, 1977).

Injection of meaning involves denying the clear meaning of another's message and substituting another meaning. The person who sent the original message can, with a persistent injector around, be left with two different meanings rather that one, with confusion rather than clarity, and with considerable self-doubt about perceiving reality accurately.

Concealing clear meaning is another form of communication distortion within the schizophrenic family. A person may hide information when it is clear that the information exists. Or the person may simply remain silent, failing to acknowledge a patent fact or sending blurred, vague, or fragmented messages. These tactics serve to conceal meanings and distort facts.

Denial of meaning takes several forms (Laing and Esterson, 1964; Lidz, 1975). The denial can be a deliberate lie, consciously told. Or it can involve some automatic denial, automatically presented. Or it can be the result of a thought disorder in the parents themselves, one that is so encompassing that they do not even realize that they are denying anything. One patient, for example, felt that his parents were "somehow talking" about him. They denied it. Yet, when the entire family gathered together, it was clear that the parents surreptitiously nodded and winked to one another, as if they could not be seen. They were oblivious to the fact that their communication was visible. More important, they were oblivious to the fact that their winking and nodding was a form of "talking." They denied its reality.

Injecting, concealing, and denying all serve either to block access to consensual reality or to distort it. Worse, they insidiously undermine the individual's faith in her own capacity to perceive reality. Thus, all of these tactics relate directly to the essential characteristics of schizophrenia: misperceived reality and disordered thought.

Society and Schizophrenia

Whether we are schizophrenic or non-schizophrenic, we are all members of a society that, in many ways, exerts its influence upon us. In approaching any mental disorder, scientists will take society into account.

SCHIZOPHRENIA AND SOCIAL CLASS

Schizophrenia can afflict anyone, in any society or socioeconomic class. But it happens that, particularly in large urban areas, rates of mental disturbance, and especially of schizophrenia, are significantly and inversely related to social class: the lower the class, the higher the rate of schizophrenia (see Figure 12–5). In the United States, the highest rates of schizophrenia occur in the centers of cities that, in turn, are inhabited by people of lower socioeconomic status (Faris and Dunham, 1939; Hollingshead and Redlich, 1958; Srole, Langner, Michael, Opler, and Rennie, 1962; Saugstad, 1989). Similar findings relate to occupation: rates of schizophrenia are highest in the lowest status occupations (Clark, 1948). The larger the city, the more powerful the relationship; in small cities, the relationship between schizophrenia and social class disappears (Clausen and Kohn, 1959).

FIGURE 12–5

THE PREVALENCE OF SCHIZOPHRENIA IN A CITY

In this map of Chicago in 1934, the center zone is the business and amusement section, which is uninhabited, except for transients and vagabonds. Surrounding the center, there is a slum area, largely made up of unskilled workers of low socioeconomic status, and having the highest rate of schizophrenia. The next circle is occupied by skilled workers and has a lower rate of schizophrenia than the slum. The next zone is inhabited by middle-class and upper-middle-class people. The last circle is populated by upper-middle-class commuters and shows the lowest rate of schizophrenia. (SOURCE: Gleitman, 1991, p. 762, based on data from Faris and Dunham, 1939)

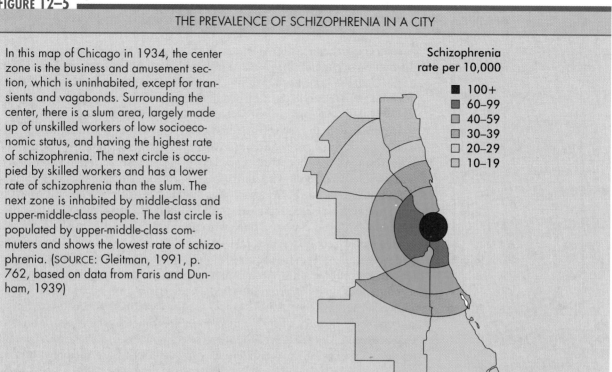

Schizophrenia rate per 10,000

■ 100+
■ 60–99
□ 40–59
□ 30–39
□ 20–29
□ 10–19

Teasing out the relationship between social class and schizophrenia is no simple matter. Do the poverty and stress associated with lower social class *cause* schizophrenia? Or do people who are predisposed to become schizophrenic drift into the lower social classes, or at least fail to rise from them? The notion that adversity and stress cause schizophrenia is termed the ***social causation*** hypothesis, while the view that genetically predisposed persons become schizophrenics and drift down or fail to rise is called the ***social selection*** hypothesis. Which is true? And if both are true, as is likely the case, which is more important in contributing to schizophrenia? The resolution of this problem is no mere academic matter, because the rate of schizophrenia is eight times as high in the lower class than it is in the middle or upper social classes.

One logical way to resolve the question would be to examine the occupational status of the fathers of schizophrenics. If schizophrenics' fathers were at the lowest occupational rung, it would be likely that the schizophrenic was born into the lower class, and that class therefore preceded psychosis. Such a finding would strengthen the view that social class produces schizophrenia. If, on the other hand, schizophrenics' fathers had higher occupational status, it would be likely that the schizophrenics were not born into the lower class, and that psychosis therefore precedes social class. This would support the view that schizophrenics drift into the lower class.

A survey of an entire county in New York State found support for both positions. The incidence of treatment for schizophrenia was remarkably high for people in the lowest occupational group, confirming the relationship between social class and schizophrenia. But the data regarding fathers' occupation was ambiguous, in that it was equally high for those whose fathers were in the lowest occupational group as it was for those whose fathers were employed in the highest occupational group. Although those schizophrenics whose fathers had been in the lowest occupational group had risen above their fathers' occupational level, they and the high occupational group stood at occupational levels lower than those of the general population (Turner and Wagenfeld, 1967).

Another way to resolve the relationship of class and schizophrenia is to conduct a study of schizophrenia in a country into which people have immigrated for reasons other than social class, and which keeps decent birth, death, and psychiatric records. The state of Israel provided such a milieu. Those who immigrated to Israel shortly after it was founded in 1948 were mainly from Europe, had gone to Israel to flee persecution, and were more heavily represented in the advantaged classes. Those who immigrated from North African and Middle Eastern countries after 1948 were more likely to be in the lower classes and were unlikely to have drifted into them for psychiatric reasons, but rather for purely economic ones. At the same time, lower-class Israelis were subject to a good deal of prejudice from those who had arrived from European countries. The social causation hypothesis would predict vast differences between the social classes in the incidence of schizophrenia, promoted wholly by the stresses that are created by prejudice. The social selection view, however, would predict fewer differences, since the differences in social class are produced by economic and educational differences, rather than prejudice.

Bruce Dohrenwend and his colleagues conducted a lengthy and careful examination into these matters (Dohrenwend, Levav, Shrout, Schwartz, Naveh, Link, Skodol, and Stueve, 1992). They found that the incidence of schizophrenia was higher among Israelis who had a European background, that is, among those in the more advantaged classes, which gave powerful support for the social selection theory. By contrast, the rates for major depression were much higher in the lower classes, especially among women, supporting the view that depression arises mainly from social sources, rather than biological ones.

While social selection is the dominant determinant of schizophrenia, it does not operate entirely alone. Membership in the lower class carries with it a host of psychological as well as economic disadvantages that may well increase an individual's vulnerability to schizophrenia. For example, one researcher observed that lower-class people attach greater value to conformity to authority than do members of the middle class (Kohn, 1973). When such lower-class people find themselves confronted with personal crises, they may be less able to cope than are people who have been more self-directed and less conforming. Solving personal problems has more to do with confronting internal pressures than it has to do with conforming to external demands. The defensive posture of the conforming person often invites attack, so the habit of conformity does little to alleviate tension. With stress unabated, the conforming person may also be more vulnerable to schizophrenia.

SCHIZOPHRENIA AND CULTURE

By now, it should be clear that schizophrenia has a strong biological component that arises both genetically and in terms of brain function. Quite as some might expect, the incidence of schizophrenia worldwide is about the same.

When diagnosticians use the same criteria, the incidence of schizophrenia is 1 percent: Biology does not change with geography!

It comes as quite a surprise, therefore, to learn that culture plays quite a role in the *outcome* of schizophrenia. Across more than two decades, the World Health Organization has been conducting cross-cultural epidemiological studies of a variety of disorders, including schizophrenia. Its most recent collaborative study examined the determinants of severe mental disorders in ten countries. Well over thirteen hundred patients were examined, the majority of whom came from urban areas and from socioeconomic circumstances that are best described as average. And while the study confirmed the ubiquitousness of schizophrenia and its similar clinical features across cultures, it provided quite a surprise with regard to outcome, with schizophrenics from *developing* nations faring far better than those from developed countries. For example, the symptoms of 63 percent of participants in developing countries remitted over the course of the two-year follow-up, while those of only 37 percent in developed nations did so. Thirty-eight percent of those in developing nations were wholly symptom free during much of the course of the follow-up, while only 22 percent of those in developed countries were symptom-free. Finally, 38 percent of those from developed countries fall into the category termed "worst possible outcome," while only 22 percent of those from developing nations were in that category (Sartorius, Jablensky, Korten, Ernberg, Anker, Cooper, and Day, 1986; Jablensky, Sartorius, Ernberg, Anker, Korten, Cooper, Day, and Bertelsen, 1992).

THE STRESSES OF MODERN LIVING

Sometimes, life events can trigger schizophrenic episodes. In a recent study, schizophrenics who had relapsed were compared to those who had not relapsed. Shortly before their relapse, the former were found to have experienced

▶ Some writers feel that the meaningless nature of modern life contributes to schizophrenia.

more stressful life events over which they had no control (Ventura, Neuchterlein, Lukoff, and Hardesty, 1989).

Society's values are often contradictory and many people find those contradictions difficult, even impossible, to live with. Searching for some meaningful purpose in life, people are often confronted with meaninglessness on every level, from the personal to the global. They find themselves running in place so as not to fall behind, working at unfulfilling jobs, often for minimal pay, simply to keep up with the body's demands for food, clothing, and shelter. Rich nations are riddled with unemployment, inflation, and other economic ills. Many are precluded from enjoying material comforts, yet materialist dreams are instilled in all.

Some theorists argue that those who are well-integrated into such an insane society are truly mad, while those who remain alienated are the most sane. Many cope with social contradictions by adjusting to them and accepting them. Others, however, may be too sensitive to the pressures and contradictions of society to cope with them at all. These people may be especially vulnerable to the meaninglessness that pervades our world. Many of them, it has been hypothesized, become schizophrenics.

The hypothesis that schizophrenia is a response to a stressful environment has been expounded by numerous theorists, and was particularly central to the thinking of the Scottish psychiatrist, R. D. Laing (1927–1990). Laing's argument is more speculative than other analyses of schizophrenia. He maintained that the schizophrenic experience arises from a person's sense that the situation can neither be lived with nor evaded. The only way to escape the contradictions and impossibilities of reality is to withdraw from the world and take refuge in schizophrenia. The schizophrenic experience, Laing argued, is potentially beneficial to those who undergo it. He wrote:

> Perhaps we will learn to accord to so-called schizophrenics who have come back to us, perhaps after years, no less respect than the often no-less-lost explorers of the Renaissance. If the human race survives, future men will, I suspect, look back on our enlightened epoch as a veritable Age of Darkness. They will presumably be able to savor the irony of this situation with more amusement than we can extract from it. The laugh's on us. They will see that what we call "schizophrenia" was one of the forms in which, often through quite ordinary people, the light began to break through the cracks in our all-too-closed minds. (Laing, 1967, p. 129)

All of the theories about the causes of schizophrenia that we have surveyed are fascinating but unsatisfactory in that they provide only part of the explanation for the emergence of schizophrenia in any one individual. Studies of twins lend credence to a fundamental genetic propensity to schizophrenia. But since perfect concordance does not exist even among MZ twins, it is likely that additional variables, particularly overproduction of neurotransmitters like dopamine and peculiarities of brain structure, play a role in vulnerability to schizophrenia. Moreover, an individual's vulnerability to schizophrenia may be heightened by social and environmental factors. While schizophrenia may "run in the family" because of a common genetic background, "schizophrenogenic" families may also create a stressful and disordered environment that may induce schizophrenia among the vulnerable (Lewis, Rodnick, and Goldstein, 1981; Roff and Knight, 1981). Similarly, very poor people whose lives are filled with the stress of maintaining a marginal subsistence may be particularly vulnerable to schizophrenia.

Nowhere is the interrelation between symptoms, biology, and family more clear than it is in a study of the conditions that predict the outcome of an episode of schizophrenia. For the first decade after the episode, premorbid functioning—that is, the individual's capacity to cope with his or her life stresses before succumbing to schizophrenia—was the most influential predictor. In the second decade, family functioning was as important as premorbid coping. Long-term outcome—twenty or more years after the episode—was best predicted by family genetics (McGlashan, 1986a).

THE TREATMENT OF SCHIZOPHRENIA

Until the mid-1950s, treatment of schizophrenia was primarily custodial or downright barbaric. Patients were warehoused for long periods of time in environments that were both boring and hopeless. Often their disorder and the hospital environment interacted to bring about behavior that required physical restraint. In 1952, however, a lucky accident changed this bleak situation, and led to a revolution in the treatment of schizophrenia.

Drug Therapy

While synthesizing new drugs called ***antihistamines*** that benefit asthmatics and those with allergies, researchers noticed the strong calming effects of these drugs. In fact, one of the drugs, promethazine, was so tranquilizing that the French surgeon Henri Laborit gave it to his patients as a prelude to anesthesia. Using a close relative of promethazine with even stronger sedative effects, French psychiatrists Jean Delay and Pierre Deniker treated various mentally disordered patients with varying results. Those who improved had a common diagnosis: schizophrenia. The drug they took was chlorpromazine. Now a

▶ Until chlorpromazine enabled the treatment of schizophrenics, they generally spent their lives in back wards such as this one.

FOCUS QUESTIONS

1. How do the neuroleptics treat the positive symptoms of schizophrenia?
2. What factors have led to the revolving door phenomenon?
3. Why does milieu therapy reduce relapse rates of schizophrenics?
4. How are schizophrenics treated in therapeutic communities?

prominent member of a class of drugs variously called **_neuroleptics, psychotropics,_** or **_tranquilizing agents,_** chlorpromazine revolutionized the treatment of schizophrenia. In 1955, there were about 560,000 patients in American psychiatric hospitals. One out of every two hospital beds was devoted to psychiatric care. It was then estimated that by 1971, 750,000 beds would be required to care for growing psychiatric populations. In fact, there were only 308,000 patients in psychiatric hospitals in 1971, less than half the projected estimate, and about 40 percent fewer than were hospitalized in 1955. By 1986, that number had declined further to 161,000, of which less than half carried the diagnosis of schizophrenia. Of course, as we shall soon see, by 1986 there had been a major shift in the administration of psychiatric service. More than 1.4 million clients (of which more than 300,000 were schizophrenic) were being seen as outpatients, and an additional 133,000, roughly half of whom were schizophrenic, were being treated in the community (Rosenstein, Milazzo-Sayre, and Manderscheid, 1990). Community-based treatment is now growing quickly. But neither it nor outpatient clinic care could have occurred without the advent of neuroleptic medications.

ANTIPSYCHOTIC EFFECTS OF DRUG THERAPY

Of the major tranquilizers, chlorpromazine, haloperidol, and clozapine are three of the most commonly used. Their most striking effect is the degree to which they "tranquilize," make peaceful, even sedate. Could it be that these antipsychotics are no different from barbiturates, whose sedative action produces no greater improvements for schizophrenia than placebos? Some evidence suggests that this is not the case. Beyond their sedative effects and even beyond their impact on anxiety, the antipsychotic drugs seem to have specific ameliorating effects on thought disorders and hallucinations. Subjective emotional experiences, such as guilt and depression, however, continue unabated despite a course of drug treatment.

The chief mode of action of neuroleptic drugs is in binding to dopamine receptors, thereby preventing dopamine itself from binding to those receptors. Once the dopamine is blocked, the positive symptoms of schizophrenia are also blocked, resulting in marked cognitive and behavioral improvement. While chlorpromazine and haloperidol seem to affect only the positive symptoms of schizophrenia, clozapine, a relatively new drug, successfully treats the negative symptoms as well and appears to be effective where other treatments fail (Breslin, 1992).

The antipsychotic drugs have been so successful in treating patients that the average hospital stay for a schizophrenic patient has declined to fewer than thirteen days, when formerly it was months, years, even a lifetime. Phenothiazines, nearly alone, have been responsible for a revolution in psychiatric care.

SIDE EFFECTS OF DRUG THERAPY

The antipsychotic drugs have a variety of unpleasant side effects that often lead patients to discontinue using them. Side effects of chlorpromazine (Thorazine), for example, frequently include dryness of mouth and throat, drowsiness, visual disturbances, weight gain or loss, menstrual disturbances, constipation, and depression. For most patients, these are relatively minor problems, but annoying enough to induce them to discontinue medications on discharge.

But there are two classes of side effects that are extremely serious. Chlor-promazine produces extra-pyramidal or Parkinson-like effects, which appear to arise because, as we have seen, antipsychotic medications affect the dopamine receptors, which are in turn implicated in Parkinson's disease. (These drugs do not cause Parkinson's disease, but they do induce analogous symptoms.) These symptoms include stiffness of muscles and difficulty in moving, freezing of facial muscles, which results in a glum or sour look, as well as an inability to smile, tremors at the extremities as well as spasms of limbs and body, and *akathesis*—a peculiar "itchiness" in the muscles which results in an inability to sit still, and an urge to pace the halls continuously and energetically (Snyder, 1974a). Other drugs can control these side effects, however.

Even more serious is a neurological disorder called *tardive dyskinesia*. Its symptoms consist of sucking, lip-smacking, and tongue movements that seem like fly-catching. Tardive dyskinesia is not reversible. Conservatively, it affects 24 percent of schizophrenics after seven years of cumulative neuroleptic exposure (Wegner, Catalano, Gibralter, and Kane, 1985; Jeste and Caligiuri, 1993). The prevalence and severity of tardive dyskinesia increases with age. And there may well be a relationship between the severity of a person's *negative* symptoms of schizophrenia and the risk of developing tardive dyskinesia (Barnes and Braude, 1985).

Clozapine often improves a patient where other neuroleptics fail and does not produce either extra-pyramidal side effects or tardive dyskinesia. Indeed, clozapine would be the treatment of choice for schizophrenia were it not for the fact that it sometimes produces a condition called *agranulocytosis,* a deficiency in granulocytes, which are produced in the bone marrow and combat infection. Because such a condition can ultimately be toxic, clozapine needs to be administered very carefully, which at present, contributes greatly to its cost (Kane and Marder, 1993).

THE REVOLVING DOOR PHENOMENON

The widespread use of psychotropic drugs promised a virtual revolution in the treatment of schizophrenia. Even if the disorder could not be cured, it seemed certain that it could be contained. No longer would thousands spend their lives in back wards. No longer would families and society be deprived of their contribution. And no longer would massive economic resources be wasted on custodial care. But the pharmaceutical revolution fell short of its promise. For, while the hospital population of schizophrenics has declined radically since 1955, the readmission rates for schizophrenics have soared. In 1972, for example, 72 percent of the schizophrenics admitted to hospitals had been there before (Taube, 1976). Another study found a 79 percent relapse rate within two years of discharge (Hogarty, Anderson, Reiss, Kornblith, Greenwald, Javna, and Madonia, 1986). One likely reason for rehospitalization is that only 15 to 40 percent of schizophrenics are able to work or care for themselves (Keith, Gunderson, Reifman, Buchsbaum, and Mosher, 1976). Another is that they return to aversive environments (Leff, 1976), and to communities that are less than welcoming. Third, they lack work skills (Gunderson and Mosher, 1976) and social skills. Indeed, when patients were given social skills training, and their families were trained to become more proficient in "family problem solving," the relapse rate among such patients declined markedly—though it did not disappear by any means (Hogarty et al., 1986). Finally, they often stop taking medications on discharge because of the drugs' aversive side effects.

▲ Many of those released into the community from mental hospitals are unable to work or care for themselves. If this man is a former mental patient, he is likely to be rehospitalized, caught in the "revolving door phenomenon."

One can interpret this "revolving-door" aspect of psychiatric hospitals both negatively and positively. On the negative side, the readmission rates are discouraging; they suggest that the attempt to treat schizophrenics is futile. But on the positive side, is it not better for a patient to be readmitted than never to have been discharged at all? This latter situation characterized the plight of many patients before the advent of the phenothiazines.

Even if one opts for the more positive response to the high readmission rate, the task of understanding its cause and of eventually reducing it remains. One thing is clear: antipsychotic drugs help ameliorate the symptoms of schizophrenia, but the symptoms of schizophrenia are by no means the entire problem. Indeed, the very fact that these drugs alter symptoms and only symptoms raises profound questions about what is meant by treatment, recovery, and cure.

Psychological Treatment

A variety of psychological approaches to schizophrenia have been tried across the decades, with unimpressive outcomes. Recently, however, a relatively structured treatment called Interpersonal Therapy (IPT) has seemed promising. IPT is a set of structured intervention programs that are derived from cognitive and behavioral principles and that attempt to remedy the cognitive and behavioral dysfunctions that are characteristic of schizophrenia. Evaluative studies of IPT suggest that as a result of the program schizophrenic patients show improvement in such elementary cognitive processes as attention, abstraction, and concept formation (Brenner, Hodel, Roder, and Corrigan, 1992; Liberman and Green, 1992). Moreover, there is reason to believe that such treatment, as well as treatments that are designed to improve social skills among schizophrenics (Liberman, Nuechterlein, and Wallace, 1982), work especially well in conjunction with drug therapy (Morrison and Bellack, 1984; Bellack, 1992).

Full Treatment: Milieu and Therapeutic Communities

Because schizophrenia arises mainly between the ages of eighteen and thirty-five, it disrupts educational and vocational training, social skills, friendships, and marriages. In addition, because the seeds of the disorder are sown before the disorder appears, both in the individual and in the family, it is a safe bet that there are problems in communication and self-esteem—in short, *psychological problems*—that the antipsychotic drugs simply do not touch. Given that these psychological problems exist and that drugs do not alleviate them, what, other than drugs, can help the schizophrenic live in the outside world? Part of the answer may lie in milieu therapy, which creates a supportive environment, and in therapeutic communities, which illustrate milieu therapy's principles.

A study of readmission rates underscores the continued importance of considering psychological problems when treating schizophrenic disorders. Patients who relapsed did not differ on their discharge examination from those who did not relapse. Apart from whether they continued their medications, two additional factors featured strongly in determining relapse rates: the emotional quality of the home, and how much time the patient spent there (Leff, 1976).

In this study, four considerations went into rating the emotional quality of the home environment: the family's hostility, overinvolvement with the patient, comments that were critical of the patient, and the family's wealth. Patients who came from families that had highly charged emotional environments had a 51 percent relapse rate. Those whose family environment was relatively uncharged had a dramatically lower relapse rate—13 percent. Moreover, for the patients from highly charged environments, the relapse rate was affected by how much time they were spending at home. Those who spent less than thirty-five hours at home—which is to say, those who had jobs or went to a day center—were much less likely to relapse than those who were at home more of the time (see Figure 12–6).

What can be done to reduce the relapse rate? For one thing, hospitals have been undergoing enormous changes: from being merely custodial warehouses to becoming centers with a variety of programs designed to increase social skills. Under the broad label of ***milieu therapy,*** patients are provided with training in social communication, in work, and in recreation (Hogarty et al., 1986; Liberman, Mueser, and Wallace, 1986). Hospitals that have incorporated such milieu treatments have successfully decreased their relapse rate. Moreover, families who have been trained to cope better with stress through greater understanding of the schizophrenic's problems and more efficacious family problem solving appear to improve the emotional quality of the home environment and to reduce the rate of relapse once patients have left hospitals

FIGURE 12–6

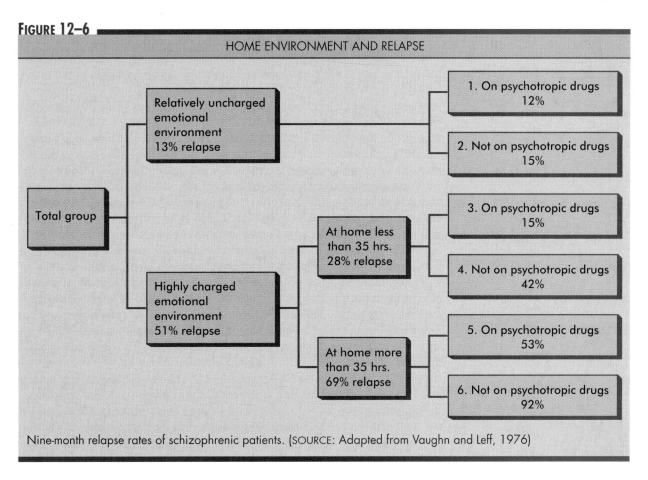

HOME ENVIRONMENT AND RELAPSE

Total group

Relatively uncharged emotional environment 13% relapse
- 1. On psychotropic drugs 12%
- 2. Not on psychotropic drugs 15%

Highly charged emotional environment 51% relapse

At home less than 35 hrs. 28% relapse
- 3. On psychotropic drugs 15%
- 4. Not on psychotropic drugs 42%

At home more than 35 hrs. 69% relapse
- 5. On psychotropic drugs 53%
- 6. Not on psychotropic drugs 92%

Nine-month relapse rates of schizophrenic patients. (SOURCE: Adapted from Vaughn and Leff, 1976)

(Vaughn, Snyder, Jones, Freeman, and Falloon, 1984; Doane, Falloon, Goldstein, and Mintz, 1985).

The ideal treatment for schizophrenia involves carefully monitored psychopharmacological interventions that are combined with psychological ones. Such treatment is now being administered increasingly in two ways: by bringing treatment to patients outside the hospital or clinic, and in group residences.

Because medication is sometimes aversive to patients, they frequently stop taking their "meds" as soon as they are discharged from the hospital. But they need medication in order to stabilize their personalities: without them, they decline psychologically and are ultimately forced to return to the hospital. One way to abort this cycle of hospitalization requires that the treatment go to the patient rather than vice versa. In New York and Michigan, for example, teams of psychologists, psychiatrists, and social workers visit with, counsel, and treat former in-patients and outpatients who are struggling with unemployment and homelessness, in addition to not taking their medications. Such programs are achieving enormous success in enabling people to stay out of psychiatric hospitals (*New York Times,* April 24, 1994).

A second form of treatment involves ***group residences.*** For example, in the late 1960s and 1970s, George Fairweather and his colleagues (1969) established the Lodge, a special residence for patients newly discharged from psychiatric hospitals. The Lodge gave residents the opportunity for task-oriented group experience, including running the household, shopping, and finding employment for each other. Over time, more and more responsibility was given to patients until finally the Lodge was taken over entirely by former patients. In order to evaluate the program's effectiveness, the seventy-five patients who volunteered for it were compared to a matched group who did not volunteer and who received the hospital's routine discharge (which included patient psychotherapy, community assistance, and foster home placement). After six months, 65 percent of the Lodge members, but only 27 percent of the comparison group, remained outside the hospital. Fifty percent of the Lodge's members and only 3 percent of the controls were employed full time during this period. Clearly, the Lodge experience was a beneficial one for those involved.

Early ***therapeutic communities*** were also established as community-based residential treatment centers that provided a home for people diagnosed as schizophrenics (Kiesler, 1980). At Soteria House, for example, nonprofessionals rather than doctors, nurses, and psychologists treated patients. The staff were selected for their ability to accept and relate to people undergoing an acute schizophrenic crisis. Schizophrenic episodes were viewed as valid, if often terrifying, experiences that have strong potential for individual growth and integration. Antipsychotic drugs were not provided at Soteria House, except in emergencies. The intense interpersonal milieu at Soteria House effectively reduced the need for medication. In a study comparing those who lived at Soteria House for five to six months with controls who remained hospitalized for less than two months in a good psychiatric hospital, it was found that six months after discharge 60 percent of Soteria House's residents were able to live independently, while only 4 percent of the controls could live apart from their families (Mosher, Menn, and Matthews, 1975; Mosher and Menn, 1978).

Today, there are thousands of group homes and apartments across the United States, so many in fact that in some states, more patients are accommodated in group homes and apartments than in state mental hospitals. These homes are located in residential neighborhoods, and upscale communities often fight to keep them out. But the overwhelming experience with such homes has been quite positive, with community fears and prejudice generally unfounded.

Today's group homes accommodate small numbers of people. They blend pharmacological interventions with a warm, understanding approach to people who are occasionally greatly distressed. Because entry and exit in these homes is voluntary, such centers cannot use coercion to compel obedient behaviors. As a result many of the distressing problems that arise in psychiatric hospitals are avoided. At the same time, the homes enable individuals to make significant progress toward living outside the hospital and being fully independent and productive (Winerip, 1994).

SUMMARY

1. The schizophrenias are marked by a *thought disorder* that is often combined with affective and behavioral anomalies. There are five clinical subtypes of schizophrenia: *paranoid, disorganized, catatonic, residual,* and *undifferentiated.* Schizophrenics can be differentiated according to whether their condition is *acute* or *chronic.* They can also be differentiated according to the kinds of symptoms they present. *Type I schizophrenia* is associated with the *positive* symptoms of the disorder, such as hallucinations, delusions, and bizarre thoughts. *Type II schizophrenia* is identified with the *negative* symptoms of the syndrome, such as withdrawal, blunted affect, and reduced motivation.

2. The schizophrenic's subjective experience is often one of being invaded by the world's stimuli, crowded by them, and unable to process them. We find this experience rooted in what appears to be a defective *cognitive filter,* itself related to serious *attentional difficulties.* The incapacity to focus attention, as well as the sense that too many stimuli are invading and capturing attention, is characteristic of many schizophrenics' experience.

3. In the cognitive domain, schizophrenics make the same errors of association that normals make, but they make many more of them. They seem especially attracted to the *dominant associations* or connotations of words, regardless of the context in which they are found. Often, their attentional difficulties seem to distract them from the ultimate goal of thought and speech. Thinking may therefore be *overinclusive,* and speech dotted with *clang associations* and *neologisms.*

4. Many schizophrenics appear to experience flattened or restricted emotion, which may make it difficult for them to experience reality meaningfully.

5. Schizophrenics seem to experience perceptual intensities or deficits that lead them to experience the world differently from others. Delusional, hallucinatory, or other cognitive experiences often bring grief or a sense of uniqueness, which they attempt to account for by constructing theories which, in form, are no different from the theories normals construct about their experiences.

6. Vulnerability to schizophrenia is a highly individual matter, but there seem to be five significant factors that promote it. First, there seems little doubt

that the schizophrenias are in part a *genetic* disorder. The schizophrenias occur much more often among MZ than DZ twins, and among biological than adoptive relatives of schizophrenics. Second, there is reason to believe that the schizophrenias are *biological* disorders. Type I schizophrenics appear to be suffering a *neurotransmission* disorder, especially involving *dopamine*. Type II schizophrenics seem to have *structural brain deficits*, including smaller frontal lobes, enlarged ventricles, and reduced cortical brain flow. Third, faulty communications within the *family* may well promote the development of schizophrenia. Fourth, schizophrenia is a disorder that affects the *poor* more than the rich, most likely because schizophrenics fail to rise from or drift down into the lower classes. Finally, the course of schizophrenia, and especially its outcome, seems to depend on the culture in which it occurs. Schizophrenia in well-developed countries appears to have a worse prognosis than the same disorder in developing nations. The stresses of modern living may negatively impact those who become schizophrenic.

7. Treatment of the schizophrenias has been revolutionized by the invention of strong antipsychotic drugs that seem to work directly on symptoms of schizophrenia. Hospitalization has become briefer, and there is a greater probability that the schizophrenic person will return to society. The effectiveness of the antipsychotic drugs, however, is limited.

8. Because schizophrenia is a psychological, as well as biological, disorder there have been increasing attempts to discover nondrug methods for treating the schizophrenias. Among these are *cognitive* and *behavioral* treatments that attempt to remedy schizophrenic deficits, as well as *therapeutic communities* that emphasize the positive aspects of the schizophrenic experience and that attempt directly to train the schizophrenic for social living. Increasingly, schizophrenics are being treated in the community, either in group residences or by bringing treatment personnel to patients, rather than requiring patients to go to the hospital or clinic.

QUESTIONS FOR CRITICAL THINKING

1. Why does a breakdown in the attentional filter cause untreated schizophrenics to have problems leading normal lives?

2. Why might there be a genetic link between creativity and schizophrenia?

3. Why are those in developed countries less likely to recover from schizophrenia than are those in developing countries?

4. Do you think that the side effects of schizophrenia are so bad that drug treatment of schizophrenics should be discontinued?

SOCIAL AND INTERPERSONAL DISORDERS

CHAPTER 13

Sexual Dysfunction and Sexual Disorder

CHAPTER ORGANIZER

FIVE LAYERS OF EROTIC LIFE: SEXUAL ORDER AND SEXUAL DISORDER
• Be able to describe the five layers of erotic life: sexual identity, sexual orientation, sexual interest, sex role, and sexual performance.

SEXUAL IDENTITY AND TRANSSEXUALISM: LAYER I
• Understand how transsexuals' sexual identity has gone awry and the radical steps they must take to resolve their disordered sexual identity.

SEXUAL ORIENTATION: LAYER II
• Learn about the origins of sexual orientation.

SEXUAL INTEREST: LAYER III
• Be able to describe the three categories of paraphilias and some treatments used to change sexual interests.

SEX ROLE: LAYER IV
• Familiarize yourself with how children categorize the world according to sex-role stereotypes.

SEXUAL PERFORMANCE: LAYER V
• Be able to describe the physiology of the human sexual response and the ways in which it may be impaired.

Notions of what is sexually normal and what is sexually abnormal change with time and place. What one society labels as deviant may well be labeled as normal by another. Although premarital sex, masturbation, oral sex, and homosexuality were all condemned by our puritanical society in the past, today most people consider these behaviors to be quite normal.

In the past, what constituted "normal sexual order" and "normal sexual function" was clearer than it is today. Ordinary sexual practices among men and women in our society seem to be more diverse today than they were in the past. And so, our concept of what sexual order is has broadened and our concept of what sexual disorder and dysfunction are has narrowed.

Attitudes toward sexuality have changed considerably with time. Surveys have found that sexual behavior is by no means restricted to intercourse during marriage (Kinsey et al., 1948, 1953; Hunt, 1974; Rozin, 1978, 1981; Billy, Tanfer, Grady, and Klepinger, 1993; Rubenstein, 1993). Sexual behavior in general increased through the 1960s and 1970s, in part probably due to the birth control pill, but also due to society's greater permissiveness. In the late 1980s, sexual adventurousness may have decreased because of apprehension about AIDS, with 40 percent of men and 18 percent of women saying they would be more sexually daring if it weren't for AIDS (Rubenstein, 1993). But AIDS seems to have made sexual attitudes more conservative, as opposed to

▲ Gustav Klimt's *The Kiss*.

creating large changes in sexual behavior (Wenger, Greenberg, Hilborne, et al., 1992; McGuire, Shega, Nicholls, et al., 1992; Roche and Ramsbey, 1993). Particular sexual practices have become more frequent over the last forty years, and a greater variety of sexual behaviors are generally considered normal today, including masturbation, premarital sex, oral sex, homosexuality, and bisexuality. Society's attitudes also have an influence on the frequency of sexual behavior and on kinds of sexual behavior engaged in, or at least on how an individual may feel about his or her behavior. Thus notions of sexual order and disorder have changed over time, and will probably change again. And such notions may well be influenced by age, subculture, and religion.

In this chapter, we will discuss the scientific study of sexual problems and their treatment. Despite changing attitudes and more permissiveness in our society, we still find many instances of sexual "disorder" and sexual "dysfunction." The sexual "disorders" are problems of sexual identity, sexual orientation, and sexual interest. The main disorder of sexual identity is transsexualism, in which a man believes he is a woman trapped in the body of a man, or a woman believes she is a man trapped in the body of a woman. Ego-dystonic homosexuality, in which the person's homosexual orientation is unwanted and distressful, is a disorder of sexual orientation. Disordered sexual interest manifests itself through sexual arousal to the unusual or bizarre, such as fetishes for panties, masochism, and exhibitionism. These are the paraphilias. The sexual "dysfunctions" are low desire, low arousal, or problems with organism. Both the sexual dysfunctions and the sexual disorders grossly impair affectionate, erotic relations between human beings, and as such, we consider them abnormal.*

FIVE LAYERS OF EROTIC LIFE: SEXUAL ORDER AND SEXUAL DISORDER

Our erotic life is organized into five layers, each grown around the layer beneath it. Sexual disorders, as well as sexual problems, can occur at each layer. At the core is sexual identity,† our awareness of being male or female. The next layer is sexual orientation, followed by sexual interest, sex role, and sexual performance.

Sexual identity is almost always consistent with our genitals. If we have a penis, we feel ourselves to be male; if we have a vagina, we feel ourselves to be female. Scientists know that sexual identity has a separate existence of its own because of the rare and astonishing dissociation of sexual identity and sexual organs. Some men (we call them men because they have penises and a pair of XY chromosomes) feel that they are women trapped in men's bodies, and some women (who have vaginas and a pair of XX chromosomes) feel that they are

*There have been long-standing controversies about what to call these sexual behaviors. Some prefer to call them "variations" and "preferences"; others label them "deviations," or even "diseases." We adopt the term "dysfunction" to refer to the sexual inabilities. We adopt the term "disorder" to refer to the paraphilias and transsexualism.
†Sexologists universally refer to these layers as "gender" identity, "gender" role, and the like (e.g., Money and Ehrhardt, 1972). We find the word "gender" in such usage unpalatable. Pronouns, but little else, can be properly said to have gender.

> Sexual identity is the most basic level of erotic life.

men trapped in women's bodies.* These individuals with the disorder "transsexualism" provide the key to understanding this deepest layer of normal sexual identity.

The stratum directly over the core sexual identity is our basic **sexual orientation.**† Do you fall in love with men or women or both? Are you heterosexual, homosexual, or bisexual? Our erotic fantasies indicate to us our sexual orientation. If you have had erotic fantasies only about the opposite sex, you are exclusively heterosexual. If you have had erotic fantasies only about members of your own sex, you are exclusively homosexual. If you have often masturbated to both kinds of fantasies, you should consider yourself bisexual. The only problem that can occur at this level is when your orientation causes you distress and confusion and you want to be rid of it. (In DSM-III this was known as "ego-dystonic homosexuality," but this category was eliminated in DSM-III-R and DSM-IV.)

The third layer is **sexual interest:** the types of persons, parts of the body, and situations that are the objects of your sexual fantasies and arousal. What parts of the body and what situations turn you on? What scenes do you masturbate about? What is on your mind at the moment of orgasm? For most men, the female face, breasts, buttocks, and legs are most arousing. For most women, the male chest and shoulders, arms, buttocks, and face are most arousing.

But these are not universal sexual interests by any means. Many people crave nonstandard objects and situations, such as feet, hair, ears, belly but-

---

*There are 23 pairs of chromosomes in both males and females. The twenty-third pair normally determines the individual's sex. In males, the two chromosomes of this pair differ—one is an X chromosome; the other a Y chromosome. In females, both are X chromosomes.

†Sexologists lump the homosexual versus heterosexual choice into the same category ("sexual object choice") as the choice of body parts, fetishistic objects, and erotic situations (sadomasochism, pedophilia, flashing, etc.). We break these into two separate categories, sexual orientation and sexual interest, because we think they are different in kind. The homosexual/heterosexual "choice" is deeper, dictated earlier in life, and more inflexible than the sexual preferences for body parts, inanimate objects, and arousing situations.

FOCUS QUESTIONS

1. What is sexual identity?
2. What are the three possible kinds of sexual orientations?
3. When are sexual interests considered sexual disorders?
4. What are sex roles?
5. What is the surface layer of erotic life?

tons; silk or rubbery textures; panties, stockings, or jeans; peeping, flashing, receiving or inflicting pain. Animals, children, urine, and even amputee's stumps are rarer and more bizarre objects of sexual interest. Murder and arranging one's own death are the most erotic situations for the extremely rare person. When these sexual turn-ons get in the way of an affectionate, erotic relationship with another consenting human being, a line has been crossed into disorder.

The fourth layer, the one next to the surface, is our **sex role.** This is the public expression of sexual identity, what an individual says or does to indicate that he is a man or she is a woman. Most people who feel that they are male adopt male sex roles, and most females adopt female sex roles. But we know of the separate existence of sex roles because men and women do not always adopt the usual male and female sex roles; some women behave aggressively and like to dominate, and some men are passive and submissive. There are no defined categories of "disorder" at this level.

The surface layer is **sexual performance**—how adequately you perform when you are with a suitable person in a suitable erotic setting. Do desire, arousal, and orgasm occur? There are a set of problems common to this stage, and these are called the sexual "dysfunctions" or "inabilities."

We have ordered erotic life into these five layers for one basic purpose—to order how easily problems at each layer will change in the natural course of life and in therapy. The deeper the layer, the harder it is to change. In this view of human sexuality, transsexuality is a problem at the core level and simply will not change; sexual orientation, the next deepest layer, very strongly resists change; sexual interests, once acquired, are strong, but some change can be wrought; sex role can change quite a bit; correcting sexual performance is not trivial, but because performance problems are at the surface layer, they will change quite readily.

SEXUAL IDENTITY AND TRANSSEXUALISM: LAYER I

Few things are more basic to what we are than our sense of what sex we are, and it is this sense that has gone awry in transsexualism. The therapy for most sexual disorders is psychologically based, but the therapy for transsexualism does not consist of changing the psychosexual identity. So basic is identity that the therapy of choice is a matter of actually changing the body to conform to the disordered identity.

Characteristics of Transsexuals

A male-to-female transsexual is a man who feels as if he is a woman trapped in a man's body, wants to be rid of his genitals, wants female sexual characteristics, and wants to live as a woman. A female-to-male transsexual is a woman who feels as if she is a man trapped in a woman's body, wants to acquire male characteristics, and wants to live as a man. Transsexuals feel, from early in life, that they were given the wrong kind of body. This body often disgusts them and the prospect of having to remain in it all their days makes them hopeless, depressed, and sometimes suicidal. They will sometimes mutilate their genitals. By their early twenties, many transsexuals will cross-dress, that it, masquerade in the clothes of the opposite sex. In effect, transsexuals often do everything they can to pass for members of the opposite sex. Unlike transvestites, such actions, particularly the cross-dressing, are not sexually exciting to them. Rather, they are the means of leading the life compatible with their sexual identity. Transvestites are decidedly not transsexual and would be horrified at the idea of changing their sex.

Before this century, transsexuals were doomed to live out their lives in a body that repelled them. In the last twenty-five years, medical procedures have been developed—although they have not been perfected—which allow transsexuals to acquire the anatomy they desire. The case of Allen-Allison shows the transsexual's problems with sexual identity:

> For the last four years, Allen has been passing as a female, but he is in reality an anatomically normal twenty-three-year-old male. He takes female hormones, and has had his facial and chest hair removed. Six months ago, he had his first operation: plastic surgery to enlarge his breasts. He expects in the next two years to undergo sex reassignment surgery to construct a vagina from his penis and scrotum.
>
> Allen says that "As early as I can recall I never had any boyish interests and always wanted to become a girl and change my name to Allison." He loved to dress in his mother's clothes and always preferred to play with "feminine" things. On one occasion, when he was given a fire engine, he threw a tantrum insisting that he wanted a doll. From about kindergarten on, he demanded acceptance from his parents as a girl and this made for constant conflict. Finally, in the fourth grade, he persuaded his parents to allow him to "be" a girl at home, except that he had to wear boys' clothes to school. For the next few years he led a double life, attending school dressed as a boy and then returning home to dress and live as a girl. By eighth grade, he began to feel very uncomfortable around people. He began to avoid school and spent a great deal of time alone.
>
> At fifteen, both school life and family life had become unbearable, and he ran away to San Francisco, where he experimented with homosexuality. He found he could not tolerate homosexual males and left after only a month. While he was attracted to men as sexual partners, only those normal heterosexual men who had accepted him as a female aroused him sexually. Soon, thereafter, he began the odyssey of physical transformation.
>
> Allen is now becoming Allison. (Adapted from Pauly, 1969)

Allen-Allison is an adult male transsexual. By age three or four, his identity as a female was well on its way to being fixed. Before puberty, most transsexual boys will play almost exclusively with girls, will act like girls, prefer to play with dolls, sew and embroider, and help their mothers with housework. They refuse to climb trees, play cowboys and Indians, or roughhouse. By puberty, they feel completely like females, they want to be accepted by society as females, and when they come to know sex-reassignment operations exist they desperately want one. This desire is so intense that, in some cases, male transsexuals actually try to cut their own genitals off (Walinder, 1967; Pauly, 1969; Stoller, 1969; Money and Ehrhardt, 1972).

Male transsexuals have four kinds of sexual histories: sexually attracted to males, females, both, or neither. In a study of seventy-two transsexuals seen at the University Clinic in Manchester, England, three-quarters had fantasies exclusively about males and roughly one-third of them engaged in sex with men (Hoenig and Kenna, 1974; Green, 1985). In this study, 15 percent of the sample were sexually attracted only to women. Finally, asexual transsexuals denied ever having any strong sexual desires and were preoccupied merely with the desire to live as women and to get rid of their male genitals. They had had little or no sexual experience.

Transsexualism is chronic. Once it has developed, it does not spontaneously disappear. A man who feels like a woman trapped in a man's body, or a woman who feels like a man trapped in a woman's body, will retain this belief for the rest of his or her life.

Transsexualism is rare. Perhaps somewhat more than 1 in 100,000 people is transsexual (Walinder, 1967; Pauly, 1974). In the Netherlands, which has quite a supportive climate for transsexuals, a prevalence of 1:11,900 for male-to-female transsexuals and 1:30,400 for female-to-male transsexuals was found (Bakker, Van Kesteren, Gooren, and Bezemer, 1993). The best estimate of the male-to-female ratio is about 2.5 to 1.

The Etiology of Transsexualism

Where does such a deep disorder come from?* What sorts of events must conspire in order for a physically normal girl to feel that she is really a boy, or a boy to feel that he is a girl? We hypothesize that most of sexual identity—both normal and transsexual—comes from an unknown hormonal process in the second to fourth month of pregnancy.

We begin with a simplified version of how a fetus becomes a male or female. The embryo has both potentials. Very early, testes or ovaries appear, but this does not set the sex of the fetus. Both sets of internal organs—male and female—are still present. The fetus goes on to become female unless the next, crucial step occurs: in male fetuses, two masculinizing hormones are secreted from the testes. The female internal organs then shrivel up, the male internal organs grow, and the external male organs develop. In the absence of the masculinizing hormones at this stage, the male internal organs shrivel up, and female internal and external organs develop. All this happens roughly at the end of the first three months of pregnancy.

PSYCHOLOGICAL EFFECTS OF FETAL HORMONES

Besides the physical effects, the masculinizing hormones also have a psychological effect on the brain. They produce male sexual identity, or in their absence, female sexual identity. In this view, the brain components of sexual identity are present in the fetus. In transsexuals, however, some as yet unknown disruption of only the sexual identity phase, but not the organ development phase, takes place (see Figure 13–1). Thus, for the male-to-female transsexual, the identity phase of masculinization does not occur, but the masculinization of the sexual organs proceeds normally. For the female-to-male transsexual, masculinization of identity occurs, but the feminization of the sexual organs proceeds normally.

In conclusion, we speculate that sexual identity—both normal and abnormal—has its origin in fundamental hormonal processes that occur around the third month of fetal development. But fetal hormones are not the only influ-

▲ Renee Richards, a tennis player and male-to-female transsexual whose name before sex-reassignment surgery was Dr. Richard Raskin.

*This theory, and much else in this chapter, is derived from M. Seligman, *What You Can Change and What You Can't*, Chapter 11 (New York: Knopf, 1993).

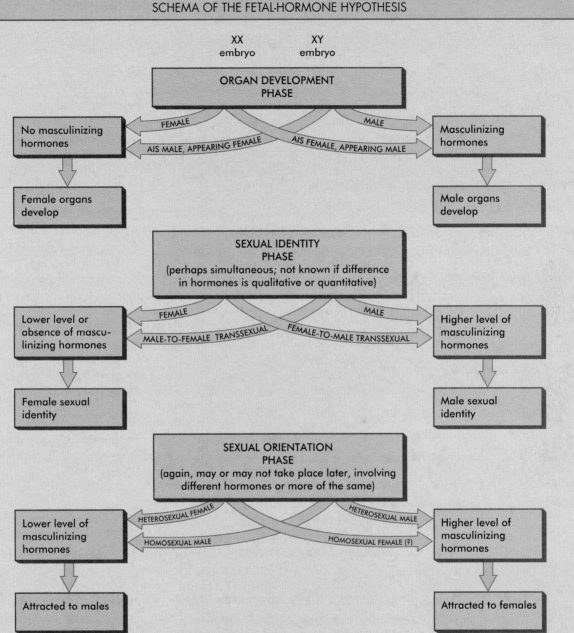

FIGURE 13–1

SCHEMA OF THE FETAL-HORMONE HYPOTHESIS

XX
embryo

XY
embryo

ORGAN DEVELOPMENT
PHASE

FEMALE

MALE

AIS MALE, APPEARING FEMALE

AIS FEMALE, APPEARING MALE

No masculinizing
hormones

Masculinizing
hormones

Female organs
develop

Male organs
develop

SEXUAL IDENTITY
PHASE
(perhaps simultaneous; not known if difference
in hormones is qualitative or quantitative)

FEMALE

MALE

MALE-TO-FEMALE TRANSSEXUAL

FEMALE-TO-MALE TRANSSEXUAL

Lower level or
absence of mascu-
linizing hormones

Higher level of
masculinizing
hormones

Female sexual
identity

Male sexual
identity

SEXUAL ORIENTATION
PHASE
(again, may or may not take place later, involving
different hormones or more of the same)

HETEROSEXUAL FEMALE

HETEROSEXUAL MALE

HOMOSEXUAL MALE

HOMOSEXUAL FEMALE (?)

Lower level of
masculinizing
hormones

Higher level of
masculinizing
hormones

Attracted to males

Attracted to females

This diagram represents a schema of how disruption of a hormonal process in the second to fourth month of pregnancy may affect organ development, sexual identity, and sexual orientation. According to this hypothesis, masculinizing hormones lead to male sexual organs, male sexual identity, and attraction to females; lower level or even absence
of the masculinizing hormones leads to female sexual organs, female sexual identity, and attraction to males. Disruptions can occur during each phase, although the different hormones involved and the timing of the process are presumably much more complex than can be shown here, and their relationship with environmental factors of childhood and
adolescence cannot be predicted. The theory is not meant to suggest that homosexuality is determined solely by events
taking place before birth, only that fetal hormones contribute to it.

ence on sexual identity. Rearing, pubertal hormones, sex organs, and stigmatization also play a role. At most, however, these later influences can reinforce or disturb the core identity that starts to develop well before the moment of birth. The early, biological origin of sexual identity is what makes it so hard to shake, and what makes psychotherapy for transsexualism useless.

Therapy for Transsexualism: Sex-Reassignment Operations

Transsexualism does not spontaneously change in the lifetime of the transsexual. Conventional psychotherapies have only very rarely been able to reverse it (see Barlow, Abel, and Blanchard, 1979, for the single report of reversal of transsexualism—by exorcism). Nevertheless, there is hope for transsexuals today. Sex-change operations (now called "sex reassignment") give transsexuals the opportunity to acquire the sexual characteristics they desire. Once a headline-making novelty, these operations are now routine; tens of thousands have been performed. Once the patient convinces the diagnosticians that the transsexual identity is unshakable, the long process of changing the body begins. Therapy for transsexuals consists of changing the sexual characteristics through surgery and hormones. This biological transformation is then supported by social, vocational, domestic, and secondary bodily changes in an attempt to shore up the new gender status. For example, in the more common male-to-female case, the person first lives for a period of time in the female role, changing his name, dressing, and acting like a woman. Often, therapists treating a transsexual who is a candidate for sex-reassignment surgery require that the person first live for two years in the new gender role. If after two years of passing for and being treated as a female or male, the individual still wants surgery, the psychological hazards of the surgery are probably lessened. Those who are schizophrenic, delusional, or otherwise emotionally disordered should probably not undertake it (Money and Ambinder, 1978).

HORMONAL TREATMENT AND SURGERY

Bodily changes are a prerequisite for sex-reassignment surgery. In male-to-female sex changes, there is a combination of hormonal treatment to make the breasts grow, electrolysis to remove facial hair, and surgery to transform the penis into a vagina. Because the skin of the penis is used to line the vagina, sexual intercourse—when the surgery is successful—is erotically pleasurable. Orgasm is a warm, sometimes spasmodic, glow through the body.

In female-to-male sex-reassignment operations, the surgery is much more complicated and extensive. It involves multiple operations that take place over several years. First, hormonal treatment suppresses menstruation, deepens the voice, and causes growth of facial and body hair. Then surgery is performed to remove the breasts, the ovaries, and, rarely, to construct a penis. The capacity of orgasm is always retained, but such a penis cannot become erect, and a prosthetic device has to be used for sexual intercourse.

FOLLOW-UP AFTER SEX-REASSIGNMENT SURGERY

Follow-up of patients who have undergone sex-reassignment surgery reveals mixed results. Some clinicians claim that when the two-year trial period in the role of the desired sex precedes the operations, patients always benefit from the

FOCUS QUESTIONS

1. Describe how a transsexual's sexual identity fails to correspond to his or her body.
2. Explain how a fetus becomes male or female, and what might go wrong in the womb to lead to transsexualism.
3. Describe the therapy for treating transsexuals.
4. What does follow-up of patients who have undergone sex-reassignment surgery reveal?

surgery, both in their sense of well-being and in their ability to love. Job status improves, sexual relationships tend to be more stable, and patients indicate that if they had to do it over again—even though the surgical outcome may have been disappointing—they would do so (Money and Ambinder, 1978; Hunt and Hampson, 1980; Pfafflin, 1992). In a study of regret, none of ninety-seven (formerly) homosexual men and women who had had sex-reassignment operations had regrets, whereas four of fourteen heterosexual men had regrets (Blanchard, Steiner, Clemmensen, and Dickey, 1989).

But there is disagreement about this. In a follow-up of fourteen patients operated on at UCLA, almost all of the patients had had surgical complications (Stoller, 1976). In a six- to twenty-five-year follow-up of thirteen male-to-female transsexuals, only one-third remained sexually active after surgery and only one-third had fair to good sexual "adjustment." Only half could reach orgasm. Four regretted having had the surgery (Lindemalm, Korlin, and Uddenberg, 1986).

As radical as sex-reassignment surgery is, long-term follow-up of hundreds of patients suggests that, while far from ideal, it is the best hope for transsexuals. Although the transsexual must cope with new problems of adjustment, the operation has become more satisfactory as surgical techniques have improved. Most patients are much happier and adapt fairly well to their new lives, living comfortably in their new bodies, dating, having intercourse, and marrying. Any children, of course, are adopted, since no surgery can transplant viable internal reproductive organs. Those patients who have the poorest surgery fare most poorly psychologically (Kuiper and Cohen-Kettenis, 1988). Because there appears to be no alternative but despair, sex-reassignment operations seem to be the therapy of choice.

SEXUAL ORIENTATION: LAYER II

Sexologists, overly fond of jargon, use the word "object choice" to denote how we come to love what we love. Gay activist groups, on the other hand, say we have no choice at all. The truth is most probably in between, although much closer to the gay activists than to the sexologists. We therefore label this layer sexual "orientation," rather than sexual "object choice." The basic sexual orientation is homosexual or heterosexual. We will focus on male homosexuality as an example of human sexual orientation as a whole. We want to emphasize that we do not view homosexuality as a disorder. Rather we discuss it now because its origins shed light on the deep roots of all human sexual orientation.

Origins of Male Homosexuality

When does a male become heterosexual or homosexual? How does it happen? Once sexually active, can he change if he wants to? We must distinguish between "exclusive" homosexuals on the one hand and bisexuals on the other. Most men who have sex with other men are bisexuals. A minority of men who are homosexual are exclusively homosexual; as far back as they can remember, they have been erotically interested only in males. They have sexual fantasies only about males. They fall in love only with males. When they masturbate or have wet dreams, the objects are always males. The orientation of the exclusive male homosexual—and of the exclusive heterosexual—is firmly made.

TIMING OF MATURATION

In late childhood and early adolescence, the content of masturbatory fantasies and nocturnal emission both probably play a role in the acquisition of a homosexual orientation. One theory proposes that the timing of the maturation of sex drive is critical. It hypothesizes that if most of your social group are of the same sex as you when you come into puberty, you will tend to become homosexual; if most are of the opposite sex when you come into puberty, you will tend toward heterosexuality. This theory predicts that early maturing males and individuals with same-sex siblings will have a higher rate of homosexuality, and this may be so (Storms, 1981).

FETAL DISRUPTION

Another major theory of the origin of homosexuality holds that the tendency is laid down much earlier—before birth—by a combination of genetic, hormonal, and neurological processes, and that this orientation is activated by hormonal changes at the onset of puberty (Ellis and Ames, 1987). Learning only alters how, when, and where homosexuality will be expressed. According to the Ellis-Ames theory, the crucial neurochemical events that control masculinization occur during the second to fourth months of pregnancy. This sequence of events is delicate and exquisitely timed and if it is disrupted, incomplete masculinization of the fetus will occur. This disruption will produce neurological feminization in a male fetus, as well as genital deformities in extreme cases. At puberty, this feminization will express itself behaviorally and psychologically as homosexuality.

We can speculate that exclusive homosexuality in males is an attenuated form of male-to-female transsexuality. In this theory, the sexual organs, sexual identity, and sexual orientation for the male (XY) may each have its own separate masculinizer, and so three separate levels of hormonal influence can occur. It might be three different hormones or it might just be a matter of how much hormone. So, for example, with complete hormonal failure, no masculinization at all occurs—the baby is a chromosomal male (XY), with external female organs, female identity, and attraction to men; when this occurs it is called the Androgen Insensitivity Syndrome (AIS). With grossly insufficient masculinizing hormone, the baby is a chromosomal male with male organs, who will tend to be attracted to men, and whose sexual identity will be female as well—a male-to-female transsexual. With somewhat insufficient hormone—a common occurrence—a chromosomal male will have male organs, male identity, but will tend to be attracted to men—an exclusively homosexual male. With sufficient masculinizing hormone, a chromosomal male, with male organs, male identity, and attraction to women tends to result.

According to this hypothesis, the subsequent hormonal events (as yet undiscovered) wherein masculinization is disrupted in those who become homosexuals occur fairly commonly during gestation: a chromosomally normal male is insufficiently masculinized. He is masculinized enough, however, to have a male identity and to have male external organs. The main effect is to change in utero just one aspect of his erotic life: sexual attraction to men rather than to women (see Figure 13–1).

This view does not assert that sexual orientation is *determined* in the womb.

FOCUS QUESTIONS

1. What defines a person as an exclusive male homosexual?
2. Describe the hypothesis that says that hormonal events in the womb may create a strong predisposition to homosexuality or heterosexuality.
3. What differences in brain structure have been found in homosexual men, heterosexual men, and women?
4. What is the concordance for homosexuality in identical twins, fraternal twins, and nontwin brothers, and what do these rates seem to indicate about a genetic contribution to homosexuality?

Rearing, role models, pubertal hormones, genes, the content of late childhood fantasies and dreams, and early sexual experiences all probably play a role in whether one becomes homosexual or heterosexual. The view does assert, however, that hormonal events in the womb, however, can create a strong predisposition to homosexuality or heterosexuality.

ANATOMICAL BASIS FOR SEXUAL ORIENTATION

Human sexual orientation may even have a basis in the anatomy of the brain. In a highly publicized and technically well-done study, brain researcher Simon LeVay (1991) examined the brains of dead homosexual men, heterosexual men, and heterosexual women. Most were AIDs victims. He focused his autopsy on one small area, the middle of the anterior hypothalamus. This area is implicated in male sexual behavior, and men usually have more tissue here than women. He found a remarkably large difference in the amount of tissue: heterosexual men have twice as much as homosexual men, who have about the same amount of tissue as women. Moreover, the anterior hypothalamus is just the area that controls male sexual behavior in rats. Also, this area develops when the brains of male rats are hormonally masculinized before birth.

In another recent study, researchers found further evidence of differing brain structure in an area unrelated to reproduction: the anterior commissure in homosexual men is significantly larger than in heterosexual women, who in turn have more tissue than heterosexual men (Allen and Gorski, 1992).

Too little research has been done on lesbians to know if the same theories might apply to female homosexuals. It is unknown if a slight masculinization of a chromosomally female fetus (XX) produces lesbians. It is possible, but still uncertain, that lesbianism is the mirror image of male homosexuality. Lesbians, unlike exclusive male homosexuals, however, commonly report choosing homosexuality after adolescence. There is also no evidence that the anterior hypothalamus is larger in lesbians than in heterosexual women. No one has looked because lesbians, fortunately, are not dying in great numbers from AIDS.

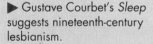

▶ Gustave Courbet's *Sleep* suggests nineteenth-century lesbianism.

TWIN DATA

It is relevant that identical twins are more concordant for homosexuality than fraternal twins and that fraternal twins are more concordant than nontwin brothers. In one study of fifty-six pairs of identical twins in which one twin was known to be homosexual, in 52 percent of the identical twins the co-twin was also found to be homosexual, as opposed to 22 percent of fraternal twins. Only 9 percent of nontwin brothers were concordant for homosexuality. The difference between the identical twins and the fraternal twins suggests a genetic component to homosexuality. But nontwin brothers and male fraternal twins share on average the same percentage (50 percent) of genes. The fact that fraternal twins, who share the same uterine world, are more concordant than nontwin brothers points to fetal hormones as an additional cause. It has also been suggested that they might be concordant for a small medial anterior hypothalamus (Ellis and Ames, 1987).

There is evidence for a sizable genetic contribution to female homosexuality: out of a sample of over 100 twins, one of whom was lesbian, the co-twin was homosexual in 51 percent of the identical twins, but only in 10 percent of the fraternal twins (Bailey, Pillard, and Agyei, 1993).

Thus there is evidence for four different sources of homosexual versus heterosexual orientation: (1) *genetic*—identical twins are more concordant than fraternal twins for homosexuality; (2) *anatomical*—the medial anterior hypothalamus is smaller in homosexual men than in heterosexual men; (3) *fetal*—homosexuality may involve incomplete hormonal masculinization of the fetus during the first three months of pregnancy; (4) *experience*—whether one's first sexual encounters are homosexual or heterosexual as one enters puberty may contribute, as well as the content of masturbatory fantasy and nocturnal emission early in puberty, which may reflect and consolidate sexual orientation.

Disordered Sexual Orientation: Ego-Dystonic Homosexuality

Up until the 1980s, the topic of homosexuality was listed in textbooks as a paraphilia or a "sexual deviation." Sexual "disorders" used to be defined as conditions that grossly impaired affectionate sexual relations between a man and a woman, and so homosexuality was, by definition, a disorder. Now there is good reason not to classify homosexuality as a disorder. DSM-IV, in fact, does not consider homosexuality a disorder. Sexual disorders are viewed as conditions that grossly impair affectionate sexual relations between two *human beings.* Homosexuality, while it may impair such relations between men and women, does not, of course, impair them between a man and a man, or a woman and a woman.

The underlying justification for not calling homosexuality a disorder distinguishes between ego-syntonic and ego-dystonic homosexuality. ***Ego-dystonic homosexuality*** is defined as a sustained pattern of homosexuality which is a source of distress and which is accompanied by the desire to acquire or increase heterosexuality. ***Ego-syntonic homosexuality,*** in contrast, is *not* a source of distress and is *not* marked by a desire to change sexual preference. When we compare ego-dystonic homosexuality to ego-syntonic homosexuality, we see that the former involves suffering and a desire to change, while the latter does not. Since these two elements count strongly toward calling a behavior disordered (see Chapter 1), we believe that ego-syntonic homosexuality is legitimately excluded from the catalogue of psychological disorders. In contrast, we believe that ego-dystonic homosexuality should be considered a sexual problem, and should be so treated.

The crux of the matter is that a significant proportion of homosexuals are satisfied with their sexual orientation, do not show signs of psychopathology, and function quite effectively at love, at work, and at play. Ego-dystonic homosexuals, on the other hand, are dissatisfied and distressed by their sexual orientation. They are depressed, anxious, ashamed, guilty, and lonely. They are also manifestly impaired in their capacity to love. On the one hand, they feel ashamed of their attraction to members of their own sex, but on the other, they are not sexually aroused by members of the opposite sex.

SOURCES OF EGO-DYSTONICITY

Part of the dissatisfaction of ego-dystonic homosexuals stems from their desire to have children and a conventional family life. Another source of dissatisfaction comes from pressures that our society puts on individuals to conform to its sexual norms. In the 1970s, 70 percent of Americans believed that homosexuals were "sexually abnormal," 50 percent believed they were "perverted," and 40 percent believed they were "mentally ill" (Weinberg and Williams, 1974). More recent surveys indicate somewhat greater tolerance, but half of Europeans think homosexuality can "never be justified," and strong negativity is still common in America, particularly among males (Jensen, Gambles, and Olsen, 1988; Herek, 1988). Against this sort of disapproval, it would be difficult to retain one's equanimity day in and day out. A major source of the distress felt by ego-dystonic homosexuals stems from rejection and disapproval by their families, their friends, and their co-workers. Moreover, they also feel distress because of their own images of "normality."

Some writers believe that the suffering that society's oppression inflicts on homosexuals raises serious ethical questions about whether a therapist should

▶ Homosexuality is no longer classified as abnormal: it does not impair affectionate relations between consenting people. When it is "ego syntonic," it does not cause distress in the homosexual person, apart from the effects of social disapproval.

FOCUS QUESTIONS

1. Distinguish between ego-dystonic and ego-syntonic homosexuality.
2. What are some of the sources of distress for ego-dystonic homosexuals?
3. Describe treatments that may help ego-dystonic homosexuals.

ever consent to treat homosexuality. When an ego-dystonic homosexual comes into therapy with a request that the therapist help him to change his sexual orientation, these writers believe that the therapist should refuse. They believe that because the self-loathing and the desire to become heterosexual are products of the oppression of homosexuals by society, the desire of the ego-dystonic homosexual to change his orientation has been coerced and is not "voluntary," and so should be disregarded (Davison, 1976, 1978). Others disagree. They believe that individual suffering is often the product of societal disapproval and rejection. Exactly how the suffering comes about is theoretical and speculative, but what is not speculative is that another human being comes into the therapist's office and voices a desire to change. The expressed desire to change is, for some, the bottom line of therapeutic decision. The therapist is first and foremost an agent of the patient. When a patient, in obvious distress, asks for help, he or she has called on the therapist's primary duties. The essence of trust between patient and therapist, just as between any two human beings, is that the expression of desires are taken seriously and, if possible, acted upon.

TREATMENT OF EGO-DYSTONIC HOMOSEXUALITY

There are two aspects of ego-dystonic homosexuality that might be treated: the dystonicity and/or the homosexuality. The anxiety, depression, guilt, shame, and loneliness that make up the dystonicity may be amenable to the treatments for anxiety and depression outlined in the anxiety and depression chapters (see Chapters 8 and 11). Cognitive therapy, assumption challenging, and progressive relaxation (see Chapter 5) should each allay the sadness and fears that make up the distress.

Traditional psychotherapy does not seem to hold much promise for changes of sexual orientation, but behavior therapy may. In two controlled studies involving seventy-one male homosexuals, a group of British behavior therapists found that sexual orientation could be changed in nearly 60 percent of the cases by using aversion therapy of the sort described below for the paraphilias (Feldman and MacCulloch, 1971; McConaghy, Armstrong, and Blaszczynski, 1981). They defined "change" as the absence of homosexual behavior, plus only occasional homosexual fantasy, plus strong heterosexual fantasy, and some overt heterosexual behavior one year after treatment.

The theory of Ellis and Ames (1987) claims that exclusive homosexuality should be almost unchangeable by therapy, since it has its origins before birth. The data are consistent with this view, since individuals who had had some heterosexual experience before therapy showed more change than exclusive homosexuals who had had no prior pleasurable heterosexual history (Mendelsohn and Ross, 1959; Marciano, 1982; Schwartz and Masters, 1984). When treatment concentrates on additional targets, such as intimacy and social skills, more change occurs (Adams and Sturgis, 1977).

Layer I (Sexual Identity) Contrasted to Layer II (Sexual Orientation)

Our sexual orientation, homosexuality or heterosexuality, is thus rather deep. Lack of change in therapy, lifelong fantasies of one sex only, small anterior hypothalamus, high concordance for homosexuality of identical twins, and fetal development all point to an almost inflexible process. Homosexuality is not quite as unchangeable as transsexualism, however. Male transsexuals never lose the feeling that they are women. They rarely marry and have natural children, whereas homosexual men sometimes marry and have children. They manage this feat by a trick of fantasy. During sex with their wives, they manage to stay aroused and climax by having fantasies about homosexual sex (just as heterosexual men restricted to homosexual release in prison do). Some measure of flexibility is thus available to exclusively homosexual men—they can choose whom they perform with sexually, but they cannot choose whom they want to perform with.

SEXUAL INTEREST: LAYER III

Sometime in the first fifteen years of life, individuals acquire their sexual interests, the objects of their erotic interest, and these objects and situations are likely to be sexually arousing to them for the rest of their lives. Most men are aroused by the female body; most women are aroused by the male body. There is a very large range of situations that men and women find sexually arousing: seductive conversation, holding a member of the opposite sex in their arms, or seeing the person naked. But other more unusual objects or situations may also be sources of sexual arousal, and it is to these that we now turn.

Types of Paraphilias

When sexual interest is so disordered that it impairs the capacity for affectionate erotic relations between human beings, it is called a ***paraphilia*** (from the Greek "love of [philia] what is beyond [para]"). The paraphilias comprise an array of unusual objects and situations that are sexually arousing to some individuals. Among the more common paraphilias are female underwear, shoes, inflicting or receiving pain, and "peeping." Among the more bizarre paraphilias are those to human feces, dead bodies, amputated limbs, and lust murder.

The paraphilias divide into three categories: (1) sexual arousal and preference for nonhuman objects, including fetishes and transvestism; (2) sexual arousal and preference for situations that involve suffering and humiliation, including sadism and masochism; and (3) sexual arousal and preference for nonconsenting partners, including exhibitionism, voyeurism, telephone scatologia, and child molesting.

The preference in a paraphilia (e.g., being spanked) may be harmless and acted out with a consenting partner. Men without a consenting partner often buy the services of prostitutes who specialize in their preference (e.g., "bondage and domination" or "rubber clothes"). In extreme form, the preference is wreaked on a nonconsenting partner and may injure the victim.

For some paraphilics, fantasies or the object itself is always included in sexual activity. For others, the paraphilia occurs only episodically, for example, during difficult periods of life. Paraphilic fantasies are common in people who do not have a paraphila. Panties, peeping, and spanking, for example, are sexually exciting fantasies for many men. The hallmarks of crossing the line to paraphilia are when the person acts on it, when the object becomes necessary

FOCUS QUESTIONS

1. What are the paraphilias?
2. Describe the three categories of paraphilias.
3. Define fetishes, transvestism, and sadomasochism.
4. Describe the paraphilias that involve sexual arousal with nonconsenting partners.

for arousal, when the person is markedly distressed by his or her actions, or when the object displaces his human partner.*

Often paraphilics are happy with their sex lives, and their only problem is the reaction of others to their sexual interests. Many other paraphilics are guilt-ridden, full of shame, and depressed by their actions, which they regard as disgusting and immoral. Sexual dysfunctions frequently accompany paraphilia, particularly when the object is absent.

FETISHES

To have a *fetish* is to be sexually aroused by a nonliving object. In many cases, it may be harmless. For example, women's panties are sexually arousing to many men. When a man fantasizes and talks erotically about panties during sexual intercourse with a mutually consenting partner, the paraphilia may be playful and lead to heightened arousal. More typically, however, his partner feels excluded; when the underwear a woman wears displaces the woman, and her partner cannot be sexually aroused unless she is wearing it, the object is no longer a means to arousal but the end of arousal.

The most common fetishes are for female underwear, shoes, boots, various textures such as rubber, fur, silk, and velvet, parts of the female body such as feet, hair, ears, and eyes. Rarer fetishes include human feces (coprophilia), human urine (urophilia), dirt (mysophilia), animals (zoophilia), and even dead bodies (necrophilia). Here is an example of a fetish, specifically a foot fetish:

> At the age of seven Leo was taught to masturbate by his older half sister. In the course of the lesson she accidentally touched his penis with her slipper. From that time on, the mere sight of a woman's shoe was enough to induce sexual excitement and erection. Now twenty-four, virtually all his masturbation occurred while looking at women's shoes or fantasizing about them. When he was at school he was unable to keep himself from grasping his teacher's shoes and in spite of punishment continued to attack her shoes. He found an acceptable way of adapting his life to his fetish. When he was eighteen, he took a job in a shop which sold ladies' shoes and was excited sexually by fitting shoes onto his customers. He was absolutely unable to have intercourse with his pretty wife unless he was looking at, touching, or thinking about her shoes at the same time. (Krafft-Ebing, 1931, case 114)

As in Leo's case, it is typical that a fetish is acquired during childhood. The object that will become the fetish accompanies early erotic play. The fetish grows in strength when it is repeatedly fantasized about and rehearsed, especially during masturbation. The fetishist often masturbates while holding, rubbing, or smelling the object, or may ask his partner to wear or hold the object during sex. A fetish may reveal itself when adult interpersonal relationships are unsatisfactory. At this point, one's childhood experience may take over and the fetishist may seek comfort in the simpler sexual pleasures of childhood instead of dealing with the complexity of another human being.

Interestingly, virtually all cases of fetishes and the vast majority of all paraphilias occur among men. Such a man is usually full of shame and guilt about his fetish, which isolates him from sexual activity with other people. Erectile dysfunction is the regular consequence of fetishism when the fetish is absent. Depression, anxiety, and loneliness often accompany the fetish. In addition to such individual problems, fetishists are occasionally in trouble with the law.

---

*We use DSM's excellent descriptive data on the different paraphilias freely in this section.

They may steal objects of the fetish, lunge for the objects in public, and they may masturbate on the objects. Some will frequently acquire a collection of the objects. One young shoe fetishist was discovered with a collection of 15,000 to 20,000 pictures of shoes.

TRANSVESTISM

Transvestism occurs when a man persistently dresses in women's clothes to achieve sexual arousal. He usually has a collection of women's clothes, and while masturbating he frequently imagines that he is done up as a woman and wearing women's clothes. Transvestism is usually carried on in secret, although a transvestite's wife may share the secret and cooperate by having intercourse with him when he is dressed as a woman. The secrecy of the act makes its prevalence difficult to estimate, but it is probably rare—occurring in fewer than 1 percent of adult men. There have been virtually no reports of transvestism in women.

Transvestism usually begins with cross-dressing in childhood, as here:

> At about the age of fourteen, I discovered in my dad's photo album a photo he had taken of me at five-and-a-half just before having my long (bobbed) hair cut off. My mother had dressed me in girls' clothes to see what I would have looked like if I had been a daughter, which is what she had wanted first. When I saw the photo I recalled the incident clearly and the sight of the photo thoroughly "shook" me, for it appeared to be a rather pretty young girl.
>
> The emotional result was twofold. It aroused my first interest in girls and also an interest in girls' clothes. I found myself compelled to go back to look at the photo again and again.
>
> One winter my wife and I were living alone. Our marital relations were good. We were spending New Year's Eve entirely alone and for some reason my wife, not knowing of my mere leanings (at the time) toward transvestism (a word I did not know then), decided to put one of her dresses on me and make up my face just as a sort of New Year's Eve prank. When she finished we sat around for a while and she asked me how I liked it. When I answered in the affirmative she became resentful and very anxious for me to take off the clothes she had put on me voluntarily. (Adapted from Stoller, 1969, subject 3)

When cross-dressing begins, only one or two items of clothing, such as panties, may be used. This item of clothing may become a fetish habitually used in masturbation and in intercourse with a cooperating partner. Such a man may wear these panties under his daily masculine garb. Cross-dressing sometimes progresses from a single item to a total costume. It may be done alone or as part of a whole group of transvestites. When dressed as a woman, the transvestite feels considerable pleasure and relaxation; he is intensely frustrated if circumstances block his cross-dressing. Sometimes sexual arousal by wearing women's clothes disappears, but the transvestite continues to dress up to relieve anxiety and depression.

A transvestite may believe he has two personalities: one male, which dominates his daily life, and the other female, which comes out when he is dressed up. In other respects, the transvestite is unremarkably masculine in appearance and conventional in his behavior.

Transvestism is often mistakenly confused with homosexuality on the one hand and with transsexuality on the other. Transvestites are decidedly not homosexual: almost three-quarters of them are married and have children, and on the average they have had less homosexual experience than the average American man (Benjamin, 1966; McCary, 1978). Further, a transvestite is aroused by his fetish, whereas a homosexual is obviously aroused by another person. While a male homosexual will occasionally dress in female clothes in order to attract another man, a homosexual, unlike a transvestite, is not sexually aroused by the fact that he is in "drag."

Since most transvestites merely want to be left alone in order to pursue their habit secretly, we must ask why it is considered a problem. Depression, anxiety, shame, and guilt often occur in transvestites; and while sexual arousal is intense during cross-dressing, affectionate sexuality is often impaired by transvestism. A transvestite will commonly be impotent unless he is wearing some female clothing, and this is often not possible when his partner objects.

SADOMASOCHISM

The second class of paraphilias involves inflicting or receiving suffering as a means to sexual excitement, and it consists of two distinct disorders that complement each other. In **sadism** the individual becomes sexually aroused by inflicting physical or psychological suffering or humiliation on another human being, while in **masochism** the individual becomes sexually aroused by having suffering or humiliation inflicted on him. These terms are greatly overused in ordinary language. We often hear individuals who cheerfully put up with suffering or hardship called masochists, and individuals who are aggressive and domineering called sadists. Much more than this is required for sadism or masochism. A sadist *repeatedly* and *intentionally* inflicts suffering on his partner, sometimes a nonconsenting partner, in order to produce sexual excitement. And a masochist repeatedly and intentionally participates in activity in which he is physically harmed, his life is threatened, or he is otherwise made to suffer in order to feel sexual excitement. Not uncommonly, the masochist and sadist will seek each other out and marry in order to engage in mutually desirable sadomasochism. Both disorders are accompanied by persistent and insistent fantasies in which torture, beating, binding, and raping are common themes producing high sexual arousal.

Many individuals who are neither sadists nor masochists have occasional sexual fantasies about humiliation and suffering. Alfred Kinsey, who studied

▼ A transvestite, Edward Hyde, Lord Cornbury, governed the colonies of New York and New Jersey.

▶ Gay men in drag are not considered transvestites because they cross-dress to attract other men, not because they find cross-dressing arousing in itself.

human sexual behavior in the 1940s and 1950s, found that about 20 percent of men and 12 percent of women reported sexual arousal when they were told stories about rape, bondage, chains, whips, and discipline (Kinsey et al., 1948, 1953). But such fantasies are hardly necessary for sexual arousal or orgasm in the great majority of individuals, and this differentiates them from sado-masochists (Gagnon, 1977; McCary, 1978). In addition to fantasies, overt acts involving suffering and humiliation in order to produce arousal must occur for sadism or masochism to be diagnosed. Nor are all overt acts that produce pain during sex play considered sadomasochistic: lightly biting a partner's earlobe or leaving scratch marks or bruises on a partner's back are common elements of sex play. The true sadist or masochist both has the relevant fantasies and engages in acts that sexually arouse him, causing more than minimal pain.

Sadism, on a physical level, involves the dominance of the sadist over the partner. Examples are forcing the partner to crawl or keeping the victim in a cage. Restraint, blindfolding, whipping, pinching, beating are common accoutrements, and burning, electrical shock, rape, cutting, strangulation, torture, mutilation, and killing are the more extreme sadistic acts and fantasies. On a psychological level, the sadist may bully, threaten, use sarcasm, and belittle. Commonly the severity of the physical acts escalates over time.

Masochistic fantasy and acts often involve being raped while bound so that there is no possibility of escape. Some masochists stick themselves with pins or give electrical shock to themselves, or with a partner (often a consenting sadist) commonly engage in physical bondage, blindfolding, paddling, whipping, pinning and piercing, being urinated or defecated upon, or being forced to crawl and bark like a dog.

Sadism takes its name from the Marquis de Sade (1740–1814), whose descriptions of sadomasochism in his novels are among the most vivid in literature.

He has harshly ordered me to be silent. I strive to melt him . . . but in vain, he strikes out savagely at my now unprotected bosom: terrible bruises are immediately writ out in black and blue; blood appears as his battering continues, my suffering wrings tears from me, they fall upon the vestiges left by the monster's rage, and render, says he, yet a thousand times more interesting. . . . He kisses those marks, he devours them and now and again returns to my mouth, to my eyes whose tears he licks up with lewd delight. (De Sade, 1791/1965, pp. 596–98)

Masochism derives its name from Leopold Sacher-Masoch (1836–1895), a very popular German novelist of the nineteenth century, whose male characters were often sexually degraded by women. Below is a description of a typical sadomasochistic interaction:

> Thomas, a masochist, and his wife enact a periodic sadomasochistic ritual, in which about once every six weeks Thomas has himself beaten by his wife. She punishes him for his "weak" and "feminine" behavior. In his daily life he is an aggressive and controlling executive, but underneath he deeply longs to be controlled. He feels he should be punished because it is wrong for him to have feelings of needing to be dominated, and so he has his wife tie him to a rack in their cellar and beat him. (Adapted from Gagnon, 1977)

Severe cases of sadism and masochism are rare, although mild forms of it occur rather frequently. About 5 percent of the men and 2 percent of the women in one survey of liberal and sexually active individuals at one time or another had gotten sexual pleasure from inflicting pain (Hunt, 1974). The incidence was greater among younger people than older people, and much greater among single men than married men. The great majority of sadists and, contrary to popular belief, masochists as well, are men; but both phenomena appear in women as well.

EXHIBITIONISM, VOYEURISM, AND PEDOPHILIA

The final category of paraphilias involves sexual arousal with nonconsenting partners. Unlike the foregoing, all of these paraphilias are crimes in our society. The criminal aspect derives from the fact that they violate the freedom of others to make unconstrained sexual decisions. **Exhibitionism** involves exposing the genitals to unwitting, and usually unwilling, strangers. **Voyeurism** involves observing the naked body, the disrobing, or the sexual activity of an unsuspecting victim. **Telephone scatologia** consists of recurrent and intense sexual urges to make obscene calls to a nonconsenting individual. **Pedophilia** involves sexual relations with children below the age of puberty, the age at which we consider it reasonable for a person to be able to give mature consent.

Rape—the sexual violation of one person by another—is the most heinous instance of sex involving nonconsenting partners. We shall not discuss rape in this section for two reasons: First, it is not clearly a paraphilia. To be a paraphilia, the act must be the individual's exclusive, or vastly preferred, mode of sexual release. The shoe fetishist does not become erect or have an orgasm unless he is fantasizing about, seeing, or touching shoes. In contrast, the vast majority of rapists, most of the time, can and do become sexually aroused and achieve sexual release in activities other than rape. While fetishism and sadism may play some role in rape, the coercive violence involved is not usually necessary for sexual arousal by the rapist.

Second, rape is a major crime, an act for which it is imperative that society hold the individual responsible, punishing him accordingly. If we were to include rape as a *disorder* in the nosology of paraphilias, there would be some tendency to excuse the act and lighten the burden of the rapist's individual responsibility—even if there was not a shred of evidence other than the rape itself that indicated psychological abnormality. The acts of murder, assault, and theft are not automatically thought of as psychological disorders unless there is additional evidence of abnormality, nor should rape be thought of as a psychological disorder. The expression "Only a crazy man could have done that," when applied to bad action seems to us deeply and insidiously confused. To call an evil person crazy or an evil act insane is not only a sloppy use of language, but it blackens the character of all the good, crazy people in the world—the fine people to whom our field is dedicated.

The distinction between "evil" and "crazy" is deeply entrenched in our language and our moral codes. Distinguishing between them is central to being able to excuse people occasionally for bad actions when they are not responsible by reason of insanity (see Chapter 18). We must not blur this distinction any further.

Exhibitionism   *Exhibitionism* consists of exposing the genitals to an unwitting stranger, on repeated occasions, in order to produce sexual excitement. The exposure itself is the final sexual act, and the exhibitionist does not go on to attempt sexual relations with his victim after exhibiting himself. A "flasher," or "flagwaver," as he is called in prison slang, typically approaches a woman with his genitals exposed. He usually has an erection, but sometimes he is flaccid. Sometimes he will ejaculate while exhibiting himself or, more commonly, he will masturbate when he is alone afterwards (Katchadourian and Lunde, 1972).

Exhibitionism is the most common sexual crime in the United States, with roughly one-third of sexual offenders arrested for it. Surprisingly enough, exhibitionism is very rare outside the United States and Europe and nonexistent in cultures such as India and Burma. Almost half of convicted exhibitionists have had four or more prior convictions for this offense (Gebhard, Gagnon, Pomeroy, and Christenson, 1965).

Exhibiting one's genitals or naked body in a public place is viewed quite differently by our society, depending on whether it is done by a man or by a woman. When a man undresses before an unsuspecting female, he is the exhibitionist and she is the victim. When a woman undresses before an unsuspecting male, he is the voyeur and she is again the victim. As Katchadourian and Lunde (1972) put it, "However badly females fare in other areas of sexual behavior, when it comes to voyeurism and exhibitionism the law is on their side." For this reason in part, exhibitionism and voyeurism are disorders mostly of men, and crimes with which mostly men are charged.

The exhibitionist has a favorite type of victim and will expose himself exclusively to female adults or exclusively to children. He wishes to shock and horrify his victim, and this is essential for the act to be gratifying. A woman who acts calmly when confronted with an exhibitionist and placidly suggests to him that he needs psychological help will usually foil the act.

Exhibitionists are usually not dangerous. The act usually takes place six to sixty feet away from the victim; very rarely is the victim touched or molested. The exhibitionist is more of a nuisance than a menace, and it is uncommon for exhibitionists to become child molesters (Gagnon, 1977; McCary, 1978).

The settings in which exhibitionists expose themselves vary. The most common are in front of girls' schools or churches, in crowds, and in parks; and in these settings, the exhibitionist may pretend he is urinating. Among the more imaginative scenarios are wearing only a raincoat in a department store, taking out a whistle and blowing it, and as the female shoppers look in the direction of the whistler, opening the raincoat; rapping on the window of a house with one's erect penis; sitting down near women in darkened movie theaters and masturbating. All these situations have one important element in common: they are public and it is very unlikely that sexual intercourse could possibly take place. These points provide clues to the dynamics of an exhibitionist: The exhibitionist needs to display his masculinity without the threat of having to perform in an adequate sexual role (Kaplan, 1974).

What is the typical exhibitionist like? Most exhibitionists are married, but there is conflicting evidence about whether or not their sexual relationships with their wives are poor or good (Maletzky, 1974; Rooth and Marks, 1974; McCary, 1978). The exhibitionist is usually between the ages of thirteen and forty, with the peak being about twenty-five. Exhibitionism may begin any time from preadolescence to about age forty. When onset occurs after forty, it is usually associated with another, more severe, condition like senility. Exhibitionism may be an impulsive response to transitory stress like being slighted by a woman, or it may be compulsive, insistent, and ritualistic. Overall, however, the words that best characterize exhibitionists are "irresponsible" and "immature" (Levin and Stava, 1987).

Voyeurism   In the eleventh century Leofric, the Lord of Coventry, agreed to lower taxes if his wife, Lady Godiva, would ride unclothed on a white horse through the town. As a friend of the poor, Lady Godiva consented, and everyone in town shuttered their windows and hid their eyes out of respect and gratitude. Only Tom, the tailor, peeked; and he went blind, becoming our legendary peeping Tom, the "original" voyeur.

Voyeurs are individuals who repeatedly seek out situations in which they can look at unsuspecting women who are naked, disrobing, or engaged in sexual activity. The acts of a peeping Tom are secret. The voyeur will masturbate during these acts or while fantasizing about the memory of these encounters. Watching an unsuspecting stranger is the final act, and the voyeur almost never approaches his victim for sexual contact. Visual stimulation is commonly erotic both to men and women, but merely being aroused by seeing a naked woman or a sexual act is not equivalent to voyeurism. In normal individuals, visual stimulation is usually a prelude to further sexual activity. In contrast to voyeurs, normal men do not need to watch an unsuspecting stranger in order to become aroused. The illegal, secretive nature of his peeping is itself arousing to the voyeur.

Almost all information about voyeurs comes from those cases in which they are caught. The act is a crime, and many of the problems—such as shame and danger to reputation—that it produces come only in the aftermath of the arrest and exposure. In addition to shame, voyeurs sometimes fall off window ledges, are shot as burglars, and are assaulted by couples who catch them peeping.

What is the typical voyeur like? The data on this must be viewed with caution, since we know only a selected sample—those who have been caught and convicted by the court. These data may reflect the difference between the caught and the uncaught as much as the difference between voyeurs and non-voyeurs. (The same caveat holds for exhibitionists and pedophiles as well.) Typically the voyeur is a man, although FBI reports indicate that one out of nine individuals arrested for voyeurism are women (McCary, 1978). Through adolescence, the typical voyeur had fewer girlfriends and was slower to begin premarital sex than his peers. Between one-third and one-half of voyeurs are married, and the quality of their marriages does not differ strikingly from the quality of the marriages of the rest of the male population. Finally, 30 percent of convicted voyeurs (more than any other group of sexual offenders) had also been convicted as juveniles of a variety of nonsexual minor offenses (Gebhard, Gagnon, Pomeroy, and Christenson, 1965).

Pedophilia   The ***pedophile,*** sometimes called the child molester, prefers sexual activity with prepubescent children and acts out his preference repeatedly. Society feels a special sense of horror and reserves special fury for the child molester. Other than lust murder, pedophilia is the most heavily punished crime of the paraphilias. About 30 percent of all convictions for sex offenses are for child molesting, but it is probably even more common than generally supposed. Between one-quarter and one-third of all adults *report* that when they were children they had been approached sexually by an adult (Kinsey et al., 1948; McConaghy, 1969; McCary, 1978; Erickson, Walbek, and Seely, 1988).*

There are probably two reasons society consigns pedophiles to a special hell. First, we do not consider a child capable of consenting to sexual activity in the same way a mature adult can, and so the child's freedom is seen as being grossly violated in such circumstances. Second, there is a common, but unsubstantiated, belief in sexual imprinting; the child's attitude toward future sexuality may be warped by these early sexual contacts.

In spite of the fact that the child molester is so despised, physical violence probably occurs in no more than 3 percent of all cases of child molesting, and in only about 15 percent of all cases does threat or coercion occur. Provocation and active participation by the victim may occur in about 10 percent of the cases (Swanson, 1968; McCary, 1978).

The molested child is twice as likely to be a girl as a boy. Pedophiles generally desire children of a particular age, which may be as specific as a range of only one or two years. Those attracted to girls usually prefer eight- to ten-year-olds, while those attracted to boys usually prefer slightly older children. Many desire both young boys and young girls.

The child molester may just undress the child and look, exposing himself, masturbating in front of the child, or gently touching and fondling the child. Some go further and have oral, anal, or vaginal sex with the child, sometimes using force. Penetration probably occurs in only about 10 percent of the cases of child molestation. The pedophile often rationalizes his actions by saying that they have "educational value" for the child or that the child "seduced" him. Generally, after being molested, the child is emotionally upset and frightened, but usually less so than the parents. The intense reaction of parents and other adults to the incident may amplify the trauma of the molested child and may even interfere with natural healing. Children involved in lengthy court cases

*We emphasize "report," rather than actuality, because of the ease with which memories of sexual molestation in childhood can be confabulated (Loftus, 1993).

are ten times more likely to remain disturbed than children whose cases are quickly resolved (Runyan, Everson, Edelsohn, et al., 1988).

Society's image of the child molester as a dirty stranger lurking in the shadows is far from the truth. Most acts of convicted pedophiles take place between the child and a family acquaintance, neighbor, or relative. The acts usually occur in the child's own home or during a voluntary visit of the child to the home of the pedophile. The relationship is not usually particularly intimate, nor is it prolonged. It typically ends when the child begins to protest or reports it to the parents. As with exhibitionism and voyeurism, however, our picture of the pedophile comes from those who have been caught and convicted, and therefore it may not accurately represent those who have successfully evaded capture.

Some child molesters threaten the child to keep her silent. Others obtain children by marrying a woman with an attractive child, trading children with other pedophiles, or, rarely, kidnapping children.

While some convicted molesters are mentally retarded, senile, or schizophrenic, the vast majority are not. The convicted molester is typically older than those in any other class of sex offenders, with the average age being thirty-seven. The majority of those convicted are married. Older offenders seek out younger children in the eight- to ten-year-old age range whereas younger offenders seek out preadolescents of ten to twelve years old. Molesters are often beset with conflicts about religious piety versus sexuality, are guilt-ridden, and feel doomed. They often lack ordinary adult social skills (Overholser and Beck, 1986), lack confidence, and may be uneasy in adult social and sexual relations and feel more comfortable with children than adults (Levin and Stava, 1987). The disorder is usually chronic, especially in those attracted to boys. For habitual child molesters, the frequency of paraphilic behavior often fluctuates with psychosocial stress. Occasionally, isolated acts of sexual behavior with children by nonpedophilic individuals will be precipitated by a stressor, most commonly upon discovering that one's wife or girlfriend has been unfaithful. In other cases, child molesters may be substituting child contact for adult contact that they have been unable to get (Gagnon, 1977).

The Causes of Paraphilias

There are some objects that we treat as means to certain ends that merely symbolize other, more important, objects. Money, for example, stands for the things it can buy and the pleasures it can bring. Similarly, some of our acquaintances are merely contacts we value, not for themselves, but because of what they do for us. Other objects serve no other master and become an end in themselves: stamps for the stamp collector, work for a "workaholic," power for some politicians. Above all, the objects of sexual choice become ends in themselves: women for most men, shoes for a shoe fetishist, inflicting suffering for a sadist, shocking an unsuspecting woman for the exhibitionist. This is the stuff out of which human passion is made.

Where does it begin and how do these processes go awry to produce the paraphilias? Two schools of thought, the psychodynamic and the behavioral, have wrestled with the problem of the origin of paraphilias. While neither has been completely successful, both have contributed to our understanding.

THE PSYCHODYNAMIC VIEW OF PARAPHILIAS

According to Freud, the concepts of "fixation," "object-cathexis," and "sexual object choice" are attempts to describe and explain how certain objects become imbued with erotic attraction for certain individuals as they grow up. ***Cathexis*** refers to the charging of a neutral object with psychical energy, either positive or negative. In the case of a "positive cathexis," the libido, or the sexual drive, attaches to the object, and it becomes loved. In the case of a "negative cathexis," the object becomes feared.

Freud described the case of the typical foot fetishist who recalled that when he was six, his governess, wearing a velvet slipper, stretched her foot out on a cushion. Although it was decently concealed, this kind of foot, thin and scraggy though it was, thereafter became his only sexual interest (Freud, 1917/1976, p. 348). The fetishist had cathected onto this kind of foot. Freud considered this cathexis to be a concentration of very high psychical energy, bounded and protected by a shield of dead layers. This protection against external stimuli allowed the cathected object to retain its erotic power through life, and only traumatic experiences could breach the protective gates.

Cathected paraphilias have the same three properties as other objects of sexual interest: (1) they have their beginnings in childhood experience; (2) they resist change, particularly rational change; and (3) they last and last—usually remaining for a lifetime. Thus, for example, a foot fetish begins in childhood; telling a foot fetishist that feet don't ordinarily signal sexual pleasure does not diminish their attractiveness; and generally a foot fetish will endure for a lifetime.

While the concept of cathexis is useful descriptively, it is not a satisfactory explanation, for as Freud acknowledged, it is unknown why it strikes one individual rather than another. And this is the main question that concerns us here. The psychodynamic view is content to describe as an acquired cathexis the origins of passion for the fetishist, the transvestite, the sadist, the masochist, the exhibitionist, the voyeur, and the pedophile. But it only describes the fact that for all of these individuals their sexual object choice is not a means to an end but an end in itself, that it is persistent, and that it does not yield to reason. Cathexis does not explain how this happens.

THE BEHAVIORAL VIEW OF PARAPHILIAS

The learning theories, too, have wrestled with the problem of erotic attachment. The most common account is Pavlovian. Recall the case of Leo, whose foot fetish began when, as a seven-year-old, his half sister's slipper touched his penis. The conditioned stimulus (CS) here is the sight of the slipper. It is paired with the unconditioned stimulus (US) of genital stimulation and the unconditioned response (UR) of sexual pleasure. As a result, in the future slippers come to produce the conditioned response (CR) of sexual arousal. Such an account explains how cathexis might occur to odd objects in childhood, and it supplements the Freudian account by providing a mechanism.

But this account leaves unanswered the question: Why do paraphilias persist? Recall that the Pavlovian account of phobias had the same problem (see Chapter 8, pp. 227–29). Once a conditioned stimulus has been paired with an unconditioned stimulus, it usually extinguishes readily when it occurs without the original unconditioned stimulus. When the shoe no longer signals that his sister will touch his penis, Leo should once again come to find shoes unin-

1. What is the psychodynamic view of the paraphilias?
2. Describe the behavioral view of the paraphilias in terms of CS, US, UR, and CR.
3. How do learning theories explain the persistence of the paraphilias?
4. Describe aversion therapy and explain how it is used to treat the paraphilias.

teresting—just as the dog, who used to have the clicking sound paired with food but who no longer experiences food following the clicking, will stop salivating to the click.

To explain the persistence of phobias, we could make the following argument: once the phobic object became fearful, it was avoided so completely that the phobic never found out that the phobic object was no longer paired with the original trauma. The phobic object remained frightening because it was untested behind its protective wall. But the paraphilic does not avoid the newly erotic object. On the contrary, he continues to seek it, embraces it, fantasizes about it, *and he masturbates to it.*

This latter fact explains the persistence of the paraphilia, once conditioned. Once the fetishistic object has been paired with erotic stimulation and the paraphilic masturbates in the presence of the fantasy of the object or in the presence of the very object itself, he provides himself with additional Pavlovian conditioning trials, thereby greatly strengthening the connection between the object and the unconditioned response of sexual pleasure. So an adolescent who experienced the sight of panties originally paired with sexual teasing by the girl next door may greatly strengthen his attachment to panties when he masturbates to orgasm while fantasizing about panties (McGuire, Carlisle, and Young, 1965; Storms, 1981).

There is a bit of laboratory evidence to supplement the case histories, which suggests that Pavlovian conditioning may be at the origin of paraphilias. S. J. Rachman and Ray Hodgson of Maudsley Hospital, University of London, attempted to condition a fetish. Pictures of boots (CS) were paired in time with pictures of naked women (US)—the latter causing their male subjects to have erections (UR). After several dozen pairings, the pictures of the boots (CS) themselves caused erections (CR). So a previously neutral object became erotic following Pavlovian sexual conditioning. But the erotic arousal to boots quickly extinguished when boots were no longer followed by the pornographic pictures—in all but one of the six subjects. Perhaps if the subjects had repeatedly masturbated to boots in fantasy the fetish might have resisted extinction (Rachman and Hodgson, 1968).

There is another factor, ***preparedness,*** which was brought up in explaining phobias and which might also help to account for the irrationality and resistance to extinction of fetishes. Phobias are not arbitrary—only several dozen human phobias exist (see Chapter 8). There are no lamb phobias, no tree phobias. Evolution seems to have allowed only a certain class of objects that were actually dangerous at one time or another in evolutionary history to become potentially phobic. A parallel argument may hold for paraphilias. There are a limited set of objects that actually become paraphilic. Why are paraphilias about parts of the body and about dominance and submission common, but paraphilias about windows, pillows, or yellow walls nonexistent, despite the fact that such objects are often paired with sexual stimulation in childhood? If there is a special class of objects that are *prepared* to take on an erotic character once the objects have been paired with unconditioned sexual stimuli, then the other properties of preparedness should follow. Such objects, once conditioned, should be irrational, robust, and easily learned. These facts describe both the paraphilias and phobias.

Thus, both psychodynamic thinking and learning theory may contribute to the explanation of paraphilias. Pairing of certain objects with actual sexual stimulation in childhood eroticizes these objects. They can be described as "cathected" because they are irrational and they resist extinction. The process by which they become cathected may be explained by Pavlovian conditioning, in which a prepared object is paired with an erotic object. Paraphilias and normal sexual object choices will resist extinction because fantasies (CS) about them are paired repeatedly with sexual arousal and orgasm (US) produced by masturbation and by wet dreams.

Changing Sexual Interest

In the natural course of life, your adolescent sexual interests abide, though new ones can be added. Bisexuals, for example, may often have only heterosexual experience. In their twenties or thirties, however, they may begin to act on their secret fantasies, happen into an encounter, and become actively bisexual. Married couples are introduced to group sex by other "swingers" and sometimes acquire a taste for it.

Sexual interests, however, which rarely die of their own accord, can—with explicit therapy—sometimes be altered. There are extensive studies of therapy to change sexual interest, but they come mostly from atypical men: sex offenders. An exhibitionist (flasher) or a pedophile (child molester) may be arrested and then have therapy mandated in addition to, or instead of, jail. So, our knowledge of therapy outcomes for changing sexual interest, unlike most areas of therapy, comes only from people who are under strong external pressure to change.

Behavior therapists have reported some favorable results in changing the paraphilias, but the success rate is far from perfect (Maletzky, 1974; Rooth and Marks, 1974; Blair and Lanyon, 1981). If paraphilias arise by conditioning during fantasy and masturbation, it might be sufficient for **aversion therapy** to concentrate on fantasy. The use of imagined sexual stimuli followed by aversive US's is called **covert sensitization** (Cautela, 1967; LaMontagne and LeSage, 1986). The treatment of exhibitionists is typical, and all of the following are used extensively, alone or in combination:

- Electric shock or chemical nauseants—The patient reads aloud, in the first person, an exciting sequence of vignettes about flashing. When he gets to the climax of exposing his erect penis, painful shock or chemical nauseants are delivered. As the climactic act becomes aversive, the aversive stimulus is now delivered earlier and earlier in the sequence.
- Orgasmic reconditioning—The man masturbates, narrating his fantasies aloud. As he reaches climax, he substitutes a more acceptable scene for the flashing fantasy.
- Masturbatory satiation—He continues to masturbate for half an hour after ejaculation—a deadly task—while rehearsing every variation of flashing aloud.

These are mildly effective. In one study with a six-year follow-up, only 40 percent of treated men continue to flash, whereas 60 percent of untreated men reoffend.

Behavior therapists also use social skills training and imagery-stopping techniques to modify paraphilias. Although some success has been reported using these techniques with exhibitionists (Maletzky, 1974), these procedures have also been known to fail (McConaghy, 1969).

More recently, therapists have started to treat this problem cognitively. For example, the patient carries cards with exciting vignettes about flashing. On the back of each card is a horrible consequence of flashing and getting caught. Whenever he is tempted to flash, the patient is instructed to read the sequence, turn the cards over, and then ruminate on the awful consequences. This may reduce the rate of reoffending to about 25 percent (Marshall, Eccles, and Barbaree, 1991).

What is changing here? Patients report changes both in their overt behavior and in their desire to flash as well. What they do is substantially changed. We believe, however, that what they want is largely unchanged. It is very much in the interest of the offender to tell the therapist, the judge, the probation officer, and the world that he no longer wants to flash, and so his reports about desire are not completely reliable. Nevertheless, the behavioral record documents that he actually does flash less. We suspect the offender learns in therapy to restrain himself from acting on his desires, which are unchanged. While not a cure, this is all to the good. It also suggests that some change—perhaps not in desire but in action—can occur with sexual interests.

It should not go unnoted that there is a substantially more effective way to curtail brutal sex offenders: castration. It is used in Europe for very serious offenses—brutal rape and child molestation. Castration is done surgically—cutting off the testicles—or, more commonly, with drugs that neutralize the hormone that the testicles produce. In four studies of over 2,000 offenders followed for many years, the reoffense rate dropped from around 70 percent to around 3 percent. Drug castration, which unlike surgery is reversible, works as well as surgical castration (Bradford, 1988). In America, castration is considered "cruel and unusual punishment," and is thus not performed. When we consider all the wasted years in prison, the high likelihood of repeated offense, and the special hell that other prisoners reserve for child molesters, however, castration seems to us less cruel than the "usual" punishment.

Layer III (Sexual Interest) Compared to Layers I (Sexual Identity) and II (Sexual Orientation)

Sexual orientation—heterosexual or homosexual—is a close neighbor of sexual identity in its depth and inflexibility, and both are deeper than sexual interest. Once identity and orientation are dictated largely by biology, the sexual interests are elaborated around them largely by environmental stimuli: breasts or bottoms, peeping, lace panties, calves or feet, rubber textures, the missionary position or oral sex, sadism, blond hair, bisexuality, spanking, or high-heeled shoes. These interests are not easily shelved once acquired. Unlike exclusive heterosexuality or homosexuality, they surely do not arise in the womb. Rather our sexual interests have their beginnings in late childhood as the first hormones of puberty awaken the dormant brain structures that were laid down in the womb and the child has encounters with potential sexual objects. With repeated masturbation and fantasy, these biologically prepared objects become strong but not wholly unchangeable life goals.

Sex role is the public expression of sexual identity—what one says and what one does to indicate being a man or a woman. In today's more tolerant world there are no "disorders" of sex role. Compassionate men and tough women, male nurses and female construction workers are not deemed to suffer from any sexual problem. We discuss the issue of sex role now—in spite of there being no sex role disorders—because sex role fills out and illuminates the layers of our sexual existence. What role we adopt is elaborated around our sexual identity, our sexual orientation, and our sexual interests.

The word "role" is misleading. As a term of the theater, it makes it sound as if sex role is a costume we can take off or put on at will—an arbitrary convention of how we are socialized. While sex role is partly learned and is more plastic than sexual interest, which is in turn more plastic than orientation and identity, it is not arbitrary.

There are huge sex-role dissimilarities between very young boys and girls (Huston, 1985; Sedney, 1987; Maccoby and Jacklin, 1974):

- By age 2 boys want to play with trucks and girls want to play with dolls.
- By age 3 children know the sex stereotypes for dress, toys, jobs, games, tools, and interests.
- By age 3 children want to play with peers of their own sex.
- By age 4 most girls want to be teachers, nurses, secretaries, and mothers, while most boys want to have "masculine" jobs.

In most cultures, young children categorize the world according to sex and organize their lives around these categories. No one has to teach them sex-role stereotypes: they spontaneously invent them. The usual explanation is that they learn sex roles from their parents. After all, parents decorate the rooms of girls in pink and put dolls in their cribs, while boys get blue cribs and toy guns.

What is surprising is that children reared "androgynously" (from the Greek for "both male and female") display their stereotypes as strongly as children not so reared. Young children's stereotypes bear no relationship to their parents' attitudes or to their parents' education, class, employment, or sexual politics. Children's play is strongly sex-stereotyped, even when their parents are androgynous in politics and behavior.

It is not that boys are merely indifferent to lessons about "androgyny." Boys don't just ignore being told it's okay to play with dolls; they actively resist. Having a teacher try to persuade a child to give up a "sex-appropriate" toy produces resistance, anxiety, and backlash, particularly among boys. Watching videotapes of other kids playing joyfully with sex-inappropriate toys doesn't work either. Intensive home programs incorporating androgynous toys, songs, and books with mother as the teacher produce no changes. Extensive classroom intervention produces no changes in androgyny—outside the classroom (Huston, 1985; Sedney, 1987).

These findings seem to disprove the belief that social pressure creates sex roles in the first place. If social pressure creates it, intense social pressure by committed parents and teachers should diminish it. But it has not been demonstrated to do so.

FOCUS QUESTIONS

1. Describe some of the sex-role dissimilarities between very young boys and girls.
2. What are the two lines of evidence that indicate that fetal hormones may play a role in creating sex roles?
3. Why may sex-role stereotypes diminish as children mature?

Since social pressure does not play a measurable role in creating sex roles, one determinant could, at least in part, be fetal hormones. There are two lines of evidence for this: In one study, seventy-four mothers had taken prescription drugs to prevent miscarriage during their pregnancies in the 1970s. These drugs had the common property of disrupting the masculinizing hormone, androgen. When the children were ten years old, the games they liked to play were compared to the games enjoyed by matched controls. The boys' games were less masculine, and the girls' games were more feminine.

A second line of evidence is a disease (Congenital Adrenal Hyperplasia, or CAH) that bathes female fetuses with extra androgen. As young children, CAH girls like male-stereotyped toys and rough and tumble play, and they are more tomboyish than matched controls. These findings suggest that one source of boys' wanting to play with guns and girls' wanting to play house originates in the womb (Money and Ehrhardt, 1972; Meyer-Bahlburg, Feldman, Cohen, and Ehrhardt, 1988; Berenbaum and Hines, 1992).

In light of this evidence, one might be tempted to leap to the conclusion that sex roles are biologically deep and unchangeable. This, however, is not true. As children grow up, the stereotypes get weaker and easier to defy. In late childhood, children begin to have stereotypes about crying, dominance, independence, and kindness, but they are much weaker than the toy and job stereotypes of early childhood.

Although pressuring kids to become androgynous does not work immediately, it may have a "sleeper" effect. As children mature into adults, sex-role stereotypes start to melt away. When children grow up, the ones who were raised by androgynous parents tend to become androgynous themselves. Supporting intellectual interests for daughters and warmth and compassion for sons, exposing children to a range of roles, may work after all—but only in the long run (Reinisch, 1992).

This is important, and it makes sense. Young children see the world in black and white terms. "I'm either a boy or a girl. There's nothing in between. If I like dolls, I'm a sissy." These are deeply held convictions. Young children seem to have a drive to conform which may have its roots in the fetal brain. As a child matures, however, considerations of morality, of justice, of fairness enter. Tolerance starts to displace blind conformity. He or she now chooses how to behave. Decisions about androgyny, about unconventionality, about rebellion are conscious choices based on a sense of what is right and what the adolescent individual wants for his or her own future. As such, the choice of androgyny requires a mature mind and a conscience; it is not a product of mechanical childhood socialization.

SEXUAL PERFORMANCE: LAYER V

Assume that the first four layers of your sexuality are in good order. You have a clear sexual identity and orientation, you have clear sexual interests, and a well-entrenched sex role. You are alone with an appropriate, consenting partner. What can now go wrong? In what ways can the surface layer of erotic life—sexual performance—be impaired?

The Physiology of the Human Sexual Response

In both men and women, the sexual response consists of three phases: the first is ***erotic desire and arousal,*** in which a variety of stimuli—tactile, visual, and more subtle ones such as fantasy—produce arousal. The second phase, ***physical excitement,*** consists of penile erection in the male and of vaginal lubrication and swelling in the genital area of the female. The third phase is ***orgasm.*** We shall review these phases in some detail because sexual dysfunction can disrupt any of them.

MALE SEXUAL RESPONSE

In men, erotic arousal results from a wide variety of events. Being touched on the genitals or looking at and touching a sexually responsive partner are probably the most compelling stimuli. In addition, visual stimuli, smells, a seductive voice, and erotic fantasies, among many others, all produce arousal.

The second phase of excitement is intertwined with the first phase of erotic arousal. In the male, it consists of penile erection. Sexual excitement stimulates parasympathetic nerves in the spinal cord, and these nerves control the blood vessels of the penis. These vessels widen dramatically and highly oxygen-rich blood streams in, producing erection. The blood is prevented from leaving by a system of valves in the veins. When the parasympathetic fibers are inhibited, the vessels empty, and rapid loss of erection occurs.

Orgasm in men consists of two stages that follow each other very rapidly—emission and ejaculation. Unlike arousal and erection, orgasm is controlled by the sympathetic nervous system, as opposed to the parasympathetic nervous system. When sufficient rhythmic pressure on the head and shaft of the penis occur, the stage of orgasmic inevitability is reached and orgasm arrives. Orgasm is engineered to deposit sperm deep into the vagina near the head of the uterus, maximizing the possibility of fertilization. Emission (the discharge of semen) occurs when the reproductive organs all contract. This is followed very rapidly by ejaculation, in which powerful muscles at the base of the penis contract vigorously, ejecting sperm from the penis. During ejaculation, these muscles contract by reflex at intervals of 0.8 seconds. This phase of orgasm is accompanied by intense pleasure. After orgasm has occurred, a man, unlike a woman, is "refractory," or unresponsive to further sexual stimulation for some interval. This interval varies from a few minutes to a few hours, and it lengthens as the man gets older.

FEMALE SEXUAL RESPONSE

The sexual response of a woman transforms the normally tight and dry vagina into a lubricated, perfectly fitting receptacle for the erect penis. The stimuli that produce arousal in women are similar to those that produce arousal in men. Kissing and caressing, visual stimuli, and a whole host of subtle cues are usually effective as sexually arousing stimuli. In our culture, at least, there appear to be some gender differences in what is arousing, with subtle stimuli and gentle touch more initially arousing to women than direct stimulation.

Once a woman is aroused, the excitement or "lubrication-swelling" phase begins. When at rest, the vagina is collapsed, pale in color, and rather dry. When arousal occurs, the vagina balloons exactly enough to "glove" an erect penis, regardless of its size. At the same time, the clitoris, a small knob of tissue

FOCUS QUESTIONS

1. What are the three phases of the human sexual response?
2. What is sexual dysfunction and in what areas of the sexual response can it occur?
3. Describe the subjective and physiological symptoms of sexual unresponsiveness in women.
4. Describe the different possible kinds of erectile dysfunctions and orgasmic dysfunctions in men.

located forward of the vagina, swells. Lubrication occurs on the walls of the vagina, making penile insertion easier. As excitement continues, the walls of the uterus fill with blood, and the uterus enlarges. This engorgement of blood and swelling greatly add to erotic pleasure and set the stage for orgasm.

Orgasm in women consists of a series of reflexive contractions of the muscles surrounding the vagina. These contract rhythmically at 0.8 second intervals against the engorged tissue around the vagina, producing the ecstatic sensation of orgasm. Both the clitoris and the vagina itself play a role: orgasm is triggered by stimulation of the clitoris, and then expressed by contraction of the vagina.

Thus, similar stimuli produce erotic arousal in both sexes. Blood flow under the control of the parasympathetic nervous system produces physical excitement and penile erection and both the lubrication and swelling phases of the vagina. Orgasm consists of powerful muscular contractions at 0.8 second intervals, produced by rhythmic pressure on the head and shaft of the penis in the man and of the clitoris of the woman. These parallels are lovely and deep. Before they were known, it was easy to fall prey to the belief that chasms separated the experience of sex between men and women. To learn that one's partner is probably experiencing the same kind of joys that you are is powerful and binding knowledge.

Impairment of Sexual Performance

When the normal mechanism of desire, arousal, or orgasm goes awry, we say an individual suffers a sexual dysfunction. Dysfunction can occur in any or all of the three areas of sexual response: (1) Erotic arousal may be dysfunctional if fantasies about and interest in sexual activity are low or nonexistent. (2) When in an appropriate sexual situation, failure to have or maintain an erection in men and lack of vaginal lubrication and genital swelling in women may occur. (3) In women, orgasm may fail to occur altogether; in men, ejaculation may be premature, occurring with minimal sexual stimulation, or retarded, occurring only after prolonged, continual stimulation, if at all.

Impairment may occur in only one of these three areas of sexuality, or in all three in the same individual. The impairment may be lifelong or acquired, it may be limited to only one situation or occur in all situations, and it may occur infrequently or all the time. For example, the failure to maintain an erection can develop after years of satisfactory intercourse, or it can occur from the very first attempt at sexual intercouse. It can occur only with one partner or with all women. It can occur only once in a while or it can occur every time the individual tries to have intercourse.

SEXUAL UNRESPONSIVENESS IN WOMEN

Because erotic desire and physical excitement are so intertwined, we will treat them together. In women, lack of sexual desire and impairment of physical excitement in appropriate situations is called ***sexual unresponsiveness*** (formerly "frigidity"). Some of the symptoms are subjective: the woman may not have sexual fantasies, she may not enjoy sexual intercourse or stimulation, or she may consider sex an ordeal. Other symptoms are physiological: when she is sexually stimulated, her vagina does not lubricate, her clitoris does not enlarge, her uterus does not swell, and her nipples do not become erect. Frequently, she becomes a spectator rather than losing herself in the erotic act. When she finds herself unstimulated, she begins to worry about her own sexual adequacy and what her partner is thinking about her. She thinks, "He must think I'm frigid." "Is he getting pleasure?" "Will I climax?" She remains outside the act, observing and studying how she and her partner are reacting. Fear of failure, scanning for cues of failure, and presiding as a judge at one's lovemaking can diminish pleasurable sex and worsen the problems of arousal and of orgasm. The woman may be unresponsive in all situations or only in specific ones. For example, if the problem is situational, she may be enraged or nauseated by the sexual advances of her husband, but she may feel instantly aroused and may lubricate when an attractive, unavailable man touches her hand. Such a woman may have problems with orgasm as well, but it is not uncommon for a "sexually unresponsive" woman—whose arousal and excitement are impaired—to have orgasm easily once intercourse takes place.

Women's reaction to this problem varies. Some patiently endure unexciting sexual intercourse, using their bodies mechanically and hoping that their partner will ejaculate quickly. But this is often a formula for resentment. Watching her husband derive great pleasure from sex over and over while she feels little pleasure may be frustrating and alienating for a woman. And eventually some women may attempt to avoid sex, pleading illness or deliberately provoking a quarrel before bedtime (Kaplan, 1974).

The man's reaction to the woman's sexual unresponsiveness also varies. Some men may accept it and indeed may expect it, based on a false belief that women don't or aren't supposed to enjoy sex. Other men may attribute their mate's lack of arousal to inadequate performance on their part and feel that they are poor lovers. Still others may pressure their wife to perform anyway and this, of course, will only make her more unresponsive. Many other couples seem to have good marriages in spite of this and spend a lifetime together without the woman ever responding to her husband sexually.

ERECTILE DYSFUNCTION IN MEN

In men, global impairment of desire (DSM-IV calls it "hypoactive sexual desire" or "sexual aversion") occurs, but it is much rarer than in women. Rather, the most common dysfunction is one of excitement, called ***erectile dysfunction*** (formerly "impotence"). It is defined as a recurrent inability to have or maintain an erection for intercourse. This condition can be humiliating, frustrating, and devastating since male self-esteem across most cultures involves good sexual performance. When erection fails, feelings of worthlessness and depression often ensue.

Here, as with the other sexual dysfunctions, the man becomes a spectator during sex. He mentally steps back and thinks, "Will I fail to get an erection this time too?" "She probably thinks I'm not really a man." "Is she really getting pleasure or just pretending?" These fears make it even more difficult for him to maintain an erection.

Erectile dysfunction in the male can be either primary or secondary, situation specific or global. Men who have had ***primary erectile dysfunction*** have never been able to achieve or maintain an erection sufficient for intercourse; whereas men who have ***secondary erectile dysfunction*** have lost this ability. When the dysfunction is ***situation specific,*** a man may be able to maintain an erection with one partner, but not with another. Some men may become erect during foreplay, but not during intercourse. When the dysfunction is **global,** a man cannot achieve an erection with any partner under any circumstances. It is important and reassuring for a man to know that a single failure in no way implies "erectile dysfunction," which is, by definition, recurrent. Virtually every man on one occasion or another—particularly when upset or fatigued—cannot get an erection or keep it long enough for intercourse.

Here is a case of primary impotence that begins with a particularly sordid circumstance surrounding the man's first attempt at intercourse:

> Sheldon was nineteen when his teammates from the freshman football team dragged him along to visit a prostitute. The prostitute's bedroom was squalid; she seemed to be in her mid-fifties, and had an unattractive face, a fat body, and foul-smelling breath. He was to be the last of a group of five friends scheduled to perform with her. Sheldon had never had intercourse before and had been anxious to begin with. His anxiety increased as his teammates returned one by one to describe in detail their heroic successes. When his turn arrived, the other four decided to watch and cheer him on, and Sheldon could not get an erection. His teammates shouted that he should hurry up and the prostitute was obviously impatient. He was pressured beyond any ability to perform and ran out of the room.
>
> After this incident, he avoided all erotic contact with women for five years, fearing that he would fail again. At age twenty-four, when his fiancée pressured him to have sex, he was overwhelmed with fears that he would fail, remembering his humiliating failure with the prostitute. This brought Sheldon into therapy for primary erectile dysfunction. (Adapted from Masters and Johnson, 1970)

ORGASMIC DYSFUNCTION IN WOMEN

Some women do not achieve the third phase of sexual response: orgasm. How easily different women can achieve orgasm lies on a continuum. At one extreme are the rare women who can have an orgasm merely by having an intense erotic fantasy, without any physical stimulation at all. Then there are women who climax merely from intense foreplay, women who have orgasm during intercourse, and women who need long and intense clitoral stimulation in order to climax. At the other extreme are approximately 10 percent of adult women who have never had an orgasm in spite of having been exposed to a reasonable amount of stimulation.

Nonorgasmic women frequently have a strong sexual drive (Andersen, 1983). They may enjoy foreplay, lubricate copiously, and love the sensation of phallic penetration. But as they approach climax, the woman may become self-conscious; she may stand apart and judge herself. She may ask herself, "I wonder if I'll climax." "This is taking too long; he's getting sick of it." Frustration, resentment, and the persistent erosion of a couple's erotic and affectionate relationship bring nonorgasmic women into therapy (Kaplan, 1974; McCary, 1978).

Failure to have an orgasm may be primary, with orgasm never having occurred, or secondary, with loss of orgasm. It may be situation specific, with orgasm occurring, for example, in masturbation when alone but not in intercourse, or it may be global.

ORGASMIC DYSFUNCTION IN MEN

In men, there are two kinds of orgasmic difficulties and they are opposite problems: premature ejaculation and retarded ejaculation.

Premature Ejaculation Most men have ejaculated occasionally more quickly than their partner would like, but this is not equivalent to premature ejaculation. ***Premature ejaculation*** is the recurrent inability to exert any control over ejaculation such that once sexually aroused, the man reaches orgasm very quickly. This is probably the most common of male sexual problems.

Premature ejaculation can wreak havoc with a couple's sex life. A man who is worrying about ejaculating as soon as he becomes aroused may have trouble being sensitive and responsive to his lover. He may be self-conscious, and his partner may feel rejected and perceive him as cold and insensitive. Not uncommonly, secondary erectile dysfunction often follows untreated premature ejaculation.

Retarded Ejaculation ***Retarded ejaculation,*** which is less common than premature ejaculation, is defined by great difficulty reaching orgasm during sexual intercourse. Frequently, the man may be able to ejaculate easily during masturbation or foreplay, but intercourse may last for a half hour or more with no ejaculation. Contrary to popular myth, the staying power of the retarded ejaculator does not place him in an enviable position. His partner may feel rejected and unskilled. He may feign orgasm, and he may have high anxiety accompanied by self-conscious thoughts like, "She must think something is wrong with me." The retarded ejaculator finds his own touch most arousing, and he may be numb to his partner's touch on his penis. His psychological arousal does not keep pace with his physiological, erectile arousal (Apfelbaum, 1980). Secondary erectile dysfunction sometimes follows.

It is unwise to attach time numbers to both retarded ejaculation and premature ejaculation, saying, for example, that premature ejaculation occurs whenever ejaculation persistently takes less than thirty seconds and retarded ejaculation occurs whenever ejaculation persistently takes more than half an hour. This misses the important point that the definition of the sexual problem, both orgasmic and arousal, is always relative to your own and your partner's expectations. Many couples are able to work out quite satisfactory erotic relationships even when one partner climaxes very quickly or very slowly, and it would be inappropriate to label these individuals as having sexual dysfunction.

The Causes of Sexual Dysfunction

PHYSICAL CAUSES

Impairment of sexual desire in both men and women can stem from aging, drug use that impairs sexual hormones (e.g., alcohol, barbiturates, narcotics, and marijuana), and prescription drugs (e.g., antihypertensives, major and minor tranquilizers, MAO inhibitors, and antihistamines) (Schiavi et al., 1984). A woman's capacity for sexual arousal may be impaired by injuries, physical anomalies of the genitals, hormonal imbalances, neurological disorders, and inflammations (Kaplan, 1974; McCary, 1978). Male sexual dysfunctions may be caused by excessive alcohol or drugs, vascular problems, aging, exhaustion, or anatomical defect. Poor circulation resulting in insufficient oxygen in the blood in the penis and low testosterone may be responsible for some erectile dysfunction problems. Out of 105 patients, 35 percent had disorders of the pituitary-hypothalamic-gonadal axis, and 90 percent of these had potency restored with biological therapy (Spark, White, and Connelly, 1980).

FOCUS QUESTIONS

1. What are some of the physical causes of sexual dysfunction in men and women?
2. Describe the psychoanalytic view of the causes of sexual dysfunction.
3. Describe the behavioral view of the causes of sexual dysfunction.
4. What are some cognitions that may interfere with sexual performance?
5. Describe how direct sexual therapy is used to treat sexually dysfunctional patients.

Nevertheless, physical causes probably account for a minority of the problems of sexual dysfunction in both men and women. There is a useful way of distinguishing between which men are physically and which men are psychologically unable to have erections. All of us dream approximately 100 minutes a night. In the male, dreaming is almost invariably accompanied by an erection (in the female, by vaginal lubrication). We are not certain why this occurs, but it does tell us if a man is physically capable of erection. If a man who is otherwise "impotent" gets erections during dreaming or has an erection upon waking in the morning, the problem is of psychological, not physical, origin.

PSYCHOLOGICAL CAUSES

Psychological problems probably cause the clear majority of the sexual dysfunctions. Negative emotional states impair sexual responsiveness. Earlier, we spoke of the sensitive interplay of physiological and psychological factors. The physiological part of the sexual response is autonomic and visceral; essentially it is produced by increased blood flow to the genitals under the control of the autonomic nervous system. But certain autonomic responses, sexual arousal among them, are inhibited by negative emotions. If a woman is frightened or angry during sex, visceral responding will be impaired. Similarly, if a man is frightened or feeling pressured during sex, there may not be sufficient blood flow to cause erection.

The Psychoanalytic View   What are the sources of the anxiety and anger that might cause sexual unresponsiveness in women? From a psychoanalytic point of view, one cause may be unresolved unconscious conflict: a woman unconsciously hostile toward her husband might express her hostility by withholding her sexual response, just as a consciously hostile woman would.

Psychoanalysts also express a view about male sexual dysfunctions. They claim that erectile dysfunction is a defense against castration anxiety. According to Freud, a boy between the ages of three and five wishes to possess his mother and, in his own mind, becomes a hated rival to his father. He fears that his father will castrate him in retaliation. When this Oedipal conflict is unresolved, erectile dysfunction may later ensue. By failing to have an erection, he wards off the anxiety of castration. That is, he will not commit the act with his "mother" and thereby not be castrated by his "father." These psychoanalytic formulations have not been tested in the laboratory and indeed are quite difficult to test.

There are other, more straightforward sources of anxiety and anger, all of which can interfere with sexual arousal in men and women. A woman may fear that she will not reach orgasm, or she may feel helpless or exploited. Some men and women feel shame and guilt, or they may believe that sex is a sin; they may have grown up in situations where sex was seen as dirty and bad, and they may have trouble ridding themselves of feelings of shame and guilt even in the shelter of marriage. Some women may expect physical pain in intercourse and therefore dread it. Many men fear rejection and become self-conscious, thereby inhibiting an otherwise normal physiological potential. And often there is the fear of pregnancy.

Negative emotions arising in relationships must not be overlooked either. Relationships do not always progress well. People change, sometimes developing different living habits and preferences. Their partner may not change accordingly, and conflict may then ensue, bringing about negative feelings between the couple. Understandably, it is often difficult to discard these feelings when the couple enters the bedroom. In such cases, one or both partners may develop a sexual dysfunction, probably specific in nature.

The Behavioral View The behavioral school offers an explanation of the causes of sexual dysfunction based on learning theory. For men, erectile dysfunction may result from an early sexual experience. A particularly traumatic first sexual experience will condition strong fear to sexual encounters. Recall Sheldon's first and formative sexual encounter. Heterosexual activity was the conditioned stimulus (CS), which resulted in a humiliating, public failure to have an erection (US) and an unconditioned response (UR) of ensuing shame and anxiety. Future exposures to the CS of sexual encounters produced the conditioned response (CR) of anxiety, which in turn blocked erection. This formulation fits many of the instances in which there is an early traumatic experience, and it also explains the success of direct sexual therapy with erectile dysfunction. It fails to account for those cases in which no traumatic experience can be discovered, and it also does not account for why certain individuals are more susceptible to sexually traumatic experiences than others. For every individual who undergoes an initial sexual experience that is a failure (such as Sheldon's) and develops erectile dysfunctions, there are many who encounter similar initial failures but do not.

The Cognitive View In addition to psychodynamic and behavioral accounts of sexual dysfunctions, the cognitive view suggests other important considerations as well (see Table 13–1). We saw that for both the orgasmic and the arousal dysfunctions, what an individual thinks can greatly interfere with performance. Men and women with orgasm difficulties become "orgasm watchers." They may say to themselves, "I wonder if I'll climax this time." "This is taking much too long; he must think I'm frigid." Individuals who have arousal dysfunctions may say to themselves, "If I don't get an erection, she'll laugh at me." "I'm not going to get aroused this time either." These thoughts produce anxiety, which in turn blocks the parasympathetic responding that is the basis of the human sexual response. Such thoughts get in the way of abandoning oneself to erotic feelings. Thus, therapy for the sexual dysfunctions can

TABLE 13–1

VIEWS OF ERECTILE AND ORGASMIC DYSFUNCTION		
Psychoanalytic View	*Behavioral View*	*Cognitive View*
Origin Unresolved unconscious conflict in women; castration anxiety in men	Traumatic early sexual experience	Traumatic sexual experience in someone with a certain cognitive style
Process Unconscious conflict or castration anxiety produces anxiety during sex	Conditioned fear of failure produces anxiety during sex	Person observes and judges him- or herself during sex, interfering with enjoyment and producing anxiety
Result Anxiety leads to sexual unresponsiveness	Anxiety blocks erection or orgasm	Anxiety blocks erection or orgasm

deal with problems at four levels: physical, behavioral, psychodynamic, and cognitive, for difficulties at any of these levels can produce human sexual dysfunction.

Treatment of Sexual Dysfunctions

It has been estimated that half of American marriages are flawed by some kind of sexual problem (Masters and Johnson, 1970; Frank, Anderson, and Rubenstein, 1978; Oggins, Leber, and Veroff, 1993). Sexual problems usually occur in the whole context of a relationship between two human beings. When sex goes badly, many other aspects of the relationship may go badly, and vice versa. Sex—often, but not always—mirrors the way two people feel about and act toward each other overall. Sex therapists often find that underneath the sexual problems are more basic problems of a relationship—love, tenderness, respect, honesty—and that when these are overcome, a fuller sexual relationship may follow (Jacobson, 1992).

In the last twenty years, substantial progress has been made in treating those problems of arousal and orgasm that stem from psychological causes. Overall, only about 25 percent of individuals with these problems fail to improve with a brief course of therapy. Let's look at one case:

> When they came to therapy, Carol, age twenty-nine, and Ed, age thirty-eight, had been married for three-and-a-half years and had one child. When they were first married, Carol had achieved orgasm almost every time they made love, but now orgasm was rare for her. She was feeling more and more reluctant to have intercourse with Ed. Ed had a strong sex drive and wanted to have intercourse every day. But Carol had made rules about sex, stating what Ed could and could not do.
>
> As time went on, Carol found it more and more difficult to keep her part of the bargain. Carol's headaches, fatigue, and quarrels deterred Ed's effective initiation of lovemaking. When he did make love to her, Carol would complain about his lovemaking technique. This effectively ended the encounter.
>
> When they first sought out sexual therapy, they were having intercourse once every two weeks, but Carol was becoming progressively more reluctant and intercourse was becoming even more of a dreaded ordeal for her. (Adapted from Kaplan, 1974, case 22)

DIRECT SEXUAL THERAPY

William Masters and Virginia Johnson, researchers who brought the study of sexual behavior into the laboratory and who have worked to discover the nature and treatment of sexual dysfunction, founded ***direct sexual therapy*** with sexually dysfunctional patients like Ed and Carol. Such therapy differs in three important ways from previous sexual therapy. First, it defines the problem differently: sexual problems are not labeled as "neuroses" or "diseases" but rather as "limited dysfunctions." Direct sexual therapy formulates the problem as local rather than global. A woman like Carol is not labeled as "hysterical," defending against deep intrapsychic conflicts by "freezing" her sexual response, as psychodynamic therapists claim. Rather, she is said to suffer from "inhibition of arousal." Second, and most dramatic, through direct sexual therapy, the clients explicitly practice sexual behavior with the systematic guidance of the therapists. A couple like Carol and Ed first receives education and instruction about their problem, then an authoritative prescription from Masters and Johnson about how to solve it, and most importantly, accompanying sexual practice sessions together. Their third major departure is that people are treated not as individual patients but as couples. In treating individuals, Masters and Johnson had often found that sexual problems do not reside in one individual, but in the interaction of the couple. Carol's lack of interest in sex is not only her problem. Her husband's increasing demands, rage, and frustration contribute to her waning interest in sex. By treating the couple together, Ed and Carol's deteriorating sexual interaction could be reversed.

Sensate focus is the major strategy of direct sexual therapy for impaired excitement in females and erectile dysfunction in males. The basic premise of sensate focus is that anxiety occurring during intercourse blocks sexual excitement and pleasure. In the female, anxiety blocks the lubrication and swelling phase; in the male, it blocks erection. The overriding objectives of treatment are to reduce this anxiety and to restore confidence. The immediate goal is to bring about one successful experience with intercourse. This is accomplished, however, in a way in which the demands associated with arousal and orgasm are minimized. Sensate focus has three phases: "pleasuring," genital stimulation, and nondemand intercourse (Masters and Johnson, 1970; Kaplan, 1974). Let us look at the sensate focus treatment for Carol and Ed.

In the "pleasuring" phase, Carol and Ed were instructed not to have sexual intercourse and not to have orgasm during these exercises. Erotic activity was limited to gently touching and caressing each other's body. Carol was instructed to caress Ed first, and then the roles were to be reversed and Ed was to stroke Carol. This was done to permit Carol to concentrate on the sensations later evoked by Ed's caresses without being distracted by guilt over her own selfishness. It also allowed her to relax knowing that intercourse was not going to be demanded of her.

After three sessions of pleasuring, Carol's response was quite dramatic. She felt freed from pressure to have an orgasm and to serve her husband, and she experienced deeply erotic sensations for the first time in her life. Further, she felt that she had taken responsibility for her own pleasure, and she discovered that she was not rejected by her husband when she asserted herself. They then went on to phase two of sensate focus—"genital stimulation." In this phase, light and teasing genital play is added to pleasuring, but the husband is cautioned not to make orgasm-oriented caresses. Orgasm and intercourse are still forbidden. The woman sets the pace of the exercises and directs the husband both verbally and nonverbally, and then the roles are reversed.

The couple's response was also very positive here. Both felt deep pleasure and were aroused and eager to go on to the next step, "nondemand intercourse." In this final phase, after Carol had reached high arousal through pleasuring and genital stimulation, she was instructed to initiate intercourse. Ed and Carol were further instructed that there was to be no pressure for Carol to have an orgasm.

In spite of—or because of—the instruction, Carol had her first orgasm in months. At this point, Ed and Carol were able to work out a mutually arousing and satisfactory style of lovemaking. Carol and Ed's improvement was typical: only about 25 percent of patients fail to improve with sensate focus for female sexual unresponsiveness or for male erectile dysfunction (Masters and Johnson, 1970; Kaplan, 1974; McCary, 1978).

Evaluation of Sexual Therapy

Direct sexual therapy seems to be quite effective in alleviating the dysfunctions of arousal and orgasm in both men and women (Marks, 1981; Heiman and LoPiccolo, 1983). In addition to good success with erectile dysfunction and female unresponsiveness, failure to improve occurs only in 2 percent of cases of premature ejaculation, and in 20 percent of the remaining orgasmic disorders. Moreover, systematic desensitization may also be effective in enhancing desire and orgasm, particularly in women with sexual anxiety (Andersen, 1983). Caution is required in two respects, however. First, the Masters and Johnson reports of success are not as well documented as many would like. Masters and Johnson do not report percentages of *successes*, but rather they report percentages of *failures*. So, for example, they report that only 24 percent of females "failed to improve" following sensate focus training for arousal dysfunction. This is not equivalent to a 75 percent *cure* rate. What "failure to improve" means is not well defined. Moreover, the percentage of patients showing only mild improvement, great improvement, or complete cure is not reported. While direct sex therapy techniques are far superior to what preceded them, well-controlled replications with explicit criteria for sampling and for improvement will be needed before they can be considered definitive (Zilbergeld and Evans, 1980).

The second caution is that while the therapeutic techniques seem effective, the reasons for their good effects are not wholly clear. As has often been the case in psychology and in medicine, effective cure often precedes understanding, and this seems to be the case for sexual dysfunctions as well.

In conclusion, we can see that the idea of *increasingly deep layers* organizes our erotic life and how changeable it is. Sexual identity and sexual orientation are very deep and don't change much, if at all. Sexual interest and sex role are of middling depth and accordingly change somewhat. Sexual dysfunction is a surface problem and with proper treatment can change readily.

SUMMARY

1. Human sexuality is composed of five layers, each grown around the layer beneath it. This five-layer organization corresponds to depth. The deeper the layer, the harder it is to change.

2. The first and deepest layer of erotic life is *sexual identity,* the awareness of being male or female. This layer has its origin in fetal hormones. *Transsexualism,* a disorder of sexual identity, occurs in men who believe they are really women trapped in men's bodies and in women who feel that they are really men trapped in women's bodies. These individuals seek to get rid of their genitals and live in the opposite sex role. *Sex-reassignment operations* provide some relief for this most distressing condition.

3. The second deepest layer is *sexual orientation,* that is, whether you are sexually attracted to men or women. One's erotic and masturbatory fantasies re-

veal one's sexual orientation. *Ego-dystonic homosexuality* may occur when an individual's homosexuality causes him intense distress.

4. *Sexual interest* is the next layer of human sexuality, dealing with the types of persons, parts of the body, and situations that are the objects of sexual fantasy and arousal. When the object of a person's arousal impairs an affectionate erotic relationship with another consenting human being, the line between normal and disordered sexual interest has been crossed. The *paraphilias* consist of sexual desire for unusual and bizarre objects. Three categories are: sexual arousal to nonhuman objects—most commonly *fetishes* and *transvestism;* sexual arousal in situations that produce suffering and humiliation—*sadomasochism;* and sexual arousal with nonconsenting partners—*exhibitionism, voyeurism, telephone scatologia,* and *pedophilia.* The paraphilias are often lifelong, and they may have their origin in *cathexes,* or emotional bonding, which is then reinforced and potentiated by masturbatory fantasies about the object. It is difficult to change the paraphilias in therapy, but recent behavior therapy techniques have had some success.

5. *Sex role* comprises the fourth layer. This is the public expression of sexual identity, what an individual does to indicate that he is a man or she is a woman. There are no disorders of sex role. Although sex-role stereotypes are rigid in young children, they weaken with age.

6. The layer closest to the surface is *sexual performance,* how adequately an individual performs with a suitable person in a suitable erotic setting. The human sexual response is similar in both men and women and consists of three phases: *erotic desire and arousal; excitement,* which consists of penile erection or vaginal lubrication; and *orgasm.* The *sexual dysfunctions* consist of impairment of desire, excitement, or orgasm. In women, these are manifested by insufficient desire, lack of excitement in sexual intercourse, and infrequent or absent orgasm. In men, there is lack of erection, *premature ejaculation* and *retarded ejaculation.* All these conditions are quite treatable. The *direct sexual therapy* of Masters and Johnson, which uses *sensate focus* to treat couples, suggests that many, if not most of these sexual dysfunctions may be curable or greatly improved in a short period of time.

QUESTIONS FOR CRITICAL THINKING

1. Why do you think sex-reassignment is the only therapy that is effective for treating transsexuals? Do you think that those who undergo such surgery are ultimately happier and more adjusted after the surgery?

2. What are the implications of LeVay's study of the brains of homosexual men, heterosexual men, and heterosexual women for societal attitudes toward homosexuality?

3. Describe how the notion of preparedness can be applied to the paraphilias.

4. Why do you think young children categorize the world according to sex and organize their lives around these categories? Why do rigid sex-role stereotypes often weaken with maturity?

CHAPTER 14

Psychoactive Substance Use Disorders

Ann E. Kelley

CHAPTER ORGANIZER

DIAGNOSING AND DEFINING DRUG ABUSE
- Learn how the social and cultural context of drug use affects definitions of addiction or dependence, and how DSM-IV and WHO currently define psychoactive substance dependence.

SUBSTANCE DEPENDENCE
- Be able to describe the basic effects of drugs and several theories and models of drug dependence.

ALCOHOL
- Learn about the effects of alcohol and the factors that predispose an individual to alcoholism.

STIMULANTS
- Familiarize yourself with the effects of the stimulants, including how they activate the brain's central reinforcement system.

OPIATES (NARCOTICS)
- Be able to describe the effects of the opiates and how the brain contains its own neurotransmitters and receptors that are similar to the opiate drugs.

HALLUCINOGENS
- Learn about the hallucinogens, including LSD, PCP, and MDMA.

MARIJUANA
- Familiarize yourself with the effects of marijuana.

NICOTINE AND CIGARETTE SMOKING
- Be able to describe the effects of nicotine and theories and treatments of nicotine dependence.

SEDATIVE-HYPNOTICS AND TRANQUILIZERS (BARBITURATES, BENZODIAZEPINES)
- Learn about the psychological and physical effects of the barbiturates and benzodiazepines.

FUTURE DIRECTIONS IN TREATMENT AND PREVENTION OF SUBSTANCE ABUSE
- Become aware of current and potential efforts to combat drug dependence, including law enforcement, drug abuse education, treatment programs, and research.

Humans have used drugs for thousands of years, to cure diseases, alleviate pain, and relieve mental suffering. People have often sought, in the words of Shakespeare, "some sweet oblivious antidote" to the hardships of living *(Macbeth)*. But the role of psychoactive drugs in our present society is very complex and often associated with highly charged, emotional debate. People use psychoactive drugs to alter their mental states; for example, such drugs can improve mood, cause euphoria, alter perception, or reduce anxiety. Explanations and theories of drug use have emerged from many fields of study, including medicine, psychiatry, psychology, law, and biology (Babor, 1990). There are many aspects of drug-taking behavior that we do not understand despite considerable research efforts, and many paradoxes in terms of the way our society views drugs. For example, it is generally accepted that nicotine is highly addictive, yet we probably would refrain from calling a smoker a drug addict. Alcoholism is one of the most clear examples of drug dependence, yet many people drink alcohol throughout their lives with no dependence problem. People have little problem condoning the benefits of drugs to treat physical diseases, and yet the use of drugs to treat mental conditions is still associated with controversy.

Substance abuse is *the* major health problem in the United States. The costs to society in terms of death, disease, and injury attributable to alcohol and nicotine abuse alone are enormous, and the emotional toll on the lives of abusers and their families is immeasurable. Abuse of alcohol, cigarettes, and other drugs results in nearly $200 billion annually in economic costs to society, a truly staggering number. Yet paradoxically, our society tacitly condones drug use, since the two drugs that cause the most suffering, alcohol and nicotine, are the ones that are legal. Why do people risk their lives to abuse these substances and what makes society seemingly blind to these problems? In this chapter, we will explore these questions and examine the powerful motivating properties of drugs.

DIAGNOSING AND DEFINING DRUG ABUSE

In the context of abnormal behavior, it is important to focus our discussion on the abnormal or *excessive* use of drugs. In our society, the use of certain psychoactive substances, such as coffee or moderate amounts of alcohol, is considered normal and appropriate behavior. When does drug taking become inappropriate and maladaptive? How do we actually define drug abuse? These are difficult questions that have posed a considerable challenge to mental health professionals, and the definitions and diagnoses have changed over the decades. Like many psychiatric disorders for which there is no obvious physical abnormality or laboratory diagnostic test, what actually constitutes dependence is somewhat a matter of opinion, and often controversial.

Historical Concepts of Drug Use and Dependence

Consideration of the historical and cultural aspects of drug use provides a useful framework for current concepts of substance use disorders. How a society views use of a particular drug has an important influence on how we might attempt to define addiction or dependence. People have used mind-altering drugs for centuries for social, religious, medicinal, and recreational purposes. For example, opium has been used in various societies for over 3,000 years. In the nineteenth century in this country and in England, various opium preparations were widely available and used, even for children. Middle-class consumption of opium was very common, and it was not considered a major social problem or an "addiction." It was only later in this century that use of opiates came to be associated with addiction, crime, and moral degeneration. Hallucinogenic drugs too have been viewed in different ways depending on the societal context. Plants containing powerful hallucinogens have been used for reli-

FOCUS QUESTIONS

1. What does it mean to say that drug-taking behavior can best be understood in terms of "drugs, set, and setting"?
2. Describe the three characteristics of the DSM-IV criteria for psychoactive substance dependence.
3. How does the World Health Organization define the dependence syndrome?

gious, ritual, or ceremonial purposes by many primitive societies (Schultes, 1987). Alcohol has also had mixed reviews, depending on the culture or the historical period. During Prohibition in this country, in the 1920s, manufacture and sale of alcohol was illegal. It was widely believed at that time that alcohol was associated with debauchery and weak moral character. Today alcohol is not only legal and widely available, but also associated with many positive features as displayed in many beer and wine commercials. These examples illustrate the point that the social and cultural context of drug use is an important part of understanding addiction. Addiction researcher Norman Zinberg emphasized that drug-taking behavior best be understood in terms of "drugs, set, and setting," meaning that it is the *interactions* between the chemical substance, personality or individual characteristics, and social setting that determine controlled use or compulsive, destructive use of a drug (Zinberg, 1984).

The concept of addiction has undergone considerable evolution throughout recent history. Central to the development of this notion has been the role of volition or "will" of the addicted individual and personal responsibility. Before the nineteenth century, addictions were generally considered as vice, sin, or moral failings. Certainly it was recognized that addictive substances led to undesirable "habits," but it was generally thought that drinking was something over which the individual had final control; that is, that drinking to excess was an individual choice.

The notion that alcoholism (and eventually, drug addiction) was more like a disease than willful immoral behavior has its roots in the nineteenth century. Thomas Trotter wrote in 1804 that "the habit of drunkenness is a disease of the mind." In 1791, Benjamin Rush argued that drunkenness began as an act of free will but descended into a disease or "derangement of the will" (cited in Berridge, 1990).

In this century, the **medical model** of alcoholism and other drug addictions has been most influential. The addict is viewed as a victim or patient with a disease, in need of medical or psychiatric treatment. It should be noted that the disease theory of dependence has its detractors. For example, Stanton Peele has argued that the disease concept has actually caused addictive behavior to increase because it excuses uncontrolled behaviors and allows people to interpret their lack of control as the expression of a disease they can do nothing about (Peele, 1985).

DSM-IV Criteria

Traditionally, the appearance of a physical withdrawal syndrome was essential in determining if someone was "addicted" to a substance. For example, some years ago cocaine was not thought to be addictive because users experienced no apparent withdrawal syndrome during abstinence from the drug. Today, physical signs of addiction are still important but not necessary for diagnosis. The DSM-IV criteria for psychoactive substance dependence emphasize clusters of symptoms or behavioral manifestations that clearly indicate distress or disability. These criteria, which are listed in Box 14–1, reflect behavioral changes that would be considered as extremely undesirable in all cultures. There are three basic characteristics to this set of criteria: (1) loss of control over the use of the substance; (2) impairment in daily functioning and continued use of substance despite adverse consequences; and (3) physical or emo-

Box 14–1

SUBSTANCE USE DISORDERS

Substance Dependence

A maladaptive pattern of substance use, leading to clinically significant impairment or distress, as manifested by three (or more) of the following, occurring at any time in the same twelve-month period:

(1) tolerance, as defined by either of the following:

   (a) a need for markedly increased amounts of the substance to achieve intoxication or desired effect

   (b) markedly diminished effect with continued use of the same amount of the substance

(2) withdrawal, as manifested by either:

   (a) the characteristic withdrawal syndrome for the substance (refer to Criteria A and B or the criteria sets for withdrawal from the specific substances)

   (b) the same (or a closely related) substance is taken to relieve or avoid withdrawal symptoms

(3) the substance is often taken in larger amounts or over a longer period than was intended

(4) there is a persistent desire or unsuccessful efforts to cut down or control substance use

(5) a great deal of time is spent in activities necessary to obtain the substance (e.g., visiting multiple doctors or driving long distances), use the substance (e.g., chain-smoking), or recover from its effects

(6) important social, occupational, or recreational activities are given up or reduced because of substance use

(7) the substance use is continued despite knowledge of having a persistent or recurrent physical or psychological problem that is likely to have been caused or exacerbated by the substance (e.g., current cocaine use despite recognition of cocaine-induced depression, or continued drinking despite recognition that an ulcer was made worse by alcohol consumption)

Substance Abuse

A. A maladaptive pattern of substance use leading to clinically significant impairment or distress, as manifested by one (or more) of the following, occurring within a twelve-month period:

   (1) recurrent substance use resulting in a failure to fulfill major role obligations at work, school, or home (e.g., repeated absences or poor work performance related to substance use; substance-related absences, suspensions, or expulsions from school; neglect of children or household)

   (2) recurrent substance use in situations in which it is physically hazardous (e.g., driving an automobile or operating a machine when impaired by substance use)

   (3) recurrent substance-related legal problems (e.g., arrests for substance-related disorderly conduct)

   (4) continued substance use despite having persistent or recurrent social or interpersonal problems caused or exacerbated by the effects of the substance (e.g., arguments with spouse about consequences of intoxication, physical fights)

B. The symptoms have never met the criteria for Substance Dependence for this class of substance.

SOURCE: DSM-IV, 1994.

---

tional adaptation to the drug, such as in the development of tolerance or a withdrawal syndrome. It is sometimes helpful to think of the essentials of drug dependence being defined by the "three C's": loss of control regarding drug use, continued use in the face of adverse consequences, and compulsion (or need) to use the drug (Shaffer and Jones, 1985). The criteria for substance abuse, also shown in Box 14–1, reflect a maladaptive, harmful pattern of drug use but do not include physical dependence or compulsive use.

WHO Definition

The problem of defining drug abuse has also been considered by the World Health Organization (WHO) from the point of view of public health policy. The WHO model was instrumental in formulating the "dependence syndrome" concept, which has gradually come to replace the terms "drug addiction" and "drug abuse." In 1981, the WHO committee defined the dependence syndrome as "a cluster of physiological, behavioral, and cognitive phenomena in which the use of a substance or a class of substances takes on a much higher priority for a given individual than other behaviors that once had higher value. A central descriptive characteristic of the dependence syndrome is the desire (often strong, sometimes overpowering) to take drugs, alcohol or tobacco" (Edwards, Arif, and Hodgson, 1981). This model also emphasizes the high frequency of maladaptive behaviors, loss of control, and neglect of alternative pleasures or interests in favor of substance use. Incorporated into the WHO definition is the concept of neuroadaptation, in which the constant presence of the drug somehow induces long-lasting changes in the brain.

As is clear from both the DSM-IV and WHO criteria, modern concepts of drug dependence tend to emphasize the *behavior* of the individual and the adverse consequences of such behavior; they do not attempt to explain the dependence. These definitions fall within the framework of psychiatry and public health, and reflect current society's general acceptance of drug dependence as a medical problem or disease.

SUBSTANCE DEPENDENCE

Many people have experimented with psychoactive drugs, yet only a small proportion go on to become drug abusers. What are the factors that determine or contribute to the development of addiction? Why is relapse to drug use so pervasive, despite months or years of abstinence? Many individuals undergo detoxification and stop using drugs for an extended period of time, and yet revert to drug use at some future point. Recidivism rates are high even among people who are motivated and have the resources to get treatment. Noted alcoholism researcher George Vaillant remarked, ". . . to a remarkable degree, relapse to drugs is independent of conscious free will and motivation" (Vaillant, 1992). Figure 14–1 shows a remarkably similar pattern across a spectrum of addictive behaviors. Nearly 80 percent of people relapse following treatment, a rather discouraging figure. We will first discuss the basic effects of drugs, and then go on to an examination of theoretical models of drug dependence.

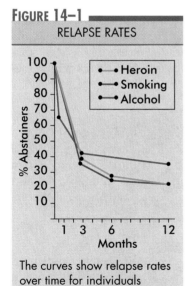

FIGURE 14–1

RELAPSE RATES

The curves show relapse rates over time for individuals treated for heroin, smoking, and alcohol addiction. (SOURCE: Hunt, Barnett, and Branch, 1971)

Basic Effects of Drugs

It is useful to consider what we mean by the term "drug." A drug is any chemical substance that has the ability to alter a biological system. The drugs we discuss in this chapter are psychoactive drugs, which affect brain function, mood, and behavior. Although different drugs often have very different effects on the brain, they also share many common properties and characteristics. Thus, the effectiveness and potency (the amount of a drug that must be given in order to obtain a particular response) of all drugs are influenced by: (1) the route of administration, (2) the ability of the drug to enter the brain, (3) how well a drug interacts with receptors in the brain, and (4) how quickly the drug is deactivated.

ROUTE OF ADMINISTRATION

For a drug to affect mental states, it must first reach the brain. All drugs are carried into the brain via the circulatory system, or blood supply to the brain.

1. What is meant by the term "drug"?
2. Describe how different routes of administration of drugs and lipid (fat) solubility of the drug affect how quickly the drug will reach the brain.
3. How do psychoactive drugs affect the chemistry and activity of the brain?
4. Define the following terms:
   • blood-brain barrier
   • neuroadaptation
   • tolerance
   • physical dependence
   • withdrawal syndrome

There are different ways that people deliver or administer drugs to achieve this purpose. Understanding these different routes is important because very often the route of administration determines how much of the drug reaches the brain, how quickly a drug effect occurs, and in some cases, the actual subjective response to the drug. For example, in smokers, nicotine enters the body through inhalation. The surface area of the lungs is great and in close contact with the circulatory system. Thus, relatively large amounts of nicotine enter the blood and hence the brain rather quickly. In smokers trying to quit, nicotine gum is often ineffective in reducing the "craving" because oral delivery of nicotine does not produce the same subjective or physiological effects as smoking nicotine. If a drug is taken orally (for example, alcohol) it must first pass through the gastrointestinal tract where it will slowly be absorbed into the circulatory system. Drugs taken this way are also absorbed by the liver, which has enzymes that may deactivate the drug. Thus, drugs taken orally often reach the brain slowly and in relatively low concentrations. In contrast, direct injection of the drug into a vein (known as "mainlining" in street jargon) would result in the drug reaching the brain quite quickly. This is a route preferred by many heroin addicts. Other routes of administration include intranasal and intraoral delivery, in which the drug is absorbed through the lining of these tissues into the circulatory system. An example of intraoral drug delivery is that of chewing tobacco.

LIPID SOLUBILITY

All drugs must cross several biological membranes (for example, the stomach lining or the capillaries in the lungs) before reaching their target, the brain. *Lipid (fat) solubility* is an important factor in whether and how fast a drug reaches the brain. Since cell membranes are composed primarily of fatty substances, a relatively more lipid soluble drug will be absorbed more quickly. For example, a small chemical modification of morphine results in heroin, which is considerably more lipid soluble than morphine. Heroin is preferred to morphine by opiate addicts because it reaches the brain more quickly and in higher concentrations. Certain general anesthetics are highly lipid soluble, reaching the brain and causing loss of consciousness within a matter of seconds.

BLOOD-BRAIN BARRIER

The most important membrane or "barrier" that a drug must cross to exert a psychoactive effect is the *blood-brain barrier.* This barrier is composed of specialized cells that prevent certain compounds in the circulatory system from entering the brain. It allows certain drugs to pass through and affect brain cells, and excludes others, depending on the size and chemical characteristics of the drug molecule.

DRUG-RECEPTOR-NEUROTRANSMITTER INTERACTIONS

All psychoactive drugs have various effects upon neurotransmitter systems in the brain. The brain contains many different types of transmitters, all of which are important for the brain's chemical signaling mechanisms. One principal way for a drug to have a psychoactive effect is to interact with receptors in the brain. Receptors are complex protein molecules embedded in the membranes of neurons. Normally they help to conduct messages by recognizing a specific neurotransmitter much the way a lock fits a certain key. The neurotransmitter

FIGURE 14–2

SYNAPTIC SITES OF ACTION OF PSYCHOACTIVE DRUGS

Drugs can cause neurotransmitter molecules to leak out of vesicles (A); crowd neurotransmitters out of storage vesicles (B); block release of neurotransmitter into the synapse (C); inhibit enzymes that synthesize the neurotransmitter (D); block neurotransmitter reuptake (E); block enzymes that degrade neurotransmitters (F); bind to postsynaptic receptors and either mimic or block the action of the neurotransmitter (G). (SOURCE: Snyder, 1986, p. 15)

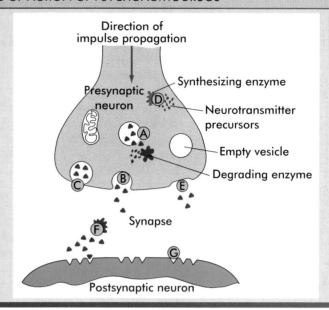

molecule activates the receptor and causes a biological response, such as stimulating or inhibiting the neuron. Drugs mimic neurotransmitters by interacting with the brain's receptor molecules. There are a number of ways that drugs can do this, and different drugs have different effects at the synapse, which is the gap between two communicating neurons. There are several basic mechanisms that are common to all synapses, as shown in Figure 14–2. A neurotransmitter must be synthesized from basic building blocks such as amino acids. It then is stored in vesicles within the nerve terminal. When the neuron fires, it releases the transmitter into the synaptic space, where it can affect receptors on the postsynaptic neuron. After the transmitter has its effect, it is removed from the synapse via two mechanisms: reuptake, which involves the transmitter molecule being taken back up by the presynaptic terminal, and deactivation, which involves the breakdown of the neurotransmitter by enzymes. Thus, psychoactive drugs affect the chemistry and activity of the brain by interacting with these different mechanisms.

ADAPTATION TO DRUGS: TOLERANCE AND PHYSICAL DEPENDENCE

Neuroadaptation refers to the complex biological changes that occur in the brain with repeated or chronic exposure to a drug. Drugs by their very definition induce some change in the neurochemical environment of the brain; one exposure to a particular drug will cause a specific effect (for example, increased levels of a particular neurotransmitter). However, with repeated exposure, the body and brain often adapt to the presence of the drug. Through homeostatic or "self-corrective" mechanisms, the nervous system attempts to compensate for the effects of the drug. ***Tolerance*** is one form of this adaptation. Tolerance refers to a state of decreased response to a drug following prior or repeated exposure to that drug. Progressively more drug is needed in order to obtain the same effect. Compared with inexperienced drinkers, people who regularly consume alcohol often show a high degree of tolerance to its behavioral effects. Tolerance may be accompanied (although not necessarily) by ***physical dependence.*** Physical dependence is characterized by the need for the presence of the drug in order to function normally, and by the appearance of a withdrawal syndrome upon cessation of the drug. The ***withdrawal syndrome*** (also called abstinence syndrome) is usually characterized by observable, physical signs such as marked changes in body temperature or heart rate, seizures, tremors, or vomiting. Such a syndrome may occur, for example, following abrupt cessation of chronic heavy drinking. It is important to note that in some forms of dependence, such as that associated with cocaine or nicotine, the so-called withdrawal syndrome may not be easily observable; it may take the form of severe depression, irritability, or craving.

Theoretical Models of Drug Dependence

There are many approaches, ideas, and theories pertaining to drug addiction, and in this small space we could not possibly discuss them all. However, an overview of several theories or models that have been influential can provide a useful framework for understanding drug dependence. The most important point to keep in mind is that drug dependence is a complex phenomenon that results from an interaction of many factors. The goal is not to develop a unitary theory of dependence, but rather to understand as much as possible the psychological, social, and biological conditions that contribute to substance use disorders.

PERSONALITY AND PSYCHOLOGICAL MODELS

For many years it was believed that a so-called "addictive" personality existed. It was thought that substance abusers had some personality flaw that made them vulnerable to use and become addicted to drugs. Attempts to demonstrate an addictive personality empirically have not been successful. However, considerable research has examined the comorbidity of specific psychiatric disorders with substance abuse disorders. Antisocial personality disorder is the most prevalent coexisting psychiatric disorder among males with substance abuse disorder (Hesselbrock, Meyer, and Hesselbrock, 1992). Antisocial personality disorder is characterized by a pattern of irresponsible, destructive, antisocial behaviors beginning in childhood or early adolescence and continuing to adulthood. While the prevalence of this diagnosis is 2 to 3 percent in the general population, it ranges from 16 to 49 percent in studies of alcoholics, cocaine, and heroin addicts (Gerstley, Alterman, McLellan, and Woody, 1990). It is likely that antisocial personality disorder is a risk factor for the development of alcoholism and other addictive disorders. Why this might be so is uncertain, but it may be that such individuals are more likely to be exposed to drugs, to experiment more, and to ignore their adverse consequences (see Chapter 15).

Psychodynamic views have also contributed to psychological perspectives of drug dependence. The general notion here is that drug use is seen as a means to compensate for defective ego functions (Treece and Khantzian, 1986). Early views tended to focus on "oral dependency" and libidinal drives, but more modern notions view addictions as representative of major deficits in ego development and affect. Drugs are used to reduce painful emotional states

FOCUS QUESTIONS

1. Describe some psychological and biological factors that may put people at risk for developing substance dependence.
2. Explain opponent-process theory.
3. How do positive reinforcement models explain drug use?
4. Explain how psychoactive drugs may activate neurotransmitters and receptors that play a fundamental role in natural rewards.
5. What are "drug cues" and how do they induce craving for the drug and trigger relapse?

or as a defense mechanism in relation to an internal conflict. According to one user's view, "Cocaine was a way of numbing out feelings. . . . Being stoned is like having a layer between me and reality, like doing things with gloves on. I dealt with emotions by avoiding them" (Shaffer and Jones, 1985). Disruption of early life development, particularly regarding relationships to others may increase vulnerability. Need for drugs is also seen as reflecting object deficits; in this view, the drug functions as an external aid or transitional object in order to maintain a sense of well-being. If there has been little experience in developing positive relationships during developmental years, relating intimately during adulthood can be particularly stressful. The use of drugs to cope with the anxiety associated with intimacy, especially during adolescence, has been noted by several theorists (Hendin, 1974).

BIOLOGICAL VULNERABILITY

People may be at risk for developing substance dependence because of biological factors that may be inherited. Most of the evidence for this viewpoint comes from research on alcoholism. Children of alcoholics are four times more likely to become alcohol-dependent than people in the general population. This risk factor is true even for children who were adopted away from the alcoholic family into nondependent families, suggesting that some genetic predisposition may be at work. Of course, these findings do not mean that there are "alcoholic genes" but rather that certain complex genetic factors may determine a person's biological response to alcohol. We do not yet know what these factors are; but they may involve deficits or dysfunctions in certain neurochemical systems. In fact, one view of substance abuse is that it is a form of "self-medication"; people take drugs to correct (unknowingly) some predisposing biochemical imbalance in the brain. Certain psychoactive drugs might alleviate the emotional distress associated with such states.

OPPONENT-PROCESS THEORY

The opponent-process theory of acquired motivation has strongly influenced notions of addictive behavior (Solomon and Corbit, 1974). The idea of opponent process is based on the theory that systems react and adapt to stimuli by opposing their initial effects. Although the theory was meant to explain many types of acquired motives such as love, social attachments, thrill seeking, and food craving, it is particularly relevant to drug addictions. The theory is best introduced with an example, that of eating a potato chip. As we all know, it's difficult to "eat just one." After consuming one chip, the motivation to eat more increases. If the bag is taken away, the craving for more chips remains for a period of time and gradually dissipates. It is as though the pleasurable experience with one chip sensitizes feelings or needs that were not there before tasting the chip. The same phenomenon is true for psychoactive drugs. A desire or craving for a drug, which clearly did not exist before experience with the substance, increases with exposure to it.

The opponent-process theory attempts to explain this increased motivation to continue drug use. It is based on three important phenomena that are common to all drugs that produce dependence. First, the pharmacological effect of drugs following initial use results in a hedonic (emotional) state known as ***affective pleasure.*** Different drugs arouse different subjective states but overall these states are associated with positive affect. For example, alcohol may provide a sense of relaxation and relief from stress while cocaine results in feelings of arousal and energy. Second, with repeated exposure, **affective tolerance** develops. As we saw earlier, tolerance refers to the diminution of a drug effect with repeated exposure. In the present case, tolerance develops to the affective, euphoriant effects of the drug. The rush or pleasurable feelings are not as intense as they were with initial administration. In order to achieve the same subjective effect, the user needs to take progressively higher doses of the drug. The third phenomenon, which is related to tolerance, is known as **affective withdrawal.** It is proposed that this state, which arises upon removal of the drug reinforcer, is the hedonic opposite of affective pleasure. For example, heroin produces feelings of euphoria and calmness, while withdrawal from heroin is associated with dysphoria (discomfort), panic, and anxiety.

Solomon's theory is represented schematically in Figure 14–3. The positive emotions that are caused by initial drug use are termed Process A. The duration and intensity of Process A depend on several factors, such as dose, duration of action, and route of administration. Process A also stimulates a compensatory reaction or "after-effect" which is opposite to Process A, called Process B. There are many examples of compensatory reactions in biological systems. A neuron that is initially inhibited by a drug may increase its basal firing rate with repeated exposures, in order to overcome or neutralize the effects of the drug. When the drug is removed, the cell continues to fire at an abnormally high rate. In any case, the model assumes that the intensity of Process A diminishes over time and with repeated drug exposure and that Process B grows in strength with repeated stimulations. The subjective experience of these two states produces what is called **affective contrast.** With continuing drug exposures, the negative, unpleasant state comes to dominate and contrasts sharply with the memory of the positive state. Despite the fact that little

FIGURE 14–3

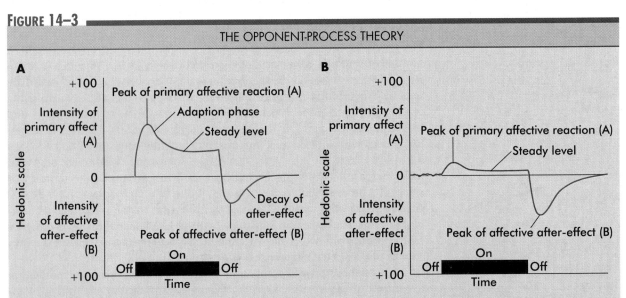

This figure shows the standard pattern of affective dynamics, based on opponent-process theory. (A) This graph shows what happens after the first few stimulations; this is the standard pattern produced by a relatively novel unconditioned stimulus. (B) This graph shows what happens after many stimulations; this is the standard pattern produced by a familiar, frequently repeated stimulus. (SOURCE: Solomon and Corbit, 1974)

pleasure is now derived from the drug, the cycle of addictive behavior continues in order to achieve at least a steady-state or neutral level.

The opponent-process theory is primarily based on the notion of negative reinforcement; people continue to take drugs and become addicted to relieve the withdrawal craving associated with B states. Moreover, the B state may be the affective expression of fundamental biological changes that take place in the brain with repeated drug exposure. However, this theory does not explain the motivation to initiate drug use when no B process is present, or why many people (and animals) engage in controlled drug use.

POSITIVE REINFORCEMENT MODELS

The positive reinforcement models focus on the pleasurable, euphoriant effects of drugs and posit that these powerful rewarding effects are the primary explanation for drug use. These models were developed in the tradition of behaviorism and operant psychology. Many years ago, it was found that animals would make an operant response, such as lever pressing, to obtain an intravenous injection of a drug. In 1964, Thompson and Shuster showed that monkeys would reliably give themselves morphine. This was a landmark experiment because until that time it was thought that drug taking was a uniquely human behavior, indicative of psychological or social stress. Soon after it was observed that monkeys would self-administer many of the drugs abused by humans: morphine, codeine, cocaine, amphetamine, pentobarbital, ethanol, and caffeine (Deneau, Yanagita, and Seevers, 1969). Most importantly, in that experiment it was shown that physical dependence was not a necessary condition for the animals to self-administer drugs. In the nearly thirty years that have passed since those experiments, a large body of research has confirmed that animals will self-administer nearly all of the drugs abused by humans, with the exception of hallucinogens. When given continuous access, the pattern of drug-taking behavior is remarkably similar for humans and animals. When given limited access, animals show stable self-administration without developing signs of toxicity or dependence. Such observations suggest that drugs are powerful reinforcers, even in the absence of physical dependence, and that a preexisting psychopathology or addictive vulnerability is not necessary for initial or continued drug taking (Jaffe, 1985). The self-administration model has been extremely useful for learning about the neurochemical systems involved in drug reinforcement.

The fact that many psychoactive drugs are powerful positive reinforcers raises the question of which brain systems are involved in their behavioral effects. For many years behavioral neuroscientists have studied specific brain regions and neurotransmitters that may be involved in both natural (food, sex) and artificial (drugs, electrical brain stimulation) rewards. Perhaps not surprisingly, many of the systems that are known to mediate natural rewards are also those affected by reinforcing drugs (Koob and Bloom, 1988). In particular, a brain region called the ***nucleus accumbens*** and the pathways connected to it have received a great deal of attention (see Figure 14–4). This nucleus, located deep in the basal forebrain, receives input from limbic areas that process information relating to emotion and mood. One of the inputs contains the neurotransmitter dopamine. Drugs that cause strong euphoria, such as cocaine and amphetamine, induce a large increase in the amount of synaptic dopamine. This occurs in a number of brain regions, but the increase in the nucleus accumbens appears to be critical for the reinforcing effects. Several

FIGURE 14–4

DRUG REWARD PATHWAYS IN THE BRAIN

The drug reward pathways (indicated in blue) are closely associated with the limbic system. The nucleus accumbens and the pathways connected to it mediate natural rewards and are affected by reinforcing drugs. (SOURCE: Adapted from Bloom, Lazerson, and Hofstadter, 1985, p. 148, and from Barnes, 1988, p. 416)

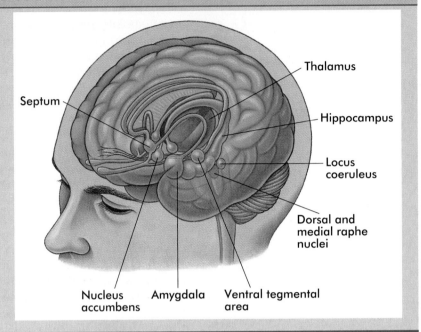

hypotheses ascribe primary importance of dopamine in the nucleus accumbens not only to psychostimulants but to a wide range of addictive substances, including alcohol, opiates, nicotine and barbiturates (Wise and Bozarth, 1987; Di Chiara and Imperato, 1988). For example, Wise and Bozarth propose that all biological reinforcers (including many drugs) activate a common neural mechanism associated with approach, or appetitive, behaviors. Di Chiara and Imperato implanted a probe in a rat's brain that can measure the amount of neurotransmitter released from nerve terminals, while the rat is awake and freely moving. All the drugs of abuse they tested, despite belonging to differing chemical classes, were able to activate the accumbens dopamine system. Other drugs not self-administered did not produce such effects.

Although activation of dopamine may be a common property of many psychoactive drugs, other neurochemical systems may also play a role. For example, the brain contains its own "morphine-like" substances, termed **endogenous opioids.** There are several types of opioid compounds, such as enkephalins, endorphins, and dynorphins, which are found in various networks throughout the brain. These compounds are released from neurons and activate opiate receptors. It is thought that the opioid system also plays a fundamental role in biological reinforcement and affect. For example, opioids may regulate food intake and the affective response to sweet taste, and they are also believed to mediate the response to emotional and physical stress (Lester and Fanselow, 1985; Kalin, Shelton, and Barksdale, 1988; Cooper and Kirkham, 1993). Opiate (narcotic) drugs such as morphine and heroin undoubtedly produce their psychoactive effects by acting on central opiate receptors, and alcohol may also involve the opioid system. It is interesting that opiate receptors in the nucleus accumbens may be particularly involved in the opiate "high." In animals trained to self-administer opiates, the reinforcing signal is reduced or blocked by infusion of the opiate antagonist naloxone directly into this structure (Vaccarino, Bloom, and Koob, 1985). Although dopamine and opioids are leading candidates for modulating the reinforcing effects of drugs, it is important to realize that psychoactive drugs have complex effects on many neurotransmitter systems.

CONDITIONING AND LEARNING MODELS

The pleasurable states that drugs induce and the relief they bring to aversive withdrawal states are important factors underlying drug-seeking behavior. However, as we have emphasized, the greatest problem in substance abuse treatment is keeping the individual abstinent. Weeks, months, or even years following successful detoxification, the patient may yield to uncontrollable drug cravings and may relapse. The conditioning and learning models provide a framework for understanding this aspect of substance dependence. These models embrace the notion that a drug is an unconditioned stimulus that becomes associated with many signals in the user's environment: sights, sounds, feelings, situations. These signals become powerful conditioned stimuli through their repeated pairing with the drug state, and may contribute to the reinstatement of drug-seeking behavior.

The acknowledged father of conditioning models is Abraham Wikler (1973). At the Public Health Service Hospital in Lexington, Kentucky, Wikler was observing opiate addicts in a group therapy session. These particular patients had been free of drugs for several months, and there were certainly no signs of opiate withdrawal. However, when the patients began talking about drugs, Wikler noticed that some of them began to show signs of withdrawal, such as tearing eyes, runny nose, sweating, and yawning. He labeled this phenomenon "conditioned withdrawal" and also noted its occurrence when the former addicts returned to neighborhoods where they had previously used drugs. Wikler suggested that through classical conditioning, environmental stimuli acquire the ability to elicit the signs of withdrawal. Moreover, these **drug cues,** or drug "reminders," induced craving for the drug as well and played an important role in triggering relapse.

There is much evidence, both from human studies and animal research, to support Wikler's theories. Charles O'Brien and his colleagues at the Addiction Research Center at the University of Pennsylvania have shown in the laboratory setting that presentation of drug-related stimuli to patients in treatment induces strong signs of physiological arousal and self-reports of drug craving (O'Brien, Childress, McLellan, and Ehrman, 1992). Their research suggests that conditioned cues elicit "drug-opposite" responses (perhaps similar to the B state in the opponent-process theory) that reinstate the overwhelming need for the drug. This may be true for a variety of psychoactive substances and situations. For example, passing a bar or arriving at a cocktail party may induce a strong desire for a drink (even in a social, moderate drinker), and the smell of smoke or sight of cigarettes can induce a strong craving in smokers trying to quit.

Learning processes may also govern animal drug-seeking behavior. Many years ago, Davis and Smith (1976) did an experiment in which rats were trained to lever-press for intravenous morphine. In some groups the morphine delivery was associated with a stimulus (a buzzer). These animals continued to lever-press vigorously even when the morphine was no longer available, as long as their responses resulted in presentation of the buzzer. The conditioned stimulus was controlling the drug-seeking behavior. Physiological conditioned responses have been shown in many studies by Shepard Siegel and colleagues, in which the usual drug administration ritual is presented in the absence of the drug (Poulos, Hinson, and Siegel, 1981). This work has demonstrated conditioned responses that are *opposite* in direction to the acute effects of the drug. For example, animals that have experienced repeated morphine injections, with their analgesic effects, show a conditioned hyperalgesic reaction (increased response to pain) during placebo testing. Animals that have repeatedly experienced alcohol-induced hypothermia display conditioned hyperthermia when given saline in place of alcohol. Siegel has labeled such phenomena drug-compensatory conditioned responses, and they have been shown to occur for many drug effects and many types of drugs. Such responses develop, as a kind of adaptation, in order to neutralize the pharmacologically induced homeostatic imbalance experienced in the presence of the drug. Cues that signal impending drug delivery can trigger these mechanisms. Drug-induced compensatory responses in animals may model conditioned withdrawal and craving in humans. Siegel also suggests that such mechanisms can explain drug tolerance, since the physiological effects of the drug would become progressively less.

ALCOHOL

For reasons that are probably social or cultural, we often do not classify alcohol as a drug. For example, people often speak of "drugs and alcohol," and the term "substance abuse" is used to include both drug abuse and alcoholism. However, alcohol is indeed a psychoactive drug with many of the characteristics of other drugs of abuse; it causes effects on the brain and behavior, and it has considerable potential for addiction and adverse consequences. In fact, if one excludes cigarette smoking, alcoholism is by far the most serious drug problem in the United States. At the same time, our society accepts and even condones its controlled use. Alcohol has a long history of this "love-hate" relationship with human society (Ray and Ksir, 1987). While in some societies, moderate alcohol drinking is considered by many as a pleasurable activity and an important part of certain social rituals, other societies or groups (such as certain religions) look upon it as an evil substance and ban its use. In American culture, odds are that fifteen of twenty adults drink moderately or occasionally and two or three of those twenty drink to the point where their drinking is a problem or compulsive (Grilly, 1989). Americans spend over $50 billion a year on alcohol products. Since its use is so pervasive, it is important to take a close look at this substance.

Effects of Alcohol

Alcohol is somewhat unusual in comparison with many other psychoactive drugs. It is not very potent, requiring several grams to exert measurable effects (most psychoactive drugs are effective in milligram quantities). A blood alcohol content (BAC) of approximately 20 to 50 mg of ethanol per 100 milliliters of blood is necessary for alcohol to have noticeable effects in most individuals.

▲ Psychoanalytic views of drug and alcohol use consider it a defense against painful internal conflicts. Perhaps Degas meant to suggest the same view in his painting *The Absinthe Drinker.*

This would be equivalent to a BAC of 0.025 to 0.05 percent. A BAC of 0.1 percent is considered to be legally intoxicating in most states. Alcohol is consumed as a beverage and is absorbed from the stomach and small intestine. The concentration of the alcohol is the primary factor in determining the rate of absorption, but other factors can influence the rate, such as food in the stomach or whether the alcohol is dissolved in a carbonated beverage. Food slows absorption of alcohol, and carbonation increases it. The amount of alcohol required to reach a particular blood alcohol concentration very much depends on the weight of the person and proportion of body fat. Alcohol is excreted in very small amounts in breath, urine, sweat, and feces, but over 90 percent is metabolized by the liver. Chronic users often suffer from liver damage, because the liver spends so much time trying to metabolize the alcohol.

BEHAVIORAL EFFECTS

Unlike most of the drugs discussed in this chapter, most of us are quite familiar with the behavioral and subjective effects of alcohol. People have used it for millenia to stimulate feelings of pleasure and relaxation, to quell anxieties and worries, and to increase their sense of self-confidence and power. From the psychopharmacological point of view, the effects of alcohol on human behavior and performance are complex and very much dependent on a number of factors, such as dose and previous experience with alcohol. At low to moderate doses of alcohol, most people experience a sense of relaxation and mild euphoria. Although alcohol is classified as a sedative-hypnotic drug, because of its obvious depressant properties, in low doses it can act as a stimulant. People become more talkative, more outgoing, and less constrained by social inhibitions. These effects are in large part due to ***disinhibition.*** Disinhibition refers to a state in which people do things they wouldn't normally do for fear of adverse consequences. The behaviors that are released from inhibition depend on the history or personality of the individual. For example, a shy, reserved person may become gregarious, or a normally passive person may become aggressive or belligerent. As some of us unfortunately might know from experience, people may do or say things under the influence of alcohol that they would never do when sober. There is a close relationship between the blood alcohol level and the nature of the behavioral effects of alcohol. A colorful description of this relationship is provided by Bogen (as cited in Ray and Ksir, 1987):

At less than 0.03%, the individual is dull and dignified
At 0.05%, he is dashing and debonair
At 0.1%, he may become dangerous and devilish
At 0.2%, he is likely to be dizzy and disturbing
At 0.25%, he may be disgusting and disheveled
At 0.3%, he is delirious and disoriented and surely drunk
At 0.35%, he is dead drunk
At 0.6%, the chances are he is dead

Higher doses of alcohol are associated with depressant effects and considerable impairment of sensory and motor functions. There are decreases in visual acuity and in sensitivity to taste and smell. Reflexes are slowed, and movement and speech may be sluggish. Reaction time is slowed by blood alcohol levels of 0.08 to 0.1 percent; complex reaction time tests, which require the subject to inte-

▶ High doses of alcohol debilitate sensory and motor functions, and severe withdrawal can be life-threatening.

grate information from several sources before responding, show that even at lower doses, both speed and accuracy are decreased (McKim, 1986). Memory processes are also disrupted by alcohol. Attention to stimuli, ability to encode new information, and short-term memory are all decreased. In heavy drinkers, "blackouts" may occur during periods of high consumption. As the name may suggest, these are periods where the individual has no recollection of events surrounding the drinking episode.

CENTRAL NERVOUS SYSTEM EFFECTS

Alcohol produces a variety of complex effects on brain function. In contrast to most psychoactive drugs that have relatively specific effects at the synapse, alcohol affects many neurotransmitter systems and many aspects of neuronal function. It has long been known that one of the principal effects of alcohol is a nonspecific interaction with neuronal membranes (Chin and Goldstein, 1977). The alcohol "dissolves" in the membrane and alters the physical state of the membrane lipids by making them more fluid. This in turn interferes with the ability of the neuron to conduct action potentials, thus reducing neuronal activity. The debilitating effects of high doses of alcohol on sensory and motor functions is largely due to this general depressant action. However, alcohol also affects a number of neurotransmitter systems, in particular the biogenic amines (norepinephrine, dopamine, and serotonin) and gamma-aminobutyric acid (GABA). Alcohol's influence on these systems may be related to its mood-altering, reinforcing, and anxiety-reducing effects. For example, alcohol enhances the inhibitory actions of GABA, which is the most important inhibitory transmitter in the brain (Nestoros, 1980; Suzdak, Schwartz, Skolnick, and Paul, 1986). Alcohol acts at the same GABA receptor complex as the benzodiazepine anti-anxiety drugs (Librium, Valium, etc.), and it is believed that this action is responsible for the anxiety-relieving properties of alcohol (Lister and Durcan, 1989; Koob, Mendelson, Schafer, Wall, Britton, and Bloom, 1989). Dopamine may be particularly involved in the rewarding and stimulant effects of low doses of alcohol. Dopamine levels in the nucleus accumbens are greatly

FOCUS QUESTIONS

1. Describe the behavioral and central nervous system effects of alcohol.
2. What are three kinds of tolerance to alcohol?
3. What factors predispose an individual to alcoholism?
4. Differentiate between Type 1 and Type 2 alcoholics.

increased in animals who have orally self-administered alcohol; moreover, in rats genetically selected for alcohol preference, this increase is much greater than in rats that do not like alcohol (Weiss, Lorang, Bloom, and Koob, 1993).

ALCOHOL TOLERANCE AND PHYSICAL DEPENDENCE

Tolerance develops to many of the effects of alcohol. In colloquial terms, someone who is able to "hold his liquor" is displaying tolerance to alcohol. There are several phenomena associated with tolerance to alcohol. The first is *metabolic* tolerance, in which the liver produces more metabolizing enzymes and breaks down alcohol at a faster rate. This mechanism does not account for most of the tolerance observed with chronic alcohol use, although it certainly contributes to liver damage. Behavioral tolerance and cellular tolerance are probably more important. *Behavioral* tolerance occurs when the individual learns to function under the influence of the drug. For example, there are some alcoholics who appear to work and perform activities normally at blood alcohol levels that would seriously impair most individuals. Behavioral tolerance can be demonstrated in laboratory rats. When given a motor coordination task (running a treadmill) under the influence of alcohol, rats quickly learned to overcome the disruptive effects of the drug. Yet, a group of rats given the same amount of alcohol after, rather than during, the treadmill sessions did not show any tolerance when tested under the influence of alcohol (Wenger, Tiffany, Bombardier, Nicholls, and Woods, 1981). *Cellular* tolerance, in which neurons adapt to the presence of the drug, can also be demonstrated. In the cerebellum, a region implicated in the motor-intoxicating effects of alcohol, neurons respond to intravenous alcohol by increasing their firing rate. However, this pattern of activation returns to normal following long-term exposure to alcohol (Rogers, Siggins, Schulman, and Bloom, 1980). During withdrawal from alcohol, there is a marked decrease in the firing rate.

Physical dependence develops quite rapidly with alcohol. In fact, anyone who has experienced a hangover after a bout of binge drinking has experienced a form of alcohol withdrawal. For this reason, there is actually some truth in the saying that drinking will cure a hangover. True physical dependence, however, develops with prolonged heavy use of alcohol, and the severity of the withdrawal syndrome varies with the level and duration of drinking. As is true with most depressant drugs, the withdrawal syndrome can be quite severe and sometimes life-threatening if not treated. Symptoms usually appear eight to twelve hours following the last drinking bout. Early symptoms may include nausea, weakness, anxiety, tremors, rapid heartbeat, and disturbed sleep. In severe cases, the syndrome progresses to include hallucinations, disorientation, confusion and agitation. In the worst cases, tremors, seizures, and severe delirium—known as delirium tremens, or the "D.T.s"—may develop within two to four days. If left untreated, the syndrome will subside in about seven to ten days (Jaffe, 1985). However, in most cases, alcohol withdrawal is treated pharmacologically to reduce the mortality rate and ease the symptoms. Several treatments, most prominently with the benzodiazepine drugs, are very successful in this regard (Bohn, 1993). Alcohol also relieves the withdrawal state at any stage. The obviously aversive physical and emotional aspects of withdrawal are strong motivation for the dependent individual to resume drinking, thus setting in motion the addictive cycle.

Defining Alcoholism

It is well recognized that alcoholism is a leading public health problem in the United States and in many parts of the world. However, defining alcoholism is not easy. Excessive alcohol intake follows many different patterns. We would all agree that the man who drinks to drunkenness every day, loses his job, suffers from liver problems, and experiences delirium tremens if he does not drink is an alcoholic. However, what about the high-powered, successful executive who has several martinis at business lunches and several more in the evening? Or the student who binge drinks every weekend but abstains during the week? Although there is no perfect definition of alcoholism, clinicians and researchers have tried to develop objective diagnostic criteria that attempt to encompass these different patterns of behavior. The diagnosis for alcoholism is based on the general criteria for substance dependence, shown in Box 14–1. In general, the individual diagnosed as an alcoholic has been drinking heavily over an extended period of time, and has consequently suffered from major multiple life problems. There is often compulsive drinking and an inability to stop although there may be repeated efforts to stop drinking. Consumption is often high, exceeding a fifth of liquor or its equivalent in wine or beer. Alcohol dependence can range from mild to severe. If there is recurrent drinking with adverse consequences, but the symptoms have not met the criteria for dependence (for example, no evidence of withdrawal or compulsive use), a diagnosis of alcohol abuse may be given. The following personal account illustrates the pervasive loss of control and physical dependence that characterize excessive drinking (cited in Orford, 1985):

> Although beer by day and liquor by night satisfied me while I [had been] busy . . . , now my nerves demanded more. I switched from morning beer to a jigger of liquor first thing after I awoke. It seemed a good formula. I improved upon it by pouring two ounces of bourbon into my breakfast orange juice so [my husband] was none the wiser.
>
> . . . I realized that I could never go out of the house again without liquor. Orange juice and bourbon in the morning was not enough. The physical demand was growing. I would need liquor most often—not because I wanted it, but because my nerves required it. Soon I was slipping down doorways, vanishing into ladies rooms, anywhere I could gain privacy, to take a swift drink . . . the two-ounce bottles graduated to six-ounce, and then to a pint, and in the last years of my marriage . . . wherever I went, I carried a fifth of liquor in my bag. (From Lilian Roth, *I'll Cry Tomorrow*)

Etiology of Alcoholism

Who becomes an alcoholic? Well over half the adult U. S. population uses alcohol regularly, but only a small fraction of those people become dependent. Half of all the alcohol drunk in this country is consumed by 10 percent of the population (Cloninger, 1987). There are many theories concerning the etiology of alcoholism. We can begin with the caveat that there is no one environment, upbringing, personality, or gene that causes alcoholism. Alcoholism is found in all socioeconomic classes and in all walks of life. As in all substance dependence, the development of pathological alcohol-related behavior is the result of the interaction of many factors. Research focuses on vulnerability factors—the factors that predispose an individual to alcoholism.

BIOLOGICAL VULNERABILITY TO ALCOHOLISM

There is strong evidence that alcoholism is a genetically influenced disorder (Schuckit, 1987). It has been known since the nineteenth century that alcoholism was associated with familial clustering. In this century, over 100 studies have shown that alcoholism is three to five times as frequent in the parents, siblings, and children of alcoholics as in the general population (Cotton, 1979). Research using rigorous methodologies suggests that the risk factor is a heritable trait. Given that identical twins share 100 percent of their genes and fraternal twins share only 50 percent, the rate of alcoholism in the identical twin of an alcoholic should be significantly higher than in the fraternal twin of an alcoholic if alcoholism is genetically based. In fact, twin studies provide evidence of the concordance rate being much higher in identical twins than in fraternal twins, although it never reaches 100 percent, suggesting that the heritability factor cannot be explained by simple genetic mechanisms (Kaij, 1960; Hrubec and Omenn, 1981). Adoption studies put any genetic hypothesis to the most stringent test, and here too the evidence is quite convincing. A study of Danish adopted-away sons of alcoholics revealed a rate of alcoholism at the age of thirty of 18 percent, compared with a rate of 5 percent in adopted-away control subjects (Goodwin, Schulsinger, Hermansen, Guze, and Winokur, 1973), and the amount of alcoholism in the adopted children of alcoholics does not vary with whether the adoptive parent is alcoholic or not (Goodwin, Schulsinger, Moller, Hermansen, and Winokur, 1974). A fourfold higher rate of alcoholism was shown in adopted-away daughters of alcoholic mothers (10.3 percent) than in controls (2.8 percent) (Bohman and Sigvardsson, 1981).

In view of the evidence for a genetic influence on alcoholism, researchers have attempted to identify a ***trait marker,*** or some observable, biological indication of the genetic predisposition. Marc Schuckit and his colleagues at the University of California at San Diego have studied populations at high risk for alcoholism for many years (Schuckit, 1984, 1987). This work is particularly compelling because the studies are of individuals who are at risk but who have not yet become alcoholic. The researchers analyzed reactivity to alcohol on a number of measures in two cohorts of subjects: those with a positive family history of alcoholism and those with a negative family history (no alcoholism). The subjects were carefully matched for other demographic, socioeconomic, and physical factors. The subjects were college-age, drinking but not yet alcoholic males, who were either sons of alcoholics or sons of nonalcoholics. The subjects were given alcohol at various intervals and were asked to rate the intensity of different aspects of intoxication, such as overall drug effect, dizziness, "high," etc. Although both groups developed similar patterns of blood alcohol level over time, the sons of alcoholics rated themselves as significantly less intoxicated following drinking a moderate dose of alcohol than the men with no alcoholism in the family. Moreover, when alcohol was given to subjects before they took a psychomotor test, the alcohol produced fewer bodily effects in the sons of alcoholics than in the sons of nonalcoholics. When subjects are asked to stand still, with hands at sides and feet together, the amount of upper body sway is normally increased by alcohol. Men with the positive family history showed much less body sway changes induced by alcohol (see Figure 14–5). We can interpret these results to suggest that people at risk for developing alcoholism may need to drink more alcohol to experience the same subjective effects as most people, and that a decreased sensitivity to low doses might make it more difficult for individuals to discern if they are becoming drunk (Schuckit, 1987; Pollock, 1992). Subtle EEG abnormalities have also been found in sons of alcoholics, even in preadolescent boys before they have ever had a drink (Begleiter, Porjesz, Bihari, and Kissen, 1984; Ehlers and Schuckit, 1990). Thus, brain wave alterations may also be trait markers for alcoholism.

To test the validity of these markers for alcoholism, it is important to show an association between the identified marker and the subsequent development of alcoholism. Utilizing a longitudinal design, Schuckit followed up the young men he had studied ten years previously (Schuckit, 1994). The men were now at the age of peak risk for alcohol dependence and abuse (average age thirty-two). Remarkably, it was found that a low level of response to alcohol at age twenty was associated with a fourfold higher likelihood of alcoholism in both the sons of alcoholics and the comparison group. For example, 56 percent of the sons of alcoholics with the low level of response developed alcoholism,

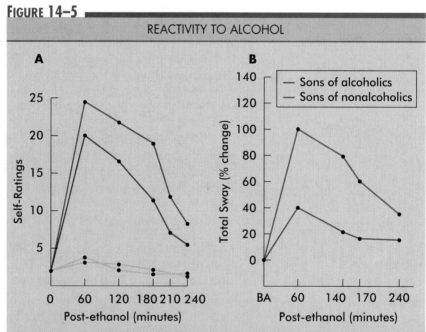

FIGURE 14–5

REACTIVITY TO ALCOHOL

The curves show the responses to a low dose of alcohol (0.75 ml/kg of ethanol; indicated in dark red and blue) and to a placebo (indicated in light red and blue) for twenty-three matched pairs of sons of alcoholics and controls (sons of nonalcoholics). Both groups developed similar patterns of blood alcohol level over time, but (A) the sons of alcoholics rated themselves on a scale of 0 (none) to 36 (great) as feeling less intoxicated following alcohol consumption than did the controls, and (B) alcohol produced less body sway changes in sons of alcoholics than in sons of nonalcoholics. (SOURCE: Schuckit, 1984)

compared to 14 percent of the men in this group who had highly sensitive alcohol responses. These results seem to indicate that a relatively low physiological and subjective response to alcohol may be a powerful predictor of future alcoholism.

PERSONALITY AND PSYCHOLOGICAL FACTORS

Psychological theories of alcoholism tend to emphasize associations between psychological or environmental variables and the development of alcoholism. One major problem with evaluating psychological differences between alcoholics and controls is that many of the differences observed could be due to the effects of years of drinking, rather than the cause of alcoholism. Therefore, investigators have attempted to study what factors predate the onset of heavy drinking and may predispose the individual to alcoholism.

As is true for substance abuse in general, a specific type of personality disorder has been frequently found to be associated with alcoholism. A diagnosis of antisocial personality disorder is a risk factor for the development of alcoholism, independent of having a family history of the disorder (Drake and Vaillant, 1988; Cadoret, O'Gorman, Troughton, and Heywood, 1985; Hesselbrock, Meyer, and Hesselbrock, 1992). In addition, antisocial personality affects the age of onset, the course, treatment response, and relapse in alcoholism. In a large sample of alcoholics, individuals with antisocial personality were found to have an earlier onset of drinking and a more rapid development of alcoholism once drinking began (Hesselbrock, Meyer, and Hesselbrock, 1992). The relapse rate is higher in these subjects compared with treated alcoholics without antisocial personality disorder.

Tension reduction has also been suggested to account for alcoholism. People drink to reduce anxiety or stress, and in some cases progress to abuse or dependence. Perhaps people who drink to excess suffer from high levels of anxiety or tension. Since alcohol has clear anti-anxiety effects, this hypothesis has much intuitive appeal. For example, clinical observations reveal a strong association between anxiety and alcoholism, and phobic patients report that they use alcohol to cope with their phobias (Mullaney and Trippet, 1982). Moreover, stressful life events are often associated with relapse to drinking (Marlatt and Gordon, 1985; Linsky, Straus, and Colby, 1985). However, the relationship between tension reduction and alcohol is complex. Although alcoholics and social drinkers report that alcohol helps them to relax and boosts their confidence, actual observation of the behavior of alcoholics while drinking reveals them to be anxious, depressed, and nervous (Tamerin and Mendelson, 1970). Although a relationship between anxiety or stress and alcoholism has not been proven, a recent study with rhesus monkeys suggests that early adverse life experiences may be associated with increased alcohol intake (Higley, Hasert, Suomi, and Linnoila, 1991). Monkeys who were reared in the absence of their mother (peer-reared) showed much higher levels of alcohol consumption later in life than monkeys who were reared by their mother. The peer-reared monkeys showed higher signs of stress such as increased plasma cortisol and increased fear-related behaviors. Moreover, acute stress (via social separation) in normal (mother-reared) monkeys increased their alcohol intake levels as well. This could represent a promising model to explore the environmental antecedents of alcohol abuse.

Clinical Subgroups of Alcoholics

Because of the complexity of the causal factors of alcoholism, researchers have attempted to define clinical subtypes of alcoholics based on genetics, personality, development and family history, and clinical course of the disorder. Many years ago, Jellenek (1960) proposed multidimensional typologies of alcoholics, based on differences in drinking patterns, and socioeconomic and cultural factors. Recent theories of alcoholic typologies have developed these early notions and have incorporated the interactive effects of personality, genetic predisposition, psychopathology, and drinking patterns (Cloniger, 1987; Bohn and Meyer, 1994). Cloniger reviewed studies of alcoholics that examined personality traits, antisocial behavior, criminality, and self-perception about alcoholics, and proposed two prototypic groups of alcoholics. Type 1 alcoholism affects both males and females (although women develop Type 1 predominantly), has an age of onset after twenty-five, and is associated with personality traits characteristic of persons with passive-dependent personality: high reward dependence, high harm avoidance, and low novelty seeking. This individual would typically be emotionally dependent, sensitive to social cues, apprehensive and inhibited, and not likely to engage in dangerous or disorderly behavior. Type 1 alcoholics can abstain from drinking alcohol but develop loss of control once drinking has been initiated, and feel guilty about their dependence. Analysis of adoption studies indicates that Type 1 alcoholism is "milieu-limited"; that is, its expression depends on both genetic predisposition *and* a family environment marked by heavy recreational drinking.

Type 2 alcoholism occurs only in males ("male-limited"), and is typified by personality traits opposite to those of Type 1: low reward dependence, low harm avoidance, and high novelty seeking. This individual would be impulsive, excitable, confident and uninhibited, and would tend to be socially detached and tough-minded. The Type 2 alcoholic has problems with alcohol before the age of twenty-five, drinks heavily and cannot abstain, and typically has experienced fighting while drinking, arrests, auto accidents, and other antisocial behavior. The risk of Type 2 alcoholism is high in adopted-away sons of Type 2 alcoholics regardless of environmental background.

It should be emphasized that these typologies are not discrete disease entities and that there is overlap between the features of each subtype in many alcoholics. Moreover, there may be other subgroups with differing features; for example, developmentally limited alcoholism occurs in socially stable individuals during young adulthood, and "negative affect" alcoholism occurs primarily in women with a family history of depression (Zucker, 1987). However, the acknowledgment that alcoholism is a heterogenous disorder with multiple etiologies and risk factors may contribute to better understanding of this disorder and improvements in treatment (Bohn and Meyer, 1994).

Treatment

The goal of treatment, as is true for any drug addiction, is prevention of relapse. Most alcoholics have tried to stop drinking and have remained abstinent for periods of time, but eventually relapse. Detoxification (the reduction and removal of alcohol from the body) is important initially in severely dependent

FOCUS QUESTIONS

1. What are the cognitive-behavioral model's three main strategies for treating alcoholism?
2. What is AA and what is its philosophy?
3. How can therapeutic drugs be used to treat alcoholics?
4. Describe four factors that may contribute to a positive outcome and recovery from alcoholism.

people, in order to treat the alcohol withdrawal syndrome. This is usually done in a hospital or treatment center under medical supervision. Following detoxification there is an active treatment phase. In general, rehabilitation for alcoholism utilizes the strategies employed to treat other behavioral or psychological disorders. These techniques may include psychotherapy, counseling, or behavioral therapy, often carried out in groups. Many programs emphasize development of coping skills, enhancement of self-esteem, behavior change, and finding strategies to cope with the possibility of relapse. The cognitive-behavioral model of treatment emphasizes three main strategies (Marlatt and Gordon, 1985): skill training, cognitive restructuring, and lifestyle intervention (see Figure 14–6). Skill-training techniques include teaching the patient to identify and cope effectively with "high-risk" situations in which the loss of control or threat of relapse is increased. Examples of such situations are negative emotional states (depression, frustration, anxiety), social pressure, or interpersonal conflict. The therapist's aim is to instill a sense of mastery or perception of self-control in these situations. This notion of self-efficacy is described as a kind of "I know I can handle it" feeling. Cognitive restructuring involves changing the individual's perception of violation of abstinence, or a "slip." If a relapse does occur, instead of reacting to the lapse as a personal failure characterized by guilt and internal attributions, the individual is taught "to reconceptualize the episode as a single, independent event and to see it as a mistake rather than a disaster that can never be undone" (Marlatt and Gordon, 1985, p. 59). The principal goal of lifestyle intervention is to develop ac-

FIGURE 14–6

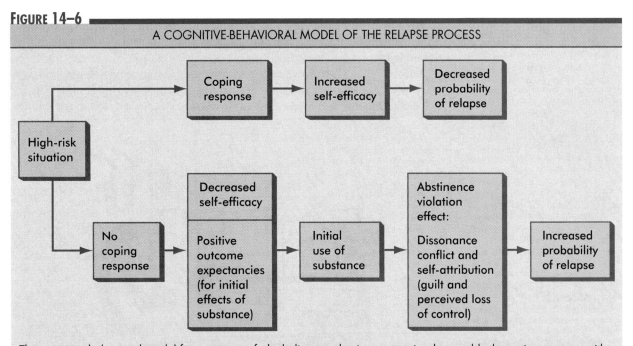

A COGNITIVE-BEHAVIORAL MODEL OF THE RELAPSE PROCESS

The cognitive-behavioral model for treatment of alcoholism emphasizes strategies that enable the patient to cope with high-risk situations. These include skill training, cognitive restructuring, and lifestyle intervention. When the patient uses these coping strategies, he is less likely to relapse than he would be if he had no strategies for dealing with high-risk situations. (SOURCE: Marlatt and Gordon, 1985)

tivities that offset sources of stress in daily life, or to replace negative addictions with "positive addictions," such as exercise, relaxation, or meditation.

Some alcoholics seek the support of the organization known as Alcoholics Anonymous (AA). AA is a self-help program that was started in 1936 by two recovering alcoholic men, and it has grown to be the world's largest self-help network. An estimated 800,000 alcoholics attend meetings of 23,000 groups in ninety countries (Goodwin, 1988). Its philosophy is based not upon scientific research but rather on experience gained through extensive work with alcoholics. AA views alcoholism as a progressive disease that cannot be controlled without the help of a higher being and the support of fellow members, and it believes that complete abstinence is required to deal with the disease. Education about alcohol and its consequences is provided, and testimonials of individuals with alcohol problems are shared.

DRUG TREATMENT

A further approach to the treatment of alcoholism is to use therapeutic drugs. Disulfiram (Antabuse) is a drug that inhibits the enzyme that aids the metabolism of alcohol. If alcohol is drunk in the presence of this drug, there is a buildup of acetaldehyde in the body and the person will feel very sick. The rationale underlying this treatment is that the fear of or prior experience with this unpleasant result will deter the individual from drinking further. It is frequently prescribed in treatment programs as an adjunct to therapy, although there is little evidence that abstinence is increased by disulfiram over the long term. However, disulfiram may lower the frequency of drinking in patients who have difficulty remaining abstinent (Bohn, 1993).

Recent clinical trials suggest that treatment with another drug, naltrexone, may be effective in reducing craving and preventing relapse. Naltrexone is an opiate antagonist that blocks or reduces opioid transmission in the brain. A double-blind, placebo-controlled study comparing naltrexone with a placebo indicated that naltrexone was very effective in reducing relapse and self-reports of alcohol craving (Volpicelli, Alterman, Hayashida, and O'Brien, 1992). The authors suggest that naltrexone may actually reduce the motiva-

"A GOOD THROW BY CAMPBELL, WHO IS IN A DRUG-REHABILITATION PROGRAM, AND IT'S CAUGHT BY SANCHEZ, WHO HASN'T HAD A DRINK IN SIX WEEKS."

tion to drink since it was particularly effective in subjects who sampled alcohol or had one "slip"; that is, naltrexone helped to stop the resumption of binge drinking typically seen in placebo-treated subjects. These promising results, which have been corroborated by other research groups, suggest that endogenous opioids may play a role in alcohol-seeking behavior (O'Malley, Jaffe, Chang, Schottenfeld, Meyer, and Rounsaville, 1992; Bohn, 1993). Moreover, they support experiments showing that administration of opiate receptor blocking drugs reduces alcohol consumption in animals (Volpicelli, Davis, and Olgin, 1986).

PROGNOSIS

How effective is treatment? What are the chances of recovering from alcoholism? Unfortunately, not very good. No single inpatient, outpatient, counseling, self-help, or drug treatment has been shown to reduce relapse rates significantly over the long term. When researchers evaluate treatment over a short period, like six months, they are likely to see positive results. Approximately 65 percent of people are still abstinent for this long after treatment (Seligman, 1993). Long-term studies reveal a different picture, however. A survey of hundreds of studies done on thousands of patients indicates that no one type of treatment is more effective than another, and most surprisingly, that treatment is not superior to no treatment (Emrick, 1982; Goodwin, 1988; Seligman, 1993). The most extensive studies of alcoholism and its course throughout the life cycle have been conducted by George Vaillant, a Harvard researcher who has followed a cohort of 700 individuals over fifty years (Vaillant, 1983, 1992). He has consistently found, as have other researchers, that about one-third of alcoholics recover whether or not treatment programs are followed. He states a "one-third" rule for alcoholism: by age sixty-five, one-third are dead or in awful shape, one-third are abstinent or drinking socially, and one-third are still trying to quit (cited in Seligman, 1993). However, Vaillant has also found that certain factors are strongly predictive of a positive outcome and recovery from alcoholism. These four factors are: (1) experiencing a strongly aversive experience related to drinking (e.g., having a serious medical emergency or condition), (2) finding a substitute dependency to compete with alcohol use (e.g., meditation, overeating, exercise) (3) obtaining new social supports (e.g., an appreciative employer or new marriage), and (4) joining an inspirational group (e.g., a religious group or AA). Vaillant finds a strong association between these factors and relapse prevention.

Medical and Social Complications

The medical and social complications of alcohol use and alcoholism are extensive. Measured in terms of accidents, lost productivity, crime, death, or damaged health, the economic cost of problem drinking in the United States is over 100 billion dollars annually (Jaffe, 1985). Drunken driving accounts for many motor vehicle deaths and injuries in this country. Alcohol intoxication is present in nearly half of all suicides, homicides, and accidents, and about 40 percent of all hospital admissions are alcohol related. Medical costs of alcohol and detriment to health form a long list. Cirrhosis of the liver, damage to the nervous system, heart, and digestive system, and cancer are all associated with chronic alcohol use. Chronic use of alcohol in pregnancy can result in ***fetal*** *alcohol syndrome,* in which the offspring has distinct physical and mental abnormalities. Sadly, fetal alcohol syndrome carries the costs of alcohol abuse to the next generation.

STIMULANTS

Although cocaine and amphetamine are the prototypical illicit stimulants, stimulating drugs are also found in coffee, tea, soft drinks, cigarettes, chocolate, and in many nonprescription medicines. If one includes all of these sources, stimulants are by far the most widely used psychoactive drug. Cocaine and amphetamine are the most commonly used illegal stimulants. Since cocaine is the drug most associated with medical problems and addiction, our discussion will focus mainly on this drug. In the mid-1980s, the National Institute on Drug Abuse declared it was the greatest drug problem facing this country. From 1976 to 1986, there was a fifteen-fold increase in the number of emergency room visits attributed to cocaine, in cocaine-related deaths, and in the number of people seeking treatment for cocaine addiction (Gawin and Ellinwood, 1988). At that time, it was estimated that nearly 3 million people used cocaine regularly. The number of people who had tried cocaine at least once in their lifetime rose from 5 million in 1974 to 22 million in 1985. In 1993, the National Household Survey on Drug Abuse* indicated that this figure had reached about 23 million, suggesting that although the number of new users had increased, it had slowed considerably.

Cocaine is prepared from the leaves of the coca plant, which grows wild and has been cultivated in South America for thousands of years. The custom of chewing the leaves by the native peoples of the Peruvian Andes dates back at least 5,000 years. The plant played an integral role in the Incan religious and social system, where it was considered a divine and highly prized plant. Incan corpses would have their cheeks stuffed with leaves, to "ease their journey to the next world" (Grinspoon and Bakalar, 1976). Cocaine was introduced into mainstream Western society in the last two decades of the nineteenth century, in various tonics, patent medicines, and remedies. In 1886, a Georgia pharmacist introduced what was to become the most famous drink of all time, Coca-Cola, which had extract of coca leaves. Cocaine's most famous proponent was Freud, who wrote extensively of its supposed virtues. He actually believed it could cure morphine and alcohol addiction! Not surprisingly, Freud struggled with a severe addiction to cocaine.

Amphetamine is a synthetic drug that was developed in the early part of this century as a treatment for asthma. In fact, it was a synthetic substitute for a drug called ephedrine, which was an extract of a plant used in ancient Chinese remedies. It was available for many years under the brand name of Benzedrine, in inhalant form for asthma. It was not until 1959 that the FDA banned the use of amphetamine in inhalants. By that time, however, the stimulant and euphoriant properties of the drug had become widely known. Vari-

*The National Household Survey on Drug Abuse, published by the National Institute on Drug Abuse, is a series of studies that provides basic information about the use of illicit drugs, alcohol, and tobacco in the United States. The 1993 report summarizes a survey of 32,594 individuals from the U. S. population conducted in 1991.

ous forms of amphetamines known as "speed" in street jargon, became very popular in the 1960s hippie drug culture. With the rising popularity of cocaine in the 1970s and 1980s, that drug became the preferred "upper" among drug abusers, and amphetamine use decreased.

Effects of Stimulants

Cocaine induces profound changes in behavior and psychological state as well as alterations in bodily physiology. It is administered in a variety of ways, but most commonly it is injected intravenously, snorted intranasally, or smoked in its free base form ("crack"). Cocaine has marked sympathomimetic properties, which means that it activates the sympathetic nervous system. It is a potent vasoconstrictor and increases heart rate and blood pressure. Cocaine may cause cardiac arrhythmias, which may have been the cause of sudden death in such cases as Len Bias, the basketball star who died of an overdose the day after he was drafted by the Boston Celtics. Cocaine also induces changes in mood and emotional state. In general, cocaine produces feelings of stimulation, well-being, vigor, and euphoria. Enhanced alertness, increased sexuality, heightened energy, and deepening of emotions may accompany the cocaine high. In contrast to some drugs, cocaine does not appear to alter perceptual processes or distort reality. It has been said that cocaine and other stimulants produce a neurochemical magnification of the pleasure experienced in most activities (Gawin and Ellinwood, 1988). In his autobiography Malcolm X wrote that ". . . cocaine produces . . . an illusion of supreme well-being, and a soaring over-confidence in both physical and mental ability. . . ."

There have been a number of attempts to quantify the subjective effects of cocaine in a laboratory setting. These investigations allow careful observation and quantification of drug effects in a controlled clinical laboratory setting, while minimizing the medical risks of cocaine. Sherer (1988) studied addicts during an initial intravenous dose of cocaine, followed by a four-hour continuous infusion. The subjects conducted self-ratings of two mood states, "rush" and "high," throughout the session. "High" was assessed using ratings of both "good" and energetic." This study found that ratings of "rush" and "high" were markedly increased by the cocaine infusion. However, "rush" was associated only with the loading dose of cocaine, reflecting perhaps the initial, rapid change in plasma (and brain) concentrations of cocaine.

It is clearly these positive properties that attract people to cocaine and underlie its addictive properties. However, cocaine can also induce negative emotional states and severe disruptions of behavior. High doses of stimulants can cause dysphoria and intense anxiety, and chronic use can result in hyperaggressiveness, complete insomnia, irritability, impulsiveness, and panic. Cocaine intoxication in extreme cases is characterized by paranoid psychosis and violent behavior. In the study by Sherer noted above, nurses blind to experimental treatment made brief psychiatric evaluations of these subjects following cocaine injection and found increased paranoia and suspiciousness.

COCAINE AND REINFORCEMENT

Cocaine is a potently reinforcing drug. In fact, of all the drugs that are self-administered by animals and humans, it may well be the most reinforcing. The cocaine addict will engage in behavior that entails extraordinary risks to health and social stability. The extreme desire to obtain the drug has been shown in animal studies of cocaine use. Rats and monkeys rapidly acquire self-administration behavior when given access to intravenous cocaine via a lever-press (see Figure 14–7). In fact, the pattern of drug-taking strongly resembles the bingeing behavior in human cocaine addicts. In a classic study by Aigner and Balster (1978), monkeys who had previously self-injected cocaine were given a choice between food and cocaine every fifteen minutes for eight days. The animals almost exclusively chose cocaine, resulting in weight loss and other signs of toxicity. A similar result was found by Bozarth and Wise (1985) in rats. Rats given unlimited access to cocaine lost 47 percent of their body weight, ceased grooming, and exhibited a marked deterioration in health. By thirty days, 90 percent of the animals had died. (Rats given unlimited access to heroin, in contrast, administered the drug but did not show signs of deterioration.) Such unlimited access studies are no longer conducted, but measurements in other behavioral paradigms clearly show the strong motivation that cocaine can induce. In the progressive ratio paradigm, an animal must make progressively more responses in order to obtain intravenous cocaine reinforcement. It has been shown that a monkey will make up to 6,000 lever-presses to obtain one infusion of cocaine (Yaganita, 1976). Thus, many animal studies have demonstrated that the rewarding effects produced by cocaine are indeed a powerful motivator of drug-seeking behavior. Moreover, studies in human subjects have indicated that people consistently prefer to press a lever that delivers intravenous cocaine rather than placebo (Fischman and Schuster, 1982).

NEUROCHEMICAL MECHANISMS

Since the cocaine epidemic reached its peak in the 1980s, researchers have confronted a fundamental question: What is it about cocaine's effects on the

FIGURE 14–7

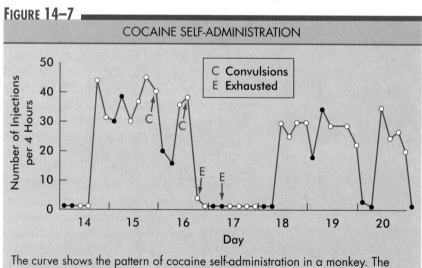

The curve shows the pattern of cocaine self-administration in a monkey. The monkey self-administered the cocaine for a period of 21 days. The graph shows the intake for four-hour periods for days 14 through 21. Note the periods of intake and abstinence. Also note that the bingeing and crashing pattern is similar to the pattern of cocaine intake in humans. (SOURCE: Deneau, Yaganita, and Seevers, 1969)

brain that makes it so rewarding and so addictive? Research suggests that cocaine and amphetamine are powerful activators of the brain's central reinforcement system. As we noted earlier, it seems that all drugs of abuse that are self-administered by humans and animals share an ability to activate dopaminergic synapses. However, most of these drugs, such as alcohol, nicotine, and opiates, have many other significant pharmacological effects. With psychostimulants, activation of the dopamine system is the *primary* pharmacological effect. Moreover, release of dopamine in the nucleus accumbens appears to be directly linked to the rewarding properties of these drugs. Animals that have undergone lesions of the dopamine projection to the nucleus accumbens are not interested in self-administering cocaine or amphetamine (Roberts, Corcoran, and Fibiger, 1977; Lyness, Friedle, and Moore, 1979). In view of the hypothesis that the nucleus accumbens may be critical for "natural" rewards (e.g., food, sex, positive emotions), the notion that cocaine amplifies pleasure may actually have a neurochemical basis.

Cocaine Dependence

Cocaine addition reached peak levels in the 1980s, and continues to be a major problem in the 1990s. In 1991, it was estimated that there were approximately 2 million regular cocaine users in the United States. Curiously, before the 1980s, cocaine was considered to be a safe, nonaddicting stimulant drug. This belief existed for a number of reasons. Before that time, cocaine was very expensive and its use was relatively infrequent. There was very little research on cocaine abuse, and there appeared to be no overt physical symptoms that would constitute a withdrawal syndrome. The spread of "crack" cocaine in the 1980s changed this perception. Crack (solid, free-base cocaine) was much cheaper than powdered cocaine and became widely available, particularly to the poor. The smoking of the drug leads to a rapid, short-lasting but profound euphoria that is extremely addictive. It rapidly became clear that the criteria for substance abuse disorder were easily met with cocaine. Compulsive use, loss of control, and a withdrawal syndrome began to be clearly recognized. Although cocaine dependence can occur with intravenous and (less frequently) with intranasal administration, it was the widespread practice of smoking crack that led to the cocaine epidemic.

Distinct phases of cocaine use and dependence have been described in detail by Gawin and Ellinwood (1988, 1989). Early experiences with the drug result in increased pleasure in many daily activities, and include heightened energy and alertness, increased self-esteem and confidence, magnified positive social interactions. The positive affective state induced by cocaine, combined with the relative lack of negative consequences, makes such early cocaine experiences extremely seductive. With repeated use, the dose of cocaine is often increased and the drug experience is intensified. Eventually, the user focuses on the intense euphoric, physical sensations produced by cocaine intoxication, rather than the enhancement of normal, external activities. Pursuit of this state becomes so dominant that the user begins to ignore signs of mounting personal problems. A number of factors may contribute to the development of compulsive "bingeing" behavior, in which the individual repeatedly administers high doses of cocaine. Increased availability and a switch in the route of administration (from intranasal to smoking) increase likelihood of dependence. The pattern of use at this stage is most often characterized by continuous bingeing followed by several days of abstinence. There is a complete preoccupation with the cocaine high and with obtaining more cocaine, and ". . . nourishment, sleep, survival, money, loved ones, and responsibility all lose significance" (Gawin and Ellinwood, 1989).

A "triphasic" abstinence pattern generally follows a cocaine binge (Gawin and Ellinwood, 1988). The first phase is termed the "crash," which lasts from hours to days. The crash is characterized by a sharp decrease in mood and energy, agitation, anxiety, depression, and craving for cocaine. There is an extreme need for sleep, which is usually met by the ingestion of sedatives, alcohol, or opiates. The next phase, "withdrawal," can last for many weeks and is characterized primarily by an intense dysphoric syndrome. Depression and anhedonia (inability to experience pleasure) contrast with memories of stimulant-induced euphoria and often lead to a repetition of the bingeing cycle. If the user continues to be abstinent, the third phase emerges, "extinction." During this phase, normal mood and energy are restored. However, the user may experience occasional cravings for cocaine for months or even years after the last binge. The cravings are usually invoked by stimuli or memories associated with the cocaine experience.

Treatment

The obstacles to successful treatment of cocaine dependence are similar to those for other drug addictions. Although motivation to quit cocaine may be very high initially, relapse is a major problem, particularly in the period when depression and anhedonia are present. A number of different strategies have been tried in treatment programs, with varying outcomes. These strategies include a range of psychotherapeutic techniques as well as pharmacotherapies. In one study, cocaine abusers were treated with desmethyimpramine (DMI), a commonly used antidepressant (Gawin, Kleber, Byck, Rounsaville, Kosten, Jatlow, and Morgan, 1989). This was a randomized, double-blind clinical trial. Both cocaine use and subjective craving scores were substantially decreased by the treatment. During the six-week study period, 59 percent of the DMI-treated subjects were abstinent for at least three to four weeks, compared with only 17 percent of a group on a placebo. The mechanisms underlying this effect are not completely understood, but they may relate to relief of the dysphoria associated with the cocaine withdrawal phase.

Although pharmacological strategies may be useful in achieving initial cocaine abstinence, counseling and intensive psychotherapy are important for long-term success. One promising clinical study reported marked success with a behavioral therapy treatment approach over a twenty-four week period (Higgins, Budney, Bickel, Hughes, Foerg, and Badger, 1993). Cocaine-dependent patients in an outpatient treatment program were divided into two groups. One group received behavioral therapy based on the contingency-management approach. Several times a week, patients' urine was screened for cocaine metabolites. If the urine was negative, the subject received points that were recorded as vouchers for future purchase of retail items in the community. The number of points increased with each consecutive negative urine specimen, or decreased if a positive specimen was noted. Individuals who remained abstinent for a twelve-week period could obtain nearly $1,000 worth of retail goods. This system was supplemented with the community reinforcement approach, in which a spouse, friend, or family member participates in counseling. The control group received standard drug abuse counseling based on the disease model of dependence. There was a marked difference in cocaine abstinence in these two groups (see Figure 14–8). The percentages of subjects in the behavioral and standard counseling groups who achieved at least eight and sixteen weeks of continuous abstinence, respectively, were 68 percent versus 11 percent, and 42 percent versus 5 percent. These results suggest that availability and emphasis of alternative rewards can increase the motivation of the user to abstain from cocaine.

Another treatment approach is based on the learning model of addiction. As discussed earlier, exposure to drug-related cues in the environment can trigger cravings and induce relapse even in long-abstinent individuals. These powerful drug-associated stimuli can elicit clear changes in physiological responses, such as in heart rate or skin conductance. When recovering addicts were exposed to cocaine-associated stimuli, an involuntary physiological response (lowered skin temperature) was induced. The aim of the treatment based on the learning model is to eliminate these conditioned responses through repeated exposure to drug-related stimuli in a safe, controlled setting. By repeatedly exposing the patient to cocaine "reminders" without cocaine, it should be possible to extinguish the conditioned responses (arousal, craving) that could lead to relapse (O'Brien, Childress, McLellan, and Ehrman, 1992). These researchers treated patients in the course of fifteen extinction sessions in

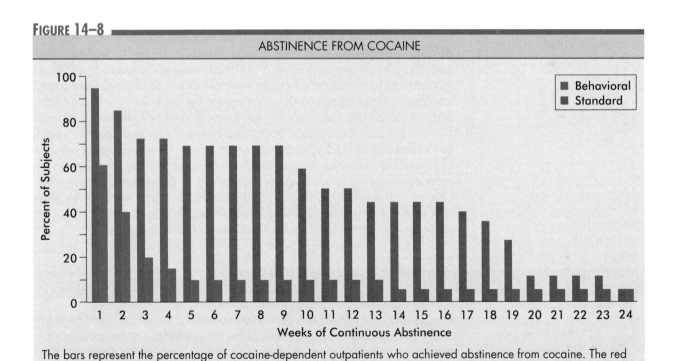

FIGURE 14–8

ABSTINENCE FROM COCAINE

The bars represent the percentage of cocaine-dependent outpatients who achieved abstinence from cocaine. The red bars are for patients given behavioral therapy based on the contingency-management approach. The blue bars are for patients given standard drug abuse counseling. (SOURCE: Higgins, Budney, Bickel, Hughes, Foerg, and Badger, 1993)

▲ Crack cocaine's low price and easy availability have contributed to a wide range of social problems, including affecting the fetuses of pregnant women who continue to smoke crack while pregnant. This woman later gave birth to twins, who were taken into a state agency's custody because the addicted mother was unable to care for them.

which the subjects were exposed to audiotapes and videotapes of cocaine-related stimuli (e.g., drug paraphernalia, someone shooting up) and engaged in a simulated cocaine ritual (preparation of drug, handling of syringe). Over the course of the extinction sessions, the craving for cocaine was reduced. Although the physiological responses were also somewhat reduced by the last session, they were surprisingly resistant to extinction. There was also a higher number of patients continuing with outpatient treatment and higher proportion of clean urines in the extinction group, compared with control groups (standard psychotherapy or drug abuse counseling).

In summary, for successful treatment of cocaine addiction, the cycle of dependence must first be broken. During the withdrawal phase, relief of depression may be aided by antidepressants or dopamine agonists. Behavioral therapeutic approaches may increase the motivation of the patient to stay abstinent. Extinction of the conditioned craving and physical responses elicited by drug reminders may be very important for avoidance of relapse.

Medical and Social Complications

The medical and social complications of cocaine use are considerable. Many adverse effects on the body occur with chronic use of this drug (as well as with other stimulants such as amphetamine). Heavy cocaine use can result in episodes of psychosis and paranoid behavior, profound irritability, and attention and concentration problems. Sleeping and eating patterns may be disturbed, and weight loss is common. As mentioned earlier, cocaine can have toxic effects on the heart and can cause sudden death. Death may also occur by cerebral hemorrhage. This is particularly dangerous because the lethal dose varies considerably among individuals; some people may be very sensitive to the toxic effects of cocaine. Panic attacks have been shown to be precipitated with cocaine (Aronson and Craig, 1986). Heavy use of stimulants by pregnant women may have adverse effects on the fetus, although the long-term consequences of stimulant use on the offspring are not yet known. In social terms, costs to individuals and to society are great. A cocaine habit can cost up to $500 a day, and most addicts resort to illegal activities and crime to enable procurement. The crack epidemic of the 1980s was associated with a substantial rise in violent crimes, arrests, and family disruptions. The most serious adverse consequence of intravenous cocaine use is the acquired immunodeficiency syndrome (AIDS). Shared needles contribute to the spread of the virus that causes AIDS. AIDS contracted in this manner accounts for the highest proportion of AIDS-related deaths in the heterosexual population.

OPIATES (NARCOTICS)

The opiate drugs consist of a class of compounds that are extracted from the poppy plant (Papaver somniferum), including opium, morphine, and codeine, as well as synthetic derivatives such as heroin and meperidine (Demerol). Traditionally, this group of drugs has also been called *narcotics*, after the Greek word for stupor. This term was originally meant to distinguish narcotic analgesics, drugs which relieve pain and cause sleepiness, from non-narcotic analgesics such as aspirin. However, this term is somewhat misleading since many laypeople and law enforcement officials refer to all addicting, illegal substances as narcotics. For the present purposes, we will use the term **opiate,** which refers to any compound that interacts with opiate receptors in the brain.

Like many of the psychoactive compounds, opiates have long been used in human society. In fact, use of the extracts of the poppy plant for its psychological and medicinal properties may date back over 5,000 years. These substances have been known for their ability to relieve pain and suffering, and they have played an important role in many ancient cultures. References to opium use are found in the writings of early Egyptian, Greek, Roman, Arabic, and Chinese cultures. In the nineteenth century, opium (in the form of laudanum, a potion containing opium) became an important part of the pharmacopeia in England and America.

While the pain-relieving effects of opiates were much appreciated, the dangers and addictive properties also became clear as its use spread throughout society. In the early part of this century in the United States, opiate drugs became illegal except through prescription. Heroin, the most commonly used illicit opiate, is not available even by prescription in this country (it is in Britain in certain circumstances).

Today, heroin addiction remains a major drug problem facing our country, although heroin use is far more rare than marijuana or cocaine use. The number of addicts who use heroin regularly is estimated at approximately 500,000, and this number has remained stable in recent years. Viewed another way, 1.3 percent of the population in the National Household Survey reported ever having used heroin, while 33 percent reported having used marijuana at least once. In the 1980s, drug users sometimes combined intravenous heroin and cocaine (the so-called "speedball"). Moreover, a recent phenomenon has been documented that suggests that highly pure, smokable heroin is making its way through certain middle- and upper-class circles associated with the film, rock, and fashion industries (Gabriel, 1994). It has been suggested that this is now the "chic" drug among such people much as cocaine was the cocktail of choice for the affluent in the early 1980s.

Effects of Opiates

The primary active ingredient of opium is morphine, named after the Greek god Morpheus, the god of dreams. Morphine is widely used for pain relief in medicine. Heroin is a semisynthetic opiate made by adding two acetyl groups to the morphine molecule. It was first made and promoted by Bayer Laboratories (the same company that makes Bayer aspirin) in 1898. It originally was marketed as a nonaddictive substitute for codeine. However, as use spread, it soon became apparent that heroin was the most addictive of all the opiates. The minor chemical modification makes heroin much more potent than morphine, because it is more lipid soluble and reaches the brain more quickly and in higher concentrations. Among the opiate addict population, heroin is the drug of choice. It is usually injected into the veins (intravenously), although it is also injected beneath the skin, which is known as "skin-popping." When injected intravenously, heroin is absorbed very rapidly and reaches the brain in a matter of seconds. Subjective accounts by addicts of the heroin high or "rush" describe a warm flushing of the skin and sensations described in intensity and

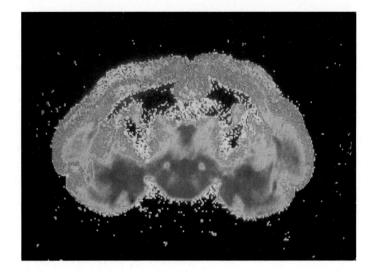

▶ This PET scan shows the distribution of opiate receptors in a guinea pig brain. Red indicates the highest density of receptors; yellow indicates moderate density; blue indicates low density; purple and white indicate very low densities.

quality as a "whole-body orgasm" (Jaffe, 1985). This initial effect lasts for less than a minute. Tolerance often develops to this euphoric effect of the drug. Opiates also can induce general feelings of well-being, calmness, and a sleepy dream-like state known as "twilight sleep." Feelings of anxiety, hostility, and aggression are reduced by opiates. Indeed, in addition to the pleasurable feelings they induce, the ability to blunt psychological pain may be an important motivation for taking these drugs.

PHYSIOLOGICAL EFFECTS

A number of physiological symptoms result from opiate administration, which is a consequence of the drug acting in several brain regions. The main physical effects these drugs have is to reduce pain perception. Opiates commonly cause nausea and vomiting, particularly with initial use. They also cause a marked constriction of the pupil, known as "pinpoint pupil." This sign is commonly seen in heroin addicts. Opiates slow the movement of food through the digestive tract and thus cause constipation. In fact, opiates have been used for thousands of years to treat diarrhea and dysentery, and they are still used for that purpose. Effects on the autonomic nervous system are more subtle than the effects of the stimulant drugs; there is not much effect on the heart, but the drugs do lower blood pressure and cause sweating. Although the initial subjective effect of heroin is likened to sexual orgasm, chronic use is associated with decreased sexual drive and sexual dysfunction. The most serious physiological effect is respiratory depression; respiratory arrest is the most common cause of death from overdose.

PHARMACOLOGICAL EFFECTS AND SITES OF ACTION

One of the most interesting aspects of opiate drugs, as we noted earlier, is the fact that the brain contains a system of neurotransmitters and corresponding receptors that are remarkably similar to the opiate drugs. The diverse effects of these drugs on psychological and physiological functions are likely due to direct stimulation of opiate receptors in many areas of the brain. High levels of enkephalins and endorphins are found in the brain in forebrain regions mediating emotion and mood, as well as in lower brainstem centers controlling autonomic functions and pain transmission. The subjective, pleasurable effects of opiates may be caused by stimulation of opiate receptors in limbic regions, such as the amygdala, nucleus accumbens, and hypothalamus (see Figure 14–9). Endogenous opioids are hypothesized to modulate a variety of affective experiences, in particular the response to stress. For example, administration of opiates to infant monkeys suppresses the signs of distress observed when they are separated from their mothers (Kalin, Shelton, and Barksdale, 1988). Thus, taking opiates may help to alleviate stressful psychological states by acting on the brain's own "coping" system. Animals will readily learn to self-administer opiates via intravenous injection. The reinforcing effects may be at least partially due to activation of opiate receptors in the nucleus accumbens, as noted earlier.

Opiate Dependence

Opiate dependence may develop in susceptible individuals in a number of situations. One pattern of drug use begins with recreational or experimental use, usually with intravenous heroin. First use is often introduced or encouraged by a drug-using friend, and with continued use a compulsive habit may develop. In this case the addict may need three to four injections per day, and obviously must obtain the heroin from illegal sources. Consequently, a great deal of time is spent trying to procure the drug. By far the most common group of users in this category are young males in poor, urban environments. There are several other patterns of use that are less common. There is a small subgroup of addicts whose dependence began with medically prescribed oral painkillers, and who continue to obtain them somehow. Moreover, the incidence of opiate dependence among physicians, nurses, and other health professionals is higher than in people of similar background in other occupations (Jaffe,

FIGURE 14–9

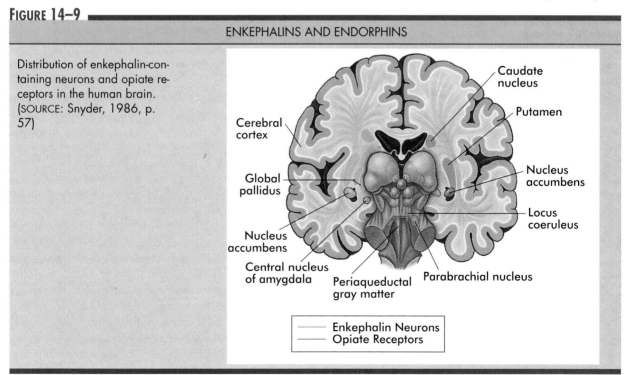

ENKEPHALINS AND ENDORPHINS

Distribution of enkephalin-containing neurons and opiate receptors in the human brain. (SOURCE: Snyder, 1986, p. 57)

▲ Celebrities who died young as a result of drug use: *(left)* Jimi Hendrix, *(middle)* Janis Joplin, and *(right)* River Phoenix.

1985). These groups have easier access to the drugs and may start using them for a variety of reasons, such as relief of a physical ailment or to alleviate depression.

TOLERANCE AND WITHDRAWAL SYNDROME

Opiate dependence may be associated with a high degree of tolerance and physical dependence. With repeated use, the dose taken by the user gradually becomes higher. After continued use of fairly high doses, some users can administer doses up to fifty times what would kill a nontolerant individual (Grilly, 1989). However, tolerance develops to some effects of opiates and not to others. For example, a remarkable degree of tolerance may be exhibited to the respiratory depressant, sedative, analgesic, nauseating, and euphoric effects while little tolerance is seen to the constipating and pupil-decreasing effects. Physical dependence is also classically associated with opiate addiction, and a withdrawal syndrome results in dependent individuals upon cessation of the drug. The degree of severity of this syndrome, however, very much depends on the type and amount of opiate taken.

There are several stages that characterize heroin withdrawal, which consists of clearly observable signs and symptoms that are in general opposite to those that are produced by the drug. It starts approximately eight to twelve hours after the last dose, reaches its peak at about forty-eight to seventy-two hours, and completely subsides in seven to ten days. At first, the addict experiences restless sleep, followed by dilated pupils, irritability, loss of appetite, and tremor. At peak intensity, the individual experiences insomnia, violent yawning, excessive tearing, and sneezing. Muscle weakness and depression may be pronounced. Piloerection, resulting in "goosebumps," gives the skin the appearance of a plucked turkey; hence the expression "cold turkey" given to signify abrupt withdrawal. Gastrointestinal distress, characterized by cramps and diarrhea, is also apparent. Dehydration and weight loss may result from the failure to take food and fluids and from vomiting, sweating, and diarrhea. The syndrome can be immediately reversed at any stage by readministration of an opiate. Gradually, the acute phase subsides although mild physiological alterations may be present for weeks. A common misperception is that the syndrome is always very severe and aversive; in fact, in most cases it is rarely life-threatening and seldom more disruptive than a bad case of the flu.

Nevertheless, avoidance of the dysphoria that accompanies this state is an important motivating factor for continuing opiate use, although it cannot account for initial use nor for relapse long after the syndrome has subsided.

DETERMINANTS OF OPIATE ADDICTION

It is not known what particular factors determine whether a person, once exposed to opiates, will become dependent. As is true with all drugs with abuse potential, some people can experiment or be exposed to opiates and not develop a habit, while others become addicted. Many factors, including social environment, drug availability, and psychological state may determine the pattern of drug use. One of the most well-known studies of opiate addiction was conducted by Lee Robins in the early 1970s, among returning Vietnam veterans (Robins, Helzer, Hesselbrock, and Wish, 1977). Heroin was easily available, cheap, and 95 percent pure in Vietnam during the war years (compared with 5 percent purity in the United States). It was estimated that up to 15 percent of the American troops were addicted to heroin. However, when the servicemen returned home, the vast majority stopped using heroin. It was found that only 1 to 2 percent were using opiates eight to twelve months after returning. This study was very surprising because at the time it was believed that once exposed to heroin, compulsive use was inevitable. This was clearly not true. Opiate use may have relieved the anxiety, boredom, or unhappiness associated with the war situation; the need for the drug decreased, however, when the person was removed from that environment. Another example of controlled opiate use exists, termed "chipping" in drug jargon. Heroin "chippers" engage in occasional heroin use, much as one might occasionally smoke marijuana or drink alcohol (Zinberg, Harding, and Winkeller, 1977). These people may have stable lives, jobs, and families, but nevertheless they may use heroin on weekends or with certain groups of friends.

Treatment

The problem of treatment for opiate addiction has challenged researchers and clinicians for many years. Although some compulsive opiate users eventually stop drug use on their own, most chronic users need some form of treatment or therapy in order to overcome dependence. There have been several approaches to this problem. In the 1960s, a number of therapeutic communities were established, sometimes by former addicts. Programs such as Synanon, Phoenix House, or Odyssey House are meant to provide a community of support while helping the individual to stay free of drugs. The philosophy of many of these communities is complete abstinence from all psychotropic drugs and, like AA, they believe that there is no "cure," just control of an illness. Group therapy sessions are meant to enable patients to face their drug problems and foster a sense of self-esteem and responsibility. While such an approach may be helpful in the short term, there is little evidence that long-term abstinence is achieved by these programs.

MAINTENANCE THERAPIES

For the past thirty years, the primary treatment for opiate addiction has been pharmacological. Maintenance or substitution therapy has involved substituting an oral synthetic opiate, usually methadone, for the intravenous heroin.

Methadone maintenance was first described in 1966 by clinicians at Rockefeller University (Dole, Nyswander, and Kreek, 1966). These researchers found that following rather high doses of methadone, heroin addicts reported a notable decrease in their craving for narcotics. There was also a marked decrease in heroin use and in drug-related crimes, and an increase in their general social functioning. Follow-up studies have supported these findings (Kosten, Rounsaville and Kleber, 1986). There are a number of reasons why methadone is preferable to heroin (see Table 14–1). First, it can be taken orally and thus intravenous injection is avoided. Second, methadone is longer acting than heroin and prevents the onset of withdrawal symptoms for up to twenty-four hours. Third, little or no euphoria is produced by methadone. Although there is an abstinence syndrome that results from withdrawal from methadone, it is less severe in intensity than withdrawal from heroin. Moreover, methadone seems to block the effects of heroin. Several studies both in the laboratory and in street settings have shown that the heroin addict does not experience the same rush or euphoria if he does take heroin while on methadone, probably because methadone is already occupying the opiate receptors (Kreek, 1992). Since the reinforcing effects of heroin are diminished and the unpleasant withdrawal state is avoided, methadone therapy is successful in getting users off heroin.

There are several other advantages to methadone treatment. To obtain methadone, patients must come to the local clinic daily and receive the methadone drink. Thus, the clinic provides social support and structure to the addict's daily life, and helps in limiting or removing drug-related, illegal activities. Kreek (1992) has noted that several factors are important for a favorable outcome in methadone maintenance. A well-trained, supportive staff providing diverse services tailored to individual patients increases the retention rate (e.g., the percentage of people remaining in treatment), as does use of an adequate dose of methadone (60 mg per day). She notes that there are approximately 100,000 heroin addicts currently in voluntary treatment in the United States. The voluntary retention rate in clinics varies from 45 to 80 percent, and at good clinics the use of illicit opiates while on treatment is less than 10 percent. The theory underlying such treatment is that once the individual is stabilized, he or she can be "weaned" from methadone with very little discomfort. However, on a more pessimistic note, the relapse to illicit opiate use among former methadone patients is 70 to 80 percent. In other words, once methadone is stopped, the chances of long-term abstinence are very low. These

TABLE 14–1

HEROIN VERSUS METHADONE		
	Heroin	*Methadone*
Route of administration	Intravenous	Oral
Onset of action	Immediate	30 minutes
Duration of action	3–6 hours	24–36 hours
Euphoria	First 1–2 hours	None (with appropriate dose)
Withdrawal symptoms	After 3–4 hours	After 24 hours

SOURCE: Kreek, 1992.

Box 14-2

Although intravenous drug use is associated with many medical risks, the most deadly is Acquired Immunodeficiency Syndrome (AIDS). The virus that causes AIDS, human immunodeficiency virus (HIV), is transmitted only by sharing intimate sexual contact or blood. Thus, intravenous (IV) drug users who share needles run a substantial risk of acquiring the virus. By the end of 1993, the total cumulative number of AIDS cases in the United States was approximately 183,000 (HIV/AIDS Surveillance Report). Twenty-four percent, or about 81,000 cases, were IV drug users, and 6 percent, or about 12,000 cases, were the sexual partners of IV drug users. As of 1992, there had been 35,000 total deaths from AIDS since 1982. Thus, it can be estimated that about 10,500 deaths due to AIDS in the past decade are associated with drug use. Women partners of IV drug users are particularly susceptible because the virus is transmitted more easily from males to females; moreover, children born to HIV positive women are also at risk. Since there are still no vaccines against HIV or treatments for AIDS, the only effective protection against infection in these high-risk groups is by behavioral changes. There is a critical need for education about avoiding promiscuous sex and the sharing of dirty needles. Unfortunately, it is particularly difficult to reach people very involved in IV drug use; their compulsive need for drugs often overshadows any concern about health and life-threatening risks.

SOURCE: HIV/AIDS Surveillance Report, U. S. Department of Health and Human Services, Centers for Disease Control and Prevention, Atlanta, GA, Vol. 5 (1993), pp. 3–17.

rather dismal figures once again underscore the extreme difficulty in remaining completely drug-free. Many methadone patients choose to remain on methadone indefinitely, which is certainly medically possible.

Medical and Social Complications

In contrast to certain other psychoactive substances such as alcohol or cocaine, there are surprisingly few medical complications or toxic effects from long-term use of opiates per se. Of course, use of needles is associated with a whole host of dangers, including the transmission of the AIDS virus (see Box 14–2). Moreover, women who continue to use heroin while pregnant run substantial risks to the health of the unborn fetus. Such babies may undergo physical withdrawal signs when born. Death from overdose, which can cause respiratory depression, can occur from opiates, but this is actually relatively rare. In fact, most deaths among addicts can be attributed to drug interactions or reactions to impurities or adulterants.

Social complications are another matter. Narcotics are expensive and illegal. It may cost over $100 a day to support a heroin habit. Although the drug itself does not increase aggressive or criminal behavior, many addicts must engage in crimes such as robbery or prostitution in order to procure their drugs.

HALLUCINOGENS

This group of compounds consists of a number of different drugs with varying chemical structures and behavioral effects. The feature that distinguishes these drugs from other classes of drugs is their ability markedly to alter sensory perception, awareness, and thoughts. In 1931, Lewin wrote about a class of drugs he called *phantasticants*, that is, drugs that could produce a world of fantasy. Other terms that have been used to describe these drugs are *psychedelic* (mind-expanding), and *psychotomimetic* (inducing a psychotic state). All of these terms refer to the ability of the drugs to distort reality and affect self-perception. Today the most common term for these drugs is **hallucinogens,** since they all have the ability to produce vivid and unusual sensory experiences. Drugs such as LSD, mescaline, and psilocybin are examples of such compounds. Use of hallucinogens is relatively low according to the National Household Survey. In 1991, 8 percent of the population reported using hallucinogens at some point in their lifetime, while 0.3 percent reported use in the past month.

Use of Hallucinogens

Most of the hallucinogens are derived from plant substances and are very similar in chemical structure to the biogenic amines in the brain (serotonin, norepinephrine, dopamine). Because of their remarkable effects upon the mind, these substances were used in religious ceremonies and folk medicine by the early cultures that discovered them. Mescaline is derived from the cactus plant peyote, and has been used for centuries in the mystical religious practices of the Mexican Indians; the Aztecs regarded the plant as sacred. Psilocybin is found in several species of mushroom, popularly known as the "magic mushroom." Stone sculptures of psychoactive mushrooms found in central America date well before 500 B.C. (Snyder, 1986). Its Indian name meant "food of the gods," and it was used in secret religious rituals among the Indians. R. Gordon Wasson, a New York banker who became interested in the mushroom in the 1950s, established a rapport with a native group and partook in one of their ceremonies. He wrote, ". . . it permits you to travel backwards and forward in time, to enter other planes of existence, even (as the Indians say), to know God . . . ." (Wasson, 1979).

LSD also has an interesting history, although much more recent. LSD (D-lysergic acid diethylamide) is a synthetic drug, but it is related chemically to a number of compounds found in the ergot fungus that infects grains, especially rye. Ergotamine is one of these compounds, which causes contractions of blood vessels and other smooth muscles such as the uterus. (It had been used for centuries in obstetrics.) In the 1940s, the chemist Albert Hofmann at Sandoz Drug Company in Basel, Switzerland, was experimenting with various derivatives of ergot compounds in hopes of finding new medicines. He synthesized a series of compounds, one of which was LSD. At the time, he had no idea he was dealing with potent hallucinogenic drugs. In 1943, after conducting several experiments, he was forced to stop work because of peculiar sensations. He recorded these impressions in his laboratory notebook and suspected they were due to accidental ingestion of LSD. Several days later he deliberately tested his theory by ingesting 0.25 mg of the substance (we know now that this is a massive dose, since LSD is an extremely potent drug). His impressions were duly recorded in his notebook:

> I had a great difficulty in speaking coherently, my field of vision swayed before me, and objects appeared distorted like images in curved mirrors. I had the impression of being unable to move from the spot, although my assistant told me afterwards that we had cycled at a good pace. . . .

By the time the doctor arrived, the peak of the crisis had already passed. As far as I remember, the following were the most outstanding symptoms: vertigo, visual disturbances; the faces of those around me appeared as grotesque, colored masks; marked motor unrest, alternating with paresis; an intermittent heavy feeling in the head, limbs, and the entire body, as if they were filled with metal; cramps in the legs, coldness, and loss of feeling in the hands; a metallic taste on the tongue; dry, constricted sensation in the throat; feeling of choking; confusion alternating between clear recognition of my condition, in which state I sometimes observed, in the manner of an independent, neutral observer, that I shouted half insanely or babbled incoherent words. Occasionally I felt as if I were out of my body. The doctor found a rather weak pulse but an otherwise normal circulation. Six hours after ingestion of the LSD-25 my condition had already improved considerably. Only the visual disturbances were still pronounced. Everything seemed to sway and the proportions were distorted like the reflections in the surface of moving water. Moreover, all objects appeared in unpleasant, constantly changing colors, the predominant shades being sickly green and blue. When I closed my eyes, an unending series of colorful, very realistic and fantastic images surged in upon me. A remarkable feature was the manner in which all acoustic perceptions (e.g., the noise of a passing car) were transformed into optical effects, every sound causing a corresponding colored hallucination constantly changing in shape and color like pictures in a kaleidoscope. At about 1 o'clock I fell asleep and awakened the next morning somewhat tired but otherwise feeling perfectly well. (Hofmann, 1968, pp. 185–86)

Reports on LSD eventually found their way into the scientific literature. Although pharmacologists and psychologists were very interested in its effects, research indicated that there was little therapeutic value to the compound. In the early 1960s, the drug became illegal, although soon after, in the late 1960s and early 1970s, its use in the "hippie" subculture reached its peak.

PSYCHOLOGICAL EFFECTS

The psychological effects of the hallucinogenic drugs are difficult to describe because they are so subjective, varying with the individual and the person's expectations and experience with the drug. One of most common reports is that of profound changes in sensory perception, including visual, tactile, or auditory distortions. Images and sounds may be remarkably vivid or bizarre. Aesthetic experiences, such as viewing art or listening to music, can be enhanced. The sense of time is also extremely altered. The neuropharmacologist Solomon Snyder, upon having ingested LSD, noted that "two hours after having taken the drug, I felt as if I had been under its influence for thousands of years. The remainder of my life on the planet Earth seemed to stretch ahead into infinity, and at the same time I felt infinitely old" (Snyder, 1986). Sensations may be transposed from one mode to another, a phenomenon known as synesthesia. Snyder wrote: "I clapped my hands and saw sound waves passing before my eyes." Emotions and the sense of self are often affected, with a feeling of depersonalization or loss of ego boundaries. In many cases, users report that they develop special insights into themselves or the world. In some instances, this feeling is experienced as positive; for others, it can be quite disturbing and result in profound dysphoria.

There are a number of important differences between hallucinogens and other drugs of abuse. Unlike drugs such as cocaine, amphetamine, or heroin, hallucinogens do not cause a rush or strong feeling of pleasure. People seem to desire these drugs uniquely for their complex effects on the mind, rather than for euphoriant or relaxing properties. It is possible that the hallucinogens do

▼ Effects of LSD may include a feeling of depersonalization or loss of ego boundaries, which some users welcome and others find deeply disturbing.

not affect the brain reward system the way most other drugs of abuse do. Animals cannot be taught to self-administer these compounds; they seem to lack true reinforcing effects in both animals and humans. Use of hallucinogens is not continual or chronic; people generally take these compounds on infrequent occasions. Moreover, people do not develop physical dependence or become addicted to them. Although they are illegal, hallucinogens do not induce cravings or compulsions.

NEUROPHYSIOLOGICAL MECHANISMS

Because of their very unusual psychological and sensory effects, researchers have long been interested in how these substances affect the brain. In fact, although there has been much research conducted, the neurophysiological mechanisms associated with these drugs are not well understood. The chemical structures of most of the compounds in this class are remarkably similar to the neurotransmitters serotonin and norepinephrine, and it is likely that they have potent effects on these neural systems. George Aghajanian and his research team at Yale University found that hallucinogens have strong inhibitory effects on the serotonin system and indirect activating effects on the norepinephrine system. The excitatory effect that external sensory stimulation has on the firing rate of norepinephrine-containing neurons is greatly enhanced by LSD and mescaline (Rasmussen and Aghajanian, 1986). Since both serotonin and norepinephrine affect brain regions concerned with sensation and emotion, it is likely that the mental phenomena induced by hallucinogens are due to interactions with these systems (Jacobs, 1987).

Medical and Social Complications

The hallucinogens have not received a great deal of attention as a medical or public health problem because of their low rates of use; moreover, since they are not injected intravenously, there is little risk of AIDS associated with their use. The most commonly used hallucinogens, such as LSD, mescaline, and psilocybin have very few toxic effects. Deaths attributed to direct effects of LSD are unknown (Jaffe, 1985). However, consumption of hallucinogens is not without potential adverse consequences. Most common is an acute psychotic reaction or "bad trip," in which the user experiences a severe panic reaction due to the feeling that he or she is going insane. In rare but tragic cases, the perceptual alterations may cause suicide; in the 1960s, stories appeared about young LSD users jumping out of windows because they believed they could fly. Another serious side effect of LSD is a phenomenon known as "flashbacks," brief episodes of drug effects that occur long after the last exposure. No one knows what causes flashbacks, which happen in approximately 15 percent of users, but they can be quite disturbing and recur intermittently even for years after LSD exposure.

PCP and MDMA

Several other drugs in this class deserve mention because of their increasing abuse in recent years. **PCP** (phencyclidine, also known as "angel dust") and the related drug ketamine were originally developed in the 1950s as anesthet-

▶ In PCP panic, the user may be convinced that he or she is going insane.

ics. People anesthetized with these drugs were awake but appeared disconnected from their environment. For this reason, they are classified as ***dissociative anesthetics.*** However, it was soon discovered that they had similar properties to hallucinogens, and their use was discontinued in humans. PCP was synthesized illicitly in the 1970s, when its use as a recreational drug was popular. The drug is smoked, snorted, or injected intravenously. Ingestion results in subjective feelings of intoxication, warmth, a tingling feeling, and sense of numbness in the extremities. Unlike the visual hallucinations that characterize LSD intoxication, distortions in body image and feelings of extreme depersonalization are typical of the PCP state. With increasing doses, confused, excited intoxication may develop or there may be stupor or coma. In some people a schizophrenia-like psychosis appears, which may persist for weeks or months. Although its use has declined sharply in recent years, there is still cause for concern because its use has been linked to violence and aggressive behavior, suicides, and depression.

MDMA (3,4-methylenedioxymethamphetamine), known as "Ecstasy" in street language, is a drug chemically related to amphetamine. However, it is principally classified as a hallucinogen and not a stimulant because it causes changes in perceptual awareness. Recreational users say that MDMA causes feelings of euphoria, tingling, and a sense of increased sociability. Users claim that even after the acute effects of the drug have subsided, they feel more insightful, empathetic, and aware. In the early 1980s, before it became illegal, a number of psychiatrists claimed they had been discretely using it to aid the therapeutic process and claimed it facilitated communication and expression of emotions (Greer and Tolbert, 1986; Grinspoon and Bakalar, 1986). Unfortunately, it is also now known that MDMA has neurotoxic effects on the brain, most notably on the central serotonin neurons (Stone, Merchant, Hanson, and Gibb, 1987).

In contrast to the hallucinogens, marijuana continues to be a relatively popular illicit drug. As of 1991, about one-third of the target population in the National Household survey reported that they had used marijuana one or more times in their lifetime; about 10 percent had used it within the last year. These figures translate into nearly 70 million people who have used marijuana at least once. Among teenagers and young adults, use is more prevalent; nearly 25 percent of this age group reported having used it within the past year and 50 percent reported use in their lifetime. However, as is true for other illicit drugs, use is markedly down from the late 1970s, when marijuana use peaked.

Marijuana is a preparation of the leaves from the hemp plant, or *Cannabis sativa*. It is not known where the plant originated, but it is likely that it was somewhere in central Asia. It is now cultivated in many areas of the world. Use of cannabis in human societies predates recorded history. It was used in China as an intoxicant as early as 6,000 years ago. In the Western world, the hemp plant was grown for its medicinal properties and fiber (for making rope), without its intoxicating effects being widely recognized. In the nineteenth century, European physicians expounded the usefulness of hemp as an appetite stimulant and anticonvulsant, and in treating a wide variety of ills such as migraine, asthma, and painful menstruation. It is believed that marijuana smoking for recreational purposes was introduced into this country by Mexican laborers in the early twentieth century (McKim, 1986). Use spread slowly and eventually stirred the concerns of people who thought that its use was associated with moral degeneration and violent crime. By the end of the 1930s, marijuana was illegal in most states.

Effects of Marijuana

The psychoactive ingredient in cannabis is delta-9-tetrahydrocannabinol (THC), which is concentrated in the resin of the plant. The concentration of this substance varies with different preparations of the plant (it can vary from 0.5 to 11 percent). Marijuana is a preparation of the leaves and buds; hashish is almost pure resin and therefore much more potent. Marijuana and hashish are usually smoked, and as we know, this is a very efficient way of delivering the drug to the brain. Psychoactive effects begin after a few minutes and reach their peak after about thirty minutes. People sometimes take this drug orally, baked in cookies or brownies. Since absorption through the GI tract is much slower, effects are not felt before two to three hours. THC is highly lipid soluble. It is taken up and stored in the fatty tissues of the body. This characteristic results in THC remaining in the body for long periods of time, for as long as one month following one dose of THC.

PSYCHOLOGICAL EFFECTS

Knowledge of the behavioral and cognitive effects of marijuana is based on both reports of users and a considerable amount of laboratory research in both animals and humans. It is difficult to describe precisely the psychological changes caused by marijuana because individuals may have differing reactions depending on dose, experience with drug, expectations, and so on. In an

FOCUS QUESTIONS

1. Differentiate between marijuana and hashish.
2. Describe the behavioral and cognitive effects of marijuana on experienced users.
3. What is the abstinence syndrome that may occur following abrupt cessation of chronic high doses of THC?
4. What are the potential hazards associated with chronic marijuana use?

▶ About half of teenagers and young adults, as of 1991, reported that they had tried marijuana at least once.

experienced user, marijuana typically elicits feelings of well-being and mild euphoria, usually referred to as "being high." An initial stimulating effect may be replaced by feelings of tranquility and dreaminess. Rapid mood changes or exaggerated emotions may occur. Often, when marijuana is consumed socially, there is frequent laughter and hilarity. Perceptual and sensory changes may occur, but generally these are mild exaggerations of pleasurable experiences. For example, music or tastes may be enhanced. However, following very high doses of THC, hallucinations and feelings of paranoia may occur.

The cognitive deficits induced by smoking marijuana are also variable, but there is general agreement that there are rather striking deficits in short-term memory, in which information is held actively in the brain for short periods. Following cannabis intoxication, users may show what has been called temporal disintegration; that is, they may lose the ability to retain and coordinate information for a purpose (McKim, 1986). It is common, for example, for people to start a sentence and fail to finish it because they forgot what they started to say. It is thought that this may be due to the intrusion of irrelevant associations (Hooker and Jones, 1987). Moreover, as with hallucinogens, there is a distortion in the sense of time, which seems to pass much more slowly.

TOLERANCE AND DEPENDENCE

Tolerance occurs to some of the effects of marijuana, although users often claim that there is a reverse tolerance, or sensitization to the drug. In one laboratory study in which subjects were given oral doses of THC every four hours for several weeks, tolerance developed to the effects on heart rate, to the subjective effects, and to the disruptive effects on cognitive and motor performance (Jones and Benowitz, 1976). It is likely that high, chronic doses of marijuana are needed for tolerance to develop. The impression of sensitization in experienced users may result primarily from learning to inhale and thus to increase more effectively blood concentrations of THC, as well as from learning what to expect from the drug-induced subjective state.

Physical dependence is very unlikely with marijuana. The majority of social users smoke it occasionally, not daily. Even smoking one marijuana cigarette a day for twenty-eight days does not cause withdrawal symptoms (Frank,

Lessin, Tyrrel, Hahn, and Szara, 1976). However, it is now recognized that following abrupt cessation of chronic high doses of THC, an abstinence syndrome can occur. This syndrome is characterized by irritability, restlessness, weight loss, insomnia, tremor, and increased body temperature (Jones and Benowitz, 1976). Psychological dependence is more common with marijuana, although even here most experts would agree that compulsive use and craving is considerably less than that associated with other drugs such as cocaine, opiates, and alcohol. Nevertheless, certain individuals may meet the DSM-IV criteria for Cannabis Dependence, in which they use very potent cannabis for months or years and spend considerable time acquiring and using the substance.

PHYSIOLOGICAL AND NEUROCHEMICAL EFFECTS

Researchers have been very interested in investigating the pharmacological and neurochemical effects of cannabinoids, but in contrast to other drugs of abuse, remarkably little is understood about the neural basis of THC's psychoactive effects. Until several years ago, it was not even known whether THC interacted with a receptor. Part of the lack of understanding is due to THC's unusual characteristics as a drug (Martin, 1986). THC is extremely lipid soluble and is absorbed by all tissues. It affects nearly all biological systems and has a "fluidizing" effect on biomembranes (similar to the effects of alcohol). Therefore, for many years, it was thought to be "nonspecific" pharmacologically. However, recently a unique receptor that binds cannabinoids was characterized and localized in specific brain structures (Herkenham, Lynn, Little, Johnson, Melvin, de Costa, and Rice, 1990), so this may be a specific site where THC acts. There is also speculation that THC has anticholinergic activity (disrupting functions of the neurotransmitter acetylcholine), which may underlie the memory deficits induced by the drug, and some of the physiological effects such as dry mouth (Miller and Branconnier, 1983).

Medical and Social Complications

There are a number of potential hazards associated with chronic marijuana use. Perhaps most important are the effects on the lungs, which are not due to THC itself but rather to inhalation of tars and other substances found in the smoke of the marijuana cigarette (Hollister, 1986). Bronchitis and asthma have long been known to be associated with marijuana smoking. Cannabinoids are also known to suppress immune responses in animals, although the clinical significance of this result is unclear. Over the years, many other adverse effects have been suggested to be associated with heavy marijuana use, none of which have been definitively proved. It is unlikely that there are serious health consequences of occasional marijuana use, although intoxication with marijuana could certainly impair judgment in such situations as driving.

Occasionally, when a young person starts smoking marijuana regularly, there may be quite marked changes in the person's lifestyle, personality, and ambitions. Chronic marijuana users may exhibit dullness, apathy, cognitive and memory impairments, and loss of interest in personal appearance and pursuit of conventional goals (McGlothlin and West, 1968). These changes have collectively been called the "amotivational syndrome." Although this syndrome is clearly a cause for concern, it is not apparent whether use of marijuana is the causal factor or whether the psychological and motivational changes precede drug use. As is true for alcohol, it is exceedingly difficult to separate the psychological effects of the drug from the psychological factors that led to its use to begin with. The syndrome does not develop in all heavy users of marijuana. Cessation of heavy use may lead to gradual improvement over several weeks or months. There is no evidence for permanent brain damage or long-lasting cognitive impairment from heavy use of marijuana.

NICOTINE AND CIGARETTE SMOKING

Tobacco has been used by humans for several thousand years. Native peoples in North and South America were the first to grow the tobacco plant and smoked its leaves for its psychoactive effects. New World explorers first observed tobacco smoking in the time of Columbus, and it was introduced into Western cultures and other parts of the world in the sixteenth century. The plant was named Nicotiana tabacum after the French ambassador Jean Nicot, who promoted its development and believed that it had medicinal values. In colonial times, tobacco was smoked in pipes, chewed, or ground into a powder and used as snuff. In the mid-nineteenth century, the cigarette was developed, which produced a smoke so mild (compared to cigars or pipes) that it could be inhaled. Although its use rapidly spread through many cultures, even as its consumption became popular its role in society was debated. King James I of England viewed cigarette smoking as a vile, immoral habit, stating that it was "harmefull to the braine, dangerous to the lungs" and Sir Francis Bacon believed that smoking was similar to opium or alcohol compulsions (cited in Henningfield and Goldberg, 1985).

In our present society, smoking is a common, legal, and (relatively) socially acceptable form of psychoactive drug consumption. Although there are over 3,000 chemical components in cigarette smoke, it is now believed that nicotine is the active and addictive ingredient. Thus, nicotine is one of the most widely consumed psychoactive drugs in the world. A one pack-per-day smoker will administer hundreds of nicotine doses to himself daily (about 200 puffs), which amounts to over 70,000 doses of nicotine per year. Levels of smoking in the population have declined in recent years; the National Household Survey reports that smoking has decreased from about 40 percent of the target population to 27 percent over the past twenty years. Although these are encouraging figures, people continue to smoke despite current widespread knowledge of the adverse health consequences of smoking. In fact, most people who smoke would like to quit. It is paradoxical that in a society that condemns drug use, nicotine consumption is a legal activity and a $30 billion a year industry. However, it is important to realize that a major difference between cigarette smoking and other drugs such as cocaine or alcohol is that chronic use of nicotine, even in high quantities, does not result in impairment of mental functioning. Although nicotine is certainly a "psychoactive" drug, its effects on the brain and behavior are subtle.

Effects of Nicotine

Nicotine can be administered in a variety of ways, but smoking is by far the most common route of administration. As smoke is drawn into the lungs via

FOCUS QUESTIONS

1. What are the effects of nicotine?
2. Describe the withdrawal syndrome that occurs when someone tries to give up smoking.
3. What are three motives for smoking?
4. Why is nicotine replacement an effective treatment for those who wish to quit smoking?

particles of "tar" (condensate), nicotine is absorbed rapidly into the circulatory system. Blood concentrations rise rapidly, and it is estimated that nicotine enters the brain in approximately seven seconds. Ingestion of nicotine via oral routes (chewing tobacco, nicotine gum, oral snuff) results in a much slower rise in blood nicotine concentrations, and levels persist for longer periods. Nicotine has a variety of complex effects on the peripheral and central nervous system. It can act as both a stimulant and a depressant. In studies of subjective effects of smoking, people say that they smoke for both its arousing and relaxation effects. The two principle actions of nicotine on neurotransmitters involve effects at cholinergic and aminergic synapses. Nicotine stimulates cholinergic receptors in the autonomic nervous system, and at the neuromuscular junction. Nicotine also induces the release of catecholamines, which results in cardiovascular activation (accelerated heart rate, increased blood pressure and cardiac output, and vasoconstriction). In the central nervous system, exposure to nicotine results in activation of several central nervous system pathways, leading to the release of acetylcholine, norepinephrine, serotonin, dopamine, and in effects on the endocrine system (Benowitz, 1988).

Tolerance develops to many of the effects of nicotine. The first smoke one experiences as a teenager often produces nausea, vomiting, pallor, and dizziness. Tolerance rapidly occurs to these aversive effects with continued smoking. A certain degree of tolerance also develops to the arousing and subjective effects of nicotine. Presumably, at least in susceptible individuals, the positive effects of smoking outweigh the unpleasant side effects, such that smoking behavior is repeated. Physical dependence may then develop, which is discussed below.

Nicotine Dependence

As recently as 1994, executives of tobacco companies claimed that smoking and nicotine were not addictive (Hilts, 1994). A vast amount of scientific evidence suggests otherwise. Two of the leading experts in drug research compared nicotine to five other drugs; both ranked nicotine low as far as the level of intoxication it produces, but highest as far as dependence (see Table 14–2). Of those smokers trying to quit, approximately 70 percent relapse within three months. Figure 14–1 shows that relapse to smoking follows a similar pattern to other drugs such as heroin and alcohol. The Surgeon General has proclaimed nicotine as addictive as heroin, which might seem shocking given that nicotine is a legal drug. However, it comes as no surprise to people who have tried numerous times to quit. As Mark Twain quipped, "I can quit smoking if I tried; I've done it a thousand times" (cited in Volpicelli, 1989). What is nicotine dependence, and why is it so difficult to give up, often despite high levels of motivation?

If we review some of the major criteria for drug dependence disorder, we find that cigarette smoking meets these criteria in most individuals who smoke: compulsive drug use, overwhelming involvement with the use of the drug, concern with the securing of its supply, and a high tendency to relapse after its withdrawal. Of course, some people smoke very little or only occasionally, but that situation is relatively rare. Smoking cessation often results in a distinct withdrawal syndrome, although it may vary from person to person in its intensity and specific symptoms. The most common signs and symptoms

TABLE 14–2

NICOTINE COMPARED TO OTHER DRUGS

Withdrawal Presence and severity of characteristic withdrawal symptoms.

Reinforcement A measure of the substance's ability, in human and aimal tests, to get users to take it again and again, and in preference to other substances.

Tolerance How much of the substance is needed to satisfy increasing cravings for it, and the level of stable need that is eventually reached.

Dependence How difficult it is for the user to quit, the relapse rate, the percentage of people who eventually become dependent, the rating users give their own need for the substance and the degree to which the substance will be used in the face of evidence that it causes harm.

Intoxication Though not usually counted as a measure of addiction in itself, the level of intoxication is associated with addiction and increases the personal and social damage a substance may do.

Dr. Jack E. Henningfield of the National Institute on Drug Abuse and Dr. Neal L. Benowitz of the University of California at San Francisco ranked six substances based on five problem areas.

1 = Most serious   6 = Least serious

HENNINGFIELD RATINGS

Substance	Withdrawal	Reinforcement	Tolerance	Dependence	Intoxication
Nicotine	3	4	2	1	5
Heroin	2	2	1	2	2
Cocaine	4	1	4	3	3
Alcohol	1	3	3	4	1
Caffeine	5	6	5	5	6
Marijuana	6	5	6	6	4

BENOWITZ RATINGS

Substance	Withdrawal	Reinforcement	Tolerance	Dependence	Intoxication
Nicotine	3*	4	4	1	6
Heroin	2	2	2	2	2
Cocaine	3*	1	1	3	3
Alcohol	1	3	4	4	1
Caffeine	4	5	3	5	5
Marijuana	5	6	5	6	4

*Equal ratings
SOURCE: Philip J. Hilts, Is Nicotine Addictive? It Depends on Whose Criteria You Use. *New York Times*, August 2, 1994, p. C3.

are irritability, anxiety, restlessness, impaired concentration, and a strong craving for tobacco. Headaches, drowsiness, insomnia, and gastrointestinal complaints are also common. Neuropsychological tests in smokers undergoing withdrawal show decreases in vigilance, attention, psychomotor performance, and increases in hostility. The syndrome gradually subsides within days or weeks, but the craving and desire for a cigarette often far outlast the physical complaints. Increased appetite and weight gain are extremely common problems associated with smoking cessation. (Smokers as a group weigh less than nonsmokers.) Research in animals and humans has shown this to be due to a number of metabolic changes, although the strong desire for a "substitute" oral behavior may also contribute. The fear of gaining weight after stopping smoking may contribute to a lowered motivation to quit, particularly among women.

THEORIES OF NICOTINE DEPENDENCE

Why do people smoke? Social factors are probably very important in the teenage years, when smoking dependence most often develops. Peer pressure, parental modeling, and experimentation may contribute to initiation of the behavior. When the habit is well established, it is likely that other factors related

► Roy Carruthers' *Three Smokers.*

to the biological effects of nicotine contribute to the maintenance of the behavior. Perhaps most important of these are nicotine's positive reinforcing effects. Like all drugs of abuse, nicotine affects mood, emotion, and cognitive functions. Self-administration tests in animals have shown that rats and monkeys will press a lever to deliver intravenous nicotine (Henningfield and Goldberg, 1983; Corrigall and Coen, 1991). Nicotine presumably has pleasurable properties for people who smoke; laboratory studies in humans have shown this to be the case (Henningfield and Jasinski, 1983). One study in England found that subjects rated smoking as an activity with both "pleasurable-relaxation" and "pleasurable-stimulation" effects (Warburton, 1988). However, it does not appear that nicotine produces the powerful euphoria or "rush" that is experienced with other drugs that are smoked or delivered intravenously, such as heroin or cocaine.

A further important model of smoking behavior is the coping model. This notion is related to the idea that people take drugs to relieve distress, or to help them cope with stresses or challenges of daily life. Many studies have found that people smoke more when worried, nervous, or anxious, and that they find smoking helps to relieve these feelings. For example, a study of students found that they smoked more and inhaled more strongly during examination periods (Warburton, 1988). Other work has found that autonomic responsivity, such as skin conductance, is blunted by smoking, thus providing evidence that smoking is able to reduce the stress response (Gilbert and Hagen, 1980).

The "functional" model focuses on nicotine's ability to improve performance, and emphasizes that people smoke to control their psychological state and to gain optimal mental functioning. It appears that the mild stimulant properties of nicotine indeed can improve performance. In tests of vigilance, attention, memory, or information processing, smoking or oral nicotine results in improved scores. These effects are present even in nonsmokers given oral nicotine (Warburton and Wesnes, 1978; Wesnes and Warburton, 1984a, 1984b). Thus, people may smoke because of the beneficial effects nicotine provides to performance of the many tasks of everyday life.

It is important to remember that there are many motives for smoking. The three models discussed are not mutually exclusive; many people smoke for a combination of factors, principally because of the mild pleasurable effects produced by nicotine, the alleviation of negative psychological states, and the improvement in daily functioning.

Treatment

▲ The coping model holds that people use smoking to combat the difficulties and anxieties of everyday life.

Most smokers who successfully quit do so without assistance from counseling programs, groups, or pharmacotherapies (Fiore, Novotny, Pierce, Giovino, Hatziandrev, Newcomb, Surawicz, and Davis, 1990). About two-thirds of smokers make serious attempts to quit each year, but most relapse within weeks or months. Although behavioral therapy, group counseling, or physician advice may be helpful in some cases, there is little evidence that these strategies work in the absence of nicotine replacement therapy. Nicotine replacement, via nicotine gum or transdermal patch (a patch placed on the skin that slowly releases nicotine, which is then absorbed by the skin into the body), has been shown to be effective in smokers unable to quit by alternative methods. The rationale underlying this approach is similar to that used in treating opiate addiction with methadone. The aim is to eliminate smoking behavior while still making nicotine available for a limited period of time. Nicotine delivered this way does not result in the same blood levels or psychoactive effects of smoking but does reduce the severity of the withdrawal symptoms and craving. The transdermal nicotine patch is a recent development that shows much promise. It is easier to use and causes fewer side effects that nicotine gum. A recent meta-analysis of seventeen studies involving more than 5,000 smokers showed that about 25 percent of smokers who used transdermal patches were abstinent six months later, compared with only 10 percent of smokers who were given dummy patches (Fiore, Smith, Jorenby, and Baker, 1994). This study, conducted at the Center for Tobacco Research and Intervention at the University of Wisconsin, also found that counseling made little difference in the rate that patch users stopped smoking. Moreover, the patch was just as effective when worn for six to eight weeks as for the recommended ten to eighteen weeks.

Medical and Social Complications of Smoking

According to the U. S. Surgeon General, smoking is the "chief, single most avoidable cause of death in our society and the most important public health issue of our time" (Surgeon General's Report, 1984). The statistics indeed are overwhelming. It has been estimated that there are 350,000 smoking-related deaths per year in this country. (For purposes of comparison, there are approximately 100,000 alcohol-related deaths, and 35,000 deaths due to AIDS annually.) Disease and death due to smoking results in over $70 billion in annual smoking-related costs to society, including health care costs and lost productivity. There are a number of diseases causally linked to smoking, including lung cancer, coronary heart disease, hypertension, and chronic lung diseases such as emphysema. The likelihood of developing these disorders increases with the amount of exposure; chronic smoking shortens the life span. It is estimated that smoking contributes to 30 percent of all cancer deaths and to 30 percent of all deaths due to cardiovascular disease. Although nicotine is the addictive component in smoke, these serious diseases are primarily caused by exposure to carbon monoxide and the many known carcinogens in smoke. However, nicotine itself, particularly with long-term exposure, may aggravate a number of cardiovascular conditions because of its stimulatory effects. Smoking during pregnancy also has adverse effects on the unborn fetus. Babies born to smokers have lower birth weight than babies born to nonsmokers.

SEDATIVE-HYPNOTICS AND TRANQUILIZERS (BARBITURATES, BENZODIAZEPINES)

Barbiturates and benzodiazepines are ***sedative-hypnotic drugs*** ("downers"); that is, their principal effects are to depress the activity of the central nervous system. In this way, they are similar to alcohol, which is also a sedative-hypnotic, but there are some important differences as well. In contrast to many of the abused drugs that have been used for thousands of years, barbiturates and benzodiazepines are drugs that were developed in this century for therapeutic purposes. The barbiturates were first synthesized in Germany in the early 1900s, and many of them are still prescribed today for anesthesia, sedation, and control of seizure disorders. Examples of barbiturates are pentobarbital (Nembutal), secobarbital (Seconal), amobarbital (Amytal), and phenobarbital (Luminal). These compounds differ slightly in chemical structure and duration of action. Benzodiazepines were introduced in the 1960s as safer alternatives to the barbiturates, particularly in the treatment of anxiety states and insomnia. Well-known benzodiazepines include alprazalam (Xanax), diazepam (Valium), chlordiazepoxide (Librium), triazolam (Halcion), and oxazepam (Tranxene). Valium is one of the most commonly prescribed drugs in the United States. Although both the barbiturates and benzodiazepines have important medical uses, they are also abused drugs.

Effects of Sedatives

FOCUS QUESTIONS

1. What are the psychological and physical effects of the barbiturates?
2. Describe the psychological and physical effects of the benzodiapines and how they differ from those of the barbiturates.
3. Describe the withdrawal syndrome that can occur when chronic use of barbiturates is stopped.

The psychological and physical effects of barbiturates are very similar to alcohol. At low or moderate doses, barbiturates cause mild euphoria, lightheadedness, and loss of motor coordination. Higher doses may cause severe intoxication characterized by difficulty in thinking, slurred speech, poor comprehension and memory, emotional lability, and aggressive behavior. Loss of consciousness may occur, and breathing is slowed. With large enough doses, as in accidental or intentional overdose, breathing ceases altogether. Indeed, barbiturates are the favored drug for committing suicide. More than 15,000 deaths per year result from overdose, and the majority of these are suicides. Unintentional deaths may result from combining alcohol with barbiturates or benzodiazepines, since the effects of these drugs are additive.

Psychological and physical effects of benzodiazepines share some characteristics with the barbiturates, but in general they have milder effects and much lower toxicity. In therapeutic doses they have anxiolytic (anxiety-relieving) effects, although at these doses there are few discernible effects in non-anxious individuals. At moderate doses, they can cause mild pleasurable feelings and paradoxical stimulant effects, similar to low doses of alcohol. In fact, both benzodiazepines and barbiturates are self-administered by animals, indicating their reinforcing effects. Higher doses of benzodiazepines cause sedation and sleep, but respiration rate is not nearly as affected as with the barbiturates. Since the margin of safety is very high with these drugs, these are the preferred drugs for treatment of anxiety and insomnia. Death from overdose of benzodiazepines is virtually unheard of, although the combination of these drugs with alcohol is dangerous.

Several potential side effects of the benzodiazepines are of considerable concern. Memory deficits may be associated with benzodiazepine use, and cases of complete amnesia induced by the short-acting benzodiazepines such as triazolam have been reported (Lister, 1985). Increased hostility or aggression can occur in some individuals who take these drugs chronically.

NEUROCHEMICAL MECHANISMS

Researchers have made considerable progress in understanding the neural mechanisms underlying the psychoactive effects of barbiturates and benzodiazepines. These studies are particularly interesting because they provide insight into the neural basis of anxiety and anxiety disorders. Although these compounds interact with many neurotransmitter systems, the one most affected is GABA. As mentioned earlier, GABA is an inhibitory neurotransmitter found in many parts of the brain. Barbiturates, benzodiazepines, and alcohol all interact with GABA receptors. The GABA receptor is actually a molecular complex of several binding sites, including one for GABA, one for benzodiazepines, and one for barbiturates and alcohol. GABA normally causes inhibition of the neuron it affects. In the presence of benzodiazepines or sedative-hypnotics, GABA becomes even more effective, and the inhibitory action is enhanced. It is thought that the anxiety-relieving effects of these drugs are due to direct effects on the GABA receptor complex. Moreover, abnormal activity of GABA and the systems that it modulates may be involved in anxiety states (Ninan, Insel, Cohen, Cook, Skolnick, and Paul, 1982).

Sedative Dependence

While abuse and dependence on sedatives have decreased in recent years, they are nevertheless significant problems. In 1991, about 5 percent of the population reported nonmedical use of sedatives or tranquilizers at some point in their lives. People dependent on other drugs, such as opiates or alcohol, sometimes use sedatives as well. Although sedatives can be obtained through illicit sources, often the first contact is through a physician's prescription. In these individuals, the development of the problem may be gradual, beginning with habitual use for insomnia or anxiety, and progressing to increased dosage several times a day (Jaffe, 1985).

Tolerance and dependence develop with both classes of sedatives. Barbiturate dependence and its corresponding withdrawal syndrome have been problems since the drugs were first developed. The symptoms are similar to alcohol withdrawal and can be life-threatening in extreme cases. Tremors, anxiety, insomnia, delirium, and seizures can occur following cessation of chronic use of barbiturates. After the benzodiazepines were developed it was thought for many years that chronic use of these compounds, at least in therapeutic doses, was not associated with a withdrawal syndrome. All the benzodiazepines have less addiction potential than the barbiturates, but in recent years it has been recognized that an abstinence syndrome can result from withdrawal. Even at relatively low doses, benzodiazepine withdrawal is associated with increases in anxiety and sleep disturbances, heightened sensitivity to stimuli, and EEG changes (Petursson and Lader, 1981; Lader, 1988). Treatment of barbiturate or benzodiazepine dependence consists primarily of management of the withdrawal syndrome, usually through a gradual reduction of dosage over a period of weeks or months, combined with supportive psychotherapy.

FUTURE DIRECTIONS IN TREATMENT AND PREVENTION OF SUBSTANCE ABUSE

Although there has been a substantial and significant decline in drug use in recent years, drug abuse remains one of the most critical problems facing the United States. Drug abuse is linked to neglect of children, family violence, crime, homelessness, AIDS, enormous health care and economic costs, urban decay, and many other social problems (Kleber, 1994). Herbert Kleber, an expert on drug abuse and treatment, observes that most people are poor judges of their own susceptibility to addiction. In the thirty years he has treated drug addicts, he notes that few anticipated addiction when they started using drugs. Most believed they had the will power to use drugs occasionally or casually. Although many people do use drugs or alcohol in a controlled or socially acceptable manner, many others become entrapped in a destructive cycle of dependence. The disease model of dependence has fostered a sense of social obligation to help dependent individuals, and on a larger scale, to reduce or prevent addiction in our society. But what should be the goals and philosophy of drug abuse prevention? How should government funds be distributed among law enforcement, drug abuse education, and treatment programs and research?

Limiting Drug Availability

Limiting drug availability is one approach to combating drug dependence. If there were no drug, there would be no drug dependence. If there were no alcohol, as is true in some Islamic societies, there would be no alcoholism. Use of legal drugs—alcohol, nicotine, caffeine—is by far greater than use of illicit drugs. In general, as availability of a substance increases, so does the substance use disorder. When the legal drinking age was lowered in some states to eighteen in the 1970s, drinking and alcohol-related traffic fatalities among youth increased greatly. When the legal limit was raised again, fatalities dropped. The period of lowest alcohol consumption in this country was during Prohibition (1920–1933). Nevertheless, despite the clear association between availability and addiction, our society does not seem prepared to do away with drugs altogether. After all, laws could be enacted that make alcohol and cigarettes illegal, but that scenario seems unlikely. Rather, policies that reduce consumption (and therefore addiction) are needed. For example, the federal tax on

FOCUS QUESTIONS

1. Describe the association between availability and addiction to drugs.
2. How can drug education programs reduce drug use?
3. What kind of research is needed to improve long-term outcome in recovering addicts?

alcohol and cigarettes could be greatly increased, and this would cut consumption and the number of deaths related to these substances.

Drug Education and Prevention

It is now recognized that one of the most effective deterrents to drug use is education and dissemination of knowledge about drugs, alcohol, and their effects. This is particularly important for children and adolescents. Broad-based community programs, in schools, or in youth services, or in religious organizations, as well as media campaigns and parent programs are critical for providing this information. For example, many public schools, even at the elementary level, have drug education programs, and many have the "drug-free zone" symbol posted on the school property. Such initiatives increase awareness of the drug problem at a very young age. However, warning about the dangers of drug use is a necessary, but not sufficient, component of prevention (Kleber, 1994). Teaching adolescents decision-making skills and techniques for confronting peer pressure to use drugs are also thought to be very important (Ellickson, 1994). The success of the anti-smoking and anti-drunk driving campaigns gives cause for optimism. Overall rates of smoking cigarettes have declined in the past twenty years from 40 to 27 percent of the adult population. Over the past fifteen years, the incidence of driver intoxication in fatal crashes has been cut by almost a third (Ayres, 1994). In the 1980s, the government's "Be Smart! Don't Start! Just Say No!" advertising campaign may have contributed to the substantial decline in illicit drug use. Thus, although progress is slow, aggressive and widespread education campaigns can be effective in reducing drug abuse.

Improved Treatment and Research

There is a critical need for more effective and expanded treatment programs. Both the number of treatment programs and their effectiveness remain woefully inadequate. Currently, approximately 1.7 million addicts are in treatment programs, but 2.5 to 3 million need treatment. Thus, more funding is needed from federal and state governments to expand resources and the number of treatment centers. If this need is incorporated into the current agenda for health care reform, billions of dollars may be saved in medical and economic costs. However, treatment methods and research on improving treatment must also be expanded. As we saw earlier, many treatments fail to keep people off drugs or alcohol. Yet, some people do recover from severe dependence. We need much more research about the determinants of successful treatment and the factors involved in relapse. Basic biological research, for example, may lead to development of better drug therapies for reducing craving in the recovering addict. Further research into behavioral and cognitive treatment methods could result in improved long-term outcome. However, research on drug abuse is currently less than 5 percent of the entire federal budget for drug control (Kleber, 1994). It is proposed that a restructuring of priorities (for example, less money for drug law enforcement, more for research and treatment) would significantly enhance prevention efforts.

1. Substance abuse is *the* major health problem in the United States. The costs to society are enormous, and yet our society continues to have an ambivalent attitude about psychoactive drugs.

2. The diagnosis of drug dependence is made if the person exhibits: (1) loss of control over the use of the substance; (2) impairment in psychological and social functioning, and (3) physical or emotional adaptation to the drug.

3. The greatest problem in substance abuse treatment is prevention of relapse. Even after very long periods of abstinence, most patients yield to uncontrollable drug cravings and revert to drug use.

4. The effectiveness of psychoactive drugs depends on several important factors, such as the route of administration, the ability of the drug to enter the brain, how well the drug interacts with the brain's receptors, and how quickly the drug is deactivated.

5. Psychological, social, and biological factors contribute to the development of substance use disorders. A diagnosis of antisocial personality disorder is a risk factor for drug and alcohol addiction. Genetic factors may also influence vulnerability to addiction.

6. The opponent-process theory suggests that drugs may cause *affective pleasure*, which diminishes with *affective tolerance* (lessened response to the drug). *Affective withdrawal*, the opposite of affective pleasure, results when the drug is removed, and avoidance of this negative state may explain continued drug taking.

7. Positive reinforcement models of addiction posit that the powerful rewarding effects of drugs are the primary explanation for their use. Research using these models shows that animals self-administer many of the drugs abused by humans. There are several brain systems thought to play a critical role in drug reinforcement: the dopamine and opioid systems, and the nucleus accumbens.

8. The conditioning and learning models of addiction postulate that a drug state is an unconditioned stimulus that becomes associated with many signals in the user's environment. These signals become powerful conditioned stimuli and may contribute to the reinstatement of drug-seeking behavior.

9. Alcohol dependence is a very common mental disorder. Chronic use of alcohol results in impaired mental functioning and physical damage to organs. Physical dependence develops rapidly with excessive alcohol use. There is convincing evidence that alcoholism is a genetically influenced disorder. Most alcoholics do not recover; however, certain factors such as social stability, a substitute dependency, and membership in a supportive group have positive influences on outcome.

10. Amphetamine and cocaine are the most commonly used illegal stimulants, and cocaine dependence is a serious problem in the United States. Cocaine, and particularly its more potent form crack, produces profound

euphoria and is extremely addictive. Cocaine use is associated with many medical and social problems. Chronic use can cause psychosis and paranoia, and withdrawal from cocaine is accompanied by dysphoria and depression.

11. Opiate drugs produce their pharmacological effects by binding to opiate receptors in the brain. Most opiate addicts are intravenous heroin users, and therefore at risk for being infected with the HIV virus. Opiate use is associated with a high degree of tolerance and physical dependence. Maintenance therapy with a synthetic opiate, methadone, is the primary treatment for opiate addiction.

12. Hallucinogens distort reality and alter self-perception. LSD is the prototypical hallucinogen. People take hallucinogens for their complex sensory and perceptual effects, rather than for euphoric or relaxing properties. Physical dependence does not develop with hallucinogens.

13. Marijuana is a commonly used illicit drug and causes mild perceptual changes and feelings of well-being.

14. People smoke cigarettes for the mild pleasurable effects produced by nicotine, for stress reduction, and for improvement in cognitive functioning. Nicotine is highly addictive and the majority of smokers are not able to stop smoking permanently. The costs of cigarette smoking to personal health and to society are staggering.

15. Barbiturates and benzodiazepines are depressants of the central nervous system. People take them to relieve anxiety and insomnia. Abuse of barbiturates has decreased in recent years, but benzodiazepine abuse and dependence has been increasingly recognized as a problem. The benzodiazepines increase the effectiveness of GABA, the principal inhibitory neurotransmitter in the brain.

16. Drug education, prevention programs, widespread media campaigns, expanded treatment programs, and more research can all contribute to reducing drug abuse in our society. Limiting drug availability can also lower rates of drug use and dependence.

QUESTIONS FOR CRITICAL THINKING

1. Explain why the social and cultural context of drug use affects whether drug users are considered "addicts" and how they are treated.

2. Does disruption of early life development and/or genetic predisposition to alcoholism inevitably lead to alcoholism? Why or why not?

3. What has led to the crack epidemic and how does crack use affect the user, the family, and society?

4. Do you think that substituting methadone dependence for heroin dependence is a worthwhile treatment for opiate addiction? Why or why not?

5. Do you think that more government funds should be used for law enforcement, for education, for treatment, or for research on drug use and abuse?

CHAPTER 15

Personality Disorders

CHAPTER ORGANIZER

THE ANTISOCIAL PERSONALITY DISORDER
- Understand the idea of a disorder of will.
- Be able to characterize the antisocial personality disorder and to identify the sources of sociopathy.

OTHER PERSONALITY DISORDERS
- Familiarize yourself with the range of personality disorders.

- Understand what the central characteristics of each disorder are.

THE PERSONALITY DISORDERS: AN EVALUATION
- Review the problems of diagnosing and treating personality disorders.

People who cheat needlessly and lie without reason are a diagnostic dilemma. So are those who are always suspicious of others' intentions. And so too are people who always respond passively to all provocation, regardless of source or intensity. Such people are hardly psychotic, for they have a good grip on reality. Nor are they necessarily dominated by unwarranted fears, sexual difficulties, addictions, and the like. Nevertheless, their behaviors strike observers as odd, as deviant, or as abnormal. Theirs seems to be a disorder of personality, which impairs their ability to function across many domains (Herbert, Hope, and Bellack, 1992). Their characteristic ways of perceiving and thinking about themselves and their environment are inflexible, and a source of social and occupational maladjustment. In addition, their behaviors may well be a source of distress for themselves and others. Their disorders are called ***personality disorders.***

Consider a young employee who is up for promotion. She knows she has done a good job, and that she probably deserves appropriate credit. But, she feels anxious, thinking perhaps that one of her colleagues is trying to undercut her achievements. When they learn of her fears, her friends call her "paranoid," pointing out that she is probably imagining the situation. Oddly reassured by that characterization, she is able to go about her business. Most of us have had similar concerns. Our worries are ones that grow out of specific situations. They are time-limited and easily dispelled. But some people's worries are not so easily relieved. Indeed, they spend much of their lives scanning the environment for cues that validate their paranoid feelings. Unlike the employee who has a few "paranoid" moments, individuals with the ***paranoid personality disorder*** are always suspicious of others' motives. While they are able to function and are not psychotic, they are continually troubled by deep distrust.

The personality disorders have provided a fascinating source of psychological study across the decades because they ascribe a stability and sturdiness to personality and behavior that extends across time and context. The personality disorders are fundamentally disorders of *traits,* that is, disorders that are reflected in the individual's tendency to perceive and respond to the environment in broad and maladaptive ways. Perhaps the most fascinating of these disorders is the ***antisocial personality disorder.*** Known also as **sociopathy** and **psychopathy,** this disorder has been studied extensively and is the best understood of the personality disorders.

THE ANTISOCIAL PERSONALITY DISORDER

People who suffer from the psychological disorders that were examined in earlier chapters create distress for their families and friends, but mainly they themselves are the ones who suffer. In contrast, the suffering in an individual with the antisocial personality disorder is muted. The hallmark of the disorder is a rapacious attitude toward others, a chronic insensitivity and indifference to the rights of other people that is marked by lying, stealing, cheating, and worse. Whereas those who suffer other psychological difficulties may be unpleasant, contact with antisocial personalities may be downright dangerous, for many of them are outright criminals. Because their numbers are not small, they constitute a major social and legal problem, as well as a psychological one.

The prevalence of antisocial behavior is roughly 2 to 3 percent, with men accorded that diagnosis as much as four times more often than women (Warner, 1978; Regier, Myers, Kramer, Robins, Blayer, Hough, Easton, and Locke, 1984; Cadoret, 1986). But does this difference reflect a sex bias in the eyes of diagnosticians, or a true base-rate difference in the prevalence of this disorder? Present evidence strongly supports a sex bias. In one study, mental health professionals were asked to offer a diagnosis on a hypothetical case history. They were offered eight possible diagnoses, among them histrionic personality disorder and antisocial personality disorder. When the client was described as female, therapists were inclined to diagnose her as hysterical or histrionic. But when the same hypothetical client was described as male, diagnostic perceptions shifted in the direction of the antisocial personality (Warner, 1978). Another study confirmed the inclination of diagnosticians to perceive women as more histrionic, even when the case features were biased toward antisocial personality disorder, and to fail to diagnose the histrionic personality disorder in men (Ford and Widiger, 1989). Thus, the sex bias in these diagnoses may be generated by the stereotypic expectations of the diagnostician, especially about women, rather than by substantive differences among the clients themselves.

Disorders of Will

People with the antisocial personality disorder steal and cheat. But they are not the only ones. "Normal" people filch, forge, and embezzle, too. When nor-

FOCUS QUESTIONS

1. What is a disorder of will?
2. What are the three areas that encompass the characteristics of a person with an antisocial personality disorder?
3. Describe the role of the family and social context as possible causes of sociopathy.
4. What defects in learning may underlie sociopathic behavior?

mal people steal and cheat, we call them criminals and their acts, crime. Why should we regard those who are diagnosed as having the antisocial personality disorder any differently?

The fact is that for the longest time antisocial personalities were *not* thought about in psychological terms. Throughout most of history, criminals were criminals and the only distinctions that were made had to do with the severity of their crimes. But in the nineteenth century especially, the idea developed that certain kinds of criminal behavior might arise from conditions over which the individual had no control—that is, from social, psychological, or biological sources. Their crimes then were not acts of will, but rather the result of circumstances beyond their control. Much as noncriminal but clearly dysfunctional behaviors might be caused by psychological experiences over which the individual had little control, so too might criminal, antisocial ones.

In the nineteenth century, such antisocial people were said to be afflicted by ***moral insanity.*** This disorder was distinguished from other psychological disorders by the English psychiatrist J. C. Prichard (1837), who wrote:

> Intellectual faculties appear to have sustained little or no injury, while the disorder is manifest principally or alone, in the state of the feelings, temper, or habits . . . the moral and active principles of the mind are strangely perverted and depraved; the power of self-government is lost or greatly impaired; and the individual is found to be incapable, not of talking or reasoning upon any subject proposed to him, for this he will often do with great shrewdness and volubility, but of conducting himself with decency and propriety in the business of life. (Prichard, 1837, p. 15)

Moral insanity then, was viewed as a disorder of the *will.* Although the term moral insanity has been displaced by "antisocial personality disorder" today, it continues to be viewed as a disorder of will. Whether for biological, social, or psychological reasons, these people are found "to be incapable . . . of conducting [themselves] with decency and propriety in the business of life." Where people are *capable* of exercising will and of conducting themselves properly, but simply *choose* not to do so, they continue to be called criminals.

How does a disorder of will develop? We are not yet certain, but there has been some interesting theoretical speculation. Robert Kegan (1986) suggests that people who have antisocial personality disorders most resemble ten-year-old children in their psychological makeup. Neither can handle responsibility, both have difficulty understanding others, and both are awfully concrete-minded. Some of the latter is represented in the following interchange between a reporter and the famous bank robber, Willy Sutton:

> Why do you rob all these banks, Willy?
> Because that's where they keep the money.
>
> (Kegan, 1986)

There is often debate about whether or not a person is actually suffering a personality disorder, and that debate arises from the very nature of the disorder itself. The antisocial personality disorder is a disorder of will, and will is not an all-or-nothing matter. One does not either have or not have will. Rather, like most other psychological functions, will exists on a continuum: normal people have more or less of it, but those who suffer this disorder have even less. The line that divides those who suffer disorders from the rest of us is arbitrary. Because of this, we diagnose this disorder with caution.

Also, like anxiety, will is *inferred.* One does not see will. Rather, its presence is inferred from behaviors that are believed to reflect it. Unless one examines those specific behaviors, judging whether someone does or does not suffer a personality disorder can be hazardous. For that reason, DSM-IV offers behavioral diagnostic criteria for the antisocial personality disorder.

Characterizing the Antisocial Personality Disorder

Antisocial behavior alone is not sufficient for the diagnosis of antisocial personality disorder. Such behavior would merely qualify as "adult antisocial behavior," which in DSM-IV is ruled out as a mental disorder. In order to qualify as a personality disorder, the antisocial behaviors must meet two primary criteria. First, the behavior has to be longstanding. Although the diagnosis cannot be applied to a person who is under eighteen, current diagnostic criteria require substantial evidence of a conduct disorder before the age of fifteen. Such evidence can include habitual lying, early and aggressive sexual behavior, destructiveness, theft, vandalism, and chronic rule violation at home and at school. Second, the present antisocial behavior must be manifested in at least three classes of behavior, among which are: repeated aggressiveness; recklessness that endangers others; deceitfulness, lack of remorse, and consistent irresponsibility as seen by such behaviors; a failure to honor financial obligations. The antisocial personality disorder then is defined by sustained antisocial behaviors that, having begun by adolescence, continue in a variety of areas during adulthood (see Table 15–1).

These criteria make clear who can be diagnosed as having an antisocial personality disorder and who should not (Hare, Hart, and Harpur, 1991). What personality characteristics are reflected in such behaviors? Hervey Cleckley, a lifelong student of these behaviors and people, described some of their characteristics in *The Mask of Sanity* (1964). Cleckley lists sixteen features of the sociopath's personality. These sixteen characteristics can be reduced to three broad categories: inadequately motivated antisocial behavior, the absence of a conscience and sense of responsibility to others, and emotional poverty.

TABLE 15–1

THE ANTISOCIAL PERSONALITY DISORDER			
Definition	*Childhood Antecedents*	*Adult Behaviors*	*Influencing Factors*
Longstanding antisocial behavior manifested across a spectrum of activities, among which are aggressiveness, irresponsibility, recklessly endangering others, failure to honor financial obligations	Habitual lying Theft Aggressive sexuality Vandalism Truancy	Deceitfulness Irritability and repeated aggressiveness Repeated arrests Failure to plan ahead Lack of remorse	Deficiencies in social learning abilities, especially in avoidance learning Emotional underarousal Genetic predisposition to criminality Brain abnormalities

INADEQUATELY MOTIVATED ANTISOCIAL BEHAVIOR

Crime "makes sense" for normal criminals. We understand what they are doing and why, and so do they. They want to get rich—quick—and they may want status. These are motivations we can understand, however much we disapprove of the behaviors. But the crimes of sociopaths often seem aimless, random, and impulsive. We do not understand why they did what they did, and neither do they understand it. They seem not to be motivated by any rational purpose, but rather seem perversely impulsive, as shown in the following case:

> On October 7, 1976, Gary Gilmore was sentenced to death by a Utah court after a seemingly purposeless crime spree, and on January 7, 1977, he became the first person to be executed in the United States since 1966. During a psychological evaluation to determine whether Gilmore was competent to stand trial, it was determined that he suffered an antisocial personality disorder. Gilmore's activities provide an interesting example of crime without understandable motives.
>
> Gilmore had been released from prison only six months earlier, after serving time for armed robbery. He promptly violated parole by leaving the state. His probation officer gave him another chance. But shortly thereafter, following a heated argument with his girlfriend, Gilmore stole a stereo. Once again, he persuaded the police not to bring charges. Gilmore himself described the next events: "I pulled up near a gas station. I told the service station guy to give me all his money. I then took him to the bathroom and told him to kneel down and then I shot him in the head twice. The guy didn't give me any trouble but I just felt like I had to do it."
>
> The very next morning, Gilmore left his car at another service station for minor repairs and walked to a motel. "I went in and told the guy to give me the money. I told him to lay on the floor and then I shot him. I then walked out and was carrying the cash drawer with me. I took the money and threw the cash drawer in a bush and I tried to push the gun in the bush too. But as I was pushing it in the bush, it went off and that's how come I was shot in the arm. It seems like things have always gone bad for me. It seems like I've always done dumb things that just caused trouble for me."

ABSENCE OF A CONSCIENCE AND A SENSE OF RESPONSIBILITY TO OTHERS

The absence of shame or remorse for past misdeeds, of any sense of humiliation for egregious ones, is one of the most common characteristics of sociopaths. They lack conscience, and with it, any deep capacity to care about other people (Hare, 1980; Williamson, Hare, and Wong, 1987). Their relationships, therefore, tend to be quite shallow and exploitative. They lack a capacity for love and sustained attachment and are unresponsive to trust, kindness, or affection. They lie shamelessly and can mercilessly abuse those who have trusted them. Gary Gilmore did not have a serious relationship until several weeks before he committed the two murders. He was then thirty-six years old. Describing the affair, he said that it was "probably the first close relationship that I ever had with anyone. I just didn't know how to respond to her for any length of time. I was very insensitive to her . . . I was thoughtless in the way I treated her. . . . [H]er two children bugged me and sometimes I would get angry at them and slap them because they were so noisy."

EMOTIONAL POVERTY

One of the major differences between the normal person who is a criminal and the sociopath lies in the depth of experienced emotion. Ordinary criminals pre-

▲ If DSM-IV had been available, convicted killer Gary Gilmore would have been diagnosed with an antisocial personality disorder.

sumably experience the same emotions as other normal people. But sociopaths experience very shallow emotions. They seem to lack the capacity for sustained love, anger, grief, joy, or despair. During a psychiatric interview, Gilmore observed that "I don't remember any real emotional event in all my life. . . . When you're in the joint, you stay pretty even all the time . . . I'm not really excitable you know. I don't get emotional." Indeed, their incapacity to experience emotion may be significantly related to their lack of conscience and to the ease with which they violate the expectations of others (Hare, Williamson, and Harpur, 1988; Patrick, Bradley, and Cuthbert, 1990; Patrick, Cuthbert, and Lang, 1990).

The Sources of Sociopathy

Personality disorders are long-lived. The antisocial personality disorder originates in childhood or early adolescence as a conduct disorder (see Chapter 16), and then continues into adulthood. Once again, Gary Gilmore is a case in point. Examining his childhood, we find that he had been suspended from school on several occasions for truancy and for alleged thefts from his classmates. When he was fourteen, he was spent to a correctional youth facility for auto theft. By the time of his last arrest, Gilmore had spent fifteen of his sixteen adult years behind bars.

What factors give rise to such continuously antisocial behavior? Four potential sources have been given considerable attention: (1) the family and social context, (2) defects in learning, (3) genetics, and (4) physiological dysfunctions in the central nervous system.

THE FAMILY AND SOCIAL CONTEXT

Because the sociopath seems not to have internalized the moral standards of the larger society, it is natural to examine the agents of socialization, particularly the family and social context, for clues about sociopathy. There is evidence, for example, that sociopaths who grew up in the lower social classes experienced more difficult childhoods than other people from those same social strata. A number of studies indicate that losing a parent through desertion, divorce, or separation (rather than through death or chronic hospitalization) is highly correlated with the later development of sociopathic behavior (Gregory, 1958; Greer, 1964; Oltman and Friedman, 1967). Moreover, the more severe the sociopathic behavior, the more likely it is that the sociopath experienced parental deprivation. Most writers believe, however, that it is not the parental deprivation per se that promotes sociopathy—otherwise the findings would include deprivation through death and hospitalization. Rather it is the emotional climate that precedes the divorce—the arguments and violent fights, the blatant promiscuity, alcoholism, parental instability, the neglectful father—which is implicated in socialization for sociopathy (Smith, 1978).

Similar but substantially enlarged findings emerged from a study of a large group of people who had been seen at a child guidance clinic between 1924 and 1929 (Robins, 1966). Fortunately, the clinic had maintained careful psychological and sociological records on the presenting problems and family circumstances of its clients. When these children grew up, they were carefully interviewed, along with a control group that had never been seen at the clinic. About 22 percent of the clinic referrals qualified for the adult diagnosis of sociopathic personality, while only 2 percent of the control group received that diagnosis.

What early experiences were correlated with the diagnosis of antisocial personality disorder in adulthood? First, as children, these sociopaths had been referred to that child guidance clinic for antisocial behaviors. Theft, truancy, and school discipline problems dot their clinic records. Second, they tended more often than the control group to come from impoverished homes and from homes that were broken by divorce or separation. Their fathers themselves were often antisocial persons who may well have served as sociopathic models for their children (Bandura and Walters, 1963), while simultaneously creating the marital discord that may spawn sociopathic development (Robins, 1966). Again taking Gary Gilmore's life as an example, we find that although Gilmore's parents were never formally separated, his father spent so much of his time away from home that Gilmore considered himself to have been raised by "a single parent." During some of that time, his father was in prison, serving eighteen months on a bad check charge. His mother was simultaneously overindulgent and neglectful: Gilmore was often left to fend for himself. Reflecting on his family, he described it as "typical" and noted that "there wasn't much closeness in it."

The children who later became sociopaths were referred to juvenile court and were subsequently sent to correctional institutions much more often than other children. In such institutions, they very likely picked up some of the habits of their antisocial peers. These findings, however, should not be interpreted to mean that *all* punishment for juvenile offenses is necessarily harmful to the child. Indeed, one study revealed that children who were apprehended and *moderately* punished for juvenile crimes have a lower recidivism rate than those who were apprehended and released without punishment (McCord, 1980). In order for children to be deterred from further crime, they must be given a clear message that what they did was wrong. The message is clearest when it comes as punishment. *Too* clear a message—one that results in sending children to penal institutions—may teach that crime is wrong, but it may also put them in an environment where they can learn from their peers how to pursue a criminal career successfully.

Other longitudinal studies underscore the relationship of the home environment and subsequent criminality in delinquent boys. Once again, whether the father was absent or present was not a key determinant of subsequent criminality. The factors that did influence whether delinquent boys became criminal adults were maternal affection and self-esteem, parental supervision, harmony within the household, and the father's deviance. Indeed, separation and divorce do not lead to criminal behavior so long as the mother is affectionate and self-confident, the child is supervised, the level of discord between the parents is minimal, and the father is nondeviant (McCord, 1979).

DEFECTS IN LEARNING

Many clinicians have been struck by the seeming inability of the sociopath to learn from experience. Prichard (1837) called them "moral imbeciles." Cleckley (1964) observed that they failed especially to learn from punishing experiences, and as a result, had poor judgment. But sociopaths are often "savvy" and intelligent. If they suffer a defect in learning, it must be a fairly subtle one. What form might such a defect take?

Deficiencies in Avoidance Learning   Cleckley's observations, in particular, suggested that sociopaths were especially deficient in *avoidance* learning. Ordinary people rapidly learn to anticipate and avoid punitive situations. But sociopaths, perhaps because they are underaroused and underanxious, fail to do so. To examine this possibility, sociopaths and normal people were taken into the laboratory to test their ability to master a certain task (Lykken, 1957). The task involved learning to press a "correct" lever, but the idea was to find out which group learned to avoid punishment.

Participants sat in front of a panel that had four levers. Immediately above each lever was a red light and a green light (see Figure 15–1). The subject's task was to find and press the lever that turned on the green light on each of a series of twenty trials. Since the correct lever changed on each trial, the subjects had to remember their sequence of responses from the first trial to the one they were now working on. A certain pattern had to be learned, and it was quite a complicated task, a veritable mental maze.

On each trial, the subject had four choices, only one of which turned on the green light. Two of the levers turned on a red light—clearly a wrong response—while the third delivered electric shock. Having two kinds of wrong responses, one that simply says "wrong" and the other that delivers physical punishment, enabled the investigator to answer a telling question. Is it that sociopaths cannot learn from negative experience, or are there particular negative experiences, namely *avoidance* experiences, from which they cannot learn?

As expected, there were no differences in the total number of mistakes made by sociopaths and nonsociopaths. But whereas nonsociopaths quickly learned to avoid the electrified levers, the sociopaths made the most errors that led to shock, suggesting that their particular learning defect was an inability to learn from painful experiences (Lykken, 1957). In effect, punishment or threat of punishment does not seem to influence a sociopath's behavior.

FIGURE 15–1

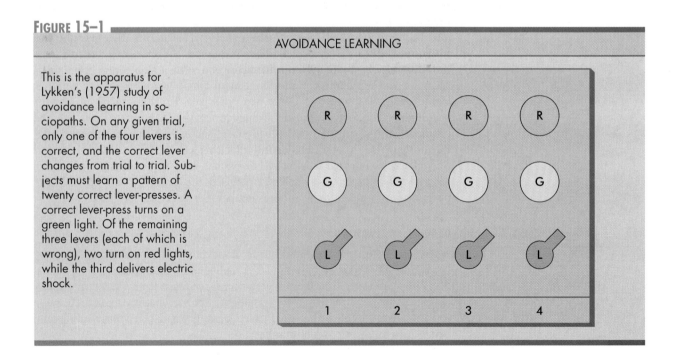

AVOIDANCE LEARNING

This is the apparatus for Lykken's (1957) study of avoidance learning in sociopaths. On any given trial, only one of the four levers is correct, and the correct lever changes from trial to trial. Subjects must learn a pattern of twenty correct lever-presses. A correct lever-press turns on a green light. Of the remaining three levers (each of which is wrong), two turn on red lights, while the third delivers electric shock.

Why should sociopaths be deficient in avoidance learning? One possibility is that sociopaths do not avoid shock because they do not find shock as noxious as do normal people, and they do not find shock as noxious because they are chronically *underaroused*. Put differently, sociopaths may actually seek stimulation in order to elevate arousal to an optimal level. Indeed, it has often seemed to clinical observers that that is the case (Cleckley, 1964). Gary Gilmore, the sociopath who was described earlier, may well have experienced underarousal and the need for stimulation as a child. Gilmore said, "I remember when I was a boy I would feel like I had to do things like sit on a railroad track until just before the train came and then I would dash off. Or I would put my finger over the end of a BB gun and pull the trigger to see if a BB was really in it. Sometimes I would stick my finger in water and then put my finger in a light socket to see if it would really shock me."

To examine the sociopath's possible need for stimulation, sociopathic and normal subjects were injected either with adrenaline, which heightens arousal, or with a placebo and tested on the "mental maze" described above. Once again, in both the adrenaline and placebo conditions, sociopaths made no more errors than normals. But sociopaths who received the placebo failed to learn to avoid shock. Only when they were given adrenaline was their characteristic underarousal overcome. Being already aroused by the adrenaline, the sociopaths avoided the electrified lever just as the normals did in the placebo condition (Schachter and Latane, 1964).

Cleckley's observation that sociopaths are emotionally flat was confirmed in this experiment, and has been confirmed in subsequent efforts (Williamson, Harpur, and Hare, 1990). Because they are underaroused in general, the emotions that ordinarily inhibit criminal behavior are not sufficiently aroused in sociopaths. At the same time, the emotions that propel people into crimes of passion are also absent. Sociopaths are mainly responsible for "cool" crimes such as burglary, forgery, and con games. When they are involved in violence, as Gilmore was, it tends to be impulsive and irrational violence, and perverse because it so lacks in feeling.

There are several kinds of punishment (see Table 15–2). There is *physical* punishment to which sociopaths do not respond as the above experiments suggest. But there is also *tangible* punishment such as the loss of money, and *social*

TABLE 15–2

AVOIDANCE LEARNING IN NORMALS AND SOCIOPATHS		
Stimulus	*Normals*	*Sociopaths*
Electric shock	Learn quickly to avoid; anxious while anticipating	Have trouble learning to avoid, unless injected with adrenaline; less anxious while anticipating
Social disapproval (red light)	Learn to avoid	Have trouble learning to avoid
Loss of a quarter	Learn to avoid	Learn more quickly than normals to avoid

punishment such as disapproval. Are sociopaths as unresponsive to the latter kinds of punishment as they are to physical punishment? The same "mental maze" was used to examine this question. But this time, if one of the wrong levers was pressed, the subject lost a quarter. If another was pressed, the subject received social disapproval, and the third wrong lever brought electric shock. Once again, sociopaths learned the task as quickly as nonsociopaths. And again, they were considerably less responsive to physical punishment than were normals. They were also less responsive to social disapproval. But they quickly learned to avoid the lever that would cost them a quarter. Indeed, they avoided this lever somewhat more than normals, indicating that sociopaths can learn to avoid punishment provided that the punishment is noxious to *them* (Schmauk, 1970).

The Immediacy of Consequences   The greater the interval between the time a behavior occurs and its consequences, the more difficult it is to learn the relationship between that behavior and its consequences. Some people generally have greater difficulty seeing a relationship between two events across time than do others. It may be that sociopaths have greater difficulty than most people. If this is the case, it would explain why sociopaths are not deterred from crime by the anticipation of punishment, since the punishment usually occurs long after the crime has been committed.

An experiment was devised to determine whether individuals with antisocial personality disorders anticipated punishment in different ways than did normals. In this experiment, three groups of subjects were used: (1) criminals who had been diagnosed as sociopaths; (2) criminals who had been diagnosed as nonsociopaths; and (3) noncriminals. These subjects were presented with the numbers "1" through "12," one at a time and consecutively. They were told that they would receive an electric shock when the number "8" appeared. In order to determine the level of anxiety experienced, the galvanic skin response (GSR), which is one measure of experienced anxiety, was assessed for each subject throughout the experiment. Both normals and nonsociopathic criminals displayed fear of the anticipated electric shock from the start. Moreover, their anxiety, as measured by the GSR, mounted markedly as the number "8" drew closer, and it plummeted afterwards. In contrast, sociopathic subjects exhibited dramatically lower anxiety levels throughout the experiment, and their measured fear did not increase as the number "8" approached. Even when the shock was administered, their arousal and GSR activity levels were far lower than those in the other two groups (Hare, 1965).

When the data on avoidance learning are combined with those on family and social antecedents of sociopathy, an interesting picture emerges. The antisocial personality disorder does not arise simply from harsh circumstances. Nor is its development deterred by physical punishment or even by imprisonment. Neither poverty nor parental deprivation necessarily led to sociopathy. But affectionate parents and parental supervision can inhibit the development of sociopathy. So, too, can punishment when it is *felt* to be painful and abhorrent, rather than when it is merely automatically applied.

GENETICS AND CRIMINALITY

The possibility that sociopathy has a genetic basis has long been attractive. In the popular imagination, sociopathy and antisocial behavior have long been associated with the "bad seed," and particularly the bad seed that came from a

FOCUS QUESTIONS

1. What do twin studies indicate about the genetic influence on criminal behavior?
2. Describe how adoption studies have been used to determine whether there is a genetic component to criminal behavior.
3. Why might XYY's be more likely to be convicted of crime than are "normal" male criminals?

family of bad seeds. That view, however, is hard to assess. The problems of sorting environmental from genetic influences are as difficult here as elsewhere. But the task here is further compounded by the fact that it is *criminals*—those who have been apprehended and convicted of a crime—who come to our attention, not those who have eluded apprehension. Not all criminals are sociopaths, of course, nor are all sociopaths criminals.

The data on the biology of sociopathy are fascinating for, though they are complex, they appear to indicate that both genetics and environment play strong roles in the development of sociopathy. We begin by considering twin and adoption studies, and then examine studies of men with an extra Y chromosome. But before doing so, one thing should be made clear. Most of these studies are concerned with the relations between biology and *criminality*. Criminality, as we indicated earlier, is not synonymous with sociopathy. Where the studies permit, we will distinguish between the two.

Twin Studies   One way to examine the relative influence of genetic and environmental factors in sociopathy is to study the concordance of sociopathic behavior in twins. Recall again that monozygotic or identical (MZ) twins each have exactly the same genetic heritage, while dizygotic (DZ) or fraternal twins are as genetically dissimilar as ordinary siblings (see Chapter 3). The environments of MZ and DZ twins are *nearly* the same. (These environments are nearly the same, rather than downright identical, because individuals contribute to their environments, and no two contributions are exactly the same.) This allows us to look at the other variable, genetics. If concordance for sociopathy or criminality is higher for MZ than for DZ twins, one can infer that genetic factors play a role.

According to the series of studies that examine the rates of criminality among MZ and DZ twins, there is a strong relationship between zygosity and criminality. In a total of 216 MZ pairs and 214 same-sex DZ pairs, 69 percent of the MZ but only 33 percent of the DZ pairs were concordant for criminality (Christiansen, 1977). By themselves, these studies would strongly suggest that genetic influences are powerful in criminality.

There are two sources of evidence that suggest that such a conclusion would be premature. First, such high concordance for criminality among MZ twins was only marginally higher than for DZ twins (Dalgard and Kringlen, 1976). The latter finding can be explained by the fact that MZ twins share a more similar environment than DZ twins. Monozygotic twins, being identical, are more likely to be treated the same by parents and others than are dizygotic twins. Indeed, they are often confused for each other. Second, and even more interesting, are the data regarding *opposite-sex* DZ pairs. Opposite-sex twins are no different genetically than same-sex DZ twins, though patently they share different environments. If criminality is determined by heredity and heredity alone, the data for opposite-sex twins should be identical to the data for same-sex DZ twins. But they are not. The concordance for criminality among opposite-sex twins is only 16 percent, less than half of what it is for same-sex twins. This difference in concordance rates underscores the environmental influences on criminality (Cloninger, Christiansen, Reich, and Gottesman, 1978; Sigvardsson, Cloninger, Bohman, and von Knorring, 1982). Moreover, it is clear that heredity plays no role in transmitting tendencies toward *violent* crime (Mednick, Brennan, and Kandel, 1988), though as we will shortly see, it does play a significant role in crime generally.

TABLE 15–3

CRIMINALITY OF ADOPTED SONS ACCORDING TO THE CRIMINALITY OF THEIR ADOPTIVE AND BIOLOGICAL FATHERS

Father		Percentage of sons who are criminal offenders	Number
Biological	Adoptive		
No registered offense	No registered offense	10.5	333
No registered offense	Criminal offense	11.5	52
Criminal offense	No registered offense	22.0	219
Criminal offense	Criminal offense	36.2	58
Total			662

SOURCE: Modified from Hutchings and Mednick, 1977, p. 132.

Adoption Studies When children are raised by their natural parents, it is impossible to separate the effects of genetics from those of environment on their development. But studies of children who have been adopted at an early age allow these influences to be separated. These studies also provide evidence for the influence of heredity in both criminality and sociopathy. One study examined the criminal records of adopted persons in Denmark (Hutchings and Mednick, 1977; Mednick, Gabrielli and Hutchings, 1984). Their names were drawn from the Danish Population Register, which records the names of both the adoptive and the biological parents of these adoptees. Thus, it is possible to compare the criminal records of the adopted children with those of both sets of parents. These comparative data are shown in Table 15–3. The incidence of crime among these offspring was lowest when neither the biological nor the adoptive fathers had been convicted of a criminal offense. Nearly indistinguishable from that low rate was the rate among adoptees whose adoptive fathers had been convicted, but whose biological fathers were "clean." The incidence of criminal conviction among adoptees jumped dramatically, however, when the natural father had a criminal record, but the adoptive father had none, providing clear support for the view that the tendency to engage in criminal acts is hereditary. But highest of all was the incidence of criminality among adoptees when both their natural *and* adoptive fathers had criminal records, underscoring again the combined influence of heredity and environment on criminality. These individuals probably inherited a tendency toward criminality from their biological fathers and learned criminal behavior from their adoptive fathers (Cloninger and Gottesman, 1987). As we mentioned, however, criminality is not identical with sociopathy. But when a measure of sociopathy rather than criminality was used, similar findings were obtained (Schulsinger, 1972).

Sex Differences in the Genetics of Criminality? In crimes against property such as stealing (as opposed to violent crimes), there appears to be strong evidence for both genetic and environmental influences. But oddly, although women in Denmark were less likely than men to become registered criminals, *children* of convicted women were at greater risk for criminal conviction than children of criminal men. Convicted females seem to have a larger genetic predisposition than convicted males (Cloninger, Reich, and Guze, 1975; Baker, Mack, Moffitt, and Mednick, 1989).

Why should that be? One reasonable explanation rests on the observation that stealing is something that men are more likely to do than women. In order for women to engage in such criminal behavior, they may require a stronger genetic predisposition, as well as more adverse environmental circumstances, than do their brothers (Baker, Mack, Moffitt, and Mednick, 1989).

XYY: An Extra Chromosome?   A person's sex is determined by a pair of chromosomes. Women have two X chromosomes (XX). Men have a single X and a single Y chromosome (XY). But some men have an extra Y chromosome (XYY). Since it is the Y chromosome that defines the male, the XYY is sometimes considered a "supermale." Such a person, for example, is especially tall—much taller than the ordinary male. It is also widely believed that the XYY is especially violent and often prone toward criminal behavior.

These beliefs are difficult to verify. Not all tall men are XYY's. Nor, of course, are all criminals XYY's. Indeed, not more than 1.5 percent of criminals and delinquents who have been tested have this additional chromosome (Rosenthal, 1970b). Some of the studies take their evidence from a few or even single cases, and they often fail to include normal control groups. Until recently, a definite relationship between the XYY syndrome and violence could neither be demonstrated nor disconfirmed.

One study examined the criminal records of all men who were born in Copenhagen between 1944 and 1947 (Witkin et al., 1976). Once again, the Danish Population Register provides very complete data on Danish citizens, and therefore permits this kind of thorough study. The investigators began with a group of 31,436 men, of whom 4,591 were at least six feet tall. Since XYY's are tall, the latter group promised to produce the maximum number of XYY's. In that group, twelve XYY's were discovered, yielding a prevalence of 2.9 XYY's per thousand population. Of those twelve, five or 42 percent had been convicted of one or more criminal offenses, as against 9.3 percent of ordinary XY males who were six feet tall or more. While the data support the view that XYY men are more likely to be convicted of a crime, they do not confirm the view that XYY's engage in *violent* crime. Only one of the five committed an act of violence against another person, and that act was relatively mild. Otherwise, nearly all of the crimes involved property. Indeed, of the 149 offenses for which the five XYY's were convicted, fully 145 were against property—usually crimes of theft.

But while XYY's are not more violent, the evidence from this study indicates that they are convicted of crime much more frequently than are "normal" male criminals. Why should that be? One interesting bit of information that emerged from the above study is that, compared to XY criminals, XYY's have markedly lower intelligence. Conceivably, lower intelligence itself leads to criminal activity, perhaps because the less intelligent find it more difficult to get jobs or to resist temptations. Alternately, these findings may not reflect differences in the incidence of crime, but merely differences in *apprehension* and *conviction.* With lower intelligence, XYY's may stand a greater chance of being apprehended, convicted, and sentenced.

FOCUS QUESTIONS

1. What problems at birth may predispose an individual toward later criminal behavior?
2. What physiological differences between sociopaths and normals have been found?

PROBLEMS AT BIRTH

There may well be a host of factors that occur at birth or before that, above and beyond genetic contributions, that predispose individuals toward violent behavior later on. For example, there is evidence that infants with low birth weight, whose parents engage in—and therefore, model—physical aggression, are more likely themselves to become criminally violent, than are infants of normal birth weight (Shanok and Lewis, 1981; Mednick, Brennan, and Kandel, 1988). Low birth weight often results from malnutrition and other problems during pregnancy that commonly affect brain development and subsequent maturation and therefore may be implicated in criminal behavior.

PHYSIOLOGICAL DYSFUNCTIONS

To whatever extent genetics and perinatal problems are related to criminality and sociopathy, the relationship is not likely a direct one. One does not directly acquire from genes the skills and disposition to engage in crime. What then is it that *is* acquired genetically? What is passed down through the genes that makes one more likely to engage in sociopathic activities?

A number of investigators have sought to discover physiological differences between sociopaths and normal people. And a good number of such differences have been discovered. For example, a substantial proportion of sociopaths have abnormal electroencephalograms (EEG's). This is especially true of the most violent and aggressive sociopaths. The abnormalities are of two kinds. First, sociopaths show the slow brain waves that are characteristic of children and that suggest brain immaturity. Second, a sizable proportion of sociopaths show positive spiking in their brain waves. Positive spikes are sudden and brief bursts of brain wave activity. These spikes occur in the EEG's of 40 to 45 percent of sociopaths as compared to about 1 to 2 percent of the general population (Kurland, Yeager, and Arthur, 1963). Positive spiking is itself associated with impulsive, aggressive behavior. Most individuals who commit aggressive acts and who also manifest positive spiking report no guilt or anxiety about their actions.

These findings are of interest for several reasons. First, the possibility that sociopaths suffer cortical immaturity (Hare, 1978) suggests that as they get older (and their cortexes become more mature) sociopaths should engage in less antisocial behavior. That is precisely what has been found. Particularly between the ages of thirty and forty, a substantial proportion of sociopaths show marked behavioral improvements (Robins, 1966).

Second, those positive spikes—the sudden and brief bursts of brain wave activity—appear to reflect a dysfunction in the brain's limbic system, precisely the system that controls emotion and motivation. And what emotion might be affected by this physiological dysfunction? Some theorists speculate that it is *fear*, the very emotion that is thought to be implicated in the phenomena of socialization and self-control (Cleckley, 1964). The sociopath's inability to inhibit behaviors and delay gratifications is generally thought to be similar to that of animals who have suffered lesions in the brain's septal region (Gorenstein and Newman, 1980). Thus, the sociopath's failure to learn from punishing experiences may be the product of faulty physiology. Biology, rather than malice, may be the wellspring of the antisocial personality disorder (see Box 15–1).

Box 15-1

PHINEAS GAGE AND ALTERED MORAL BEHAVIOR

On September 13, 1848, Phineas P. Gage, a twenty-five-year-old construction foreman, became a victim of a bizarre accident. He was part of a team that was laying railroad tracks across Vermont. He was in charge of detonations. He drilled holes in the stones, partially filled them with explosive powder, covered the powder with sand, and, using a fuse and tamping rod, triggered explosions in the rock. On the fateful day, however, Gage was momentarily distracted and began tamping directly over the powder, before it had been covered with sand. The result was a powerful explosion away from the rock and toward Gage. The 3-cm-thick, 109-cm-long tamping iron was hurled like a rocket though his face, skull, brain, and then into the sky. Gage was momentarily stunned, but regained full consciousness immediately. He was able to talk, even to walk with the help of his men. The tamping iron landed many yards away.

Phineas Gage survived the accident but survived as a different man. Before the accident, Gage had been a responsible, intelligent and sociable person, a favorite with peers and elders. He had made progress at work, showed promise, and was deemed "the most efficient and capable" man in the construction company's employ. But during his convalescence and surely afterwards, he was radically transformed. He remained as able-bodied and astute as before. He suffered no impairment of either movement or speech. Neither was his capacity to learn or conventional intelligence impaired. But he became irreverent and capricious. His respect for social conventions vanished. His profanity regularly offended. Most troubling, he had lost his sense of responsibility. He could not be trusted to honor his commitments. He lost his job, became a wanderer, and died in San Francisco some twelve years later. The tamping rod that had gone through his skull was buried alongside him.

His physician, John Harlow, recognized the relationship between the damage to Gage's frontal lobes, and his altered moral behavior. He suspected that much as there are language and motor centers in the brain, so is there a neural basis for moral reasoning and social behavior. But in those days, there was no way to ascertain such a view, especially since the relevant portion of Gage's brain had been blown away.

Harlow learned of Gage's death about five years after it occurred. He contacted the family, and asked to have Gage's corpse exhumed so that his skull could be recovered and preserved as a medical record. The family concurred, and as a result, Gage's skull and the tamping rod that did him in have resided in the Warren Anatomical Medical Museum at Harvard University.

Enter now Hanna and Antonio Damasio and their colleagues, better than a century later. They carefully photographed and X-rayed Gage's skull, and using modern image-processing techniques, reconstituted in minute detail the possible entry and exit points of the tamping rod, in order to determine where the rod might have torn the brain. They concluded that Gage "fits a neuroanatomical pattern that we have identified today in twelve patients . . . with frontal damage. Their ability to make rational decisions in personal and social matters is invariably compromised and so is their processing of emotion. On the contrary, their ability to tackle the logic of an abstract problem, to perform calculations, and to call up appropriate knowledge and attend to it remains intact."

SOURCE: Damasio, Grabowski, Frank, Galaburda, and Damasio, 1994.

▶ Electronic images of Phineas Gage's skull after the bizarre brain trauma that spared his life but dramatically changed his personality.

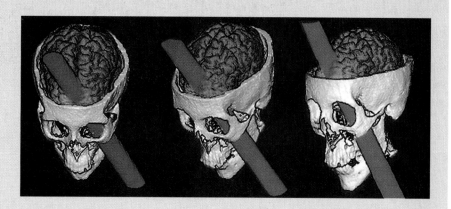

The Antisocial Personality Disorder: An Overview

The sociopath has been given many different names over the decades, but the symptoms remain remarkably the same. Sociopathy originates in childhood, where it is characterized by such things as truancy, persistent lying, theft, and vandalism. Similar behaviors persist into adulthood, taking the forms of assaults against persons and property, defaulting on major debts and financial responsibilities, and involvement in the underworld. Sociopaths share a group of personality traits, which include the absence of a sense of shame or remorse, failure to learn from past experience, and impoverished emotions.

Thus, we come full circle. Clinical observations lead us to believe that sociopaths are deficient in the ability to experience emotion and in the degree to which conscience controls their behavior. These clinical observations are confirmed by laboratory studies, which indicate that physical punishment is particularly ineffective with sociopaths. Further studies suggest that physical punishment may be ineffective because sociopaths are underaroused, a condition that may be due to aberrant limbic function. While the effects of environment are clearly evident in the development of sociopathy, there is evidence that genetics, too, plays a role. And speculation that genetic factors influence brain function, especially limbic function, is consistent with data that indicate that sociopaths are underaroused (see Figure 15–2).

OTHER PERSONALITY DISORDERS

The antisocial personality disorder is the best known and best studied of the personality disorders, but it is not the only one. People who are characteristically suspicious and distrustful, or passive, or inappropriately emotional, or overly dependent upon others, or enormously compulsive and orderly may also be suffering from a personality disorder.

Paranoid Personality Disorder

> After his wife died, Seymour moved to a retirement community in Florida. Healthy and attractive, he immediately joined a folk dancing group, a current events discussion group, and a ceramics class. Within six weeks, however, he had dropped out of all the programs, complaining to his children that other residents were talking about him behind his back, that he was unable to find a dancing partner, ignored in the current events group, and given improper instruction in ceramics.
>
> Before his retirement, Seymour had been a physicist. He had always been closed-mouth about his work. His home study had always been locked. He had not permitted anyone to clean it, and he had become angry if anyone entered it without his permission. His son reported that his parents had been extremely close and affectionate, but that his father had had few other friends. He had been wary of new faces and concerned about the motives of strangers.
>
> A hard worker throughout his life, he was now gripped by fear. He spent much of his time overseeing his investments, fearful that his broker would give him poor advice, or neglect to tell him when to buy and when to sell.

FIGURE 15–2

SOURCES OF THE ANTISOCIAL PERSONALITY DISORDER

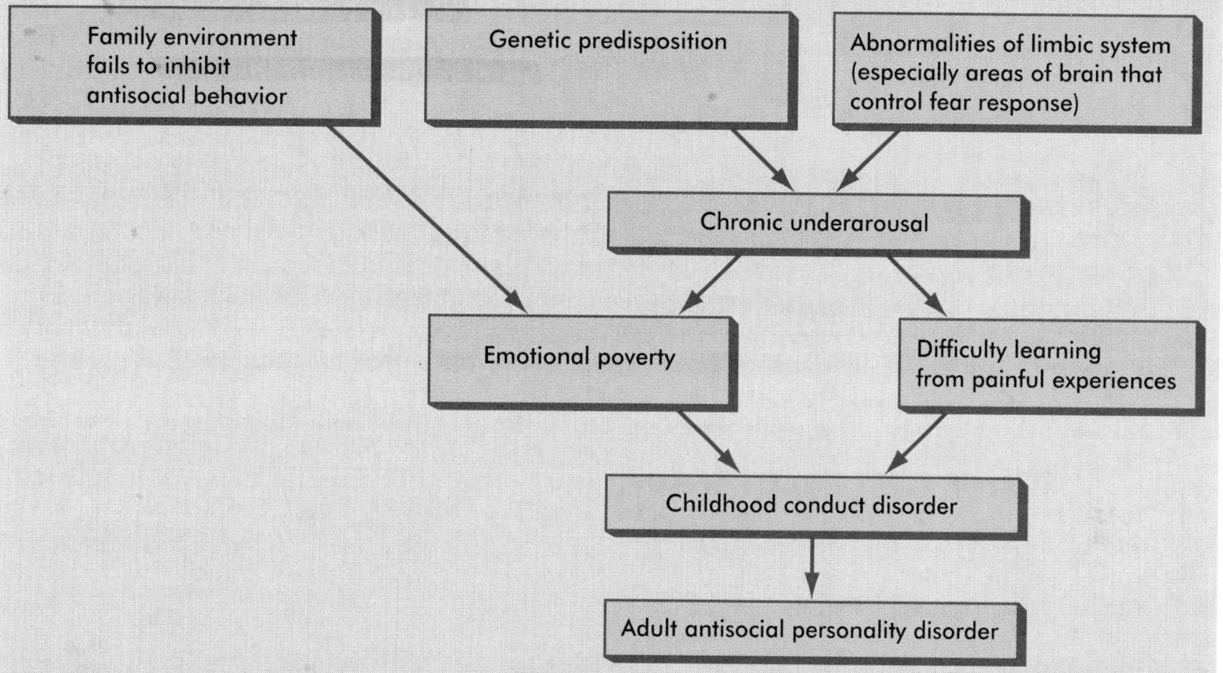

Both genes and environment play a role in whether someone will develop antisocial personality disorder. Family and social context may lead to emotional poverty in an individual. This in combination with a genetic predisposition to chronic underarousal, which may be caused by a dysfunction in the brain's limbic system, may lead to difficulties in learning, as well as emotional poverty, resulting in childhood conduct disorder and ultimately antisocial personality disorder.

FOCUS QUESTIONS

1. How is the paranoid personality disorder best characterized?
2. Describe people who have a histrionic personality disorder.
3. What is the central feature of the narcissistic personality disorder and how does this lead to disturbances in interpersonal relationships?
4. Describe the vicious cycle that characterizes the lives of those with avoidant personality disorder.

The prominent characteristics of the ***paranoid personality disorder*** are a pervasive and longstanding distrust and suspiciousness of others; hypersensitivity to slight; and a tendency to scan the environment for, and to perceive selectively, cues that validate prejudicial ideas and attitudes. Those who suffer from the paranoid personality disorder are often argumentative, tense, and humorless. They seem ready to attack. They tend to exaggerate, to make mountains out of molehills, and to find hidden motives and special meanings in the innocuous behavior of others. They tend to blame others for whatever difficulties they experience, and they cannot themselves accept any blame or responsibility for failure. Recent evidence suggests that those with a paranoid personality disorder and those with a schizophrenic disorder share a common genetic structure (Kendler and Gruenberg, 1982).

Because such people tend to externalize blame and guilt, they are rarely seen in clinics or psychiatric hospitals. Thus, it is difficult to estimate how prevalent this problem is. Generally, however, it is felt to be a problem that tends to afflict men more than women (Kass, Spitzer, and Williams, 1983). As might be expected from their tendency to externalize, the prognosis for this disorder is guarded indeed.

Histrionic Personality Disorder

People who have long histories of drawing attention to themselves and of engaging in excited emotional displays that are caused by insignificant events are captured in the diagnosis of **histrionic personality disorder.** Such people are apt to be superficially charming, warm, and gregarious, but they are often viewed by others as insincere and shallow. They seem to be seeking admiration by playing continually to unknown audiences. Once they form relationships, they become demanding and inconsiderate, egocentric, and self-absorbed. They can be enormously flirtatious or coquettish, yet their sexual adjustment is as often naive or frigid, suggesting that their flirtatious behavior serves the ends of attention-getting much more than those of sexuality. This disorder occurs more commonly among women (Kass, Spitzer, and Williams, 1983), but it is also seen among men and is then termed "machoism" (Chodoff, 1982).

> At forty-two, Michael entered therapy after his second marriage failed. He strikes you as every bit the college professor: pipe-smoking, tweedy, facile with words, and somewhat theatrical. His difficulties are gripping, and they extend beyond his marriage. He has been the victim of muggings and robberies, of badly diagnosed ailments, and wrongly prescribed drugs. His scholarly papers are often rejected by journal editors, and his colleagues seem not to appreciate his genius. For all of this, he seems clearly a charming man, though one who is more interested in the therapist's reactions than in understanding his own plight.
>
> Michael reports that he has an interesting social life, though he complains in passing that people often do not invite him to dinner a second time. Nor do they lend him money or allow him to borrow their car. Some probing reveals that Michael has frequently failed to repay loans, and that he has often been involved in accidents with other people's cars ("well, they're insured . . ."). He is prone to cancel social engagements at the last minute if something more interesting comes up. Indeed, he calls often to change his scheduled therapy sessions and is upset when those changes cannot be arranged.

▶ Histrionic personalities seem to live their lives as elaborate emotional shows played continuously to unknown audiences.

If, upon perusing Michael's history, you have the sense that the diagnosis is not entirely clear, that it seems to overlap with other personality disorders, perhaps especially with the borderline personality (see below), or even the antisocial personality disorder—you may well be right. There seems to be considerable overlap between the histrionic personality disorder and other disorders (Pfohl, 1991; Grueneich, 1992).

Narcissistic Personality Disorder

The central feature of the **_narcissistic personality disorder_** is an outlandish sense of self-importance. It is characterized by continuous self-absorption, by fantasies of unlimited success, power and/or beauty, by exhibitionistic needs for constant admiration, and by the use of a substantially more benign standard for evaluating self than for judging others (Kernberg, 1975; Tangney, Wagner, and Gramzow, 1992). Criticism, the indifference of others, and threats to esteem characteristically receive exaggerated responses of rage, shame, humiliation, or emptiness. Of course, the near-total preoccupation with self massively disturbs interpersonal relationships in a variety of ways. Such people may simply lack the ability to recognize how others feel. They may have an exaggerated sense of "entitlement," expecting that the world owes them a living without assuming reciprocal responsibilities. They may simply be exploitative, taking advantage of others to indulge their own desires. When they are able to establish a relationship, they may vacillate between the extremes of overidealization and enormous devaluation of the other person.

There is reason to believe that, perhaps as a result of parental training, those who suffer the narcissistic personality disorder simply _expect_ too much from others (Benjamin, 1987). And self theorists (see Chapter 4) would suggest that these expectations arise because empathic relationships with caregivers failed to develop (Kohut, 1971, 1977, 1978), resulting in a fragmented sense of self that is especially vulnerable to feelings of emptiness and low self-esteem, and the compensatory behaviors that these generate, as the following case illustrates.

▲ The narcissistic personality disorder arises from an exaggerated sense of self-importance, such as we might imagine in Louis XIV of France, crowned as a young child.

Marion is a bit player who, at twenty-four, has not had a major theatrical role since her high school play. She has just been turned down for the lead in a new musical. Plagued with self-doubt, she is simultaneously furious with the casting director, a man with whom she has studied acting for the past three years. In her view, she should have gotten the part—both because she was every bit as good as the young woman who ultimately did get it, and because she was owed the support of the director who encouraged her and took her money for years. Marion is certain that the other actress got the part because she slept with the director. But her own time will come, Marion believes, and when it does, her own name will be displayed on the theater marquee.

Beyond her vocational difficulties, Marion also has difficulty in establishing and maintaining friendships. Slender, beautifully dressed, and seemingly self-assured, she has no trouble attracting men. At first, she enthusiastically envisions great times with them. But shortly thereafter she drops them, terming them "duds," "sexually unexciting," or "just plain boring." Women seem to fare no better. Marion gave a friend a ticket to see her in a play. Instead, her friend visited a hospitalized aunt. Marion fumed and viewed her friend's absence as a "betrayal."

Avoidant Personality Disorder

At the core of the ***avoidant personality disorder*** is a *turning away:* from people, from new experiences, and even from old ones. The disorder often combines a fear of appearing foolish with an equally strong desire for acceptance and affection. Individuals who experience this disorder want very much to enter into social relationships or new activities, but they may find themselves unwilling to take even small risks unless they are given strong guarantees of uncritical acceptance. They are shy (Zimbardo, 1977). The slightest hint of disapproval by others and the slightest whiff of potential failure lead them to withdraw. They may interpret apparently innocuous events as ridicule. People suffering from this disorder are likely to be distressed by their relative inability to relate comfortably to others, which adds to their low self-esteem, which in turn makes them even more sensitive to criticism and humiliation—an especially vicious cycle. But is the avoidant personality disorder truly a separate disorder, or is it indistinguishable from generalized social phobia that we examined in Chapter 8? The available evidence suggests that, by and large, the diagnosis of avoidant personality disorder tells us little more than is told by the Axis I diagnosis of social phobia (Herbert, Hope, and Bellack, 1992; Holt, Heimberg, and Hope, 1992; Turner, Beidel, and Townsley, 1992). To the extent that there is a difference between those two diagnoses, it may lie in the possibility that those with the avoidant personality disorder are more anxious in social situations and possess inferior social skills to cope with them (Turner, Beidel, Dancu, and Keys, 1986; Widiger, 1992).

> Elaine became quite distraught when her co-worker and close friend left to train as a nurse-practitioner. Her replacement was "nice enough," but Elaine feared the new woman would find her boring. At twenty-one, Elaine has only one other friend, her married sister. But her sister is "too busy with her family right now," and so Elaine spends very little time with her. Her social life in high school was quite restricted, and at present, she has no social life at all. At work, she eats lunch alone and is viewed by other workers as unfriendly.

▼ Deference and fearfulness characterize the dependent personality disorder.

Dependent Personality Disorder

The central characteristic of the ***dependent personality disorder*** involves allowing others to make the major decisions, to initiate the important actions, and to assume responsibility for significant areas of one's life. People with this disorder often defer to spouse, parent, or friend regarding where they should live, the kind of job they should have, and who their friends should be. They subordinate their own needs to the needs of the people upon whom they are dependent, feeling that any assertion of their own needs may jeopardize the relationship. Such people will often tolerate enormous physical and/or psychological abuse for fear that they will be abandoned. Correspondingly, when they are alone even for brief periods of time, they may experience intense discomfort and helplessness. Thus, they often seek companionship at great cost. They lack self-esteem, and they often refer to themselves as stupid or helpless. The disorder may have its origin in parental behavior that is both overprotective and authoritarian. Such behavior may well be synergistic. Overprotective parents encourage dependency in children, and such dependent behavior brings forth comforting protectiveness for parents (Hunt, Browning, and Nave, 1982; Bornstein, 1992). The dependent personality disorder occurs more frequently among women than among men (Kass, Spitzer, and Williams, 1983).

The mother of two small children, Joyce was brought to the emergency room with multiple facial abrasions and a fractured jaw. She was no stranger to the hospital staff. Eight months earlier, she had been treated for two broken ribs and assorted bruises. Joyce was reluctant to give the details of her injuries. But the neighbor who brought her to the hospital reported that Joyce had been physically assaulted by her husband. According to the neighbor, Joyce's husband frequently abused her verbally and "slapped her around" on a number of occasions. Although Joyce feared for her own safety and that of her children, she was unresponsive to suggestions that she move out and separate from her husband.

The middle child of three, Joyce was given neither great responsibility nor great attention during her childhood. Her father was a man of strong opinions and made all the decisions in the family. He believed adamantly that women belonged at home, and joked often and coarsely about "buns in the oven and bums in bed." He controlled the family finances, and delegated no responsibility in that area.

Apart from a course in typing, Joyce learned no vocational skills in high school, and dropped out to get married. Indeed, other than baby-sitting and summer jobs as a mother's helper, Joyce had no work experience at all.

During the five years of her marriage, Joyce left all decisions to her husband, even to the point of agreeing to the purchase of a sofa that she really disliked. Her husband was intensely jealous of her friendships, and she therefore abandoned all of them. Indeed, except for visits to her mother who lived in the neighborhood, she went nowhere without her husband.

This disorder is common, especially in women. Pregnant women who suffer this disorder are much more anxious at the time of birth if their husbands are not in the delivery room, whereas women who do not suffer the disorder seem unaffected by their husbands' absence during delivery (Keinan and Hobfoll, 1989; Bornstein, 1992). Moreover, the disorder impairs occupational functioning if the nature of the job requires independent decision making. Social relations may be restricted to the few people upon whom the person is dependent. And when the dependent relationship is threatened, vast depression may ensue (Bornstein, 1992).

Obsessive-Compulsive Personality Disorder

The *obsessive-compulsive personality disorder* is characterized by a pervasive pattern of striving for perfection. Those with the disorder demand perfection in themselves as well as others. Nothing they do seems to please them, however excellent the outcome. And because they anticipate being unable to meet their own unattainable standards, they often procrastinate in important matters, allocating their time poorly and leaving the things that mean most to them to the very last. While they prize work and productivity over pleasure and interpersonal relationships, they get overly involved in details, in lists and rules and schedules. They have great trouble making work-related decisions and are excellent at postponing pleasure-related ones. People who suffer this disorder tend to have difficulty expressing emotion, and they are often seen by others as formal, stiff, overly conscientious, and moralistic. The disorder is common among both sexes, but somewhat more frequent among men.

> Laura and Steve began to see a marriage counselor because Steve insisted on it. He had become extremely distressed by Laura's unavailability and perfectionism. At thirty-seven, Laura was a partner in one of the nation's largest accounting firms. She worked long hours at the office, brought work home, was unwilling to go out more than once a week, and resisted taking vacations. At home, she snapped out orders to the children about housework and schoolwork. She could not tolerate an unwashed dish or a jacket on the sofa and was critical and demanding of household help. Much of the time, Steve found her sexually unresponsive.
>
> Laura did not believe she had a "marriage problem," though she freely acknowledged feeling harassed at work and at home. She attributed her long hours at work to the demands of her profession. Snapping at the children and nit-picking about domestic order were, she insisted, the result of being the person who had to clean up after everyone else. Laura did not consider herself sexually unresponsive, but she did think she was often tense and fatigued. The only child of upwardly striving immigrant parents, Laura had been encouraged to excel. She was valedictorian of her high school class and among the top ten of her college graduating class. The social milieu in which she grew up put great stress on the value of close family relationships. Laura never doubted that she would be a wife and mother, and she married soon after graduating college.

Schizoid Personality Disorder

The central feature of the **schizoid personality disorder** is a defect in the capacity to form social relationships, as reflected in the absence of desire for social involvements, indifference to both praise and criticism, insensitivity to the feelings of others, and/or lack of social skills. Such people have few, if any, close friends. They are withdrawn, reserved, and seclusive. Others see them as "in a fog" and absent-minded. In short, they are extreme introverts. Their feelings tend to be bland and constricted; they seem to lack warm feelings or the capacity for emotional display and are therefore perceived as cold, aloof, or distant. Sometimes, and especially in jobs that require a good deal of social isolation, these characteristics can be assets. But more often, the very poverty of social skills restricts occupational and social success.

> A thirty-eight-year-old chemical engineer, Homer was forced into marriage counseling by his wife who complained of his failure to join in family activities or to take an interest in the children, his general lack of affection and responsiveness, and his disinterest in sex. His failure to relate socially to others extended also to his job, where colleagues characterized him as either shy and reticent, or as cold and aloof.
>
> Homer's history revealed longstanding social indifference and little emotional responsiveness. He recalled that he was indifferent to the idea of marrying, but did so to please his parents. His wife tried repeatedly to arrange social situations that might be of interest to him, but to no avail.

Schizotypal Personality Disorder

The **schizotypal personality disorder** is described mainly by longstanding oddities in thinking, perceiving, communicating, and behaving—oddities that are severe enough to be noticed, but not serious enough to warrant the more serious diagnosis of schizophrenia (McGlashan, 1987). Odd thinking can be manifest in extreme superstitiousness, or in the sense that one is especially noticed by others. The latter sense, which is technically called an ***idea of reference,*** can also be a fertile breeding ground for suspiciousness and paranoia. Depersonalization—a sense of estrangement from oneself and from one's environment—may be present. Communication may be odd, but not downright peculiar. It may be tangential, digressive, vague, or overly elaborate, but it is not loose or incoherent. Finally, people suffering from this disorder may also experience constricted or inappropriate feelings, with the result that they are unable to maintain rapport in face-to-face interactions.

The schizotypal personality disorder seems genetically related to schizophrenia (Kety, 1974; Kendler and Gruenberg, 1984; Baron, Gruen, Kane, and Amis, 1985). Indeed, many of the disturbances described here are similar to those seen among chronic schizophrenics, but here the disturbances appear in milder forms. It is an error, however, to identify this disorder wholly with the schizophrenias because differences of degree are very important differences as far as psychological distress and prognosis are concerned (McGlashan, 1986b). As we do not confuse the poor and the rich, even though both have some money, so must the schizotypal personality disorder be distinguished from its more intense relatives, the schizophrenias.

> At twenty-one, Mark complains that he feels "spaced out" and "creepy" much of the time. Unemployed, he lives with his parents and spends much of his time watching television or staring into space. He says that he often feels as if he is outside himself, watching himself through a TV screen, or running through a script that someone else has written. Mark has had several jobs, but none has lasted more than a month. He was fired from his last position as a toy salesman after several customers had complained that he had talked to them in vague terms about irrelevant things.
>
> Mark is convinced that people do not like him, but he does not understand why. He is certain that people change their seats on buses to avoid sitting next to him. He is unhappy about his loneliness and isolation, but he has made no attempt to re-establish old relationships.
>
> Several months ago, Mark learned that one of his parents' friends planned to open a chain of athletic shoe discount stores. Although he has no experience or training in business, Mark is "waiting" for an offer to manage one of these stores.

Borderline Personality Disorder

Borderline personality disorder is a very broad category whose essential feature is *instability* in a variety of personality areas, including interpersonal relationships, behavior, mood, and self-image. These areas are not necessarily related and, indeed, are themselves so broad that people with quite different problems are likely to be considered for this diagnosis.

The borderline personality disorder diagnosis is, by far, the most prevalent of the personality disorder diagnoses in both inpatient and outpatient settings (Grueneich, 1992). Yet, clearly, any diagnosis that is so broad and potentially inclusive runs the risk of becoming a "kitchen sink" diagnosis. In order to increase the validity of the borderline diagnosis, as well as limit its use to a restricted range of people, DSM-IV requires that evidence for at least five of the following problems be present before the diagnosis can be made:

FOCUS QUESTIONS

1. Describe the central characteristic of the dependent personality disorder and how it may originate.
2. Why do those with the obsessive-compulsive personality disorder often procrastinate and have trouble making decisions?
3. What is the central feature of the schizoid personality disorder?
4. Describe what may cause the instability and unpredictability that characterize borderline personality disorder.

- frantic efforts to avoid real or imagined abandonment;
- a pattern of intense, yet unstable, interpersonal relationships characterized by alternating between extremes of idealization and devaluation;
- persistent and markedly disturbed, distorted, or unstable self-image, or identity;
- impulsivity in at least two areas that are self-damaging, such as sex, substance abuse, spending, reckless driving, or binge eating;
- recurrent suicidal behavior, threats of such behavior, or self-mutilating gestures;
- chronic feelings of emptiness;
- emotional instability due mainly to a marked reactivity of mood that lasts for a few hours to a few days;
- lack of control over anger;
- transient, stress-related paranoid thoughts, or severe dissociative symptoms.

What causes the instability and unpredictability that is so characteristic of the borderline personality disorder? Both empirical evidence and intelligent speculation suggest that the person who suffers borderline personality disorder is, to begin with, a *gifted* person. She is gifted with unusual perceptiveness about, and insight into, the feelings that other people have (Park, Imboden, Park, Hulse, and Unger, 1992). She is, moreover, particularly empathic (Ladisch and Feil, 1988) and quite sensitive to nonverbal nuances (Frank and Hoffman, 1986). Such gifts would ordinarily augur well for her social development were it not for the fact that she has regularly been exposed to psychological abuse in the form of devaluation and blame (Zanarini, Gunderson, Marina, Schwartz, and Frankenberg, 1989; Stone, 1990), and often to sexual and physical abuse. It is her intuitive brilliance that is assaulted, rather than vaunted, by the abusive parent (Park, Imboden, Park, Hulse, and Unger, 1992). In order to maintain a "secure" emotional base, she rejects herself and her gifts, while absolving the abusive parent (Bowlby, 1988; Crittenden and Ainsworth, 1989).

Moreover, modern self theorists (see Chapter 4, pp. 82–86) speculate that it is a failed self-object relationship in childhood that leads to adult instability of this sort (Kohut, 1977). (Failed self-object relationships in *adulthood* have only transitory effects. An unwanted ending of a love relationship, for example, may generate a variety of painful experiences such as loss of self-esteem, depression, and even some acting-out. But these behaviors and feelings commonly pass, and are therefore not characteristic of the personality disorders, which are made up of enduring problem behaviors.) In particular, the self is especially sensitive to failures in the growth of esteem during the development of the subjective self, as well as failures in the development of the sense of agency during the formative stages of the core or physical self. These result in protracted fragmentation of the self, and with it the sense that one is losing control or "coming apart." The following case illustrates some of the difficulties of the borderline personality.

Thomas Wolfe was a writer whose first work was published in 1929 and who died less than ten years later, before he was forty. In that brief decade, he was a literary sensation, hailed by the greatest novelists of his time. He was enormously productive and driven. And he was painfully unhappy. Wolfe was described as ner-

▲ Thomas Wolfe (1900–1938).

vous, surly, suspicious, given to brooding, to drinking, to violent outbursts, and sometimes even to fears that he was going mad. He was rude and dislikable. He said of himself that he was afraid of people and that he sometimes concealed his fear by being arrogant and by sneering magnificently.

It was hard for him to begin writing on any particular day, but once he began it was harder still for him to stop. The words would simply pour out of him. He would sleep late, gulp down cup after cup of black coffee, smoke innumerable cigarettes, pace up and down—and write endlessly. He would scrawl down the words on sheet after sheet of yellow paper, so hastily and hugely that the pages often contained only twenty words apiece, and those in abbreviated scrawl. At night, he would prowl the streets, drinking heavily, or spending hours in a phone booth, calling friends, and accusing them of having betrayed him. The next day, overcome with remorse, he would call again and apologize.

For all his writing, he had difficulty putting together a second book after *Look Homeward Angel.* Although he had written a million words, ten times that of an average novel, it still was not a book. He was fortunate to have as his editor Maxwell Perkins, who had discovered his talent and who cared to nurture it. Wolfe wrote: "I was sustained by one piece of inestimable good fortune. I had for a friend a man of immense wisdom and a gentle but unyielding fortitude. I think that if I was not destroyed at this time by the sense of hopelessness . . . it was largely because of . . . Perkins . . . I did not give in because he would not let me give in." Perkins recognized that Wolfe was a driven man, and feared that he would suffer either a psychological or physical breakdown, or both. He proposed to Wolfe that, having written a million words, his work was finished: it only remained for both of them to sit down and make a book out of his effort.

That collaboration was difficult. A million words do not automatically make a book. Wolfe was reluctant to cut. Most of the editing, therefore, fell to Perkins. And as Perkins slowly made a book out of Wolfe's words, Wolfe's resentment of Perkins increased. The work was not perfect, Wolfe felt. And it upset him to bring forth a book that did not meet his standards.

Until the book was published, Wolfe believed it would be a colossal failure. The reviews were magnificent, however. But although Wolfe was at first heartened by the reviews, he gradually began to feel again that the book was less than perfect, a matter for which he held Perkins responsible. His relationship with Perkins deteriorated. He became suspicious, even paranoid. Yet, apart from Perkins, he had no close friends. He became increasingly unpredictable, yielding easily to incensed anger, unable to control it. Ultimately, he broke with Perkins. Rosenthal (1979) has suggested that Wolfe's emotional liability, his inability to control his anger, the difficulties he had in being alone, his many self-damaging acts, as well as his identity problems point to the diagnosis of a borderline personality disorder. At the same time, Wolfe also had personality features that were consistent with the schizotypal personality disorder, especially his ideas of reference that made him so suspicious and paranoid.

THE PERSONALITY DISORDERS: AN EVALUATION

Laboratory experiments, naturalistic studies, and longitudinal surveys all converge to support the existence of the antisocial personality disorder. On a variety of specific criteria, individuals with the disorder are demonstrably different from normal people. However, the legitimacy of the other personality disorders is far more problematic. No matter how convincing the descriptions of these disorders seem to be, the documentation for their existence as reliable and

FOCUS QUESTIONS

1. Why do the personality disorders present diagnostic and therapeutic challenges to researchers and clinicians?
2. What are potential sources of error in making diagnoses of personality disorders?

valid syndromes is often, at bottom, anecdotal. It has grown out of clinical lore, and while it is not to be lightly dismissed for that reason, neither can it be easily accepted. For despite the effort that has gone into tightening the various categories of personality disorders they are still particularly prone to a variety of errors that easily erode their usefulness.

Alternative Views of the Personality Disorders

Because personality disorders are characterized by the presence of enduring **traits** that often originate in childhood or early adolescence, evidence for their existence needs to be accumulated across a considerable period of time. As a result, distortions of memory and failure to obtain and properly assess facts are powerful potential sources of error for these diagnoses. Consider Seymour, who was held to be suffering from a paranoid personality disorder (p. 584). The behavioral facts relating to his difficulties were quite accurate. But subsequently, a careful investigation of the sources of his difficulties yielded a quite different picture. It turned out that Seymour had been experiencing a marked hearing loss. He had not mentioned it during his early interviews both because he underestimated its extent and because he dreaded wearing a hearing aid. He had difficulty getting dancing partners because, while he heard the music, he often missed the instructor's calls and was commonly out-of-step. In the discussion group, he often repeated comments that had already been made by others or, worse, misheard others' comments, such that his own were inappropriate and disruptive. Similar difficulties pervaded his experience in the ceramics class. Moreover, his seeming distrust of others, which had been manifested in the locking of his study and in not talking about his work, takes on a somewhat different meaning when one learns that as a physicist, he had spent his entire career working on classified military problems. In addition, like many professionals of the 1950s and 1960s, Seymour had moved a great deal. Making new friends in each new location required a heavy expenditure of time and energy. Precisely because he had a close relationship with his wife and because he was deeply involved in his work, Seymour was simply unwilling to invest himself in new, but transient, relationships.

Thus, the possibility of misinterpreting lifelong behaviors is potentially dangerous because the contexts in which those behaviors developed may not be readily retrievable now. But even when considerable information *is* available, therapists of different theoretical persuasions may arrive at different diagnostic conclusions as far as the personality disorders are concerned. Consider Laura (p. 590) who appeared to have all of the characteristics of an obsessive-compulsive personality disorder. Might not a feminist therapist who is sensitive to the conflicts that arise from the competing demands of gender and work roles, see the case differently? Laura, who was traditional in her attitudes toward family and home, was simultaneously ambitious in her professional life. In attempting to fulfill both roles with excellence, she unwittingly aspired to the impossible: to be a "superwoman." She wanted her house neat, her children at the top of their class, and herself at the top of her male-dominated profession. Her carping and her insistence that the house be spotless reflected this competition between roles, for if the house was not spotless, to whom would it fall to clean it up? Similarly, in her refusal to take holidays and her long working hours, she was behaving like the ambitious men in her profession.

Finally, there are theorists who question whether the psychological predispositions that presumably underlie the personality disorders really exist and, therefore, whether the personality disorders themselves are real (Mischel, 1973; Mischel and Peake, 1982). Although the notion that traits exist is nearly as old as the notion of personality itself, it has proved quite difficult to obtain evidence that people are consistent in their dispositions and perceptions across different situations. To say that someone suffers a dependent personality disorder, for example, is to say that she manifests the traits of passivity and dependence in a variety of different contexts. Evidence for that assertion is, in fact, very hard to find. Nearly all studies that have attempted to verify the cross-situational assumptions behind the notion of traits have failed. If the notion of traits has little merit, then the personality disorders that are built upon them have shaky foundations indeed. It is no wonder then that, in DSM-IV, with the exception of the antisocial personality disorder, whose coefficient of reliability (see Chapter 6) ranges between .65 and .87, inter-judge reliability of the remaining personality disorders is uncertain, often plummeting as low as .26. Some attempts to improve the reliability and validity of personality disorder diagnoses, however, are promising (Stangl, Pfohl, Zimmerman, Bowers, and Corenthal, 1985; Loranger, Susman, Oldham, and Russakoff, 1987).

SUMMARY

1. The personality disorders are fundamentally disorders of *traits,* that is, disorders that are reflected in the individual's tendency to perceive and respond to the environment in broad and maladaptive ways. The notion of a personality disorder assumes that people respond consistently across different kinds of situations.

2. Of all of the personality disorders, the *antisocial personality disorder* is the most widely studied. It is a disorder that is characterized clinically by inadequately motivated antisocial behavior, emotional poverty, and the apparent lack of conscience or shame.

3. The antisocial personality disorder originates in childhood or early adolescence, where it takes the form of truancy, petty thievery, and other rule-violating behavior. As children, those who suffer the disorder often come from emotionally deprived backgrounds and marginal economic circumstances. Moreover, there is evidence that their antisocial behaviors have a genetic basis that may be manifested in a constitutional brain defect. This defect makes them underaroused emotionally, and therefore less able to learn from punishment or to control their impulses.

4. While severe punishment in childhood, such as sending a boy to a penal institution, increases the likelihood that the boy will subsequently engage in criminal activities, so too does no punishment at all. Moderate punishment—enough to make the boy take the consequences seriously, but not so much as to send him to places where he can learn to be a criminal—has a genuine deterrent effect.

5. The remaining personality disorders each center on a striking personality trait. *Paranoia, dependency, narcissism, avoidance,* and *obsessive-compulsiveness*

are traits that have become so dominant that they merit the personality disorder designation. In addition, some personality disorders, such as *schizotypal,* reflect many of the symptoms that are found in the corresponding Axis I disorder, but in lesser degree and without the florid thought disorder.

6. With the exception of the antisocial personality disorder, there is genuine disagreement regarding whether the personality disorders truly and reliably exist. To some extent, the disagreement arises from the low reliability of the personality disorder diagnoses. But to a larger degree, the disagreement is rooted in the scientific debate about the existence of personality traits. If traits play a relatively minor role in personality organization, then the personality disorders cannot play a large role in abnormal psychology, for they are based on the notion of traits.

QUESTIONS FOR CRITICAL THINKING

1. How may underarousal lead to sociopathic behavior and what kind of punishment is most effective with sociopaths?

2. Why may women be more likely to suffer from dependent personality disorder than men, and are changes in the role of women likely to lead to fewer women who suffer from this disorder?

3. What distinguishes the schizotypal personality disorder from the schizophrenias, and why is this distinction so important?

4. Why may people be misdiagnosed as suffering from personality disorders when their behavior is viewed out of context?

7

ABNORMALITY ACROSS THE LIFESPAN

CHAPTER 16

Childhood Disorders and Mental Retardation

Susan Nolen-Hoeksema

CHAPTER ORGANIZER

CLASSIFYING CHILDREN'S DISORDERS
- Familiarize yourself with the four categories of childhood disorders.

DISRUPTIVE BEHAVIOR DISORDERS
- Learn about conduct disorders, oppositional defiant disorder, and attention-deficit hyperactivity disorder.

EMOTIONAL DISORDERS
- Be able to describe several childhood emotional disorders and how they differ from adult disorders.

HABIT DISORDERS AND EATING DISORDERS
- Learn about the habit and eating disorders and how they are treated.

DEVELOPMENTAL DISORDERS
- Familiarize yourself with how mental retardation is defined, the different levels of retardation, and the causes of mental retardation.
- Be able to describe the learning disorders.
- Understand the deficits involved in autism, as well as theories of its causes and how it is treated.

AREAS FOR FURTHER CONSIDERATION
- Be able to explain why areas for further consideration include better classification of childhood disorders, identification of children with serious psychological problems, and long-term prognosis for children with psychological problems.

n this chapter, we turn to the problems of children and adolescents—problems that are often more difficult to understand than those of adults.

First, children's problems occur in the context of growing up, of psychological development. But normal psychological development proceeds at different rates for different children. As a result, it is often difficult to distinguish a genuine psychological problem that requires attention from one that merely reflects a developmental lag. For example, most children are toilet-trained by the time they are three years old. Of those who are not, some are merely developmental "laggards," while for others, continued bed-wetting reflects deeper emotional insecurities. Distinguishing problems that reflect the variability in rates of psychological development from those that suggest deep emotional difficulties is an issue one faces with children that is entirely absent among adults.

Second, children often cannot communicate a problem directly through language. Instead, their distress is often manifested indirectly through maladaptive behaviors. Then it is up to parents and teachers correctly to identify behaviors in children that are indicative of severe problems. This is usually not a simple task. Often adults will mislabel a child's behavior as a "psychological problem" when it is merely something that will pass with time. At other times,

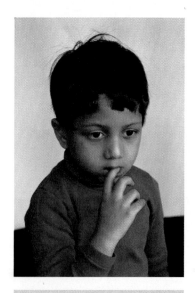

▲ Young children may not be able to communicate problems through language, but show distress through behavior. This boy may be in a pensive mood, or he may be withdrawn because of an anxiety he cannot express in words.

adults will ignore children's problem behaviors, believing the child will grow out of these behaviors, when the child really does need adult intervention. One large study of children in the general population found that only 29 percent of those qualifying for a diagnosis of a DSM-type psychological disorder had ever been taken by their parents to a teacher or mental health professional for help (Anderson, Williams, McGee, and Silva, 1987). Because children are so dependent on adults' interpretations of their problems, we often know less about children with problems than we do about the adults who care for them.

Finally, children's problems are often quite specific to particular situations and contexts. Children may be aggressive at home, but not at school. Even overactivity—a common complaint of teachers—depends on the circumstances and situations. One study found that 75 percent of children who were allegedly overactive in school were not overactive at home or in the clinic (Klein and Gittelman-Klein, 1975).

We will examine several kinds of children's problems. All are psychological disorders, not only because the child deviates from what is expected of a particular age and sociocultural context, but also for two other reasons: (1) the problem is persistent and severe, and (2) it impairs the child or others. Either the child must be suffering, as when a child with an animal phobia is paralyzed with fear, or the child is making others suffer, as when the child's aggression is turned on schoolmates or pets.

How common are DSM-type psychological disorders in children? Several large-scale epidemiological studies conducted in the United States, Europe, and Australia have sought to answer this question by administering a clinical interview to children from the general population (see Brandenburg, Friedman, and Silver, 1990). On the basis of information from these clinical interviews, researchers estimate that between 14 and 20 percent of children suffer from moderate to severe psychological problems.

What distinguishes a childhood disorder from normal variation in development is often only a matter of degree. With few exceptions, these disorders are not qualitatively different from normal, and minor variations of these problems can be found in many essentially normal children (Rutter, 1985). Thus, the temper tantrums that occur in most children once a month would hardly be labeled a psychological disorder. But if the tantrums were much more frequent, or they occurred in peculiar circumstances, or for a very long time, then the behavior might be considered abnormal. The timing during development of behavior problems also is important. For example, most preschoolers show anxiety about separating from their parents, particularly just before they are to begin school. This separation anxiety is seldom persistent or predictive of future problems. But separation anxiety occurring much later in childhood is more likely to be persistent and associated with more severe malfunctioning in a child (Rutter, 1985). Before going into the specifics of any one disorder, let's look at the system by which all childhood disorders are broadly classified.

CLASSIFYING CHILDREN'S DISORDERS

As a road map for viewing the scope of childhood disorders, consider Table 16–1. The disorders can be divided into four categories. *Disruptive behavior disorders* are characterized by symptoms such as hyperactivity, inattention, ag-

TABLE 16-1

MAJOR CLUSTERS OF CHILDHOOD DISORDERS	
Disruptive behavior disorders	Attention-deficit hyperactivity disorder Conduct disorder Oppositional defiant disorder
Emotional disorders	Separation anxiety disorder Reactive attachment disorder Childhood depression Phobias
Habit and eating disorders	Elimination disorders (e.g., bed-wetting) Speech disorders (e.g., stuttering) Tic disorders Anorexia nervosa Bulimia nervosa
Developmental disorders	Mental retardation Learning disorders Autistic disorder

SOURCE: Adapted from DSM-IV.

gressiveness, destructiveness, and defiance of authorities. *Emotional disorders* are those in which symptoms of fear, anxiety, sadness, and poor attachment predominate. *Habit and eating disorders* include a rather wide variety of disorders that are characterized by the repetitive acting out of maladaptive or nonfunctional behaviors. Examples include bed-wetting, stuttering, motor tics, and eating large quantities of food then forcing oneself to vomit. *Developmental disorders* are characterized by marked deficiencies in the child's development of important intellectual capabilities and social skills. This category includes the several levels of mental retardation as well as less severe learning disorders (such as developmental reading disorder). The category also includes autistic disorder, which is characterized by severe deficits in communication skills and social responsiveness. Note that one of the most severe of the adult disorders, schizophrenia, does not appear in Table 16–1. It is very rare for children to show signs of schizophrenia, although adolescents who will develop the disorder in adulthood sometimes show the early symptoms of schizophrenia (social withdrawal, increasingly eccentric behavior, poor hygiene). When a young person is showing signs of schizophrenia, the adult criteria for the diagnosis of the disorder may be applied.

Similarly, the criteria for diagnosing depressive disorders in children are essentially the same as those for the adult diagnosis. Major depressive disorder is uncommon in children compared to adults. Milder forms of depression in children appear to be just as common as in adults, however (Nolen-Hoeksema, 1988).

Many children who receive one of the diagnoses listed in Table 16–1 will receive one or more other diagnoses as well. For example, in one study of children in the general population (Anderson et al., 1987), 55 percent of the disorders diagnosed occurred in combination with one or more other disorders. It was particularly common in this study for a child with a disruptive behavior disorder also to show an emotional disorder (see also Bird et al., 1988).

FOCUS QUESTIONS

1. What are the four categories of childhood disorders?
2. Why is schizophrenia not considered a childhood disorder?

George, whose case is described below, qualifies for diagnoses of both major depressive disorder and conduct disorder.

George is a sixteen-year-old who was admitted to the hospital from a juvenile detention center following a serious suicide attempt. He had, in some way, wrapped shoelaces and tape around his neck, causing respiratory impairment. When found, he was cyanotic and semiconscious. He had been admitted to the detention center earlier that day. It had been noted there that he was quite withdrawn.

On admission, he was reluctant to speak, except to say that he would kill himself and nobody could stop him. He did, however, admit to a two-week history of depressed mood, difficulty sleeping, decreased appetite, decreased interest, guilt feelings, and suicidal ideation.

According to his parents, George was without emotional difficulties until, at age 13, he became involved in drugs, primarily LSD, marijuana, and other non-opioid substances. His grades dropped drastically, he ran away from home on several occasions after arguments, and he made a suicide gesture by overdosing on aspirin. A year later he was expelled from school following an argument with the principal. Unable to control his behavior, his parents had him declared a child in need of assistance. He was then evaluated in a mental health clinic, and a recommendation was made for placement in a group home. He apparently did well in the group home, and his relationships with his parents improved immensely with family counseling. He was quite responsible in holding a job and attending school and was involved in no illegal activities, including use of drugs. However, six months ago he again became involved in drugs and, over a course of two weeks, engaged in ten breaking-and-enterings, all of which he did alone. He remembers being depressed at this time, but cannot recall whether the mood change was before or after reinvolvement with drugs. He was then sent to the juvenile detention center where he did well, so that he had been discharged to his parents' care three weeks ago. One day after returning home, he impulsively left with his buddies in a stolen car for a trip to Texas. His depression began shortly thereafter; and according to him, his guilt about what he had done to his parents led to his suicide attempt. (From Spitzer, Skodol, Gibbon, and Williams, 1981, pp. 129–30)

DISRUPTIVE BEHAVIOR DISORDERS

There are three types of *disruptive behavior disorders. Conduct disorders* are characterized by persistent behaviors that seriously violate the rights of others and basic societal norms. Children with conduct disorders often get in trouble with the law and career criminals. *Attention-deficit hyperactivity disorder* is characterized by marked impulsivity, inattention, and hyperactivity. Children with this disorder are often very disruptive at school and at home. A third disorder in this category is *oppositional defiant disorder.* Children with this disorder show a pattern of negativistic, hostile, and defiant behavior, but do not show the more serious violations of others' rights as do children with conduct disorders.

Conduct Disorders

Most children, at one time or another, transgress important rules of conduct. A survey of 1,425 British boys aged thirteen to sixteen years, from all socioeconomic groupings, found that 98 percent of them admitted to keeping something that did not belong to them (Belson, 1975). In only 40 percent of the instances were the goods worth more than two dollars, but even so the rate of dishonesty in children is quite high. Similar results are reported from other countries. In Norway and Sweden, 89 percent of children aged nine to fourteen confessed to petty illegal offenses (Elmhorn, 1965). For better or worse, it seems that stealing is a part of almost every child's development. But there are some children whose conduct persistently violates very basic norms for interpersonal behavior. These children are often physically aggressive and cruel to others. They will habitually lie and cheat. When adolescents, they may engage in muggings, armed robberies, and even rapes and homocides. When a child chronically shows such behavior, he or she may be diagnosed as having a *conduct disorder*. The following case is representative of a child with one type of conduct disorder:

> Alan is the sort of teenager who makes all caring professionals despair. He has been in and out of trouble since he was six years old. At that early age, he truanted from school, and by the time he was twelve Alan had been excluded from ordinary schools and had been brought into juvenile court for persistent stealing. Within his neighborhood gang, he was popular with both boys and girls, and he was sexually active before he was fourteen. But he was quick to pick fights with boys who did not belong to his gang.
>
> At fourteen his criminal career seemed set. He had been sentenced several times for stealing cars, and no end of this activity was in sight. His probation officer had the sense of standing by impotently until either maturation or a heavy prison sentence altered Alan's behavior.
>
> Alan seemed to have all the cards stacked against him. He was the youngest of a large family. His father had himself been in and out of prison before finally deserting his mother when Alan was four. The mother struggled to keep the family together, but she frequently became depressed, during which times Alan spent long periods in foster homes. School was no refuge from these difficulties. Despite being of near-average ability, Alan had experienced considerable difficulty learning to read and spell. At fourteen, he could scarcely write a letter home.

The persistence of antisocial and aggressive tendencies from childhood into early adulthood that Alan shows is common in children with conduct disorders (Olweus, 1979; Huesmann, Eron, Lefkowitz, and Walder, 1984). Indeed, conduct disturbances and aggressivity are unusually stable characteristics across childhood and adolescence, particularly among boys (Offord et al., 1992). Approximately 35 to 40 percent of children with conduct disorder develop antisocial personality disorder as adults, and about 75 to 85 percent of these children experience as adults significant problems in social functioning, such as chronic unemployment, unstable personal relationships, impulsive physical aggression, and spouse abuse (Zoccolillo, Pickles, Quinton, and Rutter, 1992).

Alan's criminal behavior is typical of children with conduct disorders. About half of these children are eventually classified as juvenile delinquents in adolescence. And over half of juvenile delinquents commit serious crimes by the age of twenty-five (Ross and Wirt, 1984). Some of the strongest predictors of which disruptive children will go on to engage in serious criminal behavior are: (1) high frequency of deviant acts as a child, (2) greater variety of deviant acts, (3) deviant acts performed across multiple settings, and (4) early onset of deviant acts (Loeber, 1990).

Fortunately, although most children will show minor, transient conduct disturbances, only between 3 and 7 percent will be as disturbed as Alan and will qualify for a diagnosis of conduct disorder (Robins, 1991). The disorder is over three times more common in boys. Amazingly, only about 23 percent of children showing conduct disorders such as Alan's, or the less severe oppositional defiant disorder, appear to be referred for counseling (Anderson, Williams, McGee, and Silva, 1987). Apparently, even when children are being extraordinarily disruptive, parents are reluctant to seek out mental health professionals.

POSSIBLE ORIGINS OF CONDUCT DISORDERS

What causes a child to develop patterns of aggressivity and criminal behavior? First we shall consider the influence of the social environment on the development of conduct disturbances. Then we shall investigate the possible genetic origins of these disorders.

Social Sources of Conduct Disorder Children with aggressive disorders often come from social environments that are unpleasant. Like Alan's family, their families tend to be those in which affection is lacking and discord is rampant, where discipline is harsh and inconsistent, where children's activities are poorly supervised and monitored, where the family has parted through divorce or separation, or where the children have been placed outside the home during times of family crisis (Rutter, 1975; Farrington, 1978; Hetherington and Martin, 1979; Loeber and Dishion, 1983; Loeber, 1990). Patterns of interaction between family members are often characterized by coercive, even physically violent behaviors and a lack of reinforcement for prosocial behaviors (Patterson, DeBaryshe, and Ramsey, 1989). In turn, children with conduct disorders are often rejected by peers (Coie and Kupersmidt, 1983; Dodge, 1983) or become members of deviant peer groups (often called gangs) that supply the child with the motivation and rationalizations to support delinquent acts, as well as opportunities for engaging in such acts (Elliott, Hulzinga, and Ageton, 1985; Patterson, DeBaryshe, and Ramsey, 1989).

Several studies suggest that many children who show conduct distur-

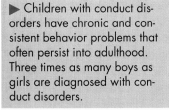

▶ Children with conduct disorders have chronic and consistent behavior problems that often persist into adulthood. Three times as many boys as girls are diagnosed with conduct disorders.

FOCUS QUESTIONS

1. Describe conduct that would lead to a diagnosis of a conduct disorder.
2. What are the strongest predictors of which disruptive children will go on to engage in serious criminal behavior?
3. Explain the possible origins of conduct disorders.
4. Describe the goals and interventions derived from social learning theory that are used to treat children diagnosed with conduct disorders.

bances also have problems in maintaining attention (Quay, 1986; Anderson, Williams, McGee, and Silva, 1987). Thus, they often do poorly in school, rendering them not only restless in the classroom during the long school day but also unavailable to the kinds of self-esteem socialization and feelings of competence that proper school performance engenders.

Family difficulties are argumented by poverty. Delinquency is particularly prevalent within inner cities. And even there, different schools, different housing areas, or different parts of town are associated with enormous variation in rates of conviction. Areas of high delinquency are characterized by high unemployment, poor housing, and poor schooling. Moreover, delinquency is highly related to indices of social pathology, such as illegitimate births, drug dependence, and venereal disease (Loeber, 1990).

Genetic Influences on the Development of Conduct Disorders   While family and social factors strongly influence the development of aggressive patterns in children, they are not wholly responsible. There may be genetic factors that play a role in determining which children have conduct problems and which do not. Most genetic studies have examined rates of criminal behavior rather than diagnoses of conduct disorders. Twin studies find the concordance rate for criminality to be 26 to 51 percent in MZ twins versus 13 to 22 percent in DZ twins (Rutter, Quinton, and Hill, 1990). Studies comparing the criminal records (rather than the clinical diagnoses) of adopted children with those of their natural and adoptive fathers have found that the criminal records of adopted sons bear stronger resemblance to those of their biological fathers, with whom they never lived, than to the records of their adoptive fathers (Crowe, 1983; Cloninger and Gottesman, 1987; Mednick, Gabriella, and Hutchings, 1987).

Such evidence cannot be ignored, for it strongly suggests that biological endowment plays a part in determining who becomes delinquent. But how might that come about? Surely one does not inherit criminal *behaviors,* for those must be *learned.* What then is inherited?

What may be inherited and what may influence subsequent criminality is the failure to experience high emotional arousal (see Figure 16–1). Because of such failure, boys with conduct disorders are less responsive than others to praise and encouragement (Patterson, 1975; Robins, 1991). Psychophysiologically they manifest low arousal and show a learning deficit in fear avoidance situations (Davies and Maliphant, 1971; Trasler, 1973)—precisely those situations that encourage stabilization and that discourage social rule violation. It is this inability to become emotionally aroused that may be inherited and that may interfere with the ability to respond to the praises and punishments that encourage socialization (see Chapter 15). Conversely, genetic inheritance may account for the fact that some children from very difficult circumstances fail to become delinquents. Because they have inherited the capacity to be aroused by social stimuli, they avoid delinquency by becoming socialized.

Several studies suggest that children who are genetically at risk to develop conduct disorder, or more specifically to become criminals, are unlikely to do so unless they are also exposed to the types of environments described above that promote antisocial behavior (Cadoret, 1986; Cloninger and Gottesman, 1987; Rutter, Quinton, and Hill, 1990; Rutter et al., 1990). This suggests that even children who are genetically predisposed to conduct disorder might be successfully treated with environmental interventions.

FIGURE 16–1

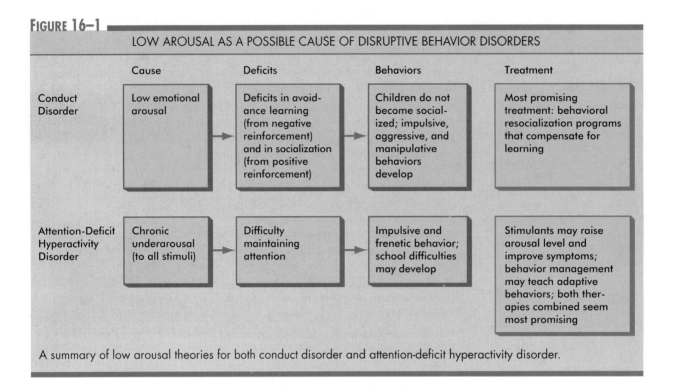

LOW AROUSAL AS A POSSIBLE CAUSE OF DISRUPTIVE BEHAVIOR DISORDERS

	Cause	Deficits	Behaviors	Treatment
Conduct Disorder	Low emotional arousal	Deficits in avoidance learning (from negative reinforcement) and in socialization (from positive reinforcement)	Children do not become socialized; impulsive, aggressive, and manipulative behaviors develop	Most promising treatment: behavioral resocialization programs that compensate for learning
Attention-Deficit Hyperactivity Disorder	Chronic underarousal (to all stimuli)	Difficulty maintaining attention	Impulsive and frenetic behavior; school difficulties may develop	Stimulants may raise arousal level and improve symptoms; behavior management may teach adaptive behaviors; both therapies combined seem most promising

A summary of low arousal theories for both conduct disorder and attention-deficit hyperactivity disorder.

TREATING THE CONDUCT DISORDERS

Historically, treatment of conduct disorders has focused on interventions derived from social learning theory (see Lochman, White, and Wayland, 1991). Goals of such interventions include: (1) teaching a child how to identify situations that trigger aggressive or antisocial behavior, (2) teaching the child how to take the perspective of others and care about this perspective, (3) reducing the aggressive child's tendency to overattribute hostility in others, and (4) teaching the child adaptive ways of solving conflicts with others, such as negotiation. Each of these goals is accomplished by reinforcing positive behaviors and punishing negative behaviors in the child and by modeling and observational learning procedures (see Chapter 5). Often a child's family will be involved in treatment, since the dynamics of the family may actually be supporting the child's conduct disorder. Interventions such as these have proven promising in outcome research, although it may be crucial for these interventions to take place soon after the child begins to exhibit antisocial behavior, and to include the child's parents or family, for the interventions to have long-term positive effects (Lochman, White, and Wayland, 1991).

As an example of the application of these interventions, consider John, whose conduct disorder stemmed from communication problems with his parents:

> John was fourteen when he was referred to a treatment center because he had been stealing from his mother. He frequently stole large sums of money, often in excess of twenty dollars. His mother, however, knew precisely how much money she had, and there was no way in which John could pretend that his stealing would go unnoticed.

Interestingly, during early discussions with the therapist, it became clear that John respected his parents, and that they loved him. The problem was that they could no longer discuss things together. John's stealing had driven a wedge of distrust between them, such that his parents could think of nothing else, yet John resented not being trusted.

In fact, stealing was simply the most irritating of a group of problems that typically arise during adolescence and that neither John nor his parents knew how to discuss and resolve. Among these problems were conflicts over curfew, neatness, personal cleanliness, and table manners.

Recognizing that these conflicts were by no means trivial irritants, the therapist arranged a series of contracts between John and his parents, whereby the rewards and penalties for meeting or violating explicit agreements were clear to both sides. In these contracts, John acknowledged that his lateness might be a source of great concern to his parents, while they recognized that his room was his own "space" which, subject only to fundamental rules of sanitation, was his to do with as he pleased. At the same time, the therapist encouraged John and his father to role-play how they might settle differences of opinion at home. After the first meeting, stealing was never discussed nor was it targeted as an area for contract or discussion. Nevertheless, it stopped altogether and long before the eight-week treatment terminated.

Sometimes a child's behavior is so disruptive, or his family environment is so dysfunctional, that he will be sent to a treatment home such as Achievement Place. At Achievement Place, which began at the University of Kansas and is now in several locations around the country, two professionally trained "teaching parents" live together in a family-style arrangement with six to eight delinquent adolescent children. Often the children's homes are in the same community, and they can continue to attend their regular school and visit in their own homes.

The aim of Achievement Place is to teach prosocial behaviors. The teaching parents develop a mutually reinforcing relationship with their charges and model, role-play, and reinforce the kinds of social skills they want the children to acquire. They emphasize skills such as responding appropriately to criticism, as well as the academic skills that are necessary to make school interesting and to obtain employment afterwards. Moreover, Achievement Place emphasizes self-government, whereby the children take increasing responsibility for their own behavior and for helping their housemates (Wolf, Phillips, and Fixsen, 1975; Kirigin, Wolf, Braukmann, Fixsen, and Phillips, 1979).

How successful has the Achievement Place approach been? One measure of success is to look at what happens to adolescents during and after Achievement Place compared to a similar group that spent time in a traditional facility. One such study found that the Achievement Place children showed greater improvement in conduct (Kirigin, Braukmann, Atwater, and Wolf, 1982). During the year of treatment, 56 percent of the boys and 47 percent of the girls assigned to Achievement Place were involved in a criminal offense, compared to 86 percent of the boys and 80 percent of the girls in more traditional institutions. One year following treatment, the Achievement Place children continued to be somewhat less likely to be in trouble with the law than the other children. One reason so many of the children in both types of treatment got into trouble when they were released was that many had to return to difficult home environments that may have undermined the effects of the treatment. Even so, the Achievement Place model remains the most effective type of intervention for children with conduct disorders. In addition, keeping a child at Achievement Place costs barely a third of what it would cost to send such a child to a state institution. Generally, then, both the efficacy and relative cost of behavioral resocialization programs generate optimism regarding the prognosis for delinquents.

Attention-Deficit Hyperactivity Disorder (ADHD)

Parents and teachers often complain that children are overactive and restless, that they won't sit still and cannot concentrate for long. What they usually mean is that the children won't concentrate for as long as *adults* would like, forgetting that attention span and concentration increase with age. But there are cases in which children do show gross overactivity, both at home and at school, and these children can truly be regarded as having an ***attention-deficit hyperactivity disorder*** (ADHD). Their behavior is marked by developmentally inappropriate inattention, impulsiveness, and motor hyperactivity. In the classroom, their attentional difficulties are manifested in their inability to stay with a specific task. They have difficulty organizing and completing work. They often give the impression that they are not listening or that they have not heard what they have been told, and they seem unable to sit still. These children do not appear to have specific problems with processing information (such as reading deficits); instead their problems lie in self-regulation (Henker and Whalen, 1989). In interactions with peers, these children are hapless and disorganized, often rejected by others as annoying and intrusive. Similarly, at home they are described as failing to follow through on parental requests and instructions and failing to sustain activities, including play, for periods of time that are appropriate for their age. A good example of an attention-deficit hyperactivity disorder is provided in the following case:

James was four years old when he was first admitted to a children's psychiatric ward as a day patient. Ever since infancy he had made life difficult for his elderly parents. As soon as he could crawl, he got into everything. He had no sense of danger. He slept very little at night and was difficult to pacify when upset. It was only because he was their only child and they could devote all of their time to him that his parents managed to maintain him at home.

His problems were noticed by others just as soon as James began preschool at age three. He made no friends among the other children. Every interaction ended in trouble. He rushed around all day, and could not even sit still at story time. His flitting from one activity to another completely exhausted his teachers. After some eighteen months of trying, his teachers suggested that he be referred to the hospital for assessment and treatment.

On examination, no gross physical damage could be found in his central nervous system. Psychological examinations revealed that James had a nearly average intelligence. In the hospital, he was just as hyperactive as he had been in school and at home. He climbed dangerously to the top of the outdoor swings. He ran from one plaything to another and showed no consideration for other children who were using them. Left to his own devices, he was constantly on the move, tearing up paper, messing with paints—all in a nonconstructive manner.

James was placed in a highly structured classroom, with two teachers and five other children. There his behavior was gradually brought under control. He was given small tasks that were well within his ability, and he was carefully shown how to perform them. His successes were met with lavish praise. Moreover, patience and reward gradually increased the length of time he would spend seated at the table.

Ultimately, James was placed in a small, structured, residential school. By age sixteen, he had settled down a great deal. He was no longer physically overactive, but his conversation still flitted from one subject to another. He had no friends among his peers although he could relate reasonably well to adults. He showed little initiative in matters concerning his own life, and his prospects for gaining employment were not good.

James's behavior is typical of children with attention-deficit hyperactivity disorder. He is hyperactive, always on the go, with apparently boundless energy. He is impulsive, doing whatever comes to mind, often without regard to physical danger. And he has problems maintaining his attention on any one task without a great deal of support from teachers. As with James, children with ADHD often show these problems in very early childhood. The prevalence of attention-deficit disorders in preadolescents is about 6.7 percent, with over five times more boys than girls having this diagnosis (Anderson et al., 1987). Some children "grow out" of the symptoms, but as many as 50 to 80 percent continue to show symptoms into adolescence (Barkley, Fischer, Edelbrock, and Smallish, 1990; Fischer, Barkley, Fletcher, and Smallish, 1993). Hyperactive children are also prone to conduct disturbances. Follow-up studies of children with ADHD find that 45 to 60 percent develop conduct disorders, delinquency, and drug abuse, compared to about 16 percent of a control group of children (Gittelman, Mannuzza, Shenker, and Bonagura, 1985; Moffitt and Silva, 1988; Barkley, Fischer, Edelbrock, and Smallish, 1990). Not surprisingly, hyperactive children also tend to do very poorly in school, and as adults, are prone to interpersonal disharmony, frequent job changes, traffic accidents, marital disruptions, and legal infractions (Henker and Whalen, 1989).

POSSIBLE CAUSES OF ATTENTION-DEFICIT HYPERACTIVITY DISORDER

Most theories of the etiology of attention-deficit hyperactivity disorder have focused on mechanisms in the central nervous system that control arousal (see Douglas, 1983). Some theorists argue that hyperactive children suffer from

▶ Most children occasionally have trouble sitting still, following directions, and paying attention. If such behavior is pervasive and chronic in one of these boys, however, he might be diagnosed with attention-deficit hyperactivity disorder.

FOCUS QUESTIONS

1. Describe the usual behavior of a child diagnosed with attention-deficit hyperactivity disorder (ADHD).
2. What are some possible causes of ADHD?
3. Describe the two main therapies for treating children with ADHD.

chronic overarousal. This seems intuitively plausible, although the fact that hyperactive children actually are made more calm by stimulant drugs seems paradoxical from this viewpoint. More recently, theorists have suggested that hyperactive children suffer from chronic *underarousal* (see Figure 16–1), which makes it more difficult for them to maintain attention (Zentall and Zentall, 1983).

The neurological impairments that ADHD children show may sometimes be due to environmental toxins. Children exposed to high levels of lead (e.g., through ingesting lead-based paints) showed higher rates of hyperactivity, distractability, impulsiveness, and problems following simple instructions (Fergusson, Horwood, and Lynskey, 1993). Some studies find that hyperactive children have been exposed to more disruptions in their families, such as frequent changes in residence or parental divorce, than control groups (Barkley, Fischer, Edelbrock, and Smallish, 1990). Whether these family disruptions are causes or merely correlates of ADHD is unclear. The fathers of ADHD children are more prone to irresponsible and antisocial behavior, but it is unclear whether these fathers influenced their children's behavior through either genetic or environmental routes (Barkley, Fischer, Edelbrock, and Smallish, 1990).

TREATMENT

When very young, children with ADHD are very difficult to deal with. They quickly exhaust their teachers and parents, and they often cannot be taught in ordinary school classes. The two main therapeutic approaches are drug therapy and behavior management.

Drug Therapy   Paradoxically, hyperactive children are made worse by tranquilizers. Instead, most hyperactive children show decreases in hyperactive behavior when given stimulant drugs (Henker and Whalen, 1989). The most common stimulant is an amphetamine called methylphenidate (whose trade name is Ritalin). Children taking this drug show decreases in demanding, disruptive, and noncompliant behavior, plus increases in interpersonal responsiveness and goal-directed efforts. There are significant side effects of Ritalin, however, such as insomnia, headaches, and nausea. In addition, the gains ADHD children make when taking stimulants are short-lived, and children who receive these medications do not have a better long-term prognosis than children who do not (Henker and Whalen, 1989). Moreover, there are large differences between children in their responses to these drugs. Some children respond rapidly and to small doses of Ritalin, whereas others respond only to large doses.

Behavior Management   Operant conditioning programs have been relatively effective in treating overactivity and its associated attentional deficits, particularly in the short run. Several investigators have used these techniques to extinguish the hyperactive child's problem behaviors—for example, distracting others—while simultaneously extending the amount of time the child attends. In one case, for example, after carefully establishing how overactive a nine-year-old boy was—that is, his base rate of overactive behavior—the boy was rewarded for sitting still. For every ten seconds that he sat quietly, he earned a penny. The first experimental session lasted only five minutes. But by the eighth session, the boy's overactivity had virtually ceased and, at follow-up four months later, his teacher reported that not only was he much quieter but he was also progressing in reading and making friends. Thus, the straightforward use of attention and tangible reinforcers can produce significant and rapid changes when they are systematically applied (Pelham, 1989; Barkley, 1990).

Several researchers have argued that the most effective treatment for ADHD is a combination of drug therapy and behavioral therapy (Pelham, 1989; Rapport, 1987; DuPaul and Barkley, 1993). Medications may make it easier for children to learn from behavioral interventions. It is clear, however, that children's responses to both stimulant medications and behavior therapy are highly idiosyncratic (DuPaul and Barkley, 1993). An effective dose of either stimulant medications or behavior therapy for one child may be an ineffective dose for another. Thus, clinicians must carefully monitor children's responses to these interventions and vary dosage levels and techniques to meet an individual child's needs.

EMOTIONAL DISORDERS

The rubric, **emotional disorders,** loosely describes those emotional abnormalities that are not accompanied by a loss in the sense of reality. Their symptomatology is frequently similar to that seen in adult emotional disorders (see Chapters 8, 9, and 10)—feelings of inferiority, self-consciousness, social withdrawal, shyness, fear, overattachment, chronic sadness, and the like. These complaints result in diagnoses that include anxiety states, depressive disorders, obsessive-compulsive conditions, phobias, and hypochondriasis.

But there are several important differences between childhood emotional disorders and adult emotional disorders. For example, adult emotional disorders are more common among women, while many childhood emotional disorders occur equally among boys and girls and only begin to be more common among girls at the onset of adolescence. In addition, many childhood emotional disorders are age-specific, that is, they occur or terminate at particular ages. Animal phobias, for example, always begin in early childhood, while agoraphobia is rarely experienced before adulthood.

Because the emotional disorders of childhood do bear a strong resemblance to those of adulthood, we do not review all of the emotional disorders here. Rather, we shall discuss what appear to be the most common childhood emotional disorders. First, we review two disorders that are characterized by heightened levels of anxiety in children: separation anxiety and phobias. Then we review the emerging literature on childhood depression. Finally, we discuss the treatments that are currently used for emotional disorders in children.

Separation Anxiety Disorder

Most of us can remember an incident sometime in our childhood in which we suddenly realized we had been separated from our parents and could not find them. We felt terror about being alone; we wondered if they would ever return. Eventually we were reunited with our parents, with great relief. For a short period after the incident, we were somewhat anxious about again being separated from our parents, and tried to stay close to them when in stores or other

FOCUS QUESTIONS

1. Describe the symptoms of separation anxiety.
2. What is school phobia?
3. What are the risk factors for depression in children?
4. Describe the therapies used for treating each of the childhood emotional disorders.
5. What are some of the effects of childhood sexual abuse, and what is the focus of treatment for those who have been abused?

big places. But for the most part, the separation was an isolated incident that we soon forgot.

There are some children who live every minute of the day with terror that they might be separated from their families. They worry that terrible things will happen to their parents, siblings, or other loved ones. They refuse to be separated from loved ones, and become panicked if they must be separated. They have nightmares with themes of separation. They cling to loved ones and follow them around the house constantly. They may show continual physical symptoms of anxiety, such as headaches, stomach aches and nausea, particularly on days that they must be separated from parents (such as school days). Children who show such symptoms for at least two continuous weeks may be suffering from *separation anxiety.*

Separation anxiety appears to be the most common of childhood emotional disorders, with a prevalence of 3.5 percent among preadolescents (Anderson et al., 1987). It is nearly twice as common in girls as in boys. In its severe form, separation anxiety can be incapacitating for children, preventing them from attending school or extracurricular activities. Also, these children often undergo repeated physical examinations as a result of their frequent complaints of aches and pains (APA, 1987). Episodes of separation anxiety often occur repeatedly over childhood and adolescence for children with this diagnosis.

A first episode of separation anxiety often occurs after some traumatic event in the child's life, such as the death of a relative or pet, being hospitalized, or moving to a new town. Children whose parents suffer from an anxiety disorder, particularly agoraphobia, are at an increased risk for separation anxiety (Gittelman and Klein, 1984). In addition, children with this disorder tend to come from very close-knit families.

Phobias

Fears are very common throughout childhood, much more so than adults realize or remember from their own early years. Forty-three percent of children

▶ Children suffer from many more fears and worries than they will probably remember as adults. A twelve-year-old drew this vision of a nuclear holocaust.

aged six to twelve years old have at least *seven* fears or worries at any one time (Lapouse and Monk, 1959). The nature of those fears often varies with age. Preschool children tend to be afraid of tangible objects, such as animals and insects. For example, Little Hans, you may recall from Chapter 8, developed his fear of horses at about age five. Tangible fears can continue throughout childhood and into adulthood, but they rarely begin after age five. As children grow older, so grow their fears of imaginary creatures, of disastrous events, and of the dark. Ghosts, murderers, and hidden dangers populate their imaginations. School-connected fears begin at age five or six when children are first enrolled in school, and they increase markedly between the ages of nine and twelve. From about age twelve and on through adolescence, children's fears begin to resemble those of adults, including fears about social relationships and anxieties about identity.

Fears become phobias when, as we saw in Chapter 8, the fear is out of proportion to the reality of the danger that an object presents (p. 217). The prevalence of simple phobias in preadolescents is about 2.4 to 9 percent, with twice as many girls as boys showing the disorder (Anderson et al., 1987; Rutter, 1989). The following case demonstrates the transition of fear to phobia:

> Sometimes children's phobias develop in complex and unpredictable ways. Sara was referred for treatment of her phobias when she was thirteen. The referring physician indicated that the girl was afraid of airplanes and bees, but Sara, like so many such children, found it hard to put in words just what she was scared of. She acknowledged that, beyond airplanes and bees, she was also afraid of elevators, but nothing more. Yet, after she came to know and trust her therapist, it emerged that there was a fear that underlay and linked all the others: that was a fear of anesthesia. The link between airplanes, elevators, bees, and anesthesia was not immediately obvious, and it took some care to piece the following history together.
>
> A number of years earlier, Sara had to have a tooth extracted. The dentist used a general anesthetic. As she "went under," everything went black, but Sara could still hear voices and rushing noises. (In fact, this is an almost universal experience since, physiologically, the nerves controlling vision are affected seconds before the nerves controlling hearing.) Sara was not prepared for these sensations, and they terrified her. Ever since, she has studiously avoided putting herself in a situation where she *might* be injured and therefore might be rushed to a hospital, where she *might* be given an anesthetic. Airplanes crash. So do elevators. Bees sting. Any one of these might land her in the hospital.
>
> Like everyone else, Sara's parents did not understand the connection between her phobias and what gave rise to them. Rather, they tended to see her globally, simply as a fearful child. The therapist explained that what Sara had originally experienced, though unexpected and unpleasant, was hardly incomprehensible and very treatable. He then trained Sara in relaxation techniques that could be used in situations of high anxiety. By focusing on her fears of elevators, the therapist demonstrated to Sara that she could conquer one fear and could go on and conquer the others by herself. Within three months, Sara had reported no more difficulties.

Sara's shifting fears were complicated, but not unusual. In her case, a plausible traumatic event was easily identified. But such events are often more difficult to trace. In many children, phobias are often associated with general anxiety or emotional disturbance, and with having parents who are phobic (see Rutter and Garmezy, 1983).

School phobia is a childhood disorder that creates significant distress in both children and their parents. School refusal is seen in about 5 percent of all clinic-referred children and 1 percent of children in the general population (Burke and Silverman, 1987). Adolescents who refuse to go to school tend to be more severely impaired and less responsive to treatment than younger children. Adults who, as children or adolescents, refused to go to school are at risk for several problems including agoraphobia, job difficulties, and personality disorders (see Burke and Silverman, 1987).

Not very long ago, it was assumed that all children who were absent from school, except those who were physically ill and could prove it, were playing hooky and were therefore truants. Yet, there seemed to be a subgroup of such absentees who differed markedly from the "real" truants who tended to be antisocial, underachieving children. In contrast, the subgroup tended to be children who were achieving very well at school, who said that they wanted to return to school, but who described all manner of anxiety symptoms whenever they set out to attend school. For example, they needed to go to the toilet frequently and they often felt sick and sweated profusely when the topic of school was brought up. Unlike the truants whose parents were often unaware that their offspring were not at school, these children stayed at home during their prolonged absences, and their parents knew exactly where they were (see Table 16–2). Consider the following case:

> Richard was a twelve-year-old who had been out of school almost continuously for five months. The previous summer he had won a scholarship to a well-known private school. He did exceedingly well in his first term. Then, just after the beginning of the second term, he contracted severe influenza which left him feeling very weak. He was worried that he would lose ground academically, and his anxious parents shared that concern. He tried to go back to school, but once in the classroom, he had a panic attack and ran home. Thereafter, he worried increasingly about what to say to the other boys and how to explain his flight and long absence. He was brought to a therapist for help in overcoming his fear.
>
> Richard was given some training in relaxation and was accompanied to his school in graded stages during the summer vacation. He and his therapist rehearsed what he would say to his friends when he returned in the fall. The therapist accompanied him to school for the first three mornings, but thereafter, he was on his own. Follow-up during the two years revealed no further difficulty. (Yule, Hersov, and Treseder, 1980)

School phobia presents a serious challenge because it is so puzzling to teachers, to parents, and to the child who suffers from it. The situation is made more tragic by the fact that the child previously was a good attender and was doing well in school when, suddenly and for no apparent reason, he stopped going to school. Careful investigation often reveals many reasons for school refusal. In Richard's case and in most others, threats to self-esteem and an unrealistically high level of aspiration play significant roles in refusal. To a child who regularly receives straight A's, the threat of even a "B" can be highly aversive and anxiety-producing.

TABLE 16–2

SCHOOL PHOBIA COMPARED WITH TRUANCY		
	School Phobia	*Truancy*
Cause	Often severe anxiety without specific traumatic event	Distaste for school, and poor performance there
Characteristics of condition	Children are usually high achievers who want to return to school but are made acutely anxious by it	Usually a form of antisocial behavior, without characteristics of phobia
Treatment	Therapy to reduce anxiety as well as conditioned fear	Disciplinary measures

Childhood Depression

Clinicians formerly assumed that pre-pubescent children would be unlikely to develop depression, because their sense of self and of the future was too immature for them to develop low self-esteem, guilt, or hopelessness (Rie, 1966). Research over the last two decades has shown, however, that pre-pubescent children can and do develop the symptoms that make up the syndrome of depression (Kovacs, Gatsonis, Paulauskas, and Richards, 1989). Certainly, the prevalence of major depression in children is lower than in adults; most studies find a prevalence of less than 3 percent in the general population of children (Fleming and Offord, 1990). This prevalence increases sharply in adolescence, however, to about double that in childhood.

▶ A nine-year-old painted this picture to describe a recurring nightmare she had of being trapped in a hole. The milder forms of depression are as common in children as they are in adults, although major depression appears less often in children.

The risk factors for depression in children are similar to those for adults: low self-esteem, pessimistic attitudes, and family dysfunction (Kovacs, Gatsonis, Paulauskas, and Richards, 1989; Fleming and Offord, 1990; Angold, 1994). Family dysfunction may be an especially potent source of depression for children. Many clinicians believe that they cannot treat depression in children without treating the family as a whole.

Although many children who become depressed recover quickly when positive changes in their environment are made, a substantial minority of them remain depressed for months, perhaps even years (Nolen-Hoeksema, Girgus, and Seligman, 1992). In turn, a bout of depression in childhood may so affect a child's functioning during critical periods in the development of skills and self-concept as to leave long-lasting scars on his or her beliefs about the self and the world.

Treatment of Emotional Disorders

Increasingly, biologically oriented clinicians are using psychotropic drugs, usually antidepressants, to treat emotional disorders in children. Outcome studies on the effectiveness of these drugs have shown mixed results, however (Harrington, 1992). Some studies suggest that tricyclic antidepressants can be helpful for separation anxiety and depression, but others find them no more helpful than placebos. The possible toxic side effects of these drugs in children and adolescents have caused concern for many clinicians.

Phobias in children, like those in adults, respond best to behavioral treatments, especially modeling (Bandura, 1969; Gelfand, 1978; Rosenthal and Bandura, 1979). In these treatments, children are exposed to, and encouraged to imitate, models who are both attractive and relatively fearless. The use of such models enables children to overcome their fears quickly. Specific fears, such as fear of animals, respond best to such treatment.

Treatment of school refusal also often follows a behavioral approach (Burke and Silverman, 1987). Sometimes this disorder is treated like a simple phobia, with systematic desensitization and modeling techniques. In other cases, school refusal is seen as the result of secondary reinforcements from parents, and interventions focus on reducing the reinforcements parents give children for avoiding school and more generally improving parents' skills at managing positive behaviors in their children.

Cognitive therapies like those designed by Aaron Beck (see Chapter 11) are increasingly being used to treat emotional disorders in older children and adolescents (Meyers and Craighead, 1984). Obviously, cognitive therapy must be adapted to the language level of the child being treated. Outcome studies of cognitive therapies for depressed children and adolescents have indicated that these therapies can be effective (e.g., Reynolds and Coats, 1986; Lewinsohn, Clarke, Hops, and Andrews, 1990; Stark, 1990). Again, however, many clinicians believe that children with emotional disorders such as depression need to be treated in the context of their entire family, since family stress or dysfunction is so frequently related to the child's disorder.

Childhood Sexual Abuse

We pause here to consider not a specific disorder, but the potential source of a range of disorders in children and adults: childhood sexual abuse. Children who are the victims of inappropriate sexual interactions with adults (e.g., fondling of genitals, intercourse) are at increased risk of developing emotional disorders, including anxiety disorders, depression, and post-traumatic stress disorder, and behavioral disorders such as conduct disorder and substance abuse (Kilpatrick, Resnick, and Veronen, 1981; Stein et al., 1988; Cutler and Nolen-Hoeksema, 1991). The effects of childhood sexual abuse on psychological health are often long-lasting. Many victims continue to suffer from severe emotional or behavioral problems long into adulthood. For example, in a large study of adults in the general population of Los Angeles, Burman and colleagues (1988) found that 18 percent of those who had been sexually abused as children were still suffering from major depression and 20 percent were suffering from drug abuse as adults. Women who had been abused were most likely to develop an emotional disorder such as depression, whereas men who had been abused were most likely to develop a behavioral problem such as drug abuse.

There has been increasing attention paid to childhood sexual abuse by mental health professionals and the lay public in the last few years. This is, in part, due to new studies showing that abuse occurs across the full range of socioeconomic groups, even in the "best" of families. In addition, however, many questions have been raised about children's ability to report accurately on experiences of abuse, following highly publicized accusations of child abuse levied against child-care workers, public figures, and parents. Some studies suggest that very young children can be led to fabricate detailed descriptions of traumatic events that never happened to them (Loftus, 1991). Of course, this does not mean that every child, or any one child, who describes sexual abuse is fabricating his or her description. It simply means that it can be very difficult to ascertain the accuracy of children's reports. This problem is multiplied many times when the report of sexual abuse is not made until long after it happened (see Chapter 18 for a discussion of adults who claim to recall repressed memories of child abuse decades after it occurred). The bottom line, however, is that when childhood sexual abuse does occur, the effects on a child's functioning and development can be devastating and enduring.

Treatments for children, or adults, who have been abused tend to focus on the survivor's self-evaluations and understanding of the abuse experience. The therapist looks for signs that the abuse survivor is blaming herself or himself for the abuse, or more generally, has developed a negative view of the self as a result of the abuse. Then, the therapist works to help the survivor develop a more realistic and positive view of the self. Therapists also often work with survivors to help them recognize, express, and understand the range of feelings they have about the abuser. When children have been abused by a family member, especially a parent, obviously the therapist must ensure that the abuser cannot harm the child further. Sometimes the child must be removed from his or her home. Sometimes the entire family enters therapy, often in the form of group therapy.

HABIT DISORDERS AND EATING DISORDERS

The **habit disorders** and **eating disorders** comprise a group of diagnoses that are united by a single fact: the troublesome behavior has a habitual physical component. They include the elimination disorders (enuresis and encopresis), speech disorders (stammering and stuttering), motor tics, and eating disorders (anorexia and bulimia). While the causes of these disorders are not entirely clear, their psychological consequences are dramatic. To be a bed wetter or a stutterer in Western society is to be stigmatized and to have to deal regularly with the taunts of others and assaults on one's self-esteem. Below we shall discuss in detail one of the elimination disorders, enuresis, then stuttering, and then the eating disorders.

Enuresis

Enuresis is arbitrarily defined as involuntary voiding of urine at least twice a month for children between five and six, and once a month for those who are older. Most children gain bladder control between eighteen months and four years of age. Thereafter, the proportion of children who have difficulty containing urine, either during the day or while in bed, drops markedly. At age twelve, 8 percent of boys and 4 percent of girls are enuretic (Friman and Warzak, 1990).

As with the other physical disorders, the problems of the enuretic are compounded by the social consequences of the disorder. Parents object to soiled clothes and bedding and commonly stigmatize the enuretic as immature. Schoolmates and friends are likely to tease the child who has an occasional "accident," the more so when those accidents are regular occurrences. Enuretics find it nearly impossible to accept overnight invitations from friends or go to camp. These social consequences may create a fertile ground for other more serious psychological problems.

CAUSES OF ENURESIS

The social consequences of enuresis are especially unfortunate because little is known about its causes. A distinction is made between primary enuresis, which is caused by a biological abnormality, and secondary enuresis, which has psychological causes such as anxiety. There is evidence that the predisposition to enuresis often is inherited. Approximately 75 percent of enuretic children have first-degree relatives who are or were enuretic, and the concordance for enuresis is higher in identical (MZ) than in fraternal (DZ) twins. That is, the more similar a person's genetic blueprint is to an enuretic's, the more likely the individual will also be enuretic (APA, 1980).

TREATMENT

Some drugs, such as the antidiuretics or imipramine, suppress bed-wetting temporarily. Usually children begin to bed wet again once the drug is stopped. However, even so, a few dry nights can be an enormous morale-booster to an enuretic child, particularly if it allows the child to visit friends overnight or go to camp without fear of embarrassment. Recall, however, that these drugs may have significant side effects that may outweigh their usefulness, including toxic death (Rohner and Sanford, 1975).

Behavioral treatments have been quite successful with enuresis, far more successful than drug treatment (Houts, 1991). Most common is a procedure that was first described over fifty years ago (Mowrer and Mowrer, 1938). The child sleeps in his or her own bed. Beneath the sheets is a special pad which, when moistened by urine, completes a harmless electric circuit that sounds a bell and awakens the child, who then goes to the toilet. A number of studies

FOCUS QUESTIONS

1. What are causes and treatments for enuresis?
2. Describe three treatments for stuttering and explain how they work.
3. What are the main symptoms and causes of anorexia and bulimia?
4. Describe some treatments for the eating disorders.

have shown that approximately 75 percent of children treated by the "bell and pad" method gain bladder control during the two-week treatment period. There is a relapse rate of up to 35 percent, but that can be reduced to 15 to 25 percent by giving a longer treatment period or by offering an additional "booster" dose of treatment (Lovibond and Coote, 1970; Shaffer, 1976; Doleys, 1979; Houts, 1991).

Stuttering

Stuttering or stammering is a marked disorder in speech rhythm. While most children go through transient periods of hesitating over particular words, the dysrhythmia is both more pronounced and more prolonged in those who are regarded as stutterers. Often, it is the initial consonants in certain words, particularly explosive sounds, that cause real problems. "I d-d-d . . . don't know what to d-d-d-do!" is a typically problematic sentence that is often accompanied by a flushed or pained face.

About 1 percent of all children are stutterers, and another 4 to 5 percent experience transient stuttering for a period of up to six months. For unknown reasons, boys outnumber girls as stutterers by four to one.

The causes of stuttering are still unclear, but as in other physical disorders, the consequences are enormous. Stutterers tax the patience of other children and teachers. They are often taunted and ostracized by peers. Teachers may avoid calling on them in class, with the result that their academic interest and performance may flag.

TREATMENT

By the time a stutterer seeks help, he or she is likely experiencing considerable tension that both results from the speech problem and magnifies it. Consequently, most treatments of stuttering combine psychotherapeutic counseling with specific reeducational techniques. The latter serve to distract the stutterer from his own speech while training him to speak fluently.

Three techniques seem particularly promising. The first is called **delayed auditory feedback** and involves hearing one's own speech played back over earphones at about a .1 second delay. When fluent speakers hear their own speech delayed in this manner, they stutter enormously. But when stutterers receive delayed auditory feedback, they become nearly fluent. These paradoxical findings suggest that feedback from their own speech is what maintains stuttering, and that any interference in that feedback will reduce it. The problem, of course, is affecting feedback outside of the treatment situation. Delayed auditory feedback works quite well in the clinic but transfers hardly at all outside of the clinic.

Shadowing is a variant of the delayed auditory feedback technique. Here, the therapist reads from a book, and the stutterer repeats the therapist's words shortly after the latter has spoken them (and without reading the words). This requires the stutterer to concentrate carefully on what the therapist is saying, and in the process, to ignore his own stuttering. Several studies indicate that shadowing may be useful in alleviating stuttering (Cherry and Sayers, 1956; Kondas, 1967).

A third method, called **syllable-timed speech,** requires stutterers to speak in time to a metronome or beeper that sounds in an earpiece. This procedure, too, may have the effect of distracting the stutterer from his own stuttering.

Combined with a system of rewards for maintaining nonstuttering, this procedure has been found relatively effective in reducing stuttering (Meyer and Mair, 1963; Ingham, Andrews, and Winkler, 1972). None of these three techniques, however, can be described as more than "promising."

Eating Disorders: Anorexia and Bulimia

There are two primary types of eating disorders, anorexia and bulimia. Although these two disorders have distinct features, they share some common symptoms, and to some degree, possibly common etiologies (see Table 16–3).

The main symptoms of ***anorexia nervosa*** are the refusal to maintain body weight at or above a minimally normal weight for one's age and height, an intense fear of gaining weight despite being much underweight, and a distorted body image. Even when they are emaciated, anorexics often feel fat. There appear to be two subtypes of anorexics: restricters and purgers. Restricters are thin primarily because they refuse to eat. Purgers also refuse to eat much of the time, but when they do eat, use vomiting and laxatives to purge what they have eaten. Often, the disorder is accompanied by a variety of other physical changes. Amenorrhea, the absence of menstrual periods, is common among female anorexics. Blood pressure may be lowered, life-threatening cardiac arrhythmias may occur, body temperature is low, bone growth is retarded, and anemia is common.

About 95 percent of anorexics are female. The prevalence of this disorder appears to be rising, such that about 1 in 100 females succumb (Fairburn, Welch, and Hay, 1993). The reason anorexia is considered a disorder of childhood is that its onset is usually in early to late adolescence, although it can begin at any age.

The following case illustrates some of the common features of anorexia:

> Frieda had always been a shy, sensitive girl who gave little cause for concern at home or in school. She was bright and did well academically, although she had few friends. In early adolescence, she had been somewhat overweight and had been teased by her family that she would never get a boyfriend unless she lost some weight. She reacted to this teasing by withdrawing and becoming very touchy. Her parents had to be careful about what they said. If offended, Frieda would throw a tantrum and march off to her room—hardly the behavior they expected from their bright and sensitive fifteen-year-old.
>
> Frieda began dieting. Initially, her family was pleased, but gradually her parents sensed that all was not well. Mealtimes became battletimes. Frieda hardly ate at all. Under pressure, she would take her meals to her room and later, having said that she had eaten everything, her mother would find food hidden away untouched. When her mother caught her deliberately inducing vomiting after a meal, she insisted they go to the family physician. He found that Frieda had stopped menstruating a few months earlier. Not fooled by the loose, floppy clothes that Frieda was wearing, he insisted on carrying out a full physical examination. Her emaciated body told him as much as he needed to know, and he arranged for Frieda's immediate hospitalization.

The consequences of anorexia can be severe. Most importantly, the low level of serum potassium caused by starvation can lead to irregularities in the heart rate that cause death.

TABLE 16-3

MODELS OF EATING DISORDERS		
Model	*Proposed cause*	*Effect or process*
Sociocultural model of anorexia and bulimia	Cultural emphasis on thinness as ideal, combined with increase in women's average weight in recent years, leads to poor body image in many	Some women respond by dieting excessively; the overweight and those who enter puberty early may be especially vulnerable
Stress reduction model of bulimia	Stress and anxiety	Those who develop bulimia seek short-term relief of stress in eating, then relief through purging of the distress caused by eating
Autonomy/control model of anorexia	Overcontrolling family leads to fierce need for autonomy and difficulty communicating emotions	Eating becomes the one area of her life the anorexic can control; her control over it defines her self-esteem

People with **bulimia** often wish they could restrict their food intake better, and many were on highly restrictive diets before they developed bulimia. But people with this disorder find themselves bingeing, often on large quantities of food, with a sense that they completely lack control over their eating. Now, everyone binges occasionally. As many as 30 percent of college students say they binge at least twice a month, and 16 to 20 percent say they binge once per week (Schotte and Stunkard, 1987). People with bulimia, however, are excessively self-critical about their binges, and more generally about their physical appearance. As a result, they attempt to purge after a binge, by self-induced vomiting, by misusing laxatives, diuretics, or other medications, by fasting, or by excessive exercising. Often the binge/purge episodes take hours out of each day of a bulimic's life, and begin to control her life. The sense of shame, distress, and helplessness that follows these episodes is often overwhelming. Many bulimics also suffer from severe depression.

As with anorexia, most people who suffer from bulimia are women. Although poor eating patterns may be rampant among adolescents and young adults, only about 1 percent of patients in this age range will qualify for a diagnosis of bulimia (Schotte and Stunkard, 1987; Drewnowski, Hopkins, and Kessler, 1988; Fairburn and Wilson, 1993). Some bulimics are excessively thin, but many are of normal weight. Bulimia is still a very dangerous disorder physically, however. Frequent vomiting and other types of purging can lead to severe loss of body fluids and electrolytes, and the stomach acid vomited up can lead to severe tooth decay (Fairburn and Wilson, 1993). Many bulimic women also experience menstrual problems.

THEORIES OF ANOREXIA AND BULIMIA

Some researchers believe that both anorexia and bulimia are variants of a mood disorder (see Agras and Kirkley, 1986). Dysphoria and depression are common among both anorexics and bulimics, and the families of people with eating disorders often have histories of affective disorders (Hudson, Pope,

▶ Anorexics are preoccupied with body image, as illustrated in this painting made by an anorexic during the severest stage of her illness.

Jonas, and Yurgelun-Todd, 1987). Whether depression is a cause or consequence of eating disorders is unclear, however. Similarly, although the metabolic changes that occur in anorexia have led some researchers to suggest that a malfunction of the hypothalamus causes this disorder, it is unclear whether changes in hypothalamic functioning precede or follow self-starvation by anorexics (Mitchell, 1986).

There are a number of psychosocial theories of the eating disorders. The facts that both anorexia and bulimia have increased in prevalance in recent decades and are more common in developed countries than underdeveloped countries have led some researchers to argue that modern cultural norms play a role in the etiology of these disorders (Garfinkel and Garner, 1982; McCarthy, 1990). There is no doubt that thinness is considered a virtue in our society, especially for females. The "ideal" shape for women, as indicated by television stars, fashion models, and winners of beauty pageants has become more and more thin over the last thirty years. Over the same time period, there has been an increase in the average weight of women due to improvements in nutrition. Thus, women are being told to become thin when it is increasingly hard to do.

Some women succumb to this pressure by going on extremely restrictive diets. These women may be especially sensitive to society's messages about thinness because they are naturally slightly heavier than their peers. In addition, girls who enter puberty earlier than their peers also appear more vulnerable to a poor body image (Brooks-Gunn, 1988). Restrained eating can lead to both perceived and real physical deprivation, however, which in turn leads to a breakdown of restraint and overeating (Herman and Mack, 1975). Many women who develop bulimia have a history of going on extremely restrictive diets, which are chronically stressful and frustrating. These women, when they break their dietary rules, tend to lose their sense of control over their eating and end up bingeing. Then the guilt and fear of fatness that follow the bingeing can lead them to purge (Polivy, 1976; Rosen and Leitenberg, 1982; Garner, 1993). Stress reduction models of bulimia suggest that bingers eat when faced with stressful circumstances to escape anxiety and distress (Heatherton and Baumeister, 1991). They focus on the short-term gratification of food in lieu of their long-term goals for weight control, and end up eating large amounts of food even though they are not hungry. Purging is then a way of reducing the distress that the binge has caused.

Most of the psychosocial theories of anorexia suggest that it arises from a deep need for autonomy, which comes from being in an overcontrolling family (Minuchin, Rosman, and Baker, 1980; Bruch, 1982). The parents of anorexic girls are characterized as overinvolved in their daughters' lives, not allowing them adequate independence or a sense of self apart from their role in the family. These families also tend to restrict shows of emotion or conflict and to demand perfection from their children, so that the adolescent girl is not allowed to express her needs or her anger at her parents. Eventually, the adolescent girl may discover that she can control at least one aspect of her life—her eating. Gaining complete control over her food intake becomes all important, the way the girl defines her self-esteem. Some females who develop eating disorders have a history of sexual abuse, usually by a family member (Kanter, Williams, and Cummings, 1992). In these cases, the eating disorder may develop as a result of a distorted body image or low self-esteem caused by the abuse, or out of a need to control some aspect of their lives. In the meantime, her weight loss may lead to expressions of concern from her parents—attention that the girl may not be getting in any other way.

TREATMENT FOR EATING DISORDERS

Antidepressant drugs have been helpful for some people with eating disorders (Mitchell and de Zwaan, 1993). Whether these drugs relieve an underlying biological dysfunction that is the cause of the eating disorder, or simply make it easier for the woman to participate in psychotherapy and to change her eating habits is unclear.

Most clinicians agree that psychotherapy is necessary for eating disorders, even for people who are taking antidepressant drugs. Cognitive-behavioral therapies have proven effective for eating disorders, especially bulimia (Agras, 1993). They teach patients to identify environmental triggers for bingeing, to introduce feared foods into their diets while controlling the amount they eat, and to identify and change distorted cognitions about food intake, weight, and body shape. One study found that 56 percent of bulimic patients ceased bingeing and purging by the end of treatment with a cognitive-behavioral therapy (Agras, Schneider, Arnow, Raeburn, and Telch, 1989a, 1989b).

Family therapies focusing on the ways family members control each other and express conflict are often recommended for anorexia (Minuchin, Rosman, and Baker, 1980). Unfortunately, however, families with an anorexic member often do not enter therapy until the anorexia reaches a crisis point at which time the anorexic is dangerously ill. It may be necessary to hospitalize the anorexic patient to stabilize her health. Even then, some anorexics will protest that they have no problem, and as many as 30 percent will refuse treatment (Crisp, 1980). Obviously, force-feeding an anorexic patient in the hospital can tap into the very autonomy issues that are supporting her anorexia. The family may also deny that there is anything wrong within the family, identifying the anorexic as their only "problem." Thus, anorexia can be a difficult disorder to treat. Clinicians and researchers are continuing to explore combinations of drug and psychological therapies that will be most effective.

According to DSM-IV, the essential feature of developmental disorders is that the predominant disturbance is in the acquisition of cognitive, language, motor, or social skills. . . . The course of developmental disorders tends to be chronic, with some signs of the disorder persisting in a stable form into adult life. However, in many mild cases, adaptation or full recovery may occur.

Mental Retardation

Mental retardation is a disorder that afflicts three out of every hundred children, two-thirds of them boys. Thus, it is a widely prevalent disorder, often heartbreaking in its emotional costs to families and in the lifelong economic burdens it imposes on them and on society. For all of its prevalence, however, and despite the fact that everyone feels they know what metal retardation is, it is a difficult disorder to define precisely and to diagnose accurately. In part, the difficulty arises from the stereotypes that people have about mental retardation. But in larger measure, the difficulty occurs because the notion of intelligence is at the heart of mental retardation, and intelligence is very difficult to define (Kamin, 1974; Gould, 1981).

The definition of mental retardation most used in the United States is the one provided by the American Association on Mental Retardation (AAMR): "Mental Retardation refers to substantial limitations in present functioning. It is characterized by significantly subaverage intellectual functioning, existing concurrently with related limitations in two or more of the following applicable adaptive skill areas: communication, self-care, home living, social skills, community use, self-direction, health and safety, functional academics, leisure, and work. Mental retardation manifests before age eighteen" (Luckasson, Coulter, Polloway, Reiss, Schalock, Snell, Spitalnik, and Stark, 1992). This definition has been incorporated into the DSM-IV as criteria for diagnosing mental retardation.

MEASURES OF MENTAL RETARDATION

Several measures have been developed to assess the abilities of mentally retarded individuals for the purposes of diagnosis and intervention planning. Factors that have contributed to the development of these tests include the AAMR definition of retardation and the passage of the Education For All Handicapped Children Act (PL94-142). The diagnosis of mental retardation can only be made when low IQ is accompanied by deficits in ability to cope with the demands of daily life. Similarly, the requirements of PL94-142 state that the classification of students must be based on a comprehensive evaluation and that assignment to special education classes cannot be made on the basis of IQ tests alone.

Adaptive behavior scales assess the degree to which an individual meets the standards of personal independence and social responsibility expected for a child's age or cultural group (Grossman, 1983). One difficulty with this type of assessment is that standards of behavior and achievement are determined by an individual's society. However, the skills typically assessed by adaptive behavior scales are based on standards that are relatively universal, such as toilet training, control of aggression, and respect for authority figures.

The Vineland Adaptive Behavior Scale (Sparrow, Balla, and Cicchetti, 1984) is a revision of one of the oldest and most widely used adaptive behavior scales, the Vineland Social Maturity Scale developed by Edgar Doll in the 1930s. The Vineland covers four domains: *communication* (receptive, expressive, written); *daily living skills* (personal, domestic, community); *socialization* (interpersonal relationships, play and leisure time, coping skills); and *motor skills* (gross, fine; primarily for young children). Other adaptive behavior scales include the Adaptive Behavior Inventory for Children (Mercer and Lewis, 1978), the AAMD Adaptive Behavior Scale, School Edition (Nihira, Foster, Shellhaas, Leland, Lambert, and Windmiller, 1981), and the Scales of Independent Behavior (Bruininks, Woodcock, Weatherman, and Hill, 1984).

The System of Multicultural Pluralistic Assessment (SOMPA) was developed by Jane Mercer (1979), based on Mercer's belief that all cultural groups have the same average potential, and in response to concern about the misclassification of minority group children as mentally retarded based solely on their IQ test scores. The SOMPA is unique in its integration of three assessment components: a medical component that assesses the physical health conditions that affect a child's learning ability; a social system component that measures a child's social-adaptive behaviors; and a pluralistic component that evaluates a child's sociocultural background. The SOMPA uses a variety of measures, including a health history, interviews with the child and his or her parents, the Bender-Gestalt, the Wechsler Intelligence Scale for Children, Revised (WISC-R) or the Wechsler Preschool and Primary Scale of Intelligence (WPPSI), and the Adaptive Behavior Inventory for Children (ABIC). An Estimated Learning Potential (ELP) score is derived that is used to compare the child's WISC-R or WPPSI score with the score predicted for children having similar backgrounds and characteristics. The ELP also assists in estimating the potential benefit of programs designed for the child's background. A major problem with the SOMPA is that the standardization sample was based on children living in California only, and therefore may not be appropriate for children living in other areas. In addition, studies have shown that the ability of the ELP to predict academic success is no better than that of the regular Wechsler IQs (Figueroa and Sassenrath, 1989).

An IQ score of less than 70 remains the long accepted criterion of mental retardation. The WISC-R and other intelligence tests continue to be regarded as acceptable measures to provide a meaningful criterion of mental retardation. One problem with the use of IQ tests is that there are not enough easy items for children with severe impairments. One possible solution to this problem would be to use infant scales such as the Bayley with children who are beyond the test's age range but who have mental ages that are within the age range (Sullivan and Burley, 1990). In addition, correlations between intelligence tests and adaptive behavior scales where parents serve as the informants are moderate to low (Kamphaus, 1993). This finding implies that psychologists should not expect much agreement between test scores and parent-reported adaptive behavior scores. It further implies that adaptive behavior scales are adding information to the diagnostic process that is different from intelligence tests. It is likely that adaptive behavior will continue to become more important in the diagnosis and intervention planning of mental retardation.

Intelligence tests developed for use with infants and preschool children typically are performance tests that measure a variety of motor, social, and cognitive skills. Tests for infants are designed to assess sensorimotor development, communication skills, and social responsivity. Tests for preschoolers assess a wider range of abilities, including perceptual and motor skills, immediate memory, ability to follow directions, simple discrimination, recognition of incongruities, identification of body parts, and identification of common objects and their functions. These tests typically use a developmental approach whereby the test items distinguish children at different developmental levels. Tests commonly used with infants and preschoolers include the Bayley Scales of Infant Development, the Gesell Developmental Schedule (GDS), the Denver Developmental Screening Test (DDST), the McCarthy Scales of Children's Abilities (MSCA), the Cattell Infant Intelligence Scale, the Kaufman Assessment Battery, Piagetian Scales, and the Wechsler Primary and Preschool Scale of Intelligence (WPPSI). Because of the instability of abilities at young ages and because the nature and composition of intelligence changes with age, these tests, especially the infant tests, have little validity for predicting future intellectual ability.

LEVELS OF RETARDATION

The various levels of mental retardation and their associated IQ scores on a standard test of intelligence are shown in Table 16–4. What do these levels of retardation mean?

Mild Mental Retardation   The largest group of retarded children, about 85 percent of them, fall into this category. These children develop social and communication skills just like all others and at quite the same times. In fact, their retardation is often not noticed until they are in the third or fourth grade, when they begin to have academic difficulties. Without help, they can acquire academic skills through the sixth grade; with help, they can go beyond that level. In all other respects, their needs and abilities are indistinguishable from those of other children. Special education programs often enable these children to acquire the vocational skills that are necessary for minimal self-support. When under social or economic stress, they may need guidance and supervision, but otherwise they are able to function quite adequately in unskilled and semi-skilled jobs.

Moderate Mental Retardation   Children in this category make up 10 percent of the mentally retarded. Like other children, they learn to talk and communicate during the preschool period. But unlike other children, the moderately re-

TABLE 16–4

| SEVERITY LEVELS OF MENTAL RETARDATION | | |
Level	Percent of Retarded People	Weschler IQ
Mild	85	50–70
Moderate	10	35–49
Severe	4	20–34
Profound	>1	below 20

▶ The mildly and moderately retarded can learn to take care of themselves and perform unskilled and semiskilled jobs. These girls in a turn-of-the-century school for the retarded are doing laundry.

tarded have difficulty learning social conventions. During the school-age period, they can profit from training in social and occupational skills, but they are unlikely to go beyond the second-grade level in academic subjects. Physically, they may be clumsy and occasionally they may suffer from poor motor coordination. They may learn to travel alone in familiar places and can often contribute to their own support by working at semiskilled or unskilled tasks in protected settings.

Severe Mental Retardation   Before they are five, the severely retarded provide considerable evidence of poor motor development, and they develop little or no communicative speech. At special schools, they may learn to talk and can be trained in elementary hygiene. Generally, they are unable to profit from vocational training, though as adults, they may be able to perform simple and unskilled job tasks under supervision.

Profound Mental Retardation   Children in this category are severely handicapped in adaptive behavior and are unable to master any but the simplest motor tasks during the preschool years. During the school years, some development in motor skills may occur, and the child may respond in a limited way to training in self-care. Severe physical deformity, central nervous system difficulties, and retarded growth are not uncommon. Health and resistance to disease are poor, and life expectancy is shorter than normal. These children require custodial care.

CAUSES OF MENTAL RETARDATION

Our knowledge of the causes of mental retardation is ever expanding. Mental retardation is a symptom, not a specific disease, and there are a multitude of causes. The more severely impaired an individual, the more likely a cause can be found. Mental retardation may result from infections and intoxications, physical trauma leading to brain damage, metabolism or nutrition problems, gross brain disease, unknown prenatal influences, chromosomal disorders,

TABLE 16–5

PHYSICAL CAUSES OF MENTAL RETARDATION		
Genetic abnormalities	*Infectious conditions*	*Traumatic conditions*
Down's Syndrome	Rubella	Rh Factor
Phenylketonuria (PKU)	Syphilis	Malnutrition
Tay-Sachs Disease	Toxoplasmosis	Lead Poisoning
Klinefelter's Syndrome	Encephalitis	Irradiation
Fragile X Syndrome	Meningitis	Anoxia
	Herpes Simplex	Head Injuries
		Drugs

gestational disorders, and psychosocial disadvantages. Table 16–5 presents some common causes of mental retardation.

About 1 in every 800 children born in the United States suffers from **Down's syndrome,** a form of moderate-to-severe mental retardation that is named after Langdon Down, who recognized it in 1886. Down's childrens' eyes are almond-shaped and slanted, and their round faces have an Asian cast, so much so that this syndrome is often called **mongolism,** and the children mongoloids. (The similarity between these features and true Asian ones is superficial at best. The condition is as easily recognizable among Asian as Caucasian children.) Children suffering from this disorder also suffer from numerous physical anomalies, among them heart lesions and gastrointestinal difficulties. About one-fourth of these children do not survive the first few years of life. And because they are uncommonly friendly, cooperative, and cheerful, their early death touches parents and siblings very deeply.

Down's syndrome arises because there are forty-seven chromosomes, rather than the usual forty-six, in the cells of these children. The disorder itself does not seem to be inherited, but the reason for this chromosomal abnormality is not presently known. Interestingly, while the risk for the disorder is about 1 in 1,500 for children born to mothers in their twenties, it increases to 1 in 40 when the mother is over forty. Other chromosomal abnormalities associated with mental retardation include Fragile X syndrome, trisomy 13, and trisomy 18. Fragile X syndrome is caused when a tip of the X chromosome breaks off. The syndrome is characterized by severe to profound mental retardation, autistic behaviors (see pp. 633–41), and speech defects. In addition, males with Fragile X syndrome have large ears, long faces, and enlarged testes. Trisomy 13 and trisomy 18 are caused when chromosomes 13 and 18 are present in triplicate rather than in pairs. Both disorders cause more severe retardation than Down's syndrome, and a shorter life expectancy.

It is possible to detect chromosomal problems through **amniocentesis,** a test that is administered to the mother after the thirteenth week of pregnancy. In this procedure, a small amount of amniotic fluid (the fluid that surrounds the fetus) is drawn off and examined for the presence of abnormal chromosomes. When they are found, mothers have the option of continuing the pregnancy or undergoing an abortion. A newer test, known as **chorionic villus sampling (CVS),** can be done earlier in a pregnancy, between the eighth and twelfth weeks, to test for Down's syndrome and other chromosomal abnormalities. A sampling of cells is taken via the mother's vagina and cervix, or through her abdominal wall. The advantage of CVS is that earlier detection of birth defects is possible, allowing for an earlier and perhaps less complicated abortion, if the mother chooses one. The disadvantage of CVS is that it is somewhat less accurate than amniocentesis.

There are a number of metabolic diseases that are associated with mental retardation, including Tay-Sachs disease, Nieman-Pick disease, and phenylketonuria (Carter, 1970). A child affected by Tay-Sachs disease appears normal until age three to six months, when mental and physical deterioration begins. Tay-Sachs disease is uniformly fatal within the first six years of life, and no effective treatment has been developed.

Phenylketonuria (PKU) is a rare metabolic disease that occurs in roughly 1 out of 20,000 births. PKU results from the action of a recessive gene that is inherited from each parent. The infant cannot metabolize phenylalanine, an amino acid that is an essential component of proteins. As a result, phenylalanine and its derivative, phenyl pyruvic acid, build up in the body and rapidly poison the central nervous system, causing irreversible brain damage. About a third of such children cannot walk; nearly two-thirds never learn to talk; and more than half have IQs that are below 20.

Carriers of PKU can be identified through biochemical tests and receive genetic counseling (Stern, 1981). In addition, affected babies can be identified by a simple test of their urine about three weeks after birth. Provided they are kept on a diet that controls the level of phenylalanine in their system until age six, when the brain is nearly fully developed, their chances of surviving with good health and intelligence are fairly high.

For approximately two-thirds of retardates, there is no clear injury or disease that caused their retardation. Rather, there seem to be factors in their genetic backgrounds that have contributed to their condition.

Cognitive ability (as measured by the IQ) appears, to some extent, to be passed through the genes. The IQs of identical (MZ) twins reared together correlate between .80 and .95, whereas the IQs of DZ twins correlate much lower, from .40 to .70 (Schwartz and Johnson, 1985). Even MZ twins reared apart have more similar IQs than DZ twins reared together (Scarr, 1975). The IQs of adopted children correlate more powerfully with the IQs of their biological par-

▶ Down's syndrome is a form of moderate to severe mental retardation.

▶ Premature birth and low birth weight are risk factors for mental retardation.

ents (.48) than their adoptive parents (.19) (Munzinger, 1975). These data suggest that intelligence is partly inherited.

Recent studies indicate that a wide range of disorders in intellectual functioning, including mental retardation and autism, co-occur in families at a high rate (Quay, Routh, and Shapiro, 1987). But there may not be a genetic predisposition specifically to mental retardation. Rather, it may be intellectual ability in general that is partially influenced by genetics.

Environment also appears to play an extremely important role in the development of intelligence. The prenatal environment to which the fetus is exposed can have a profound effect on intellectual development. Some chronic medical conditions in the mother, such as high blood pressure or diabetes, if untreated, can interfere with fetal brain development. In addition, drugs that the mother takes while pregnant can affect fetal development. Fetal alcohol syndrome (FAS) is a condition involving a variety of physical defects and deformities and mental retardation in fetuses exposed to alcohol through the mother's drinking during pregnancy. Children whose mothers severely abused alcohol during pregnancy have an average IQ in the 60s (Streissguth, Grant, and Barr, 1991). It is unclear whether there is a safe amount of alcohol mothers can ingest during pregnancy.

One of the tragedies of the emergence of crack cocaine in recent decades is "crack babies," infants born to mothers who took crack while pregnant. Crack, or any form of cocaine, constricts the mother's blood vessels, leading to reduced oxygen and blood flow to the fetus. Crack babies are born with a variety of neurological deficits, and are irritable and difficult to soothe.

Lower-class mothers are more likely to give birth to premature infants with low birth weights, and low birth weight is a risk factor for retardation (Kiely, Paneth, and Susser, 1981). Children from impoverished backgrounds also face a number of postnatal environmental challenges to intellectual growth. Some of these children ingest toxic levels of lead by eating fragments of lead-based paint that peel off the walls of the old buildings in which they live. In turn, exposure to lead is associated with retarded intellectual growth. In addition, children from lower-class families are more likely than upper-class children to be malnourished, to receive poor health care, and to suffer from a variety of illnesses across childhood. Such an environment inhibits the full development of the intellectual abilities a child does have.

Physical abuse of children and accidental falls or blows to the head can also cause brain damage and mental retardation. Brain trauma can occur if an infant is simply shaken hard, because the infant's head is large and heavy compared to her body, and her neck muscles are too weak to control her head movements. The infant's soft brain literally bangs against the inside of the skull, causing bruising.

Early intervention studies have focused on enriching the environment of lower-class children who are at risk for mental retardation. The results of these studies have not yielded conclusive results regarding the long-term effects of environment enrichment. Some investigators suggest that earlier interventions offer the best possible outcome, while others propose that later interventions are also effective (Clarke and Clarke, 1979). Most agree that involving the parents in the treatment strategy is important for maximum success (Garber, 1988).

TREATMENT

Mentally retarded children often have defects in language skills that manifest themselves even before the child enters school. Training in language necessitates that the required sounds be demonstrated, and that the child be rewarded for closer and closer approximations to normal speech. Such training, whether conducted by professionals (Baer and Guess, 1971; Garcia, Guess, and Brynes, 1973), or by parents who have been trained to do such teaching (Cheseldine and McConkey, 1979), can be very useful in helping the child communicate more effectively. Behavioral training methods have also been used successfully to teach self-care skills to retardates (Watson and Uzzell, 1981).

As we indicated earlier, many children, particularly those who are mildly handicapped, are not identified as requiring assistance until they enter school. There is considerable continuing controversy about the kind of remedial help they need once they are in school. One view holds that they should be "mainstreamed," that is educated with other school children, in the same classes and with the same teachers, since after all the vast majority of them will ultimately live with their "normal" peers. Another view holds that the needs of the retarded are so different that they need to be educated separately, with separate teaching methods and different schedules and curricula. According to this view, the education of mentally retarded children proceeds best when they are segregated in different institutions, or at least in separate classes. The fact is that neither mainstreaming, or segregation has proven particularly effective in training mentally retarded children (Cegelka and Tyler, 1970; MacMillan and Semmel, 1977). Segregation to special institutions, however, has other deleterious effects that arise from conditions within institutions for the retarded, and from the educational deficits that develop there and that prevent the children from living effectively outside the institution (Ohwaki and Stayton, 1978; Birenbaum and Rei, 1979; Chinn, Drew, and Logan, 1979). Generally, then, the issue of how the mentally retarded are best educated is unresolved. Many educators feel that until it becomes absolutely clear that the child cannot function in the normal classroom, she should remain there for humanistic as well as educational reasons.

▼ About 95 percent of retarded children fall into the "mildly" or "moderately" retarded categories. Pictured here is Christopher Burke, an actor with Down's syndrome, who starred in the TV show *Life Goes On*. The show reflected growing public recognition that the outlook for such children is no longer uniformly bleak.

Learning Disorders

Much more common than mental retardation are the ***learning disorders,*** difficulties that reflect enormous developmental tardiness and mainly affect the development of language and academic skills. Learning disorders occur frequently in combination with other difficulties, and in fact, may spawn them.

To survive in adult life, people must be able to learn a language, to learn to read, and to do simple arithmetic. Because of this, most modern industrial societies make education compulsory for about ten years of a child's life. As in most developmental matters, children progress in their education at different speeds. A certain amount of lagging behind is to be expected of some children some of the time. But when a child is significantly below the expected level, as indexed by the child's schooling, age, and IQ, then the matter is viewed as a psychological problem. For children between the ages of eight and thirteen—the critical ages for the acquisition and implementation of academic skills—a significant problem may exist if a child is more than two years behind his or her age level.

READING DIFFICULTIES

Of all the learning disorders, reading difficulties have been studied most. As a group, poor readers were late in acquiring language, and they have more of a history of reading difficulty in their families. Most children who have reading difficulties also have trouble with other domains of learning. More than three times as many boys as girls suffer serious reading difficulties. Children with severe reading difficulties at age ten have an increased risk of other psychological disorders, particularly behavior disorders.

A combination of training in reading skills and behavior therapy designed to maintain a child's interest in learning has proven effective for many children with reading disabilities. This training must start early in a child's school career and be maintained throughout the school years for the child to sustain the gains that have been made and to continue to improve. Unfortunately, children's reading difficulties often are not detected until quite late in childhood.

The social implications of serious reading problems are alarming. Poor readers who are of average intelligence rarely read books or newspapers. They aspire to little that involves reading and, therefore, they often fail to graduate high school. Retarded readers emerge from the school system handicapped educationally, socially, and economically, in the sense that their employment opportunities have been significantly constricted (Yule and Rutter, 1976).

AN EDUCATIONAL OR PSYCHOLOGICAL DISORDER?

The learning disorders are often correlated with, or give rise to, a host of distinctly psychological symptoms. It is mainly for this reason that these developmental disorders are considered *psychological,* rather than educational. But fundamentally, these are skills disabilities; they are in the domain of education rather than psychology and psychiatry. And many believe that they should continue to be viewed that way (cf. Garmezy, 1977a).

The argument is not without merit. There is no evidence, for example, that psychological treatment or drugs have any positive effect on say, the developmental reading disorder. Calling the difficulty a *psychological* disorder in fact may lead teachers to believe that reading disability is outside of their sphere,

▼ Children's rates of development naturally vary, but if a child lags more than two years behind his age group, an underlying disorder may be the cause. Learning disorders such as reading difficulties are associated not only with poor school performance but with low self-esteem and other psychological problems.

leaving the child helped neither by the teacher nor by the psychologist. Moreover, terming reading retardation a psychological disorder may stigmatize the child without contributing a solution to the problem. Indeed, it may simply compound the difficulties. Consider the case of Nelson Rockefeller, former governor of New York and Vice President of the United States. Rockefeller had a severe reading disability that handicapped him from childhood through adulthood. Even as an undergraduate, friends and others had to read his textbooks to him. Throughout his career, he much preferred oral communications to written ones. His problems were difficult enough to deal with. Would his life have been made easier if those difficulties had been described as a severe psychological disorder of childhood? Indeed, could he have been elected to high office if he had been so diagnosed?

Pervasive Developmental Disorders: Autism

There may be some question about whether the specific developmental disorders are psychological disorders at all, but no such question attaches to pervasive developmental disorders. For the latter are all-encompassing, involving difficulties of such magnitude and across so many modalities—language attention, responsiveness, perception, motor development—that little doubt remains about the psychological devastation they create. The primary type of pervasive developmental disorder is autism.

The essential feature of **autism** is that the child's ability to respond to others does not develop within the first thirty months of life. Even at that early age, gross impairment of communicative skills is already quite noticeable, as are the bizarre responses these children make to their environment. They lack interest in and responsiveness to people, and they fail to develop normal attachments. In infancy, these characteristics are manifested by their failure to cuddle, by lack of eye contact, or downright aversion to physical contact and affection. These children may fail entirely to develop language, and if language is acquired, often it will be characterized by **echolalia**—the tendency to repeat or echo immediately or after a brief period precisely what one has just heard—or **pronominal reversals**—the tendency to use "I" where "you" is meant, and vice-versa. Such children also react very poorly to change, either in their routines or in their environments. These symptoms will be taken up at greater length momentarily. But first, some of the difficulties created by autism can be seen in the following case:

> Looking at family photographs of John, one sees a good-looking, well-built, sandy-haired ten-year-old. He looks like thousands of other ten-year-olds—but he's not. If one saw a movie of John it would be immediately obvious that his *behavior* is far from normal. His social relationships seem peculiar. He seems distant, aloof. He seldom makes eye contact. He rarely plays with other children, and when he does, he plays like a three-year-old, not like someone who is ten.
>
> Some things fascinate him, and his most recent fascination has been with shiny leather belts. He carries one around with him nearly always and at times whirls it furiously, becoming more and more excited in the process. At the height of his excitement, he lets out high-pitched, bird-like noises, jumps up and down on the spot, and flaps his hands at eye level. At other times, John appears to be living in a world of his own, entirely impervious to what is happening around him. A car can backfire near him, but he doesn't flinch. He stares into space, gazing at nothing in par-

FOCUS QUESTIONS

1. What is the central feature of autism?
2. Describe the difficulties that autistic children have with communication, including their problems with language.
3. Explain the psychogenic and biological theories of the causes of autism.
4. How is autism treated?

ticular, occasionally flicking his fingers at something in the periphery of his vision.

In addition to the peculiar squeaks, John's speech is most unusual. He can follow a few simple instructions, but only if he is in familiar surroundings. He will say, "Do you want a drink?," and his parents will know that he means *he* wants a drink. Often, he will repeat complex phrases that he has heard a few days before; television commercials particularly feature in this sort of meaningless speech. At other times, he will echo back large chunks of his parents' speech, but they have realized that this is a signal that he has failed to understand them. He can ask for some things, but even simple requests come out muddled. When he fails to get meaning across—and this can be several times a day—he will fly into temper tantrums that can become quite wild.

John's parents are both intelligent, articulate, professional people who, right from the early months after John was born, were convinced that something was wrong with him. But since John was their first child, they shrugged off their worries and attributed them to inexperience. So, too, did their family physician. But gradually, no amount of bland reassurance that John would soon "grow out of it" gave any comfort. John was still too good, too quiet, yet too little interested in them as people, and entirely unwilling to be cuddled.

Worried still, they brought John to child specialists. Again the opinions were reassuring. But as John approached age two and was not yet speaking, the experts' views began to change. Words like "slow," "backward," and "retarded" began to be used more frequently. Finally, John was formally tested by a psychologist, and a surprising fact emerged. Although he was grossly retarded in language development, he was advanced for his age on nonverbal puzzles. Difficulties with hearing were ruled out, and it was during these investigations that autism was first suggested.

Oddly, merely knowing that what was wrong with John had a name, provided his parents with some relief. But it was only momentary, for as they read popular accounts of autism, they found that many experts blamed the parents for the child's bizarre problems. Damning accounts of obsessional, emotionally remote parents—dramatized as "refrigerated mothers"—soon had them questioning whether they were fit parents. Their relationship to each other, as well as to John, was undermined.

John's parents managed to get him into a small class in a school for children with learning handicaps. The teacher took a special interest in John and, encouraged by his parents, she adopted a firm, structured approach to teaching him. To everyone's surprise, he took to some aspects of schoolwork readily. He loved counting things and could add, subtract, multiply, and divide by the time he was seven. Moreover, he learned to read fluently—except that he could not understand a single word of what he read. This was brought home to his parents when he picked up a foreign language journal of his father's and read a whole page in phonic French—without, of course, understanding a word! At about this time, he began talking. He referred to himself as "John," got his personal pronouns in a dreadful muddle, and learned to say "no." He used telegraphic sentences of a sort more appropriate to a boy many years younger than he, but at least he was beginning to make himself understood.

He seemed to cherish all kinds of monotonous routines. His diet consisted of a very restricted selection of foods, and he could not be induced to try new foods. He went to school by a prescribed and invariable route, watched television from the same armchair, and strenuously resisted change. Taking him outside was a nightmare, for there was no anticipating when he might throw an embarrassing tantrum. Try as she might, his mother could not help but be hurt by the glares and comments from passersby as she struggled to get John out of the supermarket or into their car. "If only he looked *abnormal*," she often said, "people would be more understanding."

▲ Autistic children shut out everything that goes on outside themselves as in Odilon Redon's *Silence*. This condition has been called extreme autistic aloneness.

SYMPTOMS OF AUTISM

The central feature of autism, according to Leo Kanner, a child psychiatrist who was the first to recognize this disorder as a distinct syndrome, is the "inability to relate . . . in the ordinary way to people and situations . . . an *extreme autistic aloneness* that, whenever possible, disregards, ignores, shuts out anything that comes to the child from outside" (Kanner, 1943). This striking aloneness takes a variety of forms in the areas of language, behavior, intellectual and cognitive development, and in social relationships.

Language Development   One of the striking features of autistic children is how poorly their understanding and use of spoken language develops. Most parents report that the language of autistic children is delayed and deviant right from the beginning. Toward the end of the second year, when normal children are babbling in a characteristically varied way, autistic children frequently show decidedly abnormal and idiosyncratic patterns. Speech falters badly in these children because they fail to imitate or to initiate imaginative play, both of which are crucial for early language development. For example, they show little skill in such simple social imitations as "waving bye-bye." And their later use of small toys in imaginative play is severely limited if, indeed, it ever develops. Unlike deaf children, who understand the ideas of communication and who have developed nonverbal skills for communicating, autistic children do not use gestures and mime to make their needs known. They may point to objects they need, but if the object is not immediately present, their ability to communicate about it is very much restricted.

It is in their very peculiar use of sounds and words that autistic children's difficulties are most noticeable. About half of the autistic children never learn to use simple words. Those who do show many characteristic abnormalities. In the early stages, the child often uses a high-pitched, bird-like squeaking voice, as John did. Again, like John, both immediate and delayed echolalia occur for long periods after speech develops. The child latches on to a phrase from, say, a television commercial, and echoes it for weeks on end.

When speech does develop, autistic children show many of the same sorts of grammatical errors that normal children do. But with autistic children, these errors are more long-lasting and peculiar. We will look at two of these errors; pronoun reversal and the misuse of the rule for adding *-ing*.

Autistic children tend to reverse the pronouns *I* and *you*. For example, when the child wants a candy, he may say "Do *you* want a candy?" instead of "*I* want a candy." Why is this pronominal reversal so typical in autistic children? Two suggestions have been offered. Psychoanalysts have interpreted this reversal as either an unawareness or a denial of personal identity. The child refuses to say *I* because unconsciously he does not accept his own existence (Creak, 1961; Bettelheim, 1967). Others suggest a more parsimonious explanation that rests on the high correlation between echoing and pronominal reversal. Since personal pronouns occur more frequently at the beginning of sentences, and since autistic children have difficulty processing long sentences, they tend to echo the last few words only. When they are given artificial sentences with "I" and "me" placed at the end (for example, "give candy to me"), they do not reverse pronouns (Bartak and Rutter, 1974). Thus, pronominal reversal can be understood as an integral part of a more general language disorder, rather than as a symptom of emotional problems in identity formation.

▲ Autistic children often have severe temper tantrums, particularly when their environments change suddenly.

▼ An autistic boy.

While both normal and autistic children misuse the *-ing* rule, autistic children are older when the errors arise and the errors persist long after the age when normal children learn the rule. One nine-year-old autistic girl described a man smoking a pipe as "Daddy piping," while a boy blowing bubbles was "boy bubbling" (Wing, 1976). Autistic children also often identify objects by their use, such as "make-a-cup-of-tea" for kettle, and "sweep-the-floor" for broom.

These are but two of the kinds of language errors made by autistic children. For many of these children, language development proceeds no further. Even the small proportion of autistic children who do learn to talk continue to use language in a noticeably peculiar way. Often it is *too perfect, too* grammatical, rather like a person using a foreign language learned artificially. There is a lack of colloquialism. Conversation is stilted. These children can maintain a concrete question-and-answer interchange, but the subtleties of emotional tone are lost on them. They seem to know the formal rules of language, but they do not comprehend the idea of communication. This defect extends to the nonverbal aspects of communication as well.

Insistence on Sameness   Many normal children react badly to changes in their environment, particularly if those changes are sudden. But for reasons that are not at all clear, autistic children show this trait in greatly exaggerated form. For example, some autistic children will have severe temper tantrums if the furniture in the house is moved around. Others insist on being driven to school over the same route every day. Parents find that what begins as a harmless routine becomes so rigid that it seriously interferes with everyday life.

Insistence on sameness is seen in other ways. Autistic children frequently use toys and other objects to make long lines or complex patterns. They seem more interested in the pattern than in the functional or imaginative play qualities of the objects. Frequently, these children become intensely attached to one or more objects. John, you recall, carried around a long belt and gyrated it. Other children may refuse to part from a grubby piece of toweling. These intense attachments interfere with normal development and everyday living in a number of ways. If the object is lost, life is made unbearable for the child and the rest of the family. If it is a large object, it prevents hand-eye coordination since the child's hands are not free to play with other objects. As can be seen in Box 16–1, however, it is possible to reduce these abnormal attachments and promote normal development (Marchant, Howlin, Yule, and Rutter, 1974).

Social Development   One other striking characteristic of the autistic child is aloofness, a physical and emotional distance from others that is especially troublesome to parents and quite noticeable by others. John was clearly aloof, and his mother particularly was troubled by it. This aloofness reflects a fundamental failure to develop social attachments. This is shown by the fact that when autistic children can choose where to spend their time, they will spend more time near a nonreacting adult than near an empty chair (Hermelin and O'Connor, 1970). Thus, active avoidance (which would have been shown by choosing to be near the empty chair) is not the case for autistic children. Recent evidence suggests that autistic children have fundamental problems in understanding expressions of emotions in others and in using their own faces, voices, and gestures to communicate their own emotions (Hobson, 1986).

Box 16–1

TREATING INSISTENCE ON SAMENESS

One of the less obvious consequences of many autistic children's insistence on sameness is the direct interference with their already limited cognitive development. Many children become compulsively attached to unusual objects. Some carry small stones clenched tightly in their fists; one child refused to be parted from a metal wire filing basket; and others carry discs they can spin. Any attempt by their parent or teachers to remove these objects is met with an immediate and violent temper tantrum. In these circumstances, adults often give in to the child's wishes. The result can be that the child wanders aimlessly around with his hands fully occupied by the object. In turn, this means that his hands are not free to pick up other things and generally to interact with his physical environment so as to allow hand-eye coordination to develop. Missing out on this stage of normal development may interfere with the development of later, more complex cognitive skills.

Some professionals have advised parents not to interfere with their child's unusual object attachment, in the belief that the object somehow represents the parent and that to intervene will mean damaging an already precarious relationship. In contrast, Marchant and her colleagues argue that these objects fulfill different functions from other attachment objects and that intervention is desirable to promote cognitive growth.

Marchant reports on the case of a five-year-old non-speaking autistic boy who constantly carried around a large (2 foot by 2 foot) blanket. This effectively meant that he had only one arm free for all activities. His mother attempted to prevent him from carrying the blanket everywhere, but to no avail.

It was decided to use a graded-change approach. His mother was asked to cut a small piece off the blanket each night and to increase the amount cut off. The blanket was quickly reduced from 4 square feet to a small bundle of five threads. At this point, the boy was able to abandon for awhile what was left of the blanket. Soon the boy took to carrying other objects. Where these were deemed inappropriate, they were dealt with in the same way. In fact, he appeared to enjoy watching them being cut up! Within four months, he carried a wider range of objects and his interest in any one of them was short-lived. Objects that were of play value were not destroyed, rather he was praised for playing with them appropriately. A year later, he spontaneously abandoned objects for long periods of time and, by then, his comprehension skills as well as his social behavior were improving markedly.

This case illustrates that a direct behavioral approach can be helpful in dealing with one of the major behavioral problems presented by many autistic children.

SOURCE: Based on Marchant, Howlin, Yule, and Rutter, 1974.

Many autistic children gradually improve in their social relationship beginning at about age five, provided that they have not been institutionalized in unstimulating surroundings. Ultimately, however, the relationships these children establish are difficult at best. Their social skills show themselves in their lack of cooperative group play with other children, their failure to make personal friendships, and in the enormous difficulty they have in recognizing and responding appropriately to other people's feelings.

Intellectual Development While autistic children do poorly on tests that require verbal ability, they may perform far above average on tests that involve rote memory or spatial tasks. Moreover, they may be quite talented in music or drawing. But despite evidence of islands of intelligence, autistic children function quite poorly in the cognitive domain. Only about 25 to 40 percent of them have IQ scores above 70, and those scores appear to be quite stable over a ten-year period (Ritvo et al., 1989). In fact, the child's measured IQ is one of the best predictors of later progress: those with higher IQ scores do better in a variety of educational and remedial settings (Mittler, Gillies, and Jukes, 1966; Gittleman and Birch, 1967; Lockyer and Rutter, 1969; DeMeyer, Barton, Alpern, Kimberlin, Allen, Yang, and Steel, 1974).

PREVALENCE OF AUTISM

Fortunately, the severe disorders of childhood are rare. Yet, the total number of children suffering from autism is considerable. It occurs in about 4 cases per 10,000, about as frequently as deafness occurs among children, and twice as commonly as blindness (Ritvo et al., 1989). With regard to sex differences, boys outnumber girls by about three to one. The disorder does not appear to be related to socioeconomic status or race. The prevalence of autism appears to be similar across several different countries (Ritvo et al., 1989).

CAUSES OF AUTISM

The sorts of behavior associated with autism are so far removed from people's expectations of normal development that most now believe that there must be some biological abnormality underlying the syndrome. The professional climate has not always been so biologically oriented, however. Those who first studied the disorder tended to focus on the parents and *their* abnormal traits (Kanner, 1943). By examining these traits, they hoped to come up with possible psychological causes of autism. Since the evidence on parental traits is now fairly clear, let us examine this first.

Psychogenic Theories To some psychodynamic and behaviorist theorists, the parents of autistic children seemed to be introverted, distant, intellectual, and meticulous (Ferster, 1961; Bettelheim, 1967). These children seemed to be reared under conditions of "emotional refrigeration." The introvertedness of the parents was reflected in their offspring; parental distance was seen in the child's aloofness, while parental meticulousness was mirrored in the child's repetitive behaviors. Even if one accepts the evidence, however, to conclude that the parents' behavior *caused* the child's disorder is not logical. It is equally plausible that, faced with such an unusual child, parental attitudes and behaviors became unusual. This alternative hypothesis was overlooked in the rush to demonstrate parental culpability.

There is little evidence to suggest that the parents of autistic children do behave very differently than the parents of normal children behave toward them. No confirmation of extremely damaging parental behavior exists. Few autistic children actually come from broken homes, and most have not experienced early family stresses. Their parents turn out not to be overly introverted or obsessional, nor do they show any excess of thought disorder. Most autistic children experience the normal range of parental attitudes and child-rearing practices (Cantwell, Baker, and Rutter, 1978).

Biological Theories Because psychogenic theories have not been substantiated and because many autistic children appear also to suffer from a variety of physiological deficits, increasing attention has been directed to the possible biological origins of autism. During adolescence, nearly 30 percent of autistic children develop epileptic seizures even though they had shown no clear evidence of neurological disorder when they were younger. Furthermore, electroencephalographic (EEG) studies—that is, studies that examine the electrical activity of the brain—reveal that autistic children have a higher rate of abnormal brain waves than do normal children. A variety of other structural and functional differences between the central nervous systems of autistic and nonautistic children have been found, suggesting that there are multiple bio-

▲ From a very early age, many autistic children avoid physical affection and seem unable to form attachments to people.

logical causes of autism, or several subtypes of autism, each with different causes (Prior, 1987).

One area of focus for biological studies of autism involves the neurotransmitters. When neurotransmission is faulty, the brain is unable to pass messages efficiently from one neuron to another. As a result, both perception and learning are interfered with, and patchy cognitive development results. A variety of neurotransmitters could be at fault in the development of autism. Several studies have found differences between autistic and nonautistic children in levels of serotonin and dopamine (Ritvo et al., 1978; Winsberg et al., 1980; Gilberg and Svennerholm, 1987). But the majority of autistic children do not show any neurotransmitter difficulties. Moreover, such abnormalities are found in several other disorders. Thus, imbalances in neurotransmitter levels may be one cause of autism, but there are clearly other causes, too.

Another focus for biological studies of autism involves whether there is a genetic component to the disorder. Because autism is a relatively rare condition, however, it is difficult to gather extensive data on the genetics of this disorder. But one study found that about 10 percent of families with one autistic child have at least one other autistic child (Ritvo et al., 1989). The specific syndrome of autism may be only weakly transmitted genetically. Instead, a more general vulnerability to several types of cognitive impairment, only one of which is manifested as autism, seems to run in the families, and specifically the identical twins, of autistic children (Quay, Routh, and Shapiro, 1987). A significant percentage of autistic children also experience other severe, sometimes chromosome-linked, biological disorders, such as Fragile X syndrome, phenylketonuria, rubella, encephalitis, and epilepsy (Prior, 1987). Finally, autism is associated with a higher rate of obstetric and neonatal complications (Goodman, 1990). Whether these other disorders are causes of autism or simply caused by another underlying biological abnormality that also causes autism is unknown (Gilberg, 1991).

TREATING AUTISM

Drug treatments, including neuroleptics and lithium, have been used with mixed results in autistic children (Gilberg, 1991). Instead, current treatment

▶ Behavioral techniques may successfully treat specific deficits caused by autism. These autistic children receive positive reinforcement for hugging each other.

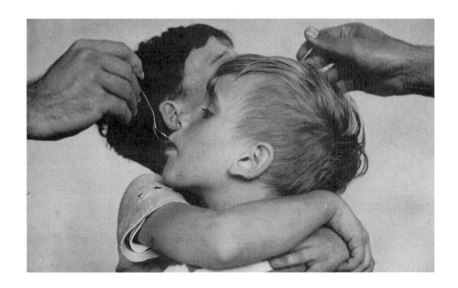

efforts arise mainly from behavioral sources that focus on the specific deficits that are engendered by autism. Considerable effort, for example, has focused on language development, on the grounds that the inability to communicate properly is so central to this disorder. In these treatments, children's vocalizations are reinforced by the therapist until they occur very frequently. Next, the children are rewarded for imitating the sounds produced by the therapist, and simultaneously punished for producing meaningless sounds. When imitation is established, children are taught to label everyday objects. And finally, the same techniques are used to teach them to ask questions (Lovaas, 1966; Risley and Wolf, 1967). Early studies of the effectiveness of these methods engendered considerable optimism that these behavioral techniques might enable children to overcome the deficits associated with autism. But this optimism was tempered somewhat by the studies showing that gains made during treatment often disappear when the children are returned to institutional care (Lovaas, 1973). One study, however, suggests that if autistic children are given intensive behavioral treatment for a significant period of time (i.e., forty hours per week for at least two years) at an early age, long-term prognosis can be good (Lovaas, 1987). In this study, 47 percent of the autistic children receiving such intensive treatment achieved normal intellectual and educational functioning by age six to seven, compared to only 2 percent of autistic children who received minimal, institutional care. Furthermore, when parents participate in treatment programs, both their behaviors and those of the children undergo change. And the more the parents are involved in the treatment program, the more likely are the language gains to be maintained (Hemsley, Howlin, Berger, Hersov, Holbrook, Rutter, and Yule, 1978).

In conjunction with behavioral approaches, direct structured educational approaches have also proven beneficial to autistic children (Hung, Rotman, Consentino, and MacMillan, 1983). These approaches zero in on the specific cognitive, motor, and perceptual handicaps of these children. A carefully designed educational program minimizes the kinds of distractions that accompany ordinary teaching, making it possible for these children to concentrate. For example, when normal children are taught to read, some texts and teaching materials print vowels in one color and consonants in another. While this helps normal children differentiate between vowels and consonants, it confuses children with pervasive developmental difficulties (Schreibman, 1975). Generally, structured education aimed at overcoming the specific handicaps of the disorder seems to be the best method presently available for helping these children. Again, including parents in these treatments, teaching them how to overcome their child's specific deficits, increases the effectiveness of the treatments.

PROGNOSIS

Long-term follow-up studies of autistic children indicate that the prognosis for them is not favorable. Close to 60 percent will be unable to lead an independent life as adults (Gilberg, 1991). Only about 4 percent will eventually recover to a point where they are indistinguishable from normal children. The remaining children will make some progress in developing skills but will still manifest a host of odd behaviors.

As mentioned earlier, the autistic child's IQ score turns out to be one of the most sensitive early indices of later outcome. In the main, the higher the autistic child's IQ, the better his prognosis. Another good prognostic indicator is the presence of some useful spoken language before the age of five. Finally, autistic children who do not develop seizures have a better outcome than those who do (Gilberg, 1991). While the outlook for such children is slowly improving as treatment slowly improves, most autistic adolescents and young adults will still need access to residential facilities.

AREAS FOR FURTHER CONSIDERATION

We have much yet to learn about the disorders discussed in this chapter. Throughout the chapter, we have pointed out gaps in our knowledge about each of the disorders. There are at least three broad sets of questions about childhood psychopathology in general that also need to be addressed over the next few years. First, does the current DSM-IV classification system for childhood disorders accurately represent the breakdown of childhood syndromes? Children's problems are extremely difficult to translate into specific syndromes with clear-cut criteria for diagnosis. This is because the symptom configuration of any disorder may change with the child's development. Also, some symptoms, such as aggressive behavior, are associated with many different disorders. The classification of children's disorders is one area that experts expect to undergo much revision in the next decade.

The second question is related to the first: How can we better identify children who have serious psychological problems and how can we assess their particular problems? At the beginning of this chapter, we mentioned that we must rely on the adults in a troubled child's life to bring that child to the attention of clinicians. In addition, children's underdeveloped language skills make it difficult to obtain information from them about their condition. We need to know how to ask better questions of parents, teachers, and children that will provide the information clinicians need to access children's psychological health.

The final question is about the long-term prognosis for children who have a psychological problem. We mentioned that children with autism or a conduct disorder appear to be at high risk for psychological disturbance in adulthood.

FOCUS QUESTIONS

1. Why are children's psychological problems so difficult to classify?
2. Why is it so difficult to identify children who have serious psychological problems?
3. Why is there a need for longitudinal studies of children with psychological problems?

▶ Because children's language skills are not fully developed, successful therapy often relies on methods other than language. This child's painting of the forbidding school he hated may communicate more about his feelings than he could have conveyed using words.

We know very little about the long-term prognosis of many of the other disorders, however. There have just been too few studies that follow children all the way into adulthood. We also know very little about the long-term effects of different types of therapy for children, especially drug therapies. What therapies are the most effective at helping a child to recover from a given problem and at preventing the recurrence of that problem in later years? Longitudinal studies of the outcome of children with different types of problems, who under different types of therapy, will be expensive, but the need for them is obvious.

SUMMARY

1. Children's psychological disorders are often difficult to distinguish from the relatively common problems of growing up because they occur in a developmental context, because children cannot communicate a problem directly through language, and because children's problems are often specific to particular situations and contexts.

2. On the whole, children's problems can be divided into four areas: disruptive behavior disorders, emotional disorders, habit and eating disorders, and developmental disorders.

3. The disruptive behavior disorders, including conduct disorder, oppositional defiant disorder, and atttention-deficit hyperactivity disorder, appear to be quite persistent from childhood into adulthood. Children with these disorders often show criminal behavior, drug abuse, and low educational and occupational attainment.

4. The most common emotional disorder in children is separation anxiety disorder. Children with this disorder have a marked fear of separation form loved ones. Phobias, such as school phobia, are also common among children.

5. The habit disorders and eating disorders include bed-wetting, stuttering, tics, and two eating disorders, anorexia and bulimia. The prevalence of the two eating disorders appears to be increasing.

6. The developmental disorders range from learning disabilities in specific areas such as reading or math to various levels of mental retardation to autism. Autism is the most severe of these because it involves both intellectual retardation and severe disturbances in the abilities to have social and emotional experiences. The development disorders are more likely than any other class of disorders to persist into adulthood.

7. There is still much to be learned about childhood disorders, and especially about their treatment. Drug therapies have been used for some disorders, but there is great concern about the toxicity of drugs in children. Behavioral treatments seem effective for several disorders, including attention-deficit hyperactivity disorder, separation anxiety disorder, phobias, bed-wetting, stuttering, and some symptoms of autism. Many therapists also advocate involving a child's parents in therapy in order to facilitate a child's recovery from a disorder and to reverse any negative effects the parents might be having on the child.

1. What are the indications that children with conduct disorder or attention-deficit hyperactivity disorder may be suffering from chronic underarousal?

2. Describe some reasons for school refusal and why children who suffer from school phobia may be at risk for agoraphobia, job difficulties, and personality disorders as adults.

3. How do genes and environment interact to produce more or less severely retarded children?

4. Why should involving parents in treatment strategies for mental retardation and autism increase the effectiveness of the treatments?

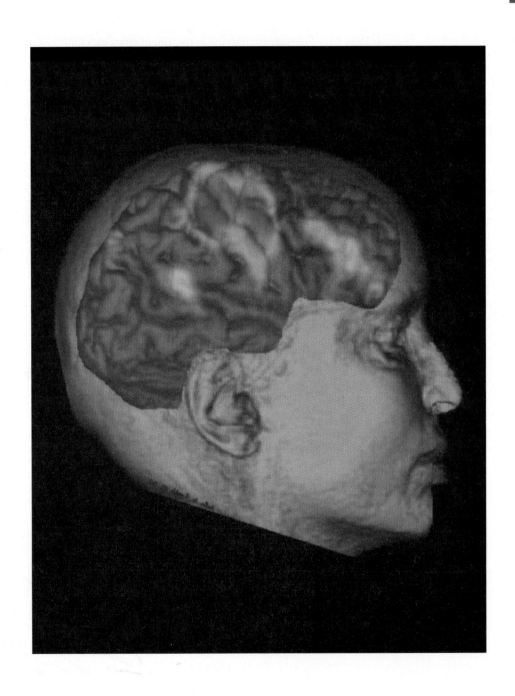

CHAPTER 17

Disorders of the Nervous System and Psychopathology

Morris Moscovitch and Paul Rozin

CHAPTER ORGANIZER

ORGANIZATION OF THE NERVOUS SYSTEM IN RELATION TO ORGANIC DISORDERS
- Learn how basic principles of the structure and function of the nervous system can account for a variety of disorders of mind and behavior.

DAMAGE TO THE NERVOUS SYSTEM
- Be able to describe how damage to the nervous system is expressed.

ASSESSING BRAIN DAMAGE
- Familiarize yourself with how neurologists make diagnoses and with brain-imaging techniques.

SOME SELECTED DISORDERS OF THE NERVOUS SYSTEM
- Learn about the aphasias, dyslexia, the amnesic syndrome, dementia, and disorders related to the frontal lobes.

THE TREATMENT OF DISEASES OF THE NERVOUS SYSTEM
- Become familiar with how disorders of the nervous system may be treated.

THE EXPANSION OF THE NEUROLOGICAL/NEUROCHEMICAL APPROACHES
- Understand how some disorders that were believed to be functional disorders have been found to have an organic basis.

THE VIRTUES AND LIMITATIONS OF THE NEUROLOGICAL APPROACH
- Understand both the advantages and disadvantages of finding or proposing neurological or neurochemical accounts of psychopathology.

The human brain is the most complex biological structure on earth. We may know more about the human brain, its anatomy and physiology, than about any other structure in the human body. But that is partly because there is so much to know. It is also true that there is more that we *don't* know about the human brain than about any other human structure.

Most scientists believe that all of the phenomena of behavior and the mind, whether they are normal or abnormal, have a basis in the activities of the nervous system. Modern medicine, however, distinguishes between two broad classes of abnormal behaviors: ***organic syndromes,*** which are caused by known pathology in the structure or function of the nervous system, and

functional syndromes, which are believed to be caused by abnormal experience imposed upon normal brain mechanisms.

There is an analogy between the organic-functional distinction and the hardware-software distinction in computer science. Hardware (corresponding to the structure of the nervous system) refers to the fixed, factory-produced components and wiring of the computer. Software is information (programs) fed into the system. The performance of the computer is the result of the interaction of software and hardware. The software is physically real and assumes an electrical form, but is quite distinct from the hardware. The software can be modified from the outside by loading a new program, whereas modification or repair of the hardware requires dealing directly with components inside the computer. Computer programmers, who design, improve, or debug software, do not usually design or repair hardware. Roughly, the distinction between organic/hardware and functional/software is generally represented by two branches of of medicine: neurology and psychiatry. In psychology, there is a corresponding split between neuropsychology, devoted to studying organic syndromes, and clinical psychology, which is concerned more with functional syndromes.

The distinction between these disciplines and the syndromes they study is not hard and fast. One reason is that experience (which corresponds to software in the nervous system) is less independent of the brain (hardware) than is the case in computers. For example, one can erase all the software in a computer, in which case the hardware returns to the original state. However, experience "loaded" into the brain usually changes the brain itself. All experiences that leave a lasting imprint must do so by modifying the brain. As a result, it is impossible to erase the effect of experience (software) on the brain (hardware). As we will see later, although amnesic patients have no recollection of recent experiences, these experiences leave a lasting impression in their brains. In fact, the software/hardware distinction in the nervous system is more like a continuous dimension.

As knowledge of the nervous system expands, there has been a tendency to reinterpret functional (near the software end) syndromes in terms of organic deficits (nearer the hardware end). Recently, developments in understanding the physiology of the synapses and the role of the neurotransmitters have, as in the cases of schizophrenia and depression, caused us to reconceptualize some disorders as having a greater organic component. Nonetheless, the distinctions remain useful, at least at the extremes.

Clinicians are often forced to make a determination of organic or functional disorder. This decision will have broad implications. It will determine the type of medical-psychological care that the patient receives, and the extent of insurance coverage for the costs of treatment and loss of income. It will also affect the way the patient views herself and the way others view her. Our judgment of a person's behavior is affected by whether we believe it is part of a neurological disorder or an aspect of the individual's personality.

We offer the following case histories to provide a sense of the type of complex symptoms that can result from neurological damage:

> A twenty-year-old man was an excellent student, relatively conservative, and quite ambitious. He had enrolled in a university to become an engineer, and was doing well, a fact that pleased his wealthy family. Upon returning home from a summer job as a waiter at a resort, however, he seemed to have lost his purposeful-

ness and motivation in general, and his behavior seemed more erratic. He announced to his family that he no longer wanted to study engineering, and wished to become a head waiter instead. An epileptic seizure alerted his family to the possibility that this change in personality was not the normal rebelliousness of youth. Subsequent neurological and neuropsychological investigation revealed that he had a malformation of the blood vessels in the frontal area of the brain. This was congenital, but its effects had just appeared. These types of symptoms often accompany damage to the frontal lobes. (Case history from the files of Morris Moscovitch)

Before the onset of her disorder, a woman had worked for years as a fish-filleter. She began to experience difficulty in doing her job. She did not seem to know what to do with her knife. She would stick the point in the head of a fish, start the first stroke, then come to a stop. In her own mind, she knew how to fillet fish, but yet she could not execute the maneuver. The foreman accused her of being drunk and sent her home for mutilating fish. She subsequently was diagnosed as having damage to the parietal lobes in her cortex, which caused a disorder of movement. (Critchley, 1966, pp. 158–59)

Before being diagnosed as having organic disorders, functional causes were suspected in both of these cases. In the case of the student with frontal-lobe damage, rebelliousness was suspected; in the case of the woman with damage to the parietal lobes, drunkenness was suspected. Neurological examination in both cases revealed the organic disorders.

Traditionally, two main sources of information have been sufficient to establish an organic or functional origin: (1) a detailed case history, including pattern of onset of the symptoms, and (2) consistency of the symptoms with a pattern of deficits that would be expected from damage to a particular neural structure. For example, a patient with sudden onset of loss of feeling in the left arm and left leg is very likely to have had a stroke in the part of the right cerebral cortex that receives input from both the left arm and leg. More recently, with the development of high-powered imaging techniques, a more direct determination can often be made by isolating neural damage in a brain scan.

Not all cases are as easy to diagnose, however, as those of the patients we've just discussed. In cases with a slow onset of symptoms and involving complex behaviors, such as those related to memory or personality, it may be quite difficult to distinguish organic from functional disorders. It is sometimes the case that patients with brain damage may have no obvious physical symptoms—e.g., no paralysis, no loss of sensation, no gross defects in language or thinking, no difficulties in solving problems. Only the presence of additional symptoms that have nothing to do with personality—e.g., difficulty drawing simple figures like cubes or clocks or loss of memory for a particular time period or failure to pay attention to events or stimuli occurring on one side of the patient—suggests to the clinician that there is a neurological disorder (Ross, 1981, 1983).

The fact that it is difficult to determine whether some syndromes are organic or functional is only one reason why a person interested in psychopathology should know something about neurology. In the future, it is likely that once we understand more about their underlying pathology, some disorders now considered to be functional will be reclassified as neurological. This has already occurred for the case of the paralysis and dementia syndrome caused by syphilis (see Chapter 3), and it may also occur for some of the major psychoses. Furthermore, neurology is based on a body of knowledge about the structure and function of the nervous system, and uses a set of advanced diagnostic techniques that compare very favorably to what is available in many other branches of medicine. As a result, neurologists work with diagnostic tools that are sophisticated and precise, and a classificatory scheme that is more clear-cut than what psychologists and psychiatrists have available to them in DSM-IV. Neurology provides an opportunity to view an advanced discipline that deals with phenomena similar to those that are the focus of abnormal psychology.

ORGANIZATION OF THE NERVOUS SYSTEM IN RELATION TO ORGANIC DISORDERS

In this section, we will show how some basic principles of the structure and function of the nervous system can account for a variety of disorders of mind and behavior.

Structural and Functional Units: Neurons, Glia, Synapses, and Neurotransmitters

Neurons are the "units" of the nervous system (Figure 17–1A). Neurons communicate with one another by releasing neurotransmitter substances into the *synapse,* the gap separating one neuron from another (Figure 17–1B). These transmitters either increase (excite) or decrease (inhibit) the activity of other neurons.

Defects in the basic structure and function of synapses have been suggested as causes of some major mental illnesses. You will recall the dopamine hypothesis of schizophrenia (see Chapters 3 and 12), which holds that an excess of the neurotransmitter dopamine and postsynaptic cell dopamine receptors causes schizophrenia (see Figure 17–1B).

Some of the pathology of the nervous system derives from damage to the supportive tissue of the nervous system, particularly the glia cells that are dispersed throughout the brain and that are much more numerous than neurons. Many tumors and other disorders originate in the glia cells. Multiple sclerosis is a disorder of the glia cells that manufacture and maintain the myelin

▶ Photomicrograph (magnified about 60X) of motor neurons of the spinal cord. The numerous small dots are nuclei of glial cells, indicating the large number of glia with respect to neurons.

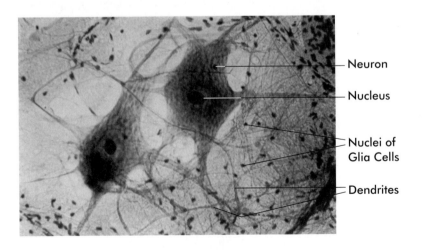

— Neuron

— Nucleus

— Nuclei of Glia Cells

— Dendrites

FIGURE 17–1

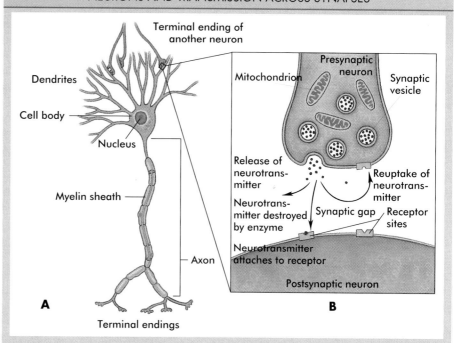

NEURONS AND TRANSMISSION ACROSS SYNAPSES

(A) Schematic diagram of the principal parts of a neuron. Neurons vary in form. The neuron pictured is a motor neuron from the spinal cord. The terminal endings of another presynaptic neuron are shown at the top, to illustrate synaptic endings. (SOURCE: Modified from Katz, 1952) (B) Schematic diagram of a synapse in the central nervous system. The generalized synapse will be described here for the specific case of the neurotransmitter dopamine (called a dopaminergic synapse). Dopamine (or any other neurotransmitter) is manufactured in the presynaptic neuron, and stored in synaptic vesicles. Release of the neurotransmitter in the synaptic gap is normally stimulated by nerve impulses in the presynaptic neuron. Some of the dopamine diffuses across the synaptic gap, attaches to receptors on the postsynaptic neuron membrane, and induces electrical changes in the postsynaptic neuron. Some of the dopamine secreted into the synapse is destroyed by an enzyme, monoamine oxidase, present in the synaptic gap. Some of the dopamine is subject to reuptake into the presynaptic neuron. (SOURCE: Modified from Gardner, 1975, p. 47)

sheath that surrounds the axons of many neurons. The result is impaired function of neurons, often leading to weakness, loss of sensation, and even mental disorders. Other pathologies may derive from damage to the sensory or motor neurons themselves. In amyotrophic lateral sclerosis (ALS), "Lou Gehrig's disease," there is selective degeneration of the motor neurons, with progressive loss of movements in the limbs, body, and head (see Box 17–1).

The Biochemical Organization of the Brain

Neurons have specific biochemical identities. They can be differentiated according to which chemicals are in their cell membranes and which neuro-

Box 17–1

LOU GEHRIG: THE IRON HORSE OF BASEBALL STRICKEN BY AMYOTROPHIC LATERAL SCLEROSIS

It is ironic that the most durable of all baseball players, Yankee Lou Gehrig, who had a major league record of playing in 2,130 consecutive games, was stricken by one of the most debilitating of all diseases, amyotrophic lateral sclerosis (ALS). The motor neuron degeneration that characterizes ALS produces weakness and a loss of the motor control that is especially necessary in athletics. In keeping with the specificity of this disease, Gehrig's first symptoms were a deterioration in batting performance. He played only the first eight games of 1939, batting only .143, an enormous drop for a consistent (lifetime .340 batting average) hitter. On May 2, 1939, Gehrig withdrew himself from the Yankee starting lineup, breaking his consecutive games' string, on the grounds of poor performance. In June, he went to the Mayo Clinic for diagnosis, and the following announcement was made to the startled press and public on June 21, 1939: "After a careful and complete examination, it was found that he is suffering from amyotrophic lateral sclerosis. This type of illness involves the motor pathways. . . . The nature of this trouble makes it such that Mr. Gehrig will be unable to continue his active participation as a baseball player. . . ." (Hubler, in Voigt, 1987, p. 185). Thus ended one of the greatest careers in baseball. Gehrig's uniform number, 4, was retired so that no other Yankee can ever wear it. In one of the most moving events in baseball history, 60,000 fans turned out to honor him in Yankee Stadium on July 4, 1939. To say his goodbye, Gehrig shuffled to the microphone, with a gait already hampered by the affliction of ALS. His closing remarks were: "I may have been given a bad break, but I've an awful lot to live for. With all this, I consider myself the luckiest man on the face of the earth."

Gehrig took a job working for the Parole Board in New York City, and he continued at this until he was unable to function. As is characteristic of ALS, his mind remained clear, but he gradually lost his ability to walk or move in other ways, and he lost his ability to speak clearly. Gehrig died on June 2, 1941, about two years after diagnosis of the disease.

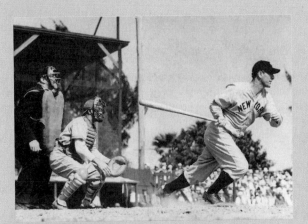 

▲ (A) Lou Gehrig connecting for a homer in 1938, his last full season. (B) Lou Gehrig being honored at Yankee Stadium on July 4, 1939, shortly after his treatment and affliction with ALS was announced.

transmitters they produce. Neurons with similar biochemical properties tend to be located near one another, or in identifiable clusters of neurons running through the nervous system. Neurons serving the same function have certain biochemical similarities in their membranes. Because of this, toxins, certain infectious agents such as viruses, or other influences may specifically affect particular types of neurons. In the case of ALS, there may be an infectious agent that recognizes and specifically attacks motor neurons.

FIGURE 17–2

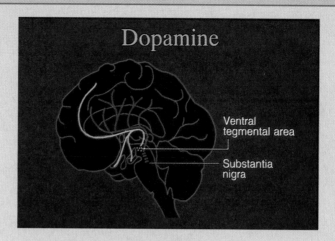

DOPAMINE PATHWAYS IN THE BRAIN

Dopamine pathways from the substantia nigra to the basal ganglia and from the ventral tegmental area to the frontal lobe are both involved in Parkinson's disease. Cell loss in these areas causes a depletion of dopamine and produces such symptoms of Parkinson's disease as tremor, physical and mental rigidity, and difficulty initiating movements. (SOURCE: Cummings, 1993)

Parkinson's disease is a disorder of movement and cognition that has a biochemical basis. At the motor level, it is characterized by tremor of the hands, rigidity, and difficulty in initiating movements. At the cognitive level, there are parallel symptoms such as mental rigidity (Brown and Marsden, 1990). It afflicts, in some degree, about 1 percent of the people over fifty in the United States. It is caused by degeneration of specific neurons, which causes depletion of the neurotransmitter dopamine in certain structures in the brain (see Figure 17–2). Although there is now no cure for the disease, its symptoms can be effectively relieved by administration of the drug L-DOPA, which is converted into dopamine in the brain (Adams, 1989). There is also evidence that schizophrenia is caused by an excess of dopamine in the brain (see Chapter 12). Given that Parkinson's disease and schizophrenia are associated with opposite disturbances in dopamine, it should not be surprising that treating Parkinson's disease patients with high levels of L-DOPA can induce the symptoms of schizophrenia, and treating schizophrenics with drugs that reduce dopamine activity can lead to the appearance of the symptoms of Parkinson's disease (Gilman, Goodman, Rall, and Murad, 1985).

Obsessive-compulsive disorder (OCD) manifests itself across a rather narrow class of behaviors or concerns, most commonly issues related to cleanliness. Despite the fact that OCD involves "styles" of thought and behavior, it has been suggested that it has a biochemical component just as does depression. Changing the level of neurotransmitters with drugs has been shown to reduce the symptoms of OCD, as in the following case:

> An eighteen-year-old high school girl from a small town in Maine was brought to a psychiatrist by her mother because of her excessive showering and dressing rituals. Showers lasted two hours; it took a half hour to dress. Each act of dressing was counted and had to be repeated precisely seventeen times. These behaviors had

begun gradually at age fifteen years, causing chronic tardiness at school; two months of counseling with the school psychologist was not helpful. When the psychiatrist was consulted, the patient's circle of friends and activities had narrowed, and she was missing school one or two times a week.

She had been an outgoing, popular girl, with average grades, who had not previously exhibited unusual concern for neatness, expressed odd thoughts or preoccupations, or presented any behavioral problems of note. When interviewed, she was embarrassed, discussing her washing and counting behaviors. She said she "knew it was crazy" but said "I just have to do this—I don't know why." Her behavior was otherwise quite unremarkable; most striking was her claim that she struggled against the symptoms continually but without success. She had never heard of anyone else who had this problem.

The patient was referred to a psychologist for behavior therapy, but would not cooperate with treatment, insisting she *had* to continue these rituals. The psychiatrist applied for enrollment of the patient through a new drug protocol. After three months, the process was complete. Clomipramine hydrochloride was administered at a dosage of 150 mg/d for three months. After about three weeks of drug therapy, the urges to wash and to count had faded sufficiently so that the patient could cooperate with her family and psychologist in further reducing her strange behaviors. After three months of treatment, because of drowsiness and constipation, the dosage was lowered to 50 mg/d. On three separate occasions the dosage was lowered still further, but the washing and counting rituals resumed each time. (Rapoport, 1988)

The effectiveness of clomipramine in the treatment of OCD has now been confirmed in a number of controlled studies (Rapoport, 1988). Other drugs, such as Prozac (fluoxetine), now also seem effective in reducing the symptoms of OCD. It seems that the common effect of these drugs is biochemical; they inhibit the selective reuptake of the neurotransmitter serotonin.

The Spatial Organization of the Brain: Localization of Function

The brain is spatially organized; that is, neurons in different regions of the brain perform different functions. Furthermore, neurons close to one another are likely to perform related functions. This spatial organization of the nervous system (*localization of function*) allows a neurologist to determine the location of damage in the nervous system by just examining behavioral symptoms. Most damage to the nervous system affects a moderately well-defined area, as would clearly be the case for damage resulting from strokes, bullet wounds, or tumors.

The nervous system contains areas in which nerve cell bodies are concentrated, called *gray matter,* and areas in which axons are concentrated into tracts, called *white matter,* because of the white myelin surrounding many axons. Tissue damage can occur in either or both regions. Functionally, we can think of the gray matter as processing centers where neurons interact, and the white matter as tracts that connect areas of gray matter. Some disorders may result from loss of a processing center (gray matter); others from disconnection of processing centers as a result of damage to tracts. Consider a person who cannot move his left hand in response to a verbal command. This deficit could result from damage to the processing centers that deal with language or hand movement, or from the severing of the connection between language processing areas and hand movement areas.

One of the most fascinating and revealing aspects about the organization of the brain is that the effects of damage are almost always circumscribed (restricted). Some functions are severely affected, whereas others are relatively spared, so much so that sometimes they are indistinguishable from normal. For example, a person with severe neglect (see p. 655) caused by parietal damage may still have normal verbal memory and language, whereas a patient with left frontal lesions and Broca's aphasia (see p. 666) will not have spatial attention deficits. This combination of spared and preserved memory function following damage to a particular structure is the evidence on which the idea of *localization of function* is based: specific functions are localized to different regions of the brain.

A *double dissociation* experiment is a formal application of the idea of preserved and impaired function following brain damage to a particular structure. In this type of experiment, it is shown that damage to structure "X" leads to a deficit on test "X" but not on test "Y," whereas the reverse holds for damage to structure "Y." Having shown that these two structures or areas of the brain have different, but quite specific effects on behavior, subsequent research can concentrate on determining exactly what function each of these areas serves. For example, knowing that damage to a region causes language deficits does not tell you what specific function is involved—is it motor aspects of language or comprehension, and if comprehension, does it relate only to deciphering speech or to the very concepts that speech conveys. In reading about the disorders of the nervous system such as aphasia and frontal-lobe damage, keep in mind that despite having the deficits we describe, each type of patient probably has a wide range of relatively preserved abilities outside the area of his or her impairment. Rehabilitation builds on these preserved abilities.

Based on evidence of double dissociation, the current view is that the brain is organized into large functional systems made up of separate components or modules, each serving a different function. In other words, the organization of the brain is modular in much the same way that an audio system or computer is modular. Removing a module or altering or interfering with its function will affect the entire system. Areas of gray matter correspond to modules, and areas of white matter to the connections (equivalent to the wires in an audio system) between the modules. Modules can be more or less restricted in their domain of operation. Some operate over a wide domain, such as gathering or evaluating information that might be required for planning or problem solving. Other modules operate on only limited sensory information, such as those involved in processing faces. Damage to the face module causes a specific deficit in recognizing faces (prosopagnosia), but not in recognizing other complex visual forms. On the basis of observations of abnormal behavior, neurologists can determine where malfunctions have occurred, and which modules of the brain have been affected.

There are three basic dimensions of spatial organization of the brain, corresponding to the three axes that describe any three-dimensional object: front-back, left-right, and up-down. We will consider the organizing principle of each axis, and the implications for organic pathology.

FOCUS QUESTIONS

1. Describe the evidence for a biochemical basis to Parkinson's disease, schizophrenia, and obsessive-compulsive disorder.
2. What is localization of function and how does it explain the symptoms of left-sided neglect?
3. Describe the differences in function and symptoms after damage to the left and right hemispheres of the brain.
4. How is action affected at the lower and higher levels of the neural hierarchy?

FRONT-BACK ORGANIZATION OF THE BRAIN

In general, both the brain and spinal cord are organized so that motor functions are in the front and sensory functions are in the back. Therefore, the damage involved in most sensory disorders occurs further back in the nervous system than that involved in motor disorders. As we ascend to the cerebral cortex, the motor-sensory distinction is preserved, but the scope is expanded.

Alexander Luria (1973), the eminent Russian neuropsychologist, distinguished between two broad domains of the "higher" function of the human brain: information processing and planning-verification-action. The information-processing system corresponds to the expanded sensory system and is located in the back (posterior) portion of the cerebral cortex. It handles the representation of the inputs from each of the senses and the integration of information from the senses, in the service of building a useful representation of the world. Within the system are the primary projection areas, the parts of the brain that receive inputs from the skin, ears, eyes, nose, and mouth. These areas are located in the parietal, temporal, and occipital lobes (see Figure 17–3A); damage to them causes loss of sensation. Other parts of the parietal and temporal lobes receive input from these projection areas, which they process and integrate into higher-order perceptual units. Damage to these areas leads to such symptoms as poor representation of space, inability to recognize meaningful objects like combs and hammers (a disorder called ***agnosia***) and inability to name objects (a disorder called ***anomia***). Some pa-

FIGURE 17–3

ANATOMY OF THE HUMAN BRAIN

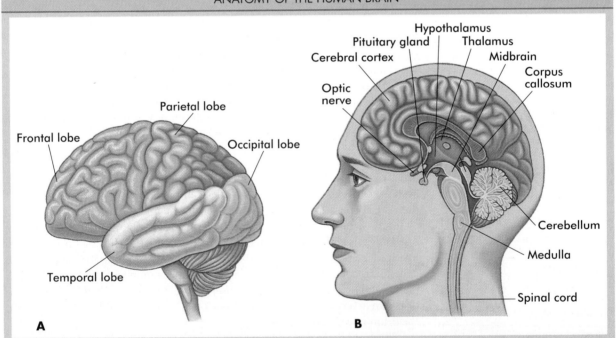

(A) Diagram of the left hemisphere, showing the major lobes of the cerebral cortex. The front of the brain is at the left. (B) Diagram of the human brain cut on the mid-line (dividing the brain into equal left and right halves). (SOURCE: Modified from Kandel, Schwartz, and Jessel, 1991)

FIGURE 17–4

BRAIN DAMAGE LEADING TO LEFT-SIDED NEGLECT

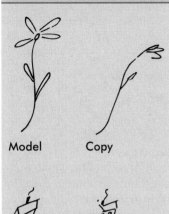

Model   Copy

These are copies of two drawings made by a patient with damage to the right hemisphere of the brain, showing the symptoms of neglect of the left side of space. (SOURCE: Hecaean and Albert, 1978, p. 219)

tients with right parietal damage may exhibit socially inappropriate behavior. They may be poor at expressing or interpreting social cues that are conveyed by tone of voice or facial movement. They may miss the point of stories and jokes. Nuances, which are fundamental to social interactions, may escape them.

A particularly interesting syndrome, **left-sided neglect,** which involves disturbance of higher-order perceptual functions, results from damage to the right parietal area (Mesulam, 1981). Patients with this syndrome neglect the left half of their body and the left side of space in front of them. When dressing, they fail to put the left hand into their shirt sleeve, or the left leg into their pants. When writing, they may only use the right side of the page, and when copying a figure, they may omit the part on the left side (Figure 17–4).

Even when they shut their eyes and imagine a scene, say of a town square or of a particular room in their house, they describe what is to the right of the vantage point they have assumed, and they neglect the left side (Bisiach and Luzzatti, 1978). Posner and his colleagues (Posner, Walker, Friedrich, and Rafal, 1984) have suggested that the deficit in this neglect syndrome arises because patients have difficulty in disengaging their attention automatically from the right side, not because they cannot shift their attention voluntarily to the left. Thus, if told to attend to the left side of a page or an imagined scene, patients with neglect can usually do so. If, however, they are already attending to the right side, and something occurs on the left side, they cannot spontaneously redirect their attention to the left.

The expanded motor system, which corresponds to Luria's planning-verification-action system, is located in the front (anterior) part of the brain, in the frontal lobes. It is primarily involved in acting upon the world. It plans and executes action, and it verifies the outcome of the action. A particular higher-order function mediated by the frontal lobes is the transition from one action to another. After frontal damage, the isolated components are intact, but the smooth sequencing is disturbed. A striking clinical sign of this deficit is **perseveration,** a difficulty in making transitions between one action and the next, or in simply terminating a dominant behavior or response (see Figure 17–5). It is often expressed as excessive repetition. Perseveration appears at many levels of function. Frontal patients have a tendency to grasp objects and then to be unable to let go. Similarly, they may repeat an action over and over, and have great difficulty in alternating two actions. This problem can be graphically illustrated by looking at what these patients do when told to draw a sequence of

FIGURE 17–5

FRONTAL DAMAGE AND PERSEVERATION

Drawings made by two patients with damage to the frontal lobes, in response to the instruction printed above each drawing. Each row represents the sequence of requests made to one patient. The tendency to repeat the previous response is called perseveration. (SOURCE: Luria, 1970, p. 239)

Cross   Circle   Cross   Circle   Cross   Circle

Patient Kryl. Intracerebral tumor of the left frontal lobe.

Circle   Square   Circle   Square   Circle   Circle   Circle

Patient Giash. Intracerebral tumor of the left frontal lobe.

alternating figures. Typically, they continue to draw the original figure, and they cannot shift. This perseverative tendency is also manifested at higher levels, in the planning and execution of strategies. Thus, frontal patients are particularly poor at abandoning a strategy they have learned, even after it ceases to work. In a test of card sorting (the Wisconsin Card Sorting test) that requires formulating hypotheses and then changing them once they are no longer valid, patients with frontal damage manage to formulate an initial hypothesis, but find it difficult to abandon it once it is no longer useful (Milner, 1964). This "fixedness" or "inflexibility" in behavior has a clear neurological origin in damage to the frontal lobes. There is growing evidence that other examples of inflexibility, such as obsessions and compulsions, might share a common pathology, or at least a common site of action (Rapoport, 1989).

Additional effects of frontal-lobe damage are revealed by testing patients on laboratory and clinical tasks that are highly controlled yet that capture features of real-life situations. In a test that requires them to suppress powerful competing responses, such as naming the color in which a word is written rather than the word itself, frontal patients perform much more poorly than patients with damage to other cortical areas.

Perseveration results from a deficit in the system that selects and monitors action, termed the supervisory-attentional system by Shallice (1988). A deficit in such a system often also leads to heightened distractibility and impulsivity. Thus, patients with frontal damage are highly distracted by irrelevant stimuli when they are searching for a target among other alternatives. In solving mazes, patients with frontal damage do not always plan their moves appropriately and end up in blind alleys. Even once they have learned to solve the maze, they will make impulsive mistakes, including breaking such rules as not touching the boundaries of the maze, or following new paths simply to find out where they lead rather than attempting to solve the puzzle (Milner, 1964; Stuss and Benson, 1986).

A classical case that gives the flavor of frontal damage on an entire personality is that of Phineas Gage (Harlow, 1868; Damasio, Grabowski, Frank, Galaburda, and Damasio, 1994). This case was first mentioned in Chapter 15, but we present the case again here to remind you of the accident and the symptoms that resulted from the damage to Gage's brain.

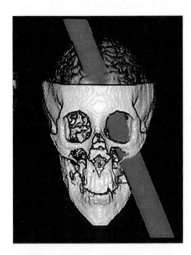

▲ Skull of Phineas Gage showing the hole in the frontal bone made by the iron rod blown through his head; the bar entered below the left eye and passed through the skull. Recently, a reconstruction of the injury to Phineas Gage's brain was made using careful measurements of the surviving skull, reconstruction of the path of the rod through the brain, and computer simulation.

> Phineas Gage was the twenty-five-year-old foreman of a group of men working on railroad track in Vermont in 1848. An explosion caused an iron bar, over an inch in diameter, to pass through the front of his skull, damaging a large part of the frontal area of his brain. Miraculously, Gage survived, with no more than a few moments of loss of consciousness. After recovery, he reapplied for his job as foreman. His contractors, who had regarded him as the most efficient and capable foreman in their employ previous to his injury, considered the change in his mind so marked that they could not give him his place again. The equilibrium or balance, so to speak, between his intellectual faculties and animal propensities, seemed to have been destroyed. He was fitful, irreverent, indulging at times in the grossest profanity (which was not previously his custom), manifesting but little deference for his fellows, impatient of restraint or advice when it conflicted with his desires, at times perniciously obstinate, yet capricious and vacillating, devising many plans of future operations, which are no sooner arranged than they are abandoned in turn for others. . . . his mind was radically changed, so decidedly that his friends and acquaintances said he was "no longer Gage." (Harlow, 1868, pp. 339–40)

Like other frontal patients, Phineas was impulsive, easily distracted, and unable to follow through on plans or evaluate their consequences. The emotional and personality changes that he underwent may have had similar causes. He could no more control, modulate, inhibit, or evaluate his emotional response than he could his actions. We will discuss other cases like this in the section on disorders associated with frontal-lobe dysfunction (see pp. 680–84).

LEFT-RIGHT ORGANIZATION OF THE BRAIN

Among all vertebrates, the left half of the brain receives most of the input from the right side of the body, and the left half controls action primarily on the right side. This "contralateral" projection is of powerful diagnostic value. In almost all cases, if weakness, paralysis, or loss of sensation on one side of the body results from damage to the brain, the damage is on the side of the brain opposite to the afflicted body part.

The human brain, more than the brain of any other species, is differentiated on a left-right basis. There is a qualitative difference in the functioning of the two human cerebral hemispheres. The full significance of this difference is best illustrated by the split-brain syndrome. (For the rest of this chapter, assume that all statements refer to right-handers, unless otherwise indicated. Left-handers are less consistent than right-handers in hemispheric organization.)

The split-brain syndrome is a by-product of a surgical procedure (Bogen and Vogel, 1975) in which the corpus callosum (Figures 17–3B and 17–6) and other major connections between the hemispheres are cut to prevent the transmission of epileptic seizures (discussed later in the chapter) from one side of the brain to the other. As a result of the operation, the two hemispheres cannot communicate with each other; the patients appear to have two consciousnesses in one head. The left brain is the only half that can speak, and it has a much more sophisticated understanding of language. The right brain is superior to the left brain in tasks involving spatial abilities and the recognition of complex forms that are difficult to describe in words, such as faces (Gazzaniga, 1970; Levy, 1972, 1980; Sperry, 1974; Benson and Zaidel, 1985; Springer and Deutsch, 1993).

FIGURE 17–6

DIFFERENCES BETWEEN THE LEFT AND RIGHT HEMISPHERES

Schematic diagram of the human brain, as seen from above, to illustrate the corpus callosum and the specialized functions of each hemisphere. (SOURCE: Modified from Levy, 1972, p. 163)

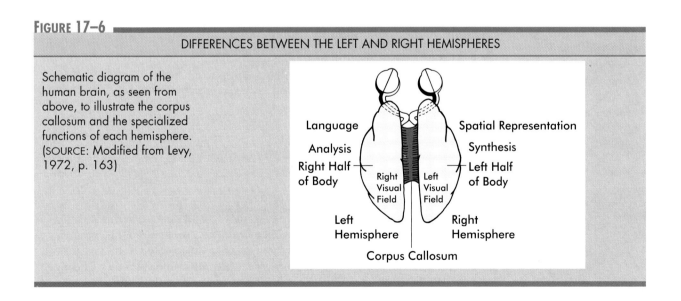

FIGURE 17–7

HEMISPHERIC DIFFERENCES AND SPATIAL REPRESENTATION

Split-brain patients were asked to make copies of various examples—one copy was made by the left hand (right hemisphere); the other by the right hand (left hemisphere). These results illustrate the superior spatial orientation capacity of the right hemisphere. Patients with damage to the right parietal lobe show, with either hand, the type of deficit seen in the right-hand drawings. (SOURCE: Gazzaniga, 1970, p. 47)

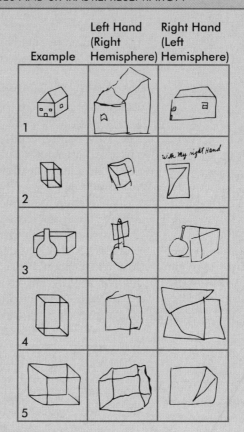

The differences between the hemispheres are well illustrated by the performance of the right hand (left hemisphere) and left hand (right hemisphere) in copying simple figures (Figure 17–7). The drawings of the right hand suggest a general deficit in the organization of the spatial world. The three-dimensional aspect of the figures is lost, whereas it is preserved in the drawings by the left hand. One way to summarize the hemispheric differences is to say that the left hemisphere is better at analyzing inputs and breaking inputs or outputs into sequences over time, while the right hemisphere is better at synthesizing components into wholes and making spatial representations (Levy, 1980; Bradshaw and Nettleton, 1981).

These differences have many clinical implications. Language disorders are much more common with left hemisphere damage (for right-handers), while disorders in getting around in space or recognizing faces and other complex configurations occur much more frequently with right hemisphere damage.

UP-DOWN (HIERARCHICAL) ORGANIZATION OF THE NERVOUS SYSTEM

The brain is organized vertically in a hierarchical structure. This means that particular functions (e.g., control of movement) are carried out at a number of different levels in the nervous system, from spinal cord to cerebral cortex. The higher levels are generally more abstract, cognitive, and voluntary. The higher levels build on or modulate the lower levels. Nineteenth-century British neu-

FIGURE 17-8
THE BABINSKI RESPONSE

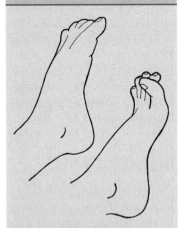

On the upper left is the normal response to scratching on the sole of the foot. On the lower right is the pathological Babinski response to this same stimulation. The Babinski response results from release of inhibition caused by damage to higher levels of the motor system. (SOURCE: Gardner, 1975)

rologist John Hughlings Jackson claimed that the higher levels are more vulnerable than the lower levels, and more often than not are the first systems to malfunction in general diseases of the whole nervous system (Jackson, 1884, in Taylor, 1958). This is illustrated by a common sequence of symptoms seen in some old adults as senility progresses: first there is a a loss of higher cortical functions that produces difficulty in dealing with new situations, problems with chronological ordering of events, and loss of powers or narration with patchy memory. Subsequently, there is a loss of subcortical functions, leading to failures in the performance of bodily functions (Barbizet, 1970).

Higher levels of the nervous system often inhibit lower levels. When the higher levels are damaged, there is a release of inhibition. A particularly clear example of release is the **Babinski response,** a reflex normally shown only by infants. When the bottom of the foot is irritated, the toes fan out (Figure 17–8). This reflex disappears early in life. The circuits that mediate it remain intact, however, inhibited by higher centers. Severe damage to higher motor centers releases this reflex; this is one of the cardinal signs of damage to the higher parts of the motor system.

Because of the neural hierarchy, damage at any number of levels can compromise function. The programming of action is a prime example of hierarchical organization. At the lower levels, the motor system operates with the unit of specific muscles. Damage to motor nerves or spinal motor centers that directly control movement usually leads to weakness or paralysis in particular muscles. At the higher levels, damage to some areas of the cortex, particularly in the frontal or parietal lobes, leads to defects in the planning or sequencing of movements (called **apraxia**), or defects in the linkage of movements with thought and language (Luria, 1973; Geschwind, 1975; Heilman, 1979; Roy, 1982; Kolb and Whishaw, 1990; Schwartz, Reed, Montgomery, Palmer, and Mayer, 1991). Yet, each of the particular movements in the sequence may be executed normally (see, for example, the case history of the fish filleter on p. 647).

DAMAGE TO THE NERVOUS SYSTEM

In this section, we will discuss the causes of damage to the nervous system, the way that damage expresses itself as a symptom, and susceptibility and resistance to damage.

Agents of Damage to the Nervous System

The agents of damage to the nervous system may produce acute or chronic symptoms. They may act locally, or throughout the body and nervous system. They may produce behavioral symptoms suddenly or gradually. We briefly review here the agents of disease.

Widespread disorders often result from deficiencies in nutrients—minerals like calcium, vitamins, amino acids; from lack of oxygen—resulting from reduced blood supply caused by narrowing of the arteries, or atherosclerosis, or from suffocation. Ingested toxins, infections, trauma to the head, and general degeneration of neurons can also produce diffuse damage. Because of differing

FOCUS QUESTIONS

1. What are some agents of damage to the nervous system?
2. What disorder is an example of the positive symptoms of damage to the nervous system and what are two reasons that positive symptoms may occur?
3. Give examples of some functions of the brain that are more vulnerable to damage than others.
4. Why is the nervous system often able to function despite damage?

vulnerabilities, symptoms may appear only, or at first, in specific systems. Many general disorders of this type affect level of consciousness and memory. A clearly localized site of damage may also produce widespread symptoms. For example, a tumor may cause a build-up in pressure of cerebrospinal fluid, thus affecting the whole brain and causing symptoms like headache, drowsiness, nausea, and dizziness.

More localized symptoms are often produced by tumors, or disorders in blood supply produced by either **stroke** (occlusion of blood vessels), or **hemorrhage** (ruptured arteries that leak blood), or localized infections, or specific genetic malformations, or degeneration of cells in a specific area.

The Expression of Damage in the Nervous System

The kinds of symptoms that may appear after nervous system damage can be positive or negative. Common sense suggests that damage should result in negative symptoms—loss or deficiency in the function that the damaged area serves. This is true much, but not all of the time. Sometimes, there are "positive" symptoms, which may occur for two reasons. First, damage can cause irritation and can increase the activity of neurons in the injured area. Second, if damage decreases the activity of an area that inhibits another area, there will be an increase of activity due to release from inhibition (e.g., the Babinski sign). In either case, the symptoms are positive in the sense that there is more activity in the nervous system and more behavior in the organism.

Epilepsy is the best example of a disorder whose primary symptoms are "positive." Epilepsy is a common disorder that affects over one million Americans. Damage to neural tissue produced by any of a number of different agents of disease may leave the tissue irritable and may lead to increased synchronized activity because of damage to inhibitory systems or because the residue of the damage (e.g., scar tissue) excites neighboring neurons. The excessive activity that is produced, known as seizures, leads to an exaggerated expression of the function of the area. Seizures occur intermittently, with sudden discharge of neurons. These may be widespread, leading to muscle contraction throughout the body and loss of consciousness, or they may be much more localized. The part of the brain or type of mental event that appears first in the seizure is an indicator of the location of the primary damage in the brain. Depending on the location of the irritable tissue, the primary symptoms may be sensory (e.g., an hallucination), motor (e.g., twitches or larger muscle contractions), or emotional (e.g., fear or laughing). Sometimes, the initial events of the seizure produce an aura, or mild symptoms such as unusual sensations or feelings related to the site of damage. Some seizures spread progressively from the original site to other parts of the brain. Epilepsy can be treated by controlling the agent of disease that caused it, by drugs that reduce the irritability of neurons, or by surgery that takes out the irritated nervous tissue (Adams, 1989).

Susceptibility to Damage: Vulnerable Systems

Some functions of the brain are more vulnerable to damage than others. A consequence of this is that general stress to the nervous system, by vitamin deficiencies, blows to the head, or toxins, can produce surprisingly specific symptoms.

FIGURE 17-9

BLOOD SUPPLY AND DISTRIBUTION OF CEREBRAL ARTERIES

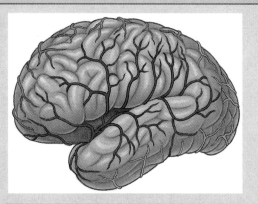

Branches of anterior cerebral artery
Branches of middle cerebral artery
Branches of posterior cerebral artery

Some parts of the brain are more vulnerable than others because of poorer blood supply. Note that three main arteries of the cerebral cortex supply the lateral surface of the brain: the middle cerebral artery (red), the anterior cerebral artery (blue), and the posterior cerebral artery (green). Surface areas located at the end of the arterial "tree" receive relatively less blood. Thus, the surface near the top of the brain, between the principal areas covered by the middle and anterior cerebral arteries gets relatively poor circulation and is subject to damage when circulation is compromised or blood oxygen levels are low. It is damage to this area that produces transcortical sensory aphasia. (SOURCE: Gray's Anatomy, 1984)

A group of neurons may be more vulnerable because it has a relatively poor blood supply. Not all parts of the brain are equal in terms of blood supply (see Figure 17–9). Some neurons, because they are especially large or active, have higher requirements for oxygen or nutrients. Thus, one of the earliest symptoms of vitamin B1 deficiency is deficits in sensation and motor control in the hands and feet (peripheral neuropathy). The vitamin deficiency affects all neurons. But the long axons of the neurons controlling the hands and feet place an extra load on the maintenance of these cells, making them more vulnerable. Other neurons are more vulnerable because they are located in a place where a stroke is more likely to occur.

Resistance to Damage: Redundancy in the Nervous System

Redundancy and the existence of alternative pathways are common in the nervous system. Redundancy occurs throughout vital biological systems. Humans can function well with only one kidney, one eye, or without a majority of their liver cells. To a lesser extent, this is true of the brain, as well.

The loss of some of the neurons that serve a particular function may not produce symptoms of damage. For example, even though there is a steady degeneration (without replacement) of the cells that respond to odors, most people in their seventies are still able to detect and identify odors fairly well and some remain professional wine tasters or perfumers. All systems, however, do not show this type of redundancy.

Where there are alternative pathways that can accomplish the same end, damage to one pathway may be circumvented. Thus, although movement of the right side of the body is primarily handled by neurons originating in the left brain, there is a small pathway leading from the right brain that allows people with split brains, or people with left hemisphere damage, to exert some control over the right side of their body, but not over fine finger movements.

The availability of alternative strategies also has the effect of reducing the symptoms resulting from tissue damage. For example, a person who has damage to the right hemisphere, which effects his ability to recognize faces holistically, might be able to recognize faces by relying more on explicit, verbally described features of the face (wears glasses, has thin lips). Alternative strategies can also be facilitated by cultural inventions. For a person who is unable to walk, crutches or wheelchairs make the arms into organs of locomotion.

Finally, because of redundancy, it is common to see normal function in partially damaged systems when conditions are optimal. But as the environmental challenges become greater, as they do under stress or with fatigue, performance falls apart. Fatigue often brings on latent symptoms of diseases as varied as multiple sclerosis and senile dementia. For similar reasons, demented people often function better intellectually in the morning than later in the day. In general, more redundant systems are less vulnerable.

ASSESSING BRAIN DAMAGE

Now that we have examined the organization of the nervous system as well as potential causes and expressions of damage in the nervous system, we turn to questions of diagnosis, and ask how damage is diagnosed and what techniques are used to make the diagnosis.

The Neurological Diagnosis

Diagnosis is more advanced in neurology than in psychology because of extensive knowledge of the structure and function of the nervous system, and because it is possible to verify diagnoses objectively with sophisticated measurements of the living brain, or at autopsy. The first task of the neurologist is to determine whether the patient is indeed suffering from a disease of the nervous system. This may be extremely difficult, as we noted in the beginning of this chapter. Having some reason to believe that the symptoms are caused by a disease of the nervous system, the neurologist assumes that *one* disease process and/or *one* lesion can account for all of the symptoms. His problem is to determine what agent of disease, acting in what location, could produce the full pattern of symptoms, and *no other* symptoms. Thus, if a patient is paralyzed on the left side of the body, it is necessary to account both for this paralysis and the lack of any paralysis or other symptoms on the right side of the body.

The neurologist has three sources of information: the history of the symptoms as described by the patient and family, the neurological examination,

1. What are three sources of information used by a neurologist to make a neurological diagnosis?
2. How does a CAT scan construct a three-dimensional representation of the brain?
3. What is magnetic resonance imaging?
4. How do PET scans and SPECT scans differ from CAT scans and MRIs?

FIGURE 17–10

MEASURING ELECTRICAL CHANGES IN THE BRAIN

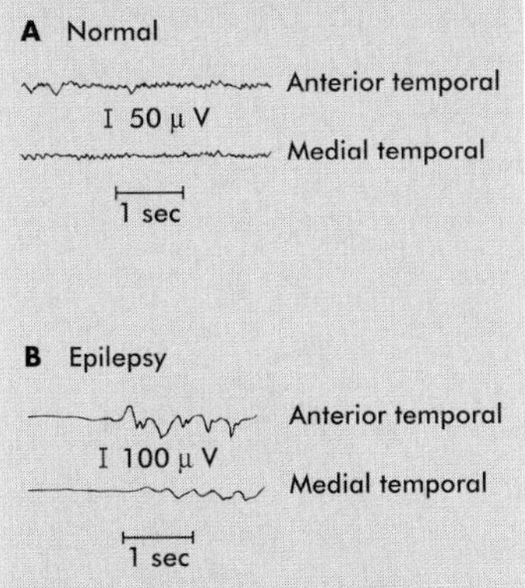

A Normal

$50 \mu V$

Anterior temporal

Medial temporal

1 sec

B Epilepsy

$100 \mu V$

Anterior temporal

Medial temporal

1 sec

Selections from (A) a normal EEG, and (B) an EEG from an epileptic patient. Note that the records from the epileptic patient use a smaller voltage scale. Thus, the difference in amplitude between normal and epileptic EEGs is even greater than it appears to be. (SOURCE: Adams and Victor, 1981, pp. 19–20)

which consists of an interview and observation of the patient, and the use of special diagnostic techniques to gain direct information about events in the nervous system.

The interview and observation (examination) of the patient may be sufficient to make a diagnosis. Information about the onset of symptoms coming from the history related by the patient (or his family) is particularly informative about the cause of the pathology: rapid onset of symptoms suggests a trauma (such as a blow to the head), a stroke, hemorrhage, or seizure activity, while gradual onset suggests a degenerative process. The quality and location of the symptoms suggest both the neural system that is damaged and the level of the nervous system that is damaged, in accordance with our discussion of the front-back, left-right, and top-bottom (hierarchical) organization of the nervous system. Consider a patient presenting with inability to voluntarily move his left arm and hand, with minimal other symptoms. If we can elicit reflexes in the left arm and hand, then we know the damage must be above the level of the spinal cord. The symptoms then suggest right hemisphere damage (by the left-right reversed projection of motor and sensory control) and damage toward the front of the brain, since the disorder is motor rather than sensory. Under some circumstances, precise conclusions may be drawn about location from this type of information.

Samples of cerebrospinal fluid, taken from the base of the spine, can reveal evidence for internal bleeding, infection, and other sources of disease. Abnormal pressure of the fluid is suggestive of tumors or other obstructions. A whole family of techniques, including a dazzling array of computer hardware, allows visualization of what is going on in the living brain, from the outside. These techniques depend on the fact that abnormal brain tissue, e.g., a tumor, damaged or dead neurons or scar tissue, is different from normal tissue. Electrical differences are detected by the ***electroencephalogram (EEG),*** which records electrical events occurring in the brain by using wires taped to the surface of the head and scalp. This technique can often record the electrical changes that occur in particular parts of the brain during epileptic seizures, as well as other electrical changes in abnormal tissue (Figure 17–10).

Neuroimaging

The greatest advance in neurological diagnosis in recent years has been in the development of new brain-imaging techniques. These allow visualization of the human brain from the outside. ***Computerized-axial tomography (CAT*** or ***CT)*** scans are an extension of the much older X-ray technique, supplemented by modern computing power. The X-ray itself is based on the principle that abnormal tissue absorbs X-rays to a different degree than bone or normal brain tissue. From a series of X-rays of the brain taken at different angles, the computer constructs a three-dimensional representation of the brain, and abnormal tissue can be located.

Magnetic resonance imaging (MRI) is another technique that is more sensitive than the CAT scan. In MRI, a magnetic field is imposed on the brain to determine the distribution of any particular chemical element (e.g., hydrogen), by detecting its resonant frequency. The results are reconstructed by a computer as an image representing the concentration of that element in different parts of the brain. In contrast to the CAT scan, which reveals the density of tissue, the MRI shows the composition of cells and their surroundings. Damaged areas of the brain have a different concentration of an element than normal areas, and they appear differently in the MRI (see Figure 17–11). The MRI is painless and harmless as far as we know.

Both the CAT scan and the MRI provide images of static brain structures. Other techniques are sensitive to the metabolic activity of the brain. The ***positron emission tomography (PET scans)*** and ***single photon emission computerized tomography (SPECT scans)*** are based on measurements of cerebral blood flow. In the PET scan procedure, a radioactive substance—usually glucose, oxygen, or water—is injected into a person, and its rate of delivery and uptake to various brain regions is measured. The technique measures the increase in blood flow to more active brain areas. Based on the same principles as MRI, an even newer technique, called ***functional MRI (fMRI),*** measures the oxygen level in the blood, which increases with local brain activity.

FIGURE 17–11

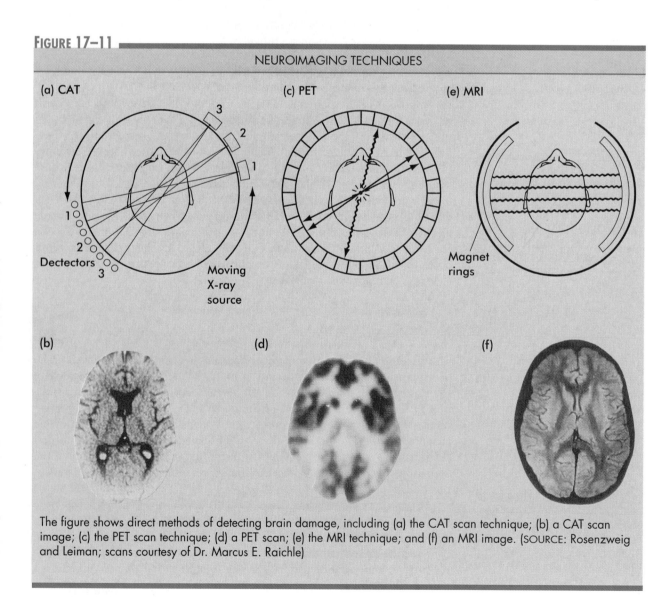

The figure shows direct methods of detecting brain damage, including (a) the CAT scan technique; (b) a CAT scan image; (c) the PET scan technique; (d) a PET scan; (e) the MRI technique; and (f) an MRI image. (SOURCE: Rosenzweig and Leiman; scans courtesy of Dr. Marcus E. Raichle)

FIGURE 17-12

IMAGE SUBSTRACTION AND AVERAGING

In functional brain imaging, researchers must determine relative changes in activation that accompany particular tasks. They can do this, for example, by taking a PET scan of a patient at rest (in a control state) and then a PET scan of a patient doing a task (task state) and determining the difference in the images (top row). The technique is then further refined to eliminate chance fluctuations by averaging the images from different subjects (middle row) and coming up with a mean difference image (bottom row). (SOURCE: Posner and Raichle, 1994)

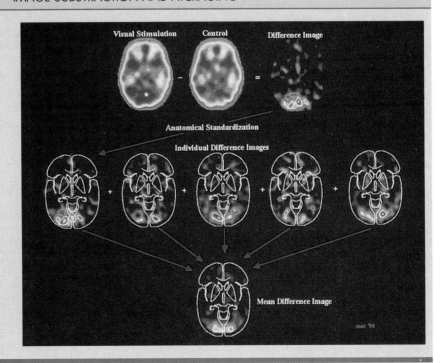

Most regions of the brain are active most of the time. In order to visualize relative changes in activation that accompany particular tasks, a "subtraction" technique is used, as described in Figure 17–12. This technique is further refined by a process that averages the results from the brain scans of a number of persons.

Up to this time, the greatest advantages in functional neuroimaging have been in the understanding of the moment-to-moment operation of the normal brain. However, most of the potential for diagnosis has yet to be tapped.

SOME SELECTED DISORDERS OF THE NERVOUS SYSTEM

In the following section, we consider a few disorders of the nervous system in some detail. We selected these disorders because they are common and well-studied. We begin with the disorders of language.

Disorders of Language: The Aphasias

Language is a uniquely human activity, and of vital importance to thought, communication, and social life. Hence, disturbances in language are particularly upsetting. Most major disorders of language have a well-defined neurological basis, and are called aphasias. We begin our discussion of the aphasias by presenting the classical view, widely held until the last decade or two.

THE CLASSICAL VIEW OF APHASIA

Aphasias illustrate particularly well the principles of spatial and left-right organization (see Geschwind, 1972; Saffran, 1982; Caplan, 1992; Kolb and Whishaw, 1990, for general discussion of aphasia). We have already pointed out that most language functions are localized in the left hemisphere of right-handers; hence, aphasias in 95 to 98 percent of right-handers are almost always the result of damage to the left hemisphere. Speech is controlled primarily by neurons located in the part of the frontal lobe designated Broca's area, in honor of the nineteenth-century neurologist, Paul Broca, who first described this syndrome (see Figure 17–13). Damage in this area leads to difficulties in expression, as indicated in the following case history:

> This fifty-five-year-old, right-handed housewife while working in her garden at 10:00 A.M. on the day of the admission suddenly developed a weakness on her right side and was unable to speak. Apparently, the right-sided weakness mainly affected her face and arm since she was still able to walk. Neurological examination revealed the following: The patient was alert. She had no spontaneous speech and could not use speech to answer questions and could not even use yes or no answers. She could not repeat words. The patient was, however, able to indicate answers to questions by nodding or shaking her head if questions were posed in a multiple-choice situation. In this manner, it was possible to determine that she was grossly oriented for time, place, and person. The patient was able to carry out spoken commands and simple written commands. There was greater loss of strength in the right arm, which suggested that the damage was in the left hemisphere. The fact that all of the symptoms were in action, as opposed to sensation, suggested a forward location of the lesion, as did the fact that the language problem was in expression, rather than in comprehension of speech. The patient showed recovery over the following days. A significant amount of strength returned to the right hand within twenty-four hours, and by forty-eight hours, she could speak single words, but there was still no spontaneous speech. Some weeks later, she still had an expressive problem: her speech was slow and labored. (Curtis, Jacobson, and Marcus, 1972, pp. 526–28)

FIGURE 17–13

BROCA'S APHASIA

CAT scan and diagram of a patient with Broca's aphasia. Note the darker area in the upper left (left frontal area) indicating brain damage. In describing a picture of a boy flying a kite, this patient says, "Waving and uh . . . the . . . oh dear . . . and the kite and boy and . . . and eeth . . . uh barking and a . . . a lil boy and a bigs. . . ." (SOURCE: Kertesz, 1982, p. 35)

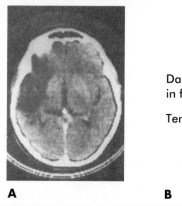

A

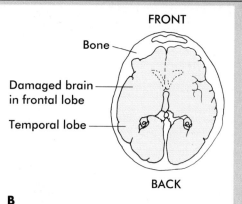

B

FRONT

Bone

Damaged brain in frontal lobe

Temporal lobe

BACK

FIGURE 17–14

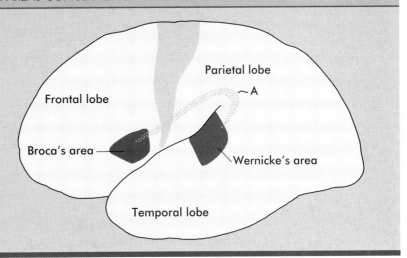

BRAIN AREAS CONCERNED WITH LANGUAGE

Schematic side view of the left hemisphere of the human brain, showing parts of the brain concerned with language. The tract connecting Wernicke's area to Broca's area is labeled *A*. When this tract is destroyed (as at *A*), the result is conduction aphasia. (SOURCE: Modified from Geschwind, 1975, p. 189)

In such a patient, perception and comprehension of language are often more or less intact, but speech is halting, labored, and ungrammatical. Many of the common small words are omitted. This pattern of symptoms is described as an **expressive aphasia.**

The perception of speech is accomplished primarily in a part of the left temporal lobe called Wernicke's area (see Figure 17–14). Damage to this area results in a **receptive aphasia,** often without any loss in ability to hear nonspeech sounds. The patient has difficulties in perceiving and/or comprehending speech, and so has difficulty following instructions. Speech is also disordered in a manner that is consistent with a comprehension deficit. The speech disorder, in contrast to the disorder of patients with damage to Broca's area, is characterized by fluent and grammatical speech that consists of many empty words, circumlocutions, paraphasias (word or sound substitutions), and neologisms (new, made-up words). The damage is usually caused by a stroke, that is, a critical reduction in the blood supply to Wernicke's area. Note that in accord with the motor-front, sensory-back principle, the speech production area is in front of the speech reception area. Furthermore, Broca's aphasia is frequently accompanied by weakness or paralysis on the left side. This is rarely the case with Wernicke's aphasia. Consider the following case of Wernicke's aphasia:

> A patient suddenly developed severe comprehension problems. She was unable to comprehend the simplest words or sentences. When addressed, she responded with grammatically correct but meaningless sentences spoken in a pleasant manner with the intonation and inflection of someone recounting a story to friends over coffee. She was unaware that what she was saying was often gibberish, nor was she sensitive to the responses of the person to whom she addressed her remarks. For example, when asked to describe a picture, she replied, "Yeh, about . . . mmmm . . . that is all. It's a bramblejite. I was at work at soler baks and baks. I did a lot of litins in England. . . . Well, kurly re retin han just the han junikin saddle. We'd nothin to sigh in England, tenah we'd come off the durlin a lot."

Her speech was no different during unstructured interviews. When one of us interviewed her, it was noted that her responses and reactions were unchanged when she was addressed in a foreign language that she did not understand or even when spoken to in a made-up gibberish. In fact, two such patients will happily exchange utterances with each other as if they are having a perfectly normal chat. (Case history courtesy of the Communication Department, Baycrest Hospital, Toronto, Ontario)

Both Broca's and Wernicke's areas are connected to other parts of the brain that allow for the extraction of the meaning of language. There is also, however, a direct connection from Broca's area to Wernicke's area (Point A in Figure 17–14). Damage to this nerve tract, a classic example of a ***disconnection syndrome,*** often leaves speech production, speech perception, and the comprehension of language more or less intact. But in the absence of the direct connection from speech perception to speech production, these patients sometimes are unable to repeat verbatim sentences that they hear, a condition called ***conduction aphasia*** (Geschwind, 1965). They are still able, however, to extract the meaning of the sentence, and thus they can follow verbal instructions. (See McCarthy and Warrington, 1990, for a reinterpretation of conduction aphasias as a deficit in verbal short-term memory.)

There is another striking but rare aphasia that is just the opposite of conduction aphasia. In this disorder, called ***transcortical aphasia,*** Broca's area, Wernicke's area, and the connection between them are intact, but the speech perception and production unit that they make up is cut off from the rest of the brain, due to extensive brain damage. This damage occurs because the "ring" of brain tissue surrounding Broca's area, Wernicke's area, and their connection is relatively far from the main artery that supplies blood to it (see Figure 17–14). This "ring" is therefore more vulnerable to the effects of low levels of oxygen or other nutrients which result from exposure to some toxins, lung disease, and other causes. These patients are much more compromised in language function than are the conduction aphasics because they cannot really use or comprehend language, although they can do the one thing conduction aphasics fail to do: repeat sentences verbatim (Geschwind, Quadfasel, and Segarra, 1968).

NEUROPSYCHOLOGICAL ANALYSIS OF BROCA'S APHASIA

In the last decade or two, there has been an explosion of interest in the analysis of the nature of the cognitive deficit resulting from different types of brain damage. The rapidly developing disciplines of cognitive science and neuroscience converge on this problem. Often, in the wake of these advances, old and clear distinctions become muddied, and the full complexity of phenomena is uncovered. This has happened in the study of the neurological aspects of language. We review here some of these advances, with respect to the classical syndrome of Broca's aphasia. This exercise will give us a sense of how neurologists and neuropsychologists attempt to understand a syndrome in terms of fundamental cognitive processes. A crucial aspect of this approach is the importance of showing what functions are preserved as well as what functions are impaired in any syndrome.

First we ask whether Broca's aphasia is truly a linguistic disorder. Might the linguistic symptoms be explained by a nonlinguistic deficit? Broca's area lies close to the motor area of the tongue and other speech musculature. Per-

FOCUS QUESTIONS

1. What are the symptoms and cause of expressive aphasia?
2. What are the symptoms and cause of receptive aphasia?
3. Which abilities are preserved and which are destroyed in patients with conduction aphasia?
4. What findings indicate that the expressive deficit in Broca's aphasia affects all domains?

haps the deficit is motoric rather than linguistic. Patients with Broca's aphasia, however, can move their lips and tongue with sufficient agility to speak. They sometimes can even sing the very words that they cannot otherwise say.

Can the disorder result from a generalized intellectual impairment? This is a little more difficult to discount, because language enters into so much of our thinking and reasoning, even when the problem does not appear to be verbal. Nonetheless, it has been shown that the performance of many Broca's aphasics (including the case illustrated in Figure 17–13) on tests of nonverbal intelligence and visuo-spatial problem solving is normal (Kertesz, 1982).

So far the evidence indicates that what is damaged is a module whose function is necessary for expressive language. We next ask whether Broca's aphasia is limited to speech, or whether it extends to other expressive domains. Writing may be as severely compromised as speaking (Kertesz, 1982). Deaf-mutes who use American sign language and suffer damage to the anterior region that includes Broca's area become aphasic in their use of signs in a manner that resembles the speech of Broca's aphasics (Poizner, Klima, and Bellugi, 1987). In light of these findings, we may conclude that the expressive deficit in Broca's aphasia affects all domains.

For over a hundred years after Broca's discovery, it was generally believed that Broca's aphasia was primarily expressive. Recent studies, however, have shown that just as Broca's aphasics have difficulty in producing grammatically correct speech they also have difficulty comprehending sentences in which grammar is essential for understanding. For example, to understand the sentence: "the woman drove the man home," syntactic (grammatical) knowledge is needed in order to determine who did the driving. The same type of syntactic knowledge is needed to understand that "the man was driven home by the woman" has the same meaning. In contrast, a sentence like "The woman drove the truck home" can be understood without extensive syntactic knowledge. For example, if the sentence is scrambled into: "the truck woman home drove," one can still extract its basic meaning (Schwartz, Saffran, and Marin, 1980; Saffran, 1982).

Matters are yet more complex. It has recently been shown that Broca's aphasics can judge whether sentences are grammatical or not, even though they cannot accurately comprehend them. Thus, they confuse "put the ball on the box" with "put the box on the ball," but they know that both are grammatical sentences, as opposed to "put the ball the box" (Lineberger, Schwartz, and Saffran, 1983). Hence, it appears that comprehension and production of syntactic utterances are defective in Broca's aphasia, but that judgments of grammaticality are preserved.

We have argued that a syntactic disorder is part of Broca's aphasia and that Broca's aphasia is, at its core, linguistic. The linguistic deficit involves phonological as well as syntactic systems, with perhaps a greater emphasis on expressive than on receptive processes. Within the larger picture we have drawn of brain function, it is appropriate that Broca's area is part of the frontal lobes, which are generally involved in sequencing and planning. Both functions are central to syntactic processing.

Dyslexia

Learning disabilities are a common disorder of childhood. One subtype, ***developmental dyslexia,*** consists of a difficulty in learning to read that is out of

FOCUS QUESTIONS

1. Distinguish between developmental dyslexia and acquired dyslexia.
2. Describe the three routes from print to meaning and relate those to phonological dyslexia and surface dyslexia.

proportion to the child's intellectual and emotional development. The incidence of dyslexia varies greatly as a function of both the precise definition employed and the country or locality in question. Estimates vary from about 1 percent to over 10 percent. About 75 percent of dyslexics are male (Rutter, 1978). Because literacy is so important in our society, a great deal of attention has been paid to this problem.

Acquired dyslexia is a disorder in reading that occurs in adults who once knew how to read well. As a result of a stroke or some other injury, they lose this ability. Acquired dyslexia is much rarer than developmental dyslexia, but because it is usually associated with clear damage to the nervous system, it has been a major source of information about the neural control of reading.

The natural route for language is from mouth to ear. Reading is a cultural invention that allows for representation of language in the visual modality. In alphabetic writing systems, a set of visual units or graphemes (called letters in English) corresponds to the individual sounds (phonemes) that underlie the stream of speech (Gleitman and Rozin, 1977; Rozin and Gleitman, 1977; Coltheart, 1985; Crowder and Wagner, 1992).

Many beginning readers sound out a written word that they have never seen before, recognize this sound as a familiar word, and then have access to all of its meanings. As readers become more fluent, the sounding-out process seems to recede. Some very common words may be recognized directly by their overall shapes. More importantly, readers seem able to convert written letter sequences directly into meanings, as if they had created an internal dictionary (or lexicon). The lexicon has information about both the meaning and pronunciation of all letter sequences that are entered in it. Readers learn about regularities in the sequences of letters: *u* regularly follows *q, w* never follows *v*. Knowledge of these regularities allows for rapid perception of words. Sounding out cannot always produce the correct pronunciation of words, for example, "yacht" or "sword." These types of words have to be read at least in part by sight.

For adult English readers, there seem to be three routes from print to meaning: one via conversion to sound and then to meaning, a second via direct conversion from letter sequence to meaning, and a third from word shape to meaning. Indeed, some children learn to read without going through direct training in sounding out words; they may directly learn the letter sequences that correspond to meanings, though they almost always also learn to sound out words even if they weren't so instructed. There are reading disorders corresponding to damage in two of these pathways.

In **phonological dyslexia,** there is damage to the system involved in reading by sound, typically a result of a specific lesion in the posterior part of the left temporal lobe. Because the visual route is available, such a patient may not make too many mistakes reading aloud. But these patients are unable to pronounce a written word that they have never seen even if it corresponds to a spoken word they know. Lacking the ability to convert even familiar written words to their sound directly, that is, through grapheme-phoneme correspondence, such patients will also be unable to determine whether visually presented non-words rhyme with each other. Asked to choose which two of the following three words rhyme ("rite," "kight," and "rit") they are likely to guess that the first and third rhyme, because they resemble each other visually (Beauvais and Derouesne, 1979; Coltheart, 1985).

Patients with **surface dyslexia** cannot read words by sight; they read the words only by sounding them out. Although they can sound out words they have never seen before, there are many familiar words that they cannot read correctly; these are the words that violate standard rules of pronunciation, such as "have," "yacht," "bread," "sew," and "sword." Such patients usually have a lesion in the left posterior temporal/parietal region (Patterson, Marshall, and Coltheart, 1985).

Among people who read non-alphabetic languages, some of these reading disorders take on characteristically different forms. Japanese has two basic writing systems. One is a syllabary, in which each of about forty-eight symbols represents a different spoken syllable, for example, "ka" or "ta." Words are formed by combining the sounds of each of these syllables. Indeed, one of the two Japanese syllabaries is called Ka-ta-ka-na, expressed as four syllabic symbols. The other writing system, Kanji, is ideographic; each symbol stands for an entire word. Written Japanese text is a mixture of these two systems, both normally within the same sentence. In Japanese, phonological dyslexia is manifested by a severe impairment in reading the syllabic script but preserved ability in reading the ideographic one. The converse is true of Japanese surface dyslexics (Sasanuma and Fujimura, 1971).

A number of investigators have tried to apply the findings from research on acquired dyslexia to children with developmental dyslexia. There is no doubt that at least a subset of dyslexic children show evidence of abnormal neuronal development in the posterior left hemisphere, where lesions have been shown to produce reading disorders in adults (Galaburda, Sherman, Rosen, and Geschwind, 1985). The underlying cause of the developmental disorder does not always correspond clearly to the cause of the acquired dyslexias. Some children behave like phonological dyslexics, in that they have severe deficits in sounding out words. Although at first one might be tempted to teach these children to read using only the sight method, such an approach would be limited in value, since there are just too many English words to learn to recognize. A better therapy might involve an intensive program of teaching the child how to parse words into their phonemic constituents, which would provide them with the foundation on which to apply rules for sounding out words (Rozin and Gleitman, 1977).

FOCUS QUESTIONS

1. Describe some causes of amnesia.
2. Which structures of the nervous system are affected in amnesics?
3. Differentiate between anterograde and retrograde amnesia.
4. Describe the difference between implicit and explicit memory and how there can be impairment in one and not the other.
5. How can amnesia be treated?

A Disorder of Memory: The Amnesic Syndrome

We have considered the varieties of pathology that can cause disorders in language and reading. We now turn to one specific and common disorder, the amnesic syndrome.

We are now at what will be, in but a moment, a memory. It is this memory of our past experiences, the idea that it is "me" who has passed through all of these experiences, the yesterdays and years ago, that gives continuity to the self. Amnesia strikes at this junction between the present and the past (see Rozin, 1976; Moscovitch, 1982a; Squire, 1987; Squire and Butters, 1992, for more detailed reviews of amnesia).

To convey the character of this syndrome, we will describe H.M., who is probably the most studied neurological case in history (Scoville and Milner, 1957; Milner, 1970). His case is an example of as "pure" an amnesic syndrome as has ever been described.

H.M. was a blue-collar worker suffering from severe epileptic seizures. They became progressively worse, and by age twenty-seven he was unable to work. Neurosurgeons removed parts of both temporal lobes (the source of the seizures) to control the seizures in 1953. H.M. was carefully evaluated prior to the operation, and had a normal memory and an I.Q. of 112. On the return of consciousness following surgery, he could no longer recognize the hospital staff, apart from Dr. Scoville, whom he had known for many years. He could not remember or learn his way around the hospital. He could not remember important events that occurred in the few years before the surgery, such as the death of his uncle, but his early memories appeared clear and vivid. His short-term memory appeared normal, and he could carry on a normal conversation. However, he could not remember any events that occurred after the operation, once they passed out of his direct attention (short-term memory). He did the same puzzles day after day and reread the same newspapers and magazines. Each time he learned of the death of his uncle, he became very moved, treating it as a new occurrence. H.M. is still alive. His epilepsy is under control, but he still shows the same amnesic syndrome. He is dimly aware of his father's death, which occurred some years ago. He has aged normally in appearance, but is surprised whenever he sees himself in a mirror, since he remembers himself as he was at twenty-seven. (In 1994, he is now about sixty-six.) Remarkably, H.M.'s "intelligence" remained intact; over many years his IQ did not decrease. He has some realization that he has a memory deficit. He says: "Every day is alone in itself, whatever enjoyment I've had, and whatever sorrow I've had. . . . Right now, I'm wondering, have I done or said anything amiss? You see, at this moment everything looks clear to me, but what happened just before? That's what worries me. It's like waking from a dream. I just don't remember." As you might expect, H.M. is able to remember something if he can keep it "in mind." He can retain a number, say 584, by constantly repeating it to himself, or repeatedly adding up the three digits. However, after being interrupted with another task for less than a minute, he is unable to recall either the number or the fact that he had been rehearsing it for some minutes. (Adapted from Milner, 1970)

CAUSES OF AMNESIA: A VULNERABLE SYSTEM

The memory "systems" that are damaged in the amnesic syndrome are *the* prime example of vulnerable systems. The range of pathological agents that can produce the syndrome is astounding. In addition to the usual causes of specific neurological syndromes such as strokes and tumors, a variety of generally harmful agents can cause amnesia. For example, infections can produce amnesia: when the herpes simplex virus attacks the nervous system, it seems to have a predilection for a few structures, including the hippocampus, an area critical for memory. Toxins and nutritional deficiencies can also cause amnesia. Chronic alcoholics get a good portion of their calories from alcohol, an essentially vitamin-free food source. They sometimes develop a deficiency in vitamin B1 (thiamine), a critical component of metabolic processes in all cells of the body. It is believed that, for some reason, a few groups of cells in the memory system are particularly vulnerable to this deficiency. They are the first to be destroyed, leading to the amnesia of Korsakoff's syndrome. Here is a case of Korsakoff's syndrome:

The patient, aged sixty, was admitted to the hospital with a history of excessive alcohol consumption for many years. His memory had been deteriorating, and on admission he was amnesic and disoriented. Even though it was 1963, he said the

A concussion or other severe blows to the skull, as often happens in automobile accidents, and occasionally in sports and other activities, not infrequently produces an amnesic syndrome that is usually transient but can last for years. Amnesia rarely occurs unless there was loss of consciousness. A similar, though usually shorter lasting syndrome is observed in the clinic in patients given electroconvulsive therapy for depression, a treatment that consists of passing an electric current across their skull, which throws their brain into a temporary seizure (Squire, Slater, and Miller, 1981; see Chapter 11). Finally, memory failures are among the most common features of aging.

THE ANATOMY OF THE AMNESIC SYNDROME

Although we don't understand the process of memory formation, there are clear relations between a set of interconnected brain structures that make up the limbic system and amnesic syndromes (Victor, Adams, and Collins, 1971; Mishkin and Appenzeller, 1987). In most cases of Korsakoff's syndrome, there is bilateral (both sides) damage to the mammillary bodies and/or the dorsomedial nucleus of the thalamus (see Figure 17–15). In cases resulting from surgery, viral attacks, and other sources, there is bilateral damage to the hip-

FIGURE 17–15

THE LIMBIC SYSTEM AND MEMORY

The structures of the limbic system are involved in memory. Damage to the mammillary bodies, the dorsomedial nucleus of the thalamus, and to cells in the hippocampus can lead to amnesic syndromes. (SOURCE: Adapted from Bloom, Lazerson, and Hofstadter, 1985)

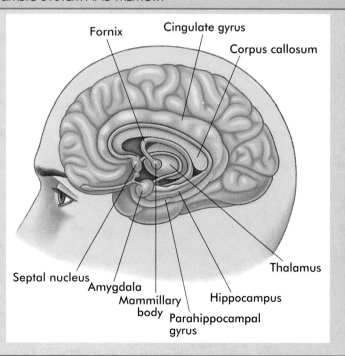

FIGURE 17-16

IMPLICIT LEARNING IN AMNESICS

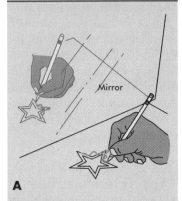

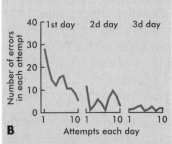

Amnesics who are not able to recall and recognize events since the onset of their amnesia are able to learn motor skills. (A) In a mirror-drawing task, the subject must trace a line between the double outline of a star while viewing the star and his hand in a mirror. The task is difficult for both normal and amnesic subjects. (B) An amnesic subject's learning curve indicates that the subject improves with practice. Although the amnesic does not consciously remember performing the task before, he retains the skill on subsequent days and improves, showing implicit (rather than explicit) learning. (SOURCE: Kolb and Whishaw, 1990, p. 542)

pocampus, in the temporal lobe. Damage to a layer of cells in the hippocampus is sufficient to produce a full-blown amnesic syndrome (Zola-Morgan, Squire, and Amaral, 1986; Squire, 1992), but in cases of damage to the temporal lobes where there is no bilateral damage to the hippocampus, memory loss is minimal (Milner, 1972).

Bilateral damage must occur to produce the full syndrome. It is usually caused by general insults to the brain, such as traumatic accidents, poisoning, vitamin deficiencies, infections, or degenerative processes. In contrast, tumors, strokes, and externally induced wounds almost always occur in one continuous spatial location, and hence they are likely to affect only one side.

Careful analysis of patients with unilateral damage to the critical memory structures reveals a more limited memory deficit, of just the type one would predict given the specialized functions of the two hemispheres. Left temporal damage (in right-handers, of course) leads to a memory impairment primarily for verbal materials, and right temporal damage leads to deficits in memory for visual and other forms of "nonverbal" memory (Milner, 1972).

THE MEMORY DEFICIT OF THE AMNESIC SYNDROME

The nature of the memory defect in the amnesic syndrome has been explored in great detail (reviewed in Milner, 1972; Rozin, 1976; Moscovitch, 1982a; Squire, 1987). It has been found that there is more or less normal short-term memory (that is, memory for that which is currently at the forefront of one's consciousness), as measured by **digit span,** the number of digits a person can remember immediately after he hears them. But there are severe deficits in recall and recognition of events experienced since onset of the disease (**antero-grade amnesia**); this is the core of the amnesic syndrome. Or there may be loss of recall and recognition for events that occurred for a period of time *prior* to the onset of the syndrome (**retrograde amnesia**). The retrograde amnesia typically runs back in time from the onset of the illness or accident, and covers recent events (days, months, years) but not usually early events of life. In most accident cases, the retrograde amnesia is eventually reduced to a period of seconds or minutes preceding the injury (Russell, 1959). One professional quarterback, following a head injury on the field, returned to the huddle and called plays that came from his previous team; he showed temporary retrograde amnesia for the period in which he had learned his new team's plays.

The amnesic syndrome is characterized by a lack of a sense of familiarity ("I've seen it before") when re-presented with recently experienced events. Nonetheless, some specific types of learning and memory are preserved in amnesics (Moscovitch, Vriezen, and Goshen-Gottstein, 1994). Thus, amnesics can be taught new perceptuo-motor skills, such as making drawings while looking in a mirror (Milner, 1972; see Figure 17–16). Generally, the preserved skills are described as **implicit learning.**

Severely amnesic patients have no recall or recognition of events that occurred even a few minutes ago, but they have some type of record of them. That record can be revived if the patient is cued in particular ways and encouraged to respond without reflecting on the past. The procedure that elicits this performance is called **priming.** For example, when asked to remember a series of words, like "metal" or "carpet," after a brief delay, amnesics failed miserably. When prompted with partial cues (e.g., "met" or "car"), however, and encouraged to say the first word that came to mind, they guessed the words quite accurately, though claiming no sense of familiarity with the words they had uttered (Warrington and Weiskrantz, 1973; Diamond and Rozin, 1984; Schacter, 1992; Moscovitch, Vriezen, and Goshen-Gottstein, 1994).

A number of theories have been proposed to explain why amnesics can't remember. Consolidation block theory holds that the basic deficit is in the formation and storage of long-term memories (memory for that which is no longer in the forefront of consciousness) (Milner, 1966; Squire, Cohen, and Nadel, 1984). This view, however, has trouble explaining retrograde amnesia, priming, and skill acquisition. If no new memories are formed, how can performance be normal on priming and skill acquisition? If memories were consolidated long before the illness, why can't they be recalled?

Retrieval failure theory holds that new memories are formed (there is no consolidation block), but that there is a deficit in the retrieval process (Warrington and Weiskrantz, 1973). Such a deficit might explain why performance on priming tests and skill acquisition (both of which provide the patient with extensive cues to retrieve memories that are available but temporarily inaccessible) is normal. But retrieval theory cannot account for the patient's lost sense of familiarity, even when memory performance is normal.

Thus, neither theory alone accounts for all of the aspects of the amnesic syndrome. This has led investigators to propose that long-term memory is comprised of different components or subsystems that mediate performance on different types of memory tests. In amnesia, only some of these components are damaged, leading to severe memory impairment on some tests but preserved memory on others. The emerging consensus is that it is important to distinguish between at least two broad classes of memory and memory tests: ***explicit*** and ***implicit*** (Graf and Schacter, 1985; Schacter, 1987; Roediger and McDermott, 1993; Moscovitch, Vriezen, and Goshen-Gottstein, 1994). Explicit tests of memory, such as recall and recognition, are those that require conscious recollection of past experiences. On implicit tests of memory, the subject is never asked to reflect on the past, but merely to perform. Memory for the past is inferred from changes in performance with experience or practice. Tests of priming and skill acquisition are implicit tests of memory. In amnesia, it is primarily performance on explicit tests of long-term memory—namely, recognition, recall, and the sense of familiarity—that is impaired.

The attribution of pastness or familiarity to an event depends on the individual's ability to re-create, at retrieval, critical aspects of the event that were encoded and consolidated when the event was first experienced (spatio-temporal markers). The event thus becomes a part of the experiences that constitute one's past. Amnesia may result from the failure to record or retrieve these spatio-temporal markers (Rozin, 1976). These markers may be especially vulnerable because they are, by their nature, unique, one-time occurrences. The hippocampus and related limbic structures may be necessary for encoding the unique spatio-temporal aspects of events as they occur so that they can be retrieved at a later time, and thus they may be necessary for making newly acquired information available to conscious awareness. Without these spatio-temporal markers, conscious recollection would not be possible.

Theories of consolidation deficits and theories of retrieval failure apply only to performance on explicit tests of memory. Conscious recollection is not a necessary component on *implicit* tests such as priming or skill learning. In implicit tests, performance is driven by a retrieval cue that reactivates, without our awareness, only that portion of a stored event that fits with the cue, and not the spatio-temporal context that locates the event in one's experience. As a result, the individual may emit the target word in response to a highly specific cue, or perform a task faster or more efficiently with practice, but he will have no sense of familiarity or personal reference to past history in doing so (Moscovitch, 1989, 1994).

TREATMENT OF AMNESIA

Patients with amnesias produced by head trauma typically recover completely, and the main function of medical treatment is to maintain the health of the patient in the acute phase of the illness. Occasional cases caused by tumors or infections may be treated surgically or with drugs, with possible alleviation of some symptoms. At this time, there is no treatment that will arrest or slow down the degeneration of neurons that causes the amnesias associated with senile dementia (see discussion of Alzheimer's disease, below). Although neural structures cannot be repaired, treatment programs can be designed that use the structures that remain intact. This is one of the forms of redundancy that we referred to earlier. Although this mode of treatment has been used for other disorders, few have used it to deal with memory disorders. At the Unit for Memory Disorders at the University of Toronto, a treatment was devised that capitalizes on the fact that amnesic patients perform well on implicit tests of memory (Glisky, Schacter, and Tulving, 1986). The technique used was the method of vanishing cues; it converts an explicit, conscious learning task into an implicit task. A response is elicited to a cue, and gradually more and more of the cue is removed, until only minimal cues are necessary for eliciting the appropriate response. By carefully linking a series of such cues, an entire behavioral repertoire can be taught. To test this technique, severely amnesic patients with no computer experience were taught to write simple programs on the computer. One patient, having demonstrated her ability on the laboratory task, was taught to enter data into a computer, a skill that is valued and for which she is now well paid. As with laboratory tests, performance on these real-life implicit tests is situation-specific. That is, learning does not transfer easily, if at all, to other situations. Moreover, after the patients had mastered their skill, they had little or no awareness of having acquired it and were unable to provide any but the most rudimentary description of what they had learned.

Memory disorders can also be treated as problems in living. Family members can accommodate to and compensate for some of the problems. Adjustments in living and working conditions can be made. Sometimes, memory tricks such as simply writing notes on a pad can help. We must remember that there is a little memory loss in all of us. As we grow older, it becomes more severe in most people. Intelligent people compensate in their lifestyle and in the memory support or crutches they develop for themselves. This is graphically illustrated by a study that compared memory in sixty- to seventy-year-old University of Toronto alumni and current University of Toronto students (Moscovitch, 1982b). Subjects from each age group were told they were in a study of memory, and that the task was simply to remember to call a particular phone number on a particular day and at a particular time (some weeks ahead), simply leaving their name. All agreed to do it. About half of the students failed to call, whereas almost all of the older group remembered to call. It appears that at least part of the result is due to different approaches to remembering. The student subjects, interviewed after the study, said they were confident they would remember the task, and they made no special effort to remind themselves. The older people thought they would forget, wrote the date down in their date books, put notes by the phone, and so on. Old age would be a lot less tolerable if these compensations did not occur.

FUNCTIONAL AMNESIA

There are also functional amnesias, such as hysterical or dissociative amnesias, that occur in cases of multiple personalities or in fugue states in which the patient has lost all memory, including personal identity (Schacter, Wang, Tulving, and Freedman, 1982). In these cases, there is often a history of psychological disturbance, along with an absence in the history or clinical examination of any signs of neurological damage. In both organic and functional amnesias, learned skills tend to remain intact, and personal memories are most affected. The retrograde amnesia in functional amnesias, however, tends to extend back into childhood; people with the neurologically based amnesic syndrome rarely forget their childhood or their name, unless they are at the end of a long period of senile degeneration, in which they lose the ability for intelligent performance on any task.

Dementia

Our concern so far has been to describe and understand the effects of focal (well-localized) lesions on behavior. Many neurological disorders, however, result from damage that is widespread, affecting more than one region of the brain. Some progressive degenerative disorders are of this type. Sometimes the disorder begins in a localized area, as in Parkinson's disease (see p. 651), but its effects gradually spread. We can apply what we have learned from studying the effects of focal lesions to understanding the effects of diffuse damage. By noting the symptoms, we can determine which structures are damaged, and vice versa. If the diffuse damage, however, is of slow onset, compensatory neurological and psychological changes may mask the extent of the damage. Conversely, once the damage is severe and appears in behavior, the symptoms may be exaggerated in comparison to focal lesions of the same area because there is less healthy tissue, in a sense, less redundancy, to compensate for the damage. With these qualifications in mind, we will turn our attention to Alzheimer's disease, the most common of all degenerative disorders.

ALZHEIMER'S DISEASE

Dementia is a progressive loss of a variety of higher mental functions usually occurring in old age. Whether or not Alzheimer's disease should be viewed as accelerated or pathological aging, it is a disease of major proportions. About 5 percent of American adults over sixty-four years of age suffer from this disorder, and about one-third of these people are severely handicapped (Terry and Davies, 1980). The beginning of this decline is sometimes seen in people in their fifties. About half of all old people diagnosed as demented probably have Alzheimer's disease. There is accumulating evidence that Alzheimer's disease is inherited in a small proportion of people. The risk of Alzheimer's disease in first-degree relatives (immediate family) of patients with the disease converges on 50 percent by age ninety compared to a risk of about 25 percent in the population at large in this age range (Mohs, Breitner, Silverman, and Davis, 1987). Here is a case of Alzheimer's disease:

FOCUS QUESTIONS

1. What are the symptoms of Alzheimer's disease?
2. Describe the dysfunctional brain pathology found in Alzheimer's patients.
3. What are some of the hypotheses about the causes of Alzheimer's disease?
4. What are early symptoms of AIDS dementia?

For two or three years, Mary's memory was slipping, but she compensated by writing things down. At first, she found herself groping for a word she had always known, and noticed that she often lost the thread of a conversation. Though she worried that her mind might be slipping away, she didn't want to think about getting old and, most important, she didn't want to be treated as if she were senile. She was still enjoying life and able to manage.

Then Mary got pneumonia and had to be taken to the hospital. In those strange surroundings, she could no longer compensate for her forgetfulness. People told her where she was, but she forgot. She complained that her daughter-in-law never visited her, though she had been there in the morning.

Although the fever and infection passed, the illness had focused attention on the seriousness of her condition. Her family realized she could no longer live alone. She was taken to live with her son's family where she was given a room. Because only some of her things were there, she thought that perhaps the rest were stolen while she was sick even though she had been told many times where her things were. She got lost in the neighborhood and often could not find her way around the house. . . .

Mary continued to deteriorate. Dressing became an insurmountable ordeal. Because of her apraxia, she no longer knew how to button buttons, to unzip zippers. Mary gradually lost the ability to interpret what she saw and heard. Words and objects began to lose their meaning. Sometimes she would react with terror and panic, or with anger. Her things were gone, her life seemed gone. She could not understand the explanations that were offered or, if she understood, she could not remember them. . . . However, Mary's social skills remained so that when she finally relaxed she was personable and engaging. She also loved music and sang old familiar songs. Music seemed to be embedded in a part of her mind that she retained long after much else was lost.

The time finally came when the physical and emotional burden of caring for Mary became too much for her family, and she went to live in a nursing home. After the initial days of confusion and panic passed, the reliability of the routine comforted her and gave her a measure of security.

Mary was glad when her family came to visit. Sometimes she remembered their names; more often she did not. . . . (Source: Adapted from Mace and Robins, 1981)

Alzheimer's disease may have early onset, but generally it begins gradually in old age. Its initial symptoms include loss of initiative, forgetfulness, naming disability, apraxia, and spatial disorientation. Different symptoms predominate in different patients. In many patients, an amnesic syndrome will be the prominent symptom; in other patients, naming or spatial disorders are the primary symptoms (Martin, 1987; Schwartz, Baron, and Moscovitch, 1990). With time, the nervous system in Alzheimer's patients deteriorates further. In many patients, sleep is severely disturbed, wandering occurs, maintaining basic hygiene and cleanliness become problematic. People with Alzheimer's disease may be incontinent of urine and feces; other unmanageable behaviors, such as screaming, aggression, and refusal to eat or drink, may appear. There are problems in walking and balance that lead to falls and injuries. As the disease progresses, more and more severe deficits appear, in more and more systems. Thus, over a period ranging from a few to ten years, it leads to severe deterioration of intellectual and basic maintenance functions. In the final stages, the person may be confined to bed, incontinent and inert. The immediate cause of death is often a complicating condition such as pneumonia, malnutrition, dehydration, or infection.

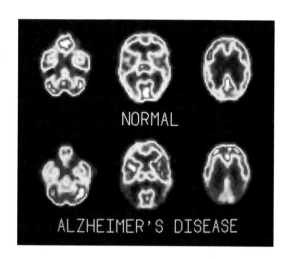

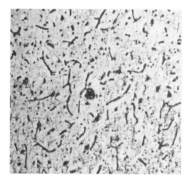

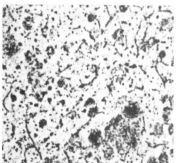

(A) PET scan of a normal brain, and (B) PET scan of an Alzheimer's patient's brain. The darker the color, the lower the metabolism. Note the generally low level of metabolism in the Alzheimer patient's brain. The only areas of normal metabolic rate are the primary motor and sensory areas, including the visual projection area in the occipital lobe at the bottom of the middle Alzheimer's scan.

▲ Photomicrographs of brain tissue from the cortex of (top) a normal patient, and (bottom) a patient with Alzheimer's disease. Note the small number of senile plaques (the darker areas) in the normal patient, and the larger number of plaques in the Alzheimer patient.

A distinctive brain pathology has been identified in Alzheimer's patients: malformations of neurons (senile plaques) and loss of cells in a number of areas of the nervous system. Neural malformations in Alzheimer's patients are particularly common in the hippocampus (Hyman, Van Hoesen, Damasio, and Barnes, 1984). The main component of the senile plaques is the protein beta amyloid, a starch-like substance. The neurons of Alzheimer's patients also contain neurofibrillary tangles, which are distorted remnants of microtubules that transport nutrients and other materials from the body of the cell to the dendrites and axons in the periphery. Together, the plaques and tangles constitute the neuropathological features that confirm a diagnosis of Alzheimer's disease at biopsy or autopsy. One hypothesis suggests that the beta amyloid leads to the formation of the tangles and to cell death (Hardy and Higgins, 1992). It suggests that Alzheimer's disease can be ameliorated by substances that retard or interfere with the accumulation of beta amyloid or prevent it from reacting on neurons.

A biochemical deficit has also been suggested: an abnormally low level of an enzyme that is critical in the synthesis of acetylcholine, a brain neurotransmitter that is known to be important in memory (Coyle, Price, and DeLong, 1983). The number of malformed neurons and the degree of the neurotransmitter deficit are related to the degree of dementia.

The causes of Alzheimer's disease are not known. One hypothesis is that it is caused by an increase in aluminum in the body, which concentrates in parts of the brain and causes the neural malformations that have been observed (Crapper, Karlik, and DeBoni, 1978).

Currently, the most widely held hypothesis is that Alzheimer's disease is caused by one or more chromosomal abnormalities. Familial Alzheimer's disease, which typically has early onset, is inherited. St. George-Hyslop and his colleagues (1987) found a defective gene in patients with familial Alzheimer's disease that was located on the same region of chromosome 21, which carries the defective gene for Down's syndrome. (And in fact, all people with Down's syndrome who live past forty-five years of age develop Alzheimer's disease.) Further investigations have isolated the defect to a mutation of a gene that is involved in forming amyloid; this mutation leads to the formation of beta amyloid, one of the pathogenic substances in Alzheimer's disease. Another rare mutation of the same gene has also been found on chromosome 14, but its defective product has not been isolated (St. George-Hyslop, Haines, Rogaev, et al., 1992).

Although Alzheimer's disease runs in families to some extent, and there is evidence that there is a genetic basis for this, family histories of Alzheimer's disease are not present in the majority of cases. Nonetheless, spurred by the finding of an association between Alzheimer's disease and chromosomal abnormalities, investigators have searched for a possible chromosomal defect in late-onset, nonfamilial forms of the disease. Such late-onset Alzheimer's disease has now been linked with a defect on a gene on chromosome 19 (the allele APOE-4). Eighty-four percent of those with familial and 64 percent of those with nonfamilial, late-onset Alzheimer's disease have at least one APOE-4 allele. As the number of APOE-4 alleles increases from 0 to 2, so does the risk for Alzheimer's disease, and the age of onset decreases from eighty-four to sixty-eight years. Having both APOE-4 alleles was virtually sufficient to cause Alzheimer's disease by age eighty (Corder, Saunders, Strittmatter, et al., 1993; Saunders, Strittmatter, Schmechel, et al., 1993).

AIDS DEMENTIA

It is now recognized that clinically observable neurological disorders occur in about 40 percent of adult AIDS patients, and pathological changes in the nervous system have been noted in 80 to 90 percent of cases that have come to autopsy (Snyder, Simpson, Nielson, et al., 1983). Some of the changes may be caused by tumors or bacterial infections that accompany AIDS. In a significant number of cases, however, there is a syndrome of acquired dementia, called AIDS dementia complex, that cannot be explained as secondary to tumor growth or bacterial infection.

The early symptoms of AIDS dementia complex include word-finding difficulty, verbal memory deficits, psychomotor slowing, impaired problem-solving ability, and poor fine motor control. AIDS was only first recognized as a syndrome in 1981, and the dementia that sometimes accompanies it was not noted until a few years later. It is therefore too early to know exactly which brain regions are affected. But consistent with the behavioral symptomatology, the affected region is initially subcortical; later, there is cortical involvement, particularly in the region of the frontal lobes (Price, Brew, Sidtis, et al., 1988; Gray, Huag, Chimelli, et al., 1991).

More controversial is whether there are any cognitive deficits in individuals who are HIV positive but who show no clinical symptoms of AIDS. Early reports of extensive deficits have been disconfirmed (Horter, 1989; Janssen, Saykin, Cannon, et al., 1989; McArthur, Cohen, Selnes, et al., 1989; Law, Martin, Mapou, et al., 1994). The consensus now is that these individuals are normal except for some psychomotor slowing on reaction-time tests, which may be indicative of subtle central nervous system involvement (Martin, Heyes, Salazar, Law, and Williams, 1993).

Disorders Related to the Frontal Lobes

The frontal lobes comprise about one-third of the cortex in humans. They probably constitute the areas of the human cerebral cortex that are most different in size and structure from comparable areas in nonhuman primates. The frontal lobe is not a homogeneous structure but consists of a number of distinct regions that together receive a variety of inputs from other cortical areas as well as from many subcortical structures (Goldman-Rakic, 1987; Pandya and Barnes, 1987). Given the strong connections so many regions have with the frontal lobes, it should not be surprising to learn that symptoms indicative of frontal-lobe dysfunction are associated with many disorders that do not affect the frontal lobes directly, such as Parkinson's and Huntington's disease, as well as obsessive-compulsive disorder and attention-deficit hyperactivity disorder.

Based on the symptoms associated with schizophrenia, it is suspected that this disorder is also associated with frontal dysfunction. Recent neuroimaging studies have provided evidence consistent with this hypothesis. On the basis of neurological, behavioral, and EEG evidence, neuropsychological theories of depression have also implicated the left frontal lobe (Davidson, 1993). PET and SPECT scans have confirmed that there is lowered metabolic activity in the left frontal lobe of people who are depressed and that this activity returns to normal levels in patients who have been treated successfully (George, Kettler, and Post, 1993).

Because the frontal lobes are the last structures to mature in childhood and the first to deteriorate with old age, young children and old adults exhibit behaviors in real life and on psychological tests that are indicative of frontal dysfunction (Diamond, 1991; Smith, Kates, and Vriezen, 1991; Moscovitch and Winocur, 1992).

THE FRONTAL LOBES, PERSONALITY, AND SOCIAL CONDUCT

As the case of Phineas Gage illustrated, reports of changes in personality and difficulties in interpersonal relationships after frontal lesions are not uncommon, especially if the ventromedial part of the lobe is affected. Aberrant social behavior and altered personality may appear in the absence of the cognitive deficits that are indicative of frontal-lobe damage (Eslinger and Damasio, 1985; Shallice and Burgess, 1991), though typically cognitive and personality changes occur together. The social disorder may be so severe in some patients that it complies with the DSM-IV diagnostic criteria for antisocial personality disorder. Here is a description of such a patient:

> By age thirty-five, E.V.R. was a successful professional, happily married, and the father of two. He led an impeccable social life, and was a role model to younger siblings. Because a meningioma (tumor of the meninges, the covering of the brain) was found on the ventromedial frontal lobes, a bilateral excision (removal) of the region was necessary.
>
> E.V.R.'s intelligence, memory, and other cognitive functions were not compromised by the surgery. In stark contrast, E.V.R.'s social conduct was profoundly affected. Over a brief period of time, he entered disastrous business ventures (one of which led to predictable bankruptcy), and was divorced twice. (The second marriage, which was to a prostitute, lasted only six months.) He has been unable to hold any paying job since the time of surgery, and his plans for future activity are defective. He now lives in a sheltered environment, unable to support himself or his family. (Damasio, Tranel, and Damasio, 1990, pp. 81–82)

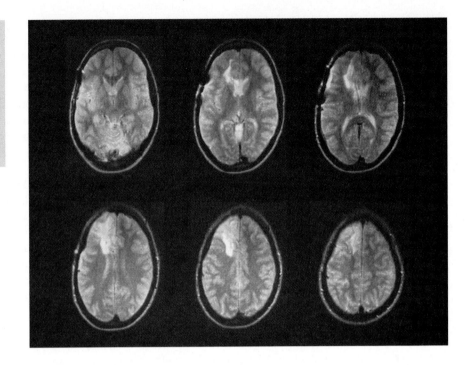

▶ Magnetic resonance imaging scan showing deep left prefrontal lobe lesions in a woman who is now thirty-three years old but who sustained damage at age seven. As a result of this frontal-lobe damage, she displays sociopathic behavior throughout her life.

When this type of damage is sustained in childhood, significant changes in personality and disturbances in social behavior occur and persist, and even worsen over time. Children who were good-natured and even-tempered become moody, surly, and given to uncontrollable rage. Despite average or superior intelligence, these children have behavioral and academic problems in school and later have erratic work histories. In the social realm, adolescence is marked by noncooperative relationships and alienation from peers. This condition continues into adulthood, manifested as a failure to establish lasting, meaningful relationships. On tests of psychosocial development and empathy, one patient scored below the first percentile on many aspects, even though she was evaluated twenty-six years after she sustained her injury at age seven (Hogan, 1969; Hawley, 1988; Grattan and Eslinger, 1992). On Kohlberg's (1969) moral judgment interview, she was at the level of an early adolescent.

Like other people who display sociopathic behavior, people with frontal-lobe lesions have full knowledge of what constitutes normal social behavior and are aware of the consequences of violating laws or social conventions (Saver and Damasio, 1991). Yet they seem unwilling or unable to act on their knowledge, just as they do not refrain from breaking rules in learning a tactile maze. Even their autonomic responses to social stimuli, such as pictures of mutilated bodies or nude people, are deficient (Damasio, Tranel, and Damasio, 1990).

Although the link between frontal-lobe damage and disorders of personality and social behavior is now being established, the processes that lead to these disorders are still poorly understood. One proposal emphasizes the impairment in activating somatic and autonomic states associated with specific social situations (see Chapter 15), so that these states can be used to anticipate outcomes of social responses (Damasio, Tranel, and Damasio, 1990, 1991). Another focuses on the possible cognitive underpinning of social conduct. Eslinger and his colleagues believe that despite normal or superior levels of mea-

FOCUS QUESTIONS

1. What are some disorders whose symptoms indicate frontal-lobe dysfunction?
2. Describe how damage to the frontal lobes can alter personality.
3. Why do some patients with frontal-lobe damage confabulate?

sured intellect, people with ventromedial frontal lesions have subtle, but pervasive, executive and self-regulatory impairments (Eslinger, Grattan, Damasio, and Damasio, 1992). These subtle deficits may not hamper performance on standard tests of frontal function, but they are picked up by new problem-solving tasks that involve organizing and planning (Shallice and Burgess, 1991). Yet a third possibility is that, just as there are modules for perception and memory, there are modules dealing with social behavior, and these seem to be absent from birth in autistic children (Frith, 1993), requiring an intact ventromedial frontal cortex in order to function properly.

THE FRONTAL LOBES AND MEMORY IMPAIRMENT

The frontal lobes' role in memory is similar to its role in other domains. People with frontal-lobe damage or dysfunction are impaired in memory sequencing, that is, they have difficulty placing remembered events in the proper temporal order with respect to one another, even though memory for the events themselves is preserved. They also have difficulty in organizing information so that they will remember it better, and in devising and implementing proper retrieval strategies. For example, if asked to search their memory for a personal event associated with the cue "letter" or "broken" or a historical event having to do with "a battle," people with frontal-lobe damage often draw a blank unless they are given more specific, direct cues to guide them (e.g., did you ever have any broken bones or teeth or did you break something valuable as a child?). People with frontal-lobe damage also do not monitor or evaluate their memories normally to determine whether they are genuine or appropriate.

The most extreme example of the failure of frontal function with respect to memory is noted in some patients who **confabulate,** that is, make up stories. They do not distort the truth deliberately but instead they are "honest liars" in the sense that they are trying to tell the truth as best they can but miss the mark without any awareness that they have done so. Confabulations are not pure fabrications, rather they consist of disorganized memories that the patients have recovered. Accurately remembered elements of one event are combined with those of another without regard to their internal consistency or even plausibility. Sometimes events are recalled but placed in inappropriate context or in impaired temporal order, as in this case:

Mr. W. is sixty-one years old and has had frontal damage caused by an aneurysm (an expanded blood vessel) of the anterior communicating artery. He has been married for over thirty years to the same woman and has four children ranging in age from twenty-seven to thirty-four years.

Clinician: How long have you been married?
Patient: About four months.
Clinician: What is your wife's name?
Patient: Martha.
Clinician: How many children do you have?
Patient: Four. (He laughs.) Not bad for four months.
Clinician: How old are your children?
Patient: The eldest is thirty-two; his name is Bob. The youngest is twenty-two; his name is Joe.
Clinician: How did you get these children in four months?
Patient: They're adopted. (He laughs again.)

Mr. W. responds correctly, or nearly so, regarding his wife's name and the age of his children. Yet he confabulates about how long he's been married. Then to make sense of the inconsistencies, he concocts a story about adoption. Failure to search for a proper reply, monitor the answer, and evaluate it to make sure it is consistent with his other knowledge accounts for confabulation.

The frontal lobes have been termed "working-with-memory" structures (Moscovitch, 1992; Moscovitch and Winocur, 1992). They operate on the information encoded in memory and recovered from it. The frontal lobes are necessary for converting remembering from a stupid, reflexive act triggered by a cue to an intelligent, reflective, goal-directed activity that is under voluntary control, much like solving a problem. In trying to place a person that looks familiar or to determine where you were during the last week of July, the appropriate memory does not emerge automatically but must be ferreted out, often laboriously, by retrieval strategies, and the output must be monitored and evaluated. As the confabulating patient demonstrated, even a simple question such as how long have you been married, may involve the "working-with-memory" functions of the frontal lobes.

FRONTAL LOBE DEMENTIA

When progressive neuronal degeneration principally affects the frontal lobes, it produces dementia with characteristic frontal signs. Unlike patients with Alzheimer's dementia, which in its initial stages affects primarily the temporal and parietal lobes, patients with frontal lobe dementia (called Pick's disease, in some cases) show variable, often mild memory deficits and little or no visuospatial impairment. Indeed, many patients present with symptoms similar to those of Phineas Gage: marked changes in personality, disinhibition, unconcern, language problems, and socially inappropriate behavior. The following case illustrates this condition:

> A fifty-year-old shop manager suffered a gradually progressive change in his personality. He became outspoken, rude, and callous, lacking in initiative, self-care, and responsibility towards his family. His mood would fluctuate between facetiousness and jocularity and negativism and irritability, with verbal and physical aggression thought to be totally out of character.
>
> On examination, he was free of neurological signs. He was generally courteous, although mildly disinhibited, talking excessively loudly, and giving frequent and inappropriate guffaws of laughter. His speech was normal. There was no evidence of impaired comprehension. He was left/right oriented, and no word finding difficulty was evident. Repetition tasks elicited perseverations of previous responses. He could read and write, although spelling was poor. He showed substantial difficulty in calculating. He had no difficulty in perceptual identification of objects, line drawings, and faces of celebrities. He was fully oriented and displayed preserved memory for day-to-day events.
>
> Over a four-year follow-up period his behavior became increasingly rigid and inflexible, and violent outbursts were more common. He was inert and lacked initiative. Stereotyped mannerisms were increasingly evident. His cognitive performance remained qualitatively similar, although increasing impulsivity, carelessness and lack of attention to the task resulted in reduced performance accuracy. (Neary, Snowden, Northern, and Goulding, 1988)

The prognosis and treatment of diseases and disorders of the nervous system are determined in large part by some of the basic principles we stated at the beginning of this chapter: the very limited ability to make new neurons, the possibility for damaged neurons to recover and for new connections to be formed, the principle of redundancy. The course and effectiveness of treatment depend on the nature of the disease or disorder, the spatial extent of the pathology (generalized or highly localized), and the specific location of the pathology (whether it is accessible to surgery, for example) (Adams, 1989).

Many neurological symptoms are produced by damage to, but not destruction of neurons. Such reversible damage can be produced by lowered oxygen and nutrient supply resulting from atherosclerosis or lung disease, and by acute pressure produced by swelling of the brain after head trauma, infection, or a tumor that impedes circulation of cerebrospinal fluid. Since damaged or nutrient-deprived neurons can recover, intervention can produce a cure. This would be the case for infections, which can be treated with antibiotics, for acute cases of high intracranial pressure, which can be relieved by draining some of the fluid, or for certain tumors, which can be removed. Since the nervous system has some ability to repair itself, a large part of the treatment of some acute disorders consists in maintaining the patient's health, to allow his nervous system to recover from the shock of trauma. Partial recovery from strokes occurs for this reason. For most of the degenerative diseases, however, as well as many of the cases of stroke or hemorrhage, there is little that can be done that would constitute a cure.

A second line of treatment, when cure is impossible, is to take medical measures to contain the problem or to treat the symptoms. The use of L-DOPA to replace the deficiency in neurotransmitters in the basal ganglia in someone with Parkinson's disease is an example of this. The L-DOPA does not cure the disease, but it reduces symptoms such as tremor and rigidity.

The situation of many people with neurological damage can also be improved by restructuring their patterns of living. Family members can compensate for deficits, by taking over or assisting in those functions that are compromised. It is sometimes possible to teach them ways around their deficit: Braille for the blind, memo pads for those with bad memories. And, more and more, specific devices, from wheelchairs to mini-computers, are becoming available that compensate for deficits.

When a patient is referred to a neurologist, he is often anxious, because he doesn't want to have a disorder of the nervous system. A "psychological" disorder is preferable to most people. In fact, much of what neurologists do is to discover that common neurological symptoms, such as tingling of the fingers, muscle twitches, and headaches, are *not* indicative of disorders of the nervous system. Although they may be early signs of neurological disorder, they are often either functional problems or minor disorders of unknown origin that will neither progress nor seriously compromise the life of the patient. In other words, some patients leave the care of the neurologist cured, some leave improved, some cannot be helped, and quite a few leave with the confidence that there is really nothing serious that is wrong with them, neurologically.

FOCUS QUESTIONS

1. What are the factors that affect the course and effectiveness of treatment of neurological disorders?
2. What medical measures can be taken while the nervous system repairs itself or when cure is impossible.
3. How can people with neurological damage restructure their patterns of living?

For the moment, the triumph of neurology is in diagnosis. It is a frustration to the neurologist that she can understand many disease processes and disorders, but she cannot cure them. Although neurologists know a lot about the nervous system, they still have only limited abilities to repair it, and none to replace it. Dramatic cures of neurological disorders can be produced by neurosurgery, and many symptoms can be relieved with drugs. It is much more common, however, to have understanding without successful treatment in neurology than in psychology. Our present ability to repair functional disorders is probably better than our ability to repair the nervous system.

Because of rapid advances in neuroscience, the prospects for successful treatment of more diseases of the nervous system are very good. The steady stream of important findings on neurotransmitters, and the operation of the immune system, as well as surgical innovations, have already made some impact on neurology. For example, research with rats has demonstrated that tissue from fetal brains or adrenal glands can be transplanted to the brain of adult rats, where it survives, forms viable connections, and releases neurotransmitters (Sladek and Shoulson, 1988). When introduced into a damaged area, the fetal transplants lead to recovery of function. Recently, similar procedures have been tried with human patients suffering from Parkinson's disease. Although initial reports are encouraging, it is too soon to pass judgment on this promising approach.

Much of the treatment of neurological disorders falls to psychiatrists and nonmedical health practitioners, such as psychologists, speech therapists, and physical therapists. As we noted in the case of treating patients with amnesia, the therapist's job involves helping the patient make maximum use of remaining abilities. Although functions can recover spontaneously, the evidence suggests that recovery is better following treatment, whether the disorder involves speech, movement, or attention.

Because neurological deficits are, by definition, organic, people rarely pay attention to the functional syndromes that often accompany neurological disorder. Many neurological patients suffer from depression, insecurity, or fear. Their feelings can exacerbate their neurological symptoms and prevent recovery. Psychotherapy can be valuable for these patients in this context.

THE EXPANSION OF THE NEUROLOGICAL/NEUROCHEMICAL APPROACHES

The last few decades have been a period of extraordinary progress in understanding the structure and function of the nervous system. Brain-imaging techniques have become more accurate and less intrusive every year. The number of identified neurotransmitters has grown massively in the last few decades, and understanding of the operation of synapses has advanced rapidly. Of those areas of science that have a direct impact on the understanding of abnormal behavior, the neurosciences are both the best understood and the most rapidly advancing,

At the same time, advances in molecular biology and genetics have made isolation of genetic contributions to abnormal behavior easier to study and identify. The result of all of these advances has been a substantial move toward the organic/hardware side of the functional-organic dimension. That is, more and more disorders that were originally believed to be purely functional have been discovered to have a genetic, neurotransmitter, or structural basis. Some decades ago, a prudent scientist could well have concluded that while brain or hardware deficits would likely be behind disorders of perception, action, and some cognitions, disorders related to mood, personality, self-esteem, and values would surely fall squarely in the domain of experience and software. Now, strong genetic influences have been found in the mood disorders and in personality. Such genetic effects must, somehow, be represented in the hardware of the nervous system, or in levels of hormones or neurotransmitters.

As we said in the introduction to this chapter, the hardware/software distinction is difficult to apply strictly to the nervous system, since most experience leaves a permanent imprint on the nervous system. Furthermore, are we to consider the level of a brain neurotransmitter a feature of hardware or software? Surely, it seems more organic than functional. It is in the area of neurotransmitters that some of the most remarkable progress has occurred. There are literally hundreds of neurotransmitters already identified, and most are localized in particular areas or systems, and are involved in particular types of behavior or brain function.

We can understand without too much difficulty, how neurotransmitters are involved in the regulation of action in Parkinson's disease, of attention in schizophrenia, or of mood in depression and mania. By raising or lowering neurotransmitter levels, behavior or mood is altered along a single dimension. It is more difficult to accept or imagine how single neurotransmitters can alter personality. Yet, exactly this kind of evidence has been accumulating in the last decade, as in cases involving clomipramine and treatment of obsessive-compulsive disorders (see p. 279), and Prozac and treatment of depression.

The psychiatrist, Peter Kramer, in his best-selling book, *Listening to Prozac* (1993), illustrates with case studies some remarkable personal transformations accomplished on people who were not functioning optimally, though certainly not diagnosable under any of the categories discussed in this book. People report a striking change in well-being, self-esteem, command, and loss of shyness which allows them to accomplish things they had thought impossible for themselves. They seem to be, according to their own testimony, "better than well." These claims have yet to be substantiated scientifically. The idea that Prozac and other drugs that are selective serotonin reuptake inhibitors are altering the sense of self must be treated with caution.

A clue to how these drugs can alter personality, if indeed they do, comes from our observation that damage to the frontal lobes often causes a change in personality. It is significant that the frontal lobes are implicated in depression and OCD. Frontal disorders are also observed in schizophrenia, which may be considered a disease that affects personality. The drugs that are effective in changing aspects of personality may all operate by influencing frontal-lobe function directly or indirectly. However, our current understanding of psychology and brain function makes it difficult to understand how something as global as self-esteem, or something as specific as concern for cleanliness, might be mediated by "hardware," and linked to specific neurotransmitter systems.

It is not possible to say, at this time, what the limits of the advance of neuroscience into abnormal psychology will be. Surely there are things, like patriotic devotion, attitudes to abortion or democracy, that are part of our culture and experience, and unlikely to become linked to a neurotransmitter system or brain area. However, returning to our hardware/software analogy, one can now buy computers with factory installation of what used to be software and is now effectively part of the hardware. In the nervous system, innately programmed circuitry, keyed to specific neurotransmitters and/or specific brain

FOCUS QUESTIONS

1. What advances have led to better understanding of the structure and functions of the nervous system?
2. What is the evidence that neurotransmitter levels can alter personality?

loci might produce some of the phenomena we have been discussing. In any event, the experiences of the last decade are sobering, and we can only wait with anticipation to see where the marching advance of neuroscience will take it.

THE VIRTUES AND LIMITATIONS OF THE NEUROLOGICAL APPROACH

The rapidly growing field of neuropsychology has as one of its principal aims the understanding of normal function. Just as pathology has been a powerful tool in the study of normal biological function in other areas, it can be used as a tool to understand normal behavior and mental function. Thus, researchers study disorders of the nervous system, particularly in the areas of language, cognition, perception, and action, to understand normal function. Since the nervous system is organized in a meaningful way, damage often breaks complex systems apart at their "joints." Thus, the study of split brains has contributed to our understanding of different modes of thought, and the study of amnesics has contributed to our understanding of normal memory.

There is a certain respectability that a psychopathological syndrome gains as a disease when it has a definite underlying neuropathology. Some definitions of disease include underlying biological pathology as a critical feature. Thus, the intrusion of neurological explanations into what were previously thought to be functional disorders dispels some of the lingering uncertainty we have about how to classify a variety of forms of mental illness. There is something to be said for this, but there are also serious intellectual and social problems raised by these advances. We devote our closing section to this problem.

First, we must realize that a form of psychopathology is not more serious because it has a demonstrable or likely neurological basis. From the point of view of the individual or society, some of the most painful and debilitating disorders currently fall outside of the domain of neurology. Agoraphobia, a variety of addictions, and anorexia nervosa are salient examples.

Second, discovery of a neurological basis for psychopathology does not necessarily improve the chances for treatment. On the contrary, given the limited capacity of the nervous system to repair itself, the prospects for treatment are often discouraging. Psychotherapy for certain disorders, such as phobias, is probably much more successful than treatments for the great majority of organic disorders. Moreover, there is the danger that physicians and patients may become overzealous in their search for a quick neurological cure to a functional disorder. The disastrous history of frontal lobotomies as a treatment for frank psychiatric disorders should serve as a warning (Valenstein, 1986).

Third, the linkage between neurological damage and disease is weaker than one might imagine. Insofar as a notion of disease includes maladaptiveness, one must consider cultural context in determining whether a disease is present. Consider the case of reading disorders. Dyslexia is a crippling disorder in our literate society. Today, reading ability is almost a prerequisite to success. One hundred years ago, however, literacy was a capacity pretty much limited to an economically and culturally privileged few. At that time, society was not built around the assumption of literacy, as ours is today. A person with severe reading disorders resulting from pathologies in the linkages between the visual system and the language system would not have been considered sick one hundred years ago, nor would such a person be considered sick today in a pri-

FOCUS QUESTIONS

1. Why doesn't the discovery of a neurological basis for psychopathology necessarily improve the chances for treatment?
2. Give an example of the dangers of searching for a quick neurological cure for a functional disorder.
3. Describe how cultural context can affect how debilitating a disorder is to an individual.

marily illiterate culture. Furthermore, as we indicated in our discussion of reading disorders, different writing systems, produced by different cultures, make different cognitive demands on the reader, and hence engage different brain mechanisms. The English alphabet is a system built on the sounds of speech, while the Chinese writing system is not. As a result, there is more reliance on phonological decoding mechanisms in reading English than in reading Chinese; brain damage that may have a small effect on a Chinese reader may seriously compromise a reader of English, and vice versa. Thus, cultural institutions increase the importance of certain skills and decrease the importance of others. Reading disability is devastating for most people in our society, and physical weakness is not. The reverse is true in some hunter-gatherer societies. It would not be surprising if the enormous influence of computers in modern life leads to realization of new deficits, perhaps with a neurological basis, that currently go unnoticed.

The same issue arises with respect to the effect of neurological diseases on different individuals in the same culture. Consider the effect of amyotrophic lateral sclerosis (ALS) on two accomplished figures, baseball great Lou Gehrig and theoretical physicist Stephen Hawking. The progressive muscular weakness that is the hallmark of ALS was absolutely devastating, even at early stages, to Lou Gehrig, a man whose accomplishments were based on physical strength and coordination. On the other hand, Hawking's purely mental efforts, the core of his professional accomplishments, have continued in the face of the extensive paralysis or weakness of the later stages of this disease.

Fourth, and most critically, one should not expect too much from the neurological approach to psychopathology. There are some types of pathology that may not have a basis in neuropathology because they involve the interaction of a particular set of experiences with a normal brain. They are no doubt represented in some way in brain circuitry, but not in any way that a neuroscientist would be able to detect. It is unlikely that fearing versus liking dogs would be diagnosable with even the most sophisticated possible brain-scanning device.

Furthermore, even for cases where there is definable neuropathology, the identification of this pathology does not usually account for the psychopathology, in the sense that it fully explains its manifestations. Knowing that depres-

▼ (A) Stephen Hawking, a distinguished British physicist, suffers from amyotrophic lateral sclerosis and is almost completely paralyzed. (B) Even so, Hawking is able to produce scientific writings of major import through the use of a personal computer.

sion is "caused" by low levels of norepinephrine does not tell us what depression is like, nor that depressives have a characteristic attributional style. Neither the pain and frustration of having expressive deficits nor the precise structure of the grammatical breakdown in Broca's aphasia are explained by locating the lesion in the left frontal lobes.

Many human phenomena are most usefully explained or dealt with at the level of mental events or behavior. There may be a biochemical basis for mother love, but mother love is best described, for some purposes, as a mental state. In the same way, one can describe one's word-processing program in terms of machine language code, but terms such as "delete," "insert," and "search" seem much more appropriate for comprehending and using it.

In short, there are dangers of both over- and under-neurologizing. This alone is an important reason to have a chapter on neurology in a textbook on abnormal psychology. There are important neurological components in some types of psychopathology, and there is much to be learned from neurology as an advanced area of medicine. We hope this chapter has convinced you of that. It is also important that the neurological approach occupies only one or a few chapters, and not the whole book. We hope that this chapter, and the others in this book have convinced you of *that*.

SUMMARY

1. Although all mental illnesses are in some sense represented in the nervous system, one group of these illnesses can be traced to specific defects in the structure and function of the nervous system. This group, which can be thought of as organic disorders, falls in the domain of neuropsychologists and neurologists, while the remaining functional disorders fall in the domain of clinical psychologists and psychiatrists.

2. Basic principles of the structure and function of the nervous system can account for many organic syndromes.

3. Principles of synaptic physiology and the action of neurotransmitters account for a number of disorders, including some types of depression.

4. The spatial (modular) and biochemical organization of the nervous system account for the fact that damage at specific sites or by specific toxins produces specific and distinctive symptoms.

5. In the nervous system, in general, structures at the front represent motor functions, and those at the back represent sensory functions. In the cerebral cortex, this front-back distinction is represented in an expanded way. The parietal and temporal lobes, located toward the back of the brain, are involved in information processing, while the frontal lobes, located at the front, are involved in the organization of action. Damage to the parietal lobes produces inabilities to represent the world visuo-spatially and/or neglect (inattention to) certain parts of the world. Frontal damage leads to disruption of strategies or plans for action, problems in negotiating the transition from one action to another, and difficulties in impulse control.

6. The left-right organization of the brain explains why damage to the left hemisphere often produces verbal deficits, while damage to the right hemisphere often leads to disorders in spatial representation.

7. The up-down (hierarchical) organization of the nervous system explains how similar symptoms can be produced by damage at different levels of the nervous system. The fact that balance among various centers in the nervous system is produced by inhibition explains the appearance of symptoms by release of inhibition from a damaged area.

8. There are many causes of diseases of the nervous system, including nutrient deficiencies, strokes, degenerative diseases, and head trauma. The symptoms of damage can be negative (a deficit) or positive (an increase in activity), resulting from release of inhibition or irritability, as in the case of epilepsy.

9. Some parts of the nervous system, such as parts involved in the formation of memories, are particularly vulnerable to damage. As a result, specific symptoms may result from general trauma to the nervous system, as in exposure to toxins or blows to the head.

10. The principle of redundancy accounts for the paucity of symptoms and recovery of function following some kinds of brain damage.

11. The diagnosis of damage to the nervous system is a well-developed science and art, based on history of the disorder, current symptoms, and highly sophisticated electrophysiological and brain-imaging techniques that allow direct measurement of brain structures and metabolism.

12. According to the classical view, disorders of language can be subdivided in terms of whether reception, comprehension, or production of language is primarily affected. They illustrate two principles of spatial organization of the brain: (1) left-right specialization (language functions on the left), and (2) the front-back principle, since receptive aphasias result from lesions near the back of the brain and expressive aphasias result from lesions near the front.

13. The classical view has been modified by recent studies based on advances in cognitive psychology and linguistics. Thus, Broca's aphasia, traditionally considered as an expressive disorder, also comprises a grammatical disorder that affects both comprehension and production of language.

14. Acquired dyslexia is a disorder of reading caused by brain damage. The symptoms of dyslexia will vary depending on which reading processes are disturbed. Phonological dyslexics are impaired at sounding out words, whereas surface dyslexics have a deficit in identifying words by their visual form.

15. The most common disorder of memory, the amnesic syndrome, most frequently results from aging (senile dementia, such as Alzheimer's disease), head trauma, or chronic alcoholism (Korsakoff's psychosis). The symptoms result from damage to a few particularly vulnerable areas of the brain, on both sides. The major feature of the amnesic syndrome is the inability to recall or recognize recent events, although new information can be "acquired" and retained without any awareness of these new memories.

16. Parkinson's disease and Alzheimer's disease both represent degenerative disorders and are associated with old age. Alzheimer's disease, the principal form of senile dementia, is characterized by progressive loss of mental functions, with memory disorders and problems in spatial relations often the most prominent early symptoms. A distinctive pathology of neurons is associated with this disorder, especially in the hippocampus.

17. The frontal lobes can be considered as part of an expanded motor system. They are involved in planning, organizing, and coordinating actions and thoughts, in monitoring their outcome to determine if goals are achieved, and in devising alternate strategies if they are not. Frontal-lobe functions are also apparent in social and emotional behavior. As a result, frontal-lobe damage or dysfunction may lead to changes in personality, to memory impairment, and to a type of dementia, as sometimes occurs in patients with Parkinson's disease, Huntington's disease, schizophrenia, and depression.

18. Because new neurons rarely, if ever, arise in adult humans, the prospects for treatment of neurological illness are limited. But recovery occurs because damaged neurons can recover. In addition, symptoms can be treated by drugs and by teaching the patient strategies that help him to minimize deficits. These strategies often involve enlisting the help of friends or family, and/or special devices such as wheelchairs or computers.

19. There has been an expansion of the neurological/neurochemical approaches due to advances in molecular biology, genetics, and neuroimaging techniques. Several disorders that were originally believed to be functional have subsequently been found to have a genetic, neurotransmitter, or structural basis.

20. Diseases of the nervous system account for some instances of abnormal behavior or thought. In some cases, discovery of a neurological basis for psychopathology may improve prospects for treatment, but in other cases, it may not because of the limited ability of the nervous system to recover. The maladaptiveness of neurological syndromes depends on the cultural context and the individual life context within which they are manifested.

QUESTIONS FOR CRITICAL THINKING

1. What do memory deficits in patients suffering from amnesia tell you about the structures involved in conscious and nonconscious memory storage and retrieval?

2. Describe some of the findings that have led us to reinterpret disorders that were once believed to be functional as organic disorders.

3. What physical, mental, and social symptoms may indicate frontal-lobe damage?

4. Why is there redundancy in the nervous system?

5. Where cure is impossible, what medical measures can be taken to contain the problem or treat the symptoms? Take one disorder and indicate the possible benefits (and problems, if any) of using medical measures to treat it.

8 ABNORMALITY, THE LAW, AND CHOOSING A PSYCHOTHERAPY

CHAPTER 18

The Law and Politics of Abnormality

CHAPTER ORGANIZER

INVOLUNTARY COMMITMENT AND TREATMENT
- Familiarize yourself with the criteria and standards of proof used to commit individuals.
- Understand the due process rights of mental patients both before and after their involuntary commitment.

CRIMINAL COMMITMENT
- Understand what various insanity defenses are.
- Be able to explain what happens when people are found incompetent to stand trial and when they are found guilty but mentally ill.

IDENTITY, MEMORY, AND THE NATURE OF EVIDENCE
- Understand the problems that can arise when a person with multiple personalities is being tried in a criminal case, and those that may arise in relation to the recovery of repressed memories.

THE SOCIAL AND POLITICAL ABUSE OF ABNORMAL PSYCHOLOGY
- Understand how the potential for abuse of diagnoses of mental disorder can arise from changing conceptions of abnormality.

There are two perspectives from which psychological distress can be examined. The first is the perspective of the individual who is suffering: how he or she might have acquired the disorder, what the present experience is like, and what remedies are available to ameliorate that condition. Until now, that has been the perspective of this book.

But there is another way to examine abnormality, and that is from the viewpoint of society. In this chapter, we examine the ways in which society protects its members from the consequences of psychological suffering. The conditions under which society moves to protect and the forms that such protection takes often involve options that are costly in terms of human rights as well as monetarily. In choosing between public protection and the civil liberties of the mentally ill, as exemplified in laws concerning civil and criminal commitment, society must make difficult and often painful choices (Steadman, 1981). Those choices concern us here.

In addition to the issues associated with involuntary and criminal commitment, we will discuss two kinds of abuse of abnormal psychology. First, we will look at how a state or government abuses what we know about psychology and psychiatry by removing dissident (but sane) individuals or groups from society, or controlling their behavior. Second, we will look at a more general problem: the stigma that is cast over an individual when that individual is labeled "mentally ill." In any profession, there are often conflicts between the requirements of practice and those of society. The practice of psychology and psychiatry is no exception.

No societal response to psychological suffering has received more attention during the past several decades than has ***involuntary commitment,*** the process whereby the state hospitalizes people for their own good, and even over their vigorous protest. In effect, the state acts as parent to those who have "lost their senses," doing for them what they might do for themselves if they had their wits about them, and uses its police power to protect the public from the foreseeable and avoidable danger that the mentally disordered may present.

Involuntary Commitment and Perceptions of Abnormality

Consider the following situations in which the state might seek to commit an individual involuntarily, and in which most people would agree that the state is right in doing so:

- As the result of a toxic psychosis, a young man wants to throw himself from the roof of a very tall building. In twenty-four hours, both the impulse and the psychosis will have passed—if he remains restrained now.
- A young man is despondent over the termination of his first love. To him, there is currently no alternative to suicide. A month from now, he may think differently.
- An attorney is overcome by irrational guilt. She calls two of her clients and informs them that she has not handled their cases properly, and that she has stolen from them. Of course, this is untrue. She would have called the rest of her clients had the state, through her family, not intervened and hospitalized her against her will.
- Following the birth of two previous children, a woman suffered a post-partum depression, and attempted to murder the infants. She is about to give birth again, and is experiencing the same impulse. To protect those young lives, the state hospitalizes the mother involuntarily.

For most people, these cases are compelling arguments for involuntary hospitalization. Where there is clear-cut danger to self or to others, most people agree that some intervention is necessary. But most cases are not nearly so clear-cut. Indeed, many cases test the very meaning of normality and abnormality that were discussed in Chapter 1. Abnormal by whose standard? Recall that some people believe themselves depressed for good reason, but "society" finds them "mentally ill" and in need of treatment. Others enjoy the relaxation and "highs" conferred by recreational drugs, yet society views them as addicts who require psychiatric attention. Still others radically alter their lifestyles on discovering a "true religion," but society may designate that discovery as psychotic and commit the discoverer to a psychiatric facility. *Mayock* v. *Martin** illustrated this issue well:

*Mayock v. Martin, 157 Conn, 56, 245A. 2d 574 (1968).

Mr. Mayock was hospitalized in July 1944 after he had removed his right eye. He was subsequently diagnosed paranoid schizophrenic, eventually released on probation, and finally discharged three years later. Three days after discharge, Mayock removed his right hand, and was committed once again to the state hospital. At the time of trial, some twenty years later, Mayock was still confined involuntarily to the state hospital with the diagnosis of paranoid schizophrenia.

At his trial, Mayock insisted that there was nothing mysterious or crazy about his self-maiming. Rather, he is a deeply religious man who believes that society's attempts to establish peace by force are entirely misguided. God's way, he says is to encourage peace through love. If society continues on its present path, many lives will be lost through war. Mayock believes that one man has been chosen to make a peace offering to God: that he, Mayock, is that man, and that it is better for one person to accept a message from God to sacrifice an eye or a hand than it is for society to suffer a great loss of human life.

During the twenty years that he had been hospitalized, Mayock had had complete freedom of the hospital grounds. He had not once maimed himself. Yet, he acknowledged that he would gladly do so again either as a significant freewill offering or in response to divine revelation.

Beyond this single symptom, there was no further evidence that Mayock was disturbed. He had risen to a position of considerable responsibility in the hospital, running the recreation center for parole-privileged patients, as well as the hospital news stand. There was ample evidence that he could handle financial matters and take care of himself in all other respects.

Psychiatrists at the hospital contended that his prophetic view of himself was "grandiose," that his religious beliefs were "grossly false," and that the diagnosis of paranoid schizophrenic was entirely warranted by the facts. Mayock contended that he is religious, not mentally ill, and that his First Amendment constitutional rights ("Congress shall make no law respecting an establishment of religion or prohibiting the free exercise thereof . . .") had been violated.

Mayock lost. Some will feel that he should have lost, for only the truly mad would gouge out their eyes and chop off their arms. Others will feel that Mayock's loss is tragic, for he was acting with courage upon deeply held religious beliefs and harming no one but himself. Perhaps the tragedy lies in that ambiguity, for Mayock can be seen as quite abnormal by some standards, and not abnormal at all by others. Given a large area of doubt, how did it happen that he was involuntarily hospitalized, and for so long?

In general, the use of involuntary hospitalization of people who are believed to be dangerous to themselves ought to be guided by the "thank you" test (Stone, 1975). This test asks: Will the person, once recovered, be grateful for that hospitalization, however much it was protested? The test would likely be passed by people who are severely depressed and suicidal and who, once the depression lifted, would be grateful to be alive.

But the informal social conventions that regulate who should and who should not be hospitalized because they are dangerous to themselves are sometimes inconsistent and ambiguous. People who seem to be experiencing similar degrees of danger to themselves may be seen as good candidates for commitment in one case but not in another, as the following two cases demonstrate:

Case 1: Emma Lake. At sixty, Emma Lake was involuntarily committed to St. Elizabeth's Hospital after she was found wandering the streets of Washington, D.C. At the commitment hearing, two psychiatrists testified that she was unable to care adequately for herself. At a subsequent hearing, she was held to be suffering from "chronic brain syndrome with arteriosclerosis (hardening of the arteries). . ." She was prone to "wandering away and being out exposed at night or any time that she is out." On one occasion, it was related, Mrs. Lake left the hospital and was missing for about thirty-two hours. She was brought back after midnight by a policeman who found her wandering the streets. She thought she had only been gone for a few hours, could not tell where she had been, and suffered a minor injury, that she attributed to having been chased by boys.

Mrs. Lake acknowledged that there were times when she lost track of things. Nevertheless, she felt able to be at liberty and willing to run the requisite risks. Her husband and sister were eager for her release and willing to provide a home for her. Moreover, she was willing to endure some form of confinement at home rather than the total confinement of a psychiatric hospital.

Ultimately the court concurred with her psychiatrist and required that she be hospitalized. She spent the last five years of her life in a psychiatric hospital, during the last year of which she received no visitors (Chambers, 1972). Often, family that would willingly provide a home for a patient are unable or unwilling to visit a psychiatric hospital regularly.

Case 2: Robert Jackson. At the age of sixty-two, Justice Robert Jackson suffered a severe heart attack while serving on the United States Supreme Court. The Court's work is arduous and taxing. His doctors gave him the choice between years of comparative (though not, by any means, total) inactivity off the Court, and the risk of death at any time by continuing his work on the Court. Jackson chose to remain on the Court. He suffered a fatal heart attack shortly thereafter.

No court interfered with the Justice's decision, nor was it ever suggested that he was dangerous to himself and therefore in need of psychiatric care. Quite the contrary: his decision to continue the work of the Court was widely praised. Many people would choose to do the same: take their chances with the things they enjoy doing rather than be cooped up, inactively, for the rest of their lives.

What distinguishes Mrs. Lake's case from Justice Jackson's? For both, the choices jeopardized their lives, Jackson's even more than Lake's. Why was Lake involuntarily committed and Jackson never questioned? The major difference between Mrs. Lake's case and Justice Jackson's is that Mrs. Lake's request to live out her years at home, and with people who loved her, was "psychiatrized." That is, her choice was believed to arise from mental illness ("chronic brain syndrome"), while Justice Jackson's was not. The fact that she suffered "chronic brain syndrome" obscured the similarities between her choice and others. If Mrs. Lake's case serves to teach anything, it is that once behavior is described or "explained" in terms of psychological abnormality, it encourages people to think of a different set of "solutions" than they would if it had been explained as the product of rational decision making. Now, it is clearly the case that some psychologically distressed persons suffer thought disorders of such magnitude that they are rarely, if ever, lucid. But that was not the case with Mrs. Lake, nor is it the case for most psychiatric patients, all of whom enjoy long periods of clarity during which they are as capable as others of making significant choices between the risks of liberty and the security of incarceration (Dershowitz, 1968).

In order to understand the thousands of commitments that occur involuntarily, be they cases like that of Mr. Mayock or Mrs. Lake or cases that appear to be more clear-cut instances of mental disorder, we need to know something about the laws that regulate commitment procedures. Our focus will be on laws in the United States.

Procedures to Commit

The issues associated with civil commitment have been dominated by intense controversy historically. Commitment procedures have varied through the years and from state to state. There is no simple federal law concerning commitment procedures, and states differ enormously in the procedures that are used to commit people, and in the safeguards those procedures provide.

COMMITMENT CRITERIA

The exact nature of the criteria for involuntary commitment varies from state to state, having evolved in accord with popular opinion and contemporary social policy, and with repeated attempts to clarify and improve procedures. But three elements remain the same across all statutes: In order to be committed, an individual must be (1) mentally disordered, (2) dangerous to self or others, and (3) gravely disabled. In addition, the American Psychiatric Association has proposed a fourth criterion, "likely to suffer substantial mental or physical deterioration," and has been trying to convince state legislatures to include such a criterion in their commitment procedures (American Psychiatric Association, 1983; Monahan and Shah, 1989). This criterion is fundamentally a predictive one that encourages civil commitment when, as evidenced by recent behavior, if not treated, a person will "suffer or continue to suffer severe and abnormal mental, emotional, or physical distress [which] . . . is associated with significant impairment of judgment, reason, or behavior causing a substantial deterioration of his previous ability to function on his own (APA, 1983, p. 673).

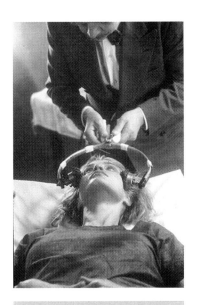

▲ In the movie *Frances*, Jessica Lange plays Frances Farmer, whose involuntary commitment was based on "impaired judgment."

Mental Disorder   All states require that an individual be ***mentally disordered,*** that is, suffering from a psychological disability, variously termed "mental illness," "mental disease," or "mental disability." But often these phrases are not specifically defined, leaving unclear which disabilities qualify and which do not. Definitions of mental disorder vary widely across the states. Perhaps the most thoughtful is that offered by the American Psychiatric Association, which would restrict civil commitment only to those with *severe* mental disorders. A severe mental disorder is defined as "an illness, disease, organic brain disorder, or other condition that (1) substantially impairs the person's thought, perception of reality, emotional process, or judgment, or (2) substantially impairs behavior as manifested by recent disturbed behavior." Roughly speaking, a severe mental disorder corresponds to a psychotic disorder.

Dangerousness to Self or Others   Many states require that there be some evidence that the individual is dangerous, either to himself or to others. And indeed, more involuntary hospitalizations are justified on these grounds than on any others. In some state statutes, the definition of dangerousness is vague. Alabama, for example, provides for commitment when a person "poses a real and

A person society considers dangerous to himself or others may be involuntarily committed. But the definition of "dangerous" may be vague, based on the prediction that a mental patient may behave dangerously in the future, rather than on an act he has already committed.

present threat of substantial harm."* Florida, on the other hand, is more specific: a mentally disordered individual can be hospitalized if "[t]here is substantial likelihood that in the near future he will inflict serious bodily harm on himself or another person, as evidenced by recent behavior causing, attempting, or threatening such harm."†

But regardless of how carefully or vaguely it is defined, two serious problems arise from the notion of dangerousness, one legal and the other scientific. The legal problem is straightforward. Incarcerating people because they are *predicted* to be dangerous creates a dilemma because Western legal traditions generally mandate the deprivation of liberty only *after* a crime has been committed, not before. The mere fact that someone is expected to violate the law is not sufficient reason for incarceration.

The scientific problem is whether dangerousness can ever be predicted so precisely that only the dangerous will be hospitalized, while the not dangerous will not be. Clearly, the ability to predict dangerous behavior lies at the very heart of civilized and rational civil commitment procedures. Yet, over the past two decades scientists have thought the capacity to predict dangerousness more elusive than real (Diamond, 1974; Ennis and Litwack, 1974; Stone, 1975). One of the most interesting of these studies arose out of the case of *Baxstrom v. Herold*‡ (Steadman and Keveles, 1972, 1978).

> After serving more than two years for second-degree assault, Johnnie K. Baxstrom was certified as insane by a prison physician and transferred to a prison-hospital. Baxstrom's sentence was about to end, however, but because he was still in need of psychiatric care, the director of the prison-hospital petitioned that Baxstrom be committed involuntarily to an ordinary psychiatric hospital. That petition was denied for administrative reasons. Baxstrom, therefore, was forced to remain where he was.
>
> Baxstrom went to court with the following contention: If he was sane, he deserved to be discharged as soon as he completed his sentence. And if he was not sane, he should be transferred to an ordinary psychiatric hospital. Thus, he argued, his constitutional rights were being violated insofar as he was required to remain in prison beyond the termination of his sentence.

The United States Supreme Court agreed. And as a result, "Operation Baxstrom," which was designed to effect the rapid release of 967 similarly confined patients from New York State's prison-hospitals was launched. These people were not merely predicted to be dangerous to others on the basis of their "insanity." They were considered to be **criminally insane,** held to be violent now and in the future because they had been violent in the past and because, additionally, they were psychologically distressed. Would those predictions hold up?

In fact, there were abundant false positives—individuals who did not act out violently—as well as false negatives—individuals released as nonviolent who later committed violent crimes. After four years, Steadman and Keveles (1972) reported that only 2.7 percent of those released patients had behaved dangerously and were either in a correctional facility or back in a hospital for

*Ala. Code SS22-52-1(a) (1977).
†West's Fla. Stats. Ann. SS394.467 (1986).
‡Baxstrom v. Herold, 383 U.S. 107 (1966).

FOCUS QUESTIONS

1. What is involuntary commitment?
2. Describe the definition of "mental disorder" as given by DSM-IV.
3. What are two problems that arise from the notion of dangerousness of an individual to self or others?
4. Describe what is meant by "grave disability" and explain why this criterion may lead to errors.

the criminally insane. Careful examination of those who were dangerous revealed no "set of factors that could have selected these returnees from all the Baxstrom patients without a very large number of false positives" (Steadman, 1973, p. 318).

Recently, however, there have been some improvements in our ability to predict violent behavior (Monahan, 1992). For example, there is mounting evidence that although past violent behavior may not be an indicator of future violent behavior, many of the mentally disordered *are* dangerous to others, particularly those who are experiencing psychotic symptoms (Monahan, 1992; Link, Cullen, and Andrews, in press). Moreover, some studies have indicated that clinicians, even inexperienced ones, can detect which male patients will become violent toward others, much better than chance and substantially better than they might have predicted had they relied only on the actuarial characteristics (e.g., age, race, and sex) of the patients (Lidz, Mulvey, and Gardner, 1993). (Unfortunately, they did not fare nearly as well in predicting female violent behavior.) Thus, it is not unreasonable for society to ask mental health professionals to attend to those who are believed to be dangerous to others. But such a request makes sense if, and only if, mental health professionals are truly able to predict who will become violent. Until such predictions become much more accurate, involuntary commitment on the basis of dangerousness to others will necessarily be a questionable procedure (Melton, Petrila, Poythress, and Slobogin, 1987).

Grave Disability   Many states permit commitment of distressed individuals when, as the result of their mental state (and for no other reason), they are unable to provide for their basic needs for food, shelter, clothing, health, and safety. Thus incapacitated, they become "passively dangerous," that is, dangerous to themselves, not because they might actively attempt suicide or mutilation, but because they will not do those things that seem necessary to stay alive and healthy.

California defines "grave disability" as "a condition in which a person, as a result of mental disorder, is unable to provide for his basic personal needs for food, clothes, or shelter."* But where those needs can be met through the willing assistance of relatives, as in the case of Emma Lake (see p. 698), should we deprive people of their liberty?

The real dangerousness of the grave disability criterion lies, of course, in the clause that makes the disability the result of their (prior) mental state. For how shall we know whether the disordered mental state that we presently see *arose* from the inability to provide for one's own basic needs, or *gave rise* to that inability? Homeless people, in particular, may well suffer psychological distress that *results from* their homelessness, quite apart from the distress that gives rise to homelessness. Therefore, estimates of the number of homeless people who suffer from psychological disorders—currently estimated at 30 percent (Morrissey and Levine, 1987; Koegel, Burnam, and Farr, 1988)—and who may require hospitalization, are likely to be substantially overstated.

DUE PROCESS OF LAW

Involuntary commitments are not entirely unlike imprisonment insofar as deprivation of liberty is concerned. Yet, few of the procedures that protect an al-

*Cal. Welfare and Institutional Code SS5008.

leged criminal defendant have been available to the psychologically distressed. They can be involuntarily hospitalized on an emergency basis for as little as twenty-four hours (in Georgia) to as long as twenty-eight days (in Oklahoma), entirely without a trial or judge, and often on the allegation of a spouse or friend. In some jurisdictions, hospitalizations can be extended indefinitely, simply on the word of a physician who deems the individual in need of further observation or treatment. And even when the matter is subjected to judicial review, the courts often rubber-stamp the physician's view, on the grounds that the hospitalization is being undertaken with the patient's best interests in mind. Thus, at many such judicial reviews, the patient need not be present, and commonly is not afforded an attorney. Many writers, and especially psychiatrist Thomas Szasz (1963), see in the involuntary commitment process an enormous and needless abuse of constitutional protection. Yet, no "plot" to deprive patients of their rights is intended in these procedures. Rather, because patients are held to be "sick," and because they are being sent to a hospital, the ordinary protections of criminal law have not been deemed necessary.

It seems only reasonable, however, to provide the psychologically distressed with the same privileges that are afforded to anyone whose liberty is threatened by state action—to criminal defendants, for example. These rights and privileges are collectively called "due process of law" and include:

- The right to be notified of trial in a timely manner
- The right to trial by jury
- The right to be present at one's own trial
- The right to legal counsel and the appointment of counsel in a timely manner
- The right to exclude unreliable evidence, such as hearsay evidence, from the testimony
- The right to challenge witnesses
- The privilege against self-incrimination
- The right to counsel at all interviews, including psychiatric interviews
- The right to know, with considerable precision, which laws one has violated and under which laws one stands accused.

In one case, *Lessard* v. *Schmidt*, Alberta Lessard complained that these very rights and privileges had been violated in her own involuntary commitment. Moreover, she argued that she had been detained without benefit of a hearing for better than three weeks, and could have been detained for as long as 145 days. The court held that Ms. Lessard's rights had been grossly violated and that all of her complaints were justified.* Commitment to a psychiatric hospital, the court held, may involve a serious restriction of individual rights. Those adjudged to be mentally ill, for example, like convicted felons, are unable to vote and may not serve on a jury. They may not drive a car. Their right to practice certain professions is restricted, as are their rights to make contracts, to sue, and to be sued. Those restrictions distinguish psychiatric from other kinds of medical care, and require that special attention be paid to due process issues.

In further support of its view that the psychologically distressed are entitled to due process, in the *Lessard* case the court pointed out that psychiatric hospitalization may not be an entirely therapeutic experience.

*Lessard v. Schmidt, 349 F. Supp. 1078 (E.D. Wis. 1972). The Wisconsin court's judgment was vacated by the U. S. Supreme Court in 1974, on procedural rather than substantive grounds.

Perhaps the most serious possible effect of a decision to commit an individual lies in the statistics which indicate that an individual committed to a mental institution has a much greater chance of dying than if he were left at large. Data compiled in 1966 indicate that while the death rate per 1,000 persons in the general population in the United States each year is only 9.5, the rate among resident mental patients is 91.8. . . . Figures for Wisconsin are similar. [One] study showed a death rate for the Wisconsin populace in general of 9.7 per 1,000 population per year (or less than 1 percent) and a death rate in Wisconsin mental institutions of 85.1 per thousand (or 8.51 percent).*

STANDARD OF PROOF

Throughout this section, we have emphasized that involuntary hospitalization involves a significant deprivation of liberty. The degree of deprivation may vary: some patients are permitted freedom on the hospital grounds, while others are locked into the ward, day and night. But even those in the former group experience a restriction on their liberty, in that they must be in the hospital rather than elsewhere. In order to so restrict a person's freedom one must prove that, in accord with the law, they belong in a psychiatric hospital. Mere allegation is insufficient. What standard of proof should be required? Generally speaking, three standards of proof are available in law: preponderance of evidence, beyond a resonable doubt, and clear and convincing proof.

Often called the 51 percent standard, ***the preponderance of evidence*** standard requires just enough proof to shift the weight of evidence to one side. This is the standard used in civil cases, where penalties are often monetary and do not involve deprivation of liberty.

Beyond a reasonable doubt is the most severe standard of proof and requires that the evidence be so compelling as to convince a reasonable listener beyond a reasonable doubt. This standard is used in criminal law, where the presumption of a defendant's innocence is very strong, and the cost of wrongful incarceration of an innocent person high indeed. It is often termed the 90

*Ibid, p. 1089.

FOCUS QUESTIONS

1. What are the three standards of proof available in law and which standard did the Supreme Court decide should be used in cases of involuntary commitment?
2. What rights do the courts believe should be accorded to patients who have been involuntarily committed?
3. What is the usual duration of civil commitment and what are the alternatives to hospitalization of those who are mentally disordered?
4. Describe the patients' rights movement.

percent or 99 percent standard, implying that the weight of evidence must be such that people would be willing to stake high odds on the guilt of the defendant.

Clear and convincing proof is an intermediate standard that is not quite so severe as that requiring proof beyond a reasonable doubt, but not as lenient as the 51 percent standard that requires the mere preponderance of evidence. Consider it the 75 percent standard.

Recalling what you have read here regarding the validity of predictions of dangerousness, and what you have learned in Chapter 7 on the reliability and validity of psychiatric diagnoses generally, what standard of proof should be invoked in order to commit a person involuntarily? In 1979, the matter was taken up by the Supreme Court in *Addington* v. *Texas.**

> Frank O'Neal Addington had been hospitalized seven times between 1967 and 1975. His mother now petitioned the court to have him involuntarily committed because he was both dangerous to himself and dangerous to others. In accord with Texas law, a jury trial was held to determine if he required hospitalization. The judge instructed the jury to determine whether there was "clear, unequivocal and convincing evidence"—the 75 percent standard—that Addington was mentally ill and required hospitalization for his protection and for the safety of others. The jury so found, but Addington appealed the decision to the U. S. Supreme Court on the grounds that the appropriate standard of proof should have been a tougher one—beyond a resonable doubt—the 90 percent standard.
>
> The Supreme Court held that the 90 percent standard was simply too severe. Given the uncertainties of psychiatric diagnosis and prediction, requiring proof beyond a reasonable doubt would render the state unable to commit many truly distressed people who were much in need of treatment. The preponderance of evidence standard, on the other hand, was much too lenient. If the state wanted to deprive a person of liberty, it needed to bear a greater burden of proof than that implied in the 51 percent standard. The Supreme Court therefore upheld the original decision, maintaining that the presentation of clear and convincing evidence—roughly 75 percent certainty—is the minimum standard for involuntary commitment and that states may not commit below this minimum standard (though they are free to fix standards that are higher than this required minimum).

Treatment

THE RIGHT TO TREATMENT

The *Lessard* and *Addington* cases dealt with the rights people can exercise and the standard of proof that is required before they can be involuntarily committed. What about after they have been committed? Is there a "right to treatment" for those who have been deprived of their liberty, presumably because they required psychiatric treatment? Oddly, and with few exceptions, the courts have been very cautious on this matter. They are understandably reluctant to invent new "rights." Yet, deprivation of liberty is a serious matter in a democratic society, and the courts have occasionally been responsive to cases in which hospitalization has occurred without the person receiving adequate treatment. Thus, in *Rouse* v. *Cameron*,† Judge David Bazelon clearly enunciated a right to treatment that was rooted in federal statute. He wrote:

---

*Addington v. Texas, 99 S. Ct. 1804 (1979).
†Rouse v. Cameron, 373 F. 2d 451 (D.C. Cir. 1966).

The purpose of involuntary hospitalization is treatment, not punishment . . . absent treatment, the hospital is transform[ed] . . . into a penitentiary where one could be held indefinitely for no convicted offense. (*Rouse v. Cameron,* 1966, p. 453)

Not all "treatments" count as treatment, however, Bazelon said:

The hospital need not show that the treatment will cure or improve him but only that there is a bona fide effort to do so. This requires the hospital to show that initial and periodic inquiries are made into the needs and conditions of the patient with a view to providing suitable treatment for him. . . . Treatment that has therapeutic value for some may not have such value for others. For example, it may not be assumed that confinement in a hospital is beneficial "environment therapy" for all. (*Rouse v. Cameron,* 1966, p. 456)

In *Wyatt v. Stickney,** Judge Frank Johnson insisted that the constitutional right to treatment is accorded to every person who has been involuntarily hospitalized. In his opinion, Johnson wrote:

To deprive any citizen of his or her liberty upon the altruistic theory that the confinement is for humane therapeutic reasons and then fail to provide adequate treatment violates the very fundamentals of due process.

▲ Conditions such as the starkness of this environment caused the courts to stipulate minimal objective standards of care in psychiatric hospitals.

In a later opinion,† Judge Johnson recognized that the absence of therapeutic regimens in the Alabama state hospitals was less a matter of simple neglect than it was one of personnel and facilities. He therefore stipulated minimal objective standards of care, standards, by the way, that were far below those recommended by the American Psychiatric Association. Thus, he required that for every 250 patients, there should be at least two psychiatrists, three additional physicians, twelve registered nurses, ninety attendants, four psychologists, and seven social workers. While these may seem a large number of personnel for every 250 patients, remember that patients are in the hospital twenty-four hours a day, seven days a week, and that personnel are needed to take care of them on a continuous basis.

In that same opinion, Judge Johnson made clear that patients have a right to privacy and dignity, to the least restrictive regimen necessary to achieve the purposes of commitment, and to freedom from unnecessary or excessive medication. He affirmed their right to send sealed mail and to use the telephone—privileges that are often denied patients on the grounds that they might say things that they would later have cause to regret. Finally, Johnson said that each patient was entitled to an individual treatment plan, and to periodic review of his or her plan and progress.

Judge Bazelon's and Judge Johnson's opinions have been hailed by civil libertarians and mental health professionals alike as major steps forward in the treatment of the psychologically distressed. Although other courts have not concurred that there is a right to treatment, these opinions have had far-reaching effects (see Box 18–1).

DURATION OF CIVIL COMMITMENT

It is very difficult to obtain recent statistics regarding the length of time civilly committed individuals spend in the hospital. Data from 1980 (Rosenstein,

*Wyatt v. Stickney, 325 F. Supp. 781 (M.D. Ala. 1971).
†Wyatt v. Stickney, 344 F. Supp. 343 (M.D. Ala. 1972).

Box 18–1

KENNETH DONALDSON'S SAGA

Perhaps Kenneth Donaldson needed treatment. But did he get it?

Kenneth Donaldson was already forty-eight years old when his parents, themselves in their seventies, petitioned for his commitment to Florida State Hospital at Chattahoochee. His life had not been an easy one until then, Donaldson frankly points out in his book, *Insanity Inside Out* (1976). He had had one psychiatric hospitalization of three-months' duration some thirteen years earlier. It was a hospitalization that followed him, and marred his life subsequently. Afterwards, his marriage had failed, his relationship with his children had cooled, he had had difficulty holding a job, and sometimes he had felt that people were out to get him. But he was not dangerous to himself, had never been dangerous to others (although his father had alleged he was in order to get him committed), and he emphatically did not want to be committed to Chattahoochee. One hospitalization was more than enough.

The judge who committed Donaldson told him that he would be in the hospital for "a few weeks." A progress note written less than three months after he was admitted indicated that he appeared to be in remission. And because his first hospitalization had been brief, there was every reason to expect this one to be brief too. Nevertheless, Donaldson remained in Florida State Hospital for fourteen-and-half years.

Donaldson is a Christian Scientist. Medication and electric shock treatments were both offered to him, but he refused them on religious grounds. What care and treatment did he get then? None. He rarely saw Drs. O'Connor or Gumanis, his physicians, and then only briefly. Grounds privileges and occupational therapy were denied him during the first ten years of his hospitalization. Some six years after he had been hospitalized, Helping Hands, Inc., a reputable organization that operates halfway houses for mental patients, offered to care for Donaldson. But his psychiatrist, Dr. O'Connor, refused to release him to anyone but his parents. By this time, his parents were too old and infirm to accept that responsibility, and presumably Dr. O'Connor knew that. Finally, a college friend made four separate attempts to have Donaldson released in his custody. His requests were either refused outright or frustrated.

During this period, Donaldson smuggled letters out of the hospital to anyone who might help. Often, however, mail sent through hospital channels would be opened or simply thrown out. Donaldson's teenage daughter wrote "Daddy, I know you are not sick. But why don't you write?" "I was writing," Donaldson says. "Then her letters stopped." (Donaldson, 1976, p. 84). As a result, he acquired a reputation for being a difficult person. But he had much to be difficult about. Day after day was spent in a locked crowded room with sixty other people, nearly one-third of whom had undergone criminal commitments. At night, some of the patients would have fits. It was frightening. Some of the beds in this crowded room were so close together that they touched. Donaldson lived in constant fear that someone would jump him during the night.

Donaldson sought the help of the Mental Health Law Project, a Washington, D.C., group of lawyers who serve the legal needs of the mentally distressed. And, finally, in 1971, Donaldson sued for his release and for damages from Drs. O'Connor and Gumanis, alleging "intentional, malicious, and reckless disregard of Donaldson's constitutional rights." The jury awarded Donaldson compensatory and punitive damages from both physicians. The physicians appealed, and the case went up to the Supreme Court, where many of the justices were simply outraged over Donaldson's incarceration (Woodward and Armstrong, 1979). On January 26, 1975, the Court unanimously wrote in *O'Connor* v. *Donaldson:*

A state cannot constitutionally confine . . . a nondangerous individual who is capable of surviving safely in freedom by himself or with the help of willing and responsible family members or friends.*

*O'Connor v. Donaldson, 422 U.S. 563, 95 S.Ct 2486 (1975).

▲ Kenneth Donaldson after the Supreme Court ruled in his favor.

Steadman, MacAskill and Manderscheid, 1986) indicate that there were more than 300,000 involuntary civil commitments, whose median length of hospitalization in general medical facilities was ten days, and in state and county mental hospitals, twenty-five days. Those who were diagnosed as suffering brain disorders or schizophrenia, as one might expect, remained hospitalized substantially longer. A recent study of civil commitment in California (there are no national data here) found that roughly 60 percent of those committed were held to be dangerous to themselves, 49 percent were dangerous to others, and 32 percent were gravely disabled (Segal, Watson, Goldfinger, and Averbuck, 1988). As you might well imagine, a substantial proportion of mentally disordered people are committed because they meet more than one criterion.

RELEASING MENTAL PATIENTS

Opinions written in such cases as *Rouse* v. *Cameron* and *Wyatt* v. *Stickney* have alerted people to the plight of psychiatric patients, and promise to improve their fate. But unfortunately, they have also had a major unintended consequence. Faced with the prospect of pouring more money into psychiatric care, many states have taken the least expensive route and have simply discharged patients from psychiatric hospitals, and closed the hospitals. During the seventies, for example, California closed a majority of its psychiatric hospitals and cut back severely on funding of mental health programs. Other states followed suit. As a result, thousands of people who were formerly housed in psychiatric hospitals were shunted to "board and care" homes in local communities. The new visibility of these people has frequently created a harsh and angry community reaction. The powerful stigma associated with those labeled mentally ill, and particularly the violence and unpredictability that is often erroneously attributed to mental patients, creates enormous community fear and backlash.

Are patients better off in board and care facilities than in psychiatric hospitals? We don't yet know. Psychiatric hospitals have yet to establish their ability to improve substantially the lives of involuntarily committed patients (Kiesler, 1982a, 1982b). Moreover, informal conversations with these patients strongly indicate that they prefer being in the community to being warehoused in psychiatric hospitals, and there is evidence that they are no worse off in the community than in hospitals (Lamb, 1979). But neither are they as well off as they would like to be or should be. Many find employment difficult to procure, and social relationships difficult to establish. They react strongly to community stereotypes about them. Given these facts, a policy that establishes and supports *community-based* treatment is clearly called for.

The Patient's Rights Movement

The wholesale release of patients into the community has had some positive effects. In many communities, former psychiatric patients have established self-help organizations which, in addition to providing social networks and employment opportunities, also have given the mentally ill a political base. A Presidential Commission on Mental Health, appointed by President Carter in 1978, led to the passage of Section 501 of the Mental Health Systems Act of 1980, otherwise known as the Patients' Bill of Rights (see Box 18–2). While this law is only advisory in nature, most states provide at least some of those rights, and some states provide all of them.

Box 18–2

SUMMARY OF THE PATIENTS' BILL OF RIGHTS

The right to appropriate treatment and related services in a setting which is most supportive and least restrictive of a person's liberty.

The right to an individualized, written treatment or service plan.

The right, consistent with one's capabilities, to participate in and receive a reasonable explanation of the care and treatment process.

The right not to receive treatment without informed, voluntary, written consent, except in a documented emergency or as permitted under applicable law for someone who has been civilly committed.

The right not to participate in experimentation in the absence of informed, voluntary, written consent.

The right to be free from restraint or seclusion except in an emergency situation pursuant to a contemporaneous written order by a responsible mental health professional.

The right to a humane treatment environment that affords reasonable protection from harm and appropriate privacy.

The right to confidentiality of personal records.

The right to have access to personal mental health records and have a lawyer or legal representative have reasonable access to records if the patient provides written authorization.

The right to private conversations, reasonable access to telephones and mail, and to visitation during regular visiting hours.

The right to timely and meaningful information about one's rights at the time of and after admission.

The right to assert grievances with regard to the infringement of rights.

The right to have a fair, timely, and impartial grievance procedure provided.

The right of access to, including private communications with, any available rights protection service or qualified advocate.

The right to exercise other rights without reprisal, including denial of appropriate treatment.

The right to referral as appropriate to other providers of mental health services upon discharge.

The right to confidentiality of and access to records continues following one's discharge.

The patient has a right that his attorney or legal representative has reasonable access to the patient/client, the facility at which the patient resides and, with written authorization, the patient's medical and service records.

SOURCE: Adapted from the Mental Health Systems Act, 1980.

To assure that the rights of the mentally ill are protected, former patients, their families, and others have joined to form a network of patients' rights advocates, such as NAMI (National Alliance for the Mentally Ill) or CAMI (California Alliance for the Mentally Ill). These advocates work for changes in state laws, monitor mental health facilities, and in some cases, provide legal representation for patients. Their efforts have resulted in considerable improvement in the conditions under which patients are housed and treated.

Abolish Involuntary Hospitalization?

Involuntary commitment gives rise to serious problems. Coerced hospitalization and coercive treatment please no one and require that one ask whether involuntary hospitalization should be abolished altogether. Thomas Szasz is one

▶ Patients who have been re-leased from mental hospitals may remain unable to take care of themselves and end up walking and sleeping on the streets.

of the most critical analysts of the nature of psychiatry and its role in society today. Szasz points out that mental illness is different from physical illness. There are no clear or generally accepted criteria of mental illness. "[L]ooking for evidence of such illness is like searching for evidence of heresy: Once the investigator gets into the proper frame of mind, anything may seem to him to be a symptom of mental illness" (Szasz, 1963, p. 225). As a result, Szasz believes that psychiatry has a great potential for social abuse, particularly as it lends itself, through involuntary commitment, to ridding society of all manner of deviants and eccentrics, all in the name of treating mental illness. Szasz is not opposed to voluntary hospitalization, provided patients are frankly told whether or not they will receive the best treatment. But he believes involuntary hospitalization should be abolished.

Some critics of psychiatry oppose not only involuntary hospitalization, but involuntarily treatment as well. Citing the adverse side effects of many antipsychotic medications, patients in a number of jurisdictions have sued to assert the right to refuse the "chemical straitjacket." Holding that medications may be administered to nonconsenting patients only in an emergency or after a full, fair adversary hearing, the Colorado Supreme Court recognized the risk involved in the use of antipsychotic drugs:

> Although the decision to forcibly medicate a patient with antipsychotic drugs undoubtedly involves an aspect of professional medical judgment in connection with psychiatric diagnosis and treatment alternatives, the fact remains that the decision itself directly implicates the patient's legal interests in personal autonomy and bodily integrity. Antipsychotic medications, either alone or in combination, can cause numerous and varied side effects and carry with them the risk of serious and possibly permanent disabilities in the patient. . . . The effects of these drugs can be far more debilitating to the patient than the physical restraint incident to the involuntary commitment process.*

*People v. Medina, 705 P.2d 961, 968 (Colorado Supreme Court, 1985).

Involuntary commitment is sometimes called **civil commitment,** the process used to hospitalize people who have committed no crime. **Criminal commitment,** on the other hand, refers to the coerced psychiatric hospitalization of people who have acted harmfully but are not legally responsible because they lack a "guilty mind" or *mens rea.* "Where there is no *mens* (i.e., mind) there can be no *mens rea*" the legal maxim goes (Fingarette and Hasse, 1979, p. 200). In the eyes of the law, such people are insane, and the legal defense used in their cases is called the **insanity defense.**

The Insanity Defense

The insanity defense requires that the defendant was wholly or partially irrational *when the crime took place,* and that this irrationality affected his or her behavior. The psychologist or psychiatrist who serves as an expert witness in this matter is required to reconstruct the defendant's state of mind as it was before and during the crime. This is not a simple task. If diagnostic opinions are often unreliable for *present* behavior, as we saw in Chapter 7, how much more unreliable are they for speculative reconstructions of the past? No wonder, then, that experts for the defense are often contradicted by equally capable experts for the prosecution, and that judges and jurors will disagree on the defendant's state of mind when he committed the crime (Low, Jeffries, and Bonnie, 1986).

Popular opinion notwithstanding, the insanity defense is not widely used. It is invoked in fewer than 1 out of 400 homicide cases that come to trial, even more rarely in nonhomicide trials. And it is successful in many fewer cases than that, mainly by agreement between the prosecutor and defense attorneys. Even when successful, the defense usually leads to long-term incarceration in an institution for the criminally insane, a fate sometimes worse than incarceration in prison. Nevertheless the role and meaning of the insanity defense is one of the most hotly debated issues in criminal law. Why should that be?

While the insanity defense is something of a bother in the criminal law, "we must put up with [it] . . . because to exclude it is to deprive the criminal law of its chief paradigm of free will" (Packer, 1968). Thus, the insanity defense is the exception that proves the rule: the notion that each of us is responsible for his or her behavior is strengthened by the recognition that some of us patently are not (Stone, 1975; Rosenhan, 1983). Below are three cases in which the insanity defense has been used (adapted from Livermore and Meehl, 1967). Is there *mens rea* in each of these defendants?*

> **Case 1: The Pigtail Snipper.** Victor Weiner, a hair fetishist, was charged with assault for snipping off a girl's pigtail while standing on a crowded bus. His experience before cutting off the pigtail (which was corroborated by psychiatric testimony and by an acquaintance with whom he had discussed this problem several

*51 Minn L. Rev. 789, 833–55 (1967).

days earlier) was one of mounting tension, accompanied by a feeling that was close to anxiety and erotic excitement. He made various efforts to distract himself and place himself in situations where he would be safe from performing this act, but finally he gave in to the impulse and boarded the bus with a pair of scissors in his pocket. Victor was diagnosed "sociopathic personality disturbance, sexual deviation, fetishism."

Case 2: The Axe-handle Murderer. Arthur Wolff, a fifteen-year-old, was charged with murdering his mother.* During the year preceding the crime, Wolff "spent a lot of time thinking about sex." He made a list of the names and addresses of seven girls in his community whom he planned to anesthetize and then either rape or photograph nude. One night, about three weeks before the murder, he took a container of ether and attempted to enter the house of one of these girls through the chimney. But he became wedged in and had to be rescued. In the ensuing weeks, Wolff apparently decided that he would have to bring the girls to his house to achieve his sexual purposes, and that it would therefore be necessary to get his mother (and possibly his brother) out of the way first.

On the Friday or Saturday before he murdered his mother, Wolff obtained an axe handle from the family garage and hid it under the mattress of his bed. On Sunday, he took the axe handle from its hiding place and approached his mother from behind, raising the weapon to strike her. She sensed his presence and asked him what he was doing; he answered that it was "nothing," and returned to his room and hid the axe handle under his mattress again. The following morning, Wolff ate the breakfast that his mother had prepared, went to his room, and took the axe handle from its hiding place. He returned to the kitchen, approached his mother from behind, and struck her on the back of the head. She turned around screaming. He hit her several more times, and they fell to the floor fighting. He got up to turn off the water running in the sink, and she fled through the dining room. He gave chase, caught her in the front room, and choked her to death with his hands.

Wolff then took off his shirt and hung it by the fire, washed the blood off his face and hands, read a few lines from the Bible or prayer book lying upon the dining room table, and walked down to the police station to turn himself in. He told the desk officer, "I have something I wish to report . . . I just killed my mother with an axe handle." The officer testified that Wolff spoke in a quiet voice and that "his conversation was quite coherent in what he was saying and he answered everything I asked him right to a T."

At his trial, four expert witnesses testified that Arthur Wolff had been suffering from schizophrenia when he murdered his mother.

Case 3: The Delusional Informer. Calvin Ellery was a paranoid schizophrenic who experienced delusions and hallucinations, and who believed that the Masons were plotting to take over the government. He believed, moreover, that the Masons had learned that he was aware of their intentions, and that because he was a potential informer, the Masons had determined to do away with him.

As a result of delusional misinterpretation of certain things he had heard on a news broadcast, Ellery believed that "today is the day for his execution." When a salesman with a Masonic button on his lapel came to the front door, he was sure that the salesman had been sent to kill him. When the salesman reached into his pocket for his business card, Ellery was convinced that he was reaching for a revolver. Ellery drew his own weapon and shot first in self-defense.

*People v. Wolff, 61 Cal. 2d 795, 800.

TABLE 18–1

		ACQUITTAL UNDER THE VARIOUS INSANITY DEFENSES				
Case	Diagnosis	M'Naghten "right-wrong" test	Durham "product of mental disease" test	American Law Institute (ALI) "appreciate and conform" test	Guilty but mentally ill	Insanity Defense Reform Act
Victor Weiner (Pigtail snipper)	Fetishist	Guilty—he knew it was wrong.	Not guilty—fetishism is a mental disease according to DSM-IV.	Maybe—depends on court's assessment of his ability to conform his conduct to law.	Guilty	Guilty
Arthur Wolff (Axe-handle murderer)	Schizo-phrenic	Guilty—he knew it was wrong.	Probably acquitted—if he were not schizo-phrenic, he probably would not have murdered.	Probably guilty if affectively, he knew murder was wrong.	Guilty	Guilty
Calvin Ellery (Delusional informer)	Paranoid schizo-phrenic	Not guilty—he thought he was shooting in self-defense.	Not guilty—the killing was clearly the product of his delusions.	Not guilty—he could appreciate the criminality of his conduct.	Guilty	Not guilty

TESTS FOR DETERMINING SANITY

What determines if the insanity defense can be used? (see Table 18–1). When is a person considered to be so insane in the eyes of the law that the ordinary cannons of criminal law do not apply? Because the answer to these questions is crucial to the very meaning of criminal law, the questions themselves have generated hot dispute. Historically, there have been three views of the insanity defense: the M'Naghten rule, the Durham test, and the American Law Institute rule. And recently, under the Insanity Defense Reform Act, another standard has been introduced (see Figure 18–1).

M'NAGHTEN: THE "COGNITIVE" FORMULA

In 1843, Daniel M'Naghten came to London for the purpose of killing Sir Robert Peel, the British Prime Minister. In so doing, M'Naghten was responding to a "voice of God," which had instructed him to kill the Prime Minister. Peel, however, was traveling with Queen Victoria on that day, and Edward Drummond, Peel's secretary, was in the Prime Minister's carriage. Drummond caught M'Naghten's bullet and was killed. During the trial, M'Naghten testified that:

> The tories in my native city have compelled me to do this. They follow and persecute me wherever I go and have entirely destroyed my peace of mind. . . . I cannot sleep at night in consequent of the course they pursue towards me. . . . They have accused me of crimes of which I am not guilty; they do everything in their power to harass and persecute me; in fact they wish to murder me.

The trial was remarkable in that M'Naghten's defense counsel relied heavily on *Medical Jurisprudence of Insanity* (1838), a recently published work by Dr. Isaac Ray. M'Naghten, the defense counsel argued, was clearly deranged, in that he suffered delusions of persecution (and, in modern terms, command hallucinations). It was one of the first times that psychiatric testimony had been permitted in a murder trial, and the judges were so impressed that the Lord Chief Justice practically directed a verdict for M'Naghten. But subsequently, Queen Victoria, who had been subject to attempted assassination

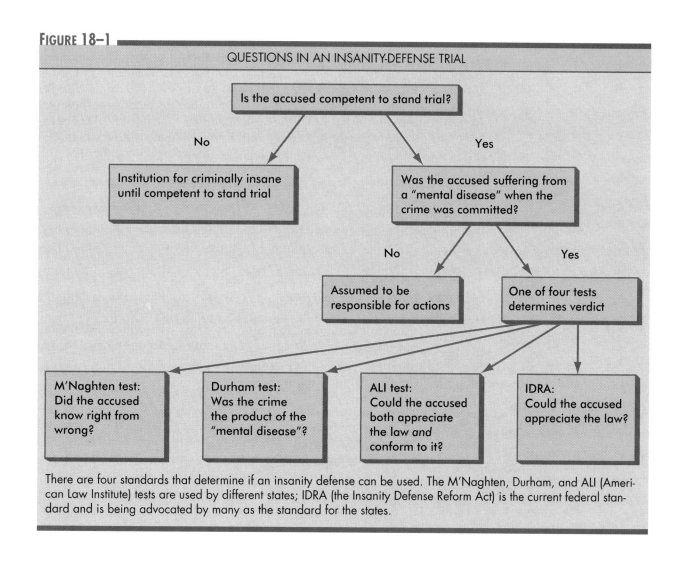

FIGURE 18–1

QUESTIONS IN AN INSANITY-DEFENSE TRIAL

Is the accused competent to stand trial?

No → Institution for criminally insane until competent to stand trial

Yes → Was the accused suffering from a "mental disease" when the crime was committed?

No → Assumed to be responsible for actions

Yes → One of four tests determines verdict

M'Naghten test: Did the accused know right from wrong?

Durham test: Was the crime the product of the "mental disease"?

ALI test: Could the accused both appreciate the law *and* conform to it?

IDRA: Could the accused appreciate the law?

There are four standards that determine if an insanity defense can be used. The M'Naghten, Durham, and ALI (American Law Institute) tests are used by different states; IDRA (the Insanity Defense Reform Act) is the current federal standard and is being advocated by many as the standard for the states.

FOCUS QUESTIONS

1. What is criminal commitment?
2. Describe the insanity defense.
3. What are the historical standards for determining sanity, and what is the standard that has been mandated by the Insanity Defense Reform Act?
4. What does it mean when a defendant is found incompetent to stand trial?

three times in the preceding two years, called in the Lord Chief Justice, as well as the other fourteen justices, and reproved them. They buckled quickly and wrote what has since been known as the **M'Naghten rule,** under which Daniel M'Naghten would clearly have been convicted! According to that rule,

> It must be clearly proved that, at the time of the committing of the act, the party accused was laboring under such a defect of reason, from disease of the mind, as not to know the nature and quality of the act he was doing; or, if he did know it, that he did not know he was doing what was wrong.

The M'Naghten test is widely used in the United States. Nearly half of the states use it alone as the yardstick for insanity, while other states use the M'Naghten rule in conjunction with other rules (see Box 18–3). It is a relatively narrow test, which relies merely on whether the accused suffered "a disease of the mind," what he understood about the nature of his actions, and whether he understood that those actions were wrong. But while the test is narrow, it taxes everything we have learned about abnormal psychology. What, for example, are diseases of the mind? Do they really exist, or are they simply metaphoric? And how do we know whether someone understood his actions when he attempted murder, and whether he knew that murder was "wrong"?

Under the M'Naghten rule, only Calvin Ellery, the delusional informer, would be acquitted, for only he clearly did not "know the nature and quality of the act he was doing," believing that he was acting in justifiable self-defense. The axe-handle murderer's behavior was clearly bizzare, yet because there was no evidence that he failed to distinguish right from wrong, he could not be acquitted according to the M'Naghten rule. Similarly, Weiner, the pigtail snipper, though clearly disturbed and seemingly caught up in an impulse that ultimately overcame his best efforts at suppression, could not be acquitted under the M'Naghten rule. He, too, knew right from wrong.

DURHAM: "THE PRODUCT OF MENTAL DISEASE"

In *Durham* v. *United States,*[*] Judge David Bazelon broadened the insanity defense to state that "an accused is not criminally responsible if his unlawful act was the product of mental disease or mental defect." Notice the difference between the Durham "mental disease" and the M'Naghten "right-wrong" test. In the **Durham test,** incapacitating conditions, such as the inability to tell right from wrong are not specified. One goes directly from "mental disease" to the act (Brooks, 1974a), leaving it to advanced knowledge in psychiatry and psychology to determine whether the act was or was not a product of mental disease or mental defect. Under the Durham rule, the axe-handle murderer would probably have been acquitted on the grounds that, absent his schizophrenic condition, he would not have murdered his mother. Likewise, defining fetishism as a "mental disease," the pigtail snipper, too, would have been acquitted on the grounds that were he not a fetishist, he would not have had such a prurient interest in little girls' pigtails. And of course, Calvin Ellery, the delusional informer, would also have been acquitted under the "mental disease" test (he was paranoid schizophrenic), as well as under the M'Naghten "right-wrong" test.

*Durham v. United States, 214 F. 2d 862 (D.C. Cir. 1954).

As Justice Bazelon maintained, the Durham rule was an experiment, one that extended for some eighteen years, from 1954 until 1972, and during which time, a view of criminal responsibility and nonresponsibility was developed. Fundamentally, the Durham rule was withdrawn for two reasons: (1) it relied too heavily on the expert testimony of psychiatrists, rendering judge and jury wholly dependent upon psychiatric testimony for the determination of criminal responsibility, and (2) it was as difficult then as it is now to know and attain agreement about what constituted a "mental disease." The metaphor itself left much to be desired, implying a distinct and verifiable organic state. Moreover, one could never be sure which of the disorders listed in the *Diagnostic and Statistical Manual of Mental Disorders* qualified. Should stuttering, tobacco dependence, and sociopathy all be considered mental diseases that can produce unlawful acts? The seeming breadth of the Durham rule created problems that were difficult to adjudicate and that ultimately, led to its near demise. Only one state, New Hampshire, still uses the *Durham* test.

THE AMERICAN LAW INSTITUTE (ALI) RULE: "APPRECIATE AND CONFORM"

In *United States* v. *Brawner,** some eighteen years after the *Durham* case, the Durham mental disease test was succeeded by a modification of the insanity defense that had earlier been propounded by the American Law Institute. That rule is considerably more specific than the Durham rule, and yet not so narrow as the M'Naghten rule. It states:

> 1. A person is not responsible for criminal conduct if, at the time of such conduct, as a result of mental disease or defect, he lacks substantial capacity either to appreciate the criminality (wrongfulness) of his conduct or to conform his conduct to the requirements of law.
> 2. As used in the Article, the terms "mental disease or defect" do not include an abnormality manifested only by repeated criminal or otherwise antisocial conduct. (American Law Institute, 1985, p. 62).

*United States v. Brawner, 471 F. 2d 969 (D.C. Dir. 1972).

In the *Brawner* case, the court tried to further narrow the meaning of "mental disease." Citing an earlier case,* it wrote:

> [A] mental disease or defect includes any abnormal condition of the mind which substantially affects mental or emotional processes and substantially impairs behavior controls.

The **ALI rule,** as modified in the *Brawner* case, is used in twenty-one state courts. Under that standard, Calvin Ellery would, of course, be acquitted. Convinced that the Masons were both plotting to take over the government and asassinate him, Ellery clearly lacked "substantial capacity. . . to appreciate the criminality (wrongfulness) of his conduct." The verdict with regard to Victor Weiner, the pigtail snipper, would depend on whether the court was willing and able to assess the strength of Weiner's desire and, therefore, his ability "to conform his conduct to the requirements of law."

The outcome of the case of Arthur Wolff, who murdered his mother because she seemed in the way of his sexual schemes, depends wholly on how a jury would interpret the word *appreciate* in the section of the ALI rule that says ". . . he lacks substantial capacity . . . to appreciate the criminality (wrongfulness) of his conduct. . . ." Wolff, "knew" he did wrong in killing his mother, for he confessed immediately at the police station. But did he really *appreciate* that this was wrong? Did he "feel it in his heart" affectively, or did he merely "know" cognitively? If the latter, he would be acquitted under the ALI rule. If the former, he would be convicted of murdering his mother.

THE INSANITY DEFENSE REFORM ACT

On June 21, 1982, a federal jury found John W. Hinckley, Jr., not guilty by reason of insanity in his attempted assassination of President Reagan. The jury's verdict was based on its perception that Hinckley was unable "to conform his conduct to the requirements of the law," which is the "volitional" standard of the ALI rule. But the public was simply outraged about that verdict. Only three days after the jury acquitted Hinckley, the Subcommittee on Criminal Law of the Committee of the Judiciary of the United States Senate began hearings on limiting the insanity defense. And over the next two and a half years, similar hearings were conducted in the legislative hearing rooms of many states.

At issue was the volitional prong (whether the criminal impulse could be resisted) of the ALI standard. Was it truly an *irresistible* impulse, or simply an impulse not resisted? Whether volition itself was a useful notion was a matter about which psychologists and psychiatrists could not agree, raising serious questions about whether the law should even include it. Ultimately, in 1984, President Reagan signed the Insanity Defense Reform Act, which eliminated the volitional prong of the insanity defense in federal courts. The new federal standard states that:

> It is an affirmative defense to a prosecution under any federal statute that, at the time of the commission of the acts constituting the offense, the defendant, as a result of a severe mental disease or defect, was unable to appreciate the nature and quality or the wrongfulness of his acts. Mental disease or defect does not otherwise constitute a defense.

*McDonald v. United States, 312 F. 3d 847 (D.C. Cir. 1962).

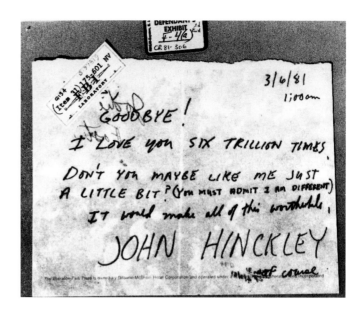

The Sheraton-Park Plaza is owned by Gilbane-McShain Hotel Corporation and operated under license [...] Hotel [...] Incorporated

► John Hinckley, Jr., successfully used the insanity defense at his trial for the attempted assassination of former President Ronald Reagan.

It had previously been the task of the prosecution to prove sanity, and sanity of course is very difficult to prove. With the new federal standard, the burden of proving by clear and convincing evidence that the defendant was insane, and hence not responsible for his actions, was placed on the defendant.

GUILTY BUT MENTALLY ILL (GBMI)

Perhaps as the result of public perceptions that defendants are "beating the rap" by entering insanity pleas, some states have abolished the "not guilty by reason of insanity" verdict, replacing it with the verdict of "guilty but mentally ill" (GBMI). A finding that a defendant is guilty but mentally ill results in commitment to a mental institution rather than to a prison.*

The GBMI verdict is an instance of a legislative rush to action, and it is mistaken on at least two counts. In the first place, the insanity defense is rarely invoked and much more rarely successful. The public impression of its usefulness arises nearly wholly from sensational news stories, not from accurate estimates of incidence. Moreover, the GBMI verdict is a contradiction in its own terms. In order to be guilty, one needs to have been able to form a morally coherent intent to harm (*mens rea*—see p. 710). But mental illness exonerates one precisely because one is held to be *unable* to form such an intent. How then can one be simultaneously guilty and mentally ill?

Clearly, enormous effort has gone into defining the meaning of insanity and limiting its effects in criminal trials. But that effort has not yet paid off in terms of outcome. Regardless of which definition of insanity is used, people seem to convict and acquit in pretty much the same proportions (James, 1959; Finkel, 1989; Steadman, McGreevy, Morrissey, Callahan, Robbins, and Cirincione, 1993). One possible reason for this disappointing outcome is that the law typically gives jurors only two choices: guilty (for whatever reason), or not guilty (for whatever reason). But when jurors in simulated trials were permitted to distinguish among several shades and types of insanity, they were con-

*Thirteen states had adopted this standard by 1985.

siderably more able to tailor their verdicts to the requirements of law (Finkel, 1990, 1991).

Competence to Stand Trial

For every defendant found not guilty by reason of insanity, at least a hundred defendants are found incompetent to stand trial and are sent to institutions for the criminally insane until they are able to be tried (Bacon, 1969). The average confinement of people committed as incompetent is 6.4 months, according to the most recent data available (Steadman, Monahan, Hartstone, Davis, and Robbins, 1982), and that is likely a high estimate for today. Yet, it occasionally happens that people alleged to be incompetent to stand trial, such as Mr. Junius Wilson (see Chapter 1) are remanded to institutions for the criminally insane for decades, and simply forgotten. At one such institution, three people among those who were now fully able to stand trial but who had been "overlooked" had been incarcerated for forty-two, thirty-nine, and seventeen years respectively—this, before any determination of their guilt had been made! (McGarry and Bendt, 1969). Moreover, even when treatment is accorded, there is mounting evidence that neither the competency evaluations nor the treatments within psychiatric hospitals are worth much (Melton, Weithorn, and Slobogin, 1985). As a result, many states are turning toward community- rather than hospital-based competency evaluation and treatment.

What does "incompetent to stand trial" mean? Most statutory definitions are similar to New York's, which defines an "incompetent person" as one "who as a result of mental disease or defect lacks capacity to understand the proceedings against him or to assist in his own defense."* The intent of the statute is noble, growing out of the English common law tradition that forbids a trial in absentia. While the defendant may be physically present, when he is judged incompetent to stand trial, he is believed to be ***psychologically absent,*** and the trial is delayed until he can participate in his own defense.

Until 1972, there were no limits on *how long* people could be committed until judged competent to stand trial. What if they would *never* be competent to stand trial? Such a dilemma arose tragically in *Jackson* v. *Indiana.*†

> Theon Jackson was a mentally defective deaf-mute. He could not read, write, or otherwise communicate except through limited sign language. In May, 1968, at the age of twenty-seven, Jackson was charged with separate robberies of two women, both of which robberies were alleged to have occurred in the previous July. The first robbery involved a purse and its contents; the total value was four dollars. The second concerned five dollars in cash. Jackson entered a plea of not guilty through his attorney.
>
> Had he been convicted, Jackson would likely have received a sentence of sixty days. But he could not be tried because, in accord with Indiana law, Jackson was examined by two psychiatrists who found that he lacked the intellectual and communicative skills to participate in his own defense, and that the prognosis for acquiring them was dim indeed. Moreover, Jackson's interpreter testified that Indiana had no facilities that could help someone as badly off as Jackson to learn minimal

*New York Criminal Code S730.10(1) (1993).
†Jackson v. Indiana, 406 U.S. 715 (1972).

Theon Jackson's case resolved one issue—that a person who would never be competent to stand trial could not be detained indefinitely. Many others are still unresolved. What of a person who might some day be competent to stand trial. How long may he or she be held? Some states set no limits. Other states limit the duration of hospitalization to the time of the maximum sentence the individual would have received if he had been competent to stand trial and found guilty. Others, like New York, limit incarceration, depending upon the charge. Federal courts require release after eighteen months. But do even those limited periods violate a person's right to bail and and to a speedy trial? And should they count against time served if convicted? Can a person be required to take medications against his or her will in order to be competent to stand trial? Practices in these matters vary enormously across states and are unlikely to be systematically resolved in the near future because such defendants, by definition, often lack the resources to press their claims vigorously.

As a result, some have urged that the notion of incompetence to stand trial be abolished on the grounds that even if impaired, the defendant is better off tried. "Withholding trial often results in an endless prolongation of the incompetent defendant's accused status, and his virtually automatic civil commitment. This is a cruelly ironic way by which to ensure that the permanently incompetent defendant is fairly treated" (Burt and Morris, 1972, p. 75). This view, however, violates the Supreme Court's dictum in *Pate* v. *Robinson* that "the conviction of an accused person while he is legally incompetent violated due process . . ."*

IDENTITY, MEMORY, AND THE NATURE OF EVIDENCE

Insanity and its various defenses are not the only psychological issues that confront the courts. There are two phenomena that are likely to capture a great deal of attention during the coming years because they raise important questions about responsibility and about evidence. They are: ***multiple personality*** and ***recovered memories.***

*Pate v. Robinson, 383 U.S. 375, 378 (1966).

Multiple Personality

Ordinarily, when someone is accused of a crime, at issue is whether the person committed the crime or not. But consider the following case:

> James Carlson stood trial for rape, theft, forgery and kidnapping. He claimed that he had eleven different personalities and was suffering from a multiple-personality disorder. Among those personalities were Jim, who committed the rape; Woofie, a fifteen-year-old boy; Jimmy, a seven-year-old; and Laurie Burke, a seventeen-year-old lesbian prostitute. In fact, at one point during the trial, Carlson took the witness stand as Laurie, wearing a skirt, black tights, pink sweater, high-heel shoes, press-on nails, and a wedding band.
>
> In her summation, Carlson's lawyer put the issue to the jury as follows. "James Carlson's body committed the crimes. But James was not in control of the body when any of the acts occurred." The prosecutor put the matter differently. "Your Honor, the statements [Carlson's confession] were made by a human being, sitting here today. The charges are not brought against any one [personality]. They are brought against the human being."
>
> As is commonly the case in such trials, there was a battle of experts. One psychologist testified that Carlson suffered a multiple personality disorder that developed after Carlson had been molested in kindergarten. Another psychologist thought Carlson was faking, and faking badly.
>
> The jury convicted Carlson. After the trial, Carlson acknowledged that he had read about multiple personalities in a psychology textbook and faked his performance, both because he wanted to avoid prison, and because he had fallen in love with his attorney. She "would see more of me when I was a multiple than if I was just myself." (*Arizona Republic*, 1994)

Carlson's case raises three very dramatic questions. First, does the multiple personality disorder really exist? Is it possible for separate personalities to exist within the same skin, and not know each other? Second, if multiple personalities do exist, how can we know them? How do we distinguish real from faked multiple personalities? And third, assuming the defendant is convicted, how can we punish the whole person for the acts of only one of his personalities? Fortunately, none of these questions had to be answered in Carlson's case.

Recovered Memories

The idea of repression is central to many views of personality, and especially to psychodynamic views (cf. Chapter 4). Experiences and memories that evoke shame, guilt, humiliation, or self-deprecation are often repressed, especially when those experiences conflict with one's self-image. When a memory is repressed, however, that memory does not disappear. It continues to exist and is simply inaccessible to consciousness, at least for the present. When psychological conditions change, the memory may reappear and the individual may become aware again of experiences long forgotten (Loftus, 1993, 1994).

The renewed awareness, however, is quite problematic. First, when you recover the memory of an event that transpired, say, twenty years ago, how can you be sure what you are recalling actually occurred? For some memories, that's hardly a problem. If you suddenly remember that you were lost in a department store when you were five years old, you can often find confirmation

▲ James Carlson took the witness stand dressed as a woman during his 1994 trial in Arizona. He pleaded not guilty on the grounds that he suffered from multiple personality disorder and that his other personalities had committed his crimes. He was later found to be faking MPD.

FOCUS QUESTIONS

1. What are the problems that arise when a person who claims to have multiple personalities is on trial for a crime?
2. What is the delayed discovery doctrine?
3. What are some of the problems surrounding the recovery of repressed memories?

(or disconfirmation) by turning to your parents or siblings. But what if the event recalled occurred privately and to your shame? What if the event concerned sexual molestation, for which there was no witness? How, then, do we determine whether what is "recalled" occurred? The conviction with which the belief is held is, unfortunately, no sure guide. A person who now vividly "recalls" having been sexually abused by her father may well have a father who, just as vividly, has absolutely no recollection of the alleged events. That person may confuse an event that was only imagined or suggested with a true one, incorporating elements of the truth, such that this imagined memory has the feeling of authenticity (see Box 18–4).

Box 18–4

RECOVERED MEMORIES AND SUGGESTIBILITY

Paul Ingram had been widely respected in Olympia, Washington, and not without reason. He was chairman of the local Republican party, chief civil deputy in the sheriff's department, and an active member of his church. His personnel file was filled with commendations from ordinary citizens who thanked him for his courtesy. Across seventeen years, no letter of complaint had ever been received about him. His wife Sandy operated a day-care center out of their home. Neighbors described them as strict but loving parents to their children.

But on November 28, 1988, fifteen minutes after he arrived at work, Sheriff Gary Edwards summoned Ingram to his office and relieved him of his automatic pistol. Ericka and Julie Ingram, then twenty-two and eighteen respectively, had accused their father of sexual molestation. While Ingram could not remember ever having molested his daughters, he added, "there may be a dark side of me that I don't know about." By the end of the day, Ingram confessed. "I really believe that the allegations did occur and that I did violate them and abuse them and probably for a long period of time. I've repressed it." Asked why he was confessing if he couldn't remember the violations, Ingram replied, "Well, number one, my daughters know me. They wouldn't lie about something like this."

Ingram's daughters' allegations had first surfaced some three months earlier. They were at a religious retreat when the leader told the sixty girls in attendance that she had a vision of someone in the audience who had been molested by a relative. There are a number of conflicting stories concerning how this occurred, but according to the leader, she simply prayed over Ericka and felt herself prompted by the Lord to say "You have been abused as a child, sexually abused." Ericka wept quietly. The leader received another divine prompting, and said, "It's by her father, and it's been happening for years." Ericka then began to sob hysterically. The leader urged her to obtain counselling in order to work through the memories that were causing her so much pain. Later, Ericka's memories included her brothers, as well as her father's friends among those who had molested her. Later still, her mother and brothers were included, not only in sexual abuse, but in satanic rituals that involved, among other things, sacrificing a baby.

After each of these allegations, Paul Ingram would go into a trancelike state, and would retrieve vivid recollections of these events. Encouraged by his pastor and detectives in his own department, Ingram found more and more to confess to. Nearly everyone, except his accused friends and one social psychologist, seemed convinced that Ingram was precisely as his children had described him: utterly corrupt.

The psychologist, Dr. Richard Ofshe, was intrigued by Ingram's ability to imagine scenes of abuse, and then come to feel, with great confidence, that they had actually occurred. This seemed to Ofshe more like suggestibility than anything else, and that hypothesis was worth testing. Ofshe told Ingram that one of his sons and one of his daughters had reported that Ingram had made them have sex together. At first, Ingram, quite correctly, couldn't remember having done that. Then he closed his eyes and acknowledged that he could see his son and daughter. The next time Ofshe visited, Ingram said he now had clear memories of his children having sex. And at their third meeting, Ingram proudly produced a three-page confession that described how he had directed his children to have sex with each other, and what they had done.

Of course, none of this was true. By the time Mr. Ingram realized that his visualizations had been fantasies, not real memories, he obtained a new lawyer and filed to retract his confessions on the grounds that they had been coerced by his investigators. But it was too late to stop the legal process, and Ingram was convicted. And in a sad footnote to a painful case, Ericka Ingram appeared at her father's leniency hearing, to demand that the judge give him the most severe sentence possible. Paul Ingram was sentenced to twenty years.

Second, the recovery of long-buried memories creates significant problems for the statute of limitations, which requires that claims for injuries must be instituted promptly. That requirement insures that memories remain fresh, and that witnesses can be examined. But where the incidents have been forgotten, how can one institute legal proceedings if one can't remember the harmful events?

Because there has been a rise in the incidence of recovered memories where the alleged crime consists of physical and sexual abuse, a substantial number of states have made an exception to the statute of limitations for such cases, much as they do for certain medical malpractice cases. If, for example, a surgeon left a roll of tape in a patient's stomach, but the tape was not discovered until many years later when the patient had a physical examination, the doctor can nevertheless be sued for malpractice under the ***delayed discovery doctrine,*** which holds that the statute of limitations does not begin to toll until all the facts that are essential to the complaint have been discovered. Similarly, when memories of sexual abuse have been repressed, no cause of action can be filed until they are recovered. The statute of limitations begins to toll from that point.

Those problems aside, it is clear that recovered memories are not merely a "family affair," but rather touch on many lives and on the nature of psychological treatment, as the following case indicates:

> Holly Ramona was nineteen years old when she consulted Marche Isabella for treatment. Holly's problem was bulimia and depression. Ms. Isabella suggested that bulimia might be rooted in childhood sexual abuse. Soon, Holly had terrifying flashbacks in which she recalled her father repeatedly molesting her between the ages of five and sixteen. In order to confirm her own memory, she undertook a "truth serum" interview. Reassured of the accuracy of her memory, she instituted legal proceedings against her father.
>
> Holly's father, Gary, was just as convinced that the sexual abuse had never occurred, but was rather suggested to Holly by her therapist. He sued the therapist, contending that Holly's allegation had caused his wife to seek a divorce, alienated him from his other children, and led directly to the loss of his job as an executive. The jury returned a verdict in his favor.
>
> According to the jury's foreman, the jury had not explored the efficacy of recovered memories, but had concentrated on the therapist's alleged negligence. Holly Ramona, however, remains convinced of the truth of her memories and feels that she benefited greatly from her therapy. And Gary Ramona remains equally convinced that "Holly's supposed memories are the result of the [the therapist's] drugs and quackery, not anything I did." (*New York Times,* 1994.)

THE SOCIAL AND POLITICAL ABUSE OF ABNORMAL PSYCHOLOGY

The ideal underlying clinical psychology and psychiatry is to help humankind, but in various societies at various times, these professions have been used toward political ends. In order to confine or control individuals holding dissident views, some political leaders have sanctioned abuses of personal liberties in the name of psychiatry. In large part, the potential for abuse arises from the very definition of abnormality that was discussed in Chapter 1. There we suggested that whether or not people are seen as abnormal depends on whether they possess a "family resemblance" to other abnormal people. There need not be an identity, or perfect match, between the behaviors of those people and the behaviors of abnormal people; so as long as *some* elements are similar, individuals might be considered abnormal by society. Among the behaviors or elements of abnormality are: whether the person produces discomfort in others, the degree to which his or her behavior is unconventional, and the degree to which the behavior violates idealized standards. If an individual's behavior triggers these criteria, he or she may be labeled abnormal, even though other criteria of abnormality, such as intense suffering, are absent. People who hold different views from those of a society's leaders might be seen (or made to be seen) as unconventional, or in violation of idealized standards. It is therefore easy to consider them abnormal and to overlook the fact that they fail to meet any of the other criteria for abnormality.

Beyond the political abuse that relies on the definitional ambiguities of abnormality, the potential for abuse arises from the fact that the meanings of abnormality change dramatically over time. For example, in DSM-II, which was approved by the American Psychiatric Association in 1968, homosexuality was listed as a mental disorder. But new information revealed that as many as 10 percent of the adult population practice homosexuality. The behavior, therefore, was no longer as unconventional as it had seemed, nor did it violate community standards as intensely as it had earlier. Consequently, in 1976, by a vote of its membership, the association decided that homosexuality was no longer a mental disorder. Similarly, in 1966, the American Association for Mental Deficiency reduced the IQ required for designating a person "mentally retarded" from 80 to 70, thereby releasing more than a million people from the retarded category (Bryan and Bryan, 1975).

Attitudes toward work, sexuality, manners, the opposite sex, marriage, clothing—indeed, toward most of the significant aspects of social life—have changed over the decades and will continue to change. Canons of appropriate behavior and attitude are fundamental to judgments of normality and abnormality. As these canons change, so will change our notions of what is normal, and what is abnormal.

Potential for abuse arises also from the fact that society endows psychologists and psychiatrists with enormous power. Perry London (1986) says they constitute a "secular priesthood"; Thomas Szasz (1963) sees (and decries) the rise of the "therapeutic state." But any general reservations we might have about psychiatry and psychology often dissolve when our own lives are touched by psychological distress. We tend to accept the views of "experts." Our personal reliance on a practitioner, and our vulnerability to the practitioner's judgments and recommendations, make all clients of psychiatry and psychology particularly vulnerable to abuse. Below we will distinguish broadly between two kinds of potential abuse: abuse by state and abuse by society.

Abuse by State

Psychiatric diagnoses, involuntary hospitalization, and treatment with neuroleptic drugs have been used in many places to stifle political dissent. Political psychiatry was heavily relied upon in the former Soviet Union. Anatoli Koryagin, a Soviet psychiatrist who emigrated to the West, described the Soviet use of psychiatric hospitals and drugs to punish political activists. At least 210 *sane* people—others claim higher figures (Podrabenek, in Fireside, 1979)—

FOCUS QUESTIONS

1. How have psychiatric diagnoses been used to stifle political dissent?
2. How does society stigmatize ordinary people who have sought psychiatric care?

▼ Pyotr Grigorenko

were interned in Soviet prison-hospitals for political reasons (Bloch and Reddaway, 1977). Pyotr Grigorenko, a distinguished general who had served in the Red Army for thirty-five years, provides a case in point. At the age of fifty-four, he began to question the policies of the Communist party of which he was a member. Ultimately, he was remanded for psychiatric examination at Moscow's Serbsky Institute, where his diagnosis read "paranoid development of the personality, with reformist ideas arising in the personality, with psychopathic features of the character and the presence of symptoms of arteriosclerosis of the brain." Shortly thereafter, he underwent an examination by a second group of psychiatrists who found him admirably sane and vigorous. But a third commission overruled the second and, as a result, Grigorenko spent six years in three of the most difficult Soviet "psychoprisons" before he was permitted to emigrate to the United States (Fireside, 1979).

While such abuses were especially well documented in the former Soviet Union, which had developed a psychiatric nomenclature especially for political dissidents (Medvedev and Medvedev, 1971; Fireside, 1979), they also existed in the United States, as shown in the case of Ezra Pound:

> When the Second World War was over, Ezra Pound, the eminent poet, was taken into custody by the American troops in Italy, returned to the United States, and charged with treason. Pound had lived in fascist Italy during the war and had supported Mussolini. It was alleged that the broadcasts that Pound made from Rome were treasonous. Pound denied the charge, but he never came to trial. Instead, the government and his attorneys agreed that he was incompetent to stand trial. He was therefore remanded to St. Elizabeth's Hospital in Washington, D.C., and effectively imprisoned without trial. Thirteen years later, in 1958, he was still considered "insane," incurably so, but not dangerous to others. He was therefore released.

All his life, Pound had been an eccentric: enormously conceited, flamboyant, sometimes downright outrageous. But he had never had a brush with the law, nor had he been remanded for psychiatric care. But because his politics were aversive, his eccentricities were invoked to indicate that he was not of sane mind and therefore that he could not stand trial (Torrey, 1983). As you saw in Chapter 7, relatively innocent behaviors change meaning drastically when observed in a diagnostic context. In Pound's case, conceit and flamboyance became "grandiosity of ideas and beliefs," contributing to the psychiatric impression that he was of unsound mind.

It has occasionally been argued (P. Suedfeld, personal communication) that Pound was *protected* by psychiatry, without which he would have faced a worse fate: prison. That may well have been the case, though without a trial, there is no way to know whether and for how long Pound would have been imprisoned. But even if one grants that Pound was protected from prison by psychiatric intervention, his case remains an illustration of the political use of psychiatry in the United States.

Abuse of psychology and psychiatry by the state occurs when the state is threatened by the actions of the individual. Fear underlies the state's abuse. It also underlies abuse by society, to which we now turn.

Abuse by Society

During the 1972 presidential campaign, George McGovern, the front-running Democratic nominee, proposed Senator Thomas Eagleton as his vice-presidential running mate. Eagleton apparently neglected to tell McGovern that he had been treated for depression, either because he viewed that as a private matter or because the stigma of such treatment might deprive him of the candidacy. In the latter, he was right: the press soon learned that Eagleton had undergone treatment and made a national story of it. After much pressure, McGovern took Eagleton off the ticket. There was no question of Eagleton's effectiveness: he had served splendidly as a senator from Missouri. Rather, there was considerable fear that he would weaken the ticket. He was, after all, stigmatized (Rosenhan, 1975; Reich, 1986).

Society stigmatizes ordinary people who have sought psychiatric care, often to the disadvantage of both the individual and society, as the following case indicates:

> Myra Grossman had had a difficult childhood and adolescence. Yet she managed to survive well enough to graduate high school, enter college, and be at the very top of her class during her first two years. Conflicts with her parents, however, and a nagging depression continued unabated and, during her third year, she left school to seek treatment. She began seeing a psychotherapist and subsequently entered a private psychiatric hospital. During that year, Myra developed considerable ability to deal with her own distress and her family conflicts. She returned to college, continued to major in both chemistry and psychology, earned her Phi Beta Kappa in her junior year, and graduated magna cum laude.
>
> During her senior year, she applied to medical school. Her Medical College Aptitude Test (MCAT) scores were extraordinarily high, and she had won a New York State Regent's Medical Scholarship. But she was rejected by all thirteen schools to which she had applied.
>
> She consulted an attorney, and they jointly decided to concentrate on the "easiest" school that had rejected her. During the trial, it became known that fewer than 8 percent of those admitted to this school had won the Regent's Medical Scholarship, that none had been admitted to Phi Beta Kappa, and that she possibly had the highest MCAT scores of any applicant. She was an attractive person, obviously well

motivated, clearly bright. Why then had she been rejected? Clearly, it was because of her prior psychiatric hospitalization.

Ms. Grossman and her attorney marshaled clear evidence that she was quite well integrated psychologically. Five psychiatrists and a psychologist testified in effect that she was the better for her prior troubles, and that they had no doubt that she could successfully complete medical school and become a first-rate doctor. She and her attorney successfully demolished the contention that she might still suffer from her prior "illness." But still, the judge ruled against her. Ms. Grossman might have appealed that decision, and might well have won her appeal had not a far better medical school admitted her when the ruling came down. (Ennis, 1972)

SUMMARY

1. The constitutional privileges that are available to ordinary citizens are not extended to the severely distressed, who can be deprived of liberty through *involuntary commitment,* often without trial.

2. There is no one federal standard for involuntary commitment, but all state statutes require that individuals who are committed must be mentally disordered, dangerous to themselves or others, or suffering from a "grave disability." The notion of dangerousness, especially, is rife with scientific, legal, and moral problems.

3. Involuntary commitment deprives a person of liberty. Before it occurs, *clear and convincing* evidence must be marshaled that indicates that the person requires hospitalization.

4. Several significant court decisions have held that those committed to psychiatric hospitals have a *right to treatment* that includes individual diagnosis and the preparation of a treatment plan that is periodically reviewed. One negative consequence of right-to-treatment decisions has been the decline in support for mental health programs, as the states often prefer to cut back their support for these programs rather than incurring the additional costs of implementing proper treatment. A positive result of deinstitutionalization, however, has been the growth of the patients' rights movement, including self-help organizations and patients' rights advocates.

5. *Criminal commitment* can occur either because a person was "insane" at the time of the crime, or because he or she is presently psychologically incompetent to stand trial.

6. The *insanity defense* requires that the defendant was wholly or partially irrational when the crime took place, and that this irrationality affected his or her behavior. While the insanity defense seemingly protects those who commit crimes while distressed, such people are commonly sent to prison-hospitals, where care is worse than in prisons themselves, and incarceration longer. Because being indefinitely committed to a psychiatric hospital is often worse than going to prison, the insanity defense is rarely used.

7. Historically, there have been three views of the insanity defense: the M'Naghten "right-wrong" test, the Durham "product of mental disease" test, and the American Law Institute (ALI) "appreciate and conform" rule. The modern standard, which is now used in all federal courts, was insti-

tuted in 1984 as the *Insanity Defense Reform Act.* It requires only that the defendant "was unable to appreciate the nature and quality or the wrongfulness of his acts." Yet another standard, termed *guilty but mentally ill* is used in some states, but is a contradiction in terms. Today there is not a uniform standard in Western countries. In the United States, a growing number of states have increasingly favored the insanity defense as described in the Insanity Defense Reform Act.

8. The notion of *competence to stand trial* is rooted in the right of every person to defend himself against accusations. A person judged incompetent to stand trial is sent to an institution for the criminally insane until he is able to be tried, which often means a long incarceration. The courts have decided that people who can never become competent to stand trial need not be "hospitalized" forever. But there is still no uniform practice regarding how long those who are treatably incompetent may be committed, and whether the time spent in such commitment is later to be subtracted from the defendant's sentence.

9. Multiple personality disorders constitute a perplexing problem for the legal system. If one personality has no knowledge, or control, of the perpetrating personality, who is to be punished? Moreover, if one personality is guilty, are *all* personalities to be punished? Fortunately, proving that one suffers a multiple personality disorder has been sufficiently difficult that the courts have not had to deal with the issues of guilt and punishment.

10. Memories that were once repressed and are now available raise difficult issues of proof, mainly because the events often transpired decades before the memory of those events was recovered. Juries have been willing to convict on the basis of such recollections, though recent testimony has increasingly come under scrutiny.

11. Psychiatry and psychology are particularly prone to social and political abuses. In the United States and elsewhere, people who should have been given their day in court have been summarily committed to psychiatric hospitals, there to languish, often for many years.

12. Considerable stigma attaches to seeking or requiring psychological care.

QUESTIONS FOR CRITICAL THINKING

1. What does it mean to "psychiatrize" a case and how does this cause people to come up with different solutions than they might have if the case had not been psychiatrized?

2. What are the problems of committing an individual based on the criterion of dangerousness to self and others and on the grave disability criterion?

3. Describe some recent cases in which defendants have been found guilty but mentally ill. Should those who are guilty and able to form an intent to commit a crime be excused for their actions?

4. Should a person with multiple personalities be held responsible when one of those personalities is found guilty of committing a crime?

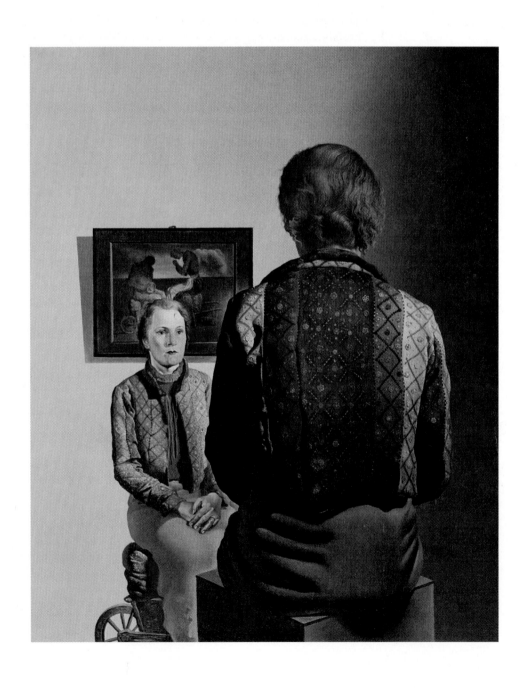

CHAPTER 19

A Consumer's Guide to Psychological Treatment

CHAPTER ORGANIZER

WHO TREATS?

- Know the variety of people who treat psychological difficulties.

THE COMMON INGREDIENTS OF THERAPY

- Be able to describe the common treatment factors and how they affect the outcome of therapy.

THE VARIETY OF TREATMENT

- Understand the differences between specific and global therapies.

THE CHOICE OF TREATMENT

- Be able to describe how specific treatments are able to alleviate specific symptoms such as those arising from anxiety, depression, and schizophrenia, and how global treatments are used to deal with "problems of self."

OUTREACH AND PREVENTION: THE HOPES OF COMMUNITY PSYCHOLOGY

- Understand how community efforts to prevent and contain psychological disorders can reduce the need for expensive professional treatment.

Where does one turn when psychological problems arise? The answer to that question has changed with the times. A century ago, people with problems might have been sent off to a good friend, a relative, or perhaps a clergyman who would have offered them sympathy, wisdom, and prayer. But today, as one writer observes, we have a "secular priesthood," a panoply of professional and nonprofessional counselors and therapists, all of whom stand ready to deal with the psychological troubles that were once the province of family and church (London, 1986). One in five people will seek the advice of these therapists sometime during their lives, fully half of them for problems that are quite serious and painful. How should they go about it? From the many available therapists and therapies, how should they choose the ones that are most likely to help, and help quickly?

In this chapter, we bring together a group of issues associated with treatment, often issues that have been remarked upon earlier. First, we describe those who treat psychological difficulties. We then consider the ingredients that all good therapies have in common, regardless of whether they are biological, psychodynamic, cognitive, behavioral, or humanistic, and regardless of whether they are practiced by highly trained professionals or by nonprofessionals. Understanding these ingredients should enable anyone to make a better choice of a therapist, and also to avoid the pitfalls of poorly practiced treatments (which are also described in this chapter). Subsequently, we recommend the best treatments for certain kinds of problems. Our recommendations are based on good evidence where that exists and on clinical wisdom where it does not. Finally, we discuss community psychological approaches that are concerned with prevention as much as treatment, and with social and economic remedies as much as psychological ones.

WHO TREATS?

A large number of people and disciplines are concerned with treating psychological difficulties, and it is sometimes hard to distinguish among them (see Figure 19–1). Some professional training takes many years to acquire, while training in other skills may require just a few months. Some therapists are certified and licensed in the states in which they reside. Others are not. A potential client is always entitled to inquire carefully about the training, licenses, certificates, and experience of anyone he or she consults. Do not be embarrassed to do this. It is equivalent to looking carefully at all the rooms in a house before purchasing or renting it. Professionals and nonprofessionals alike respect these questions; they spare all concerned from making costly mistakes.

Psychologists who offer psychological assessment and therapeutic services have obtained advanced graduate training in clinical, counseling, or school psychology. Usually, but not invariably, they hold a Ph.D. (Doctor of Philosophy) or a Psy. D. (Doctor of Psychology) degree. The former is a *scientific* degree. It emphasizes training in research, as well as clinical diagnosis and psychotherapy. The Psy. D. is an *applied* degree that certifies training mainly in diagnosis and treatment. Both degrees require a minimum of four or five years of study *beyond* the bachelor's degree, and include, or are immediately followed by, an extensive applied internship. In addition, nearly all states require psychologists to pass a licensing or certification examination.

Not all psychologists are qualified to assess and treat. Only those trained in clinical, counseling, or school psychology should be consulted. **Clinical psychologists** work mainly with people who suffer psychological difficulties, **counseling psychologists** deal with vocational problems as well, while **school psychologists** focus on academic difficulties, mainly with young people.

Psychiatrists are physicians who, after completing college, have earned a medical degree, and have completed a three-year residency in a mental health facility. Subsequently, many but not all psychiatrists take an examination in psychiatry and become board-certified. Psychiatrists are the only psychological professionals who can prescribe medications and administer such treatments as electroshock. Of course, psychiatrists often make use of psychological treatments as well.

Psychiatric social workers have completed a two-year postgraduate program in individual and group social work techniques, which includes extensive training in interviewing and in treatment.

Psychiatric nurses are centrally concerned with the care of hospitalized psychiatric patients. Beyond their basic courses in nursing, they receive training in psychiatry and psychology, as well as supervised experience on a psychiatric unit. On any psychiatric ward, the nurse is usually the person in charge of ward management, housekeeping, and recreation, as well as the one who administers medication.

FOCUS QUESTIONS

1. Distinguish among clinical, counseling, and school psychologists.
2. Which psychological professionals can prescribe psychotropic medications?
3. What additional training must psychoanalysts receive?
4. What are some examples of nonprofessional peer self-help groups and how do they attempt to help people?

FIGURE 19–1

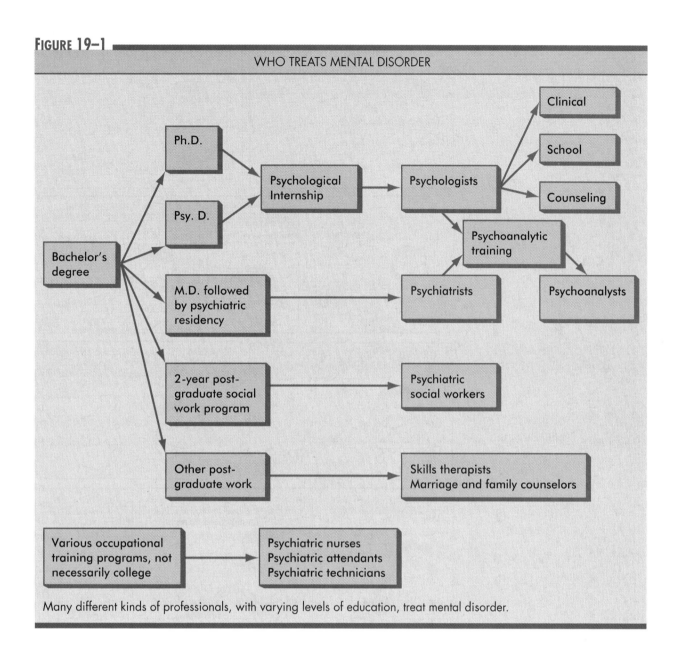

WHO TREATS MENTAL DISORDER

Many different kinds of professionals, with varying levels of education, treat mental disorder.

Psychoanalysts are fully trained mental health professionals—psychiatrists mainly, but also psychologists, social workers, and sometimes clergy—who have undertaken further training in a specific treatment approach, psychoanalysis and psychoanalytic psychotherapy. Such training is offered in psychoanalytic training institutes, and requires several years to complete. Psychoanalysts-in-training must undergo their own personal psychoanalysis, as well as treat several clients psychoanalytically, before they are considered fully accredited.

The ***clergy,*** that is, ministers, rabbis, and priests, are increasingly being trained to do personal counseling, not only with problems of a distinctly religious nature, but often with problems that go quite beyond those. While the

quality of training in pastoral counseling, as it is sometimes called, is highly variable, many clergy augment their seminary training in graduate departments of psychology or social work, and in postgraduate institutes.

Psychiatric attendants or ***aides*** are paraprofessionals who work exclusively in psychiatric hospitals. Their training can vary widely. Some are high school graduates. Others have attended community colleges, many of which train mental health paraprofessionals to work on psychiatric wards. Most attendants receive brief on-the-job training to work with the severely disturbed. From the viewpoint of hospitalized patients, the attendants are the most important people in their day-to-day lives. It is the attendants with whom they interact most, and who determine whether their experience in the hospital will be pleasant or unpleasant.

Skills therapists also work in psychiatric hospitals and have special abilities in the work-related, recreational, or artistic realms. These include occupational, art, and educational therapists, music and dance therapists, as well as recreational therapists of all kinds. These therapists enable patients to pass time pleasantly and constructively. They also provide a setting for developing psychosocial skills and for expressing personal problems. A dance therapist, for example, may enable a person to express through dance feelings that cannot otherwise be expressed verbally.

Marriage and family counselors deal with relationship problems that arise within the family. These therapists usually have postgraduate training, but commonly they do not possess doctoral degrees. The quality of their training is highly variable.

The provision of therapeutic services has become a big business that has spawned a host of nonprofessional therapists during the past decade or two. Massage therapists, hypnotherapists, primal therapists, Zen therapists, and bioenergetic therapists, are among those who, for want of a better term, we call **miscellaneous therapists.** Becoming one or another of these therapists may require little or much training. But it is not formal training at a recognized academic or medical institution. Commonly, the government neither licenses these therapists nor certifies their skills, nor are there professional organizations that control their activities. Finally, by and large what they offer has not been evaluated for therapeutic effectiveness. As a result, *caveat emptor*—client, beware!

A young man had been "tight and tense" for more than two years when he began to experience paranoid delusions and hallucinations. He was referred by a friend to a massage therapist, who treated the client with deep massage while encouraging him to recall "the memories that are stored in your muscles and bones." This treatment continued for eighteen months. The man's condition deteriorated until finally he became so discouraged and disordered that he required hospitalization. Had he been seen earlier by a trained therapist, there seems little doubt that a combination of drugs and counseling would have brought about improvement in short order.

Several nonprofessional peer self-help groups exist to help overcome specific problems, although their effectiveness varies. These include Alcoholics Anonymous (AA), Weight Watchers, TOPS (Take Off Pounds Sensibly), as well as specialized support groups. These latter groups originally grew out of the political needs of minority groups and now include advocacy groups for women, the handicapped, older adults, retired individuals, those with alternate lifestyles, and those who have been committed to mental institutions. Fundamentally, such advocacy groups are political and intellectual. Through the common exploration of "personal" problems, group members come to understand that their difficulties are often shared by others. The recognition that painful individual problems are neither unique nor idiosyncratic encourages members to seek larger solutions to these problems, often through social and political action.

Jane Williams experienced enormous discomfort at her office. Her boss continually put his arm around her and frequently suggested that they see each other after work. At first, Jane felt that she had somehow provoked his interest. Resolving to put an end to his advances, she dressed conservatively for work and kept a professional distance. To no avail. Finally, with great embarrassment, she mentioned the problem at a meeting of a women's group to which she belonged, and she was surprised to find that many of her friends had had the same experience. The fact that the problem was not idiosyncratic gave her considerable comfort, and subsequently, a diplomatic visit to the personnel office brought about a much-hoped-for transfer to another department.

THE COMMON INGREDIENTS OF THERAPY

Psychological therapy consists of a systematic series of interactions between a trained therapist who has been authorized by society to minister to psychological problems, and one or more clients who are troubled, or troubling others, because of such problems. The goal of psychological therapy is to produce cognitive, emotional, and behavioral changes that will alleviate those problems. While professional therapists are trained for the job, and paid as well, that should not blind us to the fact that there are strong similarities between the ways they function and the manner in which friends, relatives, and clergy dealt with those problems in earlier times and continue to deal with them today.

In fact, it would be a serious mistake to identify treatment wholly with the training of the therapist and the nature of the treatment he or she dispenses, for there is much more to treatment than that. In order for treatment to be maximally effective, a therapeutic relationship needs to be established, one that is voluntary and cooperative and that maximally fulfills the expectations of each participant. Only rarely do clients enter treatment suddenly or lightly. The decision to seek professional help is commonly preceded by agonizing conflict, conflict that may last for months or years. To begin with, most people try to solve their problems by themselves. Then, they may seek out parents, teachers, ministers, and friends. But often, it is only when all else fails that they seek professional treatment. And then, they come with a headful of hopes, expectations, and information; some of it accurate, some inaccurate, and much of it likely to affect the course of treatment.

Unlike many other transactions, the effectiveness of the therapeutic relationship depends heavily for its success on the free choices, hopes, expectations, and relationships of the participants. You can have your shoes redone by the neighborhood cobbler and neither your personal view of him nor his of you matters for the success of that venture; only his cobbling skill counts. Not so in psychological treatment. There, a host of "common treatment factors" play a large role in determining outcome (Kazdin, 1979). The success of highly skilled therapists is augmented massively, or greatly reduced, by the interplay of such common treatment factors as the free choices of the client, his or her hopes and expectations, the personal qualities of the therapist, and the match between those qualities and the needs of the client. We begin with the matter of free choice because choice affects the therapeutic relationship from the very outset.

FOCUS QUESTIONS

1. How does free choice in entering treatment affect the therapeutic experience?
2. How does the Role Induction Interview positively affect psychological treatment?
3. What personal characteristics of therapists play a central role in treatment?
4. What is a therapeutic alliance?

Free Choice and Treatment

You can bring a horse to water, the saying goes, but you can't make it drink. That adage holds for psychological treatment, too. Clinical experience strongly suggests that children who are dragged unwillingly into treatment, spouses who enter marriage therapy under threat of divorce, and patients who are involuntarily committed to psychiatric hospitals, all suffer substantial deficits in motivation and understanding that make treatment less effective. Sometimes coercive encouragement is all that is available, but the best way to enter treatment is willingly and fully informed; any other way substantially diminishes the likelihood of successful outcome, regardless of the kind of therapy.

The role of choice and volition in therapeutic outcome was splendidly demonstrated by Devine and Fernald (1973). Clients who suffered snake phobias were shown films of four possible treatments. Some clients were permitted to choose the treatment they preferred; others were randomly assigned to treatment: and yet a third group was required to undergo a nonpreferred treatment. Those who received the treatment they preferred had the more successful therapeutic experience. In selecting their own treatment, clients were able to exercise control over a portion of the therapy process, and this sense of control (see Chapter 5) may well have influenced therapeutic outcome.

Clients who are forced into treatment likely will view it as a mere exercise in compliance, or a punishment. Unless time and effort are taken to convince them otherwise, treatment will fail. Conversely, those who enter treatment of their own free choice are more likely to benefit from it. Their hopes and expectations are themselves curative, greatly augmenting the effectiveness of any treatment. We therefore turn to the nature of hopes and expectations in therapy.

Hopes and Expectations

A unique characteristic of humans is that their expectations about the future powerfully affect their experiences and behaviors in the present (Frank, 1978). The hope of eventual salvation has sustained countless people, enabling them to endure lifetimes of misery. For others, as we saw in Chapter 11, the belief that the future is hopeless has intensified their depression. In similar fashion, expectations strongly affect psychological treatment. "Expectation . . . coloured by hope and faith," Freud wrote, "is an effective force with which we have to reckon . . . in *all* our attempts at treatment and cure" (Freud, 1905/1976, p. 289).

MOLDING CLIENT EXPECTATIONS

Clients and therapists often have distorted expectations of each other that may impede therapeutic progress. Insight therapists, for example, expect clients to talk about their feelings, experiences, and often, their dreams. But clients, especially those from lower-class backgrounds, tend to talk about their psychological symptoms much as they might describe a sore throat to a physician. Their expectations about how therapists behave are frustrated when they are asked about feelings and dreams. Conversely, therapists gain the impression that clients will not profit from treatment when the clients persist in merely describing their ailments and when they continue to be reluctant to discuss feelings and dreams. One result of these jointly disappointed expectations is that lower-class clients drop out of insight therapy at a considerably higher rate than middle- and upper-class clients.

To deal with this problem, Jerome Frank and his colleagues devised a Role Induction Interview, during which clients' expectations about treatment could be molded (Hoehn-Saric, Frank, Imber, Nash, Stone, and Battle, 1964; Nash, Hoehn-Saric, Battle, Stone, Imber, and Frank, 1965; Orne and Wender, 1968). In a controlled study, lower-class clients were interviewed briefly before entering treatment and told what they could expect. Psychotherapy, they were told, is a way of learning to deal more effectively with life's problems, but it takes time and practice to implement what is learned. They were told that four months would be needed before improvement was seen, and even then, that they would still have problems, though they would be coping more effectively. Further, they were told that the therapist would talk very little, but would listen carefully and try to understand the problems. They were advised that they were to talk freely, describe fantasies and daydreams, express feelings, and especially, feelings toward the therapist. The concept of resistance was explained in everyday language and was described to them as evidence that the client was approaching and dealing with issues that were both significant for progress and difficult to face. Such difficulties were to be viewed as a positive sign of progress. A second group of clients was given no information on what they might expect during treatment.

The therapeutic results for clients who participated in the brief interview were remarkable. First, their drop-out rate declined precipitously. Therapists were behaving the way they were supposed to behave, so clients experienced less need to terminate. Second, therapist ratings of clients' improvement were considerably higher for these clients than for the control group that had not gone through the Role Induction Interview. Finally, clients who had experienced the Role Induction Interview rated themselves as considerably more improved on their target complaints than did those who had not participated in the interview.

The Role Induction Interview may have brought client expectations in line with their therapists' expectations, led clients to behave in ways that increased therapist optimism about, and liking for them. These considerations correlate highly with clients' tendency to remain in therapy (Rosenzweig and Forman, 1974; Shapiro, 1974), and with therapist ratings of client improvement (Shapiro, Struening, Shapiro, and Barten, 1976).

Anticipatory socialization of the sort that is conveyed in such interviews has been found to affect clients and therapists in a wide variety of settings. Hospitalized and nonhospitalized lower-class patients benefit from it (Heitler, 1973; Strupp and Bloxom, 1973), as do clients in group therapy (Yalom, Houts, Newell, and Rand, 1967; Covi, Roth, and Lipman, 1982). Moreover, patients who are in treatment for drug and alcohol abuse respond especially well to such socialization procedures (Stark and Kane, 1985; Rovndal and Vaglum, 1992). Furthermore, films that portray therapy sessions, and even tape recordings of therapy sessions, work as well as informative interviews to prepare clients for treatment (Truax, Shapiro, and Wargo, 1968; Strupp and Bloxom, 1973). In short, any information that enables clients to develop reasonable expectations about treatment facilitates treatment.

While shared expectations of clients and therapists regarding the process of treatment clearly affect its outcome, so too do expectations regarding the outcome itself. Indeed, the belief that treatment will be effective is itself such a powerful treatment that the mere anticipation of cure often brings at least momentary relief and, not uncommonly, permanent gains. Such cures are termed "placebo effects."

THE PLACEBO EFFECT

In medicine, a placebo is a pharmacologically inert substance, and the **placebo effect** describes positive treatment outcomes that result from the administration of such substances. But placebo effects, as we have seen in Chapter 6, occur with surprising regularity in a variety of settings and may be produced not only by inert substances but also by a patient's belief that treatment of any kind has been undertaken. Beecher (1961) reported that about 40 percent of patients who were suffering from a painful heart disease called angina pectoris experienced marked relief from their symptoms after merely undergoing a mock operation! In a later study, Ross found that 60 percent of patients who had undergone surgery to improve their blood circulation showed clinical improvement, even though the surgery may have left the blood supply to the heart unchanged and, in fact, may have reduced it (Ross, 1976, cited in Frank, 1978).

Placebos are sometimes as effective as psychotropic medications in treating psychological disorders, with their dosage curves showing similar characteristics. In the first part of a double-blind study, about 35 percent of patients who were given either drugs or placebos at a particular dosage level improved. Subsequently, the dosages of drugs and placebos were doubled in the second part of the study, and improvement rates jumped to 66 percent for patients on active drugs, and 76 percent for those on placebos (Lowinger and Dobie, 1969).

What is it that makes the placebo, a mere inert substance, so powerful? The power of the placebo resides in the expectation that positive results will accrue from a particular treatment (Cousins, 1979). So long as the client believes that the treatment works, it will likely have some positive effect. In no way are these effects shams or fakes, or merely the results of the gullibility of impressionable clients. Rather, they appear to be powerful treatments in themselves for reasons that are not yet fully understood. Current speculation suggests that placebos work on the immune system and that their effects are mediated through a group of enzymes called endorphins. Endorphins have been called "the brain's opiates." They affect how individuals subjectively experience pain and mood, and they may be produced when one expects to become well and able to cope.

Characteristics of Therapist-Client Interactions

Free choice, rational expectations, and effective hope are crucial for therapeutic success. But they are not sufficient. The therapist's personal characteristics, and how those characteristics fulfill the needs and expectations of the clients, are necessary ingredients for successful therapy. Not all characteristics play a central role in treatment, but some, such as empathy, warmth, and genuineness seem absolutely necessary. We turn to those characteristics now.

THERAPIST EMPATHY, WARMTH, AND GENUINENESS

Therapist empathy, warmth, and personal genuineness facilitate the therapeutic relationship and, presumably, increase the likelihood of a positive outcome.

▶ Much of the movie *Ordinary People* centered around the relationship between the main character and his psychiatrist.

Empathy describes the "ability of the therapist accurately and sensitively to understand experiences and feelings and their meaning to the client during the moment-to-moment encounter of psychotherapy" (Rogers and Truax, 1967, p. 104). *Warmth* is manifest in the therapeutic relationship when "the therapist communicates to his client a deep and genuine caring for him as a person with human potentialities, a caring uncontaminated by evaluations of his thoughts, feelings, or behaviors" (Rogers and Truax, 1967, p. 102). Therapist *genuineness* means precisely that: the therapist avoids communicating in a phony, "professional," or defensive manner. He is "freely and deeply himself" (Truax and Carkhuff, 1967). Obviously, a therapist can neither be empathic nor warm if he or she is not being genuine. Obviously, too, when shopping for a therapist, genuineness may be one of the first things to look for.

It is generally believed that warmth, empathy, and genuineness are necessary preconditions for successful therapy, though they do not guarantee it (Gurman, 1977; Mitchell, Bozarth, and Krauft, 1977). These characteristics would seem to apply to all kinds of therapists, regardless of their orientation. For example, with regard to behavior therapy (which concentrates on changing immediate behavior rather than the exploration of feelings), Marks and Gelder (1966) have argued that the single most important ingredient in determining outcome is the relationship between client and therapist. Moreover, Morris and Suckerman (1974a, 1974b) have shown that "warm" therapists are far more effective than "cold" ones in utilizing the behavioral techniques of desensitization for snake phobias.

THERAPIST EXPERIENCE

Beyond warmth, empathy, and genuineness, are there other therapist characteristics that facilitate treatment? There probably are, but their meaning is not entirely clear. Consider the matter of experience. Some studies find that experienced therapists promote greater improvement among their clients than do inexperienced ones (Katz, Lorr, and Rubinstein, 1958; Cartwright and Vogel, 1960; Barrett-Lennard, 1962; Strupp, Wallach, and Wogan, 1964; Scher, 1975; Hall and Heather, 1991; Modestin, Schwarzenbach, and Wurmle, 1992). To the extent that empathy and genuineness are requisites for therapeutic progress, they are likely to be found in greater quantity among experienced therapists, if only because experience makes one more comfortable and competent in that role. Other studies, however, have found no relationship between therapist experience and client outcome (Fiske, Cartwright, and Kirtner, 1964; Fiske and Goodman, 1965; Strupp, Fox, and Lessler, 1969; Auerbach and Johnson, 1977). Relatively inexperienced therapists may bring enormous enthusiasm to treatment, thereby compensating for the fact that they are relatively "green." Conversely, experienced therapists may become tired and less empathic with time. Experience, then, is no uniform guarantor of excellence in therapy, although there are no studies in which inexperienced therapists were more successful than experienced ones.

THE HELPING ALLIANCE

A powerfully significant determinant of the outcome of psychotherapy is the therapist's capacity to establish with the patient a ***therapeutic alliance,*** a joint sense of the goals of therapy and how they can best be achieved (Alexander and Luborsky, 1984; Luborsky, McLellan, Woody, O'Brien, and Auerbach, 1985). Regardless of therapeutic orientation, therapists who are able to engender such a cooperative spirit about the shared goals of treatment are much more likely to have successful outcomes.

The client's ability to form trusting and mutual relationships is important and of course adds to the development of a therapeutic alliance. Thus, couples in a group marital skills training program who were able to form a strong therapeutic alliance had a better prognosis for successful treatment (Bourgeois, Sabourin, and Wright, 1990). These findings are consistent with growing evidence that if a productive therapeutic alliance is developed and maintained early on within a therapy session, treatment is more likely to be effective (Horvath and Greenberg, 1989; Horvath and Luborsky, 1993). Social support from family may also strengthen the therapeutic alliance. Thus, a study of elderly depressed clients showed that elderly clients who receive more social support from their families may be more likely to become committed to treatment (Gaston, Marmor, Thompson, and Gallagher, 1988).

OTHER CONCERNS

Other factors that might possibly influence therapeutic outcome, such as gender, race, social class, sexual preference, religious involvement, and marital status, have not been fully investigated yet. And in fact the traditional paradigm of American psychology represents largely white, middle-class, male values and world view, ignoring issues of culture, race, ethnicity, and gender (Marcos, 1988, Flaskerud and Liu, 1990; Sue and Sue, 1992). Some studies have found that opposite-sex dyads communicate more effectively with each other (Brooks, 1974b; Jones and Zoppel, 1982; Orme and Boswell, 1991); others (e.g., Mendelsohn and Geller, 1963; Flaskerud, 1990) have suggested that this is not the case. These are matters where good sense is more important than research findings. A woman whose problems touch on matters of feminism, for example, may want to see a female therapist. But because all female therapists are not feminists nor even sympathetic to feminist concerns, a sensitive male therapist may be as effective (Rawlings and Carter, 1977). Gender alone is not a certain guide to insight and understanding.

A good therapist may well be sensitive to, and understanding of, a wide variety of concerns and issues that reach beyond the therapist's own gender, sex-

▼ Therapy is a series of intimate conversations, which if treatment is to succeed usually require empathy, warmth, and personal genuineness.

ual orientation, religious preference, and the like. But if a particular type of therapist is wanted, demand may exceed supply. Therapists come mainly from the upper middle class; clients from all classes. Nearly all therapists are white, but clients come in all colors. In a very large city, a black woman who wants to consult a black feminist therapist may be lucky enough to find one. And people in small cities and towns, where few qualified therapists practice, are not likely to be lucky enough to find therapists with all the desired characteristics, as the following case demonstrates:

> She is the intelligent, well-educated mother of two small children, wife of a popular internist in a small, remote town. Increasingly, she finds herself depressed. Worse, she finds herself jealous of her husband, who gets all of the community rewards ("Oh Dr. Barker—isn't he just wonderful . . .") while she gets the diapers. The very intensity of her feelings troubles her. With the passage of time, she hurts more and more and understands less and less. She tries to talk to her husband—really, her best friend—but he reacts guiltily and defensively. He really does love his work and finds it hard to understand that his pleasure and success should cause her such pain.
>
> What to do? Somehow, she feels this is a "woman's problem" and would prefer to see a woman. In fact, she would prefer to see a woman who is a feminist, one who understands something of the social and political aspects of womanhood, in addition to the psychological ones. Most of all, she wants someone to reassure her that though she is quite upset, she is not crazy, and that her feelings have some basis in reality.
>
> There are two therapists in her town, both men, both colleagues of her husband. One of them is "fresh out" of his residency. She finds him too young. The other is well into his seventies. He seems too old. She has other concerns about these therapists as well, but already her dilemma is clear. There are no nonprofessional alternatives in town: no women's groups in which these matters could be discussed, no sympathetic clergy. What should she do?
>
> Perhaps you can find a solution to her dilemma. We cannot. Some problems simply do not lend themselves to easy solutions, and this is one of them. She might try one of the therapists in town, and begin by discussing her reservations and discomforts about working with him. He *might* be able to get her over these hurdles, but then again he might not. Alternately, she might wait until spring thaws the mountain snow, and travel some three hours to a larger city. Even then, there is no guarantee that the help she wants would be found. For some problems there are no easy solutions.

Nonetheless, for all that one may prefer a therapist of a particular gender or ethnicity, the research evidence is that ethnic, cultural, or gender differences between clients and therapists do *not* consistently appear to affect the therapist's treatment of a client or the client's response to treatment (Flaskerud, 1990).

AVOIDING THE "PSYCHONOXIOUS" THERAPIST

Most therapists are professionals in whom one can trust. A few, however, are not. Whether from defects of training, character, or personality, they are unlikely to help and more likely to harm. In addition, there are therapists who, while useful to some, are harmful to others. Below follow some ways in which to detect such therapists (Segal, 1968; Haley, 1969).

Never Work with a Therapist Whose Personality Is Distasteful   If you find the therapist is aggressive, frequently angry or sadistic, impatient, challenging, or nasty, find another! Such therapists, regardless of their reputation, are unlikely to be able to do any good, and can often do considerable harm, as in the following case:

> One therapist spent two years mocking a client's passivity, appearing to retch every time she said something sweet. It was his conviction that this client needed to know how others felt about her, and he feigned retching in order to demonstrate. But the effects on the client were simply disastrous. Intimidated by him as she was by others, she became all the more sweetly passive, hoping thereby to avert yet another disaster. Only the insistence of friends made her terminate the treatment. While one ought not to expect a therapist to be constantly agreeable and protective, a therapist should appear to respect the client and to care for his or her well-being.

Beware of Sexual Exploitation   A substantial minority of psychologists and psychiatrists acknowledge having had a sexual relationship with one or more clients (Keith-Spiegel, 1977). Occasionally, such relationships are rationalized by the therapists on the grounds that they teach clients to enjoy "intimacy" or simply to make love. But these practices have more to do with the needs of the therapists and their own psychological immaturity than any treatment goal. There is no evidence that physical intimacy with one's therapist works for the client's benefit. In fact, close to 20 percent of the malpractice suits against therapists, and nearly half of the payouts are occasioned by allegations of sexual impropriety (Bales, 1987). When intimacy is suggested, the client should terminate treatment.

Avoid Suspiciously High Fees   One of the most self-serving myths among psychologists and psychiatrists is that the more the client pays, the more progress he or she makes in treatment. Pure nonsense! Some of the finest clinicians work in colleges and community clinics where fees are low or nonexistent. If you feel you are being overcharged, discuss the matter with your therapist. If you can't reach a comfortable understanding, seek help elsewhere.

Know Your Medicines   If a psychiatrist has prescribed psychoactive drugs (and only a physician can prescribe such drugs), you deserve to know the names of the drugs that are being prescribed, what symptoms they are supposed to treat, how long it will be before effects are seen, how long you will have to take them, and what the short-term and long-term side effects of these drugs are. Discuss these matters carefully with the psychiatrist, and read about them in a current edition of a lay text on medication, such as *The Essential Guide to Prescription Drugs*, published by Consumers Union (Long, 1992). Anything less than a frank and open response to your inquiries by the therapist violates the requirements of effective treatment that were discussed earlier, and may be dangerous to your health besides.

Be Free to Question   Sometimes treatment bogs down. Clients, and often therapists, feel that insufficient progress is being made. If you feel that way, raise the matter openly with the therapist. Often progress is blocked because the client has hit a *resistance:* a transient inability to deal with a significant issue. Such resistances may seem insurmountable, but they are commonly signs that progress is about to be made. Talking about feelings openly often helps to overcome resistances.

But sometimes progress is blocked, not by resistance, but by the therapist's lack of skill. Not all therapists can help all clients all the time. A therapist may occasionally lack the ability to help the client surmount particular kinds of difficulties. Again, open discussion of the stalemate can yield insight and resolution. If it does not, ask for a consultation with another professional. An objective third party can frequently shed light on the causes of stalemate, enabling client and therapist to continue their progress.

If the therapist refuses a consultation, however, seek help elsewhere. And surely if at any time during treatment the therapist forbids discussing treatment with anyone else, question the therapist carefully. Such admonitions, often given on the grounds that therapy is a private matter, are equally often self-serving. They may be designed to protect the therapist, not you.

Specify Treatment Goals The goals of treatment should be specified early in the treatment process. Otherwise, the treatment risks floundering. Many therapists arrive at an agreement with clients, not only regarding goals of treatment, but also how long treatment will last. That agreement is put in the form of a contract that serves to remind each party of their aims and obligations. Though not universal by any means, such contracts appear to hasten progress in treatment, especially when time seems to be running out. Then, clients really bend their energies toward getting the most out of what time is left. When a therapist cannot specify the goals of treatment fairly concretely, or when client and therapist do not share a common understanding of these matters, it may be wiser to seek help elsewhere.

Avoiding the wrong therapist reduces the probability of dissatisfaction and harm. And finding the right therapist, one who fulfills expectations and promotes effective hope, goes a long way toward ensuring therapeutic progress. But it does not guarantee such progress by any means. Beyond the personal qualities of the therapist are the techniques that he or she employs. Some of these techniques are highly effective for certain kinds of problems. Others are less effective.

Therapeutic Effectiveness

Therapists vary in their effectiveness (Luborsky, Crits-Cristoph, McLellan, Woody, Piper, Liberman, Imber, and Pilkonis, 1986). Broadly speaking, there are three ways in which one can assess the effectiveness of therapy (see Table 19–1). First, one can collect opinions regarding satisfaction with treatment from the client, as well as from his or her family, friends, and employers. Second, one can examine changes on a variety of personality measures, some of which were discussed in Chapter 7. Third, one can look at target behaviors—the behaviors that brought the client into treatment and that treatment is supposed to change. In a proper evaluation study, several measures of each of these types will be used. But some of these measures seem weaker than others.

PERSONAL SATISFACTION

Consider satisfaction. The fact of the matter is that most clients express considerable satisfaction with treatment. Indeed, it is rare to encounter someone who says that his therapy did him or her no good. Yet, client satisfaction, while im-

TABLE 19-1

	MEASURING THERAPEUTIC EFFECTIVENESS	
Yardstick	Researcher	Patient
Patient (client) satisfaction	Wants to know if patient feels therapy succeeded in solving presenting problem.	Because unwilling to believe time and money were spent for nothing, may be willing to see achievement of results not stated as goals as evidence of success.
Personality change in client	Wants to know if "underlying" problem has been solved—i.e., assumes patient's personality ultimately brought him or her into therapy.	Generally wants to solve "overlying" problem, usually not interested in personality change; unlikely to work to effect it or to see it as evidence of success.
Behavior change in client	Wants to know if presenting problem has been resolved, and if client has learned new behaviors that make the problem less likely to recur.	Wants to resolve presenting problem and to learn new behaviors that make the problem less likely to recur.

portant, cannot be a significant criterion of effectiveness. People can be satisfied for a variety of reasons having little or nothing to do with whether they were changed in significant ways. They may be inclined to indicate that they were satisfied merely because they had spent a good deal of time and money on treatment. It would make them quite uncomfortable to believe that it had all been for nought. Because their investment is so large, they may be motivated to seek genuine reasons for satisfaction, such as "I learned a lot about myself," even though those reasons are unrelated to the ones that brought them into treatment in the first place.

PERSONALITY CHANGE

Global assessments of personality change are a second index of the effectiveness of treatment. Such measures are taken at the outset of therapy, often during therapy, and surely at the end of it, with "improvement" (or "deterioration") being attributed to the effects of the treatment.

There is often, however, a mismatch between what the patient wants to change and what therapy does change: people rarely enter treatment to have their personalities changed (London, 1986). Rather, they seek help because they suffer a particular problem: they find it difficult to find and hold a job, hard to sustain a loving relationship, uncomfortable to be in school. They present *problems*, and it is those problems that they want to eliminate. Were it demonstrable that their problems arose from underlying personality difficulties, much as fever arises from an underlying virus, one would have little to complain about. But the relationship between presenting problems and the global personality characteristics that are said to underlie them has yet to be demonstrated.

Even if a patient consciously did want to have his personality changed, this would be a difficult task. Rather, the therapist is better able to focus on treating behaviors or feelings, and this may indirectly lead to personality change. Thus, a person who is unassertive may also experience low self-esteem. Merely training him or her to be more assertive may have dramatically positive effects on self-esteem.

Examining the impact of treatment on target behaviors, thoughts, and feelings is one of the most effective ways to assess treatment outcome. This criterion involves a careful assessment of the problems the client presents at the outset of treatment, with further similar assessments during and at the end of treatment. These assessments may be conducted jointly by client and therapist, and they may also be conducted by outside "blind" evaluators. Their hallmark, however, is that they are precise and replicable, and they stay quite close to the client's initial complaints.

These kinds of assessments are the benchmark of the action therapies, and they are increasingly being used with the insight therapies. But these assessments are not entirely without hazards. Some behaviors are elusive and difficult to measure with precision and reliability. Problems of meaning are among these. Some complaints, moreover, are very complex and intertwined. The presence of multiple phobias, for example, which extend over a range of environments and stimuli, makes assessment complex and difficult. In the main, however, behavioral change, where it can be assessed, is the "kingpin" of measures of therapeutic effectiveness.

THE VARIETY OF TREATMENT

It has been estimated that clients can choose from among 130 different "brands" of therapy (Parloff, 1976). Each year the number of therapies grows. And, of course, each "therapy" has its loyal adherents who confidently proclaim its efficacy for a host of problems. Behavior modification, Rolfing, insight therapy, rebirthing, cognitive therapy, lithium, flooding—these and dozens more are possible choices. Unfortunately, it is extremely difficult to make informed choices. Claims for success are broad but the evidence is slim. Only a few controlled tests have been conducted to assess the effectiveness of particular therapies, and even fewer tests have been done to compare the relative efficacy of various treatments. Equally important, little is known about the possible harmful effects a therapy might have. There is no protection for the consumer of therapy analogous to the protection afforded the consumer of drugs. The Federal Drug Administration imposes stringent testing procedures on all new drugs *before* they can be marketed: they must be effective; they must be relatively harmless; side effects must be clearly stated. No governmental agency acts as watchdog in the case of psychotherapy. Claims can be made with no concern for evidence.

Nonetheless, choices have to be made. In the following section, we discuss some of the more prevalent forms of psychotherapy. After a description of the unique goals and methods of particular therapies, we turn to an examination of the kinds of problems that are best addressed by one or another treatment. Although not an encyclopedic guide to all existing therapies, this overview will provide familiarity with the issue to consider when a choice must be made.

It is rare that clients enter psychotherapy solely to explore themselves. More likely, clients are brought to treatment by one or more painful problems with which they are unable to cope. Loneliness, anxiety, vague or specific fears, addictions, consuming anger, these and other problems drive people to seek therapeutic help. *All* therapies share the goal of ridding the client of distress.

FOCUS QUESTIONS

1. For what disorders have drug therapies been successful?
2. What is the main shortcoming of drug therapies?
3. Describe the following behavioral treatments:
   - systematic desensitization
   - flooding
   - modeling
   - aversion therapy
4. What are the basic assumptions and treatments of Ellis's rational-emotive therapy and Beck's cognitive therapy?

But all therapies do *not* share the belief that ridding the client of immediate distress is the exclusive, or even primary, goal of treatment.

Therapies may be divided into two broad categories: those that are designed to treat specific problems and those that seek to encourage personal insight. **Specific therapies** attempt to resolve psychological problems without altering underlying personality problems. **Insight** or **global therapies** are quite different. They treat presenting problems as the symptoms of underlying personality distress and therefore seek to change those deeper personality patterns. Obviously, there is often overlap between these approaches. The insight therapist who ignores the concrete problems that brought the client into therapy is likely to fail because the client will be impatient and dissatisfied (Haley, 1969). Similarly, the behavioral or cognitive therapist who ignores an underlying problem that spawns a host of behavioral difficulties reduces his or her chances of therapeutic success.

We have discussed the details of many global and specific therapies in earlier chapters. But in order to make our therapeutic recommendations clear and meaningful, it is useful to review the kinds of treatment that are available and useful. We will not describe *all* of the treatments that are presently offered: that would require a book in itself. Rather, we will restrict ourselves to those that have proven useful or are very popular.

Specific Therapies

Specific therapies deal with specific problems. Those problems can often be defined quite narrowly and precisely, such as a fear of heights. Or the specific problem may be a broad one, such as depression which, as discussed in Chapter 11, encompasses a heterogeneous group of symptoms, among them fatigue, loss of appetite, somatic concerns, and the like. The important thing about specific therapies is that they take one or more target problems and seek to resolve them without going deeply into other aspects of personality or unconscious processes.

There are two classes of specific therapies: biological treatments and specific psychological therapies, including behavioral treatment and cognitive restructuring. We examine these in turn.

BIOLOGICAL THERAPIES

Among the biological therapies, drug treatments are by far the most popular. Psychoactive drugs are more often prescribed than others; among these, Prozac and Valium are among the most commonly prescribed drugs in the United States. Drug therapies have been successful with a variety of common disorders, including anxiety, unipolar and bipolar depression, and schizophrenia. They can often have quite specific effects. For example, certain drugs may affect schizophrenic thought, while others may influence schizophrenic emotion.

Another form of biological therapy is **electroconvulsive shock therapy,** or **ECT.** It consists of sending a pulse of electricity through the brain, thereby producing a minor convulsion. The treatment may be repeated six to ten times. As mentioned in Chapter 11, ECT is a fast and effective treatment for unipolar depression but it can have serious side effects.

Like all therapies, biological treatments are most effective with willing and cooperative clients. But unlike psychological treatments, many biological ones can be administered against the client's will and still have moderate effects. One of the major sources of failure in drug treatment, however, resides in the client's failure or refusal to take the prescribed medications. That failure often arises from the fact that the client is unwilling to take the treatment, fails to understand how it will help, thinks the negative side effects are worse than the positive effects, or has not developed the helping alliance with the therapist that is necessary for successful treatment.

Biological therapies are designed to provide immediate relief for immediate problems. They cannot teach clients to alter their behaviors, to avoid stressful difficulties, or to cope better in the future. Nor do they try to bring about greater insight or understanding into the causes of personal difficulties. They affect biology, not learning. But their effects are not at all trivial, for problems tend to breed further problems. In reducing current anxiety, arousal, or depression, biological treatments prevent additional troubles from arising.

BEHAVIORAL TREATMENT

The behavioral treatments see the roots of clients' distress, not in physiological processes gone awry, but in behavior itself (see Chapter 5). Distressing behavior is learned, and what is learned can be unlearned and replaced by more constructive modes of coping and adaptation. Behavior therapists therefore deal directly with the problem that the client is experiencing, and seek to resolve that specific difficulty (see Table 19–2).

TABLE 19–2

STRATEGIES OF BEHAVIOR THERAPY

Technique	Outcome
Contingency management	Altering the consequences of a behavior in order to change the frequency of the behavior.
Contingency contracting	Increasing desired behaviors, and decreasing undesired ones, by drawing up a contract that stipulates rewards and punishments for the relevant behaviors.
Stimulus control	Increasing the likelihood of a behavior by magnifying the stimuli that promote the desired behavior and eliminating the stimuli that undercut it.
Systematic desensitization	Training a person to engage in behavior that makes the unwanted behavior difficult or impossible to perform. Systematic desensitization eliminates anxiety, as it is difficult to experience anxiety during a state of relaxation.
Implosion	Extinguishing anxiety by inducing the client to imagine intensely anxiety-provoking scenes that, because they produce no harmful consequences, lose their power to induce fear.
Flooding	Extinguishing anxiety by exposing the clients to actual fear-producing situations that, because they produce no harmful consequences, lose their power to produce fear.
Modeling	Exposing clients to desired behavior that is modeled by an other person, and rewarding the client for imitating that behavior.
Aversion therapy	Eliminating an unwanted behavior by pairing it with powerfully aversive consequences.
Covert sensitization	Inducing an aversion for an unwanted behavior by pairing that behavior with vividly imagined aversive consequences.
Time out	Suppressing an unwanted response by removing the client to a "neutral" environment when that response is manifested.

Although behavior treatments have become popular only in the past quarter century, many of them have their roots in an ageless folk wisdom. Consider the child who fears darkness. At first, parents will naturally accede to the child's demand that the bedroom remain lit. Over time, however, the overhead light will be replaced by a low-wattage night-light. And finally, that too will be extinguished. Used therapeutically, that process is one form of in vivo **systematic desensitization** (see Chapters 5 and 8). Introduced by Joseph Wolpe in 1958, it is used primarily to treat phobias and specific anxieties. The client is first reassured and relaxed, and then exposed to stimuli that are minimally anxiety producing. Because one cannot be relaxed and tense simultaneously, the anxiety dissipates, and gradually, the client is trained to remain relaxed in the presence of stimuli that were formerly associated with increasing anxiety. Over time and training, stimuli that formerly induced panic are now greeted with calm.

Flooding treats anxiety in quite the opposite manner (see Chapters 5 and 8). Instead of gradually approaching the anxiety-provoking stimulus, clients are encouraged to experience the full force of the anxiety storm. Because by definition phobias are irrational fears, they are unlikely to elicit reinforcement. Consequently, like any unreinforced behavior, they will extinguish. Someone who is agoraphobic and afraid to leave home, for example, would be encouraged to spend an hour in the park, and thus be flooded with anxiety. Gradually, through the process of extinction, that anxiety would abate.

Modeling is yet another form of behavioral treatment that has helped clients to overcome fears and acquire new standards for their behaviors (see Chapters 5 and 8). Here, for example, a client who is painfully shy might observe and gradually imitate the behavior of a model who both enjoys being outgoing and is rewarded for it. Combined with rehearsal and practice, modeling treatments are quite effective in overcoming fears and inhibitions (Bandura, 1969).

Aversion therapy aims to rid a client of undesired behavior by pairing that behavior with aversive consequences (see Chapters 5 and 14). If alcohol is paired with a nausea-inducing drug, or a sexually deviant impulse is paired with electric shock, the expected result is that the client will avoid the undesired behavior.

Behavioral treatments often can be very effective in speedily eliminating sources of distress. As we will shortly see, they have been used quite successfully for a variety of psychological troubles. But their virtues are also their limitations, for they often fail to deal with the thoughts and feelings that promote irrational behaviors in the first place. For these thoughts and feelings, cognitive therapies are quite useful.

COGNITIVE RESTRUCTURING

Treatments that involve cognitive restructuring are predicated on the assumption that irrational thoughts breed irrational behaviors. Such thoughts are by no means rare, for they commonly arise from the fundamental attribution errors that people make about their own behaviors (Nisbett and Ross, 1980). Consider the person who says "I have no friends because I am boring." That would be an irrational thought on the part of a young man newly arrived at a college campus, irrational because insufficient time had passed for him to meet people and test that belief. It would also be an irrational thought, but a different sort, by a rude and critical member of a typing pool. Cognitive therapies seek to illuminate these thoughts, to make clear their irrational basis, and thereby, to change them.

Rational-emotive therapy is one of the more effective and popular cognitive therapies (see Chapter 5). Developed by Albert Ellis (1962), it questions the faulty philosophical assumptions that are made by individuals and that generate irrational behaviors. The notion, for example, that it is absolutely necessary for an adult to be loved by each and every significant person in his or her community, is a widely held irrational assumption. So, too, is the assumption that in order to consider oneself worthwhile, one needs to be thoroughly competent, adequate, and fully achieving in all possible respects. These and other assumptions are vigorously challenged and attacked in rational-emotive therapy, with the aim of laying bare and ultimately changing these cognitions and the behaviors they promote.

Cognitive therapy is quite similar to rational-emotive therapy. It was initially used in the treatment of depression and anxiety (Beck, 1976; Beck and Emery, 1985), where it was found to be superior to pharmacotherapy (Elkin, Shea, Watkins, Imber, Sotsky, Collins, Glass, Pilkonis, Leber, Docherty, Fiester, and Parloff, 1989), both immediately and after a considerable period of time (Blackburn, Eunson, and Bishop, 1986). Subsequently, it was found to be particularly effective with panic disorders (Sokol, Beck, Greenberg, Wright, and Berchick, 1990) and with eating disorders (Fairburn, Jones, Peveler, Carr, Solomon, O'Connor, Burton, and Hope, 1991; Agras, Rossiter, Arnow, Schneider, Telch, Raeburn, Bruce, Perl, and Koran, 1992; Wilson and Fairburn, 1993). Beck's cognitive therapy works to identify and change such negative cognitions as self-devaluation, a negative view of life experience, and a pessimistic view of the future as leading to depression (see Chapter 11).

Acquiring and maintaining realistic cognitions is no easy task. Cognitive restructuring therapies use psychological tasks that gradually become psychologically more challenging and complex, often done as "homework" outside of the therapy session, to yield a succession of mastery and success experiences. Like biological and behavioral therapies, cognitive therapies can be used to eliminate a specific problem, and to eliminate it quickly. They differ from those

▶ Specific therapies aim to treat a fairly well-defined problem such as a phobia, depression, or a difficult situation: in this case, the patient was a 10-year-old with behavioral problems connected to his younger sister's terminal illness.

treatments, however, in the requirement that, in order to alleviate a particular problem, one needs to understand and change the thoughts that promote it. And they differ from the global therapies, to which we now turn, both in their insistence on staying "close" to the client's presenting problem, and because they find it unnecessary to explore why the relevant cognitions were distorted in the first place.

Global Therapies

Cognitive and behavioral therapies are specific treatments for quite specific problems. Those therapies assume that the presenting problem *is* the problem that requires treatment, and that nothing else requires treatment. Global therapies, on the other hand, all assume that the presenting problem is merely the symptom of some larger, underlying disorder. Much as fever is not itself the entire illness but rather a symptom of a deeper malaise, so are psychological symptoms merely the outcropping of underlying conflicts and erroneous perceptions. It is the latter that require treatment because they tend to radiate a host of cognitive and behavioral difficulties.

Global therapies are mainly those that are derived from the psychodynamic approaches. Each of these therapies assumes that psychological distress arises because something is *fundamentally* wrong with the client's personality. They differ, as we will shortly see, in their view of precisely what is wrong and how it can best be remedied.

CLASSICAL PSYCHOANALYSIS

As we saw in Chapter 4, the heartland of psychological distress in the psychoanalytic view lies in the anxiety and self-defeating postures that are generated by unacceptable impulses. These impulses are repressed and otherwise restrained from consciousness by the host of coping mechanisms that can be generated by an enormously creative and flexible mind. But ultimately, these defenses are costly, for they sap the strength of the ego and continue to leave residual anxieties that render individuals miserable. The solution for Freud, and for those who followed his tradition, was to make conscious the unconscious impulses so that acceptable means of gratifying them could be found.

With the help of the therapist, the client seeks to define his or her unconscious motivations. Classical psychoanalysts require their clients to lie on a couch in order to minimize their attention to the therapist, relax them, and enable them to engage in ***free association.*** Clients are instructed to say whatever comes to mind, regardless of how ridiculous or embarrassing it is, and without attempting to censor. The rationale behind this procedure is that the unconscious has a logic of its own that is manifested in these seemingly disconnected and meaningless associations. If the client associates freely, the unconscious motives and conflicts will reveal themselves through these disconnected verbal threads. The analysis of dreams proceeds in the same manner. There, the client associates to the content and theme of the dream and, in the process, uncovers its unconscious meaning.

Unconscious impulses and conflicts do not yield easily or readily to this form of exploration. As the client begins to confront a conflict, he or she is likely to resist going further. Such resistance can take many forms, such as changing the subject, starting an argument with the therapist, coming late, and even missing appointments. Trained not to take these matters personally,

FOCUS QUESTIONS

1. What procedures do classical psychoanalysts use to encourage clients to make conscious what have been unconscious impulses and conflicts?
2. How do modern dynamic psychotherapies resemble and differ from classical psychoanalysis?
3. Describe the following techniques that are often used by existential therapists:
   • paradoxical intervention
   • dereflection
4. What are the goals and methods of treatment of family therapists?

the therapist patiently interprets the resistance just as any other symptoms might be interpreted. These interpretations bring the client back to the "work of analysis."

As a psychoanalysis progresses, clients find themselves revealing things to their therapists that they had never revealed to anyone before, not even to themselves. Understandably, the relationship to the therapist becomes richly emotional and complex. And although the therapist remains impassive, clients react to him or her with intense love, dependency, biting anger, or rebellion, and often all at once. As we saw in Chapter 4, psychoanalysts view this behavior as the ***transference*** of conflicts and frustrations that were experienced with parents during early childhood, onto the therapist. The analysis of transference, because it is immediate and real, is a major opportunity for self-understanding and growth during psychoanalysis.

MODERN DYNAMIC PSYCHOTHERAPIES

Psychoanalysis is a time-consuming, costly, and cumbersome method of treatment. Moreover, as discussed in Chapter 4, not all therapists believe in all of its basic assumptions. As a result, a variety of psychodynamically oriented therapies have been developed which are collectively called ***dynamic psychotherapies*** (Luborsky, Barber, and Beutler, 1993). All of them retain the notion that unconscious impulses and conflicts spawn anxiety and other forms of human misery, and that insight into those conflicts is the goal of treatment. But the kinds of impulses that are examined, and the ways in which they can be made conscious, vary enormously from therapist to therapist. In general, modern psychodynamic therapies differ from classical psychoanalysis in three ways. First, the therapist is much more active, not merely in interpreting unconscious material, but also in offering advice and suggesting constructive options. Second, these therapies are more efficient and less time-consuming. Whereas classical psychoanalysis required the client to lie on the couch five times a week for several years, modern psychodynamic therapies are conducted face-to-face, commonly no more than once or twice a week, and for a briefer duration. Third, perhaps because they are briefer, the newer psychodynamic therapies concentrate on the present rather than the past, and emphasize current social relationships rather than earlier ones.

The very content of these therapies may differ widely, according to the orientation of the therapist. Whereas classical psychoanalysis is concerned mainly with the dynamics of sexual and aggressive impulses, Jungian therapists take a larger view of the psyche and may, as we saw in Chapter 4, allude to a variety of archetypes, unconscious materials, and dynamics. Adlerian therapists stress the will to superiority, and Sullivanian therapists examine current social relationships. Many psychodynamic therapists are eclectic, meaning that they use insights from each school of treatment in accord with the needs of individual cases. These newer and briefer forms of treatment are among the most widely practiced and available today (Parloff, 1976; Strupp and Binder, 1984; Svartberg and Stiles, 1991; Horowitz, Rosenberg, and Bartholomew, 1993). Moreover, because they are concerned with integrating the most valuable aspects of treatment, they often seek to match treatment to the special needs of the client. Indeed, the attempt to locate characteristics of treatment that are most useful for a specific client is the hallmark of these eclectic treatments (Shoham-Salomon, 1991; Shoham-Salomon and Hannah, 1991; Smith and Sechrest, 1991; Snow, 1991).

EXISTENTIAL THERAPIES

Existential therapists stress the importance of freedom and free choice. They believe that these are gradually acquired through the individual's struggles with responsibility. They encourage clients to view their psychological problems as being of their own making: individuals themselves are the source of their own difficulties. Viktor Frankl (1975) first described two techniques that are now often used by existential therapists. The first is **paradoxical intervention,** wherein the therapist encourages clients to indulge in and even exaggerate their symptoms. For example, someone who "just can't resist ice cream" will be encouraged to eat massive amounts of it in order to be convinced that he really does control his intake. Paradoxical interventions, particularly those that accord positive connotations to symptoms ("you're mildly depressed because you're in touch with your feelings"), are especially effective with severe symptoms (Shoham-Salomon and Rosenthal, 1987). The second, **dereflection,** involves directing the client's attention away from his symptoms and pointing out how much he could be doing and enjoying if he were not so preoccupied with his troubles. As a result of taking responsibility for themselves, clients become more aware of their choices and values, and their lives and interpersonal relations become more open, honest, and meaningful.

COUPLES AND FAMILIES IN THERAPY

Until this point, our attention has been directed to individuals seen in therapy alone or in groups. But in the past three decades, people have been seen increasingly in therapy with **significant others,** either as couples or in families. The promise of such treatment arises from the notion that symptoms are not wholly the result of individual learning, nor do they inflict suffering on individuals alone. Rather, symptoms may themselves arise from, and be maintained by, the attitudes and behaviors of significant others. And they may well cause intense suffering to significant others. Indeed, it is difficult to imagine an unpleasant symptom that does not impinge directly on the lives of others, especially intimates. Depression affects individuals, but it also deeply affects children and spouses. Impotence affects partners. Anorexia and bulimia create painful problems in families. Moreover, the reciprocal interactions of family members may well spawn, and can surely maintain those symptoms. Thus, it seemed sensible to consider couples and families as the unit of treatment, rather than individuals alone.

Seen in this light, the family substitutes for the individual as the unit of analysis. The way the *family* functions, the way it organizes and maintains its own homeostasis and its habitual patterns of interaction become the focus of assessment. Changing that homeostasis and those patterns of interaction becomes the goal of treatment. What is called the "client" or the "patient" in individual therapy becomes in family therapy the "identified patient," the one whom the family system nominated for patienthood, and who perhaps has volunteered to carry the heaviest burdens of family homeostasis.

Some family therapists take seriously the notion that individual symptoms reflect something that has gone wrong in the family system. They seek to reduce individual malfunction and pain, while simultaneously changing the ways in which the family is organized and interacts (e.g., Minuchin, 1974; Nichols, 1984). They are best described as *systemic* family therapists. But others, who are often described as *strategic* family therapists (Nichols, 1984) bring families to the consulting room with a different view in mind. For them, couples and families are powerful instruments for effecting individual change. They often use techniques that were found to be effective in individual treatment in the family context. Thus, *behavioral* family therapists seek to bring the powerful array of behavioral treatment techniques to bear on individual problems that seem to occur in the family (e.g., Patterson, 1971; Jacobson, 1981; Hahlweg and Markman, 1988; Halford, Sanders, and Behrens, 1993). *Psychoanalytic* family therapists (e.g., Meissner, 1978) similarly seek to apply insights gained from individual psychoanalytic treatment to problems that occur in families.

Both the relative newness of family therapies and their diversity (perhaps especially within the strategic dimension) make studies of the effectiveness of these therapies difficult to conduct. Nevertheless, despite the relative paucity of research findings, a recent examination of nearly all of the research efforts suggests that family treatments are particularly effective in reducing the symptoms of the identified patient (Jacobson and Addis, 1993). And family therapy may also be effective in altering family interactions (Hazelrigg, Cooper, and Borduin, 1987; Markman, Renick, Floyd, Stanley, and Clements, 1993).

With this brief overview of treatment modalities behind us, we now turn to the treatments that are especially useful for particular kinds of psychological problems.

THE CHOICE OF TREATMENT

Some problems lend themselves easily to relatively clear definition. Fear of public speaking is one such problem. Compulsions are another. Although there are important exceptions, the more specific the problem, the greater the likelihood that it can be treated successfully. It is common, therefore, for therapists to encourage clients to define their problems as carefully as possible. Such definition unfortunately does not guarantee therapeutic success, but it surely increases the likelihood that the outcome of treatment will be positive.

Specific Treatments

Once a problem is defined, it may become especially amenable to treatment by the specific behavioral and cognitive therapies, as well as biological ones. These therapies address symptoms primarily. But this is surely no shortcoming, for as we have seen earlier in this chapter, the symptoms often *are* the problem and, in any event, they are fully capable of breeding more intense and intractable problems. Symptoms treatments are, therefore, significant treatments, made all the more so by their comparative likelihood of succeeding. We turn to these first.

TREATMENTS FOR ANXIETIES, FEARS, PHOBIAS, AND PANIC

The border between the everyday anxieties that afflict all of us, and the anxieties that merit diagnostic designations for some of us is not a very clear one.

As a result, it is useful to start with ways of dealing with anxiety that are low in cost and easily acquired and that can greatly improve the quality of life for everyone. ***Progressive relaxation*** is a treatment that is very useful and blissfully inexpensive. By alternately tightening and relaxing the major muscle groups of the body, progressive relaxation induces a physical mellowness that wins out over anxious arousal. It is a relatively easy technique to teach oneself. Performed twice a day for ten-minute sessions it can provide considerable release from body tensions. (For a detailed description of the technique, see Benson, 1975.)

A second technique for reducing ordinary anxiety is ***transcendental meditation.*** Best performed twice a day for twenty minutes in a very quiet setting, it consists of closing your eyes and repeating a simple syllable or brief word (a "mantra") to yourself. Whereas progressive relaxation produces muscle responses that are incompatible with anxiety, meditation blocks the thoughts that often engender anxiety. Performed consistently, and especially in tandem with progressive relaxation, meditation can substantially reduce anxiety, even anxieties that are quite intense (Eppley, Abrams, and Shear, 1989; Kabat-Zinn, Massion, Kristeller, et al., 1992; Seligman, 1993).

Progressive relaxation and transcendental meditation are worth exploring before psychotherapy is sought, or in conjunction with psychotherapy. Ultimately, if psychotherapy proves necessary, there are three additional treatments that are quite effective in reducing fears and anxieties. Perhaps the oldest, and surely the most studied of these, is ***systematic desensitization,*** which is useful for overcoming complex social anxieties, agoraphobias, and even insomnia (Steinmark and Borkevic, 1974). It is, in fact, so successful that it has become the yardstick against which the effectiveness of new treatment techniques is measured (Kazdin and Wilson, 1978). Another study, however, suggests that cognitive and cognitive-behavioral therapies are as effective as systematic desensitization (Miller and Berman, 1983).

The second psychological treatment that seems particularly effective in reducing fears is ***modeling,*** which consists of observing a nonfearful model perform the task that generates fear in the client (Bandura, Blanchard, and Ritter, 1969; Bandura, 1977b). Modeling appears to work as well as do desensitization and flooding in alleviating both mild and severe phobias (Rachman, 1978).

Finally, as you recall from Chapter 8, there has been a major scientific breakthrough in the psychological treatment of panic disorder. While cognitive therapy is generally effective in the treatment of anxiety, it is especially effective with panic disorder, and has the added advantages of being quite rapid and low in cost (McNally, 1990; Margraf, Barlow, Clark, and Telch, 1993). In the treatment of phobias, cognitive therapy is more effective than any other treatment, including drug treatment (Seligman, 1993).

In combination with psychological treatment, biological treatments such as Valium are often useful for alleviating anxiety, especially anxiety that is manifest in body tensions. Untreated, such body tensions tend to accumulate and mount, rendering a person continually anxious. Antidepressants such as imipramine and phenelzine have been shown to alleviate phobic behavior. Unlike psychological treatments, however, these biological treatments do not teach people to *cope* with anxiety; they merely alleviate the symptoms that present circumstances have generated. If active coping techniques are not learned, new troubling circumstances will probably bring further anxiety

1. What are progressive relaxation and transcendental meditation and how do they reduce ordinary anxiety?

2. When psychotherapy is needed to treat fears and anxiety, what are the three most effective treatments that are used?

3. How do exposure and response prevention lead to relief for obsessive-compulsives?

4. What is the advantage of cognitive therapy over drug treatment and ECT in treating unipolar depression?

symptoms and require further treatment. Biological treatments, therefore, are relatively transient and passive treatments that minimize present symptoms and prevent new ones from developing during a particular crisis.

TREATMENTS FOR COMPULSIONS AND OBSESSIONS

Compulsions and obsessions were once refractory to every form of psychological and psychopharmacological treatment. Neither systematic desensitization, the various insight therapies, nor chemotherapy appeared to have much effect. Two treatments, one biological and the other behavioral however, have been found to be effective. Neither is perfect. Not everyone responds positively to these treatments. But they are effective for many people.

Clomipramine is a drug that is used in a variety of psychological disorders. It is especially effective with obsessions and compulsions, rendering the former less intrusive and the latter easier to resist. Unfortunately, the drug has substantial side effects (including drowsiness, constipation, and loss of sexual interest), such that it is unacceptable to many people. And, of course, it does not permanently alleviate obsessions or compulsions. Once the drug is terminated, for whatever reasons, the symptoms return (Katz, DeVeaugh-Geiss, and Landau, 1990a; Trimble, 1990).

Exposure and ***response prevention*** are particularly effective treatments. From a behavioral view, compulsions are an errant response to anxiety. But compulsive actions reduce anxiety only momentarily, and in so doing, generate repertoires of uncontrollable behaviors. Preventing those momentary responses in the face of anxiety should have the ultimate effect of reducing the anxiety by extinction, and preventing the useless repertoire from developing. Indeed, exposure and response prevention apparently provide relief for half to two-thirds of those who receive such treatment. However, even among the fortunate ones, the obsessive thoughts and compulsive impulses continue to lurk and are never fully stilled. Moreover, a substantial minority fails to improve at all (Rachman and Hodgson, 1980; DeSilva and Rachman, 1992).

TREATMENTS FOR UNIPOLAR AND BIPOLAR DEPRESSION

Four treatments, two of which are biological and two psychological, are known to work moderately well with unipolar depression. Drug treatments, particularly Prozac (fluoxetine) and Zoloft, take about three weeks to work and appear to relieve depression in about two-thirds of the people who take them. But these drugs have moderate side effects (including nausea, nervousness, and insomnia) for many people. Moreover, roughly a quarter of those who are depressed either cannot or will not take these drugs. Finally, there is often substantial relapse when the drug is terminated (Hollon, DeRubeis, and Evans, 1990).

Especially for very deep depressions, ***electroconvulsive shock therapy*** (ECT) is particularly effective. It relieves depression in about three-fourths of the cases, and it does so in just a few days. ECT has a much more frightening reputation than it deserves, especially when one considers the abiding pain of depression. But it is not without significant side effects, among them memory loss, confusion, and cardiovascular changes. Moreover, it provides no guarantee against recurrence (Fink, 1979; Janicak, Davis, Gibbons, Ericksen, Chang, and Gallagher, 1985).

Cognitive therapy focuses on how the depressed person thinks about defeat, failure, loss, and helplessness. It provides relief to about 70 percent of depressed people and is about as effective as drug treatment, and somewhat less effective than ECT. But it has one terrific advantage: by teaching people new ways to think about their situations, it *lowers* the risk that they will become depressed in the future (Elkin, Shea, Watkins, Imber, Sotsky, Collins, Glass, Pilkonis, Leber, Docherty, Fiester, and Parloff, 1989; Hollon, DeRubeis, and Evans, 1990).

Cognitive therapy may work best for those suffering moderate, rather than severe depression. Moreover, nearly all the studies of cognitive therapy have involved patients who are educated and aware of how their thinking affects their emotions. We know little about whether and how cognitive therapy works with less sophisticated people (Seligman, 1993).

Interpersonal therapy (IPT) deals with depression as it results from interpersonal difficulties: fights, role transitions, grief, and social deficits. It, too, is brief and inexpensive, requiring no more than a few months (Klerman, Weissman, Rounsaville, and Chevron, 1984; Elkin, Shea, Imber, Pilkonis, Sotsky, Glass, Watkins, Leber, and Collins, 1986). IPT has no known side effects, and it is apparently just as effective as cognitive therapy. Its major shortcoming is that there are very few therapists who practice IPT. Treatment, therefore, is difficult to find.

There is good reason to believe that the *combination* of drug treatment and psychological therapies is more effective than either by themselves, apparently because the drugs lift depression sufficiently so that psychological interventions can be meaningful and effective (Weissman, Klerman, Prusoff, Sholomskas, and Padian, 1981; Klerman, 1990).

The treatment of choice for bipolar depression and for mania itself is lithium carbonate, a simple inorganic salt. The symptoms of 80 percent of bipolar depressives are either fully or partially remitted as a result of lithium administration (Depue, 1979). Repeated administration to individuals who are predisposed to bipolar depression may prevent the occurrence of that disorder or alleviate its severity. Lithium, however, has serious side effects that can be lethal unless its administration is carefully supervised by a knowledgeable physician throughout the entire course of treatment. Moreover, because some people find the effects of lithium mildly annoying (it cuts out the joyous "highs" from the manic phase of the bipolar disorder), and therefore terminate the treatment quite prematurely, lithium treatment should always be accompanied by supportive psychotherapy.

TREATMENTS FOR SEXUAL DYSFUNCTION

There are, as we learned in Chapter 13, several levels of sexual disorder, ranging from the deep problems of identity to the relatively superficial problems of function. The more superficial the problem, the better the available treatment. Thus, there is no reliable treatment for problems of sexual identity. But for the host of problems that generate sexual dysfunction, including fear of sexuality, lack of sexual pleasure, and premature ejaculation, the treatments of choice, as we saw in Chapter 13, are those that are based on the work of Masters and Johnson (1970). Indeed, few psychological treatment programs, with the exception of systematic desensitization for phobias, have been quite as successful as the Masters and Johnson therapy regimen. They have reported that better than 80 percent of nearly 800 people who entered their two-week treatment program were greatly improved, and that nearly 75 percent of them maintained that improvement after a five-year follow-up. Similar findings have been

1. Why are drop out and relapse such important problems in treatment of addiction?
2. Why does group support to stop drinking or smoking often lead to positive effects in controlling these addictions?
3. What are some of the disadvantages to using aversive techniques or methadone to treat drug addictions?
4. What is dietary cycling and what is the risk associated with it? Why is exercise a more effective long-term solution to losing weight?
5. Describe cognitive-behavioral treatment for bulimia, anorexia, and bingeing.

reported by other workers who have evaluated these techniques (Hartman and Fithian, 1972; Kaplan, 1974).

TREATMENTS FOR ADDICTIONS

The addictions—alcoholism, smoking, and drug dependence—are difficult to treat. The solid treatment techniques that are available for phobias, compulsions, depression, and sexual dysfunction are not yet available here. For the soul of addiction is temptation, rather than fear and incompetence, and temptation does not seem to yield to either the rational reasoning of cognitive therapies, the control of behavioral treatments, or the insight of global psychodynamic ones. Most treatment programs, whether conducted by professionals or nonprofessionals (such as Alcoholics Anonymous, Weight Watchers, TOPS, or Daytop Village for drug addicts), are subject to two overlapping problems: drop out and relapse. Those who drop out of a treatment program almost always fail to change. And those who go through a treatment program but then resume old habits often suffer slights to their sense of hope and efficacy. This corrosion of hope and self-efficacy makes them unavailable for further treatment for a considerable period of time. Thus, in this area, researchers have begun to describe their techniques as "*more* effective" rather than "*very* effective," their typical gains as "*modest* rather than impressive," and their outcomes as "*variable* rather than consistent" (Mahoney and Mahoney, 1976).

Alcoholism   The treatment of choice for most of the addictions is abstention. But unfortunately, abstention is more easily recommended than achieved and, as a result, a multiplicity of behavioral and cognitive approaches to the addictive disorders have been suggested.

Treatments that evoke enthusiasm, hope, and commitment from participants are seen again in the help provided by Alcoholics Anonymous (AA). AA describes itself as "a fellowship of men and women who share their experiences, strength and hope with each other that they may solve their common problem and help others to recover from alcoholism." By the time an alcoholic makes first contact with AA, he or she has already acknowledged that alcohol is a problem—an enormous first step. Subsequently, two members of AA meet with the alcoholic and invite him or her to join the group. The group stresses self-help, underscoring that the alcoholic controls the drinking problem, and not vice versa. It offers group support during the struggle to control drinking, and hope—for after all, many of the other members of the group were once alcoholics and are now entirely abstinent. And while receiving support from others helps one to control the urge to drink, *giving support* to people with similar problems serves much the same purpose. Indeed, in looking back over the AA experience, reformed alcoholics rate altruism and group cohesiveness as two of its most helpful aspects (Emrick, Lassen, and Edwards, 1977).

Although testimonials to AA are a commonplace, however, the treatment has never been evaluated properly. We know next to nothing about the dropout rate from AA—those who found the procedures distasteful and simply quit—or the rate of backsliding into alcoholism again once individuals leave the group. Neither do we know how effective AA is in comparison with drug treatments such as disulfiram, which seems to be a promising drug for treating alcoholism. Carefully controlled efforts indicate that disulfiram is particularly effective with regard to preventing relapse (Johnsen and Morland, 1991).

Smoking Smoking is no less a puzzle than alcoholism. Little is known about why people smoke in the first place or why smoking persists in being so popular (Jarvik, 1979). Unlike eating, it is difficult to know what is reinforcing in smoking behavior. But whatever reinforces smoking, it does so powerfully. The pack-a-day smoker who averages ten puffs to a cigarette will have taken some 70,000 shots of nicotine and tar in a year, a frequency unmatched by any other form of addiction (Russell, 1977).

Unhooking the long-term smoker is no easy matter. The best procedures utilize a broad spectrum of behavioral strategies. One study, utilizing a combination of aversion therapy, contractual management, booster sessions, and group contact and support, resulted in a 76 percent abstinence rate six months after treatment (Lando, 1977). Unfortunately, such impressive long-term results are seldom replicated. Even rapid smoking, a most successful aversion therapy in the short term, results in high rates of relapse in the long run (Danaher, 1977; Hall, Rugg, Tunstall, and Jones, 1984).

In fact, as is the case for most addictions, relapse rates have been the bane of treatments for smoking. Within a year, 75 percent of reformed smokers can be expected to be puffing once again (Marlatt and Gordon, 1980). To combat relapse, cognitive and behavioral treatments aimed at relapse prevention have been added to successful short-term therapies. Oddly, these treatments have not fared well. Although they are associated with some long-term reduction in smoking, these relapse-prevention treatments fail to maintain meaningful abstinence levels (Danaher, 1977; Brown, Lichtenstein, McIntyre, and Harrington-Kostur, 1984; Hall et al., 1984).

Smokers prefer to quit without intensive professional assistance (Curry, 1993; Fiore, Novotny, Pierce, Giovino, Hatziandrev, Newcomb, Surawicz, and Davis, 1990). As a result, recent efforts have been directed toward defining programs that involve minimal assistance but are yet comprehensive enough to enable participants to cease smoking. Televised self-help programs have become quite popular during the past decade, and are moderately effective (Flay, 1987; Gruder, Warnecke, Jason, Flay, and Peterson, 1990). As might be expected, the efficacy of such televised programs is substantially enhanced when a social support system is instituted. Having a buddy to turn to, especially in times of distress and temptation, combined with the relative absence of policing and nagging, seemed particularly responsible for the positive effect (Gruder, Mermelstein, Kirkendol, Hedeker, Wong, Schreckengost, Warnecke, Burzette, and Miller, 1993).

Drug Abuse For drug abuse, and especially for heroin addiction, three forms of treatment have shown some modest success. The first pairs aversive stimulation, such as shock, with the client's verbal descriptions of his or her need for the drug and consumption of it. Such direct interference with the pleasures of the drug is often combined with relaxation training and systematic desensitization to reduce the tension that promotes drug taking in the first place. But aversive techniques such as these (which were popularized in Anthony Burgess's novel and film *A Clockwork Orange*) have serious shortcomings. In the first place, they often fail to generalize from the therapists' office to the social world in which the addict lives. Second, while the theory underlying aversive techniques indicates that when shock has been paired with desire, people should feel anxious, in fact they commonly feel merely neutral. Thus, the procedure does not evoke a response that is strong enough to resist the social and personal pressures that lead to drug addiction in the first place. Finally, there are ethical considerations. Often, drug addicts are required by law to undergo treatment. Is it really fair to force them to undergo such harsh treatment?

Some of these concerns have led people to favor a second form of treatment for drug addiction, one that substitutes a different drug, methadone, for the heroin that is being consumed. Methadone is a synthetic narcotic that can be taken orally, does not cloud consciousness, lasts longer than heroin, and partially blocks the "rush" that comes if the addict resumes the heroin habit. Early results of methadone maintenance programs indicated that they reduced incarcerations by 98 percent and criminal activities (which support drug purchases) by 94 percent (Dole and Nyswander, 1965). Moreover, because methadone leaves the addict with a relatively clear consciousness, this study revealed that former addicts found new interest in life and were able to take and retain jobs.

The remarkable success of the early programs, however, was not maintained in later studies. Although present evidence indicates that at least 50 percent of enrolled addicts remain in the program for a year, relapse rates are high. Moreover, methadone itself is an addicting drug, for which a secondary black market now exists. It is also a dangerous drug; an increasing number of deaths from methadone overdose have been reported (Platt and Labate, 1976). In addition, many heroin addicts who live in the ghettos and barrios feel that methadone is "establishment medicine," a palliative for the poverty that often leads people to seek the thrills of heroin, and an addicting way of controlling these people (Senay and Renault, 1972). Finally, the same ethical objection to aversive techniques applies here: Is it fair to require heroin addicts to become addicted to another drug, methadone?

A third kind of treatment consists of self-help, live-in programs conducted by such groups as Odyssey House, Daytop Village, and Synanon. Admission to these therapeutic communities is voluntary and selective. Drugs are prohibited. Addicts are required to avoid former friends and family, to become involved in the social structure of the community, and to "begin at the bottom," performing menial labor at the outset and earning their way up the labor ladder with good performance and drug-free behavior. All residents participate in intensive group therapy, which can be very aggressive and confronting. Finally, therapeutic communities vary in their goals. Some, such as Synanon, require residents to remain within the community indefinitely. Others, such as Odyssey House, emphasize returning addicts to the community.

The therapeutic community approach to treatment has, however, serious limitations. Addicts often find the program unappealing, and the drop-out rate is therefore appallingly high. In one study, only 3.7 percent of those who were enrolled completed the program (New York Legislative Commission on Expenditure Review: Narcotics Drug Control, 1971). A more recent study found that residential treatment is about as effective as methadone maintenance for heroin addicts, and both are more effective than no treatment at all, especially for heavy heroin users (Simpson, Savage, and Sells, 1978).

TREATMENTS FOR EATING DISORDERS

Obesity Obesity is an even more intractable problem than alcoholism. Obesity in modern times seems to have arisen from humans' hunter-gatherer days when people struggled to survive and needed to store up fats for scarcer times.

When humans found themselves in the midst of plenty, obesity might result. The resulting oral excesses could create devastating social and medical problems, for eating the right foods and in the right amounts comes hard for most people.

If alcoholism is a difficult problem to control, obesity is even more intractable. Everyone eats. Temptation, therefore, is a constant in nearly everyone's life. And while one can gain some control over what and how much one eats in the short run, it is obviously much more difficult to gain such control in the long run. Given those simple facts, the results of many studies of dieting are precisely as you would expect them to be: People find it relatively easy to take off weight, but quite difficult to keep it off (Brownell and Kramer, 1989; Brownell and Wadden, 1992; Wadden and Bell, 1990). Thus, the many reports of "diet breakthroughs" that clamor for attention on radio and television prove to be quite premature, if not downright unsubstantiated, when clients are followed up over longer periods.

Because the long-term effects of dieting are so pessimistic, those who diet are likely to regain their original weight (and then some) and then initiate another diet. Such **dietary cycling,** however, is not without hazard. In fact, the weight fluctuations that characterize repeated cycling may engender a strong risk of heart disease, a risk that is much greater than the risk associated with being obese (Stamler, Dyer, Shakelle, Neaton and Stamler, 1993).

Notwithstanding the justifiable pessimism that surrounds dieting, there may be something to be said for *modest* (i.e., less than 10 percent of body weight) weight loss. While it is the case that most dieters want to be permanently thin, some want (or can be persuaded) to lose a bit of weight for special purposes: an upcoming wedding, a job interview, and especially to normalize blood pressure and reduce cardiovascular risks. For those whose goals are *modest*, there are many ways to achieve them: appetite suppressants; low- and very-low-calorie diets; self-help groups, such as Weight Watchers or TOPS; as well as cognitive and behavioral therapy. All are approximately equal in effectiveness, though some (appetite suppressants and very-low-calorie diets) work faster than others.

Often, what drives people to endless dieting has less to do with health, and much more to do with being attractive. But if attractiveness is the goal, there are more effective ways to achieve it than dieting. Regular exercise is more likely to firm the body, and to firm it more effectively than dieting. Moreover, exercise not only avoids the risks of dieting, but has health advantages of its own. Moderate exercise, for example, may well reduce blood pressure (Blair, Goodyear, Gibbons, and Cooper, 1984; Dubbert, 1992); heart disease (Blair, Kohl, Paffenbarger, Clark, Cooper, and Gibbons, 1989), and diabetes (Laws and Reaven, 1991; Dubbert, 1992). Exercise, moreover, has remarkable psychological effects, particularly on mood (Plante and Rodin, 1990; Dubbert, 1992).

Finally, among people who are 100 percent or more overweight (meaning that they weigh twice or more than their normal weight), one drastic treatment seems to have relatively durable effects: surgery (Yale, 1989). Of course, there are risks associated with surgery. But those risks may well be lower than the risks associated with extreme obesity.

Bulimia Bulimia combines a morbid fear of obesity with an equally compelling passion for eating. The intense dieting, vomiting, and laxative abuse, the constant preoccupation with food and eating, the sensitivity to changes in body shape, the frequent weighing—or the absolute avoidance of weighing—are not merely symptoms of the disorder but are important in maintaining it (Fairburn, 1985). Cognitive-behavioral therapies enable the client to understand the disorder. They especially enable her to develop the core behavioral abilities that encourage accurate tracking of eating habits and accurate assessment of situations that trigger binges and purges. Clients come to understand how the disorder operates in their particular case, and to identify dysfunctional thoughts regarding weight, body shape, and eating (Agras, Schneider, Arnow, Raeburn, and Telch, 1989a, 1989b; Wilson and Fairburn, 1993). Finally, treatment focuses on strategies that prevent relapse (Marlatt and Gordon, 1985). At present, cognitive-behavioral therapy seems more effective than other approaches, including drug treatment, though the combination of cognitive-behavioral therapy with drugs needs further and deeper investigation (Fairburn, Agras, and Wilson, 1992; Wilson and Fairburn, 1993).

Anorexia Nervosa   Anorexia nervosa involves serious cognitive distortions about body image, as well as irrational beliefs about food and weight gain (see Chapter 16). The disorder is more than a compulsion to be thin. It demands minute-to-minute attention in order to achieve such near-death levels of food intake. Cognitive and behavioral therapies offer some promise in the treatment of anorexia. Techniques such as behavior rehearsal, scheduling of pleasant events, and modeling of proper eating make up the behavioral side of treatment. The cognitive approach concerns the evaluation of thoughts and beliefs and their underlying irrational assumptions, as well as the reinterpretation of body image (Garner and Bemis, 1982). Together, these techniques have helped anorexics to gain and maintain a reasonable weight; at follow-up, however, it appears that many "recovered anorexics" still maintain serious distortions of body image despite their weight gain.

Bingeing   Newly listed as a disorder in DSM-IV, binge eating is common enough to warrant special attention. Characterized simply by recurrent overeating in the absence of the strategies for weight control used by bulimics and anorexics, bingeing accompanies obesity in a substantial proportion of people. Here, too, cognitive-behavioral therapies that focus on the conditions that stimulate bingeing seem to be promising (Telch, Agras, Rossiter, Wilfley, and Kenardy, 1990; Smith, Marcus, and Kaye, 1992; Wilson and Fairburn, 1993).

TREATMENTS FOR THE SCHIZOPHRENIAS

The schizophrenias are the most puzzling and profound of the psychological disorders, and it is not surprising that they have been the most refractory to treatment. The age of hope with regard to the schizophrenias began nearly forty years ago with the advent of the **neuroleptics,** a class of antipsychotic drugs that seemed to have dramatic calming effects on the symptoms of these disorders. Until then, individuals afflicted with these disorders were considered hopeless and warehoused in the back wards of psychiatric hospitals.

Faith in neuroleptics—chlorpromazine, fluphenazine, and haloperidol, among them—gave hope that those with schizophrenia could be cured and released from the psychiatric wards. But unmitigated support for the neuroleptics has declined considerably in recent years, especially since it has been found that those treated with the neuroleptics and released from hospitals are

FOCUS QUESTIONS

1. What are the advantages and disadvantages of treating schizophrenics with neuroleptic drugs?
2. How can psychosocial therapies, especially family therapies, complement drug treatments of schizophrenics?
3. Why can brief hospitalization of schizophrenics sometimes be useful while extended hospitalization of schizophrenics is generally detrimental?

often shortly rehospitalized—the so-called "revolving door phenomenon." Moreover, the side effects that accompany neuroleptic treatment are often quite onerous.

Most neuroleptic treatments have not improved over the past decades. They seem only to control certain symptoms, mainly the positive symptoms of the schizophrenias (see Chapter 12). They are not sufficient to remedy the broad array of cognitive, affective, and social symptoms that these disorders seem to generate. Each year brings a new generation of more focal and powerful neuroleptics to the market, and with them, renewed optimism. But it seems altogether clear that medications alone will not suffice in treating the schizophrenias. Indeed, most researchers and clinicians continue to believe that improvement for those suffering from the schizophrenias, either through treatment or in the natural course of the disorder, is rather unlikely (May, Tuma, Dixon, Yale, Thiele, and Kraus, 1981).

One exception to this generally pessimistic view arises in connection with a relatively new medication, clozapine. Clozapine has proved to be particularly useful for people with whom other treatments have failed (Kane, Honigfeld, Singer, and Meltzer, 1988; Kane and Marder, 1993), and among those with whom other treatments have produced drastic side effects (Lieberman, Saltz, Johns, Pollack, Borenstein, and Kane, 1991). Clozapine has its own set of side effects, especially agranulocytosis—a severe decrease in the blood cells that contain cytoplasm—but if those risks can be identified or reduced, clozapine is likely to be the pharmacological treatment of choice for the schizophrenias (Kane and Marder, 1993).

Today, comprehensive psychosocial treatment may complement these psychopharmacological treatments, amplifying the hope available to those who suffer from the schizophrenias. Psychosocial therapies apply a diathesis-stress model to the schizophrenias. They posit that socioenvironmental stressors exacerbate schizophrenic symptoms in individuals who are biologically predisposed to the schizophrenic disorders (Falloon and Liberman, 1983; Bellack and Mueser, 1993). Indeed, a variety of studies have clearly linked stress, in the form of high tension levels in the family, with relapse into schizophrenia following successful maintenance on neuroleptics alone (Brown, Birley, and Wing, 1972; Vaughn and Leff, 1976) or on psychotherapy and antipsychotic drugs (Doane, Falloon, Goldstein, and Mintz, 1985).

Because schizophrenia is marked especially by deficits in social skills and in cognitive processing, one would expect training in those areas to be especially effective. Social skills training is, in fact, an effective and durable teaching strategy for improving social interaction (Hogarty, Andersen, Reiss, Kornblith, Greenwald, Ulrich, and Carter, 1991), although the degree to which it actually affects functioning within the community still needs to be assessed (Benton and Schroeder, 1990). Treatment of cognitive deficits, however, has been pursued through a variety of methods, none of which yet seems especially promising (Bellack and Mueser, 1993; Brenner, Kraemer, Hermanutz, and Hodel, 1990).

Of the psychosocial interventions for the schizophrenias, none has been more effective than the variety of *family therapies.* These therapies respond to the fact that, in many families, the behavior of the patient makes the family react with criticism, hostility, or emotional overinvolvement, which, in turn, has deleterious effects upon the schizophrenic person. The family therapies commonly take a larger view of the schizophrenias, and are designed to ameliorate the suffering of schizophrenics *and* of their families (Lefley, 1989; Mueser and Glynn, 1990). Several of these therapies are behavioral in nature, concerned with examining families in a functional manner and utilizing behavioral training strategies (Falloon, McGill, Boyd, and Pederson, 1987; Tarrier and Barrowclough, 1990). They aim to reduce family tension by combining education, communication skills training, and problem-solving methods, along with stabilizing neuroleptic medication in long-term intervention (Falloon, Boyd, and McGill, 1984). Results have been heartening: those who receive family therapy function better socially and suffer fewer major exacerbations of schizophrenic symptoms than do those treated with a more traditional individual-oriented approach (Falloon, Boyd, McGill, Williamson, Razani, Moss, Gilderman, and Simpson, 1985). Recent studies show that behavioral family treatment results in markedly lower relapse rates, fewer rehospitalizations, improvement in the patient's social functioning, and substantially lower levels of family burden and distress (Bellack and Mueser, 1993).

But behavioral family therapy is conducted almost exclusively on an experimental basis in research studies, and it is therefore not widely available for outpatient treatment. Instead, individual therapy is the most commonly available treatment for outpatients. There is little evidence, however, to support the efficacy of psychodynamic or client-centered individual or group psychotherapy (Mosher and Keith, 1980).

Because the schizophrenias are such severe disorders, those with schizophrenic symptoms more than occasionally seem to require hospitalization. Brief hospitalizations can be quite useful in that they may allow for a careful evaluation of the patient's symptoms, as well as prescription of psychotropic medication. Moreover, such hospitalizations often take the pressure off the patient, as well as the immediate family, affording the momentary relief that allows all parties to recoup strength and perspective.

Extended hospitalizations, however, are very costly psychologically (and often monetarily, too). The longer the hospitalization, the greater the probability of merely marginal adjustment after discharge. Those who are hospitalized over long periods of time often lose emotional contact with their families, their jobs, and the "real world" in which all of us live, making return and recontact quite difficult. Moreover, psychiatric hospitals, perhaps because they are understaffed and underfinanced, are often dangerous places where death and disability rates are substantially higher than might ordinarily be expected. In fact, since publication of a study that is now more than two decades old (Rosenhan, 1973), no studies on the experience of psychiatric hospitalization have been initiated. Combined with the reduction of governmental allocations for psychiatric hospitals, the absence of attention to such institutions suggests an abandonment that has pessimistic implications for each patient.

Less restrictive alternatives to long-term hospitalization may lead to a better prognosis for patients. Supervised halfway houses are especially attractive as therapeutic alternatives because they minimally disrupt the contact between the patients and their social environment, and because, unlike psychiatric hospitals, they are so patently temporary residences. Day hospitals, which provide daytime care for patients and return them to their families in the evenings, are sometimes also alternatives to full hospitalization.

The dangers of hospitalizing children and adolescents, especially for long periods of time, however, cannot be overstated. There are differences between hospitals for children, of course: some are better, some worse. But those differences need to be investigated and demonstrated, rather than taken for granted on the basis of reputation and advertising. To the extent that psychiatric hospitals generally are underfunded and understaffed, hospitals for children are even more so. Thus, many hospitals for adults, adolescents, and children come quickly to rely on medication for controlling, rather than treating, large numbers of patients. Children, because they are young and lack legal control of their lives, seem especially vulnerable to the callousness of such institutions (U. S. House of Representatives, Select Committee on Children, Youth, and Families, 1992; Armstrong, 1993).

Specific treatments, where they exist, are the quickest and most effective way of treating specific problems. Unfortunately, however, there continue to be problems for which no specific treatment is really effective. Severe autism is one such problem, and some forms of schizophrenia are others. Such problems are presently untreatable, but the future holds promise for their treatment. Most of the specific biological and psychological treatments that were described here and in earlier chapters simply did not exist thirty years ago. Progress in this area has been explosive and likely will accelerate further in coming years.

Global Treatments

Besides specific problems, there are also problems that are global and that resist specification. Among these are problems of meaning, where people ask about the purpose of their lives, and problems in loving. The latter, while specific enough, is an affective problem for which, unless it is promoted by fear, no specific treatment remedies exist. For global problems, global treatments may be the only remedy.

Global treatments include those that were discussed in Chapter 4: the psychodynamically oriented therapies, as well as the existential ones. These therapies seek to explore, strengthen, and change the *self*—not merely the individual's *image* of self, but the host of traits, abilities, beliefs, attitudes, and broad dispositions that give rise to self. They may even try to help people develop a sense of self, to know who they are, and what they believe. The goals of self-exploration and changing the self in accord with that knowledge are the goals of these global therapies.

THE SEARCH FOR SELF

The problems of self—of the meaning of life and work, of loving, and of commitment—are fundamental problems that everyone faces, or avoids, throughout life. These problems need not be considered abnormal, for we are not put in this world with a script that tells us "what it's all about." Each of us discovers that for himself or herself. This process is often as complicated and painful as it is fascinating, and one simply may want a professional guide to lead one through the forests and around the dead ends.

Traditional vehicles for self-exploration have been Freudian or Jungian psychoanalysis and their many psychodynamic offshoots. These psychodynamic therapies are more than treatments for distress. They are methods of self-examination. In "Psychoanalysis: Terminable or Interminable," Freud (1905/1976) concluded that the process of self-exploration is an interminable

▼ Global treatments may help individuals to explore, strengthen, and change the self.

one for which psychoanalysis can serve as a useful adjunct throughout life. In fact, the ideal psychoanalytic client is still captured by the acronym YAVIS—young, attractive, verbal, intelligent, and successful—someone who may have some problems but, on the spectrum of these matters, is surely experiencing no real desperation. The YAVIS client benefits from psychoanalysis to the extent that he or she develops deep understandings of self that, in turn, lead to greater change and self-fulfillment.

Do these therapies work? The answer to this question is complex. When global treatments are used to facilitate the search for self, questions about effectiveness lose much of their meaning, for here, notions of "cure" and of "symptoms remission" are entirely inappropriate. To the extent that the question has any meaning at all, the answer must be a private one, entirely dependent upon whether the client *believes* it has been meaningful. When asked, close to 90 percent of such clients reported themselves satisfied with the outcomes of such treatment (Strupp, Fox, and Lessler, 1969).

The treatments that have been discussed in this section apply to problems that are full-grown. Such problems already will have taken their toll in human misery, long before they come to the attention of professional therapists. Once they do, moreover, treatment will be expensive and time-consuming, and outcomes will not always be optimistic. Can anything be done to prevent problems from arising in the first place? And if they do arise, can their effects be minimized and contained? Finally, are there alternatives to the kinds of treatment that have been discussed in this section, alternatives that utilize community rather than professional resources? Because, as an old adage tells us, it is the squeaky wheel that gets the oil, clinical psychology and psychiatry have attended mainly to those who are in need of treatment, often desperately in need of it. But plain common sense makes clear that the squeaky wheel principle is wrong. If problems were prevented in the first place, or minimized before they flowered, both human misery and the need for expensive professional treatment would be greatly reduced. In the next section, we turn to efforts to prevent and contain human distress, as well as alternative modes of treatment in the community.

OUTREACH AND PREVENTION: THE HOPES OF COMMUNITY PSYCHOLOGY

Traditional psychological treatment suffers two major liabilities. First, as we have seen, it arrives only *after* a problem has entailed untold misery for the client. And second, there are simply not enough professional therapists to treat all those who are in need. As a result, psychologists and psychiatrists have become increasingly involved in *community* efforts to *prevent* and *contain* psychological disorders. Because they are allied with others, the efforts of psychologists can now influence the psychological well-being of a much larger proportion of the population than is possible through traditional treatment.

These collaborative efforts between psychologists and the community take place on three fronts: prevention, containment, and alternative modes of treatment and rehabilitation. We take these areas up in turn.

Prevention programs such as community outreach projects, Headstart and preschool interventions are intended to reduce the overall incidence of mental illness, rather than treating it only when it arises.

Prevention

An ounce of prevention is worth a pound of cure, we are told. And a review of the chapters that deal with anxiety, depression, crime and delinquency, and children's disorders, makes clear that many of the multiple causes of these distresses could well have been prevented. Unfortunately, our society budgets much less for preventive efforts than for treatment, largely because of the squeaky-wheel principle. But it has chosen to invest resources in three areas that are significant for prevention: child-care facilities, preschool preparation, and job training.

CHILD CARE

Imagine a mother raising three children, all of them under five. Worse yet, imagine her as a single parent, responsible for the economics, as well as the psychological welfare of her brood.

> I had to work at night, while the children slept. If one of them was sick and needed me, and the neighbor's kid wasn't free to baby-sit, I missed work and pay. There was one year when I was fired from four jobs because Julie and Richard were sick a lot and needed me. Finally, I just couldn't take it.

Such mothers are hardly rare in our society. In 1990, 61.4 percent of working mothers had children under the age of eighteen. And more than 54 percent had children under age six. Indeed, even among married couples, more than half reported that both spouses were working (Bureau of National Labor Affairs, 1990). Either their own needs, or those of their children, and commonly both, are neglected.

Child-care facilities provide a safe and healthy environment for young children, one that parents and children can count on. Not only do they reduce familial pressures, but often they provide children with experiences that simply could not be gotten at home, such as learning to socialize with other children and to respond to adults other than parents. These experiences are likely beneficial for children when they begin school.

1. How do good child-care facilities, preschool interventions, and job-training programs help to prevent psychological problems?
2. Give some examples of containment services and explain why they are effective at limiting the consequences of psychological crises.
3. What are some alternatives to the traditional mental hospital and why have they often been beneficial to patients?
4. Describe some of the accomplishments of the self-help groups organized by former mental patients.

PRESCHOOL INTERVENTIONS

The early school years are fertile ground for psychological problems. Once a child falls behind in work, fails to make friends, or becomes disruptive in the classroom or playground, the likelihood is high that these problems will endure and grow. Often, such problems develop because children are ill-prepared for the school experience, either intellectually or socially. Preschool programs, such as Operation Headstart, are intended to encourage the development of cognitive and intellectual skills necessary for kindergarten and the early school grades.

JOB TRAINING AND RETRAINING

Poverty and unemployment take enormous tolls on people, and they probably spawn more social problems than any other cause. Simple economic need often drives people to crime and violence. Training the unemployed in the host of skills necessary both to find a job and keep it goes a long way toward preventing psychological problems.

It is important to note that psychologists do not usually establish or control child-care, preschool, or job-training facilities. Rather, their contribution is made through *consultation* and *collaboration* with members of the community who want to establish these centers in the first place. They often and successfully consult in schools to increase communication between teachers, students, and their families (Sarason, 1974). They may even consult with urban renewal organizations regarding creating new cities that are psychologically stimulating and that encourage neighborliness and conviviality (Lemkau, 1969). And often they consult with legislators, policymakers, and the courts on such issues as school desegregation and detention of juveniles, issues whose resolution can eventually prevent the development of psychological difficulties. By collaboration with other members of the community, the resources of psychologists can be utilized more broadly and effectively than would be possible in traditional professional roles.

How effective are these efforts at prevention? The evidence with regard to preschool programs such as Operation Headstart suggests that they are not as good in some regards as had earlier been hoped, and that they surpass expectations, often in quite surprising directions, in others (Zigler, Taussig, and Black, 1992). Child-care facilities and job training, on the other hand, have not yet been evaluated for their impact on psychological distress. Relative to other alternatives (such as the poverty that might result without child care, or the psychological pressure on parents who are unable to afford such care or obtain such job training) they are effective, but *how* effective is not yet clear. The entire area of prevention, however, is still in its infancy, still more of a hope than a reality (Cowen, 1977a, 1977b; Price, Cowen, Lorion, and Ramos-McKay, 1989); it may yet be too early to expect full and careful evaluation of these efforts.

Containment

Psychological crises often have immediate consequences. A heated argument may result in violence; a painful rejection, in suicide; an overwhelming impulse, in rape, murder, or drunkenness. **Containment services** are designed to limit the consequences of such crises, as they affect the individual, the potential or actual victim, and their families. In the main, these services are charac-

► Containment services are designed to limit the consequences of crises. Here a person who has attempted to commit suicide is being counseled.

terized by three features. First, treatment is delivered quickly. The potential Friday night suicide, for example, need not wait until Monday morning when the clinics open; by then, it may be too late. He or she can immediately go to a crisis intervention center, or phone a "hot-line" for counseling. Second, services are delivered to a broad range of people, including many who would never seek traditional psychological help. And third, they are located in the community and offered by the community, rather than through hospitals, clinics, or professionally trained therapists. Their very visibility and availability ensures their use.

"HOT-LINES"

The telephone **hot-line** is a twenty-four-hour phone service for people who are undergoing deep distress. The first of these hot-lines was established in 1958 by Norman Farberow and Edwin Schneidman as part of the Los Angeles Suicide Prevention Center (Farberow, 1974).

In the main, hot-lines are staffed by carefully trained nonprofessional volunteers. The primary functions of the volunteer are to establish a sympathetic relationship with the caller, to help him clarify his problem, and to formulate a constructive plan that immediately mobilizes the individual's resources as well as those of family, friends, and community. Volunteers will often attempt to assess the suicidal potential of their caller (see Chapter 11), as well as whether the suicide has already been attempted. This kind of work is exceedingly stressful for the volunteers, for they, too, are on the "hot seat." The results of their efforts often determine whether someone will continue to live, yet because callers often hang up without leaving their name or phone number, the volunteers rarely learn to what extent they have helped. As a result, volunteers often become discouraged on this job, and frequently burn out quickly.

Beyond offering instant counseling, hot-lines serve to educate callers about available treatment resources. Often, callers will be referred to a community mental health center, where the causes of the crisis can be explored and treated in greater depth. The emphasis, however, is not on long-term treatment, but on crisis intervention and speedy referral.

Such emergency treatment appears effective in reducing suicide rates. Among 8,000 high-risk callers to the Suicide Prevention Center in Los Angeles, Farberow (1970) reports that fewer than 2 percent committed suicide,

HE SAID HE'D NEVER HIT YOU AGAIN . . .

BUT THAT'S WHAT HE SAID LAST TIME.
Stop the cycle of violence.
For help, call (401) 861-2760
V-TDD

▲ The Providence (Rhode Island) Domestic Abuse Network operates a shelter, a twenty-four hour telephone hotline, support services, and community outreach to victims of domestic violence. This poster and others like it in both English and all major immigrant languages aims to stop the cycle of domestic violence by showing battered women that there is help for them.

▶ These women and their children are in a shelter for battered women. Much of community psychiatry is designed to educate people and limit the consequences of problems when they arise—here, by letting women in abusive relationships know their options.

compared to the estimated 6 percent overall rate of suicide among such persons.

Today, nearly every large city, and many small ones, have suicide hot-lines. Moreover, hot-line services have been extended to people who are experiencing many different kinds of crises, including hot-lines for distressed employees, runaways, troubled families, abused and abusive spouses. For example, child-abuse hot-lines seek to cool parental rage before harm is done to children. Other hot-lines exist to defuse impulses to drink, take drugs, gamble, and engage in violent behavior. Finally, there are yet others that have no particular focus or specialty, but that attempt to provide a listening ear and immediate counsel to whoever calls.

Hot-line users are often ashamed of their behavior and their lack of control. The fact that they are assured of anonymity encourages them to call in the first place; that may be one of the hot-line's greatest strengths. For while hot-line services neither cure nor provide long-term solutions, they diffuse crises and head off serious and immediate losses. That is no small virtue.

SHORT-TERM TREATMENT

In many cases, distraught individuals may be unable to undertake long-term treatment, but they may be able to go for short-term **crisis treatment.** Such treatment rarely requires more than six sessions. In it, the therapist is extremely active, helping the client to focus on his or her problem, providing support and reassurance, and devising constructive solutions (Golan, 1978). Such crisis intervention often enables a person to resume her life without hospitalization or disruption of employment.

HELP FOR VICTIMS AND THEIR FAMILIES

Being the victim of brutality often has enormous psychological consequences that, if left unattended, can be long-lasting. Immediately after being raped, for example, women experience considerable psychological disorganization, including feelings of insecurity and loneliness and rampant fear, and they are subject to heightened influence by others. Depending on their prior experi-

▶ Here a clinical psychologist is consulting police on how to handle hostage situations. He is providing them with psychological cues for police negotiations and actions in such situations.

ences and background, these fears and insecurities can develop into stable patterns of avoidance (Burgess and Holmstrom, 1974). Their spouses and families, moreover, often experience changes in these women's attitudes and affection that can be directly traced to these traumatic experiences (Bard and Sangrey, 1979). As described in Chapter 8, political hostages, too, have similar reactions to the trauma and humiliation that result from being held against their will (Sank, 1979). Short-term crisis interventions may range from support and counseling, to brief behavioral treatments that are useful in alleviating and containing these symptoms.

Battered wives and children once had no recourse except to "take it," or perhaps to turn to the police and courts. As their numbers have become known, however, concern for these victims has heightened and has led to the establishment of shelters for battered women. Such shelters provide temporary sanctuary for women and their children, enabling them to take some time out to recover from abuse and plan their futures. Staffed almost entirely by nonprofessionals, their central function is protection. Unfortunately, shelters are often dangerous and unhappy places—dangerous because of possible retaliation from still-angry husbands, and unhappy because these women are beset with doubts about themselves and their futures.

EARLY DETECTION OF PSYCHOLOGICAL DIFFICULTIES

Several programs have been concerned with detecting behavioral problems in school children. Some programs have trained teachers to detect the early signs of maladjustment (Zax and Cowen, 1969; Levine and Graziano, 1971), while others have used brief tests that can be easily scored (Cowen, 1973; Price, Cowen, Lorion and Ramos-McKay, 1989). Both types of programs seek to identify early signs of maladjustment so that children can be referred for remediation before their problems become relatively insurmountable.

CONSULTATION

Psychologists and psychiatrists are often consulted by a variety of other professionals and organizations. They may be consulted by teachers on how to increase children's motivation, or about how to handle a particular child's problem in the classroom rather than at the clinic. They will often be consulted by industry about how to make working conditions more pleasant, and how to reduce executive stress.

One ingenious example of consultation has arisen in the training of police who are often called to mediate family quarrels. Family quarrels are a major source of assaults and homicides. They are dangerous, not only for the participants, but also for those who intervene. Many police have been assaulted while attempting to calm family conflicts. In one New York City precinct, police were given extensive training by psychologists on how to intervene in these family quarrels, and then worked as family crisis intervention teams in that precinct. In contrast to the police in the neighboring precinct, who were not given such training and who both suffered and witnessed the same amount of violence that is usually associated with such calls, the trained police fared much better. In the next 1,388 calls to intervene in family crises, trained team members did not suffer an assault, did not witness a family homicide, and were able to markedly reduce the number of assaults on family members (Bard, 1970). The enormous success of this program in New York City has led to its wider adoption. The positive results strongly support the idea of providing psychological consultation for other service agencies.

Rehabilitation

Treatment and rehabilitation of those who are seriously distressed was once exclusively in the hands of professional psychologists and psychiatrists and was conducted mainly in psychiatric hospitals. But partly because of shortages of fully qualified personnel, and partly because hospitals have serious shortcomings as treatment centers for the psychologically distressed, community psychologists have devised other settings in which such people and problems can be treated. They have trained nonprofessionals to deal with these problems. They have established alternative treatment centers such as halfway houses, residential treatment programs, and day and night hospitals. And they have encouraged patients and former patients to establish self-help groups, designed to find employment for and combat discrimination against, those who suffer or have suffered serious psychological distress.

TRAINING NONPROFESSIONALS

It takes a long time to become a psychologist, psychiatrist, or social worker. Not many people have the time or resources to undertake such training, and as a result, there are far too few trained people to meet current need. Recently, there have been increasing efforts to train paraprofessionals in this area. Whether through on-the-job training, or in undergraduate and junior colleges, these paraprofessionals are trained to take over some of the functions of the professional. Trained paraprofessionals can interview, test, make home visits, and often handle social and vocational rehabilitation under the supervision of psychologists or psychiatrists. They can serve as aides and attendants in psychiatric hospitals. And indeed, some studies have shown that paraprofessionals can be trained to be good therapists (Rioch, 1967). Though their training is narrower than that of fully qualified professionals, and though they can perform fewer tasks, a variety of studies have indicated that what they do, they do quite well (Rioch, 1967; Brown, 1974). Moreover, they vastly increase the number of people who can be treated, enabling professionals to reserve their skills for complicated problems, for consultation and supervision, and for training.

ALTERNATIVE TREATMENT CENTERS

The search for alternatives to the traditional mental hospital is an ongoing one. As we have seen, long-term patients in such hospitals tend to become habituated to that environment, and subsequently unable to function outside of it. Even short-term patients suffer enormously after discharge; they have difficulty finding adequate employment and establishing satisfying social lives. As a result, psychologists and psychiatrists try not to hospitalize in the first place, and to use partial care centers and transitional facilities. Such facilities maintain patients in the community where they can often retain old friendships and establish new ones, and where they can be trained for job responsibilities.

Day and night hospitals are intended to serve as transition points for fully hospitalized patients, as well as treatment centers for those who were never hospitalized. In day hospitals, patients are treated during the day, and then permitted to join their families at night and over the weekend. Night hospitals are for patients who either have daytime employment, or families with whom they are comfortable and supported. Such patients return to the hospital in the evening to continue their treatment. Participation in day and night treatment is often brief, just long enough to enable the former patient to get his or her feet on the community ground.

Halfway houses or community lodges are also designed as transition experiences between hospital and community. Optimally, these residences house no more than twenty people. With only paraprofessionals in residence, and a psychologist or psychiatrist on call, halfway houses serve to train patients to govern themselves after they have been governed by the hospital. Here patients make decisions about running the house. They often establish small businesses to support themselves, and they receive training both in vocations and in the skills necessary for holding a job. Former patients who have resided in halfway houses before fully entering the community are less likely to be rehospitalized than those who have entered the community directly from the hospital.

Residential treatment centers attempt to avoid the hospital entirely. Here, distressed people are treated in the community, either by families who are will-

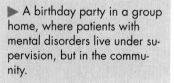

▶ A birthday party in a group home, where patients with mental disorders live under supervision, but in the community.

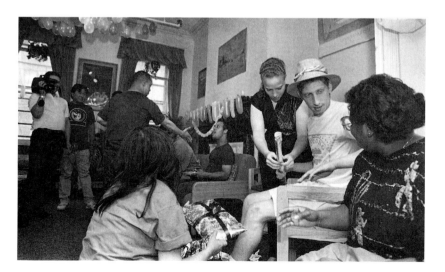

ing to take them in (Stein, Test, and Marx, 1975; Polak and Kirby, 1976; Mosher and Menn, 1978), or in residences established for these purposes. Such treatment commonly takes more time than does traditional drug-oriented therapy. But its consequences are commonly more beneficial. People in these settings emerge without a "record" of psychiatric hospitalization, which enables them to find employment more easily and to establish social relationships with greater ease and less stigma. The evidence, moreover, suggests that residential treatment centers cost less to operate than traditional hospitals (Kiesler, 1982a).

SELF-HELP GROUPS

Funds for treating the psychologically distressed, which never were plentiful, are much less available today than a decade ago. Many psychiatric hospitals have closed. Many patients have been discharged, often to "board and care" facilities. One would expect that the closing of psychiatric hospitals would free funds for community treatment, but that has not been the case. Rather, patients have been thrown on their own resources—and some have done some fairly remarkable things without much help from government and society.

One focus of self-help groups has been to establish a community where patients can associate with and help each other. Because they often reside in the marginal areas of cities, former patients have been plagued by poverty and dislocation in addition to their own psychological difficulties. Self-help groups have established cooperatives where members can obtain food and services at affordable prices. Using their political strength—for they now constitute a sizable voting minority in some neighborhoods—they have been able to locate community facilities in which to meet. Increasingly, they have turned to the law to remedy the abuses of discrimination that they face. Such groups as NAPA (Network Against Psychiatric Assault), moreover, have sought to correct what they perceive to be abuses in patient care. Increasingly, members of such groups are invited to the professional meetings of psychologists and psychiatrists, to "tell their story" and to alert professionals to the difficulties that present and former patients experience.

SUMMARY

1. The kinds of people who offer help for psychological problems, and the kinds of help they offer, are difficult to enumerate, and harder still to catalog properly. Most people are familiar with the names of one or two kinds of traditional therapists: psychologists, psychiatrists, psychiatric social workers, and psychiatric nurses. But the available help for psychological problems extends far beyond those narrow confines and includes friends, teachers, parents, clergy, and self-help groups, to name a few.

2. Psychotherapy is an active collaborative process in which both therapist and client work to overcome the client's problems. While outcome of the process clearly depends on the competence of the therapist, it depends equally on the hopes and expectations of the client.

3. The therapeutic relationship is facilitated when the therapist shows empathy, warmth, and genuineness. It is also enhanced when the client trusts

and feels free to question and when treatment goals are specified early in the treatment process.

4. The effectiveness of therapy can be assessed by considering the client's satisfaction with the treatment, by measuring the extent of the client's personality change, and by examining the impact of treatment on target behaviors.

5. After finding a therapist whom one likes, and avoiding poorly trained or simply immature therapists, one is ready to consider the type of treatment that will be most useful. Generally, the more specific the problem, the better the chance that it can be resolved through specific treatments. The less specific the problem, the more likely global treatment will be called upon.

6. There are psychological problems that are quite treatable today that could not be resolved a decade ago. Great strides have been made in behavioral treatment of fears, panic attacks, phobias, and compulsions, in cognitive treatment of depression, and in pharmacological treatment of bipolar depression. But some forms of schizophrenia are still difficult problems to cope with.

7. Psychologists and psychiatrists have become increasingly involved in community efforts to prevent and contain psychological disorders. Three significant areas in which funds have been invested in an effort to prevent psychological disorders from developing are: child-care facilities, preschool interventions, and job training and retraining. Areas in which containment services have been designed to limit the consequences of psychological crises include hot-lines, short-term crisis treatment centers, and shelters for battered wives.

8. Because some treatments have powerful side effects, and because some treatment settings, such as hospitals, create undesired difficulties for patients, increasing effort has been directed toward finding treatment alternatives. Paraprofessionals are being trained to take on many of the tasks that were once the exclusive province of professionals. Residential treatment centers and halfway houses often supplement the traditional psychiatric hospital. And former patients are gradually collecting into self-help groups.

QUESTIONS FOR CRITICAL THINKING

1. Why does administering the Role Induction Interview before treatment contribute to client improvements as a result of therapy?

2. Why do therapist empathy, warmth, and genuineness matter toward a successful therapeutic outcome?

3. Explain why drug treatments are considered relatively transient rather than long-term solutions for alleviating anxiety.

4. Why are extended hospitalizations of schizophrenics often detrimental to them, and what do you think are the best alternatives to such hospitalization?

5. What is the value of community psychology?

NUMERICAL LISTING OF DSM-IV DIAGNOSES AND CODES

To maintain compatibility with ICD-9-CM, some DSM-IV diagnoses share the same code numbers. These are indicated in this list by brackets.

NOS = Not Otherwise Specified

290.0	Dementia of the Alzheimer's Type, With Late Onset, Uncomplicated
⌐ 290.10	Dementia Due to Creutzfeldt-Jakob Disease
│ 290.10	Dementia Due to Pick's Disease
└ 290.10	Dementia of the Alzheimer's Type, With Early Onset, Uncomplicated
290.11	Dementia of the Alzheimer's Type, With Early Onset, With Delirium
290.12	Dementia of the Alzheimer's Type, With Early Onset, With Delusions
290.13	Dementia of the Alzheimer's Type, With Early Onset, With Depressed Mood
290.20	Dementia of the Alzheimer's Type, With Late Onset, With Delusions
290.21	Dementia of the Alzheimer's Type, With Late Onset, With Depressed Mood
290.3	Dementia of the Alzheimer's Type, With Late Onset, With Delirium
290.40	Vascular Dementia, Uncomplicated
290.41	Vascular Dementia, With Delirium
290.42	Vascular Dementia, With Delusions
290.43	Vascular Dementia, With Depressed Mood
⌐ 291.0	Alcohol Intoxication Delirium
└ 291.0	Alcohol Withdrawal Delirium
291.1	Alcohol-Induced Persisting Amnestic Disorder
291.2	Alcohol-Induced Persisting Dementia
291.3	Alcohol-Induced Psychotic Disorder, With Hallucinations

291.5	Alcohol-Induced Psychotic Disorder, With Delusions
⌐ 291.8	Alcohol-Induced Anxiety Disorder
│ 291.8	Alcohol-Induced Mood Disorder
│ 291.8	Alcohol-Induced Sexual Dysfunction
│ 291.8	Alcohol-Induced Sleep Disorder
└ 291.8	Alcohol Withdrawal
291.9	Alcohol-Related Disorder NOS
⌐ 292.0	Amphetamine Withdrawal
│ 292.0	Cocaine Withdrawal
│ 292.0	Nicotine Withdrawal
│ 292.0	Opioid Withdrawal
│ 292.0	Other (or Unknown) Substance Withdrawal
└ 292.0	Sedative, Hypnotic, or Anxiolytic Withdrawal
⌐ 292.11	Amphetamine-Induced Psychotic Disorder, With Delusions
│ 292.11	Cannabis-Induced Psychotic Disorder, With Delusions
│ 292.11	Cocaine-Induced Psychotic Disorder, With Delusions
│ 292.11	Hallucinogen-Induced Psychotic Disorder, With Delusions
│ 292.11	Inhalant-Induced Psychotic Disorder, With Delusions
│ 292.11	Opioid-Induced Psychotic Disorder, With Delusions
│ 292.11	Other (or Unknown) Substance-Induced Psychotic Disorder, With Delusions
│ 292.11	Phencyclidine-Induced Psychotic Disorder, With Delusions
└ 292.11	Sedative-, Hypnotic-, or Anxiolytic-Induced Psychotic Disorder, With Delusions
⌐ 292.12	Amphetamine-Induced Psychotic Disorder, With Hallucinations

292.12 Cannabis-Induced Psychotic Disorder, With Hallucinations
292.12 Cocaine-Induced Psychotic Disorder, With Hallucinations
292.12 Hallucinogen-Induced Psychotic Disorder, With Hallucinations
292.12 Inhalant-Induced Psychotic Disorder, With Hallucinations
292.12 Opioid-Induced Psychotic Disorder, With Hallucinations
292.12 Other (or Unknown) Substance-Induced Psychotic Disorder, With Hallucinations
292.12 Phencyclidine-Induced Psychotic Disorder, With Hallucinations
292.12 Sedative-, Hypnotic-, or Anxiolytic-Induced Psychotic Disorder, With Hallucinations
292.81 Amphetamine Intoxication Delirium
292.81 Cannabis Intoxication Delirium
292.81 Cocaine Intoxication Delirium
292.81 Hallucinogen Intoxication Delirium
292.81 Inhalant Intoxication Delirium
292.81 Opioid Intoxication Delirium
292.81 Other (or Unknown) Substance-Induced Delirium
292.81 Phencyclidine Intoxication Delirium
292.81 Sedative, Hypnotic, or Anxiolytic Intoxication Delirium
292.81 Sedative, Hypnotic, or Anxiolytic Withdrawal Delirium
292.82 Inhalant-Induced Persisting Dementia
292.82 Other (or Unknown) Substance-Induced Persisting Dementia
292.82 Sedative-, Hypnotic-, or Anxiolytic-Induced Persisting Dementia
292.83 Other (or Unknown) Substance-Induced Persisting Amnestic Disorder
292.83 Sedative-, Hypnotic-, or Anxiolytic-Induced Persisting Amnestic Disorder
292.84 Amphetamine-Induced Mood Disorder
292.84 Cocaine-Induced Mood Disorder
292.84 Hallucinogen-Induced Mood Disorder
292.84 Inhalant-Induced Mood Disorder
292.84 Opioid-Induced Mood Disorder
292.84 Other (or Unknown) Substance-Induced Mood Disorder
292.84 Phencyclidine-Induced Mood Disorder
292.84 Sedative-, Hypnotic-, or Anxiolytic-Induced Mood Disorder
292.89 Amphetamine-Induced Anxiety Disorder
292.89 Amphetamine-Induced Sexual Dysfunction
292.89 Amphetamine-Induced Sleep Disorder
292.89 Amphetamine Intoxication

292.89 Caffeine-Induced Anxiety Disorder
292.89 Caffeine-Induced Sleep Disorder
292.89 Cannabis-Induced Anxiety Disorder
292.89 Cannabis Intoxication
292.89 Cocaine-Induced Anxiety Disorder
292.89 Cocaine-Induced Sexual Dysfunction
292.89 Cocaine-Induced Sleep Disorder
292.89 Cocaine Intoxication
292.89 Hallucinogen-Induced Anxiety Disorder
292.89 Hallucinogen Intoxication
292.89 Hallucinogen Persisting Perception Disorder
292.89 Inhalant-Induced Anxiety Disorder
292.89 Inhalant Intoxication
292.89 Opioid-Induced Sleep Disorder
292.89 Opioid-Induced Sexual Dysfunction
292.89 Opioid Intoxication
292.89 Other (or Unknown) Substance-Induced Anxiety Disorder
292.89 Other (or Unknown) Substance-Induced Sexual Dysfunction
292.89 Other (or Unknown) Substance-Induced Sleep Disorder
292.89 Other (or Unknown) Substance Intoxication
292.89 Phencyclidine-Induced Anxiety Disorder
292.89 Phencyclidine Intoxication
292.89 Sedative-, Hypnotic-, or Anxiolytic-Induced Anxiety Disorder
292.89 Sedative-, Hypnotic-, or Anxiolytic-Induced Sexual Dysfunction
292.89 Sedative-, Hypnotic-, or Anxiolytic-Induced Sleep Disorder
292.89 Sedative, Hypnotic, or Anxiolytic Intoxication
292.9 Amphetamine-Related Disorder NOS
292.9 Caffeine-Related Disorder NOS
292.9 Cannabis-Related Disorder NOS
292.9 Cocaine-Related Disorder NOS
292.9 Hallucinogen-Related Disorder NOS
292.9 Inhalant-Related Disorder NOS
292.9 Nicotine-Related Disorder NOS
292.9 Opioid-Related Disorder NOS
292.9 Other (or Unknown) Substance-Related Disorder NOS
292.9 Phencyclidine-Related Disorder NOS
292.9 Sedative-, Hypnotic-, or Anxiolytic-Related Disorder NOS
293.0 Delirium Due to . . . [Indicate the General Medical Condition]
293.81 Psychotic Disorder Due to . . . [Indicate the General Medical Condition], With Delusions

293.82	Psychotic Disorder Due to . . . *[Indicate the General Medical Condition]*, With Hallucinations
293.83	Mood Disorder Due to . . . *[Indicate the General Medical Condition]*
293.89	Anxiety Disorder Due to . . . *[Indicate the General Medical Condition]*
293.89	Catatonic Disorder Due to . . . *[Indicate the General Medical Condition]*
293.9	Mental Disorder NOS Due to . . . *[Indicate the General Medical Condition]*
294.0	Amnestic Disorder Due to . . . *[Indicate the General Medical Condition]*
294.1	Dementia Due to . . . *[Indicate the General Medical Condition]*
294.8	Amnestic Disorder NOS
294.8	Dementia NOS
294.9	Cognitive Disorder NOS
294.9	Dementia Due to HIV Disease
295.10	Schizophrenia, Disorganized Type
295.20	Schizophrenia, Catatonic Type
295.30	Schizophrenia, Paranoid Type
295.40	Schizophreniform Disorder
295.60	Schizophrenia, Residual Type
295.70	Schizoaffective Disorder
295.90	Schizophrenia, Undifferentiated Type
296.00	Bipolar I Disorder, Single Manic Episode, Unspecified
296.01	Bipolar I Disorder, Single Manic Episode, Mild
296.02	Bipolar I Disorder, Single Manic Episode, Moderate
296.03	Bipolar I Disorder, Single Manic Episode, Severe Without Psychotic Features
296.04	Bipolar I Disorder, Single Manic Episode, Severe With Psychotic Features
296.05	Bipolar I Disorder, Single Manic Episode, In Partial Remission
296.06	Bipolar I Disorder, Single Manic Episode, In Full Remission
296.20	Major Depressive Disorder, Single Episode, Unspecified
296.21	Major Depressive Disorder, Single Episode, Mild
296.22	Major Depressive Disorder, Single Episode, Moderate
296.23	Major Depressive Disorder, Single Episode, Severe Without Psychotic Features
296.24	Major Depressive Disorder, Single Episode, Severe With Psychotic Features
296.25	Major Depressive Disorder, Single Episode, In Partial Remission
296.26	Major Depressive Disorder, Single Episode, In Full Remission
296.30	Major Depressive Disorder, Recurrent, Unspecified
296.31	Major Depressive Disorder, Recurrent, Mild
296.32	Major Depressive Disorder, Recurrent, Moderate
296.33	Major Depressive Disorder, Recurrent, Severe Without Psychotic Features
296.34	Major Depressive Disorder, Recurrent, Severe With Psychotic Features
296.35	Major Depressive Disorder, Recurrent, In Partial Remission
296.36	Major Depressive Disorder, Recurrent, In Full Remission
296.40	Bipolar I Disorder, Most Recent Episode Hypomanic
296.40	Bipolar I Disorder, Most Recent Episode Manic, Unspecified
296.41	Bipolar I Disorder, Most Recent Episode Manic, Mild
296.42	Bipolar I Disorder, Most Recent Episode Manic, Moderate
296.43	Bipolar I Disorder, Most Recent Episode Manic, Severe Without Psychotic Features
296.44	Bipolar I Disorder, Most Recent Episode Manic, Severe With Psychotic Features
296.45	Bipolar I Disorder, Most Recent Episode Manic, In Partial Remission
296.46	Bipolar I Disorder, Most Recent Episode Manic, In Full Remission
296.50	Bipolar I Disorder, Most Recent Episode Depressed, Unspecified
296.51	Bipolar I Disorder, Most Recent Episode Depressed, Mild
296.52	Bipolar I Disorder, Most Recent Episode Depressed, Moderate
296.53	Bipolar I Disorder, Most Recent Episode Depressed, Severe Without Psychotic Features
296.54	Bipolar I Disorder, Most Recent Episode Depressed, Severe With Psychotic Features
296.55	Bipolar I Disorder, Most Recent Episode Depressed, In Partial Remission
296.56	Bipolar I Disorder, Most Recent Episode Depressed, In Full Remission
296.60	Bipolar I Disorder, Most Recent Episode Mixed, Unspecified

296.61	Bipolar I Disorder, Most Recent Episode Mixed, Mild
296.62	Bipolar I Disorder, Most Recent Episode Mixed, Moderate
296.63	Bipolar I Disorder, Most Recent Episode Mixed, Severe Without Psychotic Features
296.64	Bipolar I Disorder, Most Recent Episode Mixed, Severe With Psychotic Features
296.65	Bipolar I Disorder, Most Recent Episode Mixed, In Partial Remission
296.66	Bipolar I Disorder, Most Recent Episode Mixed, In Full Remission
296.7	Bipolar I Disorder, Most Recent Episode Unspecified
296.80	Bipolar Disorder NOS
296.89	Bipolar II Disorder
296.90	Mood Disorder NOS
297.1	Delusional Disorder
297.3	Shared Psychotic Disorder
298.8	Brief Psychotic Disorder
298.9	Psychotic Disorder NOS
299.00	Autistic Disorder
299.10	Childhood Disintegrative Disorder
⌈ 299.80	Asperger's Disorder
⎢ 299.80	Pervasive Developmental Disorder NOS
⌊ 299.80	Rett's Disorder
300.00	Anxiety Disorder NOS
300.01	Panic Disorder Without Agoraphobia
300.02	Generalized Anxiety Disorder
300.11	Conversion Disorder
300.12	Dissociative Amnesia
300.13	Dissociative Fugue
300.14	Dissociative Identity Disorder
300.15	Dissociative Disorder NOS
300.16	Factitious Disorder With Predominantly Psychological Signs and Symptoms
⌈ 300.19	Factitious Disorder NOS
⎢ 300.19	Factitious Disorder With Combined Psychological and Physical Signs and Symptoms
⌊ 300.19	Factitious Disorder With Predominantly Physical Signs and Symptoms
300.21	Panic Disorder With Agoraphobia
300.22	Agoraphobia Without History of Panic Disorder
300.23	Social Phobia
300.29	Specific Phobia
300.3	Obsessive-Compulsive Disorder
300.4	Dysthymic Disorder
300.6	Depersonalization Disorder

⌈ 300.7	Body Dysmorphic Disorder
⌊ 300.7	Hypochondriasis
⌈ 300.81	Somatization Disorder
⎢ 300.81	Somatoform Disorder NOS
⌊ 300.81	Undifferentiated Somatoform Disorder
300.9	Unspecified Mental Disorder (nonpsychotic)
301.0	Paranoid Personality Disorder
301.13	Cyclothymic Disorder
301.20	Schizoid Personality Disorder
301.22	Schizotypal Personality Disorder
301.4	Obsessive-Compulsive Personality Disorder
301.50	Histrionic Personality Disorder
301.6	Dependent Personality Disorder
301.7	Antisocial Personality Disorder
301.81	Narcissistic Personality Disorder
301.82	Avoidant Personality Disorder
301.83	Borderline Personality Disorder
301.9	Personality Disorder NOS
302.2	Pedophilia
302.3	Transvestic Fetishism
302.4	Exhibitionism
⌈ 302.6	Gender Identity Disorder in Children
⌊ 302.6	Gender Identity Disorder NOS
302.70	Sexual Dysfunction NOS
302.71	Hypoactive Sexual Desire Disorder
⌈ 302.72	Female Sexual Arousal Disorder
⌊ 302.72	Male Erectile Disorder
302.73	Female Orgasmic Disorder
302.74	Male Orgasmic Disorder
302.75	Premature Ejaculation
302.76	Dyspareunia (Not Due to a General Medical Condition)
302.79	Sexual Aversion Disorder
302.81	Fetishism
302.82	Voyeurism
302.83	Sexual Masochism
302.84	Sexual Sadism
302.85	Gender Identity Disorder in Adolescents or Adults
302.89	Frotteurism
⌈ 302.9	Paraphilia NOS
⌊ 302.9	Sexual Disorder NOS
303.00	Alcohol Intoxication
303.90	Alcohol Dependence
304.00	Opioid Dependence
304.10	Sedative, Hypnotic, or Anxiolytic Dependence
304.20	Cocaine Dependence
304.30	Cannabis Dependence
304.40	Amphetamine Dependence
304.50	Hallucinogen Dependence
304.60	Inhalant Dependence

304.80	Polysubstance Dependence		307.9	Communication Disorder NOS

304.80 Polysubstance Dependence
304.90 Other (or Unknown) Substance Dependence
304.90 Phencyclidine Dependence
305.00 Alcohol Abuse
305.10 Nicotine Dependence
305.20 Cannabis Abuse
305.30 Hallucinogen Abuse
305.40 Sedative, Hypnotic, or Anxiolytic Abuse
305.50 Opioid Abuse
305.60 Cocaine Abuse
305.70 Amphetamine Abuse
305.90 Caffeine Intoxication
305.90 Inhalant Abuse
305.90 Other (or Unknown) Substance Abuse
305.90 Phencyclidine Abuse
306.51 Vaginismus (Not Due to a General Medical Condition)
307.0   Stuttering
307.1   Anorexia Nervosa
307.20 Tic Disorder NOS
307.21 Transient Tic Disorder
307.22 Chronic Motor or Vocal Tic Disorder
307.23 Tourette's Disorder
307.3   Stereotypic Movement Disorder
307.42 Insomnia Related to . . . [Indicate the Axis I or Axis II Disorder]
307.42 Primary Insomnia
307.44 Hypersomnia Related to . . . [Indicate the Axis I or Axis II Disorder]
307.44 Primary Hypersomnia
307.45 Circadian Rhythm Sleep Disorder
307.46 Sleep Terror Disorder
307.46 Sleepwalking Disorder
307.47 Dyssomnia NOS
307.47 Nightmare Disorder
307.47 Parasomnia NOS
307.50 Eating Disorder NOS
307.51 Bulimia Nervosa
307.52 Pica
307.53 Rumination Disorder
307.59 Feeding Disorder of Infancy or Early Childhood
307.6   Enuresis (Not Due to a General Medical Condition)
307.7   Encopresis, Without Constipation and Overflow Incontinence
307.80 Pain Disorder Associated With Psychological Factors
307.89 Pain Disorder Associated With Both Psychological Factors and a General Medical Condition

307.9   Communication Disorder NOS
308.3   Acute Stress Disorder
309.0   Adjustment Disorder With Depressed Mood
309.21 Separation Anxiety Disorder
309.24 Adjustment Disorder With Anxiety
309.28 Adjustment Disorder With Mixed Anxiety and Depressed Mood
309.3   Adjustment Disorder With Disturbance of Conduct
309.4   Adjustment Disorder With Mixed Disturbance of Emotions and Conduct
309.81 Posttraumatic Stress Disorder
309.9   Adjustment Disorder Unspecified
310.1   Personality Change Due to . . . [Indicate the General Medical Condition]
311   Depressive Disorder NOS
312.30 Impulse-Control Disorder NOS
312.31 Pathological Gambling
312.32 Kleptomania
312.33 Pyromania
312.34 Intermittent Explosive Disorder
312.39 Trichotillomania
312.8   Conduct Disorder
312.9   Disruptive Behavior Disorder NOS
313.23 Selective Mutism
313.81 Oppositional Defiant Disorder
313.82 Identity Problem
313.89 Reactive Attachment Disorder of Infancy or Early Childhood
313.9   Disorder of Infancy, Childhood, or Adolescence NOS
314.00 Attention-Deficit/Hyperactivity Disorder, Predominantly Inattentive Type
314.01 Attention-Deficit/Hyperactivity Disorder, Combined Type
314.01 Attention-Deficit/Hyperactivity Disorder, Predominantly Hyperactive-Impulsive Type
314.9   Attention-Deficit/Hyperactivity Disorder NOS
315.00 Reading Disorder
315.1   Mathematics Disorder
315.2   Disorder of Written Expression
315.31 Expressive Language Disorder
315.31 Mixed Receptive-Expressive Language Disorder
315.39 Phonological Disorder
315.4   Developmental Coordination Disorder
315.9   Learning Disorder NOS
316   . . . [Specified Psychological Factor] Affecting . . . [Indicate the General Medical Condition]

317	Mild Mental Retardation	780.9	Age-Related Cognitive Decline
318.0	Moderate Mental Retardation	787.6	Encopresis, With Constipation and Overflow Incontinence
318.1	Severe Mental Retardation	799.9	Diagnosis Deferred on Axis II
318.2	Profound Mental Retardation	799.9	Diagnosis or Condition Deferred on Axis I
319	Mental Retardation, Severity Unspecified	995.2	Adverse Effects of Medication NOS
332.1	Neuroleptic-Induced Parkinsonism	995.5	Neglect of Child (if focus of attention is on victim)
333.1	Medication-Induced Postural Tremor		
333.7	Neuroleptic-Induced Acute Dystonia	995.5	Physical Abuse of Child (if focus of attention is on victim)
333.82	Neuroleptic-Induced Tardive Dyskinesia		
333.90	Mediciation-Induced Movement Disorder NOS	995.5	Sexual Abuse of Child (if focus of attention is on victim)
333.92	Neuroleptic Malignant Syndrome	995.81	Physical Abuse of Adult (if focus of attention is on victim)
333.99	Neuroleptic-Induced Acute Akathisia		
347	Narcolepsy	995.81	Sexual Abuse of Adult (if focus of attention is on victim)
607.84	Male Erectile Disorder Due to . . . [Indicate the General Medical Condition]		
608.89	Male Dyspareunia Due to . . . [Indicate the General Medical Condition]	V15.81	Noncompliance With Treatment
		V61.1	Partner Relational Problem
608.89	Male Hypoactive Sexual Desire Disorder Due to . . . [Indicate the General Medical Condition]	V61.1	Physical Abuse of Adult
		V61.1	Sexual Abuse of Adult
		V61.20	Parent-Child Relational Problem
608.89	Other Male Sexual Dysfunction Due to . . . [Indicate the General Medical Condition]	V61.21	Neglect of Child
		V61.21	Physical Abuse of Child
625.0	Female Dyspareunia Due to . . . [Indicate the General Medical Condition]	V61.21	Sexual Abuse of Child
		V61.8	Sibling Relational Problem
625.8	Female Hypoactive Sexual Desire Disorder Due to . . . [Indicate the General Medical Condition]	V61.9	Relational Problem Related to a Mental Disorder or General Medical Condition
		V62.2	Occupational Problem
625.8	Other Female Sexual Dysfunction Due to . . . [Indicate the General Medical Condition]	V62.3	Academic Problem
		V62.4	Acculturation Problem
780.09	Delirium NOS	V62.81	Relational Problem NOS
780.52	Sleep Disorder Due to . . . [Indicate the General Medical Condition], Insomnia Type	V62.82	Bereavement
		V62.89	Borderline Intellectual Functioning
780.54	Sleep Disorder Due to . . . [Indicate the General Medical Condition], Hypersomnia Type	V62.89	Phase of Life Problem
		V62.89	Religious or Spiritual Problem
		V65.2	Malingering
780.59	Breathing-Related Sleep Disorder	V71.01	Adult Antisocial Behavior
780.59	Sleep Disorder Due to . . . [Indicate the General Medical Condition], Mixed Type	V71.02	Child or Adolescent Antisocial Behavior
		V71.09	No Diagnosis on Axis II
780.59	Sleep Disorder Due to . . . [Indicate the General Medical Condition], Parasomnia Type	V71.09	No Diagnosis or Condition on Axis I

GLOSSARY

acquired dyslexia Difficulty in reading experienced by those who had been able to read well.

acquisition In Pavlovian conditioning, the learning of a response based on the contingency between a conditioned stimulus and an unconditioned stimulus.

acting out The direct expression of unconscious impulses.

acute schizophrenia A condition characterized by the rapid and sudden onset of very florid symptoms of schizophrenia.

addiction Dependence on a drug, resulting in tolerance and withdrawal symptoms when the addict is deprived of the drug. *See also* tolerance, withdrawal.

adoptive study The study of offspring and biological and adoptive parents to see whether the occurrence of a trait is related to genes or environment. This method is one of two widely used methods (the other is the twin study) for quantifying the relative contribution of genetic to nongenetic determinants of psychological traits.

adrenaline (or epinephrine) A hormone secreted by the adrenal glands, which causes increase in blood pressure, release of sugar by the liver, and a number of other physiological reactions to threat.

adrenergic A descriptive term for the nerve cells that use adrenaline and noradrenaline as chemical transmitters. The sympathetic nervous system is an andrenergic system.

affective disorders A class of mental disorders characterized by a disturbance of mood. Includes unipolar depression, bipolar depression, and mania.

affective pleasure An effect of drug use in the opponent-process model of addiction. Affective pleasure is the pleasant emotional state that is the initial pharmacological effect produced by the drug.

affective tolerance An effect of drug use in the opponent-process model of addiction. With continued use, the addictive drug tends to lose its affective pleasure.

affective withdrawal An effect of drug use in the opponent-process model of addiction. The sudden termination of narcotic use often produces the opposite affective state of the initial pleasant one.

agnosia Inability to recognize meaningful objects.

agoraphobia An anxiety disorder characterized by fear of situations in which one might be trapped and unable to acquire help, especially in the event of a panic attack. Agoraphobics will avoid crowds, enclosed spaces (such as elevators and buses), or large open spaces. From the Greek "fear of the marketplace."

akathesis A side effect of chlorpromazine in which an itchiness in the muscles occurs and results in an inability to sit still.

alexia Acquired inability to read resulting from brain damage, with vision intact.

alexithymia The word literally means "no words for feelings" and is used to describe people who have difficulty expressing their feelings.

altruistic suicide Suicide required by the society (as defined by Durkheim; for example, hari-kari).

Alzheimer's disease Degenerative disease of late middle or old age, in which mental functions deteriorate. An amnesic syndrome is often the major feature of this disorder. Its initial symptoms include loss of initiative, extreme forgetfulness, memory disability, and spatial disorders. It progresses to severe deteriorations of intellect and basic maintenance functions that lead to death.

amenorrhea Loss of the menstrual period. A common occurrence in women anorexics.

American Law Institute (ALI) rule A legal test for insanity that holds that a person is not responsible for his criminal conduct if, at the time of the crime and as a result of mental disease or defect, he lacks substantial capacity to appreciate the criminality of the conduct or to conform his conduct to the law.

amnesia A dissociative disorder characterized by loss of memory of happenings during a certain time period, or loss of memory of personal identity. Includes generalized amnesia, retrograde amnesia, post-traumatic amnesia, anterograde amnesia, and selective amnesia.

amnesic syndrome A disorder of memory, of organic origin, in which memory for recent events (events occurring after the brain damage) is very poor or completely absent.

amphetamine A stimulant that causes agitation, increase in energy and activity, hyper-responsiveness to the environment, euphoria, and a number of physiological signs of hyperactivation.

amyotrophic lateral sclerosis (ALS) Also known as Lou Gehrig's disease, this disorder is characterized by weakness and a loss of motor control produced by motor neuron degeneration, and by gradual loss of ability to move; it eventually leads to death.

anaclitic depression A depression experienced by some infants between the ages of six and eighteen months who have been separated from their mothers for prolonged periods. This disorder is characterized by apathy, listlessness, weight loss, susceptibility to illness, and sometimes death.

anal character traits Traits such as orderliness, stinginess, and stubbornness which, according to psychoanalytic theory, result from fixation during the anal stage of psychosexual development.

anal stage The second stage of psychosexual development whose principal foci, according to psychodynamic theorists, are pleasure and the parental control involved in toilet training.

androgen A hormone that is principally responsible for the morphological development of the external genitals of the male.

androgen insensitivity syndrome A syndrome in which the fetus lacks the receptors for the sex hormone, androgen, and which produces neurological females in male fetuses.

animalism The belief that the insane were like animals and that as such, like animals, they could not control themselves and needed to be severely controlled, were capable of violence suddenly and without provocation, and could live without protest in miserable conditions.

animism The belief in premodern societies that everyone and everything has a "soul" and that mental disturbance was due to animistic causes, e.g., an evil spirit had taken control of an individual and was controlling that individual's behavior.

animal phobias   Specific phobias in which an individual has a fear of a particular animal, usually cats, dogs, birds, rats, snakes, and insects.

anomia   Inability to name objects.

anomic suicide   Suicide precipitated by a shattering break in an individual's relationship to his society (as defined by Durkheim).

anorexia nervosa   A disorder in which the individual has an intense fear of becoming fat, eats far too little to sustain herself, and has a distorted body image.

anterograde amnesia   Difficulty learning new material after a traumatic event.

antigens   Invaders of the immune system.

anti-reductionism   A philosophy that holds that at least some psychological phenomena exist that cannot be reduced to biological phenomena.

antisocial personality disorder (or **psychopathy, sociopathy**)   A personality disorder in which the individual has a rapacious attitude toward others and a chronic insensitivity and indifference to the rights of other people. The behavior must be longstanding and must be manifested in at least three classes of behavior, among which are: repeated aggressiveness; recklessness that endangers others; deceitfulness, lack of remorse, and consistent irresponsibility; failure to honor financial obligations.

anxiety   Fear characterized by the expectation of an unspecified danger, dread, terror, or apprehension, often leading to an emergency reaction and "flight or fight" behavior. As used in psychoanalytic theory, the psychic pain that results from conflicts among the various personality processes.

anxiety disorders   A class of mental disorders characterized by chronic and debilitating anxiety. Include agoraphobia, generalized anxiety disorder, panic disorder, phobias, and post-traumatic stress disorder.

aphasia   Disorders of language resulting from damage to certain areas of the cerebral cortex.

applied tension   A technique in which, upon seeing blood, blood phobics tense the muscles of their arms, legs, and chest, thereby raising their blood pressure and heart rate, which prevents them from fainting at the sight of blood.

appraisal   Evaluation of short-term mental events, a target of cognitive therapy.

apraxia   A disorder of movement in the absence of muscle weakness or inability to perform any specific movement.

arbitrary inference   Reaching a conclusion for which there is little or no evidence. According to Beck, depressives are prone to making arbitrary inferences.

archetypes   As used by Jung, universal ideas about which we are knowledgeable even at birth.

arteriosclerosis   A building up of fat on the inner walls of the coronary arteries; this clogging blocks blood from reaching the heart muscle, and heart attack and sudden death can result.

assimilative projection   Attribution to another of beliefs, attitudes, or feelings that we are quite unaware of experiencing ourselves.

attention-deficit hyperactivity disorder   A disorder characterized by marked impulsivity, inattention, and hyperactivity.

attention withdrawal   A process facilitating repression, wherein the individual withdraws attention and redirects it away from painful images and memories.

attribution   An assignment of cause for an event; a short-term mental event, and a target of cognitive therapy.

autism   A childhood disorder whose central feature is the failure to develop the ability to respond to others within the first thirty months of life.

automatic thoughts   Discrete sentences, negative in character, that a person says to himself, quickly and habitually. According to Beck, depressives typically engage in automatic thoughts.

autonomic nervous system   The system that regulates the internal environment of the body, including the heart, stomach, adrenals, and intestines. The autonomic nervous system is divided into the sympathetic and parasympathetic nervous systems.

aversion therapy   A behavior therapy that seeks to rid a client of undesired behavior by pairing that behavior with aversive consequences.

avoidance-approach conflict   A conflict between a desire to approach an object or situation that has some positive value, and a desire to avoid that object or situation because it has been associated with harm. According to traditional learning theory, this conflict is a root of anxiety.

avoidance responding   The act of getting out of a situation that has been previously associated with an aversive event, thereby preventing the aversive event. Differs from escape responding, which is getting out of the aversive event itself.

avoidant personality disorder   A disorder whose central feature is social withdrawal combined with hypersensitivity to rejection.

Babinski sign   A change in the reflex response to scratching of the bottom of the foot that indicates damage to upper levels of the motor system.

barbiturates   A class of drugs depressing the central nervous system, decreasing anxiety and blunting sensitivity to the environment. Includes phenobarbital, pentobarbital, secobarbital, and benzodiapines.

behavior therapy   A therapy that is rooted in the view that psychological distress results from learned behavior that can be unlearned; the therapy seeks to replace the distressing behavior with more constructive modes of coping and adaptation.

behavioral assessment   A record of behaviors and thoughts one wishes to change, including their time of occurrence, duration, and intensity.

behavioral disorder   A disorder in which something behavioral, rather than emotional, is amiss, such as hyperactivity, attentional problems, and aggressive, destructive, and dishonest behaviors.

behavioral school   The school of abnormal psychology that claims that behavior is shaped by the environment, and that behavior can be changed by changing the environment. According to the behavioral theorists, the symptomatic behavior of a mental disorder is the disorder, and is that which should be treated.

benzodiazepines   A group of mild tranquilizers producing muscle relaxation, decreased anxiety, and sedation. Includes Librium, Valium, and Dalmane.

beta cells   Lymphocytes that come from bone marrow and that have receptors on their surface for specific antigens.

beta-endorphins   Large proteins that are produced in the body and that are opiate-like compounds.

biofeedback   Therapeutic technique in which the individual is given electronically amplified information on certain (somewhat) controllable physiological systems (such as heart rate and blood pressure) and trained to control that response system.

biogenic amines   Neurochemicals that facilitate neural transmission, including catecholamines and indoleamines.

biological psychiatry   The area of psychiatry specializing in the drug treatment, the biochemistry, neuroanatomy, and genetics of mental disorder.

biomedical model of abnormality   The school of abnormal psychology that claims that mental disorders are illnesses of the body resulting from an underlying physiological pathology such as a virus, disordered biochemistry or genes, or a dysfunctional organ.

bipolar depression (or **manic-depressive disorder**)   An affective disorder characterized by alternating periods of depression and mania.

bisexuality   Desire for sexual relations with members of both sexes.

blitz rape   Sudden and unexpected rape, as contrasted to acquaintance rape, often leading to PTSD.

blood-brain barrier   A barrier in the brain composed of specialized cells that prevent certain compounds in the circulatory system from entering the brain.

blood phobia   A specific phobia in which the individual becomes highly anxious in situations involving the sight of blood, injections, and injuries.

borderline personality disorder   A broad Axis-II diagnostic category that designates people whose salient characteristic is instability in a variety of personality areas, including interpersonal relationships, behavior, mood, and self-image.

brain imaging   Techniques such as PET scans and CAT scans that capture the way that the brain looks and functions.

breakdown   One of the ways in which norepinephrine is reduced during neural transmission; the enzyme monoamine oxidase (MAO) and other enzymes chemically break down the norepinephrine in the synaptic gap and render it inactive.

Briquet's syndrome   *See* somatization disorder.

bulimia   A disorder in which people alternately gorge themselves with enormous quantities of food, and then purge themselves of that food by vomiting, or using laxatives or diuretics.

caffeine   A drug that stimulates the central nervous system and the skeletal muscles, lengthening the time it takes to fall asleep, decreasing fatigue, and aiding the individual in doing physical work.

castration anxiety   Fear of having one's penis removed or harmed; part of the basis for the Oedipus conflict.

catecholamines   Hormones involved in neural transmission in the brain. Includes norepinephrine, epinephrine, and dopamine.

categorical amnesia   *See* selective amnesia.

catharsis   In psychoanalytic theory, the uncovering and reliving of early traumatic conflicts.

CAT scan   *See* computerized axial tomography.

cathexis   Charging of a neutral object with psychical energy, either positive or negative. Psychoanalytic basis of acquired fears and lusts.

central nervous system (CNS)   That part of the nervous system that coordinates all of the activity of the nervous system. In vertebrates, the CNS is made up of the brain and the spinal cord. All sensory inputs are transmitted to the CNS and all motor impulses are transmitted from the CNS.

cerebral cortex   The outermost layer (gray matter) of the cerebral hemispheres.

cerebrospinal fluid   A clear fluid, like blood plasma, that accounts for some of the circulation in the brain and spinal cord.

cholinergic   A descriptive term for the nerve cells that use acetylcholine as a chemical transmitter. The parasympathetic nervous system is a cholinergic system.

chronic fatigue syndrome (CFS)   A disorder of persistent and severe fatigue, which is thought to be a long-term sequelae of Epstein-Barr virus. Fifteen percent of CFS patients also have somatization disorder.

civil commitment   The process used to hospitalize mentally disordered people who have committed no crime.

clang associations   Associations produced by the rhyme of words. Commonly found in schizophrenics.

classical conditioning   *See* Pavlovian conditioning.

client-centered therapy   The therapy developed by Carl Rogers; it emphasizes unconditional positive regard and therapist empathy.

clinical case history   The record of part of the life of an individual seen in therapy.

cocaine   The psychoactive agent in the coca plant. Cocaine increases energy, combats fatigue and boredom, and enhances the individual's responsiveness to things in his environment.

cognitions   Beliefs, thoughts, attitudes, expectations, and other mental events.

cognitive-behavioral therapy   A therapeutic technique in which therapists attempt to alter both the maladaptive thoughts and maladaptive behaviors of a client through restructuring of maladaptive belief systems and re-training behavior.

cognitive (or selective) filter   A mechanism for sorting out stimuli to determine which ones will be admitted and which ones barred; something seems wrong with this filter in schizophrenics.

cognitive model   The school of abnormal psychology that claims that many disorders result from maladaptive beliefs or thought styles.

cognitive restructuring   Treatments that are predicated on the assumption that irrational thoughts create irrational behaviors, which can be eliminated by changing the underlying thoughts.

cognitive therapy   Used primarily in the treatment of depression, this therapy seeks to change the cognitive triad of (a) self-devaluation, (b) a negative view of life experience, and (c) the pessimistic view of the future, as the determining cognitions for depression.

cognitive triad   According to Beck, a group of cognitions characterizing depressives. These cognitions include (a) negative thoughts about the self, (b) negative thoughts about ongoing experience, and (c) negative thoughts about the future.

collective unconscious   As used by Jung, the memory traces of the experience of past generations.

communication deviance   Unclear messages and conversations arising when a parent is unable to establish and maintain a shared area of attention with a child.

compulsion   A repetitive, stereotyped, and unwanted action that can be resisted only with difficulty. It is usually associated with obsessions.

compulsive personality disorder   A disorder that is characterized by the long-term inability to express warm emotions, combined with an inappropriate preoccupation with trivial rules and details.

computerized axial tomography (CAT or CT scan)   An X-ray technique, used in neurological diagnosis, for constructing three-dimensional representations of the X-ray density of different areas of the brain.

concordant   When both of two twins have a disorder such as schizophrenia, they are called concordant for that disorder. *See also* discordant.

conditioned response (CR)   A response that is evoked by a certain stimulus (conditioned stimulus) once that stimulus has become associated with some other stimulus (unconditioned stimulus) that naturally evokes the unconditioned response. *See also* Pavlovian conditioning.

conditioned stimulus (CS)   A stimulus that, because of its having been paired with another stimulus (unconditioned stimulus) that naturally provokes an unconditioned response, is eventually able to evoke that response. *See also* Pavlovian conditioning.

conduct disorders   A cluster of children's behavioral disorders consisting mainly of aggressive and rule-breaking behaviors.

confabulation   Making up stories based on recovered but disorganized memories.

confound   A factor other than the experimentally controlled independent variable that might produce an experimental effect.

congenital adrenal hyperplasia (CAH)   A disease that bathes female fetuses with extra androgen. As young children, CAH girls like male-stereotyped toys, rough and tumble play, and are more tomboyish than matched controls.

consolidation block   Failure to establish (consolidate) short-term memories. This is a mechanism proposed as an explanation of the amnesic syndrome.

containment services   Services designed to limit the consequence of crises as they affect the individual, the potential or actual victim, and their families; these services are characterized by quick delivery to a broad range of people and are located in and offered by the community.

contiguity   Conjunction in time and place.

contingency   A conditional relationship between two objects or events, describable by the probability of event A given event B, along with the probability of event A in the absence of event B. A positive contingency between A and B obtains when A is more likely in the presence of B than in the absence of B. *See also* Pavlovian conditioning.

continuous reinforcement   Provision of reinforcement every time a subject makes a response. *See also* reinforcement.

control group   A group of subjects similar to those in an experimental group, who experience everything the experimental group does, except the independent variable.

conversion (or **hysterical conversion**)   A somatoform disorder characterized by the loss of functioning of some part of the body not due to any physical disorder, but apparently due to psychological conflicts. The loss is not under voluntary control.

coping strategies   As used by psychoanalytic theorists, the process by which people alter the meaning and significance of troublesome drives and impulses in order to eliminate anxiety.

core self   The self that develops first, between the second and sixth month of an infant's life. It embraces the infant's awareness that she and her caregiver are *physically separate.*

coronary heart disease (CHD)   Heart or circulatory problems often caused by arteriosclerosis; it can often lead to heart attack and sudden death.

corpus callosum   The largest tract in the brain, connecting corresponding areas of the two hemispheres.

correlation   Pure observation without manipulation to determine the relationship between two classes of events.

correlation coefficient   A statistic indicating the degree of contingency between two variables.

corticospinal tract   A tract of axons from cell bodies in the motor cortex that innervates motor neurons in the spinal cord, and mediates (among other things) voluntary movements of the hands.

cosmetic psychopharmacology   A change in personality, rather than mere change in mood, that is brought about by drugs.

co-twin   As used in psychological research, one of a pair of twins whose sibling is seen at a psychiatric clinic in order to diagnose a psychological problem.

counterconditioning   A therapeutic technique for phobias in which a phobic patient is helped to relax while imagining fear-provoking situations (usually the least fear-provoking situation first, then gradually more and more fear-provoking situations). The relaxation response to the imagined situation is incompatible with the fear the patient has previously associated with the situation, and the fear is thus extinguished.

counterphobia   The pursuit of precisely those activities that are deeply feared.

covert sensitization   A behavioral therapy for changing sexual interest; it uses imaged sexual stimuli followed by aversive US's to treat such paraphilias as exhibitionism.

criminal commitment   The coerced psychiatric hospitalization of mentally disordered people who have acted harmfully but are not legally responsible because they lack *mens rea*, or a "guilty mind."

cross tolerance   When tolerance to one drug produces tolerance to other drugs.

defense mechanisms   *See* coping strategies.

delayed auditory feedback   Used in the treatment of stuttering, this technique involves hearing one's own speech played back over earphones at about a one-second delay.

delirium tremens   A dangerous syndrome of withdrawal from alcohol, which is characterized by psychomotor agitation, hyperactivity of the autonomic nervous system, anxiety, loss of appetite, delusions, amnesia, and convulsions.

delusions   False beliefs that resist all argument and are sustained in the face of evidence that normally would be sufficient to destroy them.

delusions of control   Beliefs that one's thoughts or behaviors are being controlled from without.

delusions of grandeur   Unsubstantiable convictions that one is especially important.

delusions of persecution   Groundless fears that individuals, groups, or the government has malevolent intentions and is "out to get me."

delusions of reference   Incorrect beliefs that the casual remarks or behaviors of others apply to oneself.

demand characteristics   Aspects of the experimental setting that induce the subject to invent and act on a hypothesis about how one should behave.

dementia   A more or less general deterioration of mental function, found most commonly in old people. Alzheimer's disease is a common form of dementia.

denial   As used in psychoanalytic theory, the process by which distressing external facts are eliminated.

dendrites   A usually highly branched part of a neuron that is stimulated by neurotransmitters produced by receptors or other neurons.

dependent personality disorder   A disorder wherein people allow others to make major decisions, to initiate important actions, and to assume responsibility for the significant areas of their life.

dependent variable   The factor that the experimenter expects will be affected by changes in the independent variable.

depersonalization   Feeling detachment from oneself; just going through the motions or looking at oneself from the outside.

depression   An affective disorder characterized by (a) sad affect and loss of interest in usually satisfying activities, (b) a negative view of the self and hopelessness, (c) passivity, indecisiveness, and suicidal intentions, and (d) loss of appetite, weight loss, sleep disturbances, and other physical symptoms.

deprivation dwarfism   A disorder marked by retarded bone age without evidence of primary medical disease in children. The disorder can be reversed by removing the child from her family environment and placing her in an emotionally supportive hospital setting.

derealization   Feeling as if the world, not the self, seems unreal.

dereflection   Used by existential therapists, this technique involves directing the client's attention away from his symptoms and pointing out how much he could be doing and enjoying if he were not so preoccupied with his troubles.

descriptive validity   The ability of a system of diagnosis to facilitate communication by accurately describing patients and differentiating patients in one category from another.

developmental disorders   A cluster of disorders of childhood that may consist of deficits in language comprehension, speech, and responses to others that can result in such serious disorders as autism or childhood schizophrenia.

developmental dyslexia   Difficulty in learning to read out of proportion to intellectual and emotional development.

diathesis   Physical vulnerability or predisposition to a particular disorder.

diathesis-stress model   A general model of disorders that postulates that an individual develops a disorder when he both has some constitutional vulnerability (diathesis) and when he experiences psychological disturbance (stress).

direct sexual therapy   A therapeutic method developed by Masters and Johnson, in which (a) sexual dysfunctions are clearly and simply defined, (b) clients explicitly practice sexual behavior under the systematic guidance of therapists, and (c) clients are treated as couples, not as individuals.

disconnection syndrome   A disorder accounted for by severing of or damage to tracts connecting specific areas of the brain.

discordant   When only one of two twins has a disorder such as schizophrenia, they are called discordant for that disorder. *See also* concordant.

discriminative stimulus   A signal indicating that reinforcement is available if a certain operant response is made.

disinhibition   An increase in some reaction resulting from release of inhibition.

disorganized schizophrenia   A schizophrenic disorder whose most striking behavioral characteristic is apparent silliness and incoherence. Behavior is jovial but quite bizarre and absurd, suggesting extreme sensitivity to internal cues and extreme insensitivity to external ones, but without systematic delusions or hallucinations.

disowning projection   A process whereby feelings and experiences that one personally denies having and that are usually repressed are attributed to others.

displacement   A cognitive alteration of reality that involves replacing the true object of one's emotions with one that is more innocent and less threatening.

disruptive behavior disorders   A cluster of disorders characterized by symptoms such as hyperactivity, inattention, aggressiveness, destructiveness, and defiance of authority.

dissociation   A situation in which two or more mental processes co-exist or alternate without being connected or influencing each other, with some area of memory split off or dissociated from conscious awareness.

dissociative amnesia   A loss of personal memory caused by severe trauma such as the death of a child or the dashing of a career. (Formerly known as psychogenic amnesia.)

dissociative disorders   A group of mental disorders characterized by fragmentation of an individual's identity. Dissociative disorders include amnesia, fugue, multiple personality, and depersonalization disorder.

dissociative identity disorder (or multiple personality disorder)   The occurrence of two or more personalities in the same individual, each of whom is sufficiently integrated to have a relatively stable life of its own and recurrently to take full control of the person's behavior.

diversiform disorder   A type of somatization disorder in which individuals have some back problems but tend to complain about the rest of the body.

dizygotic twins   Fraternal twins, or twins who developed from separate eggs, and whose genes are no more alike than are those of any pair of non-identical-twin siblings.

dopamine   A catecholamine that facilitates neural transmission.

dopamine hypothesis   The theory that schizophrenia results from an excess of the neurotransmitter dopamine.

double-blind experiment   An experiment in which both the subject and experimenter are blind as to whether the subject has received an experimental treatment or a placebo.

double depression   A major depressive episode superimposed on an underlying chronic depression.

Down's syndrome (or mongolism)   A disorder that results from the fact that an individual has forty-seven rather than the usual forty-six chromosomes in his or her cells.

drug cues   Drug reminders, such as settings in which drugs were taken, that induce craving for the drug and can trigger relapse in those who have been free of drugs.

drug dependence   The regular use of drugs acting on the brain that leads to maladaptive behavioral changes that would be seen as maladaptive in any culture. Three criteria characterize the disorder: (a) a pattern of pathological use of a drug, (b) impairment in occupational, social, physical, or emotional functioning, and (c) evidence of affective or physical adaptation to the drug.

drug tolerance   The need to use increased amounts of the drug to get the desired effect.

drug withdrawal   Characteristic affective and physical symptoms that follow drug use after the drug is discontinued.

DSM-IV   Published in 1994, this is the fourth edition of the *Diagnostic and Statistical Manual of Mental Disorders* of the American Psychiatric Association.

Durham test   A legal test for insanity which provides that an accused is not criminally responsible if his unlawful act was the product of mental disease or mental defect.

dysfunction   Impairment of functioning.

dyslexia   *See* acquired dyslexia, developmental dyslexia, phonological dyslexia, surface dyslexia.

dysphoria   An unpleasant emotional state experienced during drug withdrawal; the opposite of euphoria.

dysthymic disorder   Chronic depression in which the individual has been depressed for at least two years without having had a remission to normality that lasted more than two months.

efficacy expectation   According to Bandura, a person's belief that he can successfully execute the behavior that will produce a desired outcome.

ego   The self.

ego-dystonic homosexuality   Homosexuality that is incongruent with the individual's desire for sexual preference, and which the individual wants to change.

ego-syntonic homosexuality   Homosexuality that is congruent with the individual's desire for sexual preference, and which the individual does not want to change.

egoistic suicide   Suicide resulting when the individual has too few ties to his fellow humans (as defined by Durkheim).

electroconvulsive shock treatment (ECT)   A therapeutic treatment for depression, in which metal electrodes are taped to either side of the patient's head, and the patient is anesthetized. A high current is passed through the brain for a half second, followed by convulsions lasting almost one minute.

electroencephalogram (EEG)   A record of the electrical activity of cells in the brain (primarily the cortex) obtained from wires placed on the skull, and used in neurological diagnosis.

emergency reaction   A reaction to threat in which the sympathetic nervous system mobilizes the body for action. The blood pressure rises, heart rate increases, breathing becomes deeper, perspiration increases, and the liver releases sugar for use by the muscles.

emotional disorders   A cluster of disorders in which symptoms of fear, anxiety, inhibition, shyness, and overattachment predominate.

empathy   The gift and tool that enables us to understand others.

empiricism   The school of philosophy that claims that all that people are and all that they know are the result of experiences.

endogenous depression   A depression resulting from disordered biology. From the Greek "arising from within."

endorphins   Endogenous morphine-like substances.

enkephalins   Small amino acid compounds that are endogenous opioids.

enuresis (or bed-wetting)   A disorder that is manifested by regular and involuntary voiding of urine.

environmentalism   The first assumption of behaviorism; it states that all organisms, including humans, are shaped by the environment.

epidemiological evidence   Evidence from many individuals.

epilepsy   A disorder of the brain that expresses itself as excessive neuronal discharge (seizure) in some parts of the brain, with appropriate sensory, mental, or motor effects, and frequently some alteration in consciousness.

epinephrine   *See* adrenaline.

epiphenomenon   A process, which while not causal, reflects the underlying process, which is causal.

episodic depression   Depression that has a clear onset and that lasts less than two years.

erectile dysfunction (or impotence)   In males, recurrent inability to have or to maintain an erection for intercourse.

erogenous zones   Pleasure centers.

erotic arousal   Excitement of sexual desire.

escape responding   The act of getting out of an ongoing harmful situation. *See also* avoidance responding.

etiology   Causal description of the development of a disorder.

exhibitionism   A psychosexual disorder in which the individual is sexually aroused primarily by exposing his genitals to unwitting strangers.

exhortative will   The will whereby we force ourselves to work.

existential theory   A theory that holds that mental disorders result when an individual fails to confront the basic questions of life successfully. Three issues are particularly important: fear of dying, personal responsibility, and will.

existential therapy   A therapy that encourages clients to view their psychological problems as being of their own making.

exogenous depression   A depression precipitated by a life stressor. Sometimes called reactive depression. From the Greek "arising from without."

exorcism   A ceremonial ritual during which the demons and spirits possessing an individual are expelled from the victim's body.

expectations   Cognitions that extrapolate the present to the anticipation of future events.

experiment   A procedure in which a hypothesized cause (independent variable) is manipulated and the occurrence of an effect (dependent variable) is measured.

experimental effect   The change in the dependent variable as a result of the manipulation of the independent variable.

experimental group   A group of subjects who are given experience with an independent variable.

experimentalism   The behaviorist view that experiments can reveal what aspects of the environment cause behavior.

experimenter bias   The exertion of subtle influences by the experimenter on subjects' responses in an experiment.

experimenter-blind design   An experiment in which the experimenter, but not the subject, is blind as to whether a subject is receiving a drug or placebo

experiments of nature   Studies in which the experimenter observes the effects of an unusual natural event.

exposure therapy   A behavioral form of treatment for phobia and PTSD in which the patient repeatedly endures the phobic object or original trauma in vivo or in imagination. *See also* extinction, flooding.

expressed emotion   Attitudes of cynicism, hostility, or overinvolvement that an important relative expresses toward a schizophrenic person.

expressive aphasia   A language disorder that manifests itself primarily as a deficit in speech or the organization of spoken language.

external attribution   An assignment of cause for an event to a factor that is outside oneself (i.e., other people or circumstances).

extinction   In Pavlovian conditioning, cessation of a previously conditioned response to a conditioned stimulus, due to having learned that the conditioned stimulus no longer signals the onset of an aversive or desirable event. In instrumental learning, cessation of acquired operant responses due to reinforcement being discontinued. Modern theorists believe that extinction occurs when there is a negative contingency between the conditioned stimulus and the unconditioned stimulus. *See also* contingency.

factitious disorder (or **Munchhausen syndrome**)   A mental disorder characterized by multiple hospitalizations and operations precipitated by the individual's having self-inflicted signs of illness.

false alarm   In experimental analysis, accepting the hypothesis that independent and dependent variables are related, when they really are not. *See also* miss.

family resemblance approach   Assessing abnormality based on the match between an individual's characteristics and the seven elements of abnormality: suffering, maladaptiveness, incomprehensibility and irrationality, unpredictability and loss of control, vividness, observer discomfort, and violation of moral and ideal standards.

family therapy   A group of diverse psychotherapies that treat the couple or family, rather than the individual alone.

fat solubility   *See* lipid solubility.

feeling substitution   A process by which feelings that are stressful are unconsciously replaced by less painful feelings.

fetish   A psychosexual disorder characterized by a need to have an inanimate object close by in order to become sexually aroused.

fixation   Stagnation of psychological development.

flooding   A method used by behavioral therapists to treat phobias. The phobic is exposed to the situations or objects most feared for an extended length of time without the opportunity to escape. *See also* response prevention.

fluoxetine (Prozac)   A serotonin reuptake inhibitor prescribed for depression.

free association   A psychoanalytic instruction to say whatever comes to mind, regardless of how ridiculous or embarrassing it is, and without attempting to censor.

frequency distribution   The number of observations in each given class observed.

frontal lobe   A lobe in each cerebral hemisphere that includes control and organization of motor function.

fugue state   A dissociative disorder in which an individual, in an amnesic state, travels away from home and assumes a new identity.

functional analysis   A behavioral assessment that is accompanied by a description of the stimuli that are presumed either to increase or decrease the incidence of specified behaviors.

functional MRI (fMRI)   A brain-imaging technique that measures the oxygen level in the blood, which increases with local brain activity.

functional syndromes   Abnormal behaviors believed to be caused by abnormal experience imposed upon normal brain mechanisms. Psychiatry and clinical psychology study these syndromes.

fusion   Protecting oneself against the fear of death or nonbeing by fusing with others such that one becomes attached to and indistinguishable from the others.

gender identity   Awareness of being male or being female.

gender identity disorder   A class of mental disorders in which the essential feature is an incongruence between anatomic sex and gender identity. Includes transsexualism.

gender role   Public expression of gender identity; what an individual does and says to indicate that he is a man or she is a woman.

gene-environment covariance   The correlation of genetic structure with the occurrence of an environmental event such that the immediately effective causal element from the environment can sometimes be masked. Having basketball experience is an example of a proximal environmental cause for becoming a professional basketball player that covaries with tallness, a genetically determined trait.

general adaptation syndrome   According to Selye, a sequence of three stages that ensues when an individual is stressed: (a) the somatic emergency reaction is initiated, (b) the individual engages in defensive behaviors, and (c) eventually the individual's adaptative actions are exhausted.

generalized anxiety disorder   An anxiety disorder characterized by chronic tenseness and vigilance, beliefs that something bad will happen, mild emergency reactions, and feelings of wanting to run away.

general paresis   A disorder characterized by mental deterioration, paralysis, then death. This disorder is caused by a spirochete involved in syphilis.

genital stage   In psychoanalytic theory, the fifth and final stage of psychosexual development during which the adolescent learns to channel sexual energy into love and work.

Gestalt therapy   A therapy that emphasizes taking responsibility for one's life by living in the present.

global attribution   An individual's assignment of cause for an event to a factor that will affect a number of different areas of his life.

glove anesthesia   A conversion symptom in which nothing can be felt in the hand and fingers, but sensation is intact from the wrist up.

goal-directed will The will that develops out of hope, expectation, and competence, wherein we are able to work toward future goals.

grade 5 hypnotizable person That fraction of the population (5 percent) that is extremely hypnotizable, very suggestible, showing pathological compliance with their therapists and giving up critical judgment. Most MPD's are grade 5.

grave disability A legal phrase that describes an individual's psychological inability to provide food or shelter for herself, which places her in imminent danger.

gray matter That part of the central nervous system that is composed primarily of neurons and glia cell bodies.

group residences Group homes for patients discharged from psychiatric hospitals in which the patients live together and run the household, shop, and work.

habit disorders A collection of childhood disorders in which the prominent symptoms include difficulties associated with eating, movement disorders, or tics. These disorders consist of a diverse group of problems with physical manifestations such as bed-wetting, stuttering, sleepwalking and epilepsy.

half-life The length of time it takes for the level of a drug in the blood to be decreased by 50 percent.

hallucination A perception that occurs in the absence of an identifiable stimulus.

hallucinogens Chemicals that cause perceptual disorientation, depersonalization, illusions, hallucinations, and physiological symptoms such as tachycardia, palpitations, and tremors. Includes LSD, PCP, and MDMA.

health psychology The field that deals with disorders that stand at the border of psychology and medicine.

heritability coefficient The quantitative estimate of the contribution of genetic factors to a trait, relative to nongenetic factors. It can be calculated as $2 \times$ (correlation of MZ twins − the correlation of DZ twins**).**

heterosexuality Preference for sexual partners of the opposite sex.

hierarchy A form of organization, characteristic of the nervous system, in which narrower "categories" or domains of "control" are subsumed under successively broader "nodes."

high frequency somatization disorder A disorder in which individuals have frequent stomach and back pains in conjunction with psychiatric problems.

histrionic personality disorder A personality disorder in which people are shallow, egocentric, and self-absorbed and have long histories of drawing attention to themselves and engaging in excited emotional displays caused by insignificant events.

homosexuality Preference for sexual partners of one's own sex.

hopelessness theory of depression A theory that emphasizes the stable and global dimensions for negative events as determinants of hopelessness.

hormones Genes that modulate physical growth, bodily differentiation, and psychological growth.

hypertension High blood pressure.

hypomanic personality A chronic form of mania involving an unbroken two-year-long manic state. *See also* mania.

hyposomnia Greatly lessened need for sleep.

hyperactivity A disorder that is marked by developmentally inappropriate impulsiveness, inattentiveness, and excessive motor behavior. *See also* attention-deficit hyperactivity disorder.

hypochondriasis The sustained conviction, in the absence of medical evidence, that one is ill or about to become ill.

hysterical conversion *See* conversion.

id In psychoanalytic theory, the mental representation of biological drives.

ideas of reference The belief that certain events and people have special significance for him (e.g., that newscasters are speaking to him or that strangers in the street are looking at him).

identification As used by psychoanalytic theorists, the process by which the characteristics of others—their ideas, values, mannerisms, status, and power—are internalized.

identity alteration A dissociative experience in which one displays a skill that one did not know one had.

identity confusion A dissociative state in which one is confused or uncertain about who one is.

illness and injury phobias (or nosophobias) Specific phobias in which an individual fears having one specific illness or injury or death.

immunocompetence The degree to which the immune system is able to protect the organism efficiently.

immunologic memory The factor that enables those T-cells and B-cells that initially combated an antigen to multiply more rapidly the second time the antigen is spotted, such that the immune system is able to do a better job of destroying the antigen than it did the first time.

inanimate object phobias Specific phobias in which the symptoms are focused on one object, including dirt, heights, darkness, closed spaces, and travel.

incidence The rate of new cases of a disorder in a given time period.

independent variable The hypothesized cause of some effect, manipulated by the experimenter in an experiment.

index case (or proband) In psychological research, one of a pair of twins who is first seen at a psychiatric clinic.

indoleamines Hormones involved in neural transmission. Indoleamines include serotonin and histamine.

inhibition An active process through which the excitability of a particular neuron or center (group of neurons) is decreased.

injection of meaning Denying the clear meaning of another's message and substituting another meaning.

insanity defense A defense for a crime that requires that the individual was wholly or partially irrational when the crime took place, and that this irrationality affected his or her behavior.

Insanity Defense Reform Act (IDRA) A federal standard for determining whether the insanity defense can be used; it eliminates the volitional prong of the ALI standard and states that the insanity defense can be used if at the time of the crime the defendant, as a result of severe mental disease or defect, was unable to appreciate the nature and quality or wrongfulness of his act.

instrumental learning (or instrumental conditioning) A technique in which an organism must learn to perform some voluntary behavior in order to acquire a desired outcome, or to stop an undesirable event.

instrumental response A response whose probability can be modified by reinforcement; a response that an organism has learned will bring about a desired outcome, or will stop an undesired event. *See also* operant.

intellectualization A coping strategy that takes the form of repressing the emotional component of experience, and restating that experience as an abstract intellectual analysis.

inter-judge reliability When two psychologists arrive at the same impression on the basis of psychological tests and observation.

internal attribution An individual's assignment of cause for an event to a factor that is an aspect of himself.

interpersonal therapy (IPT) A therapy that deals with depression as it results from interpersonal difficulties.

intersubjectivity The sense that we understand each others' intentions and feelings, as well as the sharing of experience about things and events.

introcosm A metaphor that describes a person's internal world.

involuntary commitment The process whereby the state hospitalizes people for their own good, and even over their vigorous protest.

isolation A coping strategy in which only the affective component of an unpleasant experience is repressed while the information is retained.

Kappa A statistic that attempts to describe the extent to which observers agree about a diagnosis by taking into consideration the likelihood that such an agreement might have arisen by co-incidence.

Korsakoff's syndrome A particular form of the amnesic syndrome caused by alcoholism.

laboratory model The production, under controlled conditions, of phenomena analogous to naturally occurring mental disorders.

latency stage In psychoanalytic theory, the third stage of psycho-sexual development during which sexuality is repressed and attention is directed toward mastering social and cognitive skills.

learned helplessness A condition characterized by an expectation that bad events will occur, and that there is nothing one can do to prevent their occurrence. Results in passivity, cognitive deficits, and other symptoms that resemble depression.

learning disorders Difficulties that reflect enormous developmental tardiness and mainly affect the development of language and academic skills, including reading difficulties.

learning model The model that includes the behavioral approach, which holds that we learn abnormal behavior through conditioning and that we can unlearn these maladaptive ways of behaving, and the cognitive approach, which holds that abnormality springs from disordered conscious thought about oneself and the world.

left visual field The left half of one's visual world, that is, the part of the world that projects onto the right side of the retina and into the right hemisphere.

lesion Localized damage to (neural) tissue.

libido In psychoanalytic theory, psychic energy that can become associated with a host of pleasurable activities.

lifetime prevalence The proportion of people in a sample who have ever experienced a particular disorder.

linkage analysis A research technique in genetics that seeks to evaluate the occurrence of a familial disorder alongside a known genetic marker.

lipid (or fat) solubility Ability of a drug to be stored in fat cells; this is an important factor in whether or how fast a drug reaches the brain; more lipid soluble drugs will be absorbed more quickly.

LSD (lysergic acid diethylamide) A hallucinogenic drug that causes changes in body sensations (dizziness, weakness, nausea), perception (distorted time sense), emotion, and cognitive processes.

lycanthropy A disorder in which people believe they are wolves, and act accordingly.

lymphocytes Cells in the immune system that recognize foreign cells.

macrophages Cells in the immune system that "eat" antigens.

magnetic resonance imaging (MRI) A brain-imaging technique in which each type of atom behaves like a tiny spinning magnet, wobbling at a characteristic frequency in the magnetic field. An MRI shows the elemental composition of cells and surrounding tissue. Damaged areas of the brain have a different concentration of elements than normal areas and appear differently on an MRI.

magnification Overestimating the impact of a small bad event; error of logic made by those who are depressed.

malingering A disorder in which the individual reports somatic symptoms, but these symptoms are under the individual's control, and the individual has an obvious motive for the somatic complaints. *See also* conversion.

mania An affective disorder characterized by excessive elation, expansiveness, irritability, talkativeness, inflated self-esteem, and flight of ideas.

manic-depression *See* bipolar depression.

MAO (monoamine oxidase) An enzyme that helps to break down catecholamines and indoleamines. MAO inhibitors are used to treat depression.

marijuana A psychoactive drug that, when used chronically and heavily, causes impairment of ability to focus on a task, impulsive

and compulsive behavior, delusions, sensory-perceptual distortions, and sometimes panic reactions.

masochism A psychosexual disorder in which the individual prefers to become sexually aroused by having suffering or humiliation inflicted upon him.

maturational hierarchy Four levels of coping strategies, ranging from defenses that are primitive and immature because they distort reality to defenses that do less violence to reality and are therefore more mature.

mean Average value of a set of values.

meditation A relaxation technique in which one closes one's eyes and silently repeats a mantra; it works by blocking thoughts that produce anxiety.

melancholia Depression characterized chiefly by loss of pleasure in most activities and by somatic symptoms, including sleep loss and loss of appetite.

mental disorder In DSM-IV, a behavioral or psychological pattern that is genuinely dysfunctional and that either distresses or disables the individual in one or more significant areas of functioning.

mental retardation Substantial limitations in present functioning; characterized by significantly subaverage intellectual functioning and limitations in two or more skill areas such as communication, self-care, home living, social skills, community use, self-direction, health and safety, functional academics, leisure, and work.

mental inhibition The blocking of images or memories either intentionally or unconsciously.

meta-analysis A technique of looking at a large number of therapy outcome studies that may differ in many of their particulars (e.g., sample size, age of clients, experience of therapists, kind of therapy, duration of therapy) and that attempts to integrate them statistically by concluding whether or not the therapy works and how large an effect it has.

methadone A narcotic used in heroin treatment programs. Methadone acts as a substitute for heroin, and prevents the heroin addict from experiencing withdrawal.

milieu therapy Therapy in which patients are provided with training in social communication, work, and recreation.

Minnesota Multiphasic Personality Inventory (MMPI) A widely used personality inventory consisting of 550 test items that inquire into a wide array of behaviors, thoughts, and feelings.

minimization Downplaying good events; an error of logic in depression.

miss Rejecting a hypothesis that the independent variable and dependent variable are related, when they really are.

M'Naghten test A legal test for insanity which provides that a person cannot be found guilty of a crime if, at the time of committing the offense, due to "disease of the mind," the individual did not know the nature and quality of the act or that the act was wrong.

modeling The observation and gradual imitation of a model who exhibits behavior that the client seeks to adopt in place of an undesirable behavior.

mongolism *See* Down's syndrome.

monozygotic (MZ) twins Identical twins, or twins who developed from a single egg fertilized by a single sperm, which divided and produced two individuals who have identical genes and chromosomes.

moral anxiety As used by psychoanalytic theorists, anxiety that arises when one anticipates that one's behavior will violate one's personal standards, or when that behavior has in fact violated those standards.

moral treatment The humane, nonthreatening treatment of the insane.

MRI *See* magnetic resonance imaging.

multiple personality A dissociative disorder in which more than one distinct personality exists in the same individual, and each personality is relatively rich, integrated, and stable.

myelin A fatty substance that surrounds many axons in the peripheral and central nervous system.

mystification   A process in which people are encouraged to doubt their own feelings, perceptions, and experiences.

narcissistic personality disorder   A personality disorder whose salient characteristics are an outlandish sense of self-importance, continual self-absorption, fantasies of unlimited success, power and/or beauty, and need for constant admiration.

narcotics   A class of psychoactive drugs blocking emotional response to pain and producing euphoria, dysphoria, apathy, psychomotor retardation, drowsiness, slurred speech, and maladaptive behavior. Includes opium, morphine, heroin, and methadone.

natural killer cells   Cells in the immune system that lyse cells of a tumor.

nature-nurture issue   A major debate in psychology, concerning the relative roles of environment and heredity in the development of personality and behavior.

negative correlation   A relationship between two classes of events wherein as one increases, the other decreases.

negative reinforcer   An event whose removal increases the probability of a response that precedes it. *See also* punishment.

Neo-Freudians   Psychodynamic theorists who modified and expanded upon Freud's views.

neuroadaptation   The complex biological changes that occur in the brain with repeated or chronic exposure to a drug.

neurology   The clinical discipline that studies the diseases of the nervous system.

neuron   A nerve cell; the basic unit of the nervous system.

neurosis   Formerly, a category for disorders in which the individual experienced (a) emotionally distressing symptoms, (b) an unwelcome psychological state, (c) reasonably good reality testing, and (d) behavior that was reasonably within social norms. A neurotic disorder was not considered a transient reaction to stress or the result of organic brain damage.

neurotic anxiety   As used in psychoanalytic theory, anxiety that arises from the possibility that one will be overwhelmed by one's impulses, especially unconscious sexual and aggressive impulses.

neurotransmitter   A chemical that facilitates the transmission of electrical impulses among nerve endings in the brain.

neutrophils   Cells in the immune system that "eat" an antigen-antibody complex.

niacin (nicotinic acid)   An essential vitamin, the deficiency of which results in pellagra, a disease marked by dermatitis, diarrhea, and dementia.

nicotine   The active ingredient in tobacco that produces psychoactive effects.

norepinephrine   A neurochemical involved in neural transmission. Disturbances of the availability of norepinephrine in the brain have been associated with affective disorders.

nosophobias   *See* illness and injury phobias.

nuclear magnetic resonance imaging   *See* magnetic resonance imaging.

obsessions   Repetitive thoughts, images, or impulses that invade consciousness, are abhorrent, and are very difficult to dismiss or control; usually associated with compulsions.

obsessive-compulsive disorder   An anxiety disorder in which the individual is plagued with uncontrollable, repulsive thoughts (obsessions) and engages in seemingly senseless rituals (compulsive behaviors).

obsessive-compulsive personality disorder   A personality disorder characterized by a pervasive pattern of striving for perfection in oneself and others.

obsessive personality   A personality characterized by a rigid, methodical, moralistic personality. The individual with an obsessive personality is meticulous in dress and speech, pays much attention to detail, and often has problems making decisions.

occipital lobe   A lobe in each cerebral hemisphere which includes the visual projection area.

Oedipal conflict   The conflict between a boy's desire for his mother, and the fear of punishment by castration for that desire by the father.

operant   A response whose probability can be increased by positive reinforcement, or decreased by negative reinforcement.

operant conditioning   Training the organism to perform some instrumental response in order to escape punishment or gain reward.

operational definition   A set of observable and measurable conditions under which a phenomenon is defined to occur.

opiates (or narcotics)   Drugs that produce euphoria or dysphoria, apathy, psychomotor retardation, pupillary constriction, drowsiness, slurred speech, and impairment in attention and memory. Includes codeine, opium, morphine, heroin, and methadone.

opponent-process model of addiction   A model developed by Richard Solomon which explains the increased motivation to use a drug which occurs with continued use of that drug. According to the model, all drugs that produce dependence have three properties: affective pleasure, affective tolerance, and affective withdrawal.

oppositional defiant disorder   A disruptive behavior disorder in which children show a pattern of negativistic, hostile, and defiant behavior, but do not show the more serious violations of others' rights as do children with conduct disorders.

optimal living   The pleasures, maturities, insights, achievements, and wisdoms that constitute the positive aspects of living and that serve as a good defense against abnormality.

oral character traits   In psychoanalytic theory, traits such as dependency that result from fixation at the oral stage of psychosexual development and that persist into adulthood.

oral stage   In psychoanalytic theory, the earliest psychosexual stage of development during which pleasure arises from feeding.

organic syndromes   Abnormal behaviors caused by known pathology in structure or function of the nervous system. Neurology and neuropsychology concentrate on the study of these syndromes.

ostracism   The casting out of the person as well as his or her demons from the community.

outcome expectation   A person's estimate that a given behavior will lead to the desired outcome. *See also* efficacy expectation.

outcome validity   *See* predictive validity.

overdetermination   Behaviors that are caused or determined by more than one psychological force and with more than the requisite psychic energy.

overgeneralization   Drawing global conclusions on the basis of a single fact; an error of logic made by those who are depressed.

overinclusiveness   The tendency to form concepts from both relevant and irrelevant information; this thought defect, which is generally present in schizophrenics, arises from an impaired capacity to resist distracting information.

pain disorder (or psychalgia)   A somatoform disorder in which the individual experiences pain, not attributable to a physical cause, but to psychological conflict.

panic disorder   An anxiety disorder characterized by severe attacks of panic, in which the person (a) is overwhelmed with intense apprehension, dread, or terror, (b) experiences an acute emergency reaction, (c) thinks he might go crazy or die, and (d) engages in fight or flight behavior.

paradoxical intervention   A therapeutic technique that encourages clients to indulge and even exaggerate their symptoms in order to convince them that they really do control those symptoms.

paranoid personality disorder   A personality disorder in which the person has a pervasive and long-standing distrust and suspiciousness of others; hypersensitivity to slight; and a tendency to look for hidden motives for innocuous behavior.

paranoid schizophrenia   A form of schizophrenia in which delusions of persecution or grandeur are systematized and complex.

paraphilias   A group of psychosexual disorders in which bizarre sexual acts or imagery are needed to produce sexual arousal. Includes fetishes, masochism, exhibitionism, voyeurism, transvestism, sadism, zoophilia, and pedophilia.

parasympathetic nervous system (PNS)   That part of the autonomic nervous system which generally works to counteract arousal. *See also* autonomic nervous system, sympathetic nervous system.

parietal lobe   A lobe in each cerebral hemisphere which includes the somatosensory projection areas and is involved with many perceptual functions.

Parkinson's disease   Disorder of movement characterized by tremor of the hands, rigidity, and difficulty in initiating movement. It is caused by degeneration of specific neurons, which leads to decreased amounts of the neurotransmitter dopamine in certain structures in the brain.

partial reinforcement (or intermittent reinforcement)   Rewarding or punishing only some percentage of instrumental responses.

passive-aggressive personality disorder   A disorder that is characterized by resistance to social and occupational performance demands through procrastination, dawdling, stubbornness, inefficiency, and forgetfulness that seem to border on the intentional.

Pavlovian conditioning (or classical conditioning)   Training in which an organism is exposed to one neutral stimulus (conditioned stimulus) and a stimulus (unconditioned stimulus) that naturally provokes a certain response (unconditioned response). Through the learned association between the conditioned stimulus and the unconditioned stimulus, the conditioned stimulus is able to evoke the conditioned response. Modern theorists believe that acquisition occurs when there is a positive contingency between the conditioned stimulus and the unconditioned stimulus. *See also* contingency.

PCP (phencyclidine)   An hallucinogen that causes sensitization to all sensory inputs, depersonalization, diminished awareness of self and the environment, disorientation, muddled thinking, and impaired attention and memory.

pedophilia   A psychosexual disorder in which the individual needs to engage in sexual relations with children below the age of mature consent in order to be sexually aroused.

pellagra psychosis   The dementia that can develop from pellagra, a condition that results from a niacin deficiency.

penis envy   In psychoanalytic theory, girls' negative feelings associated with the absence of a penis and possible anger at their mothers for having created them incomplete and inferior.

peptic ulcer   A circumscribed erosion of the mucous membrane of the stomach or of the duodenum, the upper portion of the small intestine. The main symptom of a peptic ulcer is abdominal pain.

perceptual consciousness   As used by Freud, the first of three levels of consciousness that describes the small number of mental events to which the individual is presently attending.

perseveration   A tendency to repeat the same actions, and to have difficulty making transitions from one action (or idea or strategy) to another. Characteristic of frontal lobe damage.

personality disorders   Disorders in which characteristic ways of perceiving and thinking about oneself and one's environment are inflexible and a source of social and occupational maladjustment. *See also* antisocial personality disorder, avoidant personality disorder, dependent personality disorder, histrionic personality disorder, narcissistic personality disorder, obsessive-compulsive personality disorder, paranoid personality disorder, schizoid personality disorder, schizotypal personality disorder.

personalization   Incorrectly taking responsibility for bad events; an error of logic in those who are depressed.

pervasive learning disorders   Disorders that are all-encompassing, involving difficulties of great magnitude and across many modalities, including language attention, responsiveness, perception, and motor develoment. *See also* autism.

PET scan   *See* positron emission tomography.

phallic stage   In psychoanalytic theory, the third stage of psychosexual development during which the libido focuses on phallic pleasures or masturbation.

pharmacology   The study of drugs and their actions in cells and physiological processes.

phenylalanine   An amino acid that is an essential component of proteins. Children with phenylketonuria cannot metabolize phenylalanine.

phenylketonuria (PKU)   A rare metabolic disease that prevents digestion of an essential amino acid called phenylalanine. As a result of this disease, phenopyruvic acid, a derivative of phenylalanine, builds up in and poisons the nervous system, causing irreversible damage.

phobia   An anxiety disorder characterized by (a) persistent fear of a specific situation out of proportion to the reality of the danger, (b) compelling desire to avoid and escape the situation, (c) recognition that the fear is unreasonably excessive, and (d) the fact that it is not due to any other disorder.

phonological dyslexia   Inability to pronounce a written word that has never been seen before even if it corresponds to a known spoken word.

physical dependence   The need for the presence of a drug to function normally, and the appearance of the withdrawal syndrome upon cessation of the drug.

physiological   Having to do with the body.

Pick's disease   A disorder in which patients show variable memory deficits but little or no visuo-spatial impairments. Patients exhibit marked changes in personality, disinhibition, and socially inappropriate behavior.

placebo   A neutral stimulus that produces some response because the subject believes it should produce that response.

placebo effect   A positive treatment outcome that results from the administration of placebos.

pleasure principle   As used in psychodynamic theory, biological drives that clamor for immediate gratification.

population   The entire set of potential observations.

positive correlation   A relationship between two classes of events wherein when one increases so does the other.

positive reinforcer   An event that increases the probability of a response when made contingent upon it. *See also* discriminative stimulus, instrumental learning, operant.

positron emission tomography (PET) scan   A brain-imaging technique that produces a three-dimensional image of the brain. A radioactive substance, usually glucose or oxygen, is incorporated directly into the neuron in proportion to the metabolic rate. With the aid of a computer, a representation of metabolic rate in different brain regions can be shown.

post-traumatic amnesia   The inability to recall events *after* the traumatic episode.

post-traumatic stress disorder (PTSD)   An anxiety disorder resulting from having witnessed or been confronted by the threat of death, injury, or threat to the physical integrity of self or others, including rape, mugging, watching a bloody accident, or watching or committing an atrocity; the three symptoms defining the disorder are: (a) numbness to the world, (b) reliving of the trauma in dreams, flashbacks, and memories, and (c) symptoms of anxiety and arousal not present before the trauma.

preconscious   As used by Freud, the second of three levels of consciousness, consisting of information and impulses that are not at the center of attention, but that can be retrieved relatively easily.

predictive (or outcome) validity   The ability of the diagnostic categories in a system of diagnosis to predict the course and outcome of treatment.

premature ejaculation   The recurrent inability to exert any control over ejaculation, resulting in rapid ejaculation after penetration.

prepared classical conditioning   In learning theory, the concept of the organism as being biologically predisposed to learning about relationships between certain stimuli, and therefore learning the relationship very easily.

prevalence The percentage of a population having a certain disorder at a given time.

primary erectile dysfunction A disorder in which the male has never been able to achieve or maintain an erection sufficient for intercourse.

proband *See* index case.

prognosis Outlook for the future of a disorder.

progressive relaxation A technique for reducing anxiety in which one tightens and then turns off each of the major muscle groups of one's body, until the muscles are wholly flaccid; the resulting relaxation engages a response system that competes with anxious arousal.

projection Attributing private understandings and meanings to others; substituting "you" for "I."

psychalgia *See* pain disorder.

psychic energy The energies that fuel psychological life.

psychoactive drugs Drugs that affect consciousness, mood, and behavior.

psychoanalysis The psychological theory that claims that disorders are the result of intrapsychic conflicts, usually sexual or aggressive in nature, stemming from childhood fixations. Psychoanalysis is also a therapeutic method in which the therapist helps the patient gain insight into those intrapsychic conflicts behind his or her symptoms.

psychodynamic Dealing with the psychological forces that influence mind and behavior.

psychodynamic model of abnormality A model whose theorists believe that abnormality is driven by hidden conflicts within the personality.

psychogenic amnesia *See* dissociative amnesia.

psychological inventory A highly structured test containing a variety of statements that the client can answer true or false as to whether or not they apply to her; used for vocational guidance, personal counseling, or in connection with a job.

psychomotor retardation Slowing down of movement and speech; prominent in severe depression.

psychoneuroimmunology (PNI) The study of how mental state and behavior influence the immune system.

psychopharmacology That branch of pharmacology that studies drug effects on the cells of the brain and drug actions affecting consciousness, mood, and behavior.

psychosexual Concerning the relationship between the mind and pleasure.

psychosexual disorders A class of mental disorders in which psychological factors impair sexual functioning.

psychosis A mental state characterized by profound disturbances in reality testing, thought, and emotion. *See also* schizophrenia.

psychosomatic disorders A group of disorders in which actual physical illness is caused or influenced by psychological factors. The diagnosis of a psychosomatic disorder requires that the physical symptoms represent a known physical pathology and that psychologically meaningful events preceded and are judged to have contributed to the onset or worsening of the physical disorder.

punishment In psychology experiments, inflicting aversive stimuli on an organism, which reduces the probability of recurrence of certain behaviors by that organism. *See also* negative reinforcement.

Q-sort A personality inventory consisting of a large number of cards, each of which contains a statement such as "is an assertive person," "evades responsibility," or "is sensitive." The person being tested must place each statement in one of nine categories according to whether the statement is more or less characteristic of him. The number of items permitted in each category is ranged in accord with the bell-shaped normal distribution.

random assignment Assigning subjects to groups in an experiment such that each subject has an equal chance of being assigned to each group.

rape The sexual violation of one person by another.

rape trauma syndrome A woman's reaction to rape in which symptoms similar to those of post-traumatic stress disorder occur.

rapid cycling bipolar disorder A subclass of manic-depression in which four or more episodes per year occur.

rational-emotive therapy A therapy in which the therapist challenges the irrational beliefs of the client, and encourages the client to engage in behavior that will counteract his irrational beliefs.

rationalization The process of assigning to behavior socially desirable motives, which an impartial analysis would not substantiate.

reaction formation The process of substituting an opposite reaction for a given impulse.

reactive schizophrenia A schizophrenic condition precipitated by a severe social or emotional upset from which the individual perceives no escape.

realistic anxiety As used in psychoanalytic theory, the fear that arises from the expectation that real world events may be harmful to the self.

reality principle In psychodynamic theory, the way in which the ego expresses and gratifies the desires of the id in accordance with the requirements of reality.

receptive aphasia An aphasia (disorder of language) where the primary deficit is in the perception of speech.

recovered memories Memories that were repressed because of shame, guilt, humiliation, or self-deprecation but that reappear and become accessible to consciousness years later.

recurrence The return of depressive symptoms following at least six months without significant symptoms of depression.

reductionism A philosophy that holds that all psychological phenomena can be explained by and reduced to biological phenomena.

reinforcement An event that, when made contingent on a response, increases its probability. A reward or punishment.

relapse The return of depressive symptoms after drugs or psychotherapy have relieved the depression for less than six months.

relaxation response Physiological response regulated by the parasympathetic nervous system (PNS), which counteracts the emergency reaction to threat. In the relaxation response, the PNS inhibits heart action, constricts respiratory passages, and causes secretion of digestive fluids.

release from inhibition Disinhibition or removal of inhibition.

reliability The characteristic whereby an assessment device generates the same findings on repeated use.

repeatability The chance that, if an experimental manipulation is repeated, it will produce similar results.

repression A coping strategy by which the individual forces unwanted thoughts or prohibited desires out of consciousness and into the unconscious mind.

research diagnoses Hunches that may prove useful in communicating about people and treating them; not as reliable or valid as clinical diagnoses.

reserpine A powerful sedative given to lower high blood pressure. Reserpine occasionally induces depression.

residual rules Unwritten rules of behavior that no one ever teaches but that we know intuitively and that we use to guide our behavior.

residual schizophrenia A form of schizophrenia characterized by the absence of such prominent symptoms as delusions, hallucinations, incoherence or grossly disorganized behavior, but in which there is continuing evidence of the presence of two or more relatively minor but distressing symptoms.

response prevention A therapeutic technique in which a therapist prevents the individual from engaging in a behavior that the therapist wishes to extinguish. *See also* flooding.

retarded ejaculation   In men, great difficulty reaching orgasm during sexual intercourse.

retrograde amnesia   Loss of memory of events predating some disease or trauma. The loss is often confined to a period seconds or minutes prior to a trauma.

reuptake   One of the ways in which norepinephrine is inactivated during neural transmission, wherein neuron 1 reabsorbs the norepinephrine in the synaptic gap, thereby decreasing the amount of norepinephrine at the receptors of neuron 2.

reward   In psychology experiments, giving the organism positive stimuli, which increases the probability of recurrence of certain behaviors by the organism. *See also* positive reinforcer.

right visual field   The right half of one's visual world, that is, the part of the world that projects onto the left side of the retina and into the left hemisphere.

role construct repertory test (Rep test)   A personality inventory that examines the constructs that a person uses in interpreting significant events.

Rorschach test   A personality test consisting of ten bilaterally symmetrical "inkblots," some in color, some in black, gray, and white, each on an individual card. The respondent is shown each card separately and asked to name everything the inkblot could resemble. The test is supposed to elicit unconscious conflicts, latent fears, sexual and aggressive impulses, and hidden anxieties.

sadism   A psychosexual disorder in which the individual becomes sexually aroused only by inflicting physical and psychological suffering and humiliation on another human being.

sample   A selection of items or people, from the entire population of similar items or people.

schizoid personality disorder   A disorder that is characterized by the inability to form social relationships, the absence of desire for social involvements, indifference to both praise and criticism, insensitivity to feelings of others, and by lack of social skills.

schizophrenia   A group of disorders characterized by incoherence of speech and thought, hallucinations, delusions, blunted or inappropriate emotion, deterioration in social and occupational functioning, and lack of self-care.

schizophrenogenic families   Families that seem to foster schizophrenia in one or more family members.

schizotypal personality disorder   A personality disorder characterized by longstanding oddities in thinking, perceiving, communicating, and behaving.

school phobia   A persistent and irrational fear of going to school.

seasonal affective disorder (SAD)   Characterized by depression beginning each year in the fall and remitting or switching to mania in the spring.

secondary erectile dysfunction   Loss of the ability in a male to achieve or maintain an erection.

selective abstraction   Focusing on one insignificant detail while ignoring the more important features of a situation; an error of logic in those who are depressed.

selective amnesia (or categorical amnesia)   Loss of memory of all events related to a particular theme.

selective positive reinforcement   Therapeutic technique in which the therapist delivers positive reinforcement contingent on the occurrence of one particular behavior.

selective punishment   Therapeutic technique in which the therapist negatively reinforces a certain target event, causing it to decrease in probability.

self-object   Those people and things that are critically significant for personality cohesiveness.

self theory   A personality theory that addresses the fact that people feel *whole* and *unified* rather than fragmented into ego, superego, behaviors, etc. Wholeness is thought to be endowed by the *self.*

sensate focus   A strategy of direct sexual therapy that involves (a) a "pleasuring" phase during which the couple engages in nongenital erotic activity, but restrains from intercourse, then (b) a phase of "genital stimulation" in which the couple engages in genital play, but without intercourse, then (c) the phase of "nondemand intercourse" in which the couple engages in intercourse, but without making demands on each other.

separation anxiety disorder   A disorder characterized by a very strong fear of being separated from one's family. Children with this disorder become panicked if they must separate from loved ones, and they often show continual physical symptoms of anxiety.

sex role   The public expression of sexual identity, what an individual says or does to indicate that he is a man or she is a woman.

sexual dysfunction   Disorders in which adequate sexual arousal, desire, or orgasm are inhibited.

sexual identity   Generally consistent with one's genitals; feeling that one is male if one has a penis; feeling that one is female if one has a vagina.

sexual interest   The types of persons, parts of the body, and situations that are the objects of sexual fantasies, arousal, and preferences.

sexual orientation   Attraction to and erotic fantasies about men, women, or both.

sexual unresponsiveness (or frigidity)   In women, lack of sexual desire and impairment of physical excitement in appropriate situations.

shadowing   A technique used in treating stuttering which entails repeating the therapist's words shortly after the latter has spoken them.

single-blind experiment   An experiment in which the subject, but not the experimenter, is blind as to whether the subject has received an experimental treatment or a placebo.

single photon emission computerized tomography (SPECT) scan   A brain-imaging technique that measures cerebral blood flow by measuring the concentration of a radioactive substance, injected in nonharmful amounts, into the brain.

social phobias   Unreasonable fear of and desire to avoid situations in which one might be humiliated in front of other people.

soft signs   Signs of neurological disorder apparent from external, noninvasive, behavioral examination of the patient.

somatic   Having to do with the body.

somatization disorder (or Briquet's syndrome)   A somatoform disorder characterized by the experience of a large number and variety of physical symptoms for which there are no medical explanations. These symptoms are not under the voluntary control of the individual.

somatoform disorders   A group of mental disorders characterized by (a) loss or alteration in physical functioning, for which there is no physiological explanation, (b) evidence that psychological factors have caused the physical symptoms, (c) lack of voluntary control over physical symptoms, and (d) indifference by the patient to the physical loss. Includes conversion, pain disorder, somatization disorder.

specific attribution   An individual's assignment of cause for an event to a factor that is relevant only to that situation.

specific phobias   There are four classes of specific phobias: animal phobias are unreasonable fears of and desires to avoid or escape specific animals. Illness and injury phobias (nosophobias) are unreasonable fears of and desires to avoid or escape a specific illness or injury. Inanimate objects phobias are unreasonable fears of and desires to avoid certain situations or objects other than social situations, crowds, animals, illness, or injuries. Blood phobias are an unreasonable fear of blood.

stable attribution   An individual's assignment of cause for an event to a factor that persists in time.

statistical inferences   Procedures used to decide whether a sample or a set of observations is truly representative of the population.

statistically significant effect   An effect that is highly unlikely (typically less than one time in twenty) to occur solely by chance.

stigmata   Marks on the skin, usually bleeding or bruises, and often of high religious or personal significance, brought on by an emotional state.

stimulants   A class of psychoactive drugs that induces psychomotor agitation, physiological hyperactivity, elation, grandiosity, loquacity, and hypervigilance. Includes amphetamines and cocaine.

stroke   Damage to the nervous system caused by loss or severe reduction in the supply of nutrients and oxygen, resulting from damage to blood vessels (e.g., hemorrhage or occlusion by a blood clot).

subclinical   The property of being symptomatic, but more mild than a full-blown disorder.

subject   Participant in an experiment.

subject bias   The influence of a subject's beliefs about what he is expected to do in an experiment on his responses in the experiment.

subjective self   The second sense of self, which develops between the age of seven and nine months. It gives rise to the sense that we understand each others' feelings and intentions.

sublimation   In psychoanalytic theory, the transfer of libidinal energies from relatively narcissistic gratifications to those which gratify others and are highly socialized. More generally, the process of rechanneling psychic energy from socially undesirable goals to constructive and socially desirable ones.

superego   Those psychological processes that are "above the self," i.e., conscience, ideals, and morals.

surface dyslexia   Someone with surface dyslexia can only read words by sounding them out.

syllable-timed speech   Used in treating stuttering, this technique requires stutterers to speak in time to a metronome.

sympathetic nervous system (SNS)   The part of the autonomic nervous system that mobilizes the body's reaction to stress. *See also* autonomic nervous system, parasympathetic nervous system.

symptom   A sign of disorder.

synapse   The junction between neurons. Excitation or inhibition is transmitted from one neuron to another by diffusion of neurotransmitters across the synaptic gap.

syndrome   A set of symptoms that tend to co-occur.

systematic desensitization   A behavior therapy primarily used to treat phobias and specific anxieties. The phobic is first given training in deep muscle relaxation and is then progressively exposed to increasingly anxiety-evoking situations (real or imagined). Because relaxation and fear are mutually exclusive, stimuli that formerly induced panic are now greeted calmly.

tarantism   A dancing mania that occurred in Italy and was thought to have been brought on by a tarantula's bite

tardive dyskinesia   A nonreversible neurological side effect of antipsychotic drug treatment, whose symptoms consist of sucking, lip smacking, and peculiar tongue movements.

T cells   Cells in the immune system that are produced in the thymus gland. They have receptors on their surfaces for specific antigens.

telephone scatologia   A paraphilia that consists of recurrent and intense sexual urges to make obscene telephone calls to a nonconsenting individual.

temporal lobe   A lobe in each cerebral hemisphere that includes the auditory projection area and is particularly involved in memory.

tension reduction hypothesis   A hypothesis that states that people drink alcohol to reduce tension.

Thematic Apperception Test (TAT)   A personality test that consists of a series of pictures that are not as ambiguous as Rorschach cards, but not as clear as photographs either. Respondents look at each picture and make up a story about it. The test is supposed to elicit underlying psychological dynamics.

therapeutic alliance   An agreement between therapist and patient on the goals of therapy and how they can best be achieved.

tolerance   The state of drug addiction in which, after repeated use of a drug, the addict needs more and more of the drug to produce the desired reaction, and there is great diminution of the effect of a given dose.

Tourette's syndrome   A disorder characterized by motor tics and uncontrollable verbal outbursts, usually beginning in childhood.

trait marker   An observable, biological indication of a genetic predisposition.

transsexuality   A psychosexual disorder characterized by the belief that one is a woman trapped in the body of a man, or a man trapped in the body of a woman.

transvestism   A psychosexual disorder in which a man often dresses in the clothes of a woman in order to achieve sexual arousal.

tricyclic antidepressants   Antidepressant drugs that block uptake of norepinephrine, thus increasing the availability of norepinephrine.

tumor   An abnormal tissue that grows by cell multiplication more rapidly than is normal.

twin study   The study of the degree of concordance of a trait in identical versus fraternal twins. This method allows the quantification of the heritability of psychological traits. *See also* adoptive study.

Type A behavior pattern   A personality type characterized by (a) an exaggerated sense of time urgency, (b) competitiveness and ambition, and (c) aggressiveness and hostility when thwarted.

unconditioned stimulus (US)   A stimulus that will provoke an unconditioned response without training. For example, a loud noise will naturally provoke a startle response in humans.

unconscious   In psychoanalytic theory, the third level of consciousness consisting of the large mass of hidden memories, experiences, and impulses.

undifferentiated schizophrenia   A category of schizophrenia used to describe disturbed individuals who present evidence of thought disorder, as well as behavioral and affective anomalies, but who are not classifiable under the other subtypes.

unipolar depression   A disorder characterized by depression, in the absence of a history of mania.

unstable attribution   An individual's assignment of cause for an event to a factor that is transient.

validity   The extent to which a test of something is actually measuring that something.

verbal self   The third sense of self, which develops between fifteen and eighteen months of age. It is the verbal and symbolic storehouse of experience and knowledge.

voyeurism   A psychosexual disorder in which the individual habitually gains sexual arousal only by observing the naked body, the disrobing, or the sexual activity of an unsuspecting victim.

white matter   Those parts of the central nervous system composed primarily of myelinated axons. The myelin imparts a white color to these areas.

withdrawal syndrome (or abstinence syndrome)   A substance-specific syndrome that follows cessation of the intake of a substance that has been regularly used by the individual to induce intoxication; usually characterized by observable, physical signs such as marked changes in body temperature or heart rate, seizures, tremors, or vomiting.

yoking   An experimental procedure in which both experimental and control groups receive exactly the same physical events, but only the experimental group influences these events by its responding.

zoophilia (or bestiality)   A psychosexual disorder in which the individual habitually engages in sexual relations with animals in order to be sexually aroused.

References

Abrams, R., Taylor, M., Faber, R., Ts'o, T., Williams, R., & Almy, G. (1983). Bilateral vs. unilateral electroconvulsive therapy: Efficacy and melancholia. *American Journal of Psychiatry, 140,* 463–65.

Abrams, R., & Vedak, C. (1991). Prediction of ECT response in melancholia. *Convulsive Therapy, 7,* 81–84.

Abramson, L. Y. (1978). Universal versus personal helplessness. Unpublished doctoral dissertation, University of Pennsylvania.

Abramson, L. Y., Garber, J., Edwards, N., & Seligman, M. E. P. (1978). Expectancy change in depression and schizophrenia. *Journal of Abnormal Psychology, 87,* 165–79.

Abramson, L., Metalsky, G., & Alloy, L. (1989). Hopelessness depression: A theory-based subtype of depression. *Psychological Review, 96,* 358–72.

Abramson, L. Y., Seligman, M. E. P., & Teasdale, J. (1978). Learned helplessness in humans: Critique and reformulation. *Journal of Abnormal Psychology, 87,* 32–48.

ACNP-FDA Task Force. (1973). Medical intelligence—drug therapy. *New England Journal of Medicine, 130,* 20–24.

Adams, H. E., & Sturgis, E. T. (1977). Status of behavioral reorientation techniques in the modification of homosexuality: A review. *Psychological Bulletin, 84,* 1171–88.

Adams, R. D. (1989). *Principles of neurology* (3rd ed.). New York: McGraw-Hill.

Adams, R. D., & Victor, M. (1981). *Principles of neurology* (2nd ed.). New York: McGraw-Hill.

Adler, T. (1989). Integrity test popularity prompts close scrutiny. *APA Monitor, 7.*

Agras, S., Sylvester, D., & Oliveau, D. (1969). The epidemiology of common fears and phobia. *Comprehensive Psychiatry, 10* (2): 151–56.

Agras, W. S. (1993). Short-term psychological treatments for binge eating. In C. G. Fairburn & G. T. Wilson (Eds.), *Binge eating: Nature, assessment, and treatment.* New York: Guilford Press.

Agras, W. S., & Kirkley, B. G. (1986). Bulimia: Theories of etiology. In K. D. Brownell & J. P. Foreyt (Eds.), *Handbook of eating disorders: Physiology, psychology and treatment of obesity, anorexia, and bulimia.* New York: Basic Books.

Agras, W. S., Rossiter, E. M., Arnow, B., Schneider, J. A., Telch, C. F., Raeburn, S. D., Bruce, B., Perl, M., & Koran, L. M. (1992). Pharmacologic and cognitive-behavioral treatment for bulimia nervosa: A controlled comparison. *American Journal of Psychiatry, 149,* 82–87.

Agras, W. S., Schneider, J. A., Arnow, B., Raeburn, S. D., & Telch, C. F. (1989a). Cognitive-behavioral and response-prevention treatments for bulimia nervosa. *Journal of Consulting and Clinical Psychology, 57*(2): 215–21.

Agras, W. S., Schneider, J. A., Arnow, B., Raeburn, S. D., & Telch, C. F. (1989b). Cognitive-behavioral treatment with and without exposure plus response prevention in the treatment of bulimia nervosa. *Journal of Consulting and Clinical Psychology, 57,* 778–79.

Aigner, T. G., & Balster, R. L. (1978). Choice behavior in rhesus monkeys: Cocaine versus food. *Science, 201,* 534–35.

Akhtar, S., Wig. N., Varma, V. K., Pershard, D., & Verma, S. K. (1975). A phenomenological analysis of symptoms in the obsessive-compulsive neurosis. *British Journal of Psychiatry, 127,* 342–48.

Akiskal, H. S. (1979). A biobehavioral model of depression. In R. A. Depue (Ed.), *The psychobiology of depressive disorders: Implications for the effects of stress.* New York: Academic Press.

Akiskal, H. S., & McKinney, W. T. (1973). Depressive disorders: Toward a unified hypothesis. *Science, 182,* 20–29.

Akiskal, H. S., & McKinney, W. T. (1975). Overview of recent research in depression. *Archives of General Psychiatry, 32,* 285–305.

Aleksandrowicz, D. R. (1961). Fire and its aftermath on a geriatric ward. *Bulletin of the Menninger Clinic, 25,* 23–32.

Alexander, F. (1950). *Psychosomatic medicine.* New York: Norton.

Alexander, F., French, T. M., & Pollack, G. H. (1968). *Psychosomatic specificity: Experimental study and results.* Chicago: University of Chicago Press.

Alexander, L., & Luborsky, L. (1984). Research on the helping alliance. In L. Greenberg & W. Pinsof (Eds.), *The psychotherapeutic process: A research handbook.* New York: Guilford Press.

Allen, L., & Gorski, R. (1992). Sexual orientation and the size of the anterior commissure in the human brain. *Proceedings of the National Academy of Sciences, 89,* 7199–7202.

Allen, M. G. (1976). Twin studies of affective illness. *Archives of General Psychiatry, 33.* 1476–78.

Alloy, L. B., & Abramson, L. Y. (1979). Judgment of contingency in depressed and nondepressed students: Sadder but wiser? *Journal of Experimental Psychology: General, 108,* 441–85.

Alloy, L., & Clements, C. (1992). Illusion of control: Invulnerability to negative affect and depressive symptoms after laboratory and natural stressors. *Journal of Abnormal Psychology, 101,* 234–45.

Alloy, L. B., Lipman, A. J., & Abramson, L. Y. (1992). Attributional style as a vulnerability factor for depression: Validation by past history of mood disorders. *Cognitive Therapy and Research, 16*(4): 391–407.

Allport, G. W. (1937). *Personality: A psychological interpretation.* New York: Henry Holt.

Alper, J. (1993). Ulcers as an infectious disease. *Science, 260,* 159–60.

American Psychiatric Association (1980). *Diagnostic and statistical manual of mental disorders* (3rd ed.) (DSM-III). Washington, DC: Author.

American Psychiatric Association. (1983). Guidelines for legislation on the psychiatric hospitalization of adults. *American Journal of Psychiatry, 140,* 672–79.

American Psychiatric Association (1987). *Diagnostic and statistical manual of mental disorders* (3rd ed., revised) (DSM-III-R). Washington, DC: Author.

American Psychiatric Association (1994). *Diagnostic and statistical manual of mental disorders* (4th ed.) (DSM-IV). Washington, DC: Author.

Andersen, B. L. (1983). Primary orgasmic dysfunction: Diagnostic conditions and review of treatment. *Psychological Bulletin, 93,* 105–36.

Anderson, J. C., Williams, S., McGee, R., & Silva, P. A. (1987). DSM-III: Disorders in preadolescent children. *Archives of General Psychiatry, 44,* 69–76.

Anderson, J. R., & Bower, G. H. (1973). *Human associative memory.* Washington, DC: Winston.

Anderson, N. (1993). Reactivity research on sociodemographic groups: Its value to psychophysiology and health psychology. *Health Psychology, 12,* 3–5.

Andreasen, N., & Glick, I. (1988). Bipolar affective disorder and creativity: Implications and clinical management. *Comprehensive Psychiatry, 29,* 207–17.

Andreasen, N. C., Nasrallah, H. A., Dunn, V., Olson, S. C., Grove, W. M., Ehrhardt, J. C., Coffman, J. A., & Crossett, J. H. (1986). Structural abnormalities in the frontal system in schizophrenia: A magnetic resonance imaging study. *Archives of General Psychiatry, 43* (2): 136–44.

Andreasen, N. C., & Olsen, S. (1982). Negative versus positive schizophrenia: Definition and validation. *Archives of General Psychiatry, 39,* 789–94.

Andreasen, N. C., Scheftner, W., Reich, T., Hirschfeld, R. M. A., Endicott, J., & Keller, M. B. (1986). The validation of the concept of endogenous depression. *Archives of General Psychiatry, 43,* 246–51.

Angold, A. (1994). Unpublished data. Presentation to NIMH Workshop on Emergence of Sex Differences in Depression, Bethesda, MD, March 1994.

Angst, J. (1992). Epidemiology of depression. 2nd International Symposium on Moclobemide: RIMA (Reversible Inhibitor of Monoamine Oxidase Type A): A new concept in the treatment of depression. *Psychopharmacology, 106* (Suppl): 71–74.

Angst, J., Baastrup, P., Grof, P., Hippius, H., Poldinger, W., & Weis, P. (1973). The course of monopolar depression and bipolar psychoses. *Psykiotrika, Neurologika and Neurochirurgia, 76,* 489–500.

Angst, J., & Wicki, W. (1991). The Zurich Study: XI. Is dysthymia a separate form of depression? Results of the Zurich Cohort Study. *European Archives of Psychiatry and Clinical Neuroscience, 240* (6): 349–54.

Anisman, H. (1978). Aversively motivated behavior as a tool in psychopharmacological analysis. In H. Anisman & G. Binami (Eds.), *Psychopharmacology of aversively motivated behavior.* New York: Plenum.

Annau, Z., & Kamin, L. J. (1961). The conditional emotional response as a function of intensity of the US. *Journal of Comparative and Physiological Psychology, 54,* 428–32.

Ansbacher, H. L., & Ansbacher, R. (1956). *The individual psychology of Alfred Adler.* New York: Basic Books.

Apfelbaum, B. (1980). The diagnosis and treatment of retarded ejaculation. In S. A. Leiblum & L. A. Pervin (Eds.), *Principles and practice of sex therapy* (pp. 236–96). New York: Guilford Press.

Archibald, H. C., & Tuddenham, R. D. (1965). Persistent stress reaction after combat. *Archives of General Psychiatry, 12,* 475–81.

Arendt, H. (1978). *The life of the mind.* New York: Harcourt Brace Jovanovich.

Arieti, S. (1974). *Interpretation of schizophrenia.* New York: Basic Books.

Arieti, S. (1979). New views on psychodynamics of phobias. *American Journal of Psychotherapy, 33,* 82–95.

Arieti, S., & Bemporad, J. (1978). *Severe and mild depression.* New York: Basic Books.

Aronow, E., & Reznikoff, M. (1976). *Rorschach content interpretation.* New York: Grune & Stratton.

Aronow, E., Reznikoff, M., & Rauchway, A. (1979). Some old and new directions in Rorschach testing. *Journal of Personality Testing, 43,* 227–34.

Arizona Republic. (1994). Liar in drag: Rapist admits faking multiple personalities. *Arizona Republic,* April 20.

Armstrong, L. (1993). *And they call it help.* New York: Addison-Wesley.

Aronson, T. A., & Craig, T. J. (1986). Cocaine precipitation of panic disorder. *American Journal of Psychiatry, 143,* 643–45.

Asberg, M., Traskman, L., & Thoren, P. (1976). 5–HIAA in the cerebrospinal fluid. *Archives of General Psychiatry, 33,* 1193–97.

Asch, S. E. (1951). Effects of group pressure on the modification and distortion of judgments. In H. Guetzkow (Ed.), *Groups, leadership and men: Research in human relations.* Pittsburgh, PA: Carnegie Press.

Ashcroft, G., Crawford, T. B. B., Eccleston, D., Sharman, D. F., MacDougall, E. J., Stanton, J. B., & Binns, J. K. (1966). 5-hydroxylindole compounds in the cerebrospinal fluid of patients with psychiatric or neurological diseases. *Lancet, 2,* 1049–52.

Assad, G., & Shapiro, B. (1986). Hallucinations: Theoretical and clinical overview. *American Journal of Psychiatry, 143* (9): 1088–97.

Atkinson, J. W. (1958). *Motives in fantasy, action and society.* Princeton: Van Nostrand.

Auerbach, A. H., & Johnson, M. (1977). Research on the therapist's level of experience. In A. S. Gurman & A. M. Razin (Eds.), *Effective psychotherapy.* New York: Pergamon.

Averill, J. R., & Rosenn, M. (1972). Vigilant and non-vigilant coping strategies and psychophysiological stress reactions during the anticipation of an electric shock. *Journal of Personality and Social Psychology, 23,* 128–41.

Ax, A. F. (1953). The physiological differentiation between fear and anger in humans. *Psychosomatic Medicine, 15,* 433–42.

Ayllon, T., & Michael, J. (1959). The psychiatric nurse as a behavioral engineer. *Journal of the Experimental Analysis of Behavior, 2,* 323–34.

Ayres, B. D., Jr. (1994). Big gains are seen in battle to stem drunken driving. *New York Times,* May 22, p. A1.

Babor, T. F. (1990). Social, scientific and medical issues in the definition of alcohol and drug dependence. In A. Edwards & M. Lader (Eds.), *The nature of drug dependence* (pp. 19–40). New York: Oxford University Press.

Bacon, D. L. (1969). Incompetency to stand trial; commitment to an inclusive test. *Southern California Law Review, 42,* 444.

Baer, D. M., & Guess, D. (1971). Receptive training of adjectival inflections in mental retardates. *Journal of Applied Behavior Analysis, 4,* 129–39.

Bailey, J. M., & Pillard, R. (1991). A genetic study of male sexual orientation. *Archives of General Psychiatry, 48,* 1089–96.

Bailey, J. M., Pillard, R., & Agyei, Y. (1993). A genetic study of female sexual orientation. *Archives of General Psychiatry, 50,* 217–23.

Baker, L. A., Mack, W., Moffitt, T. E., & Mednick, S. (1989). Sex differences in property crime in a Danish adoption cohort. *Behavior Genetics, 19*(3).

Bakker, A., Van Kesteren, P., Gooren, L., & Bezemer, P. (1993). The prevalence of transsexualism in the Netherlands. *Acta Psychiatrica Scandinavica, 87,* 237–38.

Bales, J. (1987). A few smart habits cut malpractice risk. *The APA Monitor, 18* (8): 39.

Ballenger, J. C. (1986). Pharmacotherapy of the panic disorders. *Journal of Clinical Psychiatry, 47* (Suppl): 27–32.

Baltes, P. B., Reese, H. W., & Lipsitt, L. P. (1980). Life-span developmental psychology. *Annual Review of Psychology, 31,* 65–110.

Ban, T. A., Choi, S. M., Lamonn, H. E., & Adamo, E. (1966). Conditional reflex studies in depression. *Canadian Psychiatric Association Journal, 11,* 98–105.

Bandura, A. (1969). *Principles of behavior modification.* New York: Holt, Rinehart & Winston.

Bandura, A. (1977a). Self efficacy: Toward a unifying theory of behavioral change. *Psychological Review, 84,* 191–215.

Bandura, A. (1977b). *Social learning theory.* Englewood Cliffs, NJ: Prentice-Hall.

Bandura, A. (1978). The self system in reciprocal determinism. *American Psychologist, 33,* 344–58.

Bandura, A. (1982). Self-efficacy mechanism in human agency. *American Psychologist, 37,* 122–47.

Bandura, A. (1986). Fearful expectations and avoidant actions as coeffects of personal self-inefficacy. *American Psychologist, 41* (12), 1389–91.

Bandura, A., & Adams, N. E. (1977). Analysis of self-efficacy theory of behavioral changes. *Cognitive Therapy and Research, 1,* 287–310.

Bandura, A., Adams, N. E., & Beyer, J. (1977). Cognitive processes mediating behavioral change. *Journal of Personality and Social Psychology, 35,* 125–39.

Bandura, A., Blanchard, E. B., & Ritter, B. (1969). Relative efficacy of desensitization and modelling approaches for inducing behavioral, affective, and attitudinal change. *Journal of Personality and Social Psychology, 13,* 173–99.

Bandura, A., & Walters, R. H. (1959). *Adolescent aggression.* New York: Ronald Press.

Bandura, A., & Walters, R. H. (1963). *Social learning and personality development.* New York: Holt, Rinehart & Winston.

Barbizet, J. (1970). *Human memory and its pathology.* (D. K. Jardine, Trans.). San Francisco: Freeman.

Bard, M. (1970). *Training police as specialists in family crisis intervention.* Washington, DC: U.S. Government Printing Office.

Bard, M., & Sangrey, D. (1979). *The crime victim's book.* New York: Basic Books.

Bardhan, K. D. (1980). Cimetidinea in duodenal ulcer: The present position. In A. Torsoli, P. E. Lucchelli, & R. W. Brimbelcombe (Eds.), *H2 antagonists.* Amsterdam: Excerpta Medica.

Barefoot, J. C., Dahlstrom, W. G., & Williams, R. B. (1983). Hostility, CHD incidence, and total mortality: A 25-year follow-up study of 255 physicians. *Psychosomatic Medicine, 45* (1): 59–63.

Barefoot, J., Peterson, B., Dahlstrom, W., et al. (1991). Hostility patterns and health implications: Correlates of Cook-Medley Hostility scale scores in a national survey. *Health Psychology, 10,* 18–24.

Barkley, R. A. (1990). *Attention deficit hyperactivity disorder: A handbook for diagnosis and treatment.* New York: Guilford Press.

Barkley, R. A., Fischer, M., Edelbrock, C. S., & Smallish, L. (1990). The adolescent outcome of hyperactive children diagnosed by research criteria. I. An 8-year prospective follow-up. *Journal of the American Academy of Child and Adolescent Psychiatry, 29*(4): 546–57.

Barlow, D. H. (1986). The classification of anxiety disorders. In G. L. Tischler (Ed.), *Diagnoses and classification in psychiatry: A critical appraisal of DSM-III* (pp. 223–42). Cambridge: Cambridge University Press.

Barlow, D. H. (1988). *Anxiety and its disorders: The nature and treatment of anxiety and panic.* New York: Guilford Press.

Barlow, D. H., Abel, G. G., & Blanchard, E. B. (1979). Gender identity change in transsexuals. *Archives of General Psychiatry, 36,* 1001–1007.

Barnes, D. M. (1988). The biological tangle of drug addiction. *Science, 241,* 415–17.

Barnes, G. E., & Prosin, H. (1985). Parental death and depression. *Journal of Abnormal Psychology, 94,* 64–69.

Barnes, T. R. E., & Braude, W. M. (1985). Akathisia variants and tardive dyskinesia. *Archives of General Psychiatry, 42,* 874–78.

Baron, M., Gruen, R., Kane, J., & Amis, L. (1985). Modern research criteria and the genetics of schizophrenia. *American Journal of Psychiatry, 142,* 697–701.

Barrett-Lennard, G. T. (1962). Dimensions of therapist response as causal factors in therapeutic change. *Psychological Monographs, 76* (43, Whole No. 562).

Barsky, A. J., Wyshak, G., & Klerman, G. L. (1986). Hypochondriasis, an evaluation of the DSM-III criteria in medical outpatients. *Archives of General Psychiatry, 43,* 493–500.

Bartak, L., & Rutter, M. (1974). Use of personal pronouns by autistic children. *Journal of Autistic Children and Schizophrenia, 4,* 217–22.

Bartlett, D. L., & Steele, J. B. (1979). *Empire: The life, legend, and madness of Howard Hughes.* New York: Norton.

Bartrop, R. W., Luckhurst, E., Lazarus, L., Kiloh, L. G., & Penny, R. (1977). Depressed lymphocyte function after bereavement. *The Lancet, I,* April 16, 834–36.

Bateson, G., Jackson, D. D., Haley, J., & Weakland, J. (1956). Toward a theory of schizophrenia. *Behavioral Science, 1,* 251–64.

Bauer, M. S., & Whybrow, P. C. (1990). Rapid cycling bipolar affective disorder: II. Treatment of refractory rapid cycling with high-dose levothyroxine. A preliminary study. *Archives of General Psychiatry, 47*(5): 435–40.

Baum, A. (1990). Stress, intrusive imagery, and chronic distress. *Health Psychology, 9,* 653–75.

Baum, A., Cohen, L., & Hall, M. (1993). Control and intrusive memories as possible determinants of chronic stress. *Psychosomatic Medicine, 55,* 274–86.

Baum, M. (1969). Extinction of an avoidance response following response prevention: Some parametric investigations. *Canadian Journal of Psychology, 23,* 1–10.

Baumgold, J. (1977). Agoraphobia: Life ruled by panic. *New York Times Magazine,* December 4, p. 46.

Baxter, L., Schwartz, J., Bergman, K., Szuba, M., et al. (1992). Caudate glucose metabolic rate changes with both drug and behavior therapy for obsessive-compulsive disorder. *Archives of General Psychiatry, 49,* 681–89.

Bazelon, D. (1971). New gods for old: "Efficient" courts in a democratic society. *New York University Law Review, 46,* 653, 658–60.

Beauvais, M. F., & Derouesne, J. (1979). Phonological alexia: The dissociations. *Journal of Neurology, Neurosurgery, and Psychiatry, 42,* 1115–24.

Beasley, C., Dornseif, B., Bosomworth, J., et al. (1992). Fluoxetine and suicide: A meta-analysis of controlled trials of treatment for depression. *International Clinical Psychopharmacology, 6* (Suppl. 6): 35–57.

Beaumont, G. (1990). Adverse effects of antidepressants. *International Clinical Psychopharmacology, 5,* 61–66.

Beck, A. T. (1967). *Depression: Clinical, experimental, and theoretical aspects.* New York: Hoeber.

Beck, A. T. (1973). *The diagnosis and management of depression.* Philadelphia: University of Pennsylvania Press.

Beck, A. T. (1976). *Cognitive therapy and the emotional disorders.* New York: International Universities Press.

Beck, A. T. (1993). Cognitive therapy: Past, present, and future. *Journal of Consulting and Clinical Psychology, 61*(2): 194–98.

Beck, A.T., & Emery, G. (1985). *Anxiety disorders and phobias: A cognitive perspective.* New York: Basic Books.

Beck, A. T., & Horvich, M. J. (1959). Psychological correlates of depression. *Psychosomatic Medicine, 21,* 50–55.

Beck, A. T., Kovacs, M., & Weissman, A. (1975). Hopelessness and suicidal behavior: An overview. *Journal of the American Medical Association, 234,* 1146–49.

Beck, A. T., Rush, A. J., Shaw, B. F., & Emery, G. (1979). *Cognitive therapy of depression.* New York: Guilford Press.

Beck, A. T., Sokol, L., Clark, D., Berchick, B., & Wright, F. (1991). Focussed cognitive therapy of panic disorder: A crossover design and one-year follow-up. Manuscript.

Beck, A. T., Ward, C. H., Mendelson, M., Mock, J. E., & Erbaugh, J. K. (1962). Reliability of psychiatric diagnoses II: A study of consistency of clinical judgments and ratings. *American Journal of Psychiatry, 119,* 351–57.

Beck, T. R. (1811). An inaugural dissertation on insanity. Cited in A. Deutsch, *The mentally ill in America.* New York: Columbia University Press, 1949.

Beech, H. R., & Vaughan, M. (1979). *Behavioural treatment of obsessional states.* Chichester: Wiley.

Beecher, H. K. (1959). *Measurement of subjective responses: Quantitative effects of drugs.* New York: Oxford University Press.

Beecher, H. K. (1961). Surgery as placebo. *Journal of the American Medical Association, 176,* 1102–1107.

Begleiter, H., Porjesz, B., Bihari, & Kissen, B. (1984). Event-related brain potentials in children at risk for alcoholism. *Science, 227,* 1493–96.

Bellack, A. S. (1992). Cognitive rehabilitation for schizophrenia: Is it really possible? Is it necessary? *Schizophrenia Bulletin, 18*(1): 43–50.

Bellack, A. S., & Muesser, K. T. (1993). Psychosocial treatment for schizophrenia. *Schizophrenia Bulletin, 19*(2): 317–36.

Belson, R. (1975). The importance of the second interview in marriage counseling. *Counseling Psychologist, 5*(3): 27–31.

Benes, F. M., Davidson, J., & Bird, E. D. (1986). Quantitative cytoarchitectural studies of the cerebral cortex of schizophrenics. *Archives of General Psychiatry, 42,* 874–78.

Benjamin, H. (1966). *The transsexual phenomenon.* New York: Julian Press.

Benjamin, L. S. (1987). The use of the SASB dimensional model to develop treatment plans for personality disorders. I: Narcissism. *Journal of Personality Disorders, 1* (1): 43–70.

Benowitz, N. L. (1988). Pharmacologic aspects of cigarette smoking and nicotine addiction. *The New England Journal of Medicine, 17,* 1318–30.

Benson, D. F., & Zaidel, E. (Eds.). (1985). *The dual brain: Hemispheric specialization in humans.* New York: Guilford Press.

Benson, H. (1975). *The relaxation response.* New York: Morrow.

Benton, M. K., & Schroeder, H. E. (1990). Social skills training with schizophrenics: A meta-analytic evaluation. *Journal of Consulting and Clinical Psychology, 58*(6): 741–47.

Berenbaum, H., Gottesman, I. I. & Oltmanns, T. F. (1985). Formal thought disorder in schizophrenics and their twins. *Journal of Abnormal Psychology, 94* (1): 3–16.

Berenbaum, S., & Hines, M. (1992). Early androgens are related to childhood sex-typed toy preferences. *Psychological Science, 3,* 203–6.

Berger, F. (1970). Anxiety and the discovery of tranquilizers. In F. J. Ayd & H. Blackwell (Eds.), *Discoveries in biological psychiatry.* Philadelphia: Lippincott.

Berger, P. (1977). Antidepressant medications and the treatment of depression. In J. Barchas, P. Berger, R. Ciaranello, & G. Elliot (Eds.), *Psychopharmacology.* New York: Oxford University Press.

Bergin, A. E. (1966). Some implications of psychotherapy research for therapeutic practice. *Journal of Abnormal Psychology, 71,* 235–46.

Bergin, A. E. (1971). The evaluation of therapeutic outcomes. In A. E. Bergin & S. L. Garfield (Eds.), *Handbook of psychotherapy and behavior change* (pp. 217–70). New York: Wiley.

Bergler, E. (1949). *The basic neurosis: Oral regression and psychic masochism.* New York: Grune & Stratton.

Berkman, L. F. (1984). Assessing the physical health effects of social networks and social support. *Annual Review of Public Health, 5,* 413–32.

Berkman, L. F. (1986). Social networks, support, and health: Taking the next step forward. *American Journal of Epidemiology, 123,* 559–62.

Berman, J. S., & Norton, N. C. (1985). Does professional training make a therapist more effective? *Psychological Bulletin, 98.*

Bernheim (1886). In F. A. Pattie, A brief history of hypnotism. In J. E. Gordon (Ed.), *Handbook of clinical and experimental hypnosis.* New York: Macmillan, 1967.

Berridge, V. (1990). Dependence: Historical concepts and constructs. In A. Edwards & M. Lader (Eds.), *The nature of drug dependence* (pp. 1–18). New York: Oxford University Press.

Bettelheim, B. (1943). Individual and mass behavior in extreme situations. *Journal of Abnormal and Social Psychology, 38,* 417–52.

Bettelheim, B. (1967). *The empty fortress.* New York: The Free Press.

Bexton, W. H., Heron, W., & Scott, T. H. (1954). Effects of decreased variation in the sensory environment. *Canadian Journal of Psychology, 8,* 70–76.

Bibring, E. (1953). The mechanism of depression. In P. Greenacre (Ed.), *Affective disorders.* New York: International Universities Press.

Billy, J., Tanfer, K., Grady, W., & Klepinger, D. (1993). The sexual behavior of men in the United States. *Family Planning Perspectives, 25,* 52–60.

Binstock, J. (1974). Choosing to die. The decline of aggression and the rise of suicide. *The Luterost, 8,* 68–71.

Biran, M., & Wilson, G. T. (1981). Treatment of phobic disorders using cognitive and exposure methods: A self-efficacy analysis. *Journal of Consulting and Clinical Psychology, 48,* 886–87.

Bird, H. R., Canino, G., Rubio-Stipec, M., Gould, M. S., Ribera, J., Sesman, M., Woodbury, M., Huertas-Goldman, S., Pagan, A., Sanchez-Lacay, A., & Moscoso, M. (1988). Estimates of the prevalence of childhood maladjustment in a community survey in Puerto Rico: The use of combined measures. *Archives of General Psychiatry, 45,* 1120–26.

Bird J. (1979). The behavioural treatment of hysteria. *British Journal of Psychiatry, 134,* 129–37.

Birenbaum, A., & Rei, M. A. (1979). Resettling mentally retarded adults in the community—almost 4 years later. *American Journal of Mental Deficiency, 83,* 323–29.

Bisiach, E., & Luzzatti, C. (1978). Unilateral neglect of representational space. *Cortex, 14,* 129–33.

Black, A. (1974). The natural history of obsessional neuroses. In H. R. Beech (Ed.), *Obsessional states.* London: Methuen.

Black, D. W., Noyes, R., Goldstein, R. B., & Blum, N. (1992). A family study of obsessive-compulsive disorder. *Archives of General Psychiatry, 49,* 362–68.

Blackburn, I. M., Eunson, K. M., & Bishop, S. (1986). A two-year naturalistic follow-up of depressed patients treated with cognitive therapy, pharmacotherapy, and a combination of both. *Journal of Affective Disorders, 10,* 67–75.

Blair, C. D., & Lanyon, R. I. (1981). Exhibitionism: A critical review of the etiology and treatment. *Psychological Bulletin, 89,* 439–63.

Blair, S. N., Goodyear, N. N., Gibbons, L. W., & Cooper, K. H. (1984). Physical fitness and incidence of hypertension in healthy normotensive men and women. *Journal of the American Medical Association, 252,* 487–90.

Blair, S. N., Kohl, H. W. III, Paffenbarger, R. S., Clark, D. G., Cooper, K. H., & Gibbons, L. W. (1989). Physical fitness and all-cause mortality. *Journal of the American Medical Association, 262,* 2395–2401.

Blakemore, C. (1977). *Mechanics of the mind.* Cambridge, Eng.: Cambridge University Press.

Blanchard, R., Steiner, B., Clemmensen, L., & Dickey, R. (1989). Prediction of regrets in postoperative transsexuals. *Canadian Journal of Psychiatry, 34,* 43–45.

Blashfield, R. K. (1984). *The classification of psychopathology: NeoKraeplinian and quantitative approaches.* New York: Plenum.

Blashfield, R. K., & Draguns, J. G. (1976). Evaluative criteria for psychiatric classification. *Journal of Abnormal Psychology, 85,* 40–150.

Blashfield, R. K., & Livesley, W. J. (1991). Metaphorical analysis of psychiatric classification as a psychological test. *Journal of Abnormal Psychology, 100* (3): 262–70.

Blazer, D., Hughes, D., & George, L. (1987). Stressful life events and the onset of generalized anxiety syndrome. *American Journal of Psychiatry, 144,* 1178–83.

Bleuler, E. (1924). *Textbook of psychiatry.* New York: Macmillan.

Bleuler, M. (1984). Different forms of childhood stress and patterns of adult psychiatric outcome. In W. F. Watt, E. J. Anthony, L. C. Wynne, & J. E. Rolf (Eds.). *Children at risk for schizophrenia: A longitudinal perspective* (pp. 537–42). Cambridge: Cambridge University Press.

Bliss, E. L. (1980). Multiple personalities: Report of fourteen cases with implications for schizophrenia and hysteria. *Archives of General Psychiatry, 37,* 1388–97.

Bliss, E. L., & Jeppsen, A. (1985). Prevalence of multiple personality among inpatients and outpatients. *American Journal of Psychiatry, 142,* 250–51.

Bloch, S., & Reddaway, P. (1977). *Psychiatric terror: How Soviet psychiatry is used to suppress dissent.* New York: Basic Books.

Bloom, F. E., Lazerson, A., & Hofstadter, L. (1985). *Brain, mind, and behavior.* New York: Freeman.

Blumberg, S. H., & Izard, C. E. (1985). Affective and cognitive characteristics of depression in 10- and 11-year-old children. *Journal of Personality and Social Psychology, 49,* 194–202.

Bogen, E. (1932). The human toxicology of alcohol. In H. Emerson (Ed.), *Alcohol and man.* New York: Macmillan.

Bogen, J. E., & Vogel, P. J. (1975). Neurological status in the long term following complete cerebral commisurotomy. In F. Michel & B. Schott (Eds.), *Les syndromes de disconnexion calleuse chez l'homme.* Lyons: Hopital Neurologique.

Bogerts, B. (1993). Recent advances in the neuropathology of schizophrenia. *Schizophrenia Bulletin, 19,* 431–45.

Bohman, M., & Sigvardsson, S. C. (1981). Maternal inheritance of alcohol abuse: Cross-fostering analysis of adopted women. *Archives of General Psychiatry, 38,* 965–69.

Bohn, M. J. (1993). Pharmacotherapy: Alcoholism. In D. Dunner (Ed.), *Psychopharmacology. Volume 2: Psychiatric Clinics of North America.* New York: W. B. Saunders.

Bohn, M. J., & Meyer, R. E. (1994). Typologies of addiction. In M. Galanter & H. Kleber (Eds.), *Treatment of substance abuse.* Washington, DC: American Psychiatric Press.

Booker, J. M., & Hellekson, C. J. (1992). Prevalence of seasonal affective disorder in Alaska. *American Journal of Psychiatry, 149*(9): 1176–82.

Bootzin, R. R. (1975). *Behavior modification and therapy: An introduction.* Cambridge, MA: Winthrop.

Borkovec, T., & Costello, E. (1993). Efficacy of applied relaxation and cognitive-behavioral therapy in the treatment of generalized anxiety disorder. *Journal of Consulting and Clinical Psychology, 61,* 611–19.

Bornstein, R. F. (1992). The dependent personality: Developmental, social, and clinical perspectives. *Psychological Bulletin, 112*(1): 3–23.

Borysenko, M. (1987). The immune system: An overview. *Annals of Behavioral Medicine, 9,* 3–10.

Bouchard, T., Lykken, D., McGue, M., Segal, N., & Tellegen, A. (1990). Sources of human psychological differences: The Minnesota study of twins reared apart. *Science, 250,* 223–28.

Bouchard, T., & McGue, M. (1990). Genetic and rearing environmental influences on adult personality: An analysis of adopted twins reared apart. *Journal of Personality, 58,* 263–92.

Boulos, C., Kutcher, S., Gardner, D., & Young, E. (1992). An open naturalistic trial of fluoxetine in adolescents and young adults with treatment-resistant major depression. *Journal of Child and Adolescent Psychopharmacology, 2,* 103–11.

Bourdon, K., Boyd, J., Rae, D., & Burns, B. (1988). Gender differences in phobias: Results of the ECA community survey. *Journal of Anxiety Disorders, 2,* 227–41.

Bourgeois, L., Sabourin, L. S., & Wright, J. (1990). Predictive validity of therapeutic alliance in group marital therapy. *Journal of Consulting and Clinical Psychology, 58*(5): 608–13.

Bourgeois, M. (1991). Serotonin, impulsivity, and suicide. *Human Psychopharmacology: Clinical and Experimental, 6,* 31–36.

Bourne, H. R., Bunney, W. E., Colburn, R. W., Davis, J. M., Davis, J. N., Shaw, D. M., & Loppen, A. J. (1968). Noradrenalin, 5-hydroxytryptamine and 5-hydroxyindoleacidic in hind brains of suicidal patients. *Lancet, 2,* 805–808.

Bowlby, J. (1960). Grief and mourning in infancy and early childhood. *The Psychoanalytic Study of the Child, 15,* 9–52.

Bowlby, J. (1969). *Attachment.* New York: Basic Books.

Bowlby, J. (1988). Developmental psychiatry comes of age. *American Journal of Psychiatry, 145,* 1–10.

Boyd, J., Rae, D., Thompson, J., & Burns, B. (1990). Phobia: Prevalence and risk factors. *Social Psychiatry and Psychiatric Epidemiology, 25,* 314–23.

Bozarth, M. A., & Wise, R. A. (1985). Toxicity associated with long-term intravenous heroin and cocaine self-administration in the rat. *Journal of the American Medical Association, 254,* 81–83.

Bradford, J. (1988). Organic treatment for the male sexual offender. *Annals of the New York Academy of Sciences, 528,* 193–202.

Bradshaw, J. (1990). *Homecoming: Reclaiming and championing your inner child.* New York: Bantam.

Bradshaw, J. L., & Nettleton, N. C. (1981). The nature of hemispheric specialization in man with commentary. *The Behavioral and Brain Sciences 4,* 51–92.

Brady, J. P. (1958). Ulcers in "executive" monkeys. *Scientific American, 199,* 95–100.

Brady, J. P., & Lind D. L. (1961). Experimental analysis of hysterical blindness: Operant conditioning techniques. *Archives of General Psychiatry, 4,* 331–39.

Brady, J. P., Porter, R. W., Conrad, D. G., & Mason, J. W. (1958). Avoidance behavior and the development of gastroduodenal ulcers. *Journal of Experimental Analysis of Behavior, 1,* 69–73.

Braff, D. L., & Saccuzzo, D. P. (1985). The time course of information-processing deficits in schizophrenia. *American Journal of Psychiatry, 142* (2): 170–74.

Brandenburg N. A., Friedman, R. M., & Silver, S. E. (1990). The epidemiology of childhood psychiatric disorders: Prevalence findings from recent studies. *Journal of the American Academy of Child and Adolescent Psychiatry, 29*(1): 76–83.

Bregman E. O. (1934). An attempt to modify the emotional attitudes of infants by the conditioned response technique. *Journal of Genetic Psychology, 45,* 169–98.

Brehm, S. S., & Brehm, J. W. (1981). *Psychological reactance: A theory of freedom and control.* New York: Academic Press.

Breier, A., Charney, D. S., & Heninger, G. R. (1984). Major depression in patients with agoraphobia and panic disorder. *Archives of General Psychiatry, 41* (12): 1129–35.

Breier, A., Charney, D. S., & Heninger, G. R. (1986). Agoraphobia with panic attacks: Development, diagnostic stability, and course of illness. *Archives of General Psychiatry, 43,* 1029–36.

Brenner, H. D., Hodel, B., Roder, V., & Corrigan, P. (1992). Treatment of cognitive dysfunctions and behavioral deficits in schizophrenia. *Schizophrenia Bulletin, 18* (1): 21–26.

Brenner, H. D., Kraemer, S., Hermanutz, M., & Hodel, B. (1990). Cognitive treatment in schizophrenia. In E. Straube & K. Hahlweg (Eds.), *Schizophrenia: Models and interventions* (pp. 161–91). New York: Springer.

Breslau, N. & Davis, G. C. (1986). Chronic stress and major depression. *Archives of General Psychiatry, 43,* 309–14.

Breslau, N., & Davis, G. C. (1987). Posttraumatic stress disorder: The etiologic specificity of wartime stressors. *American Journal of Psychiatry, 144,* 578–83.

Breslin, N. H. (1992). Treatment of schizophrenia: Current practice and future promise. *Hospital and Community Psychiatry, 43,* 877–85.

Brett, C. W., Burling, T. A., & Pavlik, W. B. (1981). Electroconvulsive shock and learned helplessness in rats. *Animal Learning and Behavior, 9*, 38–44.

Brickman, A. S., McManus, M., Grapentine, W. L., & Alessi, N. (1984). Neuropsychological assessment of seriously delinquent adolescents. *Journal of the American Academy of Child Psychiatry, 23*, 453–57.

Broadbent, D. E. (1958). *Perception of communication*, London: Pergamon.

Broadbent, D. E. (1971). *Decision and stress.* New York: Academic Press.

Brodie, H. K. H., & Leff, M. J. (1971). Bipolar depression: A comparative study of patient characteristics. *American Journal of Psychiatry, 127*, 1086–90.

Broen, W. E., Jr. (1968). *Schizophrenia: Research and theory.* New York: Academic Press.

Brooks, A. D. (1974a). *Law, psychiatry and the mental health system.* Boston: Little, Brown.

Brooks, L. (1974b). Interactive effects of sex and status on self-disclosure. *Journal of Counseling Psychology, 21*, 469–74.

Brooks, N., & McKinlay, W. (1992). Mental health consequences of the Lockerbie disaster. *Journal of Traumatic Stress, 5*, 527–43.

Brooks-Gunn, J. (1986). Differentiating premenstrual symptoms and syndromes [editorial]. *Psychosomatic Medicine, 48*, 385–87.

Brooks-Gunn, J. (1988). Antecedents and consequences of variations in girls' maturational timing. *Journal of Adolescent Health Care, 9*(5): 365–73.

Brown, F. W., Golding, J. M., & Smith, G. R. (1990). Psychiatric comorbidity in primary care somatization disorder. *Psychosomatic Medicine, 52*, 445–51.

Brown, G. W., Birley, J. L. T., & Wing, J. K. (1972). Influence of family life on the course of schizophrenic disorders: A replication. *British Journal of Psychiatry, 121*, 241–58.

Brown, G. W., & Harris, T. (1978). *Social origins of depression.* London: Tavistock.

Brown, R., Colter, N., Corsellis, J. A., Crow, T. J., Frith, C. D., Jagoe, R., Johnstone, E. C., & Marsh, L. (1986). Postmortem evidence of structural brain changes in schizophrenia. Differences in brain weight, temporal horn area, and parahippocampal gyrus compared with affective disorder. *Archives of General Psychiatry, 43*(1): 36–42.

Brown, R., & Herrnstein, R. J. (1975). *Psychology.* Boston: Little, Brown.

Brown, R. A., Lichtenstein, E., McIntyre, K. O., & Harrington-Kostur, J. (1984). Effects of nicotine fading and relapse prevention on smoking sensation. *Journal of Consulting and Clinical Psychology, 52*, 307–308.

Brown, R. G., & Marsden, C. D. (1990). Cognitive function in Parkinson's disease: From description to theory. *Trends in Neurosciences, 13*, 21–29.

Brown, W. F. (1974). Effectiveness and paraprofessionals: The evidence. *Personnel and Guidance Journal, 53*, 257–63.

Brownell, K. D., & Kramer, F. M. (1989). Behavioral management of obesity. *Medical Clinics of North America, 73*, 85–201.

Brownell, K. D., & Wadden, T. A. (1992). Etiology and treatment of obesity: Understanding a serious, prevalent, and refractory disorder. *Journal of Consulting and Clinical Psychology, 60*(4): 505–17.

Bruch, H. (1978). *The golden cage: The enigma of anorexia nervosa.* Cambridge, MA: Harvard University Press.

Bruch, H. (1982). Anorexia nervosa: Therapy and theory. *American Journal of Psychiatry, 139*, 1531–38.

Bruininks, R. H., Woodcock, R. W., Weatherman, R. F., & Hill, B. K. (1984). *Scales of independent behavior: Woodcock-Johnson Psycho-Educational Battery: Part IV.* Allen, TX: DLM Teaching Resources.

Bryan, T. H., & Bryan, J. H. (1975). *Understanding learning disabilities.* New York: Alfred Publishing Co.

Bryant, R. N., & McConkey, K. M. (1989). Visual conversion disorder: A case analysis of the influence of visual information. *Journal of Abnormal Psychology, 98*, 326–29.

Buchanan, G. (1994). Explanatory style and coronary heart disease. In G. Buchanan & M. Seligman (Eds.), *Explanatory style.* Hillsdale, NJ: Erlbaum.

Buchsbaum, M. S. (1990). The frontal lobes, basal ganglia, and temporal lobes as sites for schizophrenia. *Schizophrenia Bulletin, 16*(3): 379–89.

Buchsbaum, M. S., & Heier, R. J. (1987). Functional and anatomical brain imaging: Impact on schizophrenia research. *Schizophrenia Bulletin, 13*, 115–32.

Buchwald, A. M., Coyne, J. C., & Cole, C. S. (1978) A critical evaluation of the learned helplessness model of depression. *Journal of Abnormal Psychology, 87*, 180–93.

Budzynski, T. H., Stoyva, J. M., Adler, C. S., & Mullaney, D. M. (1973). EMG biofeedback and tension headache: A controlled outcome study. *Psychosomatic Medicine, 35*, 484–96.

Bunney, W. E., Murphy, D. L., Goodwin, F. K., & Borge, G. L. (1972). The switch process in manic depressive illness. *Archives of General Psychiatry, 27*, 295.

Bunney, W. E., & Murphy, D. L. (1974). Switch processes in psychiatric illness. In N. S. Kline (Ed.), *Factors in depression.* New York: Raven Press.

Bureau of National Labor Affairs. (1990). Women in the work force. *DLR #147*, July 31, 1990.

Burgess, A. W., & Holmstrom, L. L. (1974). *Rape: Victims of crisis.* Bowie, MD: Robert J. Brady Co.

Burgess, A., & Holmstrom, L. (1979). Adaptive strategies and recovery from rape. *American Journal of Psychiatry, 136*, 1278–82.

Burke, A. E., & Silverman, W. K. (1987). The prescriptive treatment of school refusal. *Clinical Psychology Review, 7*, 353–62.

Burman, A. M. (1988). Sexual assault and mental disorders in a community population. *Journal of Consulting and Clinical Psychology, 56*(6): 843–50.

Burnett, K. F., Taylor, C. B., & Agras, W. S. (1985). Ambulatory computer assisted therapy for obesity: A new frontier for behavior therapy. *Journal of Consulting and Clinical Psychology, 53*, 698–703.

Burns, B., & Reyher, J. (1976). Activating posthypnotic conflict: Emergent, uncovering, psychopathology, repression and psychopathology. *Journal of Personality Assessment, 40*, 492–501.

Burns, D., & Mendels, J. (1977). Biogenic amine precursors and affective illness. In W. Fann, I. Karacan, A. Pikorny, & R. Williams (Eds.), *Phenomenology and a treatment of depression.* New York: Spectrum.

Burt, R. A., & Morris, N. (1972). A proposal for the abolition of the incompetency plea. *Chicago Law Review, 40*, 66–80.

Buss, A. H., & Lang, P. J. (1965). Psychological deficit in schizophrenia: Affect reinforcement and concept attainment. *Journal of Abnormal Psychology, 70*, 2–24.

Buss, D. (1989). Sex differences in human mate preferences: Evolutionary hypotheses tested in 37 cultures. *Behavioral and Brain Sciences, 12*, 1–49.

Buss, D. (1991). Evolutionary personality psychology. *Annual Review of Psychology, 42*, 439–91.

Butcher, J. D., Dahlstrom, W. G., Graham, J. R., Tellegen, A., & Kraemer, B. (1989). *Minnesota Multiphasic Personality Inventory-2: Manual for administration and scoring.* Minneapolis: University of Minnesota Press.

Butcher, J. N. (1969). *MMPI: Research developments and clinical applications.* New York: McGraw-Hill.

Butler, G., Fennell, M., Robson, P., & Gelder, M. (1991). Comparison of behavior therapy and cognitive behavior therapy in the treatment of generalized anxiety disorder. *Journal of Consulting and Clinical Psychology, 59*, 167–75.

Butler, S., Chalder, T., Ron, M., & Wessely, S. (1991). Cognitive behaviour therapy in chronic fatigue syndrome. *Journal of Neurology, Neurosurgery and Psychiatry, 54*, 153–58.

Butterfield, E. C. (1964). Locus of control, test anxiety, reaction to frustration, and achievement attitudes. *Journal of Personality, 32,* 298–311.

Butterfield, F. (1986). Judge backs discipline at institute for autistic. *New York Times,* June 5.

Bynum, W. F., Jr. (1981). Rationales for therapy in British psychiatry, 1780–1835. In A. Scull (Ed.), *Madhouses, mad-doctors, and madmen: The social history of psychiatry in the Victorian era* (pp. 35–57). Philadelphia: University of Pennsylvania Press.

Cade, J. F. J. (1949). Lithium salts in the treatment of psychotic excitement. *Medical Journal of Australia, 36,* 349–52.

Cade, W. (1970). The story of lithium. In F. J. Ayd & H. Blackwell (Eds.), *Discoveries in biological psychiatry.* Philadelphia: Lippincott.

Cadoret, R. (1986). Epidemiology of antisocial personality. In W. H. Reid, D. Dorr, J. I. Walker, & J. W. Bonner, III (Eds.), *Unmasking the psychopath: Antisocial personality and related syndromes* (pp. 28–44). New York: Norton.

Cardoret, R. J., & Cain, C. (1980). Sex differences in predictors of antisocial behavior in adoptees. *Archives of General Psychiatry, 137,* 1171–75.

Cadoret, R. J., O'Gorman, T. W., Troughton, E., & Heywood, E. (1985). Alcoholism and antisocial personality. *Archives of General Psychiatry, 42,* 161–67.

Cameron, N. (1938). Reasoning, regression and communication in schizophrenia. *Psychological Monographs, 50* (Whole No. 221).

Cameron, N. (1947). *The psychology of behavior disorders.* Boston: Houghton Mifflin.

Cantor, N., Smith, E., French, R. de S., & Mezzich, J. (1980). Psychiatric diagnosis as prototype categorization. *Journal of Abnormal Psychology, 89,* 181–93.

Cantwell, D. P., Baker, L., & Rutter, M. (1978). Family factors in the syndrome of infantile autism. In M. Rutter & E. Schopler (Eds.), *Autism: A reappraisal of concepts and treatment.* New York: Plenum.

Caplan, D. (1992). *Language: Structure, processing and disorders.* Cambridge, MA: MIT Press/ Bradford.

Carey, G. (1982). Genetic influences on anxiety neurosis and agoraphobia. In R. J. Mathew (Ed.), *Biology of anxiety* (pp. 37–50). New York: Brunner-Mazel.

Carey, G., & Gottesman, I. I. (1978). Reliability and validity in binary ratings: Areas of common misunderstandings in diagnosis and symptom ratings. *Archives of General Psychiatry, 35,* 1454–59.

Carey, G., & Gottesman, I. I. (1981). Twin and family studies of anxiety, phobic, and obsessive disorders. In D. F. Klein & J. Rabkin (Eds.), *Anxiety: New research and changing concepts* (pp. 117–36). New York: Raven Press.

Carkesse, J. (1679). Lucida intetvalla. Quoted in R. Hunter and I. Macalpine, *Three hundred years of psychiatry: 1535–1860.* London: Oxford University Press, 1963.

Carlson, G. A., Kotin, J., Davenport, Y. B., & Adland, M. (1974). Followup of 53 bipolar manic depressive patients. *British Journal of Psychiatry, 124,* 134–39.

Carmelli, D., Dame, A., Swan, G., & Rosenman, R. (1991). Longterm changes in Type A behavior: A 27-year follow-up of the Western Collaborative Group Study. *Journal of Behavioral Medicine, 14,* 593–606.

Carney, R., Freedland, K., & Jaffe, A. (1990). Insomnia and depression prior to myocardial infarction. *Psychosomatic Medicine, 52,* 603–9.

Carpenter, W. T., Jr. (1992). The negative symptom challenge [comment]. *Archives of General Psychiatry 49* (3): 236–37.

Carpenter, W. T., Jr., Strauss, J. S., & Bartko, J. J. (1973). Flexible system for the diagnosis of schizophrenia: Report from the WHO International Pilot Study of Schizophrenia. *Science, 182,* 1275–78.

Carpenter, W., Strauss, J., & Bartko, J. (1974). Use of signs and symptoms for the identification of schizophrenic patients. *Schizophrenia Bulletin, 11,* 37–49.

Carrington, R. (1959). *Elephants.* New York: Basic Books.

Carter, A. B. (1949). The prognosis of certain hysterical symptoms. *British Medical Journal, 1,* 1076–80.

Carter, C. H. (1970). *Handbook of mental retardation syndromes.* Springfield, IL: Charles C. Thomas.

Carter, R. B. (1853). *On the pathology and treatment of hysteria.* London: John Churchill.

Cartwright, R. D., & Lerner, B. (1963). Empathy, need to change, and improvement with psychotherapy. *Journal of Consulting Psychology, 27,* 138–44.

Cartwright, R., & Vogel, J. (1960). A comparison of changes in psychoneurotic patients during matched periods of therapy and no therapy. *Journal of Consulting Psychology, 24,* 121–27.

Casey, J. F., Bennett, I. F., Lindley, C. J., Hollister, L. E., Gordon, M. H., & Springer, N. N. (1960). Drug therapy and schizophrenia: A controlled study of the effectiveness of chlorpromazine, promazine, phenobarbitol and placebo. *Archives of General Psychiatry, 2,* 210–20.

Casey, R. J., & Berman, J. S. (1985). The outcome of psychotherapy with children. *Psychological Bulletin, 98* (2): 388–400.

Cautela, J. R. (1967). Covert sensitization. *Psychological Reports, 20,* 459–68.

Cegelka, W. J., & Tyler, J. L. (1970). The efficacy of special class placement for the mentally retarded in proper perspective. *Training School Bulletin, 67,* 33–68.

Chambers, D. L. (1972). Alternatives to civil commitment of the mentally ill: Practical guides and constitutional imperatives. *Michigan Law Review, 70B,* 1107–1200.

Chandler, J., & Winokur, G. (1989). How antipsychotic are antipsychotics? A clinical study of the subjective antipsychotic effect of the antipsychotics in chronic schizophrenia. *Annals of Clinical Psychiatry, 1,* 215–20.

Chapman, L. J., & Chapman, D. T. (1969). Illusory correlations as an obstacle to the use of valid psychodiagnostic signs. *Journal of Abnormal Psychology, 74,* 271–80.

Chapman, L. J., & Chapman, J. P. (1973). *Disordered thought in schizophrenia.* New York: Appleton-Century-Crofts.

Chapman, L. J., & Taylor, J. A. (1957). Breadth of deviate concepts used by schizophrenics. *Journal of Abnormal Social Psychology, 54,* 118–23.

Chappell, M. N., & Stevenson, T. I. (1936). Group psychological training in some organic conditions. *Mental Hygiene, 20,* 588–97.

Charney, D. S., & Heninger, G. R. (1985). Noradrenergic function and the mechanism of action of antianxiety treatment: The effect of long-term imipramine treatment. *Archives of General Psychiatry, 42,* 473–81.

Charney, D. S., & Heninger, G. R. (1986). Abnormal regulation of noradrenergic function in panic disorders: Effects of clonidine in healthy subjects and patients with agoraphobia and panic disorder. *Archives of General Psychiatry, 43* (11): 1042–54.

Cherry, C., & Sayers, B. McA. (1956). Experiments upon the total inhibition of stammering by external control and some clinical results. *Journal of Psychosomatic Research, 1,* 233.

Cheseldine, S., & McConkey, R. (1979). Parental speech to young Down's syndrome children: An intervention study. *American Journal of Mental Deficiency, 83,* 612–20.

Chin, J. H., & Goldstein, D. B. (1977). Drug tolerance in biomembranes: A spin label study of the effects of ethanol. *Science, 196,* 684–85.

Chinn, P. C., Drew, C. J., & Logan, D. R. (1979). *Mental retardation: A life cycle approach* (2d. ed.). St. Louis: Mosby.

Chodoff, P. (1973). The depressive personality: A critical review. *International Journal of Psychiatry, 11,* 196–217.

Chodoff, P. (1974). The diagnosis of hysteria: An overview. *American Journal of Psychiatry, 131,* 1073–78.

Chodoff, P. (1982). Hysteria and women. *American Journal of Psychiatry, 139,* 545–51.

Christiansen, K. O. (1977). A review of studies of criminality among twins. In S. A. Mednick & K. O. Christiansen (Eds.), *Biosocial bases of criminal behavior.* New York: Gardner Press.

Christodoulou, G. N., Gergoulas, A., Paploukas, A., Marinopoulou, A., & Sideris, E. (1977). Primary peptic ulcer in childhood. *Acta Psychiatrica Scandinavia, 56,* 215–22.

Cicero, J. J., Myers, R. D., & Black, W. C. (1968). Increase in volitional ethanol consumption following interference with a learned avoidance response. *Physiology and Behavior, 3,* 657–60.

Claparède, E. (1911). Recognition and "me-ness." In D. Rapaport (Ed.), *Organization and pathology of thought.* New York: Columbia University Press, 1951. (Reprinted from Recognition et moiite. *Archives de Psychologie,* 1911, *11,* 79–90.)

Clark, D. M. (1986). A cognitive approach to panic. *Behaviour Research and Therapy, 24,* 461–70.

Clark, D. M. (1988). A cognitive model of panic attacks. In S. Rachman & J. D. Maser (Eds.), *Panic: Psychological perspectives.* Hillsdale, NJ: Erlbaum.

Clark, D. (1989). Anxiety states: Panic and generalized anxiety. In K. Hawton, P. Salkovskis, J. Kirk, & D. Clark (Eds.), *Cognitive behaviour therapy for psychiatric problems: A practical guide.* Oxford, Eng.: Oxford University Press.

Clark, D., Gelder, M., Salkovskis, P., Hackman, A., Middleton, H., & Anatasiades, A. (1990). Cognitive therapy for panic: Comparative efficacy. Presented at the annual meeting of the American Psychiatric Association, New York, May 15, 1990.

Clark, R. E. (1948). The relationship of schizophrenia to occupational income and occupational prestige. *American Sociological Review, 13,* 325–30.

Clarke, A. M., & Clarke, D. D. (1979). *Early experience: Myths and evidence.* New York: Free Press.

Clarke-Stewart, K. A. (1973). Interactions between mothers and their young children: Characteristics and consequences. *Monographs of the Society for Research in Child Development, 37,* 153.

Clausen, J. A., & Kohn, M. L. (1959). Relation of schizophrenia to the social structure of a small city. In B. Pasamanick (Ed.), *Epidemiology of mental disorder.* Washington, DC: American Association for the Advancement of Science.

Cleckley, H. (1964). *The mask of sanity.* St. Louis: Mosby.

Clementz, B. A., Sweeney, J. A., Hirt, M., & Haas, G. (1990). Pursuit gain and saccadic intrusions in first-degree relatives of probands with schizophrenia. *Journal of Abnormal Psychology* 99(4): 327–35.

Clomipramine Collaborative Study Group. (1991). Clomipramine in the treatment of obsessive-compulsive disorder. *Archives of General Psychiatry, 48,* 730–38.

Cloninger, C. P. (1987). Neurogenic adaptive mechanisms in alcoholism. *Science, 236.*

Cloninger, C. R., Christiansen, K. O., Reich, T., & Gottesman, I. I. (1978). Implications of sex differences in the prevalences of antisocial personality, alcoholism, and criminality for familial transmission. *Archives of General Psychiatry, 35,* 941–51.

Cloninger, C. R., & Gottesman, I. I. (1987). Genetic and environmental factors in antisocial behavior disorders. In S. A. Mednick, T. E. Moffitt, & S. A. Strack (Eds.), *The causes of crime: New biological approaches.* Cambridge: Cambridge University Press.

Cloninger, C. R., Reich, T., & Guze, S. B. (1975). The multifactorial model of disease transmission. II. Sex differences in familial transmission of sociopathy (antisocial personality). *British Journal of Psychiatry, 127,* 11–22.

Cloninger, C. R., Sigvardsson, S., von Knorring, A., & Bohman, M. (1984). An adoption study of somatoform disorders: II. Identification of two discrete somatoform disorders. *Archives of General Psychiatry, 41,* 863–71.

Cobb, S., & Rose, R. M. (1973). Hypertension, peptic ulcer and diabetes and the traffic controllers. *Journal of the American Medical Association, 224,* 489–92.

Cohen, A. (1976). Alcohol and heroin: Structural comparison of reasons for use between drug addicts and alcoholics. *Annals of the New York Academy of Sciences, 273,* 605–12.

Cohen, B. M. (1977). Genetics of psychiatric disorders. *McLean Hospital Lecture Series.* Tape recording reproduced by Endo Laboratories, Garden City, N.Y.

Cohen, I. (1970). The benzodiazepines. In F. J. Ayd & H. Blackwell (Eds.), *Discoveries in biological psychiatry.* Philadelphia: Lippincott.

Cohen, J. A. (1960). A coefficient of agreement for nominal scales. *Educational and Psychological Measurement, 20,* 37–46.

Cohen, J. B., & Reed, D. (1985). The Type A behavior pattern and coronary heart disease among Japanese men in Hawaii. *Journal of Behavioral Medicine, 8* (4): 343–52.

Cohen, N. B., Baker, G., Cohen, R. A., Fromm-Reichmann, F., & Weigert, E. B. (1954). An intensive study of 12 cases of manic-depressive psychosis. *Psychiatry, 17,* 103–37.

Cohen, S., Tyrrell, D., & Smith, A. (1993). Negative life events, perceived stress, negative affect, and susceptibility to the common cold. *Journal of Personality and Social Psychology, 64,* 131–40.

Cohn, N. R. C. (1975). *Europe's inner demons: An enquiry inspired by the great witch-hunt.* Chatto, Eng.: Heinemann for Sussex University Press.

Coie, J. D., & Kupersmidt, J. B. (1983). A behavioral analysis of emerging social status in boys' groups. *Child Development, 54,* 1400–16.

Coltheart, M. (1985). Cognitive neuropsychology and the study of reading. In M. I. Posner & O. S. M. Marin (Eds.), *Attention and Performance XI.* Hillsdale, NJ: Erlbaum.

Cook, W. W., & Medley, D. M. (1954). Proposed hostility and pharisaic-virtue scales for the MMPI. *Journal of Applied Psychology, 38,* 414–18.

Cooke, G., Johnston, N., & Pogany, E. (1973). Factors affecting referral to determine competency to stand trial. *American Journal of Psychiatry, 130*(8): 870.

Coons, P., Bowman, E., Pellow, T., & Schneider, P. (1989). Post-traumatic aspects of the treatment of victims of sexual abuse and incest. *Psychiatric Clinics of North America, 12,* 325–35.

Cooper, A. F., Garside, R. F., & Kay, D. W. (1976). A comparison of deaf and non-deaf patients with paranoid and affective psychoses. *British Journal of Psychiatry, 129,* 532–38.

Cooper, A. F., & Porter, R. (1976). Visual acuity and ocular pathology in the paranoid and affective psychoses. *British Journal of Psychiatry, 129,* 532–38.

Cooper, G. (1988). The safety of fluoxetine—An update. *British Journal of Psychiatry, 153,* 77–86.

Cooper, S. J. & Kirkham, T. C. (1993). Opioid mechanisms in the control of food consumption and taste preferences. In A. Herz (Ed.), *Handbook of experimental pharmacology, 104/II* (pp. 239–62). Berlin: Springer-Verlag.

Coppen, A., Prange, A. J., Whybrow, P., & Noguera, R. (1972). Abnormalities of indoleamines and affective disorders. *Archives of General Psychiatry, 26,* 474–78.

Corballis, M. C. (1991). *The lopsided age.* New York: Oxford University Press.

Corder, E. H., Saunders, A. M., Strittmatter, W. J., et al. (1993). Gene dose of apolipoprotein E type 4 allele and the risk of Alzheimer's disease in late onset families. *Science, 261,* 921–23.

Corrigall, W. A., & Coen, K. A. (1991). Selective dopamine antagonists reduce nicotine self-administration. *Psychopharmacology, 104,* 171–76.

Coryell, W., & Norten, S. (1981). Briquet's Syndrome and primary depression: Comparison of background and outcome. *Comprehensive Psychiatry, 22,* 249–56.

Costello, C. G. (1972). Depression: Loss of reinforcers or loss of reinforcer effectiveness. *Behavior Therapy, 3,* 240–47.

Costello, C. (1982). Fears and phobias in women: A community study. *Journal of Abnormal Psychology, 91,* 280–86.

Cotton, N. S. (1979). The familial incidence of alcoholism: A review. *Journal of Studies on Alcohol, 40*, 89–116.

Cousins, N. (1979). *Anatomy of an illness: As perceived by the patient.* New York: Norton.

Covi, L., Roth, D., & Lipman, R. S. (1982). Cognitive group psychotherapy for depression: The close-ended group. *American Journal of Psychotherapy, 36*(4): 459–69.

Cowen, E. L. (1973). Social and community interventions. *Annual Review of Psychology, 24*, 423–72.

Cowen, E. L. (1977a). Baby steps toward primary prevention. *American Journal of Community Psychology, 5*, 1–22.

Cowen, E. L. (1977b). Psychologists in primary prevention: Blowing the cover story. An editorial. *American Journal of Community Psychology, 5*, 481–90.

Cowen, E. L., & Zax, M. (1968). Early detection and prevention of emotional disorder: Conceptualizations and programming. In J. W. Carter (Ed.), *Research contributions from psychology to community mental health.* New York: Behavioral Publications.

Cox, P., Hallam, R., O'Connor, K., & Rachman, S. (1983). An experimental analysis of fearlessness and courage. *British Journal of Psychology, 74*, 107–17.

Coyle, J. T., Price, D. L., & DeLong, M. R. (1983). Alzheimer's disease: A disorder of cortical cholinergic innervation. *Science, 219*, 1184–90.

Craighead, W. E., Kazdin, A. E., & Mahoney, M. J. (1976). *Behavior modification: Principles, issues and applications.* Boston: Houghton Mifflin.

Crapper, D. R., Karlik, S., & De Boni, U. (1978). Aluminum and other metals in senile (Alzheimer) dementia. In R. Katzman, R. D. Terry, K. L. Bick, *Alzheimer's disease: Senile dementia and relaxed disorders* (Aging, Vol. 7; pp. 471–85). New York: Raven Press.

Craske, M. G., Sanderson, W. C., Barlow, D. H. (1987). The relationships among panic, fear, and avoidance. *Journal of Anxiety Disorders, 1* (2): 153–60.

Creak, M. (1961). Schizophrenia syndrome in childhood: Progress report of a working party. *Cerebral Palsy Bulletin, 3*, 501–504.

Crisp, A. H. (1980). *Anorexia nervosa—Let me be.* London: Plenum.

Critchley, M. (1966). *The parietal lobes.* New York: Hafner.

Crits-Cristoph, P. (1992). The efficacy of brief psychotherapy. A meta-analysis. *American Journal of Psychiatry, 149*(2): 151–57.

Crittenden, P. M., & Ainsworth, M. D. S. (1989). Child maltreatment and attachment theory. In D. Chichetti & V. Carlson (Eds.), *Child maltreatment* (pp. 432–63). Cambridge: Cambridge University Press.

Cromwell, R. L. (1993). Searching for the origins of schizophrenia. *Psychological Science, 4*, 276–79.

Cronbach, L. J., Gleser, G. C., Nanda, H., & Rajaratnam, N. (1972). *The dependability of behavioral measurements: Theory of generalizability for scores and profiles.* New York: Wiley.

Crow, T. J. (1980). Molecular pathology of schizophrenia: More than one disease process? *British Medical Journal,* 66–68.

Crow, T. J. (1982). Two dimensions of pathology in schizophrenia: Dopaminergic and non-dopaminergic. *Psychopharmacology Bulletin, 18*, 22–29.

Crow, T. J. (1985). The two-syndrome concept: Origins and current status. *Schizophrenia Bulletin, 11* (3): 471–85.

Crowe, M. J., Marks, I. M., Agras, W. S., & Leitenberg, H. (1972). Time limited desensitization, implosion and shaping for phobic patients: A crossover study. *Behavior Research and Therapy, 10*(4): 319–28.

Crowe, R. R. (1983). Antisocial personality disorders. In R. E. Tarter (Ed.), *The child at psychiatric risk.* New York: Oxford University Press.

Crowe, R. (1990). Panic disorder: Genetic considerations. *Journal of Psychiatric Research, 24*, 129–34.

Crowder, R. G., & Wagner, R. K. (1992). *The psychology of reading: An introduction.* Oxford, England: Oxford University Press.

Cullen. (1808). Moral treatment reconsidered. In A. Scull (Ed.), *Madhouses, mad-doctors and madmen: The social history of psychiatry in the Victorian era* (pp. 105–18). Philadelphia: University of Pennsylvania Press, 1981.

Cummings, J. L. (1993). The neuroanatomy of depression. *Journal of Clinical Psychiatry, 54*, 14–20.

Currie, E. P. (1968). Crimes without criminals: Witchcraft and its controls in Renaissance Europe. *Law and Society Review, 3*, 7–32.

Curry, S. J. (1993). Self-help interventions for smoking cessation. *Journal of Consulting and Clinical Psychology, 61*(5): 790–803.

Curtis, B. A., Jacobson, S., & Marcus, E. M. (1972). *An introduction to the neurosciences.* Philadelphia: Saunders.

Cushing, H. (1932). Peptic ulcers and the interbrain. *Surgery, Gynecology and Obstetrics, 55*, 1–34.

Cutler, S., & Nolen-Hoeksema, S. (1991). Accounting for sex differences in depression through female victimization: Childhood sexual abuse. *Sex Roles, 24*, 425–38.

Cytryn, L., & McKnew, D. H. (1972). Proposed classification of childhood depression. *American Journal of Psychiatry, 129*, 149–55.

Dalgard, O. S., & Kringlen, E. (1976). A Norwegian twin study of criminality. *British Journal of Criminality, 16*, 213–32.

Damasio, A. R., Tranel, D., & Damasio, H. C. (1990). Individuals with sociopathic behavior caused by frontal damage fail to respond autonomically to social stimuli. *Behavioral Brain Research, 41*, 81–94.

Damasio, A. R., Tranel, D., & Damasio, H. C. (1991). Somatic markers and the guidance of behavior. In H. S. Levin, H. M. Eisenberg, & A. L. Benton (Eds.), *Frontal lobe function and dysfunction* (pp. 217–29). New York: Oxford University Press.

Damasio, H., Grabowski, T., Frank, R., Galaburda, A. M., & Damasio, A. R. (1994). The return of Phineas Gage: Clues about the brain from the skull of a famous patient. *Science, 264*, 1102–5.

Danaher, B. G. (1977). Rapid smoking and self-control in the modification of smoking behavior. *Journal of Consulting and Clinical Psychology, 45*, 1068–75.

Datey, K. K., Deshmuck, S. N., Dalvi, C. P., & Vinekarsl. (1969). "Shavasan": A Yogic exercise in the management of hypertension. *Angiology, 20*, 325–33.

Davenport, H. W. (1972). Why the stomach does not digest itself. *Scientific American, 226*, 86–92.

Davidson, J., Kudler, H., Smith, R., et al. (1990). Treatment of PTSD with amitriptyline and placebo. *Archives of General Psychiatry, 47*, 250–60.

Davidson, L. M., & Baum, A. (1986). Chronic stress and post-traumatic stress disorders. *Journal of Consulting and Clinical Psychology, 54*, 303–308.

Davidson, R. J. (1993). The neuropsychology of emotion and affective style. In M. Lewis & J. M. Haviland (Eds.), *Handbook of emotions* (pp. 143–54). New York: Guilford Press.

Davidson, R. J., Schaffer, C. E., & Saron, C. (1985). Effects of lateralized presentations of faces on self-reports of emotion and EEG asymmetry in depressed and non-depressed subjects. *Psychophysiology, 22* (3): 353–64.

Davies, J. C. V., & Maliphant, R. (1971). Autonomic responses of male adolescents exhibiting refractory behavior in school. *Journal of Child Psychology and Psychiatry, 12*, 115–27.

Davies, R. (1978). *One half of Robertson Davies.* New York: Penguin.

Davis, J., & Miller, N. (1963). Fear and pain: Their effect on self-injection of ambarbitol sodium by rats. *Science, 141*, 1286–87.

Davis, P. H., & Osherson, A. (1977). The current treatment of a multiple-personality woman and her son. *American Journal of Psychotherapy. 31*, 504–15.

Davis, P. J., & Schwartz, G. E. (1987). Repression and the inaccessibility of affective memories. *Journal of Personality and Social Psychology, 51* (1): 155–62.

Davis, W. M., & Smith, S. G. (1976). Role of conditioned reinforcers in the initiation, maintenance and extinction of drug-seeking behavior. *Pavlovian Journal of Biological Sciences, 11,* 222–36.

Davison, G. C. (1976). Homosexuality: The ethical challenge. *Journal of Counseling and Clinical Psychology, 44,* 157–62.

Davison, G. C. (1978). Not can but ought: The treatment of homosexuality. *Journal of Consulting and Clinical Psychology, 46,* 170–72.

Davison, G. C., & Wilson, G. T. (1972). Critique of "Desensitization: Social and cognitive factors underlying the effectiveness of Wolpe's procedure." *Psychological Bulletin, 78*(1): 28–31.

DeAngelis, T. (1990). Cambodians' sight loss tied to seeing atrocities. *APA Monitor,* July, pp. 36–37.

Dekker, E., Pelse, H., & Groen, J. (1957). Conditioning as a cause of asthmatic attacks: A laboratory study. *Journal of Psychosomatic Research, 2,* 97–108.

DeMeyer, M. K., Barton, S., Alpern, G. D., Kimberlin, C., Allen, J., Yang, E., & Steel, R. (1974). The measured intelligence of autistic children. *Journal of Autistic Children and Schizophrenia, 4,* 42–60.

Deneau, G., Yanagita, T., & Seevers, M. H. (1969). Self-administration of psychoactive substances by the monkey. *Psychopharmacologia (Berl.), 16,* 30–48.

Department of International Economic and Social Affairs. (1985). Demographic Yearbook (37th ed.). New York: United Nations.

Depue, R. (1979). *The psychobiology of the depressive disorders: Implications for the effect of stress.* New York: Academic Press.

Depue, R. H., & Monroe, S. (1978). The unipolar-bipolar distinction in depressive disorders. *Psychological Bulletin, 85,* 1001–29.

Depue, R. A., & Monroe, S. M. (1986). Conceptualization and measurement of human disorder in life stress research: The problem of chronic disturbance. *Psychological Bulletin, 99,* 36–51.

Dershowitz, A. M. (1968). Psychiatry in the legal process: "A knife that cuts both ways." *Trial, 4,* 29.

De Sade, Marquis. (1791). *Justine, Philosophy in the Bedroom, and Other Writings.* (Richard Seaver & Austryn Wainhouse, Trans.). New York: Grove, 1965.

De Silva, P., & Rachman, S. J. (1992). *Obsessions and compulsions: The facts.* Oxford: Oxford University Press.

De Silva, P., Rachman, S., & Seligman, M. E. P. (1977). Prepared phobias and obsessions: Therapeutic outcome. *Behaviour Research and Therapy, 15*(1): 65–77.

Deutsch, A. (1949). *The mentally ill in America.* New York: Columbia University Press.

Devanand, D., Sackeim, H., & Prudic, J. (1991). Electroconvulsive therapy in the treatment-resistant patient. *Electroconvulsive Therapy, 14,* 905–23.

Devine, P. A., & Fernald, P. S. (1973). Outcome effects of receiving a preferred randomly assigned or nonpreferred therapy. *Journal of Consulting and Clinical Psychology, 41*(1): 104–107.

Diamond, A. (1991). Some guidelines for the study of brain-behavior relationships during development. In H. Levin, H. Eisenberg, & A. Benton (Eds.), *Frontal lobe function and dysfunction* (pp. 189–211). New York: Oxford University Press.

Diamond, B. L. (1974). Psychiatric prediction of dangerousness. *University of Pennsylvania Law Review, 123,* 439–52.

Diamond, E. L. (1982). The role of anger and hostility in essential hypertension and coronary heart disease. *Psychological Bulletin, 92,* 410–33.

Diamond, R. G., & Rozin, P. (1984). Activation of existing memories in anterograde amnesia. *Journal of Abnormal Psychology, 93,* 98–105.

Di Chiara, G., & Imperato, A. (1988). Drugs abused by humans preferentially increase synaptic dopamine concentrations in the mesolimbic system of freely moving rats. *Proceedings of the National Academy of Sciences, 85,* 5274–78.

Diekstra, R. (1992). The prevention of suicidal behavior: Evidence for the efficacy of clinical and community-based programs. *International Journal of Mental Health, 21,* 69–87.

Diggory, J. C. (1976). United States suicide rates, 1933–1968: An analysis of some trends. In E. S. Shneidman (Ed.), *Suicidology: Contemporary developments.* New York: Grune & Stratton.

Dimsdale, J. E., Pierce, C., Schoenfeld, D., Brown, A., Zusman, R., & Graham, R. (1986). Suppressed anger and blood pressure: The effects of race, sex, social class, obesity, and age. *Psychosomatic Medicine, 48,* 430–36.

DiPalma, J. R. (1971). Introduction: Brief history. In J. R. DiPalma (Ed.), *Drill's pharmacology in medicine.* New York: McGraw-Hill.

Doane, J. A., Falloon, I. R. H., Goldstein, M. J., & Mintz, J. (1985). Parental affective style and the treatment of schizophrenia: Predicting the course of illness and social functioning. *Archives of General Psychiatry, 42,* 34–42.

Dodge, K. A. (1983). Behavioral antecedents of peer social status. *Child Development, 54,* 1386–99.

Dohrenwend, B. S., & Dohrenwend, B. P. (Eds.). (1974). *Stressful life events: Their nature and effects.* New York: Wiley.

Dohrenwend, B. P., Levav, I., Shrout, P. E., Schwartz, S. , Naveh, G., Link, B. G., Skodol, A. E., & Stueve, A. (1992). Socio-economic status and psychiatric disorders: The causation-selection issue. *Science, 255,* 946–52.

Dohrenwend, B. S., & Martin, J. L. (1978, February). Personal vs. situational determination of anticipation and control of the occurrence of stressful life events. Paper presented at the annual meeting of AAAS, Washington, D.C.

Dohrenwend, B. P., & Shrout, P. E. (1985). "Hassles" in the conceptualization and measurement of life stress variables. *American Psychologist, 40,* 780–85.

Dole, V. P., & Nyswander, M. E. (1965). Heroin addiction—a metabolic disease. *Archives of Internal Medicine, 120,* 19–24.

Dole, V. P., Nyswander, M. E., & Kreek, M. J. (1966). Narcotic blockade. *Archives of Internal Medicine, 118,* 304–9.

Doleys, D. M. (1979). Assessment and treatment of childhood enuresis. In A. J. Finch, Jr., & P. C. Kendall (Eds.), *Clinical treatment and research in child psychopathology* (pp. 207–33). New York: Spectrum.

Donaldson, D. (1976). *Insanity inside out.* New York: Crown.

Dorsey, M. F., Iwata, B. A., Ong, P., & McSween, T. (1980). Treatment of self-injurious behavior using a water mist: Initial response suppression and generalization. *Journal of Applied Behavior Analysis, 13,* 343–53.

Dorworth, T. R. (1971). The effect of electroconvulsive shock on "helplessness" in dogs. Unpublished doctoral dissertation, University of Minnesota.

Dostoyevsky, D. (1864). *Notes from the underground.* New York: Dell, 1960.

Douglas, M. (Ed.). (1970). *Witchcraft: Confessions and accusations.* London: Tavistock.

Douglas, V. I. (1983). Attentional and cognitive problems. In M. Rutter (Ed.), *Developmental neuropsychiatry* (pp. 280–329). New York: Guilford Press.

Drake, R., & Vaillant, G. E. (1988). Predicting alcoholism and personality disorder in a 30–year longitudinal study of children of alcoholics. *British Journal of Addiction, 83,* 799–807.

Drewnowski, A., Hopkins, S. A., & Kessler, R. C. (1988). The prevalence of bulimia nervosa in the U.S. college student population. *American Journal of Public Health, 78*(10): 1322–25.

Drossman, D. A. (1982). Patients with psychogenic abdominal pain: Six years' observation in the medical setting. *American Journal of Psychiatry, 139,* 1549–57.

Drummond. (1875). In R. Carrington, *Elephants.* New York: Basic Books, 1959.

Dubbert, R. M. (1992). Exercise in behavioral medicine. *Journal of Consulting and Clinical Psychology, 60*(4): 613–18.

Dunbar, H. F., & Arlow, J. (1944). Criteria for therapy in psychosomatic disorders. *Psychosomatic Medicine, 6,* 283–86.

Dunner, D. L., Gershom, E. S., & Goodwin, F. K. (1976). Heritable factors in the severity of affective illness. *Biological Psychiatry, 11*, 31–42.

DuPaul, G. J., & Barkley, R. A. (1993). Behavioral contributions to pharmacotherapy: The utility of behavioral methodology in medication treatment of children with attention deficit hyperactivity disorder. *Behavior Therapy, 24*, 47–65.

Dworkin, S. F., Von Korff, M., & LeResche, L. (1990). Multiple pains and psychiatric disturbance: An epidemiologic investigation. *Archives of General Psychiatry, 47*, 239–44.

Eaker, E., Haynes, S., & Feinleib, M. (1983). Spouse behavior and coronary heart disease. *Activitas Nervosa Superior, 25*, 81–90.

Early, L. S., & Lisschutz, J. E. (1974). A case of stigmata. *Archives of General Psychiatry, 30*, 197–200.

Eastman, C. I., Lehmeyer, H. W., Watell, L. G., & Good, G. D. (1992). A placebo-controlled trial of light treatment for winter depression. *Journal of Affective Disorders, 26*(4): 211–21.

Eberhard, G. (1968). Personality in peptic ulcer: Preliminary report of a twin study. *Acta Psychiatrica Scandinavia, 203*, 131.

Edwards, G., Arif, A., & Hodgson, R. (1981). Nomenclature and classification of drug- and alcohol-related problems: A WHO memorandum. *Bulletin of the World Health Organization, 59*, 225–42.

Egeland, J. A., & Hostetter, A. M. (1983). Amish study, I: Affective disorders among the Amish, 1976–1980. *American Journal of Psychiatry, 140*, 56–61.

Egeland, J. A., & Sussex, J. N. (1985). Suicide and family loading for affective disorders. *Journal of the American Medical Association, 254*, 915–18.

Ehlers, C. L., & Schuckit, M. A. (1990). EEG fast frequency activity in the sons of alcoholics. *Biological Psychiatry, 27*, 631–41.

Eidelson, J. I. (1977). Perceived control and psychopathology. Unpublished doctoral dissertation, Duke University.

Eisenberg, L. (1956). The autistic child in adolescence. *American Journal of Psychiatry, 112*, 607–12.

Eisenberg, L. (1977). Psychiatry and society: A sociobiological synthesis. *New England Journal of Medicine. 29*, 903–10.

Ekman, P., & Friesen, W. V. (1975). *Unmasking the face.* Englewood Cliffs, NJ: Prentice-Hall.

Ekman, P., Friesen, W. V., & Ellsworth, P. (1972). *Emotion in the human face.* New York: Pergamon.

Elashoff, J. D., & Grossman, M. I. (1980). Trends in hospital admissions and death rates for peptic ulcer in the United States from 1970 to 1978. *Gastroenterology, 78*, 280–85.

Elkin, I., Shea, T., Imber, S., Pilkonis, P., Sotsky, S., Glass, D., Watkins, J., Leber, W., & Collins, J. (1986). NIMH treatment of depression collaborative research program: Initial outcome findings. Paper presented at meetings of the American Association for the Advancement of Science, May 1986.

Elkin, I., Shea, M. T., Watkins, J. T., Imber, S. D., Sotsky, S. M., Collins, J. F., Glass, D. R., Pilkonis, P. A., Leber, W. R., Docherty, J. P., Fiester, S. J., & Parloff, M. B. (1989). National Institute of Mental Health Treatment of Depression Collaborative Research Program: General effectiveness of treatments. *Archives of General Psychiatry, 46*(11): 971–82.

Ellenberger, H. F. (1970). *The discovery of the unconscious: The history and evolution of dynamic psychiatry.* New York: Basic Books.

Ellickson, P. L. (1994). School-based drug prevention: What should it do? What has been done? In R. Coombs & D. Ziedonis (Eds.), *Handbook on drug abuse prevention.* Englewood Cliffs, NJ: Prentice-Hall.

Elliott, D. S., Hulzinga, D., & Ageton, S. S. (1985). *Explaining delinquency and drug use.* Beverly Hills, CA: Sage.

Ellis, A. (1962). *Reason and emotion in psychotherapy.* New York: Lyle Stuart.

Ellis, L., & Ames, M. A. (1987). Neurohormonal functioning and sexual orientation: A theory of homosexuality-heterosexuality. *Psychological Bulletin, 101* (2): 233–58.

Ellis, L., Ames, M. A., Peckham, W., & Burke, D. (1988). Sexual orientation of human offspring may be altered by severe maternal stress during pregnancy. *Journal of Sex Research, 25* (1): 152–57.

Ellis, A., & Harper, R. A. (1975). *A new guide to rational living.* Englewood Cliffs, NJ: Prentice-Hall.

Ellison, G. D. (1977). Animal models of psychopathology. *American Psychologist, 32*, 1036–55.

Ellsworth, P. C., & Carlsmith, M. J. (1968). Effects of eye contact and verbal content on affective response to dyadic interactions. *Journal of Personality and Social Psychology, 10*, 15–20.

Elmhorn, K. (1965). Study in self-reported delinquency among school children. In *Scandinavian studies in criminology.* London: Tavistock.

Emmelkamp, P., Hoekstra, R., & Visser, S. (1985). The behavioral treatment of obsessive-compulsive disorder: Prediction of outcome at 3.5 years follow-up. In P. Pichot, A. Brenner, R. Wolf, & K. Thau (Eds.), *Psychiatry: The state of the art* (Vol. 4). New York: Plenum.

Emmelkamp, P., & Kuipers, A. (1979). Agoraphobia: A follow-up study four years after treatment. *British Journal of Psychiatry, 134*, 352–55.

Emrick, C. D., Lassen, C. L., & Edwards, M. T. (1977). Nonprofessional peers as therapeutic agents. In A. S. Gurman & A. M. Razin (Eds.), *Effective psychotherapy.* New York: Pergamon Press.

Emrick, D. C. (1982). Evaluation of alcoholism therapy methods. In E. M. Pattison & E. Kaufman (Eds.), *Encyclopedic handbook of alcoholism.* New York: Gardner Press.

Endicott, J., & Spitzer, R. L. (1978). A diagnostic interview: The schedule for affective disorders and schizophrenia. *Archives of General Psychiatry, 35*, 837–44.

Endler, N. S., Magnusson, D., Ekehammar, B., & Okada, M. O. (1975). The multidimensionality of state and trait anxiety. Reports from the Department of Psychology, University of Stockholm.

Enkelmann, R. (1991). Alprazolam versus busiprone in the treatment of outpatients with generalized anxiety disorder. *Psychopharmacology, 105*, 428–32.

Ennis, B. J. (1972). *Prisoners of psychiatry: Mental patients, psychiatrists, and the law.* New York: Harcourt Brace Jovanovich.

Ennis, B. J., & Litwack, T. R. (1974). Psychiatry and the presumption of expertise: Flipping coins in the courtroom. *California Law Review, 62*, 693.

Ennis, B., & Siegel, L. (1973). *The rights of mental patients: The basic ACLU guide to a mental patient's rights.* New York: Discus Books.

Eppley, K., Abrams, A., & Shear, J. (1989). Differential effects of relaxation techniques on trait anxiety: A meta-analysis. *Journal of Clinical Psychology, 45*, 957–74.

Erdelyi, M. H. (1985). *Psychoanalysis: Freud's cognitive psychology.* New York: Freeman.

Erickson, W. D., Walbek, N. H., & Seely, R. K. (1988). Behavior patterns of child molesters. *Archives of Sexual Behavior, 17*(1): 77–86.

Erikson, K. (1976). *Everything in its path: Destruction of community in the Buffalo Creek flood.* New York: Simon & Schuster.

Eslinger, P. J., & Damasio, A. R. (1985). Severe disturbance of higher cognition after bilateral frontal lobe ablation: Patient E.V.R. *Neurology, 35*, 1731–41.

Eslinger, P. J., Grattan, L. M., Damasio, H., & Damasio, A. R. (1992). Developmental consequences of childhood frontal damage. *Archives of Neurology, 49*, 764–69.

Evans, M. D., Hollon, S. D., DeRubeis, R. J., Piasecki, J., Grove, W. M., & Tuason, V. B. (1989). Differential relapse following treatment for depression: IV. A two-year follow-up at the cognitive-pharmacotherapy project.

Evans, M. D., Hollon, S. D., DeRubeis, R. J., & Piasecki, J. M. (1992). Differential relapse following cognitive therapy and pharmacotherapy for depression. *Archives of General Psychiatry, 49*(10): 802–8.

Exline, R., & Winters, L. C. (1965). Affective relations and mutual glances in dyads. In S. Tomkins & C. E. Izard (Eds.), *Affect, cognition and personality.* New York: Springer.

Exner, J. E. (1974). *The Rorschach: A comprehensive system.* New York: Wiley.

Exner, J. E. (1978). *The Rorschach: A comprehensive system: Vol. 2. Current research and advanced interpretation.* New York: Wiley.

Eysenck, H. J. (1952). The effects of psychotherapy: An evaluation. *Journal of Consulting Psychology, 16,* 319–24.

Eysenck, H. J. (1961). The effects of psychotherapy. In H. J. Eysenck (Ed.), *Handbook of abnormal psychology: An experimental approach* (pp. 697–725). New York: Basic Books.

Eysenck, H. J. (1979). The conditioning model of neurosis. *Communications in Behavioral Biology, 2,* 155–99.

Fairburn, C. G. (1985). The management of bulimia nervosa. *Journal of Psychiatric Research, 19,* 465–72.

Fairburn, C. G., Agras, W. S., & Wilson, G. T. (1992). The research on the treatment of bulimia nervosa: Practical and theoretical implications. In G. H. Anderson & S. H. Kennedy (Eds.), *The biology of feast and famine: Relevance to eating disorders* (pp. 318–40). San Diego: Academic Press.

Fairburn, C. G., Jones, R., Peveler, R. C., Carr, S. J., Solomon, R. A., O'Connor, M. E., Burton, J., & Hope, R. A. (1991). Three psychological treatments for bulimia nervosa. *Archives of General Psychiatry, 48,* 463–69.

Fairburn, C. G., Welch, S. L., & Hay, P. J. (1993). The classification of recurrent overeating: The "binge eating disorder" proposal. *International Journal of Eating Disorders, 13*(2), 155–59.

Fairburn, C. G., & Wilson, G. T. (1993). Binge eating: Definition and classification. In C. G. Fairburn & G. T. Wilson (Eds.), *Binge eating: Nature, assessment, and treatment.* New York: Guilford Press.

Fairweather, G. W., Sanders, D. H. Cressler, D. L., & Maynard, H. (1969). *Community life for the mentally ill.* Chicago: Alpine.

Falloon, I. R. H. (1988). Editorial: Expressed emotion: Current status. *Psychological Medicine, 18,* 269–74.

Falloon, I. R. H., Boyd, J. L., & McGill, C. W. (1984). *Family care of schizophrenia: A problem-solving approach to the treatment of mental illness.* New York: Guilford Press.

Falloon, I. R. H., Boyd, J. L., McGill, C. W., Williamson, M., Razani, J., Moss, H. B., Gilderman, A. M., & Simpson, G. M. (1985). Family management in the prevention of morbidity in schizophrenia. *Archives of General Psychiatry, 42,* 887–96.

Falloon, I. R. H., & Liberman, R. P. (1983). Interactions between drug and psychosocial therapy in schizophrenia. *Schizophrenia Bulletin, 9,* 543–55.

Falloon, I. R. H., McGill, C., Boyd, J., & Pederson, J. (1987). Family management in the prevention of morbidity of schizophrenia: Social outcome of a two-year longitudinal study. *Psychological Medicine, 17,* 59–66.

Fancher, R. (1973). *Psychoanalytic psychology: The development of Freud's thought.* New York: Norton.

Farber, L. H. (1966). *The ways of the will: Essays toward a psychology and psychopathology of will.* New York: Basic Books.

Farberow, N. L. (1970). Ten years of suicide prevention—past and future. *Bulletin of Suicidology, 6,* 6–11.

Farberow, N. L. (1974). *Suicide.* Morristown, NJ: General Learning Press.

Faris, R. E. L., & Dunham, H. W. (1939). *Mental disorders in urban areas.* Chicago: University of Chicago Press.

Farmer, A. E., McGuffin, P., & Gottesman, I. I. (1987). Twin concordance for DSM-III schizophrenia: Scrutinizing the validity of the definition. *Archives of General Psychiatry, 44,* 634–41.

Farrington, D. P. (1978). The family background of aggressive youths. In L. A. Hersov & D. Shaffer (Eds.), *Aggression and antisocial behavior in childhood and adolescence.* New York: Pergamon.

Fawcett, J., Maas, J., & Dekirmenjian, H. (1972). Depression and MHPG excretion: Response to dextroamphetamine and tricyclic antidepressants. *Archives of General Psychiatry, 26,* 246–51.

Fawzy, F., Fawzy, N., Hyun, C., et al. (1993). Malignant melanoma: Effects of an early structured psychiatric intervention, coping, and affective state on recurrence and survival 6 years later. *Archives of General Psychiatry, 50,* 681–89.

Feinberg, I. (1962). A comparison of the visual hallucinations in schizophrenics with those induced by mescaline and LSD. In L. J. West (Ed.), *Hallucinations.* New York: Grune & Stratton.

Feinberg, T. E., Rifkin, A., Schaffer, C., & Walker, E. (1986). Facial discrimination and emotional recognition in schizophrenia and affective disorders. *Archives of General Psychiatry, 43,* 276–79.

Feldman, M. P., & MacCulloch, M. J. (1971). *Homosexual behaviour: Theory and assessment.* Oxford: Pergamon.

Fenichel, O. (1945). *The psychoanalytic theory of neurosis.* New York: Norton.

Fenton, W. S., & McGlashan, T. H. (1991). Natural history of schizophrenia subtypes. I. Longitudinal study of paranoid, hebephrenic, and undifferentiated schizophrenia. *Archives of General Psychiatry, 48*(11): 969–77.

Fergusson, D. M., Horwood, L. J., & Lynskey, M .T. (1993). Early dentine lead levels and subsequent cognitive and behavioural development. *Journal of Child Psychology and Psychiatry, 34,* 215–27.

Ferster, C. B. (1961). Positive reinforcement and the behavioral deficits of autistic children. *Child Development, 32,* 437–56.

Ferster, C. B. (1974). Behavioral approaches to depression. In R. J. Friedman & M. M. Katz (Eds.), The *psychology of depression: Contemporary theory and research.* Washington, DC: Winston.

Fieve, R. R. (1975). *Mood swing.* New York: Morrow.

Figueroa, R. A., & Sassenrath, J. M. (1989). A longitudinal study of the predictive validity of the System of Multicultural Pluralistic Assessment (SOMPA). *Psychology in the Schools, 26,* 1–19.

Fine, C. G. (1991). Treatment stabilization and crisis prevention. Pacing the therapy of the multiple personality disorder patient. *Psychiatric Clinics of North America, 14,* 661–75.

Fingarette, H., & Hasse, A. (1979). *Mental disabilities and criminal responsibility.* Berkeley: University of California Press.

Fink, M. (1979). *Convulsive therapy: Therapy and practice.* New York: Raven Press.

Fink, P. (1992). Physical complaints and symptoms of somatizing patients. *Journal of Psychosomatic Research, 36,* 125–36.

Finkel, N. J. (1989). The Insanity Defense Reform Act of 1984: Much ado about nothing. *Behavioral Sciences and the Law, 7,* 403–19.

Finkel, N. J. (1990). De facto departures from insanity instructions: Toward the remaking of common law. *Law and Human Behavior, 14,* 105–22.

Finkel, N. J. (1991). The insanity defense: A comparison between verdict schemas. *Law and Human Behavior, 15,* 533–55.

Fiore, M. C., Novotny, T. E., Pierce, J. P., Giovino, G. A., Hatziandrev, G. A., Newcomb, E. J., Surawicz, T. S., & Davis, R. M. (1990). Methods used to quit smoking in the United States: Do cessation programs help? *Journal of the American Medical Association, 263,* 2760–65.

Fiore, M. C., Smith, S., Jorenby, D., & Baker, T. B. (1994). The effectiveness of the nicotine patch for smoking cessation: A meta-analysis. *Journal of the American Medical Association, 271* (24): 1940–47.

Fireside, H. (1979). *Soviet psychoprisons.* New York: Norton.

Fischer, M., Barkley, R.A., Fletcher, K.E., & Smallish, L. (1993). The adolescent outcome of hyperactive children: Predictors of psychiatric, academic, social, and emotional adjustment. *Journal of the American Academy of Child and Adolescent Psychiatry, 32,* 324–32.

Fischman, M. W., & Schuster, C. R. (1982). Cocaine self-administration in humans. *Federation Proceedings 41 (2):* 241–46.

Fisher, J., Epstein, L. J., & Harris, M. R. (1967). Validity of the psychiatric interview: Predicting the effectiveness of the first Peace Corps volunteers in Ghana. *Archives of General Psychiatry, 17,* 744–50.

Fisher, S., & Greenberg, R. P. (1977). *The scientific credibility of Freud's theories and therapy*. New York: Basic Books.

Fiske, D., Cartwright, D., & Kirtner, W. (1964). Are psychotherapeutic changes predictable? *Journal of Abnormal and Social Psychology, 69*, 418–26.

Fiske, D., & Goodman, G. (1965). The post-therapy period. *Journal of Abnormal Psychology, 70*, 169–70.

Flaskerud, J. H. (1990). Matching client and therapist ethnicity, language, and gender: A review of research. *Issues in Mental Health Nursing, 11*, 321–36.

Flaskerud, J. H., & Liu, P. Y. (1990). Influence of therapist ethnicity and language on therapy outcomes of Southeast Asian clients. *International Journal of Social Psychiatry, 36*(1): 18–29.

Flavell, J. H. (1977). *Cognitive development*. Englewood Cliffs, NJ: Prentice-Hall.

Flay, B. R. (1987). Mass media and smoking cessation: A critical review. *American Journal of Public Health, 77*, 153–60.

Fleiss, J. L. (1971). Measuring nominal scale agreement among many raters. *Psychological Bulletin, 76*, 378–82.

Fleming, J. E., & Offord, D. R. (1990). Epidemiology of childhood depressive disorders: A critical review. *Journal of the American Academy of Child and Adolescent Psychiatry, 29*(4): 571–80.

Flood, R., & Seager, C. (1968). A retrospective examination of psychiatric case records of patients who subsequently commit suicide. *British Journal of Psychiatry, 114*, 443–50.

Foa, D. B., & Kozak, M. J. (1986). Emotional processing of fear: Exposure to corrective information. *Psychological Bulletin, 99*, 20–35.

Foa, E., & Kozak, M. (1993). Obsessive-compulsive disorder: Long-term outcome of psychological treatment. In M. Mavissakalian & R. Prien (Eds.), *Long-term treatments of anxiety disorders*. Washington, DC: American Psychiatric Press.

Foa, E., Rothbaum, B., Riggs, D., & Murdock, T. (1991). Treatment of post-traumatic stress disorder in rape victims: A comparison between cognitive-behavioral procedures and counseling. *Journal of Consulting and Clinical Psychology, 59*, 715–23.

Fodor, O., Vestea, S., & Urcan, S. (1968). Hydrochloric acid secretion capacity of the stomach as an inherited factor in the pathogenesis of duodenal ulcer. *American Journal of Digestive Diseases, 13*, 260.

Ford, M. R., & Widiger, T. A. (1989). Sex bias in the diagnosis of histrionic and antisocial personality disorders. *Journal of Consulting and Clinical Psychology, 57*(2): 301–5.

Foster, D. W., & Wilson, J. D. (Eds.). (1985). *William's textbook of endocrinology* (7th ed.). Philadelphia: Saunders.

Foucault, M. (1965). *Madness and civilization: A history of insanity in the age of reason*. New York: Random House.

Fowler, R. D. (1986). Howard Hughes: A psychological autopsy. *Psychology Today, 20*, 22–33.

Fowles, D. C., & Gersh, F. (1979). Neurotic depression: The endogenous-neurotic distinction. In R. A. Depue (Ed.), *The psychobiology of the depressive disorders: Implications for the effects of stress*. New York: Academic Press.

Frank, E., Anderson, B., Stewart, B., Dacu, C., et al. (1988). Efficacy of cognitive behavior therapy and systematic desensitization in the treatment of rape trauma. *Behavior Therapy, 19*, 403–20.

Frank, E., Anderson, C., & Rubenstein D. (1978). Frequency of sexual dysfunction in "normal" couples. *New England Journal of Medicine, 299*, 111–15.

Frank, H., & Hoffman, N. (1986). Borderline empathy: An empirical investigation. *Comprehensive Psychiatry, 2*, 387–95.

Frank, I. M., Lessin, P. J., Tyrrell, E. D., Hahn, P. M., & Szara, S. (1976). Acute and cumulative effects of marihuana smoking on hospitalized subjects: A 36–day study. In M. C. Braude & S. Szara (Eds.), *Pharmacology of marihuana* (Vol. 2, pp. 673–80). New York: Academic Press.

Frank, J. D. (1978). Expectation and therapeutic outcome—The placebo effect and the role induction interview. In J. D. Frank, R. Hoehn-Saric, S. D. Imber, B. L. Liberman, & A. R. Stone (Eds.), *Effective ingredients of successful psychotherapy*. New York: Brunner/Mazel.

Frank, J., Kosten, T., Giller, E., & Dan, E. (1988). A randomized clinical trial of phenelzine and imipramine for post-traumatic stress disorder. *American Journal of Psychiatry, 145*, 1289–91.

Frankl, V. E. (1975). Paradoxical intention and dereflection. *Psychotherapy: Theory, Research and Practice, 12*, 226–37.

Frederick, C. J. (1973). *Suicide, homicide and alcoholism among American Indians*. (DHEW Publication No. ADM 24-42). Washington, DC: U.S. Government Printing Office.

Frederick C. J. (1978). Current trends in suicidal behavior in the United States. *American Journal of Psychotherapy, 32*, 172–200.

Freud, A. (1936). *The ego and mechanisms of defense* (rev. ed.). New York: International Universities Press, 1967.

Freud, S. (1884). Letter to his fiancée. In N. Taylor, *Flight from reality*. New York: Duell, Sloan, & Pearce, 1949.

Freud, S. (1894). The neuro-psychoses of defense. In J. Strachey (Ed. and Trans.), *The complete psychological works* (Vol. 3). New York: Norton, 1976.

Freud, S. (1905). Psychical (or mental) treatment. In J. Strachey (Ed. and Trans.), *The complete psychological works* (Vol. 7). New York: Norton, 1976.

Freud, S. (1909a). Some general remarks on hysterical attacks. In J. Strachey (Ed. and Trans.), *The complete psychological works* (Vol. 9). New York: Norton, 1976.

Freud, S. (1909b). Notes upon a case of obsessional neurosis. In J. Strachey (Ed. and Trans.), *The complete psychological works* (Vol. 10). New York: Norton, 1976.

Freud, S. (1917). Introductory lectures on psychoanalysis, Part III. In J. Strachey (Ed. and Trans.), *The complete psychological works* (Vol. 16). New York: Norton, 1976.

Freud, S. (1923). The ego and the id. In J. Strachey (Ed. and Trans.), *The complete psychological works* (Vol. 19). New York: Norton, 1976.

Freud, S. (1933). New introductory lectures on psychoanalysis. In J. Strachey (Ed. and Trans.), *The complete psychological works* (Vol. 22). New York: Norton, 1976.

Freud, S. (1936). A disturbance of memory on the Acropolis. In J. Strachey (Ed. and Trans.), *The complete psychological works* (Vol. 22). New York: Norton, 1976.

Freud, S. (1937). Analysis terminable and interminable. In J. Strachey (Ed. and Trans.), *The complete psychological works* (Vol. 23). New York: Norton, 1976.

Friedman, M. (1988). Toward rational pharmacotherapy for post-traumatic stress disorder: An interim report. *American Journal of Psychiatry, 145*, 281–85.

Friedman, M., & Rosenman, R. H. (1974). *Type A behavior*. New York: Knopf.

Friman, P. C., & Warzak, W. J. (1990). Nocturnal enuresis: A prevalent, persistent, yet curable parasomnia. *Pediatrician, 17*, 38–45.

Frith, U. (1993). Autism. *Scientific American, 268*(6): 108–14.

Frumkin, K., Nathan, R., Prout, M., & Cohen, M. (1978). Nonpharmacologic control of essential hypertension in men: A critical review of the experimental literature. *Psychosomatic Medicine, 40*, 294–320.

Fuche, C. Z., & Rehm, L. P. (1977). A self-control behavior therapy program for depression. *Journal of Consulting and Clinical Psychology, 45*, 206–15.

Gabbard, G. O. (1992). Psychodynamic psychiatry in the "Decade of the Brain." *American Journal of Psychiatry, 149*(8):991–98.

Gabriel, T. (1994). Heroin finds a new market along the cutting edge of style. *New York Times*, May 8, p. A1.

Gagnon, J. H. (1977). *Human sexuality*. Chicago: Scott, Foresman.

Galen. In Veith, I. *Hysteria: The history of a disease*. Chicago: University of Chicago Press, 1965.

Galaburda, A. M., Sherman, G. F., Rosen, G. D., & Geschwind, N. (1985). Developmental dyslexia: Four consecutive cases with cortical anomalies. *Annals of Neurology, 18,* 222–33.

Ganaway, G. K. (1989). Historical versus narrative truth: Clarifying the role of exogenous trauma in the etiology of MPD and its variants. *Dissociation: Progress in the Dissociative Disorders, 2,* 205–20.

Garber, H. L. (1988). *The Milwaukee Project: Preventing mental retardation in children at risk.* Washington, DC: American Association of Mental Retardation.

Garcia, J., Ervin, F. R., & Koelling, R. A. (1967). Toxicity of serum from irradiated donors. *Nature, 213,* 682–83.

Garcia, E., Guess, D., & Brynes, J. (1973). Development of syntax in a retarded girl using procedures of imitation, reinforcement, and modelling. *Journal of Applied Behavior Analysis, 6,* 299–310.

Garcia, J., & Koelling, R. A. (1966). Relation of cue to consequence in avoidance learning. *Psychonomic Science, 4,* 123–24.

Gardner, E. (1975). *Fundamentals of neurology: A psychophysiological approach* (6th ed.). Philadelphia: Saunders.

Gardner, H. (1974). *The shattered mind.* New York: Vintage.

Garfinkel, P. E., & Garner, D. M. (1982). *Anorexia nervosa: A multidimensional perspective.* New York: Brunner/Mazel.

Garmezy, N. (1971). Vulnerability research and the issue of primary prevention. *American Journal of Orthopsychiatry, 41,* 101–16.

Garmezy, N. (1974). Children at risk: The search for the antecedents of schizophrenia: Part II. Ongoing research programs, issues, and intervention. *Schizophrenia Bulletin, 9,* 55–125.

Garmezy, N. (1977a). DSM III: Never mind the psychologists—Is it good for the children? *The Clinical Psychologist, 31,* 3–4.

Garmezy, N. (1977b). The psychology and psychopathology of Allenhead. *Schizophrenia Bulletin, 3,* 360–69.

Garner, D. M. (1993). Binge eating: Definition and classification. In C. G. Fairburn, G. T. Wilson, C. G. Fairburn, & G. T. Wilson (Eds.), *Binge eating: Nature, assessment, and treatment.* New York: Guilford Press.

Garner, D. M., & Bemis, K. M. (1982). A cognitive-behavioral approach to anorexia nervosa. *Cognitive Therapy and Research, 6,* 123–50.

Garner, D., & Wooley, S. (1991). Confronting the failure of behavioral and dietary treatments for obesity. *Clinical Psychology Review, 11,* 729–80.

Garrison, C. Z., Addy, C. L., Jackson, K. L., McKeown, R. E., & Waller, J. L. (1992). Major depressive disorder and dysthymia in young adolescents. *American Journal of Epidemiology, 135* (7): 792–802.

Garrity, T. F., Somes, G. W., & Marx, M. B. (1977). Personality factors in resistance to illness after recent life changes. *Journal of Psychosomatic Research, 21,* 23–32.

Gaston, L., Marmar, C. R., Thompson, L. W., & Gallagher, D. (1988). Relation of patient pretreatment characteristics to the therapeutic alliance in diverse psychotherapies. *Journal of Consulting and Clinical Psychology, 56*(4): 483–89.

Gawin, F. H., & Ellinwood, E. H. (1988). Cocaine and other stimulants. *New England Journal of Medicine, 318,* 1173–82.

Gawin, F. H., & Ellinwood, E. H. (1989). Cocaine dependence. *Annual Review of Medicine, 40,* 149–61.

Gawin, F. H., Kleber, H. D., Byck, R., Rounsaville, B. J., Kosten, T. R., Jatlow, P. I., & Morgan, C. (1989). Desipramine facilitation of initial cocaine abstinence. *Archives of General Psychiatry, 46,* 117–21.

Gay, P. (1988). *Freud: A life for our time.* New York: Norton.

Gazzaniga, M. (1970). *The bisected brain.* New York: Appleton-Century-Crofts.

Gebhard, P. H., Gagnon, J. H., Pomeroy, W. B., & Christenson, C. V. (1965). *Sex offenders.* New York: Harper & Row.

Gelenberg, A. J., & Klerman, G. L. (1978). Maintenance drug therapy in long-term treatment of depression. In J. P. Brady & H. K. H. Brodie (Eds.), *Controversy in psychiatry.* Philadelphia: Saunders.

Gelfand, D. M. (1978). Social withdrawal and negative emotional states: Behavioral treatment. In B. B. Wolman, J. Egan, & A. O. Ross (Eds.), *Handbook of treatment of mental disorders in childhood and adolescence.* Englewood Cliffs, NJ: Prentice-Hall.

George, M. S., Kettler, T. A., & Post, R. M. (1993). SPECT and PET images in mood disorders. *Journal of Clinical Psychiatry, 54* (Suppl): 6–12.

George, M., Trimble, M., Ring, H., et al. (1993). Obsessions in obsessive-compulsive disorder with and without Gilles de la Tourette's syndrome. *American Journal of Psychiatry, 150,* 93–97.

Gergen, K. J. (1982). *Toward transformation in social knowledge.* New York: Springer Verlag.

Gerstley, L. J., Alterman, A. I., McLellan, A. T., & Woody, G. E. (1990). Antisocial personality disorder in patients with substance abuse disorders. *American Journal of Psychiatry, 147,* 481–87.

Geschwind, N. (1962). The anatomy of acquired disorders of reading. In J. Money (Ed.), *Reading disability* (pp. 115–30). Baltimore: Johns Hopkins University Press.

Geschwind, N. (1965). Disconnection syndromes in animals and man. *Brain, 88,* 237–94, 585–640.

Geschwind, N. (1972). Language and the brain. *Scientific American, 226,* 76–83.

Geschwind, N. (1975). The apraxias: Neural mechanisms of disorders of learned movement. *American Scientist, 188,* 188–95.

Geschwind, N., Quadfasel, F. A., & Segarra, J. M. (1968). Isolation of the speech area. *Neuropsychologia, 6,* 327–40.

Gilberg, C. (1991). Outcome in autism and autistic-like conditions. *Journal of the American Academy of Child and Adolescent Psychiatry, 30*(3): 375–82.

Gilberg, C., & Svennerholm, L. (1987). CSF monoamines in autistic syndromes and other pervasive developmental disorders in childhood. *British Journal of Psychiatry, 151,* 89–94.

Gilbert, D. G., & Hagen, R. L. (1980). The effects of nicotine and extraversion on self-report, skin conductance, electromyographic, and heart responses to emotional stimuli. *Addictive Behavior, 5,* 247–57.

Gilberstadt, H., & Duker, J. (1965). *A handbook for clinical and actuarial MMPI interpretations.* Philadelphia: Saunders.

Gillham, J., Reivich, K., Jaycox, L., & Seligman, M. (1994). Prevention of depressive symptoms in school children: Two-year follow-up. Submitted.

Gilman, A. G., Goodman, L. S., Rall, T. W., & Murad, F. (Eds.). (1985). In A. J. Goodman & L. S. Gilman (Eds.), *The pharmacological basis of therapeutics.* New York: Macmillan.

Girelli, S., Resick, P., Marhoefer-Dvorak, S., & Hutter, C. (1986). Subjective distress and violence during rape: The effects on long-term fear. *Violence and Victims, 1,* 35–46.

Gittelman, R., & Klein, D. F. (1984). Relationship between separation anxiety and panic and agoraphobic disorders. *Psychopathology, 17,* 56–65.

Gittelman, R., Mannuzza, S., Shenker, R., & Bonagura, N. (1985). Hyperactive boys almost grown up. *Archives of General Psychiatry, 42,* 937–47.

Gittleman, M., & Birch, H. G. (1967). Childhood schizophrenia: Intellect, neurologic status, perinatal risk, prognosis and family pathology. *Archives of General Psychiatry, 17,* 16–25.

Gittleson, N. L. (1966). Depressive psychosis in the obsessional neurotic. *British Journal of Psychiatry, 122,* 883–87.

Glass, D. C. (1977). *Behavior pattern stress in coronary disease.* Hillsdale, NJ: Erlbaum.

Glazer, H. I., & Weiss, J. M. (1976). Long-term interference effect: An alternative to "learned helplessness." *Journal of Experimental Psychology: Animal Behavior Processes, 2,* 202–13.

Gleitman, H. (1981). *Psychology.* New York: Norton.

Gleitman, H. (1991). *Psychology* (3rd ed.). New York: Norton.

Gleitman, L. R., & Rozin, P. (1977). The structure and acquisition of reading: I. Relations between orthographics and the structure of language. In A. S. Reber & D. Scarborough (Eds.), *Toward a psychology of reading* (pp. 1–53). Potomac, MD: Erlbaum.

Gleser, G. C., Green, B. L., & Winget, C. (1981). *Prolonged psychosocial effects of disaster*. New York: Academic Press.

Glisky, E. L., Schacter, D. L. & Tulving, E. (1986). Computer learning by memory-impaired patients: Acquisition and retention of complex knowledge. *Neuropsychologia, 24,* 313–28.

Golan, N. (1978). *Treatment in crisis situations*. New York: The Free Press.

Gold, J. M., Randolph, C., Carpenter, C. J., Goldberg, T. E., & Weinberger, D. R. (1992). Forms of memory failure in schizophrenia. *Journal of Abnormal Psychology, 101*(3): 487–94.

Golden, C. J. (1981). The Luria-Nebraska Children's Battery: Theory and formulation. In G. W. Hynd & J. E. Obrzut (Eds.), *Neuropsychological assessment and the school-age child: Issues and procedures*. New York: Grune & Stratton.

Golden, C. J., Hammeke, T. A., & Puriosch, A. D. (1980). *Manual for the Luria-Nebraska Neuropsychological Battery*. Los Angeles: Western Psychological Services.

Goldfried, M. R., & Davison, G. C. (1976). *Clinical behavior therapy*. New York: Holt, Rinehart & Winston.

Goldfried, M. R., Decenteceo, E., & Wineburg, L. (1974). Systematic rational restructuring as a self-control technique. *Behavior Therapy, 3,* 398–416.

Goldfried, M. R., Linehan, M. M., & Smith, J. L. (1978). Reduction of test anxiety through cognitive restructuring. *Journal of Consulting and Clinical Psychology, 46,* 32–39.

Golding, J. M., Smith, G. R., & Kashner, T. M. (1991). Does somatization disorder occur in men? Clinical characteristics of women and men with unexplained somatic symptoms. *Archives of General Psychiatry, 48,* 231–35.

Goldman-Rakic, P. S. (1987). Circuitry of primate prefrontal cortex and regulation of behavior by representational memory. In F. Plum (Ed.), *Handbook of physiology: The nervous system* (Vol. 5, pp. 373–417). Bethesda, MD: American Physiological Society.

Goldstein, J. M. (1988). Gender differences in the course of schizophrenia. *American Journal of Psychiatry, 145,* 684–89.

Goldstein, M .J., Strachan, A. M., & Wynne, L .C. (1994). DSM-IV literature review: Relational problems with high expressed emotion. In T. A. Widiger, A. J. Frances, H. A. Pincus, W. Davis, & M. First (Eds.), *DSM-IV sourcebook*. Washington, DC: American Psychiatric Association.

Goodman, L., & Gilman, A. (1941). *The pharmacological basis of therapeutics*. New York: Macmillan.

Goodman, R. (1990). Technical note: Are perinatal complications causes or consequences of autism? *Journal of Child Psychology and Psychiatry, 31*(5): 809–12.

Goodwin, D. W. (1988). Alcoholism: Who gets better and who does not. In R. M. Rose & J. Barrett (Eds.), *Alcoholism: Origins and outcomes* (pp. 281–92). New York: Raven Press.

Goodwin, F., Brodie, H., Murphy, D., et al. (1970). L-dopa, catecholamines and behavior: A clinical and biochemical study in depressed patients. *Biological Psychiatry, 2,* 341–66.

Goodwin, D. W., Schulsinger, F., Hermansen, L., Guze, S. B., & Winokur, G. (1973). Alcohol problems in adoptees raised apart from alcoholic biological parents. *Archives of General Psychiatry, 28,* 238–43.

Goodwin, D. W., Schulsinger, F., Moller, N., Hermansen, L., & Winokur, G. (1974). Drinking problems in adopted and non-adopted sons of alcoholics. *Archives of General Psychiatry, 31,* 164–69.

Gorenstein, E. E., & Newman, J. P. (1980). Disinhibitory psychopathology: A new perspective and a model for research. *Psychological Review, 87,* 301–15.

Gottesman, I. I. (1991). *Schizophrenia genesis: The origins of madness*. New York: Freeman.

Gottesman, I. I. (1993). Origins of schizophrenia: Past as prologue. In R. Plomin & G. E. McClearn (Eds.), *Nature, nurture, and psychology* (pp. 231–44). Washington, DC: American Psychological Association.

Gottesman, I. I., McGuffin, P., & Farmer, A. E. (1987). Clinical genetics as clues to the "real" genetics of schizophrenia (a decade of modest gains while playing for time). *Schizophrenia Bulletin, 13,* 23–47.

Gottesman, I. I., & Shields, J. (1972). *Schizophrenia and genetics: A twin study vantage point*. New York: Academic Press.

Gottesman, I. I., & Shields, J. (1982). *Schizophrenia: The epigenetic puzzle* (pp. xiii and 258). Cambridge: Cambridge University Press.

Gould, S. J. (1981). *The mismeasure of man*. New York: Norton.

Gove, W. R. (1975). Labelling and mental illness: A critique. In W. R. Gove (Ed.), *The labelling of deviance: Evaluating a perspective*. New York: Sage.

Grace, W. J., & Graham, D. T. (1952). Relationship of specific attitudes and emotions to certain bodily disease. *Psychosomatic Medicine, 14,* 243–51.

Graf, P., & Schacter, D. L. (1985). Implicit and explicit memory for new associations in normal and amnesic subjects. *Journal of Experimental Psychology: Learning, Memory, and Cognition, 11,* 501–18.

Graham, D., Lew, G., Klein, P., et al. (1992). Effect of treatment of Heliobacter pylori infection on the long-term recurrence of gastric or duodenal ulcer: A randomized, controlled study. *Annals of Internal Medicine, 116,* 705–8.

Graham, R. B. (1990). *Physiological psychology*. Belmont, CA: Wadsworth.

Granville-Grossman, K. L. (1968). The early environment and affective disorder. In A. Coppen & A. Walk (Eds.), Recent developments in affective disorders. *British Journal of Psychiatry*. (Special Publication No. 2).

Grattan, L. M., & Eslinger, P. J. (1992). Long-term psychological consequences of childhood frontal lobe lesion in patient D.T. *Brain and Cognition, 20,* 185–95.

Gray, F., Huag, H., Chimelli, L., et al. (1991). Prominent cortical atrophy with neuronal loss as correlate of human immunodeficiency virus encephalopathy. *Acta Neuropathologica, 82,* 229–33.

Gray's Anatomy (30th edition). (1984). Malvern, PA: Lea & Febiger.

Green, B., Grace, M., Lindy, J., et al. (1990). Buffalo Creek survivors in the second decade: Comparison with unexposed and nonlitigant groups. *Journal of Applied Social Psychology, 20,* 1033–50.

Green, B., Lindy, J., Grace, M., & Leonard, A. (1992). Chronic posttraumatic stress disorder and diagnostic comorbidity in a disaster sample. *Journal of Nervous and Mental Diseases, 180,* 760–66.

Green, R. (1985). Gender identity in childhood and later sexual orientation: Follow-up of 78 males. *American Journal of Psychiatry, 142,* 339–41.

Greenberg, S. (1989). *Immunity and survival: Keys to immune system health*. New York: Human Sciences Press.

Greene, R. L. (1991). *The MMPI-2/MMPI: An interpretive manual*. Boston: Allyn & Bacon.

Greenspoon, J. (1955). The reinforcing effect of two spoken sounds on the frequency of two responses. *American Journal of Psychology, 68,* 409–16.

Greer, G., & Tolbert, R. (1986). Subjective reports of the effects of MDMA in a clinical setting. *Journal of Psychoactive Drugs, 18,* 319–27.

Greer, S. (1964). Study of parental loss in neurotics and sociopaths. *Archives of General Psychiatry, 11,* 177–80.

Greer, S., Morris, T., & Pettingale, K. W. (1979). Psychological response to breast cancer: Effect on outcome. *The Lancet, II,* October 13, 785–87.

Gregor, T. (1985). *Anxious pleasures: The sexual lives of an Amazonian people*. Chicago: University of Chicago Press.

Gregory, I. (1958). Studies on parental deprivation in psychiatric patients. *American Journal of Psychiatry, 115,* 432–42.

Gregory, R. (Ed.). (1987). *Oxford companion to the mind*. Oxford, Eng.: Oxford University Press.

Greist, J. (1990). Treating the anxiety: Therapeutic options in obsessive-compulsive disorder. *Journal of Clinical Psychology, 51,* 29–34.

Grilly, D. M. (1989). *Drugs and human behavior* (pp. 135–68). Boston: Allyn & Bacon.

Grimshaw, L. (1964). Obsessional disorder and neurological illness. *Journal of Neurology, Neurosurgery and Psychiatry, 27,* 229–31.

Grinspoon, L., & Bakalar, J. B. (1976). Cocaine. New York: Basic Books.

Grinspoon, L, & Bakalar, J. B. (1986). Can drugs be used to enhance the psychotherapeutic process? *American Journal of Psychotherapy, 40,* 393–404.

Gross, H. J., & Zimmerman, J. (1965). Experimental analysis of hysterical blindness: A follow-up report and new experimental data. *Archives of General Psychiatry, 13,* 255–60.

Grossman, H. J. (Ed.) (1973). *Manual on terminology and classification in mental retardation.* Washington, DC: American Association of Mental Deficiency. (Special Publication Series, No. 2).

Grossman, H. J. (1983a). *Classification in mental retardation.* Washington, DC: American Association of Mental Deficiency.

Grossman, H. J. (Ed.). (1983b). *Manual on terminology and classification in mental retardation.* Washington, DC: American Association of Mental Deficiency.

Grove, W. M., & Andreasen, N. C. (1985). Language and thinking in psychosis. *Archives of General Psychiatry, 42,* 26–32.

Gruder, C. L., Mermelstein, R. J., Kirkendol, S., Hedeker, D., Wong, S. C., Schreckengost, J., Warnecke, R. B., Burzette, E., & Miller, T. Q. (1993). Effects of social support and relapse prevention training as adjuncts to a televised smoking-cessation intervention. *Journal of Consulting and Clinical Psychology, 61,* 113–20.

Gruder, C. L., Warnecke, R., Jason, L. A., Flay, B. R., & Peterson, P. (1990). A televised, self-help, cigarette smoking cessation intervention. *Addictive Behaviors, 15,* 505–16.

Grueneich, R. (1992). The Borderline Personality Disorder Diagnosis: Reliability, diagnostic efficiency, and covariation with other personality disorder diagnoses. *Journal of Personality Disorders, 6*(3): 197–212.

Gualtieri, C. (1991). *Neuropsychiatry and behavioral pharmacology.* New York: Springer-Verlag.

Grunbaum, A. (1984). *The foundations of psychoanalysis: A philosophical critique.* Berkeley: University of California Press.

Gunderson, J. G., & Mosher, L. R. (1975). The cost of schizophrenia. *American Journal of Psychiatry, 132,* 901–906.

Gur, R. E., Gur, R. C., Skolnick, B. E., Caroff, S., Obrist, W. D., Resnick, S., & Reivich, M. (1985). Brain function in psychiatric disorders: III. Regional cerebral blood flow in unmediated schizophrenia. *Archives of General Psychiatry, 42,* 329–34.

Gurman, A. S. (1973a). Instability of therapeutic conditions in psychotherapy. *Journal of Counseling Psychology, 20,* 16–24.

Gurman, A. S. (1973b). The effects and effectiveness of marital therapy: A review of outcome research. *Family Process, 12,* 145–70.

Gurman, A. S. (1977). Therapist and patient factors influencing the patient's perception of facilitative therapeutic conditions. *Psychiatry, 40,* 218–31.

Guze, S. B., & Robins, E. (1970). Suicide and primary affective disorders. *British Journal of Psychiatry, 17,* 437.

Hackmann, A., & McLean, C. (1975). A comparison of flooding and thought-stopping treatment. *Behavior Research and Therapy, 13,* 263–69.

Hahlweg, K., & Markman, H. J. (1988). The effectiveness of behavioral marital therapy: Empirical status of behavioral techniques in preventing and alleviating marital distress. *Journal of Consulting and Clinical Psychology, 56,* 440–47.

Halbreich, U., Endicott, J., & Nee, J. (1983). Premenstrual depressive changes. *Archives of General Psychiatry, 40,* 535–42.

Halbury's Statutes of England and Wales. (1994). *Criminal law* (Vol. 12). London: Butterworths.

Haley, J. (1969). *The power tactics of Jesus Christ.* New York: Grossman.

Halford, W. K., Sanders, M. R., & Behrens, B. C. (1993). A comparison of the generalization of behavioral marital therapy and enhanced behavioral marital therapy. *Journal of Consulting and Clinical Psychology, 61*(1): 51–60.

Hall, C. S., & Lindzey, G. (1970). *Theories of personality.* New York: Wiley.

Hall, J. (1988). Fluoxetine: Efficacy against placebo and by dose—An overview. *British Journal of Psychiatry,* 59–63.

Hall, R. V., Fox, R., Willard, D., Goldsmith, L., Emerson, M., Owen, M., Davis, T., & Porcia, E. (1971). The teacher as observer and experimenter in the modification of disputing and talking-out behaviors. *Journal of Applied Behavior Analysis, 4,* 141–49.

Hall, S. M., Rugg, D., Tunstall, C. & Jones, R. T. (1984). Preventing relapse to cigarette smoking by behavioral skill. *Journal of Consulting and Clinical Psychology, 52,* 372–82.

Hall, W., & Heather, N. (1991). Issues of statistical power in comparative evaluations of minimal and intensive controlled drinking evaluations. *Addictive Behaviors, 16*(2): 83–87.

Halpern, J. (1977). Projection: A test of the psychoanalytic hypothesis. *Journal of Abnormal Psychology, 86,* 536–42.

Hamilton, J. W. (1973). Voyeurism: Some therapeutic considerations. *International Journal of Psychotherapy, 2,* 77–91.

Hammen, C. L. & Glass, D. R. (1975). Expression, activity, and evaluation of reinforcement. *Journal of Abnormal Psychology, 84,* 718–21.

Hammen, D. L., & Padesky, C. A. (1977). Sex differences in the expression of depressive responses on the Beck Depression Inventory. *Journal of Abnormal Psychology, 86,* 609–14.

Hanada, K., & Takahashi, S. (1983). Multiaxial-institutional collaborative studies of diagnostic reliability of DSM-III. In R. Spitzer, J. Williams, & A. Skodal (Eds.), *International perspectives on DSM-III* (pp. 273–90). Washington, DC: American Psychiatric Press.

Hannum, R. D., Rosellini, R. A., & Seligman, M. E. P. (1976). Retention of learned helplessness and immunization in the rat from weaning to adulthood. *Developmental Psychology, 12,* 449–54.

Harburg, E., Erfurt, J. C., Hauenstein, L. S., Chape, C., Schull, W. J., & Schork, M. A. (1973). Socio-ecological stress, suppressed hostility, skin color, and black-white male blood pressure: Detroit. *Psychosomatic Medicine, 35,* 276.

Hardy, J. A., & Higgins, G .A. (1992). Alzheimer's disease: The amyloid cascade hypothesis. *Science, 256,* 184.

Hare, R. D. (1965). Temporal gradient of fear arousal in psychopaths. *Journal of Abnormal Psychology, 70,* 442–45.

Hare, R. (1970). *Psychopathy: Theory and research.* New York: Wiley.

Hare, R. D. (1978). Electrodermal and cardiovascular correlates of sociopathy. In R. D. Hare & D. Schalling (Eds.), *Psychopathic behavior: Approaches to research.* New York: Wiley.

Hare, R. D. (1980). A research scale for the assessment of psychopathy in criminal populations. *Personality and Individual Differences, 1,* 111–19.

Hare, R. D., Hart, S. D., & Harpur, T. J. (1991). Psychopathy and the DSM-IV criteria for antisocial personality disorder. *Journal of Abnormal Psychology, 100,* 391–98.

Hare, R. D., Williamson, S. E., & Harpur, T. J. (1988). Psychopathy and language. In T. E. Moffitt & S. A. Mednick (Eds.), *Biological contributions to crime causation* (pp. 68–92). Dordecht, the Netherlands: Martinuus Nijhoff.

Hartlage, L., Asken, M., & Hornsby, J. (1987). *Essentials of neuropsychological assessment.* New York: Springer.

Harlow, J. M. (1868). Recovery from the passage of an iron bar through the head. *Publications of the Massachusetts Medical Society, 2,* 327.

Harrington, R. (1992). Annotation: The natural history and treatment of child and adolescent affective disorders. *Journal of Child Psychology and Psychiatry, 33*(8): 1287–1302.

Harris, B. (1979). Whatever happened to little Albert? *American Psychologist, 34,* 151–60.

Harris, E. L., Noyes, R., Crowe, R. R., & Chaudry, D. R. (1983). Family study of agoraphobia. *Archives of General Psychiatry, 40,* 1061–64.

Harrison, R. (1965). Thematic apperceptive methods. In B. B. Wolman (Ed.), *Handbook of clinical psychology.* New York: Wiley.

Hartman, W. E., & Fithian, M. A. (1972). *Treatment of sexual dysfunction.* New York: Jason Aronson.

Hartmann, H. (1958). *Ego psychology and the problem of adaptation.* New York: International Universities Press.

Hasin, D. S., & Grant, B. F. (1987). Assessment of specific drug disorders in a sample of substance abuse patients: A comparison of the DIS and the DADS-L procedures. *Drug and Alcohol Dependence, 19,* 165–76.

Hathaway, S. R., & McKinley, J. C. (1943). *MMPI manual.* New York: Psychological Corporation.

Haynes, S. G., Feinleib, M., & Kannel, W. B. (1980). The relationship of psychosocial factors to coronary heart disease in the Framingham study: III. Eight years incidence in coronary heart disease. *American Journal of Epidemiology, 3,* 37–85.

Hawley, G. A. (1988). *Measures of psychosocial development: Professional manual.* Odessa, FL: Psychological Assessment Resources.

Hazell, P., & Lewin, T. (1993). An evaluation of postvention following adolescent suicide. *Suicide and Life-Threatening Behavior, 23,* 101–9.

Hazelrigg, M. D., Cooper, H. M., & Borduin, C. M. (1987). Evaluating the effectiveness of family therapies: An integrative review and analysis. *Psychological Bulletin, 101* (3): 428–42.

Heatherton, T. F., & Baumeister, R. F. (1991). Binge eating as escape from self-awareness. *Psychological Bulletin 110*(1): 86–108.

Hecaen, H., & Albert, M. L. (1978). *Human neuropsychology.* New York: Wiley.

Hecker, M., Chesney, M., Black, G., & Frautschi, N. (1988). Coronary-prone behaviors in the Western Collaborative Group Study. *Psychosomatic Medicine, 50,* 153–64.

Heider, F. (1958). *The psychology of interpersonal relationships.* New York: Wiley.

Heilbrun, A. B., Jr. (1993). Hallucinations. In C. G. Costello (Ed.), *Symptoms of schizophrenia* (pp. 56–91). New York: Wiley.

Heilman, K. M. (1979). The neuropsychological basis of skilled movement in man. In M. Gazzaniga (Ed.), *Handbook of behavioral neurobiology: Vol. 2. Neuropsychology* (pp. 447–61). New York: Plenum.

Heiman, J. R., & LoPiccolo, J. (1983). Clinical outcome of sex therapy. *Archives of General Psychiatry, 40,* 443–49.

Heinicke, C. M. (1973). Parental deprivation in early childhood: A predisposition to later depression. In J. P. Scott & E. C. Senay (Eds.), *Separation and depreciation.* Washington, DC: American Association for the Advancement of Science.

Heitler, J. (1973). Preparation of lower class patients for expressive group psychotherapy. *Journal of Consulting and Clinical Psychology, 41,* 260–61.

Hellekson, C. J., Kline, J. A., & Rosenthal, N. E. (1986). Phototherapy for seasonal affective disorder in Alaska. *American Journal of Psychiatry, 143,* 1035–37.

Helsing, K. J., Szklo, M., & Comstock, G. W. (1981). Factors associated with mortality after widowhood. *American Journal of Public Health, 71,* 802–809.

Hemsley, R., Howlin, P., Berger, M., Hersov, L., Holbrook, D., Rutter, M., & Yule, W. (1978). Treating autistic children in a family context. In M. Rutter & E. Schopler (Eds.), *Autism: A reappraisal of concepts and treatment.* New York: Plenum.

Hendin, H. (1969). Black suicide. *Archives of General Psychiatry, 21,* 407–22.

Hendin, H. (1974). Students on heroin. *Journal of Nervous Mental Disorders, 156,* 240–55.

Henker, B., & Whalen, C. K. (1989). Hyperactivity and attention deficits. *American Psychologist, 44*(2): 216–23.

Henningfield, J. E. (1984). Pharmacological basis and treatment of cigarette smoking. *Journal of Clinical Psychiatry, 45,* 24–34.

Henningfield, J. E., & Goldberg, S. R. (1983). Nicotine as a reinforcer in human subjects and laboratory animals. *Pharmacology, Biochemistry and Behavior, 19,* 989–92.

Henningfield, J. E., & Goldberg, S. R. (1985). Stimulus properties of nicotine in animals and human volunteers: A review. In L. Seiden & R. L. Balster (Eds.), *Behavioral pharmacology: The current status* (pp. 433–49). New York: Alan Liss.

Henningfield, J. E., & Jasinski, D. R. (1983). Human pharmacology of nicotine. *Psychopharmacological Bulletin, 19,* 413–15.

Henry, J. (1992). Toxicity of antidepressants: Comparison with fluoxetine. *International Clincial Psychopharmacology, 6* (Suppl. 6): 22–27.

Hentschel, E., Brandstetter, G., Dragosics, B., et al. (1993). Effect of rantidine and amoxicillin plus metronidazole on the eradication of Heliobacter pylori and the recurrence of duodenal ulcer. *New England Journal of Medicine, 328,* 308–12.

Herbert, J. D., Hope, D. A., & Bellack, A. S. (1992). Validity of the distinction between generalized social phobia and avoidant personality disorder. *Journal of Abnormal Psychology, 101*(2): 332–39.

Herek, G. (1988). Heterosexuals' attitudes toward lesbians and gay men: Correlates and gender differences. *Journal of Sex Research, 25,* 451–77.

Herkenham, M., Lynn, A. B., Little, M. D., Johnson, M. R., Melvin, L. S., de Costa, B. ., & Rice, K. C. (1990). Cannabinoid receptor localization in brain. *Proceedings of the National Academy of Sciences U.S.A., 87,* 1932–36.

Herman, C. P., & Mack, D. (1975). Restrained and unrestrained eating. *Journal of Personality, 43,* 647–60.

Hermelin, B., & O'Connor, N. (1970). *Psychological experiments with autistic children.* Oxford: Pergamon.

Herrnstein, R. (1969). Method and theory in the study of avoidance. *Psychological Review, 76,* 49–69.

Herson, M., Eisler, R. M., Alford, G. S., & Agras, W. S. (1973). Effects of token economy on neurotic depression: An experimental analysis. *Behavior Therapy, 4,* 392–97.

Hersov, L. (1976). Emotional disorders. In M. Rutter & L. Hersov (Eds.), *Child psychiatry: Modern approaches.* Oxford: Blackwell.

Hesselbrock, V., Meyer, R., & Hesselbrock, M. (1992). Psychopathology and addictive disorders: The specific case of antisocial personality disorder. In C. P. O'Brien & J. H. Jaffe (Eds.), *Addictive states.* New York: Raven Press.

Heston, L. L. (1966). Psychiatric disorders in foster home reared children of schizophrenic mothers. *British Journal of Psychiatry, 112,* 819–25.

Heston, L. L. (1970). The genetics of schizophrenia and schizoid disease. *Science, 167,* 249–56.

Heston, L. L., & Denney, D. (1968). Interactions between early life experience and biological factors in schizophrenia. In D. Rosenthal & S. S. Kety (Eds.), *The transmission of schizophrenia* (pp. 363–76). New York: Pergamon.

Hetherington, E. M., & Martin, B. (1979). Family interaction. In H. C. Quay & J. S. Werry (Eds.), *Psychopathological disorders of childhood.* New York: Wiley.

Higgins, S. T., Budney, A. J., Bickel, W. K., Hughes, J. R., Foerg, F., & Badger, G. (1993). Achieving cocaine abstinence with a behavioral approach. *American Journal of Psychiatry, 150* (5): 763–69.

Higley, J. D., Hasert, M. F., Suomi, S. J., & Linnoila, M. (1991). Nonhuman primate model of alcohol abuse: Effects of early experience, personality and stress on alcohol consumption. *Proceedings of the National Academy of Sciences U.S.A., 88,* 7261–65.

Hilgard, E. R. (1965). *Hypnotic susceptibility.* New York: Harcourt Brace Jovanovich.

Hilgard, E. R. (1977). *Divided consciousness: Multiple controls in human thought and action.* New York: Wiley.

Hill, P. O. (1972). Latent aggression and drug-abuse: An investigation of adolescent personality factors using an original cartoon-o-graphic aggressive tendencies test. *Dissertation Abstracts International, 33,* 1765.

Hilts, P. J. (1994a). Cigarette makers dispute reports on addictiveness. *New York Times,* April 15, p. A1.

Hilts, P. J. (1994b). Is nicotine addictive? It depends on whose criteria you use. *New York Times,* August 2, pp. C1, C3.

Hiroto, D. S. (1974). Locus of control and learned helplessness. *Journal of Experimental Psychology, 102,* 187–93.

Hiroto, D. S., & Seligman, M. E. P. (1975). Generality of learned helplessness in man. *Journal of Personality and Social Psychology, 31,* 311–27.

Hirst, W. (1982). The amnesic syndrome: Descriptions and explanations. *Psychology Bulletin, 91,* 1480–83.

Hobson, R. P. (1986). The autistic child's appraisal of expressions of emotion. *Journal of Childhood Psychology and Psychiatry, 27,* 321–42.

Hodgson, R., Rachman, S., & Marks, I. (1972). The treatment of chronic obsessive-compulsive neurosis. *Behavior Research and Therapy, 10,* 181–89.

Hoehn-Saric, R., Frank, J. D., Imber, S. D., Nash, E. H., Stone, A. R., & Battle, C. C. (1964). Systematic preparation of patients for psychotherapy I. Effects on therapy behavior and outcome. *Journal of Psychiatric Research, 2,* 267–81.

Hoenig, J., & Kenna, J. C. (1974). The nosological position of transsexualism. *Archives of Sexual Behavior, 3,* 273–87.

Hoffman, J. L., & Frank, H. (1987). Borderline empathy and borderline pathology: Constitutional considerations. *Comprehensive Psychiatry, 28,* 412–15.

Hofmann, A. (1968). Psychotomimetic agents. In A. Burger (Ed.), *Drugs affecting the central nervous system* (Vol. 2). New York: Marcel Dekker.

Hogan, R. (1969). Development of an empathy scale. *Journal of Consulting and Clinical Psychology, 33,* 307–16.

Hogarty, G. E., Anderson, C. M., Reiss, D. J., Kornblith, S. J., Greenwald, D. P., Javna, C. D., & Madonia, M. J. (1986). Family psychoeducation, social skills training and maintenance chemotherapy in the aftercare treatment of schizophrenia: I. One-year effects of a controlled study on relapse and expressed emotion. *Archives of General Psychiatry, 43,* 633–42.

Hogarty, G. E., Anderson, C. M., Reiss, D. J., Kornblith, S. J., Greenwald, D. P., Ulrich, R. F., & Carter, M. (1991). Family psychoeducation, social skills training, and maintenance chemotherapy in the aftercare treatment of schizophrenia: II. Two-year effects of a controlled study on relapse and adjustment. *Archives of General Psychiatry, 48,* 340–47.

Hokanson, J. E. (1961). The effects of frustration and anxiety on aggression. *Journal of Abnormal and Social Psychology, 62,* 346.

Hokanson, J. E., & Burgess, M. (1962). The effects of three types of aggression on vascular processes. *Journal of Abnormal and Social Psychology, 65,* 446–49.

Hokanson, J. E., Willers, K. R., & Koropsak, E. (1968). Modification of autonomic responses during aggressive interchange. *Journal of Personality, 36,* 386–404.

Holden, C. (1986a). Manic-depression and creativity. *Science, 233,* 725.

Holden, C. (1986b). Youth suicide: New research focuses on a growing social problem. *Science, 233,* 839–41.

Holden, C. (1987). Creativity and the troubled mind. *Psychology Today, 21,* 9–10.

Hollander, E., Schiffman, E., Cohen, B., et al. (1990). Signs of central nervous system dysfunction in obsessive-compulsive disorder. *Archives of General Psychiatry, 47,* 27–32.

Hollingshead, A. B., & Redlich, F. C. (1958). *Social class and mental illness: A community study.* New York: Wiley.

Hollister, L. E. (1962). Drug-induced psychoses and schizophrenic reactions: A critical comparison. *Annals of the New York Academy of Sciences, 96,* 80–89.

Hollister L. E. (1973). *Clinical uses of psychotherapeutic drugs.* Springfield, IL: Charles C. Thomas.

Hollister, L.E. (1986). Health aspects of cannabis. *Pharmacological Reviews, 38,* 1–20.

Hollon, S. D., DeRubeis, R. J., & Evans, M. D. (1990). Combined cognitive therapy and pharmacotherapy in the treatment of depression. In D. W. Manning & A. J. Frances (Eds.), *Combined pharmacotherapy and psychotherapy for depression.* Washington, DC: American Psychiatric Press.

Hollon, S. ., DeRubeis, R. J., Evans, M. D., & Weimer, M. J. (1992). Cognitive therapy and pharmacotherapy for depression: Singly and in combination. *Archives of General Psychiatry 49* (10): 774–81.

Hollon, S. D., & Kendall, P. C. (1980). Cognitive self-statements in depression: Development of an automatic thoughts questionnaire. *Cognitive Therapy and Research, 4,* 383–95.

Hollon, S. D., Kendall, P. C., & Lumry, A. (1986). Specificity of depressotypic cognitions in clinical depression. *Journal of Abnormal Psychology, 95,* 52–59.

Holmes, D. (1990). The evidence for repression: An example of sixty years of research. In J. Singer (Ed.), *Repression and dissociation: Implications for personality theory, psychopathology, and health* (pp. 85–102). Chicago: University of Chicago Press.

Holmes, G. (1935). Treatment of syphilis of the nervous system. *British Medical Journal, 3909,* 1111–14.

Holmes, T. H., & Rahe, R. H. (1967). The social readjustment ratings scale. *Journal of Psychosomatic Research, 11,* 213–18.

Holt, C. S., Heimberg, R. G., & Hope, D. A. (1992). Avoidant personality disorder and the generalized subtype in social phobia. *Journal of Abnormal Psychology, 102,* 318–25.

Holtzman, W. H. (1961). *Inkblot perception and personality: Holtzman Inkblot Technique.* Austin: University of Texas Press.

Hooker, W. D., & Jones, R. T. (1987). Increased susceptibility to memory intrusions and the Stroop interference effect during acute marijuana intoxication. *Psychopharmacology, 91,* 20–24.

Hope, H., Jonas, J., & Jones, B. (1982). Factitious psychosis: Phenomenology, family history, and long-term outcome of nine patients. *American Journal of Psychiatry, 139,* 1480–83.

Horne, A. S., & Snyder, S. H. (1971). Chlorpromazine and dopamine: Conformational similarities that correlate with the antischizophrenic activity of phenothiazine drugs. *Proceedings of the National Academy of Sciences, 68,* 2325–28.

Horne, R. L., & Picard, R. S. (1979). Psychosocial risk factors for lung cancer. *Psychosomatic Medicine, 41,* 503–14.

Horney, K. (1945). *Our inner conflicts: A constructive theory of neurosis.* New York: Norton.

Horowitz, L. M., Post, D. L., French, R. de S., Wallis, K. D., & Seigelman, E. Y. (1981). The prototype as a construct in abnormal psychology: 2. Clarifying disagreement in psychiatric judgments. *Journal of Abnormal Psychology, 90,* 568–74.

Horowitz, L. M., Rosenberg, S. E., & Bartholomew, K. (1993). Interpersonal problems, attachment styles, and outcome in brief psychotherapy. *Journal of Consulting and Clinical Psychology, 61*(4): 549–60.

Horowitz, M. (1975). Intrusive and repetitive thoughts after experimental stress. *Archives of General Psychiatry. 32,* 1457–63.

Horowitz, M., Stinson, C., Curtis, D., et al. (1993). Topic and signs: Defensive control of emotional expression. *Journal of Consulting and Clinical Psychology, 61,* 421–30.

Horter, D. H. (1989). Neuropsychological status of asymptomatic individuals seropositive to HIV-1. *Annals of Neurology, 26,* 589–91.

Horvath, A. D., & Greenberg, L. D. S. (1989). Development and validation of the working alliance inventory. *Journal of Consulting and Clinical Psychology, 36,* 223–33.

Horvath, A. D., & Luborsky, L. (1993). The role of the therapeutic alliance in psychotherapy. *Journal of Consulting and Clinical Psychology, 61* (4): 561–73.

Houts, A. C. (1991). Nocturnal enuresis as a biobehavioral problem. *Behavior Therapy, 22,* 133–51.

Hrubec, Z., & Omenn, G. S. (1981). Evidence of genetic predisposition to alcohol cirrhosis and psychosis: Twin concordances for alcoholism and its biological end points by zygosity among male veterans. *Alcoholism: Clinical and Experimental Research, 5,* 207–12.

Hudson, J. I., Pope, H. G., Jonas, J. M., & Yurgelun-Todd, D. (1987). A controlled family history study of bulimia. *Psychological Medicine, 17*(4): 883–90.

Huesmann, L. R., Eron, L. D., Lefkowitz, M. M., & Walder, L. O. (1984). Stability of aggression over time and generations. *Developmental Psychology, 20,* 1120–34.

Hugdahl, K., & Ohman, A. (1977). Effects of instruction on acquisition and extinction of electrodermal response to fear-relevant stimuli. *Journal of Experimental Psychology: Human Learning and Memory, 3*(5): 608–18.

Hung, D. W., Rotman, Z., Consentino, A., & MacMillan, M. (1983). Cost and effectiveness of an educational program for autistic children using a systems approach. *Education and Treatment of Children, 6*(1): 47–68.

Hunt, C., & Singh, M. (1991). Generalized anxiety disorder. *International Review of Psychiatry, 3,* 215–29.

Hunt, D. D., & Hampson, J. L. (1980). Transsexualism: A standardized psychosocial rating format for the evaluation of results of sex reassignment surgery. *Archives of Sexual Behavior, 9,* 225–63.

Hunt, D. D., & Hampson, J. L. (1980). Follow-up of 17 biologic male transsexuals after sex-reassignment surgery. *American Journal of Psychiatry, 137,* 432–38.

Hunt, E., Browning, P., & Nave, G. (1982). A behavioral exploration of dependent and independent mildly mentally retarded adolescents and their mothers. *Applied Research in Mental Redardation, 3,* 141–50.

Hunt, J. McV., & Cofer, C. N. (1944). Psychological deficit. In J. McV. Hunt & C. N. Cofer (Eds.), *Personality and the behavior disorders* (Vol. 2, pp. 971–1032). New York: Ronald.

Hunt, M. (1974). *Sexual behavior in the 1970's.* New York: Dell.

Hunt, W. A., Barnett, L. W., & Branch, L. G. (1971). Relapse rates in addiction programs. *Journal of Clinical Psychology, 27,* 455–56.

Hunter, R., & McAlpine, I. (1963). *Three hundred years of psychiatry.* London: Hogarth Press.

Huston, A. (1985). The development of sex typing: Themes from recent research. *Developmental Review, 5,* 1–17.

Hutchings, B., & Mednick, S. A. (1977). Criminality in adoptees and their adoptive and biological parents: A pilot study. In S. A. Mednick & K. O. Christiansen (Eds.), *Biosocial bases of criminal behavior* (pp. 127–41). New York: Gardner Press.

Hygge, S., & Ohman, A. (1978). Modeling processes in the acquisition of fear: Vicarious electrodermal conditioning to fear-relevant stimuli. *Journal of Personality and Social Psychology, 36* (3): 271–79.

Hyler, S. E., & Spitzer, R. T. (1978). Hysteria split asunder. *American Journal of Psychiatry, 135,* 1500–1504.

Hyman, B. T., Van Hoesen, G. W., Damasio, A. R., & Barnes, C. L. (1984). Alzheimer's disease: Cell-specific pathology isolates the hippocampal formation. *Science, 225,* 1168–70.

Iacono, W. G., Moreau, M., Beiser, M., Fleming, J. A. E., & Lin, R. Y. (1992). Smooth-pursuit eye tracking in first-episode psychotic patients and their relatives. *Journal of Abnormal Psychology, 101,* 104–16.

Imber, S. D., Pilkonis, P. A., Sotsky, S. M., & Elkin, I. (1990). Mode-specific effects among three treatments for depression. *Journal of Consulting and Clinical Psychology 58*(3): 352–59.

Imboden, J. B., Cantor, A., & Cluff, L. E. (1961). Convalescence from influenza: The study of the psychological and clinical determinants. *Archives of Internal Medicine, 108,* 393–99.

Ingham, R. J., Andrews, G., & Winkler, R. (1972). Stuttering: A comparative evaluation of the short-term effectiveness of four treatment techniques. *Journal of Communicative Disorders, 5,* 91–117.

Insel, T. R. (1992). Toward a neuroanatomy of obsessive-compulsive disorder. *Archives of General Psychiatry, 49,* 739–44.

Ironson, M., Taylor, F., Boltwood, M., et al. (1992). Effects of anger on left ventricle rejection fraction in coronary artery disease. *American Journal of Cardiology, 70,* 281–85.

Irwin, M., Daniels, M., Bloom, E. T., Smith, T. L., & Weiner, H. (1987). Life events, depressive symptoms, and immune function. *American Journal of Psychiatry, 144,* 437–41.

Ishii, N., & Nishihara Y. (1985). Pellagra encephalopathy among tuberculous patients: Its relation to isoniazid therapy. *Journal of Neurology, Neurosurgery, and Psychiatry, 48,* 628–38.

Iverson, S. D., & Iverson, L. L. (1975). *Behavioral pharmacology.* New York: Oxford University Press.

Jablensky, A., Sartorius, N., Ernberg, G., Anker, M., Korten, A., Cooper, J.E., Day, R., & Bertelsen, A. (1992). Schizophrenia: Manifestations, incidence, and course in different cultures. A World Health Organization ten-country study. *Psychological Medicine* (Monograph Supplement 20): 1–97.

Jackson, J. H. (1884). Croonian lectures on evolution and dissolution of the nervous system. *British Medical Journal, 1,* 591.

Jacobs, B. L. (1987). How hallucinogenic drugs work. *American Scientist, 75,* 386–92.

Jacobs, W. J., & Nadel, L. (1985). Stress-induced recovery of fears and phobias. *Psychological Review, 92,* 512–31.

Jacobson, E. (1971). *Depression: Comparative studies of normal, neurotic and psychotic conditions.* New York: International Universities Press.

Jacobson, N. S. (1981). Behavioral marital therapy. In A. S. Gurman & D. P. Kniskern (Eds.), *Handbook of family therapy.* New York: Brunner/Mazel.

Jacobson, N. (1992). Behavior couple therapy: A new beginning. *Behavior Therapy, 23,* 493–506.

Jacobson, N. S., & Addis, M. E. (1993). Research on couples and couple therapy: What do we know? Where are we going? *Journal of Consulting and Clinical Psychology, 61*(1): 85–93.

Jaffe, J. H. (1985). Drug addiction and drug abuse. In A. J. Goodman & L. S. Gilman (Eds.), *The pharmacological basis of therapeutics.* New York: Macmillan.

Jahoda, M. (1958). *Current concepts of positive mental health.* New York: Basic Books.

James, R. M. (1959). Jurors' assessment of criminal responsibility. *Social Problems, 7,* 58–67.

James, W. (1890). *The principles of psychology.* New York: Henry Holt.

Janicak, P. G., Davis, J. M., Gibbons, R. D., Ericksen,S., Chang, S., & Gallagher, P. (1985). Efficacy of ECT: A meta-analysis. *American Journal of Psychiatry, 142,* 297–302.

Janssen, R. S., Saykin, A. J., Cannon, L., et al. (1989). Neurological and neuropsychological manifestation of HIV-1 infection: Association with AIDS-related complex but not asymptomatic HIV-1 infection. *Annals of Neurology, 26,* 592–600.

Jarvik, M. F. (1979). Biological influences on cigarette smoking. In N. A. Krasnegor (Ed.), *The behavioral aspects of smoking.* Washington, DC: National Institute on Drug Abuse.

Jaycox, L., Reivich, K., Gillham, J., & Seligman, M. (1994). Prevention of depressive symptoms in school children. *Behaviour Research and Therapy,* in press.

Jaynes, J. (1977). *The origin of consciousness in the breakdown of the bicameral mind.* Boston: Houghton Mifflin.

Jefferson, J. (1990). Lithium: The present and the future. *Journal of Clinical Psychiatry, 5,* 4–8.

Jeffrey, R., Adlis, S., & Forster, J. (1991). Prevalence of dieting among working men and women: The healthy worker project. *Health Psychology, 10,* 274–81.

Jellenek, E. (1960). *The disease concept of alcoholism.* Highland Park, NJ: Hillhouse.

Jenike, M., Baer, L., Ballantine, T., et al. (1991). Cingulotomy for refractory obsessive-compulsive disorder. *Archives of General Psychiatry, 48,* 548–55.

Jenike, M., Baer, L., Summergrad, P., et al. (1989). Obsessive-compulsive disorder: A double-blind, placebo-controlled trial of clomipramine in 27 patients. *American Journal of Psychiatry, 146,* 1328–30.

Jenkins, C. D. (1982). Psychosocial risk factors for coronary heart disease. *Acta Medica Scandinavia Supplimentum, 660,* 123–36.

Jenkins, C. D., Rosenman, R. H., & Friedman, M. (1967). Development of an objective psychological test for the determination of the coronary prone behavior pattern in employed men. *Journal of Chronic Disease, 20,* 371–79.

Jens, K. S., & Evans, H. I. (1983, April). The diagnosis and treatment of multiple personality clients. Workshop presented at the Rocky Mountain Psychological Association, Snowbird, Utah.

Jensen, L., Gambles, D., & Olsen, J. (1988). Attitudes toward homosexuality: A cross-cultural analysis of predictors. *The International Journal of Social Psychiatry, 34,* 47–57.

Jerome, J. (1880). Intern's syndrome. In *Three men in a boat, not to mention the dog.*

Jerome, J. (1979, January 14). Catching them before suicide. *The New York Times Magazine.*

Jeste, D. V., & Caligiuri, M. P. (1993). Tardive dyskinesia. *Schizophrenia Bulletin, 19,* 303–15.

Johnsen, J., & Morland, J. (1991). Disulfiram implant: A double-blind placebo controlled follow-up on treatment outcome. *Alcoholism: Clinical and Experimental Research, 15,* 532–38.

Johnson, H., Olafsson, K., Andersen, J., Plenge, P., et al. (1989). Lithium every second day. *American Journal of Psychiatry, 146,* 557.

Jones. (1955). In W. F. Bynum, Jr., Rationales for therapy in British psychiatry, 1780–1835. In A. Scull (Ed.), *Madhouses, mad-doctors, and madmen: The social history of psychiatry in the Victorian era* (pp. 35–57). Philadelphia: University of Pennsylvania Press.

Jones, E. E., & Zoppel, C. L. (1982). Impact of client and therapist gender on psychotherapy process and outcome. *Journal of Consulting and Clinical Psychology, 50,* 259–72.

Jones, R. T., & Benowitz, N. (1976). The 30–day trip: Clinical studies of cannabis tolerance and dependence. In M. C. Braude & S. Szara (Eds.), *Pharmacology of marihuana* (Vol. 2, pp. 627–42). New York: Academic Press.

Jourard, S. M. (1974). *Healthy personality: An approach from the viewpoint of humanistic psychology.* New York: Macmillan.

Joyce, P., Bushnell, J., Oakley-Browne, M., & Wells, J. (1989). The epidemiology of panic symptomatology and agoraphobic avoidance. *Comprehensive Psychiatry, 30,* 303–12.

Junginger, J., Barker, S., & Coe, D. (1992). Mood themes and bizarreness of delusions in schizophrenia and mood psychosis. *Journal of Abnormal Psychology, 101*(2): 287–92.

Kabat-Zinn, J., Massion, A., Kristeller, J., et al. (1992). Effectiveness of meditation-based stress reduction program in the treatment of anxiety disorders. *American Journal of Psychiatry, 149,* 937–43.

Kaffman, M. (1986). The Israeli high-risk study: Some critical remarks. *Schizophrenia Bulletin, 12,* 151–57.

Kahn, M. (1973). Social class and schizophrenia: A critical review and a reformulation. *Schizophrenia Bulletin, 1,* 60–74.

Kahoe, M., & Ironside, W. (1963). Studies on the experimental evocation of depressive responses under hypnosis. II. The influence of depressive responses on the secretion of gastric acid. *Psychosomatic Medicine, 25,* 403.

Kaij, L. (1960). *Studies on the etiology and sequels of abuse and alcohol.* Lund, Sweden: University of Lund.

Kalin, N. H., Shelton, S. E., & Barksdale, C. M. (1988). Opiate modulation of separation-induced distress in non-human primates. *Brain Research, 440,* 285–92.

Kamen-Siegel, L., Rodin, J., Seligman, M., & Dwyer, J. (1991). Explanatory style and cell-mediated immunity in elderly men and women. *Health Psychology, 10,* 229–35.

Kamin, L. J. (1974). *The science and politics of IQ.* Potomac, MD: Erlbaum.

Kamphaus, R. W. (1993). *Clinical assessment of children's intelligence.* Boston: Allyn & Bacon.

Kandel, E., Schwartz, J. H., & Jessel, T. M. (Eds.). (1991). *Principles of neural science* (3rd ed). New York: Elsevier.

Kane, J. M., Honigfeld, G., Singer, J., & Meltzer, H. Y. (1988). Clozapine for the treatment-resistant schizophrenic: A double-blind comparison with chlorpromazine. *Archives of General Psychiatry, 45,* 789–96.

Kane, J. M., & Marder, S. R. (1993). Psychopharmacologic treatment of schizophrenia. *Schizophrenia Bulletin, 19,* 287–302.

Kanfer, F. H., & Grimm, L. G. (1976). The future of behavior modification. In W. E. Craighead, A. E. Kazdin, & M. J. Mahoney (Eds.), *Behavior modification: Principles, issues and applications.* Boston: Houghton Mifflin.

Kanfer, F. H., & Karoly, P. (1972). Self-control. A behavioristic excursion into the lion's den. *Behavior Therapy, 3,* 398–416.

Kanfer, F. H., & Saslow, G. (1969). Behavioral analysis. In C. M. Franks (Ed.), *Behavior therapy: Appraisal and status.* New York: McGraw-Hill.

Kanner, A. D., Coyne, J. C., Schaefer, C., & Lazarus, R. S. (1981). Comparison of two modes of stress measurement: Minor daily hassles and uplifts vs. major life events. *Journal of Behavioral Medicine, 4,* 1–39.

Kanner, L. (1943). Autistic disturbances of affective contact. *Nervous Child, 2,* 217–50.

Kanter, R. A., Williams, B. E., & Cummings, C. (1992). Personal and parental alcohol abuse, and victimization in obese binge eaters and nonbingeing obese. *Addictive Behaviors, 17*(5): 439–45.

Kaplan, H. S. (1974). *The new sex therapy.* New York: Brunner/Mazel.

Kaplan, S. M., Gottschalk, L. A., Magliocco, D., Rohobit, D., & Ross, W. D. (1960). Hostility in hypnotic "dreams" of hypertensive patients. (Comparisons between hypertensive and normotensive groups and within hypertensive individuals.) *Psychosomatic Medicine, 22,* 320.

Karasek, R., Baker, D., Marxer, F., Ahlbom, A., & Theorell, T. (1981). Job decision latitude, job demand, and cardiovascular disease: A prospective study of Swedish men. *American Journal of Public Health, 71,* 694–705.

Karlsson, J. L. (1972). An Icelandic family study of schizophrenia. In A. R. Kaplan (Ed.), *Genetic factors in schizophrenia* (pp. 246–55). Springfield, IL: Charles C. Thomas.

Kasl, S. V. (1983). Pursuing the link between stressful life experiences and disease: A time for reappraisal. In C. L. Cooper (Ed.), *Stress research: Issues for the eighties.* New York: Wiley.

Kasl, S. V., & Cob, S. (1979). Blood pressure changes in men undergoing job loss: A preliminary report. *Psychosomatic Medicine, 32,* 19–38.

Kaslow, N. J., Tannenbaum, R. L., Abramson, L. Y., Peterson, C., & Seligman, M. E. P. (1983). Problem solving deficits and depressive symptoms among children. *Journal of Abnormal Child Psychology.*

Kass, F., Spitzer, R. L., & Williams, J. B. W. (1983). An empirical study of the issue of sex bias in the diagnostic criteria of DSM-III axis II personality disorders. *American Psychologist, 38,* 799–801.

Katchadourian, H. A., & Lunde, D. T. (1972). *Fundamentals of human sexuality.* New York: Holt, Rinehart & Winston.

Katz, B. (1952). The nerve impulse. *Scientific American, 187,* 55–64.

Katz, M., Lorr, M., & Rubinstein, E. (1958). Remainder patient attributes and their relation to subsequent improvement in psychotherapy. *Journal of Consulting Psychology, 22,* 411–13.

Katz, R. J., DeVeaugh-Geiss, J., & Landau, P. (1990a). Clinical predictors of treatment response in obsessive-compulsive disorder: Explanatory analyses from multicenter trials of clomipramine. *Psychopharmacology Bulletin, 26,* 54–59.

Katz, R., DeVeaugh-Geiss, J., & Landau, P. (1990b). Clomipramine in obsessive-compulsive disorder. *Biological Psychiatry, 28,* 401–14.

Kaufman, I. C., & Rosenblum, L. A. (1967). Depression in infant monkeys separated from their mothers. *Science, 155,* 1030–31.

Kazdin, A. E. (1979). Nonspecific treatment factors in psychotherapy outcome research. *Journal of Consulting and Clinical Psychology, 47,* 846–51.

Kazdin, A. E., & Wilcoxon, L. A. (1976). Systematic desensitization and nonspecific treatment effects: A methodological evaluation. *Psychological Bulletin, 83*(5): 729–58.

Kazdin, A. E., & Wilson, G. T. (1978). *Evaluation of behavior therapy: Issues, evidence, and research strategies.* Cambridge, MA: Ballinger.

Keck, P., Cohen, B., Baldessarini, R., & McElroy, S. (1989). Time course of antipsychotic effects of neuroleptic drugs. *American Journal of Psychiatry, 146,* 1289–92.

Keefe, J. A., & Magaro, P. A. (1980). Creativity and schizophrenia: An equivalence of cognitive processing. *Journal of Abnormal Psychology, 89,* 390–98.

Keeton, W. T. (1980). *Biological science* (3rd ed.). New York: Norton.

Kegan, R. (1986). Pathology in moral development. In W. H. Reid, D. Dorr, J. I. Walker, & J. W. Bonner, III (Eds.), *Unmasking the psychopath: Antisocial personality and related syndromes.* New York: Norton.

Kehoe, M., & Ironside W. (1963). Studies on the experimental evocation of depressive responses using hypnosis: II. The influence upon the secretion of gastric acid. *Psychosomatic Medicine, 25,* 403–19.

Keinan, G. & Hobfoll, S. E. (1989). Stress, dependency and social support: Who benefits from husbands' presence in delivery? *Journal of Social and Clinical Psychology, 8,* 32–44.

Keith, S. J., Gunderson, J. G., Reifman, A., Buchsbaum, S., & Mosher, L. R. (1976). Special report: Schizophrenia, 1976. *Schizophrenia Bulletin, 2,* 510–65.

Keith-Spiegel, P. (1977). Violation of ethical principles due to ignorance or poor professional judgment versus willful disregard. *Professional Psychology, 8,* 288–96.

Keller, M. B., & Baker, C. A. (1991). Bipolar disorder: Epidemiology, course, diagnosis, and treatment. *Bulletin of the Menninger Clinic, 55*(2): 172–81.

Keller, M. B., Beardslee, W. R., Dorer, D. J., Lavori, P. W., Samuelson, H., & Klerman, G. R. (1986). Impact of severity and chronicity of parental affective illness on adaptive functioning and psychopathology in children. *Archives of General Psychiatry, 43,* 930–37.

Keller, M. B., Lavori, P. W., Mueller, T. I., Endicott, J., et al. (1992). Time to recovery, chronicity, and levels of psychopathology in major depression: A 5-year prospective follow-up of 431 subjects. *Archives of General Psychiatry, 49*(10):809–16.

Keller, M., & Shapiro, R. (1982). "Double depression": Superimposition of acute depressive episodes on chronic depressive disorders. *American Journal of Psychiatry, 139,* 438–42.

Kelley, H. H. (1967). Attribution theory in social psychology. In D. Levine (Ed.), *Nebraska Symposium on Motivation* (pp. 192–240). Lincoln: Dot Nebraska Press.

Kendall, P., Williams, L., Pechacek, T., Graham, L., Shisslac, C., & Hertzoff, N. (1979). Cognitive, behavioral and patient education interventions in cardiac catheterization procedures: The Palo Alto medical psychology project. *Journal of Consulting and Clinical Psychology, 47,* 49–58.

Kendell, R. E. (1991). Relationship between the DSM-IV and the ICD-10. *Journal of Abnormal Psychology, 100*(3): 297–301.

Kendler, K. S., & Diehl, S. R. (1993). The genetics of schizophrenia. *Schizophrenia Bulletin, 19,* 261–86.

Kendler, K. S., & Gruenberg, A. M. (1982). Genetic relationship between paranoid personality disorder and the "schizophrenic spectrum" disorders. *American Journal of Psychiatry, 139,* 1185–86.

Kendler, K. S., & Gruenberg, A. M. (1984). An independent analysis of the Danish adoption study of schizophrenia: VI. The relationship between psychiatric disorders as defined by DSM-III in the relatives and adoptees. *Archives of General Psychiatry, 41,* 555–64.

Kendler, K. S., Kessler, R., Neale, M., Heath, A., & Eaves, L. (1993). The prediction of major depression in women: Toward an integrated etiologic model. *American Journal of Psychiatry, 150,* 1139–48.

Kendler, K., Neale, M., Kessler, R., & Heath, A. (1992). Generalized anxiety disorder in women: A population-based twin study. *Archives of General Psychiatry, 49,* 267–72.

Kenyon, F. E. (1965). Hypochondriasis: A survey of some historical, clinical and social aspects. *British Journal of Psychiatry, 38,* 117.

Kernberg, O. F. (1975). *Borderline conditions and pathological narcissism.* New York: Jason Aronson.

Kerr, T. A., Roth, M., Schapira, K., & Gurney, C. (1972). The assessment and prediction of outcome in affective disorders. *British Journal of Psychiatry, 121,* 167.

Kertesz, A. (1982). Two case studies: Broca's brain and Wernicke's aphasia. In M. A. Arbib, D. Caplan, & J. C. Marshall (Eds.), *Neural models of language processes.* New York: Academic Press.

Kessler, R., McGonagle, K., Zhao, S., et al. (1994). Lifetime and 12-month prevalence of DSM-III-R psychiatric disorders in the United States: Results from the National Comorbity Survey. *Archives of General Psychiatry, 51,* 8–19.

Kety, J. (1974). Biochemical and neurochemical effects of electroconvulsive shock. In M. Fink, S. Kety, & J. McGough (Eds.), *Psychology of convulsive therapy.* Washington, DC: Winston.

Kety, S. S. (1974). From rationalization to reason. *American Journal of Psychiatry, 131,* 957–63.

Kety, S., Rosenthal, D., Wender, P. H., & Schulsinger, F. (1968). The types and prevalence of mental illness in the biological and adoptive families of adopted schizophrenics. In D. Rosenthal & S. S. Kety (Eds.), *The transmission of schizophrenia.* New York: Pergamon Press.

Kiecolt-Glaser, J., Dura, J., Speicher, C., Trask, J., & Glaser, R. (1991). Spousal caregivers of dementia victims: Longitudinal changes in immunity and health. *Psychosomatic Medicine, 53,* 345–62.

Kiecolt-Glaser, J. K., Garner, W., Speicher, C., Penn, G. M., Holliday, J., & Glaser, R. (1984). Psychosocial modifiers of immunocompetence in medical students. *Psychosomatic Medicine, 46,* 7–14.

Kiecolt-Glaser, J. K., & Glaser, R. (1987). Psychosocial moderators of immune function. *Annals of Behavioral Medicine, 9,* 16–20.

Kiely, J. L., Paneth, N., & Susser, M. (1981). Low birthweight, neonatal care and cerebral palsy: An epidemiological review. In P. J. Mittler & J. M. deJong (Eds.), *Frontiers in mental retardation: II: Biomedical aspects.* Baltimore, MD: University Park Press.

Kiesler, C. A. (1980). Mental health policy as a field of inquiry for psychology. *American Psychologist, 35,* 1066–80.

Kiesler, C. A. (1982a). Mental hospitals and alternative care: Noninstitutionalization as potential public policy for mental patients. *American Psychologist, 37,* 349–60.

Kiesler, C. A. (1982b). Public and professional myths about mental hospitalization: An empirical reassessment of policy-related beliefs. *American Psychologist, 37,* 1323–39.

Kilpatrick, D., Resnick, P., & Veronen, L. (1981). Effects of a rape experience: A longitudinal study. *Journal of Social Issues, 37,* 105–22.

Kilpatrick, D., Saunders, B., Amick-McMullan, A., et al. (1989). Victim and crime factors associated with the development of crime-related post-traumatic stress disorder. *Behavior Therapy, 20,* 199–214.

Kilpatrick, D., Saunders, B., Veronen, L., Best, C., & Von, J. (1987). Criminal victimization: Lifetime prevalence, reporting to police, and psychological impact. *Crime and Delinquency, 33,* 479–89.

King, S., & Phillips, S. (1985). Problem-solving characteristics of process and reactive schizophrenics and affective-disordered patients. *Journal of Abnormal Psychology, 94*(1): 17–29.

Kinsey, A. C., Pomeroy, W. D., & Martin, C. E. (1948). *Sexual behavior in the human male.* Philadelphia: Saunders.

Kinsey, A. C., Pomeroy, W. D., Martin, C. E., & Gebhard, P. H. (1953). *Sexual behavior in the human female.* Philadelphia: Saunders.

Kirigin, K., Wolf, M. M., Braukman, C. J., Fixsen, D. L., & Phillips, E. L. (1979). Achievement Place: A preliminary outcome evaluation. In J. S. Stumphauzer (Ed.), *Progress in behavior therapy with delinquents.* Springfield, IL: Charles C. Thomas.

Kirigin, K. A., Braukmann, C. J., Atwater, J. D., & Wolf, M. M. (1982). An evaluation of teaching-family (Achievement Place) group homes for juvenile offenders. *Journal of Applied Behavior Analysis, 15,* 1–16.

Kirk, S. A., & Kutchins, H. (1992). *The selling of DSM: The rhetoric of science in psychiatry.* New York: Aldine de Gruyter.

Kirmayer, L. J., & Robbins, J. M. (1991). Three forms of somatization in primary care: Prevalence, co-occurrence, and sociodemographic characteristics. *Journal of Nervous and Mental Disease, 179,* 647–55.

Kittel, F., Kornitzer, M., de Backer, G., & Dramaix, M. (1982). Metrological study of psychological questionnaires with reference to social variables: The Belgian Heart Disease Prevention Project (BHDPP). *Journal of Behavioral Medicine, 5*(1): 9–35.

Kleber, H. D. (1994). Our current approach to drug abuse: Progress, problems, proposals. *The New England Journal of Medicine, 330*(5): 361–64.

Klein, D. F., & Gittelman-Klein, R. (1975). Are behavioral and psychometric changes related in methylphenidate treated, hyperactive children? *International Journal of Mental Health, 14*(1–2): 182–98.

Klein, D. F., Ross, D. C., & Cohen, P. (1987). Panic and avoidance in agoraphobia, application of path analysis to treatment studies. *Archives of General Psychiatry, 44,* 377–85.

Klein, D. N., Depue, R. A., & Slater, J. F. (1985). Cyclothymia in the adolescent offspring of parents with bipolar affective disorder. *Journal of Abnormal Psychology, 94,* 115–27.

Kleinknecht, R., & Lenz, J. (1989). Blood/injury fear, fainting and avoidance of medically related situations: A family correspondence study. *Behaviour Research and Therapy, 27,* 537–47.

Klerman, G. L. (1990). Depression and panic anxiety: The effect of depressive co-morbidity on response to drug treatment of patients with panic disorder and agoraphobia. *Journal of Psychiatric Research, 24* (Suppl. 2): 27–41.

Klerman, G. L., Endicott, J., Spitzer, R., & Hirschfeld, R. (1979). Neurotic depressions: A systematic analysis of multiple criteria and meanings. *American Journal of Psychiatry, 136,* 57–61.

Klerman, G. L., Lavori, P. W., & Rice, J., et al. (1985). Birth cohort trends in rates of major depressive disorder among relatives of patients with affective disorder. *Archives of General Psychiatry, 42* (7): 689–93.

Klerman, G. L., Rounsaville, B., Chevron, E., Neu, C., & Weissman, M. M. (1979). *Manual for short-term interpersonal therapy (IPT) of depression (fourth draft preliminary).* New Haven-Boston Collaborative Depression Project.

Klerman, G. L., Schildkraut, J., & Hassenbush, J. (1963). Clinical experience with dihydroxyphrenylalanine (dopa) in depression. *Journal of Psychiatric Research, 1,* 289–97.

Klerman, G. L., Weissman, M. M., Rounsaville, N. B., & Chevron, E. (1984). *Interpersonal psychotherapy of depression.* New York: Basic Books.

Kline, N. (1970). Monoamine oxidase inhibitors: An unfinished picaresque tale. In F. J. Ayd & H. Blackwell (Eds.), *Discoveries in biological psychiatry.* Philadelphia: Lippincott.

Klosko, J., Barlow, D., Tassarini, R., & Cerny, J. (1988). Comparison of alprazolam and cognitive behavior therapy in the treatment of panic disorder: A preliminary report. In I. Hand & H. Wittchen (Eds.), *Treatment of panic and phobias: Modes of application and variables affecting outcome.* Berlin: Springer-Verlag.

Kluft, R. (1984). Treatment of multiple personality. *Psychiatric Clinics of North America, 7,* 9–29.

Kluft, R. P. (1987). An update on multiple personality disorder. *Hospital and Community Psychiatry, 38,* 363–73.

Kluznik, J. C., Speed, N., Van Valkenberg, C., & Magraw, R. (1986). Forty-year follow-up of United States prisoners of war. *American Journal of Psychiatry, 143,* 1443–46.

Kobasa, S. C. (1979). Stressful life events, personality, and health: An inquiry into hardiness. *Journal of Personality and Social Psychology, 37,* 1–11.

Koegel, P., Burnam, A., & Farr, R.K. (1988). The prevalence of specific psychiatric disorders among homeless individuals in the inner city of Los Angeles. *Archives of General Psychiatry, 445,* 1085–92.

Koh, S. D., & Peterson, R. A. (1974). Perceptual memory for numerousness in "nonpsychotic schizophrenics." *Journal of Abnormal Psychology, 83,* 215–26.

Kohlberg, L. (1969). Stage and sequence: The cognitive developmental approach to socialization. In D. A. Goslin (Ed), *Handbook of socialization: Theory and research* (pp. 347–480). New York: Rand McNally.

Kohn, M. L. (1973). Social class and schizophrenia: A critical review and a reformulation. *Schizophrenia Bulletin, 7,* 60–79.

Kohut, H. (1971). *The analysis of the self.* New York: International Universities Press.

Kohut, H. (1977). *The restoration of the self.* New York: International Universities Press.

Kohut, H. (1978). *The search for self.* New York: International Universities Press.

Kohut, H. (1984). How does analysis cure? In P. E. Stepansky & A. Goldberg (Eds.), *Kohut's legacy: Contributions to self psychology.* Hillsdale, NJ: Analytic Press.

Kolb, B, & Whishaw, I.Q. (1990). *Fundamentals of human neuropsychology* (3rd ed). New York: Freeman.

Kolvin, I., Miller, F., Fleeting, M., & Kolvin, P. (1988). Social and parenting factors affecting criminal-offence rates: Findings from the Newcastle Thousand Family Study (1947–1980). *British Journal of Psychiatry, 152,* 80–90.

Kondas, O. (1967). The treatment of stammering in children by the shadowing method. *Behavior Research and Therapy, 5*(4): 325–29.

Koob, G. F., & Bloom, F. E. (1988). Cellular and molecular mechanisms of drug dependence. *Science, 242,* 715–23.

Koob, G. F., Mendelson, W. B., Schafer, J., Wall, T. L., Britton, K. T., & Bloom, F. E. (1989). Picrotoxin receptor ligand blocks antipunishment effects of alcohol. *Alcohol, 5,* 437–43.

Korchin, S. J. (1976). *Modern clinical psychology: Principles of intervention in the clinic and the community.* New York: Basic Books.

Korsakoff, S. S. (1889). Etude medicopsychologique sur une forme des maladies de la memoire. *Revue Philosophique, 5,* 501–30.

Kosten, T. R., Rounsaville, B. J., & Kleber, H. D. (1986). A 2.5-year follow-up of treatment retention and reentry among opioid addicts. *Journal of Substance Abuse Treatment, 3,* 181–89.

Kotsopoulos, S., & Snow, B. (1986). Conversion disorders in children: A study of clinical outcome. *Psychiatric Journal of the University of Ottawa, 11,* 134–39.

Kovacs, M., & Beck, A. T. (1977). An empirical-clinical approach towards a definition of childhood depression. In J. G. Schulterbrand & A. Raven (Ed.), *Depression in childhood: Diagnosis, treatment, and conceptual models.* New York: Raven Press.

Kovacs, M., Gatsonis, C., Paulauskas, S.L., & Richards, C. (1989). Depressive disorders in childhood: IV. A longitudinal study of comorbidity with and risk for anxiety disorders. *Archives of General Psychiatry, 46*(9): 776–82.

Kovacs, M., Rush, A. J., Beck, A. T., & Hollon, S. D. (1981). Depressed outpatient treatment with cognitive therapy or pharmaco therapy: A one year follow-up. *Archives of General Psychiatry, 38,* 33–39.

Kraepelin, E. (1919). *Dementia praecox and paraphrenia.* New York: Robert E. Krieger.

Krafft-Ebing, R. von. (1931). *Psychopathia sexualis.* New York: Physicians & Surgeons Book Co.

Kramer, P. D. (1993). *Listening to Prozac.* New York: Penguin-Viking.

Krantz, D., Helmers, K., Bairey, N., et al. (1991). Cardiovascular reactivity and mental stress-induced myocardial ischemia in patients with coronary artery disease. *Psychosomatic Medicine, 53,* 1–12.

Kraupl Taylor, F. (1966). *Psychopathology: Its causes and symptoms.* London: Butler Wells.

Kreek, M. J. (1992). Rationale for maintenance pharmacotherapy of opiate dependence. In C. P. O'Brien & J. H. Jaffe (Eds.), *Addictive states* (pp. 205–30). New York: Raven Press.

Krieckhaus, E., Donahoe, J., & Morgan, M. (1992). Paranoid schizophrenia may be caused by dopamine hyperactivity of CA1 hippocampus. *Biological Psychiatry, 31,* 560–70.

Kriegman, D., & Solomon, L. (1985). Cult groups and the narcissistic personality: The offer to heal defects in the self. *International Journal of Group Psychotherapy, 35* (2): 239–61.

Kringlen, E. (1965). Obsessional neurotics. A long-term follow-up. *British Journal of Psychiatry, 111,* 709–22.

Krull, F., & Schifferdecker, M. (1990). Inpatient treatment of conversion disorder: A clinical investigation of outcome. *Psychotherapy and Psychosomatics, 53,* 161–65.

Krystal, H. (1968). *Massive psychic trauma.* New York: International Universities Press.

Kuch, K., & Cox, B. (1992). Symptoms of PTSD in 124 survivors of the Holocaust. *American Journal of Psychiatry, 149,* 337–40.

Kugelmass, S., Marcus, J., & Schmueli, J. (1985). Psychophysiological activity in high-risk children. *Schizophrenia Bulletin, 11,* 66–73.

Kuiper, B., & Cohen-Kettenis, P. (1988). Sex reassignment surgery: A study of 141 Dutch transsexuals. *Archives of Sexual Behavior, 17,* 439–57.

Kupfer, D. J., Berger, P. A., Conger, J. J., Endicott, J., Gergen, J. A., Guze, S. B., Hollister,L. E., Keller, M. B., Laska, E. M., Prior, R. E., Robbins, H. H., Rush, A. J., & Schorr, L. B. (1984). Mood disorders: Pharmacologic prevention of recurrences. *NIH Consensus Development Conference Consensus Statement, 5* (4).

Kupfer, D., Frank, E., Perel, J., et al. (1992). Five-year outcome for maintenance therapies in recurrent depression. *Archives of General Psychiatry, 49,* 769–73.

Kurland, H. D., Yeager, C. T., & Arthur, R. J. (1963). Psychophysiologic aspects of severe behavior disorders. *Archives of General Psychiatry, 8,* 599–604.

Kutchins, H., & Kirk, S. A. (1986). The reliability of DSM-III: A critical review. *Social Work Research and Abstracts,* 3–12.

Lacey, J. I. (1950). Individual differences in somatic response patterns. *Journal of Comparative and Physiological Psychology, 43,* 338–50.

Lachman, S. J. (1972). *Psychosomatic disorders: Behavioristic interpretations.* New York: Wiley.

Lader, M. (1988). The psychopharmacology of addiction: Benzodiazepine tolerance and dependence. In M. Lader (Ed.), *The psychopharmacology of addiction.* New York: Oxford University Press.

Ladisich, W., & Feil, W.B. (1988). Empathy in psychiatric patients. *British Journal of Medical Psychology, 61,* 155–62.

Laing, R. D. (1965a). Mystification, confusion and conflict. In I. Boszormeny-Nagy & J. L. Framo (Ed.), *Intensive family therapy.* New York: Hueber Medical Division, Harper & Row.

Laing, R. D. (1965b). *The divided self.* Baltimore: Penguin.

Laing, R. D. (1967). *The politics of experience.* New York: Pantheon Books.

Laing, R. D. (1970). *Knots.* New York: Pantheon Books.

Laing, R. D., & Esterson, A. (1964). *Sanity, madness, and the family.* London: Tavistock.

Lamb, H. R. (1979). The new asylums in the community. *Archives of General Psychiatry, 36,* 129–34.

Lambert, M. J., Bergin, A. E., & Collins, J. L. (1970). Therapist-induced deterioration in psychotherapy. In A. S. Gurman & A. M. Razin (Eds.), *Effective psychotherapy: A handbook of research.* New York: Pergamon.

Lamiell, J. T. (1987). *The psychology of personality: An epidemiological inquiry.* New York: Columbia University Press.

LaMontagne, Y., & LeSage, A. (1986). Private exposure and covert sensitization in the treatment of exhibitionism. *Journal of Behavior Therapy and Experimental Psychiatry, 17* (3): 197–201.

Lamy, R. E. (1966). Social consequences of mental illness. *Journal of Consulting Psychology, 30,* 450–55.

Lando, H. A. (1977). Successful treatment of smokers with a broad-spectrum behavioral approach. *Journal of Consulting and Clinical Psychology, 45,* 361–66.

Lang, P. (1967). Fear reduction and fear behavior. In J. Schlein (Ed.), *Research in psychotherapy.* Washington DC: American Psychological Association.

Lang, P. J. (1977). Imagery in therapy: An information processing analysis of fear. *Behavior Therapy, 8* (5): 862–86.

Lang, P. J. (1979). A bio-informational theory of emotional imagery. *Psychophysiology, 92* (3): 276–306.

Langer, E. J., & Abelson, R. P. (1974). A patient by any other name . . . : Clinician group difference in labelling bias. *Journal of Consulting and Clinical Psychology, 42,* 4–9.

Langer, E. J., Janis, I., & Wolfer, J. (1975). Effects of a cognitive coping device and preparatory information on psychological stress in surgical patients. *Journal of Experimental Social Psychology, 11,* 155–65.

Langer, E. J., & Rodin, J. (1976). Effects of choice and enhanced personal responsibility for the aged: A field experiment in an institutional setting. *Journal of Personality and Social Psychology, 34,* 191–99.

Langman, M. (1974). The changing nature of the duodenal ulcer diathesis. In C. Waspell (Ed.), *Westminister Hospital Symposium on chronic duodenal ulcer* (pp. 3–12). London: Butterworth.

Lanzetta, J. T., & Orr, S. P. (1980). Influence of facial expressions on the classical conditioning of fear. *Journal of Personality and Social Psychology, 39,* 1081–87.

Lapouse, R., & Monk, M. (1959). Fears and worries in a representative sample of children. *American Journal of Orthopsychiatry, 29,* 803–18.

Laughlin, H. P. (1967). *The neuroses.* Washington, DC: Butterworth.

Law, W. A., Martin, A., Mapou, R. L., Roller, T.L., Salazar, A. M., Temoshack, L.R., & Rundell, J. R. (1994). Working memory in individuals with HIV infection. *Journal of Clinical and Experimental Neuropsychology, 16,* 173–82.

Laws, A., & Reaven, G. M. (1991). Physical activity, glucose tolerance, and diabetes in older adults. *Annals of Behavioral Medicine, 13,* 125–32.

Lazarus, A. A. (1971). *Behavior therapy and beyond.* New York: McGraw-Hill.

Lazarus, A. A. (1976). *Multimodal behavior therapy.* New York: Springer.

Lecompte, D. (1989). Psychotherapy in non-organic somatization: A comparative study. *European Journal of Psychiatry, 3,* 82–90.

Leff, J. P. (1976). Schizophrenia and sensitivity to the family environment. *Schizophrenia Bulletin, 2,* 566–74.

Leff, M. J., Roatch, J. F., & Bunney, W. E. (1970). Environmental factors preceding the onset of severe depressions. *Psychiatry, 33,* 293–311.

Lefley, H. P. (1989). Family burden and family stigma in major mental illness. *American Psychologist, 44*(3): 556–60.

Lehman, D. R., Wortman, C. B., & Williams, A. F. (1987). Long-term effects of losing a spouse or child in a motor vehicle crash. *Journal of Personality and Social Psychology, 52,* 218–31.

Lehmkuhl, G., Blanz, B., Lehmkuhl, U., & Braun-Scharm, H. (1989). Conversion disorder (DSM-III 300.11): Symptomatology and course in childhood and adolescence. *European Archives of Psychiatry and Neurological Sciences, 238,* 155–60.

Leiberman, M. A., Yalom, I. D., & Miles, M. B. (1973). *Encounter groups: First facts.* New York: Basic Books.

Lelliott, P., Marks, I., Monteiro, W., et al. (1987). Agoraphobics 5 years after imipramine and exposure: Outcome and predictors. *Journal of Nervous and Mental Diseases, 175,* 599–605.

Lemkau, P. V. (1969). The planning project for Columbia. In M. F. Shore & F. V. Mannino (Ed.), *Mental health and the community: Problems, programs and strategies.* New York: Behavioral Publications.

Lenane, M., Swedo, S., Leonard, H., et al. (1990). Psychiatric disorders in the first degree relatives of children and adolescents with obsessive compulsive disorder. *Journal of the American Academy of Child and Adolescent Psychiatry, 29,* 407–12.

Leonard, H. , Lenane, M., Swedo, S., et al. (1992). Tics and Tourette's disorder: A 2- to 7-year follow-up of 54 obsessive-compulsive children. *American Journal of Psychiatry, 149,* 1244–51.

Leonard, H. L., Swedo, S., Lenane, M., et al. (1991). A double-blind desipramine substitution during long-term clomipramine treatment in children and adolescents with obsessive-compulsive disorder. *Archives of General Psychiatry, 48,* 922–27.

Leonard, H., Swedo, S., Lenane, M., et al. (1993). A 2- to 7-year follow-up study of 54 obsessive-compulsive children and adolescents. *Archives of General Psychiatry, 50,* 429–39.

Lesser, I. M. (1985). Current concepts in psychiatry: Alexithymia. *New England Journal of Medicine, 312,* 690–92.

Lester, D. (1977). Multiple personality: A review. *Psychology, 14,* 54–59.

Lester, D. (1993). The effectiveness of suicide prevention centers. *Suicide and Life-Threatening Behavior, 23,* 263–67.

Lester, L. S., & Fanselow, M. S. (1985). Exposure to a cat produces opioid analgesia in rats. *Behavioral Neuroscience, 99,* 756–59.

LeVay, S. (1991). A difference in the hypothalamic structure between heterosexual and homosexual men. *Science, 253,* 1034–37.

Levin, A., Scheier, F., & Liebowitz, M. (1989). Social phobia: Biology and pharmacology. *Clinical Psychology Review, 9,* 129–40.

Levin, S., & Stava, L. (1987). Personality characteristics of sex offenders: A review. *Archives of Sexual Behavior, 16,* 57–79.

Levine, M., & Graziano, A. M. (1971). Intervention programs in elementary schools. In S. E. Golann & C. Eisdorfer (Eds.), *Handbook of community psychology.* New York: Appleton-Century-Crofts.

Levy, J. (1972). Lateral specialization of the human brain. Behavioral manifestations and possible evolutionary basis. In J. A. Kiger, Jr. (Ed.), *The biology of behavior* (pp. 159–80). Corvallis, OR: Oregon State University Press.

Levy, J. (1980). Cerebral asymmetry and man and the psychology of man. In M. Wittrock (Ed.), *The brain and psychology.* New York: Academic Press.

Lewine, R. R. J. (1981). Sex differences in schizophrenia: Timing or subtypes. *Psychological Bulletin, 90,* 432–44.

Lewinsohn, P. M. (1975). Engagement in pleasant activities and depression level. *Journal of Abnormal Psychology, 84,* 718–21.

Lewinsohn, P. M. (1977). The behavioral study and treatment of depression. In M. Hersen, R. M. Eisler, & P. M. Miller (Eds.), *Progress in behavior modification.* New York: Academic Press.

Lewinsohn, P. M., Clarke, G. N., Hops, H., & Andrews, J. (1990). Cognitive-behavioural treatment for depressed adolescents. *Behaviour Therapy, 21,* 385–401.

Lewinsohn, P. M., Mischel, W., Chaplin, W., & Barton, R. (1980). Social competence and depression: The role of illusory self-perceptions. *Journal of Abnormal Psychology, 89,* 203–12.

Lewinsohn, P. M., Rohde, P., Seeley, J. R., & Fischer, S. A. (1993). Age-cohort changes in the lifetime occurrence of depression and other mental disorders. *Journal of Abnormal Psychology, 102* (1): 110–20.

Lewis, J. M., Rodnick, E. H., & Goldstein, M. J. (1981). Interfamilial interactive behavior, parental communication deviance, and risk for schizophrenia. *Journal of Abnormal Psychology, 90,* 448–57.

Lewis, V., & Money, J. L. (1983). Gender identity/role: GI/R Part A: XY (androgen insensitivity) syndrome and XX (Rokitansky) syndrome of vaginal atresia compared. In L. Dennerstein & G. Burrows (Eds.), *Handbook of psychosomatic obstetrics and gynecology.* New York: Elsevier.

Lewy, A. J., Sack, L., Miller, S., & Hoban, T. M. (1987). Antidepressant and circadian phase-shifting effects of light. *Science, 235,* 352–54.

Lhermitte, F. (1983). Utilization behaviour and its relation to lesions of the frontal lobe. *Brain, 106,* 237–55.

Liberman, R. P., & Green, M. F. (1992). Whither cognitive-behavioral therapy for schizophrenia? *Schizophrenia Bulletin, 18*(1): 27–35.

Liberman, R. P., Mueser, K. T., & Wallace, C. J. (1986). Social skills training for schizophrenic individuals at risk for relapse. *American Journal of Psychiatry, 143* (4): 523–26.

Liberman, R. P., Neuchterlein, K. H., & Wallace, C. J. (1982). Social skills training and the nature of schizophrenia. In J. P. Curran & P. M. Monti (Eds.), *Social skills training: A practical handbook* (pp. 5–56). New York: Guilford Press.

Lichtenstein, E., et al. (1973). Comparison of rapid smoking, warm smoky air, and attention placebo in the modification of smoking behavior. *Journal of Consulting and Clinical Psychology, 40,* 92–98.

Lick, J., & Bootzin, R. (1975). Expectancy factors in the treatment of fear: Methodological and theoretical issues. *Psychological Bulletin, 82,* 917–31.

Lidz, T. (1975). *The origin and treatment of schizophrenic disorders.* London: Hutchinson.

Lidz, C. W., Mulvey, E. P., & Gardner, W. (1993). The accuracy of predictions of violence to others. *Journal of the American Medical Association, 269*(8): 1007–11.

Lieberman, J. A., & Koreen, A. R. (1993). Neurochemistry and neuroendocrinology of schizophrenia. *Schizophrenia Bulletin, 19,* 371–430.

Lieberman, J. A., Saltz, B. L., Johns, C. A., Pollack, S., Borenstein, M., & Kane, J. M. (1991). The effects of clozapine on tardive dyskinesia. *British Journal of Psychiatry, 158,* 503–10.

Liebowitz, M. R., Fyer, A. J., Gorman, J. M., Dillon, D., Davies, S., Stein, J. M., Cohen, B. S., & Klein, D. F. (1985). Specificity of lactate infusions in social phobia versus panic disorders. *American Journal of Psychiatry, 142,* 947–50.

Liebowitz, M. R., Gorman, J. M., Fyer, A. J., Levitt, M., Dillon, D., Levy, G., Appleby, I. L., Anderson, S., Palij, M., Davies, S. O., & Klein, D. F. (1985). Lactate provocation of panic attacks: II. Biochemical and physiological findings. *Archives of General Psychiatry, 42,* 709–19.

Lindemalm, G., Korlin, D., & Uddenberg, N. (1986). Long-term follow-up of "sex change" in 13 male-to-female transsexuals. *Archives of Sexual Behavior, 15,* 187–210.

Lindemann, E. (1944). The symptomatology and management of acute grief. *American Journal of Psychiatry, 101,* 141–48.

Linden, L. L., & Breed, W. (1976). The demographic epidemiology of suicide. In E. S. Shneidman (Ed.), *Suicidology: Contemporary developments.* New York: Grune & Stratton.

Lineberger, M., Schwartz, M. F., & Saffran, E. M. (1983). Sensitivity to grammatical structure in so-called agrammatic aphasics. *Cognition, 13,* 361–92.

Link, B., Cullen, F., & Andrews, H. (in press). Violent and illegal behavior of current and former mental patients compared to community controls. *American Sociological Review.*

Linsky, A. S., Straus, M. A., & Colby, J. P. (1985). Stressful events, stressful conditions, and alcohol problems in the United States, a partial test of Bale's Theory. *Journal of Studies on Alcohol, 33,* 979–89.

Lipowski, Z. J. (1990). Chronic idiopathic pain syndrome. *Annals of Medicine, 22,* 213–17.

Lippold, S., & Claiborn, J. M. (1983). Comparison of the Wechsler Adult Intelligence Scale and the Wechsler Adult Intelligence Scale-Revised. *Journal of Consulting and Clinical Psychology, 51,* 315.

Lipsey, M., & Wilson, D. (1993). The efficacy of psychological, educational, and behavioral treatment. *American Psychologist, 48,* 1181–1209.

Lister, R. G. (1985). The amnesic action of benzodiazepines in man. *Neuroscience and Biobehavioral Reviews, 9,* 87–94.

Lister, R. G., & Durcan, M. J. (1989). Antagonism of the intoxicating effects of ethanol by the potent benzodiazepine receptor ligand Ro 19–4603. *Brain Research, 482,* 141–44.

Littlefield, C. H., & Rushton, J. P. (1986). When a child dies: The sociobiology of bereavement. *Journal of Personality and Social Psychology, 51,* 797–802.

Livermore, J. M., & Meehl, P. E. (1967). The virtues of M'Naghten. *Minnesota Law Review. 51,* 789–856.

Livingston, H., Livingston, M., Brooks, D., & McKinlay, W. (1992). Elderly survivors of the Lockerbie air disaster. *International Journal of Geriatric Psychiatry, 7,* 725–29.

Lochman, J. E., White, K. J., & Wayland, K. K. (1991). Cognitive-behavioral assessment and treatment with aggressive children. In P. C. Kendall (Eds.), *Child and adolescent therapy.* New York: Guilford Press.

Lockyer, L., & Rutter, M. (1969). A five-to fifteen-year follow-up study of infantile psychosis. *British Journal of Psychiatry, 115,* 865–82.

Loeber, R. (1990). Development and risk factors of juvenile antisocial behavior and delinquency. *Clinical Psychology Review, 10,* 1–41.

Loeber, R., & Dishion, T. J. (1983). Early predictors of male delinquency: A review. *Psychological Bulletin, 94,* 68–99.

Loewenstein, R. J., & Ross, D. R. (1992). Multiple personality and psychoanalysis: An introduction. *Psychoanalytic Inquiry, 12,* 3–48.

Loftus, E. (1991). Made in memory: Distortions of recollection after misleading information. In G. Bower (Ed.), *Psychology of learning and motivation* (Vol. 27, pp. 187–215). New York: Academic Press.

Loftus, E. (1993). The reality of repressed memories. *American Psychologist, 48,* 518–37.

Loftus, E. (1994). The repressed memory controversy. *American Psychologist, 49,* 443–45.

Logue, C. M., & Moos, R. H. (1986). Premenstrual symptoms: Prevalence and risk factors. *Psychosomatic Medicine, 48,* 388–414.

London, P. (1969). *Behavior control.* New York: Harper & Row.

London, P. (1986). *The modes and morals of psychotherapy.* New York: Hemisphere.

London, P., & Rosenhan, D. L. (1968). Mental health: The promise of behavior science. In P. London & D. L. Rosenhan (Eds.), *Foundations of abnormal psychology* (pp. 599–619). New York: Holt, Rinehart & Winston.

Long, J. W. (1992). *The essential guide to prescription drugs.* Mount Vernon, NY: Consumers Union.

Looney, J. G., Lipp, M. G., & Spitzer R. L. (1978). A new method of classification for psychophysiological disorders. *American Journal of Psychiatry, 135,* 304–308.

Loranger, A., & Levine, P. (1978). Age of onset of bipolar affective illness. *Archives of General Psychiatry, 35,* 1345–48.

Loranger, A. W., Susman, V. L., Oldham, J. M., & Russakoff, L. M. (1987). The personality disorder examination: A preliminary report. *Journal of Personality Disorders, 1* (1): 1–13.

Losonczy, M. F., Song, I. S., Mohs, R. C., Mathe, A. A., Davidson, M., Davis, B. M., & Davis, K. L. (1986). Correlates of lateral ventricular size in chronic schizophrenia: II. Biological measures. *American Journal of Psychiatry, 143*(9): 1113–17.

Lovaas, O. I. (1966). A program for the establishment of speech in psychotic children. In J. K. Wing (Ed.), *Early childhood autism.* New York: Pergamon.

Lovaas, O. I. (1973). *Behavioral treatment of autistic children.* Morristown, NJ: General Learning Press.

Lovaas, O. I. (1987). Behavioral treatment and abnormal education and intellectual functioning in young autistic children. *Journal of Consulting and Clinical Psychology, 55,* 3–9.

Lovaas, O. I., & Simmons, J. Q. (1969). Manipulation of self-destruction in three retarded children. *Journal of Applied Behavior Analysis, 2,* 143–57.

Lovibond, S. H., & Coote, M. A. (1970). Enuresis. In C. G. Costello (Ed.), *Symptoms of psychopathology.* New York: Wiley.

Low, P. W., Jeffries, Jr., J. C. , & Bonnie, R. J. (1986). *The trial of John W. Hinckley, Jr.: A case study in the insanity defense.* Mineola, NY: Foundation Press.

Lowinger, P., & Dobie, S. (1969). What makes the placebo work? A study of placebo response rates. *Archives of General Psychiatry, 20,* 84–88.

Luborsky, L. (1972). Another reply to Eysenck. *Psychological Bulletin, 78,* 406–408.

Luborsky, L. (1984). *Principles of psychoanalytic theory: A manual for supportive expressive treatment.* New York: Basic Books.

Luborsky, L., Barber, J. P., & Beutler, L. (1993). Introduction to special section: A briefing on curative factors in dynamic psychotherapy. *Journal of Consulting and Clinical Psychology, 61*(4): 539–41.

Luborsky, L., Crits-Cristoph, P., McLellan, A. T., Woody, G., Piper, W., Liberman, B., Imber, S., & Pilkonis, P. (1986). Do therapists vary much in their success? Findings from four outcome studies. *American Journal of Orthopsychiatry, 56* (4): 501–12.

Luborsky, L., McLellan, A. T., Woody, G. E., O'Brien, C. P., & Auerbach, A. (1985). Therapist success and its determinants. *Archives of General Psychiatry, 42* (6): 602–11.

Luborsky, L., Singer, B., & Luborsky, L. (1975). Comparative studies of psychotherapies. *Archives of General Psychiatry, 32,* 995–1008.

Luckasson, R., Coulter, D.L., Polloway, E.A., Reiss, S., Schalock, R.L., Snell, M.E., Spitalnik, D.M., & Stark, J.A. (1992). *Mental retardation: Definition, classification, and systems of support.* Washington, DC: American Association on Mental Retardation.

Luria, A. (1970). The functional organization of the brain. *Scientific American, 222,* 66–78.

Luria, A. (1973). *The working brain.* New York: Basic Books.

Lykken, D. T. (1957). A study of anxiety in the sociopathic personality. *Journal of Abnormal and Social Psychology, 55,* 6–10.

Lyness, W. H., Friedle, N. M., & Moore, K. E. (1979). Destruction of dopaminergic nerve terminals in the nucleus accumbens: Effect on d-amphetamine self-administration. *Pharmacology, Biochemistry and Behavior, 11,* 553–56.

Maas, J. W. (1975). Biogenic amines and depression. *Archives of General Psychiatry, 32,* 1357–61.

Mace, N., & Rabins, P. V. (1981). *The thirty-six hour day.* Baltimore: Johns Hopkins Press.

Maccoby, E., & Jacklin, C. (1974). *The psychology of sex differences.* Stanford: Stanford University Press.

MacDonald, M. *Mystical bedlam: Madness and healing in seventeenth-century England.* Unpublished doctoral dissertation, Stanford University.

MacDonald, N. (1960). Living with schizophrenia. *Canadian Medical Association Journal, 82,* 218–21.

MacFarland, J. W., Allen, L., & Honzik, N. P. (1954). *A developmental study of the behavior problems of normal children between 21 months and 14 years.* Berkeley and Los Angeles: University of California Press.

Mackay, A. V. P. (1980). Positive and negative schizophrenic symptoms and the role of dopamine. *British Journal of Psychiatry, 137,* 379–86.

MacMillan, D. L., & Semmel, M. I. (1977). Evaluation of mainstreaming programs. *Focus on Exceptional Children, 6* (4): 8–14.

Madakasira, S., & O'Brien, K. (1987). Acute post-traumatic stress disorder in victims of a natural disaster. *Journal of Nervous and Mental Disease, 175,* 286–90.

Magaro, P. A. (1981). The paranoid and the schizophrenic: The case for distinct cognitive style. *Schizophrenia Bulletin, 7,* 632–61.

Maher, B. A. (1966). *Principles of psychopathology: An experimental approach.* New York: McGraw-Hill.

Maher, B. A. (1971). The language of schizophrenia: A review and interpretation. *British Journal of Psychiatry, 120,* 3–17.

Maher, B. A. (1974). Delusional thinking and cognitive disorder. In H. London & R. E. Nisbett (Eds.), *Thought and feeling: Cognitive alteration of feeling states.* Chicago: Aldine.

Maher, W. B., & Maher, B. (1982). The ship of fools: *Stultifera Navis* or *Ignis Fantuus? American Psychiatrist, 37,* 756–61.

Mahler, M. (1979). *The selected papers of Margaret Mahler* (Vol. 1, 2, 3). New York: Jason Aronson.

Mahoney, M. J. (1971). The self-management of covert behavior: A case study. *Behavior Therapy, 2,* 575–78.

Mahoney, M. J. (1974). *Cognition and behavior modification.* Cambridge, MA.: Ballinger.

Mahoney, M. J., & Mahoney, K. (1976). *Permanent weight control: A total solution to the dieter's dilemma.* New York: Norton.

Mahoney, M. J., & Thoresen, C. E. (1974). *Self-control: Power to the person.* Belmont, CA: Brooks/Cole.

Maier, S. F., Laudenslager, M., & Ryan, S. M. (1985). Stressor controllability, immune function, and endogenous opiates. In F. Bush & J. B. Overmier (Eds.), *Affect, conditioning, and cognition.* Hillside, NJ: Erlbaum.

Maier, S. F., & Seligman, M. E. P. (1976). Learned helplessness: Theory and evidence. *Journal of Experimental Psychology, 105* (1): 3–46.

Maier, S. F., Seligman, M. E. P., & Solomon, R. L. (1969). Pavlovian fear conditioning and learned helplessness: Effects on escape and avoidance behavior of (a) the CS-US contingency and (b) the independence of the US and voluntary responding. In Campbell & Church (Eds.), *Punishment and aversive behavior.* New York: Appleton.

Malarkey, W., Kiecolt-Glaser, J., Pearl, D., & Glaser, R. (1994). Hostile behavior during marital conflict alters pituitary and adrenal hormones. *Psychosomatic Medicine, 56,* 41–51.

Maletzky, B. M. (1974). "Assisted" covert sensitization in the treatment of exhibitionism. *Journal of Consulting and Clinical Psychology, 42,* 34–40.

Malitz, S., et al., (1984). Low dosage ECT: Electrode placement and acute physiological and cognitive effects. Special Issue: Electroconvulsive therapy. *American Journal of Social Psychiatry, 4* (4): 47–53.

Malmo, R. B., & Shagass, C. (1949). Physiological study of symptom mechanism in psychiatric patients under stress. *Psychosomatic Medicine, 11,* 25–29.

Malt, U., & Weisaeth, L. (1989). Disaster psychiatry and traumatic stress studies in Norway. *Acta Psychiatrica Scandinavica, 80,* 7–12.

Mann, J., Arango, V., & Underwood, M. (1990). Serotonin and suicidal behavior. *Annals of the New York Academy of Sciences, 600,* 476–85.

Manu, P., Lane, T. J., & Matthews, D. A. (1989). Somatization disorder in patients with chronic fatigue. *Psychosomatics, 30,* 388–95.

Marchant, R., Howlin, P., Yule, W., & Rutter, M. (1974). Graded change in the treatment of the behavior of autistic children. *Journal of Child Psychology and Psychiatry, 15,* 221–27.

Marciano, T. D. (1982). Four marriage and family texts: A brief (but telling) array. *Contemporary Sociology, 11,* 150–53.

Marcos, L. R. (1988). Understanding ethnicity in psychotherapy with Hispanic patients. *American Journal of Psychoanalysis, 48*(1): 35–42.

Marengo, J. T., Harrow, M., & Edell, W. S. (1993). Thought disorder. In C. G. Costello (Ed.), *Symptoms of schizophrenia* (pp. 27–55). New York: Wiley.

Margraf, J., Barlow, D., Clark, D., & Telch, M. (1993). Psychological treatment of panic: Work in progress on outcome, active ingredients, and follow-up. *Behaviour Research and Therapy, 31*(1): 1–8.

Margraf, J., & Schneider, S. (1991). Outcome and active ingredients of cognitive-behavioural treatments for panic disorder. Paper presented at the annual meeting of the Association for the Advancement of Behavior Therapy, New York, November 26, 1991.

Marin, O. S. M., Saffran, E., & Schwartz, M. (1976). Dissociation of language in aphasia: Implications for normal function. *Annals of the New York Academy of Science, 280,* 868–84.

Markman, H.J., Renick, M.J., Floyd, F.J., Stanley, S.M., & Clements, M. (1993). Preventing marital distress through communication and conflict management training: A 4– and 5–year follow-up. *Journal of Consulting and Clinical Psychology, 61*(1): 70–77.

Marks, I. M. (1969). *Fears and phobias.* New York: Academic Press.

Marks, I. M. (1976). The current status of behavioral psychotherapy: Theory and practice. *American Journal of Psychiatry, 133,* 253–61.

Marks, I. (1977). Phobias and obsessions: Clinical phenomena in search of laboratory models. In J. Maser & M. E. P. Seligman (Eds.), *Psychopathology: Experimental models.* San Francisco: Freeman.

Marks, I. M. (1981). Review of behavioral psychotherapy: II. Sexual disorders. *American Journal of Psychiatry, 138,* 750–56.

Marks, I. M. (1986a). Epidemiology of anxiety. *Social Psychiatry, 21,* 167–71.

Marks, I. M. (1986b). Genetics of fear and anxiety disorders. *British Journal of Psychiatry, 149,* 406–18.

Marks, I., Boulougouris, J., & Marset, P. (1971). Flooding versus desensitization in the treatment of phobic patients: A crossover study. *British Journal of Psychiatry, 119,* 353–75.

Marks, I. M., & Gelder, M. G. (1966). Common ground between behavior therapy and psychodynamic methods. *British Journal of Medical Psychology, 39,* 11–23.

Marks, I. M., Gray, S., Cohen, D., Hill, R., Mawson, D., Ramm, E., & Stern, R. S. (1983). Imipramine and brief therapist-aided exposure in agoraphobics having self-exposure homework. *Archives of General Psychiatry, 40,* 153–62.

Marks, I. M., & Rachman, S. J. (1978). Interim report to the Medical Research Council.

Marks, I., & Tobena, A. (1990). Learning and unlearning fear: A clinical and evolutionary perspective. *Neuroscience and Biobehavioral Reviews, 14,* 365–84.

Marlatt, G. A. (1983). The controlled drinking controversy: A commentary. *American Psychologist, 38,* 1097–1110.

Marlatt, G. A., & Gordon, J. R. (1980). Determinants of relapse: Implications for the maintenance of behavior change. In P. O. Davison & S. M. Davidson (Eds.), *Behavioral medicine: Changing health lifestyles.* New York: Brunner/Mazel.

Marlatt, G. A., & Gordon, J. R. (1985). *Relapse prevention.* New York: Guilford Press.

Marsella, A. J. (1982). Culture and mental health: An overview. In A. J. Marsella & G. M. White (Eds.) *Cultural conceptions of mental health and therapy* (pp. 359–88). Dordecht, Holland: D. Reidel.

Marshall, C. D. (1976). The affective consequences of "inadequately explained" physiological arousal. Unpublished doctoral dissertation, Stanford University.

Marshall, E. (1980). Psychotherapy faces test of worth. *Science, 207,* 35–36.

Marshall, W., Eccles, A., & Barbaree, H. (1991). The treatment of exhibitionists: A focus on sexual deviance versus cognitive and relationship features. *Behaviour Research and Therapy, 29,* 129–35.

Martin, A. (1987). Representation of semantic and spatial knowledge in Alzheimer's patients: Implications for models of preserved learning in amnesia. *Journal of Clinical and Experimental Neuropsychology, 9,* 191–224.

Martin, A. (1990). Neuropsychology of Alzheimer's disease: The case for subgroups. In M. F. Schwartz (Ed.), *Modular deficits in Alzheimer's-type dementia.* Cambridge, MA: MIT Press.

Martin, A., Heyes, M. P., Salazar, A. M., Law, W. A., & Williams, J. (1993). Impaired motor-skill learning, slowed reaction time, and elevated cerebro-spinal fluid guinolinic acid in a subgroup of HIV-infected individuals. *Neuropsychology, 7,* 149–57.

Martin, B. (1977). *Abnormal psychology.* New York: Holt, Rinehart & Winston.

Martin, B. (1986). Cellular effects of cannabinoids. *Pharmacological Reviews, 38,* 45–74.

Marx, M. B., Garrady, T. F., & Bowens, F. R. (1975). The influence of recent life experience on the life of college freshmen. *Journal of Psychosomatic Research, 19,* 87–98.

Maslow, A. H. (1954). *Motivation and personality.* New York: Harper & Row.

Mason, J. W. (1971). A re-evaluation of the concept of "non-specificity" in stress theory. *Journal of Psychiatric Research, 8,* 323–33.

Mason, J. W. (1975). A historical view of the stress field, Part I. *Journal of Human Stress, 1,* 6–12.

Masters, W. H., & Johnson, V. E. (1970). *Human sexual inadequacy.* Boston: Little, Brown.

Matarazzo, J. D. (1983). The reliability of psychiatric and psychological diagnosis. *Clinical Psychology Review, 3,* 103–45.

Matthews, A., & MacLeod, C. (1986). Discrimination of threat cues without awareness in anxiety states. *Journal of Abnormal Psychology, 95,* 131–38.

Matthews. K. A. (1981). Psychological perspectives on the Type A behavior pattern. *Psychological Bulletin, 90,* 293–323.

Matthews, K. A., & Haynes, S. G. (1986). Type A behavior pattern and coronary disease risk: Update and critical evaluation. *American Journal of Epidemiology, 123,* 923–60.

Matthysse, S. (1973). Antipsychotic drug actions: A clue to the neuropathology of the schizophrenias. *Federation Proceedings, 32,* 200–205.

Matthysse, S. (1977). The role of dopamine in schizophrenia. In E. Usdin, D. A. Homburg, & J. D. Barkus (Eds.), *Neuroregulators and psychiatric disorders* (pp. 3–13). New York: Oxford University Press.

Mattick, R., Andrews, G., Hadzi-Pavlovic, D., & Christensen, H. (1990). Treatment of panic and agoraphobia: An integrative review. *Journal of Nervous and Mental Disease, 178,* 567–78.

Mavissakalian, M., Jones, B., Olson, S., & Perel, J. (1990). Clomipramine in obsessive-compulsive disorder: Clinical response and plasma levels. *Journal of Clinical Psychopharmacology, 10,* 261–68.

Mavissakalian, M., & Michelson, L. (1986). Two-year follow-up of exposure and imipramine treatment of agoraphobia. *American Journal of Psychiatry, 143,* 1106–12.

Mavissakalian, M., Perel, J., Bowler, K., & Dealy, R. (1987). Trazodone in the treatment of panic disorder and agoraphobia with panic attacks. *American Journal of Psychiatry, 144,* 785–91.

May, P. R. A., Tuma, A. H., Dixon, W. J., Yale, C., Thiele, D. A., & Kraus, W. H. (1981). Schizophrenia: A follow-up study of the results of five forms of treatment. *Archives of General Psychiatry, 38,* 776–84.

May, R. (1953). *Man's search for himself.* New York: Norton.

McArthur, J. C., Cohen, B. A., Selnes, O. A., et al. (1989). Low prevalence of neurological and neuropsychological abnormalities in otherwise healthy HIV-1–infected individuals. Results from the multicenter AIDS cohort study. *Annals of Neurology, 26,* 601–10.

McCarthy, M. (1990). The thin ideal, depression, and eating disorders in women. *Behaviour Research and Therapy, 28*(3): 205–15.

McCarthy, R., & Warrington, E. K. (1990). *Cognitive neuropsychology.* London: Academic Press.

McCary, J. L. (1978). Human sexuality: Past present and future. *Journal of Marriage and Family Counseling, 4,* 3–12.

McClearn, G. E. (1968). Genetics and motivation of the mouse. In W. J. Arnold (Ed.), *Nebraska Symposium on Motivation.* Lincoln: University of Nebraska Press.

McClelland, D. C. (1979). Inhibited power motivation and high blood pressure in men. *Journal of Abnormal Psychology, 88,* 182–90.

McClelland, D. C., Atkinson, J. W., Clark, R. A., & Lowell, E. L. (1953). *The achievement motive.* New York: Appleton.

McConaghy, N. (1969). Subjective and penil plethysmograph response following aversion-relief and apomorphine aversion therapy for homosexual impulses. *British Journal of Psychiatry, 115,* 723–30.

McConaghy, N., Armstrong, M., & Blaszczynski, A. (1981). Controlled comparison of aversive therapy and covert sensitization in compulsive homosexuality. *Behaviour Research and Therapy, 19,* 425–34.

McConnell, R. B. (1966). *Genetics of gastro-intestinal disorders.* London: Oxford University Press.

McCord, J. (1979). Some child-rearing antecedents of criminal behavior in adult men. *Journal of Personality and Social Psychology, 37,* 1477–86.

McCord, J. (1980, November 5–8). Myths and realities about criminal sanctions. Paper presented at the annual meetings of the American Society of Criminology, San Francisco, CA.

McFarlane, A. (1970). *Witchcraft in Tudor and Stuart England: A regional and comparative study.* New York: Harper & Row.

McFarlane, A. (1989). The aetiology of post-traumatic morbidity: Predisposing, precipitating, and perpetuating factors. *British Journal of Psychiatry, 154,* 1221–28.

McGarry, A. L., & Bendt, R. H. (1969). Criminal vs. civil commitment of psychotic offenders: A seven year follow-up. *American Journal of Psychiatry, 125,* 1387–94.

McGhie, A. (1969). *Pathology of attention.* London: Penguin.

McGhie, A., & Chapman, J. S. (1961). Disorders of attention and perception in early schizophrenia. *British Journal of Medical Psychology, 34,* 103–16.

McGlashan, T. H. (1986a). Predictors of shorter-, medium-, and longer-term outcome in schizophrenia. *American Journal of Psychiatry, 142* (10): 50–55.

McGlashan, T. H. (1986b). Schizotypal personality disorder. Chestnut Lodge follow-up study: VI. Long-term follow-up perspectives. *Archives of General Psychiatry, 43,* 329–34.

McGlashan, T. H. (1987). Testing DSM-III symptom criteria for schizoptypal and borderline personality disorders. *Archives of General Psychiatry, 44,* 143–48.

McGlashan, T. H., & Fenton, W. S. (1992). The positive-negative distinction in schizophrenia: Review of natural history validators. *Archives of General Psychiatry, 49*(1): 63–72.

McGlothin, W. H., & West, L. J. (1968). The marihuana problem: An overview. *American Journal of Psychiatry, 125,* 370–78.

McGue, M. (1992). When assessing twin concordance, use the probandwise not the pairwise rate. *Schizophrenia Bulletin, 18,* 171–76.

McGue, M., Gottesman, I. I., & Rao, D. C. (1985). Resolving genetic models for the transmission of schizophrenia. *Genetic Epidemiology, 2,* 99–110.

McGuffin, P., & Katz, R. (1989). The genetics of depression and manic-depressive disorder. *British Journal of Psychiatry, 155,* 294–304.

McGuire, E., Shega, J., Nicholls, G., et al. (1992). Sexual behavior, knowledge, and attitudes about AIDS among college freshmen. *American Journal of Preventive Medicine, 8,* 226–34.

McGuire, R. J., Carlisle, J. M., & Young, B. G. (1965). Sexual deviation as conditioned behavior. *Behaviour Research and Therapy, 2,* 185–90.

McIntosh, J. (1989). Trends in racial differences in U.S. suicide statistics. *Death Studies, 13,* 275–86.

McKim, W. A. (1986). *Drugs and behavior.* Englewood Cliffs, NJ: Prentice-Hall.

McKinney, W. T., Suomi, S. J., & Harlow, H. F. (1972). Repetitive peer separations of juvenile age rhesus monkeys. *Archives of General Psychiatry, 27,* 200–203.

McKnew, D. H., Jr., Cytryn, L., & Yahraes, H. (1983). *Why isn't Johnny crying?* New York: Norton.

McLeod, D., Hoehn-Saric, R., Zimmerli, W., & De Souza, E. (1990). Treatment effects of alprazolam and imipramine: Physiological versus subjective changes in patients with generalized anxiety disorder. *Biological Psychiatry, 28,* 849–61.

McMillan, M. J., & Pihl, R. O. (1987). Premenstrual depression: A distinct entity. *Journal of Abnormal Psychology, 96.* 149–54.

McNally, R. J. (1987). Preparedness and phobias: A review. *Psychological Bulletin, 101,* 283–303.

McNally, R. M. (1990). Psychological approaches to panic disorder: A review. *Psychological Bulletin, 108*(3): 403–19.

McNeal, E. T., & Cimbolic, P. (1986). Antidepressants and biochemical theories of depression. *Psychological Bulletin, 99* (3): 361–74.

McNitt, P. C., & Thornton, D. W. (1978). Depression and perceived reinforcement: A consideration. *Journal of Abnormal Psychology, 87,* 137–40.

Medley, E. S. (1978). Peptic ulcer disease in children. *Journal of Family Practice, 7,* 281–84.

Mednick, B. R. (1973). Breakdown in high-risk subjects: Familial and early environmental factors. *Journal of Abnormal Psychology, 82,* 469–75.

Mednick, S. A., Brennan, P., & Kandel, E. (1988). Predisposition to violence. *Aggressive Behavior, 14,* 25–33.

Mednick, S. A., Cudeck, R., Griffith, J. J., Talovic, S. A., & Schulsinger, F. (1984). The Danish high-risk project: Recent methods and findings. In N. F. Watt, E. J. Anthony, L. C. Wynne, & J. E. Rolf (Eds.), *Children at risk for schizophrenia: A longitudinal perspective* (pp. 21–42). Cambridge: Cambridge University Press.

Mednick, S. A., Gabriella, W. F., & Hutchings, B. (1984). Genetic influences in criminal convictions: Evidence from an adoption cohort. *Science, 224,* 891–94.

Mednick, S. A., Gabriella, W. F., & Hutchings, B. (1987). Genetic factors and etiology of criminal behavior. In S. A. Mednick, T. E. Moffitt, & S. A. Stack (Eds.), *Causes of crime: New biological approaches* (pp. 74–91). New York: Cambridge University Press.

Mednick, S. A., Parnas, J., & Schulsinger, F. (1987). The Copenhagen high-risk project, 1962–1986. *Schizophrenic Bulletin, 13,* 485–95.

Mednick, S. A., & Schulsinger, F. (1968). Some premorbid characteristics related to breakdown in children with schizophrenic mothers. In D. Rosenthal & S. S. Kety (Eds.), *The transmission of schizophrenia.* Elmsford, NY: Pergamon.

Medvedev, Z. A., & Medvedev, R. A. (1971). *A question of madness.* New York: Knopf.

Meehl, P. E. (1986). Diagnostic taxa as open concepts: Metatheoretical and statistical questions about reliability and construct validity in the grand strategy of nosological revision. In T. Millon & G. L. Klerman (Eds.), *Contemporary directions in psychopathology: Toward the DSM-IV* (pp. 215–31). New York: Guilford Press.

Meichenbaum, D. (1977). *Cognitive-behavior modification.* New York: Plenum.

Meichenbaum, D., Gilmore, B., & Fedoravicius, A. (1971). Group insight vs. desensitization in treating speech anxiety. *Journal of Consulting and Clinical Psychology, 36,* 410–21.

Meissner, W. W. (1978). The conceptualization of marriage and family dynamics from a psychoanalytic perspective. In T. J. Paolino & B. S. McCrady (Eds.), *Marriage and marital therapy.* New York: Brunner/Mazel.

Mellsop, F. & Varghese, F. (1983). An Australian study reflecting on the reliability and validity of Axis II. In R. Spitzer, J. Williams, & A. Skodal (Eds.), *International perspectives on DSM-III.* Washington, DC: American Psychiatric Press.

Melton, G.B., Petrila, J., Poythress, N.G., & Slobogin, C. (1987). *Psychological evaluations for the courts.* New York: Guilford Press.

Melton, G. B., Weithorn, L. A., & Slobogin, C. (1985). *Community mental health centers and the courts.* Lincoln, NE: University of Nebraska Press.

Melzack, R. (1973). *The puzzle of pain.* New York: Basic Books.

Mendels, J. (1970). *Concepts of depression.* New York: Wiley.

Mendels, J., & Cochran, C. (1968). The nosology of depression: The endogenous-reactive concept. *American Journal of Psychiatry, 124,* Supplement 1–11.

Mendelsohn, F., & Ross, M. (1959). An analysis of 133 homosexuals seen at a university health service. *Diseases of the Nervous System, 20,* 246–50.

Mendelsohn, G. A., & Geller, M. H. (1963). Effects of counselor-client similarity on the outcome of counseling. *Journal of Counseling Psychology, 10,* 71–77.

Mendelsohn, G. A., & Geller, M. H. (1967). Similarity, missed sessions, and early termination. *Journal of Counseling Psychology, 14,* 210–15.

Mercer, J. (1979). *The system of multicultural pluralistic assessment: Conceptual and technical manual.* New York: The Psychological Corporation.

Mercer, J. R., & Lewis, J. E. (1978). *Adaptive behavior inventory for children.* New York: The Psychological Corporation.

Merikangas, K. R., Leckman, J. F., Prusoff, B. A., Pauls, D. L., & Weissman, M. M. (1985). Familial transmission of depression and alcoholism. *Archives of General Psychiatry, 42,* 367–72.

Merton, R. K. (1957). *Social theory and social structure.* Glencoe, IL: Free Press.

Mesulam, M. M. (1981). A cortical network for directed attention and unilateral neglect. *Annals of Neurology, 10,* 309–24.

Metalsky, G. I., Halberstadt, L. J., Abramson, L. Y. (1987). Vulnerability to depressive mood reactions: Toward a more powerful test of the diathesis-stress and causal mediation components of the reformulated theory of depression. *Journal of Personality and Social Psychology, 52* (2): 386–93.

Meyer, C. B., & Taylor, S. E. (1986). Adjustment to rape. *Journal of Personality and Social Psychology, 50,* 1226–34.

Meyer, V. (1966). Modification of expectations in cases with obsessional rituals. *Behaviour Research and Therapy, 4,* 273–80.

Meyer, V., & Mair, J. M. M. (1963). A new technique to control stammering: A preliminary report. *Behavior Research Therapy, 1,* 251–54.

Meyer-Bahlburg, H., Feldman, J., Cohen, P., & Ehrhardt, A. (1988). Perinatal factors in the development of gender-related play behavior: Sex hormones versus pregnancy complications. *Psychiatry, 51,* 260–71.

Meyers, A. W., & Craighead, W. E. (Eds.) (1984). *Cognitive behavior therapy with children.* New York: Plenum Press.

Mezzich, J. E., Fabrega, H., Coffman, G. A., & Haley, R. (1989). DSM-III disorders in a large sample of psychiatric patients: Frequency and specificity of diagnoses. *American Journal of Psychiatry, 146,* 212–19.

Michelson, L., & Marchione, K. (1989). Cognitive, behavioral, and physiologically based treatments of agoraphobia: A comparative outcome study. Paper presented at the annual meeting of the American Association for the Advancement of Behavior Therapy, Washington, DC, November 1989.

Midelfort, H. C. E. (1972). *Witch-hunting in Southwestern Germany, 1562–1684.* Stanford, CA: Stanford University Press.

Miklowitz, D. J. (1994). Family risk indicators in schizophrenia. *Schizophrenia Bulletin, 20,* 137–49.

Miklowitz, D. J., Strachan, A. M., Goldstein, M. J., Doane, J. A., Snyder, K. S., Hogarty, G. E., & Falloon, I. R. H. (1986). Expressed emotion and communication deviance in the families of schizophrenics. *Journal of Abnormal Psychology, 95* (1): 60–66.

Miller, D., & Dawson, W. H. (1965). Effects of stigma on reemployment of ex-mental patients. *Mental Hygiene, 49,* 281–87.

Miller, L. (1986). Talking or signing ups blood pressure. *Psychology Today,* June, p. 18.

Miller, L. L., & Branconnier, R. J. (1983). Cannabis: Effects on memory and the cholinergic system. *Psychological Bulletin, 93,* 441–56.

Miller, N. E. (1969). Learning of visceral and glandular responses. *Science, 163,* 434.

Miller, N. E. (1985). The value of behavioral research on animals. *American Psychologist, 40,* 423–40.

Miller, R. C., & Berman, J. S. (1983). The efficacy of cognitive behavioral therapies: A quantitative review of the research. *Psychological Bulletin, 94,* 39–53.

Miller, S. M. (1978). Controllability in human stress. In M. E. P. Seligman & J. G. Garber (Eds.), *Human helplessness: Theory and application.* New York: Academic Press.

Miller, W. R., & Seligman, M. E. P. (1975). Depression and learned helplessness in man. *Journal of Abnormal Psychology, 84,* 228–38.

Miller, W. R., & Seligman, M. E. P. (1976). Learned helplessness, depression, and the perception of reinforcement. *Behavior Research and Therapy, 14,* 7–17.

Milner, B. (1964). Some effects of frontal lobectomy in man. In J. M. Warren & K. Akert (Eds.), *The frontal granular cortex and behavior.* New York: McGraw-Hill.

Milner, B. (1966). Amnesia following operation on the temporal lobes. In C. W. M. Whitty & O. L. Zangwill (Eds.), *Amnesia.* London: Butterworth.

Milner, B. (1970). Memory and the medial temporal regions of the brain. In K. H. Pribram & D. E. Broadbent (Eds.), *Biology of memory.* New York: Academic Press.

Milner, B. (1972). Disorders of learning and memory after temporal lobe lesions in man. *Clinical Neurosurgery, 19,* 421–46.

Mineka, S. (1985). Animal models of anxiety-based disorders: Their usefulness and limitations. In A. H. Tuma & J. D. Maser (Eds.), *Anxiety and the anxiety disorders* (pp. 199–244). Hillsdale, NJ: Erlbaum.

Mineka, S., Davidson, M., Cook, M., & Keir, R. (1984). Observational conditioning of snake fear in rhesus monkeys. *Journal of Abnormal Psychology, 93* (4): 355–72.

Minuchin, S. (1974). *Families and family therapy.* Cambridge, MA: Harvard University Press.

Minuchin, S., Rosman, B. L., & Baker, L. (1980). *Psychosomatic families: Anorexia nervosa in context.* Cambridge: Harvard University Press.

Miranda, J., Perez-Stable, E. J., Munoz, R. F., Hargreaves, W., et al. (1991). Somatization, psychiatric disorder, and stress in utilization of ambulatory medical services. *Health Psychology, 10,* 46–51.

Mirsky, A. F., & Duncan-Johnson, C. (1984). Nature versus nurture in schizophrenia—the struggle continues. *Integrative Psychiatry, 2,* 137–48.

Mirsky, A. F., Silberman, E. K., Latz, A., & Nagler, S. (1985). Adult outcomes of high-risk children: Differential effects of town and kibbutz rearing. *Schizophrenia Bulletin, 11,* 150–54.

Mirsky, I. A. (1958). Physiologic, psychologic, and social determinants of the etiology of duodenal ulcer. *American Journal of Digestive Diseases, 3,* 285–314.

Mirsky, I. A., Futterman, P., & Kaplan, S. (1952). Blood plasma pepsinogen. II. The activity of the plasma from "normal" subjects, patients with duodenal ulcer and patients with pernicious anemia. *Journal of Laboratory and Clinical Medicine, 40,* 198–99.

Mischel, H. N., & Mischel, W. (1973). *Readings in personality.* New York: Holt, Rinehart & Winston.

Mischel, W. (1968). *Personality and assessment.* New York: Wiley.

Mischel, W. (1973). Toward a cognitive social learning reconceptualization of personality. *Psychological Review, 80,* 252–83.

Mischel, W. (1976). *Introduction to personality* (2nd ed.). New York: Holt, Rinehart & Winston.

Mischel, W., & Baker, N. (1975). Cognitive transformations of reward objects through instructions. *Journal of Personality and Social Psychology, 31,* 254–61.

Mischel, W., & Ebbesen, E. (1970). Attention in delay of gratification. *Journal of Personality and Social Psychology, 16,* 329–37.

Mischel, W., Ebbesen, E., & Zeiss, A. R. (1972). Cognitive and attentional mechanisms in delay of gratification. *Journal of Personality and Social Psychology, 21,* 204–18.

Mischel, W., & Peake, P. K. (1982). Beyond deja vu in the search for cross-situational consistency. *Psychological Review, 89,* 730–55.

Mishkin, M., & Appenzeller, T. (1987). The anatomy of memory. *Scientific American, 256* (6): 80–89.

Mishra, S. P., & Brown, K. H. (1983). The comparability of WAIS and WAIS-R IQs and subtest scores. *Journal of Clinical Psychology, 39,* 754–57.

Mitchell, J. E. (1986). Anorexia nervosa: Medical and psychological aspects. In K. D. Brownell & J. P. Foreyt (Eds.), *Handbook of eating disorders: Physiology, psychology, and treatment of obesity, anorexia, and bulimia.* New York: Basic Books.

Mitchell, J. E., & de Zwaan, M. (1993). Pharmacological treatments of binge eating. In C. G. Fairburn & G. T. Wilson (Eds.), *Binge eating: Nature, assessment, and treatment.* New York: Guilford Press.

Mitchell, K. M., Bozarth, J. D., & Krauft, C. C. (1977). A reappraisal of the therapeutic effectiveness of accurate empathy, nonpossessive warmth, and genuineness. In A. S. Gurman & A. M. Razin (Eds.), *Effective psychotherapy: A handbook of research.* New York: Pergamon.

Mittelmann, B., Wolff, H. G., & Scharf, M. (1942). Emotions in gastroduodenal functions. *Psychosomatic Medicine, 4,* 5–61.

Mittler, P., Gillies, S., & Jukes, E. (1966). Prognosis in psychotic children. Report of follow-up study. *Journal of Mental Deficiency Research, 10,* 73–83.

Model Penal Code and Commentaries, Sec. 4.01 (Part I). (1962). Philadelphia, PA: American Law Institute, 1980.

Modell, W. (1967). Mass catastrophes and the roles of science and technology. *Science, 156,* 346–51.

Modestin, J., Schwarzenbach, F. A., & Wurmle, O. (1992). Therapy factors in treating severely ill psychiatric patients. *British Journal of Medical Psychology, 65* (2): 149–56.

Moffitt, T. E., & Silva, P. A. (1988). Self-reported delinquency, neuropsychological assessment, and history of attention deficit disorder. *Journal of Abnormal Child Psychology, 16,* 553–69.

Mohler, H., & Okada, T. (1977). Properties of 3H-diazepam binding to benzodiazepine receptors in rat cerebral cortex. *Life Science, 20,* 2101–10.

Mohs, R. D., Breitner, J. C. S., Silverman, J. M., & Davis, K. L. (1987). Alzheimer's disease: Morbid risk among first-degree relatives approximates fifty percent by ninety years of age. *Archives of General Psychiatry, 44,* 405–408.

Monahan, J. (1976). *Community mental health and the criminal justice system.* New York: Pergamon.

Monahan, J. (1992). Mental disorder and violent behavior. *American Psychologist, 47,* 511–21.

Monahan, J., & Shah, S. A. (1989). Dangerousness and commitment of the mentally disordered in the United States. *Schizophrenia Bulletin, 15* (4): 541–53.

Monahan, J., & Wexler, D. (1978). A definite maybe: Proofs and probability in civil commitment. *Law and Human Behavior, 2,* 37–42.

Money, J., & Ambinder, R. (1978). Two-year, real-life diagnostic test: Rehabilitation vs. cure. In J. P. Brady & H. K. H. Brodie (Eds.), *Controversy in psychiatry.* Philadelphia: Saunders.

Money, J., & Ehrhardt, A. A. (1972). *Man and woman, boy and girl.* Baltimore: The John Hopkins University Press.

Moody, R. L. (1946). Bodily changes during abreaction. *The Lancet, 2,* 934–35.

Moras, K., Telfer, L., & Barlow, D. (1993). Efficacy and specific effects data on new treatments: A case study strategy with mixed anxiety and depression. *Journal of Consulting and Clinical Psychology, 61,* 412–20.

Morris, P., Robinson, R., Andrzejewski, P., et al. (1993). Association of depression with 10–year post-stroke mortality. *American Journal of Psychiatry, 150,* 124–29.

Morris, R. J., & Suckerman, K. R. (1974a). The importance of the therapeutic relationship to systematic desensitization. *Journal of Consulting and Clinical Psychology, 42,* 142.

Morris, R. J., & Suckerman, K. R. (1974b). Therapist warmth as a factor in automated systematic desensitization. *Journal of Consulting and Clinical Psychology, 42,* 244–50.

Morrisey, J. P., & Levine, I. S. (1987). Conference Report: Researchers discuss latest findings, examine needs of homeless mentally ill persons. *Hospital and Community Psychiatry, 38,* 811–12.

Morrison, R. L., & Bellack, A. (1984). Social skills training. In A. S. Bellack (Ed.), *Schizophrenia, treatment, management, and rehabilitation* (pp. 247–79). Orlando, FL: Grune & Stratton.

Moscovitch, M. (1982a). Multiple dissociations of function in amnesia. In L. S. Cermak (Ed.), *Human memory and amnesia.* Hillsdale, NJ: Erlbaum.

Moscovitch, M. (1982b). A neuropsychological approach to perception and memory in normal and pathological aging. In F. I. M. Craik & S. Trehub (Eds.), *Aging and cognitive processes.* New York: Plenum.

Moscovitch, M. (1989). Confabulation and the frontal lobes: Strategic vs. associative retrieval in neuropsychological theories of memory. In H. L. Roediger III & F. I. M. Craik (Eds.), *Varieties of memory and consciousness: Essays in Honor of Endel Tulving* (pp. 133–60). Hillsdale, NJ: Erlbaum.

Moscovitch, M. (1992). Memory and working-with-memory: A component process model based on modules and central systems. *Journal of Cognitive Neuroscience, 4,* 257–67.

Moscovitch, M. (1994). Models of consciousness and memory. In M. S. Gazzaniga (Ed.), *The cognitive neurosciences.* Cambridge, MA: MIT Press.

Moscovitch, M., Vriezen, E., & Goshen-Gottstein, Y. (1994). Implicit trots of memory in patients with focal lesions and degenerative brain disorders. In F. Boller & J. Grafman (Eds.), *Handbook of neuropsychology.* Amsterdam: Elsevier.

Moscovitch, M., & Winocur, G. (1992). The neuropsychology of memory and aging. In F. I. M. Craik & T. A. Salthouse (Eds.), *The handbook of aging and cognition.* Hillsdale, NJ: Erlbaum.

Mosher, L. R., & Keith, S. J. (1980). Psychosocial treatment: Individual, group, family, and community support approaches. *Schizophrenia Bulletin, 6*(1): 10–41.

Mosher, L. R., & Menn, A. Z. (1978). Community residential treatment for schizophrenia: Two year follow-up. *Hospital and Community Psychiatry, 29,* 715–23.

Mosher, L. R., Menn, A., & Matthews, S. (1975). Soteria: Evaluation of a home-based treatment for schizophrenia. *American Journal of Orthopsychiatry 45,* 455–67.

Mowrer, O. H. (1947). On the dual nature of learning—A reinterpretation of "conditioning" and "problem-solving." *Harvard Educational Review, 17,* 102–50.

Mowrer, O. H. (1948). Learning theory and the neurotic paradox. *American Journal of Orthopsychiatry, 18,* 571–610.

Mowrer, O. H., & Mowrer, W. M. (1938). Enuresis: A method for its study and treatment. *American Journal of Orthopsychiatry, 8,* 436–59.

Mueser, K. T., Bellack, A. S., Morrison, R. L., & Wade, J. H. (1990). Gender, social competence, and symptomatology in schizophrenia: A longitudinal analysis. *Journal of Abnormal Psychology, 99*(2): 138–47.

Mueser, K. T., & Glynn, S. M. (1990). Behavioral family therapy for schizophrenia. In M. Hersen, R. M. Eisler, & P. M. Miller (Eds.), *Progress in behavior modification* (Vol. 26, pp. 122–49). Newbury Park, CA: Sage.

Mullaney, J. A., & Trippett, C. J. (1982). Alcohol dependence and phobias: Clinical description and relevance. *British Journal of Psychiatry, 135,* 565–73.

Munoz, R., Hollon, S., McGrath, E., Rehm, L., & VandenBos, G. (1994). On the AHCPR depression in primary care guidelines: Further considerations for practitioners. *American Psychologist, 49,* 42–61.

Munzinger, H. (1975). The adopted child's IQ: A critical review. *Psychological Bulletin, 80,* 623–29.

Murphy, D., Brodie, K., Goodwin, F., & Bunney, W. E. (1971). Regular induction of hypomania by L-dopa in "bipolar" manic-depressive patients. *Nature, 229,* 135–36.

Murphy, J. M., Sobol, A. M., Neff, R. K., Olivier, D. C., & Leighton, A. H. (1984). Stability of prevalence: Depression and anxiety disorders. *Archives of General Psychiatry, 41,* 990–97.

Murray, H. A. (1951). Forward. In H. H. Anderson & G. L. Anderson (Eds.), *An introduction to projective techniques.* Englewood Cliffs, NJ: Prentice-Hall.

Murstein, B. I. (1965). New thoughts about ambiguity and the TAT. *Journal of Projective Techniques and Personality Assessment, 29,* 219–25.

Musetti, L., Perugi, G., Soriani, A., & Rossi, V. (1989). Depression before and after age 65: A re-examination. *British Journal of Psychiatry, 155,* 330–36.

Myers, J. K., Weissman, M. M., Tischler, G. L., Holzer, C. E., Leaf, P. J., Orvaschel, H., Anthony, J. C., Boyd, J. H., Burke, J. D., Kramer, M., & Stolzman, R. (1984). Six-month prevalence of psychiatric disorders in three communities: 1980 to 1982. *Archives of General Psychiatry, 41,* 959–67.

Nagler, S., & Glueck, Z. (1985). The clinical interview. *Schizophrenia Bulletin, 11,* 38–47.

Nagy, A. (1987). Possible reasons for a negative attitude to benzodiazepines as antianxiety drugs. *Nordisk Psykiatrisk Tidsskrift, 4,* 27–30.

Nash, E. H., Hoehn-Saric, R., Battle, C. C., Stone, A. R., Imber, S. D., & Frank, J. D. (1965). Systematic preparation of patients for short-term psychotherapy. II. Relation to characteristics of patient, therapist and the psychotherapeutic process. *Journal of Nervous and Mental Disorders, 140,* 374–83.

Nathan, P. E. (1988). The addictive personality is the behavior of the addict. *Journal of Consulting and Clinical Psychology, 56,* 183–88.

National Household Survey on Drug Abuse. (1991). *Highlights 1991.* Washington, DC: Department of Health and Human Services.

Neary, D., Snowden, J. S., Northern, B., & Goulding, P. (1988). Dementia of frontal lobe type. *Journal of Neurology, Neurosurgery and Psychiatry, 51,* 353–61.

Nelson, C., Mazure, C., & Jatlow, P. (1990). Does melancholia predict response in major depression? *Journal of Affective Disorders, 18,* 157–65.

Nemiah, J. C. (1971). The psychophysiologic management: A treatment of patients with peptic ulcer. *Advances in Psychosomatic Medicine, 6,* 169–85.

Nesse, F. M., Cameron, O. G., Curtis, G. C., McCann, D. S., & Huber-Smith, M. J. (1984). Adrenergic function in patients with panic anxiety. *Archives of General Psychiatry, 41,* 771–76.

Nestel, P. J. (1969). Blood pressure in catecholamine excretion after mental stress in labile hypertension. *Lancet, 1*(2): 692–94.

Nestoros, J. N. (1980). Ethanol specifically potentiates GABA-mediated neurotransmission in the feline cerebral cortex. *Science, 209,* 708–10.

New York Times. (1994a). Albany plans house calls to monitor the mentally ill. *New York Times,* April 24, 1994.

New York Times. (1994b). Father who fought "memory therapy" wins damage suit. *New York Times,* May 14, 1994.

Nicol, S. E., & Gottesman, I. I. (1983). Clues to the genetics and neurobiology of schizophrenia. *American Scientist, 71,* 398–404.

Nichols, M. (1984). *Family therapy: Concepts and methods.* New York: Gardner.

Nihira, K., Foster, R., Shellhaas, M., Leland, H., Lambert, N., & Windmiller, M. (1981). *AAMD adaptive behavior scale* (school edition). Monterey, CA: Publisher's Test Service.

Ninan, P., Insel, T., Cohen, R., Cook, J., Skolnick, P., & Paul, S. (1982). Benzodiazepine receptor-mediated experimental "anxiety" in primates. *Science, 218,* 1332–34.

Nisbett, R., & Ross, L. (1980). *Human inference: Strategies and shortcomings of social judgment.* Englewood Cliffs, NJ: Prentice-Hall.

Noel, N. E., & Lisman, S. A. (1980). Alcohol consumption by college women following exposure to unsolvable problems: Learned helplessness or stress-induced drinking? *Behaviour Research and Therapy, 18,* 429–40.

Nolen-Hoeksema, S. (1988). Life-span views on depression. In P. B. Baltes, D. L. Featherman, & R. M. Lerner (Eds.), *Life span development and behavior* (Vol. 9). New York: Erlbaum.

Nolen-Hoeksema, S. (1990). *Sex differences in depression.* Stanford: Stanford University Press.

Nolen-Hoeksema, S., Girgus, J., & Seligman, M. E. P. (1986). Learned helplessness in children: A longitudinal study of depression, achievement, and explanatory style. *Journal of Personality and Social Psychology, 51,* 435–42.

Nolen-Hoeksema, S., Girgus, J., & Seligman, M. (1992). Predictors and consequences of childhood depressive symptoms: A 5-year longitudinal study. *Journal of Abnormal Psychology, 101*(3): 405–22.

Noyes, R., Chaudry, D., & Domingo, D. (1986). Pharmacologic treatment of phobic disorders. *Journal of Clinical Psychiatry, 47,* 445–52.

Noyes, R., Clarkson, C., Crowe, R., & Yates, W. (1987). A family study of generalized anxiety disorder. *American Journal of Psychiatry, 144,* 1019–24.

Noyes, R., Garvey, M., Cook, B., & Samuelson, L. (1989). Problems with tricyclic anti-depressant use in patients with panic disorder or agoraphobia. *Journal of Clinical Psychiatry, 50,* 163–69.

Noyes, R., Kathol, R. G., Fisher, M. M., & Phillips, B. M. (1993). The validity of DSM-III-R hypochondriasis. *Archives of General Psychiatry, 50* (12): 961–70.

Noyes, R., & Kletti, R. (1977). Depersonalization in response to life-threatening danger. *Comprehensive Psychiatry, 18,* 375–84.

Nyman, A. K., & Jonsson, H. (1983). Differential evaluation of outcome in schizophrenia. *Acta Psychiatrica Scandinavica, 68,* 458–75.

O'Brien, C. P., Childress, A. R., McLellan, A. T., & Ehrman, R. (1990). Integrating systematic cue exposure with standard treatment in recovering drug-dependent patients. *Addictive Behaviors, 15,* 355–65.

O'Brien, C. P., Childress, A. R., McLellan, A. T., & Ehrman, R. (1992). A learning model of addiction. In C. P. O'Brien & J. H. Jaffe (Eds.), *Addictive states* (pp. 157–78). New York: Raven Press.

Odier, C. (1956). *Anxiety and magical thinking.* New York: International Universities Press.

Offord, D. R., Boyle, M. D., Racine, Y. A., Fleming, J. E., Cadman, D. T., Blum, H. M., Byrne, C., Links, P. S., Lipman, E. L., MacMillan, H. L., Grant, N. I., Rae, D., Sanford, M. N., Szatmari, P., Thomas, H., & Woodward, C. A. (1992). Outcome, prognosis, and risk in a longitudinal follow-up study. *Journal of the Academy for Child and Adolescent Psychiatry, 31*(5): 916–23.

Oggins, J., Leber, D., & Veroff, J. (1993). Race and gender differences in Black and White newlyweds' perception of sexual and marital relations. *Journal of Sex Research, 30,* 152–60.

Ohman, A. (1979). Fear relevance, autonomic conditioning and phobias: A laboratory model. In S. Bates, W. K. Dockens, K. G. Blotesharm, L. Melin, & P. O. Sjoden (Eds.), *Trends in behavior therapy.* New York: Academic Press.

Ohman, A., Anders, E., & Olafson, C. (1975). One trial learning and superior resistance to extinction of autonomic responses conditioned to potentially phobic stimuli. *Journal of Comparative and Physiological Psychology, 88* (88), 619–27.

Ohman, A., Fredrikson, M., & Hugdahl, K. (1978). Orienting and defensive responding in the electrodermal system: Palmar-dorsal differences and recovery rate during conditioning to potentially phobic stimuli. *Psychophysiology, 2,* 93–102.

Ohman, A., Fredrikson, M., Hugdahl, K. & Per-Arne, R. (1974). A dimension of preparedness in human learning: The effect of poten-

tially phobic stimuli as CS's in electro-dermal conditioning. *Biological Psychology, 2,* 85–93.

Ohman, A., Fredrikson, M., Hugdahl, K., & Rimmo, P. (1976). The premise of equipotentiality in human classical conditioning: Conditioned electrodermal responses to potentially phobic stimuli. *Journal of Experimental Psychology-General, 105* (4): 313–37.

Ohman, A., Nordby, H., & d'Elia, G. (1986). Orienting and schizophrenia: Stimulus significance, attention, and distraction in a signaled reaction time task. *Journal of Abnormal Psychology, 95* (4): 326–34.

Ohwaki, S., & Stayton, S. E. (1978). The relation of length of institutionalization to the intellectual functioning of the profoundly retarded. *Child Development, 49,* 105–109.

Oi, M., Oshida, K., & Sugimura, A. (1959). Location of the gastric ulcer. *Gastroenterology, 36,* 45–56.

O'Leary, S. G., & Pelham, W. E. (1978). Behavior therapy and withdrawal of stimulant medication in hyperactive children. *Pediatrics, 61,* 211–17.

Olivieri, S., Cantopher, T., & Edwards, J. (1986). Two hundred years of anxiolytic drug dependence. *Neuropharmacology, 25,* 669–70.

Oltman, J., & Friedman, S. (1967). Parental deprivation in psychiatric conditions. *Diseases of the Nervous System, 28,* 298–303.

Oltmanns, T. F., & Maher, B. A. (1988). *Delusional beliefs.* New York: Wiley.

Olweus, D. (1979). Stability of aggressive reaction patterns in males: A review. *Psychological Bulletin, 86,* 852–75.

O'Malley, S., Jaffe, A. J., Chang, G., Schottenfeld, R. S., Meyer, R. E., & Rounsaville, B. (1992). Naltrexone and coping skills therapy for alcohol dependence. *Archives of General Psychiatry, 49,* 881–87.

Orenstein, H. (1989). Briquet's syndrome in association with depression and panic: A reconceptualization of Briquet's syndrome. *American Journal of Psychiatry, 146,* 334–38.

Orford, J. (1985). *Excessive appetites: A psychological view of addictions.* Chichester: John Wiley & Sons Ltd.

Orgel, S. (1985). Effects of psychoanalysis on the course of peptic ulcer. *Psychosomatic Medicine, 20,* 117–23.

Orne, M. T. (1962). On the social psychology of the psychological experiment: With particular reference to demand characteristics and their implications. *American Psychologist, 17,* 776–83.

Orne, D. R., & Boswell, D. (1991). The pre-intake drop-out at a community mental health center. *Community Mental Health Journal, 27*(5): 375–79.

Orne, M. T., Dinges, D. F., & Orne, E. C. (1984). On the differential diagnosis of multiple personality in the forensic context. *International Journal of Clinical and Experimental Hypnosis, 32,* 118–69.

Orne, M. T., & Wender, P. H. (1968). Anticipatory socialization for psychotherapy. *American Journal of Psychiatry, 124,* 1202–11.

Ornitz, E. M. (1978). Biological homogeneity or heterogeneity. In M. Rutter & E. Schopler (Eds.), *Autism: A reappraisal of concepts and treatment.* New York: Plenum.

Osler, W. (1897). *Lectures on angina pectoris and allied states.* New York: D. Appleton and Company.

Osmond, H., & Smythies, J. R. (1952). Schizophrenia: A new approach. *Journal of Mental Science, 98,* 309–15.

Öst, L.-G. (1987). Applied relaxation: Description of a coping technique and review of controlled studies. *Behaviour Research and Therapy, 25,* 397–410.

Öst, L.-G. (1991). Cognitive therapy versus applied relaxation in the treatment of panic disorder. Paper presented at the annual meeting of the European Association of Behavior Therapy, Oslo, September 1991.

Öst, L.-G., & Hugdahl, K. (1981). Acquisition of phobias and anxiety response patterns in clinical patients. *Behaviour Research and Therapy, 19,* 439–48.

Öst, L.-G., Sterner, U., & Fellenius, J. (1989). Applied tension, applied relaxation, and the combination in the treatment of blood phobia. *Behaviour Research and Therapy, 27,* 109–21.

O'Sullivan, G., Noshirvani, H., Marks, I., et al. (1991). Six-year follow-up after exposure and clomipramine therapy for obsessive-compulsive disorder. *Journal of Clinical Psychiatry, 52,* 150–55.

Overholser, J. C., & Beck, S. (1986). Multimethod assessment of rapists, child molesters, and three control groups on behavioral and psychological measures. *Journal of Consulting and Clinical Psychology, 54* (5): 682–87.

Overmier, J. B., & Seligman, M. E. P. (1967). Effects of inescapable shock upon subsequent escape and avoidance learning. *Journal of Comparative and Physiological Psychology, 63,* 23–33.

Packer, H. (1968). *The limits of the criminal sanction.* Stanford: Stanford University Press.

Palmer, R. L. (1980). *Anorexia nervosa.* New York: Penguin.

Pandya, D. N., & Barnes, C. L. (1987). Architecture and connections of the frontal lobe. In E. Perecman (Ed.), *The frontal lobes revisited* (pp. 41–72). Hillsdale, NJ: Erlbaum.

Park, L. C., Imboden, J. B., Park, T. J., Hulse, S. H., & Unger, H. T. (1992). Giftedness and psychological abuse in borderline personality disorder: Their relevance to genesis and treatment. *Journal of Personality Disorders, 6,* 226–40.

Parker, G., & Hadzi-Pavlovic, D. (1993). Prediction of response to antidepressant medication by a sign-based index of melancholia. *Australian and New Zealand Journal of Psychiatry, 27,* 56–61.

Parkes, M. C. (1964). Recent bereavement as a cause of mental illness. *British Journal of Psychiatry, 110,* 194–204.

Parkes, M. C., Benjamin, B., & Fitzgerald, R. G. (1969). Broken heart: A statistical study of increased mortality among widowers. *British Medical Journal, 1,* 740–43.

Parloff, M. B. (1976). Shopping for the right therapy. *Saturday Review, 21*(February): 14–20.

Parloff, M. B. (1979). Can psychotherapy research guide the policymaker? A little knowledge may be a dangerous thing. *American Psychologist, 34,* 296–306.

Parloff, M. B. (1982). Psychotherapy research evidence and reimbursement decisions: Bambi meets Godzilla. *American Journal of Psychiatry, 139,* 718–27.

Parloff, M. B., Waskow, I. E., & Wolfe, B. E. (1978). Research on therapist variables in relation to process and outcome. In S. L. Garfield & A. E. Bergin (Eds.), *Handbook of psychotherapy and behavior change: An empirical analysis* (2nd ed.). New York: Wiley.

Parnas, J., Cannon, T. D., Jacobsen, B., Schulsinger, H., Schulsinger, F., & Mednick, S. A. (1993). Lifetime DSM-IIIR diagnostic outcomes in the offspring of schizophrenic mothers. Results from the Copenhagen high-risk study. *Archives of General Psychiatry, 50,* 707–14.

Pasner, M. I., Walker, J. A., Friedrich, F. J., & Rafal, R. D. (1984). Effects of parietal lobe injury on covert orienting of visual attention. *Journal of Neuroscience, 4,* 1863–74.

Pato, M., Piggott, T., Hill, J., et al. (1991). Controlled comparison of buspirone and clomipramine in obsessive-compulsive disorder. *American Journal of Psychiatry, 148,* 127–29.

Pato, M., Zohar-Kadouch, R., Zohar, J., & Murphy, D. (1988). Return of symptoms after discontinuation of clomipramine in patients with obsessive-compulsive disorder. *American Journal of Psychiatry, 145,* 1521–25.

Patrick, C. J., Bradley, M., & Cuthbert, B. N. (1990). The criminal psychopath and startle modulation. *Psychophysiology, 27* (Suppl. 4A): 87.

Patrick, C. J., Cuthbert, B. N., & Lang, P. J. (1990). Emotion in the criminal psychopath: Fear imagery. *Psychophysiology, 27*(Suppl. 4A): 55.

Patterson, G. R. (1971). *Families: Applications of social learning theory to family life.* Champaign, IL: Research Press.

Patterson, G. R. (1973). Reprogramming the families of aggressive boys. In C. Thoreson (Ed.), *Behavior modification in education: 72nd Year Book, Part I.* Chicago: University of Chicago Press.

Patterson, G. R. (1975). *Families: Applications of social learning theory to family life* (2nd ed.). Champaign, IL: Research Press.

Patterson, G. R., DeBaryshe, B. D., & Ramsey, E. (1989). A developmental perspective on antisocial behavior. *American Psychologist, 44,* 329–35.

Patterson, G. R., Weiss, R. L., & Hops, H. (1976). Training of marital skills: Some problems of concepts. In H. Leitenberg (Ed.), *Handbook of behavior modification and behavior therapy.* Englewood Cliffs, NJ: Prentice-Hall.

Patterson, K., Marshall, J. C., & Coltheart, M. (Eds.). (1985). Surface dyslexia: *Cognitive and neuropsychological studies of phonological reading.* Hillsdale, NJ: Erlbaum.

Patterson, T., Spohn, H. E., Bogia, D. P., & Hayes, K. (1986). Thought disorder in schizophrenia: Cognitive and neuroscience approaches. *Schizophrenia Bulletin, 12* (3): 460–72.

Pattie, F. A. (1967). A brief history of hypnotism. In J. E. Gordon (Ed.), *Handbook of clinical and experimental hypnosis.* New York: Macmillan.

Paul, G. L. (1966). Insight vs. desensitization in psychotherapy. Stanford: Stanford University Press.

Paul, G. L. (1967). Insight vs. desensitization in psychotherapy two years after termination. *Journal of Consulting Psychology, 31* (4): 333–48.

Pauly, I. B. (1969). Adult manifestation of male transsexualism. In R. Green & J. Money (Eds.), *Transsexualism and sex reassignment.* Baltimore: The Johns Hopkins Press.

Pauly, I. B. (1974). Female transsexualism. *Archives of Sexual Behavior, 3,* 487–526.

Pavel, O. (1990). *How I came to know fish* (trans. J. Baclai & R. McDowell). New York: Story Line Press/New Directions.

Paykel, E. S. (1973). Life events and acute depression. In J. P. Scott & E. C. Senay (Eds.), *Separation and depression.* AAAS.

Paykel, E. S. (1974a). Recent life events and clinical depression. In E. K. E. Gunderson & R. H. Rahe (Eds.), *Life stress and illness* (pp. 150–51). Springfield, IL: Charles C. Thomas.

Paykel, E. S. (1974b). Life stress and psychiatric disorder: Application of the clinical approach. In B. P. Dohrenwend & B. S. Dohrenwend (Eds.), *Stressful life events: Their nature and effects* (pp. 135–49). New York: Wiley.

Paykel, E. S., Meyers, J. K., Dienelt, M. N., Klerman, J. L., Lindenthal, J. J., & Pfeffer, M. P. (1969). Life events and depression. *Archives of General Psychiatry, 21,* 753–60.

Payne, R. W. (1966). The measurement and significance of over-inclusive thinking and retardation in schizophrenic patients. In P. H. Hoch & J. Zubin (Eds.), *Psychopathology of schizophrenia* (pp. 77–79). New York: Grune & Stratton.

Payne, R. W., & Hewlett, J. H. G. (1960). Thought disorder in psychotic patients. In H. J. Eysenck (Ed.), *Experiments in personality* (Vol. 2, pp. 3–104). London: Routledge & Kegan Paul.

Pecknold, J., Swinson, R., Kuch, K., & Lewis, C. (1988). Alprazolam in panic disorder and agoraphobia: Results from a multicenter trial: III. Discontinuation effects. *Archives of General Psychiatry, 45,* 429–36.

Pedersen, N., McClearn, G., Plomin, R., Nesselroade, J., Berg, J., & DeFaire, U. (1994). The Swedish adoption/ twin study of aging: An update. *Acta Geneticae Medicae et Gemellologiae,* in press.

Peele, S. (1985). *The meaning of addiction: Compulsive experience and its interpretation.* Lexington, MA: Lexington Books.

Pelham, W.E. (1989). Behavioral therapy, behavioral assessment, and psychostimulant medication in the treatment of attention deficit disorder: An interactive approach. In J. Swanson & I. Bloomingdale (Eds.), *Attention deficit disorder: IV. Current concepts and emerging trends in attentional and behavioral disorders of childhood* (pp. 169–95). New York: Pergamon.

Pennebaker, J. W. (1985). Traumatic experience and psychosomatic disease: Exploring the roles of behavioural inhibition, obsession, and confiding. *Canadian Psychology, 26,* 82–95.

Pennebaker, J. (1990). *Opening up.* New York: Morrow.

Perkins, K. A., & Reyher, J. (1971). Repression, psychopathology and drive representation: An experimental hypnotic investigation of impulse inhibition. *American Journal of Clinical Hypnosis, 13,* 249–58.

Perley, M. J., & Guze, S. B. (1962). Hysteria: The stability and usefulness of clinical criteria. *New England Journal of Medicine, 266,* 421–26.

Perris, C. (1968). The course of depressive psychosis. *Acta Psychiatrica Scandinavica, 44,* 238–48.

Perry, S., Frances, A., & Clarkin, J. (1990). *A DSM-III-R case book of treatment selection.* New York: Brunner/Mazel.

Persons, J. B. (1986). The advantages of studying psychological phenomena rather than psychiatric diagnoses. *American Psychologist, 41,* 1252–60.

Peterson, C., Luborsky, L., & Seligman, M. E. P. (1983). Attributions and depressive mood shifts: A case study using the symptom-context method. *Journal of Abnormal Psychology, 92,* 96–103.

Peterson, C., Maier, S., & Seligman, M. (1993). *Learned helplessness.* New York: Oxford University Press.

Peterson, C., & Seligman, M. E. P. (1984). Explanatory style and depression: Theory and evidence. *Psychological Review.*

Peterson, C., & Seligman, M. E. P. (1987). Explanatory style and illness. Special Issue: Personality and physical health. *Journal of Personality, 55* (2): 237–65.

Peterson, C., Seligman, M. E. P., & Vaillant, G. (1988). Pessimistic explanatory style as a risk factor for physical illness: A 35-year longitudinal study. *Journal of Personality and Social Psychology, 55,* 23–27.

Peterson, D. R. (1978). *The clinical study of social behavior.* New York: Appleton.

Petursson, H., & Lader, M. H. (1981). Withdrawal from long-term benzodiazepine treatment. *British Medical Journal, 283,* 643–45.

Petzel, T. P., & Johnson, J. E. (1972). Time estimation by process and reactive schizophrenics under crowded and uncrowded conditions. *Journal of Clinical Psychology, 28*(3): 345–47.

Pfafflin, F. (1992). Regrets after sex reassignment surgery. Special Issue: Gender dysphoria: Interdisciplinary approaches in clinical management. *Journal of Psychology and Human Sexuality, 5*(4): 69–85.

Pfohl, B. (1991). Histrionic personality disorder: A review of available data and recommendations for DSM-IV. *Journal of Personality Disorders, 5*(2): 150–66.

Phares, E. J. (1976). *Locus of control in personality.* Morristown, NJ: General Learning Press.

Phares, E. J., Wilson, K. G., & Klyrer, N. W. (1971). Internal-external control and the attribution of blame under neutral and distractive conditions. *Journal of Personality and Social Psychology, 18,* 286–88.

Piggott, T., Pato, M., Bernstein, S., et al. (1990). Controlled comparisons of clomipramine and fluoxetine in the treatment of obsessive-compulsive disorder. *Archives of General Psychiatry, 47,* 926–32.

Place, E. J. S., & Gilmore, G. C. (1980). Perceptual organization in schizophrenia. *Journal of Abnormal Psychology, 89,* 409–18.

Plante, T. G., & Rodin, J. (1990). Physical fitness and enhanced psychological health. *Current Psychology: Research and Reviews, 9,* 3–24.

Platt, J. J., & Labate, C. (1976). *Heroin addiction.* New York: Wiley.

Plomin, R., Corley, R., DeFries, J., & Fulker, D. (1990). Individual differences in television viewing in early childhood: Nature as well as nurture. *Psychological Science, 1,* 371–77.

Plomin, R., Scheier, M., Bergeman, C., Pedersen, N., Nesselroade, J., & McClearn, G. (submitted). Optimism, pessimism, and mental health: A twin/adoption analysis.

Poizner, H., Klima, E. S., & Bellugi, U. (1987). *What the hands reveal about the brain.* Cambridge, MA: MIT/Bradford Books.

Pokorny, A. D. (1964). Suicide rates and various psychiatric disorders. *Journal of Nervous and Mental Diseases, 139,* 499–506.

Polak, P. R., & Kirby, M. W. (1976). A model to replace psychiatric hospitals. *Journal of Nervous and Mental Diseases, 162,* 13–22.

Polivy, J. (1976). Perception of calories and regulation of intake in restrained and unrestrained subjects. *Addictive Behaviors, 1,* 237–44.

Pollack, J. M. (1979). Obsessive-compulsive personality: A review. *Psychological Bulletin, 86,* 225–41.

Pollard, C., Bronson, S., & Kenney, M. (1989). Prevalence of agoraphobia without panic in clinical settings. *American Journal of Psychiatry, 146,* 559.

Pollit, J. D. (1960). Natural history studies in mental illness: A discussion based on a pilot study of obsessional states. *Journal of Mental Science, 106,* 93–113.

Pollock, V.I. (1992). Meta-analysis of subjective sensitivity to alcohol in sons of alcoholics. *American Journal of Psychiatry, 149,* 1534–38.

Pomerleau, O. F., & Pomerleau, C. S. (1984). Neuroregulators and the reinforcement of smoking: Towards a biobehavioral explanation. *Neuroscience and Biobehavioral Reviews, 8,* 503–13.

Pope, H. G., Jonas, J. M., & Jones, B. (1982). Factitious psychosis: Phenomenology, family history, and long-term outcome of nine patients. *American Journal of Psychiatry, 139,* 1480–83.

Porsolt, R. D., Anton, G., Blavet, N., & Jalfre, M. (1978). Behavioral despair in rats: A new model sensitive to antidepressant treatments. *European Journal of Pharmacology, 47,* 379–91.

Posner, M.I., & Raichle, M.E. (1994). *Images of mind.* New York: Scientific American Library/Freeman.

Posner, M. I., Walker, J. A., Friedrich, F. J., & Rafal, R. D. (1984). Effects of parietal lobe injury on covert orienting of visual attention. *Journal of Neuroscience, 4,* 1863–74.

Post, R., Kotin, J., Goodwin, F. K., & Gordon, E. K. (1973). Psychomotor activity and cerebrospinal fluid amine metabolites in affective illness. *American Journal of Psychiatry, 130,* 67–72.

Post, R. M., Kramlinger, K. G., Altshuler, L. L., & Ketter, T. (1990). Treatment of rapid cycling bipolar illness. *Psychopharmacology Bulletin, 26*(1): 37–47.

Poulos, C. X., Hinson, R. E., & Siegel, S. (1981). The role of Pavlovian processes in drug tolerance and dependence: Implications for treatment. *Addictive Behaviors, 6,* 205–11.

Powell, K. E., Thompson, P. D., Caspersen, C. J., & Kendrick, J. S. (1987). Physical activity and the incidence of coronary heart disease. *Annual Review of Public Health, 8,* 253–87.

Power, K., Simpson, R., Swanson, V., & Wallace, L. (1990). A controlled comparison of cognitive-behavior therapy, diazepam, and placebo, alone or in combination, for the treatment of generalized anxiety disorder. *Journal of Anxiety Disorders, 4,* 267–92.

Prange, A. J., Wilson, J. C., Knox, A., McClane, T. K., & Lipton, M. A. (1970). Enhancement of imipramine by thyroid stimulating hormone: Clinical and theoretical implications. *American Journal of Psychiatry, 127,* 191–99.

Premack, D. (1959). Toward empirical behavior laws: I. Positive reinforcement. *Psychological Review, 66,* 219–33.

Preskorn, S., & Jerkovich, G. (1990). Central nervous system toxicity of tricyclic antidepressants: Phenomenology, course, risk factors, and the role of drug monitoring. *Journal of Clinical Psychopharmacology, 10,* 88–95.

Price, K. P., Tryon, W. W., & Raps, C. S. (1978). Learned helplessness and depression in a clinical population: A test of two behavioral hypotheses. *Journal of Abnormal Psychology, 87,* 113–21.

Price, R. H., Cowan, E. L., Lorion, R. P., & Ramos-McKay, J. (1989). The search for effective prevention programs: What we learned along the way. *American Journal of Orthopsychiatry, 59*(1): 49–58.

Price, R. W., Brew, B., Sidtis, J., et al. (1988). The brain in AIDS: Central nervous system HIV-1 infection and AIDS dementia complex. *Science, 239,* 586–92.

Prichard, J. C. (1837). *Treatise on insanity and other disorders affecting the mind.* Philadelphia: Haswell, Barrington & Haswell.

Prior, M. R. (1987). Biological and neuropsychological approaches to childhood autism. *British Journal of Psychiatry, 150,* 8–17.

Public Health Service. (1984). *The health consequences of smoking: Chronic obstructive lung disease. A report of the surgeon general.* Washington, DC: Government Printing Office.

Purcell, D., Brady, K., Chai, H., Muser, J., Molk, L., Gordon, N., & Means, J. (1969). The effect of asthma in children during experimental separation from the family. *Psychosomatic Medicine, 31,* 144–64.

Putnam, F. (1989). *Diagnosis and treatment of multiple personality.* New York: Guilford Press.

Putnam, F. W. (1991). Recent research on multiple personality disorder. *Psychiatric Clinics of North America, 14,* 489–502.

Putnam, F. W., Guroff, J. J., & Silberman, E. K., et al. (1986). The clinical phenomenology of multiple personality disorder: Review of 100 recent cases. *Journal of Clinical Psychiatry, 47* (6): 285–93.

Putnam, F., & Loewenstein, R. (1993). Treatment of multiple personality disorder: A survey of current practices. *American Journal of Psychiatry, 150,* 1048–52.

Putnam, F. W., Zahn, T. P., & Post, R. M. (1990). Differential autonomic nervous system activity in multiple personality disorder. *Psychiatry Research, 31,* 251–60.

Quade, H. C. (1986). A critical analysis of DSM-III as a taxonomy of psychopathology in childhood and adolescence. In T. Millon & G. L. Klerman (Eds.), *Contemporary directions in psychopathology: Toward the DSM-IV* (pp. 151–66). New York: Guilford Press.

Quay, H. C. (1986). Conduct disorders. In H. C. Quay & J. S. Werry (Eds.), *Psychopathological disorders of childhood* (pp. 35–62). New York: Wiley.

Quay, H. C., Routh, D. K., & Shapiro, S. K. (1987). Psychopathology of childhood: From description to validation. *Annual Review of Psychology, 38,* 491–532.

Quiggle, N., Garber, J., Panak, W., & Dodge, K. (1992). Social information processing in aggressive and depressed children. *Child Development, 63,* 1305–20.

Rabavilos, A. D., Boulougouris, J. C., & Stefanis, C. (1976). Duration of flooding session in the treatment of obsessive-compulsive patients. *Behaviour Research and Therapy, 14,* 349–55.

Rachman, S. J. (1965). Aversion therapy: Chemical or electrical? *Behaviour Research Therapy, 2,* 289–99.

Rachman, S. J. (1971). *The effects of psychotherapy.* Oxford: Pergamon.

Rachman, S. J. (1976). Therapeutic modeling. In M. Felman & A. Broadhurst (Ed.), *Theoretical and experimental bases of behavior therapy.* Chichester: Wiley.

Rachman, S. J. (1978). *Fear and courage.* New York: Freeman.

Rachman, S. J., Cobb, J., Grey, S., MacDonald, B., Mawson, C., Sartory, G., & Stern, R. (1979). The behavioral treatment of obsessive-compulsive disorders, with and without domipramine. *Behaviour Research and Therapy, 17,* 467–78.

Rachman, S. J., & Hodgson, R. J. (1968). Experimentally induced "sexual fetishism": Replication and development. *Psychological Records, 18,* 25–27.

Rachman, S. J., & Hodgson, R. J. (1980). *Obsessions and compulsions.* Englewood Cliffs, NJ: Prentice-Hall.

Rachman, S. J., & Hodgson, R. J. (1987). *Obsessions and compulsions* (2nd ed.). New York: Appleton-Century-Crofts.

Rachman, S. J., Hodgson, R., & Marks, I. M. (1971). The treatment of chronic obsessional neurosis. *Behaviour Research and Therapy, 9,* 237–47.

Rachman, S. J., Marks, I., & Hodgson, R. (1973). The treatment of chronic obsessive-compulsive neurosis by modeling and flooding in vivo. *Behaviour Research and Therapy, 11,* 463–71.

Rachman, S., & Maser, J. (Eds.). (1988). *Panic: Psychological perspectives.* Hillsdale, NJ: Erlbaum.

Rachman, S. J., & Wilson, G. T. (1979). *The effects of psychotherapy.* Oxford: Pergamon.

Rack, P. (1977). Clinical experience in the treatment of obsessional states. *Journal of International Medical Research, 5,* 81–91.

Radloff, L. S. (1975). Sex differences in depression: The effects of occupation and marital status. *Sex Roles, 1,* 249–65.

Rado, S. (1928). Psychodynamics of depression from the etiological point of view. In W. Galen (Ed.), *The meaning of despair.* New York: Science House.

Raichle, M. E. (1994). Visualizing the mind. *Scientific American, 270*(4): 58–64.

Rapee, R. (1991). Generalized anxiety disorder: A review of clinical features and theoretical concepts. *Clinical Psychology Review, 11,* 419–40.

Rapoport, J. L. (1988). The neurobiology of obsessive-compulsive disorder. *Journal of the American Medical Association, 260,* 2888–90.

Rapoport, J. L. (1989). The biology of obsessions and compulsions. *Scientific American,* March, pp. 83–89.

Rapoport, J. L. (1990). *The boy who couldn't stop washing.* New York: Plume.

Rapport, M. D. (1987). Attention deficit disorder with hyperactivity. In M. Hersen & V. B. Van Hasselt (Eds.), *Behavior therapy with children and adolescents* (pp. 325–62). New York: Wiley.

Raps, C. S., Peterson, C., Reinhard, K. E., Abramson, L. Y., & Seligman, M. E. P. (1982). Attributional style among depressed patients. *Journal of Abnormal Psychology, 91,* 102–103.

Raps, C. S., Reinhard, K. E., & Seligman, M. E. P. (1980). Reversal of cognitive and affective deficits associated with depression and learned helplessness by mood elevation in patients. *Journal of Abnormal Psychology, 89,* 342–49.

Raskin, A., Crook, T. H., & Herman, K. D. (1975). The psychiatric history and symptom differences in black and white depressed patients. *Journal of Consulting and Clinical Psychology, 43,* 73–80.

Raskind, M. A. (1976). Helping the elderly psychiatric patient in crisis. *Geriatrics, 31,* 51–56.

Rasmussen, K., & Aghajanian, G. K. (1986). Effects of hallucinogens on spontaneous and sensory-evoked locus coeruleus unit activity in the rat: Reversal by selective antagonists. *Brain Research, 385,* 395–400.

Rattan, R. B., & Chapman, L. J. (1973). Associative intrusions in schizophrenic verbal behavior. *Journal of Abnormal Psychology, 82,* 169–73.

Rawlings, E. I., & Carter, D. K. (1977). *Psychotherapy for women.* Springfield, IL: Charles C. Thomas.

Ray, O., & Ksir, C. (1987). *Drugs, society, and human behavior.* St. Louis: Times Mirror/Mosby.

Ray, W. J., & Katahn, M. (1968). Relation of anxiety to locus of control. *Psychological Reports, 23,* 1196.

Redmond, D. E., Maas, J. W., Kling, A., & DeKirmenjian, H. (1971). Changes in private school behavior after treatment with alpha-methyl-para-tyrosine. *Psychosomatic Medicine, 33,* 97–113.

Regier, D., Myers, J., Kramer, M., Robins, L., Blayer, D., Hough, R., Eaton, W., & Locke, B. (1984). The NIMH Epidemiological Catchment Area program: Historical context, major objectives, and study population characteristics. *Archives of General Psychiatry, 41,* 934–41.

Regier, D. A., Narrow, W. E., & Rae, D. S. (1990). The epidemiology of anxiety disorders: The Epidemiological Catchment Area (ECA) experience. Symposium: Benzodiazepines: Therapeutic, biologic, and psychological issues. *Journal of Psychiatric Research 24* (Suppl 2): 3–14.

Rehm, L. (1977). A self-control model of depression. *Behavior Therapy, 8,* 787–804.

Rehm, L. P. (1978). Mood pleasant events, and unpleasant events: Two pilot studies. *Journal of Consulting and Clinical Psychology, 46,* 854–59.

Rehyer, J., & Smyth, L. (1971). Suggestibility during the execution of a posthypnotic suggestion. *Journal of Abnormal Psychology, 78,* 258–65.

Reich, L. H., Davies, R. K., & Himmelhoch, J. M. (1974). Excessive alcohol use in manic-depressive illness. *American Journal of Psychiatry, 131*(1): 83–86.

Reich, T., Van Eerdewegh, P., Rice, J. P., & Mullaney, J. (1987). The familial transmission of primary major depressive disorder. *Journal of Psychiatric Research, 21* (4): 613–24.

Reich, W. (1986). Diagnostic ethics: The uses and limits of psychiatric explanation. In L. Tancredi (Ed.), *Ethical issues in epidemiological research.* New Brunswick, NJ: Rutgers University Press.

Reid, W. H., Dorr, D., Walker, J. I., & Bonner, III, J. W. (Eds.). (1986). *Unmasking the psychopath: Antisocial personality and related syndromes.* New York: Norton.

Reiman, E., Raichle, M., Robins, E., et al. (1986). The application of positron emission tomography to the study of panic disorder. *American Journal of Psychiatry, 143,* 469–77.

Reinisch, J. (1992). Unpublished study cited in C. Gorman, Sizing up the sexes. *Time, 139,* 45–46.

Reisen, M. F., Brust, A. A., & Farris, E. B. (1951). Life situations, emotions and the course of patients with arterial hypertension. *Psychosomatic Medicine, 13,* 133.

Reisenger, J. J. (1972). The treatment of "anxiety-depression" via positive reinforcement and response. *Journal of Applied Behavior Analysis, 5,* 125–30.

Reiss, S., Peterson, R. A., Erron, L. D., & Reiss, N. M. (1977). *Abnormality: Experimental and clinical approaches.* New York: Macmillan.

Reitan, R. M., & Davison, L. A. (1974). *Clinical neuropsychology: Current status and applications.* Washington, DC: Winston and Sons.

Rennie, M. A., & Wollensheim, J. P. (1979). Cognitive therapy, stress management training and the Type A behavior pattern. *Cognitive Therapy and Research, 3* (1): 61–73.

Rescorla R. A., & Solomon, R. L. (1967). Two-process learning theory: Relationship between Pavlovian conditioning and instrumental learning. *Psychological Review, 74,* 151–82.

Rescorla, R. A., & Wagner, A. R. (1972). A theory of Pavlovian conditioning: Variations in the effectiveness of reinforcement and nonreinforcement. In A. Black & W. F. Prokasy (Eds.), *Classical conditioning II.* New York: Appleton-Century-Crofts.

Resick, P., Jordan, C., Girelli, S., Hutter, C., et al. (1988). A comparative outcome study of behavioral group therapy for sexual assault victims. *Behavior Therapy, 19,* 385–401.

Reynolds, W. M., & Coats, K. I. (1986). A comparison of cognitive-behavioral therapy and relaxation training for the treatment of depression in adolescents. *Journal of Consulting and Clinical Psychology, 54,* 653–60.

Rice, J., Reich, T., Andreasen, N. C., Endicott, J., Van Eerdewegh, M., Fishman, R., Hirschfeld, R. M. A., & Klerman, G. L. (1987). The familial transmission of bipolar illness. *Archives of General Psychiatry, 44,* 441–47.

Richter, C. P. (1957a). Hormones and rhythms in man and animals. *Recent Progress in Hormone Research, 13.*

Richter, C. P. (1957b). On the phenomenon of sudden death in animals and men. *Psychosomatic Medicine, 19,* 191–98.

Ricks, D. F. (1974). Supershrink: Methods of a therapist judged successful on the basis of adult outcome of adolescent patients. In D. Ricks, M. Roff, & A. Thomas (Eds.), *Life history research in psychopathology* (Vol. 3). Minneapolis: University of Minnesota Press.

Rie, H. E. (1966). Depression in childhood: A survey of some pertinent contributions. *Journal of the American Academy of Child Psychiatry, 5,* 653–85.

Rief, W., Schaefer, S., Hiller, W., & Fichter, M.M. (1992). Lifetime diagnoses in patients with somatoform disorders: Which came first? *European Archives of Psychiatry and Clinical Neuroscience, 241,* 236–40.

Rihmer, Z., Barsi, J., Arato, M., & Demeter, E. (1990). Suicide in subtypes of primary major depression. *Journal of Affective Disorders, 18* (3): 221–25.

Rihmer, Z., Barsi, J., Veg, K., & Katona, C. (1990). Suicide rates in Hungary correlate negatively with reported rates of depression. *Journal of Affective Disorders, 20,* 87–91.

Rimm, D. C., & Masters, J. C. (1974). *Behavior therapy: Techniques and empirical findings.* New York: Academic Press.

Rioch, M. J. (1967). Pilot projects in training mental health counselors. In E. L. Cowen, E. A. Gardner, & M. Zax (Eds.), *Emerging approaches to mental health problems.* New York: Appleton-Century-Crofts.

Risley, T., & Wolf, M. (1967). Establishing functional speech in echolalic children. *Behavior Research and Therapy, 5,* 73–88.

Rittenhouse, J. D. (1976). Selected themes of discussion. In J. D. Rittenhouse (Ed.), *The epidemiology of heroin and other narcotics.* Menlo Park, CA: Stanford Research Institute.

Ritvo, E. R., Freeman, B. J., Pingree, C., Mason-Brothers, A., Jorde, L., Jenson, W. R., McMahon, W. M., Petersen, P. B., Mo, A., & Ritvo, A. (1989). The UCLA-University of Utah Epidemiology Survey of Autism: Prevalence. *American Journal of Psychiatry, 146*(2): 194–99.

Ritvo, E. R., Rabin, K., Yuwiler, A., Freeman, B. J., & Geller, E. (1978). Biochemical and hematogic studies: A critical review. In M. Rutter & E. Schopler (Eds.), *Autism: A reappraisal of concepts and treatment.* New York: Plenum.

Roache, J. (1990). Addiction potential of benzodiazepines and non-benzodiazepine anxiolytics. *Advances in Alcohol and Substance Abuse, 9,* 103–28.

Robbins, T. W. (1990). The case of frontostriatal dysfunction in schizophrenia. *Schzophrenia Bulletin, 16* (3): 391–402.

Roberts, D. C. S., Corcoran, M. E., & Fibiger, H. C. (1977). On the role of ascending catecholaminergic systems in intravenous self-administration of cocaine. *Pharmacology: Biochemistry and Behavior, 6,* 615–20.

Roberts, M., & Hanaway, J. (1970). *Atlas of the human brain in section.* Philadelphia: Lea & Febiger.

Robertson, M., Trimble, M., & Lees, A. (1988). The psychopathology of Gilles de la Tourette syndrome. *British Journal of Psychiatry, 152,* 383–90.

Robins, E., & Guze, S. B. (1972). Classification of affective disorders: The primary-secondary, the endogenous-reactive, and the neurotic-psychotic concepts. In T. A. Williams, M. M. Katz, & J. A. Shields (Eds.), *Recent advances in the psychobiology of the depressive illnesses* (pp. 283–93). Washington, DC: U.S. Government Printing Office.

Robins, L. N. (1966). *Deviant children grow up.* Baltimore: Williams & Wilkins.

Robins, L. N. (1985). Epidemiology: Reflections on testing the validity of psychiatric interviews. *Archives of General Psychiatry, 42,* 918–24.

Robins, L. N. (1991). Conduct disorder. *Journal of Child Psychology and Psychiatry, 32,* 193–212.

Robins, L. N., & Helzer, J. E. (1986). Diagnosis and clinical assessment: The current state of psychiatric diagnosis. *Annual Review of Psychology, 37,* 409–32.

Robins, L. N., Helzer, J. E., Hesselbrock, M., & Wish, E. D. (1977). Vietnam veterans three years after Vietnam: How our study changed our views of heroin. In L. Harris (Ed.), *Problems of drug dependence.* Richmond, VA: Committee on Problems of Drug Dependence.

Robins, L. N., Helzer, J. E., Weissman, M. M., Orvaschel, H., Gruenberg, E., Burke, J. D., & Regier, D. A. (1984). Lifetime prevalence of specific psychiatric disorders in three sites. *Archives of General Psychiatry, 41*, 949–58.

Robinson, D. S., Davis, J., Nies, A., Ravaris, C., & Sylvester, D. (1971). Relation of sex in aging to monoamine oxidase activity in human brain, plasma, and platelets. *Archives of General Psychiatry, 24*, 536.

Roche, J., & Ramsbey, T. (1993). Premarital sexuality: A five-year follow-up study of attitudes and behavior by dating stage. *Adolescence, 28*, 67–80.

Rodin, J., & Langer, E. J. (1977). Long-term effects of control intervention with the institutionalized patient. *Journal of Personality and Social Psychology, 12*, 897–902.

Rodnick, E. H., Goldstein, M. J., Lewis, J. M., & Doane, J. A. (1984). Parental communication style, affect, and role as precursors of offspring schizophrenia-spectrum disorders. In N. F. Watt, E. J. Anthony, L. C. Wynne, & J. E. Rolf (Eds.), *Children at risk for schizophrenia: A longitudinal perspective* (pp. 81–92). Cambridge: Cambridge University Press.

Roediger, H. L. III, & McDermott, K. B. (1993). Implicit memory in normal human subjects. In F. Boller & J. Grafman (Eds.), *Handbook of neuropsychology.* Amsterdam: Elsevier.

Roediger, H., Weldon, M., & Challis, B. (1989). Explaining dissociations between implicit and explicit measures of retention: A processing account. In H. Roediger & F. Craik (Eds.), *Varieties of memory and consciousness: Essays in honor of Endel Tulvin,* (pp. 3–14). Hillsdale, NJ: Erlbaum.

Roff, J. D., & Knight, R. (1981). Family characteristics, childhood symptoms, and adult outcomes in schizophrenia. *Journal of Abnormal Psychology, 90*, 510–20.

Rogers, C. (1951). *Client-centered therapy.* Boston: Houghton-Mifflin.

Rogers, C. (1961). *On becoming a person.* Boston: Houghton Mifflin.

Rogers, C. (1977). *Carl Rogers on personal power.* New York: Delacorte.

Rogers, C. R., & Dymond, R. (Eds.). (1954). *Psychotherapy and personality change.* Chicago: University of Chicago Press.

Rogers, C. R., & Truax, C. B. (1967). The therapeutic conditions antecedent to change: A theoretical view. In C. R. Rogers (Ed.), *The therapeutic relationship and its impact: A study of psychotherapy with schizophrenics.* Madison: University of Wisconsin Press.

Rogers, J., Siggins, G. R., Schulman, J. R., & Bloom, F. E. (1980). Physiological correlates of ethanol intoxication tolerance, and dependence in rat cerebellar Purkinje cells. *Brain Research, 196*, 183–98.

Rogerson, H. L. (1951). Venerophobia in the male. *British Journal of Venereal Disease, 27*, 158–59.

Rohner, J. J., & Sanford, E. J. (1975). Imipramine toxicity. *Journal of Urology, 114*, 402–403.

Rooth, F. G., & Marks, I. M. (1974). Persistent exhibitionism: Short-term responses to aversion, self-regulation, and relaxation treatment. *Archives of Sexual Behavior, 3*, 227–48.

Roper, G., Rachman, S., & Marks, I. M. (1975). Passive and participant modeling in exposure treatment of obsessive compulsive neurotics. *Behaviour Research and Therapy, 13*, 271–79.

Rosellini, R. A., Binik, Y. M., & Seligman, M. E. P. (1976). Sudden death in the laboratory rat. *Psychosomatic Medicine, 38*, 55–58.

Rosen, J. C., & Leitenberg, H. (1982). Bulimia nervosa: Treatment with exposure and response prevention. *Behavior Therapy, 13*, 117–24.

Rosenberg, C. M. (1967). Personality and obsessional neurosis. *British Journal of Psychiatry, 133*, 471–77.

Rosenhan, D. L. (1969). Some origins of concern for others. In P. Mussen, J. Langer, & M. Covington (Eds.), *Trends and issues in developmental psychology* (pp. 132–53). New York: Holt, Rinehart & Winston.

Rosenhan, D. L. (1970). The natural socialization of altruistic social autonomy. In J. Macaulay & L. Berkowitz (Eds.), *Altruism and helping behavior* (pp. 251–68). New York: Academic Press.

Rosenhan, D. L. (1973). On being sane in insane places. *Science, 179*, 250–58.

Rosenhan, D. L. (1975). The contextual nature of psychiatric diagnosis. *Journal of Abnormal Psychology, 84*, 462–74.

Rosenhan, D. L. (1983). Psychological abnormality and law. In C. J. Scheirer & B. L. Hammonds (Eds.), *Psychology and the law* (pp. 89–118). Washington, DC: American Psychological Association.

Rosenman, R. H., Brand, R. J., Jenkins, C. D., Friedman, M., Straus, R., & Wurm, M. (1975). Coronary heart disease in the Western Collaborative Group study: Final follow-up experience at $8\frac{1}{2}$ years. *Journal of the American Medical Association, 233*, 872–77.

Rosenstein, M. J., Milazzo-Sayre, L. J., & Manderscheid, R. W. (1990). Characteristics of persons using specialty inpatient, outpatient, and partial care programs in 1986. In R. W. Manderscheid & M. A. Sonnenschein (Eds.), *Mental health in the United States* (pp. 139–72). Washington, DC: U.S. Government Printing Office.

Rosenstein, M. J., Steadman, H. J., MacAskill, R. L., & Manderscheid, R. W. (1986). *Legal status of admissions in three inpatient psychiatric settings, United States, 1980.* Statistical Note No. 178. DHHS Publication No. (ADM) 86-1484. Washington, DC: Superintendent of Documents, U.S. Government Printing Office.

Rosenthal, D. (1970a). Genetic research in the schizophrenic syndrome. In R. Cancro (Ed.), *The schizophrenic reactions* (pp. 245–58). New York: Brunner/Mazel.

Rosenthal, D. (1970b). *Genetic theory and abnormal behavior.* New York: McGraw-Hill.

Rosenthal, D. (1974). Issues in high risk studies of schizophrenia. In D. F. Ricks, A. Thomas, & M. Roff (Eds.), *Life history research in psychopathology* (Vol. 3, pp. 25–41). Minneapolis: University of Minnesota Press.

Rosenthal, D. (1979). Was Thomas Wolfe a borderline? *Schizophrenia Bulletin, 5*, 87–94.

Rosenthal, D., Lawlor, W. G., Zahn, T. P., & Shakow, D. (1960). The relationship of some aspects of mental set to degree of schizophrenic disorganization. *Journal of Personality, 28*, 26–38.

Rosenthal, N. E., Carpenter, C. J., James, S. P., Parry, B. L., Rogers, S. L. B., & Wehr, T. A. (1986). Seasonal affective disorder in children and adolescents. *American Journal of Psychiatry, 143*, 356–86.

Rosenthal, N. E., Moul, D. E., Hellekson, C. J., & Oren, D. A. (1993). A multicenter study of the light visor for seasonal affective disorder: No difference in efficacy found between two different intensities. *Neuropsychopharmacology, 8*(2): 151–60.

Rosenthal, N. E., Sack, D. A., Gillin, J. C., Lewy, A. J., Goodwin, F. K., Davenport, Y., Mueller, P. S., Newsome, D. A., & Wehr, T. A. (1984). Seasonal affective disorder: A description of the syndrome and preliminary findings with light therapy. *Archives of General Psychiatry, 41*, 72–80.

Rosenthal, P. A., & Rosenthal, S. (1984). Suicidal behavior by preschool children. *American Journal of Psychiatry, 141*, 520–25.

Rosenthal, T. L., & Bandura, A. (1979). Psychological modeling: Theory and practice. In A. Bergin & S. Garfield (Eds.), *Handbook of psychotherapy and behavior change.* New York: Wiley.

Rosenzweig, M., & Leiman, A. (1989). *Physiological psychology* (2nd ed.). New York: Random House.

Rosenzweig, S. P., & Forman, R. (1974). Patient and therapist variables affecting premature termination in group psychotherapy. *Psychotherapy: Theory, research and practice, 11*, 76–79.

Rosman, B., Minuchin, S., Liebman, R., & Baker, Y. (1976). Input and outcome of family therapy in anorexia nervosa. In J. L. Claghorn (Ed.), *Successful therapy.* New York: Brunner/Mazel.

Ross, C. A. (1991). Epidemiology of multiple personality disorder and dissociation. *Psychiatric Clinics of North America, 14*, 503–17.

Ross, C. A., Anderson, G., Fleisher, W. P., & Norton, G. R. (1991). The frequency of multiple personality disorder among psychiatric inpatients. *American Journal of Psychiatry, 148*, 1717–20.

Ross, C. A., Heber, S., Norton, G. R., & Anderson, G. (1989a). Differences between multiple personality disorder and other diagnostic groups on structured interview. *Journal of Nervous and Mental Disease, 177,* 487–91.

Ross, C. A., Heber, S., Norton, G. R., & Anderson, G. (1989b). Somatic symptoms in multiple personality disorder. *Psychosomatics, 30,* 154–60.

Ross, C. A., Miller, S. D., Reagor, P., Bjornson, L., et al. (1990). Structured interview data on 102 cases of multiple personality disorder from four centers. *American Journal of Psychiatry, 147,* 596–601.

Ross, E. D. (1981). The aprosodias: Functional-anatomic organization of the affective components of language in the right hemisphere. *Archives of Neurology, 38,* 561–69.

Ross, E. D. (1983). Right-hemisphere lesions in disorders of affective language. In A. Kertesz, *Localization in neuropsychology.* New York: Academic Press.

Ross, J. D., & Wirt, R. D. (1984). Childhood aggression and social adjustment as antecedents of delinquency. *Journal of Abnormal Child Psychology, 12*(1): 111–26.

Ross, L. (1977). The intuitive psychologist and his shortcomings: Distortions in the attribution process. In L. Berkowitz (Ed.), *Advances in experimental social psychology* (Vol. 10). New York: Academic Press.

Ross, L., Greene, D., & House, P. (1977). The false consensus phenomenon: An attributional bias in self perception and social perception processes. *Journal of Experimental Social Psychology, 13,* 279–301.

Ross, M., & Need, J. (1989). Effects of adequacy of gender reassignment on psychological adjustment: A follow-up of fourteen male-to-female patients. *Archives of Sexual Behavior, 18,* 145–53.

Roth, L. (1954). *I'll cry tomorrow.* New York: Fell.

Rothaus, P., Hanson, P. G., Cleveland, S. E., & Johnson, D. L. (1963). Describing psychiatric hospitalization: A dilemma. *American Psychologist, 18,* 85–89.

Rothbaum, B., Foa, E., Riggs, D., Murdock, T., & Walsh, W. (1992). A prospective examination of post-traumatic stress disorder in rape victims. *Journal of Traumatic Stress, 5*(3): 455–75.

Rothbaum, F., Weisz, J. R., & Snyder, S. S. (1982). Changing the world and changing the self: A two-process model of perceived control. *Journal of Personality and Social Psychology, 42,* 5–37.

Rothblum, E. D., Solomon, L. J., & Albee, G. W. (1986). A sociopolitical perspective of DSM-III. In T. Millon & G. L. Klerman (Ed.), *Contemporary direction in psychopathology: Toward the DSM-IV* (pp. 167–89). New York: Guilford Press.

Rothman, D. (1971). *The discovery of the asylum.* New York: Harper & Row.

Rotter, J. (1954). *Social learning and clinical psychology.* Englewood Cliffs, NJ: Prentice-Hall.

Rotter, J. B. (1966). Generalized expectancies for internal versus external control of reinforcement. *Psychological Monographs, 80*(1).

Rotter, J. B., Chance, J. E., & Phares, E. J. (1972). *Applications of a social learning theory of personality.* New York: Holt, Rinehart & Winston.

Rovndal, E., & Vaglum, P. (1992). Different intake procedures: The influence of treatment start and treatment response: A quasi-experimental study. *Journal of Substance Abuse and Treatment, 9,* 53–58.

Roy, E. A. (1982). Action and performance. In A. Ellis (Ed.), *Normality and pathology in cognitive function* (pp. 265–98). London: Academic Press.

Rozin, P. (1976). The psychobiological approach to human memory. In M. R. Rosenzweig & E. L. Bennett (Eds.), *Neural mechanisms of learning and memory* (pp. 3–46). Cambridge, MA: MIT Press.

Rozin, P. (1978). *Personal communication.* Based on data collected in the introductory course of psychology at the University of Pennsylvania.

Rozin, P. (1981). *Personal communication.* Based on data collected in the introductory course of psychology at the University of Pennsylvania.

Rozin, P., & Gleitman, L. R., (1977). The structure and acquisition of reading: II. The reading process and the acquisition of the alphabetic principle. In A. S. Reber & D. Scarborough (Eds.), *Toward a psychology of reading* (pp. 55–141). Potomac, MD: Erlbaum.

Rozin, P., & Kalat, J. (1971). Specific hungers and poison avoidance as adaptive specializations of learning. *Psychological Review, 78,* 459–86.

Rubenstein, C. (1982, May). What's good. *Psychology Today, 16,* 62–72.

Rubenstein, C. (1993). Generation sex. *Mademoiselle,* June 1993, pp. 130–37.

Rubin, R., Villanueva-Meyer, J., Ananth, J., et al. (1992). Regional xenon 133 cerebral blood flow and cerebral technetium 99m HMPAO uptake in unmedicated patients with obsessive-compulsive disorder and matched normal control subjects. *Archives of General Psychiatry, 49,* 739–44.

Runyan, D., Everson, M., Edelsohn, D., et al. (1988). Impact of legal intervention on sexually abused children. *Journal of Pediatrics, 113,* 647–53.

Rush, H. A., Beck, A. T., Kovacs, M., & Hollon, S. (1977). Comparative efficacy of cognitive therapy and pharmacotherapy in the treatment of depressed outpatients. *Cognitive Research and Therapy, 1,* 17–37.

Ruskin, A., Beard, O. W., & Schaffer, R. L. (1948). "Last hypertension": Elevated arterial pressure in victims of the Texas City disaster. *American Journal of Medicine, 4,* 228.

Russek, L., King, S., Russek, S., & Russek, H. (1990). The Harvard mastery of stress study 35-year follow-up: Prognostic significance of patterns of psychophysiological arousal and adaptation. *Psychosomatic Medicine, 52,* 271–85.

Russell, M. (1977). Smoking problems: An overview. In M. Jarvik, J. Cullen, E. Gritz, T. Vogt, & L. West (Eds.), *Research on smoking behavior.* Rockville, MD: National Institute on Drug Abuse.

Russell, W. R. (1959). *Brain, memory, learning: A neurologist's view.* Oxford, England: Oxford University Press.

Rutter, M. (1968). Concepts of autism: A review of research. *Journal of Child Psychology and Psychiatry, 9,* 1–25.

Rutter, M. (1975). *Helping troubled children.* New York: Plenum.

Rutter, M. (1978). Prevalence and types of dyslexia. In A. L. Benton & D. Pearl, *Dyslexia: An appraisal of current knowledge.* New York: Oxford University Press.

Rutter, M. (1985). Family and school influence on behavioural development. *Journal of Child Psychology and Psychiatry, 26,* 349–68.

Rutter, M. (1989). Isle of Wight revisited: Twenty-five years of psychiatric epidemiology. *Journal of the American Academy of Child and Adolescent Psychiatry, 28*(5): 633–53.

Rutter, M., & Garmezy, N. (1983). Developmental psychopathology. In P. H. Mussen (Ed.), *Handbook of child psychology, Vol. 4: Socialization, personality, and social development.* New York: Wiley.

Rutter, M., Macdonald, H., Le Couteur, A., Harrington, R., Bolton, P., & Bailey, A. (1990). Genetic factors in child psychiatric disorders: II. Empirical findings. *Journal of Child Psychology and Psychiatry, 31*(1): 39–83.

Rutter, M., Quinton, D., & Hill, J. (1990). Adult outcome of institution-reared children: Males. In L. Robins & M. Rutter (Eds.), *Straight and devious pathways from childhood to adulthood* (pp. 135–57). New York: Cambridge University Press.

Saccuzzo, D. P., & Braff, D. L. (1986). Information processing abnormalities: Trait- and state-dependent components. *Schizophrenia Bulletin, 12* (3): 447–59.

Sack, R., & De Fraites, E. (1977). Lithium and the treatment of mania. In J. Barchas, P. Berger, R. Ciaranello, & G. Elliot (Eds.), *Psychopharmacology.* New York: Oxford University Press.

Sack, W., Clarke, G., Him, C., & Dickason, D. (1993). A 6–year follow-up study of Cambodian refugee adolescents traumatized as children. *Journal of the American Academy of Child and Adolescent Psychiatry, 32*, 431–37.

Sackheim, H. A., Greenberg, M. S., Weiman, A. L., Gur, R. C., Hunger-Buhler, J. P., & Geschwind, N. (1982). Hemispheric asymmetry in the expression of positive and negative emotions: Neurological evidence. *Archives of Neurology, 39*, 210–18.

Sackheim, H. A., Nordlie, J. W., & Gur R. C. (1979). A model of hysterical and hypnotic blindness: Cognitions, motivation and awareness. *Journal of Abnormal Psychology, 88*, 474–89.

Sackheim, H., Prudic, J., Devanand, D., et al. (1993). Effects of stimulus intensity and electrode placement on the efficacy and cognitive effects of electroconvulsive therapy. *New England Journal of Medicine, 328*, 839–46.

Saffran, E. M. (1982). Neuropsychological approaches to the study of language. *British Journal of Psychology, 73*, 317–37.

Sakai, T. (1967). Clinico-genetic study on obsessive compulsive neurosis. *Bulletin of Osaka Medical School,* Supplement XII, 323–31.

Sakamoto, K., Kamo, T., Nakadaira, S., & Tamura, A. (1993). A nationwide survey of seasonal affective disorder at 53 outpatient university clinics in Japan. *Acta Psychiatrica Scandinavica, 87*(4): 258–65.

Salzman, L., & Thaler, F. (1981). Obsessive-compulsive disorders: A review of the literature. *American Journal of Psychiatry, 138*, 286–96.

Sanchez-Craig, M., Annis, H. M., Bornet, A. R., & MacDonald, K. R. (1984). Random assignment to abstinence and controlled drinking: Evaluation of a cognitive-behavior program for problem drinkers. *Journal of Clinical and Consulting Psychology, 52*, 390–403.

Sandler, J., & Hazari, A. (1960). The "obsessional": On the psychological classification of obsessional character traits and symptoms. *British Journal of Medical Psychology, 33*, 113–22.

Sank, L. I. (1979). Community disasters: Primary prevention and treatment in a health maintenance organization. *American Psychologist, 34*, 334–38.

Sarason, S. B. (1974). *The psychological sense of community: Prospects for a community psychology.* San Francisco: Jossey-Bass.

Sartorius, N., Jablensky, A., Korten, A., Ernberg, G., Anker, M., Cooper, J. E., & Day, R. (1986). Early manifestations and first-contact incidence of schizophrenia in different cultures. *Psychological Medicine, 16*, 909–28.

Sasanuma, S., & Fujimura, O. (1971). Selective impairment of phonetic and nonphonetic transcription of words in Japanese aphasic patients: Kana versus Kanji in visual recognition and writing. *Cortex, 7*, 1–18.

Saugstad, L. F. (1989). Social class, marriage and fertility in schizophrenia. *Schizophrenia Bulletin, 15*, 9–43.

Saunders, A. M., Strittmatter, M. D., Schmechel, M. D., et al. (1993). Association of apolipoprotein E allele type 4 with late-onset familial and sporadic Alzheimer's disease. *Neurology, 43*, 1467–72.

Saver, J. L., & Damasio, A. R. (1991). Preserved access and processing of social knowledge in a patient with acquired sociopathy due to ventromedial frontal damage. *Neuropsychologia, 29*, 1241–49.

Sawrey, W. L., Conger, J. J., & Turrell, E. S. (1956). An experimental investigation of the role of psychological factors in the production of gastric ulcers in rats. *Journal of Comparative and Physiological Psychology, 49*, 457–61.

Sawrey, W. L., & Weiss, J. D. (1956). An experimental method of producing gastric ulcers. *Journal of Comparative and Physiological Psychology, 49*, 269.

Scarr, S. (1975). Genetics and the development of intelligence. In F. D. Horowitz (Ed.), *Child development research* (Vol. 4). Chicago: University of Chicago Press.

Schachter, S., & Latane, B. T. (1964). Crime, cognition, and the autonomic nervous system. In D. Levine (Ed.), *Nebraska Symposium on Motivation.* Lincoln: University of Nebraska Press.

Schachter, S., Silverstein, B., Kozlowski, L. T., Perlick, D., Herman, C. P., & Liebling, B. (1977). Studies of the interaction of psychological and pharmacological determinants of smoking. *Journal of Experimental Psychology—General, 106*, 3–40.

Schachter, S., & Singer, J. E. (1962). Cognitive, social and physiological determinants of emotional state. *Psychological Review, 69*, 379–99.

Schacter, D. L. (1987). Implicit memory: History and current status. *Journal of Experimental Psychology: Learning, Memory and Cognition, 13*, 501–18.

Schacter, D. L. (1992). Priming and multiple memory systems: Perceptual mechanisms of implicit memory. *Journal of Cognitive Neuroscience, 4*, 244–56.

Schacter, D. L., Wang, P. L., Tulving, E., & Freedman, M. (1982). Functional retrograde amnesia: A quantitative case study. *Neuropsychologia, 20*, 523–32.

Schaefer, H., & Martin, P. (1977). *Behavioral therapy* (2nd ed.). New York: McGraw-Hill.

Scheff, T. J. (1966). *Being mentally ill: A sociological theory.* Chicago: Aldine.

Scher, M. (1975). Verbal activity, sex counselor experience and success in counseling. *Journal of Counseling Psychology, 22*, 97–101.

Schiavi, R. C., et al. (1984). Pituitary-gonadal function during sleep in men with erectile impotence and normal controls. *Psychosomatic Medicine, 46* (3): 239–54.

Schildkraut, J. J. (1965). The catecholamine hypothesis of affective disorders: A review of supporting evidence. *American Journal of Psychiatry, 122*, 509–22.

Schildkraut, J. J., & Kety, S. S. (1967). Biogenic amines and emotion. *Science, 156*, 21–30.

Schlichting, U. U., Goldberg, S. R., Wuttke, W., & Hoffmeister, F. (1970). D-amphetamine self-administration by rhesus monkeys with different self-administration histories. *Proceedings of the European Society for the Study of Drug Toxicity, 220*, 62–69.

Schmale A., & Iker, H. (1966). The psychological setting of uterine cervical cancer. *Annals of the New York Academy of Sciences, 125*, 807–13.

Schmauk, F. J. (1970). Punishment, arousal, and avoidance learning in sociopaths. *Journal of Abnormal Psychology, 76*, 443–53.

Schneider, R. A., & Zangori, V. N. (1951). Variations in clotting time, relative viscosity and other physiochemical properties of the blood accompanying physical and emotional stress in the normotensive and hypertensive subject. *Psychosomatic Medicine, 13*, 289–303.

Schneier, F., Johnson, J., Hornig, C., et al. (1992). Social phobia: Comorbidity and morbidity in an epidemiologic sample. *Archives of General Psychiatry, 49*, 282–88.

Schotte, D. E., & Stunkard, A. J. (1987). Bulimia vs. bulimic behaviors on a college campus. *Journal of the American Medical Association, 258*, 1213–15.

Schreiber, F. R. (1974). *Sybil.* New York: Warner Books.

Schreibman, L. (1975). Effects of within-stimulus and extra-stimulus prompting on discrimination learning in autistic children. *Journal of Applied Behavioral Analysis, 8*, 91–112.

Schuckit, M. A. (1984). Subjective responses to alcohol in sons of alcoholics and controls. *Archives of General Psychiatry, 41*, 879–84.

Schuckit, M. A. (1987). Biological vulnerability to alcoholism. *Journal of Consulting and Clinical Psychology, 55*, 301–309.

Schuckit, M. A. (1994). Low level of response to alcohol as a predictor of future alcoholism. *American Journal of Psychiatry, 151*, 184–89.

Schulberg, H., & Rush, A. J. (1994). Clinical practice guidelines for managing major depression in primary care practice. *American Psychologist, 49*, 34–41.

Schulsinger, F. (1972). Psychopathy, heredity and environment. *International Journal of Mental Health, 1*, 190–206.

Schulterbrand, J. G., & Raven, A. (Eds.). (1977). *Depression in childhood: Diagnosis, treatment, and conceptual models.* New York: Raven Press.

Schultes, R. E. (1987). Coca and other psychoactive plants: Magico-religious roles in primitive societies of the new world. In S. Fisher et al. (Eds.), *Cocaine: Clinical and biobehavioral aspects.* New York: Oxford University Press.

Schuyler, D. (1974). The evaluation of the suicidal patient. In J. R. Novello (Ed.), *Practical handbook of psychiatry.* Springfield, IL: Charles C. Thomas.

Schuyler, D., & Katz, M. M. (1973). *The depressive illnesses: A major public health problem.* Washington, DC: U.S. Government Printing Office.

Schwab, J. J., Bialow, M., Holzer, C. E., Brown, J. M., & Stevenson, B. E. (1967). Socio-cultural aspects of depression in medical inpatients. *Archives of General Psychiatry, 17*, 533–43.

Schwartz, B. (1984). *Psychology of learning and behavior* (2nd ed.). New York: Norton.

Schwartz, G. E. (1973). Biofeedback as therapy. Some theoretical and practical issues. *American Psychologist, 29*, 633–73.

Schwartz, G., & Weiss, S. M. (1977). What is behavioral medicine? *Psychosomatic Medicine, 39*, 377–81.

Schwartz, M. F., Baron, J., & Moscovitch, M. (1990). Symptomatology of Alzheimer-type dementia: Report on a survey-by-mail. In M. F. Schwartz (Ed.), *Modular deficits in Alzheimer-type dementia.* Cambridge, MA: MIT Press/Bradford.

Schwartz, M. F., & Masters, W. H. (1984). The Masters and Johnson treatment program for dissatisfied homosexual men. *American Journal of Psychiatry, 141* (2): 173–81.

Schwartz, M. F., Reed, E. S., Montgomery, M., Palmer, C., & Mayer, N. H. (1991). The quantitative description of action disorganization after brain damage: A case study. *Cognitive Neuropsychology, 8*, 381–414.

Schwartz, M. F., Saffran, E. M., & Marin, O. S. M. (1980). The word order problem agrammatism: I. Comprehension. *Brain and Language, 10*, 249–62.

Schwartz, S., & Johnson J. H. (1985). *Psychopathology of childhood: A clinical-experimental approach.* New York: Pergamon.

Schweizer, E., Rickels, K., Csanalosi, I., & London, J. (1990). A placebo-controlled study of enciprazine in the treatment of generalized anxiety disorder. *Psychopharmacology Bulletin, 26*, 215–17.

Scott, R. A. (1985). *Rational uses of irrationality: Insanity as a resource for coping in total institutions.* Unpublished manuscript.

Scovern, A. W., & Killman, P. R. (1980). Status of electroconvulsive therapy: Review of the outcome literature. *Psychological Bulletin, 87*, 260–303.

Scoville, W. B., & Milner, B. (1957). Loss of recent memory after bilateral hippocampal lesions. *Journal of Neurology, Neurosurgery and Psychiatry, 20*, 11–21.

Scull, A. (1981). Moral treatment reconsidered: Some sociological comments on an episode in the history of British psychiatry. In A. Scull (Ed.), *Madhouses, mad-doctors and madmen: The social history of psychiatry in the Victorian era* (pp. 105–18). Philadelphia: University of Pennsylvania Press.

Searles, H. F. (1959). The effort to drive the other person crazy! An element in the aetiology and psychotherapy of schizophrenia. *British Journal of Medical Psychology, 32*, 1–18.

Sears, R. R. (1936). Experimental studies of projection: I. Attribution of traits. *Journal of Social Psychology, 7*, 151–63.

Secunda, S., Katz, M. M., & Friedman, R. (1973). *The depressive disorders in 1973.* National Institute of Mental Health. Washington, DC: U.S. Government Printing Office.

Sedney, M. (1987). Development of adrogyny: Parental influences. *Psychology of Women Quarterly, 11*, 321–26.

Seeman, P., Lee, T., Chau-Wong, M., & Wong, K. (1976). Antipsychotic drug doses and neuroleptic/dopamine receptors. *Nature, 261*, 717–19.

Segal, J. (1968). Finding the right therapy for you. *Cosmopolitan, 304*, 262–77.

Segal, S., Watson, M., Goldfinger, S., & Averbuck, D. (1988). Civil commitment in the psychiatric emergency room: II. Mental disorder indicators and three dangerousness criteria. *Archives of General Psychiatry, 45*, 753–58.

Seligman, M. E. P. (1968). Chronic fear produced by unpredictable shock. *Journal of Comparative and Physiological Psychology, 66*, 402–11.

Seligman, M. E. P. (1970). On the generality of the laws of learning. *Psychological Review, 77*, 406–18.

Seligman, M. E. P. (1975). *Helplessness: On depression, development, and death.* San Francisco: Freeman.

Seligman, M. E. P. (1978). Comment and integration. *Journal of Abnormal Psychology, 87*, 165–79.

Seligman, M. E. P. (1980). Harris on selected misrepresentation: The selected misrepresentation of Seligman. *American Psychologist, 35*, 214–15.

Seligman, M. E. P. (1991). *Learned optimism: The skill to conquer life's obstacles, large and small.* New York: Random House.

Seligman, M. E. P. (1993). *What you can change and what you can't: The ultimate guide to self-improvement.* New York: Knopf.

Seligman, M. E. P., Abramson, L. Y., Semmel, A., & von Baeyer, C. (1979). Depressive attributional style. *Journal of Abnormal Psychology, 88*, 242–47.

Seligman, M. E. P., & Binik, Y. M. (1977). The safety signal hypothesis. In H. Davis & H. Hurwitz (Eds.), *Pavlovian operant interactions.* Hillsdale, NJ: Erlbaum.

Seligman, M. E. P., & Hager, J. (Eds.). (1972). *Biological boundaries of learning.* New York: Appleton-Century-Croft.

Seligman, M. E. P., & Johnston, J. C. (1973). A cognitive theory of avoidance learning. In F. J. McGuigan, & D. B. Lumsden (Eds.), *Contemporary approaches to conditioning and learning.* Washington, DC: Winston.

Seligman, M. E. P., & Maier, S. F. (1967). Failure to escape traumatic shock. *Journal of Experimental Psychology, 74*, 1–9.

Selye, H. (1956). *The stress of life.* New York: McGraw-Hill.

Selye, H. (1975). Confusion and controversy in the stress field. *Journal of Human Stress, 1*, 37–44.

Semans, J. H. (1956). Premature ejaculation: A new approach. *Southern Medical Journal, 49*, 353–58.

Senay, E. C., & Renault, P. F. (1972). Treatment methods for heroin addicts. In D. E. Smith & G. R. Gay (Eds.), *It's so good, don't even try it once.* Englewood Cliffs, NJ: Prentice-Hall.

Serling, R. J. (1986). Curing a fear of flying. *USAIR*, 12–19.

Shaffer, D. (1976). Enuresis. In M. Rutter & L. Hersov (Eds.), *Child psychiatry: Modern approaches.* Oxford: Blackwell.

Shaffer, H. J., & Jones, S. B. (1985). *Quitting cocaine: The struggle against impulse.* Lexington, MA: Lexington Books.

Shah, D. R., Pandey, S. K., & Rathi, R. (1972). Psychiatric manifestation in pellagra. *Journal of Association of Physicians of India, 20*, 573–78.

Shallice, T. (1988). *From neuropsychology to mental structure.* Cambridge: Cambridge University Press.

Shallice, T., & Burgess, P. W. (1992). Deficits in strategy applications following frontal-lobe damage in man. *Brain, 114*, 727–41.

Shanok, S. S., & Lewis, D. O. (1981). Medical histories of female delinquents. *Archives of General Psychiatry, 38*, 211–13.

Shapiro, A. K., Struening, E., Shapiro, E., & Barten, H. (1976). Prognostic correlates of psychotherapy in psychiatric outpatients. *American Journal of Psychiatry, 133*, 802–808.

Shapiro, D. (1965). *Neurotic styles.* New York: Basic Books.

Shapiro, D. A., & Shapiro, D. (1982). Meta-analysis of comparative therapy outcome studies: A replication and refinement. *Psychological Bulletin, 92,* 581–604.

Shapiro, D. A., & Shapiro, D. (1983). Comparative therapy outcome research: Methodological implications of meta-analysis. *Journal of Consulting and Clinical Psychology, 51,* 42–53.

Shapiro, R. J. (1974). Therapist attitudes and premature termination in family and individual therapy. *Journal of Nervous and Mental Diseases, 159,* 101–107.

Shea, M. T., Elkin, I., Imber, S. D., & Sotsky, S. M. (1992). Course of depressive symptoms over follow-up: Findings about the National Institute of Mental Health Treatment of Depression Collaborative Research Program. *Archives of General Psychiatry, 49*(10): 782–87.

Shea, S. C. (1990). Contemporary psychiatric interviewing: Integration of DSM-III-R, psychodynamic concerns and mental status. In G. Goldstein & M. Hersen (Eds.), *Handbook of psychological assessment* (2nd ed.). New York: Pergamon.

Sheehan, D. V. (1984). Delineation of anxiety and phobic disorders responsive to monoamine oxidase inhibitors: Implications for classification. *Journal of Clinical Psychiatry, 45* (7): 29–36.

Shekelle, R. B., Gale, M., Ostfeld, A. M., & Paul, O. (1983). Hostility, risk of coronary heart disease, and mortality. *Psychosomatic Medicine, 45* (2): 109–14.

Shekelle, R. B., Hulley, S. B., Neaton, J. D., et al. (1985). The MRFIT behavior study. Type A behavior and incidence of coronary heart disease. *American Journal of Epidemiology, 122,* 559–70.

Sher, K. J., Mann, B., & Frost, R. O. (1984). Cognitive dysfunction in compulsive checkers: Further explorations. *Behaviour Research and Therapy, 22,* 493–502.

Sherer, M. A. (1988). Intravenous cocaine: Psychiatric effects, biological mechanisms. *Biological Psychiatry, 24,* 865–85.

Sherman, A. D., & Petty, F. (1980). Neurochemical basis of the action of antidepressants on learned helplessness. *Behavioral and Neurological Biology, 30,* 119–34.

Sherman, A. D., & Petty, F. (1982). Additivity of neurochemical changes in learned helplessness and imipramine. *Behavioral and Neurological Biology, 35* (4): 344–53.

Shields, J. (1972). *Monozygotic twins brought up apart and brought up together.* Oxford: Oxford University Press.

Shneidman, E. (1976). Suicide among the gifted. In E. S. Shneidman (Ed.), *Suicidology: Contemporary developments.* New York: Grune & Stratton.

Shoham-Salomon, V. (1991). Introduction to special section on client-therapy interaction research. *Journal of Consulting and Clinical Psychology, 59*(2): 203–4.

Shoham-Salomon, V., & Hannah, M. T. (1991). Client-treatment interaction in the study of differential change processes. *Journal of Consulting and Clinical Psychology, 59,* 217–25.

Shoham-Salomon, V., & Rosenthal, R. (1987). Paradoxical interventions: A meta-analysis. *Journal of Consulting and Clinical Psychology, 55* (1): 22–28.

Shore, J. E., Tatum, E. L., & Vollmer, W. M. (1986). Psychiatric reaction to disaster: The Mount St. Helens experience. *American Journal of Psychiatry, 143* (5): 590–95.

Siegel, D., & Wissler, T. (1986). Family environment as a predictor of psychiatric rehospitalization. *American Journal of Psychiatry, 143*(1): 56–60.

Siegel, S. (1977). Morphine tolerance as an associative process. *Journal of Experimental Psychology: Animal Behavior Processes, 3,* 1–13.

Siegal, S. (1979). The role of conditioning in drug tolerance and addiction. In J. D. Keehn (Ed.), *Psychopathology in animals: Research and treatment implications.* New York: Academic Press.

Sifneos, P. E. (1973). The prevalence of "alexithymic" characteristics in psychosomatic patients. *Psychotherapy and Psychosomatics, 22,* 255–62.

Sigvardsson, S., Cloninger, C. R., Bohman, M., & von Knorring, A. L. (1982). Predisposition to petty criminality in Swedish adoptees. III: Sex differences and validation of the male typology. *Archives of General Psychiatry, 39,* 1248–53.

Silverman, J. (1964). The problem of attention in research and theory in schizophrenia. *Psychological Review, 71,* 352–79.

Silverman, L. H. (1976). Psychoanalytic theory: The reports of my death are greatly exaggerated. *American Psychologist, 31*(9): 621–37.

Silverstone, J. T., & Salkind, M. R. (1973). Controlled evaluation of intravenous drugs in the specific desensitization of phobias. *Canadian Psychiatric Association Journal, 18*(1): 848–50.

Simon, G. E., & Von Korff, M. (1991). Somatization and psychiatric disorder in the NIMH Epidemiological Catchment Area Study. *American Journal of Psychiatry, 148,* 1494–1500.

Simpson, D. D., Savage, L. J., & Sells, S. B. (1978). *Data book on drug treatment outcomes.* Fort Worth: Institute of Behavioral Research.

Skinner, B. F. (1971). *Beyond freedom and dignity.* New York: Knopf.

Sladek, J. K., Jr., & Shoulson, I. (1988). Neural transplantation: A call for patience rather than patients. *Science, 240,* 1386–88.

Sloane, R. B., Cristol, A. H., Pepernik, M. C., & Staples, F. R. (1970). Role preparation and expectation of improvement in psychotherapy. *Journal of Nervous and Mental Diseases, 150,* 18–26.

Sloane, R. B., Staples, F. R., Cristol, A. H., Yorkston, N. J., & Whipple, K. (1975). *Psychoanalysis versus behavior therapy.* Cambridge: Harvard University Press.

Smith, B., & Sechrest, L. (1991). Treatment of aptitude × treatment interactions. *Journal of Consulting and Clinical Psychology, 59,* 233–44.

Smith, D., Marcus, M. D., & Kaye, W. (1992). Cognitive-behavioral treatment of obese binge eaters. *International Journal of Eating Disorders, 12,* 257–62.

Smith, J. C., Glass, G. V., & Miller, T. I. (1980). *The benefits of psychotherapy.* Baltimore: The Johns Hopkins Press.

Smith, M. L., & Glass, G. V. (1977). Meta-analysis of psychotherapy outcome studies. *American Psychologist, 32,* 752–60.

Smith, M. L., Kates, M. H., & Vriezen, E. R. (1991). The development of frontal-lobe functions. In S. J. Segalowitz & I. Rapin (Eds.), *Handbook of neuropsychology, Vol. 7: Child neuropsychology.* Amsterdam: Elsevier.

Smith, R. E., Sarason, I. G., & Sarason, B. R. (1982). *Psychology: The frontiers of behavior.* New York: Harper & Row.

Smith, R. J. (1978). *The psychopath in society.* New York: Academic Press.

Smith, T. (1992). Hostility and health: Current status of a psychosomatic hypothesis. *Health Psychology, 11,* 139–50.

Snow, R. E. (1991). Aptitude-treatment interaction as a framework for research on individual differences in psychotherapy. *Journal of Consulting and Clinical Psychology, 59,* 205–16.

Snyder, S. H. (1974a). Catecholamines as mediators of drug effects in schizophrenia. In F. O. Schmitt & F. G. Worden (Eds.), *The neurosciences: Third study program.* Cambridge, MA: MIT Press.

Snyder, S. H. (1974b). *Madness and the brain.* New York: McGraw-Hill.

Snyder, S. H. (1977). Opiate receptors and internal opiates. *Scientific American, 236,* 44–56.

Snyder, S. H. (1981). Dopamine receptors, neuroleptics and schizophrenia. *American Journal of Psychiatry, 138,* 460–64.

Snyder, S. H. (1986). *Drugs and the brain.* New York: Scientific American Library.

Snyder, S. H., Banerjee, S. P., Yamamura, H. I., & Greenberg, D. (1974). Neurotransmitters and schizophrenia. *Science, 184,* 1243–53.

Snyder, W. D., Simpson, D. M., Nielson, S., et. al., (1983). Neurological complications of Acquired Immune Deficiency Syndrome: Analysis of 50 patients. *Annals of Neurology, 14,* 403–18.

Sohlberg, S. C., & Yaniv, S. (1985). Social adjustment and cognitive performance of high-risk children. *Schizophrenia Bulletin, 11*, 61–64.

Sokol, L., Beck, A. T., Greenberg, R. L., Wright, F. D., & Berchick, R. J. (1989). Cognitive therapy of panic disorder: A nonpharmacological alternative. *Journal of Nervous and Mental Diseases, 177*(12): 711–16.

Solomon, R. L. (1977). An opponent process theory of acquired motivation: The affective dynamics of addiction. In J. Maser & M. Seligman (Eds.), *Psychopathology: Experimental models*. San Francisco: Freeman.

Solomon, R. L., & Corbit, J. D. (1974). An opponent process theory of motivation. *Psychological Reviews, 81*(2): 119–45.

Solomon, R. L., Kamin, L. J., & Wynne, L. C. (1953). Traumatic avoidance learning: The outcomes of several extinction procedures with dogs. *Journal of Abnormal Social Psychology, 48*, 291–302.

Solomon, Z., Kotler, M., & Mikulincer, M. (1988). Combat-related post-traumatic stress disorder among second-generation Holocaust survivors: Preliminary findings. *American Journal of Psychiatry, 145*, 865–68.

Solomon, Z., Laor, N., Weiler, D., & Muller, U. (1993). The psychological impact of the Gulf War: A study of acute stress in Israeli evacuees. *Archives of General Psychiatry, 50*, 320–21.

Solomon, Z., Oppenheimer, B., Elizur, Y., & Waysman, M. (1990). Exposure to recurrent combat stress: Can successful coping in a second war heal combat-related PTSD from the past? *Journal of Anxiety Disorders, 4*, 141–45.

Sontag, S. (1978). Disease as political metaphor. *New York Review of Books, 25*, 33.

Southard, D. R., Coates, T. J., Kolodner, K., Parker, F. C., Padgett, N. E., & Kennedy, H. L. (1986). Relationship between mood and blood pressure in the natural environment: An adolescent population. *Health Psychology, 5*, 469–80.

Spanos, N. P., Weekes, J. R., & Bertrand, L. D. (1985). Multiple personality: A social psychological perspective. *Journal of Abnormal Psychology, 94*, 362–76.

Spark, R. F., White, R. A., & Connelly, P. B. (1980). Impotence is not always psychogenic. *Journal of the American Medical Association, 243*, 750–55.

Sparrow, S. S., Balla, D. A., & Cicchetti, D. V. (1984). *Vineland adaptive behavior scales*. Circle Pines, MN: American Guidance Service.

Sperry, R. W. (1974). Lateral specialization in the surgically separated hemispheres. In F. O. Schmitt & F. G. Worden (Eds.), *The neurosciences: Third study program*. Cambridge, MA: MIT Press.

Spielberger, C. D., Gorsuch, R. C., & Lushene, R. E. (1970). *Manual for the state-trait anxiety inventory*. Palo Alto, CA: Consulting Psychologists Press.

Spiegel, D. (1984). Multiple personality as a post-traumatic stress disorder. *Psychiatric Clinics of North America, 7*, 101–10.

Spiegel, D. (1990). Dissociating dissociation: A commentary on Dr. Garcia's article. *Dissociation: Progress in the Dissociative Disorders, 3*, 214–15.

Spiegel, D., Bloom, J., Kraemer, H., & Gottheil, E. (1989).Effect of psychosocial treatment on survival of patients with metastatic breast cancer. *The Lancet*, October 14, pp. 888–91.

Spiegel, D., & Cardena, E. (1991). Disintegrated experience: The dissociative disorders revisited. *Journal of Abnormal Psychology, 100*, 366–78.

Spiegel, R. (1989). *Psychopharmacology* (2nd ed.). New York: Wiley.

Spierings, C., Poels, P. J., Sijben, N., Gabreels, F. J., et al. (1990). Conversion disorders in childhood: A retrospective follow-up study of 84 inpatients. *Developmental Medicine and Child Neurology, 32*, 865–71.

Spies, T. D., Aring, C. D., Gelperin, J., & Bean, W. B. (1938). The mental symptoms of pellagra. Their relief with nicotinic acid. *American Journal of the Medical Sciences, 196*, 461–75.

Spitz, R. A. (1946). Anaclitic depression. *The Psychoanalytic Study of the Child, 2*, 313–47.

Spitzer, R. L. (1975). On pseudoscience in science, logic in remission and psychiatric diagnosis: A critique of Rosenhan's "On being sane in insane places." *Journal of Abnormal Psychology, 84*, 442–52.

Spitzer, R. L. (1991). An outsider-insider's views about revising the DSMs. *Journal of Abnormal Psychology, 100* (3): 294–96.

Spitzer, R. L., & Endicott, J. (1969). Diagno II: Further developments in a computer program for psychiatric diagnosis. *American Journal of Psychiatry, 125*, 12–21.

Spitzer, R. L., Endicott, J., Robins, E., Kuriansky, J., & Gurland, B. (1975). Preliminary report of the reliability of research diagnostic criteria applied to psychiatric case records. In A. Sudilofsky, B. Beer, & S. Gershon (Eds.), *Prediction in psychopharmacology*. New York: Raven Press.

Spitzer, R. L., & Fleiss, J. L. (1974). A reanalysis of the reliability of psychiatric diagnosis. *British Journal of Psychiatry, 125*, 341–47.

Spitzer, R., Forman, J., & Nee, J. (1979). DSM-III field trials: I. Initial inter-rater diagnostic reliability. *American Journal of Psychiatry, 136*, 815–17.

Spitzer, R., Gibbon, M., Skodol, A., Williams, J., & First, M. (1989). *DSM-III-R case book*. Washington, DC: American Psychiatric Press.

Spitzer, R. L., Skodol, A. E., Gibbon, M., & Williams, J. B. W. (1981). *DSM-III casebook*. Washington, DC: American Psychiatric Association.

Spitzer, R. L., & Wilson, P. T. (1975). Nosology and the official psychiatric nomenclature. In A. Freedman & H. Kaplan (Eds.), *Comprehensive textbook of psychiatry*. New York: Williams & Wilkins.

Springer, S. P., & Deutsch, G. (1993). *Left brain, right brain* (3rd ed.). New York: Freeman.

Squire, L. R. (1982). The neuropsychology of memory. *Annual Review of Neuroscience, 5*, 241–73.

Squire, L. R. (1986). Memory functions as affected by electroconvulsive therapy. *Annals of the New York Academy of Sciences, 462*, 307–14.

Squire, L. R., (1987). *Memory and brain*. New York: Oxford University Press.

Squire, L. R. (1992). Memory and the hippocampus: A synthesis from findings with rats, monkeys, and humans. *Psychological Review, 79*, 195–231.

Squire, L. R.., & Butters, N. (Eds.). (1992). *The neuropsychology of memory* (2nd ed.). New York: Guilford Press.

Squire, L. R., Cohen, N. J., & Nadel, L. (1984). The medial temporal region and memory consolidation: A new hypothesis. In H. Weingarten & E. Parker (Eds.), *Memory consolidation: Towards a psychobiology of cognition* (pp. 185–210). Hillsdale, NJ: Erlbaum.

Squire, L. R., Slater, P. C., & Miller, P. L. (1981). Retrograde amnesia and bilateral electroconvulsive therapy: Long-term follow-up. *Archives of General Psychiatry, 38*, 89–95.

Srole, L., Langner, T. S., Michael, S. T., Opler, M. K., & Rennie, T. A. (1962). *Mental health in the metropolis: The midtown Manhattan study*. New York: McGraw-Hill.

Staats, A. W. (1978). *Child learning intelligence and personality* (rev. ed.). Kalamazoo, MI: Behaviordela.

Stamler, J., Dyer, A. R., Shakelle, R. B., Neaton, J., & Stamler, R. (1993). Relationship of baseline major risk factors to coronary and all-cause mortality, and to longevity: Findings from long-term follow-up of Chicago cohorts. *Cardiology, 82*, 191–222.

Stampfl, T. G. (1967). Implosive therapy. In S. G. Armitage (Ed.), *Behavior modification techniques in the treatment of emotional disorders*. Battle Creek, MI.: V.A. Publication.

Stampfl, T. G., & Levis, D. J. (1967). Essentials of implosive therapy: A learning-theory-based psychodynamic behavioral therapy. *Journal of Abnormal Psychology, 72*, 496–503.

Stangl, D., Pfohl, B., Zimmerman, M., Bowers, W., & Corenthal, R. (1985). A structured interview for the DSM-III personality disorders: A preliminary report. *Archives of General Psychiatry, 42,* 591–96.

Stark, K.D. (1990). *Childhood depression: School-based intervention.* New York: Guilford Press.

Stark, M. J., & Kane, B. J. (1985). General and specific psychotherapy role induction with substance-abusing clients. *International Journal of Addiction, 20*(8): 1135–41.

Steadman, H. J. (1973). Follow-up on Baxstrom patients returned to hospitals for the criminally insane. *American Journal of Psychiatry, 3,* 317–19.

Steadman, H. J. (1981). The statistical prediction of violent behavior: Measuring the costs of a public protectionist versus a civil libertarian model. *Law and Human Behavior, 5,* 263–74.

Steadman, H. J. (1983). Predicting dangerousness among the mentally ill: Art, magic, and science. *International Journal of Law and Psychiatry, 6,* 381–90.

Steadman, H. J., & Keveles, G. (1972). The community adjustment and criminal activity of the Baxstrom patients: 1966–1970. *American Journal of Psychiatry, 129,* 304–10.

Steadman, H., & Keveles, G. (1978). The community adjustment and criminal activity of Baxstrom patients. *American Journal of Psychiatry, 135,* 1218–20.

Steadman, H. J., McGreevy, M. A., Morrissey, J. P., Callahan, L. A., Robbins, P. C., & Cirincione, C. (1993) *Before and after Hinckley: Evaluating insanity defense reform.* New York: Guilford Press.

Steadman, H. J., Monahan, J., Hartstone, E., Davis, S. K., & Robbins, P. C. (1982). Mentally disordered offenders: A national survey of patients and facilities. *Law and Human Behavior, 8*(1): 31–37.

Stein, J. A., Golding, J. M., Siegel, J. M., Burnam, M. A., Sorenson, S. B., & Powell, G. J. (1988). Long-term psychological sequelae of child sexual abuse: The Los Angeles epidemiologic catchment area study. In G. E. Wyatt (Ed.), *Lasting effects of child sexual abuse.* Newbury Park, CA: Sage.

Stein, L. (1968). Chemistry of reward and punishment. In D. Efron (Ed.), *Psychopharmacology: Review of progress, 1957–1967* (pp. 105–23). Washington, DC: U.S. Government Printing Office.

Stein, L. I., Test, M. A., & Marx, A. J.(1975). Alternative to the hospital: A controlled study. *American Journal of Psychiatry, 132,* 517–21.

Steinberg, L. (1986). Stability and instability of Type A behavior from childhood to young adulthood. *Developmental Psychology, 22,* 393–401.

Steinberg, M., Rounsaville, B., & Cicchetti, D. V. (1990). The structured clinical interview for DSM-III-R dissociative disorders: Preliminary report on a new diagnostic instrument. *American Journal of Psychiatry, 147,* 76–82.

Steinhausen, H. C., Göbel, D., Breinlinger, M., & Wohlleben, B. (1986). A community survey of infantile autism. *Journal of the American Academy of Child Psychiatry, 25,* 186–89.

Steinmark, W. W., & Borkevic, T. D. (1974). Active and placebo treatment effects on moderate insomnia under counter-demand and positive demand instructions. *Journal of Abnormal Psychology, 83,* 157–63.

Stern, D. (1985). *The interpersonal world of the infant.* New York: Basic Books.

Stern, J. (1981). Brain dysfunction in some hereditary disorders of amino acid metabolism. In P. J. Mittler, & J. M. deJong (Eds.), *Frontiers of knowledge in mental retardation: Vol II. Biomedical aspects.* Baltimore, MD: University Park Press.

Stewart, D. E. (1990). Emotional disorders misdiagnosed as physical illness: Environmental hypersensitivity, candidiasis hypersensitivity, and chronic fatigue syndrome. *International Journal of Mental Health, 19,* 56–68.

St. George-Hyslop, P., et al., (1987). The genetic defect causing familial Alzheimer's disease maps on chromosome 21. *Science, 235,* 885–90.

St. George-Hyslop, P., Haines, J., Rogaev, E., et al. (1992). Genetic evidence for a novel familial Alzheimer's disease locus on chromosome 14. *Nature Genetics, 2,* 330–34.

Stinnett, J. (1978). Personal communication.

Stoller, R. J. (1969). Parental influences in male transsexualism. In R. Green & J. Money (Eds.), *Transsexualism and sex reassignment.* Baltimore: The Johns Hopkins Press.

Stoller, R. J. (1976). *Sexual gender—the transsexual experiment* (Vol. II). New York: Jason Aronson.

Stone, A. A. (1975). *Mental health and law: A system in transition.* Rockville, MD.: National Institute of Mental Health, Center for Studies of Crime and Delinquency.

Stone, D. M., Merchant, K. M., Hanson, G. R., & Gibb, J. W. (1987). Immediate and long-term effects of 3, 4-methylenedioxymethamphetamine (MDMA) on serotonin pathways in brain of rat. *Neuropharmacology, 26,* 1677–83.

Stone, G. C., Weiss, S. M., Matarazzo, J. D., Miller, N. E., Rodin, J., Belar, C. K., Fullick, M., & Singer, J. E. (Eds.). (1987). *Health Psychology: A discipline and a profession.* Chicago: University of Chicago Press.

Stone, M. H. (1990). Abuse and abusiveness in borderline personality disorder. In P. S. Links (Ed.), *Family environment and borderline pesonality disorder* (pp. 131–48). Washington, DC: American Psychiatric Press.

Storms, M. D. (1981). A theory of erotic orientation development. *Psychological Review, 88,* 340–53.

Strauss, M. E., Foureman, W. C., & Parwatikar, S. D. (1974). Schizophrenics' size estimations of thematic stimuli. *Journal of Abnormal Psychology, 83*(2): 117–23.

Streissguth, A. P., Grant, T. M., & Barr, H. M. (1991). Cocaine and the use of alcohol and other drugs during pregnancy. *American Journal of Obstetrics and Gynecology, 164,* 1239–43.

Strober, M., Lampert, C., Schmidt, S., & Morrell, W. (1993). The course of major depressive disorder in adolescents: I. Recovery and risk of manic switching in a follow-up of psychotic and nonpsychotic subtypes. *Journal of the American Academy of Child and Adolescent Psychiatry 32*(1): 34–42.

Strupp, H. H. (1963). The outcome problem in psychotherapy revisited. *Psychotherapy: Theory, Research and Practice, 1,* 1–13.

Strupp, H. H., & Binder, J. (1984). *Psychotherapy in a new key: Time limited dynamic psychotherapy.* New York: Norton.

Strupp, H. H., & Bloxom, A. (1973). Preparing lower-class patients for group psychotherapy: Development and evaluation of a role induction film. *Journal of Consulting and Clinical Psychology, 41,* 373–84.

Strupp, H. H., Fox, R., & Lessler, K. (1969). *Patients view their psychotherapy.* Baltimore: The Johns Hopkins Press.

Strupp, H. H., Hadley, S. W., & Gomes-Schwartz, B. (1977). *Psychotherapy for better or worse: An analysis of the problem of negative effects.* New York: Jason Aronson.

Strupp, H. H., Wallach, M., & Wogan, M. (1964). Psychotherapy experience in retrospect: Questionnaire survey of former patients and their therapists. *Psychological Monographs, 78* (11, Whole No. 588).

Stuart, R. B. (1969). Operant-interpersonal treatment for marital discord. *Journal of Consulting and Clinical Psychology, 33,* 675–82.

Stunkard, A. J. (1976). Anorexia nervosa. In J. P. Sanford (Ed.), *The science and practice of clinical medicine* (pp. 361–63). New York: Grune & Stratton.

Stunkard, A. J., & Penick, S. B. (1979). Behavior modification and treatment of obesity. *Archives of General Psychiatry, 36,* 801–11.

Sturdevant, R. A. L. (1976). Epidemiology of peptic ulcer: Report of a conference. *American Journal of Epidemiology, 104,* 9–14.

Stuss, D. T., & Benson, D. F. (1986). *The frontal lobes.* New York: Raven Press.

Suarez, J. M., & Pittluck, A. T. (1976). Global amnesia: Organic and functional considerations. *Bulletin of the American Academy of Psychiatric Law, 3,* 17–24.

Suddath, R. L., Christison, M. D., Torrey, E. F., Casanova, M., & Weinberger, D. R. (1990). Anatomic abnormalities in the brains of monozygotic twins discordant for schizophrenia. *New England Journal of Medicine, 322,* 789–94.

Sue, D. W., & Sue, D. (1992). *Counseling the culturally different* (2nd ed.). New York: Wiley.

Sullivan, P. M., & Burley, S. K. (1990). Mental testing of the hearing-impaired child. In C. R. Reynolds & R. W. Kamphaus (Eds.), *Handbook of psychological and educational assessment of children.* New York: Guilford Press.

Summers, M. (1971). *Witchcraft and black magic.* New York: Grand River Books.

Susser, M. (1967). Causes of peptic ulcer: A selective epidemiological review. *Journal of Chronic Disabilities, 20,* 435–56.

Suzdak, P. P., Schwartz, R. D., Skolnick, P., & Paul, S. M. (1986). Ethanol stimulates gamma-aminobutyric acid receptor-mediated chloride transport in rat brain synaptoneurosomes. *Proceedings of National Academy of Sciences U.S.A, 83,* 4071–75.

Svartberg, M., & Stiles, T. C. (1991). Comparative effects of short-term psychodynamic psychotherapy. *Journal of Consulting and Clinical Psychology, 59*(5): 704–14.

Svebak, S., Cameron, A., & Levander, S. (1990). Clonazepam and imipramine in the treatment of panic attacks. *Journal of Clinical Psychiatry, 51,* 14–17.

Swanson, D. W. (1968). Adult sexual abuse of children: The man and circumstances. *Diseases of the Nervous System, 29*(10): 677–83.

Swanson, W. C., & Breed, W. (1976). Black suicide in New Orleans. In E. S. Shneidman (Ed.), *Suicidology: Contemporary developments.* New York: Grune & Stratton.

Swedo, S., Pietrini, P., Leonard, H., et al. (1992). Cerebral glucose metabolism in childhood-onset obsessive-compulsive disorder. *Archives of General Psychiatry, 49,* 690–94.

Sweeney, P. O., Anderson, K., & Bailey, S. (1986). Attributional style in depression: A meta-analytic review. *Journal of Personality and Social Psychology, 50*(5): 974–91.

Sweeney, J. A., Haas, G. L., & Li, S. (1992). Neuropsychological and eye movement abnormalities in first-episode and chronic schizophrenia. *Schizophrenia Bulletin, 18*(2): 283–93.

Szasz, T. S. (1961). *The myth of mental illness.* New York: Dell.

Szasz, T. S. (1963). *Law, liberty and psychiatry: An inquiry into the social uses of mental health practices.* New York: Macmillan.

Szasz, T. S. (1970). *The manufacture of madness.* New York: Dell.

Szasz, T. S. (1974). The ethics of suicide. *Bulletin of Suicidology* (Vol. 9). Philadelphia: Charles Press.

Tagiuri, R., Bruner, J. S., & Blake, R. R. (1958). On the relation between feelings and the perception of feelings among members of small groups. In E. E. Maccoby, T. M. Newcomb, & E. L. Hartley (Eds.), *Readings in social psychology* (pp. 110–16). New York: Holt, Rinehart & Winston.

Talovic, S. A., Mednick, S. A., Schulsinger, F., & Falloon, I. R. H. (1981). Schizophrenia in high-risk subjects: Prognostic maternal characteristics. *Journal of Abnormal Psychology, 89,* 501–504.

Tamerin, J. S., & Mendelson, J. (1970). Alcoholic's expectancies and recall of experiences during intoxication. *American Journal of Psychiatry, 126,* 1697–1704.

Tangney, J. P., Wagner, P., & Gramzow, R. (1992). Proneness to shame, proneness to guilt, and psychopathology. *Journal of Abnormal Psychology, 101*(3): 469–78.

Tarrier, N., & Barrowclough, C. (1990). Family interventions for schizophrenia. *Behavior Modification, 14,* 408–40.

Taube, C. A. (1976). Readmissions to inpatient services of state and county hospitals 1972. Statistical note 110. (DHEW Publications No. ADM 76–308). Rockville, MD: National Institute of Mental Health.

Taubee, E. S., & Wright, H. W. (1971). A psychosocial behavioral model for therapeutic intervention. In C. D. Spielberger (Ed.), *Current topics in clinical and community psychology* (Vol. 3). New York: Academic Press.

Taylor, J. A. (1951). The relationship of anxiety to the conditioned eyelid responses. *Journal of Experimental Psychology, 41,* 81–92.

Taylor, J. A. (1953). A personality scale of manifest anxiety. *Journal of Abnormal and Social Psychology, 48,* 285–90.

Taylor, J. (Ed.). (1958). *Selected writings of John Hughlings Jackson.* New York: Basic Books.

Taylor, W. S., & Martin M. F. (1944). Multiple personality. *Journal of Abnormal and Social Psychology, 39,* 281–300.

Teasdale, J. D. (1985). Psychological treatments for depression: How do they work? *Behaviour Research and Therapy, 23,* 157–65.

Teasdale, J. D., & Rezin, V. (1978). The effect of reducing frequency of negative thoughts on the mood of depressed patients: Test of a cognitive model of depression. *British Journal of Social and Clinical Psychology, 17,* 65–74.

Teicher, M., Glod, C., & Cole, J. (1990). Emergence of intense suicidal preoccupation during fluoxetine treatment. *American Journal of Psychiatry, 147,* 207–10.

Telch, C. F., Agras, W. S., Rossiter, E. M., Wilfley, D., & Kenardy, J. (1990). Group cognitive-behavioral treatment for the nonpurging bulimic: An initial evaluation. *Journal of Consulting and Clinical Psychology, 58,* 629–35.

Telch, M. J. (1988). Combined pharmacological and psychological treatments for panic sufferers. In S. Rachman & J. D. Maser (Eds.), *Panic: Psychological perspectives.* Hillsdale, NJ: Erlbaum.

Telch, M., Agras, S., Taylor, C., et al. (1985). Combined pharmacological and behavioral treatment for agoraphobia. *Behaviour Research and Therapy, 23,* 325–35.

Temerlin, M. K. (1970). Diagnostic bias in community mental health. *Community Mental Health Journal, 6,* 110–17.

Tennant, C. C., Goulston, K. J., & Dent, O. F. (1986). The psychological effects of being a prisoner of war: Forty years after release. *American Journal of Psychiatry, 143,* 618–21.

Terenius, L. (1978). Endogenous peptides and analgesia. *Annual Review of Pharmacology and Toxicology, 18,* 189–204.

Terry, R. D., & Davies, P. (1980). Dementia of the Alzheimer type. *Annual Review of Neuroscience, 3,* 77–95.

Tesar, G. (1990). High potency benzodiazepines for short-term management of panic disorder: The U.S. experience. *Journal of Clinical Psychiatry, 51,* 4–10.

Teuber, H. L., & Powers, E. (1953). Evaluating therapy in a delinquency prevention program. *Psychiatric Treatment, 21,* 138–47.

Theodor, L. H., & Mandelcorn, M. S. (1978). Hysterical blindness: A case report and study using a modern psychophysical technique. *Journal of Abnormal Psychology, 82,* 552–53.

Theorell, T., & Rahe, R. H. (1971). Psychosocial factors in myocardial infarction. I. An inpatient study in Sweden. *Journal of Psychosomatic Research, 15,* 25–31.

Thigpen C. H., & Cleckley, H. (1954). A case of multiple personality. *Journal of Abnormal and Social Psychology, 49,* 135–51.

Thomas, K. (1971). *Religion and the decline of magic.* New York: Charles Scribner's Sons.

Thompson, J., Burns, B., Bartko, J., et al. (1988). The use of ambulatory services by persons with and without phobias. *Medical Care, 26,* 183–98.

Thompson, T., & Dews, P. B. (1985). *Advances in behavioral pharmacology* (Vol. IV). New York: Academic Press.

Thompson, T., & Schuster, C. R. (1964). Morphine in self-administration, food-reinforced, and avoidance behaviors in rhesus monkeys. *Psychopharmacologia, 5,* 87–94.

Thoren, P., Asberg, M., Chronholm, B., et al. (1980). Clomipramine treatment of obsessive-compulsives. *Archives of General Psychiatry, 37,* 1281–85.

Tien, A., Pearlson, G., Machlin, S., et al. (1992). Oculomotor performance in obsessive-compulsive disorder. *American Journal of Psychiatry, 150,* 641–46.

Tienari, P. (1991). Interaction between genetic vulnerability and family environment: The Finnish adoptive family study of schizophrenia. *Acta Psychiatrica Scandinavica, 84,* 460–65.

Thornhill, N. (1989). *Behavioral and Brain Sciences, 12,* 35–36.

Tinklenberg, J. (1977). Anti-anxiety medications and the treatment of anxiety. In J. Barchas, P. Berger, R. Ciaranello, & G. Elliot (Eds.), *Psychopharmacology.* New York: Oxford.

Tizard, J., & Venables, P. H. (1956). Reaction time responses by schizophrenics, mental defectives, and normal adults. *American Journal of Psychiatry, 112,* 803–807.

Tobias, L. L., & MacDonald, M. L. (1974). Withdrawal of maintenance drugs with long-term hospitalized schizophrenics: A critical review. *Psychological Bulletin, 81,* 107–25.

Tomasson, K., Kent, D., & Coryell, W. (1991). Somatization and conversion disorders: Comorbity and demographics at presentation. *Acta Psychiatrica Scandinavica, 84,* 288–93.

Tomes, N. (1984). *A generous confidence.* London: Cambridge University Press.

Tonks, C. M., Paykel, E. S., & Klerman, J. L. (1970). Clinical depressions among Negroes. *American Journal of Psychiatry, 127,* 329–35.

Torgersen, S. (1983). Genetic factors in anxiety disorders. *Archives of General Psychiatry, 40,* 1085–89.

Torgersen, S. (1986a). Genetic factors in moderately severe and mild affective disorders. *Archives of General Psychiatry, 43,* 222–26.

Torgersen, S. (1986b). Genetics of somatoform disorders. *Archives of General Psychiatry, 43,* 502–505.

Torrey, E. F. (1983). *The roots of treason: Ezra Pound and the secret of St. Elizabeth's.* New York: McGraw-Hill.

Torrey, E.F. (1992). Are we overestimating the genetic contribution to schizophrenia? *Schizophrenia Bulletin, 18* (2): 159–70.

Tourney, G. (1967). A history of therapeutic fashions in psychiatry, 1800–1966. *American Journal of Psychiatry, 124,* 784–96.

Traskman-Bendz, L., Alling, C., Alsen, M., et al. (1993). The role of monoamines in suicidal behavior. *Acta Psychiatrica Scandinavica, 87,* 45–47.

Trasler, G. (1973). Criminal behavior. In H. J. Eysenck (Ed.), *Handbook of abnormal psychology.* London: Pitman Medical.

Treece, C., & Khantzian, E. J. (1986). Psychodynamic factors in the development of drug dependence. *Psychiatric Clinics of North America, 9,* 399–412.

Treiber, F., Davis, H., Musante, L., et al. (1993). Ethnicity, gender, family history of myocardial infarction, and hemodynamic responses to laboratory stressors in children. *Health Psychology, 12,* 6–15.

Trevor-Roper, H. (1970). *The European witch-craze of the sixteenth and seventeenth centuries.* New York: Harper & Row.

Trimble, M. (1990). Worldwide use of clomipramine. *Journal of Clinical Psychiatry, 51,* 51–58.

Trotter, R. J. (1986, May). The making of a Type A. *Psychology Today,* p. 12.

Truax, C. B., & Carkhuff, R. R. (1967). *Toward effective counseling and psychotherapy: Training and practice.* Chicago: Aldine.

Truax, C. B., & Mitchell, K. M. (1971). Research on certain therapist interpersonal skills in relation to process and outcome. In A. E. Bergin & S. L. Garfield (Eds.), *Handbook of psychotherapy and behavior change.* New York: Wiley.

Truax, C. B., Shapiro, J. G., & Wargo, D. G. (1968). Effects of alternate sessions and vicarious therapy pretraining on group psychotherapy. *International Journal of Group Psychotherapy, 18,* 186–98.

True, W., Rice, J., Eisen, S., et al. (1993). A twin study of genetic and environmental contributions to liability for post-traumatic stress symptoms. *Archives of General Psychiatry, 50,* 257–64.

Tryon, W. W. (1976). Models of behavior disorder. *American Psychologist, 31,* 509–18.

Tuke, S. (1813). Description of the Retreat, an institution near York for insane persons of the Society of Friends. Cited in Foucault, M., *Madness and civilization: A history of insanity in the age of reason.* New York: Random House, 1965.

Tulving, E. (1985). How many memory systems are there? *American Psychologist, 40,* 385–98.

Turgay, A. (1990). Treatment outcome for children and adolescents with conversion disorder. *Canadian Journal of Psychiatry, 35,* 585–89.

Turner, R. J., & Wagenfeld, M. O. (1967). Occupational mobility and schizophrenia. *American Sociological Review, 32,* 104–13.

Turner, S. M., Beidel, D. C., Dancu, C. V., & Keys, D. J. (1986). Psychopathology of social phobia and comparison to avoidant personality disorder. *Journal of Abnormal Psychology, 95,* 389–94.

Turner, S. M., Beidel, D. C., & Townsley, R. M. (1992). Social phobia: A comparison of specific and generalized subtypes and avoidant personality disorder. *Journal of Abnormal Psychology, 101*(2): 326–31.

Tyrer, P., Murphy, S., Kingdon, D., et al. (1988). The Nottingham study of neurotic disorder: Comparison of drug and psychological treatment. *Lancet,* 235–40.

Ullman, L. P., & Krasner, L. (1965). *Case studies in behavior modification.* New York: Holt, Rinehart & Winston.

Understedt, V. (1971). Stereotoxic mapping of the monoamine pathways in the rat brain. *Acta Psychiatrica Scandinavica, 10,* 1–48.

Upham, Charles W. (1867). Salem witchcraft. Cited in A. Deutsch, *The mentally ill in America.* New York: Columbia University Press, 1949.

Urbina, S. P., Golden, C. J., & Ariel, R. N. (1982). WAIS/WAIS-R: Initial comparisons. *Clinical Neuropsychology, 4,* 145–46.

U.S. Department of Health and Human Services. (1987). Vital Statistics of the United States, 1984. Volume II-Mortality. National Center for Health Statistics, Hyattsville, MD.

U.S. House of Representatives, Select Committee on Children, Youth, and Families. (1992). *The profits of misery: How inpatient psychiatric treatment bilks the system and betrays our trust.* Washington, DC: U.S. Government Printing Office.

Vaccarino, F. J., Bloom, F. E., & Koob, G .F. (1985). Block of nucleus accumbens opiate receptors attenuates intravenous heroin reward in the rat. *Psychopharmacology, 86,* 37–42.

Vaillant, G. E. (1977). *Adaptation to life.* Boston: Little, Brown.

Vaillant, G. E. (1978). Natural history of male psychological health: IV. What kinds of men do not get psychosomatic illness. *Psychosomatic Medicine, 40,* 420–31.

Vaillant, G. E. (1983). *The natural history of alcoholism.* Cambridge, MA: Harvard University Press.

Vaillant, G. E. (1986). *Empirical studies of ego mechanisms of defense.* Washington, DC: American Psychiatric Press.

Vaillant, G. E. (1992). Is there a natural history of addiction? In C. P. O'Brien & J. H. Jaffe (Eds.), *Addictive states.* New York: Raven Press.

Vaillant, G. E., Bond, M., & Vaillant, C. O. (1986). An empirically validated hierarchy of defense mechanisms. *Archives of General Psychiatry, 43,* 786–94.

Valenstein, E. S. (1973). *Brain control.* New York: Wiley.

Valenstein, E. S. (1986). *Great and desperate cures.* New York: Basic Books.

Valentine, C. W. (1930). The innate bases of fear. *Journal of Genetic Psychology, 37,* 394–419.

Valins, S., & Nisbett, R. E. (1976). Attribution processes in the development and treatment of emotional disorders. In J. T. Spence, R. C. Carson, & J. W. Thibaut (Eds.), *Behavioral approaches to therapy.* Morristown, NJ: General Learning Press.

VandenBos, G. R., & Karon, B. P. (1971). Pathogenesis: A new therapist personality dimension related to therapeutic effectiveness. *Journal of Personality Assessment, 35,* 252–60.

Vanderlinden, J., Van Dyck, R., Vandereycken, W., & Vertommen, H. (1991). Dissociative experiences in the general population in the Netherlands and Belgium: A study with the Dissociative Questionnaire (DIS-Q). *Dissociation: Progress in the Dissociative Disorders, 4,* 180–84.

Van Dyke, C., Zilberg, N. J., & McKinnon, J. A. (1985). Post-traumatic stress disorder: A thirty-year delay in a World War II veteran. *American Journal of Psychiatry, 142,* 1070–73.

Van Kempen, G. M., Zitman, F. G., Linssen, A. C., & Edelbroek, P. M. (1992). Biochemical measures in patients with somatoform pain disorder, before, during, and after treatment with amitriptyline with or without flupentixol. *Biological Psychiatry, 31,* 670–80.

Van Praag, H., Korf, J., & Sheet, D. (1973). Cerebral monoamines and depression: An investigation with the probenecid technique. *Archives of General Psychiatry, 28,* 827–31.

Varnik, A., & Wasserman, D. (1992). Suicides in the former Soviet republics. *Acta Psychiatrica Scandinavica, 86,* 76–78.

Vaughn, C. E., & Leff, J. P. (1976). The influence of family and social factors on the course of psychiatric illness: A comparison of schizophrenic and depressive-neurotic patients. *British Journal of Psychiatry, 129,* 127–37.

Vaughn, C. E., Snyder, K. S., Jones, S., Freeman, W. B., & Falloon, I. R. H. (1984). Family factors in schizophrenic relapse: Replication in California of British research on expressed emotion. *Archives of General Psychiatry, 41,* 1169–77.

Veiel, H. (1993). Detrimental effects of kin support networks on the course of depression. *Journal of Abnormal Psychology, 102,* 419–29.

Veith, I. (1965). *Hysteria: The history of a disease.* Chicago: University of Chicago Press.

Venables, P. (1964). Input dysfunction in schizophrenia. In B. A. Maher (Ed.), *Progress in experimental personality research.* New York: Academic Press.

Ventura, J., Neuchterlein, K. H., Lukoff, D., & Hardesty, J. P. (1989). A prospective study of stressful life events and schizophrenic relapse. *Journal of Abnormal Psychology, 98*(4): 407–11.

Versiani, M., Mundim, F., Nardi, A., et al. (1988). Tranylcypromine in social phobia. *Journal of Clinical Psychopharmacology, 8,* 279–83.

Victor, M., Adams, R. D., & Collins, G. H. (1971). *The Wernicke-Korsakoff syndrome. A clinical and pathological study of 245 patients, 82 with post-mortem examinations.* Philadelphia: Davis.

Videbech, T. (1975). A study of genetic factors, childhood bereavement, and premorbid personality traits in patients with anancastic endogenous depression. *Acta Psychiatrica Scandinavica, 52,* 178–222.

Vogel, G. W. (1975). A review of REM sleep deprivation. *Archives of General Psychiatry, 32,* 96–97.

Voigt, D. Q. (1987). *Baseball: An illustrated history.* University Park, PA: Pennsylvania State University Press.

Volpicelli, J. R. (1989). Psychoactive substance use disorders. In D. L. Rosenhan & M. E. P. Seligman (Eds.), *Abnormal psychology.* New York: Norton.

Volpicelli, J. R., Alterman, A. I., Hayashida, M., & O'Brien, C. P. (1992). Naltrexone in the treatment of alcohol dependence. *Archives of General Psychiatry, 49,* 876–80.

Volpicelli, J. R., Davis, M. A., & Olgin, J. E. (1986). Naltrexone blocks the post-shock increase of ethanol consumption. *Life Sciences, 38,* 841–47.

Wadden, T. A., & Bell, S. T. (1990). Obesity. In A. S. Bellack, M. Hersen, & A. Kazdin (Eds.), *International handbook of behavior modification and therapy* (Vol. 2, pp. 449–73). New York: Plenum Press.

Wadden, T., Stunkard, A., & Smoller, J. (1986). Dieting and depression: A methodological study. *Journal of Consulting and Clinical Psychology, 54,* 869–71.

Wakefield, J. C. (1992a). Disorder as harmful dysfunction: A conceptual critique of DSM-III-R's definition of mental disorder. *Psychological Review, 99,* 232–47.

Wakefield, J. C. (1992b). The concept of mental disorder: On the boundary between biological facts and social values. *American Psychologist, 47,* 373–88.

Wakefield, J. C. (1993). The limits of operationalization: A critique of Spitzer and Endicott's proposed operational criteria of mental disorder. *Journal of Abnormal Psychology, 102,* 160–72.

Walker, E., Hoppes, E., Emory, E., Mednick, S., & Schulsinger, F. (1981). Environmental factors related to schizophrenia in psychophysiologically high-risk males. *Journal of Abnormal Psychology, 90*(4): 313–20.

Waller, N., Kojetin, B., Bouchard, T., Lykken, D., & Tellegen, A. (1990). Genetic and environmental influences on religious interests, attitudes, and values. *Psychological Science, 1,* 138–42.

Wallerstein, J. S., & Kelly, J. B. (1980). California children of divorce. *Psychology Today, 13.*

Walinder, J. (1967). *Transsexualism.* Goteburg: Scandinavian University Books.

Warburton, D. M. (1988). The puzzle of nicotine use. In M. Lader (Ed.), *The psychopharmacology of addiction* (pp. 27–49). New York: Oxford University Press.

Warburton, D. M., & Wesnes, K. (1978). Individual differences in smoking and attentional performance. In R. E. Thornten (Ed.), *Smoking behavior: Physiological and psychological influence* (pp. 19–43). Edinburgh: Churchill-Livingstone.

Ward, C. H., Beck, A. T., Mendelson, M., Mock, J. E., & Erbaugh, J. K. (1962). The psychiatric nomenclature: Reasons for diagnostic disagreement. *Archives of General Psychiatry, 7,* 198–205.

Warheit, G., Holzer, C., & Schwab, J. (1973). An analysis of social class and racial differences in depressive symptom etiology: The community study. *Journal of Health and Social Behavior, 4,* 921–99.

Warner, R. (1978). The diagnosis of antisocial and personality disorders: An example of sex bias. *Journal of Nervous and Mental Disease, 166,* 839–45.

Warrington, E. K., & Weiskrantz, L. (1973). An analysis of short-term and long-term memory defects in man. In J. A. Deutsch (Ed.), *The physiological basis of memory* (pp. 365–96). New York: Academic Press.

Wasson, R. G. (1979). The divine mushroom of immortality. In P. T. Furst (Ed.), *Flesh of the god* (pp. 185–200). New York: Praeger.

Watkins, G. (1960). The incidence of chronic peptic ulcer sounded necropsy: The study of 20,000 examinations performed in Leeds in 1930 to 1949 and in England and Scotland in 1956. *Gut, 1,* 14.

Watson, C. G., & Buranen, C. (1979). The frequency of conversion reaction. *Journal of Abnormal Psychology, 88,* 209–11.

Watson, J. B., & Rayner, R. (1920). Conditioned emotional reactions. *Journal of Experimental Psychology, 3,* 1–14.

Watson, L. S. (1973). *Child behavior modification: A manual for teachers, nurses, and parents.* New York: Pergamon.

Watson, L. S., & Uzzell, R. (1981). *Handbook of behavior modification with the mentally retarded.* New York: Plenum.

Watt, N. F., Anthony, E. J., Wynne, L. C., & Rolf, J. E. (Eds.). (1984). *Children at risk for schizophrenia: A longitudinal perspective.* Cambridge: Cambridge University Press.

Watts, F. N., McKenna, F. P., Sharrock, R., & Trezise, L. (1986). Colour naming of phobia-related words. *British Journal of Psychology, 77,* 97–108.

Watzlawick, P., Beavin, J. H., & Jackson, D. D. (1967). *Pragmatics of human communication.* New York: Norton.

Wegner, J. T., Catalano, F., Gibralter, J., & Kane, J. M. (1985). Schizophrenics with tardive dyskinesia. *Archives of General Psychiatry, 42,* 860–65.

Wehr, T. A., Sack, D. A., & Rosenthal, N. E. (1987). Sleep reduction as a final common pathway in the genesis of mania. *American Journal of Psychiatry, 144,* 201–204.

Weinberg, M., & Williams, C. J. (1974). *Male homosexuals: Their problems and adaptations in three societies.* New York: Oxford University Press.

Weinberger, D. R. (1988). Schizophrenia and the frontal lobes. *Trends in Neuroscience, 11,* 367–70.

Weinberger, D. R., Berman, K. F., & Zec, R. F. (1986). Physiologic dysfunction of dorsolateral prefrontal cortex in schizophrenia. I. Regional cerebral blood flow evidence. *Archives of General Psychiatry, 43* (2): 114–24.

Weiner, B. (1972). *Theories of motivation: From mechanism to cognition.* Chicago: Rand McNally.

Weiner, B. (Ed.) (1974). *Achievement motivation and attribution theory.* Morristown, NJ: General Learning Press.

Weiner, H. M. (1977). *Psychology and human disease.* New York: Elsevier.

Weiner, H., Failer, M., Reiser, M. F., & Mirsky, I. A. (1957). Ideology of duodenal ulcer. I. Rise in specific psychological characteristics to rate of gastric secretion (serum pepsinogen). *Psychosomatic Medicine, 19,* 1.

Weiner, I. (1969). Effectiveness of a suicide prevention program. *Mental Hygiene, 53,* 357.

Weintraub, S., & Mesulam, M. M. (1989). Neglect: Hemispheric specialization, behavioral components and anatomical correlates. In F. Boller & J. Grafmann (Eds.), *Handbook of neuropsychology* (Vol. 2). Amsterdam: Elsevier.

Weisaeth, L. (1989). A study of behavioural responses to industrial disaster. *Acta Psychiatrica Scandinavia, 80,* 13–24.

Weiskrantz, L., Warrington, E. K., Sanders M. D., & Marshall, J. (1974). Visual capacity of the hemianopic field following a restricted occipital ablation. *Brain, 97,* 709–28.

Weisman, A. D. (1956). A study of the psychodynamics of duodenal ulcer exacerbations. *Psychosomatic Medicine, 18,* 2–42.

Weiss, F., Lorang, M. T., Bloom, F. E., & Koob, G. F. (1993). Oral alcohol self-administration stimulates dopamine release in the rat nucleus accumbens: Genetic and motivational determinants. *Journal of Pharmacological and Experimental Therapy, 267,* 250–58.

Weiss, J. M. (1968). Effects of predictable and unpredictable shock on the development of gastrointestinal lesion in rats. *Proceedings of the 76th Annual Convention of the American Psychological Association, 3,* 263–64.

Weiss, J. M. (1970). Somatic effects of predictable and unpredictable shock. *Psychosomatic Medicine, 32,* 397–409.

Weiss, J. M. (1971). Effects of coping behavior in different warning signaled conditions on stress pathology in rats. *Journal of Comparative and Physiological Psychology, 77,* 1–13.

Weiss, J. M., Glazer, H. I., & Pohoresky, L. A. (1976). Coping behavior and neurochemical change in rats: An alternative explanation for the original "learned helplessness" experiments. In G. Serban & A. King (Eds.), *Animal models in human psychobiology.* New York: Plenum.

Weiss, J. M., Pohoresky, L. A., Salman, S., & Gruenthal, M. (1976). Attenuation of gastric lesions by psychological aspects of aggression in rats. *Journal of Comparative Physiological Psychology, 90,* 252–59.

Weiss, J., et al. (1981). Behavioral depression produced by an uncontrollable stressor: Relationship to norepinephrine, dopamine, and serotonin levels in various regions of the rat brain. *Brain Research Reviews, 3,* 167–205.

Weiss, J. M., Simson, P. G., Ambrose, M. J., Webster, A., & Hoffman, L. J. (1985). Neurochemical basis of behavioral depression. *Advances in Behavioral Medicine, 1,* 253–75.

Weissman, M. (1990). Panic and generalized anxiety: Are they separate disorders? *Journal of Psychiatric Research, 24,* 157–62.

Weissman, M. M., Kidd, K. K., & Prusoff, B. A. (1982). Variability in rates of affective disorders in relatives of depressed and normal probands. *Archives of General Psychiatry, 39,* 1397–1403.

Weissman, M. M., Klerman, G. L., Prusoff, B. A., Sholomskas, D., & Padian, N. (1981). Depressed patients: Results one year after treatment with drugs and/or interpersonal psychotherapy. *Archives of General Psychiatry, 38,* 51–55.

Weissman, M. M., & Paykel, E. S. (1974). *The depressed woman: A study of social relationships.* Evanston: University of Chicago Press.

Wells, K., Burnam, M., Rogers, W., & Hays, R. (1992). The course of depression in adult outpatients: Results from the Medial Outcomes Study. *Archives of General Psychiatry, 49,* 788–94.

Wender, P. H., Kety, S. S., Rosenthal, D., Schulsinger, F., Ortmann, J., & Lunde, I. (1986). Psychiatric disorders in the biological and adoptive families of adopted individuals with affective disorders. *Archives of General Psychiatry, 43,* 923–29.

Wenger, J. R., Tiffany, T. M., Bombardier, C., Nicholls, K., & Woods, S. C. (1981). Ethanol tolerance in the rat is learned. *Science, 213,* 575–76.

Wenger, N., Greenberg, J., Hilborne, L., et al. (1992). Effects of HIV antibody testing and AIDS education on communication about HIV risk and sexual behavior. *American College of Physicians, 117,* 905–11.

Werner, P. D., & Pervin, L. A. (1986). The content of personality inventory items. *Journal of Personality and Social Psychology, 51,* 622–28.

Wernicke, J. (1985). The side effect profile and safety of fluoxetine. *Journal of Clinical Psychiatry, 46,* 59–67.

Werry, J. S., Methven, J., Fitzpatrick, J., & Dixon, H. (1983). The inter-rater reliability of DSM-III in children. *Journal of Abnormal Child Psychology, 11,* 341–54.

Wertheimer, M. (1978). Humanistic psychology and the humane and tough-minded psychologist. *American Psychologist, 33,* 631–47.

Wesnes, K., & Warburton, D.M. (1984a). Effects of scopolamine and nicotine in human rapid information-processing and performance. *Psychopharmacology, 82,* 147–50.

Wesnes, K., & Warburton, D.M. (1984b). The effects of cigarettes of varying yield on rapid information processing performance. *Psychopharmacology, 82,* 338–42.

Wessely, S. (1991). Chronic fatigue syndrome. *Journal of Neurology, Neurosurgery, and Psychiatry, 54,* 669–71.

Westermeyer, J., Bouafuely, M., Neider, J., & Callies, A. (1989). Somatization among refugees: An epidemiologic study. *Psychosomatics, 30,* 34–43.

White, K., Wykoff, W., Tynes, L., Schneider, L., et al. (1990). Fluvoxamine in the treatment of tricyclic-resistant depression. *Psychiatric Journal of the University of Ottawa, 15,* 156–58.

White, R. W. (1959). Motivation reconsidered: The concept of competence. *Psychological Review, 66,* 297–333.

White, R. W. (1963). Ego and reality in psychoanalytic theory: A proposal regarding independent ego energies. *Psychological Issues, 3,* 1–210.

Widiger, T. A. (1992). Generalized social phobia versus avoidant personality disorder: A commentary on three studies. *Journal of Abnormal Psychology, 101* (2): 340–43.

Widiger, T. A., Frances, A J., Pincus, H. A., Davis, W. W., & First, M. B. (1991). Toward an empirical classification for the DSM-IV. *Journal of Abnormal Psychology, 100* (3): 280–88.

Wikler, A. (1973). Dynamics of drug dependence. *Archives of General Psychiatry, 28,* 611–16.

Wilkins, M. A. (1971). Comparisons of attitudes toward childrearing of parents of certain exceptional and normal children. *Dissertation Abstracts International, 31* (11–A): 5894.

Wilkins, W. (1979). Expectancies in therapy research: Discriminating among heterogeneous nonspecifics. *Journal of Consulting and Clinical Psychology, 47,* 837–45.

Wilkinson, C. (1983). Aftermath of a disaster: The collapse of the Hyatt Regency Hotel skywalks. *American Journal of Psychiatry, 140,* 1134–39.

Williams, R. B., Barefoot, J. C., & Shekelle, R. B. (1985). The health consequences of hostility. In M. Chesbney & R. Rosenman (Eds.), *Anger and hostility in cardiovascular and behavioral disorders.* New York: McGraw-Hill/Hemisphere.

Williams, R., Lane, J., Kuhn, C., et al. (1982). Type A behavior and elevated physiological and neuroendocrine responses to cognitive tasks. *Science, 218,* 483–85.

Williamson, S., Hare, R. D., & Wong, S. (1987). Violence: Criminal psychopaths and their victims. *Canadian Journal of Behavioral Science, 19,* 454–62.

Williamson, S., Harpur, T. J., & Hare, R. D. (1990). *Sensitivity to emotional valence in psychopaths.* Paper presented at the 98th Annual Convention of the American Psychological Association, Boston, MA.

Willis, M. H., & Blaney, P. H. (1978). Three tests of the learned helplessness model of depression. *Journal of Abnormal Psychology, 87,* 131–36.

Willner, A. G., Brankman, C. J., Kirigan, K. A., & Wolf, M. M. (1978). Achievement Place: A community treatment model for youths in trouble. In D. Marholin (Ed.), *Child behavior therapy.* New York: Gardner Press.

Wilner, A., Reich, T., Robins, I., Fishman, R., & Van Doren, T. (1976). Obsessive-compulsive neurosis. *Comprehensive Psychiatry, 17,* 527–39.

Wilson, G. T., & Fairburn, C. G. (1993). Cognitive treatments for eating disorders. *Journal of Consulting and Clinical Psychology, 61*(2): 261–69.

Wilson, P. H., Goldin, J. C., & Charbonneau-Powis, M. (1983). Comparative efficacy of behavioral and cognitive treatments of depression. *Cognitive Therapy and Research, 7,* 111–24.

Winerip, M. (1994). *9 Highland Road.* New York: Pantheon.

Wing, J. K., & Hailey, A. M. (Eds.). (1972). *Evaluating a community psychiatric service.* London: Oxford University Press.

Wing, L. (1976). *Diagnosis, clinical description and prognosis.* Oxford: Pergamon.

Wing, L., Yeates, S. R., Brierly, L. M., & Gould, J. (1976). The prevalence of early childhood autism: Comparison of administrative and epidemiological studies. *Psychological Medicine, 6,* 89–100.

Winnicott, D. W. (1971). *Playing and reality.* New York: International Universities Press.

Winokur, G. (1972). Family history studies VIII: Secondary depression is alive and well and . . . . *Diseases of the Nervous System, 33,* 94–99.

Winokur, G., & Coryell, W. (1992). Familial subtypes of unipolar depression: A prospective study of familial pure depressive disease compared to depression spectrum disease. *Biological Psychiatry, 32*(11): 1012–18.

Winokur, G., Scharfetter, C., & Angst, J. (1985). The diagnostic value in assessing mood congruence in delusions and hallucinations and their relationship to the affective state. *European Archives of Psychiatry and Neurological Science, 234,* 299–302.

Winokur, G., & Tanna, V. L. (1969). Possible role of X-link dominant factor in manic-depressive disease. *Diseases of the Nervous System, 30,* 89.

Winsberg, B. G., Sverd, J., Castells, S., Hurwic, M., & Perel, J. M. (1980). Estimation of monoamine and cyclic-AMP turnover and amino acid concentrations of spinal fluid in autistic children. *Neuropediatrics, 11,* 250–55.

Wirz-Justice, A., Graw, P., Krauchi, K., et al. (1993). Light therapy in Seasonal Affective Disorder is independent of time of day or circadian phase. *Archives of General Psychiatry, 50,* 929–40.

Wise, R. A., & Bozarth, M. A. (1987). A psychostimulant theory of addiction. *Psychological Review, 94,* 469–92.

Witkin, H. A., Mednick. S. A., Schulsinger, F., Bakkestrom, E., Christiansen, K. O., Goodenough, D. R., Hirschhorn, K., Lundsteen, C., Owen, D. R., Philip, J., Rubin, D. B., & Stocking, M. (1976). Criminality in XYY and XXY men: The elevated crime rate of XYY males is not related to aggression. *Science, 193,* 547–55.

Wittgenstein, L. (1953). *Philosophical investigations.* New York: Macmillan.

Wolf, M. M., Phillips, E. L., & Fixsen, D.C. (1975). *Achievement Place, phase II: Final report.* Kansas: Department of Human Development, University of Kansas.

Wolf, S., Cardon, P. V., Shepard, E. M., & Wolff, H. G. (1955). *Life stress and essential hypertension.* Baltimore: Williams & Wilkins.

Wolf, S., & Wolff, H. G. (1947). *Human gastric function.* New York: Oxford University Press.

Wolff, S. (1965). *The stomach.* New York: Oxford University Press.

Wollheim, R. (1974). *Freud: A collection of critical essays.* Garden City, NY: Anchor/Doubleday.

Wolpe, J. (1958). *Psychotherapy by reciprocal inhibition.* Stanford: Stanford University Press.

Wolpe, J. (1969). Basic principles and practices of behavior therapy of neuroses. *American Journal of Psychiatry, 125*(5): 1242–47.

Wolpe, J. (1971). Neurotic depression: Experimental analogue, clinical syndromes and treatment. *American Journal of Psychotherapy, 25,* 362–68.

Wolpe, J., & Lazarus, A. A. (1969). *The practice of behavior therapy.* New York: Pergamon.

Wolpe, J., & Rachman, S. (1960). Psychoanalytic "evidence": A critique based on Freud's case of Little Hans. *Journal of Nervous and Mental Disease, 131,* 135–47.

Wong, D., Horng, J., et al. (1974). A selective inhibitor of serotonin uptake: Lilly 110140, 3-(p-trifluoromethylphenoxy-N-Methyl-3-Phenylpropylamine). *Life Sciences, 15,* 471–79.

Wong, D. F., Wagner, H. N., Tune, L. E., Dannals, R. F., Pearlson, G. D., Links, J. M., Tamminga, C. A., Broussolle, E. P., Ravert, H. T., Wilson, A. A., Toung, J. K. T., Malat, J., Williams, J. A., O'Tuama, L. A., Snyder, S. H., Kuhar, M. J., & Gjedde, A. (1986). Positron emission tomography reveals elevated D_2 dopamine receptors in drug-naive schizophrenics. *Science, 234,* 1558–63.

Woodruff, R. A., Clayton, P. J., & Guze, S. B. (1971). Hysteria: Studies of diagnosis, outcome and prevalence. *Journal of the American Medical Association, 215,* 425–28.

Woodruff, R. A., Goodwin, D. W., & Guze, S. B. (1974). *Psychiatric diagnosis.* New York: Oxford University Press.

Woodward, B., & Armstrong, A. (1979). *The brethren: Inside the Supreme Court.* New York: Simon & Schuster.

Wrobel, T. A., & Locher, D. (1982). Validity of the Wiener subtle and obvious scales for the MMPI: Another example of the importance of inventory-item content. *Journal of Consulting and Clinical Psychology, 50,* 469–70.

Wynne, L. C. (1970). Communication disorders and the quest for relatedness in families of schizophrenics. *American Journal of Psychoanalysis, 30,* 100–14.

Wynne, L. C., Rykoff, I. M., Day, J., & Hirsch, S. I. (1958). Pseudomutuality in the family relations of schizophrenics. *Psychiatry, 21,* 205–20.

Wynne, L. C. Singer, M. T., Bartko, J. J., & Toohey, M. L. (1977). Schizophrenics and their families: Recent research on parental communication. In J. M. Tanner (Ed.), *Developments in psychiatric research.* London: Hodder & Stoughton.

Yaganita, T. (1976). Some methodological problems in assessing dependence-producing properties of drugs in animals. *Pharmacological Reviews, 27,* 503–9.

Yager, T., Laufer, R., & Gallops, M. (1984). Some problems associated with war experience in men of the Vietnam generation. *Archives of General Psychiatry, 41,* 327–33.

Yale, C. (1989). Gastric surgery for the morbidly obese. *Archives of Surgery, 124,* 941–46.

Yalom, I. D. (1980). *Existential psychotherapy.* New York: Basic Books.

Yalom, I. D., Houts, P. S., Newell, G., & Rand, K. H. (1967). Preparation of patients for group therapy. *Archives of General Psychiatry, 17,* 416–27.

Yates, A. (1966). *Theory and practice in behavior therapy* (2nd ed.). New York: Wiley.

Youkilis, H. D., & DeWolfe, A. S. (1975). The regression hypothesis and scales classification in schizophrenia. *Journal of Abnormal Psychology, 84,* 36–40.

Yule, W., Hersov, L., & Treseder, J. (1980). Behavioral treatments of school refusal. In L. Hersov & I. Berg (Eds.), *Out of school: Modern perspectives in truancy and school refusal.* New York: Wiley.

Yule, W., & Rutter, M. (1976). Epidemiology and social implication of specific reading retardation. In R. M. Knights & D. J. Bakker (Eds.), *The neuropsychology of learning disorders.* Baltimore: University Park Press.

Zafiropoulou, M., & McPherson, F. M. (1986). "Preparedness" and the severity and outcomes of clinical phobias. *Behavior Research and Therapy, 24,* 221–22.

Zahn, T. P., & Rosenthal, D. (1965). Preparatory set in acute schizophrenia. *Journal of Nervous and Mental Disease, 141,* 352–58.

Zaidel, E. (1978a). Auditory language comprehension in the right hemisphere following cerebral commisurotomy and hemispherectomy: A comparison with child language and aphasia. In A. Caramazza & E. B. Zurif (Eds.), *Language acquisition and language breakdown: Parallels and divergences.* Baltimore, MD: Johns Hopkins University Press.

Zaidel, E. (1978b). Lexical organization in the right hemisphere. In P. Buser & A. Rougeul-Buser (Eds.), *Cerebral correlates of conscious experience.* Amsterdam: Elsevier.

Zanarini, M. C., Gunderson, J. G., Marina, M. F., Schwartz, E. O., & Frankenberg, F. R. (1989). Childhood experiences of borderline patients. *Comprehensive Psychiatry, 30,* 18–25.

Zangwill, O. L. (1966). The amnesic syndrome. In C. W. M. Whitty & O. L. Zangwill (Eds.), *Amnesia.* London: Butterworth.

Zax, M., & Cowen, E. L. (1969). Research on early detection and prevention of emotional dysfunction in young school children. In C. D. Spielberger (Ed.), *Current topics in clinical and community psychology* (Vol. 1, pp. 67–108). New York: Academic Press.

Zentall, S. S., & Zentall, T. R. (1983). Optimal stimulation: A model of disordered activity and performance in normal and deviant children. *Psychological Bulletin, 94,* 446–71.

Ziegler, F. J., & Imboden, J. B. (1962). Contemporary conversion reactions: II. A conceptual model. *Archives of General Psychiatry, 6,* 279–87.

Ziegler, D. K., & Paul, N. (1954). Hysteria. *Diseases of the Nervous System, 15,* 30.

Zigler, E., & Levine, J. (1981). Age on first hospitalization of schizophrenics: A developmental approach. *Journal of Abnormal Psychology, 90,* 458–67.

Zigler, E., & Phillips, L. (1961). Psychiatric diagnosis and symptomatology. *Journal of Abnormal and Social Psychology, 63,* 69–75.

Zigler, E., Taussig, C., & Black, K. (1992). Early childhood intervention: A promising preventative for juvenile delinquency. *American Psychologist, 47*(8): 997–1006.

Zilbergeld, B., & Evans, M. (1980). The inadequacy of Masters and Johnson. *Psychology Today, 14,* 28–43.

Zilboorg, G., & Henry, G. W. (1941). *A history of medical psychology.* New York: Norton.

Zimbardo, P. G. (1977). Shy murderers. *Psychology Today, 148,* 66–76.

Zimbardo, P. G., Andersen, S. M., & Kabat, L. G. (1981). Induced hearing deficit generates experimental paranoia. *Science, 212,* 1529–31.

Zimmerman, M. (1990). Is DSM-IV needed at all? *Archives of General Psychiatry, 47,* 974–76.

Zinberg, N. E. (1984). *Drugs, set, and setting.* New Haven, CT: Yale University Press.

Zinberg, N. E., Harding, W. M., & Winkeller, M. (1977). A study of social regulatory mechanisms in controlled illicit drug users. *Journal of Drug Issues, 7,* 117–33.

Zitrin, C. M., Klein, D. F., Woerner, M. G., & Ross, D. C. (1983). Treatment of phobias I. Comparison of imipramine hydrochloride and placebo. *Archives of General Psychiatry, 40,* 125–38.

Zoccolillo, M., Pickles, A., Quinton, D., & Rutter, M. (1992). The outcome of childhood conduct disorder: Implications for defining adult personality disorder and conduct disorder. *Psychological Medicine, 22,* 971–86.

Zola-Morgan, S., Squire, L. R., & Amaral, D. (1986). Human amnesia and the medial temporal region: Enduring memory impairment following a bilateral lesion limited to the CA 1 field of the hippocampus. *Journal of Neuroscience, 6,* 2950–67.

Zubin, J., Eron, L. D., & Schumer, F. (1965). *An experimental approach to projective techniques.* New York: Wiley.

Zubin, J. E., & Spring, B. (1977). Vulnerability: A new view of schizophrenia. *Journal of Abnormal Psychology, 86,* 103–26.

Zucker, R. A. (1987). The four alcoholisms: A developmental account of the etiologic process. In P. C. Rivers (Ed.), *Alcohol and addictive behavior* (pp. 27–83). Lincoln, NB: University of Nebraska Press.

Zuckerman, M., & Lubin, B. (1965). *Manual for the Multiple Affect Adjective Check List.* San Diego, CA: Educational and Industrial Testing Service.

Zullow, H., & Seligman, M. E. P. (1985). Pessimistic ruminations predict increase in depressive symptoms: A process model and longitudinal study. Unpublished manuscript.

ACKNOWLEDGMENTS AND COPYRIGHTS

US and voluntary responding," in Campbell and Church, (Eds.), *Punishment and aversive behavior*, 1969, p. 328. Adapted by permission of Prentice-Hall, Englewood Cliffs, NJ. **Figure 11–8:** Peterson, C., Luborsky, L., & Seligman, M.E.P., Attributions and depressive mood shifts: A case study using the symptom-context method. *Journal of Abnormal Psychology*, 1983, 92: 96–103. Copyright © 1983 by the American Psychological Association. Reprinted by permission. **Figure 11–9:** Gillham, J., Reivich, K., Jaycox, L., and Seligman, M.E.P., Prevention of depressive symptoms in school children: Two-year follow-up, 1994. Submitted. **Figure 11–10:** Bunney, W.E., & Murphy, D.L., "Switch processes in psychiatric illness" in N.S. Kline (Ed.), *Factors in depression*. New York: Raven Press, 1974. **Figure 11–11:** Rosenthal, N.E., Sack, D.A., Gillin, J.C., Lewy, A.J., Goodwin, F.K., Davenport, Y., Mueller, P. S., Newsome, D.A., & Wehr, T.A., Seasonal affective disorder: A description of the syndrome and preliminary findings with light therapy. *Archives of General Psychiatry*, 1984, 41: 72–80. Copyright © 1984, American Medical Association. Reprinted by permission. **Figure 12–2:** From *Schizophrenia genesis: The origins of madness* by Irving Gottesman. Copyright © 1991 by Irving I. Gottesman. Used with permission of W.H. Freeman and Company. **Figure 12–3:** From *Drugs and the brain* by Solomon H. Snyder. Copyright © 1986 by Scientific American Books, Inc. Used with permission of W.H. Freeman and Company. **Figure 12–5:** From *Psychology*, 3rd ed., by Henry Gleitman, by permission of W.W. Norton & Company, Inc. based on a figure from Faris and Dunham, *Mental disorders in urban areas*. Chicago: University of Chicago Press, 1939. **Figure 12–6:** Vaughn, C.E., and Leff, J. P., The influence of family and social factors on the course of psychiatric illness: A comparison of schizophrenic and depressive-neurotic patients. *British Journal of Psychiatry*, 1976, 129: 127–37. Adapted by permission. **Figure 14–1:** Hunt, W.A., Barnett, L. W., and Branch, L.G., Relapse rates in addiction programs. *Journal of Clinical Psychology*, 1971, 27, 455–56. Copyright © 1971 by the American Psychological Association. Reprinted by permission. **Figure 14–2:** From *Drugs and the brain* by Solomon H. Snyder. Copyright © 1986 by Scientific American Books, Inc. Used with permission of W.H. Freeman and Company. **Figure 14–4:** From *Brain, mind, and behavior* by Bloom, F.E., Lazerson, A., and Hofstadter, L., Copyright © 1985 by Educational Broadcasting Corporation. Used by permission of W.H. Freeman and Company. Also from Barnes, D.M., The biological tangle of drug addiction. *Science*, 241: 415–417. Copyright © 1988 by the Association for the Advancement of Science. **Figure 14–5:** Schuckit, M.A., Subjective responses to alcohol in sons of alcoholics and controls. *Archives of General Psychiatry*, 1984, 41: 879–84. Copyright © 1984, American Medical Association. Reprinted by permission. **Figure 14–6:** Marlatt, G.A., and Gordon, J.R., *Relapse prevention: Maintenance strategies in the treatment of addictive behaviors*, Figure 1–4. New York: Guilford Press, 1985, page 38. **Figure 14–7:** Deneau, G., Yaganita, T., & Seevers, M.H., Self-administration of psychoactive substances by the monkey. *Psychopharmacologia* (Berlin), 1969, 16: 30–48. Copyright © 1969 by Springer-Verlag Berlin-Heidelberg. **Figure 14–8:** Higgins, S.T., Budney, A.J., Bickel, W.K., Hughes, J.R., Foerg, F., & Badger, G., Achieving cocaine abstinence with a behavioral approach. *American Journal of Psychiatry*, 1993, 150 (5): 763–69. Copyright © 1993 by The American Psychiatric Association. Reprinted by permission. **Figure 14–9:** From *Drugs and the brain* by Solomon H. Snyder. Copyright © 1986 by Scientific American Books, Inc. Used with permission of W.H. Freeman and Company. **Figure 15–2:** Lykken, D.T., A study of anxiety in the sociopathic personality. *Journal of Abnormal and Social Psychology*, 1957, 55: 6–10. Copyright © 1957 by the American Psychological Association. Reprinted by permission. **Figure 17–1:** Katz, B., The nerve impulse. *Scientific American*, November 1952, 187: 164–65. Copyright © 1952 by Scientific American, Inc. All rights reserved. **Figure 17–1 (inset):** Adapted from Gardner, Ernest, *Fundamentals of neurology: A psychological approach*, 6th edition. Copyright © 1975 by W.B. Saunders & Company. **Figure 17–2:**

From J.L. Cummings, The neuroanatomy of depression, *Journal of Clinical Psychiatry*, Vol. 54 (1993), p. 15, Courtesy Dr. J.L. Cummings. **Figure 17–3 (B):** Modified from Kandel, E., Schwartz, J.H., and Jessel, T.M. (Eds.), *Principles of neural science*, 3rd edition. New York: Elsevier Publishing Company, 1991. Copyright © 1991 by Elsevier Publishing Company. **Figure 17–4:** Hecaen, M., and Albert, M.L., *Human neuropsychology*. Copyright © 1978 by John Wiley & Sons, Inc. Reprinted by permission. **Figure 17–5:** Luria, A., The functional organization of the brain. *Scientific American*, 1970, 222: 66–78. Copyright © 1970 by Scientific American, Inc. All rights reserved. **Figure 17–6:** Modified from Levy, J., "Lateral specialization of the human brain: Behavioral manifestations and possible evolutionary basis," in J.A. Krieger, Jr. (Ed.), *The biology of behavior*. Oregon State University Press, 1972, p. 163. Reprinted by permission. **Figure 17–7:** Gazzaniga, M., *The bisected brain*. New York: Plenum Publishing Corp., 1970, p. 42. Reprinted by permission. **Figure 17–8:** Gardner, Ernest, *Fundamentals of neurology: A psychological approach*, 6th edition. Copyright © 1975 by W.B. Saunders & Company. **Figure 17–9:** Clemente, Carmine D. (Ed.), *Gray's anatomy*, 30th ed., p. 1115. Copyright © 1984 by Lea & Febiger. **Figure 17–10:** Adams, R.D., and Victor, M., *Principles of neurology*, 2nd ed. Copyright © 1981 by McGraw-Hill, Inc. Adapted by permission of McGraw-Hill Book Company. **Figure 17–11:** Rosenzweig, M., and Leiman, A., *Physiological psychology*, 2nd ed, p. 39. Copyright © 1989 by Random House, Inc. **Figure 17–12:** Posner, M., and Raichle, M., *Images of mind*, 1994, p. 65. Scientific American Library. Used with permission of W.H. Freeman. **Figure 17–13:** Kertesz, A., "Two case studies: Broca's and Wernicke's aphasia" in M.A. Arbib, D. Caplan, and J.C. Marshall (Eds.), *Neural models of language processes*. Copyright © 1982 by Academic Press. **Figure 17–14:** Geschwind, N., The apraxias: neural mechanisms of disorders of learned movement. *American Scientist*, 1975, 188: 189. Used by permission. **Figure 17–15:** From *Brain, mind, and behavior* by Bloom, F.E., Lazerson, A., and Hofstadter, L. Copyright © 1985 by Educational Broadcasting Corporation. Used by permission of W.H. Freeman and Company. **Figure 17–16:** From *Fundamentals of human neuropsychology*, 3rd ed. by Kolb, B. and Whishaw, I.Q. Copyright © 1990 by W.H. Freeman and Company.

TABLES

Table 4–4: Vaillant, G.E., *Adaptation to life*. Boston: Little, Brown and Company, 1977. Adapted by permission. **Table 5–3:** Abramson, L.T., Seligman, M.E.P., & Teasdale, J., Learned helplessness in humans; critique and reformulation. *Journal of Abnormal Psychology*, 1978, 87: 32–48. Copyright © 1978 by the American Psychological Association. Reprinted by permission. **Table 5–4:** Adapted from Lazarus, A.A., *Multimodal behavior theory*. Copyright © 1976, Springer Publishing Company, Inc. New York, 10012. Used by permission. **Table 6–2:** Robins, L.N., Helzer, J.E., Weissman, M.M., Orvaschel, H., Gruenberg, E., Burke, J.D., & Regier, D.A., Lifetime prevalence of specific psychiatric disorders in three sites. *Archives of General Psychiatry*, 1984, 41: 949–58. Copyright © 1984, American Medical Association. Reprinted by permission. **Table 6–3:** Kessler, R., McGonogle, K., Zhao, S., et al., Lifetime and 12-month prevalence of DSM-III-R psychiatric disorders in the United States: Results from the National Comorbity Survey. *Archives of General Psychiatry*, 1994, 51, 8–19. Copyright © 1994, American Medical Association. Reprinted by permission. **Table 7–1:** Butcher, J.N., *MMPI: Research developments and clinical applications*. Copyright © 1969 by McGraw-Hill, Inc., New York. Used with permission of the McGraw-Hill Book Company. **Table 7–2:** American Psychiatric Association: *Diagnostic and statistical manual of mental disorders, third edition, revised*. Washington, DC, American Psychiatric Association, 1987. **Table 8–2:** Marks, I.M., *Fears and phobias*. New York: Academic Press, 1969. Used by permission. **Table 9–1:** Rachman, S.J. and Hodgson, R.J., *Obsessions and compulsions*. Prentice-Hall, 1980. Adapted by permission of Prentice-Hall, Inc., Englewood Cliffs, N.J. **Table 9–3:** Hyler,

S.E. and Spitzer, R.T., Hysteria split asunder. *American Journal of Psychiatry*, 1978, 135 (12): 1500–4. **Table 10–1:** Weiss, J.M., Effects of coping behavior in different warning signaled conditions on stress pathology in rats. *Journal of Comparative and Physiological Psychology*, 1971, 77: 1–13. Copyright © 1971 by the American Psychological Association. Reprinted by permission of the American Psychological Association and the author. **Table 10–2:** Adapted by permission of Elsevier Science Publishing Co., Inc., from Grace, W.J. and Graham, D.T., Relationship of specific attitudes and emotions to certain bodily disease. *Psychosomatic Medicine*, 1952, 14: 243–51. Copyright © 1952 by the American Psychosomatic Society, Inc. **Table 10–3:** Holmes, T.H., and Rahe, R.H., The social readjustments ratings scale. *Journal of Psychosomatic Research*, 1967, 11: 213–18. Elsevier Science, Ltd., Pergamon Imprint, Oxford, England. Reprinted with permission. **Table 11–2:** Robins, L.N., Helzer, J.E., Weissman, M.M., Orvaschel, H., Gruenberg, E., Burke, J.D., & Regier, D.A., Lifetime prevalence of specific psychiatric disorders in three sites. *Archives of General Psychiatry*, 1984, 41: 949–58. Copyright © 1984, American Medical Association. Reprinted by permission. **Table 12–2:** From *Schizophrenia genesis: The origins of madness* by Irving Gottesman. Copyright © 1991 by Irving I. Gottesman. Used with permission of W.H. Freeman and Company. **Table 14–2:** Kreek, M.J., Rationale for maintenance pharmacotherapy of opiate dependence, in C.P. O'Brien and J.H. Jaffe (Eds.), *Addictive states*, pp. 205–30. New York: Raven Press, 1992. **Table 14–2:** Adapted from Hilts, P.J., "Is nicotine addictive? It depends on whose criteria you use," in *The New York Times*, Aug. 2, 1994. Copyright © 1994 by The New York Times Company. Reprinted by permission. **Table 15–3:** Hutchings, B., & Mednick, S.A., "Criminality in adoptees and their adoptive and biological parents: A pilot study," in Mednick and Christiansen, (Eds.), *Biosocial bases of criminal behavior.* New York: Gardner Press, 1977, p. 132. **Table 16–1:** Adapted from American Psychiatric Association: *Diagnostic and statistical manual of mental disorders, fourth edition.* Washington, DC, American Psychiatric Association, 1994.

BOXES

Box 7–1: American Psychiatric Association: *Diagnostic and statistical manual of mental disorders, fourth edition.* Washington, DC, American Psychiatric Association, 1994. **Box 8–1:** Adapted from *Psychology*, 3rd ed., by Henry Gleitman, by permission of W.W. Norton & Company, Inc. Copyright © 1991 by W.W. Norton & Company, Inc. **Box 8–2:** Endler, N.S., Magnusson, D., Ekehammar, B., & Okada, M.O., The multi-dimensionality of state and trait anxiety. Reports from the Department of Psychology, University of Stockholm, 1975. Adapted by permission of the authors. **Box 10–1:** Spiegel, D., Bloom, J., Kraemer, H., & Gottheil, E., Effect of psychosocial treatment on survival of patients with metastatic breast cancer. *The Lancet*, October 14, 1989, pp. 888–91. Reprinted by permission. **Box 11–1:** Alloy, L.B., and Abramson, L.Y., Judgment of contingency in depressed and nondepressed students. Sadder but wiser? *Journal of Experimental Psychology, General*, 1979, 108: 441–85. Copyright © 1979 by the American Psychological Association. Reprinted by permission of the author. **Box 11–3:** Seligman, M.E.P., *Learned optimism: The skill to conquer life's obstacles, large and small.* New York: Random House, © 1991. **Box 11–5:** Shneidman, E., "Suicide among the gifted," in E. Shneidman (Ed.), *Suicidology: Contemporary developments.* New York: Grune & Stratton, 1976. Adapted by permission of The Psychological Corporation and Edwin Shneidman. **Box 14–1:** American Psychiatric Association: *Diagnostic and statistical manual of mental disorders, fourth edition.* Washington, DC, American Psychiatric Association, 1994. **Box 15–1:** Damasio, H., Grabowski, T., Frank, R., Galaburda, A.M., and Damasio, A.R., The return of Phineas Gage: Clues about the brain from the skull of a famous patient. *Science*, 264, 1102–5. Copyright © 1994 by the Association for the Advancement of Science. **Box 16–1:** Adapted from Marchant, R., Howlin, P., Yule, W., & Rutter, M., Graded change in the treatment of the behavior of autistic children. *Journal of Child Psychology and Psychiatry*, 1974, 15, 221–27. Copyright © 1974 by the Association for Child Psychology and Psychiatry.

PHOTO CREDITS

Part 1 opener (p. 1): Adolf Wölfli, *The Mental Asylum Band-Hain*, courtesy Adolf Wölfli Foundation, Museum of Fine Arts, Bern. **Chapter 1 opener (p. 2):** Jacqueline Morreau, *Psyche's Burden*, 1986, courtesy Jacqueline Morreau. **p. 4:** Courtesy John Wasson. **p. 5:** *(left)* Colored-pencil drawing by Paul Duhem, courtesy Art en Marge, Brussels; *(right)* "Stressé?", illustration by Geneviève Côté. **p. 7:** The Phillips Collection. **p. 9:** ©Marcia Weinstein. **p. 12:** Motion Picture & Television Photo Archive. **p. 10:** Drawing by Sempé, ©1981 The New Yorker Magazine, Inc. **p. 17:** ©Jonathan A. Meyers. **p.18:** *(left)* Karen McClean; *(right)* Ron Chapple/FPG International. **Chapter 2 opener (p. 22) and p. 40:** Robert Fleury, *Pinel Strikes the Chains of the Insane*, Saltpétrière/Photo Bulloz. **p. 25:** *(top)* Courtesy John Verano/Smithsonian Institution; *(bottom)* The Warder Collection. **p. 26:** Rare Books and Manuscripts Division, The New York Public Library, Astor, Lenox and Tilden Foundation. **p. 28:** T.H. Matteson, *Examination of a Witch*, 1853, courtesy Peabody Essex Museum, Salem, Mass. **p. 30:** Courtesy National Library of Medicine. **p. 31:** Wellcome Institute Library, London. **p. 32:** Bettmann. **p. 34:** *St. Catherine Exorcising a Possessed Woman*, Denver Art Museum. **p. 37:** Courtesy Sir John Soane's Museum, London. **p. 38:** Rijksdienst voor de Monumentenzorg, Zeist, Netherlands. **p. 41:** The Warder Collection. **Part 2 opener (p. 45):** Rob Scholte, *Secret of the Poet*, 1987; courtesy Rob Scholte. **Chapter 3 opener (p. 46):** Frantisek Kupka, *Red and Blue Disks*, 1911(?); oil on canvas, 39" by 24", The Museum of Modern Art, New York, Inter-American Fund. **p. 48:** Courtesy Dr. Henry Wagner. **p. 49:** Copyright ©Museo del Prado, Madrid. **p. 51:** Courtesy National Library of Medicine. **p. 53:** Bettmann. **p. 56:** ©1989 Bob Sacha. **p. 57:** Drawing by Chas. Addams; ©1981, The New Yorker Magazine, Inc. **p. 58:** Courtesy Dr. Henry Wagner. **p. 63:** Courtesy State of New York Office of Mental Health. **p. 64:** Cartoon by Sidney Harris. **Chapter 4 opener (p. 70):** Berthe Morisot, *La Psyché*, ©1994 Fundación Colección Thyssen-Bornemisza, Madrid. All rights reserved. Total or partial reproduction prohibited. **p. 72:** Courtesy National Library of Medicine. **p. 73:** *(top)* Karen McClean; *(bottom)* ©Jonathan A. Meyers. **p. 74:** Suzanne Szasz. **p. 75:** ©Jonathan A. Meyers. **p. 76:** ©Jonathan A. Meyers. **p. 77:** Illustration from *Their Eyes Meeting the World* by Robert Coles, copyright ©1992 by Robert Coles. Reprinted by permission of Houghton Mifflin Co. **p. 78:** Drawing by Dana Fradon; ©1973 The New Yorker Magazine, Inc. **p. 81:** *(top)* Bettmann; *(bottom)* Courtesy Alexandra Adler. **p. 82:** *(left)* Courtesy National Library of Medicine; *(right)* The Warder Collection. **p. 83:** *(left)* Photograph by John Erikson; *(right)* Wide World Photos. **p. 84:** The Warder Collection. **p. 85:** *(top left)* Suzanne Szasz; *(top right)* ©1992 Jonathan A. Meyers; *(bottom)* Kevin Kling. **p. 88:** ©Jules Feiffer. Reprinted with permission of United Press Syndicate. All rights reserved. **p. 97:** ©British Museum. **p. 98:** Wide World Photos. **p. 99:** *(left)* ©Marcia Weinstein. *(right)* Karen McClean. **p. 100:** ©Jonathan A. Meyers. **p. 106:** Photograph by Nozizwe S. **Chapter 5 opener (p. 112):** Illustration by Eric Dinyer. **p. 115:** Kevin Kling. **p. 116:** Cartoon by Sidney Harris. **p. 117:** Courtesy Sovfoto. **p. 120:** ©Reuters/Hulton Deutsch. **p. 121:** *(all)* ©1983 Erika Stone. **p. 122:** *(top)* Courtesy National Library of Medicine; *(bottom)* Photograph by Christopher S. Johnson. **p. 123:** Suzanne Szasz. **p. 124:** Karen McClean. **p. 125:** Allan Grant. **p. 130:** *(both)* Suzanne Szasz. **p. 132:** Louis DeLuca. **p. 134:** Courtesy Institute for Rational Living. **Part 3 opener (p. 141):** Edvard Munch, *Eros and Psyche*, ©1995 The Munch Museum/The Munch-Ellingsen Group/ARS, New York. **Chapter 6 opener (p. 142):** Giorgio de Chirico, *The Song of Love*, 1914; oil on canvas, 28" by 23", The Museum of Modern Art, New York, The Nelson A. Rockefeller Bequest. **p. 146:** Source unknown. **p. 150:** Courtesy Dr. Joseph Brady.

p. 152: ©Chronicle Features, 1984. p. 153: Yale Joel, Life Magazine, ©1958 Time Inc. p. 166: AP/Wide World. Chapter 7 opener (p. 172): Winold Reiss, mural at Cincinnati Union Terminal (detail), ©1994 Estate of Winold Reiss/VAGA, New York. p. 175: ©1981 by Marcia Weinstein. p. 181: The New York Public Library. p. 182: Cartoon by Sidney Harris. p. 186: Courtesy Dr. Steve Wolf, Emory University. p. 190: (top) Theodore Géricault, Monomanie du vol, Museum of Fine Arts, Ghent; (bottom) Courtesy National Library of Medicine. p. 203: James Nachtwey/Magnum. Part 4 opener (p. 207): Drawing by Scottie Wilson, courtesy Musée de l'Art Brut, Neuilly-sur-Marne, France. Chapter 8 opener (p. 208): Marc Chagall, Nu, ©1994 Fundación Colección Thyssen-Bornemisza, Madrid. All rights reserved. Total or partial reproduction prohibited. p. 210: The Warder Collection. p. 215: The Museum of Modern Art/Film Stills Archive. p. 218: (left) Charles Mason/Black Star; (right) Wide World Photos. p. 220: ©1982 Frostie/Woodfin Camp. p. 222: ©Skjold Photos. p. 224: ©Chronicle Features, 1982. p. 226: Rufino Tamayo, Animals, 1941; oil on canvas, 36" by 28", The Museum of Modern Art, New York. p. 228: Nicholaes Maes, Girl at a Window, Rijksmuseum Amsterdam. p. 230: (top) Courtesy Dr. Joseph Wolpe; (bottom) Randy Olson. p. 231: ©Susan Rosenberg/Photo Researchers. Snake courtesy of Academy of Natural Sciences of Philadelphia. p. 235: Courtesy J. Scott Altenbach. p. 236: Scott Prior, Max Asleep, oil on canvas, 56"x72", private collection; courtesy Forum Gallery, New York. p. 240: (left) ©David Lane/The Palm Beach Post; (right) Agence France-Presse. p. 243: The Warder Collection. p. 244: (top) ©1991 Ed Kashi; (bottom) Titian, Tarquin and Lucretia, Fitzwilliam Museum, University of Cambridge. p. 245: National Archives Photo 111-SC-347803. p. 250: Wilfredo Lam, The Jungle, 1943; gouache on paper mounted on canvas, 7'10" by 7'6", The Museum of Modern Art, New York, Inter-American Fund. p. 252: Courtesy David Clark. p. 256: Edward Hopper, Rooms By the Sea, Yale University Art Gallery, bequest of Stephen Carlton Clark. p. 259: Rosalyn Benjet, The North Beach Cafes, ©1994 Rosalyn Benjet/VAGA, New York. Chapter 9 opener (p. 264): Drawing by Claire Teller, courtesy Musée d'Art Brut, Neuilly-sur-Marne, France. p. 268: Wide World. p. 274: (top) Drawing by W. Miller; ©1982 The New Yorker Magazine, Inc.; (bottom) Courtesy Dr. S.J. Rachman. p. 277: Courtesy Dr. Judith Rapoport. p. 278: Courtesy Dr. Edna Foa. p. 281: The Warder Collection. p. 284: ©1982 Jules Feiffer. Reprinted with permission of Universal Press Syndicate. All rights reserved. p. 285: UPI/Bettmann. p. 296: The Museum of Modern Art/Film Stills Archive. p. 298: Jacqueline Morreau, Divided Self I, 1982, courtesy Jacqueline Morreau. p. 301: Courtesy Dr. Eugene L. Bliss. p. 305: AP/Wide World Photos. Chapter 10 opener (p. 310): Sir Edward Burne-Jones, Laus Veneris (detail), Laing Art Gallery, Tyne and Wear Museums, Newcastle-upon-Tyne, England. p. 312: Moody, R.L., Bodily changes during abreaction. The Lancet, 1946: 2: 934–35. Reprinted by permission. p. 316: Cartoon by Sidney Harris. p. 318: AP/Wide World. p. 319: AP/Wide World. p. 320: (top) Reuters/Bettmann; (bottom) Christopher Morris/Black Star. p. 324: Sportsphoto/Hulton Deutsch. p. 329: Courtesy Dr. Curt Richter. p. 330: AP/Wide World Photos. p. 331: Adam Kufeld. p. 335: ©1986 Lennart Nilsson/National Geographic. Courtesy Bonniers Fakta, Sweden. p. 339: Chuck Nacke/Picture Group. p. 344: AP/Wide World. Part 5 opener (p. 349): Edvard Munch, Self-Portrait in the Garden at Ekely (detail), ©1995 The Munch Museum/The Munch-Ellingsen Group/ARS, New York. Chapter 11 opener (p. 350): Cézanne, Madame Cézanne in a Red Armchair, Museum of Fine Arts, Boston. p. 353: (top) Collection Vincent van Gogh Foundation/Van Gogh Museum, Amsterdam; (bottom) James Ensor, Pierrot Jaloux, Rijksmuseum Kröller-Müeller, Otterlo, Netherlands. p. 357: Jacqueline Morreau, The Artist Watching, courtesy Jacqueline Morreau. p. 364: Isabel Bishop, Nude, 1934, Collection of Whitney Museum of American Art, New York. p. 366: ©Marcia Weinstein. p. 369: ©Ed Lettau/Photo Researchers. p. 377: ©Will McIntyre/Photo Researchers. p. 378: Thomas Eakins, Mrs.

Edith Mahon, 1904, Smith College Museum of Art, Northampton, Mass. p. 380: The Warder Collection. p. 389: Rembrandt, Titus van Rijn in a Monk's Habit, Rijksmuseum Amsterdam. p. 395: ©Jonathan A. Meyers. p. 403: Courtesy Theodore Roosevelt Birthplace, New York. p. 408: Richard Bosman, Witness, 1983, courtesy Brooke Alexander. p. 410: (both) AP/Wide World. p. 412: (top) Henry Wallis, Chatterton, 1856, Tate Gallery, London/Art Resource, New York; (bottom) Jerome, J., Catching them before suicide, The New York Times Magazine, January 11, 1979. Copyright ©1979 by the New York Times Company. Reprinted by permission. p. 413: UPI/Bettmann. Chapter 12 opener (p. 418): Adolf Wölfli, Arnica Flower, 1917, courtesy Adolf Wölfli Foundation, Museum of Fine Arts, Bern. p. 420: (top) Charles Bell's "Madness" from his Essays on the anatomy of expression in painting, 1806; (bottom) Courtesy National Library of Medicine. p. 422: Drawing by Carl Lange, ©Prinzhorn-Sammlung, Universität Heidelberg/Foto Klinger Kunsthist Institute. p. 424: ©1995 C. Herscovici, Brussels/Artists Rights Society, New York. p. 426: (left) Jerry Cooke/Photo Researchers; (right) Bill Bridges/Globe Photos. p. 428: Salvador Dali, Les Eléphants, courtesy Galerie Christine et Isy Brachot, Brussels. p. 430: Courtesy Prinzhorn-Sammlung, Universität Heidelberg. p. 431: Drawing by August Klett (Klotz), courtesy Prinzhorn-Sammlung, Universität Heidelberg/Foto Zentsch. p. 434: Painting by Miguel Hernandez, courtesy Musée d'Art Brut, Neuilly-sur-Marne, France. p. 436: ©1995 The Munch Museum/The Munch-Ellingsen Group/ARS, New York. p. 447: (left) Library of Congress; (right) Bethlem Royal Hospital Archives and Museum. p. 451: Courtesy Dr. Henry Wagner. p. 452 (both): Courtesy National Institute of Mental Health. p. 457: Illustration by Elizabeth Wolf. p. 459: ©1979 Jerry Cooke/Photo Researchers. p. 462: AP/Wide World. Part 6 opener (p. 467): Painting by Jean-Marie Heyligen, courtesy Art en Marge, Brussels. Chapter 13 opener (p. 468): Isabel Bishop, The Encounter, 1940; The Saint Louis Art Museum, Eliza McMillan Trust Fund. p. 470: Klimt, The Kiss, Oesterreichische Galerie, Vienna/Art Resource. p. 471: Jacqueline Morreau, In the Mirror I, courtesy Jacqueline Morreau. p. 474: AP/Wide World. p. 479: Courbet, Sleep, Phototèque des Musées de la Ville de Paris/©SPADEM. p. 481: ©John Harrington/Black Star. p. 485: The Museum of Modern Art/Film Stills Archive. p. 486: Collection of The New-York Historical Society. p. 487: Marcia Weinstein. Chapter 14 opener (p. 510): Melissa Miller, Smokey Spirits, 1986; courtesy Melissa Miller/Texas Gallery, Houston. p. 525: Degas, The Absinthe Drinker, Musée d'Orsay, Paris; ©Photo RMN. p. 526: ©Jonathan A. Meyers. p. 534: Cartoon by Sidney Harris. p. 542: Eugene Richards/Magnum. p. 544: Courtesy Dr. Michael J. Kuhar. p. 546: (left) Amalie R. Rothschild; (center) Photofest; (right) Motion Picture & Television Photo Archive. p. 551: ©Jill Greenberg/Photonica. p. 553: Ann-Marie Rousseau, Crouching Figure, 1991, courtesy Ann-Marie Rousseau. p. 555: ©Marcia Weinstein. p. 560: Roy Carruthers, Three Smokers, courtesy Carruthers & Company/Newborn Group. p. 561: Kate Brewster. Chapter 15 opener (p. 568): ©Musée d'Art Brut, Neuilly-sur-Marne, France. p. 574: Courtesy The Salt Lake Tribune. p. 583: Damasio, H., Grabowski, T., Frank, R., Galaburda, A.M., & Damasio, A.R. (1994). The return of Phineas Gage: Clues about the brain from the skull of a famous patient. Science, 264, ©1994 by the AAAS; courtesy Hanna Damasio. p. 586: Drawing by Martha Grunenwaldt, courtesy Musée d'Art Brut, Neuilly-sur-Marne, France. p. 587: The Warder Collection. p. 588: Jacqueline Morreau, Woman Watching, 1981, courtesy Jacqueline Morreau. p. 593: The Warder Collection. Part 7 opener (p. 597): Leland Wallin, Child's Round Table with Russian Wooden Blocks, German Bisque Doll, Chinese Paper Fish Kite and American Metal Top, 1980–1982. Chapter 16 opener (p. 598): Paul Mathey, Woman and Child in an Interior, Musée d'Orsay/Photo RMN. p. 600: Marcia Weinstein. p. 604: Marcia Weinstein. p. 609: Karen McClean. p. 612: Illustration from Their Eyes Meeting the World by Robert Coles, copyright ©1992 by Robert Coles. Reprinted by permission of Houghton Mifflin Co. **p. 615:** Illustration from *Their Eyes Meeting the World* by Robert Coles, copyright ©1992 by Robert Coles. Reprinted by permission of Houghton Mifflin Co. **p. 622:** ©1982 Susan Rosenberg/Photo Researchers. **p. 627:** AP/Wide World. **p. 629:** *(left)* Nancy Kaye/Leo de Wys; *(right)* Alan Carey/The Image Works. **p. 630:** Karen McClean. **p. 631:** Bob D'Amico/ABC/Photofest. **p. 632:** ©Marcia Weinstein. **p. 635:** Odilon Redon, *Silence*, c. 1911; oil on gesso on paper, 21" by 21", The Museum of Modern Art, New York, Lillie P. Bliss Collection. **p. 636:** *(top)* Allan Grant; *(bottom)* Alan Carey/The Image Works. **p. 638:** Patrick Tehan. **p. 639:** Allan Grant. **p. 641:** Illustration from *Their Eyes Meeting the World* by Robert Coles, copyright ©1992 by Robert Coles. Reprinted by permission of Houghton Mifflin Co. **Chapter 17 opener (p. 644):** Photo courtesy of Dr. John Haller, Washington University School of Medicine. **p. 648:** Phototake. **p. 650:** *(left)* AP/Wide World; *(right)* UPI/Bettmann. **p. 656:** Damasio, H., Grabowski, T., Frank, R., Galaburda, A.M., & Damasio, A.R. (1994), The return of Phineas Gage: Clues about the brain from the skull of a famous patient, *Science*, 264, ©1994 by the AAAS; courtesy Hanna Damasio. **p. 679:** *(top)* Visuals Unlimited. *(center and bottom)* Blessed, G., Tomlinsun, B.E., & Roth, M., The association between quantitative measures of dementia and of senile change in the cerebral gray matter of elderly subjects, *British Journal of Psychiatry*, 1968, 114: 797–811. Reprinted by permission. **p. 682:** Eslinger et al., Childhood frontal lobe damage, *Archives of Neurology*, Volume 49, July 1992. Courtesy Dr. Paul Eslinger. **p. 689:** *(both)* Stephen Shames/Matrix. **Part 8 opener (p. 693):** Vincent van Gogh, *Hospital Corridor at Saint-Remy* (1889); gouache and watercolor on paper, 24"x19", The Museum of Modern Art, New York, Aby Aldrich Rockefeller Bequest. **Chapter 18 opener (p. 694):** Giorgio de Chirico, *The Enigma of a Day*, 1914; oil on canvas, 6'1 1/4" by 55", The Museum of Modern Art, New York, James Thrall Soby Bequest. **p. 699:** Photofest. **p. 700:** Painting by Marshall Arisman. **p. 703:** Raymond Depardon/Magnum. **p. 705:** Raymond Depardon/Magnum. **p. 706:** Wide World. **p. 709:** AP/Wide World. **p. 717:** AP/Wide World. **p. 720:** ©1994 M. Ging/The Phoenix Gazette. **p. 723:** The Warder Collection. **p. 724:** *(top)* ©Peter Reddaway; *(bottom)* United Press International Photos. **Chapter 19 opener (p. 728):** Salvador Dali, *Portrait of Gala*, 1935; oil on wood, 12 3/4" by 10 1/2", The Museum of Modern Art, New York, gift of Abby Aldrich Rockefeller. **p. 732:** ©1966 United Feature Syndicate, Inc. **p. 738:** Photofest. **p. 739:** Jatin Das, *Man-Woman Two Together*, ©1994 Jatin Das/VAGA, New York. **p. 748:** Randy Olson. **p. 763:** Drawing by Kathe Köllwitz, courtesy Kupferstich-Kabinett, Staatliche Kunstsammlungen Dresden, Germany. **p. 765:** Ricki Rosen/Picture Group. **p. 767:** Jeffrey Grosscup. **p. 768:** *(top)* Courtesy Women's Center of Rhode Island; *(bottom)* Ann Chwatsky/Leo de Wys. **p. 769:** Dan Cunningham for American Psychological Association. **p. 771:** Marcia Weinstein.

NAME INDEX

Aaronson, T. A., 542
Abel, G. G., 476
Abelson, R. P., 201
Abraham, K., 378
Abrams, A., 261, 753
Abrams, R., 361, 377
Abramson, L. Y., 132, 133, 168, 354, 357, 367, 387, 389, 390, 391, 392, 395
Adams, H. E., 482
Adams, N. E., 131, 231, 232
Adams, R. D., 651, 660, 673, 685
Addington, F. O., 704
Addis, M. E., 752
Addy, C. L., 366
Adland, M., 403
Adler, A. A., 81
Adler, C. S., 185
Adler, T., 178
Adlis, S., 366
Ageton, S. S., 604
Aghajanian, G. K., 552
Agras, S., 221, 258
Agras, W. S., 257, 621, 623, 748, 760
Agyei, Y., 480
Ahlbom, A., 328
Aigner, T. G., 538
Ainsworth, M. D. S., 592
Akhtar, S., 267
Akiskal, H. S., 399
Albert, M. L., 655
Alessi, N., 187
Alexander, F., 324, 340
Alexander, L., 739
Allen, J., 637
Allen, L., 225, 479
Allen, M. G., 371, 404
Alling, C., 409
Alloy, L. B., 354, 355, 357, 389
Allport, G. W., 17
Almy, G., 377
Alper, J., 316, 321
Alpern, G. D., 637
Alsen, M., 409
Alterman, A. I., 518, 534
Altshuler, L. L., 406
Amaral, D., 674
Ambinder, R., 476, 477
Ambrose, M. J., 168
Ames, M. A., 478, 480, 482
Amick-McMullan, A., 245
Amis, L., 591
Ananth, J., 277
Anastasiades, A., 254
Andersen, B. L., 502, 508
Andersen, J., 63
Andersen, S. M., 435
Anderson, B., 249

Anderson, C. M., 461, 506, 761
Anderson, G., 297, 302
Anderson, J. C., 600, 601, 604, 605, 609, 612, 613
Anderson, J. R., 88
Anderson, K., 395
Anderson, N., 325
Andreasen, N. C., 361, 404, 431, 440, 451
Andrews, G., 258, 620
Andrews, H., 701
Andrews, J., 616
Andrzejewski, P., 330
Angold, A., 616
Angst, J., 362, 370, 403, 433
Anisman, H., 398
Anker, M., 424, 427, 457
Annau, Z., 228
Ansbacher, H. L., 81
Ansbacher, R., 81
Anthony, W. A., 445
Apfelbaum, B., 503
Appenzeller, T., 673
Arango, V., 409
Archibald, H. C., 246
Arendt, H., 100
Argyll, D. M., 51
Ariel, R. N., 182
Arieti, S., 223, 225, 379, 436, 438
Arif, A., 515
Armstrong, A., 482, 706
Armstrong, L., 763
Arnow, B., 623, 748, 760
Aronow, E., 181
Arthur, R. J., 582
Asberg, M., 280, 409
Asch, S. E., 200
Asken, M., 186
Assad, G., 373, 428
Atkinson, J. W., 181
Atwater, J. D., 607
Auerbach, A. H., 739
Averbuck, D., 707
Ayllon, T., 126
Ayres, B. D., Jr., 565

Baastrup, P., 403
Babor, T. F., 512
Bacon, D. L., 718
Bacon, F., 557
Badger, G., 540, 541
Baer, D. M., 631
Baer, L., 277, 279
Bailey, J. M., 480
Bailey, S., 395
Bailly, J.-S., 31
Bairey, N., 325

Bakalar, J. B., 536, 553
Baker, C. A., 403
Baker, D., 328
Baker, L., 623, 638
Baker, L. A., 581
Baker, T. B., 561
Bakker, A., 474
Baldessarini, R., 62
Bales, J., 741
Balla, D. A., 625
Ballantine, T., 277
Ballenger, J. C., 257, 258
Balster, R. L., 538
Baltes, P. B., 166
Bandura, A., 18, 130–31, 231, 232, 237, 330, 575, 616, 747, 753
Baonagura, N., 609
Barbaree, H., 496
Barber, J. P., 750
Barbizet, J., 659
Bard, M., 769, 770
Bardhan, K. D., 321
Barefoot, J. C., 195, 324, 325
Barker, S., 433
Barkley, R. A., 609, 610, 611
Barksdale, C. M., 522, 545
Barlow, D., 157, 254
Barlow, D. H., 251, 476, 753
Barnes, C. L., 679, 681
Barnes, G. E., 368
Barnes, T.R.E., 461
Baron, J., 678
Baron, M., 591
Barr, H. M., 630
Barrett-Lennard, G. T., 738
Barrowclough, C., 762
Barsi, J., 403
Barsky, A. J., 221
Bartak, L., 635
Barten, H., 736
Bartholomew, K., 750
Bartko, J. J., 256, 436, 454
Bartlett, D. L., 268
Barton, R., 354
Barton, S., 637
Bartrop, R. W., 333
Bateson, G., 445, 453
Battle, C. C., 736
Bauer, M. S., 406
Baum, A., 340, 341
Baum, M., 228, 231, 242
Baumeister, R. F., 623
Baumgold, J., 256
Baxter, L., 59, 277
Bayle, A. L. J., 50, 52
Bazelon, D., 704–5, 714–15
Beardslee, W. R., 371

Beasley, C., 374, 375
Beaton, M. K., 761
Beaumont, G., 63, 374, 375
Beauvais, M. F., 670
Beck, A. T., 131, 132, 133, 135, 191, 252,
    254, 353, 354, 356, 357, 358, 367, 369,
    375, 380-84, 396, 410, 413, 414, 492,
    616, 748
Beck, R., 41-42
Beech, H. R., 269, 278
Beecher, H. K., 152, 737
Begleiter, H., 530
Behrens, B. C., 752
Beidel, D. C., 588
Beiser, M., 452
Belar, C. K., 311
Bell, S. T., 759
Bellack, A. S., 424, 462, 569, 588, 761, 762
Bellugi, U., 669
Belson, R., 603
Bemis, K. M., 760
Bemporad, J., 379
Bendt, R. H., 718
Benes, F. M., 452
Benjamin, B., 330
Benjamin, H., 486
Benjamin, L. S., 587
Benowitz, N., 555, 556, 558
Benson, D. F., 656, 657
Benson, H., 753
Benton, M. K., 761
Ber, L., 277, 279
Berchick, B., 254
Berchick, R. J., 748
Berenbaum, S., 498
Berg, J., 58
Bergeman, C., 58
Berger, F., 63
Berger, M., 640
Berger, P., 63, 64
Bergman, K., 59, 277
Berkman, L. F., 345
Berman, J. S., 753
Berman, K. F., 452
Bernheim, H., 33, 35
Bernstein, S., 279
Berridge, V., 513
Bertelsen, A., 427, 457
Bertrand, L. D., 306
Best, C., 245
Bettelheim, B., 91, 635, 638
Beutler, L., 750
Bexton, W. H., 153
Beyer, J., 231, 232
Bezemer, D., 474
Bialow, M., 368
Bianchi, K., 305-6
Bibring, E., 380
Bickel, W. K., 540, 541
Bihari, 530
Billy, J., 469
Binder, J., 750
Binet, A., 181
Binik, Y. M., 319
Biran, M., 131
Birch, H. G., 637
Bird, E. D., 452
Bird, H. R., 601

Bird, J., 293
Birenbaum, A., 631
Birley, J.L.T., 761
Bishop, S., 748
Bisiach, E., 655
Bjornson, L., 302
Black, D., 270
Black, G., 323
Black, K., 766
Blackburn, I. M., 748
Blackmun, H. A., 719
Blaer, D., 259
Blair, C. D., 495
Blair, S. N., 759
Blake, R. R., 92
Blanchard, E. B., 476, 753
Blanchard, R., 477
Blaney, P. H., 398
Blanz, B., 287
Blashfield, R. K., 191, 195, 198
Blaszczynski, A., 482
Blazer, D., 570
Bleuler, E., 190, 420-21, 430, 432
Bliss, E., 297, 298, 300, 301, 322
Bloch, S., 724
Bloom, E. T., 335
Bloom, F. E., 521, 523, 526, 527, 673
Bloom, J., 334
Bloxom, A., 736
Blum, N., 270
Blumberg, S. H., 367
Bogen, J., 657
Bogerts, B., 452
Bogia, D. P., 431
Bohman, M., 283, 529, 579
Bohn, M. J., 527, 532, 534, 535
Boltwood, M., 325
Bombardier, C., 527
Bond, M., 94–95
Bonnie, R. J., 710
Booker, J. M., 406
Borduin, C. M., 752
Borenstein, M., 761
Borge, G. L., 404
Borkovec, T., 261, 753
Bornstein, R. F., 589
Borysenko, M., 332
Bosomworth, J., 374, 375
Boswell, D., 739
Bouafuely, M., 291
Bouchard, T., 57, 58
Boulos, C., 374
Boulougouris, J. C., 257, 278
Bourdon, K., 220
Bourgeois, L., 739
Bourgeois, M., 409
Bower, G. H., 88
Bowers, W., 595
Bowlby, J., 367, 592
Bowler, K., 257
Bowman, E., 296
Boyd, J. L., 219, 220, 222, 256, 762
Bozarth, J. D., 738
Bozarth, M. A., 522, 538
Bradford, J., 496
Bradley, M., 574
Bradshaw, J. L., 298, 658
Brady, J. P., 292

Brady, J. V., 150, 320
Brady, K., 337
Braff, D. L., 431
Branconnier, R. J., 556
Brand, R. J., 323
Brandenburg, N. A., 600
Brandstetter, G., 316
Braude, W. M., 461
Braukmann, C. J., 607
Braun-Scharm, H., 287
Breed, W., 409, 410
Bregman, E. O., 233
Brehm, J. W., 8
Brehm, S. S., 8
Breier, A., 257
Breitner, J. C. S., 677
Brennan, P., 579, 582
Brenner, H. D., 462, 761
Breslau, N., 247, 369
Breslin, N. H., 460
Brett, C. W., 393
Breuer, J., 35, 281
Brew, B., 680
Brickman, A. S., 187
Bridgman, P., 413
Britton, K. T., 526
Broadbent, D. E., 429
Broca, P., 666, 669
Brodie, H. K. H., 403
Bronson, S., 257
Brooks, A. D., 714
Brooks, D., 243
Brooks, L., 739
Brooks, N., 243
Brooks-Gunn, J., 622
Brown, A., 324
Brown, F. W., 288
Brown, G. W., 368, 369, 394, 761
Brown, J. M., 368
Brown, K. H., 182
Brown, R. A., 452, 757
Brown, R. G., 651
Brown, W. F., 770
Brownell, K. D., 759
Browning, P., 589
Bruce, B., 748
Bruch, H., 623
Bruininks, R. H., 625
Bruner, J. S., 92
Bryan, J. H., 723
Bryan, T. H., 723
Bryant, R. N., 292
Brynes, J., 631
Buchanan, G., 331
Buchsbaum, M. S., 428, 452
Buchsbaum, S., 461
Buchwald, A. M., 398
Budney, A. J., 540, 541
Budzynski, T. H., 185
Bunney, W. E., 361, 369, 404, 405
Bunyan, J., 267
Buranen, C., 283, 291
Burgess, A., 767
Burgess, A. W., 244, 769
Burgess, M., 324
Burgess, P. W., 681, 683
Burke, A. E., 614, 616
Burley, S. K., 625

Burling, T. A., 393
Burman, A. M., 617
Burnam, A., 701
Burnam, M., 360
Burns, B., 87, 219, 220, 222, 256
Burt, R. A., 719
Burton, J., 748
Burton, R., 222
Burzette, E., 757
Bushnell, J., 251
Buss, A. H., 55
Butcher, J. D., 178
Butcher, J. N., 177
Butler, G., 259, 261, 288
Butters, N., 671
Byck, R., 540
Bynum, W. F., Jr., 39

Cade, J., 63, 404–5
Cadoret, R., 531, 570, 605
Cain, C., 605
Caligiuri, M. P., 461
Callahan, L. A., 717
Callies, A., 291
Cameron, A., 252
Cameron, N., 252, 431
Cannon, L., 680
Cannon, T. D., 166, 445
Cantopher, T., 64
Cantor, A., 360
Cantor, N., 13
Cantwell, D. P., 638
Caplan, D., 666
Cardena, E., 294
Cardon, P. V., 324
Carey, G., 195, 218, 237, 270
Carkhuff, R. R., 738
Carlisle, J. M., 494
Carlsmith, J. M., 174
Carlson, G. A., 403
Carlson, J., 720
Carmelli, D., 323
Carney, R., 332
Carpenter, C. J., 407, 452
Carpenter, W. T., Jr., 420, 436, 440
Carr, S. J., 748
Carrier, M., 28
Carrier, S., 28
Carter, A. B., 293
Carter, C. H., 629
Carter, D. K., 739
Carter, J., 707
Carter, M., 761
Cartwright, R. D., 738, 739
Casanova, M., 452
Caspersen, C. J., 329
Catalano, F., 62, 461
Cautela, J. R., 495
Cegelka, W. J., 631
Cerny, J., 254
Chai, H., 337
Chalder, T., 288
Challis, B., 295
Chambers, D. L., 698
Chandler, J., 62
Chang, G., 535
Chang, S., 754
Chaplin, W., 354

Chapman, D. T., 180, 181, 432
Chapman, J. P., 430
Chapman, J. S., 429
Chapman, L. J., 180, 181, 430, 431, 432
Charcot, J. M., 32–33, 35, 281, 291, 293, 294
Charney, D. S., 252, 257
Chaudry, D. R., 233, 257
Cherry, C., 619
Cheseldine, S., 631
Chesney, M., 323
Chevron, E., 396, 755
Chiarugi, V., 39
Childress, A., 523, 541
Chimelli, L., 680
Chin, J. H., 526
Chinn, P. C., 631
Chodoff, P., 287, 291, 586
Christensen, H., 258
Christiansen, K. O., 579
Christenson, C. V., 489, 491
Christison, M. D., 452
Christodoulou, G. N., 316
Chronholm, B., 280
Churchill, R., 52
Churchill, W., 52, 404
Cicchetti, D. V., 294, 625
Cimbolic, P., 372
Cirincione, C., 717
Claiborn, J. M., 182
Clark, D. G., 759
Clark, D. M., 252–54, 753
Clark, R. E., 454
Clarke, A. M., 631
Clarke, D. D., 631
Clarke, G., 244, 616
Clarke-Stewart, K. A., 80
Clarkin, J., 360
Clarkson, C., 259
Clausen, J. A., 454
Clayton, P. J., 286, 287, 288
Cleckley, H., 299, 572, 575, 577, 582
Clements, C., 355
Clements, M., 752
Clementz, B. A., 452
Clemmensen, L., 477
Cloninger, C. P., 528
Cloninger, C. R., 283, 287, 532, 579, 580, 581, 605
Cluff, L. E., 360
Coaper, J. E., 424
Coates, T. J., 327
Coats, K. I., 397, 616
Cobb, J., 278
Cobb, S., 318
Cochran, C., 361
Coe, D., 433
Coen, K. A., 560
Coffman, G. A., 281
Coffman, J. A., 451
Cohen, B., 62, 275
Cohen, B. A., 680
Cohen, D., 257
Cohen, I., 64
Cohen, J. B., 324
Cohen, L., 340
Cohen, N. J., 675
Cohen, P., 258, 498

Cohen, R., 563
Cohen, S., 335
Cohen-Kettenis, P., 477
Coie, J. D., 604
Colby, J. P., 531
Cole, C. S., 398
Cole, J., 63, 374, 375
Collins, G. H., 673
Collins, J. F., 395, 748, 755
Colter, N., 452
Coltheart, M., 670, 671
Comstock, G. W., 330
Conger, J. J., 318
Connolly, P. B., 503
Consentino, A., 640
Cook, B., 258
Cook, J., 563
Cook, M., 237
Cook, W. W., 324
Coons, P., 296
Cooper, A. F., 435
Cooper, G., 63, 374
Cooper, H. M., 752
Cooper, J. E., 427, 457
Cooper, K. H., 759
Cooper, S. J., 522
Coote, M. A., 618
Corbit, J. D., 404
Corbit, J. P., 519
Corcoran, M. E., 539
Corder, E. H., 680
Corenthal, R., 595
Corley, R., 57
Corrigall, W. A., 560
Corrigan, P., 462
Corsellis, J. A., 452
Coryell, W., 281, 287, 288, 371
Costello, C. G., 221, 398
Costello, E., 261
Cotton, N. S., 529
Coulter, D. L., 624
Cousins, N., 737
Covi, L., 736
Cowen, E. L., 766, 769
Cox, B., 243
Cox, P., 216
Coyle, J. T., 679
Coyne, J. C., 344, 398
Craig, T. J., 542
Craighead, W. E., 616
Crapper, D. R., 679
Creak, M., 635
Crisp, A. H., 623
Critchley, M., 647
Crits-Cristoph, P., 108, 742
Crittenden, P. M., 592
Cromwell, R. L., 442
Cronbach, L. J., 194
Crossett, J. H., 451
Crow, T. J., 439, 440, 451, 452
Crowder, R. G., 670
Crowe, M. J., 257
Crowe, R., 252, 257, 259, 605
Csanalosi, I., 259
Cudeck, R., 445
Cullen, F., 701
Cullen, W., 38
Cummings, C., 623

Currie, E. P., 25
Curry, S. J., 757
Curtis, B. A., 666
Curtis, D., 136
Curtis, G. C., 252
Cuthbert, B. N., 574
Cutler, S., 617
Cytryn, L., 367

Dacquin, J., 39
Dacu, C., 249
Dahlstrom, W. G., 178, 324, 325
Dalgard, O. S., 579
Damasio, A. R., 583, 656, 681, 682, 683
Damasio, H., 583, 656, 681, 682, 683
Dame, A., 323
Dan, E., 248
Danaher, B. G., 757
Dancu, C. V., 588
Daniels, M., 335
Darwin, C., 107
Davenport, H. W., 315
Davenport, Y. B., 403
Davidson, J., 248, 452
Davidson, L. M., 242
Davidson, M., 237
Davidson, R. J., 375, 681
Davies, J. C. V., 605
Davies, P., 677
Davies, R. K., 403
Davis, G. C., 247, 369
Davis, H., 325
Davis, J. M., 365, 754
Davis, K. L., 677
Davis, M. A., 535
Davis, P. H., 299–300
Davis, P. J., 87
Davis, R. M., 561
Davis, S. K., 718
Davis, W. M., 523
Davis, W. W., 191
Davison, G. C., 183, 482
Davison, L. A., 186
Day, R., 424, 427, 457
Dealy, R., 257
DeAngelis, T., 285
De Backer, G., 323
DeBaryshe, B. D., 604
DeBoni, U., 679
Decenteceo, E., 131
de Costa, B. R., 556
DeFaire, J., 58
De Fraites, E., 63
DeFries, J., 57-58
Dekker, E., 341
Delay, J., 61, 62, 459
d'Elia, G., 431
DeLong, M. R., 679
Demeter, E., 403
DeMeyer, M. K., 637
Deneau, G., 521, 538
Deniker, P., 62, 459
Denney, D., 447
Dent, O. F., 246
Depue, R. H., 344, 398, 403, 405, 755
Derouesne, J., 670
DeRubeis, R. J., 754, 755
Descartes, R., 113

De Silva, P., 234, 754
de Souza, E., 259
Deutsch, A., 27, 28, 38, 41, 42
Deutsch, G., 657
Devanand, D., 377
DeVeaugh-Geiss, J., 279, 754
Devine, P. A., 735
Diamond, A., 681
Diamond, B. L., 322, 324, 700
Diamond, R. G., 675
Di Chiara, G., 522
Dickason, D., 244
Dickey, R., 477
Diehl, S. R., 447
Diekstra, R., 414
Dienelt, M. N., 342, 361
Diggory, J. C., 409
Dimsdale, J. E., 324
Dinges, D. F., 306
Dishion, T. J., 604
Dixon, H., 196
Dixon, W. J., 761
Doane, J. A., 453, 464, 761
Dobie, S., 737
Docherty, J. P., 748, 755
Dodge, K. A., 389, 604
Dohrenwend, B. P., 342, 344, 424, 456
Dohrenwend, B. S., 342, 344
Dole, V. P., 548, 758
Doleys, D. M., 618
Doll, E., 625
Domingo, D., 233
Donahoe, J., 59
Donaldson, K., 706
Dorer, D. J., 371
Dornseif, B., 374, 375
Dorsey, M. F., 126
Dorworth, T. R., 393
Douglas, M., 25
Douglas, V. I., 609
Down, L., 628
Dragosics, B., 316
Draguns, J. G., 198
Drake, R., 531
Dramaix, M., 323
Drew, C. J., 631
Drewnowski, A., 621
Drossman, D. A., 283
Drummond, T., 712–13
Dubbert, R. M., 759
Duker, J., 177
Duncan-Johnson, C., 446
Dunham, H. W., 454, 455
Dunn, V., 451
Dunner, D. L., 403
DuPaul, G. J., 611
Durcan, M. J., 526
Durkheim, E., 413
DuRubeis, R. J., 391
Dwyer, C., 335
Dyer, A. R., 759

Eaker, E., 323
Eastman, C. I., 407
Eaton, W., 570
Eaves, L., 166
Eberhard, G., 316
Eccles, A., 496

Eddy, M. B., 32
Eddy, T., 42
Edelbrock, C. S., 609, 610
Edelbroek, P. M., 293
Edell, W. S., 431
Edelsohn, D., 492
Edwards, G., 515
Edwards, J., 64
Edwards, M. T., 756
Edwards, N., 357, 391
Egeland, J. A., 364, 409
Ehlers, C. L., 530
Ehrhardt, A. A., 470, 473, 498
Ehrhardt, J. C., 451
Ehrlich, P., 52
Ehrman, R., 523, 541
Eidelson, J. I., 393
Eisen, S., 248
Eisenberg, L., 52
Ekehammar, B., 260
Ekman, P., 174
Elashoff, J. D., 316
Elizur, Y., 248
Elkin, I., 395, 396, 748, 755
Ellenberger, H. F., 25, 33
Ellery, C., 711, 712, 714, 716
Ellinwood, E. H., 536, 537, 539, 540
Elliot, D. S., 604
Ellis, A., 133-35, 380, 384, 748
Ellis, L., 478, 480, 482
Ellsworth, P. C., 174
Elmhorn, K., 603
Emerick, D. C., 535
Emery, G., 252, 382, 414, 748
Emmelkamp, P., 257, 278
Emrick, C. D., 756
Endicott, J., 361, 365, 370, 404
Endler, N., 260
Enkelmann, R., 259
Ennis, B. J., 700, 726
Eppley, K., 261, 753
Epstein, L. J., 175
Erdelyi, M. H., 80
Ericksen, S., 754
Erikson, E. H., 82, 106
Erikson, K., 166, 240
Erikson, W., 491
Ernberg, G., 424, 427, 457
Eron, L. D., 181
Ervin, F. R., 237
Eslinger, P. J., 681, 682, 683
Esquirol, J., 50
Esterson, A., 453, 454
Eunson, K. M., 748
Eutsch, G., 657
Evans, H. I., 300
Evans, M. D., 391, 508, 754, 755
Everson, M., 492
Evon, L. D., 603
Exline, R., 174
Exner, J. E., 179, 181
Eysenck, H., 80, 234, 236

Faber, R., 377
Fabrega, H., 281
Fairburn, C. G., 620, 621, 748, 760
Fairweather, G., 464
Falloon, I. R. H., 445, 453, 464, 761, 762

Fancher, R., 379
Fanselow, M. S., 522
Farberow, N., 767-68
Faris, R. E. L., 454, 455
Farmer, A. E., 433, 441
Farr, R. K., 701
Farrington, D. P., 604
Fawzy, F., 334
Fawzy, N., 334
Feil, W. B., 592
Feinberg, T. E., 428
Feinleib, M., 323
Feldman, J., 498
Feldman, M. P., 482
Fellenius, J., 221, 232
Fenichel, O., 278, 379
Fennell, M., 259, 261
Fenton, W. S., 425, 439, 440
Fernald, P. S., 735
Ferster, C. B., 638
Fibiger, H. C., 539
Fiester, S. J., 748, 755
Fieve, R. R., 400, 401, 402
Figuero, R. A., 625
Fine, C. G., 303
Fingarette, H., 710
Fink, M., 377, 754
Finkel, N. J., 717, 718
Fiore, M. C., 561, 757
Fireside, H., 723, 724
First, M. B., 191, 406
Fischer, M., 609, 610
Fischer, S. A., 366
Fischman, M. W., 538
Fisher, J., 175
Fisher, M. M., 221
Fisher, S., 109
Fishman, R., 270, 404
Fiske, D., 739
Fithian, M. A., 756
Fitzgerald, R. G., 330
Fitzpatrick, J., 196
Fixsen, D. C., 607
Flaskerud, J. H., 739, 740
Flavell, J. H., 80
Flay, B. R., 757
Fleeting, M., 54
Fleisher, W. P., 297
Fleiss, J. L., 195
Fleming, J.A.E., 452
Fleming, J. E., 615, 616
Fletcher, K. E., 609
Flood, R., 410
Floyd, F. J., 752
Foa, D. B., 212, 232
Foa, E., 121, 244, 245, 249, 278, 280
Fodor, O., 316
Foerg, F., 540, 541
Folker, D., 58
Follick, M., 311
Ford, M. R., 570
Forman, R., 736
Forster, J., 366
Foster, D. W., 68
Foster, R., 625
Foucault, M., 29, 33, 36, 37, 40, 41
Foureman, W. C., 428
Fournier, A., 51

Fowler, R. D., 268
Fowles, D. C., 353, 361
Fox, R., 739, 764
Frances, A., 191, 360
Frank, E., 249, 375, 506
Frank, H., 592
Frank, I. M., 555
Frank, J., 248
Frank, J. D., 736, 737
Frank, R., 583, 656
Frankenberg, F. R., 592
Frankl, V., 751
Franklin, B., 31, 38
Frautschi, N., 323
Frederick, C. J., 410
Fredle, N. M., 539
Fredrikson, M., 235
Freedland, K., 332
Freedman, M., 677
Freeman, R. M., 600
Freeman, W. B., 464
French, R., 13
French, T. M., 324
Freud, A., 91
Freud, S., 33, 35, 62, 71–82, 86–93, 102–6,
    107–9, 144, 223–25, 230, 273, 281,
    288–90, 291, 292, 293, 378, 379, 493,
    536, 735, 749, 763–64
Friedle, N. M., 539
Friedman, M., 248, 323
Friedman, S., 574
Friedrich, F. J., 655
Friesen, W. V., 174
Friman, P. C., 618
Frith, C. D., 452
Frith, U., 683
Fromm, E., 82
Fujimura, O., 671
Fulker, D., 58
Fyer, A., 251

Gabbard, G. O., 108
Gabreels, F. J., 288
Gabriel, T., 543
Gabriella, W. F., 605
Gabrielli, W. F., 580
Gage, P., 583, 656–57, 684
Gagnon, J. H., 487, 488, 489, 491, 492
Galaburda, A. M., 583, 656, 671
Gale, M., 324
Galen, 29–30
Gallagher, D., 739
Gallagher, P., 754
Gallops, M., 247
Gambles, D., 481
Ganaway, G. K., 304, 305
Garber, H. L., 631
Garber, J., 357, 389, 391
Garcia, E., 631
Garcia, J., 234, 236, 237
Gardner, D., 374
Gardner, E., 649
Gardner, W., 701
Garfinkel, P. E., 622
Garmezy, N., 430, 613, 632
Garner, D., 165, 366
Garner, D. M., 622, 760
Garner, W., 335

Garrison, C. Z., 366
Garrity, T. F., 345
Garside, R. F., 435
Garvey, M., 258
Gaston, L., 739
Gatsonis, C., 615, 616
Gawin, F. N., 536, 537, 539, 540
Gay, P., 108
Gazzaniga, M., 657, 658
Gebhard, P. H., 489, 491
Gehrig, L., 649, 650, 689
Gelder, M., 254, 259, 261
Gelder, M. G., 738
Gelenberg, A. J., 375
Gelfand, D. M., 616
Geller, M. H., 739
George, L., 259
George, M., 276
George, M. S., 681
George III, King of England, 38
Gergen, K. J., 81, 200
Gergoulas, A., 316
Gersh, F., 353, 361
Gershom, E. S., 403
Gerstley, L. J., 518
Geschwind, N., 659, 666, 668, 671
Gibb, J. W., 553
Gibbon, M., 406, 602
Gibbons, L. W., 759
Gibbons, R. D., 754
Gibralter, J., 62, 461
Gilberstadt, H., 177
Gilbert, D. C., 560
Gilderman, A. M., 762
Gillberg, C., 639, 640, 641
Giller, E., 248
Gillham, J., 397
Gillies, S., 637
Gillin, J. C., 407
Gilman, A. G., 651
Gilmore, G. C., 430, 573, 575, 576, 577
Girelli, S., 245, 249
Giovino, G. A., 561, 757
Girgus, J., 367, 389, 616
Gittelman, M., 612, 637
Gittelman, R., 609
Gittelman-Klein, R., 600
Gittleson, N. L., 269
Glaser, R., 325, 335
Glass, D. C., 323, 326, 344, 395, 755
Glass, D. R., 162, 748
Glass, G. V., 108, 150
Glazer, H. I., 392, 398
Gleitman, H., 179, 212–13, 455
Gleitman, L. R., 670, 671
Gleser, G. C., 240
Glick, I., 404
Glisky, E. L., 676
Glod, C., 63, 374, 375
Glueck, Z., 446
Glynn, S. M., 762
Golan, N., 768
Gold, J. M., 452
Goldberg, S. R., 557, 560
Goldberg, T. E., 452
Golden, C. J., 182, 187
Goldfinger, S., 707
Goldfried, M. R., 131, 183

Golding, J. M., 288
Goldman-Rakic, P. S., 681
Goldstein, D. B., 526
Goldstein, J. M., 424
Goldstein, M. J., 453, 458, 464, 761
Goldstein, R., 270
Good, G. D., 407
Goodman, G., 739
Goodman, L. S., 651
Goodman, R., 639
Goodwin, D. W., 291, 529, 534, 535
Goodwin, F. K., 403, 404
Goodyear, N. N., 759
Gooren, L., 474
Gordon, J. R., 531, 533, 757, 760
Gordon, N., 337
Gorenstein, E. E., 582
Gorman, J. M., 251
Gorski, R., 479
Gorsuch, R. C., 260
Goshen-Gottstein, Y., 674, 675
Gottesman, I. I., 54, 195, 218, 270, 420,
    422, 424, 425, 433, 437, 440–42, 445,
    579, 580, 605
Gottheil, E., 334
Gottschalk, L. A., 324
Gould, S. J., 624
Goulding, P., 684
Goulston, K. J., 246
Grabowski, T., 583, 656
Grace, M., 241, 247
Grace, W., 341, 342
Grady, W., 469
Graf, P., 675
Graham, D., 316, 341, 342
Graham, J. R., 178
Graham, R., 324
Gramzow, R., 587
Grant, B. F., 195
Grant, T. M., 630
Grapentine, W. L., 187
Grattan, L. M., 682, 683
Graw, P., 407
Gray, F., 680
Gray, S., 257
Graziano, A. M., 769
Green, 462
Green, B., 241, 247
Green, B. L., 240
Green, M. F., 462
Green, R., 473
Greenberg, J., 470
Greenberg, L. D. S., 739
Greenberg, M. S., 375
Greenberg, R. P., 109
Greene, D., 9
Greene, R. L., 177, 178, 748
Greenspoon, J., 152
Greenwald, D. P., 461, 761
Greer, G., 553
Greer, S., 334, 574
Gregor, T., 26
Gregory, I., 574
Gregory, R., 294
Greisinger, W., 50, 51
Greist, J., 279
Grey, S., 278
Griffith, J. J., 445

Grigorenko, P., 724
Grilly, D. M., 524, 546
Grimshaw, L., 277
Grinspoon, L., 536, 553
Groen, J., 340
Grof, P., 403
Gross, H. J., 292
Grossman, H. J., 624
Grossman, M. I., 316, 725–26
Grove, W. M., 431, 451
Gruder, C. L., 757
Gruen, R., 591
Gruenberg, A. M., 585, 591
Grueneich, R., 591
Grunbaum, A., 80
Gualtieri, C., 62
Guess, D., 631
Gumanis, Dr., 706
Gunderson, J. G., 461, 592
Gur, R. C., 292
Gurman, A. S., 738
Gurney, C., 370
Guroff, J. J., 297, 302
Guze, S., 529
Guze, S. B., 286, 287, 288, 291, 369, 410,
    581

Haas, G. L., 452
Hackmann, A., 254, 278
Hadzi-Pavlovic, D., 258
Hagen, R. L., 560
Hager, J., 236
Hahlweg, K., 752
Hahn, P. M., 556
Haines, J. E., 680
Halberstadt, L. J., 390
Halbreich, U., 365
Haley, J., 453, 740, 745
Haley, R., 281
Halford, W. K., 752
Hall, C. S., 80
Hall, J., 63
Hall, M., 340
Hall, S. M., 757
Hall, W., 738
Hallam, R., 216
Hallekson, C. J., 406
Halpern, J., 89
Hammeke, T. A., 187
Hammen, C. L., 162, 358
Hampson, J. L., 477
Hanada, K., 196
Hannah, M. T., 750
Hannum, R. D., 394
Hanson, G. R., 553
Hardesty, J. P., 458
Harding, W. M., 547
Hardy, J. A., 679
Hare, R. D., 572, 573, 574, 577, 578, 582
Harlow, H. F., 367
Harlow, J. M., 656
Harpur, T. J., 572, 574, 577
Harrington, R., 616
Harrington-Kostur, J., 757
Harris, B., 227
Harris, E. L., 257
Harris, M. R., 175
Harris, T., 368, 369, 395

Harrison, R., 181
Harrow, M., 431
Hart, S. D., 572
Hartlage, L., 186
Hartman, W. E., 756
Hartstone, E., 718
Hasert, M. F., 531
Hasin, D. S., 195
Hasse, A., 710
Hathaway, S. R., 176
Hatziandrev, G. A., 561, 757
Hawking, S., 685, 689
Hawley, G. A., 682
Hay, P. J., 620
Hayashida, M., 534
Hayes, K., 431
Haynes, S. G., 323, 325
Hays, R., 360
Hazari, A., 270, 271
Hazdi-Pavlovic, D., 361
Hazell, P., 414
Hazelrigg, M. D., 752
Heath, A., 166, 259
Heather, N., 738
Heatherton, T. F., 623
Heber, S., 302
Hecaen, H., 655
Hecker, M., 323
Hedeker, D., 757
Heider, F., 133
Heier, R. J., 428
Heilbrun, A. B., Jr., 428
Heilman, K. M., 659
Heiman, J. R., 508
Heimberg, R. G., 588
Heitler, J., 736
Hellekson, C. J., 407
Helmers, K., 325
Helsing, K. J., 330
Helzer, J. E., 199, 547
Helzer, M., 163
Hemsley, R., 640
Hendin, H., 410, 519
Heninger, G. R., 252, 257
Henker, B., 608, 609, 610
Hennigfield, J. E., 557, 560
Henry, J., 374, 375
Hentschel, E., 316
Herbert, J. D., 569, 588
Herek, G., 481
Herkenham, M., 556
Herman, C. P., 622
Hermansen, L., 529
Hermanutz, M., 761
Hermelin, B., 636
Heron, W., 153
Hersov, L., 614, 640
Hesselbrock, M., 518, 531, 547
Hesselbrock, V., 518, 531
Heston, L., 444, 447
Hetherington, E. M., 604
Heyes, M. P., 680
Heywood, E., 531
Higgins, G. A., 679
Higgins, S. T., 540, 541
Higley, J. D., 531
Hilborne, L., 470
Hilgard, E. R., 93, 292

Hill, B. K., 625
Hill, J., 279, 605
Hill, P. O., 181
Hill, R., 257
Hilts, P. J., 558
Him, C., 244
Himmelhoch, J. M., 403
Hinckley, J., Jr., 716–17
Hines, M., 498
Hinson, R. E., 524
Hippius, H., 403
Hippocrates, 221–22
Hiroto, D. S., 168, 387
Hirschfeld, R. M. A., 361, 404
Hirst, W., 295
Hirt, M., 452
Hoban, T. M., 407
Hobfoll, S. E., 589
Hobson, R. P., 636
Hodel, B., 462, 761
Hodgson, R. J., 124, 266, 267, 269, 270, 271, 274, 278, 291, 494, 515, 754
Hoehn-Saric, R., 259, 736
Hoekstra, R., 278
Hoenig, J., 473
Hoffman, L. J., 168
Hoffman, N., 592
Hofmann, A., 550–51
Hofstadter, L., 673
Hogan, R., 682
Hogarty, G. E., 453, 461, 463, 761
Hokanson, J. E., 324
Holbrook, D., 640
Holden, C., 404, 413
Hollander, E., 275
Holliday, J., 335
Hollingshead, A. B., 454
Hollister, L. E., 556
Hollon, S. D., 131, 132, 375, 391, 396, 754, 755
Holmes, D., 88
Holmes, G., 225
Holmes, T., 162, 342, 343
Holmstrom, L. L., 244, 769
Holt, C. S., 588
Holtzman, W. H., 181
Holzer, C. E., 368
Honigfeld, G., 761
Honzik, N. P., 225
Hooker, W. D., 555
Hope, D. A., 569, 588
Hope, R. A., 748
Hopkins, S. A., 621
Hops, H., 616
Horne, R. L., 334
Horney, K., 81
Horng, J., 374
Hornig, C., 222
Hornsby, J., 186
Horowitz, L. M., 750
Horowitz, M., 136, 274
Horter, D. H., 680
Horvath, A. O., 739
Horwood, L. J., 610
Hostetter, A. M., 364
Hough, R., 570
House, P., 9
Houts, A. C., 618, 619

Houts, P. S., 736
Howlin, P., 636, 637, 640
Hrubec, Z., 529
Huag, H., 680
Huber-Smith, M. J., 252
Hubler, 650
Hudson, J. I., 621
Huesman, L. R., 603
Hugdahl, K., 220, 235, 236
Huges, D., 259
Hughes, H., 267
Hughes, J. R., 540, 541
Hulley, S. B., 324
Hulse, S. H., 592
Hulzinga, D., 604
Hume, D., 114
Hung, D. W., 640
Hunt, 41
Hunt, C., 259
Hunt, E., 589
Hunt, M., 469, 477, 488
Hunter, R., 267
Huston, A., 497
Hutchings, B., 57, 580, 605
Hutter, C., 245, 249
Hyde, E., 486
Hygge, S., 237
Hyler, S. E., 287
Hyman, B. T., 679
Hyun, C., 334

Iacono, W. G., 452
Iker, H., 334
Imber, S. D., 395, 396, 736, 742, 748, 755
Imboden, J. B., 290, 360, 592
Imperato, A., 522
Ingham, R. J., 620
Ingram, P., 721
Insel, T., 563
Ironside, W., 318
Ironson, M., 325
Irwin, M., 335
Isabella, M., 722
Ishii, N., 68
Iwata, E. A., 126
Izard, C. E., 367

Jablensky, A., 424, 427, 457
Jacklin, C., 497
Jackson, D. D., 453
Jackson, J. H., 659
Jackson, K. L., 366
Jackson, R., 698
Jackson, T., 718–19
Jacobs, B. L., 552
Jacobs, W. J., 235
Jacobsen, B., 166, 445
Jacobson, N., 506
Jacobson, N. S., 752
Jacobson, S., 666
Jaffe, A., 332
Jaffe, A. J., 535
Jaffe, J. H., 521, 527, 535, 544, 545–46, 552, 563
Jagoe, R., 452
Jahoda, M., 17
James, R. M., 717
James, S. P., 407

Janet, P., 281
Janicak, P. G., 754
Janis, I., 131
Janssen, R. S., 680
Jarvik, M. E., 757
Jasinski, D. R., 560
Jason, L. A., 757
Jatlow, P., 361, 540
Javna, C. D., 461
Jaycox, L., 397
Jaynes, J., 83
Jefferson, J., 63
Jeffrey, R., 366
Jeffries, J. C., Jr., 710
Jellenek, E., 532
Jenike, M., 277, 279
Jenkins, C. D., 323
Jens, K. S., 300
Jensen, L., 481
Jeppsen, A., 297
Jerkovich, G., 63
Jerome, J., 19, 411
Jeste, D. V., 461
Johns, C. A., 761
Johnsen, J., 756
Johnson, F., 705
Johnson, H., 63
Johnson, J., 222
Johnson, J. E., 428
Johnson, J. H., 629
Johnson, M., 739
Johnson, M. R., 556
Johnson, V., 502, 506–7, 508, 755
Johnson, W., 183
Johnston, J. C., 228, 279
Johnstone, E. C., 452
Jonas, J. M., 286, 622
Jones, 39
Jones, B., 279, 286
Jones, E. E., 739
Jones, R., 748
Jones, R. T., 555, 556, 757
Jones, S., 464
Jones, S. B., 514, 519
Jonsson, H., 424
Jordan, C., 249
Jorenby, D., 561
Jourard, S. M., 174
Joyce, P., 251
Juginger, J., 433
Jukes, E., 637
Jung, C., 81

Kabat, L. G., 435
Kabat-Zinn, J., 261, 753
Kaffman, M., 446
Kaij, L., 529
Kalat, J., 236
Kalin, N. H., 522, 545
Kamen, L., 335
Kamin-Siegel, L. J., 228, 624
Kamo, T., 406
Kamphaus, R. W., 625
Kandel, E., 579, 582
Kane, B. J., 736
Kane, J., 591
Kane, J. M., 62, 461, 761
Kanfer, F. H., 131

Kannel, W. B., 323
Kanner, A. D., 344
Kanner, L., 635, 638
Kanter, R. A., 623
Kaplan, H. S., 490, 501, 502, 503, 506, 507, 756
Kaplan, S. M., 324
Karasek, R., 328
Karlik, S., 679
Karlsson, J. L., 447
Karoly, P., 131
Kasl, S. V., 345
Kaslow, N. J., 367
Kass, F., 585, 586, 589
Katchadourian, H. A., 489
Kates, M. H., 681
Kathol, R. G., 221
Katz, B., 649
Katz, M., 738
Katz, R., 279, 404, 754
Kaufman, I. C., 367
Kay, D. W., 435
Kaye, W., 760
Kazdin, A. E., 230, 734, 753
Keck, P., 62
Keefe, J. A., 447
Kegan, R., 571
Kehoe, M., 318
Keinan, G., 589
Keir, R., 237
Keith, S. J., 461, 762
Keith-Spiegel, P., 741
Keller, M. B., 360, 361, 370, 371, 403
Kelley, A. E., 511–67
Kelley, H. H., 133
Kelly, J. B., 367
Kenardy, J., 760
Kendall, P. C., 131, 132
Kendell, R. E., 191
Kendler, K. S., 166, 259, 447, 585, 591
Kendrick, J. S., 329
Kenna, J. C., 473
Kennedy, H. L., 327
Kenney, M., 257
Kent, D., 281, 287
Kernberg, O. F., 587
Kerr, T. A., 370
Kertesz, A., 669
Kesey, K., 12
Kessler, R., 163, 164, 166, 259, 368, 621
Ketter, T., 406
Kettler, T. A., 681
Kety, S. S., 371, 444, 591
Keveles, G., 700
Keys, D. J., 588
Khantzian, E. J., 518
Kidd, K. K., 371
Kiecolt-Glaser, J. K., 325, 335
Kiely, J. L., 630
Kiesler, C. A., 464, 707, 772
Killman, P. R., 377
Kiloh, L. G., 333
Kilpatrick, D., 245, 617
Kimberlin, C., 637
Kindgon, D., 64
King, S., 328
Kinsey, A. C., 469, 486–87, 491
Kirby, M. W., 772

Kirigin, K., 607
Kirk, S. A., 196
Kirkendol, S., 757
Kirkhan, T. C., 522
Kirkley, B. G., 621
Kirtner, W., 739
Kissen, B., 530
Kittel, F., 323
Kleber, H. D., 540, 548, 564, 565
Klein, D. F., 257, 258, 600, 612
Klein, P., 316
Kleinknecht, R., 221
Klepinger, D., 469
Klerman, G. L., 63, 221, 342, 361, 375, 383, 395, 396, 404, 755
Klerman, G. R., 368, 371
Kletti, R., 294
Klima, E. S., 669
Kline, J. A., 407
Kline, N., 63
Klosko, J., 254
Kluft, R. P., 302, 304
Kluznik, J. C., 247
Knight, R., 458
Knorring, A. L. von, 283, 579
Kobasa, S. C., 345
Koegel, P., 701
Koelling, R. A., 234, 236, 237
Kohl, H. W., III, 759
Kohlberg, L., 682
Kohn, M. L., 454, 456
Kohut, H., 83, 86, 587, 592
Kojetin, B., 58
Kolb, B., 659, 666
Kolodmer, K., 327
Kolvin, I., 54
Kolvin, P., 54
Kondas, O., 619
Koob, G. F., 521, 523, 526, 527
Koragin, A., 723
Koran, L. M., 748
Korchin, S. J., 178
Koreen, A. R., 451
Korlin, D., 477
Kornblith, S. J., 461, 761
Kornitzer, M., 323
Koropsak, E., 324
Korten, A., 424, 427, 457
Kosten, T., 248, 540
Kotin, J., 403
Kotler, M., 248
Kotsopoulos, S., 287
Kovacs, M., 367, 396, 615, 616
Kozak, M. J., 212, 232, 280
Kraemer, B., 178
Kraemer, H., 26, 334
Kraemer, S., 761
Kraepelin, E., 190, 420–21, 430
Krafft-Ebing, R. von, 51–53, 484
Kramer, F. M., 759
Kramer, M., 570
Kramer, P. D., 375, 687
Kramlinger, K. G., 406
Krantz, D., 325
Krasner, L., 124
Krauchi, K., 407
Krauft, C. C., 738
Kraus, W. H., 761

Kreek, M. J., 548
Kretschmer, E., 190
Krieckhaus, E., 59
Kringlen, E., 277, 579
Kristeller, J., 261, 753
Krystal, H., 243
Ksir, C., 524, 525
Kuch, K., 243, 252
Kudler, H., 248
Kugelmass, S., 446
Kuhn, C., 325
Kuiper, B., 477
Kuipers, A., 257
Kupersmidt, J. B., 604
Kupfer, D., 375
Kurland, H. D., 582
Kutcher, S., 374
Kutchins, H., 196

Labate, C., 758
Laborit, H., 459
Lacey, J. I., 338
Lachman, S. J., 315, 316, 322
Lader, M. H., 564
Ladisich, W., 592
Laing, R. D., 438, 453, 454, 458
Lake, E., 698–99, 701
Lamb, H. R., 707
Lambert, N., 625
Lamiell, J. T., 80
LaMontagne, Y., 495
Lampert, C., 404
Landau, P., 279, 754
Lando, H. A., 757
Lane, J., 325
Lane, T. J., 288
Lang, P., 211, 212, 232
Lang, P. J., 574
Langer, E. J., 131, 201, 331
Langman, M., 316
Langner, T. S., 454
Lanyon, R. I., 495
Lanzetta, J. T., 213
Laor, N., 243
Lapouse, R., 613
Lassen, C. L., 756
Latane, B. T., 577
Latz, A., 446
Laudenslager, M. L., 332
Laufer, R., 247
Laughlin, H. P., 225, 250, 251, 258, 259, 268, 273, 278, 283, 286, 289, 291, 292, 295
Lavoisier, A. L., 31
Lavori, P. W., 363, 370, 371
Law, W. A., 680
Laws, A., 759
Lazarus, A., 131, 135, 136, 237
Lazarus, L., 333
Lazarus, R. S., 344
Lazerson, A., 673
Leber, D., 506
Leber, W., 395, 755
Leber, W. R., 748
Leckman, J. F., 371
Lecompte, D., 288
Lees, A., 276
Leff, J. P., 461, 462, 463

Leff, M. J., 361, 368, 403, 761
Lefkowitz, M. M., 603
Lefley, H. P., 762
Lehman, D. R., 240, 245
Lehmeyer, H. W., 407
Lehmkuhl, G., 287
Lehmkuhl, U., 287
Leiman, A., 664
Leitenberg, H., 257, 622
Leland, H., 625
Lelliott, P., 258
Lemkau, P. V., 766
Lenane, M., 276, 279
Lenz, J., 221
Leonard, A., 241
Leonard, H., 276, 277, 279
LeSage, A., 495
Lessard, A., 702, 704
Lesser, I. M., 290
Lessin, P. J., 556
Lessler, K., 739, 764
Lester, D., 300, 414
Lester, L. S., 522
Levander, S., 252
Levar, I., 456
LeVay, S., 479
Levin, A., 233
Levin, S., 490, 492
Levine, I. S., 701
Levine, J. L., 424
Levine, M., 769
Levine, P., 403
Levis, D. J., 120, 231
Levy, J., 657, 658
Lew, G., 316
Lewin, 549–50
Lewin, T., 414
Lewinsohn, P. M., 160, 354, 366, 616
Lewis, C., 252
Lewis, D. O., 582
Lewis, J. E., 625
Lewis, J. M., 453, 458
Lewy, A. J., 407
Li, S., 452
Liberman, B., 742
Liberman, R. P., 462, 463, 761
Lichtenstein, E., 757
Lidz, C. W., 701
Lidz, T., 454
Lieberman, J. A., 451, 761
Liebowitz, M., 233
Liebowitz, M. R., 251
Lin, R. Y., 452
Lincoln, A., 404
Lind, D. L., 292
Lindemalm, G., 477
Lindemann, E., 239
Linden, L. L., 409, 410
Lindenthal, J. J., 342, 361
Lindy, J., 241
Lindzey, G., 80
Lineberger, M., 669
Linehan, M. M., 131
Link, B., 701
Link, B. G., 456
Linnoila, M., 531
Linsky, A. S., 531
Linssen, A. C., 293

Lipman, A. J., 389
Lipman, R. S., 736
Lipowski, Z. J., 293
Lipp, M. G., 313
Lippold, S., 182
Lipsey, M., 150
Lipsitt, L. P., 166
Lister, R. G., 526, 563
Little, M. D., 556
Little Albert B., 227, 233
Littlefield, C. H., 369
Little Hans, 223–25, 226, 613
Litwack, T. R., 700
Liu, P. Y., 739
Livermore, J. M., 710
Livesley, W. J., 191
Livingston, M., 243
Livingston, N., 243
Lochar, D., 176
Lochman, J. E., 606
Locke, B., 570
Locke, J., 114
Lockyer, L., 637
Loeber, R., 604, 605
Loewenstein, R. J., 298, 304
Loftus, E., 88, 491, 617, 720
Logan, D. R., 631
Logue, C. M., 365
London, J., 259
London, P., 9, 723, 729, 743
Long, J. W., 741
Looney, J. G., 313
LoPiccolo, J., 508
Lorang, M. T., 527
Loranger, A. W., 403, 595
Lorion, R. P., 766, 769
Lorr, M., 738
Losonczy, M. F., 452
Lovaas, O. I., 126, 640
Lovibond, S. H., 618
Low, P. W., 710
Lowinger, P., 737
Lubin, B., 260
Luborsky, L., 135, 390, 739, 742, 750
Luckasson, R., 624
Luckhurst, E., 333
Lukoff, D., 458
Lumry, A., 132
Lunde, D. T., 489
Lunde, I., 371
Luria, A., 187, 654–55, 659
Lushene, R. E., 260
Luzzatti, C., 655
Lykken, D. T., 57, 58, 576
Lyness, W. H., 539
Lynn, A. B., 556
Lynskey, M. T., 610

Maas, J. W., 372
MacAlpine, I., 267
MacAskill, R. L., 707
Maccoby, E., 497
MacCulloch, M. J., 482
MacDonald, B., 278
MacDonald, N., 430
Mace, N., 678
MacFarland, J. W., 225
Machlin, S., 276

Mack, R. W., 622
Mack, W., 581
Mackey, A. V. P., 451
MacLeod, C., 274
MacMillan, D. L., 365, 631
Macmillan, M., 640
Madakasira, S., 294
Madonia, M. J., 461
Magaro, P. A., 447
Magliocco, D., 324
Magnusson, D., 260
Magraw, R., 247
Maher, B. A., 33, 427, 435
Maher, W. B., 33
Mahler, M., 83
Mahoney, K., 756
Mahoney, M. J., 131, 135, 184, 756
Maier, S. F., 168, 332, 385, 386, 393
Mair, J. M. M., 620
Malarkey, W., 325
Maletzky, B. M., 490, 495, 496
Maliphant, R., 605
Malitz, S., 377
Malmo, R. B., 338
Malt, U., 248
Mandelcorn, M. S., 292
Manderscheid, R. N., 460
Manderscheid, R. W., 707
Mann, J., 409
Mannuzza, S., 609
Manu, P., 288
Mapou, R. L., 680
Marchant, R., 636, 637
Marchione, K., 254
Marciano, T. D., 482
Marcus, J., 446
Marcus, L. R., 739
Marcus, M., 666
Marcus, M. D., 760
Marder, S. R., 461, 761
Marengo, J. T., 431
Margraf, J., 254, 753
Marhoefer-Dvorak, S., 245
Marin, O. S. M., 669
Marino, M. F., 592
Marinopoulou, A., 316
Markman, H. J., 752
Marks, I. M., 218, 219, 220, 221, 222, 235, 257, 258, 277, 278, 279, 490, 495, 508, 738
Marlatt, G. A., 531, 533, 757, 760
Marmar, C. R., 739
Marsden, C. D., 651
Marset, P., 257
Marsh, L., 452
Marshall, J. C., 292, 671
Marshall, W., 496
Martin, A., 678, 680
Martin, B., 432, 556, 604
Martin, J. L., 344
Martin, M. F., 297, 301
Marx, A. J., 772
Marx, K., 107
Marx, M. B., 345
Marxer, F., 328
Maser, J., 252
Maslow, A. H., 17
Mason, W., 340

Massion, A., 261, 753
Masters, W. H., 482, 502, 506–7, 508, 755
Matarazzo, J. D., 175, 311
Mather, C., 28
Mathews, A., 274
Matthews, D. A., 288
Matthews, K. A., 325
Matthews, S., 464
Matthysse, S., 59
Mattick, R., 258
Mavissakalian, M., 257, 258, 279
Mawson, D., 257, 278
May, P. R. A., 761
May, R., 19
Mayer, N. H., 659
Mayock, Mr., 697, 699
Mazure, C., 361
McArthur, J. C., 680
McCann, D. S., 252
McCarthy, M., 165, 366, 622
McCarthy, R., 668
McCary, J. L., 486, 487, 489, 490, 491, 502,
    503, 507
McClearn, G., 58
McClelland, D. C., 181, 327
McConaghy, N., 482, 491, 496
McConkey, K. M., 292
McConkey, R., 631
McConnell, R. B., 316
McCord, J., 574, 575
McDermott, K. B., 675
McElroy, S., 62
McFarlane, A., 25, 248
McGarry, A. L., 718
McGee, R., 600, 604, 605
McGhie, A., 429
McGill, C. W., 762
McGlashan, T. H., 425, 439, 440, 459, 591
McGlothin, W. H., 556
McGonigle, K., 163, 164, 368
McGovern, G., 725
McGrath, E., 375
McGreevy, M. A., 717
McGue, M., 54, 57, 58, 445
McGuffin, P., 404, 433, 441
McGuire, E., 470
McGuire, R. J., 494
McIntosh, J., 410
McIntyre, K. O., 757
McKim, W. A., 526, 554, 555
McKinlay, W., 243
McKinley, J. C., 176
McKinney, W. T., 367, 399
McKinnon, J. A., 238
McKnew, D. H., 367
McLean, C., 278
McLellan, A. T., 518, 523, 541, 739, 742
McLeod, D., 259
McManus, M., 187
McNally, C. E., 235, 237
McNally, R. M., 753
McNeal, E. T., 372
McNitt, P. C., 398
McPherson, F. M., 234
McSween, T., 126
Means, J., 337
Medley, E. S., 316, 324
Mednick, S., 57

Mednick, S. A., 166, 445, 579, 580, 581,
    582, 605
Medvedev, R. A., 724
Medvedev, Z. A., 724
Meehl, P. E., 195, 710
Meichenbaum, D., 129, 131, 135
Meissner, W. W., 752
Mellsop, F., 196
Melton, G. B., 701, 718
Meltzer, H. Y., 761
Melvin, L. S., 556
Melzack, R., 152
Mendels, J., 361, 410
Mendelsohn, F., 482
Mendelsohn, G. A., 739
Mendelson, J., 531
Mendelson, W. B., 526
Menn, A. Z., 464, 772
Mercer, J., 625
Mercer, J. R., 625
Merchant, K. M., 553
Merikangas, K. R., 371
Mermelstein, R. J., 757
Mesmer, F. A., 30-32, 35
Mesulam, M. M., 655
Metalsky, G. I., 357, 389, 390
Metcalfe, 185
Methuen, J., 196
Meyer, A., 190, 420–21
Meyer, C. B., 245
Meyer, R., 518, 531, 532, 535
Meyer, V., 278, 620
Meyer-Bahlburg, H., 498
Meyers, A. W., 616
Meyers, J. K., 342, 361
Mezzich, J., 13, 281
Michael, S. T., 454
Michel, J., 126
Michelson, L., 254, 258
Middleton, H., 254
Midelfort, H. C. E., 25
Miklowitz, D. J., 453
Mikulincer, M., 248
Milazzo-Sayre, L. J., 460
Miller, F., 54
Miller, L. L., 556
Miller, N. E., 158, 168, 311
Miller, P. L., 673
Miller, R. C., 753
Miller, S., 407
Miller, S. D., 302
Miller, T. I., 108
Miller, T. Q., 757
Miller, W. R., 358, 391
Mills, H., 40–41
Milner, B., 656, 671, 672, 674, 675
Milton, J., 86
Mineka, S., 234, 237
Mintz, J., 464, 761
Minuchin, S., 623
Mirsky, A. A., 316
Mirsky, A. F., 446
Mischel, W., 80, 181, 185, 354, 595
Mishkin, M., 673
Mishra, S. P., 182
Mitchell, J. E., 622, 623
Mitchell, K. M., 738
Mittelmann, B., 318

Mittler, P., 637
M'Naghten, D., 712–14, 715
Modestin, J., 738
Moffitt, T. E., 581, 609
Mohs, R. C., 677
Molk, L., 337
Moller, N., 529
Monahan, J., 699, 701, 718
Money, J., 470, 473, 476, 477, 498
Monk, M., 613
Monroe, S., 344, 398, 403, 755
Monteiro, W., 258
Montgomery, M., 659
Moody, R. L., 312
Moore, K. E., 539
Moos, R. H., 365
Moras, K., 157
Moreau, M., 452
Morgan, C., 540
Morgan, M., 59
Morland, J., 756
Morrell, W., 404
Morris, N., 719
Morris, P., 330
Morris, R. J., 738
Morris, T., 334
Morrison, R. L., 424, 462
Morrissey, J. P., 701, 717
Morton, 38
Moscovitch, M., 645–92
Mosher, L. R., 461, 464, 762, 772
Moss, H. B., 762
Moul, D. E., 407
Mowrer, O. H., 127, 618
Mowrer, W. M., 618
Mueller, T. I., 370
Mueser, K. T., 424, 463, 761, 762
Mullaney, D. M., 185
Mullaney, J. A., 531
Muller, U., 243
Mulvey, E. P., 701
Mundin, F., 233
Munoz, R., 375
Munszinger, H., 630
Murad, F., 651
Murdock, T., 121, 244, 245, 249
Murphy, D. L., 404, 405
Murphy, O., 279
Murphy, S., 64
Murray, H. A., 179
Murstein, B. I., 181
Musante, L., 325
Muser, J., 337
Musetti, L., 288
Myers, J. K., 362, 367, 570

Nadel, L., 235, 675
Nagler, S., 446
Nagy, A., 64
Nakadaira, S., 406
Nardi, A., 233
Narrow, W. E., 218, 251, 256
Nash, E. H., 736
Nasrallah, H. A., 451
Nave, G., 589
Naveh, G., 456
Neale, M., 166, 259
Neary, D., 684

Neaton, J. D., 324, 759
Nee, J., 365
Neider, J., 291
Nelson, C., 361
Nesse, F. M., 252
Nesselroade, J., 58
Nestoros, J. N., 526
Nettleton, N. C., 658
Neuchterlein, K. H., 458, 462
Newcomb, E. J., 561, 757
Newell, G., 736
Newman, J. P., 582
Nicholls, G., 470
Nicholls, K., 527
Nichols, M., 750
Nicot, J., 557
Nielson, S., 680
Nies, A., 365
Nihira, K., 625
Ninan, P., 563
Nishihara, Y., 68
Nisbett, R., 81, 89, 180, 435, 747
Nishihara, Y., 68
Nofstadter, 673
Nolen-Hoeksema, S., 165, 364, 365, 367,
    389, 601, 616, 617
Nordby, H., 431
Nordlie, J. W., 292
Norten, S., 288
Northen, B., 684
Norton, G. R., 297, 302
Noshirvani, H., 278, 279
Novotny, T. E., 561, 757
Noyes, R., 221, 233, 257, 258, 259, 270,
    294
Nyman, A. K., 424
Nyswander, M. E., 548, 758

Oakley-Browne, M., 251
O'Brien, C. P., 523, 534, 541, 564, 739
O'Brien, K., 294
O'Connor, Dr., 706
O'Connor, K., 216
O'Connor, M. E., 748
O'Connor, N., 636
Odier, C., 223
Offord, D. R., 603, 615, 616
Ofshe, R., 721
Oggins, J., 506
O'Gorman, T. W., 531
Öhman, A., 235, 236, 237, 431
Ohwaki, S., 631
Okada, M. O., 260
Olafsson, K., 63
Oldham, J. M., 595
Olgin, J. E., 535
Oliveau, D., 221
Olivieri, S., 64
Olsen, J., 481
Olsen, S. C., 451
Olson, S., 279, 440
Oltman, J., 574
Oltmanns, T. F., 435
Olweus, D., 603
O'Malley, S., 535
Omenn, G. S., 529
Ong, P., 126
Opler, M. K., 454
Oppenheimer, B., 248

Oren, D. A., 407
Orford, J., 528
Orgel, S., 322
Orne, M. T., 153, 305, 306, 736
Orr, S. P., 213
Ortmann, J., 371
Osherson, A., 299-300
Osler, Sir W., 322
Öst, L.-G., 220, 221, 232, 254, 261
Ostfeld, A. M., 324
O'Sullivan, G., 278, 279
Overholser, J. C., 492
Overmier, B., 385, 386

Packer, H., 710
Padesky, C. A., 358
Padgett, N. E., 327
Padian, N., 755
Paffenbarger, B. S., 759
Palmer, C., 659
Panak, W., 389
Pandya, D. N., 681
Paneth, N., 630
Paploukas, A., 316
Park, L. C., 592
Park, T. J., 592
Parker, F. C., 327
Parker, G., 361
Parkes, M. C., 330
Parloff, M. B., 744, 748, 750, 755
Parnas, J., 166, 445
Parwatikar, S. D., 428
Pato, M., 279
Patrick, C. J., 574
Patterson, G. R., 604, 605, 750
Patterson, K., 671
Patterson, T., 431
Pattie, F. A., 31, 35
Paul, O., 324
Paul, G. L., 183, 184, 230
Paul, N., 288
Paul, S. M., 526, 563
Paulauskas, S. L., 615, 616
Pauls, D. L., 371
Pauly, I. B., 473, 474
Pavel, O., 402
Pavlik, W. B., 393
Pavlov, I., 116–21, 127, 234, 385, 493,
    494, 495
Paykel, E. S., 342, 344, 361, 365, 368, 369
Payne, R. W., 431
Peake, P. K., 595
Pearl, D., 325
Pearlson, G., 276
Pearson, K., 162
Pecknold, J., 252
Pedersen, N., 58
Pederson, J., 762
Peel, R., 712, 715
Peele, S., 513
Pelham, W. E., 611
Pellow, T., 296
Pelse, H., 341
Penick, S. B., 137
Penn, G. M., 335
Pennebaker, J. W., 248–49, 290
Penny, R., 333
Perel, J., 257, 279, 375

Perkins, K. A., 87
Perkins, M., 593
Perl, M., 748
Perley, M. J., 288
Perris, C., 370
Perry, S., 360
Pershard, D., 267
Person, J., 203
Perugis, G., 288
Pervin, L. A., 177
Pery, S., 360
Peterson, B., 325
Peterson, C., 331, 333, 367, 390, 393, 398
Peterson, D. R., 181
Peterson, P., 757
Petrila, J., 701
Pettingale, K. W., 334
Petty, F., 168
Petursson, H., 564
Petzel, T. P., 428
Peveler, R. C., 748
Pfafflin, F., 477
Pfeffer, 342, 361
Pfohl, B., 595
Phillips, E. L., 607
Phillips, L., 199, 438
Piasecki, J. M., 391
Picard, R. S., 334
Pickles, A., 603
Pierce, C., 324
Pierce, J. P., 561, 757
Pietrini, P., 277
Piggott, T., 279
Pihl, 365
Pilkonis, P., 395, 742, 748, 755
Pillard, R., 480
Pincus, H. A., 191
Pinel, P., 39-40, 62, 190
Piper, W., 742
Pittluck, A. T., 296
Place, E. J. S., 430
Plante, T. G., 759
Platt, J. J., 758
Plenge, P., 63
Plomin, R., 57, 58
Podrabenek, 723
Poels, P. J., 288
Pohoresky, L. A., 392, 398
Poizner, H., 669
Pokorny, A. D., 410
Polak, P. R., 772
Poldinger, W., 403
Polivy, J., 622
Pollack, G. H., 324
Pollack, J. M., 270, 271
Pollack, S., 761
Pollard, C., 257
Pollit, J. D., 277
Pollock, V. I., 530
Polloway, E. A., 624
Pomerleau, C. S., 345
Pomerleau, O. F., 345
Pomeroy, W. D., 489, 491
Pope, H. G., Jr., 286, 621
Porjesz, B., 530
Porsolt, R. D., 393
Porter, R. W., 435
Posner, M. I., 655, 665

Post, R. M., 300, 406, 681
Poulos, C. X., 524
Pound, E., 724–25
Powell, K. E., 329
Power, K., 261
Poythress, N. G., 701
Premack, D., 125
Preskorn, S., 63
Price, D. L., 679
Price, K. P., 358, 391
Price, R. H., 766, 769
Price, R. W., 680
Prichard, J. C., 571, 575
Prior, M. R., 639
Prosin, H., 368
Prudic, J., 377
Prusoff, B. A., 371, 755
Puig-Antich, J., 411
Purcell, D., 337
Puriosch, A. D., 187
Putnam, F. W., 297, 300, 302, 304

Quadfasel, F. A., 668
Quay, H. C., 605, 630, 639
Quiggle, N., 389
Quinton, D., 603, 605

Rabavilos, A. D., 278
Rachman, S. J., 124, 211, 216, 226, 231,
    234, 252, 266, 267, 269, 270, 271, 274,
    278, 288, 291, 494, 753, 754
Rack, P., 271
Radloff, L. S., 359, 365
Rado, S., 379
Rae, D. C., 218, 219, 220, 222, 251, 256
Raeburn, S. D., 623, 748, 760
Rafal, 655
Rahe, R., 162, 342, 343
Raichle, M., 252, 665
Rakaczky, C. J., 288
Rall, T. W., 651
Ramm, E., 257
Ramona, G., 722
Ramona, H., 722
Ramos-McKay, J., 766, 769
Ramsbey, T., 470
Ramsey, E., 604
Rand, K. H., 736
Randolph, C., 452
Rao, D. C., 54
Rapee, R., 259
Rapoport, J. L., 276, 277, 652
Rapport, M. D., 611
Raps, C. S., 358, 391, 393
Rasmussen, K., 552
Rat Man, 273
Rattan, R. B., 432
Ravaris, C., 365
Raven, A., 367
Rawlings, E. I., 739
Ray, I., 713
Ray, O., 524, 525
Rayner, R., 159, 227, 233
Razani, J., 762
Reagor, P., 302
Reaven, G. M., 759
Reddaway, P., 724
Redlich, F. C., 454

Reed, D., 324
Reed, E. S., 659
Reese, H. W., 166
Regier, D. A., 218, 251, 256
Rehm, L. P., 131, 382
Rei, M. A., 631
Reich, L. H., 403
Reich, T., 270, 361, 366, 404, 579, 581
Reich, W., 725
Reifman, A., 461
Reiger, D., 570
Reiman, E., 252
Reinhard, K. E., 393
Reinisch, J., 498
Reiss, D. J., 461, 761
Reiss, S., 624
Reitan, R. M., 186
Reivich, K., 397
Renault, P. F., 758
Renick, M. J., 752
Rennie, T.A.C., 454
Rescorla, R. A., 127, 228, 235
Resick, P., 245, 249, 617
Reyher, J., 87
Reynolds, W. M., 397, 616
Rezin, V., 270
Reznikoff, M., 181
Rhazes, 292
Rice, J., 248, 363, 366, 404
Rice, K. C., 556
Richards, C., 615, 616
Richter, C., 329–30
Rickels, K., 259
Rie, H. E., 615, 616
Rienhard, K. E., 393
Rifkin, A., 428
Riggs, D., 121, 244, 245, 249
Rihmer, Z., 403
Rimmo, P., 235
Ring, H., 276
Rioch, M. J., 770
Risley, T., 640
Ritter, B., 753
Ritvo, E. R., 637, 638, 639
Roache, J., 64
Roatch, J. F., 361, 368
Robbins, P. C., 717, 718
Robbins, T. W., 452
Roberts, D.C.S., 539
Robertson, M., 276
Robin, L., 163
Robins, 678
Robins, E., 252, 369, 410
Robins, I., 270
Robins, L. E., 547
Robins, L. N., 195, 199, 362, 363, 367,
    403, 570, 574, 575, 582, 604, 605
Robins, P. V., 678
Robinson, D. S., 365
Robinson, R., 330
Robson, P., 259, 261
Roche, J., 470
Rockefeller, N., 633
Roder, V., 462
Rodin, J., 311, 331, 335, 759
Rodnick, E. H., 453, 458
Roediger, H., 295, 675
Rogaev, E., 680

Rogers, C., 86, 106–7, 738
Rogers, J., 527
Rogers, W., 360
Rogerson, H. L., 221
Rogins, E., 252
Rohde, P., 366
Rohner, J. J., 618
Rohobit, D., 324
Rolf, J. E., 445
Ron, M., 288
Rooth, F. G., 490, 495
Roper, G., 278
Rorschach, H., 179–81
Rose, R. M., 318
Rosellini, R. A., 394
Rosen, B., 622
Rosen, G. D., 671
Rosenberg, C. M., 271
Rosenberg, S. E., 750
Rosenblum, L. A., 367
Rosenhan, D. L., 9, 17, 191, 195, 198, 200,
    201, 203, 710, 725, 762
Rosenman, R. H., 323
Rosenstein, M. J., 460, 705
Rosenthal, D., 371, 442, 444, 446, 448,
    581, 593
Rosenthal, N. E., 404, 407
Rosenthal, P. A., 411
Rosenthal, R., 751
Rosenthal, S., 411
Rosenthal, T. L., 616
Rosenzweig, M., 664
Rosenzweig, S. P., 736
Rosiani, 288
Rosman, B. L., 623
Ross, 737
Ross, C. A., 297, 302
Ross, D. C., 257, 258
Ross, D. R., 298
Ross, E. D., 647
Ross, J. D., 458, 603
Ross, L., 9, 81, 89, 180, 435, 747
Ross, M., 482
Ross, W. D., 324
Rossi, V., 288
Rossiter, E. M., 748, 760
Roth, D., 736
Roth, L., 528
Roth, M., 370
Rothbaum, B., 121, 244, 245, 249
Rothbaum, F., 8
Rothman, D., 42
Rotman, Z., 640
Rotter, J. B., 8, 130, 132
Rounsaville, B., 294, 535, 540, 548
Rounsaville, E. S., 755
Rounsaville, N. B., 395, 396
Routh, D. K., 630, 639
Rovndal, E., 736
Roy, E. A., 659
Roy, O., 524, 525
Rozee, P., 285
Rozin, P., 236, 469, 645–92
Rubenstein, C., 290, 469
Rubenstein, D., 506
Rubin, R., 277
Rubinstein, E., 290, 738
Rugg, D., 757

Runyan, D., 492
Rush, A. J., 375, 382, 396, 414
Rush, B., 513
Rushton, J. P., 369
Russakoff, L. M., 595
Russek, H., 328
Russek, L., 328
Russek, S., 328
Russell, M., 757
Russell, W. R., 674
Rutter, M., 600, 603, 604, 605, 613, 632, 635, 636, 637, 638, 640, 670
Ryan, S. M., 332

Sabourin, L. S., 739
Saccuzzo, D. P., 431
Sacher-Masoch, L., 488
Sack, D. A., 404, 407
Sack, R., 63
Sack, W., 244
Sackheim, H. A., 292, 375, 377
Sade, Marquis de, 487–88
Saffran, E., 666, 669
St. George-Hyslop, P., 679–80
Sakai, T., 269
Sakamoto, K., 406
Salazar, A. M., 680
Salkovskis, P., 252–53, 254
Saltz, B. L., 761
Salzman, L., 278
Samuelson, H., 371
Samuelson, L., 258
Sanders, M. D., 292
Sanders, M. R., 752
Sandler, J., 270, 271
Sanford, E. J., 618
Sangrey, D., 769
Sank, L. I., 769
Sarason, S. B., 766
Saron, C., 375
Sartorius, N., 424, 427, 457
Sartory, G., 278
Sasanuma, S., 671
Sassenrath, J. M., 625
Saugstad, L. F., 424, 454
Saunders, A. M., 680
Saunders, B., 245
Savage, L. J., 758
Saver, J. L., 682
Sawrey, W. L., 318
Sayers, B., 619
Saykin, A. J., 680
Scarr, S., 629
Schachter, S., 577
Schacter, D. L., 675, 676, 677
Schaefer, C., 344
Schafer, J., 526
Schaffer, C. E., 375, 428
Schalock, R. L., 624
Schapira, K., 370
Scharf, M., 318
Scharfetter, C., 433
Scheff, T. J., 10
Scheftner, W., 361
Scheier, F., 233
Scheier, M., 58
Scher, M., 738
Schiavi, R. C., 503

Schiffman, E., 275
Schildkraut, J. J., 372
Schmale, A., 334
Schmauk, F. J., 578
Schmechel, M. D., 680
Schmidt, S., 404
Schmueli, J., 446
Schneider, J. A., 623, 748, 760
Schneider, L., 63
Schneider, P., 296
Schneider, S., 254
Schneidman, E., 767
Schneier, F., 222
Schoenfeld, D., 324
Schotte, D. E., 621
Schottenfeld, R. S., 535
Schreckengost, J., 757
Schreiber, F., 299
Schreibman, L., 640
Schroeder, H. E., 761
Schuckit, M. A., 529, 530
Schulberg, H., 375
Schulman, J. R., 527
Schulsinger, F., 166, 371, 444, 445, 529, 580
Schulsinger, H., 445
Schulterbrandt, J. G., 367
Schultes, R. E., 513
Schumer, F., 181
Schumlan, J. R., 527
Schuster, C. R., 538
Schuyler, D., 370, 371, 377, 409
Schwab, J. J., 368
Schwartz, 669
Schwartz, E. O., 592
Schwartz, G. E., 87
Schwartz, J., 59, 277
Schwartz, M. F., 123, 482, 659, 678
Schwartz, R. D., 526
Schwartz, S., 456, 629
Schwarzenbach, F. A., 738
Schweizer, E., 259
Scott, T. H., 153
Scovern, A. W., 377
Scoville, W. B., 671
Scull, A., 38, 42
Seager, C., 410
Searles, H. F., 453
Sears, R. R., 89
Sechrest, L., 750
Sedney, M., 497
Seeley, J. R., 366
Seely, R., 491
Seevers, M. H., 521, 538
Segal, J., 740
Segal, S., 707
Segarra, J. M., 668
Seligman, M. E. P., 8, 17, 61, 132, 133, 168, 227, 228, 234, 236, 274, 279, 319, 329, 331, 333, 335, 352, 356, 357, 358, 365, 367, 380, 385, 386, 387, 389, 390, 391, 393, 394, 395, 397, 398, 474, 535, 616, 753, 755
Sells, S. B., 758
Selye, H., 339, 340
Semmel, A., 395
Semmel, M. I., 631
Senay, E. C., 758

Seneca, M., 408
Serling, R. J., 231
Shaffer, D., 412, 618
Shaffer, H. J., 514, 519
Shafi, M., 412
Shagass, C., 338
Shah, S. A., 699
Shakelle, R. B., 759
Shallice, T., 656, 681, 683
Shanok, S. S., 582
Shapiro, A. K., 736
Shapiro, B., 428
Shapiro, D., 270, 271
Shapiro, J. G., 736
Shapiro, R., 360
Shapiro, R. J., 736
Shapiro, S. K., 630, 639
Shaw, B. F., 414
Shaw, D. W., 382
Shea, M. T., 748
Shea, S. C., 175
Shea, T., 395, 396, 755
Shear, J., 261, 753
Shega, J., 470
Shekele, R. B., 195, 324
Shellhaas, M., 625
Shelton, S. E., 522, 545
Shenker, R., 609
Shepard, E. M., 324
Sherer, M., 537
Sherman, A. D., 168
Sherman, G. F., 671
Shields, J., 441–42
Shneidman, E., 409, 410, 411, 413, 415
Shoham-Salomon, V., 750, 751
Sholomskas, D., 755
Shore, J. E., 242
Shoulson, I., 686
Shrout, P. E., 344, 456
Shuster, C. R., 521
Sideris, E., 316
Sidtis, J., 680
Siegel, S., 524
Sifneos, P. E., 290
Siggins, G. R., 527
Sigvardsson, S., 283, 529
Sijben, N., 288
Silberman, E. K., 297, 302, 446
Silva, P. A., 600, 604, 605, 609
Silver, S. E., 600
Silverman, J. M., 677
Silverman, L. H., 87
Silverman, W. K., 614, 616
Simmons, J. Q., 126
Simon, G. E., 288
Simpson, D. D., 758
Simpson, D. M., 680
Simpson, G. M., 762
Simpson, R., 261
Simson, P. G., 168, 391
Singer, J., 761
Singer, J. E., 311
Singer, M. T., 454
Singh, M., 259
Skinner, B. F., 122–26, 128
Skodol, A. E., 406, 456, 602
Skolnick, P., 526, 563
Sladek, J. K., Jr., 686

Slater, P. C., 673
Slobogin, C., 701, 718
Smallish, L., 609, 610
Smith, 681
Smith, A., 335
Smith, B., 750
Smith, D., 760
Smith, E. E., 13
Smith, G. R., 288
Smith, J. C., 108
Smith, J. L., 131
Smith, M. L., 150, 681
Smith, R., 248
Smith, R. J., 574
Smith, S., 561
Smith, S. G., 523
Smith, T., 325
Smith, T. L., 335
Smyth, L., 87
Smoller, J., 365
Snedo, S., 276, 277, 279
Snell, M. E., 624
Snow, B., 287
Snow, R. E., 750
Snowden, J. S., 684
Snyder, K. S., 453, 464
Snyder, S. H., 448, 449, 450, 461, 545,
    550, 551
Snyder, S. S., 8
Snyder, W. D., 686
Sohlberg, S. C., 446
Sokol, L., 254, 748
Solomon, R. A., 748
Solomon, R. L., 127-28, 228, 385, 404,
    519, 520
Solomon, Z., 243, 248
Somes, G. W., 345
Soranus, 29
Soriani, A., 288
Sotsky, S., 395, 396, 748, 755
Southard, D. R., 327
Spanos, N. P., 306
Spark, R. F., 503
Sparrow, S. J., 625
Speed, N., 247
Speicher, C., 335
Spence, J. T., 260
Sperry, R., 657
Spiegel, D., 294, 302, 305, 334
Spiegel, R., 62, 63, 64
Spielberger, C., 260
Spierings, C., 288
Spitalnik, D. M., 624
Spitz, R. A., 366
Spitzer, R. L., 191, 195, 287, 313, 406, 585,
    586, 589, 602
Spohn, H. E., 431
Sprenger, J., 26
Spring, B., 440
Springer, S. P., 657
Squire, L. R., 378, 671, 673, 674, 675
Srole, L., 454
Staats, A. W., 131
Stamler, J., 759
Stamler, R., 759
Stampfl, T. G., 120, 231
Stangl D., 595
Stanley, S. M., 752

Stark, J. A., 624
Stark, K. D., 616
Stark, M. J., 736
Stava, L., 490, 492
Stayton, S. E., 631
Steadman, H. J., 695, 700, 701, 707, 717,
    718
Steel, R., 637
Steele, J. B., 268
Stefanis, C., 278
Stein, J. A., 617
Stein, L., 372, 772
Steinberg, L., 323
Steinberg, M., 294
Steiner, B., 477
Steinmark, W. W., 753
Stern, D., 80, 83, 84
Stern, J., 629
Stern, R. S., 257, 278
Sterner, U., 221, 232
Stevenson, B. E., 368
Stewart, B., 249
Stewart, D. E., 288
Stiles, T. C., 750
Stinnett, J., 145, 282
Stinson, C., 136
Stoller, R. J., 473, 485
Stone, A. A., 697, 700, 710
Stone, A. R., 736
Stone, D. M., 553
Stone, G. C., 311
Stone, M. H., 592
Storms, M. D., 478, 494
Stoyva, J. M., 185
Strachan, A. M., 453
Straus, M. A., 531
Straus, R., 323
Strauss, J., 436
Strauss, M. E., 428
Streissguth, A. P., 630
Strittmatter, W. J., 680
Strober, M., 404
Struening, E., 736
Strupp, H. H., 736, 738, 739, 750, 764
Stueve, A., 456
Stunkard, A. J., 125, 137, 365, 621
Sturdevant, R. A. L., 316
Sturgis, E. T., 482
Stuss, D. T., 656
Suarez, J. M., 296
Suckerman, K. R., 738
Suddath, R. L., 452
Sue, D., 739
Sue, D. W., 739
Suedfeld, P., 725
Sullivan, H. S., 81, 396
Sullivan, P. M., 625
Summergard, P., 279
Summers, M., 26
Suomi, S. J., 367, 531
Surawicz, T. S., 561, 757
Susman, V. L., 595
Susser, M., 316, 630
Sussex, J. N., 409
Sutton, W., 571
Suzdak, P. P., 526
Svartberg, M., 750
Svebak, S., 252

Svennerholm, L., 639
Swan, G., 323
Swanson, D. W., 491
Swanson, V., 261
Swanson, W. C., 410
Swedo, S., 276, 277, 279
Sweeney, J. A., 452
Sweeney, P. O., 395
Swinson, R., 252
Sylvester, D., 221, 365
Szara, S., 556
Szasz, T. S., 67, 408, 428, 702, 708–9, 723
Szklo, M., 330
Szuba, 59

Taguiri, R., 92
Takahashi, S., 196
Talovic, S. A., 445
Tamerin, J. S., 531
Tamura, A., 406
Tanenbaum, R. L., 367
Tangney, J. P., 587
Tarrier, N., 762
Tassarini, R., 254
Tatum, E. L., 242
Taube, C. A., 461
Taussig, C., 766
Taylor, C., 258
Taylor, F., 325
Taylor, J. A., 260, 431, 659
Taylor, M., 377
Taylor, S. E., 245
Taylor, W. S., 297, 301
Teasdale, J. D., 132, 133, 270, 382, 387
Teicher, M., 63, 374, 375
Telch, C. F., 623, 748, 780
Telch, M., 254, 258, 753
Telfer, L., 157
Tellegen, A., 57, 58, 178
Temerlin, M. K., 202
Tennant, C. C., 246
Terry, R. D., 677
Tesar, G., 252
Test, M. A., 772
Thaler, F., 278
Theodor, L. H., 292
Theorell, T., 328, 342
Thiele, D. A., 761
Thigpen, C. H., 299
Thomas, K., 27
Thompson, T., 521
Thompson, J., 219, 222, 256
Thompson, P. D., 329
Thompson, L. W., 739
Thoren, P., 280
Thoresen, C. E., 131
Thorndike, E. L., 121, 122, 233
Thornhill, N., 55
Thornton, D. W., 398
Tien, A., 276
Tienari, P., 444
Tiffany, T. M., 527
Tinklenberg, J., 64
Tobena, A., 277
Tolbert, R., 553
Tomasson, K., 281, 287
Tonks, C. M., 368
Toohey, M. L., 454

Torgersen, S., 252, 287, 371
Torrey, E. F., 442, 445, 452, 725
Tourney, G., 42
Townsley, R. M., 588
Tranel, D., 681, 682
Traskman, L., 409
Traskman-Bendz, L., 409
Trasler, G., 605
Treece, C., 518
Treiber, F., 325
Treseder, J., 614
Trevor-Roper, H., 26
Trimble, M., 276, 279, 754
Trippet, C. J., 531
Trotter, T., 513
Troughton, E., 531
Truax, C. B., 736, 738
True, W., 248
Tryon, W. W., 231, 358, 391
Ts'o, T., 377
Tuddenham, R. D., 246
Tuke, S., 42
Tuke, W., 41
Tulving, E., 676, 677
Tuma, A. H., 761
Tunstall, C., 757
Turgay, A., 293
Turner, R. J., 456
Turner, S. M., 588
Turrell, E. S., 318
Tyler, J. L., 631
Tynes, L., 63
Tyrer, P., 64
Tyrrel, E. D., 556
Tyrrell, D., 335

Uddenberg, N., 477
Ullman, L. P., 124
Ulrich, R. F., 761
Understedt, V., 450
Underwood, M., 409
Unger, H. T., 592
Upham, C. W., 28
Urbina, S. P., 182
Urcan, S., 316
Uzzell, R., 631

Vaccarino, F. J., 523
Vaglum, P., 736
Vaillant, C. O., 94–95
Vaillant, G. E., 86, 93, 94–96, 331, 338,
    340, 515, 531, 535
Valenstein, E. S., 688
Valentine, C. W., 233
Vandereycken, W., 294
Vanderlinden, J., 294
Van Doren, T., 270
van Dyck, R., 294
Van Dyke, C., 238
Van Eerdewegh, M., 366, 404
Van Hoesen, G. W., 679
Van Kempen, G. M., 293
Van Kesteren, P., 474
Van Valkenberg, C., 247
Varghese, F., 196
Varma, V. K., 267
Varnik, A., 411
Vaughan, M., 269, 278, 761

Vaughn, C. E., 463, 464
Vedak, C., 361
Veiel, H., 340
Veith, I., 29, 30, 281
Venables, P. H., 435
Ventura, J., 458
Verma, S. K., 267
Veroff, J., 506
Veronen, L., 245, 617
Versiani, M., 233
Vertommen, H., 294
Vestea, S., 316
Victor, M., 651, 660, 673, 685
Videbech, T., 269
Villanueva-Meyer, J., 277
Visser, S., 278
Vogel, G. W., 148
Vogel, J., 738
Vogel, P. J., 657
Voight, D., 650
Vollmer, W. M., 242
Volpicelli, J. R., 534, 535, 558
Von, J., 245
von Baeyer, C., 395
Von Boehmel, G., 285
Von Korff, M. R., 288
Vriezen, E. R., 674, 675, 681

Wadden, T. A., 365, 759
Wade, J. N., 424
Wagenfeld, M. O., 456
Wagner, A. R., 235
Wagner, P., 587
Wagner, R. K., 670
Wakefield, J., 230
Walbek, N., 491
Walder, L. O., 603
Walinder, J., 473, 474
Walker, E., 428
Walker, J. A., 655
Wall, T. L., 526
Wallace, C. J., 462, 463
Wallace, L., 261
Wallach, M., 738
Waller, N., 58
Wallerstein, J. S., 367
Walsh, W., 244, 245
Walters, R. H., 130, 575
Wang, P. L., 677
Warburton, D. M., 560, 561
Wargo, D. G., 736
Warnecke, R., 757
Warner, R., 570
Warrington, E. K., 292, 668, 675
Warzak, W. J., 618
Wassermann, A. von, 52
Wasserman, D., 411
Wasson, R. G., 550
Watell, L. C., 407
Watkins, G., 316
Watkins, J., 395, 396, 748, 755
Watson, C. G., 283, 291
Watson, J. B., 115, 159, 227, 233
Watson, L. S., 631
Watson, M., 707
Watt, N. F., 445
Wayland, K. K., 606
Waysman, M., 248

Weakland, J., 453
Weatherman, R. F., 625
Webster, A., 168
Wechsler, D., 181
Weekes, J. R., 306
Wegner, J. T., 62, 461
Wehr, T. A., 404
Weiler, D., 243
Weimer, M. J., 391
Weinberg, M. S., 481
Weinberger, D. R., 452
Weiner, B., 132, 133
Weiner, H. M., 315, 316, 322, 335, 337
Weiner, R. D., 181
Weiner, V., 710–11, 712, 714, 716
Weisaeth, L., 248
Weiskrantz, L., 292, 675
Weisman, A. D., 314
Weiss, F., 527
Weiss, J. D., 318, 319
Weiss, J. M., 151, 168, 321, 391, 392, 398
Weiss, P., 403
Weiss, S. M., 311
Weissman, M., 163, 259
Weissman, M. M., 365, 371, 395, 396, 755
Weisz, J. R., 8
Weithorn, L. A., 718
Welch, S. L., 620
Weldon, M., 295
Wells, J., 251
Wells, K., 360
Wender, P. H., 371, 444, 736
Wenger, J. R., 527
Wenger, N., 470
Werner, P. D., 177
Wernicke, J., 63, 374
Werry, J. S., 196
Wesnes, K., 561
Wessely, S., 288
West, L. J., 556
Westermeyer, J., 291
Whalen, C. K., 608, 609, 610
Whishaw, I. Q., 659, 666
White, K., 63
White, K. J., 606
White, R. A., 503
Whybrow, P. C., 406
Wicki, W., 370
Widiger, T. A., 191, 570, 588
Wig, N., 267
Wikler, A., 523
Wilcoxon, L. A., 230
Wilfley, D., 760
Wilkinson, C., 294
Willers, K. R., 324
Williams, A. F., 240, 245
Williams, B. E., 623
Williams, C. J., 481
Williams, J., 680
Williams, J. B. W., 406, 585, 586, 589, 602,
    734
Williams, R. B., 195, 324, 325, 377
Williams, S., 600, 604, 605
Williamson, M., 762
Williamson, S., 573, 574, 577
Willis, M. H., 398
Willis, T., 50
Wilner, A., 270

Wilson, D., 150
Wilson, G. T., 131, 288, 621, 748, 753, 760
Wilson, J., 3–4, 13, 15, 718
Wilson, J. D., 68
Windmiller, M., 625
Wineburg, L., 131
Winerip, M., 465
Wing, J. K., 761
Wing, L., 636
Winget, C., 240
Winkeller, M., 547
Winkler, R., 620
Winnicott, D. W., 83
Winokur, G., 62, 365, 371, 433, 529, 681, 684
Winsberg, B. G., 639
Winters, L. C., 174
Wirt, R. D., 603
Wirz-Justice, A., 407
Wise, R. A., 522, 538
Witkin, H. A., 581
Woerner, M. G., 257
Wogan, M., 738
Wolf, M. M., 607, 640
Wolf, S., 324
Wolfe, T., 592–93
Wolfer, J., 131
Wolff, A., 711, 712, 716
Wolff, H. G., 317, 318, 324
Wolpe, J., 121, 226, 229, 230, 232, 747
Wong, D., 374
Wong, S., 573, 757
Woodcock, R. W., 625

Woodruff, R. A., 286, 287, 288, 291
Woods, S. C., 527
Woodward, B., 706
Woody, G. E., 239, 240, 518, 739, 742
Wooley, S., 165, 366
Wortman, C. B., 239, 240, 245
Wright, F., 254, 748
Wright, J., 739
Wrobel, T. A., 176
Wurm, M., 323
Wurmle, O., 738
Wykoff, W., 63
Wynne, L. C., 445, 453, 454
Wyshak, G., 221

Yager, T., 247
Yale, C., 759, 761
Yalom, I. D., 84, 97, 99, 100, 736
Yanagita, T., 521, 538
Yang, E., 637
Yaniv, S., 446
Yates, A., 431
Yates, W., 259
Yeager, C. T., 582
Young, B. G., 494
Young, E., 374
Yule, W., 614, 632, 636, 637, 640
Yurgelun-Todd, D., 622

Zaidel, E., 657
Zafiropoulou, M., 215, 234
Zahn, T. P., 300
Zaidel, E., 657

Zanarini, M. C., 592
Zangwill, O. L., 673
Zax, M., 769
Zec, R. F., 452
Zentall, S. S., 610
Zentall, T. R., 610
Zhao, S., 163, 164, 368
Ziegler, F. J., 288, 290
Zigler, E., 199, 424, 438, 766
Zilberg, N. J., 238
Zilbergeld, B., 508
Zilboorg, G., 34
Zimbardo, P. G., 435, 588
Zimberg, N. E., 547
Zimmerli, W., 259
Zimmerman, J., 292
Zimmerman, M., 191, 595
Zinberg, N. E., 547
Zitman, F. G., 293
Zitrin, C. M., 257
Zoccolillo, M., 603
Zohar, J., 279
Zohar-Kadouch, P., 279
Zola-Morgan, S., 674
Zoppel, C. L., 739
Zubin, J. E., 181, 440
Zucker, R. A., 532
Zuckerman, M., 260
Zullow, H., 365, 389
Zusman, R., 324
Zwaan, M. De, 623

SUBJECT INDEX

AA (Alcoholics Anonymous), 534, 535, 756
abnormality:
    assessment methods for, 173–88
    defining of, 4–6
    diagnosing of, 3–4, 13–15, 49–50,
        173–205
    elements of, 6–12
    family resemblance approach to, 6,
        11–12, 723
    history of approaches to, 23–43
    investigating of, 143–71
    linguistic conventions for, 10
    models of, 47–49; see also behavioral
        model; biomedical model; cognitive
        model; existential model; psychody-
        namic model
    normality vs., 4, 16–17, 78, 107, 115,
        722–23
    organic-functional distinction in, 645–59
    perceived causes of, 24–33
    perceptions of, 696–99
    as social judgment, 8, 9–11, 13–14,
        23–24, 722–23
    societal stigma and, 695, 725–26
    see also specific disorders
abnormal psychology, social and
        political abuses of, 556, 558, 695,
        722–26
abstinence syndrome, 556, 564
acetylcholine, 48, 213, 679
Achievement Place, 607–8
Acquired Immunodeficiency Syndrome, see
        AIDS
acquisition phenomena, 118, 122, 214,
        226–29, 233–35
ACTH (adrenocorticotrophic hormone), 339
acting out, 93
action-orientation, 365
activity raising, 382
adaptive behavior scales, 624–25
addictions, see alcohol dependence; drug de-
        pendence; obesity, treatment of
Addington v. Texas, 704
ADHD (attention-deficit hyperactivity disor-
        der), 600–601, 602, 608–11
Adlerian therapy, 750
adoption studies:
    on alcohol dependence, 529, 532
    on antisocial personality disorder, 580
    on criminality, 605
    on depression, 371
    on genetics, 55–58
    on IQs, 629–30
    on schizophrenia, 444–45
adrenaline (epinephrine), 213, 372, 577
adrenergic system, 213
adrenocorticotrophic hormone (ACTH), 339

Affect Adjective Checklist, 260
affective contrast, 520
affective disorders, 352–415, 621–22
    see also depression, bipolar; depression,
        unipolar; mania
affective pleasure, 519–20
affective style, 453
affective tolerance, 520
affective withdrawal, 520
age:
    and depression, 351–52, 362–63,
        366–67
    and frontal lobes, 681
    and schizophrenia, 444
    and suicide, 411–13
aggressiveness, 323, 324, 327, 544
agnosia, 654–55
agoraphobia, 7, 219, 255–58, 611, 612,
        688
    panic attacks in, 210, 255–58
    treatment of, 257–58
agranulocytosis, 461
AIDS (Acquired Immunodeficiency Syn-
        drome), 469–70, 479, 542, 549,
        552, 561, 564
    dementia complex, 680
air traffic controllers, 318
akathesis, 461
alarm reaction, 339
alcohol, 512, 513, 519, 522, 524–36, 539,
        549, 558, 562, 563, 672, 756
    dependence on, see alcohol dependence
    effects of, 524–27, 556–57
    intoxication, 524–26, 529–30, 535
    tolerance of, 527
    withdrawal, 527, 528, 533
alcohol dependence, 190, 367, 403, 515,
        518, 519, 524–36, 556, 756
    adoption studies, 529, 532
    amnesia resulting from, 295, 672–73
    biological vulnerability to, 529–31
    clinical subgroups, 532
    defining, 528
    D.T.'s and, 527, 528
    etiology of, 528–31
    family history and, 532
    genetics and, 519, 529–31, 532
    medical and social complications in, 527,
        535–36
    physical aspect of, 527
    prevalence of, 524
    psychological factors, 531, 532
    recovery prognosis, 535
    and society, 512, 513, 531, 535
    treatment of, 532–35, 756
    twin studies, 529
    Type 1 vs. Type 2, 532

Alcoholics Anonymous (AA), 534, 535, 756
alexithymia, 290–91
ALI (American Law Institute) Rule, 715
alprazolam, 233
ALS (amyotrophic lateral sclerosis), 649–50,
        689
altruism, 75, 94, 96
Alzheimer's disease, 66, 335, 676, 677–80,
        684
    aluminum and, 679
    APOE-4 alleles and, 680
    symptoms of, 678
amenorrhea, 620, 621
American Law Institute (ALI) Rule, 715
Amish, unipolar depression among, 362,
        363–64
amitriptyline, 293
amnesia, 266, 294, 671–77, 686
    and Alzheimer's disease, 676, 678–80
    anatomy of, 673–74
    anterograde, 295, 674
    causes of, 294, 295–97, 672–73
    consolidation block theory of, 675
    description of, 674–75
    digit span in, 674
    dissociative, 295–97, 307
    DSM-IV and, 298
    frontal lobes and, 683–84
    functional, 677
    global (generalized), 295
    Korsakoff's syndrome, 672–73
    in multiple personality, 300, 304, 677
    nature of memory defect in, 296, 674–75,
        678–80, 686
    neurologically based, 295–96, 671–77
    organic vs. dissociative, 295–96
    post-traumatic, 295
    retrieval failure theory of, 675–76
    retrograde, 295, 674, 675, 677
    selective (categorical), 295
    syndrome of, 671–76
    treatment of, 674–75, 676–77
amniocentesis, 628
amotivational syndrome, 556–57
amphetamine psychosis, 448, 450
amphetamines, 448, 521, 536–37, 539,
        542, 551, 553, 610, 618
    disorders treated with, 610, 618
amygdala, 545
amyotrophic lateral sclerosis (ALS), 649–50,
        689
Anafranil, 279
anal character traits, 74
anal stage, 72, 73–74
androgen, 478, 497, 498
androgen-insensitivity syndrome, 478
anger, 89–90, 318

anger (continued)
  in depression, 378–79
  hostility and, 324–25
animalism, 29, 38, 39, 40
animal magnetism, 30, 35
animal phobia, 131, 217, 219, 689
  among children, 225, 611, 613
  irrationality of, 236
  Little Albert experiment and, 159, 227
  Little Hans case and, 223–25
  selectivity of, 233–35
  therapy for, 231
animal possession, 25
animism, 24–27
anomia, 654–55
anorexia nervosa, 125, 165, 618, 620–23,
    688, 760
ANS (autonomic nervous system), 213, 682
Antabuse, 534
anti-anxiety drugs, 64, 66, 157–58,
    232–33, 252, 257, 259, 261, 304,
    526, 753
anticonvulsant drugs, 406
antidepressant drugs, 62–63, 64, 66, 148,
    168, 233, 248, 252, 257–58, 304,
    361, 371, 373–75, 393, 395–97,
    540, 542, 616, 623, 753, 754–55
antigens, 332–33, 335
antihistamines, 459
anti-mentalism, 115–16
antipsychotic drugs, 61–62, 64, 709
anti-reductionists, reductionists vs., 68
antisocial personality disorder (psychopathy;
    sociopathy), 8, 138, 306, 570–84,
    594, 595, 603, 682
  causes of, 574–84
  chronic under-arousal in, 577, 584, 605
  conscience and responsibility lacking in,
    572, 573
  criminality linked to, 571, 578–82
  diagnosing of, 572
  as disorder of will, 570–72
  and drug abuse, 518, 531, 532
  emotional poverty in, 573–74, 577
  family and social context in, 574–75
  genetic basis for, 574, 578–82, 584, 605
  inadequately motivated behaviors in, 573
  learning defects in, 574, 575–78, 605
  personality characteristics of, 572–74
  physiological dysfunctions in, 574,
    582–84
  sources of, 585
anxiety, 7, 72, 86, 209–63, 265–309, 298,
    483, 519, 537, 540, 544, 562–63
  and alcohol, 531
  alleviation of, 86–87; see also coping
    strategies
  castration, 74, 80, 109, 223, 224, 226,
    504
  cognitive therapy for, 129–30, 131–32
  components of, 215–16
  control treatment, 157–58
  about death, 97–99, 297
  and depression, 157–58
  drug treatment for, 64, 66, 157–58,
    232–33, 252, 259, 261, 304, 526,
    753
  everyday, 261

  in Freudian theory, 79–80
  gastric secretions and, 317–18, 322
  phobic, 233
  physiological correlates of, 185
  in post-traumatic stress disorder, 239, 241
  questionnaires on, 260
  as realistic, neurotic, or moral, 79–80
  separation, 612, 614
  in sexual dysfunction, 504–5, 507, 508
  as social experience, 81, 82
  state vs. trait distinction, 260
anxiety disorders, 166, 209–10, 249–61,
    306, 307, 617
  generalized, 215–16, 250, 257, 258–61,
    306
  inferred class of, 265–309; see also disso-
    ciative disorders; obsessive-compul-
    sive disorders; somatoform disorders
  panic disorder, 216, 250–55, 306
  treatment of, 64, 227, 232, 259–61,
    656–57, 752–54; see also phobia;
    post-traumatic stress disorder
aphasias (language disorders), 653, 658,
    665, 669, 689
  conduction, 668
  expressive, 667
  receptive, 667
  transcortical, 668
applied tension, 229
appraisals, 131, 134
arbitrary inference, 381–82
arousal level, 577, 584, 605
arteriosclerosis, 322
ASQ (Attributional Style Questionnaire),
    389, 390
assertiveness training, 136, 382, 393
assessment, see psychological assessment
assimilative projection, 89
asthma, 337, 341, 556
atherosclerosis, 322, 659
at-risk studies, on schizophrenia, 444,
    445–46
attentional deficits, in schizophrenics,
    429–30, 431
attention-deficit hyperactivity disorder
    (ADHD), 600–601, 602, 608–11
attention disorders, in children, 602,
    608–11
attention withdrawal, 87
Attributional Style Questionnaire (ASQ),
    389, 390
attributions:
  in cognitive therapy, 132–33, 383, 384,
    533
  of depressives, 387–92, 395, 399
  drugs for, 639–40
  global-specific dimension in, 132–33,
    389–91, 395
  internal vs. external, 132, 133, 389–91,
    395
  stable-unstable dimension in, 132,
    389–91, 395
  therapy and, 133, 383–84, 393
authenticity, 98–99
autism, 633–41, 683
  behavioral therapy for, 125, 126, 137,
    637, 640
  causes of, 638–39

  drugs for, 639–40
  insistence on sameness in, 635, 636, 637
  intellectual development in, 630, 637
  language development in, 633, 635–36,
    640
  prevalence of, 638
  prognosis for, 640–41
  social development and, 636–37
  symptoms of, 633, 635–37
  treating, 639–40
automatic thoughts, 131–32, 136, 340,
    382–84, 393
autonomic nervous system (ANS), 213, 682
autonomy, 18
aversion therapy, 482, 495–96, 747,
    757–58
avoidance-approach conflicts, 318
avoidance responding, 127–28, 214, 215
  extinction of, 228, 278–79
  learned helplessness and, 384–85
  sociopaths deficient in, 576–78, 605
avoidant personality disorder, 588
axons, 653, 661

Babinski response, 659
barbiturates, 460, 522, 562–64
basal ganglia system, 680, 685
BASIC ID technique, 135, 136
battered women, shelters for, 768–69
Baxtrom v. Herold, 700
B-cells, 332–33
Beck Depression Inventory (BDI), 389
bed-wetting (enuresis), 618–19
behavioral assessment, 183–85, 188
  therapeutic effectiveness measured by,
    744
behavioral disorders, in children, 600–11,
    617
behavioral medicine, 311–12
behavioral model, 48, 113–28, 554
  amnesia as viewed in, 297
  assumptions of, 116
  autism as viewed in, 638–39
  avoidance learning in, 127–28
  cognitive model vs., 128–29, 135–36
  drugs and, 521
  empiricism and, 113–14
  and erectile dysfunction, 505
  evaluation of, 137–38, 307
  existential psychology vs., 99
  normal vs. abnormal behavior in, 115
  obsessive-compulsive disorders as viewed
    in, 272, 274–75, 307
  operant conditioning in, 116, 121–26
  paraphilia as viewed in, 492, 493–95
  Pavlovian conditioning in, 116–21
  phobia as viewed in, 119, 223, 224,
    226–37, 307
  psychosomatic disorders as viewed in,
    337, 341–45
  sexual dysfunction as viewed in, 505
behavioral therapy, 745–47
  for agoraphobia, 257–58
  for alcoholism, 533, 756
  for anorexia nervosa, 125, 760
  assessment of, 109, 137–38
  assumptions of, 114–16
  for autism, 125, 126, 137, 637, 640

avoidance learning in, 128
for bulimia nervosa, 623, 760
for cancer, 334
client-therapist relationship in, 737–42
for cocaine dependence, 540–42
cognitive-, 135–36, 259–61, 288, 553–54, 760
for enuresis, 618–19
for foot fetishism, 117, 128
for homosexuality, 482
for hyperactivity, 610–11
for obesity, 137, 759
for obsessive-compulsive disorders, 127–28, 277, 278–79
operant conditioning in, 124–26
for paraphilias, 495–96
Pavlovian conditioning in, 118–21, 229–33
for phobia, 120–21, 224, 229–33, 616, 747
for reading disabilities, 632
for schizophrenia, 762
for school refusal, 616
for smoking, 757
behaviorism, 114–16
beliefs, 129–31, 133–34
and depressions, 356–57
irrational and illogical, 133–35
Bender Visual-Motor Gestalt Test, 186
Benzedrine, 536
benzodiazepines, 527, 562–64
bereavement:
depression after, 92, 344, 368, 378–79
normal vs. depressive reaction to, 378–79
and stress, 333, 335, 342–44
sudden death and, 329–31
beta amyloid, 679–80
beta blockers, 233
bingeing, 621, 622–23, 760
biochemistry, as etiology, 48, 49, 58–59, 61
biofeedback, 185
biogenic amines, 371–72, 377, 399
biomedical model, 27–29, 47–69, 173, 687, 688
assessment of, 61, 66–67
autism as viewed in, 638–39
biochemistry as etiology in, 48, 49, 58–59
depression as viewed in, 358–60, 370–78, 398–400, 406
genetics as etiology in, 49, 54–58, 66–67
germs as etiology in, 49, 50–53
infantile autism as viewed in, 638–39
juvenile delinquency as viewed in, 605
obsessive-compulsive disorders as viewed in, 272, 275–77
overall approach in, 49–50
principles of, 49–60
psychosomatic disorders as viewed in, 337–40
psychotherapy and, 61
schizophrenia as viewed in, 440–52
sociopathy as viewed in, 578–84
biomedical treatment:
behavioral therapy vs., 120
cognitive therapy vs., 251–55
for depression, 375–78
drawbacks of, 66–67

for general paresis, 52, 66, 67
methodology of, 49, 61–65
neuroanatomy as etiology in, 59–60
see also drug treatment
bisexuality, 471, 477
blacks, depression among, 367–68
blame, irrational, 384
blanchophobia, 219
blindness, hysterical, 144–45, 146–47, 148, 291–92
blood-brain barrier, 515, 516
blood phobias, 219, 221, 229
blood pressure, 537
in blood phobia, 221
in emergency reaction, 213, 340
see also high blood pressure
body image, 365–66, 622
borderline personality disorder, 591–93
brain, 213, 646
abnormalities and obsessive-compulsive disorder, 276–77
anatomy of, 479, 647, 649–59
biochemical organization of, 439, 649–52
blood supply to, 664
diagnostic techniques for, 662–65, 686
disordered, 59–60, 186
dopamine in, 58–59, 372, 439, 448–51, 458, 460, 651
drug use and, 515–17, 524, 539
dysfunctions of, in sociopaths, 582
front-back organization of, 654–57
hierarchical organization of, 658–59
imaging, 187, 687
information-processing system in, 652–53, 654
language center in, 657, 666–68
lateral organization of, 657–58, 666–67
left-right organization of, 657–58
movement center in, 653, 654–57, 658–59, 662
planning-verification-action system in, 655, 659
scanning, 187–88, 276–77
in schizophrenics, 448–52
seizures in, 562, 563, 638, 657, 660, 663
spatial organization of, 451–52, 652–59, 662
surgery on, 686
trauma, 275–76
tumors in, 652, 660, 663, 672, 674, 676, 680, 684
ventricles, 452
see also nervous system; neurons
brain damage, 182, 185–88, 628, 630, 631, 668, 689
assessing, 662–65
double dissociation, 653
to left vs. right hemisphere, 375, 657–58, 662, 666–67, 671, 674
movement after, 653, 654–57
neuroimaging, 663
personality changes after, 656–57, 681–84, 687
recovery of function after, 685, 686
redundancy and, 661–62, 685, 689
restrictions and, 653–65
systems vulnerable to, 660–61
unilateral neglect and, 655, 674

see also nervous system disorders
brain waves, abnormal, 638
breakdown process, 373
brief psychotherapy, 102–6
Briquet's syndrome, 282–83, 287, 288, 290–91
Broca's area, 653, 666–69, 690
bulimia nervosa, 165, 601, 618, 620, 621–23, 759–60

CAMI (California Alliance for the Mentally Ill), 708
cancer, 332, 561
susceptibility to, 334, 335–36
cannabis, see marijuana
carbon dioxide, 254
cardiac arrhythmias, 537
cardiovascular disorders, 322–32
case histories, see clinical case histories
castration, 496
castration anxiety, 74, 80, 109
in erectile dysfunction, 504
in phobia, 223, 224, 226
catatonic schizophrenia, 425, 426–27
catecholamines, 336, 371–74, 558
catharsis, 35, 104
cathexis, 493, 495
cat phobia, 217, 228
CAT (computerized-axial tomography) scan, 187–88, 663–64
causality, see etiology
CCRT (core conflictual relationship theme), 135–36
central nervous system (CNS), 212, 526–27, 558, 562, 609–10, 629
cerebral cortex, 647, 654, 658
cerebrospinal fluid, 660, 663, 685
chewing tobacco, 516
child abuse, 298, 304–5, 564, 616–17
validity of stories of, 304–5, 617
childhood disorders, 599–643
adult life related to, 600, 603, 609, 612, 616, 617, 641–42
anorexia nervosa, 125, 165, 618, 620–23, 688–760
attention-deficit hyperactivity disorder (ADHD), 600–601, 602, 608–11
autism, 125, 126, 137, 601, 630, 633–41, 683
behavioral, 600–611, 617
bulimia nervosa, 165, 601, 618, 620, 621–23, 759–60
classifying of, 600–602, 641
conduct, 574, 602–8, 641
depression, 367, 601, 615–16, 617
developmental, 600, 601, 624–41
disruptive behavior, 600–601, 602–11
eating, 298, 601, 617–18
emotional, 601, 611–17
encopresis, 617–18
enuresis, 601, 617–19
habit (physical), 601, 617–23
identifying, 641
intellectual (mental retardation), 601, 624–31
learning, 632–33
oppositional defiant, 602
parental agency and, 599–600, 640, 641

childhood disorders (*continued*)

phobia, 225, 611, 612–14

prognosis for, 641–42

reading difficulties, 601, 632

separation anxiety, 611–12, 614

situational-specificity of, 600

stuttering (stammering), 137, 601, 618, 619–20

suicide among, 411

treatment for, 616, 617

child molestation (pedophilia), 483, 488, 489, 491–92, 495, 616–17

chlorpromazine, 61, 62, 189, 460–61, 760

cholinergic system, 213

chorionic villus sampling, 628–29

chromosomes, 478, 479

abnormal, in Down's syndrome, 628–29, 679

antisocial personality disorder and, 578–79, 581

chronic fatigue syndrome, 288

chronic hypomanic disorder, 400

cigarette smoking, *see* smoking

circulatory system, 515–16

civil commitment, *see* involuntary commitment

clang associations in schizophrenia, 429

classical conditioning, *see* Pavlovian conditioning

client-centered therapy, 106–7, 751, 763–64

clinical case histories, 143, 144–47

evaluation of, as method, 145–46, 169–70

example of, 144–45

psychodynamic theory based on, 109, 114

clinical interviews, 174–75

clinical psychologists, 730

clomipramine, 277, 279, 652, 753

clozapine, 460, 761

CNS (central nervous system), 212, 526–27, 558, 562, 609–10, 629

cocaine, 513, 518, 519–21, 536, 537–42, 543, 549, 551, 556

cognitive ability, 629

cognitive-behavioral therapy, 135–36, 259–61, 288, 553–34, 760

cognitive deficits, 682

and AIDS, 680

cognitive (selective) filter, 429–30, 431

in depression, 358, 391–92

in learned helplessness, 387, 391–92

cognitive filter, 429, 431

cognitive model, 48, 115, 128–38, 554

behavioral model vs., 128–29

depression as viewed in, 370–71, 380–400, 401–2

evaluation of, 137–38

obsessive-compulsive disorders as viewed in, 272, 274–75, 307

psychosomatic disorders as viewed in, 337, 341, 342, 345

sexual dysfunction as viewed in, 505–6

cognitive processes, 130–35

appraisals, 131

attributions, 132–33

beliefs, 133–34, 356–57

expectations, 130–31

cognitive therapy, 747–49

for anorexia nervosa, 760

for anxiety, 129–30, 131–32

assessments of, 137–38, 382

biomedical therapy vs., 251–55

for bulimia nervosa, 623, 760

for depression, 129, 382–84, 391, 395–400, 616, 748–49, 754–55

for emotional disorders in children, 616

focus of, 129, 135

for homosexuality, 482

for multiple personality, 304

for obesity, 759

optimism and, 394

for panic, 753

for phobia, 131

for PNI, 336

psychodynamic therapy vs., 135–36, 382

rational-emotive therapy, 134–35

cognitive triad, 380–81

cohort trends, 363, 366

cold, common, 335

collective unconscious, 81

color obsession, 269, 275, 280

combat fatigue, 245–47

commitment, *see* criminal commitment; involuntary commitment

communication:

in autism, 633, 635–36

difficulties in, between parents and children, 453, 606

schizophrenics' attempts at, 437–38

in schizophrenogenic family, 453–54

communication deviance, 453

community reinforcement, 541, 565

competence, in optimal living, 18

competitiveness, 323, 324, 326

compulsions:

alcohol, 528

anxiety neutralized by, 269, 274–75, 280–81

cleaning rituals, 266, 267–68

defined, 267

see also obsessive-compulsive disorders

compulsive personality disorder, 589–90, 594

computerized-axial tomography (CAT) scan, 187–88, 663–64

concealment of meaning, 454

concentration camps, 91, 92

survivors of, post-traumatic stress disorder among, 238, 242–43, 245, 247

conditioned responses (CR), 117–19, 214, 226–29

conditioned stimulus (CS), 117–19, 214, 226–29, 257

conditioning, *see* operant conditioning; Pavlovian conditioning

conduct disorders, 574, 602–8

genetic influences on, 605

juvenile delinquency and, 602–5

prognosis for, 641–42

treatment of, 606–8

confabulation, 683–84

conflict, 71, 72, 86, 102, 150, 395

anxiety caused by, 79–80

avoidance-approach, 318

Oedipal, 74, 77, 109, 223–25

repressed in unconscious, 79, 88

between self-image and memory, 87

conformity, 456

confounds, 150–53

demand characteristics, 150, 152–53

experimenter bias, 150, 152

nonrandom assignment, 150

subject bias, 150, 152

conscious experience, 95–97

consciousness, 78–79, 82, 115, 660

defenses and, 86–97

constipation, 544

containment services, 766–70

hot-lines, 767–68

contamination obsession, 266–68, 275, 278, 279

continual emergency reaction, 327–28

continuous reinforcement (CRF), 123

control, 326–27, 621

and CHD, 326–27

and environment, 330–31

flexible, 9

loss of, 6, 8–9, 12, 528

parental, 73

sense of, 84

control groups, 148, 150–51, 152, 153, 155

conversions, *see* hysteria; somatoform disorders

convulsions, hysterical, 281

Cook-Medley hostility score, 324

coping strategies (defense mechanisms), 72, 81, 86–97, 102, 104

acting out, 93

denial, 92, 93, 96, 512

displacement, 90, 93, 272–73

dissociation, *see* dissociative disorders

editing processes, 88

fusion, 97–98

identification, 90–92

intellectualization, 92, 93, 96

isolation, 92, 93

maturational hierarchy of, 93–95

in obsessive-compulsive disorders, 272–73

organization of, 93–95

projection, 88–90, 93, 96

rationalization, 92–93

reaction formation, 90, 96

repression, 87–88, 92, 93, 96

specialness, 97, 98

sublimation, 75, 93, 96

core conflictual relationship theme (CCRT), 135–36

coronary heart disease (CHD), 311, 313, 345

hormonal changes and, 325

risk factors for, 322, 561, 562

studies of, 323–25, 328, 331–32

and Type A personality, 322–29

corpus callosum, 657

corpus stratum, 449, 450

correlational studies, 144, 159–65

causality unclear in, 162

evaluation of, 164–65, 169–70

example of, 159–61

relationships in, 159–60
correlation coefficient (r), 161–62
cortical-striatal-thalamic brain circuit, 276–77
counseling psychologists, 730
counterphobia, 90
counter shock, 339
covert sensitization, 495–96
crack, 537, 539, 542, 630
creativity, of schizophrenics, 447–48, 630
CRF (continuous reinforcement), 123
criminal commitment, 695, 710–19
    incompetence to stand trial and, 718–19
    insanity defense and, 710–18
criminal insanity, 700, 710–18
criminality, 564
    childhood conduct disorders and, 602, 603
    frontal-lobe damage and, 682
    genetic factors in, 54–55, 56–57, 605
    see also antisocial personality disorder
crisis interventions, 766–70
cultural differences:
    and drug abuse, 512–13
    and schizophrenia, 456–57
    and suicide, 410–11

dancing manias, 25
dangerousness:
    to others, 699–701
    prediction of, 699–701
    to self, 699–701
deactivation, 517
death, 345
    fear of, 97–99
    of spouse, 290, 330, 333, 335–36, 344
    sudden, 329–32
death phobia, 219
decision making, difficulty in, 358
defense mechanisms, see coping strategies
delayed auditory feedback, 619
delayed discovery doctrine, 722
delinquency, see juvenile delinquency
delirium tremens (D.T.'s), 527, 528
delusions, 96, 422–23
    of control, 433
    of grandeur, 50, 425, 433, 436
    normal cognitive processes and, 434–36
    of persecution, 425, 433, 436, 713
    of reference, 433–34, 435–36
    in schizophrenia, 422–23, 425, 432–36, 439, 451, 711
    somatic, 434
demand characteristics, 150, 152–53
dementia, 190, 677–80, 684
dementia praecox, 420, 421
demonic possession, 24, 33
denial, 92, 93, 96, 512
    of meaning, 454
dependent personality disorder, 588–89, 594, 595
dependent variables, 147
depersonalization, 294
depressants, barbiturates as, 460
depression, 190, 351–407, 646, 651, 681
    as element of abnormality, 7, 10
    normal vs. clinical, 352

suicide as outcome of, 352, 403, 407–8, 409–10, 413, 437, 697
treatments for, 754–55
see also depression, bipolar; depression, unipolar
depression, bipolar (manic-depression), 49, 352, 400–406
    cause of, 404
    characteristics of, 403–4
    depressive component of, 400, 403
    genetic vulnerability to, 404
    manic component of, 401–2
    suicide as outcome of, 437, 697
    symptoms of, 400–403, 405–6, 407–8
    treatment of, 63, 66, 352, 404–6, 754–55
    unipolar depression vs., 352
depression, unipolar, 298, 353–400, 407–8
    age factors in, 351–52, 362–63, 366–67
    agoraphobia and, 257
    among Amish, 362, 363–64
    anaclitic, 366
    as anger turned upon self, 378–79
    animal model of, 168
    anxiety and, 157–58
    attributional style in, 391–92, 395, 399
    biomedical model of, 358–60, 370–78, 398–400, 406
    bipolar depression vs., 352
    among blacks, 367–68
    body image and, 365–66
    bulimia nervosa and, 621–22
    causal inference, 165
    childhood or recent losses and, 91–92, 368–69, 393, 394–95, 397–98, 399
    in children, 367, 601, 615–16, 617
    cognitive deficit in, 358, 391–92
    cognitive models of, 48–49, 370–71, 380–400
    cognitive therapy for, 129, 382–84, 391, 395–400, 616, 748–49, 754–55
    course of, 369–70, 398–400
    double, 360
    dream deprivation and, 148–49, 393
    and drugs, 540
    drug treatment for, 62–63, 64, 66, 148, 168, 233, 248, 252, 257–58, 304, 361, 371, 373–75, 393, 395–97, 540, 542, 616, 623, 753, 754–55
    electroconvulsive shock treatment for, 62, 361, 371, 376–78, 393, 754
    endogenous vs. exogenous, 360–61
    episodic vs. chronic, 360
    explanatory style and, 389–91
    genetics and, 352, 363, 365, 371, 404
    helplessness perceived in, 378, 380
    integration of theories and therapies for, 398–400
    lack of pleasant events, 160–61
    learned helplessness model of, 381, 384–85, 398
    life events and, 333, 335, 368–69
    measuring symptoms of, 359
    meta-analysis and, 151
    modernity studies of, 362–64
    mood and emotional symptoms of, 352,

353–54, 359, 361, 381, 392
    motivational deficit in, 338, 353, 357–58, 372, 373, 391
    neuroanatomical basis of, 375, 687, 688
    neurochemical basis of, 371–75, 377, 398, 687, 688, 689–90
    obsessions linked to, 269–70, 274–75
    optimism and, 394
    physical symptoms of, 344, 353, 358–60, 361, 381, 398
    PNI and, 333, 335, 336
    premenstrual, 365
    prevalence of, 163–64
    preventing, 397–98
    prospective studies on, 166–67
    psychodynamic model of, 370–71, 378–80, 398–400
    psychodynamic therapy for, 361, 380, 755
    self-esteem problems in, 344, 354–56, 378, 380, 381, 592
    social class and, 367–68
    somatoform disorders and, 288
    sudden death and, 330
    symptoms of, 353–60, 399
    theories and therapies of, 370–400
    thought symptoms of, 353, 354–57, 380–84, 391–92
    twin studies and, 166–67
    for unipolar depression, 62–63, 148, 361, 371, 373–75, 391, 393, 395–97, 754, 755
    vulnerability to, 362–69, 393–95, 399
    among women vs. men, 362, 364–66
depressive personality, 379
depressogenic assumptions, changing of, 383, 384
deprivation dwarfism, 68
derealization, 294
dereflection, 751
desmethyimipramine (DMI), 540
detoxification, 532–33
developmental disorders, 600, 601, 624–41
    pervasive, 633–41; see also autism
diagnosis, 173–74, 188–203
    in biomedical model, 50
    and categorization, 203
    cluster and specific, 196–98
    context factor in, 200–201
    diagnostician's expectations and, 200, 201–2
    of drug dependence, 512–15
    DSM-IV and, 13, 163, 191–200, 203
    evaluation of, 193–203
    historical origins of, 190–93
    multiple axes approach, 192–93
    psychological vs. medical, 190, 200
    reasons for, 189–90
    research vs. clinical, 203
    self-, 19–20
    source credibility and, 200, 202
diathesis, genetics and, 315, 316, 322, 337–41
diathesis-stress model, 313, 337
    behavioral view of, 341–45
    of peptic ulcers, 316–21, 322
    psychodynamic view of, 340, 345

diathesis-stress model *(continued)*
   of schizophrenia, 761
diazepam, 261
diets, and exercise, 759
direct sexual therapy, 505–7, 508
disconnection syndromes, 668
discriminative stimuli, 122
disinhibition, 525
disorganized schizophrenia, 425, 426, 439
disowning projection, 89
displacement, 90, 93
   in obsessive-compulsive disorders, 272–73
disruptive behavior, 600–601, 602–11
dissidents, political psychiatry and, 695,
   722, 723–25
dissociative disorders, 93, 266, 294–306
   amnesia, 266, 294–97, 306, 307, 313
   anesthetics, 553
   anxiety component of, 266, 294, 297,
      306, 307
   multiple personality, *see* multiple
      personality
disulfiram, 534
divorce, childhood depression and, 367
DMI (desmethyimpramine), 540
dopamine, 372, 439, 448–51, 452,
      521–22, 523, 526–27, 539, 542,
      550, 558, 639
   Parkinson's disease and, 461, 651
   schizophrenia and, 58–59, 458
dopamine hypothesis, 448–50, 451
double-binds, 445, 453
double-blind experiments, 152
double depression, 360
Down's syndrome, 628–29, 679
dream deprivation, 148–49, 393
dreaming:
   physiological signs of, 148
   sexual excitement during, 504
   traumas relived in, 238, 240–41, 243
   unconscious revealed in, 79
drug dependence, 367, 511–67
   adaptation to, 10, 513–14, 517–18
   addictive disorders, 518–20
   AIDS and, 542
   alcohol, *see* alcohol dependence
   animals and, 521, 523–24, 527, 531,
      535, 537–38, 539, 552, 554, 560,
      563
   and availability, 564–65
   conditioning models, 523–24
   defining, 512–15
   diagnosing, 512–15
   drug effectiveness and, 515–24
   education and prevention, 565
   emotional and financial costs of, 512
   functional impairment, 513–14
   future directions in treatment and preven-
      tion, 564–65
   limiting availability, 564–65
   loss of control and, 513–14, 515
   medical model, 513
   medical professionals and, 545–46
   neuroadaptation, 515, 517
   opponent-process theory, 519–20
   physical, 517–18
   positive reinforcement, 521–23
   process A vs. process B, 520–21
   quantification of effects, 537

relapse, 515, 548–49, 558
research in, 565
society and, 512–13
theoretical models of, 518–24
tolerance of, 517–18, 558
treatment of, 540–42, 547–49, 561,
   565, 756, 757–58
vulnerability in, 515
withdrawal and, 514, 518, 520–21,
   523–24, 539, 540, 546–47, 548,
   555, 559, 563–64
drug reminder cues, 523
drugs, 49, 511–67
   addiction to, *see* drug dependence
   administration, route of, 515–17
   alcohol, 515
   amphetamines, 536–37
   anti-anxiety, 64, 66, 157–58, 232–33,
      252, 257, 259, 261, 304, 526, 753
   anticonvulsant, 406
   antidepressant, 62–63, 64, 66, 148, 168,
      233, 248, 252, 257–58, 304, 361,
      371, 373–75, 393, 395–97, 540,
      542, 616, 623, 753, 754–55
   antihistamines, 459
   antipsychotic, 61–62, 64, 709
   barbiturates, 562–64
   brain functions and, 515–17, 524
   cocaine, 513, 518, 519–21, 536,
      537–42, 543, 549, 551, 556
   depressant, 460
   effectiveness of, 515
   hallucinogens, *see* hallucinogens
   historical use of, 512–13, 549–50, 554,
      557
   intoxication and, 562
   intravenous administration of, 516, 537,
      539, 543, 545, 549
   lipid solubility, 515, 516
   marijuana, *see* marijuana
   narcotics, *see* narcotics
   nicotine, *see* nicotine; smoking
   PCP, 552–53
   pleasure of, 521, 523, 525, 539, 551,
      560
   potency of, 515
   rate of deactivation of, 516
   sedative-hypnotic, 525, 562–64
   side effects of, 62, 63, 64
   stimulants, *see* stimulants
   tolerance to, 520, 524, 546–47, 555–56
   vulnerability to, 519
drug treatment, 67, 741, 745–46
   for alcohol dependence, 534–35
   for anxiety disorders, 64, 259–61, 753
   in biomedical model, 49, 58–59, 61–65,
      67
   for bulimia nervosa, 623
   for childhood disorders, 642
   for drug abuse, 757–58
   for enuresis, 618
   for hyperactivity, 610, 611
   maintenance therapies, 547–49
   for manic-depression, 63, 352, 404–6,
      755
   for nervous system disorders, 676, 686
   for obsessive-compulsive disorder, 277,
      279

for panic attacks, 252
for peptic ulcers, 321
for phobia, 232–33
placebo effect in, 152
for PNI, 336
for post-traumatic stress disorder, 248
for schizophrenia, 61–62, 66, 189, 448,
   450, 452, 459–62, 464, 465,
   760–61
for separation anxiety disorder, 616
for unipolar depression, 62–63, 64, 66,
   148, 168, 233, 248, 252, 257–58,
   304, 361, 371, 373–75, 393,
   395–97, 540, 542, 616, 623, 753,
   754–55
DSM-I (*Diagnostic and Statistical Manual of
   Mental Disorders*, First Edition), 190,
   199
DSM-II (*Diagnostic and Statistical Manual of
   Mental Disorders*, Second Edition),
   190–91, 192, 199, 723
   DSM-III vs., 191
   reliability of, 190–91, 192, 195–96
DSM-III (*Diagnostic and Statistical Manual of
   Mental Disorders*, Third Edition):
   and diagnosis, 163
   DSM-II vs., 191
   multiple axes approach in, 191, 192
   paraphilias and, 484
   post-traumatic stress disorder in, 238,
      247
   reliability of, 192, 195–98
   schizophrenia in, 424
   somatoform disorders in, 281
DSM-III-R (*Diagnostic and Statistical Manual
   of Mental Disorders*, Third Edition—
   Revised):
   DSM-III vs., 191
   DSM-IV vs., 191, 192
   homosexuality in, 471
   multiple axes approach in, 191, 192
   reliability of, 192
DSM-IV (*Diagnostic and Statistical Manual of
   Mental Disorders*, Fourth Edition):
   amnesia and, 298
   antisocial personality disorder in, 572,
      682
   anxiety disorders and, 306
   bingeing in, 760
   borderline personality disorder in,
      591–92
   cannabis dependence criteria, 556
   childhood disorders in, 600, 641
   depression in, 168, 360, 361
   and diagnosis, 13, 163, 191–93,
      195–98, 203, 313
   drug abuse in, 513–14, 515
   DSM III-R vs., 191, 192
   frontal-lobe damage and, 682
   generalized anxiety disorder and, 258
   homosexuality in, 471
   legal definition of "mental disease" in, 715
   mental disorder defined in, 191–92
   multiple axes approach in, 192–93
   and multiple personality disorder, 297,
      298
   neurology and, 648
   post-traumatic stress disorder in, 238

premenstrual depression in, 365
reliability of, 192–93, 195–98
schizophrenia in, 422, 438
somatoform disorders in, 281
validity, 198–200
and World Health Organization, 191
Durham test, 714–15
Durham v. United States, 714
dysfunction, 191
dyslexia, 669–71, 689
acquired, 670, 671
Chinese and, 689
developmental, 669–70, 671
English and, 689
Japanese and, 671
phonological, 670
surface, 670–71
dysphoria, 537, 540, 547, 621
dysthymic disorder, 360

eating disorders, 298, 601, 617–18
anorexia nervosa, 125, 165, 618,
620–23, 688, 760
bingeing, 621, 622–23, 760
bulimia nervosa, 165, 601, 618, 620,
621–23, 759–60
obesity, 137
treatments for, 758–60
ECA (Epidemiologic Catchment Area) study,
163
echolalia, 633, 635
ECT (electroconvulsive shock therapy), 361,
371, 376–78, 393, 673, 745, 754
EEG's (electroencephalograms), 530, 564,
582, 638, 663, 681
efficacy expectation, 130–31
ego, 76–77, 79, 81, 82, 104, 105
ego-dystonic homosexuality, 480–82
sources of, 481–82
treatment of, 482
ego-syntonic homosexuality, 480–81
ejaculation, 488, 489
physiology of, 499
premature, 500, 503, 508
retarded, 500, 503
electroconvulsive shock therapy (ECT), 361,
371, 376–78, 393, 673, 745, 754
electroencephalograms (EEG's), 530, 564,
582, 638, 663, 681
electromyographs (EMG's), 185
elimination disorders, 601, 617–19
emergency reaction, 212–13, 216, 252,
258–59, 269
blood pressure and, 213, 340
evolution and, 338–39
general adaptation syndrome and,
339–40
and Type A personality, 323, 324,
327–29
EMG's (electromyographs), 185
emotional arousal, chronic deficit in, 577,
584, 605
emotional catharsis, 35, 104
emotions:
antisocial personality and, 572, 573–74,
577
core self and, 83, 84
and environment, 462–64

in existential therapies, 107
expressed, 453
negative, 533
Pavlovian conditioning and, 118–20, 121
somatoform disorder and, 290
empathy, 84, 86, 106
empiricism, 113–14, 115
encopresis, 617–18
endogenous morphine and opioids, 522,
535
endorphins, 335, 336–37, 544–45, 737
enkephalins, 544–45
enuresis, 601, 617–19
environment, 167, 462–64, 630–31
environmental competence, 17, 18
environmentalism, 114, 115
environmental model, *see* behavioral model;
cognitive model
environmental toxins, 610
enzymes, 365, 679
epidemiological evidence, 51, 163–65
Epidemiologic Catchment Area (ECA) study,
163
epilepsy, 276, 638, 657, 660, 663
epinephrine (adrenaline), 213, 372, 577
Epstein-Barr virus, 288
erectile dysfunction, 484, 500, 501–2, 503
of physical vs. psychological origin, 504
primary vs. secondary, 501
psychological causes of, 504–5
situation specific vs. global, 501, 502
therapy for, 505, 508
erection, penile, 499, 500, 503–4
erogenous zones, 73
erotic arousal:
impairment of, 500–506
physiology of, 499–500
therapy for problems of, 506–8
erotic life, five layers of, 470, 472
errors in logic, 380, 381–82
escape responding, 214–15
etiology (causality), 143
biochemistry as, 48, 49, 58–59, 61
in biomedical model, 49, 61, 251–55
in clinical case histories, 144, 146, 147
in cognitive model, 251–55
in correlation studies, 162
and epidemiology, 165
in experiments of nature, 167
genetics as, 47, 49, 54–58, 61
germs as, 49, 50–53, 61
neuroanatomy as, 59–60
in scientific experimentation, 147–50,
156–57, 168–69
suggested by diagnosis, 189
evidence (legal), nature of, 719–22
executive monkey study, 150–51, 320
exercise:
and CHD, 323, 329
diets and, 759
exhibitionism, 483, 488, 489–90, 495
exhortative will, 100, 101
existential model, 97–101
existential psychology, 97–101
fear of dying and, 97–99
responsibility central to, 99–100
will in, 100–101
existential therapy, 48, 751, 763

exorcism, 33
expectations, 130–31, 133
experimental effects, 147–48, 149
experimental groups, 148, 152, 153, 155
experimentalism, 114, 115
experimental method, 114
experimental studies, *see* scientific experimentation
experimenter bias, 150, 152
experimenter-blind design, 152
experiments of nature, 144, 165–67, 390,
391
evaluation of, 167, 169–70
prospective, 166–67
explanatory style:
and depression, 389–91
pessimistic and optimistic, 330–32, 333,
335, 389–90, 394
exposure, 754
extinction:
of avoidance responding, 228, 278–79
obsessive-compulsive disorders and, 280
as operant phenomenon, 122
as operant therapy, 126
partial reinforcement and, 124
as Pavlovian phenomenon, 118
in phobia therapies, 120–21, 229–33
post-traumatic stress disorder and, 249
in systematic desensitization, 121
see also flooding; modeling therapy; response prevention; systematic desensitization
extinction trials, 228

factitious disorders, 284, 286
family:
communication within, 453–54, 606,
623
counseling, 733, 751–52
hyperactive children and, 610
schismatic (divided), 454
schizophrenia relapse rate and, 462–63,
762
schizophrenogenic, 440, 442–46,
453–54, 458–59
family resemblance approach:
abnormality recognized by, 6, 11–12
hazards of, 13–15, 198, 723
family therapy, 293, 617, 623, 733, 751–52
fear, 209–15, 306, 307, 753
as conditioned response, 118, 119, 214,
226–27
degree of, 215
elements of, 211–15
instrumental responses to, 214
normal vs. phobic, 215–16, 226, 613
in panic attacks, 251–55
as treatment for loss of reason, 38
see also specific phobias
fear disorders, 209–10, 249–50, 753
see also phobia; post-traumatic stress disorder
feelings, *see* emotions
feeling substitution, 90
fetal alcohol syndrome, 535–36, 630
fetal hormones, 474–76, 478–79, 498
fetishes, 471–72, 484–85, 486, 488
conditioning of, 493–94

flat affect, 439, 451
flooding, 120, 747
  agoraphobia and, 257–58
  obsessive-compulsive disorders and,
      278–79
  phobia and, 120, 229, 230–31
fluoxetine, 374–75
fluphenazine, 760
fMRI (functional MRI), 664–65
foot fetishists, 117, 128, 484, 493–94
free association, 102, 105, 382, 749
frequency distribution, 154
frigidity, see sexual unresponsiveness
frontal lobes, 451, 452, 680–84
fugue states, 295, 297, 677
functional analyses, 183
functional MRI (fMRI), 664–65
fusion, 97–98

GABA (gamma-aminobutyric acid), 526,
    563
galvanic skin response (GSR), 578
gamma-aminobutyric acid (GABA), 526,
    563
gastric secretions, 315, 317–18, 322, 338,
    340
gastrointestinal tract, 516
GBMI (guilty but mentally ill) verdict,
    717–18
general adaptation syndrome, 339–40
generality, 146
generalized anxiety disorder, 210, 215–16,
    250, 257, 258–61, 306
general paresis, 203
  eradication of, 52, 66, 68, 173
  syndrome of, 50
  syphilis linked to, 50–52, 67, 68
genetics:
  abnormal behavior and, 687
  adoption studies and, 55–58
  alcoholism and, 519
  Alzheimer's disease and, 677, 679–80
  antisocial personality disorder and, 574,
      578–82, 584, 605
  autism and, 639
  criminal behavior and, 54–55, 56–57, 67
  depression and, 352, 363, 365, 371, 404
  diathesis and, 315, 316, 322, 337–41
  and drug dependence, 519
  enuresis and, 618
  as etiology, 47, 49, 54–58, 61
  homosexuality and, 478–79, 480
  juvenile delinquency and, 604, 605
  mental retardation and, 629–30
  "molar" traits and, 55
  panic attacks and, 251–52
  personality and, 54–58, 66–67
  PKU and, 629
  schizophrenia and, 53–54, 440–48, 453,
      458–59
  see also adoption studies; twin studies
genital stage, 72, 75
genital stimulation, 507
germs, as etiology, 49, 50–53, 61
glia cells, 648–49
global anxiety disorder, 255, 257
glove anesthesia, 286, 291
goal-directed will, 100–101

graded task assignment, 382
graphemes, 670
grave disability, 701
growth:
  and existential model, 97–101
  in optimal living, 17
  see also personality development
GSR (galvanic skin response), 578
guilt, 238, 241, 243, 533, 615
guilty but mentally ill (GBMI) verdict,
      717–18

habit disorders, 601, 617–23
hallucinations, 46, 423–24, 521, 555, 660
  hallucinogens and, 550–52
  in schizophrenia, 423–24, 428–29, 430,
      439, 451
  sensory deprivation and, 152–53
hallucinogens, 512–13, 549–53
  effects of, 550–52
  LSD, 550–51, 552, 553
  MDMA, 552–53
  medical and social complications of, 552
  mescaline, 550, 552
  PCP, 552–53
  psilocybin, 550, 552
  use of, 550–52
haloperidol, 460, 760
Halstead-Reitan Neuropsychological Battery,
    186
headaches, biofeedback and, 185
head trauma, 685
  amnesia caused by, 295–96, 673, 674,
      676
health psychology, 311–47
heart attacks:
  hypertension and, 322, 324, 326, 327
  among Type A vs. Type B persons, 323,
      326–27, 344
  uncontrollable life events and, 326–27,
      344
helplessness:
  attributional model of, 387–91
  immune system and, 335, 336
  perceived in depression, 378, 380
  sudden death and, 329–31
  and Type A personality, 324, 326–27
  see also learned helplessness
hermaphrodites, 446–47
heroin, 516, 518, 520, 522, 542, 543–44,
    545, 546–47, 551, 558
  methadone programs and, 758
heterosexuality, 471
  AIDS and, 542
  depth of orientation, 482–83
  transsexuality and, 473–74
high blood pressure (hypertension),
    338–39, 340, 561
  cognitions and, 341
  personality traits and, 324–25, 327, 341
  treatment of, 375
hippocampus, 672, 673–74, 675, 679
histamine, 372
histrionic personality disorder, 586
HIV, 680
homosexuality, 471, 477–83, 486
  causes of, 478–79, 480
  changeability of, 482–83

choice vs. orientation, 477
  depth of orientation, 482–83
  ego-dystonic, 480–82
  ego-syntonic, 480–81
  exclusive, 477–78
  fetal disruption and, 478–79, 480
  male, origins of, 477–80
  maturation timing and, 478
  societal attitudes toward, 481–82
  transsexuality and, 473
  twin studies and, 480
hopelessness:
  in depression, 356–57, 381, 389, 615
  immune system and, 334, 335
  sudden death and, 329–31
  and suicide, 414
hormones, 68, 325, 474–76, 478–79, 480,
    498, 686
hospitals:
  rise of, 35–37
  segregation at, 37–39
  see also psychiatric hospitals
hostility, 323, 324–25, 332, 544
hot-lines, 414, 767–68
Huntington's chorea, 681
hyperactivity, 600–601, 602, 608–11
  behavior management for, 610–11
  drug therapy for, 610
hypersensitivity tests, 333
hypertension, see high blood pressure
hyperventilation, 253, 254
hypnosis, 32–33, 93
  catharsis under, 35
  Charcot's study of, 32–33, 35
  mesmerism as precursor of, 32, 35
  self-, 302, 303, 304, 306
  in treatment of hysteria, 32–33, 35,
      144–45, 281, 293
  in treatment of multiple personality,
      302–3, 304
hypochondriasis, 93, 96, 221
hypomanic personality, 400, 404
hypothalamus, 213, 479, 480, 545
hypotheses, in clinical case histories, 146,
    147
hysteria:
  Galen's investigation of, 29–30
  historical view of, 27–33, 49–50
  hypnosis in treatment of, 32–33, 35,
      144–45, 281, 293
  paralysis, 32–33, 281, 289, 290, 293,
      297
  prevalence of, in historical periods, 23n
  see also somatoform disorders

id, 76, 79, 81, 82
ideal standards, violation of, 6, 10–11, 12,
    14
ideas:
  associations between, 113–14
  flight of, 401
  of reference, 432, 591, 593
identification:
  with aggressor, 90–92
  as coping strategy, 91
  with same-sex parent, 75
identity alteration, 294
identity confusion, 294

illnesses, *see* physical illnesses
illness phobia, 219, 220–21
imipramine, 258, 618
immigration studies, 456
immune system, 332–37, 556, 686
immunization, 333
immunocompetence, 333
immunoglobulin, 333
immunologic memory, 332–33
impotence, *see* erectile dysfunction
inanimate object phobia, 219, 220
inauthenticity, 98–99
incest, 75
incidence, 218
incompetence to stand trial, 717–19
incomprehensibility, 6, 8, 12
independent variable, 147, 159
indoleamines, 372, 374–75
infanticide obsession, 273, 278, 280
infantile autism, 547–56, 633–41
    see also autism
infections, neural damage due to, 685
information variance, 195
inhibition, 327
injection of meaning, 454
injury phobia, 219, 220–21
insanity, 3–4
insanity defense, 710–18
    "appreciate and conform" test in, 715–16
    burden of proof, 716–17
    debate over, 489, 710, 712–14
    GBMI verdict in, 717–18
    mental disease test in, 714–16
    reform act, 716–17
    "right-wrong" test in, 714, 716
instrumental conditioning, *see* operant con-
    ditioning
instrumental responses, 214
intellectualization, 92, 93, 96
Intelligence Quotient (IQ), 182
    developmental disorders and, 632, 637,
        640
    genetic factors in, 629–30
    mental retardation and, 182, 624–26,
        629–30, 723
intelligence tests, 176, 181–82, 624–26
inter-judge reliability, 193, 195
International Classification of Diseases and
    Related Health Problems, 190, 191
"intern's syndrome," 19–20
interpersonal relationships, 602
    positive, in optimal living, 17, 18–19
interpersonal therapy (IPT), 158, 395, 396,
    397, 462, 755
intersubjectivity, 84
interviews, 174–75
interview schedule, 175
intranasal drug users, 516, 537, 539
intraoral drug users, 516
intravenous (IV) drug users, 516, 537, 539,
    542, 543, 545, 549
introcosm, 83
introspection, 115
involuntary (civil) commitment, 695,
    696–709
    abolishment of, 708–9
    criteria for, 699–701
    as deprivation of liberty, 700

due process of law in, 699–700, 701–3
    release from, 705–7
    right to treatment in, 704–7
    standard of proof in, 703–4
    see also criminal commitment
IPT (interpersonal therapy), 158, 395, 396,
    397, 462, 755
IQ, *see* Intelligence Quotient
irrationality, 6, 8, 12
isolation, 81, 345
    as coping strategy, 92, 93

Jackson v. *Indiana*, 718–19
job training programs, 766
Jungian therapy, 750, 763–64
juvenile delinquency, 601
    genetic factors in, 606–8
    socialized vs. unsocialized, 603–4
    social sources of, 604–5
    treatment of, 606–8

Kappa statistic (*K*), 195, 197
ketamine, 552–53
Korsakoff's syndrome, 672–73

laboratory models, 144, 167–69
language, 84–85, 99, 109
language deficits, in autism, 633, 635–36,
    640
language disorders, *see* aphasias
latency stage, 72, 75
law, and abnormality, 695–722
law of effect, 122
L-DOPA, 449, 651, 685
learned helplessness, 365, 381, 384–95
    assessment of, 398
    attributional dimensions in, 387–89,
        391–92, 395
    cause of, 393
    cognitive deficit in, 387, 391–92
    experimental discovery of, 338–39
    in humans, 386–87, 398
    norepinephrine depletion in, 392
    passivity deficit in, 168, 385–86, 391
    prevention of, 393–95
    therapy for, 168, 393, 398
    unipolar depression compared with, 168,
        389–95
learning:
    avoidance, 127–28
    defects in, sociopathy and, 574, 575–78
    disorders, 632–33
    by operant conditioning, 121–24
    by Pavlovian conditioning, 116–21
    vicarious, 130
learning model, *see* behavioral model;
    cognitive model
left-sided neglect, 655
lesbians, 479, 480
Lessard v. *Schmidt*, 702, 704
levothyroxine, 406
libido, 72, 73, 74, 75
Librium, 64
life events:
    and alcohol, 533–34
    depression and, 333, 335, 368–69
    psychosomatic disorders and, 341–45
    stress and, 333, 335, 340, 341–42

lifespan, and stress, 338
lifetime prevalence, 163
linkage analysis, 446–47
lithium carbonate, 63, 352, 404–6, 755
Little Albert experiment, 159, 227, 233
Little Hans case:
    behavioral analysis of, 226
    psychodynamic analysis of, 223–25
liver, 516, 527, 535
lobotomies, 62, 689
Lockerbie air disaster, 243
logical errors, 381–82
loneliness, fusion and, 97–98
longitudinal studies, 166–67
Lou Gehrig's disease (amyotrophic lateral
    sclerosis), 689
lung disease, 557, 561–62
Luria-Nebraska Neuropsychological Battery,
    187
lycanthropy, 25
lymphocytes, 332
lysing, 332, 335, 336

macrophages, 332
magnetic resonance imaging (MRI),
    663–64
magnification, 382
mainlining, 516
mainstreaming, 631
maladaptiveness, 6, 7–8, 11
malingering, 284–86
Malleus Maleficarum, 26
mammillary bodies, 673
mania, 90, 190, 352, 400–403, 687
    dancing, 25
manic-depression, *see* depression, bipolar
Manifest Anxiety Scale, 260
MAO inhibitors, 63, 148, 233, 371,
    373–75, 393
marijuana, 519, 554–57
    effects of, 554–56
    medical and social complications, 556–57
    use of, 554
marriage counselors, 733
masochism, 486–88
masturbation, 74, 477, 480, 489, 490, 495,
    502
    fetishes in, 484, 485, 486, 494, 495
    normality of, 16–17
Maudsley Obsessive-Compulsive Disorder
    Inventory, 271
Mayock v. *Martin*, 696–97
mean, in statistical inference, 154
meaning, communication distortions and,
    454
medial forebrain bundle (MFB), 372
medication, psychotropic, 460, 616, 762
    see also specific medications
meditation, 261
melancholia, 30, 190, 378
    age of, 360–61, 362–64
    depression with vs. without, 360
membranes, biological, 516
memory, 556, 660, 671–77
    aging and, 676–77, 678–80
    collective unconscious and, 81
    components of, 671–72
    deficit, 674–76

memory *(continued)*
  digit span in, 674
  explicit vs. implicit, 674, 675–76
  familiarity in, 674–75, 676
  frontal lobes and, 683–84
  and information, 684
  loss of, 294–97, 378
  priming in, 674–75
  reconstruction of, 88
  recovered, the law and, 617, 720–22
  repressed, 79, 87–88
  selectivity of, 146
  short-term vs. long-term, 674–75
  skill acquisition in, 674, 675
  traumatic, 340
  vulnerability of, 672–73
  see also amnesia
mens rea, 710, 717
  see also insanity defense
menstrual cycles, 621
mental disorder:
  DSM-IV definition of, 191–92
  prevalence of, 163–64
mental inhibition, 87
mental retardation, 182, 624–31
  cultural-familial, 630–31
  definition of, 624
  Down's syndrome, 628–29, 679
  IQ and, 182, 624–26, 629–30, 723
  levels of, 626–27
  measures of, 624–26
  phenylketonuria and, 629
  treatment of, 631
mesmerism, 30–32, 35, 302–3, 304
meta-analysis, 149–50, 151
methadone maintenance programs, 758
MFB (medial forebrain bundle), 372
milieu therapy, 462–65
Miltown, 64
mind-body problem, 335–37
minimization, 382
Minnesota Multiphasic Personality
    Inventory (MMPI), 176–78, 324
M'Naghten rule, 712–14, 715
modeling therapy, 747
  for fear, 753
  for obsessive-compulsive disorders, 278
  for phobia, 131, 229, 231–32, 616, 753
models of abnormality, 48–49
  see also behavioral model; biomedical
    model; cognitive model; existential
    model; psychodynamic model
modernity, and depression, 362–64
mongolism (Down's syndrome), 628–29
moral anxiety, 80
moral insanity, 571
moral standards, violation of, 6, 10–11, 12
moral treatment, 41–42
morphine, 516, 521, 522, 523–24, 536,
    542
motivational deficits:
  as depression symptoms, 338, 353,
    357–58, 372, 373, 391
  passivity deficit and, 385–86, 391
motor tics, 601, 618
movement disorders, 296, 662
  damage to frontal or parietal lobes in,
    654–57
  lower motor neuron damage and, 658–59

upper motor neuron damage and, 659
  see also paralysis
MRFIT (Multiple Risk Factor Intervention
    Trial), 324
MRI (magnetic resonance imaging),
    663–64
multi-modal therapy, 48–49, 135
multiple personality, 87, 266, 294,
    297–306, 677
  child abuse and, 298, 304–5
  described, 298–301
  DSM-IV and, 297, 298
  etiology of, 302–3
  faking, 305–6
  incidence of, 297
  law and, 720
  personalities in, 300–301
  psychological health of individual person-
    alities in, 300–301
  psychotherapy for, 303–4
  schizophrenia vs., 301–2, 421
Multiple Risk Factor Intervention Trial
    (MRFIT), 324
Münchhausen syndrome (factitious
    disorders), 284, 286
mystification, 453

naltrexone, 534–35
NAMI (National Alliance for the Mentally
    Ill), 708
narcissism, 97
narcissistic personality disorder, 587
narcotics, 542–49
  addiction to, 547–48
  codeine, 542
  heroin, 516, 518, 520, 522, 542,
    543–44, 545, 546–47, 551, 558,
    758
  medical and social complications of, 549
  meperidine, 542
  methadone, 547–49, 758
  morphine, 516, 521, 522, 523–24, 536,
    542
  opium, 542
  tolerance to, 546–47
  treatment for, 547–49
  withdrawal from, 546–47, 548
  see also opiates
narrenschiffen, 33
National Alliance for the Mentally Ill
    (NAMI), 708
National Comorbidity Study, 163–64
National Institute of Mental Health (NIMH),
    395, 396
Natural Killer (NK) cells, 332, 333, 335
negative appraisals, 131–32
negative correlation, between depression and
    pleasant activities, 159–61
negative reinforcement, 122
  selective, 126
negativism, in catatonic schizophrenia, 427
Neo-Freudians, 71, 81–82
neologism, 429, 667
nervous system, 646
  autonomic (ANS), 213, 682
  central (CNS), 212, 526–27, 558, 562,
    609–10, 629
  gray vs. white matter in, 652–53

hardware-software analogy and, 646,
    687, 688
  hierarchical organization, 658–59
  inhibition-excitation balance in, 659
  movement controlled by, 653, 654–57,
    658–59, 662
  organization of, 648–49
  parasympathetic (PNS), 212–13, 499,
    500, 505
  recovery of function in, 685, 686
  redundancy in, 661–62, 685, 689
  structure and function of, 648–49,
    652–59
  sympathetic (SNS), 212–13, 499
  vulnerable areas in, 659–61
  see also brain; neurons
nervous system, disorders of, 662–65
  abnormal behaviors based in, 688, 689
  agents of damage in, 659–60
  assessing, 662–65
  cultural values and, 689
  diagnosing of, 686
  frontal lobes and, 680–84
  functional syndromes in, 646, 648
  language and, 653, 658, 665–69, 689
  memory and, 296, 659, 660, 671–77
  movement and, 653, 654–57, 658–59,
    662
  neuroimaging and, 663–65
  organic syndromes in, 645–47, 648
  reading and, 669–71, 689
  symptoms of, 654–57, 659–60, 661–62,
    666–67, 686
  treatment of, 685–90
neuroanatomy, 49
  as etiology, 59–60
neurochemical events, 478, 537, 538–39,
    552, 687–88
neuroleptics, 439, 448, 452, 460, 723,
    760–61
neurological signs of obsessive-compulsive
    disorder, 275–76
neurologic impairment, 186, 187
neurology:
  domain of, 646, 648, 662–65, 686
  expansion of, 687–88
  virtues and limitations of, 688–90
neurons, 527
  anatomy of, 648–49
  axons of, 653, 661
  biochemistry of, 649–50
  degeneration or damage of, 452, 526,
    650, 659–60, 661–62, 667–68,
    671, 676, 679, 685
  glia cells and, 648–49
  in gray matter, 652
  recovery of, 685, 686
  redundancy and, 661–62, 685, 689
  synapses and, 517, 648
  vulnerability of, 659–60, 661
neuropsychological testing, 185–87
neurosis:
  adult vs. childhood disorders, 600, 603,
    609, 612, 616, 617, 641–42
  anxiety and, 209, 306–7
  see also anxiety disorders; dissociative dis-
    orders; obsessive-compulsive disor-
    ders; phobia; post-traumatic stress

disorder; somatoform disorders
neurosurgery, 686
neurotic anxiety, 79–80
neurotoxic effects, 553
neurotransmitters, 48, 252, 335, 336, 439,
    448–49, 450, 452, 521–22, 523,
    526, 563, 639, 646
  brain, 679, 685, 686, 687, 688
  deficits in, 651–52
  psychoactive drugs interact with, 374,
    515, 516–17, 519, 544, 552, 556,
    558
  see also dopamine
neutrophils, 332
nicotine, 345, 512, 516, 518, 522, 539,
    557–62
  dependence, 558–61
  effects of, 557–58
  medical and social complications of,
    561–62
  treatment, 561
  use of, 557
  see also smoking
Nieman-Pick disease, 629
NIMH (National Institute of Mental Health),
    395, 396
nocturnal emission, 477, 480
norepinephrine (noradrenaline; NE), 550,
    552, 558
  depression and, 371–74, 377, 398, 690
  in emergency reaction, 213
  learned helplessness and, 392
normality:
  abnormality vs., 4, 16–17, 78, 107, 115,
    722–23
  definition of, 16
nosophobia, 220–21
Nuclear Magnetic Response Imaging (MRI),
    188
nuclear medicine, and obsessive-compulsive
    disorder, 59
nucleus accumbens, 521–22, 526, 539,
    545
nutrient deficiencies, 659, 661, 672, 674,
    685

obesity, treatment of, 137, 758–60
object deficits, 519
observations, 183–88, 195
observer disagreement, 14–15
observer discomfort, 6, 10, 12, 13
observers, actors' disagreements with,
    14–15
obsessions, 137, 656
  content of, 272–73, 280
  defined, 266–67
  depression linked to, 269–70, 274–75
  harmless vs. clinical, 267
  social context of, 267–68
obsessive-compulsive disorder, 257, 265,
    266–81, 651–52
  anxiety component of, 266, 269–70,
    273–75, 280–81
  biomedical view of, 272, 275–77
  brain activity and, 59, 687, 688
  cognitive-behavioral view of, 272,
    274–75, 307
  comparison of treatments for, 279–80

nuclear medicine and, 59
  primitive content of, 277
  psychodynamic view of, 272–73, 307
  theories of, 272–77
  treatment of, 127–28, 277–80, 754
  vulnerability to, 270–71, 273
  see also compulsions
obsessive-compulsive personality, 270–71
O'Connor v. Donaldson, 706
Odyssey House, 758
Oedipus complex, 74–75, 77, 80, 109
  in erectile dysfunction, 504
  in phobia, 223–25
operant (instrumental) conditioning, 116,
    121–26, 521
  acquisition and extinction phenomena in,
    122
  in avoidance situation, 127–28
  basic concepts of, 122
operants, 122
operant therapies, 124–26
  extinction, 122, 126
  for hyperactivity, 610–11
  Pavlovian therapies vs., 127
  principles of, 124
  selective positive reinforcement, 125
  selective punishment, 126
operational definitions, 147
opiates, 516, 522, 523, 539, 542–49, 556
  dependence, 548, 547–48
  determinants of addiction, 547
  effects of, 543–45
  endogenous, 545
  history of, 543
  medical and social complications, 549
  treatment, 547–49
  see also narcotics
opioid receptors, 548
opium, 512
opponent-process model of addiction,
    519–21
oppositional defiant disorder, 602
optimal living, 17–19
optimism, 115, 331, 333, 335, 394
oral character traits, 73
oral-dependent personality disorder, 518–19
oral stage, 72, 73, 74, 109
organ vulnerability, 338, 340
orgasm, 500, 501, 544
  dysfunctions of, 500, 502–3, 505, 508
  physiology of, 499–500
  after sex-reassignment operations, 476
ostracism, 33
outcome expectations, 130
overdetermined behaviors, 108
overgeneralization, 382
overinclusiveness, in schizophrenia, 431,
    435

pain perception, 544
panic attacks, 64, 250–55, 259, 542
  in agoraphobia, 210, 255–58
  fear elements in, 250–51
panic disorder, 210, 216, 250–55, 257–58,
    259, 306, 753–54
  etiology and therapy in, 251–55
paradoxical intention technique, 751
paralysis:

hysterical, 32–33, 281, 289, 290, 293,
    297
  malingering and, 284
  see also general paresis; movement
    disorders
"paralysis of will," 358
paranoia, 189, 542, 555
paranoid personality disorder, 537, 569–70,
    584–85, 594
paranoid schizophrenia, 425, 439, 696–97
  delusions of persecution in, 433, 711
  drug use and, 448, 450
  treatment of, 189
paraphasias, 667
paraphilias, 470, 471–72, 483–96
  behavioral view of, 492, 493–95
  causes of, 492–95
  ego-dystonic homosexuality, 480–82
  exhibitionism, 483, 488, 489–90, 495
  fetishes, 484–85, 486, 488, 493–94
  pedophilia, 483, 488, 489, 491–92, 495,
    616–17
  psychodynamic view of, 492–93, 494–95
  sadomasochism, 483, 486–88
  telephone scatologia, 488
  transvestism, 473, 483, 485–86
  treatment of, 495–96
  types of, 483–84
  voyeurism, 483, 488, 489, 490–91
parasympathetic nervous system (PNS),
    212–13, 499, 500, 505
parental control, 73, 599–600
Parkinson's disease, 448, 449–50, 461,
    651, 677, 680, 681, 685, 686, 687
partial reinforcement extinction effect, 124
passive-aggressive personality disorder, 96
passivity deficit, 385–86, 391
Pate v. Robinson, 719
patients' rights movement, 707–8
Pavlovian (classical) conditioning, 116–21
  acquisition and extinction phenomena in,
    118
  in avoidance situation, 127–28, 228
  conditioned response in, 118–19
  emotional states acquired by, 118–19,
    121, 214, 226–27, 233–37
  for foot fetishism, 117
  operant therapies vs., 127
  of paraphilias, 493–94
  of phobia, 119, 120–21, 226–33,
    493–94
  prepared, 235, 495
PCP (phencyclidine), 552–53
pedophilia (child molesting), 483, 488, 489,
    491–92, 495, 616–17
pellagra psychosis, 68
penile erection, 499, 500, 503–4
  see also erectile dysfunction
penis, sex-reassignment operations and, 476
penis envy, 74, 109
Pennsylvania Prevention Project, 397–98
pepsin, 314, 315
peptic ulcers, 311, 313–22
  animal models of, 318–21
  description of, 313–14
  diathesis-stress model of, 316–21, 322
  emotional states and, 314, 316–21, 322
  general adaptation syndrome and, 339

peptic ulcers (continued)
    personality factors in, 340
    physiological development of, 315
    prevalence of, 314, 315–16
    susceptibility to, 315–16
    symptoms of, 315
    treatment of, 321–22
perception, 86
    reconstruction of, 88
    responsibility for, 99
perceptual consciousness, 78
perceptual deficits, in schizophrenia, 427–28, 435–36, 454
peripheral neuropathy, 661
periventricular system (PVS), 372
perseveration, 655–56
personality, 48, 109
    alcohol and, 531, 532
    depressive, 379
    Freudian view of, 76–80
    genes and, 54–58, 66–67
    hypertensive, 340
    hypomanic, 400, 404
    illness and, 344–45
    marijuana and, 556
    multiple, 87, 266, 294, 297–306, 421, 677, 720
    obsessive-compulsive, 270–71
    psychodynamic view of, 82–97
    and self, 82–86
    Type A vs. Type B, 323–27
    ulcer-prone, 340
personality alterations:
    as measure of therapeutic effectiveness, 375, 742–44
    in psychodynamic treatment, 104–5
personality development:
    conflict resolution in, 72
    psychosexual stages of (Freud), 72–75
    psychosocial stages of (Erikson), 82
personality disorders, 86, 569–96, 687, 688
    avoidant, 588
    borderline, 591–93
    compulsive, 589–90, 594
    dependent, 588–89, 594, 595
    frontal lobes and, 681–83
    histrionic, 586
    interpretation discrepancies in, 594–95
    narcissistic, 587
    oral-dependent, 518–19
    paranoid, 537, 569–70, 584–85, 594
    passive-aggressive, 96
    schizoid, 590
    schizotypal, 590–91, 593
    underlying traits in, 570, 594–95
    see also antisocial personality disorder
personalization, 384
pessimism, 330–32, 333, 335, 336, 394, 616
PET (positron emission tomography) scan, 59, 188, 450, 451, 664, 665, 681
phallic stage, 72, 74–75, 104
phencyclidine (PCP), 552–53
phenothiazines, 448, 449, 450, 451, 460, 462
phenylalanine, 629
phenylketonuria (PKU), 629

phobia, 137–38, 210, 215, 216, 217–37, 249, 689
    alcohol and, 531
    anxiety and, 233
    behavioral analysis of, 119, 120–21, 224, 226–37, 307
    in childhood, 225, 611, 612–14
    among concentration camp survivors, 243
    defined, 217–18
    diagnosing of, 217–18
    drug treatment for, 232–33
    irrationality of, 233, 235–36
    Little Albert experiment and, 159, 227, 233
    Little Hans case and, 223–25, 226
    non-traumatic, 230, 233, 237
    normal fear vs., 215–16, 226, 613
    panic attacks in, 255–57
    persistence of, 227–29, 231, 493–94
    in post-traumatic stress disorder, 239
    prevalence of, 218
    psychoanalytic analysis of, 223–25, 230
    selectivity of, 233–35
    self-efficacy expectations and, 131
    societal judgment and, 218
    susceptibility to, 237
    symptom substitution in, 230
    systematic desensitization and, 121, 150, 229–30, 232, 753
    therapies for, 120–21, 131, 223, 224–25, 229–33, 616, 747, 752–53
    types of, 219–22
physical approach, 27–29, 47–48
    animalism and, 29
    hysteria and, 27–29, 34
    treatment in, 29, 33, 34, 49–50
    see also biomedical model
physical excitement:
    impairment of, 500–501, 503–4
    physiology of, 499–501
    therapy for, 506–8
physical illnesses:
    from life events and personality, 344–45
    phobia of, 219, 220–21
    PNI and, 332–37
    susceptibility to, 359–60
    undiagnosed, 282–83, 286
    see also nervous system disorders; psycho-somatic disorders; somatoform disorders
physiological correlates, 185, 212–13
Pick's disease, 684
placebo effect, 152, 395–96, 397, 737
pleasure principle, 76
PNS (parasympathetic nervous system), 212–13, 499, 500, 505
political psychiatry, 4, 723–25
population, statistical inferences and, 153–54
positive correlation, 159
positive reinforcement, 122, 521–23
    selective, 125
positive symptoms of schizophrenia, 761
positron emission tomography (PET) scan, 59, 188, 450, 451, 664, 665, 681
posthypnotic suggestion, 93

post-traumatic stress disorder, 210, 216, 237–49, 306, 307, 617
    course of, 245–47
    disability claims and, 247
    genetic predisposition for, 248
    after manmade catastrophes, 238, 242–44, 245–47, 248–49
    after naturally occurring disasters, 166, 238, 240–42, 247
    and phobias, 239
    precipitants of, 238–45
    predisposition factors, 247–48
    rape trauma syndrome, 238, 244–45
    recovery period, 239–40
    symptoms of, 238–39, 247
    treatment of, 66, 248–49
    vulnerability in, 247–48
precipitating incidents, 399
pre-consciousness, 78–79
premenstrual depression, 365
prepared classical conditioning, 233–37, 495
preschool interventions, 765–66
prevalence, 218
prevention efforts, 414, 764–66
prisoners-of-war, post-traumatic stress disorders of, 246–47
progressive relaxation, 261, 753
projection, 88–90, 93, 96
projective tests, 176, 179–81, 327
    Rorschach Test, 179–81
    Thematic Apperception Test, 179, 181, 327
prolonged exposure therapy, 249
pronominal reversals, 633
prospective studies, 166–67
Prozac, 63, 374–75, 652, 687, 745, 754
pseudopatients, diagnosis of, 200–202
psychalgia, 283, 287
psychiatric attendants (aides), 732–33
psychiatric hospitals, 3–4, 35–42, 61–62, 699–701, 760–61, 762–63
    animalism and, 29, 38, 40
    board and care facilities vs., 705–7, 771–72
    confinement as purpose of, 36–37, 39–40
    day or night care at, 771
    death rate at, 703
    English religious reforms at, 40–41
    humane treatment introduced in, 39–42
    insane abused at, 37–39
    moral treatment at, 41–42
    rise of, 35–42
    shackles and chains at, 37–38, 39–40
psychiatric nurses, as therapists, 730
psychiatric social workers, as therapists, 730
psychiatrists, as therapists, 723, 730
psychic energy, 72, 93, 102
    in id, ego, and superego processes, 76, 78
    transformed in psychosexual develop-ment, 72–75
    transmuted into somatic loss, 288–89
psychoactive substance use disorders, 511–67
    see also alcohol dependence; drug depen-dence

psychoanalysis, 72
  classical, 48, 749–50, 763–64
  see also psychodynamic therapies
psychoanalysts, as therapists, 731
psychodynamic (psychoanalytic) model, 48,
    71–111, 120, 179
  amnesia as viewed in, 297
  anorexia nervosa as viewed in, 623
  anxiety disorders and, 253–54
  anxiety role in, 79–80, 81, 102, 289–90
  assessment of, 107–9, 306–7
  autism as viewed in, 635, 638
  behavioral accounts of phobias vs., 223
  clinical cases as basis for, 109, 114
  comprehensiveness of, 108
  coping strategies in, see coping strategies
  depression as viewed in, 370–71,
    378–80, 398–400
  drug dependence and, 518–19
  existential psychology vs., 97
  faults of, 80
  Freud and, 72–80
  hostility in, 324
  multiple personality and, 298
  neo-Freudians' criticisms of, 81–82
  normal vs. abnormal behavior in, 78, 107
  obsessive-compulsive disorder as viewed
    in, 272–73, 307
  paraphilia as viewed in, 493, 494–95
  personality development in, 72–75, 81,
    104–5
  personality processes in, 76–78, 81, 82;
    see also ego; id; superego
  phobia as viewed in, 223–25, 230
  problems of proof in, 108–9
  psychosomatic disorders as viewed in,
    337, 340, 345
  scientific evidence lacking in, 109
  self in, 82–86
  sexual dysfunction as viewed in, 504–5
  situation and context underestimated in,
    108, 109
  social forces in, 82
  treatment in, 102–7
  unconscious forces in, 78–79, 81
psychodynamic (psychoanalytic) therapies,
    564, 749–50, 762
  for alcohol dependence, 533
  assessment of, 107–8
  behavioral therapy vs., 119–20, 135–36
  breast cancer and, 334
  case study in, 102–6
  catharsis in, 104
  classical psychoanalysis, 48, 749–50,
    763–64
  for cocaine dependence, 540–41
  cognitive therapy vs., 135–36, 382
  for conversion disorders, 293
  for depression, 361, 380, 755
  drugs for depression vs., 375
  focus of, 102
  free association in, 102, 105, 382
  for multiple personality, 298, 303–4
  for obsessive-compulsive disorders,
    277–78
  for peptic ulcers, 322
  personality altered in, 104–5

  for phobia, 223, 224–25
  for post-traumatic stress disorder, 248–49
  transference in, 105
  varied orientations of, 750
psychogenic approach, 29–33
  Charcot's hypnosis studies and, 32–33, 35
  Galen's theory of, 29–30
  Mesmer's cures and, 30–32, 35
  treatment based on, 33, 34–35
  see also psychodynamic model
psychological assessment, 67, 174–88
  clinical interviews in, 174–75, 195
  evaluating, 193–203
  MMPI, 176–78
  observation in, 174, 183–88, 195
  psychological inventories, 176–78
  psychological testing in, 174, 175–82
  reliability of, 188, 193–95
psychological disability, 697–98
psychological states, 332–35, 551–52
psychological testing, 174, 175–82
  intelligence tests, 176, 181–82
  projective tests, 176, 179–81, 327
  psychological inventories, 176–78
  reliability of, 181, 193–95
psychologists, as therapists, 723, 730
psychomotor retardation, 358, 361
psychoneuroimmunology (PNI), 311–12,
    332–37, 345
psychopathy, see antisocial personality
    disorder
psychopharmacology, 515
  of alcohol, 525
psychophysiological assessment, 185
psychophysiological disorders, see psychoso-
    matic disorders
psychoses, 422
  neuroses vs., 209
  see also depression, bipolar; schizophrenia
psychosexual development:
  neo-Freudians' disagreements with,
    81–82
  stages of, 72–75, 109
psychosocial development, 81, 82
psychosocial treatments, 622, 623, 761
psychosomatic disorders, 286, 311–47, 446
  behavioral model of, 337, 341–45
  biomedical model of, 337–40
  cognitive model of, 337, 341, 342, 345
  diagnosing of, 313
  evolution and, 338–39
  general adaptation syndrome and,
    339–40
  life events and, 341–45
  psychodynamic model of, 337, 340, 345
  somatoform disorders vs., 284, 286, 287,
    313
  stigmata, 312, 313
  sudden death, 329–32
  theories of, 337–45
  voluntary behavior and, 345
  see also high blood pressure; peptic ulcers
psychotropic medication, 460, 616, 762
  see also specific medications
puberty, genital stage and, 75
punishment, 122
  anticipation of, 578

  as physical, tangible or social, 577–78
  selective, 126
  sociopaths' responses to, 575–78
PVS (periventricular system), 372

questionnaires, see psychological testing

random assignment, 150
rape, 488–89
rape trauma syndrome, 244–45, 247, 249,
    768
rapid cycling bipolar disorder, 405–6
rational-emotive therapy, 134–35, 748
rationalism, 113–14
rationalization, 92–93
Rat Man case, 273
reaction formation, 90, 96
reactive crisis, 438
reading deficits, 601, 632
realistic anxiety, 79–80
reality:
  accurate perception of, 17, 18
  depressed people's perception of, 354–55
reality principle, 76
reality testing:
  by depressives, 383–84
  by phobics, 228, 230–31
  by schizophrenics, 422
reason, loss of, 38
reattribution training, 383, 384
Recovery Movement, 298
reductionism, 68
reductionists, anti-reductionists vs., 68
reinforcement:
  cocaine and, 537–38
  continuous (CRF), 123
  negative, 122, 126
  partial (intermittent), 123
  positive, 122, 125, 521–23
relapse, 532–35, 540, 542, 548–49
relapse rates, 462–64, 535
relaxation:
  progressive, 261, 753
  in systematic desensitization, 229–30
reliability, 174, 188, 193–98, 203
  acceptable degree of, 174, 195
  of DSM-III and DSM-III-R, 192
  factors influencing, 195
  high vs. low, 193–94
  inter-judge, 193, 195
  test-retest, 193–94, 195
repeatability, as methodological
    concern, 146, 155, 156, 165
repression, 75
  as coping strategy, 87–88, 92, 93, 96
  unconscious level and, 79
research diagnoses, 203
resemblance principle, 114
reserpine, 371, 374
residual rules, 10
resistances, in therapy, 741–42
resistance stage, 339
response initiation, lack of, 358
response prevention, 278–79, 754
  obsessive-compulsive disorders and,
    280–81
responsibility, 97, 109

responsibility (*continued*)
    avoidance of, 99
    in existential view, 99–100
retrospective studies, 166
reuptake process, 373, 517, 652
Ritalin, 610
Role Induction Interviews, 736
Rorschach Test, 179–81
    interpreting of, 180–81
    reliability and validity of, 181
Rouse v. Cameron, 704–5, 707

SAD (seasonal affective disorder), 400,
    406–7
sadism, 306, 486–88
sadness, as symptom of depression, 353
sadomasochism, 483, 486–88
SAD (seasonal affective disorder), 400,
    406–7
samples, statistical inference and, 153
Satanistic forces, 26–27
schizoid personality disorder, 590
schizophrenia, 23, 137, 357, 419–66, 646,
    648
    acute vs. chronic, 438–39, 448, 450
    affective disturbances in, 436–37
    attentional deficits in, 429–30, 431
    biological basis of, 58–59, 420–21,
        448–54
    brain structure in, 451–52, 681, 687,
        688
    catatonic, 425, 426–27
    causes of, 53–54, 58–59, 420–21,
        440–59
    and children, 166, 442–46, 453–54, 601
    cognitive distractibility in, 431–32
    communication attempts in, 437–38
    course of, 420–21
    creativity and, 447–48, 630
    culture and, 456–57
    dangerous behavior associated with, 421
    defining of, 421–24
    delusions in, 422–23, 425, 432–36, 439,
        451, 711
    dimensions of, 438–40
    disorganized, 425, 426, 439
    drug therapy for, 61–62, 66, 189, 448,
        450, 452, 459–62, 464, 465,
        760–61
    genetic factors in, 53–54, 440–48, 453,
        458–59
    hallucinations in, 422–23, 428–29, 430,
        439, 451
    historical survey of views on, 420–21
    hospitalization decision in, 439, 762–63
    immigration studies and, 456
    linkage analysis in, 446–47
    meaning in, 437–38
    milieu therapy and therapeutic communi-
        ties for, 462–65
    multi-modal therapy for, 135
    multiple personality vs., 301–2, 421
    myths about, 421
    negative and positive symptoms of,
        439–40, 451, 460
    neurochemical basis of, 440, 448–51,
        458, 651
    overinclusiveness in, 431, 435

perceptual difficulties in, 427–28,
    435–36, 454
prevalence and incidence of, 424
prospective studies on, 166
pseudopatients diagnosed as, 200, 201
psychological treatment for, 462
recurrent depression and, 437
residual, 427
"revolving-door" phenomenon in,
    461–62, 761
schizotypal personality disorder and,
    590–91
societal factors in, 454–59
suicide and, 437
symptoms of, 427–38, 439–40, 448,
    451, 452
thought disorder in, 8, 429–36, 454
treatments for, 189, 459–65, 760–63
two-self view of, 438
types of, 425–27, 439–40, 448, 451
undifferentiated, 425, 427
see also paranoid schizophrenia
schizophrenogenic family, 440, 442–46,
    453–54, 458–59
    communication distortions in, 453–54
schizotypal personality disorder, 590–91,
    593
school phobia (refusal), 614–15
school psychologists, 730
scientific experimentation, 143–44, 147–59
    basic method in, 147
    causality in correlation studies and, 162
    confounds in, 148, 150–53
    ethical issues in, 144, 148, 158–59
    evaluation of, as investigative method,
        158–59, 168–69
    example of, 148–50
    indirect methods of, 144, 159–67
    meta-analysis in, 149–50
    repeatability and generality in, 155–56
    with single subject, 155–58
    statistical inferences in, 153–55
scientific method, origin of, 30
seasonal affective disorder (SAD), 400,
    406–7
secondary gains, 225, 284–86
sedatives-tranquilizers, 562–64
    dependence, 563–64
    effects of, 562–64
selective abstraction, 382
selective (cognitive) filter, 429, 431
selective positive reinforcement, 125
selective punishment, 126
self, 48, 82–86, 109, 592
    Adler's view of, 81
    children and, 615, 616
    core, 83, 84
    false, 85
    search for, 763–64
    significance of, 86
    subjective, 83, 84, 86
    verbal, 83, 84–85, 86
self-acceptance, 17
self-coherence, 84
self-diagnosis, 19–20
self-esteem, low, 344, 354–56, 375, 378,
    380, 381, 533, 592, 615, 616, 687

self-help groups, 707, 733, 759, 772
self-history, 84
self-hypnosis, 302, 303, 304, 306
self-image, repression and, 87
self-objects, 85–86, 592
senile dementia, 676–77
senility, 190
sensate focus, 507
sensory deficits, 654
sensory deprivation experiments, 152–53
separation anxiety, 611–12, 614
serotonin, 372, 374, 526, 550, 552, 553,
    558, 639, 652
sex differences:
    in depression, 362, 364–66
    and schizophrenia, 424
    and suicide, 410
sex-reassignment operations, 473, 476–77
    follow-up after, 476–77
sex role, 472, 497–98
    dissimilarities in children, 497
    stereotypes, 497, 498
sexual activity, 244
sexual behavior, 469–70
    AIDS and, 469–70
    physiology of, 499–500
    scientific study, 506–7
    societal norms and, 469–70, 481–82,
        497
    see also homosexuality; masturbation
sexual crimes, 489, 490, 491–92
sexual disorders, 470–77, 483–96
    see also ego-dystonic homosexuality; para-
        philias; transsexuality
sexual dysfunctions, 137, 298, 358–59,
    470, 472, 484, 498–509
    in erotic arousal and excitement,
        500–506
    in orgasm, 500, 502–3, 505, 508
    partner's responses to, 501, 502–3
    physical causes of, 503–4
    physiological correlates of, 185
    psychological causes of, 504–6
    therapy evaluation, 508
    treatment of, 66, 505–8, 755–56
sexual energy, 72
    libido, 72, 73, 74, 75
sexual identity, 470–71, 472–77, 497
    disorders of, *see* transsexuality
    fetal development and, 474–76
    vs. sexual interest, 496
    vs. sexual orientation, 482–83
sexual intercourse, 9
    nondemand, 507
sexual interest, 471–72, 483–96, 495
    changing, 495–96
    vs. sexual identity, 496
    vs. sexual orientation, 496
sexual object choice, disorder in, *see* para-
    philias
sexual order vs. disorder, 470–72
sexual orientation, 471, 477–83, 497
    anatomical basis for, 479
    vs. sexual identity, 482–83
    vs. sexual interest, 496
    see also homosexuality
sexual performance, 472, 498–508

impairment of, 500–503
sexual response, 499–500
   female, 499–500
   male, 499, 500
sexual unresponsiveness, 500–501, 504
   therapy for, 506–8
shadowing, 619
shamans, 25, 33
single-blind experiments, 152
single photon emission computerized
      tomography (SPECT) scan, 664, 681
single-subject experiments, 155–58
skills therapists, 733
sleep disturbance, 358, 361
sleeping sickness, 276
smoking, 322, 324, 329, 345, 516, 757
   see also nicotine
snake phobia, 131, 231, 235, 237
snow phobia, 219
social causation, 455
social deviance, 191
social disorder, 682–83
social learning theory, 606
social phobia, 219, 221–22, 228
Social Readjustment Rating Scale, 342–44
social selection, 455
social skills training, 158, 495–96, 600,
      636
social support, 340, 345, 759
society:
   abnormality as judgment of, 4, 8, 9–11,
     13–14, 23–24, 695, 722–23,
     725–26
   and drug use and abuse, 512–13
   stigma of mental illness and, 695, 725–26
   well-being of, 7, 8
sociopathy, see antisocial personality disorder
sodium lactate, 251, 252, 254
somatization disorder (Briquet's syndrome),
   282–83, 287, 288, 290–91
somatoform disorders, 340
   anxiety component of, 266, 288,
     289–92, 294, 306–7
   Briquet's syndrome, 282–83, 287
   chronic fatigue syndrome and, 288
   communicative model of, 290–91
   comorbidity of, 288
   conversion, 265–66, 281–82, 286–294
   course of, 287–88
   depression and, 288
   diagnosing of, 284–86
   etiology of, 288–92
   historical trends in, 291
   hysterical blindness, 144–45, 146–47,
     148, 285, 286, 291–92
   hysterical conversions and, 281
   hysterical paralysis, 32–33, 281, 289,
     290, 293, 297
   pain disorder (psychalgia), 283, 287
   percept blocking model of, 291–92
   psychalgia (pain disorder), 283, 287
   psychodynamic view of, 288–90
   psychosomatic disorders vs., 284, 286,
     287, 313
   symptoms of, 281, 282, 283, 286, 289,
     290–91
   treatment of, 292–94

types of, 281–83
   vulnerability to, 286–87
   see also hysteria
Soteria House, 464
Soviet Union, psychiatric abuses in, 723–24
specialness, 97, 98
speech anxiety:
   behavioral assessment and, 183–84
   behavioral vs. cognitive view of, 129–30
   cognitive therapy for, 129–30, 131
spider phobia, 235, 237
spinal cord, 658, 663
spirits, possession by, 25, 33
split-brain syndrome, 657–58, 662, 688
stammering, 137, 601, 618, 619–20
Stanford-Binet Intelligence Test for
   Children, 181
state-orientation, 365
State-Trait Anxiety Inventory, 260
statistical inference, 153–55
statistical significance, 155, 162
stigmata, 312, 313
stimulants:
   addiction to, 536
   amphetamines, 448, 521, 536–37, 539,
     542, 551, 553, 610, 618
   caffeine, 536
   cocaine, 513, 518, 519–21, 536,
     537–42, 543, 549, 551, 556
   effects of, 537, 542
   medical and social complications of,
     539–40, 542
   psychopharmacology of, 536–40
   treatment of, 540–42
   withdrawal, 539, 540
straitjackets, 41
stress, 235, 242, 660
   and alcohol, 531, 534, 545
   defined, 316–17
   general adaptation syndrome and, 339
   inoculation, 249
   life events and, 333, 335, 340, 341–42
   lifespan and, 338
   of modern living, 457–59
   see also diathesis-stress model
strokes, 188
   amnesia and, 295–96
   neural damage and, 647, 652, 660, 661,
     666–67, 672, 674, 685
structured interviews, 175
stuttering, 137, 601, 618, 619–20
subject bias, 150, 152
sublimation, 75, 93, 96
substance abuse, see drug dependence
substitution, 90
   in obsessive-compulsive disorders, 272–73
sudden death, 322, 329–32, 542
   animal models of, 329–30
   after death of spouse, 330
   hopelessness and helplessness in, 329–31
   process of, 329
suffering, as element of abnormality, 6–7, 11
suicide, 352, 361, 374, 378–79, 407–15,
     437, 535, 562, 697
   altruistic, 413
   anomic, 413
   in Briquet's syndrome, 283

among children, 411
   cultural differences and, 410–11
   egoistic, 413
   hot-lines and, 767–68
   manipulative, 413–14
   motivations for, 413–14
   among older people, 413
   prevention and treatment of, 414
   statistics on, 408–9
   surcease as goal of, 413, 414
   surviving relatives and, 414
   vulnerability for, 408, 413
   among women vs. men, 410
   among young people, 412–13
Sullivanian therapy, 750
superego, 76, 77–78, 79, 82
suppression, 87
survival guilt, 238, 241, 243
syllable-timed speech, 619–20
sympathetic nervous system (SNS), 212–13,
     499
symptoms:
   diagnosis based on, 189, 190, 192, 199
   disorders equated with, 120
   organized into syndromes, 49, 50
   see also specific disorders
symptoms substitution, in phobia, 230
Synanon, 758
synapse, 517, 648
syndromes, 49, 50
syntactic knowledge, 669
syphilis, 68, 647
   general paresis linked to, 50–53, 67, 68
syphilophobia, 221
systematic desensitization, 121, 131, 747
   phobia and, 121, 150, 229–30, 232, 753
   for sexual dysfunction, 508

tarantism, 25
tardive dyskinesia, 62, 461
target behaviors, 125
taste aversions, 237
Tay-Sachs disease, 629
T-cells, 332–33, 335
tension, 86, 185, 531
test anxiety, 131
testing, see psychological testing
tetrahydrocannabinol (THC), 444, 445,
     554, 555, 556
thalamus, 673
Thematic Apperception Test (TAT), 179,
     181, 327
therapeutic alliance, 739
therapeutic communities, 547
   for drug or alcohol abusers, 547, 758
   for schizophrenics, 462–65
therapies, see treatments
therapists:
   children and, 617
   defects in, 723, 740–42
   empathy, warmth, and genuineness of,
     737–38
   experience of, 738–39
   gender and race of, 739–40
   miscellaneous, 733
   paraprofessionals, 770–71
   therapeutic alliance with, 739

therapists (continued)
   types of, 730–34
therapy outcome studies, 149
thin ideal, 365–66, 622
Thorazine, 460–61
thought disorders, 8, 439, 451
thymus gland, 332, 339
time urgency, 323, 324, 326
tobacco:
   chewing, 516
   dependence, see smoking
Tofranil (imipramine), 618
toilet training, 73, 74, 599
Tourette's syndrome, 276
toxins, neurological effects of, 668, 672
trait marker, 529–31
tranquilizers, 562–64
tranquilizing agents, 460, 562–64, 610
Transcendental Meditation (TM), 261, 753
transference, 105, 750
transsexuality, 470, 471, 472–77, 486
   characteristics of, 472–74
   etiology of, 474–76
   fetal development and, 474–76
   as homosexual, heterosexual, or asexual, 473–74
   sex-reassignment operations for, 473, 476–77
   typical life history of, 473–74
transvestism, 473, 483, 485–86
trauma, see post-traumatic stress disorder
treatments (therapies):
   alternative centers for, 707, 771–72
   animistic, 25, 26, 33
   assessing effectiveness of, 742–44
   behavioral assessment in, 183–85
   biomedical, 61–65
   choice of, 752–54
   classical, 102–7
   common ingredients of, 734–44
   consumer's guide to, 729–73
   containment services and, 776–70
   free choice and, 735
   global, 763–64
   goals set in, 742
   hopes and expectations in, 735–37
   insurance and, 189–90
   physical approach to, 29, 33, 34, 49–50
   preventive efforts and, 764–66
   psychogenic, rise of, 33, 34–35
   short-term, 768
   specific vs. insight (global), 745
   suggested by diagnosis, 189, 198, 199–200
   types of, 744–52
   see also behavioral therapy; biomedical treatment; cognitive therapy; drug treatment; existential therapy; psychiatric hospitals; psychodynamic therapies; therapists; specific disorders
trephines, 25, 27
tricyclics, 63, 148, 288, 371, 373, 374, 375, 391, 393, 395–97, 616
triphasic abstinence pattern, 540

tuberculosis, 63, 68, 373–74
tumors, 188, 335
twilight sleep, 544
twins, identical:
   fraternal vs., 53–54, 440–42, 445, 446
   maturation and upbringing of, 443–44, 445, 446
twin studies, 47
   on alcohol dependence, 529
   on antisocial personality disorder, 579
   on autism, 639
   concordance vs. discordance in, 54, 440–41
   on diathesis, 316, 338
   genetic factors and, 54–58
   on homosexuality, 480
   index case (proband) vs. co-twin in, 441–42
   on IQs, 629–30
   logic of, 54, 440–41
   on manic-depression, 371, 404
   on obsessive-compulsive disorder, 270
   on panic attacks, 251–52
   on schizophrenia, 53–54, 440–42, 443–44, 445, 458
   on unipolar depression, 166–67, 371
Type A personality, 322–29, 345
   assessment of, 324–29
   CHD and, 322–29
   defining of, 322–23
   emergency reaction and, 323, 324, 327–29
   helplessness and, 324, 326–27
   hostility and, 324–25
Type B personality, 323–27

ulcers, see peptic ulcers
unconditional positive regard, 106
unconditioned response (UR), 117–18, 119, 214, 226–29, 258
unconditioned stimulus (US), 117–19, 214, 226–29
unconscious, 78–79
   collective, 81
   explored in classical psychoanalysis, 749–50
uncontrollability:
   in learned helplessness, 168, 326, 385, 387
   psychosomatic events and, 319–21
unconventionality, 6, 9–10, 13–14
uncorrelated events, 159
undifferentiated schizophrenia, 425, 427
United States v. Brawner, 715–16
unpredictability:
   as element of abnormality, 6, 8–9, 12
   ulcers and, 318–19, 321
unstructured interviews, 174–75
UR (unconditioned response), 117–18, 119, 214, 226–29, 258
uterus:
   malfunctions of, hysteria caused by, 27–29, 30

wandering, hysteria caused by, 27–29, 34, 49, 287

vagina, sex-reassignment operations and, 476
vaginal lubrication, 504
   dysfunctions of, 500, 501
   physiology of, 499–500
validity, 174, 181, 198–200, 203
   descriptive, 198–99
   predictive (outcome), 198, 199–200
Valium, 64, 562, 745, 753
values acquired from experience, introjected values vs., 86
variables:
   in correlation studies, 160
   dependent and independent, 147, 159
   mental and physical, 336
variances, occasion and information, 195
ventromedial lesions, 682, 683
veterans, combat fatigue among, 245–47
victims, counseling for, 769
vividness, 6, 9–10, 12, 13–14
volition, loss of, 439, 451
voluntary behavior, 345
voyeurism, 483, 488, 489, 490–91

Wechsler Adult Intelligence Scale (WAIS), 181
Wechsler Adult Intelligence Scale—Revised (WAIS-R), 182
Wechsler Intelligence Scale for Children (WISC), 181
Wechsler Preschool and Primary Scale of Intelligence (WPPSI), 181–82
weight loss, 358, 758–59
well-being:
   individual, 7
   societal, 8
Wernicke's area, 667–68
will, 97, 358
   disorders of, 101, 570–72
   exhortative, 100, 101
   goal-directed, 100–101
   wishing, willing and, 101
witchcraft, 23
   abnormal behavior attributed to, 25–27
   tests for, 26–27
work:
   sexual energy channeled into, 75, 93
   therapeutic value of, 42
workaholics, 97
work ethic, 36–37, 42
World Health Organization, 190, 191, 457
   drug abuse definition, 514–15
Wyatt v. Stickney, 705, 707

Xanax, 233

Yohimbine, 254

Zoloft, 754